ENCYCLOPEDIA *of* INVESTMENTS

MARSHALL E. BLUME is Howard Butcher Professor of Finance and Chairman of the Department of Finance at the Wharton School, University of Pennsylvania. He is also Associate Director of the Rodney L. White Center for Financial Research at Wharton, and author or coauthor of numerous books, monographs, and journal articles on investments and finance. Dr. Blume is a consultant in the fields of corporate finance and investments, and has served as Associate Editor of the *Journal of Financial Economics* and the *Journal of Financial and Quantitative Analysis,* and as Managing Editor of the *Journal of Finance.* A trustee and member of Phi Beta Kappa at Trinity College, Dr. Blume received his M.B.A. and Ph.D. degrees from the Graduate School of Business at the University of Chicago.

JACK P. FRIEDMAN is Head of the Research Division of the Texas Real Estate Research Center, Texas A&M University. Dr. Friedman has written several books and monographs, and his writings have appeared in many professional journals including *Real Estate Review, Appraisal Journal, Mortgage Banker, Financial Executive,* and the *Journal of Commercial Bank Lending.* A Certified Public Accountant and a Senior Real Property Appraiser, Dr. Friedman received his M.B.A. degree from Pace University and his Ph.D. degree from Georgia State University.

ENCYCLOPEDIA *of* INVESTMENTS

Editor-in-Chief

MARSHALL E. BLUME

Howard Butcher Professor of Finance
The Wharton School
University of Pennsylvania

Associate Editor

JACK P. FRIEDMAN

Head, Research Division
Texas Real Estate Research Center
Texas A&M University

WARREN, GORHAM & LAMONT

Boston • New York

WARREN, GORHAM & LAMONT, INC.
210 SOUTH STREET
BOSTON, MASSACHUSETTS 02111

ISBN 0-88262-713-9

Library of Congress Catalog Card No. 82-50341

This publication is designed to provide accurate and authoritative information in regard to the subject matter covered. It is sold with the understanding that the publisher is not engaged in rendering legal, financial, or other professional service. If investment advice or other expert assistance is required, the services of a competent professional person should be sought.

PRINTED IN THE UNITED STATES OF AMERICA

Contributing Authors

Douglas A. Albert
Associate Municipal Note Trader, Ehrlich-Bober & Co., Inc., New York
(MUNICIPAL SECURITIES)

Kathy August
Vice-President–Treasurer, PMI Mortgage Insurance Co., San Francisco
(MORTGAGE-BACKED SECURITIES)

Michele Beiny
Vice-President, The Antique Porcelain Company, New York
(PORCELAIN)

Rotraut Beiny
President, The Antique Porcelain Company, New York
(PORCELAIN)

Peter A. Bernard
Executive Vice-President and Head, Investment Banking and Trading Group, Bache Halsey Stuart Shields, Inc., New York
(COMMON STOCK—NEW ISSUES)

Richard Blum
Vice-President, First National Bank of Chicago
(BANK CERTIFICATES OF DEPOSIT)

Marshall E. Blume
Howard Butcher Professor of Finance, The Wharton School, University of Pennsylvania
(PORTFOLIO MANAGEMENT)

John C. Bogle
President, Vanguard Group of Investment Companies, Valley Forge, Pa.
(MUTUAL FUNDS)

Q. David Bowers
Chairman, Bowers & Ruddy Galleries, Inc., Wolfeboro, N.H., and Los Angeles
(COINS)

June M. Butler
Advisory Economist, Department of Economic Analysis and Planning, Chicago Board of Trade
(FUTURES—METALS)

Thomas M. Campfield
Vice-President, Manufacturers Hanover Trust Company, New York
(FOREIGN BANK DEPOSITS)

Archie Cherkezian
President, William Cherkezian & Son, Inc., New York; Editor, Oriental Rugs
(RUGS)

Thomas C. Coleman
Vice-President and Director, Department of Economic Analysis and Planning, Chicago Board of Trade
(FUTURES—FINANCIAL; FUTURES—METALS)

J. Patrick Cooney
Assistant Vice-President, Fine Arts Management Service, Citibank, New York
(PAINTINGS)

Frank H. David
Vice-President and Associate Actuary, The Prudential Insurance Company of America, Florham Park, N.J.
(LIFE INSURANCE INVESTMENTS—SEPARATE ACCOUNTS)

Bancroft G. Davis
Late Chairman, Bancroft Convertible Fund, Inc., New York
(CONVERTIBLE SECURITIES)

Alice Levi Duncan
Director of Sculpture and Works of Art, Christie's, New York
(SCULPTURE)

J. Alastair Duncan
Vice-President, Nineteenth- and Twentieth-Century Decorative Arts, Christie, Manson & Woods International, Inc., New York
(ART NOUVEAU AND ART DECO)

Burtt R. Ehrlich
President, Ehrlich-Bober & Co., Inc., New York
(MUNICIPAL SECURITIES)

Paul H. Epstein, Esq.
Member, Proskauer Rose Goetz & Mendelsohn, New York
(THEATRICAL PRODUCTIONS)

John F. Fleming
Consultant and dealer in rare books and manuscripts, New York
(BOOKS)

Irving D. Friedman, Esq.
Registered representative, Muller and Company, Inc.; Managing Attorney, Ballon, Stoll & Itzler, New York
(Corporate Bonds)

Jack P. Friedman
Head of Research Division, Texas Real Estate Research Center, Texas A&M University
(Real Estate Limited Partnerships; Real Estate—Undeveloped Land)

Donald S. Grubbs, Jr. Esq.
Consulting Actuary, George B. Buck Consulting Actuaries, Inc., Washington, D.C.
(Retirement Income—Individual Retirement Plans; Retirement Income—Pension Plan Investments)

James E. Hamer
Trust Officer, The Northern Trust Company, Chicago
(Real Estate—Farms and Ranches)

Thomas J. Herzfeld
President, Thomas J. Herzfeld & Co., Inc., South Miami, Fla.
(Closed-End Funds)

John Holmgren
Research Analyst, PMI Mortgage Insurance Co., San Francisco
(Mortgage-Backed Securities)

Roger G. Ibbotson
Senior Lecturer in Finance and Executive Director of the Center for Research in Security Prices, Graduate School of Business, The University of Chicago
(Historical Returns on Principal Types of Investments)

William C. Ketchum, Jr.
Consultant and collector of folk art and Americana, New York
(Folk Art and Americana)

Robert G. Kirby
Chairman, Capital Guardian Trust Company, Los Angeles
(Common Stocks—Listed Issues)

Eugene M. Krader, Esq.
Managing Editor, Tax Publications, Warren, Gorham & Lamont, Inc., New York
(Tax Considerations for Collector-Investors)

Paul A. Kunkel
Associate Editor, Art & Auction, *New York*
(Period Furniture)

Nancy J. Kyle
Vice-President, Morgan Guaranty Trust Company of New York
(Foreign Equities)

Charles W. Lard
Assistant Treasurer, United Technologies Corporation, Hartford, Conn.
(Preferred Stock)

Harris Lawless
President, Harris Lawless & Associates, Sausalito, Cal.
(Real Estate—Multi-Family Rental)

Jeffrey R. Leeds
Vice-President, Chemical Bank, New York
(U.S. Treasury Bills)

Terrence L. Love
Chairman, Land Development Analysts, Atlanta
(Real Estate—Undeveloped Land)

Eugene G. Martin
Vice-President, National Investment Services, Milwaukee
(Oil and Gas)

Gordon J. Munro
Vice-President, Pension Department, New York Life Insurance Company
(Life Insurance Investments—Guaranteed Interest Contracts)

J. Marc Myers
Partner, Trammel Crow Company, Dallas
(Real Estate—Commercial and Industrial)

John B. Nicholson
President, Berryhill Associates, Washington, D.C.
(Real Estate Investment Trusts)

David Nochimson, Esq.
Member, Mitchell, Silberberg & Knupp, Los Angeles
(Motion Pictures)

Bruce E. Paine
Corporate Vice-President, Paine Webber Jackson & Curtis, Inc., New York
(U.S. Government Bonds, Notes, Agency Securities)

Anne E. Peck
Associate Professor, Food Research Institute, Stanford University
(Futures—Agricultural Commodities)

Peter M. Rexford
Vice-President, Rare Stamp and Coin Division, Newhard, Cook & Co., St. Louis
(Stamps)

R. Bruce Ricks
Real estate finance and investment counselor, Portola Valley, Cal.
(Real Estate—Single-Family Rental)

Keith B. Romney
Founder, Keith Romney Associates, Salt Lake City
(Real Estate—Condominiums, Cooperatives, Timesharing)

Ira Z. Romoff
Vice-President, Commercial Funding, Inc., New York
(Commercial Paper)

Randy Rosen
President, Artists Originals–Corporate Art Advisory Service, New York
(Prints)

Robert S. Rubinstein
Actuary, The Equitable Life Assurance Society of the United States, New York
(Life Insurance Investments—Annuities)

Myron S. Scholes
Edward Eagle Brown Professor of Banking and Finance, Graduate School of Business, University of Chicago
(Options—Puts and Calls)

Evan Schulman
Senior Vice-President, Batterymarch Financial Management, Boston
(Index Funds)

John R. Schumann
Vice-President, Trust Department, The Northern Trust Company, Chicago
(Real Estate—Farms and Ranches)

Allan M. Shapiro, Esq.
Associate Counsel, United Artists Corporation, New York
(Theatrical Productions)

Laurence B. Siegel
Research Division Manager, R.G. Ibbotson & Company, Chicago
(Historical Returns on Principal Types of Investments)

James E. Sinclair
General Partner, Sinclair Group Companies, New York
(METALS—GOLD, SILVER, PLATINUM; STRATEGIC AND CRITICAL MATERIALS)

Jeanne Cairns Sinquefield
Manager, Department of Economic Analysis and Planning, Chicago Board of Trade
(FUTURES—FINANCIAL)

Rex A. Sinquefield
Executive Vice-President and Chief Investment Officer, Dimensional Fund Advisors, Inc., Chicago
(HISTORICAL RETURNS ON PRINCIPAL TYPES OF INVESTMENTS)

Frank P. Slattery, Jr.
President, Lease Financing Corporation, Radnor, Pa.
(LEASING VENTURES)

Howard Stein
Chairman, President and Chief Executive, The Dreyfus Corporation, New York
(MONEY MARKET FUNDS)

Joan C. Terwilliger
Assistant Secretary, Morgan Guaranty Trust Company of New York
(BANK-MANAGED INVESTMENT ACCOUNTS)

John R. Thomas
Vice-President, Morgan Guaranty Trust Company of New York
(BANK-MANAGED INVESTMENT ACCOUNTS)

Rhodri Thomas
Vice-President, First Boston Corporation, New York
(FOREIGN FIXED INCOME INVESTMENTS)

Martin A. Weinstein
Vice-President, Salomon Brothers, Inc., New York
(ARBITRAGE)

Daniel Wolf
Chairman, Daniel Wolf Gallery, New York
(PHOTOGRAPHS)

Charles E. Wooley
Collectible investments consultant, Methuen, Mass.
(COLLECTIBLES)

Allan E. Young
Professor of Finance, School of Management, Syracuse University
(OPTIONS—WARRANTS)

Benjamin Zucker
Chairman, Precious Stones Company, New York
(GEMSTONES)

Preface

Investors today are considering a much wider range of investment vehicles than they did ten years ago. Part of the reason for this change is the poor performance of the stock and bond markets in the 1970s in comparison to other types of investments, like real estate or even Treasury bills. Another part of the reason is the keen competitiveness of financial institutions in responding to this situation with a large number of new and imaginative investment products. Most persons would readily recognize some of them, like money market funds, but would be less familiar with others, like financial futures or Eurodollar instruments.

The purpose of this *Encyclopedia* is to provide in a single source reliable information about a wide array of investment vehicles. In this volume the reader can turn to a basic description of nearly sixty different kinds of investments, prepared by leading bankers, brokers, investment advisers, dealers, and financial specialists. A lawyer, asked by a client about strategic metals as an investment, can quickly obtain sufficient information to provide intelligent advice. An individual investor can use the *Encyclopedia* to learn about the tax consequences of investing in options. An institutional investor can obtain a concise overview of eight kinds of real estate investments. Estate executors and trustees, whether attorneys or bankers, can compare the performance of many new and traditional kinds of investment vehicles. Investors of moderate to substantial means should find the *Encyclopedia* a continuing source of interesting ideas and challenging insights.

To make the *Encyclopedia* easy to use, the entries for each investment vehicle are extensively cross-referenced and follow, to the extent possible, a standard format. Each entry begins with a general description of the vehicle itself. Then there is a discussion of the characteristics that make it an attractive investment and those characteristics that detract from its appeal.

Each entry examines — often in depth — the practical considerations of investing in the vehicle, such as

- The primary factors that determine the monetary value of the asset;
- Its suitability for specific types of investors;
- Where to obtain professional advice;
- How to buy and sell;
- Tax implications; and
- Unusual custodial problems and how to solve them.

The *Encyclopedia* ends with three articles of broad interest to investors. The first contains the latest investment return numbers of bonds, stocks, and real estate from the well-known Ibbotson-Sinquefield studies. Some performance statistics begin as early as 1926. The authors also include performance data on a number of other, less standard, investments. This discussion utilizes many tables and charts of unusual interest. The second article describes the fundamentals of portfolio management in nontechnical terms. These fundamentals are often associated with the term "modern portfolio theory," or MPT. The discussion provides numerical examples of optimal portfolio strategies under various possible future scenarios and then examines the implications of these strategies for attaining specific investment objectives. The third article discusses the tax implications of investing in collectibles, which in some respects are critically different from investing in more traditional vehicles. The Internal Revenue Code makes important distinctions between a "dealer" and "non-dealer," and these differences are carefully explored. In addition, the reader is warned of certain pitfalls in donating collectibles to nonprofit institutions.

Readers will appreciate a further attractive feature — the publisher's commitment to ensure the *Encyclopedia's* lasting usefulness through cumulative updates that will be regularly available.

As Editor-in-Chief of this volume, I have been fortunate in working with a large number of capable and dedicated individuals. My Associate Editor, Jack P. Friedman, who prepared the initial outline for the book, provided invaluable expertise in the real estate area and, in addition, carefully reviewed every contributed piece, including my own. The staff at Warren, Gorham & Lamont was superb. At the outset, I was highly skeptical that a group of contributors of the caliber I desired could be persuaded to participate, but Eugene Simonoff was persistent in arguing that his organization could do it. Indeed, an outstanding group of authors was assembled under the efforts of Gordon Laing, who also directed the editing of the authors' contributions. The quality of the *Encyclopedia* is a direct reflection of all these persons.

Final credit, however, is due to the contributors themselves. For their arduous efforts and unfailing cooperation in meeting high editorial standards and demanding deadlines, my Associate Editor and I are deeply indebted.

MARSHALL E. BLUME

June 1982

Contents

Arbitrage

Martin A. Weinstein *

BASIC CHARACTERISTICS

Arbitrage, in its purest form, is the practice of buying something in one market and simultaneously selling it in another market in order to take advantage of price differences existing at the moment of purchase and sale without risk of loss of capital.

Riskless Arbitrage

The usual subjects of arbitrage are currencies, currency futures, securities, and precious metals. For example, the British pound may be selling in Paris at $1.80 and in Tokyo at $1.81. An arbitrageur who buys a large quantity of pounds in Paris at $1.80 and simultaneously sells a large number of pounds in Tokyo at $1.81 can make a substantial profit based on the one-cent differential. In so doing, the arbitrageur has not risked any capital, but has merely taken advantage of an inefficiency in the marketplace based on differences in time and distance. Another example of a riskless-arbitrage situation is the purchase of a security on the New York Stock Exchange for $33 a share and the simultaneous sale of the same number of shares of the same security on the Pacific Coast Stock Exchange at a higher price. This procedure may be carried out in reverse by selling the shares short on the New York Exchange and buying them at a lower price on the Pacific Coast Exchange, in order to lock in the differential in price.

Risk Arbitrage

A variant of arbitrage that in practice involves risk of capital loss is the purchase or sale of a security at a discount or premium from some announced or stated value, with the hope that the price of the security will ultimately increase or decrease to this stated value. The magnitude of the discount or premium reflects the likelihood that the security will never reach, or will greatly surpass, the stated value. A very simple example of risk arbitrage is the purchase of a stock at $33 per share when another company has announced a tender offer at $35 per share. While the investor is trying to earn the $2 differential per share by buying at the lower price and selling to the announced purchaser at the higher price, there is a risk that the proposed offer may not be successfully completed. The

* Martin A. Weinstein is a Vice-President of Salomon Brothers, Inc., New York.

material that follows deals exclusively with the various forms of risk arbitrage as practiced by specialists today.

TYPES OF RISK ARBITRAGE

Risk arbitrage may be undertaken in all forms of corporate reorganizations and capital restructurings, including tender offers, mergers, exchange offers, self-tenders and liquidations. These transactions generally require that the arbitrageur follow similar analytical procedures in deciding whether to make a purchase, but have different legal characteristics and requirements that may affect the outcome and shape of the final transaction, the price of the securities purchased when the transaction is completed, and the price of the securities during the period between the original announcement and completion of the transaction.

In order to evaluate each transaction fairly, therefore, it is necessary for the arbitrageur to know the mechanics, legal requirements, and possible pitfalls involved in each.

TRANSACTIONS

Tender Offers

A tender offer is the quickest and simplest way for one company to acquire any or all of the shares of another company. The advantages of the tender offer for the purchasing corporation are its speed, relative simplicity, and flexibility. A tender offer can be geared to acquire any specific percentage of a company that the buyer wants to purchase. In other words, Corporation A can tender for all of Corporation B or for any fixed number of shares that would result in A owning its desired percentage of B.

Mechanics of a tender offer. The purchasing company makes an offer to purchase for cash the number of shares of the company it seeks to acquire (the target company). The offer is made through an offering circular which, as required by the Securities and Exchange Commission (SEC) regulations, must disclose the salient terms of the offer, such as the source of the buyer's funds, the expiration date of the offer, the means by which an individual may withdraw the tendered shares, and where and how to redeem the stock certificates. Basic tax considerations concerning the offer are also included.

SEC regulations require that the mechanics of the tender offer commence within five business days of the public announcement of intent to purchase, and remain open for the following twenty business days. In non-regulated industries, however, no shares are actually purchased until the termination of a defined waiting period under the antitrust laws in order to give time to the Federal Trade Commission (FTC) or Antitrust Division of the Department of Justice to determine whether the combination resulting from the proposed tender offer would violate the antitrust laws. In regulated industries such as utilities, banking, insurance, and transportation, the tender offer is made contingent upon the approval of the agencies charged with regulating those industries, and the buyer cannot pay for the shares until all such approvals are received. Since this can take quite a bit of time, combinations in regulated industries are usually structured as mergers.

Partial Tender Offers

In a partial tender offer where the purchaser only attempts to acquire a certain percentage of the shares of the target company, SEC regulations require that a bidder accept all shares properly tendered and not withdrawn during at least the first ten calendar days of an offer. If the tender offer is oversubscribed in this period, then all such shares tendered must be purchased on a pro rata basis. If the offer is not oversubscribed, the bidder may accept shares in the order in which they are tendered.

Hostile Takeovers

A hostile take-over situation develops when the management or board of directors of a corporation has turned down an offer to purchase made by another corporation. The would-be acquiring corporation might then make a tender offer for all of the target company's stock or a certain portion thereof in order to get voting control of the board of directors and of the company. If the acquiring company does not get the necessary number of shares in the requisite amount of time, it may either extend the offer, increase the offering price, or abandon the offer entirely. In some instances, the target company may attempt to seek out a candidate of its own to purchase its shares at a higher price than that offered by the company engaged in the hostile takeover and recommend that the shareholders tender their shares to that corporation. This new purchaser of the target company is frequently referred to as the "white knight."

Tender offers are the preferred type of transaction for a hostile takeover of another corporation because they do not need to be approved or endorsed by the target's board of directors, nor is a vote of the target corporation's shareholders required.

Exchange Offers

In an exchange offer a purchasing corporation offers to exchange its securities for the securities of the target company. An exchange offer is similar to a cash tender offer in that a shareholder vote of the target company is not required. The shareholders of the target, in effect, vote by either accepting or not accepting the offer. A shareholder vote of the acquiring company may also be required under certain circumstances, for instance, if that company is issuing new equity securities or if the shares to be exchanged have not yet been authorized for issue by its shareholders.

An exchange offer is usually faster than a merger and offers an advantage over a cash tender offer because the buyer is not limited to cash as the form of payment for the target. The specific terms of the exchange will be contained in an exchange offering circular registered with the SEC. This will also contain detailed information on the company offering to exchange its shares, since this information must be evaluated by the target company's shareholders so they can determine whether they wish to exchange their shares. No shares can actually be exchanged before the registration statement has been declared effective by the SEC.

Since approval by the target's board is not required, exchange offers can also be used to effect a hostile acquisition, especially if the acquiring corporation lacks sufficient cash to commence a hostile cash tender offer. However, the exchange offer is not as quick as a cash tender offer and gives the target company more time to pursue defensive measures.

Mergers

A merger differs from a tender offer and an exchange offer in that the transaction must first be approved by the board of directors of the target company. The shareholders of the target company then vote on whether or not to accept the transaction. If approved by the necessary vote (which depends on the target company's state of incorporation), and if all regulatory approvals have been obtained, the merger is accomplished.

Mergers can be effected through cash or securities. They are usually done on a friendly basis after the two companies and their advisers have negotiated terms. In addition to a vote of the target company's shareholders, a vote of the purchasing company's shareholders may be required under the same circumstances as in an exchange offer.

A proxy statement containing detailed information about the target company and details of the terms of the consolidation is filed with the SEC and presented to the target's shareholders after SEC clearance. This proxy statement is designed to provide adequate information upon which the shareholders of the target company can make an informed decision. If the merger is for an exchange of securities, the proxy statement will constitute a prospectus and will also contain detailed information on the acquiring company and pro forma combined financial information.

The time period from the original announcement of the proposed merger until the proxy statement is cleared by the SEC and then presented to the shareholders can be lengthy. It should be pointed out that usually the longer a transaction takes to complete, the greater the risk of its not being consummated. Time is seldom a friend of the parties to a transaction or to an arbitrageur.

Leveraged Buy-Outs

Leveraged buy-outs have become increasingly popular during the past few years. They are similar to cash mergers in form and have essentially the same legal requirements. However, the structure of the financing of the transaction is different.

In a typical leveraged buy-out, the acquiring group puts up a small amount of its own funds (10 to 20 percent of the total value of the acquisition) and borrows the rest from lending and/or investing institutions. The assets of the acquired company are used as collateral for the loans. This type of transaction generally takes longer to close than a merger does because of the time necessary to arrange the complicated financing.

The advantage of a leveraged buy-out is that a purchaser who does not have securities to issue in payment for another company, and who does not have enough assets to use as collateral for a loan, can get access to borrowed funds.

Corporate Reorganizations

Another area of risk arbitrage investing is that of corporate reorganizations, including self-tenders, exchanges, and spin-offs.

Self-tenders. Self-tenders are usually for less than 100 percent of the stock outstanding. The arbitrageur's value analysis centers on the pro forma financial statements and the value of the stock after the tender expires. The effect of the reduction in number of shares on earnings per share and net book value per share must be determined. Given this analysis, the investor estimates where the stock will trade after the offer expires (the risk). The reward depends on the investor's ability to establish accurately the percentage of the position that will be accepted in the tender offer and hence the value of residual shares. The company's proxy statement will show management holdings and any holders of more than 5 percent of the company's stock. The offering circular will disclose management's intentions. Although it is not required, holders of large amounts of stock very often disclose their intentions as well.

The investor must keep accurate statistics on the daily trading volume from the time of the announcement of the self-tender until the earlier of the early pro rata date or expiration date of the offer as an indication of how many shares are likely to be tendered. Most of this stock will have been bought by arbitrageurs with the intention of tendering. Those shares, plus some amount of the other shares, will come in; but the total is difficult to estimate and really depends on the feel one gets from the trading activity and patterns.

Exchanges. Company exchange offers require similar analysis, with the emphasis on the value of the security being offered. These exchanges (usually debt for common stock, or preferred stock for debt) are generally for purposes of improving the balance sheet.

Spin-offs or split-ups. Another form of reorganization consists of spin-offs or split-ups of a corporation into more than one corporation, each with its own securities trading in the market. Again, the value analysis is the heart of the decision.

The investor must evaluate each of the parts into which the corporation will split. This is generally approached by taking the financial statements and recasting them as though the transaction had occurred. The next step is to compare these new companies to existing similar companies to estimate the market prices at which the newly created securities will trade.

Liquidations

The investment decision regarding announced liquidations is different from those of the various other forms of consolidation. There is very little probability risk (uncertainty about future events) but a greater amount of value risk (uncertainty about future equity worth). When a company announces that its board of directors has approved a resolution authorizing the management to present a plan of liquidation for shareholder approval, the arbitrageur must assess the potential break-up or liquidating value of the company and base the investment decision on that analysis.

Generally, a company will sell off its operations over time and pay liquidating cash dividends to its shareholders. One of the arbitrageur's analytical functions is to estimate the amount and timing of these dividends.

Liquidations generally take longer to consummate than any other risk-arbitrage transaction except acquisitions of companies in certain regulated industries. However, historically, they have proven to be the most profitable form of risk-arbitrage investing.

IMPORTANT FACTORS IN RISK-ARBITRAGE DECISIONS

The risk-arbitrage decision consists of three parts: whether to buy into one of the special situations described above; the stage of the transaction at which the purchase should be made; and the size of the position to be taken. These three factors in the decision must be viewed in the context of the type of transaction involved and the potential risk-reward relationship inherent at each stage of the transaction.

Analyzing the Transaction

Immediately upon the announcement of a proposed transaction, the arbitrageur thoroughly analyzes the announcement with regard to the form of the transaction, the stage to which it has progressed (i.e., an agreement in principal, a definitive agreement, two parties in discussions, a proposed restructuring, and so forth) and whether it is a friendly or hostile transaction.

Form and stage of transaction. The form of the transaction, if it is part of the announcement, gives a preliminary indication of the timing. The simplest case, an uncontested tender offer in a non-regulated industry, can take as little as one month from start to finish. In a hostile tender offer, the target corporation can cause some delay through filing lawsuits under various state take-over statutes or federal securities laws. However, except in the case of those legal violations that cannot be cured by additional disclosure, the target company may delay but cannot defeat the offer. This may be contrasted to a merger between two railroads or banks, which requires a significantly greater time frame.

The stage of transaction is another variable that must be considered. The most usual form of announcement is that two companies have reached an agreement in principle for some form of consolidation. The announcement also includes the proposed terms of the transaction. This is usually arrived at by the chief executive officers of both companies who, along with their respective advisers (lawyers and investment bankers), have been negotiating those terms.

The next step is to announce the transaction's approval by the respective boards of directors of the companies, which is followed by a signing of the definitive merger agreement. This last step can take a varying amount of time depending upon the number of details to be ironed out and the amount of further investigation that the two parties require. After that, the proxy statement for the shareholders' meeting is distributed (approximately one month prior to the meeting), with the deal usually closing the day of the shareholders' meeting or shortly thereafter.

Original announcement and public information. The arbitrageur also gets some feeling for the risk in the deal from the original announcement. In a sense, the longer a deal takes, the riskier it is, since there is more time for the parties to change their minds. Thus, an original announcement that states that a definitive agreement has been signed (which is very unusual) is less risky and should close faster than an announcement simply saying that ABC Company and XYZ Company are in discussions that could lead to some form of combination.

The arbitrageur also gets a feeling for the timing from whether a deal is friendly or hostile. Friendly deals consummate faster regardless of the form. In a friendly tender offer, the target would not file time-consuming lawsuits or seek delay through state take-over statutes. In a hostile exchange offer, the target can attack the purchasers' prospectus for a lack of disclosure and other securities violations. As mentioned before, such litigation rarely prevents a deal entirely if there are no violations of securities laws, but can often create delay.

After analyzing the original announcement, the arbitrageur examines the public information available on the companies involved. The first thing to consider is the industries of the respective companies to determine whether or not any extraordinary regulatory approvals will be required. This will probably be the one key determinant to the timing of the transaction. As discussed earlier, deals involving companies in regulated industries require varying levels of government agency approvals and can take in excess of two years from the time of announcement until completion. In non-regulated industries, which comprise the great majority of industrial companies, SEC and antitrust filings with the FTC and the Antitrust Division of the Department of Justice are required.

Since the SEC essentially looks for adequate disclosure of information to the shareholders, the arbitrageur need not be concerned about disclosure, but looks at the respective bankers and attorneys involved. In situations where experienced professionals are working on the transaction, there is a great likelihood that the deal will proceed according to the normal schedule for its respective form of transaction. The arbitrageur also attempts to determine whether the transaction raises potential antitrust questions that could either prohibit the deal entirely or result in a request for additional information, thereby delaying the transaction.

The arbitrageur must rely on an attorney for advice on both of these important issues.

Whether to buy. The key to the investment decision is a valuation analysis of the target company, aimed at estimating the risk-reward relationship involved in the transaction. The important point is to assess the relationship between the value of the company if the deal is completed (the reward) with the value of the company in the marketplace if the announced deal terminates (the potential risk). The arbitrageur is trying to justify the deal price and determine if a higher bidder is likely to be forthcoming.

Probably the most important tools for the arbitrageur in valuing target companies are historical records of other acquisitions of companies in the same industry. The arbitrageur can track the prices paid for companies in specific industries and relate those prices to the current target based on such criteria as price-earnings ratio, premium over last sale, price to net book value, dollars per barrel of oil in the ground, etc. While the arbitrageur should not intend to become a bona fide expert in every industry, he must attempt to establish some range of possible values or a minimum value for a company and its shares and use that determination as a basis for starting the investment decision.

Use of these records is particularly helpful when a company announces that it has been approached by another company, or is in discussions with another company, which may or may not lead to an eventual consolidation. The arbitrageur can use past pricing levels to get a feeling for the price that would probably be required to acquire the company.

Price analysis. Where a price has been announced, the historic records help the arbitrageur determine if the price is fair. If the price is too high, particularly in a merger where the buyer has time to re-evaluate the decision to purchase, there is a significant risk of the deal terminating. If the price is too low, the arbitrageur may invest in the target at prices higher than the announced terms in the hope that the target company's willingness to sell will attract other companies willing to pay a more generous price, or, in effect, a more realistic price. Thus, the potential reward may be higher than it first appears.

In using a historic basis to estimate the current value of a company, the arbitrageur must remember that no two companies are alike, even in the same industry. The arbitrageur is initially not trying to get an exact price but only trying to establish a range. In order to narrow the range, the arbitrageur would compare certain characteristics of the target company to the companies that have been acquired in the recent past. In addition, it is important to try to see if the companies that were acquired at the higher end of the range had better growth rates, or perhaps whether interest rates were lower at the time they were acquired.

It is also important to determine if there have been any major events that would have altered the value of companies in a specific industry. Such events include any legislation that has been enacted or is pending, or a changed outlook for a specific industry caused by external variables such as demographics or new competitive products.

The other part of the valuation procedure is traditional securities analysis, aimed at estimating where the security of the target company will trade should the transaction be terminated. This establishes the level of risk that the arbitrageur is assuming. The price of the security after the cancelling of a deal will often depend on the reason for the termination. However, the reason for cancelling is generally not public information, and thus the analyst tries to estimate this value by traditional means such as historic price-earnings ratios, earnings estimates, and growth rates.

It is important to monitor the target on a continuing basis since the terms of the deal are based on certain operating assumptions made by the two parties. If the operations of the target (or the buyer in an exchange-of-securities-type transaction) take a sharp turn downward, or sometimes upward, there is greater likelihood of the deal being terminated.

Probability analysis. Risk-reward relationships will never make sense without some form of probability analysis.

Example. Assume Company A is offering to acquire Company B for $45 per share in a cash tender offer and Company B is trading at $43 per share with four weeks to go before the tender offer expires. Further assume that if the deal were terminated the target's stock would trade at $30 per share. If the deal closes on time and the arbitrageur gets paid in one month, the earning would be an attractive annualized return of approximately 56 percent. Based on a simple risk-reward analysis, there is a $2 potential profit versus a $13 potential loss.

The next question would be whether the probability of earning $2 in one month on a $43 investment is greater than losing $13 on the same investment at almost any moment. Furthermore, he must evaluate, based on the value analysis, what the probability is that another company might offer a price in excess of $45.

One of the first steps in probability analysis is to attempt to justify the concept of the transaction; that is, why Company A wants to buy Company B, why Company B wants to sell, or why the two companies want to merge.

There are essentially three major reasons for a company to acquire another company: The buyer may be purchasing undervalued assets; the buyer is getting net cash-flow benefits; or the buyer wants to get into a specific business, perhaps in order to round out a product line or achieve some form of vertical integration where the cost of acquiring an ongoing business is less than the start-up costs of a similar business.

In order to justify the transaction, the arbitrageur prepares pro forma financial statements to see how the buying company's income statement and balance sheet are affected by the transaction. Whether the purchase was for the undervalued assets or for improved cash flow becomes apparent from this financial analysis. The purchaser's strategic reasons may not be determined from the financial statements but may become apparent from studying and thoroughly understanding the operations of both companies. This will help determine if increased efficiencies and higher combined earnings would result from the transaction.

Another consideration in evaluating the probability of the transaction closing is the past history of the buyer and the seller in closing deals after they are announced. This includes whether the seller has backed out of transactions in the past and, if so, why.

The arbitrageur must also look closely at the proxy statements of both companies. Where a substantial number of insiders or other persons with controlling interest in the target company have agreed to a deal, there is a greater likelihood of the deal closing.

Friendly vs. unfriendly transactions. Friendly transactions have a greater likelihood of closing than hostile transactions do. However, the potential reward for hostile transactions has proven greater. When assessing the probability of a hostile transaction closing, the arbitrageur must consult with an attorney to assess the possible legal defenses to the transaction and determine the prospects of these defenses. Since these will involve a considerable expenditure of time and money on the part of the acquiring corporation, the investor must make a determination of how badly the buyer wants the target company and whether its management is willing to undergo the expense and pressure required to bring a hostile deal to completion.

When to Buy and Price Determination

If after the foregoing analysis the arbitrageur has made a decision to buy, the timing of the investment and the price of the purchase must be decided.

In general, the arbitrageur is willing to pay a price that offers a potential reward high enough to cover carrying costs and to compensate for the perceived level of risk undertaken.

Assume, in the previous example of the cash tender at $45, that the transaction is hostile. In addition, the arbitrageur and counsel felt that there were no regulatory requirements that would stretch the timing beyond the normal period and that there were no antitrust problems. The investor would be willing to pay a price that would result in a lower potential return due to the lower perceived risk of the deal falling apart or being delayed. Under the same circumstances, the arbitrageur might also be willing to pay a price in excess of the tender price if it was felt that the only alternative for the target company would be to solicit a friendly take-over bid by another company at a higher price. The value analysis made before would be important in setting guidelines. If the arbitrageur felt that a realistic price for a corporation to pay for the target would be $50 per share, the arbitrageur might be willing to buy the stock for as high as $47 or $48. At that point, the $45 bid is reasonably secure from the first bidder. Thus, the price of $48 offers the potential of a $2-to-$3 profit if the target company can arrange a friendly takeover at $50 per share, and offers a maximum risk of $2 or $3 a share if no higher offer is forthcoming and the company is acquired at $45 per share. If the shares have been bid up to $55 per share, the arbitrageur should re-evaluate his estimate of the value of the target company, since market circumstances are suggesting that his view is incorrect. If, after a re-evaluation, the investor still thinks that $50 is the maximum price that another corporation would be willing to pay, the investment should not be made.

In a cash merger transaction, the trading decisions are somewhat different. Company A has announced an agreement in principal to acquire Company B in a cash merger valued at $50 per share of the Company B stock. The arbitrageur has done the legal and fundamental research and has concluded that there are no reasons that the transaction should not be completed. The investor estimates that it should take approximately three months before the proxy statement is sent to the shareholders and the deal would be most likely to close the day of the shareholders' meeting. Company B's stock would trade in the market at some discount from the $50 per share that the investor expects to receive in approximately four months. This discount represents the perceived risk of the transaction not consummating and the cost of funds to the investor.

In cases where the investor feels that the announced price is significantly below his appraisal of the target's value, he may buy stock at a premium from the deal price, in the hope that another buyer will emerge who shares this view. Nevertheless, if management of the target company had agreed to the $50, and obviously felt that the price was a fair one, the arbitrageur must consider that the management of the target knows the values better than he does and that a higher bid is unlikely. The arbitrageur wants to buy at a price that gives a potential high enough to compensate for his perception of the level of risk undertaken relative to the probability of the transaction closing. On a practical basis, however, the price at which the arbitrageur can buy is actually dictated by the market, which in turn reflects the collective opinion of other investors. As opinions change, the price is subject to change.

Importance of monitoring. All announced risk-arbitrage deals must be monitored constantly, both from the trading aspect and from the fundamental aspect. At certain prices, given certain circumstances, the buy, sell, and hold decisions must always be re-evaluated. The stock of any target in almost any announced deal can be an attractive investment at some price.

One form of timing management is to try to anticipate the various news announcements likely to be made to the public during the course of the transaction, and then to use these events and the reaction of the stock to these announcements as opportunities to buy or sell.

An example might be to buy a certain percentage of one's ultimate position when the companies have reached an agreement-in-principal stage, then increase the position after the respective boards have approved the transaction, and perhaps increase the holding again after the definitive agreement has been signed. Announcements such as these reduce the risk in the transaction. On the other hand, since the risk is reduced, the price of the target stock tends to approach the deal price. In other words, the spread or discount should get narrower after announcements such as these are made; although the potential risk may have decreased, so has the potential reward.

This type of trading decision can work in the opposite manner where some negative news does not stop the transaction, but adds additional uncertainty and risk by lengthening the time needed for the transaction to close. This might cause a drop in the stock of the target company, but if the arbitrageur feels that it will not ultimately pose a problem to the transaction, he can use this piece of negative news as an opportunity to increase the investment at a more favorable price. Thus, while the risk in the transaction has increased, the potential reward has also increased by presenting the opportunity to buy at a lower price.

Hedging One's Bets

The rise of the listed options markets has created several alternative means of investing and hedging in risk-arbitrage situations. As in all parts of the investment decision, the use of options requires the investor to make specific judgments on the timing and probability of the deal closing. In addition, the investor must make a decision on the level of risk to be assumed and how he wants to play the deal. (See article on Options — Puts and Calls, elsewhere in this volume.)

Example. Assume that the stock of a target company is selling at $57 with a $60 cash merger expected to be closed in approximately one month, and that the stock of the target company will sell at about $30 if the transaction does not close. If the deal closes on time, the return would be 63 percent annualized.

If, after all the previously described work had been done, the investor felt there was a high probability of the deal closing, he would buy the stock of the target company and wait. However, if he wanted to limit risk but earn a lower return, he would also buy put options (options to sell stock at a fixed price) of the target company. In this case, the $50 puts would be about $1 or $1.25 going out more than one month. Purchase of these puts would add to the cost of the position. If the deal closed on time, the annualized return would be reduced to 36 percent. However, if the deal was not consummated and the stock went to $30, the loss would be only $8.25 per share and not $27 per share because the value of the $50 puts with the stock at $30 is $20. Thus, the investor would lose $27 on the stock position, but make $18.75 on the put position. This assumes that the investor was fully hedged; that is, an equal amount of stock and puts had been purchased. Very often, depending on instincts, the investor might only hedge part of the position.

Use of call options. It is also possible to use call options (options to buy stock at a fixed price) either as a partial hedge (selling the calls against one's stock position) or as substitutes for stock. The latter approach offers less flexibility because of problems in timing. However, in-the-money options (options whose underlying stock price has reached the option price) can be purchased with the intent to exercise at the proper time and perhaps save carrying costs. Out-of-the-money options can be used as a way of increasing the rate of return if the deal closes. The decision to purchase call options is based on calculation of the timing of the deal and the premium at which the options trade, as well as the investor's feeling for the probability. However, if the deal is delayed longer than anticipated, the investor owning the nearer series of options may have in effect bought the stock at too high a price. On the other hand, by purchasing the further out series, both the potential return and the risk would be reduced.

Size of the Position

The decision on position size is part of the portfolio management function of a risk-arbitrage investor. One approach that has worked well over time is to be concerned with the overall risk management of the portfolio as opposed to investing with the emphasis on potential reward.

Since the investor has a fixed amount of investment capital, it is important to determine what percentage of capital it is advisable to have at risk at any one time. After that decision is made, the arbitrageur calculates the amount of total dollar risk to be assumed in any one particular deal. Since he has already estimated what the various investments would be worth if the respective deals were terminated, the size of any position is an easily derived figure. If the arbitrageur is willing to live with $100,000 of risk on the XYZ deal, and if he has estimated that the target's stock will sell for $10 less than his cost if the deal was terminated, then the investor should buy no more than 10,000 shares of the target.

Deciding how much risk one can assume in a particular deal, however, is not simple. The same factors of reward and probability again become the most important decisions. The investor must judge and assess the probabilities. He may be willing to assume $100,000 of risk in the XYZ deal and assume $1 million of risk in the ABC deal because he has a stronger conviction of the ABC deal closing. However, it is important not to be overinvested in any one deal that does not close, and that will outweigh the returns earned by the careful and thoughtful work put into ten deals that do close.

Stock Mergers

Many transactions are for exchanges of securities and require additional analysis of the buying company as well as the combined company. The trading decisions are more complex.

Example. Assume Company A's stock is selling at $50 per share and it announces a friendly acquisition of Company B on a share-for-share basis. The arbitrageur must pay particular attention to the combined company because that will determine how Company A's stock reacts in the market. Shares of Company B will trade at a discount from the value of Company A regardless of where Company A trades. In this case, Company A intends to pay, in effect, $50, and Company B has accepted a $50 deal. It is estimated that it will take four months for the deal to be completed.

If Company A stock goes down because the market perceives the combined company as less attractive, or the pro forma income statement shows a dilutive effect on earnings per share, the value to Company B is no longer $50, and thus there is additional risk of the transaction being terminated. On the other hand, there is a possibility that another buyer may be willing to pay hard value of $50, since the target has in effect said that a $50 price is acceptable. To compensate for this possibility, many exchanges of securities are agreed to as a fixed-dollar amount of the buyer's stock. For example, Company A would pay $50 worth of its stock for a share of Company B, but in no event less than 0.9 share or more than 1.1 shares. Thus, the price of Company A could range from $45.45 to $55.55 and the value would hold $50.

Since the amount being paid is a variable amount even if collared, the arbitrageur usually does not just buy the stock of the target, but attempts to lock in profit by simultaneously selling short the securities being offered by the buyer. Thus, the decision to set it up also includes a decision on when to sell short the acquiring company. In this example, if Company A was at $48 and Company B was at $45, the ratio would then be 1.04 shares of A ($50) for one Company B. Company B would be at a 10 percent discount and, assuming four months to completion, the annualized rate of return would be 33.3 percent.[1] If the arbitrageur believes that Company A stock has temporarily overreacted, and will shortly move higher, the investor may merely purchase Company B stock and wait a few days in the hope that Company A stock goes higher before selling it short. Market feel is very important here. As can be realized, it is unusual for the arbitrageur to only buy target company shares in an exchange-of-securities transaction and bear the dual risk of the deal terminating and a decline in the value of Company A when an attractive profit can be guaranteed by the short sale.

---

[1] Since the price of Company A will vary during the time period, the companies generally determine the final ratio based on some average price of Company A during a specific period prior to the shareholders' meeting.

Following through with the same example, the mechanics would be as follows. The arbitrageur would buy 1,000 shares of Company B for $45,000 and sell short 1,040 shares of Company A for $49,920. After the deal closes, the arbitrageur can deliver the 1,040 Company A shares received in exchange for his Company B shares, to cover the short and keep the $49,920. Hence, the Company B shares cost $45,000, and the gross profit will be $4,920 on a $45,000 investment for four months.

ATTRACTIVE FEATURES

Risk arbitrage is an attractive form of investing for several reasons. Under careful management, the gross return on investment can exceed 40 percent annually before deducting major expenses such as interest charges and legal fees. Most arbitrage investors use leverage or margin. Under the most stringent requirements, the investor would be subject to Regulation T requirements, currently 50 percent (for $1 of equity, the investor can have $2 of positions and pay interest on the borrowed $1). This can increase with the form of investment vehicle. Certain risk-arbitrage partnerships are able to leverage their equity four or five times over. Staying with the more conservative 50 percent margin, however, the investor can still earn in excess of 50 percent net on equity.

Risk-arbitrage investing can be exciting. The successful arbitrageur must be able to play several roles. The investment decision must be reached after analyzing the deal from the point of view of the corporate executive, attorney, accountant, securities analyst, trader, investment banker, and portfolio manager.

REPRESENTATIVE TYPES OF INVESTORS

Until approximately ten years ago, risk-arbitrage investing was predominantly used by a few member firms of the New York Stock Exchange (NYSE) as a profitable application of capital. While this continues to be true, publicity given to this area has caused an increasing number of member firms to establish risk-arbitrage departments, and has led to the creation of a growing number of limited partnerships set up to do risk-arbitrage investing exclusively. These limited partnerships generally become members of the NYSE and are registered broker-dealers for certain tax and capital reasons. Some of these benefits are generally not available to individual investors. In addition, costs of funds, short-sale credits, and transactions costs — not to mention legal fees — combine to create an environment that generally would place risk arbitrage beyond the scope of most investors.

Certain brokerage houses that have their own risk-arbitrage departments also take on customers. This, plus the limited partnerships mentioned above, afford the investor the opportunity to participate in the profits from a professionally managed risk-arbitrage portfolio. In neither of these cases does the investor get a chance to become involved in the investment decision-making.

GLOSSARY

arbitrage — The practice of buying and selling a security simultaneously to take advantage of price differences existing at the moment of purchase and sale.

arbitrageur — An investor who practices arbitrage.

collared offer — An exchange offer in which lower and upper limits are set for the number of shares of the offering company that will be exchanged for a share of the target company.

discount — The amount by which a security is selling below a specific value. In a tender offer at $50 per share, if the stock is selling at $48, it is at a $2 or 4 percent discount.

exchange offer — An offer by one company to exchange its securities for those of another company or for different securities of the same company.

in-the-money option — An option whose underlying stock price has reached the option price.

leveraged buy-out — A merger in which the acquiring company borrows a large part of the purchase price, using the assets of the acquired company as collateral.

merger — The acquisition of one company by another, for cash or securities, with the approval of the board of directors and the shareholders of the target company and, sometimes, of the shareholders of the purchasing company as well.

out-of-the-money option — An option whose underlying stock price has not reached the option price.

premium — The amount by which a security is selling above a specific value.

pro forma statements — Financial statements of both parties to a transaction, prepared as if the transaction had already taken place.

proxy statement — A statement containing detailed information on the basis of which parties to a proposed merger, especially shareholders of the target company, can make an informed decision.

risk arbitrage — Purchase or sale of a security at a discount or premium from a stated value with the hope that the security will eventually reach the stated value; may be undertaken in all forms of corporate reorganization and capital restructuring; unlike pure (riskless) arbitrage, involves risk of capital loss.

riskless arbitrage — Simultaneous purchase and sale of a security in different markets without risk of capital loss.

self-tender — A company tendering for some of its own shares.

spin-off or split-up — A form of corporate reorganization in which one corporation is split up into two or more corporations, each with its own securities trading in the market.

target company — A company that is the object of a take-over bid by another company.

tender offer — A bid by one company to purchase for cash or securities all or a percentage of the shares of another company.

white knight — A more desirable bidder for a target company in a hostile take-over battle; the white knight is generally selected by the target as the means of thwarting the original bidder.

SUGGESTED READING

Periodicals

"All About Arbitrage." *Economist* 270:25, March 1979.

Gillis, J.G. "Inside Information Development." *Financial Analyst Journal* 36:10-11, March 1980.

Stavrou, C.C. "Profits in Arbitrage: The Opportunities Have Rarely Been Greater." *Barrons* 59:12, January 1979.

Strickland, D.G. "How an Investment Banker Prepares a Company for a Tender Offer." *Management Accounting* 61:26-28, Fall 1980.

"Takeover Crisis." [Special Report] *Institutional Investor* 13:31-68, June 1979.

Thompson, D.N. "Brascan vs. Woolworth — It Would Have Been the Largest Hostile Takeover in History." *Business Quarterly* 44:69-79, Autumn 1979.

Welles, C. "Inside the Arbitrage Game." *Institutional Investor* 15:41-44, August 1981.

Art Nouveau and Art Deco

J. Alastair Duncan *

BASIC CHARACTERISTICS

The Art Nouveau/Art Deco market has emerged as a major area within the decorative arts during the last five years. Encompassing works of art from both the turn-of-the-century period and the 1920s, the market includes virtually every medium: jewelry, glass, furniture, posters, prints, sculpture, and architectural fixtures, for example. Only paintings fall into other specialized auction categories.

Art Nouveau

The Art Nouveau period, covering roughly the years from 1895 to the beginning of World War I, incorporates a wide range of botanical, entomological, and female forms as its principal motifs; bats, dragonflies, and scantily clad nymphs fly, swarm, and clamber across every kind of object of the period. This new art, or Art Nouveau as it was named by one of the movement's leading figures, the dealer Samuel Bing, evolved at the end of the nineteenth century from the total rejection of the pastiche of earlier styles that had dominated interior design through the 1800s.

In the nineteenth century, Classical, Gothic, Renaissance, and Medieval art, as well as Louis XIV, XV, and XVI ("all the Louis' " as Edmond de Goncourt later wrote) and Biedermeier were robbed of their most distinctive motifs; these in turn were applied together to mid- and late-nineteenth-century furnishings in a variety of styles known today euphemistically as Napoleon III or Victorian. By 1900, the cry in the decorative arts was for a renaissance, a rejection of all previous styles, a fresh start — hence the term "Art Nouveau." The concept was comprehensive; not only would all furniture and glassware, for example, incorporate the same range of themes, but an entire interior had to match. Furthermore, not only the tables, carpets, and lighting fixtures had to be harmonious, but also the façade of the house itself and all of its fine details, down to the very keyplate on the front door.

Art Nouveau was hugely popular for ten years as an international movement, reaching its high point at the 1900 Exposition Universelle in Paris and then falling from favor as exponents began to introduce wild excesses into the already exaggerated curves and volutes that characterized the style. World War I brought to a timely end an art movement that had risen and fallen with meteoric speed.

* J. Alastair Duncan is Senior Vice-President, Nineteenth- and Twentieth-Century Decorative Arts, of Christie, Manson & Woods International, Inc., New York.

Art Deco

Art Nouveau was superseded in the early 1920s by what art historians now define as the Art Deco style. Not surprisingly, in a time of post-war austerity, it was the complete antithesis of the earlier style. Gone was the exuberance; in its place were stark functionalism and geometry. No longer did the whiplash-like and organic protrusions in a Guimard or Charpentier armchair, for example, disguise the fact that it was an object in which one was supposed to sit. Art Deco captured the decorative feeling of the 1920s with top-quality materials and craftsmanship allied to design on strictly functional lines.

Art Nouveau and Art Deco as a Combined Market

In an art world that has become increasingly compartmentalized in the last ten years, it is paradoxical that the two styles are invariably grouped and sold together at auction. This often leads to confusion in the public mind as to the distinction between the two and as to which preceded which. It is also curious that two styles, one following immediately after the other, should both produce such a host of highly innovative artists, designers, and craftsmen. No other period within the decorative arts field can boast so much talent within a fifty-year span. It is for this reason that Art Nouveau and Art Deco have become so widely collectable and attractive to today's investor, even though objects of these eras cannot yet be defined as antiques (in the strict sense that an antique is 100 years old). Very few investments, either in or outside of the art world, can, for example, match the recent escalation of prices for Tiffany lamps and Gallé vases. A Tiffany lamp that sold in 1976 to a dealer for $36,000 was resold at auction in 1980 for $360,000 (excluding the 10 percent buyer's premium). Likewise, a Gallé vase that sold at auction in Paris in 1973 for $4,000 recently changed hands privately for $195,000. This unprecedented rise in value within the last five to ten years has made it difficult to distinguish between those who collect Art Nouveau and Art Deco because they appreciate it and those who collect it because it is appreciating.

Primary Areas of Investment

The primary areas of investment within the Art Nouveau/Art Deco market can be divided into three main categories: art glass, jewelry, and furniture. (For a discussion of Art Nouveau/Art Deco sculpture, see article on Sculpture, elsewhere in this volume.)

Art glass. The two main exponents of glassmaking at the turn of the century were Emile Gallé in France and Louis Comfort Tiffany in the United States. Gallé's importance from an investment standpoint is concentrated on the pieces that he made himself, as distinct from those made in his atelier. Not many of these unique pieces have survived; therefore, they have strong collector appeal and investment potential. Items incorporating his more sophisticated and innovative techniques, such as marquetry, applied work, and engraved work, represent the high point of Gallé's work. There are usually several pieces worth more than $50,000 available on the market at any one time, while a select number command prices in excess of $200,000. The investor must distinguish between pieces in these price ranges and the many hundreds of industrial wares produced in Gallé's workshop for commercial purposes, a great percentage of which were manufactured between Gallé's death in 1904 and the time the firm closed in the late 1920s. Professional advice must be sought to determine what is and is not of importance.

Tiffany's value for investment purposes lies more with his lamps than with his vases. A hierarchy of lamp models has now been established, with importance assessed according to both aesthetics and rarity. Sixteen Tiffany lamps brought more than $100,000 each at Christie's in New York between 1977 and 1981, and there is no reason to believe that the market will not continue to appreciate for the most important models, even allowing for short-term reverses. Tiffany represents the capstone of American decorative arts and, as such, will continue to command enormous prices. As with Gallé's glassware, however, it is imperative to distinguish between Tiffany's great lamps and the many hundreds of less important models that were produced in his Corona Studios and that are on the market at any one time.

Tiffany's windows have a possibly greater investment potential, as they are hugely underpriced compared with the lamps. Again, it is necessary to seek professional expertise on the types of windows that have investment value. Windows that incorporate ecclesiastical or historical themes do not tend to generate much interest; those with landscapes and flowers are more eagerly sought. Similarly, Tiffany's vases are underpriced. A superb example of a Tiffany lava or Cypriote vase still can be obtained for $20,000, a relatively low price for a unique, hand-blown work of art.

Competitors of Gallé and Tiffany, in both Europe and the United States, produced some excellent glassware. The Daum brothers in Alsace-Lorraine and Steuben in Corning, New York vied for the public's fancy; however, neither has emerged as a serious contender for top prices.

Glass of the Art Deco period is not generally considered to be as important as its Art Nouveau counterpart. Some craftsmen warrant serious consideration, however. These were the French artists Marinot, Navarre, and Thuret, all of whom produced extremely modern geometric shapes utilizing highly sophisticated glass techniques.

Jewelry. Both the Art Nouveau and Art Deco eras produced a great number of top-quality jewelers. In discussing the prominent jewelers of the earlier period, it is important to stress that it was a time when tradition was broken, if only momentarily.

Jewelry has always consisted of precious gems, such as diamonds, emeralds, and rubies, set in gold and silver mounts. The Art Nouveau era, however, saw the infusion of non-precious materials into top-quality pieces. René Lalique, for example, incorporated plique-à-jour enamel, horn, tortoiseshell, ivory, and semiprecious hardstone cabochons into his major works. These cannot, therefore, be appraised primarily at their intrinsic value. Rather, their value depends on the quality of the workmanship and on the celebrity of the designer. A purchase of one of Lalique's pieces of jewelry is essentially an investment in the Lalique name, not in the number of carats or quality of stone.

Another great jewelry designer of the period was Georges Fouquet. A Parisian like Lalique, he also embellished his necklaces, tiaras, and bracelets with the same range of female, flower, and insect motifs. The third preeminent jeweler at the turn of the century was Philippe Wolfers of Brussels. Wolfers' output was very limited; so few pieces are on the market today that it is difficult to determine their relative value. The jewelry of other contemporaries, such as the Spaniard Luis Masriera and the Parisian Henri Vever, should generally be avoided for investment purposes. Similar, if not identical, in style to the work of Lalique and Fouquet, their pieces are often of inferior quality.

The Art Deco jewelers, twenty-five years later, reverted to the traditional use of precious stones mounted in gold, platinum, and silver. Most major jewelry retailers in the 1920s and 1930s, such as Tiffany & Company and VanCleef & Arpels, marketed their own range of Art Deco-style jewelry; these also have investment potential. Names associated with the best jewelry of the period include Templier, Sandoz, and the incomparable Louis Cartier. The latter's exquisite jewelry, mystery clock, and wide range of vertu objects recently formed the nucleus of several spectacular jewelry sales in Geneva. There is a timelessness and quality about Cartier's work, however, that places it beyond the average Art Deco jewelry collector's price range into that of major jewelry; for example, $360,000 was paid for a Cartier mystery clock at Christie's in 1979.

Furniture. It is a tribute to the cabinetmakers of the Art Nouveau period that numerous examples of their work have already surpassed in value those of earlier periods. A six-piece Majorelle bedroom suite, for example, recently sold for $225,000, more than top-quality Louis XIV and XV bedroom suites tend to bring today. Majorelle's inlaid grand pianos, of which five models are known to exist, sell for upward of $100,000.

The Art Nouveau era brought two great French furniture designers to the fore: Louis Majorelle and Emile Gallé, both from Nancy. Gallé, who considered his work in glass to be more important than his furniture, brought to his cabinetmaking the same botanical and entomological motifs that covered his vases and lamps. Majorelle's work is generally considered to be finer than Gallé's. His carved and inlaid exotic woods were enhanced with boldly chased ormolu mounts cast as water lilies and orchids, providing an overall impression of richness comparable to the best of Riesener and Cressent more than 100 years earlier. Gallé's furniture tends to bring prices slightly lower than Majorelle's, although certain pieces have changed hands for more than $75,000. Other prominent Art Nouveau cabinetmakers were Vallin, Gruber, Gaillard, and Colonna. Prices range from $2,000 for a tea table to $30,000 for a buffet or console.

The 1920s produced another spate of superb furniture designers, a group whose investment value is probably greater than that of Majorelle and Gallé. Highest honors are reserved for Emile-Jacques Ruhlmann, whose furniture exemplified the Art Deco dictum that form follows function. Prices for Ruhlmann's pieces are already high, and they will continue to escalate. A few pieces have exceeded $100,000, with average prices above those for the work of his contemporaries, who include Jean Dunand, Jean Dupas, Paul Follot, Süe et Mare, André Groult, and Clément Mère. All produced furniture of superior quality.

ATTRACTIVE FEATURES

An obvious attraction to the investor in Art Nouveau and Art Deco objects is that the more important pieces are extremely beautiful, providing both investment and aesthetic value. The annual cost of home insurance to cover theft or damage, however, must be offset against an item's potential resale value. (This cost is greatly reduced if the item is placed in a bank vault.) Part of the benefit of purchasing a Lalique necklace or a Ruhlmann dressing table is, of course, intangible; the satisfaction and pride that they generate can more than offset the higher return one might receive on another type of investment.

POTENTIAL RISKS

The art market is subject to the same variances that affect all aspects of the economy, such as inflation, recession, and change of government. It has, in addition, various internal pressures, such as the impact of speculation, as exemplified by the international silver market in 1980. Short-term investment should therefore be considered extremely risky; reverses can occur virtually overnight, especially in the auction world where an infinite number of factors can affect the strength of a market. For example, adverse weather conditions can close international airports, thereby preventing major buyers from attending an auction.

Most serious collectors find that they have to stretch to pay when purchasing major objects of the period. For example, they often pay tomorrow's prices today for objects they want. The Art Nouveau market tends to catch up with high prices very quickly; no sooner has an object been bought at a high price than the market adjusts upward and the price paid is considered reasonable.

Despite this tendency of the market to adjust, the purchase of Art Nouveau pieces for investment should be on a medium- or long-term basis only. The investor should not buy today to sell tomorrow, as he is unlikely to realize a profit over a short time. It is not unusual for an item to depreciate slightly in value for two years and then to increase 40 percent in the third. This means the collector must average his investment return over the three years to eliminate the annual fluctuations. Short-term liquidity will, therefore, probably generate a loss, sometimes a substantial one. Top Art Nouveau collectors often complain, when selling to upgrade their collections, that it is a collector's privilege to buy at retail and sell at wholesale. This is a well-proved axiom.

TAX CONSEQUENCES

Profit from the sale of art held by an individual for more than one year is taxable under federal law as capital gain, not as ordinary income. In certain circumstances, works of art can be exchanged tax-free for others of equal or greater value. Donation to a qualified organization of a work of art whose market value has appreciated can be used to realize a tax deduction. (See article on Tax Considerations for Collector-Investors, elsewhere in this volume.) For specific guidance in these matters, the investor should consult a professional tax adviser.

REPRESENTATIVE TYPES OF INVESTORS

Art Nouveau and Art Deco collectors tend to fall into the category of first-generation money, successful entrepreneurs in their thirties or forties who have recently been exposed to the 1900-1925 field and for whom it is therefore new and exciting. Such collectors usually have a substantial amount of capital to invest in art; there is little of potential investment value available to the smaller investor with $5,000-$25,000 to spend. As for institutional collectors, only one or two museums in the world have funds available to purchase works of art that are, at most, eighty years old.

IMPORTANT FACTORS IN BUYING AND SELLING

Using Professional Advisers

It is vital for the uninitiated collector-investor to seek professional advice before making a purchase. The Art Nouveau/Art Deco world is relatively new and formal instruction on it cannot yet be obtained. Most universities do not provide decorative art courses, and in the event they do, the faculty of such universities generally would not appraise specific works of art. One must seek instruction from people directly involved in the field, such as top dealers or auction gallery specialists. Both should guarantee the authenticity of the items they sell and provide a money-back warranty. An investor should not make a purchase until an acknowledged expert has confirmed its value. The difference in value, for example, between two vases of identical height and seemingly identical decoration may be $200,000.

Buying at Auction

Buying at auction has recently become highly fashionable. However, it presents several potential pitfalls for the investor. First, one tends to forget in the excitement of bidding that most auction houses charge a 10 percent buyer's premium. This surcharge can affect the short-term investment value of an item considerably. Five years ago, when auctions were traditionally for dealers only and no 10 percent buyer's premium existed, an investor would have made many excellent purchases. Today, ironically, a buyer may stand an equal chance of paying a wholesale price to a dealer. People frequently overpay at auction, as they believe that it is still a wholesale market. It is no longer necessarily so, however.

Second, the collector-investor must bear in mind that a large number of the truly great items in any art field never pass through auction; they exchange hands privately, often in the most clandestine circumstances. The collector cannot, therefore, assemble a collection of masterpieces at auction. Top dealers must be alerted that a specific buyer is in the market for specific top-quality pieces, if this is so. Dealers normally charge a 15 to 20 percent commission to negotiate a purchase in this manner.

CUSTODIAL CARE

Security is, of course, essential for all works of art to protect against damage as well as theft. Art Nouveau items such as glassware require extraordinary precautions, since the slightest chip or crack in a vase can render it virtually valueless for resale purposes.

Locked vitrines, safes, and bank vaults provide security for most Art Nouveau pieces. As objects have appreciated in value, so has the likelihood of their being stolen. Many of the items of the period are unique and therefore can be identified if stolen. Others, however, create problems. Tiffany lampshades and bases, in particular, were made in editions that were designed to be interchangeable. A twenty-two-inch peony lampshade, for example, can be taken off one base and placed on another, making later identification more difficult. Repatination and the professional replacement of select sections of glass make detection increasingly difficult. Lamps that were stolen on the West Coast, for example, have found their way into collections across the country without a question of provenance being raised.

GLOSSARY

Art Deco— Art produced from World War I until the mid-1930s, characterized by stylization and geometric form. Media include jewelry, glass, and furniture.

Art Nouveau— Art glass, jewelry, and furniture produced at the turn of the century, characterized by elaborate detail and a wide range of botanical, entomological, and other motifs.

cabochon— A highly polished gem without facets.

cameo glass— Glass utilizing the technique of applying one or more layers of different colored glass on top of the initial layer; the different layers are then etched or hand engraved to provide relief decoration.

champlevé— A decorative technique of enameling applied to a recessed metal ground (and therefore opaque).

coquille d'oeuf— Crushed egg shell, frequently applied on Art Deco furniture.

Cypriote (Tiffany glass)— A Tiffany glass in which the surface is given a pock-marked iridescent texture as found frequently on excavated antique glass.

dinanderie— A technique of inlaying precious or semiprecious metals into a base metal such as brass, copper, or bronze.

enamel— Pigments of metallic oxides mixed with ground glass and used as an overglaze on glass, porcelain, and metal.

Favrile— Tiffany's patent for his hand-blown glass. It is an adaptation of the Old English word "fabrile," which meant handmade.

lava— A glass produced by Tiffany in which the surface was made to resemble the iridescence of volcanic rock.

marquetry— In furniture, the creation of floral and other patterns by inserting pieces of wood or other materials into a veneer.

objet de vertu— A curio or art object, usually antique.

ormolu— Metal mount given a gold patina.

pâte de verre— Literally, glass paste; glassware formed by firing finely ground glass particles in a mold. Several colors are frequently mixed.

patination— Application of a patina to artificially age metal or wood.

plique-à-jour— A method of enameling that enables light to pass through with an effect similar to that of stained glass.

shagreen— Closely grained and stained shark skin used as a covering on Art Deco objects, table tops, etc.

CREATORS OF ART NOUVEAU/ART DECO

Bing, Samuel— German art critic who founded the Maison d'Art Nouveau, Paris.

Cartier, Louis— Foremost Art Deco jewelry designer of the 1920s and 1930s.

Colonna, Eugène— French designer who worked for Bing and later came to America.

Dunand, Jean— Prominent worker of dinanderie and lacquerwork.

Dupas, Jean— Worked in lacquer and was prominent in Paris from the mid-1920s to 1930s.

Follot, Paul— Furniture designer who began his career at La Maison Moderne (circa 1900) and reached prominence in the 1920s.

Fouquet, Georges— Designer of Art Nouveau and Art Deco jewelry.

Gaillard, Eugène— Furniture designer who worked for Bing. Gaillard was much acclaimed at the 1900 Exposition Universelle.

Gallé, Emile— Master glassmaker and furniture designer who founded the School of Nancy in 1901.

Goncourt, Edmond de— Respected art critic who worked in the late 1800s.

Groult, André— Furniture designer who worked in Paris from the late 1920s through the 1930s.

Gruber, Jacques— Furniture maker and stained-glass artist. Member of the School of Nancy.

Lalique, René— Initially, Art Nouveau's foremost jewelry artist. After 1906, he turned to commercial glassware.

Majorelle, Louis— Art Nouveau's foremost cabinetmaker. Member of the School of Nancy.

Mère, Clément— Furniture designer in the 1920s.

Ruhlmann, Emile-Jacques— Most important furniture designer of this century and an exponent of Art Deco style.

Sandoz, Edouard— Art Deco sculptor of animal bronzes.

Süe et Mare— Louis Süe and André Mare were partners in the furniture business in the 1920s.

Templier, Edouard— Art Deco jewelry designer.

Tiffany, Louis Comfort— The great American creator of art glass, especially lamps and vases, whose more innovative techniques were exemplified in Gallé's outstanding work.

Vallin, Eugène— Furniture maker and member of School of Nancy.

Wolfers, Philippe— Belgian sculptor and jeweler during Art Nouveau period.

TRADE ORGANIZATIONS

Art Appraisers of America, New York, N.Y.

Art Dealers Association of America, New York, N.Y.

Art Nouveau Chapter of the Victorian Society in America, Philadelphia, Pa.

Royal Pavillion, Brighton, England

LEADING DEALERS

Teddy Ader, Westbury, N.Y.

Areta Galleries, Miami, Fla.

De Lorenzo Gallery, New York, N.Y.

Martin Dolin, New City, N.Y.

James Frambers, St. Louis, Mo.

Barry Friedman, New York, N.Y.

Ted Ingham, Taylor, Mich.

Gladys Koch, Stamford, Conn.

Simon Lieberman, New York, N.Y.

Lyons Den, Riverhead, N.Y.

Macklowe Gallery, New York, N.Y.

Lillian Nassau, New York, N.Y.

Alice Osofsky, Hewlett Bay Park, N.Y.
Peacock Alley, Beverly Hills, Cal.
Plantation Galleries, Davison, Mich.
Primavera Gallery, New York, N.Y.
Minna Rosenblatt, New York, N.Y.
Fred Silberman, New York, N.Y.
Team Antiques, Great Neck, N.Y.
Leonard and Gerry Trent, New York, N.Y.
United Art & Antiques, Beverly Hills, Cal.

MAJOR AUCTION HOUSES

Christie, Manson & Woods International, Inc., New York, N.Y.
Phillips, New York, N.Y.
Sotheby Parke Bernet, New York, N.Y.
Sotheby's of London, New York, N.Y.

SUGGESTED READING

Periodicals

Antique Trader. Published by Babka Publishing Co., Dubuque, Iowa
Antique World. Published by Artnews, New York, N.Y.
Architectural Digest. Published by Knapp Press, Los Angeles, Cal.
Art & Auction. Published by Auction Holdings, Inc., New York, N.Y.
Connaissance des Arts. Published by Société d'Etudes et des Publications, Paris, France
Nineteenth Century. Published by Victorian Society in America, Philadelphia, Pa.

Reference Books

Arwas, Victor. *Glass Art Nouveau to Art Deco.* London, 1977.
Austellung im Münchner Stadtmuseum. *Nancy 1900 Jugendstil in Lothringen.* Munich, 1980. (It is to this that the Munich exhibition refers.)
Bloch-Dermant, Janine. *L'Art de Verre en France 1860-1914.* Paris, 1974.
Brunhammer, Yvonne. *Le Style 1925.* Paris, 1980.
Buffet-Challié, Laurence. *Le Modern Style.* Paris, 1980.
Duncan, Alastair. *Art Nouveau and Art Deco Lighting.* New York, 1978.
Galerie des Arts Décoratifs SA. *L'Art Verrier à l'Aube du XX Siècle.* Lausanne, 1973.
Garner, Phillippe. *Gallé.* London, 1977.
Lalique, Marc. *Lalique par Lalique.* Paris, 1976.
Lesieutre, A. *The Spirit and Splendour of Art Deco.* London, 1974.

McClinton, K.M. *Lalique for Collectors.* New York, 1975.
Neuwirth, Waltraud. *Das Glas des Jugendstils.* Vienna, 1973.
Percy, Charles V. *The Glass of Lalique.* London, 1978.
Rheims, Maurice. *L'Objet 1900.* Paris, 1964.

Bank Certificates of Deposit

Richard J. Blum *

BASIC CHARACTERISTICS

Definition and Origin

Certificates of deposit, commonly known as CDs, have become one of the major sources of bank funds. A certificate of deposit is a financial instrument that evidences the placement of a sum of money with a bank for a specific time period at an agreed-upon rate of interest. It is normally quoted and sold on an interest-bearing basis and may be in either negotiable or nonnegotiable form. CDs are issued by banks of all sizes and have provided these institutions with the funds with which to substantially increase their loan and investment portfolios. As Figure 1 on page 30 indicates, the value of outstanding CDs has risen from over $26 billion at the end of 1970 to over $132 billion at the end of 1981.

Over the past twenty years, interest rates have exhibited a sharp secular increase and a rise in volatility, financial institutions have experienced growing competition for lendable funds, and federal regulations on the creation of financial instruments have been relaxed. As a result, CDs have evolved from a rather simple beginning and are now available in a variety of forms. These different forms have been developed to make the CD attractive to a wide range of investors.

The major determinant of a CD's value, regardless of the form of issuance, is the creditworthiness of the issuer. The value of a CD issued in negotiable form, however, is also dependent on its worth in the secondary market. This in turn is influenced by the CD's maturity and its rate of interest relative to prevailing market rates of interest on CDs with similar maturities.

A CD should not be confused with a time deposit or bank paper. A time deposit is an insured bank deposit not evidenced by a negotiable instrument. A bank paper is not a bank deposit, but a non-insured negotiable debt instrument issued by a bank holding company or one of its non-bank subsidiaries.

Regulatory Impact

Regulation Q of the Federal Reserve Board governs the rate of interest that banks may pay on CDs. Since 1973, Regulation Q has been suspended on amounts of $100,000 or more for all maturities. Banks, therefore, may pay whatever

* Richard J. Blum is a Vice-President of The First National Bank of Chicago.

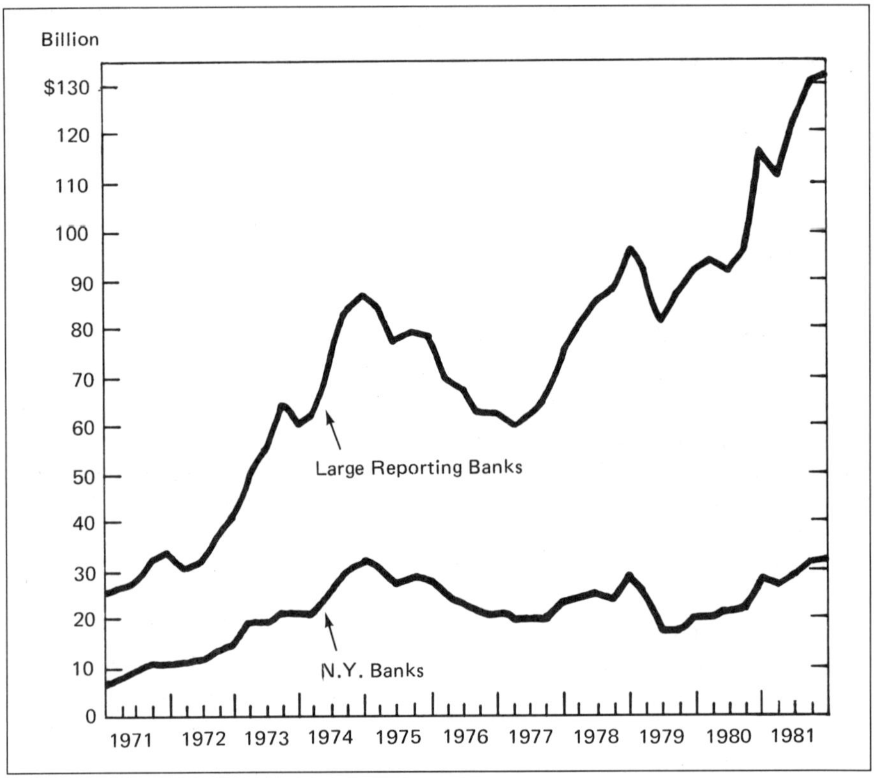

FIG. 1. Outstanding CDs of Large Reporting Banks and New York City Banks
SOURCE: *Federal Reserve Bulletin*

market rate is required to attract these large deposits. On amounts less than $100,000, Regulation Q remains in effect and limits the rate that may be paid to certain maximums. These maximums generally increase as the maturity of the CD increases.

As a result of Regulation Q, CDs are effectively divided into those that total $100,000 or more and those that total less than $100,000. CDs totaling $100,000 or more may have fixed or variable rates. Most of these CDs are in negotiable form and those of major banks may be traded in the secondary market. Smaller savings CDs in amounts less than $100,000 are nonnegotiable and thus cannot be traded in the secondary market.

Insurance on demand and savings accounts, as well as on CDs and other time accounts, is provided by the Federal Deposit Insurance Corporation (FDIC). Currently, each depositor's accounts are insured in the aggregate for $100,000.

Until 1981, interest on all CDs was subject to federal income taxes. The Economic Recovery Tax Act of 1981, however, authorized a new type of CD, which has a tax-exempt feature. The new CD, commonly called an "All-Savers Certificate," is sold to individuals and allows them to deduct the interest earned, up to certain levels, from their federal income tax returns. Interest on other CDs continues to be taxable under federal tax law.

TYPES OF CDs

The financial evolution of the CD over the past twenty years has resulted in the development of three main categories. These categories are the fixed-rate CD, the variable-rate CD, and the savings CD. The large, fixed-rate CD is the oldest and most common type, and was used by banks to compete against other fixed-rate short-term instruments such as Treasury bills and commercial paper. The variable-rate CD was designed by banks in a variety of forms to attract investors who wanted some protection against highly volatile interest rate movements. By giving investors some protection against interest rate movements, banks were able to extend the maturities of their CDs and thus take advantage at that time of lower bank reserve requirements on longer-term CDs. The savings CD has been developed in all its various forms in an attempt to appeal to individual customers with smaller sums of money and to counter the heavy competition by other financial institutions for consumer deposits. Each of these types of CD is discussed below.

Fixed-rate negotiable CDs. These are issued for a specific amount at a specific rate for a specific number of days. The rate is quoted on an interest-bearing basis, and the time factor uses actual number of days on the basis of a 360-day year.

The formula for the interest calculation is as follows:

$$I = PRT$$

where I = Interest
P = Principal amount deposited
R = Rate of interest expressed as a percentage
T = Time expressed as the exact number of days from date of deposit to maturity divided by 360

Example: Interest on a $1 million CD for 180 days at 12% equals ($1 million × .12 × 180/360) or $60,000.

A specimen negotiable CD issued according to the terms of the above example is given in Figure 2 on page 32.

Face amount. Large negotiable CDs are issued for any amount ranging from $100,000 to $1 million. Trades of $1 million are considered round-lot trades by money center banks, and individual transactions can exceed $100 million. Investors who may have to sell a CD in the secondary market prior to maturity should request $1 million denominations at the time of issuance. Negotiable CDs are

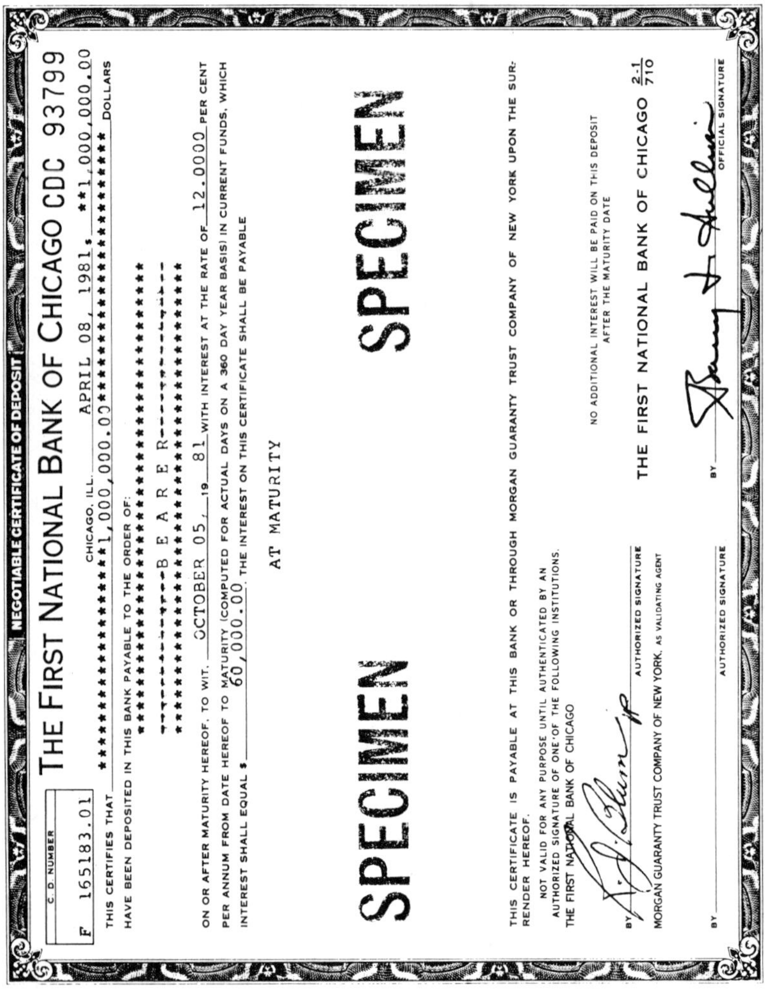

NEGOTIABLE CERTIFICATE OF DEPOSIT

C. D. NUMBER F 165183.01

THE FIRST NATIONAL BANK OF CHICAGO CDC 93799

CHICAGO, ILL. APRIL 08, 1981

THIS CERTIFIES THAT ****************1,000,000.00**************** $ **1,000,000.00 DOLLARS

HAVE BEEN DEPOSITED IN THIS BANK PAYABLE TO THE ORDER OF:

B E A R E R

ON OR AFTER MATURITY HEREOF, TO WIT, OCTOBER 05, 19 81 WITH INTEREST AT THE RATE OF 12.0000 PER CENT PER ANNUM FROM DATE HEREOF TO MATURITY (COMPUTED FOR ACTUAL DAYS ON A 360 DAY YEAR BASIS) IN CURRENT FUNDS, WHICH INTEREST SHALL EQUAL $ 60,000.00. THE INTEREST ON THIS CERTIFICATE SHALL BE PAYABLE

AT MATURITY

SPECIMEN SPECIMEN

THIS CERTIFICATE IS PAYABLE AT THIS BANK OR THROUGH MORGAN GUARANTY TRUST COMPANY OF NEW YORK UPON THE SURRENDER HEREOF.

NOT VALID FOR ANY PURPOSE UNTIL AUTHENTICATED BY AN AUTHORIZED SIGNATURE OF ONE OF THE FOLLOWING INSTITUTIONS. THE FIRST NATIONAL BANK OF CHICAGO

BY ________ AUTHORIZED SIGNATURE

MORGAN GUARANTY TRUST COMPANY OF NEW YORK, AS VALIDATING AGENT

BY ________ AUTHORIZED SIGNATURE

NO ADDITIONAL INTEREST WILL BE PAID ON THIS DEPOSIT AFTER THE MATURITY DATE

THE FIRST NATIONAL BANK OF CHICAGO 2-1/710

BY ________ OFFICIAL SIGNATURE

FIG. 2. Specimen Negotiable CD
SOURCE: Author's data.

normally issued in bearer form. Those CDs that are issued in registered form can be negotiated upon proper indorsement of the instrument.

Maturities. Maturities of negotiable CDs range from 14 days to 5 years. Most CDs, however, are issued for maturities ranging from 14 to 180 days. Investors will pick specific dates within this period in order to provide cash for tax, dividend, and other known payments. In addition, shorter-term CDs have less market risk should they have to be sold in the secondary market.

Purchase and redemption. Large negotiable CDs are usually issued at the main office of the issuing bank. Major money center banks, however, will also issue the CD through an agent bank in New York. Payment for CDs is made by the buyer in immediately available funds, and principal and interest are repaid in immediately available funds. Payment is normally effected by charging the buyer's account at the bank issuing the CD or by instructing the buyer's safekeeping agent to pay immediately available funds to the issuer upon delivery of the CD to the specified agent. CD trades are usually settled on a cash basis (same day), but regular settlement (next day) and skip-day settlement (two days forward) can also be arranged.

Maturing CDs must be presented to the issuing bank or a designated agent in order to receive payment of principal and interest. CDs that pay semiannual interest must also be presented in similar fashion in order for the investor to receive interest payments. Regulation Q does not allow banks to pay additional interest on CDs that are presented after the maturity date.

Discount CD. A discount CD is a recently developed variety of fixed-rate CD. This instrument, like a Treasury bill, is sold to investors at a cost that is less than its stated maturity value. The difference between cost and maturity value is the investor's interest. The rate of return on this instrument can be quoted on either a bank discount basis or its simple-interest equivalent. An example is given below:

- A discount CD issued for $1 million for 180 days at a bank discount rate of 12% will cost an investor $940,000. The earnings of $60,000 over the 180-day period translate into an annual simple-interest equivalent yield of 12.77%.

The physical instrument has an issue date, maturity date, and maturity value but the rate at which it was sold to the initial investor is not indicated. This type of CD appeals to dealers who can hide the rate at which it was issued from other dealers and investors. Investors who must revalue their portfolios at cost or market on a regular basis also find this instrument attractive, as the market value of a discount CD is unlikely to fall below cost unless interest rates rise very sharply soon after the CD is purchased.

Roly-poly CD. A roly-poly CD is a negotiated long-term deposit whereby a bank agrees to issue and the buyer agrees to deposit fixed amounts at periodic intervals, with the sum of the intervals equalling the total term of the deposit.

Thus, an investor may give a bank a two-year deposit in the form of four consecutive 180-day deposits. Each deposit is made at 180-day intervals with the bank giving the depositor a 180-day fixed-rate negotiable CD at the beginning of each interval. The depositor can either hold the CD to maturity or sell it in the secondary market. In return for the greater liquidity on the secondary market, the bank will pay a lower rate of interest than would be required on a standard two-year semiannual-payment CD sold without the repetitive 180-day issuance feature. CDs of this variety are sold only to large, creditworthy investors who the issuing bank feels will honor the repetitive deposit agreement.

Variable-rate CDs. This instrument was created because of the increased volatility of short-term interest rates and the former difference in reserve requirements between deposits of 180 days or more and those of 179 days or less.[1] Investors who were reluctant to invest funds for six months because of the risk of rising interest rates wanted the ability to increase their return if in fact interest rates did go higher. Banks that would pay lower reserve requirements if they could attract 180-day or longer money and that needed to fund variable-rate assets began to offer investors a variable-rate CD. The variable-rate CD and the coupon-payment CD were combined into a highly competitive instrument. The instrument normally takes on the following form: A base rate is established, which is the return on some common short-term security such as a Treasury bill or negotiable CD. The base rate used is calculated and reported by a disinterested third party so the investor is not subject to a base rate that has been determined by the issuer. To this base rate is added some negotiated spread. The payment schedule is then determined, and is usually monthly, quarterly, or semiannually.

A typical variable-rate CD is a six-month instrument whose rate is 10 to 25 basis points over the thirty-day secondary-CD rate as determined by the Federal Reserve Bank of New York. Interest is paid every thirty days. On the payment date the new rate is determined for the next thirty days. Obviously, a wide variety of bases, spreads, and payment schedules can be used depending on market conditions. Variable-rate CDs are normally sold directly to dealers who then place them with investors. Dealers normally agree with the issuing bank to buy back the CD from the investor at par on coupon change dates, and at a bid price between payment dates, thus creating a secondary market for the instrument. In the absence of such a buy-back agreement, the price of the security in the secondary market would become much more volatile. An optional variable-rate CD has

---

[1] Prior to October 30, 1980, the reserve requirements imposed on CDs under Regulation D of the Federal Reserve Board were determined by the maturity of the CD. Beginning November 2, 1978, reserves on deposits having maturities in the 30- to 179-day range were 8 percent while reserves on deposits maturing in the 180-day to four-year range were 4.50 percent. A bank paying a 12 percent simple-interest rate on a CD due in less than 180 days had an effective cost of 13.04 percent (12% ÷ 0.92). The effective cost on a 12 percent CD due in 180 days or more was only 12.57 percent (12% ÷ 0.955). Thus, banks could afford to pay a higher simple-interest rate (up to 12.46 percent) for money due in 180 days or more than they could afford to pay for money due in 179 days or less and still achieve a cost saving.

also been issued where the various spreads and bases are determined at the time of issuance, but where the maturities within the agreed-upon term are chosen by the buyer. At the end of the first maturity the investor chooses the next maturity and its associated base and spread. This process is repeated and continues until maturity.

Small savings CDs. For investors who have less than $100,000 to invest, banks have been authorized to offer a variety of nonnegotiable time deposits that are often referred to as savings CDs. All but three of these instruments (the Treasury-rate (T-rate) CD, the Small-Savers CD, and the All-Savers CD), however, operate like a passbook savings account. The rate of interest that can be paid on these passbook-type accounts increases as the maturity increases. Banks may compound the rates using a variety of formulas, which effectively increases their yield.

The methods of compounding, the minimum deposit, the number of days used as a basis for one year (360 or 365), and the interest payment schedule (monthly, quarterly, etc.) vary from bank to bank. Therefore, the investor must be careful to check the method of interest computation used by each bank in order to obtain a valid rate comparison. Interest rates on all small savings CDs are regulated by the Depository Institutions Deregulation Committee.

Six-month T-rate CD. In 1978, banks introduced the six-month T-rate CD. The rate of interest on this instrument is determined by the weekly auction average on six-month Treasury bills. The rate, carried out to three decimal places, changes on a weekly basis and is a simple rate of interest that legally may not be compounded. If the auction average for Treasury bills is 7.50 percent or higher, banks may pay up to a ¼ percent premium above the auction rate on the CD. Thus, if the Treasury bill average is 9.012 percent, a bank may pay 9.262 percent for the six-month time period. It should be pointed out the Treasury bills are sold on a discount basis, and at high rates of interest the simple-interest equivalent of this discount rate will be higher than the average plus the ¼ percent allowable premium.[2] The cost of buying Treasury bills outright should be considered when comparing the two instruments. T-rate CDs are nonnegotiable and are sold in minimum denominations of $10,000.

Small-Savers, Super-Savers, and All-Savers CDs. A two-and-a-half to four-year nonnegotiable CD, commonly referred to as a Small-Savers CD or Super-Savers CD, made its appearance in 1980. The rate on this instrument is normally pegged to the average yield on two-and-a-half-year Treasury securities as determined by the Board of Governors of the Federal Reserve System. The yield is changed biweekly, and the maximum rate that commercial banks may pay is the

---

[2] If the discount rate of a six-month Treasury bill is 12 percent, the simple-interest equivalent of that discount rate is 12.77 percent. A bank could only pay 12.25 percent simple interest or .52 percent below the comparable yield on the Treasury bill.

average yield less 25 basis points. The rate on this CD may be compounded, and thus the yield can vary considerably depending on the maturity of the instrument, the interest payment schedule, and the compounding method used.[3] No minimum denomination is required. If the biweekly average yield falls below 9.50 percent, commercial banks may pay a maximum of 9.25 percent.

The new All-Savers Certificate is of special significance to the individual investor. This instrument was authorized by the Economic Recovery Tax Act of 1981 and has a unique tax-exempt feature. Depending on the individual's filing status, lifetime income received from this source up to certain levels is exempt from federal income taxes. The instrument may be issued in minimum amounts of $500 and has a one-year maturity. The instrument can be issued during the period of October 1, 1981 to December 31, 1982. The yield that can be paid on an annual basis is 70 percent of the average investment yield on fifty-two-week Treasury bills as determined in the most recent auction. Other time certificates of deposit may be converted into the All-Savers Certificates without penalty under the following conditions: The rate on the All-Savers Certificate must be lower than that on the instrument currently held, and the maturity of the All-Savers Certificate must be greater than the maturity of the instrument currently held. The tax-exempt feature of the All-Savers Certificate is lost if it is used as collateral. If the All-Savers Certificate is paid prior to maturity, the tax-exempt feature is also lost and the normal prepayment penalty applied.

Although smaller CDs may be convenient for the consumer, the higher interest rates of recent years and federal regulations have generally made them noncompetitive on a yield basis with similar instruments sold by competing thrift institutions such as savings and loan associations and mutual savings banks. At high rates of interest, these other thrift institutions are allowed to pay at least the same rate as a bank and in many instances up to .25 percent more. Money market mutual funds have no restrictions on the rates they may pay for small deposits and have attracted billions of dollars of consumer deposits away from banks and other thrift institutions in recent years. Because of the intense competition among thrift institutions, the Depository Institutions Deregulation Committee has set 1986 as the year by which the ceilings on all small deposits will be phased out.

---

[3] The effective annual yield of a 10 percent CD compounded at different frequencies is given below.

Frequency of Compounding	*Effective Yield*
Annually	10.000%
Semiannually	10.250
Quarterly	10.381
Monthly	10.471
Weekly	10.506
Daily	10.516
Continuously	10.517

Consequently, all banks and thrift institutions will be allowed to pay market rates of interest on all their deposits.

Federal Reserve regulations regarding maximum interest rates on small CDs are subject to change. Therefore, investors should check the monthly Federal Reserve Bulletin for the current maximum rates and the maturities to which they apply.

The Primary and Secondary Markets

The primary market. A CD issued by a bank directly to the initial investor is called a primary CD. Most banks prefer to issue large negotiable CDs directly to the primary investor. Banks who issue directly to the investor have better knowledge of who owns their liabilities and increased likelihood of rolling over the CD at maturity. The rate at which a bank offers its CD directly to an investor for a specific maturity is called its primary rate. The common maturities for which banks will quote a primary CD rate are 14 to 29 days, 30 to 59 days, 60 to 89 days, 90 to 179 days, 180 to 269 days, 270 to 359 days, and one year or longer. The rates for these different maturities make up what is called a bank's primary CD scale. Banks may be willing to negotiate rates above the primary scale on large blocks of money. At money center banks, rates on a block of money above $5 million may be negotiated depending on market conditions. The primary CD scales will vary from one bank to another depending on the size and credit-worthiness of the bank, the bank's current need for funds, and the bank's outlook for interest rates.

The secondary market. A CD sold by an investor or dealer to some other dealer or investor is called a secondary CD. The secondary market came into existence for two reasons: First, primary CD holders needed liquidity and hence a market in which to sell their CDs prior to maturity; and second, banks needed another distribution network through which they could quickly sell a larger volume of CDs than their own primary network was willing to purchase. This market is composed of approximately thirty-five bank and non-bank dealers who stand ready to make a market in the CDs of the fifty largest U.S. banks and certain foreign agency banks. Today, these dealers enhance the liquidity of the CD market, and trading volume in a typical month exceeds $50 billion. (See *Leading Dealers* in this article.)

Role of dealers and brokers. Dealers in the secondary market quote bid and offered rates for CDs by the month. Thus dealers have bids or offers for June CDs or August CDs as opposed to the traditional thirty-, sixty-, ninety-day rate scale used by banks in the primary market. The spread between the bid and offered side of the market is normally 10 basis points, but this spread can narrow or widen depending on market conditions. Trades with dealers are done on a net basis with no commission added.

The minimum denomination of a CD traded in the secondary market is $1 million. Round lots are considered to be $5 million blocks. Settlement for CDs bought or sold in the secondary market is normally made on a regular basis, but cash trades can also be arranged. Settlement for CDs is in immediately available funds and delivery must be made to a bank in New York or the dealer's New York office. Dealers must make a bid on CDs but, since they cannot sell CDs short, may not have an offering rate. Dealers who underwrite a bank offering of CDs will usually charge the issuing bank a commission ranging from 2 to 10 basis points; the average for major money center banks is 5 basis points.

Brokers in CDs add liquidity to the secondary market by accepting bids and offers for CDs from a list of approved dealers. The dealer specifies the amount, the selling or buying rate, the maturity range, and the tier in which the bank's name falls. These bids and offers, which are good for a certain time period, are communicated by various means to other dealers who can sell or buy the specified securities at the broker's bid or offer price. Dealers use brokers to execute trades in a confidential manner since the dealer who consummates a trade through the broker does not know who the dealer is on the other side of the transaction. The price of buying or selling through a broker is paid by the dealer who agrees to execute a trade shown to him by the broker; the fee ranges from ½ to 2 basis points.

Yield-basis pricing. Fixed-rate CDs are sold in the secondary market on a yield basis. This yield is used to compute a dollar price and establishes the amount paid for the principal of a CD. To this amount must be added the amount of interest accrued since the date of issuance. The formula for the price of a secondary CD is as follows:

$$X = \frac{P\,(360 + R_i T_1)}{(R_s T_3 + 360)} - \frac{P R_i\, T_2}{360}$$

where X = Price of the CD in the secondary market
P = Principal of the deposit
R_i = Initial rate of the deposit expressed as a decimal
T_1 = Original term of the CD in days
T_2 = Days from issuance date to sale date
T_3 = Days from sale date to maturity date
R_s = Rate at which the CD is sold expressed as a decimal

Example: A $1 million CD issued for 180 days at a rate of 12%, which is sold at 11% after ninety days, will cost an investor $1,001,630.17. To this amount must be added $30,000 in accrued interest so that the CD costs the investor $1,031,630.17. See Table 1 on following page for other examples.

In the secondary market, banks are tiered according to how their CDs trade relative to those of the most creditworthy banks. These tierings change according

TABLE 1. Return on $1 Million CDs Sold in Secondary Market Prior to Maturity

Example	*Original Term of CD (Days)*	*Remaining Term of CD (Days)*	*Interest Rate on CD*	*Secondary Market Bid for CD*	*Principal Received*	*Accrued Interest*	*Total Proceeds*	*Per Annum Yield for Period Held*	*Gain or (Loss)*
1	180	90	12%	11%	$1,001,630.17	$30,000.00	$1,031,630.17	12.65%	$ 1,630.17
2	180	90	12	13	996,634.38	30,000.00	1,026,634.38	10.65	(3,365.62)
3	360	180	12	11	1,001,611.37	60,000.00	1,061,611.37	12.32	1,611.37
4	360	180	12	13	991,643.19	60,000.00	1,051,643.19	10.33	(8,356.81)

SOURCE: Author's data.

to various market conditions but, currently, the first tier of banks consists of the ten largest ("top ten") domestic banks. In the second tier are certain large regional banks. Other regional banks and large foreign agency banks fall into the third tier. CDs of banks in the second tier currently trade 5 to 15 basis points in yield above first-tier banks, while those of third-tier banks trade 25 to 50 basis points in yield above first-tier banks. In periods of tight money and increasing interest rates the spread between the rates paid by top ten banks and those paid by lower-tier banks expands, while in periods of easier money and declining rates this spread contracts. The tiering process also affects the rate at which banks can issue CDs in the primary market. Large investors who need the liquidity provided by the secondary market will exact the credit-risk premium at the time of purchase by requiring the issuing bank in a lower tier to pay a higher rate. Small, local-bank CDs may be excellent credit risks but, because they are not known outside their local markets, are not traded in the secondary market. Sophisticated investors may demand a liquidity premium because these local-bank CDs are less liquid. However, because these smaller banks may not compete in their local market with larger banks, or are not attempting to obtain funds from large investors, many can issue CDs at rates equal to or lower than those paid by large money center banks.

ATTRACTIVE FEATURES

Safety and Current Return

The CD provides investors with safety of principal and attractive current return. While the creditworthiness of the approximately 15,000 banks in the United States obviously varies, no investor has lost principal by investing in large CDs with major banks since their introduction in 1961. While there is no guarantee that a major bank could not fail in the future, federal regulatory agencies have in the past merged weak or failing banks with stronger partners or assisted them with large loans in order to avoid putting the institution into bankruptcy. As a result, federal regulatory agencies have not been forced to contend with the potential financial panic that could arise from a major bank failure. In addition, the FDIC insurance of $100,000 on all accounts, including CDs, has acted to build the confidence of the smaller investors and avoid the bank runs that were all too prevalent during the 1930s. This stability of the banking system over the past two decades should give investors confidence that the principal of their CDs is highly protected.[4]

The spread between the rate on ninety-day secondary CDs and the rate on like-maturity Treasury bills has averaged 118 basis points from February 1973 through April 1981. As mentioned earlier in this article, this spread has averaged

---

[4] Only $14.5 million has not been paid to depositors of the 558 insured banks that failed during the period 1934-1979. *1979 Annual Report of the Federal Deposit Insurance Corporation,* page 15.

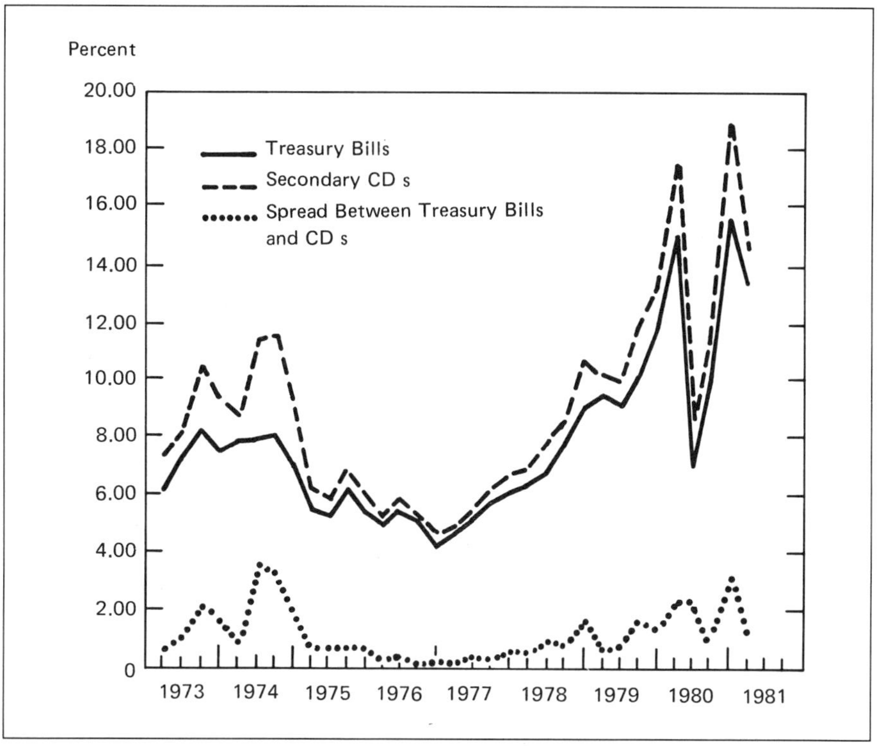

FIG. 3. Rate and Spread Table — Three-Month Treasury Bills and Secondary CDs
SOURCE: Bank of America N.T. and S.A.

as low as 25 basis points or as high as 333 basis points in various months during this period. Figure 3 shows the movement in Treasury-bill rates and secondary-CD rates over the eight-year time frame.

When yields on CDs are compared with those of other money market instruments at various maturities, the rankings from lowest yield to highest yield are generally the following: Treasury bills, U.S. government agency securities, CDs, bankers' acceptances, commercial paper, Eurodollar deposits.

Liquidity and Convenience

The liquidity of major bank CDs is provided by the large secondary market. Trades of $25 million to $50 million are quite common in this market, and investors in major bank CDs should have little problem selling them prior to maturity. As recent financial history has shown, short-term interest rates can be highly volatile, and some principal can be lost by an investor who sells a CD prior to maturity in a falling secondary market. Equally possible, however, is the gain that investors may receive if they sell a CD in a rising secondary market. See Examples 1 and 3 in Table 1 on page 39 for an illustration. Investors who wish to speculate on short-term interest rate movements will find the CD to be an excellent medium for this purpose.

A CD can also be used as collateral against a loan. The rate on the loan using CDs as collateral is determined by the lending institution. Regulation Q, however, requires that a bank lending money to customers who use their own CD as collateral must charge a minimum of one percent above the rate of interest being paid on the CD. Regulation Q does not apply if a bank loans against the CD of some other bank. A bank is allowed to prepay a CD if asked by a customer, but it has no obligation to prepay it. If the bank does pay it, provisions of Regulation Q require the customer to forfeit three months' interest, and the interest on the remaining term, if any, reverts to the savings passbook rate, which is currently 5.25 percent. If an All-Savers Certificate is used as collateral or prepaid, the tax-exempt feature is lost.

Buying a CD is a very convenient transaction to execute, particularly if the customer already has other banking relationships with the issuing bank. The investor merely has to call the institution, obtain the necessary rate quotations, and decide the amount and maturity he wishes to purchase. The bank will charge the customer's account, issue the CD, hold it in safekeeping, and credit the proceeds at maturity back to the customer's account. No visits to the bank are necessary. The statement and safekeeping receipt plus the advice of debit and credit to the investor's account give accurate data for budget and tax purposes.

POTENTIAL RISKS

Credit and Market Risks

The large negotiable CD, like all investments, is subject to a number of risks. An investor should consider the credit and market risks before buying a CD. These two risks influence the rate at which the CD is issued in the primary market and have an increased effect on the rate at which the CD can be sold in the secondary market. These risks may exist individually or collectively and may change in magnitude depending on market conditions.

Although the U.S. banking system has shown excellent financial strength since World War II, investors should examine the creditworthiness of the banks with which they place CDs. One method of analyzing a bank's credit standing is to observe the tier in which a bank's CDs trade in the secondary market. This tiering process is heavily influenced by a bank's credit standing in the national market. Another method of analyzing a bank's credit rating is to review the bond and commercial paper ratings of the holding company that owns the bank. Moody's Investor's Service, Inc. and Standard & Poor's Corporation both rate long-term bond debt and short-term commercial paper. Bank ratings published by Keefe, Bruyette & Woods, Inc., and others, enable the investor to make a comparison among individual banks. Only after he has made a credit analysis of the issuing bank can the investor determine the rate that should be received from that bank, given the rates posted by other banks in the market.

Sale in a rising-interest environment. When evaluating market risk, the investor should consider the effects that a substantial increase in interest rates will have on the value of CDs that have to be sold prior to maturity. In a rising-rate environment, an accidental or deliberate mismatch of assets and liabilities can be very costly either in terms of actual losses or in foregone opportunities. Inaccurate cash-flow projections could force investors to sell the CDs prior to maturity in order to raise necessary cash. Investors who forecast declining interest rates and buy CDs expecting to sell them at a profit prior to maturity may later find that interest rates are in fact rising, and would thus be forced to sell in order to reduce their losses. Examples 2 and 4 in Table 1 on page 39 indicate the change in value of a 12 percent CD being sold in the secondary market at a 13 percent rate. It should also be noted from Table 1 that the longer the remaining term on the CD, the greater the potential loss in principal given the same one percent increase in interest rates. As interest rates have become more volatile in recent years, the market risk on longer CDs has appreciably increased.

Analyzing the CD–Treasury bill spread. Another method of evaluating market risk is to look at the yield spread between CDs and Treasury bills. In September 1977 yields on ninety-day secondary CDs averaged 5.32 percent, and the rate on three-month Treasury bills averaged 5.06 percent, producing a yield spread of 26 basis points. In December 1980 the yield on ninety-day secondary CDs averaged 18.95 percent and the rate on three-month Treasury bills averaged 15.61 percent; in this instance, the spread was 334 basis points. While a large portion of the spread change between the two periods represents a change in investors' perception of credit risk, another portion represents a change in the investors' perception of the market risk of CDs.

During periods of tight money, the spread between Treasury bills and CDs widens as banks bid up the price for funds and investors seek increased marketability in Treasury bills. As interest rates decline, this spread narrows. Dealers are also not as willing to take on as large a block of CDs at the bid price when interest rates are rising as they are when interest rates are falling because of the increased risk of losses in a rising-rate environment. Investors who purchase the CDs of smaller banks (below the top fifty banks in the country) cannot be guaranteed marketability of the instrument in the secondary market at any time unless the local issuing bank, as agent, can arrange to find a buyer.

TAX CONSEQUENCES

The federal tax consequences of owning CDs are very straightforward. Corporations may use either a cash or an accrual method of accounting for the tax liability on interest received from fixed- or variable-rate CDs. If a corporation purchases a fixed- or variable-rate CD at a discount in the secondary market and holds it to maturity, the gain is normally taxed at the short-term capital gains rate unless the CD had a maturity date greater than one year at the time of purchase. The long-term capital gains rate will generally apply to the discount on a CD purchased on the secondary market that has a maturity greater than one year at the time of purchase. Any premium on a CD purchased in the secondary market would have to be amortized over the term of the CD.

Banks and certain other entities, which do not enjoy long-term capital gains treatment on gains realized from the sale of fixed-income securities, will have the gains treated as ordinary income. The tax law as regards original-issue discount would apply to a CD with a term exceeding one year and that is purchased at a discount directly from the issuing bank. A buyer subject to federal income taxes may have to amortize the discount over the life of the CD. If an original-issue discount CD is sold prior to maturity, the price at which it is sold would have to be compared with the amortized book value to determine gain or loss. The amount of time the CD was held would determine whether the gain was short- or long-term. Interest and/or discount on CDs is also subject to taxation by state and local governments, depending on the taxing authority of those entities. Tax-exempt entities are not normally affected by tax laws as they relate to CDs.

Individuals generally do not use the accrual method and must report CD interest as income within the year it is paid. However, individuals filing separately may take a lifetime exemption of $1,000 on interest received from All-Savers Certificates, while a married couple filing jointly may take a lifetime exemption of $2,000. Individuals who suffer an interest penalty as a result of early withdrawal of funds from a CD may use the penalty as an adjustment to income during the year of withdrawal.

Since CDs are classified as deposits, they are exempt from withholding tax when the holder is a foreign entity. While the Treasury does not require banks to issue Form 1099 to holders of large negotiable CDs, banks are required to record the tax identification number and interest payable to the initial owner. They are also required to record the tax identification number and interest paid to the presenter of the CD at maturity. This information must be released to the Treasury upon their request. Banks are required to send Form 1099 to all entities holding nonnegotiable or nontransferable CDs.

REPRESENTATIVE TYPES OF INVESTORS

Large CDs are purchased by a wide range of investors. Corporations are the largest purchasers, followed in importance by financial institutions and governmental bodies. Foreign banks and governments are also large buyers, as are nonprofit organizations and wealthy individuals.

Corporations find CDs an attractive instrument in which to invest their surplus funds. The funds are invested to mature on dates when the corporation has a known cash outflow. Maturities are chosen to coincide with tax, dividend, supplier payment, payroll, and other known payment dates. The portfolio management guidelines vary among corporations. Some corporations buy CDs to hold to maturity while others actively trade their entire portfolio.

Financial institutions are particularly large buyers of CDs. Banks, acting in the capacity of trustee, and money market mutual funds are substantial buyers. Bank trust departments find that CDs provide attractive yields to pension funds, profit-sharing funds, and other entities for which the bank acts as trustee. As of October 1981, money market mutual funds (money funds) had grown to over $166 billion by selling shares that pay large and small investors a competitive rate of return but that are not subject to the interest rate limitations that affect banks and other thrift institutions. These money funds combine the deposits lost by banks and other thrifts into large sums and then recycle a portion of these sums back to the large money center banks in the form of CD placements. On October 21, 1981 money funds held approximately $35 billion in CDs.[5]

State and local governmental units invest large sums of tax receipts in CDs. Governmental units usually receive tax payments at particular times during the year. This inflow of tax revenue must be used to pay expenses throughout the year. As a result, the governmental unit will take the tax receipts and invest a certain portion in CDs that mature during periods when tax revenues are not being received. Banks may have to secure the funds these entities place in CDs by pledging U.S. government or suitable municipal securities as collateral against the deposit. State and local laws determine which deposits must be secured and what constitutes suitable collateral.

Foreign banks and governments have become large buyers of domestic CDs over the past ten years. During this period the United States has run substantial deficits in its balance of payments. Some of the dollars accumulated by nations that have run large surpluses — particularly OPEC nations — have been deposited with major money center banks in the form of CDs. Foreign banks have found it convenient to keep a certain portion of their dollar reserves in the form of CDs.

Wealthy individuals and nonprofit organizations such as foundations and college endowment funds are also significant purchasers of bank CDs.

IMPORTANT FACTORS IN BUYING AND SELLING

Knowledge of current market conditions and correct assessment of future trends in interest rates are key factors in the successful management of a short-term portfolio. Consequently, the investor must select those banks and dealers whose sales representatives give an accurate picture of current market conditions

---

[5] *Donoghue's Money Fund Report,* 306:2-3, October 26, 1981.

and include the outlook for the near term as well. While the prediction of interest rate movements is hardly a science, certain institutions have a better track record than others. The investor must feel confident in dealing with the various sales representatives and feel that they are interested in dealing at market prices over the long term rather than exploiting any short-term advantages. The sales representative should know where his bank or dealer firm is competitive (on the market) and where it is noncompetitive (off the market). An accurate picture of market conditions for all short-term instruments should be given to the investor by the sales representative so that the investor can weigh the options of alternative investment strategies.

Shopping the Markets

Large buyers of CDs must compare rates available from banks in the primary market with rates available from dealers in the secondary market. Buyers must also compare the amounts and maturities banks are willing to write in the primary market with those available in the secondary market. Only after such comparisons have been made can the investor make the appropriate investment decision. Rates in the secondary market normally will be 5 to 10 basis points higher than the rates quoted in the primary market. However, secondary dealers may not have the bank names and maturity dates desired by the investor.

Buying in the Primary Market

An investor who has a large block of money to place may find that by the time he executes a number of trades in the secondary market this has moved the market to lower rate levels. By buying directly from a bank in the primary market, the investor may be able to execute the order in the size necessary and for the exact maturity date desired without moving the market. Certainly on large placements, investors normally should be able to negotiate a primary rate competitive with those in the secondary market. Only after obtaining the necessary market information can the investor decide where to execute transactions and thus maximize return. Sellers of CDs should evaluate the bids of a number of dealers with respect to rate and size before executing the transaction. Given the volatility of markets in recent years, the investor must make decisions quickly in order to execute transactions at the quoted rates. Investors who have large portfolios and desire to trade actively in the market need a large number of bank and dealer contacts in order to effect a wide range of portfolio transactions at competitive prices.

Avoiding Fails and Errors

Investors should confirm all details of a transaction with the bank or dealer at the time the transaction is consummated. This confirmation process eliminates errors and misunderstandings. The investor must also give his safekeeping agent equally clear instructions with respect to all aspects of the transaction. Lack of clear instructions can result in fails, incorrect accounting entries, and time-consuming negotiations over compensation. An investor who gives clear instructions to all parties involved in a transaction has the right to expect the transaction to be completed correctly and in a timely fashion.

Setting Credit and Market Risk Standards

The investor is responsible for setting risk standards for the portfolio. In setting credit risk standards, the investor must determine which bank names are acceptable and the amount of each bank name to hold. In setting market risk standards, the investor must evaluate the accuracy of the cash-flow projections and interest rate forecast. The potential profit and loss impact of meeting unforeseen needs through forced portfolio liquidation is an important ingredient in this evaluation process. The investor should never forget that the placement of money for any term is an implicit if not explicit speculation on the movement of interest rates.

Only after setting the credit and market risk standards can the investor set goals for portfolio performance that can be monitored effectively. The portfolio manager can achieve potentially higher rates of return only by increasing the market and/or credit risks within the portfolio. Portfolio managers who are willing to accept higher market risk must be able to shift their portfolios quickly between long and short maturities as their interest rate forecast changes or as market circumstances dictate. Investors who wish to minimize market risk should confine their portfolios to shorter-term maturities.

CUSTODIAL CARE

Negotiable CDs should be held by a bank acting in its capacity as a safekeeping agent. By holding CDs at a bank, the investor avoids the financial risk of loss or theft and obtains the convenience of easy payment and accurate recordkeeping. Major banks have a specific department to pay for securities upon delivery, hold them in safekeeping, and collect principal and interest on proper maturity and payment dates. Issuing banks normally do not assess a charge for holding CDs that they have sold directly to their customers. If a CD is lost, the holder normally must post an indemnification bond before the issuing bank will pay off the instrument.

By having a bank hold the certificate, the holder is assured of timely receipt of principal and interest. Because the bank credits the buyer's account on payment dates, the buyer can re-invest the proceeds on the same day and thus avoid the loss of interest that arises from failure to present the certificate on the due date or coupon payment date. Banks will not pay any CD unless it is in their own or their agent's possession, and Regulation Q does not allow banks to pay interest on CDs after maturity. Most banks will contact CD holders prior to maturity date in an attempt to roll over the CD. However, there is no legal obligation to do so and many notifications are sent out by mail. Thus, it is important that all buyers of CDs maintain proper maturity records so that they maximize their returns by not allowing the proceeds of a maturing CD to remain uninvested. In most instances the rollover and associated payment and safekeeping arrangements can be accomplished through a single phone call or letter.

Small savings CDs should be kept in a safe at a bank or held in the buyer's safe-deposit box. To the extent that these securities can be held at the bank itself, the customer avoids having to make special trips to the bank or sending securities through the mail and can re-invest the proceeds of maturing CDs by phone. This procedure makes re-investment convenient for investors who travel extensively, and merely requires that the holder keep accurate records of maturity dates. By using a bank account to handle all payments of principal and interest, the investor has a duplicate record of CD transactions on his bank statement, which can be used for budget and tax purposes.

GLOSSARY

basis point— One one-hundredth of a percent. Usually referred to as an 01, its mathematical value is .0001. On a $1,000,000 security, the value of a basis point for 360 days, 180 days, and 90 days is $100, $50, and $25, respectively.

dealer— A financial institution that stands willing to buy or sell a security at a stated price or yield.

make a market— To quote both a bid and offer price for a security.

reserve requirements— The amount, expressed as a percentage of a particular type of deposit, that banks must hold in the form of cash or a deposit at the Federal Reserve Bank as determined by Federal Reserve Regulation D.

rollover— The re-investment of the principal and/or proceeds of a maturing security in the same type of security.

roly-poly CD— A negotiated long-term fixed-rate deposit contract whereby a bank agrees to issue and the buyer agrees to deposit a specified amount at periodic intervals, the sum of the intervals equaling the total term of the deposit.

spread— A rate, usually expressed in basis points, that measures the difference between the bid and offer price of a security, or that measures the difference in yield between two securities. It is also used to measure the additional rate added to some base yield to give a final yield on a variable-rate security.

variable-rate CD— A CD that has a rate of return that fluctuates at specific intervals over its term at some fixed spread over a stated base rate — normally a published yield on a specific maturity of a short-term security such as secondary CDs or Treasury bills. Interest is paid either at maturity or at certain specified intervals.

yield— Rate of discount that makes the present values of a security equal to its current market price. An annual simple-interest yield does not take into account any effects of compounding and is effectively the annualized return on a security divided by its cost.

LEADING DEALERS

A.G. Becker Inc., New York, N.Y.

Bache Halsey Stuart Shields Inc., New York, N.Y.

Bank of America N.T. & S.A., San Francisco, Cal.

Bankers Discount Co., New York, N.Y.

Bankers Trust Co., New York, N.Y.

Briggs Schaedle & Co., Inc., New York, N.Y.

Carroll McEntee & McGinley Inc., New York, N.Y.

Chemical Bank, New York, N.Y.

Citibank, N.A., New York, N.Y.

Continental Illinois National Bank & Trust Co. of Chicago, Chicago, Ill.

Discount Corp. of New York, New York, N.Y.

Donaldson, Lufkin & Jenrette Securities Corp., New York, N.Y.

E.F. Hutton & Co., Inc., New York, N.Y.

Ehrlich Bober Government Securities Inc., New York, N.Y.

First Boston Corp., New York, N.Y.

First National Bank of Chicago, Chicago, Ill.

Goldman Sachs & Co., New York, N.Y.

Harris Trust & Savings Bank, New York, N.Y.

Kidder Peabody & Co., Inc., New York, N.Y.

Aubrey G. Lanston & Co., Inc., New York, N.Y.

Lehman Commercial Paper, Inc., New York, N.Y.

Lombard Wall, Inc., New York, N.Y.

Merrill Lynch Money Market Securities, Inc., New York, N.Y.

Morgan Guaranty Trust Co. of New York, New York, N.Y.

Morgan Stanley & Co., Inc., New York, N.Y.

Paine Webber Jackson & Curtis Inc., New York, N.Y.

Wm. E. Pollock & Co., Inc., New York, N.Y.

Salomon Brothers, New York, N.Y.

Security Pacific National Bank, Los Angeles, Cal.

Smith Barney Harris Upham & Co., Inc., New York, N.Y.

United California Bank, Los Angeles, Cal.

Dean Witter Reynolds Inc., New York, N.Y.

Wells Fargo Bank N.A., San Francisco, Cal.

TRADE ORGANIZATIONS

American Bankers' Association, Washington, D.C.

Association of Primary Dealers in U.S. Government Securities, New York, N.Y.

LEADING BROKERS

Garvin Guy-Butler, New York, N.Y.

GMS Securities, New York, N.Y.

Hilliard Farber & Co., New York, N.Y.

SUGGESTED READING

Daily Periodicals

American Banker

The New York Times

The Wall Street Journal

Weekly Periodicals

Bondweek, Published by Institutional Investor, Inc., New York, N.Y.

Monthly Periodicals

Federal Reserve Bulletin, Federal Reserve Board, Washington, D.C.

Reference Books

Darst, David M. *The Complete Bond Book.* New York: McGraw-Hill, 1975.

The First Boston Corporation. *Handbook of Securities of the United States Government and Federal Agencies and Related Money Market Instruments.* 29th Edition. New York, 1980.

Stigum, Marcia. *The Money Market: Myth, Reality and Practice.* Homewood: Dow Jones-Irwin, 1978.

Stigum, Marcia, in collaboration with John Mann. *Money Market Yield Calculations: Yields, Break-Evens, and Arbitrage.* Homewood: Dow Jones-Irwin, 1981.

Bank-Managed Investment Accounts

John R. Thomas and Joan C. Terwilliger *

BASIC CHARACTERISTICS

Bank-managed accounts are trust funds that take three general forms: commingled funds, for the exclusive use of the bank's employee benefit clients; common trust funds, available to the trusts of estates and individuals; and individually invested accounts, portfolios set up for a single investor (individual or corporate) and owned exclusively by the investor.

General Attributes

A commingled or common fund is established by a trust company solely for the use of its clients and may not legally be used by persons outside the established trust relationship. In this respect, these funds differ from mutual funds, through which investors at large may pool their resources. (As of early 1982, banks are not permitted to operate mutual funds; they are offered to the public only by investment companies or brokerage houses.)

An individually invested account, set up for an individual or an organization, consists of a number of different securities and may be balanced between fixed income and equities, or may be concentrated in one or the other depending on how conservatively the portfolio is to be invested.

The technique known as commingling involves the pooling of securities to create a fund of a certain type or classification of security. The commingling technique applies to both commingled funds and common trust funds, although only an ERISA (Employee Retirement Income Security Act of 1974) client's fund is formally designated a commingled fund. In its broadest sense, the idea of commingling or pooling securities can be compared with the mutual fund concept; in each instance participants share in the total return of a fund represented by dividends and/or interest and appreciation.

Pricing of pooled funds. Pooled funds are valued at the end of every month or more frequently, and the assigned unit (share) value is adjusted accordingly. (Mutual funds are valued on a daily basis; special valuations for pooled funds may occur when warranted by extraordinary market conditions.) Within the fund,

* John R. Thomas is a Vice-President and Joan C. Terwilliger is an Assistant Secretary at Morgan Guaranty Trust Company of New York.

public market securities are priced on the basis of market closing trades (last price), or in the case of narrowly traded securities, on a mean price (between bid and asked); private placements are priced on a matrix (valuation model) created from a composite of similar public issues and discounted for liquidity restrictions peculiar to the type of investment and its marketability. (See further discussion of pricing under *Acquiring and Retiring Pooled Fund Shares* in this article.)

The Pooling Concept

The efficiency of asset management may be greatly enhanced by the use of the pooled vehicle. The element of timing is often crucial to the execution of security trades. The pooled-fund manager has immediate access to each of the holdings in the fund and easy reference to the weighted effect of each security on the portfolio's total performance. The individually invested account manager, although he may have direct access to account holdings, must take the time to consider each account profile to determine the advisability of a purchase or sale. Furthermore, the pooling of securities makes it possible for individual trusts, through participation in the funds, to share in attractive investments of a number of companies, even though the market supply (shares or issues outstanding) may be limited. Thus, the investor can participate in a composite fund of securities consisting of many small to medium-sized companies in which it would have been impractical to invest directly on behalf of individual trusts.

The degree to which assets are invested on a pooled basis depends on the participating client and his trustee. For example, when a trust is established for an individual and his beneficiary, parameters are set for the degree of emphasis to be placed on current and/or future income, growth and capital appreciation, tax-free return, and risk tolerance. Should a decision then be made to use a common fund vehicle, a selection is made from the various equity, convertible, fixed-income, and tax-exempt funds to satisfy the needs of the client and the beneficiary.

Common stock investing. In planning a comprehensive equity portfolio, the account manager may elect to review each industry with an in-house or outside research group to determine which of the various sectors and subsectors of the economy should be emphasized and which should be eliminated from consideration. From the industries that remain, a selection of stocks is made on the basis of their short- or long-term attractiveness, as well as risk tolerance and anticipated total return (dividend payment plus appreciation). Within an industry, the portfolio may concentrate on a particular aspect of the sector or subsector, such as the area of the public served (e.g., regional banks versus money center banks) or the types of goods sold (e.g., specialty retailing versus mass marketing).

In rapidly declining or ascending markets in which the "herd instinct" seems to have overpowered the fundamental analytical approach to stock selection, the choice of specific companies may take precedence over industry considerations.

The turnover or trading in and out of securities is generally based on long-range considerations of a fundamental nature, using a two- to three-year time horizon. However, in an overvalued situation, a stock may be sold and then repurchased at a later date when its price is judged to be more in line with researched criteria peculiar to its industry or to the company itself.

Another form of equity ownership is real estate. During the 1960s and early 1970s it was necessary for a tax-exempt trust to use an indirect ownership vehicle such as a real estate investment trust to avoid the tax consequences of outright ownership in real estate. Since then, changes in the law have resolved this conflict and direct ownership-participation is actively sought. Real estate investments are generally packaged and marketed as a joint effort by the developer and institutional buyer, with the advice and assistance of legal counsel. Initial returns from equity real estate investments are a form of fixed income insofar as a contractual rate of interest is paid; the equity feature generally becomes more important after construction and remodeling has taken place and the investor receives an incremental return by participating in a percentage of the rents collected.

Fixed income investing. The fixed component of a portfolio may be structured with varying maturities to meet the basic needs of an individual and his beneficiary, to service the actuarial needs of the corporation and its employees, or to satisfy the cash-flow requirements of an institution or foundation. Good credit quality is also an important consideration; it can be determined in some instances by referring to Moody's and Standard & Poor's investment services. In-house credit committees also perform a crucial function in monitoring existing investments and establishing credit quality estimates for private placement issues, as opposed to public market issues of bonds. Highest quality issues, such as Treasury bonds and notes, Treasury bills, securities of government agencies, of the Federal National Mortgage Association (FNMA), and Federal Home Loan (FHL) bonds, may represent a small percentage of a well-diversified portfolio, or a greater percentage of a safety-of-principal portfolio consisting of short-term investments.

Most pooled funds hold a minimum issue size of $100,000; this is considered to be a round lot and is easy to trade. Smaller pieces of an issue could present a liquidity problem as they are more difficult and costly to trade. Conversely, a private placement has no issue size consideration. Since trading is of no consequence in a private placement, each participant is allocated a pro rata share of the institutional purchase and receives a proportionate share of the amortization (payback of principal and interest).

In some cases a portfolio will be a hybrid of individual public market bonds, represented by government, corporate, and finance bonds, but will have its private placement component represented by units of specialized pooled funds. Qualified pensions and institutions may find it advantageous to purchase and hold private placements through the medium of the commingled or pooled fund. This commingling increases the efficiency of servicing an issue for amortization and for the execution of consent agreements related to changes in the borrower's financial restructuring; it also affords the investor an attractive way of spreading risk among a larger number of issues.

Variety of Investments

Commingled funds. The commingled concept for the investment of pension, profit-sharing, and thrift fund assets has evolved from the establishment of the basic common stock and bond funds to the creation of a profusion of funds aimed at designated areas of investment opportunity.

Common stock funds. Large capitalization stocks (companies in which capitalization and/or sales are in excess of $750 million) are either treated by bank trustees as one common stock fund, or the companies are broken down into the four sectors of the economy: consumer and service; technology and machinery; finance, regulated industries, and transportation; natural resources and processing. Common stocks of these companies are generally considered to be core holdings with attractive current yields and growth potential.

Intermediate capitalization stocks (companies in which capitalization and/or sales are between $250 million and $750 million) are bought for their sound growth prospects and high earnings visibility, and for the potential added return from the acquisition trend prevalent to today's market.

Special situation stocks (companies in which capitalization and/or sales are under $250 million) are smaller-size companies that are perceived to have relatively high risk with potentially greater reward. Because of the high risk factor, holdings in this type of fund tend to be spread among a larger number of issues.

International equities are classified as stocks of foreign companies traded on foreign exchanges. Country weightings in an international equity fund are of significant value to that fund's performance, and these weightings are periodically changed to reflect world financial, political, and economic conditions. Past experience has shown that the market volatility of an equity portfolio can be lowered by a representative holding of international equities.

Equity real estate is synonymous with direct ownership of real estate, which has equity features such as the outright ownership of office buildings and shopping centers. Securities of this type are purchased privately under agreement with the borrower with the assistance of separate legal counsel for the lender and for the borrower.

Opportunity equities represent a further refinement of the pooled fund process. Companies classified under this heading may be considered undervalued relative to their financial condition, book value, replacement cost, or economic value.

Convertibles. Convertible issues are originated by the borrower as either public market or private placement securities. They can be of a fixed income or a preferred-stock nature. Convertibles tend to lower the volatility of a portfolio because they decline less in down markets, but they also appreciate more slowly as markets rise.

Fixed income funds. Money market funds are used by bank trustees as temporary interest-earning vehicles for monies that are earmarked for more permanent investments, or for monies to be distributed to employees in the form of retirement benefits, profit-sharing, or thrift fund payments. Included in a money market fund would be instruments such as negotiable certificates of deposit, banker's acceptances, commercial paper, and Treasury bills. Issues of this type are traded through primary dealers in U.S. government securities, including money center banks located throughout the United States and including certain broker/dealers.

Temporary investments excluded, a bond portfolio may consist of varying amounts of intermediate- and long-term maturities tailored to the risk factor of the portfolio and the future requirements of these funds. Maturity structure can fluctuate depending on the forecast of interest rates, market opportunities, and adjustments for yield curve fluctuations. Since the 1960s, constantly changing interest rates and response to inflationary pressures have led to more active trading of public market bond issues. Private placement issues, on the other hand, are not heavily traded, since they are non-public securities that tend to have a relatively short average life due to the amortization or payback of principal.

International fixed income securities may be denominated in U.S. dollars or in foreign currencies; dollar securities may be issued in the United States or in the country of origin, non-dollar securities are issued in the respective country of origin. International credit instruments of foreign obligors have been used selectively by bank trustees since the latter part of the 1970s.

Common trust funds. The common trust vehicle for the pooling of personal trust assets was originally formed to give individual trusts the advantage of diversified investing. This broadening of participation in equity and fixed income markets permitted individual trusts to have representative holdings in a greater number of issues without the expense involved in odd-lot trading of small holdings. Types of common trust funds may be classified basically as equity, fixed income, convertible, and tax-exempt.

Common trust equity fund. This may include common stocks of domestic, multinational, and foreign-based companies, or it may be a specialized fund consisting mainly of emerging growth companies and small companies of superior growth potential.

Convertible common trust fund. This kind of fund invests in fixed income and preferred issues that are convertible into common stock. A representative holding in this type of fund tends to lower a portfolio's volatility.

Fixed income fund. A fixed income fund for the common trust investor may include not only public issues of U.S. companies but also private placements, government bonds, and dollar-denominated international bonds. Other refinements of fixed income funds may be available to the common trust, such as a specialized intermediate fund, which invests in short- and intermediate-term maturities of public, private, government, and international issues.

Tax-exempt common fund. Securities that are issued by municipal, state, and governmental entities are purchased by this type of fund. The interest paid on these issues is exempt from federal income taxes. Certain refinements have been instituted by bank trustees to give the personal trust the opportunity to invest in an intermediate tax-exempt fund and a similar fund for trust beneficiaries residing in a particular state, such as New York, New Jersey, Florida, etc.

Individually invested accounts. An individually managed trust account contains a selection of individual stock and bond issues. A hypothetical trust of less than $1 million in size would not have a diversification as broad as that of a larger trust; that is, the number of issues would be less in a small trust. On the other hand, the allocation of assets between equity and fixed income for any size trust depends to a large extent on the account profile, growth orientation, yield emphasis, payout requirements, and other factors. The minimum account size generally ranges from $250 thousand to $1 million, although some banks may have a lower minimum.

Private placement securities do not usually play a role in the lesser-sized trust as the servicing of them for amortization, interest payments, consent agreements, etc., is too costly and cumbersome.

ATTRACTIVE FEATURES

Current Cash Return

To achieve a high current return, the investor may enjoy the advantages of a wide variety of securities.

The fixed income market. Money market instruments, such as banker's acceptances and commercial paper, as well as U.S. government and agency securities such as Treasury bills, Federal National Mortgage Association bonds (Fannie Maes), Government National Mortgage Association pass-through securities (Ginnie Maes), and federal home loans, pay relatively high interest rates and can be bought for short-term maturity. Investment managers offer pooled money market funds similar to those that are available through brokers. The basic purpose of bank-managed money market funds is to provide a liquid vehicle that will earn interest for short-term monies but will make those funds available to the investor on a daily basis. The interest rates on these funds are tied to current money market rates, and the funds' attractiveness to the investor is enhanced by interest rate forecasts, or histograms.[1]

The convertible market. Convertibles are attractive from the standpoint of both yield and risk. Convertible bonds and preferred stocks provide a good current rate of return from interest and/or dividends. In a declining stock market, convertibles have a stabilizing influence due to their fixed income component. They also lend a degree of stability to a portfolio during periods of rising interest rates.

The equity market. This market has a number of stocks — notably, but not exclusively, public utility stocks — that pay excellent dividends and yield the investor a return of 10 percent or better. However, a high cash dividend may not always justify the use of a stock in a portfolio. Some companies may seem to maintain a good payout ratio (dividend as a percentage of total earnings), but may be highly leveraged with frequent issuing of new debt securities or may increase the float (shares outstanding) of their stock by issuing new shares more often than the accepted norm, resulting in a dilution of current shares outstanding.

Deferred Return

Bank investment managers offer several avenues of investment to the individual or corporate investor who is not dependent on current income. Classified among deferred-return investments would be drilling and exploration programs for oil and gas, the purchasing of gold, and dealing in collectibles such as paintings. Investing in this type of deferred-income vehicle requires a good deal of expertise and is done with the assistance of professionals in the particular field.

There are investment banks and brokerage houses that specialize in structuring direct oil and gas drilling investments for the individual taxable client, and passive oil and gas programs for the tax-exempt pension fund institution and foundation. In order to achieve tax-deferred status for this type of venture, annual income must be re-invested for a minimum of three years. Insurance is essential to cover liability for possible blowouts of oil wells and other such disasters. While the active, direct investor participates in acreage acquisitions, exploratory drilling, and well development, the passive investor makes loans for these activities and for the purchase of oil and gas reserves, all with royalty interests.

A means of partially deferring returns is the real estate-equity investment. In a project involving the development and/or expansion of an office building, shopping center, hotel, or other commercial property, the initial cash flow is

---

[1] The technique of histogramming is performed by a group of fixed income professionals who give individual predictions of interest rate levels for U.S. government securities of varying maturities, namely, three months and twelve months hence. From these predictions, a yield curve is plotted and a consensus forecast is reached.

generally lower in the early years compared to regular mortgage return, but once the expansion or development has been completed, the investor benefits from the guaranteed return to the investor plus an incremental participating return in the rents collected.

The principle of deferred return also may be carried through to common stock investing by looking to companies in early stages of development that initially plow back their earnings into operations and expansion and that are regarded as potential candidates for growth of total return.

Capital Gains

The discipline of selling fully valued or overpriced securities is a difficult art to master. At the peak of the market cycle in 1972, investors could look back on a prolonged period of price-earnings ratios ranging from 10 to 20 for the well established, mature company, and ratios of 30 to 50 for the young and fast-growing company. In the market environment of that period, the investor was easily lulled into a false sense of security.

The selling of securities to realize profits is a necessary component of overall investment strategy. However, capital gains must be viewed not only from an investment perspective but also with an eye to the taxable consequences. Persons in high-income brackets may choose to avoid excessive taxes by balancing gains with realized losses. This may be accomplished by forward planning; for example, a municipal bond holding may be sold and the proceeds re-invested in a higher-quality municipal issue of similar coupon and maturity; however, it should be kept in mind that losses realized within thirty days of the sale and repurchase of an identical security (wash sale) are generally disallowed for tax purposes.

A capital gain or loss can be experienced by a pooled-fund participant in one of two ways: Within the fund itself, a security may be sold resulting in a realized profit; or the participating trust may sell shares or units held in a common trust fund at a higher price than was paid for them. In the first instance, the investor is taxed on the pro rata share of the realized gain from the sale of the security within the fund; in the second, a tax is levied on the gain realized from the sale of the units or shares of the common fund per se.

The capital gains tax is not relevant to the management of tax-exempt trusts, as there are no tax levies on these funds. Benefit payments to retired participants in a pension fund are taxed as ordinary income, but the tax rate is lower than that incurred during an active salaried employment.

Safety of Principal

Erosion of principal may occur in both stock and bond markets as these markets respond to the political, social, and economic forces that surround them. If an individual or corporation determines that a percentage of assets to be invested must not be exposed to market risk, there are several possible investment alternatives.

Bond immunization. Immunization is not a new idea, but it finally came into its own in the 1970s as an answer to market volatility. It is based on an actuarial analysis of determining bullet years for cash requirements. It is a useful tool for a corporation that wishes to set aside a portion of its pension assets in a relatively risk-free portfolio of fixed income securities with varying maturities. The maturities are tailored to the years in which retirements have been projected to occur. These projections are made by the plan actuary. It should be remembered that actuarial forecasts can only be estimates of forward cash requirements; this is why only a portion of overall funds are placed in an immunized portfolio. The concept can be applied to individual accounts when projected outflow is relatively certain, as in the case of annual gifts or donations.

Short-term government securities. A portfolio of short-term U.S. government and government agency securities is another means of providing safety of principal. These securities possess the high-quality, risk-free characteristics desired, although the return on investment is subject to fluctuating interest rates.

Hedge Against Inflation

There is no sure way for the investor to meet the challenge of inflation. The theory that common stocks are one of the best hedges against inflation has been subscribed to by numerous investment managers. However, since the peak of the market cycle in 1972, the equity portfolio manager has been hard pressed to keep his book values from being eroded, much less to preserve any kind of market stability. In some instances, managers have engaged in active turnover and swapping of securities to realize profits and to keep abreast of social, political, and economic forces in the marketplace. There have also been frequent reductions in the percentage of stocks held in favor of temporary investments in short-term money market instruments.

Much of this reaction to inflation has been guided by the threshold of pain that can be withstood by the individual or corporate client. For the client who has a low risk tolerance and/or short-term investment goals, the more comfortable investment would be the short-term money market or municipal market instruments. With the aid of the histogramming technique, the fixed income manager will use his expertise to play the yield curve by rotating invested funds among short-term (up to one year), medium-term (average maturity five to ten years), and longer-term (exceeding ten years) maturities in anticipation of market trends.

The real estate-equity type of investment is another tool being increasingly recognized by institutional investors. The immediate return from equity real estate has been in the range of 9 to 11 percent during the initial term. This rate is offered by the property owner-developer who, in effect, takes on the investor as a partner, offering an acceptable return during the primary years of the investment. Once the commercial property has been fully developed and rented, the investor receives an incremental return from a percentage of rentals and rent renewals that should increase over the years, effectively giving the investor a hedge against inflation.

POTENTIAL RISKS

Instability of Principal and Income

Stability is, first and foremost, a function of the quality of the issuer. It cannot be measured statistically. However, in the case of stocks and bonds, a judgment may be made by evaluating the corporation's ability to pay, as well as its historical soundness and capacity to perform under adverse conditions.

To determine the measure of a company's solvency and its future earnings capability, both qualitative and quantitative analysis is performed by in-house research groups, supplemented by outside broker research. This technical analysis is designed to give the investor a perspective of probability to guide him from the known quantity of past market performance into the anticipated future performance. Analytical information supplied for each company includes its expected return, earnings comparisons, market-related data such as price range and capitalization, historical and anticipated growth rates for earnings per share and dividends, return on equity, payout ratios (percentage of total earnings paid out in dividends), and comparisons of earnings-per-share estimates with brokerage house forecasts.

An important guide to fixed income investing is a company's credit rating. Moody's and Standard & Poor's services supply and update these ratings on a regular basis. As an additional safeguard, banks have established in-house credit committees to monitor and anticipate changes in credit ratings affecting corporate and municipal bond investments. An existing bond portfolio can suffer unrealized (paper) losses when interest rate forecasts and new issue rates are increasing. Bond managers have taken the precaution of shortening the maturity structure in their portfolios during periods of high inflation when interest rates tend to increase at an unusually rapid pace.

Market Volatility

To avoid wide swings in the market performance of an account, the equity manager will diversify his holdings in terms of both risk (or beta) of individual securities and of industry weighting; the fixed income manager will diversify by maturity and by credit instrument.

For the individually invested account, this is accomplished by broad selection of blue chip and well-established growth companies, perhaps with a sprinkling of smaller companies dealing in unique products or services. This stock selection is complemented by several issues of good-quality municipal (for taxable account) and corporate bonds of varying maturity, and/or several money-market-type issues to meet liquidity needs. The percentage of distribution between equities and fixed income will favor equities for a higher level of risk and will favor fixed income when the risk tolerance is low.

Convertible preferreds and bonds can be used to smooth volatility, as they tend to decline less in down markets but also increase at a slower pace in up markets.

International investments also can play an important role in smoothing performance fluctuations and reducing volatility. Investment management firms may have branch offices overseas that have developed expertise in international investing, or they may rely on foreign investment firms that have U.S. branches. Foreign markets operate quite differently from those in the United States, and they have far fewer issues available. There is also less active trading of international securities on foreign markets.

A portfolio of commingled or common trust funds can be similarly tailored to the objectives of the client by weighting the account's participation in a selection of different types of pooled funds, each of which has an assigned level of risk and expected return.

It should go without saying that market volatility, aided and abetted by investor psychology, may or may not reflect the conscientious analysis of market and company risk.

Illiquidity

The short-term investor, who needs to earn interest on his money but who must have the flexibility of cashing in a holding on a moment's notice, must turn to money market instruments such as Treasury bills, other government and government agency securities, banker's acceptances, and commercial paper. These money market instruments are usually purchased for a maturity of less than one year. Money market funds consisting of such instruments are offered by brokerage houses for the individual client and by bank and insurance company pension trustees for the corporate client.

Investments in stocks and bonds have varying degrees of liquidity. Round lots of stocks (100 shares) and bonds ($100,000 principal amount) are generally considered to be more liquid than odd lots (smaller denominations). Liquidity may also be a function of shares outstanding (issued) or the amount of bonds outstanding, which is called "float." Private placements are generally considered to be illiquid types of investment as they are not traded on any public exchange. Investor perception of the relative attractiveness of a company may influence the trading of its debt or equity securities.

The assets held in pooled funds are generally priced at the end of every month, at which time a prospective investor may purchase units or shares, and a participant may sell his interest in the fund. There are rare occasions when a fund of highly specialized investments, such as real estate, will not be in a position to take on new investors or to redeem units for existing holders without prior notice. A fund of short-term money market investments is open for purchase and sale transactions on a daily basis.

For the purposes of investment planning, the liquidity needs of the individual or corporation should be established, monitored, and provided for as an integral part of the investment package.

TAX CONSEQUENCES

Income tax treatment for the personal trust, estate, or advisory account is multifaceted and complicated. A bank trustee or investment adviser will have the support of in-house or outside tax experts to provide him with the tax liability background on which to build a trust's portfolio. A trust that is being invested in individual securities may be structured with tax-exempt bonds and low-income equities, including preferred and common stocks that are partially tax-exempt, so that the grantor or beneficiary who is already in a relatively high income tax bracket can avoid further increased liability. On the other hand, in a case where the taxability is of nominal concern, the portfolio may contain high-yielding stocks and fixed income securities that do not have tax-exempt features.

A personal trust or estate includes in the computation of its taxable income the distribution received from a common trust fund during the fund's fiscal year. Similarly, the common trust fund's capital gains and losses, although not distributed to the participating trust or estate, are includable in the computation of the trust's or estate's taxable income. The amount of undistributed capital gains and losses allocable to the trust or estate participating in a common trust fund is determined in the same fashion as the income distribution (i.e., on a pro rata basis). The tax bases for a participating account in a common trust fund are regularly adjusted for realized gains and losses. In a manner similar to mutual fund accounting, the distribution of gains and the debiting of losses for the fund's participants are eliminated in favor of the tax-basis adjustment. This avoids the possibility of duplicating the tax liability for gains and the tax credit for losses realized in the common trust fund. For income tax purposes, the treatment of the common trust fund is similar to that of a partnership: The common trust fund does not pay tax on its capital gains; rather, the participating trusts or estates bear the direct tax responsibility.

Tax planning for the individual trust or estate also may include investments in oil and gas drilling, real estate, and other enterprises that are considered to have tax-sheltering or tax-deferring advantages. This is a highly specialized field of investment in which there are varying degrees of risk and uncertain rewards. They should be entered into with caution and pursued only with advice and counsel from experienced investment managers knowledgeable about this type of vehicle.

ACQUIRING AND RETIRING POOLED FUND SHARES

Participation in pooled funds is no longer a function of an account's size, but rather of the desire to diversify assets efficiently and inexpensively. The individual or corporation will find that the trustee can construct a portfolio of units or shares in a selected group of pooled funds so that specific needs of cash flow and growth can be appropriately met.

Common Trust Fund Investors

Common trust funds, as established by law, are for the exclusive use of the individual clients of the sponsoring trust company. A co-trustee must agree to the use of these pooled funds before investments in them are made. Most individual trust agreements have interpretive general language or specific authorization that permits the assets of a trust to be invested in a common trust fund. However, certain states do not permit the use of these funds, and the state of residency of the client governs.

Commingled Fund Investors

Investments in commingled funds are made on behalf of a trust or fund for which the trust company acts as sole trustee or as investment manager. The trust must be a tax-exempt pension trust, profit-sharing trust, or other type of retirement trust, and it must be part of a plan or group of plans qualified and exempt from tax under the Internal Revenue Code. The authorization for participation in a commingled fund must be specifically contained in the trust agreement, which may have general language including all available pooled funds or specific language for one or more funds selected by the sponsoring company. A corporation or institution may elect to have a group of managers, each of whom is considered to have expertise in a specific type of investment such as fixed income, real estate, equity, and convertibles.

Mechanics and Pricing

The mechanics of acquiring or retiring units or shares for the participant's account is the responsibility of the bank trustee, who purchases (from clients wishing to redeem their holdings) and sells (to other clients) units or shares of the pooled fund based on the composite of individually priced securities within the fund. The price range of a share of a pooled fund varies considerably by the type of fund and its longevity. A new fund is generally priced at 100 (par) on its first day of existence and can vary from 20 to 30 points below par to 300 or more points above par. For example, a bond fund established in the 1950s would have a lower coupon rate associated with the individual holdings and therefore a lower unit price; a more recent bond fund would be priced close to par, either above or below, depending on interest rate fluctuations. Conversely, a special situations (small companies) stock fund, which has reaped the rewards of a wise selection of securities in its universe, may have increased in price from 100 to 400 or more per share over a ten- or fifteen-year period.

CUSTODIAL CARE

The custody and servicing of securities is provided by most investment management firms as a supportive service for in-house accounts, or an independent service for outside companies and individuals seeking professional caretaking facilities.

In many instances the custodian will interface with the Depository Trust Company (DTC), which is owned by its participating members. The DTC has a fully automated system that accepts securities on a book entry basis. Security transactions normally are cleared through DTC within the required five-day settlement period, providing evidence of ownership to the participating members without the physical movement of the securities from seller to buyer. The Federal Reserve System operates in much the same fashion by providing a book entry system for transactions in Treasury bills and government bonds.

Additional safekeeping facilities for securities and other valuables are provided in the vaults of trust companies. Specifications for the construction of these vaults are contained in the burglary prevention manual issued by the National Bureau of Casualty and Surety Underwriters. Most trust companies conform to the highest class-ten rating for the required specifications. The custodian does not assume liability as an insurer but does carry an on-premises blanket bond insurance to cover the usual risks of security loss, dishonesty of employees, burglary, robbery, destruction, or disappearance. It will also carry insurance to cover securities in transit by its own messengers. Most custodians will take the precaution of making duplicate records (on microfilm) that are transported daily to a safe-storage area far removed from trust company vaults, so that a client's account can be reconstructed if original records are destroyed. The records of trust company custodians are examined by separate internal auditors and by outside certified public accountants. They are also subject to annual examination by the state banking department and by the Federal Reserve Banks.

Securities that are left in safekeeping are registered in the name of a nominee partnership provided by the trust company to assure prompt negotiability in the event of sale or transfer. Most banks have a fully automated custodial system that provides for the crediting of interest and dividend payments to each account on the payment date. This information is supplied in advance so that the monies can be invested on the payment date.

The custodian will supply the client with the following updated information:

- Stock dividends, splits, and distributions;
- Dividend omissions;
- Dividend re-investment plans;
- Subscription offerings;
- Purchase and exchange offers;
- Tender offers for preferred stocks and bonds;
- Calls on preferred stocks and bonds;

- Conversion of preferred stock and bond issues;
- Company name changes;
- Modifications to bond indentures; and
- Government subscription and exchange offerings.

Additional safeguards provided by custodial trusts include an armed security force, alarm control systems, television surveillance, controlled access to the premises, smoke- and fire-alarm devices, certificate number control, and polygraph examinations for all secured area employees.

GLOSSARY

amortization— The return or payback of principal on a fixed income security in periodic installments to the lender.

average life— The length of time between the initial issuing of a bond and the final payback of principal by the borrower prior to the bond's stated maturity.

beta— A measure of market risk. The stock market as a whole has a beta of 1.0. Greater than 1.0 indicates higher volatility; less than 1.0 indicates lower volatility.

commingled fund— Broadly, a trust fund in which the equities of a number of investors are combined for common management; a pooled fund. Formally, a fund to which participation is legally limited to a bank's pension or employee benefits clients.

common trust fund— A pooled fund available to individual investors.

current return— Yield received by the investor from cash payments in the forms of interest on bonds and dividends on stock.

histogramming— A technique performed by a group of fixed income professionals who give individual predictions of interest rate levels for U.S. government securities of varying maturities, namely, three months and twelve months hence. From these predictions, a yield curve is plotted and a consensus forecast reached.

immunization— The investment of a fixed income portfolio using an actuarial type of analysis in the purchase of bullet maturities, each of which is targeted for future cash requirements.

individually invested account— A trust account for an individual or corporation in which all holdings are owned by the investor.

liquidity— The degree to which a security is easily traded; generally speaking, stocks with a greater number of shares outstanding are more marketable, as are short-term public market bonds such as U.S. government and government agency securities.

odd lots— Denominations of a principal amount of a bond that are not multiples of $100,000, or of shares of stock not in multiples of 100.

payout ratio— The dividend paid to stockholders as a percentage of that company's total assets.

pooled fund— See *commingled fund, common trust fund.*

private placement— A security purchased by the lender directly from the borrower.

total return — A composite of the yield from dividends and income plus the appreciation or increase of an asset's market value.

wash sale — The sale and repurchase of an identical amount of the same security.

SUGGESTED READING

Bernstein, Peter, ed. *The Theory and Practice of Bond Portfolio Management.* Vols. I and II. New York: Institutional Investor Books, 1980.

Brealey, Richard A. *An Introduction to Risk and Return From Common Stocks.* Cambridge: MIT Press, 1969.

Carosso, Vincent P. *Investment Banking in America.* Cambridge: Harvard University Press, 1970.

Cohen, Jerome B. *Investment Analysis and Portfolio Management,* 3rd ed. Homewood: Dow Jones-Irwin, 1977.

Cutler, Steven E. *Trust Investments.* Park Ridge: Bank Administration Institute, 1979.

Munn, Glenn G. *Encyclopedia of Banking and Finance.* Boston: Bankers Publishing Co., 1973.

Soldofsky, Robert M. *Institutional Holdings of Common Stock 1900-2000 — History, Projection, and Interpretation.* University of Michigan, 1971.

Books

*John F. Fleming**

BASIC CHARACTERISTICS

Determinants of Value

Rare books — including manuscripts, limited editions, and finely printed books — form a group of collectibles that offer a variety of returns for the investor. One collects books, as one collects stamps or coins, because of their intellectual value and their historical association. For example, a first edition of John Milton's *Poems* (1645) is valuable because of the light it sheds on early printing, and spelling, and on other facets of the printing trade of the time. In addition, the literary scholar looks to the first printing of a literary work (along with the manuscript, if it is available) as a primary source for the text. This same first edition of Milton's *Poems,* moreover, has intrinsic value based on its rarity, since in all probability there are no more than three dozen copies extant of this famous work.

Relative nature of rarity. Simply because only a few copies exist does not necessarily make a book valuable, although it may indeed be rare. Thus, a rare book by a minor and nearly forgotten author may have very modest value. On the other hand, that rarity is a relative matter is demonstrated in the case of the most notable single volume in English literature — the *First Folio* (1623) of Shakespeare's work. This book exists in approximately 180 copies, scattered throughout the world; many of them are in a single collection in the Folger Library in Washington, D.C. By usual book-collecting standards, this is not really a rare book; however, it is such a literary monument in terms of authorship and content that it is widely sought-after and expensive; as a result, it is indeed considered a major rare book.

Physical condition. The price that a particular copy of a rare book can command relative to other copies is determined by its condition. It is well known among more sophisticated collectors, and often learned sadly by neophytes, that most collectors cannot really afford to buy less than the best copy available of a particular book. The price of an excellent copy of a work is often many times higher in the marketplace than that of a mediocre or poor one. One month after

* John F. Fleming is a New York consultant and dealer in rare books and manuscripts. The author gratefully acknowledges material contributions to this article by Paul D. Neuthaler of Warren, Gorham & Lamont, Inc.

a splendid Shakespeare *Folio* fetched $775,000 in Paris, a similar but not nearly so well-preserved copy was sold for a mere $175,000 in London.

Points of issue. The serious collector wants his copy of a rare book to be of the earliest printing. In the course of printing a first edition, an important mistake may be noticed in the earliest copies. The presses are stopped, a correction is made, and the remainder of the edition is known as a second issue. These are less desirablc and less valuable. An example is Nathaniel Hawthorne's *Twice Told Tales* (1837), in which the leaf of contents lists the fifth story as beginning on page 78, an error that is corrected to page 77 in the second issue. Another example is Poe's *Tales of the Grotesque and Arabesque* (1840), where, in the first issue, page 213 is wrongly numbered.

Publishers' advertisements sometimes make a point of establishing priority, but they are not too dependable. In the famous case of Hawthorne's *The Scarlet Letter* (1850), the advertisements are usually dated 1850 in the first edition and 1849 in the second. It is suspected that the book's sudden success found the publishers unprepared and that, lacking a further supply of advertisements, they substituted earlier ones that they happened to have on hand. A myriad of variations in printing has been noted by bibliographers in almost every subject. This is why many collectors specialize in one author or one subject until they attain the technical bibliographical knowledge needed to go further afield.

To acquire and understand this knowledge is no easy task. The following is a sample of a bibliographical description taken from the bibliographical bible of English literature from the fifteenth to seventeenth centuries.[1]

> D.[ONNE], J.[OHN] Poems, by J.D. With Elegies on the Authors Death. London: Printed by M.[iles] F.[lesher] for John Marriot, and are to be sold at his shop in St. Dunstans Church-yard in Fleet-Street, 1633. First Edition, quarto. Collation: A^4 (the first, blank and genuine); A^2; B-Fff^4 (the last, blank and genuine); 210 leaves.
>
> Contents: blank, Sig[A]; title, recto[A2]; verso blank; Epistle, recto A3-recto[A4]; The printer to the understanders, recto A-recto A2; Hexastichon Biblipolae, signed 'Jo. (MAR.'[RIOT]), verso A2; text, pp.1-406; blank, pp. [407-8]. (P.161 is numbered 145, 164-5 are 148-9, 168 is 152, 194-5 are 164-5, 198-9 are 168-9, and 250 is 205).

Provenance. Another determinant of value in rare books is provenance, or former ownership. Volumes from great rare-book libraries of the past — those of Holford, Hoe, Heber, Kern, Pforzheimer, and Houghton — are identifiable through their book plates or other markings. Such books are much sought-after, since the great collectors usually bought or commissioned purchases of the best copies available. As collectors gain experience, they become aware of the niceties and points of condition of a rare book and seek some indication of the previous owners.

---

1 Unger, Emma, and Jackson, William A. *The Carl H. Pforzheimer Library of English Literature 1475-1700.* 3 vols. Privately printed, 1940. Excerpt from page 287, Vol. I.

Other Attributes of Rarity

Rare books is really a collective term for a number of different kinds of book collectibles. Some books are rare in the traditional sense of scarcity because they were published many, many years ago. Other books were published in limited editions; these derive their value not necessarily from age or priority but because few copies were printed, usually on special papers bound in a special way, and often containing signatures of authors, illustrators, printers, or others associated with the particular edition of the book. There is also the class of fine books or "Press" books, frequently a series of unconnected literary or other books composed and printed by a particular press, such as Nonesuch Press, Doves Press, and Ashendine Press. All of these categories which have found eager collectors through the years, have included many books of increasing financial value determined by the marketplace.

ATTRACTIVE FEATURES

Aesthetic and Historical Interest

Rare books, unlike negotiable financial instruments that merely represent value, are notable for inherent value. Scholars, indeed, have argued that a book's importance lies only in its intellectual message, not in its physical form, and, consequently, that collecting rare books for their scarcity, design, and the collector's notorious penchant for physical possession is futile and absurd. However, as an investment, books enjoy an increasingly large market among collectors seeking objects of lasting monetary worth that at the same time further their desires to identify with a notable author. Thus, among the most sought-after books is any first edition of John Milton or William Shakespeare, two of the greatest authors in the history of English literature.

Return on Investment

The investor in rare books usually (but certainly not always) makes a profit over time. However, even assuming pristine condition and legitimate and intelligent advice in purchasing, there is no guarantee that, for example, the copy of Fielding's *Tom Jones* (published in six volumes in 1749) that was bought in the 1920s for $1,500 will be worth appreciably more thirty years later. It so happens that this particular book, although one of the greatest and most renowned novels in the English language, has actually maintained, in average condition, pretty much the same value in the marketplace over the last forty to fifty years.

Hedge Against Inflation

Interesting anomalies notwithstanding, rare books in all categories are usually an excellent hedge against inflation. As they are acquired by libraries and other institutions that seldom put them on the market again, the books become more scarce, and consequently values increase. Price resistance per se is rarely a controlling factor in the market; a book is worth what collectors are willing to pay for it, and a recent auction price or other market indicator is the sole determinant of monetary value.

Intangible Benefits

Perhaps the most meaningful — but hardest to measure in terms of return on investment — benefits derived from collecting rare books are the aesthetic, intellectual, and psychological pleasures derived from associating with great objects. Beyond this is the sheer fun and pleasure of collecting, of coming suddenly upon something one has looked for and finding it all at once available. The collector sophisticated enough or lucky enough to come upon a particularly good value as well is all the more ahead. However, the collector who restricts his search to potential bargains may easily lose in the long run. It is not wise in book investments, as in any commercial venture, to put price before all other criteria.

SUCCESSFUL RARE-BOOK INVESTMENTS

Shakespeare's *First Folio*

The sales record of the *First Folio* presents a very good case for the potential investor to analyze. There are approximately 180 copies known, of which about twenty are in their original state. It is thought that 600 copies of the original edition were published, and the survival of 180 copies shows it was appreciated and sought-after more than any other book of its time. For more than a century, no monetary value was placed on it. The first known auction of the Shakespeare *First Folio* was in 1687, but the records of the auction and the *First Folio*'s price are lost. The earliest complete auction record appears in 1756, when a copy was sold for three guineas. Ten years later another copy sold for the same price. For some time three guineas was the highest price obtainable, and during the same period other copies changed hands for much less. In about 1760 the celebrated actor, David Garrick, purchased one for £1.16.

Although the price ebbed, its upward movement was never seriously checked. In 1787, Dr. Richard Wright's copy fetched £10 at auction. A big jump came in 1790 when the Duke of Roxburghe paid £35.14 at auction. It was then called the most expensive book in the English language. The same copy was re-auctioned in 1812 for £100, another record price. When the Duke of Roxburghe's library was sold at Sotheby's in 1812, his copy of the *First Folio*, which he had purchased twenty-two years earlier, advanced almost 300 percent, from twenty guineas to £100. The sale of this collection caused a sensation; it is still written and talked about today.

Upon entering the twentieth century, the pace quickens. In 1905, Mr. Bernard Buchanan George, who had purchased his *First Folio* in July 1899 for £1,700, sold it along with the second, third, and fourth editions for £10,000 ($50,000). This was the greatest advance in any six years and proved quite a successful financial investment. In March 1907 the Van Antwerp copy brought £3,600; in 1911 the Hoe copy brought £13,000. For the next twenty years, several defective copies were sold for sums in the neighborhood of £8,000. Then in 1933 in the depths of the Depression, the marvelous copy belonging to Lord Rosebery was sold for the enormous sum of £14,500 ($72,500). It was sold again at auction in 1945 for $50,000.

The Rosebery-Hogan copy was held in one collection from 1945 to 1980, when it was sold in Paris on May 20. The book-collecting world was stunned when this copy realized the enormous sum of $775,000, thus becoming the most expensive literary book in the world. The new owner, somewhat concerned about the price he had paid, asked his banker what today's relative value would be of 50,000 1945 dollars. He was informed that 50,000 1945 dollars had the purchasing power of $750,000 today.

Experience has shown that great collected books are the last commodity to feel a depression, just as they are the last to show financial gain in affluent times. The prices paid at auction for the *First Folio* are due to the excitement generated by the sale combined with the supreme egos of certain collectors and dealers who compete against each other. It was Peter Wilson, the former head and guiding genius of Sotheby's of London who once said, "If you take the theater out of the auction you have nothing."

Although few books have enjoyed the notoriety or financial success of the *First Folio,* this recapitulation of its auction history is important because it illustrates the general appreciation, over time, that rare books enjoy. It also shows some of the unexplainable vagaries of the marketplace.

The Houghton Collection

The most recent collection of superb copies of celebrated books to appear on the market is that of Arthur A. Houghton, Jr. His collection of books and manuscripts of English literature from the sixteenth to the nineteenth centuries was unsurpassed in condition and quality. The collection was dispensed of in two sales at Christie's of London in 1979 and 1980. A sample of Houghton's costs on most of the items compared to the auction price received should be a revelation to the would-be collector.

Table 1 on pages 72 and 73 shows in dollars what a few of the books cost Houghton, the dates of purchase, and what they fetched at the Houghton auctions.

Books for which Houghton paid an approximate $290,000, bought over a period of forty years, fetched $1,865,583. It would be interesting to calculate their investment value. Of course, the value to Houghton of his added fame and the joys he experienced in pursuit of the game of book collecting must be immeasur-

TABLE 1. Selected Purchase and Retail Prices — Houghton Collection

Date of Purchase	*Title*	*Price Paid by Houghton*	*Auction Price*
1932	Shakespeare, *Works* (1632)	$ 4,750	$ 10,800
1932	Shakespeare, *Works* (1623)	75,000	192,000
1933	Spenser, *Faerie Queene* (1590-1596) Shakespeare, *Poems* (1640)	15,000	53,400
1933	Oppian, *Halientica* (1478)	369	6,300
1934	Caxton, *Chronicles of England* (1480)	6,220	139,500
1935	Machiavelli, *Prince* (1640)	45	1,056
1935	Purchase, *His Pilgrimes* (1624-1625) (5 vols.)	480	14,400
1935	Ariosto, *Orlando Furioso* (1591)	985	14,625
1935	Evelyn, *Sylva* (1664) (presentation copy)	675	5,850
1935	Holinshed's *Chronicle* (1577)	975	4,950
1935	*Common Prayer Book* (1549)	16,610	112,500
1935	Donne, *Poems* (1633)	285	3,600
1935	Ford, *Broken Heart* (1633)	858	5,400
1935	Herbert, *The Temple* (1633)	4,100	15,750
1935	Milton, *Paradise Lost* (1667)	19,000	91,200
1936	Schedel, *Chronicle* (1493)	585	24,000
1936	Herrick, *A.L.S to His Uncle*	775	24,000
1941	Milton, *On Education* (1644)	850	13,200
1941	Shadwell, *Psyche* (1675)	245	6,240
1941	Blake, *Songs of Innocence & E.* (1795)	6,610	157,000
1941	Congreve, *Incognita* (1692)	500	16,875
1941	Lovelace, *Lucasta* (1649)	1,300	16,875
1941	Herrick, *Hesperides* (1648)	1,950	24,750
1941	Gascoigne, *Hundred Flowers* (1573)	2,550	54,000
1941	Gascoigne, *Poesies* (1575)	950	37,500
1941	Gascoigne, *Whole Works* (1587)	1,450	33,750
1941	Campion, *1st etc. Book of Ayres* (1610)	680	40,500
1941	Daniel, *Delia* (1592)	5,850	45,000
1941	Daniel, *Works* (1601)	850	5,850
1942	Sidney, *Astrophel & Stella* (1591) Sidney, *Pembrokes Arcadia* (1590)	5,000	74,400
1945	Brontë, *Poems* (1846)	1,800	7,875
1950	Sidney, *Sonnets* (ms.)	5,990	36,000

TABLE 1. Selected Purchase and Retail Prices — Houghton Collection (*cont'd*)

Date of Purchase	*Title*	*Price Paid by Houghton*	*Auction Price*
1956	[B.R. *Orpheus* (1595)]		$16,875
	[Barnes, *Divine Centurie* (1595)]		22,500
	[Bastard, *Chresteleres* (1598)]		13,500
	[Breton, *Workes of Young Wyt* (1577)]		42,750
	[Breton, *A Divine Poem* (1601) Breton, *Longing of a Blessed Heart* (1601) Breton, *Honour of Valour* (1605)]		49,500
	[Edwards, *Paradis* (1600)]		13,500
	[Godwyn, *Dolorous Lovers* (1520)]		38,250
	[Homer, *Georgicks* (Trans. by Chapman, Presentation) (1618)]		21,375
	[Howard, *Songs* (1557) (Shakespeare's copy)]		54,000
	[James, I., *Essayes* (1584)]		29,250
	[O.J., *Lamentations of Troy* (1594)]		12,375
	[Phillis & Flora, *Contention* (1598)]		5,850
	[Raynolds, *Primerese* (1596)]		50,400
	[Smith, *Cloris* (1592)]		16,800
	[Pettie, G., *Petite Palace* (1576)]		36,000
	[Watson, *Passionate Century* (1582)]		48,000
	[*Withal Short Dictionary* (1553)]		28,000
	LOT	42,500	576,437
1961	[Sidney, *Countess of Pembroke* (ms.)]	$ 20,000	$ 48,000
	TOTALS	$290,742	$1,865,583

SOURCE: Author's data.

able. Mr. Houghton's experience may be one of fortunate excess; however, it is seldom that a basic investment in rare books is not recoupable over time, whether or not the investor makes a profit. The investor who has bought wisely with respect to current value and condition need not be overly concerned with safety of the investment principal.

Key Books in Science and Mathematics

As an alternative to buying books of universally acknowledged value, the investor may benefit by foresight with respect to an up-and-coming area for collecting. A good example is found in books in the history of science and mathematics. Prior to 1930, medical books were very much sought-after by collectors and institutions; however, in general, key science and mathematics books held little interest for the collector. Universities basically ignored the history of science in their curricula; historians rejected it because it was science, and scientists because it was history. Surprisingly, the first Ph.D. in this field at an American university was granted as recently as 1947.

It was the atomic bomb and the general impact of science on the outcome of World War II that awakened everyone to the tremendous influence that science has on world history. Individual collections and institutional libraries sprang up everywhere. Since the 1950s, the prices of the monuments of science have risen steadily. One great collector of science books has recently complained, "Why is it every time I buy a book I pay a record price?"

The following examples typify the rise in prices over the last thirty years. Note only very acceptable copies of a few key works are included.

Euclid. *Geometry.* Venice, 1482. The basic treatise of geometry.

1952: $375	1975: $6,660
1963: $1,700	1978: $9,216
1966: $7,840	1979: $31,800

Francis Bacon. *Instauratio Magna.* London, 1620. His great work on the philosophy of science, the systematic organization of knowledge, and the inductive method.

1958: $478	1974: $8,892
1961: $896	1979: $67,840
1966: $2,184	

Robert Boyle. *The Sceptical Chymist.* London, 1661. A masterpiece of scientific literature, seeking to clarify the confused theories and vague concepts then current. Boyle claimed that there are many more elements than the four identified by Aristotle — earth, fire, air, and water — and that matter is composed of atoms and clusters of atoms in motion.

1965: $13,400 (the first copy sold since 1950)
1967: $10,000
1977: $22,750
1979: $25,440

Nicolaus Copernicus. *De Revolutionibus Orbium Coelestium.* Nuremberg, 1543. A declaration of the heretical new heliocentric theory of our planetary system, which revolutionized astronomy. This was probably the most important scientific publication of the sixteenth century. Several copies of this book were sold in the trade from 1950 to 1974 for about $10,000 each, but no fine copy was offered at auction until 1974, when a very fine presentation copy fetched $44,000. The owner had purchased it in the late 1950s for $15,000. In 1978, a fine copy brought $43,000.

POTENTIAL RISKS

Inferior Copies

One basic risk in the collecting of rare books is the possibility of purchasing a specimen of a particular book that is inferior in some way, is not a complete copy, or is otherwise damaged; this, of course, will lower the value. It is extremely important to purchase in a knowledgeable fashion.

Market Volatility

This second basic risk is not excessive, but it is nonetheless real. For example, when the songwriter Jerome Kern sold his library in 1929, he sold it at the height of an inflationary and optimistic economic period. The prices paid for some of his books have never been equalled in fifty years of continued inflation and rising values.

Illiquidity

Books are not the ideal investment for those who require relative liquidity. Long-term investment value, for the serious collector, must be accompanied by an appreciation of the pleasures of ownership.

TAX CONSEQUENCES

The tax benefits available to book collectors, as to collectors of any other appreciating art object, are limited. The taxpayer cannot depreciate an object that appreciates in value. However, it is possible to donate to a qualified charitable source books that have increased in value many times through the years as determined by current appraisal. The investor should obtain a qualified appraisal of the materials before they are donated, so that the IRS will be inclined to accept the amount that he claims the books donated are worth. The donor is then entitled to a tax deduction for the current fair market value of the books, which more often than not is far above the purchase cost or basis. When a book is sold at least one year after purchase, the profit, if any, is taxed at the capital gains rate. Separate rules apply to those who are recognized as investors by the IRS. (See article on Tax Considerations for Collector-Investors, elsewhere in this volume.) For complete guidance in these matters, readers are urged to consult a professional tax adviser.

REPRESENTATIVE TYPES OF INVESTORS

As there is no typical reader, there is really no typical collector. For centuries, books have been collected by kings and scholars for whatever reasons may have motivated them. As a pure investment, books require too much knowledge of bibliography and the market itself for one to consider collecting them on a casual or impulse basis. Yet, for the collector who holds an active interest and curiosity in a particular area, rare books offer a unique source of intellectual satisfaction and potential gain.

Of course, in addition to individual collectors, libraries and other scholarly institutions hold a substantial number of the world's rare books.

IMPORTANT FACTORS IN BUYING AND SELLING

Need for Knowledge and Interest

It is important for the potential collector to know at the outset that books, like most collectibles, require a good deal of background knowledge on market values, special characteristics of an edition or issue, and a general understanding of bibliographical techniques. In addition, the book collector should have some interest in a particular subject, writer, or genre.

Choosing a Dealer

A serious beginner will gravitate to a dealer whose taste and acumen he trusts to give him — through early purchases — an intelligent understanding of both intrinsic and extrinsic value. A reliable dealer is of invaluable help in monitoring the marketplace and providing information of previous auctions, sale records, and catalogues.

CUSTODIAL CARE

The scientific care and preservation of rare books is a relatively recent concern of the bibliographic world. Besides fire, only extreme heat or extreme dampness historically have ruined these surprisingly hardy productions.

The northern hemisphere, in which most of the world's rare books originated, has always enjoyed a relatively moderate climate that did little damage to printed books or even manuscripts, particularly if they received even minimal care. Prior to the nineteenth century, paper was made from pure linen fibers, which proved to be a durable surface for print. Indeed, one can find books dating from the 1500s that appear as fresh and bright as if they were printed yesterday. In the nineteenth century, wood pulp and chemicals were introduced into the making of paper, and, as this trend has continued to the present day, the life of book paper has become increasingly limited.

It is only in the last fifty years that scientific care has been applied to old and rare books and manuscripts. Methods for neutralizing paper acidity are a real concern for rare-book librarians, dealers, and collectors. Leather preservation, though less immediately crucial, remains a problem in both early and modern fine bindings. There are restoration specialists who address these and similar problems. Leather-bound volumes should be stored in an atmosphere that is neither too hot nor too cold, too dry nor too humid. Twice a year, the leather should be lightly treated — not soaked — with any one of a number of leather dressings such as British Museum Dressing, Lexol, or one of the preservative preparations that a dealer or bookbinder can provide. The basic aim is to keep the leather from drying out. On the other hand, if too much of a liquid preparation is used, the leather fibers may part and/or the solution may pass through the covers onto the leaves themselves. (The restorers listed at the end of this article are the best resource for maintenance information.)

GLOSSARY

as issued — The original condition of a volume, especially when an anomolous feature occurred that had not been anticipated, such as an inverted or transposed folio.

association copy — A copy that either belonged to the author or to a person whose relationship with the author (or the book's contents) bears an interesting association.

autograph — In rare-book parlance, a manuscript that the author has signed or handwritten.

boards — Sides of hard-cover books that are not bound in leather, pasteboard or cardboard.

broadside or broadsheet — Printing done on only one side of a sheet of paper.

collation — The description of the physical makeup of a book using bibliographic criteria.

editio princeps — The Latin phrase used by antiquarians for "first edition."

edition and impression — An "edition" represents all copies of a book printed from one set of type or plates; an "impression" is each printing of that edition. One edition may go through many impressions.

errata — When errors are discovered after printing, often a separate sheet is added after binding to list these mistakes for the reader.

ex-library — Any book that has been in a lending library.

foxed, foxing — Paper stained or discolored, usually from age.

leaf — Sheet of paper containing a front and back page — the single production unit.

provenance — Ownership history of a book traced in a variety of ways, which often provides an interesting sidelight to owning a particular copy of a rare book.

re-backed — A book that has been given a new spine or strip along the back to secure the front and back covers.

sophisticated — A euphemistic term for a book that has had pages added or replaced from other copies.

variants — A copy of a particular edition that is noticeably different from other copies because of misprint, changes made during printing, or other factors.

LEADING ANTIQUARIAN BOOKSELLERS AND RESTORERS

Booksellers

Argosy Book Store, Inc., New York, N.Y.
Out-of-print, early maps and prints, Americana, rare medical books, first editions.

Richard B. Arkway, Inc., New York, N.Y.
Atlases, maps, illustrated books, travel, Americana.

J.N. Bartfield, New York, N.Y.
Paintings, bindings, sets, rare books, color plate books.

Martin Breslauer, Inc., New York, N.Y.
Autographs, early illustrated books, fine bindings, incunabula, manuscripts.

The Current Company, Bristol, R.I.
Americana, rare and early literature, English and American first editions, voyages and travels, important works in all fields.

James Cummins, Bookseller, New York, N.Y.
Literature, sporting books, press books.

Dawson's Book Shop, Los Angeles, Cal.
Western Americana, books about books, miniature books, mountaineering, Oriental art.

John F. Fleming, Inc., New York, N.Y.
Rare books, first editions, manuscripts.

Anthony Garnett — Fine Books, St. Louis, Mo.
Fine printing, first editions, press books, English literature.

Edwin V. Glaser, Rare Books, Sausalito, Cal.
Early science and medicine, history of ideas, rare books in many fields.

Lucien Goldschmidt, Inc., New York, N.Y.
Fine arts, French literature, illustrated books (fifteenth–twentieth century), prints, drawings.

Goodspeed's Book Shop, Inc., Boston, Mass.
Autographs, Americana, genealogies, first editions, prints.

Lathrop C. Harper, Inc., New York, N.Y.
Incunabula, illuminated manuscripts, illustrated books, early science and medicine, all fine books before 1800.

Heritage Bookshop, Inc., Los Angeles, Cal.
Rare books, Californiana, press books, manuscripts, first editions.

John Howell — Books, San Francisco, Cal.
Rare books and manuscripts in all fields, American prints and paintings.

Joseph the Provider — Books, Santa Barbara, Cal.
Modern literature, manuscripts, letters, signed and associated copies, first editions.

H.P. Kraus, New York, N.Y.
Incunabula, history of science, cartography, Americana, medieval manuscripts.

George S. MacManus Co., Philadelphia, Pa.
English and American literature, Pennsylvania, local history, rare Americana, Western Americana.

Jeremy Norman & Co., Inc., San Francisco, Cal.
Medicine, science and technology, natural history, voyages and travels, art and illustrated books.

The Ravenstree Company, "Tor Haven," Wellton, Ariz.
English books before 1800, Americana, classics, drama, general rare and fine books.

B. & L. Rootenberg — Rare Books, Sherman Oaks, Cal.
Rare books and manuscripts, science and medicine, literary classics, first editions.

Leona Rostenberg & Madeleine B. Stein — Rare Books, New York, N.Y.
Renaissance, political theory, ephemera.

William Salloch, Ossining, N.Y.
Rare books and manuscripts, incunabula classics, Renaissance, Middle Ages.

Justin G. Schiller, Ltd. New York, N.Y.
Early children's literature, illustrated books, original drawings, decorative arts, history of education.

Charles Sessler, Inc., Philadelphia, Pa.
Rare books, prints, rare maps.

C.A. Stonehill, Inc., New Haven, Conn.
English literature and history, incunabula, manuscripts, appraisals.

W. Thomas Taylor, Austin, Tex.
American literature, typography, incunabula, press books, English literature.

Trebizond Rare Books, New York, N.Y.
English, continental, and American literature, voyages and travels, Americana.

Ximenes Rare Books, Inc., New York, N.Y.
Rare books, English and American literature, travels, science and medicine, economics.

Zeitlin & Ver Brugge, Los Angeles, Cal.
Early science, natural history, fine arts, history of medicine, fine press books.

Irving Zucker — Art Books, New York, N.Y.
Typography and printing, old and rare books, modern French illustrated, fine and applied arts, color plate books.

Specialists in Book and Manuscript Restoration

Caroline Horton, New York, N.Y.

Sky Meadow Bindery, Inc., Suffern, N.Y.

Laura Young, New York, N.Y.

SUGGESTED READING

The most comprehensive single source for general and author bibliographies is *The New Cambridge Bibliography of English Literature,* 4 vols. plus an index, published by Cambridge University, England, 1973-1976. This invaluable reference source lists numerous individual author bibliographies as well as critical and bibliographical essays on particular topics and authors.

Individual author bibliographies and topics other than literature are far too numerous to list here. The would-be collector should know, however, that almost any conceivable subject — from aeronautics to insects — has some published bibliographic listings. The quickest source to these may be found by inquiring at the reference desk of any large university or municipal library. Antiquarian book dealers, of course, will be able to refer the collector to the standard bibliographical references relating to any topics of interest.

Some particularly useful bibliographic references for collectors follow.

Blanck, J.N. *Bibliography of American Literature.* 6 vols. New Haven: Yale University Press for the Bibliographical Society of America, 1955-1963.

Bowers, Fredson. *Principles of Bibliographical Description.* Princeton: Princeton University Press, 1949. Reprinted by Russell and Russell, New York, 1962.

The Grolier Club of New York. *100 Books Famous in English Literature.* New York, 1902. Reprinted by Kraus, Millwood, N.Y.

Hayward, John. *English Poetry, A Descriptive Catalogue: First and Early Editions of Works of the English Poets from Chaucer to the Present Day.* National Book League, 1947, rev. 1950. Reprinted by Greenwood Press, Westport, Conn.

McKerrow, Ronald B. *An Introduction to Bibliography for Literary Students.* Cambridge: Oxford University Press, 1927.

Pollard, A.W., and Redgrave, G.R. *A Short-Title Catalogue of Books Printed in England, Scotland and Ireland and of English Books Printed Abroad, 1475-1640.* London: The Bibliographical Society, and Cambridge: Oxford University Press, 1962. Second edition (Vol. 2), 1976.

Sadleir, Michael. *19th Century Fiction.* 2 vols. Los Angeles: London and University of California Press, 1951.

Shawyer, N.M. *A Catalogue of the Collection of 18th Century Printed Books and Manuscripts Formed by Lord Rothschild.* London: privately printed, 1954.

Unger, Emma V., and Jackson, William A. *The Carl H. Pforzheimer Library of English Literature, 1475-1700.* 3 vols. New York: privately printed, 1940.

Wing, David. *Short-Title Catalogue of Books Printed in England, Scotland, Ireland, Wales and British America, and of English Books Printed in Other Countries, 1641-1700.* Second edition, 2 vols. New York: Index Society, Columbia University Press, and Modern Language Association, 1972 and 1981.

Closed-End Funds

Thomas J. Herzfeld *

BASIC CHARACTERISTICS

Although they are one of the oldest forms of investment, closed-end funds are among the most misunderstood and, consequently, most often overlooked investment areas today. Yet they offer investors unique values and attractive opportunities. Also known as publicly traded funds or closed-end investment trusts (CEITs), their origins can be traced to the early nineteenth century. King William I of the Netherlands generally is credited with forming the first one (in Belgium) in 1822; thereafter they flourished, particularly among English and Scottish investors in the latter 1800s. The first U.S. fund was formed in 1893 and, until the time of the stock market crash of 1929, closed-end funds remained the dominant form of publicly owned investment companies.

Distinctions Between Closed- and Open-End Funds

The dominance of closed-end funds in the market ended with the arrival of mass-appeal open-end investment companies. (See article on Mutual Funds, elsewhere in this volume.) The two groups may be thought of as first cousins in that they are as much alike in fundamental purpose as they are different in the means they use to achieve that end. Both, of course, are investment companies; that is, they are companies whose business it is to invest the capital they attract from investors in the securities markets. The stockholder of either type of fund owns an equity in assets that consist primarily of stocks and bonds. The job of either fund's management is to enhance the value of its portfolio through profitable buying, selling, and holding of these securities. That the two types differ in their appeal to investors is clear from the record: In recent years, mutual funds have, by and large, outpaced closed-end funds in the growth of both assets and shareholders. Closed-end funds are distinct from mutual funds in two basic respects: the way in which they are capitalized (hence, marketed) and how their shares are priced.

Capitalization. Unlike the standard fixed-capital structure of all closed-end funds, the mutuals have open-ended capitalizations. When an investor purchases shares of a mutual fund, the fund issues new shares and receives that new capital. Conversely, when an investor wishes to sell mutual fund shares, it is done through the fund, which redeems the shares and diminishes its capitalization in the

* Thomas J. Herzfeld is President, Thomas J. Herzfeld & Co., Inc., South Miami, Fla.

process. Thus, a mutual fund's shares are continuously increasing or decreasing, based directly on share sales and redemptions. A closed-end fund, in contrast, has a fixed capitalization just like an industrial corporation. It makes one initial issue of stock and the shares then trade in the open market (usually on the New York Stock Exchange (NYSE)), although off-board trading in the so-called third market was introduced in 1981. When an investor purchases shares in a closed-end fund, the seller is another investor rather than the fund itself. Similarly, when an investor sells shares in a closed-end fund, the buyer is another investor and not the fund.

Pricing. The other principal difference between closed- and open-end funds is the way they are priced. Mutual funds are bought and sold at prices based directly on their net asset value (NAV) per share. The NAV per share is the total net assets of the fund divided by the outstanding shares (e.g., if the fund has $15 million in net assets and one million shares outstanding, its NAV is $15.00). If the mutual fund is a no-load fund, it will issue and redeem shares at the NAV. (Load mutual funds issue shares at the NAV plus a sales charge and redeem at the NAV.) Closed-end funds are priced by the forces of supply and demand in the open marketplace. When buyers are abundant and sellers are scarce, the price will rise. When sellers predominate, the price will decline, irrespective of the fund's underlying assets.

Varieties of Closed-End Funds

Of approximately seventy closed-end funds whose shares are traded publicly, the combined market values of outstanding stock in the latter months of 1981 approached some $8 billion. That not inconsiderable sum, representing the total value of shares that (for the most part) discount the NAV of their respective portfolio holdings, may in turn be divided among five basic investment categories: stock, bond, convertible bond, specialty, and dual-purpose. (See Table 1 on page 83.)

Stock funds. This type was the first to be developed and remains the most common today, with some forty different companies trading publicly. Each limits its portfolio to primarily equity investments, and seeks appreciation (capital gains) as its primary objective. The three largest stock funds, ranked by total assets, are: Tri-Continental, $807,331,477; Madison Fund, Inc., $604,877,408; and Adams Express Co., $320,549,782.

Bond and convertible-bond funds. There are approximately twenty-seven bond funds at present, mostly formed in the 1970s, together with four convertible-bond funds of more recent vintage. All told, these account for well over $2 billion in total assets. Bond funds (of which twenty-three are listed on the NYSE) have income as their primary objective; convertible-bond funds seek to combine income with appreciation. The three largest bond funds, ranked by total assets, are:

TABLE 1. Major Closed-End Funds

Fund	*Symbol*	*Exchange*	*Type*	*Total Assets (in millions)*
Adams Express	ADX	NYSE	Stock	$320.549
American General Convertible Securities	AGS	NYSE	Convertible Bond	99.859
American General Bond Fund	AGB	NYSE	Bond	170.000
ASA, Ltd.	ASA	NYSE	Specialty	628.416
General American Investments	GAM	NYSE	Stock	211.931
John Hancock Income Securities	JHS	NYSE	Bond	104.000
Heizer	HZR	ASE	Specialty	308.945
INA Investment Securities	IIS	NYSE	Bond	58.845
Madison Fund	MAD	NYSE	Stock	604.877
Massachusetts Mutual Income Investments	MIV	NYSE	Bond	106.949
Mexico Fund	MXF	NYSE	Specialty	58.680
Niagara Share Corp.	NGS	NYSE	Stock	175.052
Pacific American Income Shares	PAI	NYSE	Bond	66.421
Petroleum & Resources	PEO	NYSE	Specialty	257.305
Tri-Continental Corp.	TY	NYSE	Stock	807.331

SOURCE: Thomas J. Herzfeld & Co., Inc.

American General Bond Fund, $170,000,000; Intercapital Income, $136,000,000; and John Hancock Income Securities, $104,000,000.

Specialty funds. These deal essentially with stock investments and specialize by limiting their portfolios to holdings in select areas of investor interest. They include such varied investments as gold and precious metal funds, venture capital investment companies, utility funds, funds with positions concentrated in a few companies, funds invested in a single country or region, and funds invested in a single industry.

Dual-purpose funds. A relative handful of these came to market in the latter 1960s, with fixed expiration dates extending in most cases into the 1980s. The dual-purpose closed-end fund has a leveraged capital structure and two classes of stock: common and preferred. Common shareholders are entitled to all of the capital gains of the company; preferred shareholders are entitled to all of the income. At a specified date, the preferred shares are redeemed at a specified price; the assets remaining belong to the common shareholders. The common shareholders then determine by vote whether to continue the company as an open-end fund or to liquidate. Examples (with expiration years) include: Leverage Fund of Boston (1982), Scudder Duo Vest (1982), Income and Capital Shares (1982), Gemini Fund (1984), and Hemisphere Fund (1985).

Fixed-unit investment trusts. These are also closed-end funds, as defined by the Investment Company Act of 1940. However, their shares are not traded publicly. Furthermore, they differ from the publicly traded closed-end funds in a fundamental respect: Their portfolios, rather than being actively managed, are frozen, comprising only those securities (often tax-exempt municipals) acquired at the outset. (See articles on Municipal Securities and Corporate Bonds, elsewhere in this volume.)

ATTRACTIVE FEATURES

Buying Stocks and Bonds at a Discount

The most obvious advantage of the closed-end fund, when purchased at a discount from NAV, is that an investor is buying something worth a dollar for seventy or eighty cents. This gives closed-end fund investors something unique in the world of investments: free leverage. In other forms of financial leverage, the buyer pays either interest (i.e., on a margin account) or premiums (i.e., call options). The closed-end fund offers, in a sense, negative cost for the leverage because the investor receives the dividends on 100 cents on the dollar, but invests only a fraction of a dollar.

Management of Investments

Closed-end funds offer all the advantages of investing in the securities of publicly held corporations — at the relatively small cost of a fee deducted from earnings — with some minimalization of the risk factors inherent in the markets for stocks and bonds. This is the result of each portfolio being under the active management of a professional investment team.

Diversification

Closed-end investment companies, like mutual funds, offer by definition a diversification of invested capital. This will vary, to be sure, depending on the type of closed-end fund and, to a lesser extent, the sheer amount of assets with which it has been entrusted. Through a single purchase, an investor is buying indirectly 50 to 100 stocks in most stock funds and a similar number of bonds in the case of a bond fund.

In some instances, the fund may own a speculative position, which an investor might be wary of buying directly, but which he can afford in a fund holding because of the principle of safety through diversification.

Regulatory Protection

Both closed-end and open-end funds offer the investor at least the promise of governmental protection — in addition to that afforded all investors by the Securities and Exchange Commission (SEC) — through SEC regulation of the funds themselves under the Investment Company Act of 1940. In practice, it is a very rare instance to find legal irregularities in investment companies.

Marketability and Investor Liquidity

The shares of closed-end funds are as marketable as are any other publicly traded securities and more so than many, since by and large they are listed on a major stock exchange or, if over the counter, in the National Association of Securities Dealers Automatic Quotation (NASDAQ) computerized daily data. All major brokerage firms execute orders in closed-end fund shares; at present only one firm [1] specializes in making off-board markets.

A fund may own a highly illiquid portfolio, but the fund's shares are not necessarily illiquid. An example of this phenomenon lies in the closed-end bond funds that own private placements.

The fund receives higher interest on its bond portfolios because it has purchased privately placed bonds. The shareholders of the fund receive the benefit of the higher interest in the form of higher dividends, with all the liquidity of an NYSE-listed stock.

TAX CONSEQUENCES

When an investment company realizes a long-term capital gain and distributes the gain to its shareholders in the form of a dividend, the shareholder treats it as a long-term capital gain. Therefore, even if an investor held the fund for only a month or two, he is taxed at the long-term capital gains tax rate on the dividend. There are opportunities to convert short-term capital gains to long-term capital gains utilizing closed-end funds. Also, in some cases it is possible to convert regular income into capital gains.

POTENTIAL RISKS

Central to any discussion of closed-end funds is the concept of the discount from NAV. As noted, the price of a closed-end fund share is based on the

[1] Thomas J. Herzfeld & Co., Inc.

open-market forces of supply and demand. Therefore, at any given time, that price could be above NAV (putting a premium on the stock), equal to NAV, or below it (at a discount). If a fund's NAV is $15 per share and the market price is $17, the fund's stock is trading at a $2 premium. But if the same fund is selling at $12, it is trading at a $3 — or 20 percent — discount from NAV. In fact, for some years now the overwhelming majority of closed-end funds have been selling at discounts, some of these quite sharp. While this is clearly disadvantageous to the long-term shareholder, it represents (in this writer's judgment) a buying opportunity for the new investor; indeed, an excessive discount presents an exceptional investment opportunity. During a sustained bull market, that discount can disappear; of course, it is likely to reappear in the course of the next downswing.

Lack of Sponsorship

A primary reason behind the closed-end fund discount is thought to be the fund's lack of a sponsor or sales agent, which leaves it bereft of promotional backing in a hotly competitive market. Most stockbrokers understandably prefer to sell mutual funds (at an 8 percent commission or load) or fixed-unit investment trusts (5 percent selling commission), instead of closed-end funds. The commission charge for buying or selling shares of a closed-end fund is the same as that for any other stock and, as elsewhere in the market, that commission has been subject to negotiated rates since 1975. Currently, it averages only about one percent. While this is a favorable factor for the customer, its effect is a disincentive for the broker. His attention is logically directed toward the open-end funds, with the probable consequence that the market for closed-end funds is inhibited, and prices are depressed.

An exception to this lack-of-sponsorship factor occurs when a new closed-end fund comes to market. It may be due to the extra commission earned by brokers when they underwrite any new issue. For instance, if a new closed-end fund issue comes to market at $12, the current underwriting spread would be approximately 80 cents, or roughly 6.7 percent. Unfortunately, such sponsorship occurs when it is needed least — when the fund, as a new issue, already is apt to be priced at a premium over NAV.

Other factors. Depending on the season, the state of the market, or the quality of the fund itself, a number of additional reasons may be cited (in varying degree) to explain the discount from NAV exhibited by any given fund. General contributory causes include year-end tax-selling, a heavy overhang of competitive issues (e.g., fixed-unit investment trusts), and the all-pervasive impact of a bear market. Specific causes affecting one fund but not necessarily another might include poor yield, sub-par performance, high expense ratios, illiquid portfolios, and potential capital gains tax liabilities. Generally speaking, however, bull markets tend to be bullish for the group. Like most other companies on the stock market, closed-end funds sell at higher prices, narrowing their discounts and even converting these to premiums.

Eliminating the Discount Through Reorganization

Shareholders of closed-end funds seem endlessly frustrated by the discount. They reason that the shareholders of mutual funds can realize full value for their shares through the normal redemption process. In contrast, closed-end fund owners usually must sell their shares below true value because of the perpetual discount from NAV. Growing numbers of them feel that they have found a solution to this dilemma: conversion of their closed-end fund to an open-end mutual fund. Such reorganization can be achieved by a shareholder proposal and the subsequent affirmative vote of a majority of the outstanding shares. Once the fund has been reorganized, it must redeem its shares at net asset value.

Pros and cons. Usually, however, the fund's management will oppose such a change in status. A principal reason is that once it has been reorganized, the fund's assets may shrink drastically from a flood of redemptions, thereby reducing management fees, which generally are based on a percentage of assets. There are other arguments pro and con as to reorganization. A fact often overlooked by both sides is that by eliminating the discount through reorganization, the shareholders are also eliminating the possibility of selling their shares at a premium. In any case, over the past two decades, at least fifteen closed-end funds have been open-ended through outright reorganization or merger into existing mutual funds.

REPRESENTATIVE TYPES OF INVESTORS

Shareholders in closed-end funds represent virtually the entire spectrum of individual and institutional investors, with the exception of other investment companies. Increasingly, however, today's shareholders are more sophisticated than the investor population at large, and include such professionals as bankers, brokers, and hedge-fund buyers.

IMPORTANT FACTORS IN BUYING AND SELLING

Deciding Between Closed-End and Open-End Funds

Most studies have found that, on average, the performance of mutual funds and closed-end funds is similar (in terms of NAV). Any decision to purchase one type over the other should focus on the relative size of the discount from NAV of the closed-end fund. During periods when such discounts are of average or deeper than average proportions, the closed-end fund shares offer superior profit potential. Alternatively, when closed-end funds in general are selling at narrow discounts, or even at premiums above NAV, the mutual fund — and, specifically, the no-load mutual — would seem to have the more attractive prospects. Assuming there is a rising stock market, consider two hypothetical examples.

(1) *Deep discounts.* This is the more favorable buying situation for closed-end funds. Suppose the following factors:

- The Dow-Jones industrial average (DJI), the market's most popular index, is at 950.
- Closed-end fund ABC, with $9.50 NAV, is selling at only $7.50, a deep discount of 21 percent.
- Mutual fund M, also with $9.50 NAV, is priced to sell at $10.26, its NAV plus the 8 percent load (sales commission).
- No-load mutual fund Q, also with $9.50 NAV, sells at $9.50.

Now let us see what happens to these prices and to an investor in each fund some time later, after the market has risen by 100 points and the asset values of all three funds have made equivalent gains:

- The DJI is up 10.5 percent, to 1050.
- Closed-end fund ABC, its NAV up proportionately to $10.50, has narrowed the discount to 10 percent as its price has risen to $9.45. Profit: $1.95, or 26 percent before commission and 21 percent net.
- Mutual fund M, with NAV at $10.50, is priced for redemption at the same $10.50. Profit: $.24, or 2.3 percent net.
- No-load mutual fund Q, at $10.50 NAV, is also redemption-priced at $10.50. Profit: $1.00, or (with no commissions) 10.5 percent net.

(2) *Narrow discount.* The clear-cut advantage to the investor who buys a deep-discounted closed-end fund in preference to either type of open-end fund is sacrificed, however, if the closed-end fund is only narrowly discounted (all else being equal). To illustrate, assume a situation with all the foregoing factors the same except for a narrower discount:

- DJI at 950.
- Closed-end fund XYZ: $9.50 NAV, price $9.25 (discount only 2.6 percent).
- Mutual fund M: $9.50 NAV, offering price (with 8 percent load) $10.26.
- No-Load mutual fund Q: $9.50 NAV, price $9.50.

Now let's look at how these investments might fare relative to one another in those same market circumstances:

- DJI up 10.5 percent to 1050.
- Closed-end fund XYZ: $10.50 NAV, price now $9.45 (same as fund ABC in the first example), a widening of its discount, to 10 percent. Profit: $.20, or 2.2 percent; but after commission, a net loss of 2.2 percent.
- Mutual fund M: $10.50 NAV, redemption price $10.50. Profit: $.24, or 2.3 percent net.

- No-load mutual fund Q: $10.50 NAV, redemption price $10.50. Profit: $1.00, or 10.5 percent net.

Other considerations. In a declining market, the typical closed-end fund also will offer better protection if purchased at a wide discount. Closed-end funds, moreover (unlike mutuals), are marginable if listed on an exchange, as most are. It should be noted, too, that while equal performances may be assumed for illustrative purposes (as in the examples above), actual performance comparisons among several different funds can never be projected with certainty.

Hedging the Closed-End Investment

Strategies. An almost infinite variety of hedging strategies has been developed and used, for the most part successfully, by imaginative investment professionals. Some require considerably greater sophistication on the part of investor/traders than might otherwise be the norm. The more popular strategies include the following:

- Buy a closed-end fund selling at an excessive discount; at the same time sell short another closed-end fund that is priced at a premium. *Point:* If a down market carries the first fund's shares still lower, it will almost surely do greater damage to the premium-priced fund, enabling the short-seller to cover at a profit that more than offsets the loss. (See article on Options — Puts and Calls, elsewhere in this volume.)
- Buy a closed-end fund at an excessive discount; meanwhile, go short on an equivalent amount of individual stocks in the same fund's portfolio. *Point:* During a rally, the NAV will rise in direct proportion to the rise in the short positions. However, the long position in the fund will outperform the rise in the funds stocks as the discount narrows.
- Buy a closed-end bond fund at an excessive discount; sell short U.S. Treasury bond futures, or a combination of U.S. Treasury and corporate bonds. *Point:* As the bond market rallies and the excessive discount of the bond fund narrows, the long position should become more profitable than the short position. The loss in the short position will mirror the performance of the overall bond market, but because of the leverage factor in buying the bond market at a discount via the fund, it will produce a larger profit than the loss on the short position.
- Buy a closed-end fund that is to be open-ended and is selling at a discount; sell short the stocks in the fund's portfolio. *Point:* This is a riskless arbitrage. As the closed-end fund approaches its self-destruct date, the discount will narrow. As an open-end fund, it will not sell at any discount — it is redeemable at NAV. The trader is locking in the discount as a profit. (See article on Arbitrage, elsewhere in this volume.)
- Buy a closed-end fund at an excessive discount; sell naked call options against the fund's portfolio positions. *Point:* This strategy (developed by the writer and known as the "Herzfeld Hedge") may be summarized as follows:

The thrust of the strategy is that if the stock market declines, the diminishing time factor of the option plus the probable erosion of the price of the underlying stock exerts pressure on the excessive premium of the option. This probably would result in a greater gain on the short option position than the resulting loss in the long position on the excessively discounted fund. If the market rises, in-the-money options will tend to lose their rich premiums and will probably not rise as fast as their underlying stocks. In addition, the diminishing time factor is working against the option. At the same time as the underlying stocks rise, the net asset value of the fund should increase, combined with the probable narrowing of its discount, possibly causing it to become more profitable than the loss developing in the options. The hedge may also result in dividends being received on the long positions in the fund.

- Sell short a closed-end fund priced at a premium; write naked put options against the fund's portfolio positions (the so-called Reverse Herzfeld Hedge).

CUSTODIAL CARE

The same precautions apply to the safekeeping of closed-end fund certificates as to stocks, bonds, and other investments. The investor may leave his certificates in the custody of a brokerage firm or may retain possession himself, taking normal precautions for physical security.

GLOSSARY

closed-end fund— An investment company having a fixed number of shares outstanding. Closed-end funds do not redeem shares at their net asset value; shares are bought and sold at the prevailing market price.

dual-purpose fund— A closed-end fund having two classes of shares, each of which comprises 50 percent of the fund's outstanding shares. Income shares receive all of the fund's income but no capital appreciation; capital shares receive none of the fund's income but all of any capital appreciation or depreciation.

fixed-unit investment trust— A closed-end fund, not traded publicly, with a frozen rather than actively managed portfolio.

mutual fund— An open-end investment company in which shares are redeemed at net asset value rather than at market-determined value, as with closed-end funds.

net asset value per share— The per-share value of the assets in an investment company's portfolio, less outstanding liabilities.

no-load fund— A mutual fund that does not impose a sales charge.

open-end fund— A mutual fund without a fixed number of shares outstanding. Shares are sold and redeemed at their net asset value at the time of the transaction.

prospectus— The formal description of a new issue of securities, as required by the Securities Act of 1933.

specialty fund— A fund that limits its portfolios to holdings in select areas or a single region or industry.

SUGGESTED READING

Periodicals

Drach Market Research. Published by Drach Market Research, Inc., Key Biscayne, Florida. A continuing review and analysis of stock market timing, useful for closed-end fund traders.

Herzfeld Weekly Closed-End Bond Fund Report. Published by Thomas J. Herzfeld & Co., Inc., South Miami, Florida. Ongoing review and analysis of one fast-growing closed-end fund group.

The Income Investor. Published by Ceryx Corp., New York, N.Y.

Articles

Bettner, Jill. "Your Money Matters," The *Wall Street Journal,* April 13, 1981, page 40, col. 1.

Grant, James. "Discount to Premium," *Barron's,* April 28, 1980, page 4.

Herzfeld, Thomas J. "Why the Widening of Closed-End Fund Discounts?" *Investment Dealer's Digest,* December 19, 1978, page 24.

Phalon, Richard. "Better Mañana," *Forbes,* June 22, 1981, page 98.

Sokoloff, Kiril. "The Open End in Closed-End Funds," *Business Week Letter,* November 29, 1976, pages 3-4.

"Sound Tactics, Bad Strategy," *Forbes,* August 4, 1980, page 69.

Reference Books

Cobleigh, Ira, and Dorfman, Bruce. *The Roaring Eighties on Wall Street.* New York: Macmillan, 1982.

Herzfeld, Thomas J. *The Investor's Guide to Closed-End Funds — The Herzfeld Hedge.* New York: McGraw-Hill, 1979.

Herzfeld, Thomas J., and Drach, Robert F. *High Return-Low Risk Investments Combining Market Timing, Stock Selection and Closed-End Funds.* New York: G.P. Putnam's Sons, 1981.

Phalon, Richard. *Your Money — How to Make it Work Harder Than You Do.* New York: St. Martin's Press, 1979.

Coins

Q. David Bowers *

BASIC CHARACTERISTICS

Coins, once the domain of the historian and student, have become popular as an investment medium. Pension funds, trusts, profit-sharing plans, investment advisers, and many individuals have purchased coins for their investment potential.

Indeed, the track record of selected coins, when viewed over the perspective of several decades, is nothing less than spectacular. Using figures published annually in R.S. Yeoman's *A Guide Book of United States Coins,* the performance of a coin can be charted easily. (See *Price Performance Tables* in this article.) An Uncirculated (or new condition) 1796 silver quarter-dollar was listed at $175 in 1950. By 1955 the price had climbed to $325. The year 1960 saw a $1,450 price, which increased to $4,250 by 1965. In 1970 a figure of $5,750 was registered, and it climbed to $12,000 in 1975 and to $23,000 in 1980. (See Table 3 on page 112.) Is such growth indicative of a one-of-a-kind situation, or is it representative of coins in general? Actually, hundreds of different U.S. coins have performed nearly as well or even better in past years. An 1834 Uncirculated quarter climbed from $5 in 1950 to $1,900 in 1980. A study of fifteen classic U.S. coins — scarce, early issues in higher-condition grades—shows that a group valued at $1,010 in 1950 was valued at $92,750 thirty years later. (See Table 3 on page 112.)

This discussion is concerned primarily with U.S. coins, as they are of greatest concern to the typical investor. However, over 2,500 years, countless varieties of coins have been issued by hundreds of different authorities, ranging from countries to cities, states, and private individuals.

Historical Background

Briefly defined, "coins" are metallic objects, usually round in shape, that serve as a medium of exchange. In modern times, coins have been struck at special government institutions called "mints," which use high-speed presses to stamp them out from designs on engraved dies. The location at which a coin was minted can sometimes affect its value and make it desirable to a collector.

In past years there have been seven different mints in the United States. The Philadelphia Mint, established in 1792 and first operated on a production basis

* Q. David Bowers is Chairman of Bowers & Ruddy Galleries, Inc., Wolfeboro, N.H., and Los Angeles. Acknowledgment is made to Richard H. Bagg, Research Associate, Bowers & Ruddy Galleries, Inc.

in 1793, is the main mint today. Over the years the institution has moved to several different buildings and locations within Philadelphia, each one larger than the last. With only a few exceptions, coins struck at the Philadelphia Mint have no mintmark or mint letter.

In 1838 three additional mints were established. The New Orleans Mint operated until 1909 and issued coins bearing "O" mintmarks. The Dahlonega (Georgia) and Charlotte (North Carolina) Mints each operated from 1838 to 1861, struck gold coins only, and issued coins with "D" and "C" mintmarks, respectively.

The San Francisco Mint, still in operation today, commenced business in 1854. Its coins bear "S" mintmarks. From 1870 through 1893 the Carson City (Nevada) Mint produced coins, mainly silver, with "CC" mintmarks, mainly using metal from the nearby Comstock Lode.

In 1906 the Denver Mint, still in operation today, commenced business. Its coins bear "D" mintmarks.

ATTRACTIVE FEATURES

Inherent Interest

Coin collecting is an interesting pursuit. As coin prices have increased over the years, many coin collectors have found that their favorite hobby has also been their best investment. Coins literally carry imprints of history. Rulers, nations, wars, monetary crises, exploration and discovery, and countless other situations have been depicted on or memorialized by coins. Imagine where a worn 1890 nickel has been and what it has seen: It may have traveled to the 1893 Columbian Exposition in Chicago, been in and out of penny arcades, furnished admission to Charlie Chaplin movies, and so on. Carson City silver dollars of the 1880s, fairly easily obtained today, are large and heavy reminders of the rip-roaring days of silver mining, when the West was truly wild.

The coin collector can share experiences with others by belonging to organizations, attending conventions, engaging in research, and becoming otherwise involved. There are countless books and periodicals to read, museums to visit, and facts to learn. After a hard day on the job, many people find solace and comfort by quietly studying metallic reminders of years ago.

Convenience

Coins are small and can be stored easily. A bank safe-deposit box can store hundreds of thousands of dollars worth of rare coins. Because of their size and light weight, coins can be moved from place to place without attracting attention. They can be safely and easily sent through the mail by registering and insuring them at the post office. Indeed, it may come as a surprise that most commercial coin transactions are handled this way. Coin buyers will travel to Los Angeles,

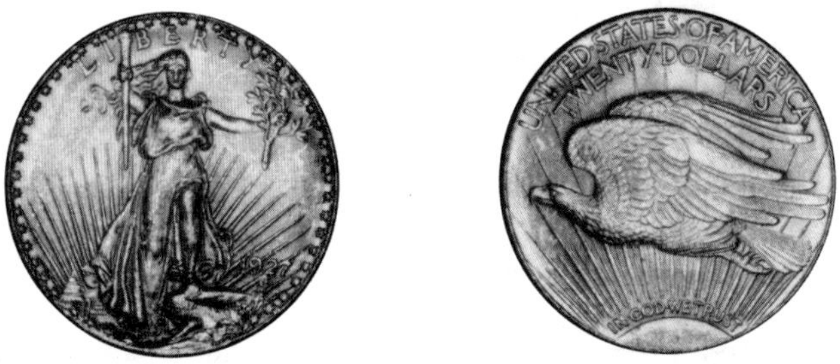

1927 $20 double eagle, the largest regularly issued U.S. coin denomination. These impressive and heavy gold coins have traditionally been favorites with collectors.

1826 half-dollar. At the time this piece was minted, over a century and a half ago, it was the largest actively circulating American silver coin. Silver dollars were rarely used at the time. Today, half-dollars of the draped bust style, minted in 1807 through 1836, are exceedingly popular with collectors and investors alike.

1898 half-dollar, representative of the style designed by Charles E. Barber and features a Liberty head. The design was produced from 1892 through 1915. There are a number of scarce and rare dates.

FIG. 1. Some Popular Rare Coins

New York, or some other location to bid in an auction and then will have their purchases shipped home by mail, simply because that is the safest way. By means of insured, registered mail, the U.S. Postal Service enables a patron to insure a valuable article (up to specified limits) and then sign for it on receipt. In addition, the Postal Service itself maintains strong internal safeguards whereby each person handling the article within the system must sign for it as it is transferred. When the Hope Diamond was sent from New York to Washington, D.C. a few years ago, a number of methods were considered to ensure its safety, including armored truck, special messenger, and mail. It was finally decided to send it by registered mail through the post office. It arrived safely.

Application of Standard Descriptions

Coin nomenclature is universal and a very valuable coin can be described briefly. For example, the description "1894-S dime, MS-65" [1] refers to a coin mentioned earlier, a Choice Uncirculated example of the 1894-S dime of which two dozen pieces were made and only about a dozen of which are known today. With such a brief description a dealer in Boston can offer a piece to another dealer in Los Angeles, give a price, and in a moment's notice a decision can be reached. There is no need for complicated and involved description or procedures. Reference books exist on almost all areas of U.S. and world coinage, so the coin buyer has a wealth of information available for research and study.

Active Market

Thousands of dealers worldwide must constantly replenish their stock to supply hundreds of thousands, if not millions, of customers. Most dealers find that buying coins, not selling them, is their greatest problem. Important collections of choice coins have always been in demand and will no doubt always continue to be so.

Demonstrated Track Record

In recent decades, coin prices have trended upwards as charted at five-year intervals. (See *Price Performance Tables* in this article.) As in any market, there have been cycles and fluctuations, and not all coins have gone up in value. For example, a roll of forty 1950-D nickels in Uncirculated grade sold for $1,200 in 1965, but in 1981 was worth only about $300. But for every U.S. coin that went down in price during that year, 100 or more went up. For example, $1,000 invested in a typical group of U.S. coins in 1948 would have increased in value to $72,237 over thirty years later (as reported in Q. David Bowers' *High Profits From Rare Coin Investment*). During the same approximate period the Dow-Jones Industrial average went from 177.30 (the last day of trading figures used

[1] "MS-65" defines the grade of the coin. The grading system is discussed in greater detail later in this article.

in 1948) to about 1,000 early in 1981. Stated another way, a $1,000 investment in the Dow-Jones averages, not including re-investment of dividends, would have yielded slightly more than $5,000 during the same time interval.

At the same time, an investment in a savings account at 5 percent interest (although such interest was not readily available in the United States during the late 1940s and 1950s), with interest compounded quarterly, would have risen from $1,000 to the $5,000 range by early 1981.

Also during the same period, inflation caused the purchasing power of the dollar to decline very sharply. According to U.S. government statistics, $1,000 in 1948 (if kept in cash) would have declined in purchasing power to less than $400.

Privacy

Coins may be collected privately. Buyers may be anonymous if they wish, and their neighbors will have no idea that their coin collections, safely stored in safe-deposit boxes, may be worth several times the price of their houses. What a buyer owns in the way of coins is no one else's business. At the same time, too much privacy is not advisable. When buying coins, a collector should always insist upon a written bill of sale and a receipt. Some very "clever" buyers of Krugerrands, who thought they were outwitting the government and everyone else by paying cash for Krugerrands that were believed to contain one ounce of gold each, did not ask for a record. A year or two later they tried to sell the pieces only to find that they were made of gold-plated base metal and were worth nothing. When the original sellers of the pieces are approached, chances are they will either be out of business or will say, "I couldn't have sold those coins. You must have bought them someplace else." It is very important that the buyer insist upon written statements for each and every piece bought.

POTENTIAL RISKS

As suggested above, all is not roses in coin collecting and investing. There are some problem areas, and it is wise to make note of them, as brochures and advertisements offering coins for sale do not always mention them.

Authenticity

There are many clever forgeries of coins, and many people are victimized each year. As mentioned above, it is important to insist upon a written receipt when buying coins, since it is protection if a coin should later be proved spurious. Dealers who are members of the Professional Numismatists Guild and the International Association of Professional Numismatists guarantee the authenticity of each and every coin they sell. If a coin is later determined to be counterfeit, the buyer's money will be refunded in full — an important protection. Although buying a counterfeit coin from a member of one of these organizations is unlikely, mistakes do happen. If an investor buys coins from a dealer who is not established in the rare-coin field, the chance of getting forgeries increases dramatically. During a trip to several European countries, hundreds of U.S. gold coins at various banks and bullion exchanges were examined. Although the pieces bore price tags indicating that they were indeed rare and authentic, less than half of them were genuine. It pays to be careful.

Grading

Under the official American Numismatic Association (ANA) Grading System, a coin is assigned a grade indicating its state of wear. (See *Determining Value* below.) Before buying, an investor should be sure the coins are graded properly, for a small difference in grade can make a big difference in price. Nearly all dealers offer a return period when coins are ordered, usually from fourteen to thirty days after receipt. Use this time to verify that the coins are indeed as described, taking them to other collectors and dealers or submitting them to the ANA Grading Service, which, for a fee, will give a grading opinion. Once the time limit has expired it may be too late to return a coin because of a grading problem. A buyer who pays $4,300 for an MS-65 1886-O silver dollar and later finds that it is only an MS-60 (and worth only $350) may be out of luck unless this is discovered soon after the coin is purchased.

TAX CONSEQUENCES

In many areas there is no property tax to be paid when coins are held. Taxes are due only when the coins are sold at a profit. If the pieces are held for more than one year, the tax will be at the low capital gains rate. The IRS has ruled that under certain conditions rare coins can be exchanged for other rare coins in a tax-free transaction, thus making it possible to upgrade a collection without a tax penalty. (See article on Tax Considerations for Collector-Investors, elsewhere in this volume.) For advice in these matters, investors are urged to consult a professional tax adviser.

IMPORTANT FACTORS IN BUYING AND SELLING

Determining Value

What determines a coin's value? Most people would think that age is the most important factor. Actually, age has very little to do with the value of a coin or its desirability to a collector. It is perhaps surprising to learn that a 2,000-year-old copper coin of ancient Rome can be purchased for five or ten dollars, while certain rare varieties of Lincoln cents that are scarcely thirty years old can cost $1,000 each or more. Among the factors that determine a coin's value are the following:

Condition (basic grades). The condition, or state of wear, of a coin is exceedingly important. With very few exceptions, the closer to new or Uncirculated grade a coin is, the more it is worth. Coins are divided into the following basic grades, as enumerated by the official ANA Grading System.

Uncirculated or mint state (MS). An Uncirculated piece is like new and represents a piece that has not been in hand-to-hand circulation as a medium of exchange. However, when coins emerge from high-speed mechanical presses they are dumped together with other coins into bins, run through mechanical sorters, put into bags, and shipped from bank to bank. Even Uncirculated coins will show some nicks and contact marks. Accordingly, Uncirculated pieces are divided into several subgrades. The ANA Scale runs from condition 1, or a piece that is worn nearly smooth, to condition 70, which is perfect. Uncirculated coins, also known as mint state, fall into the 60 to 70 range. The ANA Grading System notes that an MS-60 or Typical Uncirculated coin is one that shows numerous light surface marks and blemishes but does not show actual wear. The coin may be brilliant (as bright as when first minted) or it may have acquired toning. MS-65, or Choice Uncirculated, refers to a piece that has only a few scattered nicks and marks. Generally, MS-65 is the grade that collectors who can afford the finest aspire to own. MS-70, or Perfect Uncirculated, is a theoretical condition that does not exist for many issues more than a few decades old, simply because of the minting and handling processes described earlier. Additional Uncirculated grades are the intermediate grades of MS-67, or Gem Uncirculated, and MS-63, or Select Uncirculated.

Almost Uncirculated (AU). Once a coin has seen very light wear it may be known as Almost Uncirculated. The ANA Grading System recognizes two divisions: AU-50 and AU-55.

Extremely Fine (EF). This grade, which includes Extremely Fine-40 and Choice Extremely Fine-45 (EF-45), designates a piece that shows more wear than AU but still has nearly all of the design details sharp.

Very Fine (VF). A piece that shows even more wear than Extremely Fine. Designated as VF-20 or VF-30, depending upon the characteristics within the grade.

Fine (F). A piece that is extensively worn, but on which most of the major lettering is still readable. F-12 and F-15 are the numerical equivalents.

Very Good (VG). A piece that is considerably worn and that has some of the lettering gone, particularly on the higher spots. It is numerically designated as VG-8.

Good (G). A coin that is worn almost smooth. Most of the major letters and the date are clear, but many other design details are gone. It is abbreviated as G-4.

Poor, Fair, and About Good (P, F, and AG). Coins that are so worn that they are only of value if they are of exceedingly rare varieties (1 to 3 on numerical grading scale).

Each of the preceding grades has specific detailed definitions, which are listed in *The Official ANA Grading Guide.* This guide must be consulted in order to accurately determine a coin's condition.

Sometimes a small difference in grade can make a vast difference in price. For example, the 1981 edition of *A Guide Book of United States Coins* listed an 1886-O (New Orleans Mint) silver dollar at the following grades and values: VF-20, $22; EF-40, $23; AU-50, $50; MS-60, $350; and MS-65, $4,300. In other words, an MS-60 was listed at seven times more than the price of an AU-50 piece. Even more dramatic is the difference between MS-60 at $350 and MS-65 at $4,300. Obviously, it is crucial to know how to grade coins properly and accurately, or to buy from someone who does. If one were to purchase an MS-65 coin at $4,300 and find that the piece was really only MS-60, more than 90 percent of the investment would be lost immediately. There are many abuses in this area.

In addition to the grades mentioned above, a special grade called "Proof" designates coins made especially for collectors. They are struck from mirror-like dies with a high degree of polish created by specially prepared metallic coining blanks. These coins are produced in limited quantities on slow-speed, hand-fed presses, and have sold at a premium to collectors over the years. Although there are some exceptions, prior to 1968 most Proof coins were struck at the Philadelphia Mint. Since that time the San Francisco Mint has been the issuer. Proof coins, which are graded according to the amount of nicks and marks they have, can be classified as Proof-60 (with numerous marks), Choice Proof-65 (with just a few marks), and Perfect Proof-70. Most early Proofs are collected in Proof-65 grade, with Proof-70 examples unknown. Generally, a Proof coin is worth more than an Uncirculated example of the same issue, but there are some exceptions.

Rarity. Rarity is a prime determinant of a coin's value. If all other factors are equal, a coin of which 100 specimens are known will be worth considerably more than a coin of which there are a million examples. Most of the world's price records for rare coins are held by pieces that are extremely rare. For example, only seven pieces are known of the 1787 Brasher Doubloon, which, at $725,000 (realized in the sale of the Garrett Collection by Bowers & Ruddy Galleries in 1979), stands as the highest price ever recorded at auction for a rare coin of any type. Only fifteen examples are known of the 1804 silver dollar, a specimen of which sold for $400,000 in 1980. An Uncirculated 1894-S dime (just twenty-four were minted and only about a dozen are known today) would bring $125,000 or more if offered today. An 1876-CC twenty-cent piece in Uncirculated grade, of which about two dozen are known, is valued in the $75,000 range.

Rarity depends upon several things. The original mintage is an important factor. Generally, the more pieces that were minted, the more that are apt to survive today. As an example of this, 1,476,490 Liberty-head nickels were made in 1885. In 1911, 39,559,372 nickels of the same design were produced. As might be expected, the 1885 is a scarcer coin. An Uncirculated MS-60 example of the 1885 coin lists in catalogues for $700, while the 1911 in the same grade brings just $175. Sometimes coins were hoarded, with the result that the mintage figures are not particularly meaningful. This is especially true for silver dollars. From 1878 onward the government produced hundreds of millions of silver dollars in response to political pressures from the West. The market for silver was poor, so the government was persuaded to buy quantities of silver that it did not want and to coin them into silver dollars. Millions of these remained in Treasury vaults until the early 1960s, when they were released at face value. Included in the release were pieces dated in the 1870s, 1880s, and 1890s. There were 228,000 1885-CC silver dollars minted and, when an inventory of the Treasury holdings was taken in the 1960s, it was discovered that over half of these still remained in existence in the original bags of issue. Therefore, an Uncirculated 1885-CC dollar is common today. On the other hand, 350,000 1889-CC dollars were minted, but most of these were put into circulation or melted many years ago; consequently, perhaps no more than 5,000 to 10,000 exist today in Uncirculated grade. So although the mintage of an 1889-CC dollar is higher than it is for an 1885-CC, the 1889-CC sells for dozens of times more on today's market.

Coins can have different degrees of rarity in different grades. For example, a 1919-D half-dollar in worn condition, described as G-4, is not particularly hard to find. The catalogue listing is $11. However, an Uncirculated or MS-60 piece is very rare and is listed at $2,500. With the exception of coins that were hoarded by collectors or were not released by the government, most coin issues are scarcer in Uncirculated grade than in worn conditions.

Demand. Demand is one of the most important determinants of a coin's value. Unless someone wants a coin, it is worth only its face value, or the value of its metallic content.

Different series among American coins are collected with varying degrees of interest. Coins that are very popular (and, hence, in great demand) usually bring more than coins that are not. For example, scarce issues among one-cent pieces, nickels, dimes, quarters, half-dollars, and silver dollars tend to sell for high figures, while scarce issues in obscure series sell for less.

A 1914-D Lincoln cent, a coin of which 1,193,000 were minted, lists at $225 in Extremely Fine (EF-40) grade. There are many thousands of these in existence. However, because tens of thousands of people want to obtain one of each date and mintmark variety of these Lincoln cents, the $225 price is easily sustained. On the other hand, there may be a streetcar token of Kingston, Pennsylvania, of which just five examples are known. It too can be Extremely Fine, but because there is very little demand from collectors for rare varieties of Kingston streetcar tokens, the piece may be worth only a few dollars, even though it is thousands of times more rare than the 1914-D Lincoln cent. Demand is everything.

Demand and popularity tend to change over a period of time. Sometimes a particular type of rare coin will be in strong demand for a few years. As soon as the tastes of collectors change, the focus will be on something else. The astute investor will study patterns of demand and will try to predict future changes.

Age. As noted earlier, age is not an important determinant of a coin's value. The public often considers an old coin automatically to be valuable, but, for the collector, such considerations as condition, demand, and rarity are much more important.

Metallic content. The metallic or meltdown value of a coin can be important, particularly for pieces struck in precious metals. A $20 U.S. gold piece of the year 1928 is not particularly rare, for millions of them were minted, but it is quite valuable. Like other $20 or double-eagle pieces, it contains nearly a full ounce of gold, and its value is therefore related to the world market value for gold. Generally, a $20 piece will sell for more than its gold content. For example, if gold is selling for $600 per ounce, an Extremely Fine $20 gold piece of a common date may bring $700. If gold sells for $900, then the coin will bring $1,000. If gold sells for $300, then the coin will bring about $375.

The more common a gold coin is, the more responsive it is to bullion price movements. Among American gold coins there are certain common issues of the denominations $5, $10, and $20. On a worldwide scale, such pieces as the South African Krugerrand, the Austrian 100-corona and the Mexican 50-peso piece, all of gold, are responsive to metallic price fluctuations. Certain other denominations of U.S. gold coins (e.g., $1, $2.50, $3, and $4) are sufficiently rare that they are not affected measurably by changes in the price of gold. For example, an 1861-D (Dahlonga, Georgia, Mint) one-dollar gold piece in Uncirculated MS-60 grade lists at $23,000, although if gold were selling at $600 an ounce, the piece would have a meltdown value of about $15.

Certain silver coins (bags of worn silver dollars and bags of common American silver coins from the 1930s, 1940s, 1950s, and early 1960s) are often traded in bulk based upon the fluctuating value of silver. For investment purposes, bulk gold and silver coins are not particularly related to the rare coin market. The rise and fall of gold and silver bullion is much more of a determinant of the value of a common-date $20 gold piece than is the demand by collectors. Accordingly, investment in such pieces should be guided by the buyer's belief in the future of the metals market, not by coin-collecting considerations.

Other considerations. There are a number of other considerations that help determine a coin's value. The design may be appealing, and the coin may sell more for this reason. Or a coin might have some romantic or historical connection — with the Civil War, for example — and it may sell more for this reason. Sometimes the quality or status of a collection will add to a particular coin's value. The fabulous Garrett Collection was formed during the period from 1865 until about 1940 by the family that managed the Baltimore and Ohio Railroad, and it contained many of the finest known examples of great American rarities. When it was sold at public auction in a series of sales from 1979 through 1981, many pieces sold for much more than other pieces of the same variety would have sold for, because collectors wanted to own pieces that were once in the Garrett Collection.

Selecting a Dealer

The Professional Numismatists Guild, the leading organization of rare-coin dealers, has as its members most of the long-established leading firms, and close to 200 dealers. In addition, thousands of other people buy and sell coins in their spare time as part of a business involving stamps or antiques. There is an active market at all times. (See *Directory of Leading Dealers* in this article.)

When selecting a rare-coin dealer or professional numismatist (as they are called), it is important to check carefully and verify credentials. There are no licensing requirements to become a rare-coin dealer, and anyone who has enough money to print business cards or fancy brochures can proclaim to be "the world's best coin dealer." There have been many problems in this regard, particularly in times of intense coin-market activity. Sometimes the dealers with the most lavish brochures and the highest advertising budgets are of questionable reputation and financial strength.

A dealer who belongs to the Professional Numismatists Guild or to the International Association of Professional Numismatists is pledged to a strict code of ethics, and the buyer has certain protections should any problems arise. However, there are many reputable dealers who do not belong to these groups for various reasons, including length of time in business, insufficient capital, or simply no desire to belong. In any event, the buyer should check around, compare grades and prices, and make a decision. It is easy to avoid mistakes at the outset, but it is not easy to correct them once they have been made. "Investigate before investing" is an axiom appropriate to all areas of investment activity. It is surprising how gullible some coin buyers can be. If someone were to put up a sign in a store window saying "IBM stock at half market price" or "$100 bills for $75 each," few people would be buyers. But if someone puts up a sign saying "The greatest coin dealer offers coins at half price," customers will come flocking in.

Vast fortunes have been made in coin investments, but vast sums have been lost as well. Generally, the greatest gains have gone to those who have taken the time to learn about coins, investigate the subject carefully, and make purchases with patience. Those who have taken the losses generally have been those who have viewed coins as a get-rich-quick scheme and who have spent large sums of money without taking the time to learn even the first thing about grading (in particular), rarity, demand, and other considerations.

Buying Coins

Coins can be bought in several different ways. Many coin dealers issue price catalogues that describe and offer coins for sale. In addition, dealers will service want lists given by customers. Advertisements in *Coin World, Numismatic News,* and other periodicals also list coins for sale. Some firms offer special groups or packages to potential investors, and others have monthly or periodic investment plans.

Each year in the United States there are several dozen rare-coin auctions. Many of these are unreserved and unrestricted, and offer the buyer the chance to bid competitively for desirable coins. However, in order to bid intelligently one must have the requisite knowledge, so auctions usually are the realm of the advanced collector. Still, for the beginner, they furnish a good guide to comparative market values.

Selling Coins

Selling to a dealer. Most dealers are eager to buy choice and rare coins and will make an offer for them. The amount of the offer will depend upon the market conditions at the time, the size of the dealer's stock, economic conditions, the cost the dealer incurs when borrowing money from the bank, and the dealer's demand or desire for the coin. Not all dealers want all coins at all times. And yet, there are enough dealers to constitute a generally strong market. Most dealers will buy coins at 60 to 80 percent of the retail price, with certain high-demand pieces selling for even closer to the posted value. Generally, coins that are very inexpensive are bought for deeper discounts, simply because of the handling involved. A few illustrations follow.

A dealer may want to pay only fifty cents or one dollar for a coin that retails at two dollars, simply because a large part of that coin's value lies in dealer handling. In the 1981 edition of *A Guide Book of United States Coins,* a recent Lincoln cent, an Uncirculated 1980, listed for ten cents. This does not mean that 10,000 of these pieces, having a total face value of $100, could be sold for $1,000. Rather, the pieces would be worth just face value or slightly more. The listing of ten cents per coin, or ten times face value, reflects the dealer's handling cost.

A coin that sells for $10 may be bought for about $5 to $7 by a dealer, depending on the dealer's stock at the time. A $1,000 coin is apt to be more closely traded on a percentage basis and will wholesale for $700 to $800 in many instances.

Selling through an auction catalogue. Auction cataloguers charge a commission for their services. The fee, generally expressed in terms of a percentage, is usually all-inclusive, covering expenses of insurance, photographing important pieces for the catalogue, advertising, printing, preparing, and distributing the catalogue, and many other considerations. Most leading cataloguers with large mailing lists charge about a 20 percent commission, but there are exceptions. When selling coins through an auction catalogue, it is important to investigate what services a seller can receive. Obviously, if a dealer distributes 2,000 copies of the seller's auction catalogue, the seller's coins may be auctioned for 10 percent commission and the dealer may still make a nice profit, while a dealer who distributes 15,000 copies of a seller's catalogue and who charges 20 percent may profit less in the long run. However, it is obvious that if 15,000 people see the catalogue the seller will have a much greater chance of attracting high bids.

In recent years, some auction firms have developed a split-commission arrangement whereby the consigner of the coin is charged, say, 10 percent and the buyer at the sale is charged another 10 percent. Although the 10 percent commission charged to the seller might sound low, it should be borne in mind that people attending the sale have to pay a 10 percent premium when they pay their bill, so they may bid less in competition. The end result is equivalent to charging a 20 percent regular commission.

In view of the spread between buying and selling prices, it is wise to consider coin investment on a long-term basis. Investors who buy coins today and sell them a month or even a year from now may make a lot of money for the dealers involved, but not necessarily for themselves. On the other hand, if the investor holds coins for a long period of time, the dealer markups become less important. For example, a 1932-D Uncirculated quarter listed at $33 in 1950, $45 in 1955, $90 in 1960, $240 in 1965, $250 in 1970, $425 in 1975, and $3,000 in 1980. (See Table 4 on page 113.) Assume, for purposes of illustration, that pieces sell for precisely their catalogue value (in practice, some sell for more and some for less). An investor who paid $425 for a piece in 1975 and sold it for $3,000 in 1980, paying a 20 percent commission upon doing so, would net $2,400, or nearly six times the purchase price. Few would begrudge the dealer's profit in such a situation. On the other hand, an investor who purchased the coin in March of 1980 for $3,000 and attempted to sell it in December of the same year might find that the price did move a bit and that he had taken a $600 loss, certainly not a pleasant situation.

Deciding when to sell. How long should one hold coins? There is no hard-and-fast rule for this, although a minimum of three to five years is advisable, and ten years or longer is even better. As the Tables on pages 110 to 115 vividly demonstrate, those who have held coins for a decade or more generally have done well. The longer the coins are held, assuming the market is trending upward, the greater the profits that will be made, and the buying and selling fee will have less impact.

ACQUIRING A COIN COLLECTION

What Does the Future Hold?

The future for rare-coin investment is unknown, as is the future for investment in the stock market, real estate, the money market, and so on. The best one can do is to consider the factors and come to a reasonable decision.

The future of coin prices will depend upon demand. While investors buying coins help create a market, the ultimate consumer is the collector. If the number of true collectors increases, then the price of coins will generally increase. If the number of collectors declines, then coin prices will decline.

From all indications, coin collecting is on the increase. As of early 1981, membership in the ANA stood at nearly 40,000, an all-time record. (The organization was formed in 1891.) The current trend in our society is for more leisure time to conduct pursuits such as coin collecting, which is a favorable indication. Personal earnings are on the increase, permitting more disposable income for hobbies.

In recent years, coins have become established as an investment medium. Financial institutions have added coins to their portfolios. Many investors, particularly individuals, begin by buying coins strictly as a hedge against inflation. After they have been involved for some time they learn how fascinating coins can be from a historical, artistic, and romantic viewpoint, and then they become collectors. Once this happens, another true collector or consumer is established, and the market is strengthened.

Market Volatility

The coin market is subject to cycles. In 1979–1980 certain coins, rare and bullion-type alike, rose sharply in value, doubling and tripling in many instances. This was due to a worldwide fever for precious metals. Fortunes were made with the rising price of these metals and, as a result, dealers who made large sums of money often re-invested it in the rare-coin market, driving prices up. After the high point in the market, which came early in 1981, prices for many pieces subsided sharply; this cycle was one of several since 1953. In 1957 there was a market break, another in 1966, and another in 1975. Undoubtedly there will be many more in the future, as coin prices do move in cycles. However, by and large, the cycles trend upward, like a saw blade rotating on an angle. There are several things one can do to avoid the effects of cycles. First, when the price of a coin rises sharply, beware. It may indicate that the coin is under speculative pressure. The time to buy is when the market is rather quiet. However, during the quiet periods there is very little done in the way of promotional advertising, so it takes a measure of individual determination and fortitude to buy. The writer has always believed that working against the trend is best — the greatest profits have gone to those who have bought during dips in the cycle and not during rising periods.

Diversification also will help counter the effects of cycles. An investor should buy some gold coins, some silver coins, some copper coins, and some nickel coins, or buy some coins from the early 1800s, and some minted 150 years later. It is a good idea to buy some very scarce coins and, at the same time, some that are not so scarce; it would also be helpful to study numismatic reference books and build a diversified collection or portfolio.

An investor who studies the field before investing and buys carefully will be in a position to get the most value from investment dollars. It is important to buy with a long-term commitment in mind; as the market trends upwards as it has done in the past, an investor will be in an ideal position to take advantage of the profits.

Ways to Collect Coins

By date, mintmark, and variety. For example, Franklin half-dollars were minted from 1948 through 1963. There were several varieties minted each year, each one distinguished by a mintmark on the reverse. Thus, a complete collection of Franklin half-dollars would include such issues as 1948 (without mintmark — struck at Philadelphia), 1948-D, 1949, 1949-D, 1949-S, 1950, 1950-D, 1951, 1951-D, 1951-S, and so on through 1963 (thirty-five varieties in all).

Collections of Indian cents from the first year of issue, 1859, through the last, 1909, Liberty nickels from 1883 through 1912, Buffalo nickels from 1913 through 1938, Mercury dimes from 1916 through 1945, and other series have attracted the attention of collectors.

Certain early coins (one-cent pieces from 1793 through 1857, for example) can be collected by die varieties. During the early years, individual dies used to strike coins were hand-cut, resulting in many interesting variations. Sometimes letters were punched backwards in the die, words were misspelled, numbers were incorrectly put into the die, and so on. Each die had its own characteristic. Such studies form a fascinating area for the specialist.

The date and mintmark collector aspires to own one of each of the different dates, mintmarks, and major varieties with a series. Completing a set by finally acquiring a major scarcity or rarity in the series is akin to the feeling of putting the last word in a crossword puzzle — completion.

By design type. With the demand for coins very strong and the supply of older coins necessarily limited, no one can seriously aspire to collect one of each and every date and mintmark variety of U.S. coins from 1793 (the year the Philadelphia Mint first made coins in quantity for circulation) to the present. Even if one had the necessary financing — which would run to many millions of dollars — certain pieces simply are not available. A practical alternative is to collect by design type. Such a collector wants to obtain one of every major design. Thus, to illustrate the Franklin half-dollar in his collection, the type collector does not want thirty-five different dates and mintmarks from 1948 through 1963; rather, any Franklin half-dollar from 1948 through 1963 (a single example) will suffice. Likewise, any dime, quarter, or half-dollar from the 1892-1915 years will illustrate the Liberty head or Barber (named after the designer) style. A set of major types of U.S. coins offers a fascinating panorama of many different styles, artistic concepts, metals, and ideas.

Recommendation: It is wise to collect a type set at first. In this way, a collector will become familiar with the different types of coin designs available and, at the same time, will diversify his holdings, as he will not acquire more than one of any given type or issue.

Colonial coins. U.S. coins cover a wide collecting area. Before the establishment of the Philadelphia Mint in 1792 and its first commercial coinage production in 1793, coins were issued by many private authorities. The field of early American coins or colonials, as they are called, is rich and varied and furnishes an interesting area for study. The Massachusetts Bay Colony issued threepence, sixpence, and shilling issues in silver, including the famous Pine Tree shilling, from 1652 until 1682. The denominations were patterned after the British monetary system, for the American system of dollars and cents did not come into use until the establishment of the Philadelphia Mint.

The Rosa Americana issues in copper composition, dated 1722-1724, were made in England for circulation in America and are popular with collectors today.

Different states issued their own coinage. Vermont issued copper coins from 1785 through 1788, as did Connecticut. New Jersey produced copper coins from 1786 through 1788, and Massachusetts issued cents and half-cents in 1787 and 1788.

The 1776 so-called Continental dollar bears the name of the thirteen original colonies on the reverse and has a design authorized by the Continental Congress. Many tokens and coins honoring President George Washington were circulated during the late eighteenth century and form an interesting part of the colonial series today.

When the Philadelphia Mint opened for business in 1793 it produced coins of only two denominations: the cent and half-cent. Thus was set the stage for American coinage. As of 1981, there are six denominations of coins being produced: the cent, nickel, dime, quarter, half-dollar, and dollar. Only the first four circulate with any regularity. Half-dollars, once plentiful in circulation, are now seldom used, despite the fact that there is no shortage of them. The Susan B. Anthony dollar, introduced with much fanfare in 1979, has been a flop as far as the public is concerned, and examples are rarely seen in everyday commercial transactions.

Many different U.S. denominations have been produced over the years. These include:

- Half-cents: 1793 to 1857
- Large-size cents: 1793 to 1857
- Small-size cents: 1856 to the present time
- Two-cent pieces: 1864 to 1873
- Silver three-cent pieces: 1851 to 1873
- Nickel three-cent pieces: 1865 to 1889
- Nickel five-cent pieces: 1866 to the present time
- Half-dimes (silver five-cent pieces): 1795 to 1873

- Dimes: 1796 to the present time
- Twenty-cent pieces: 1875 to 1878
- Quarter-dollars: 1796 to the present time
- Half-dollars: 1794 to the present time
- Silver dollars: 1794 to the present (struck in metals other than silver in recent years)
- Trade dollars: 1873 to 1885
- Gold dollars: 1849 to 1889
- Gold $2.50 (quarter eagles): 1796 to 1929
- Gold $3: 1854 to 1889
- Gold $4 (patterns only): 1879 to 1880
- Gold $5 (half eagles): 1795 to 1929
- Gold $10 (eagles): 1795 to 1933
- Gold $20 (double eagles): 1849 to 1933
- Gold $50 (1915-S Panama-Pacific Commemorative issue)

Within the various denominations are many different designs. For example, the collector of half-dollars encounters the following: 1794-1795 type with flowing hair of Miss Liberty on the obverse (collectors' term for the front of a coin) and small eagle reverse; 1796-1797 great bust obverse and small eagle reverse; 1801-1807 great bust obverse and heraldic eagle reverse; 1807-1836 capped-bust-type with lettered edge; 1836-1837 capped-bust-type with reeded edge, reverse reading 50 CENTS; 1838-1839 capped-bust-type, reeded edge, reverse reading HALF DOL.; Liberty-seated-type 1839-1891, including the following subtypes: 1853 (arrows at date and rays on the reverse); 1854-1855 (arrows at date), 1873-1874 (arrows at date), all issues 1866–1891 (IN GOD WE TRUST and all caps on the reverse); 1892-1915 (Barber design); 1916-1947 (Liberty-walking design); 1948-1963 (Franklin type); 1964 to date (Kennedy type); 1776-1976 (Kennedy Bicentennial type).

In addition to the regular U.S. issues, special commemorative coins have been produced from time to time. From 1892 through 1954, forty-eight different designs of commemorative silver half-dollars were produced. These were struck at several different mints, and some were produced with minor design varieties, giving a total of 142 date, mintmark, and design varieties. Commemorated events were varied and included the 1892 Columbian Exposition, the Bicentennial of Norfolk, Virginia, the 1915 Panama-Pacific International Exposition, the Centennial of Maine, and many others. The 1893 Isabella commemorative quarter and the 1900 Lafayette commemorative silver dollar were the only commemoratives of their type ever made.

Thirteen varieties of commemorative gold dollars and quarter eagles were produced. Most impressive of all commemorative coins are the $50 issues made in octagonal (eight-sided) and round shapes for the 1915 Panama-Pacific International Exposition. These items are exceedingly rare today. Only 483 round pieces were issued, and only 645 octagonal pieces were distributed to collectors.

In addition to coinage produced at the various mints, collectors desire tokens, medals, various types of U.S. paper money, and other issues that serve as currency from time to time. Tokens, in particular, are collected avidly. While such diverse areas are not recommended for the beginning investor (as they require a certain degree of expertise to study), they are highly recommended for the advanced numismatist who seeks a challenge. As is true of many fields, the more one learns about coins, the more one finds there is to know.

CUSTODIAL CARE

Expenses such as insurance and upkeep are very low. The cost of safe-deposit box rentals is trivial compared to the value of coins stored within them, and insurance rates for coins stored in banks are likewise low. Therefore, the holding cost of coins is minimal.

Care must be taken, however, to handle coins properly. Fingerprints, bruises, scratches, or careless handling can damage a coin. For this reason, most collectors and investors prefer to keep their coins in either special transparent envelopes provided for the purpose, or lucite holders. It is also important to keep pieces away from dampness or harmful industrial fumes.

PRICE PERFORMANCE TABLES

TABLE 1. Price Performance of Ten Colonial Coins 1950-1980

	Grade	*1950*	*1955*	*1960*	*1965*	*1970*	*1975*	*1980*
Fugio Cent, 1787, Pointed Rays	Unc	$10	$15	$43	$80	$125	$350	$500
Talbot, Allum and Lee Cent, 1795	Unc	6	9	20	60	75	300	350
Kentucky, 1792 Plain Edge	Unc	8	10	33	85	125	250	375
Vermont, 1787, Bust Right	Fine	4	5	12	45	65	160	175
N.J., 1788, Horse Head Left	Fine	6	9	23	50	90	90	300
Conn., 1787, Draped Bust Left	Fine	2	3	7	15	20	30	45
Mass., 1787, Half-Cent	Fine	5	5	11	25	30	60	70
Constellatio, Nova 1785, Pointed Rays	Fine	3	4	9	20	25	50	65
Virginia, 1773, Half-Penny, Period	Unc	4	8	15	45	70	230	425
Washington Cent, 1791, Large Eagle	Unc	15	20	40	100	175	650	775
Total		$63	$88	$213	$525	$800	$2,170	$3,080

NOTE: This group contains selected examples of early American coins that circulated prior to the year 1800 and are generally known as "colonials" by collectors today.

SOURCE: R.S. Yeoman, *A Guide Book of United States Coins.* Fourth through thirty-fourth editions, 1951-1981. Racine: Western Publishing Co., with permission.

TABLE 2. Price Performance of Ten Rare Coins 1950-1980

	Grade	*1950*	*1955*	*1960*	*1965*	*1970*	*1975*	*1980*
1894-S Dime	Unc	$2,250	$2,250	$(3,625)*	$13,000	$12,250	$97,000	$97,000
1802 Half-Dime	Fine	500	500	675	2,500	3,000	4,200	10,000
1827/3 Twenty-five cents Original	Proof	2,500	2,500	(4,025)*	(12,550)*	(18,450)*	40,000	190,000
1838-O Fifty Cents	Proof	2,000	3,000	4,500	(14,055)*	14,000	41,000	62,000
1804 $1 Type 2	EF	3,125	3,125	8,000	29,000	29,000	225,000	400,000
1848 CAL $2.50	Unc	250	300	750	5,500	6,000	11,500	30,000
1875 $3	Proof	2,750	3,000	5,000	17,000	25,000	150,000	91,000
1815 $5	Unc	2,250	3,000	3,250	5,000	6,500	(36,400)*	150,000
1858 $10	Unc	2,500	3,000	4,000	6,000	6,200	(34,725)*	30,000
1927-D $20	Unc	750	850	900	4,500	32,000	150,000	225,000
Total		$18,875	$21,525	$34,725	$109,100	$152,400	$789,825	$1,285,000

NOTE: This chart includes selected major U.S. coin rarities and gives a vivid indication of price performance over the years.

*Prices not provided in source. These are estimates based on averages.

SOURCE: R.S. Yeoman, *A Guide Book of United States Coins.* Fourth through thirty-fourth editions, 1951-1981. Racine: Western Publishing Co., with permission.

TABLE 3. Price Performance of Fifteen Classic Coins 1950-1980

	Grade	*1950*	*1955*	*1960*	*1965*	*1970*	*1975*	*1980*
1793 Half-Cent	Fine	$ 50	$ 75	$ 140	$ 550	$ 650	$ 800	$ 1,500
1793 Chain One-Cent	Fine	100	125	215	625	800	1,200	2,500
1793 Wreath One-Cent	Fine	60	75	130	400	600	800	1,150
1795 Half-Dime	Unc	45	65	200	750	950	2,475	6,000
1829 Half-Dime	Unc	3	6	12	50	93	335	600
1827 Dime	Unc	9	13	28	125	180	2,000	2,100
1796 Quarter	Unc	175	325	1,450	4,250	5,750	12,000	23,000
1834 Quarter	Unc	5	13	23	100	300	1,400	1,900
1807 Bust Right Fifty-Cents	Unc	23	33	85	185	425	1,850	8,000
1815 Fifty-Cents	Unc	65	90	240	600	875	2,250	3,000
1795 Flowing $1	Unc	150	160	400	1,100	1,600	12,000	16,000
1807 $2.50	Unc	100	115	400	1,450	1,500	4,650	8,500
1800 $5	Unc	75	85	160	775	850	3,350	6,000
1812 $5	Unc	50	75	145	575	650	2,250	4,500
1801 $10	Unc	100	135	290	950	1,200	4,500	8,000
Total		$1,010	$1,390	$3,918	$12,485	$16,423	$51,860	$92,750

NOTE: Shown here are moderately scarce classic U.S. coins of the eighteenth and nineteenth centuries, with emphasis on high-conditioned pieces.

SOURCE: R.S. Yeoman, *A Guide Book of United States Coins.* Fourth through thirty-fourth editions, 1951-1981. Racine: Western Publishing Co., with permission.

TABLE 4. Price Performance of Twenty Modern Coins 1950-1980

	Grade	*1950*	*1955*	*1960*	*1965*	*1970*	*1975*	*1980*
1878 One Cent	Unc	$ 7	$ 13	$ 29	$ 100	$ 88	$ 95	$ 135
1909 SVDB One Cent	Unc	13	30	98	350	200	275	400
1914-D One Cent	Unc	20	80	275	775	560	675	750
1883 NC Five Cents	Unc	1	2	4	8	11	40	50
1926-S Five Cents	Unc	70	100	175	400	440	470	625
1910 Dime	Proof	4	8	44	80	100	185	600
1911-D Dime	Unc	4	5	15	19	23	75	275
1916-D Dime	Unc	10	150	360	750	675	950	2,500
1942 Dime	Proof	1	3	5	23	20	55	425
1895 Quarter	Proof	7	12	43	75	100	350	600
1897-O Quarter	Unc	16	50	100	145	125	325	1,500
1917 Type I Quarter	Unc	3	6	10	36	48	175	275
1930 Quarter	Unc	3	5	8	23	33	75	150
1932-D Quarter	Unc	33	45	90	240	250	425	3,000
1936-D Quarter	Unc	9	25	25	265	245	270	900
1892 Fifty Cents	Unc	4	9	20	60	100	400	800
1915 Fifty Cents	Proof	30	250	500	575	550	625	1,200
1916 Fifty Cents	Unc	6	18	25	55	110	210	400
1936 Fifty Cents	Proof	16	45	118	350	265	475	2,400
1949-S Fifty Cents	Unc	1	2	5	27	24	38	250
Total		$348	$858	$1,999	$4,316	$3,967	$6,188	$17,235

NOTE: This chart shows a variety of modern coins, most of which were minted within the past hundred years, and many of which are from the past fifty years.

SOURCE: R.S. Yeoman, *A Guide Book of United States Coins.* Fourth through thirty-fourth editions, 1951-1981. Racine: Western Publishing Co., with permission.

TABLE 5. Price Performance of Ten Silver Dollars 1950-1980

	Grade	*1950*	*1955*	*1960*	*1965*	*1970*	*1975*	*1980*
1881-S	Unc	$ 3	$ 4	$ 4	$ 3	$ 4	$ 11	$ 60
1884-S	Unc	15	20	16	30	65	750	13,500
1885	Unc	4	2	3	3	4	11	55
1889-CC	Unc	13	45	150	700	950	3,100	23,500
1892-S	Unc	25	50	125	500	1,800	12,500	18,500
1904-O	Unc	15	75	150	4	6	11	50
1921 Peace	Unc	4	8	13	40	40	135	2800
1924	Unc	3	3	3	5	5	12	75
1925	Unc	7	9	3	5	4	12	65
1934-S	Unc	15	33	60	300	275	800	10,000
Total		$104	$249	$527	$1,590	$3,153	$17,342	$68,605

NOTE: Silver dollars have always been a popular collecting field. This chart shows representative price changes of a mixture of scarce as well as common issues.

TABLE 6. Price Performance of Eight Bullion-Related Gold Coins 1950-1980

	Grade	*1950*	*1955*	*1960*	*1965*	*1970*	*1975*	*1980*
1904 $2.50	Unc	$ 14	$ 15	$ 35	$ 75	$ 65	$175	$525
1925-D $2.50	Unc	8	10	24	32	50	150	500
1901 $5	Unc	15	15	21	33	55	125	425
1909-D $5	Unc	14	12	20	35	80	225	800
1901-S $10	Unc	35	30	34	50	70	200	500
1932 $10	Unc	40	45	35	75	90	285	1,000
1904 $20	Unc	75	75	60	85	85	375	775
1927 $20	Unc	85	80	58	85	85	340	850
Total		$286	$282	$287	$470	$580	$1,875	$5,375

NOTE: The coins shown here are made of gold and respond more in relation to the price movement of precious metals than to the considerations of collecting. This is particularly true of the $5 to $20 denominations.

SOURCE: R.S. Yeoman, *A Guide Book of United States Coins*. Fourth through thirty-fourth editions, 1951-1981. Racine: Western Publishing Co., with permission.

TABLE 7. Price Performance of Ten Commemorative Coins 1950-1980

	Grade	*1950*	*1955*	*1960*	*1965*	*1970*	*1975*	*1980*
Isabella Quarter	Unc	$ 10	$ 30	$ 39	$100	$ 85	$180	$1,200
Lafayette $1	Unc	15	43	50	160	180	530	7,000
Albany Fifty Cents	Unc	6	20	28	68	50	140	625
Bridgeport Fifty Cents	Unc	4	10	12	43	28	70	400
California Fifty Cents	Unc	7	12	13	33	25	50	750
Cleveland Fifty Cents	Unc	3	5	6	28	18	40	160
Columbian Fifty Cents	Unc	2	4	5	7	9	20	120
Hawaii Fifty Cents	Unc	33	110	165	650	465	1,000	3,400
Norfolk Fifty Cents	Unc	8	20	33	90	58	160	900
Vermont Fifty Cents	Unc	7	16	28	60	38	90	1,000
Total		$ 95	$270	$379	$1,239	$956	$2,280	$15,555

NOTE: Price performances of selected silver commemorative coins over the years.

TABLE 8. Price Performance of Five Territorial Gold Coins 1950-1980

	Grade	*1950*	*1955*	*1960*	*1965*	*1970*	*1975*	*1980*
1849 Norris, Gregg and Norris, P.E. $5	Unc	$225	$225	$385	$1,000	$1,000	$4,000	$8,000
1849 Moffat $5	Unc	65	75	115	575	575	1,800	4,500
1849 Miners' Bank $10	Unc	575	750	1,500	3,500	3,500	20,000	25,000
1855 Wass Molitor $50	Unc	900	900	1,900	2,500	2,500	7,500	10,000
1860 Clark, Gruber $10	Unc	275	275	600	2,000	2,000	6,000	10,000
Total		$2,040	$2,225	$4,500	$9,575	$9,575	$39,300	$57,500

NOTE: During the developmental years of the American West, many private firms issued gold coins. This served as a convenience to the miners, who were distant from regular U.S. mints, and also served to furnish coins for use in circulation. Today these privately issued gold coins, known as territorial issues, are avidly desired.

SOURCE: R.S. Yeoman, *A Guide Book of United States Coins.* Fourth through thirty-fourth editions, 1951-1981. Racine: Western Publishing Co., with permission.

GLOSSARY

Almost Uncirculated— Showing the slightest trace of wear.

authentication— Authoritative determination of the genuineness of a numismatic item.

bag marks— Minor abrasions on an otherwise Uncirculated coin caused by handling in mint bags.

Choice— A desirable, superior, or better-than-average numismatic item.

coin— Usually a piece of metal, marked with a device, issued by a governing authority and intended to be used as money.

condition— The state of preservation of a numismatic item; same as *grade.*

counterfeit— An object made to imitate a genuine numismatic piece with the intent to deceive or defraud.

Extremely Fine— Degree of physical condition, less than Almost Uncirculated.

Fine— Degree of physical condition, less than Very Fine.

gem— A relatively flawless numismatic item of superlative quality.

good— Degree of physical condition, less than Very Good.

grade— The state of preservation of a numismatic item, expressed either adjectively (such as Very Good) or numerically (such as MS-60).

intrinsic— As applied to value, the net metallic value as distinguished from face value.

luster— The sheen or bloom on the surface of an Uncirculated numismatic object resulting from the centrifugal flow of metal caused by striking with dies.

mint— (1) A location where coins are struck, usually under the auspices of the government; (2) term for Uncirculated, a condition or grade.

mintmark— A letter or other symbol indicating the mint of origin, for example, S, for San Francisco.

mint set— Grading term referring to a coin in condition as it left the mint; Uncirculated.

numismatics— The science, study, or collecting of coins, tokens, medals, paper money, and similar objects.

numismatist— One who studies rare coins or who collects them while at the same time learning their history.

obverse— The side of a numismatic item that bears the principal design or device.

patterns— A proposed coin prepared officially by the mint or prepared unofficially by an outside entrepreneur usually for submission to a coin-issuing authority.

Proof— A piece produced by a technique involving specially prepared dies and planchets and usually special striking resulting in sharpness of detail and flawless surfaces.

prooflike— Having a surface as flawless and brilliant, or nearly so, as a Proof but struck from working dies and sold to collectors as above-average specimens.

proof set— A set of one Proof coin for each denomination issued by a recognized mint for a specific year.

restrike— A numismatic item produced from original dies at a later date.

reverse— The side opposite to that on which the head or principal figure is impressed.

type set— A collection composed of one of each coin of a given series.

Uncirculated— A numismatic item in new condition, as issued by the mint.

Very Fine— Degree of physical condition, less than Extremely Fine.
Very Good— Degree of physical condition, less than Fine.

TRADE ORGANIZATIONS

American Numismatic Association, Colorado Springs, Colo.
American Numismatic Society, New York, N.Y.
International Association of Professional Numismatists, London, England
Professional Numismatists Guild, Van Nuys, Cal.

LEADING DEALERS

Bowers & Ruddy Galleries, Inc., Los Angeles, Cal.
Kagin's, Des Moines, Iowa
A. Kosoff, Palm Springs, Cal.
Kreisberg/Cohen, Beverly Hills, Cal.
Lester Merkin, New York, N.Y.
NASCA, Rockville Centre, N.Y.
Paramount, Englewood, Ohio
Rarcoa, Chicago, Ill.
Sotheby Parke Bernet, New York, N.Y.
Stack's, New York, N.Y.
Superior Stamp & Coins, Beverly Hills, Cal.

SUGGESTED READING

Periodicals

Coin Dealer Newsletter. Published in Hollywood, Cal. Weekly.
Coin World. Published in Sidney, Ohio. Weekly.
Numismatic News. Published in Iola, Wis. Weekly.
The Numismatist. Published in Colorado Springs, Colo. Monthly.

Price Guide

Yeoman, R.S. *A Guide Book of United States Coins.* 34th edition. Racine: Western Publishing, 1980. Annually.

Reference Books

General/Historical

Bowers, Q. David. *Adventures with Rare Coins.* Los Angeles: Bowers & Ruddy Galleries, Inc., 1979.

———. *The History of United States Coins as Illustrated by the Garrett Collection.* Los Angeles: Bowers & Ruddy Galleries, Inc., 1979.

Taxay, Don. *The U.S. Mint and Coinage.* New York: Arco Publishing, 1966.

Grading Coins

Bagg, Richard A., and Jelinski, J.J., eds. *Grading Coins: A Collection of Readings.* Portsmouth: Essex Publications, 1977.

Bressett, Ken, and Kosoff, Abe, eds. *The Official American Numismatic Association Grading Standards for United States Coins.* With an Introduction by Q. David Bowers. Colorado Springs: American Numismatic Association, and Racine: Western Publishing, 1977.

Ruddy, James F. *Photograde: A Photographic Grading Guide for U.S. Coins.* 1970. Los Angeles: Bowers & Ruddy Galleries, Inc., 1979.

Investing in Rare Coins

Bowers, Q. David. *Collecting Rare Coins for Profit.* New York: Harper & Row, 1975.

———. *High Profits from Rare Coin Investment.* 1974. Los Angeles: Bowers & Ruddy Galleries, Inc., 1980.

Forman, Harry J. *How You Can Make Big Profits Investing in Coins.* New York: Nummus Press, 1972.

Hoppe, Donald J. *How to Invest in Gold Coins.* New York: Arco Publishing, 1973.

Specific Areas of Interest

Breen, Walter. *Encyclopedia of U.S. Coins.* New York: Doubleday, forthcoming.

———. *Encyclopedia of U.S. and Colonial Proof Coins.* New York: F.C.I. Press, 1977.

———. *U.S. Gold Coins.* 6 vols. 1964. Rep. Chicago: Hewitt, 1973.

Crosby, Sylvester S. *The Early Coins of America.* 1875. Rep. Lawrence: Quarterman Publications, 1974.

Judd, J. Hewitt. *United States Pattern, Experimental and Trial Pieces,* 1982. 7th edition. Racine: Western Publishing, 1977.

Kagin, Donald H. *Private Gold Coins and Patterns of the United States.* New York: Arco Publishing, 1981.

Sheldon, William H. *Penny Whimsy.* 1949. Rep. Lawrence: Quarterman Publications, 1976.

Collectibles

*Charles E. Wooley**

BASIC CHARACTERISTICS

Collectibles, as categorized below, represent the synthesis of technology and the human urge for entertainment. In the form of baseball cards and movie posters, they are the modern equivalent of the primitive amusements found in all nonindustrial societies. As such, collectibles help preserve and transmit information about American culture that would otherwise be lost. In fact, the most valuable collectibles tend to be those that use the technology of the day to implement or record current social developments. The results of this combination of factors tell us much about ourselves in a pleasing and accessible manner. The toys, games, and comic books of the past are a great aid to those who seek to understand our culture.

Investment-grade collectibles are appearing in museum collections with increasing frequency, as well as becoming an increasingly popular investment medium among the general public. An investment-grade collectible is an item that is relatively scarce, as well as historically significant within the context of the collectible genre itself and, preferably, within the larger context of the culture that produced it. Further, it should be in excellent condition and attractive to display. Since collectibles form a relatively new investment field, there is disagreement as to what objects fall into this category. Some, indeed, define a "collectible" as anything that can be collected. The definition used here is based upon entertainment.

Major Categories of Collectibles With Investment Potential

As there are numerous types of human amusements, so there are hundreds of types of collectible genres. There are collectors of arcade and pinball machines, autographs, beer cans, bottle openers, cameras, carnival plaster, carousel animals, chalkware, cigarette lighters, circus memorabilia, clothing, combs, detective fiction, drug paraphernalia, embroidery, figurines, fishing tackle, folk art, greeting cards, inkwells, magazines, magician's paraphernalia, medals, menus, musical instruments, opera mementos, pens and pencils, photographs, pipes, political souvenirs, postcards, premiums, punchboards, radios, religious items, science fiction, scrimshaw, sheet music, sound recordings, telephones, theatrical

* Charles E. Wooley is an author and consultant in the collectible investment field in Methuen, Mass.

memorabilia, World's Fair souvenirs, and many other items as well. These things are all fun to collect, and many of them will increase in value.

Few, however, possess serious investment potential, although the eight collectible fields in the following discussion have established themselves as legitimate investment media during the last twenty years. Active markets, in which investment-grade merchandise is regularly traded, exist for all of them.

Advertisements. Color printing techniques became widespread in the 1850s, and popular advertising collectibles date from that decade onward. Older advertising pieces do exist, mostly in the form of three-dimensional object signs, but these are extremely scarce and most collections of advertisements therefore commence with the introduction of color printing.

Advertising collectibles are often divided into three technological time frames. First, there are the early pieces produced from 1850 to 1890. The great majority of these are simply colorful, postcard-type scenes printed upon small sheets of paper. These pictures may or may not be related to the item being advertised. Second, there are the advertising messages printed between 1890 and 1920. Stone lithography was perfected during the 1890s, and the brilliantly rich colors that are found on advertising pieces of this era are unequaled. As technology blossomed, printers learned to print color onto metal, and the most desirable metal advertising pieces also date from this time period. Produce labels and Coca-Cola trays are examples of highly desirable items produced during this era.

Finally, collectors seek the advertising objects produced from 1920 through World War II. The color printing process known as photolithography was widely utilized by 1920. The colors produced by this technological process are not as rich as those that were previously made with stone lithography. However, the fascinating themes that occur during this period tend to compensate for the muted colors. Further, neon (and other noble gas) signs were introduced from France to this country in about 1924; choice examples of gaseous signs are scarce and in great demand.

Baseball cards. First issued during the 1860s and still marketed in quantity today, baseball cards are a clear reflection of the colorful history of America's national sport. Originally marketed primarily as premiums intended to influence the buyer's choice of cigarettes, the cards became associated with bubble gum in the 1930s. They are currently marketed both with gum and in their own right.

Over the years baseball cards were published in a variety of styles, all of which are currently collectible. The most desirable card of all, the T-206 Honus Wagner, issued sometime between 1909 and 1911, has reportedly sold at auction for $15,000, and a variety of cards, including those of superstar players issued in their rookie years, have sold for more than $1,000.

Comic books. Comic books were originally marketed as collections of comic strip reprints. F.M. Howarth's *Funny Folks,* issued in 1899, is considered by many to be the first true American comic book. Issued in a variety of shapes and covers,

FIG. 1. Front Cover of the First Modern Comic Book, Introduced in 1933

the comic book format was standardized in 1933, when Max Gaines produced *Funnies on Parade,* the first modern comic book. (See Figure 1 on page 121.) Just five years later, the comics' most successful character, Superman, made his debut in the June 1938 issue of *Action Comics # 1.* Approximately 80,000 separate comics have subsequently been issued, and the new ones continue to sell each month. There are hundreds of thousands of avid comics collectors in the United States alone, and a single comic book, *Marvel Comics #1,* sold for $13,000 in the late 1970s.

Fantasy art. Fantasy artwork includes pictorial elements such as elves and dragons, which are not found in real life. This type of art became widespread in the United States during the 1890s, when major art figures such as Aubrey Beardsley began experimenting with the genre at the same time that color printing techniques were perfected. In response, illustrators such as Parrish, Pyle, Mucha, and Wyeth created fantasy artwork for various markets, including the mainstream magazines of the day. America's fascination with the pictorially fantastic reached a peak during the 1930s with the sensuous magazine covers of Margaret Brundage (see Figure 2 on page 123), and the animation art of Disney, Fleischer, and Iwerks.

Today, Americans are still entranced by the fantastic. Books like *The Fantastic Art of Frank Frazetta, Gnomes,* and *Faeries* have been dramatically successful. Further, now that the New York Metropolitan Museum of Art has begun exhibiting works by Parrish and his contemporaries, and the Brooklyn Museum sculpture garden is including fantasy pieces, it would seem that the overall interest in fantasy art can only increase. Certain major pieces of fantasy art have already sold for sums approaching $50,000.

Games. The ancient Sumerians produced the oldest extant games thousands of years before Christ's birth, and nontechnological peoples throughout the world still produce games of their own, independent of modern influences. Most collectors, however, only purchase games that contain colorful boards or boxes. The first such game produced in the United States, *The Mansion of Happiness,* was initially offered for sale in the mid-1840s. Of great historical significance, it is credited with the creation of the basic linear progression format, in which players follow a prearranged course, which has come to be characteristic of modern games.

American games have always reflected contemporary life in a clear and dramatic manner. Just a few years after baseball was "officially" created, a version of our national pastime was marketed as a boxed game. As bicycling became a national fad in the 1890s, board games captured on pulp paper the characteristics of high-wheeling. The international sport of ping pong was created as a boxed game in about 1901. During the Depression, many games were issued that enabled the players, if only on paper, to become wealthy; the original *Monopoly* game, first issued in 1935, is a classic and valuable example of this type

FIG. 2. Margaret Brundage painting for the May 1934 cover of *Weird Tales* magazine

of game. More recently, games about space exploration have proliferated and become collectible. Currently, the most desirable games are those issued by Parker and McLoughlin Brothers during the era of perfected stone lithography (1890-1920).

Movie memorabilia. First produced about 1896, movie-related items have been collectible for many decades. As collectors discover early on, many different types of items qualify as movie memorabilia. Aside from the films themselves, the studios issued a variety of posters, cards, and glossy stills, as well as an assortment of press kits. They also granted licenses to numerous publishers and novelty promoters who issued items that either were outright movie adaptations or featured major studio stars.

Further, the studios have sold many of their own props at public auction. About 1970, a pair of Dorothy's ruby slippers (worn by Judy Garland in the 1939 MGM production of *The Wizard of Oz*) sold at the MGM auction for about $10,000. More recently, old Disney cartoon posters, which regularly sold for $4 or $5 in the 1960s, have begun selling at public auction for as much as $2,000.

It is likely, however, that Ronald Reagan material will show the most rapid appreciation in value during the 1980s. Many items from Reagan's movie career increased in value between 10 and 100 times on the evening of Election Day (November 4, 1980) alone.

Posters. Poster art, which is accessible to more people than is fine art, is becoming increasingly desirable. Prices realized at gallery auctions, as well as at quality antique and collectible shows, have dramatically increased during the last decade.

Certain posters, such as those produced for advertising purposes and by movie studios, are mentioned above. Others, however, such as the magnificent propaganda posters created during both World Wars, fit into their own unique category.

Most poster collectors feel that a poster's value lies in both its graphic design and its historical context. Largely because of this, many posters from the turn of the century are now commanding prices in the $3,000 to $6,000 range. A world record recently was set when an incomplete version of Toulouse-Lautrec's first poster, *Moulin Rouge,* sold at auction for $52,000.

Toys. Although toys have existed as long as children have, the overwhelming majority of collectors seek only those toys produced from 1840-1970. Because toys are often treated roughly by children, it is usually extremely difficult to locate examples in excellent condition. However, only toys in the best condition bring high prices at auction.

Although most quality toys still sell for less than $1,000 each, desirable examples are increasing in value daily. Almost every major toy auction features toys that crack the $1,000 barrier. Just as significantly, it has become almost impossible to purchase many fine old toys at any price. They simply are not being offered for sale.

Most toy collectors prefer to specialize in one of the following types of toys (the most desirable dates of manufacture are listed in parentheses): dolls (1840-1950), cast-iron toys and banks (1865-1900), toy trains (1880-1955), clockwork toys (1880-1965), tin toys (1890-1940), celluloid toys (1920-1940), Disney toys (1930-1960), plastic toys (1935-1955), and robot toys (1950-1970).

Special Attributes

Perishability. Most collectibles are extremely fragile, and are created for limited use. Many comic books are offered for newsstand sale for a period of only two days. Fantasy artwork that appeared in magazines such as the original *Life* was intended to survive only until the next week's issue came out. Advertisements are rarely displayed for more than a month. Movie memorabilia generally endure only until the motion picture concludes its original run. And many toys do not survive beyond Christmas morning.

Even those collectibles with better survival prospects, such as games and baseball cards, are not created to last for more than a few years. Approximately 500,000 copies of *Action Comics #1,* in which Superman first appeared, were originally printed; about forty-five still exist. Before they were perceived as legitimate investment media, collectibles survived only in curious ways, and then primarily as a result of chance. Very few have survived in fine condition.

Timeliness. The best collectibles are very timely. Baseball cards traditionally feature current players, not those who have retired. Comic book superheroes fight menaces of immediate danger to the culture: Nazis in World War II, and environmental pollution and nuclear destruction today. Just as there were few games issued during the 1930s that dealt with space exploration, so there are few new games that concern earning a fortune from a minimal investment. Investors should note that a good collectible directly reflects the contemporary culture that produced it.

Mass-market appeal. Collectibles are intended to possess widespread appeal. They generally retail for a nominal amount, and thus the producers must rely upon a large volume of sales to earn a profit. In order to accomplish this, most issuers of collectibles package their product in dramatic, even gaudy, fashion. An investment-grade collectible not only will have mass appeal when issued, therefore, but will similarly appeal to a wide variety of collectors in later years. Thus, the best collectibles make impressive display pieces, either framed or in a case.

Continuing production. The collectibles with the best investment potential mark either the beginnings or the high points of specific collectible genres that are still being produced. This is because a certain percentage of the people who enjoy the contemporary products decide that they would like to see and own significant earlier examples. In all eight of the collectible fields discussed here, new merchandise is being created today. This helps sustain and increase the value of top-grade collectible investments by generating new collectors year after year.

How Collectibles Differ From Traditional Investments

Collectibles are tangible objects. The value of collectibles lies in their physical being. They do not represent something in the way that a Treasury bill represents an obligation of the U.S. government. Rather, the collectible itself is an object of value. If one needs cash quickly, a tangible investment that can be picked up and carried to a broker may be preferable to a bond, which promises to pay a certain amount at a given time in the future. On the other hand, if one loses a Treasury bill receipt or stock certificate, the paper can be replaced. If one loses a prized collectible, however, it is unlikely that it will ever return. Further, if one accidentally creases the corner of a stock certificate, the stock retains its full value. If the corner of the only known near-mint copy of *Marvel Comics #1* were creased, however, the *Marvel Comics #1* would instantly be worth about $4,000 less.

Market is not standardized. In the stock market, anyone with sufficient cash can quickly and easily find a broker. Further, such investors realize that specific stocks are virtually always available, and can be purchased within a narrow price range. Market value, after all, seldom varies more than two points in a single day.

The purchase of investment-grade collectibles is a very different matter. Prices are not standardized, and very rare items may only be traded once or twice each decade. Further, few dealers clearly understand the history of their field or its market dynamics. This is due both to the scarcity of rare collectibles and to the rapid rise of the market.

Importance of Expertise

The acquisition of investment-grade collectibles is best accomplished in one of two ways. The lowest acquisition prices are realized by the investor who is willing to become an expert in a given field. Such a person will read the available literature and initiate contact with major dealers who are willing to impart the information they possess to the serious investor. By becoming friendly with a variety of such dealers, the investor finds that most of them are occasionally willing to sell rare collectibles at substantially below market value.

The investor who lacks the time or desire to become so intimately involved with the field should instead find a reputable dealer who is willing to sell investment-grade material at current market value. Since market value is often difficult for the nonprofessional to determine, however, it is necessary that the dealer be honest and well informed. When a dealer of known integrity agrees with a purchaser on the price of a choice collectible, they actually create fair market value by virtue of completing the sale. Thus, it is particularly important to choose a dealer whose judgment one trusts.

ATTRACTIVE FEATURES

Growth Potential

Since many people still do not consider collectibles to be particularly desirable, many outstanding investment opportunities exist. Most major museums are devoting increasing display space to collectibles; it is only a matter of time before collectibles are widely perceived as being as legitimate an investment as any of the other tangibles. As their role in our culture becomes more widely understood, the demand for choice collectibles is growing. Further, as investors increasingly perceive collectibles as legitimate investment media, new collectors enter the marketplace.

Coin and stamp collectors point with pride to the strength of their market, which they often relate to the existence of millions of numismatists and philatelists worldwide. Many investors fail to realize, however, that there are millions of comic book and toy collectors, too. As with coins and stamps, such broad interest is the hallmark of a healthy market.

Because of this worldwide demand, investment-grade collectibles are selling for ever-increasing prices. Almost every week some specific collectible sets a new price record. Beyond question, the best collectibles are being recognized worldwide as legitimate investment media. This realization in itself is certain to infuse new money into the marketplace, and that new money will compete for, and increase the value of, the best investment-grade collectibles.

Given this apparent inevitability, which is based upon past market performance and steadily increasing interest among various types of investors, it would seem that this is an excellent time to invest in fine collectibles. In a time when more traditional investment media, such as fine art and household furnishings, climb in value, collectibles may do even better than the more established tangible investment media because many more people can afford them.

Few Sophisticated Buyers

Persons who invest in widely accepted media, such as stocks, bonds, and Treasury bills, are in constant competition with other well-trained investors. At present, however, there are few sophisticated, investment-oriented buyers in the collectibles market. Given the allure of substantial values that are increasing with dramatic speed, this situation is bound to change. Those experienced investors who enter the marketplace first, however, will find little real competition.

Enjoyment

There is much fun to be had in the purchase, ownership, and sale of collectibles. Compared to that of the floor of the Chicago Board of Trade, the general level of competition is minimal, and this relatively relaxed atmosphere helps to make working conditions pleasant. Then, too, looking for an investment in a good transportation toy can be an experience that is much more enjoyable (not to mention rewarding) than looking for a good transportation stock. Similarly, inspecting a comic book for defects can be infinitely more pleasing than inspecting a New York City bond for defects. Collectibles are created to be entertaining, and investing in them usually is, too.

Relative Market Stability

Many institutional investors still perceive collectibles as a faddish investment with values liable to crash at any moment. However, at least 98 percent of all collectibles are controlled not by dealers who must trade continually to survive, but by individuals who normally resist selling under any circumstances. The market is, in that sense, very strong. Further, most collectors have been motivated to assemble their collections out of love for their chosen field and the desire to possess specific pieces. Many are aware of the investment potential present in their collectibles, but that is usually secondary to them. Their primary goal is simply to own and enjoy, on a long-term or permanent basis, the objects that comprise their collections.

Because of this, the collectibles marketplace has never experienced a general sell-off, such as that which currently occurs when the Dow Jones reaches 1,000 or when gold reaches $600 per ounce. Unlike investors who own stocks and bonds because they wish to profit from their ownership, collectors own collectibles because they wish to own the objects collected. This would seem to preclude the possibility of significant panic-selling in the collectibles market during the foreseeable future.

The collectibles market, then, seems as unlikely to crash as does the quality antiques market, and for much the same reasons. Naturally, it is possible that certain values might slide, but the possibility that a typical investment-grade collectible will lose its value during the foreseeable future is small.

POTENTIAL RISKS

Although there are tremendous profits to be made by wisely investing in collectibles, there are distinct risks.

Misrepresentation of Quality

Investors must be certain that the investment-grade collectibles they are buying are actually in the condition in which they believe them to be. One of the greatest risks faced by the non-expert is winding up with items of lower quality.

Volatility of Popular Taste

Investors also must consider the relationship between popular taste and collectible values. Collectibles that decline in popularity do not appreciate as quickly as those that must be divided among ever-growing numbers of collectors.

Even if the number of collectors increases steadily, the sale of a collectible still should be timed to take advantage of the various market cycles. Poor judgment can be costly.

Government Regulation

Government intrusion into the marketplace also may affect values adversely. Coins and stamps, which were the tangibles of choice for many trusts and Keogh plans, suddenly have found that millions of dollars have been withdrawn annually from their marketplace by government fiat. Other market disruptions are certainly possible.

Reproductions and Forgeries

Most investment-grade collectibles are printed in a variety of colors, and this makes them difficult to forge convincingly. Unscrupulous persons do attempt forgeries on occasion, but in the past these have apparently only been successfully distributed when the forged item was a black and white piece. To this writer's knowledge, no one has ever attempted to forge a complete four-color comic book.

Persons have attempted to forge cast-iron toys in the past, but in such instances the forgers, lacking access to the original master molds, were forced to make their forgeries from actual toys. This always results in loss of detail, and the forgeries, although they have fooled casual collectors, should be obvious to professional dealers.

Most collectibles, then, cannot be forged convincingly enough to fool an expert. Those investors who are not experts must rely upon either their professional dealers or their own common sense. People do try to forge black and white items and easily copied metal pieces, although these pieces must be of distinct value to make the illegal enterprise worthwhile. There are also reports that some color baseball cards have been forged. However, color and metal forgeries probably will not withstand careful scrutiny when compared with original items by professionals.

At any rate, even though a certain risk does exist, there is generally a much smaller risk of encountering forgeries in the collectibles marketplace than in most of the other tangible marketplaces. A reputable dealer should be willing to guarantee authenticity if asked to do so.

Drop in Market Due to Warehouse Finds

A warehouse find involves the discovery of a large quantity of a specific type of collectible. Usually, such finds occur when someone searches a printer's personal files or gains access to stores that have been closed, complete with contents, for a very long time. A quantity of a given collectible, heretofore unknown, might thereby emerge onto the marketplace.

If such a find is handled properly, the hoard will quietly find its way into the hands of private collectors who are happy to pay market value for the items. More often than not, this delicate situation is handled tactfully, and the market emerges stronger than ever. Occasionally, however, an inexperienced dealer runs across a warehouse find and virtually destroys all confidence in the value of a specific collectible.

Luckily, this happens only very rarely. During the 1970s, several warehouse finds made their way into the hands of comic book dealers. All but one of these finds were handled properly, however, and the market was actually strengthened in most cases. In only one instance was the market value of a comic book seriously impaired. It should be kept in mind that the risk of a warehouse find adversely affecting the value of a particular piece does exist, but that the odds of it affecting any given investment are minimal.

Physical Risks

Most collectibles are extremely fragile when produced and are intended to be used quickly and discarded. Because of this, manufacturers give little thought to producing items capable of withstanding the rigors of aging. In fact, the overwhelming majority of paper items utilize the cheapest pulp paper available. Such paper normally contains a high sulphur content which, unless prevented, destroys the cellular bonds that hold the paper fibers together. Further, temperatures of more than 60 degrees greatly accelerate this process. Thus, if left in a normal environment, pulp paper will crumble into dust in 50 to 100 years.

Most of the collectibles that are not made of paper are made, at least in part, of metal. As with paper items, metal collectibles are not intended to endure for long periods of time. They are not rust-proofed, and many fine old metal toys that are stored in a normal household eventually will begin to rust.

In addition to their intrinsic fragility or obsolescence, collectibles are subject to a variety of environmental hazards. If they are purchased in excellent condition, however, they are relatively easy to keep that way. (See *Custodial Care* in this article.)

TAX CONSEQUENCES

Capital Gains

A collectible purchased as an investment is a capital asset for federal income tax purposes. Thus, profit from the sale of such a collectible is not taxed as ordinary income, but rather as long-term capital gain, to an individual who has owned it for over a year. Since the very best short-range profits are made by investing in collectibles just as the demand for them is about to rise and selling them just as demand peaks (a process that usually takes one to two years), this type of investment takes full advantage of the long-term capital gains tax.

Controlling the Year of Taxation

Another advantage of investing in collectibles is that one can control when one is taxed. Many investors buy collectibles when their income is high and sell them when their income is lower.

Furthermore, those who invest in collectibles can increase their net profit by controlling how frequently their profits are taxed. Until the taxable sale or exchange of a collectible occurs, one need not pay any tax upon its increased value. In comparison, one usually must pay taxes upon the earnings from a bank account every year, and earnings from the bank account are necessarily smaller because of the tax owed upon it. Since the government does not tax the increased value of collectibles until they are actually sold, however, the collectibles investor is, in effect, able to realize compounded appreciation in value each year without taxation until a sale.

As compared with many investments, then, collectibles are taxed at favorable rates and give the investor some control as to when and how frequently he is taxed.

For a more detailed discussion of tax factors, including deductions for contributions of tangibles to qualified organizations, see article on Tax Considerations for Collector-Investors, elsewhere in this volume. For complete guidance in these matters, readers are urged to consult a professional tax adviser.

REPRESENTATIVE TYPES OF INVESTORS

Private Individuals

Most investors in the collectibles field are private individuals. They range from the impoverished to the wealthy, and they live in all parts of the United States, Western Europe, and Japan.

These investors are divided into three groups: those who buy collectibles primarily for fun and nostalgia (keeping a reasonable eye open for value and investment potential); those who believe that collectibles are valuable as an intrinsic part and reflection of our culture; and those who buy collectibles strictly for profit. Some, of course, collect for all these reasons; but for most, one or another motive is primary.

Universities

As universities come to realize that the popular culture of technological societies is equivalent to the myth and folklore of primitive societies, they become increasingly interested in collectibles. As such items become better appreciated as a valuable — and very accessible — subject for research, more and more papers are being written at the university level about movies, comic books, and other collectibles. Bowling Green, Syracuse, and Berkeley are currently the academic leaders in the development of popular culture resources.

Museums

Many major museums now display collectibles. The New York Metropolitan Museum of Art hung a striking paper ephemera collection in May 1976. Since this show, an ever-increasing number of museums are devoting attention to the cultural and aesthetic value of collectibles.

Corporations

Although there are currently few corporate investors active in the collectibles marketplace, many seem likely to enter into it. Certain corporations already are assembling significant collections of toys and advertisements.

IMPORTANT FACTORS IN BUYING AND SELLING

Dual Markets

All collectibles markets operate on both retail and wholesale levels simultaneously. To realize full retail price at any given moment, the seller must take a variety of factors into account. However, collectibles can always be sold immediately on the wholesale market. In that sense, collectibles are as liquid as stocks are. Prices thus realized average about one-half of retail for investment-grade items, but it is possible to liquidate a major collection on wholesale terms in just one day. The fear that collectibles can be very difficult to sell is simply not grounded in fact.

Grading

Most beginning collectors find it difficult to describe accurately the physical condition of collectibles. This descriptive process is called "grading," and its entire purpose is to define how near an item is to being in perfect condition. A collectible's age has no relationship to its grade. Since its value is based predominantly on its grade, it is important for the investor to either learn to grade collectibles or find a reputable dealer to do it.

Typically, collectibles are graded on a scale of approximately twenty points, ranging from poor to fair, good, very good, fine, very fine, near mint, mint, and pristine mint. Each of these has its own refinements. For example, the difference between fine minus and fine plus currently can amount to several thousand dollars on a key collectible.

How does someone become an accurate grader? Trial and error is the best method. The new collector should read whatever literature is available and then attempt to grade a number of items. Most price guides and specialty publications contain guidelines for grading. Once an understanding of the grading system has been developed, the collector should approach as many dealers as possible, perhaps at a specialty convention, and quiz them about the condition of various items. A certain amount of disagreement is to be found even among professionals, but each field also has a hard-core group of dealers who grade very strictly. Since grading is very important, it is advisable to locate these dealers and buy from them.

Market Cycles

Collectibles markets develop in related cycles, and it is critical that the investor understand the nature of these cycles. This is because investors whose timing is inaccurate will tie up their capital needlessly.

Collectors tend to make as many discriminations of collectibles types as they can. Thus, comic book collectors divide their field into about seventy types of comics, such as superhero, war, love, adventure, western, and horror. Baseball card collectors regularly discriminate between manufacturers, individual teams, and different styles of cards. All eight of the basic collectibles fields discussed here have numerous subcategories.

The key to understanding market cycles is to realize that collectors tend to focus their energies on one type of item at a time. These items become hot; that is, dealers cannot hold onto them. When superhero comics are hot, dealers with fair prices find that their superhero comics sell as soon as they reach the market. All of this consumer interest, and the subsequent depletion of dealers' stocks, results in a typical supply and demand situation that forces up the market value of hot items. Meanwhile, most of the other types of comics sell less quickly, each following its own market cycle.

In a major marketplace like that governing comic books, there are about seventy separate cycles operating at once. Naturally, the best time to purchase any given type of item is when the demand for that type is at its lowest ebb, as most dealers are anxious to move slow sellers. In fact, investors can often buy items at the lowest point on the demand cycle at a very favorable price.

Similarly, the best time to sell is when the demand is just about to peak. These cycles take an average of three to eight years to progress through a full turn, and full retail is realized quickly when the demand is peaking. Investors should take careful note of this, and plan to purchase and sell accordingly.

These cycles are particularly important because most collectors are unaware that they exist. Consequently, many collectors tend to buy while the demand is rising, and sell when the demand has fallen.

Investors should also note that these ostensibly separate cycles are, in fact, related to each other in an orchestrated fashion. This is true because, over the long term, relative market values seldom fluctuate widely. Investors who understand this can make dramatic short-term gains.

What happens is this: One type of comic, for example, begins a sharp upward journey in demand. This type of collectible (e.g., superhero comics) thus becomes hot. Meanwhile, other types of comics (e.g., Donald Duck comics) are apparently following their own independent market cycles. Within a period of about a year, the hot superhero comics have nearly doubled in value, while the cool Donald Duck comics have maintained the same basic price level.

At about this point, two market phenomena occur simultaneously. First, the demand for superhero comics begins to cool. Collectors, realizing that the same superhero comics cost twice as much today as they did a year ago, decide that they are unwilling to pay the ever-increasing prices that dealers are forced to ask. Thus, the demand for (though not the value of) superhero comics begins to decline.

Meanwhile, the dealers are not overly concerned, as they realize that this merely means that some other type of comic will now become hot. For example, the collectors of Donald Duck comics, which were at a low point on their own demand scale when the superhero comics were peaking, now stop to consider the current market. They realize that their favorite comic, which in the past was usually valued at half the worth of the superheroes, is now valued at only one quarter. As this realization spreads among collectors, the demand for Donald Duck comics will increase dramatically as collectors rush to purchase those comics before the market again balances. The pent-up demand of these collectors then bursts forth, and the Donald Duck comics themselves become hot as the demand for them shoots sharply upward.

Since all seventy types of comics are following their own demand curves at all times, these curves will be in varying positions relative to each other at any given moment. Over the long term, however, relative values have remained remarkably consistent, regardless of the collectibles genre, and short-term fluctuations in value have tended to eventually regain the relative market values that were established in the middle 1960s. For those who understand market cycles, knowing the best time to buy and sell becomes simple.

Price Guides

An accurate price guide is a boon to investors in any collectibles marketplace. Unfortunately, few, if any, are totally accurate. It is critical that the sophisticated investor understand the limitations under which most price guides operate. These inaccuracies occasionally occur even in generally accurate guides, such as Overstreet's *Comic Book Price Guide,* and for arguably legitimate reasons. For example, let us examine the history of the Overstreet *Price Guide* values of a very rare, anti-Communist comic book known as *Blood Is The Harvest,* which was published by the Catholic Church in 1950. First listed in the Overstreet *Price Guide* in 1973 (presumably Overstreet was unaware of its existence previously), a mint copy was valued at $2. By 1977, its value was officially $9, and in 1978 mint copies were listed at $45.

During this period various collectors discussed with Overstreet the fact that because there were only two known copies of this historically important comic, a fairer value for it would be between $500 and $1,000. However, Overstreet refused to raise his valuation significantly, as his *Price Guide* is a report of prices asked and sales made. Overstreet was worried that if he valued *Blood Is The Harvest* (*Blood*) much more highly without the justification of an actual sale, he might be blamed with attempting to manipulate the market.

As neither of the two people who owned copies of *Blood* was willing to sell them, the *Price Guide* value for 1978 increased minimally to $45. During 1979, however, a Catholic priest surfaced at a Philadelphia comic convention with approximately nine copies of *Blood,* as well as various other comics that the Catholic Church had published during the 1950s; he sold these comics to several dealers for a total of about $10,000. These dealers, aware of the true importance of *Blood,* proceeded to ask and receive an average of about $1,200 per copy. Overstreet then raised his valuation of *Blood* from $45 in 1978 to $1,200 in 1979.

In retrospect, it is clear that *Blood Is The Harvest* was worth far more than the $45 listed in Overstreet's guide in 1978. After all, even with an official *Price Guide* value of $45, dealers still managed to sell all the copies they could acquire for about $1,200 each. On the other hand, one may respect Overstreet's determination to avoid influencing the market in advance of actual sales.

To sum up, price guides are very useful tools, but they all have their limits. Investors should note carefully that the greatest profits in the collectibles field are made by those who possess the courage and foresight to predict future values, not by those who merely rely upon last year's market reports.

CUSTODIAL CARE

Preservation of Materials

As mentioned earlier, most collectibles from the popular culture were not made to last. In particular, paper is liable to disintegrate over a long period, and metal to rust. However, professional restoration experts (on staff at many major museums) can neutralize the acid content in pulp paper, thus preventing the cellular breakdown that would otherwise occur. As for metal collectibles, they tend to rust only if their environment is humid.

Collectibles can be kept in excellent condition by maintaining the humidity level at about 40 percent, and the temperature at 50 to 60 degrees. Collectibles can be stored in such a fashion for many years without requiring any further care.

Collectibles that are stored or displayed under adverse conditions constitute a different matter, however. For example, if a curator decides to display a grouping of World War II posters in a bank lobby, it may be advantageous to have the acid content of the paper neutralized before the acid is energized by the adverse effects of sunlight, heat, and air pollution.

Environmental Hazards

Collectibles are occasionally subjected to more dramatic dangers than inappropriate temperature and humidity. For example, many fine collectibles have been destroyed when basements flooded; others have been damaged by earthquake and tornado. Vermin, particularly mice and silverfish, but also cockroaches, rats, and bats, have destroyed innumerable fine pieces. Further, air pollution is as dangerous to collectibles as it is to asthmatics. Perhaps the most bizarre environmental hazard of all is that constituted by other collectibles, as acids and molds can migrate from one paper to another. Thus, choice paper items must not be stored with pieces in poorer condition.

All of the commonly used transport companies (including the post office, air freight, boats, trains, and trucks) have damaged more than their share of fine collectibles. Unfortunately, theft is also an ever-present danger. Therefore, valuable items are often stored in safe-deposit boxes.

Insurance

As with other tangible investments, valuable collectibles should be insured. Further, with prices increasing dramatically, it is advisable to have them reappraised every few years.

MARKETS FOR COLLECTIBLES

There are eight basic types of collectibles marketplaces and seven types of dealers engaged in them. A brief examination of these types will enable the investor to choose the best market situation and type of dealer.

Periodicals

There are three basic types of periodicals that serve as marketplaces for the investor. They are the general interest newspapers or magazines that carry advertisements for collectibles among many other kinds of merchandise, such as the *New York Times;* the collectors' magazines, which carry advertisements directed at collectors generally, such as *The Antique Trader;* and the specialty publications, which are directed at a very narrow audience, such as *The Buyer's Guide For Comics Fandom* or the Robert W. Skinner Inc. auction catalogues.

Mail-Order Purchases. Most of the collectibles transactions that result from a public notice in a periodical are conducted through the mail. Because of the frequency of mail fraud, it is necessary to take greater precautions with these than are normally required in face-to-face transactions. It is advisable to be certain that any item not in the condition described can be returned for a complete refund; it is also wise to put into writing that the shipper is responsible for insuring the parcel, and to try to telephone the seller before sending a check or money order. If it is impossible to contact the seller by telephone, it may be just as difficult to collect the merchandise.

Flea Markets

These affairs are conducted all over the country on a weekly basis, and are advertised in both general circulation and trade publications. They normally feature between 20 and 400 dealers, and the larger gatherings often have a tremendous array of prized collectibles. What makes flea markets so attractive to collectors is that key pieces are often available at bargain prices. This is because flea market dealers handle a vast array of material for which they pay very little and that they prefer to turn over quickly. Further, these dealers, like many other collectibles dealers, are often willing to haggle over prices.

When shopping at flea markets, it is best to arrive as early as the first dealers do. Although the collectors' frequent complaint that the best bargains sell before the public arrives is not always justified, it is true that the exceptional values normally sell to the first person who recognizes them as such.

Antique Shops

These are normally mom-and-pop operations, run by independent individuals who have a broad knowledge of many fields and an in-depth expertise in one or two. Most antique shops feature a wide assortment of merchandise, much of which is overpriced, some of which is fairly priced, and a small percentage of which is underpriced. Investors seeking to make acquisitions through the antique shop circuit should obtain antique shop directories[1] and then map out an efficient shopping tour in advance of their initial departure from home or office.

Upon entering each shop, it is advisable to quietly scout for one's chosen specialty, buying any desired items that are fairly priced or underpriced, and then to ask if the shop owner has any other interesting items. Often the owner will have desirable items in storage, or will recommend other local shops that the buyer might visit.

General Auctions

These occur throughout the country on a daily basis. Public announcements of the auction and its contents are made prior to the sale date; on the day of the auction itself the items are sold, on a nonreturnable basis, to the highest bidder.

These auctions frequently are held in order to settle an estate or a bankruptcy, or because someone who is moving does not wish to transport possessions to a new locale. Since these auctions generally feature something for every taste, they can draw a large crowd.

Such auctions usually last three to ten hours. Even though most of the items sell at bargain prices, persons interested in just a few pieces often feel that when the cost of their time is computed, the overall cost of acquisition becomes unreasonable.

---

[1] These are available through antique trade papers, flea markets, antique shops, better business bureaus, and local chambers of commerce.

Estate Sales

There are often many items in an estate that have value but are unwanted by the heirs. Notices of an estate sale are placed in a local newspaper, detailing many of the items to be sold. At the appropriate time, the public lines up outside the deceased's home, waiting for admission. The managers of the sale normally sell everything in the house within three days by pricing items very cheaply. As a result, there is keen competition for the choice items, and minor melees are not uncommon. For the hardy who appreciate a bargain, however, estate sales can be an excellent source of collectibles.

Conventions, Quality Shows, and Specialty Auctions

These gatherings, which are advertised in general, trade, and specialty publications, feature hundreds, and occasionally thousands, of fine collectibles. Since they require a minimum of the investor's time, they are favored by many. The average sale price often will be higher than at the marketplaces discussed above, but the abundance of merchandise is considered by most collectors to be more than adequate compensation for the higher prices. One should also keep in mind that many of the specialty auction houses accept mail bids.

Specialty Shops

As collectibles gain ground as legitimate investment media, specialty shops around the country that deal primarily in collectibles have opened their doors. Although most of these shops are run in only a semiprofessional manner, some are excellent. The owners of the top-quality shops usually are knowledgeable individuals who feature a wide selection of fine collectibles. Unfortunately, these owners pay fairly high prices to acquire their merchandise, and usually maintain a high overhead. Although this means that investors who purchase through these quality shops will pay top dollar, occasionally it is reasonable to do so. Knowledgeable specialty shop owners often discover the best investment-grade material and, due to their intimate contact with their chosen marketplace, can sometimes locate unique or hard-to-obtain collectibles. Such shops are usually listed in the Yellow Pages.

Fellow Collectors

As an investor becomes active in the collectibles market, he or she invariably meets fellow collectors. Most collectors, however attached to the items they own, occasionally have material to sell; often they prefer selling to a fellow collector. Where the average dealer pays about half of retail value for investment-grade collectibles, collectors sell to each other items at three-quarters of retail. The seller thus receives 50 percent more than he would from a dealer, and the buyer saves 25 percent.

TYPES OF DEALERS

The various types of dealers active in the marketplaces described above are listed, in order of increasing sophistication, below. Dealing with each has its advantages and disadvantages.

Junkmen

Junkmen seldom exhibit any genuine appreciation for the material they are handling; rather, they concentrate on converting unwanted objects into cash. Most junkmen tend to undervalue quality collectibles.

Naïve Experts

Such individuals believe that they are experts in their fields; unfortunately, they are not. At first encounter they can be somewhat convincing, however, and it is worthwhile to keep in mind that there are more alleged experts in the collectibles field than there are true authorities. Like junkmen, such individuals occasionally underprice whatever they have for sale.

Minor Collectors

The minor collector often has a well-defined collection that, although small, brings its owner great pleasure. Such people are generally accurate in their statements and tend to sell items at low prices.

Medium Collectors or Minor Dealers

This type of dealer is usually transitory. As collections grow, people generally discard their less desirable objects and acquire others that they find more interesting. Existing market dynamics make it difficult to be a small-time dealer, however, and most people in this position are somewhat surprised by the business realities that they encounter. As a result, they either return to the relatively carefree status of a minor collector or progress into the market in a significant way.

Major Collectors and Medium Dealers

Such individuals spend a fair percentage of their conscious thought on market considerations. They deal in valuable or large quantities of material, much of it investment grade. As collectors, they are important customers to major dealers; as dealers, they often introduce new collectors to the field. Their selling prices vary as their understanding of market dynamics develops.

Major Dealers

Although few in number, major dealers control the bulk of the investment-grade collectibles that are offered at public sale. They have access to large amounts of cash as well as to major collections, and their behind-the-scenes maneuverings affect many collectors. Serious investors should meet and come to know as many major dealers as possible.

Market Masters

Within their limited field, these individuals have significant power. They often control large quantities of investment-grade collectibles, and are constantly engaged in original research within their chosen field. Although they are welcome contributors to price guides, the market masters do not generally use such guides in business dealings. Rather, they create their own price levels that are based upon their interpretation of current fair market value. Market masters are recognizable by one demonstrable attribute: They are the only ones who can acquire, on short notice, any collectible that exists.

GLOSSARY

auction— A public sale where the purchaser is the highest recognized bidder.

bid— The amount offered for an item being sold at auction.

dealer— One who stands willing to buy or sell a collectible of a certain kind; prices are often negotiable.

grading scale— A 20-point scale ranging from "poor" to "pristine mint," used in evaluating investment-grade collectibles.

lot— An item or a group of items sold together at an auction.

market master— A specialist who trades large quantities of investment-grade collectibles.

LEADING DEALERS AND OTHER SOURCES

Dealers

Collector's Bookstore, Hollywood, Cal. Comic books, fantasy art, movie memorabilia, and posters.

Comic Investments, Philadelphia, Pa. Baseball cards and comic books.

Tony Dispoto, Lodi, N.J. Fantasy art.

Forbidden Planet, New York, N.Y. Comic books.

The Game Preserve, Peterborough, N.H. Games.

Hake's Americana & Collectibles, York, Pa. Advertisements (emphasizing political souvenirs) and other collectibles.

John Knight, Rockville, Md. Comic books.

Miscellaneous Man, New Freedom, Pa. Posters.

New England Auction Gallery, Methuen, Mass. Toys.

Walter Wang, Staten Island, N.Y. Baseball cards.

West Side Comics, New York, N.Y. Comic books.

Charles E. Wooley, Methuen, Mass. Comic books, fantasy art, and movie posters.

Conventions

Creation Conventions, Glen Oaks, N.Y. Comic books, baseball cards, and fantasy art. Shows held in many major cities.

Phil Seuling, Brooklyn, N.Y. Comic books and baseball cards. Monthly shows in New York City.

Museums

The Game Preserve, Peterborough, N.H. Games

Perelman Antique Toy Museum, Philadelphia, Pa.

SUGGESTED READING

For those who wish to learn about collectibles, two basic types of publications are available: the first is historical, and the second is in the form of sales catalogues and reports. Unfortunately, most of the histories of collectibles are laced with inaccuracies. One's goal in reading them is simply to obtain a generally accurate overview of the field.

As for sales catalogues, many dealers and auction houses offer both current and back issues that include value estimates and price keys (follow-up sheets of prices realized). These are useful to the more sophisticated investor in charting market trends and in gleaning factual information that is unavailable in the histories. Further, back-issue trade papers contain numerous listings that may be used to chart the value of given collectibles.

A selection of useful source material follows.

Periodicals

Antique Monthly. Published by Boone, Inc., Tuscaloosa, Ala. Monthly; fine-quality antiques and collectibles offered for sale.

Antique Toy World. Published by Dale Kelley, Chicago, Ill. Monthly; toy advertisements and articles.

Antique Trader. Published by Babka Publishing Co., Dubuque, Iowa. Weekly; features many advertisements for collectibles of all types.

The Buyer's Guide for Comics Fandom. Published by DynaPubs Enterprises, East Moline, Ill. Weekly; comic books.

Film Collector's World. Published by Alan L. Light, Rapids City, Ill. Biweekly; movie memorabilia.

Articles

Berry, Heidi L. "Mosler Collects — and Studies — Banks." *Antique Monthly,* June 1980, pages 6C, 11C.

Byrne, Janet S. "American Ephemera." *The Metropolitan Museum of Art Bulletin,* Spring 1976, pages 1-52.

Deweese-Wehen, Joy. "Corporate Collecting Is a Profitable Venture." *Antique Monthly,* June 1980, pages 1A, 8A, 22A.

Gerd, Abigail. "Collecting From the Five-and-Dime." *Americana,* February 1981, pages 54-59.

Seggerman, Helen-Louise. "Phillips Poster Sale Paces Growing Market." *Antique Monthly,* January 1980, pages 1A, 4B, 22B.

Weinstein, Bob. "Collectibles: Don't Sell Them Short." *Trusts & Estates,* September 1977, pages 590-594.

Reference Books

Beckett, Dr. James, and Eckes, Dennis W. *The Sport Americana Baseball Card Price Guide.* Lakewood, Ohio: Edgewater Book Co., 1981.

Frankel, Betsy, ed. *The Encyclopedia of Collectibles.* Alexandria, Va.: Time-Life, 1978-1980.

Overstreet, Robert M. *The Comic Book Price Guide.* Cleveland, Tenn.: Crown Publishers, annual.

Commercial Paper

Ira Z. Romoff *

BASIC CHARACTERISTICS

Brief Description

Commercial paper, or unsecured short-term promissory notes, are negotiable documents issued in denominations as low as $25,000, often with a $100,000 minimum and an average amount in excess of $2 million. They are issued by big corporations as a method of obtaining large amounts of short-term funds. When issued for no more than 270 days and used to finance current transactions, the paper is exempt from registration with the SEC, thereby reducing the issuer's expenses and providing an attractive source of short-term funds.

These own-name or unsecured notes are direct obligations of the issuer and therefore, historically, commercial paper has only been issued by the strongest, most creditworthy, companies. Over 1,000 companies and institutions sold commercial paper in 1980, with over $121 billion outstanding.[1]

During the 1970s, the supply of commercial paper grew at a 12.82 percent compounded growth rate, due in large part to borrowers using commercial paper as an alternative to often more expensive short-term bank loans. In addition, the rise in commercial paper outstanding has been due to the general substitution of short-term debt for long-term debt due to the high rate of inflation. Volatile money market rates reflected the uncertainty about the future rates of inflation that made firms hesitant to add historically high-rate long-term debt to their balance sheets. In retrospect, of course, short-term rates in general have averaged higher than long-term rates. The relatively high short-term rates have also kept investors away from the long-term debt and equity markets and have encouraged the use of money market funds. These funds, in large part, have found their way into commercial paper.

Categories of Commercial Paper

The main issuers of commercial paper fall into two categories:

1. Bank holding companies and finance companies. Commercial paper is used to support the lending activities of bank holding companies and finance companies on a continuous basis. These borrowings fluctuate with the demand for consumer

* Ira Z. Romoff is Vice-President of Commercial Funding, Inc., New York.

[1] Federal Reserve Bank of New York, Market Reports Division: *Commercial Paper Outstanding,* October 30, 1981.

and commercial loans and to the extent each institution raises long-term or intermediate-term funds.

2. Non-financial companies. Commercial paper is used to fund temporary short-term needs of non-financial companies, for example, for tax payments or seasonal fluctuations.

Smaller companies, which are good bank customers, have been able to enter the commercial paper market only by securing their paper with their banks' guarantee or letter of credit. This provides the double benefit of lower costs compared to bank borrowings for the issuer and, in times of tight money, additional fee income for the banks. Also, parent company guarantees and foreign country guarantees for state-owned companies are now entering the commercial paper market.

Savings banks have recently been allowed to issue paper, although reserve requirements have been too costly for this paper to become popular. Tax-exempt commercial paper, issued by state and municipal governments, has expanded recently due to the advent of tax-free money market funds and demand from commercial bank trust departments.

Placement

Commercial paper is placed by a few large investment brokers[2] or directly by the issuer through its own sales force. Most of the largest commercial paper issuers choose to sell commercial paper directly to avoid the one-eighth to one-quarter percent commission charged by dealers. For example, commissions of at least $125,000 per $100 million outstanding would be staggering to General Motors Acceptance Corporation, which had almost $10 billion outstanding on March 31, 1981. Most industrial/non-financial companies, however, place their paper through dealers.

ATTRACTIVE FEATURES

Liquidity

Despite the high quality and short-term nature of commercial paper, there is no regular secondary market. Only a very small percentage of outstanding commercial paper is redeemed prior to maturity. Although at first this may seem to the investor to be a disadvantage due to the fact that commercial paper can be purchased to mature on any date not to exceed 270 days from issuance, investors rarely need to request early terminations. It is noted that most paper

---

2 *Moody's Commercial Paper Record.* Vol. 1, No. 8, Aug. 1981, page 70. According to *Moody's,* the main U.S. dealers in commercial paper (ten issues or more) are: A.G. Becker, Inc.; Bankers Trust Co.; The First Boston Corp.; Goldman, Sachs & Co.; Lehman Commercial Paper, Inc.; Merrill Lynch Money Market Securities, Inc.; and Salomon Brothers. All are located in New York City.

is issued for not longer than forty-five days with the average about thirty days or less.

Back-Up Lines of Credit

Very often, issuers obtain yearly credit lines with their banks, offering further protection to investors and assuring that funds will be available upon maturity of commercial paper. The usual case is for 100 percent of the outstandings to be backed by lines of credit. Although credit lines can be withdrawn by a bank on short notice and are subject to yearly review and disapproval, this is not often the case. Recent trends have seen issuers replace bank lines with contractual agreements and/or multi-year revolving credit facilities providing investors with additional safety.

Favorable Rates of Return

As with all other money market instruments, the marketplace determines the rates for commercial paper. Some factors relating to commercial paper yields include:

- Costs of alternative funds to issuers;
- Alternative short-term instruments available to investors;
- Quality of the issuer — the ratings;
- The cost of back-up lines to issuers;
- Costs of rating services;
- Seasonal needs;
- Government controls;
- Tax consequences to purchaser; and
- The general state of the economy.

Current commercial paper rates are quoted in most major daily newspaper business sections and can be obtained from most brokers or commercial banks. While rate trends are unpredictable, it is noted that over the twelve months ending July 31, 1981, commercial paper rates have shadowed the rates of bank certificates of deposit. Figure 1 on page 146 shows a compilation of yields of various types of investments that is prepared weekly by the Federal Reserve Bank of St. Louis.

Ratings

Of the millions of businesses that exist, only just over 1,000 of the strongest issue commercial paper. In order to place their commercial paper, most issuers obtain ratings from one or more of the three companies that grade commercial paper borrowers, namely Moody's Investors Service, Standard & Poor's Corporation (S&P), and Fitch Investors Service. Most investors limit their commercial paper investments to only the highest quality graded paper; lower-graded paper

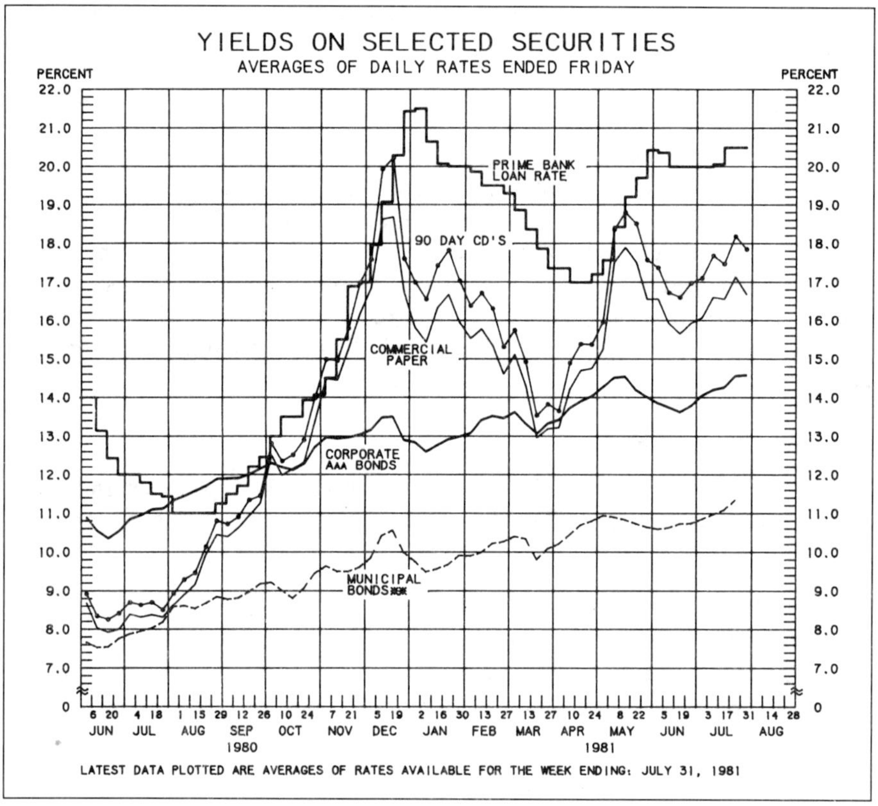

FIG. 1. Yields on Selected Securities
SOURCE: Federal Reserve Bank of St. Louis

(i.e., those commercial paper investments of lesser quality and greater risk) often are forced to pay significantly higher yields in order to attract interested investors. Before any commercial paper is purchased, the investor should have a full knowledge of the commercial paper ratings relating to the investment being made. The ratings are designated as follows.

	Highest Quality		*Lowest Quality*
Moody's	Prime-1	Prime-2	Prime-3
S&P	A-1	A-2	A-3
Fitch	F-1	F-2	F-3

Moody's employs the following three designations, all judged to be investment grade, to indicate the relative repayment capacity of rated issuers.

"*Issuers rated Prime-1* (or related supporting institutions) have a superior capacity for repayment of short-term promissory obligations. Prime-1 repayment capacity will normally be evidenced by the following characteristics:

— Leading market positions in well-established industries.

— High rates of return on funds employed.

— Conservative capitalization structures with moderate reliance on debt and ample asset protection.

— Broad margins in earnings coverage of fixed financial charges and high internal cash generation.

— Well-established access to a range of financial markets and assured sources of alternate liquidity.

"*Issuers rated Prime-2* (or related supporting institutions) have a strong capacity for repayment of short-term promissory obligations. This will normally be evidenced by many of the characteristics cited above but to a lesser degree. Earnings trends and coverage ratios, while sound, will be more subject to variation. Capitalization characteristics, while still appropriate, may be more affected by external conditions. Ample alternate liquidity is maintained.

"*Issuers rated Prime-3* (or related supporting institutions) have an acceptable capacity for repayment of short-term promissory obligations. The effect of industry characteristics and market composition may result in changes in the level of debt protection measurements and the requirement for relatively high financial leverage. Adequate alternate liquidity is maintained.

"If an issuer represents to Moody's that its Commercial Paper obligations are supported by the credit of another entity or entities, then . . . (in) assigning ratings to such issuers, Moody's evaluates the financial strength of the indicated affiliated corporations, commercial banks, insurance companies, foreign governments or other entities, but only as one factor in the total rating assessment. Moody's makes no representation and gives no opinion on the legal validity or enforceability of any support arrangement." [3]

Moody's further indicates the issuer's long-term debt rating, if any, thereby differentiating between Prime-1 paper of the highest caliber (and the lowest yield) and other Prime-1 paper that may be slightly higher in risk but still may fall within the Prime-1 grade. Moody's debt ratings for commercial paper issuers run, from highest to lowest, AAA, AA, A, and BAA. It is interesting to note that only very few commercial paper issuers are given P-3, A-3, or F-3 ratings and investor demand for this grade of investment is minimal.

POTENTIAL RISKS

As noted above, lack of a secondary market can conceivably work a hardship on the investor in certain circumstances. Also, as with many other investments, the temptation to seek top yield with marginal quality can lead to possible loss.

---

[3] *Moody's Commercial Paper Record.* Vol. 1, No. 8, Aug. 1981, page 5.

TAX CONSEQUENCES

Except for commercial paper issued by tax-exempt authorities, all commercial paper interest is fully taxable as interest income.

REPRESENTATIVE TYPES OF INVESTORS

Although no statistics are available on the categories of holders of commercial paper, by far the largest commercial paper investor group consists of corporate treasurers looking to invest temporary company funds for short-term periods. Paper is purchased to coincide with the date cash is needed, thereby ensuring full use of the available funds.

Trustees often use commercial paper as a safe and relatively risk-free short-term investment, as do smaller banks and many insurance companies. Individuals often invest in commercial paper, usually in amounts of $100,000 or more, where they perceive a minimal risk is more than outweighed by the increased yield of commercial paper as compared to alternative short-term investments such as Treasury notes. Money market managers have had substantial interest in purchasing commercial paper and appear to be continuing purchasers of these investments.

PURCHASING COMMERCIAL PAPER

Most large commercial banks and almost all brokers will accept orders for commercial paper for a small commission charge, usually not exceeding one-quarter of one percent of the purchase. (In some cases, only a service fee is charged.) Investors interested in purchasing commercial paper in large amounts should contact the investment broker [4] issuing the paper to avoid additional fees. It should be noted that many of the largest industrial commercial paper issuers sell commercial paper to the public and may be contacted directly.

CUSTODIAL CARE

Because of its short-term nature, most commercial paper is issued in directly negotiable form. For convenience, buyers almost always leave paper in the custody of the dealer or broker.

GLOSSARY

bank holding company— A controlling corporation that issues commercial paper in support of the lending activities of its subsidiary banks.

---

[4] See brokers listed at note 2, *supra.*

commercial paper— An unsecured short-term promissory note, issued by large corporations.

dealer— One of the major investment brokers through which commercial paper is bought and sold.

direct placement— Sale of paper directly to the investor through the issuer's own sales force.

finance company— An issuer of commercial paper used in support of its lending activities.

own-name paper— Commercial paper, representing the direct obligation of the issuer.

quality ratings— The credit classification system applied to issuers by any of the three companies providing rating services.

tax-exempt paper— Commercial paper used for short-term borrowing by state and municipal governments.

SUGGESTED READING

Abken, Peter A. "Commercial Paper." *Economic Review,* March/April 1981, page 11.

Hurley, Evelyn M. "The Commercial Paper Market." *Federal Reserve Bulletin,* June 1977, page 525.

Judd, John P. "Competition Between the Commercial Paper Market and Commercial Banks." *Economic Review,* Winter 1979, page 39.

Silbert, Theodore H. *Commercial Paper.* New York: Standard Financial Corporation, 1980.

Common Stocks—Listed Issues

*Robert G. Kirby**

BASIC CHARACTERISTICS

Common Stocks Compared to Other Corporate Securities

Common stocks represent the basic equity ownership of a corporation. The owners of a company's common stock share directly in the success or failure of that business enterprise. Capital contributed by the common share owners becomes a permanent part of the company's capital.

In some companies, the equity capital of the common shareholders is the only long-term capital that the business employs. Other companies may seek additional investors to contribute other forms of capital through securities such as preferred stock and long-term bonds.

Common stock compared to preferred stock. Even though preferred stock is thought of as an equity security by some investors, it is really a hybrid security. The preferred stock owner agrees to forgo any participation in the growth of the company's earnings in return for a fixed claim on the company's earnings or assets that is prior to the claim of the common stockholders.

The common stock owner is the beneficiary of the corporation's residual earnings after all prior claims of bondholders and preferred stockholders are satisfied. In a company with a considerable amount of securities senior to the common stock outstanding, substantial financial leverage is created so that the earnings available to the common shareholders fluctuate more widely than the net operating earnings of the company as a whole. Preferred stocks, on the other hand, have a fixed dividend rate; the full preferred dividend must be paid before any dividend can be paid on the common stock. The dividends paid by a company to its shareholders are determined by the board of directors, usually at quarterly intervals. But, in determining the quarterly dividend, the directors normally rely on the recommendation of the company's management, which bases its advice on its estimates of future earnings and future capital investment requirements.

In the event of the company's liquidation, the full par value of the preferred stock must be paid, to the extent possible, to the holders of the preferred stock. With most preferred stocks, there is also a cumulative dividend provision under which, if the company should be unable to pay preferred dividends for one or more years, the cumulative total must be paid to preferred shareholders before

* Robert G. Kirby is Chairman of Capital Guardian Trust Co., Los Angeles.

dividends can be resumed on the common shares.

Occasionally, companies have variations of the traditional common stock-preferred stock relationship, such as participating preferreds that receive a portion of any dividend increase for the common stock, or different classes of common stock with one class receiving a cash dividend and the other receiving a stock dividend.

Common stock compared to long-term bonds. Long-term corporate bonds are a typical debt instrument requiring the company to pay a fixed rate of interest over the life of the bond and full principal repayment on the maturity date. In contrast, the common stock owners have only a residual claim on corporate assets and earnings, and benefit from no specific or implied promise of any future payments. The common shareholders' rewards are completely dependent on the future success of the company. Bondholders are protected by the full faith and credit of the company and sometimes by the pledge of specific assets. In the event that the company defaults on the payment of interest or principal, the bondholders may institute foreclosure procedures leading to forced liquidation of company assets for the benefit of bond owners. In some cases, a company may have one or more bond issues that are subordinate to other issues in their claims on the company's assets.

Influences on Preferred Stock and Bond Prices

Because the rewards of ownership are fixed, the current market values of preferred stocks and long-term bonds are primarily influenced by two factors. The first is investment quality, that is, the degree of protection that the company's assets and earning power offer the owner of the securities. The second is the current level of interest rates, which determine the return that investors can get from newly issued securities of like quality. If interest rates decline, the market prices of existing bonds will increase, and vice versa. Except during periods when interest rates are undergoing wide fluctuation, the market values of good quality long-term bonds and preferred stocks can be expected to hold within a fairly narrow range.

Common Stock Price Behavior

Common stock prices can be expected to fluctuate in a much broader range than bonds and preferred stocks because the common shareholder represents the residual investor who participates directly in the company's success or failure.

Investor expectations. The strongest influence on common stock values is the consensus of investor expectations as to prospective level of earnings and dividends for the company in future years. Common stocks of certain kinds of companies (such as American Telephone & Telegraph), whose earnings and dividend growth tend to be stable and predictable, usually have below-average price volatility. In contrast, prices of the shares of stock in highly cyclical industries or of small companies in industries with rapidly changing technology tend to fluctuate widely. With such companies, future results are very difficult to predict and investor expectations change greatly from one period to another. Therefore, an investor who has a required level of investment returns and, thereby a limited ability to accept risk, must pay careful attention to the certainty with which future earnings and dividends can be predicted in making an investment choice.

Level of company earnings. In the short run (i.e., over a period of a few months), the price behavior of common stocks appears to be a virtually random one. In the long run, (i.e., a period of a year or two or more), common stock price changes seem to correlate most highly with changes in the company's earnings per share. The more future earnings are likely to fluctuate, the more price variability a given common stock or group of common stocks is likely to experience.

Current economic environment. Investors' perceptions of the future are always influenced by current events. If the current economic environment is unfavorable, investors' expectations for the future are apt to be pessimistic. The reverse is true if the present business environment is favorable. Normally, current common stock prices are determined first by predicted future business activity, which is subject to substantial forecasting error, and second, by investment psychology stemming from the existing business environment. With this background, the safest prediction that can be made about common stock prices in the short run is that they will fluctuate widely but without any logical or explicable basis. In the long run, common stock prices can be expected to correlate substantially with corporate earnings but, on many occasions, the investor's patience will be tried sorely before this relationship becomes apparent.

Classifications of Common Stocks

In an effort to cope with the wide variability that is an essential part of the market behavior of common stocks, investors over the years have tended to develop an informal classification system. They have attempted to identify companies with common or similar characteristics and place them in a particular category to aid in the procedure of common stock selection. The names of some of these categories, such as income stocks, growth stocks, blue chip stocks, and cyclical stocks, imply a much higher level of precision than what actually exists. However, they are probably concepts that are of some use to investors.

Income stocks. Broadly speaking, income stocks are normally the shares of companies in relatively stable industries that have reached a fair degree of maturity. These companies have been able to build up strong balance sheets that, combined with a modest need for re-investment earnings to finance future growth, permit the payout of a substantial portion of earnings in dividends. This modest earnings re-investment process limits capital growth potential and makes the stocks primarily attractive to investors in need of current income rather than future rewards.

Growth stocks. Growth stocks normally have characteristics exactly the opposite of those of income stocks. They represent companies in rapidly growing industries that offer the opportunity for substantial additional capital investment, so that the shareholders will benefit considerably in the long run if earnings are retained and re-invested to underwrite future growth. However, it is probably true that no company is inherently a growth company. Every large company was a growth company at one time or it would not have become large. The growth phase is usually a finite phase that can vary from a year or two for some companies to several decades for others. One of the key requirements to successful investing in growth stocks is to identify where a company is in its growth cycle.

Blue chip stocks. The term "blue chip stocks" applies to the shares of those companies that hold dominant domestic, and usually also international, positions in economic areas that are not subject to substantial cyclical swings. However, the blue chip stocks of one period are not those of another. Today's blue chip stocks are typified by companies such as Procter & Gamble, Johnson & Johnson, and Schlumberger. Ten or twenty years ago, the blue chip category would have included such names as General Motors, U.S. Steel, Great Atlantic & Pacific Tea Company, Sherwin Williams, and Union Carbide, all of which would fall well short of meeting the blue chip requirements of today.

Cyclical stocks. Cyclical stocks are those of companies whose fortunes depend very much on the general level of business activity. As the general economy goes through cycles and experiences changes in the gross national product, consumer disposable incomes, and the general level of employment, some industries are more directly and immediately affected than others. Two economic areas are normally affected first in a typical business recession: the first is capital equipment spending on the part of business, and the second is consumer spending for so-called big-ticket durable items such as appliances, houses, and automobiles. Companies serving these markets typically head the list of cyclical companies. Many industries move into the cyclical category from the growth category as they gain maturity. Both the chemical and the aluminum industries would have been regarded as growth categories twenty or twenty-five years ago. Today, most investors would consider them cyclical.

Imprecision of categories. As stated previously, these categories are neither precise nor mutually exclusive. A company can produce products or services that are quite sensitive to changes in the overall level of business activity (and therefore be called cyclical) and yet still have very strong growth characteristics. Also, service companies that are not capital-intensive and do not require substantial new capital to grow can pay out a high portion of earnings in dividends and continue to meet the requirements of a growth company.

Nature of Common Stock Markets

New York and American exchanges. There are approximately 5,000 publicly owned companies in the United States whose common stocks may be purchased and sold by individual investors. They range in size from American Telephone & Telegraph Company, with a total market value of approximately $40 billion and an active market in which 500,000 shares may easily change hands in a single day, to very small companies with market values of under $50,000, whose shares may change hands in small amounts only several times a year.

Approximately 2,000 companies have their shares listed on a recognized stock exchange. By far the largest of these is the New York Stock Exchange (NYSE), on which the stocks of some 1,600 companies are listed. The shares of all but a few of the largest U.S. companies are traded on the NYSE, along with the shares of some large foreign companies such as Royal Dutch Petroleum and Unilever.

The second largest stock exchange is the American Stock Exchange (AMEX), on which the shares of an additional 400 companies have a public market. As a general rule, the companies listed on the AMEX are smaller and younger than those on the NYSE. The AMEX traditionally acts as an incubator for the NYSE. Growing companies not yet of sufficient size, and lacking enough publicly traded shares to meet NYSE listing requirements, will initially list their shares on the AMEX. The company may later transfer that listing to the NYSE as it is able to meet the latter's more extensive listing requirements. However, there are exceptions to this generalization. A few large, mature companies that could easily qualify for listing on the NYSE have remained on the AMEX.

Other exchanges. There are a number of other regional exchanges, such as the Philadelphia-Baltimore Exchange, the Midwest Exchange, and the Pacific Coast Stock Exchange. On each of these exchanges, there are a few companies listed that are not listed on other exchanges. However, the bulk of activity on these so-called regional exchanges occurs in stocks that are also listed on the NYSE. Transactions on the NYSE-listed issues occur on these regional exchanges for a variety of reasons. The two primary reasons are that the buyer or seller in a transaction desires to have the trade executed by a broker who is not a member of the NYSE but is a member of the regional exchange, or that the time differential allows an order to be executed on the Midwest or the Pacific Coast Stock Exchanges, which remain open after the NYSE is closed.

Over-the-counter market. Even though the approximately 2,000 companies listed on the New York and American Stock Exchanges make up the preponderance of the market value of all publicly owned companies, there are at least another 3,000 companies with public shareholders that are not listed on any exchange. The shares of these companies are traded in the so-called over-the-counter market. The over-the-counter market is made up of hundreds of investment firms (both members of exchanges and non-members) who make markets in unlisted stocks. Some firms make markets in hundreds of over-the-counter stocks and others in just a few. These over-the-counter firms operate in the same way as dealers in stamps, rare coins, or used cars. They do not act as brokers between a buyer and a seller; they operate for their own accounts by maintaining a bid and an ask for each of the securities in which they make a market. Whenever a buyer or a seller of an unlisted security executes a transaction, he does not buy or sell from or to another investor, but rather from or to the over-the-counter market-maker in the particular stock.

Common Stock Ownership

Management shareholders. The principal difference between a privately held corporation and a publicly held corporation is often in the role and importance of professional management. In the majority of large, publicly owned corporations, the management does not own a significant or important percentage of the outstanding common stock. Among the 100 largest publicly owned companies, it would be unusual for management to hold as much as 2 or 3 percent of the outstanding shares. The chain of responsibility from the managers of a company to the shareholders or owners of a company is through the board of directors. The shareholders elect directors each year at the company's annual meeting. The directors are responsible for selecting the managers of the company, evaluating their performance, and making changes that are necessary.

Professional management evolved as founding-family ownership and control declined. In the transition, shareholders having no other relationship with the company beyond stock ownership became the dominant owners. As a result, boards of directors changed. Today, company managers often hold only two or three seats on a board of directors that may number eleven to fifteen in total. However, in medium and smaller companies — that is, those below the country's 100 largest corporations — professional managers often still have controlling influence on the board and frequently make up a majority of its members.

Limited influence of shareholders. From a practical standpoint, the shareholder of a large, publicly owned corporation, whether an individual or an institution, has very little influence on the way a company is managed. Shareholders are invited to attend annual meetings and to cast their votes directly. However, since the shareholders of large companies are scattered throughout the country and, indeed, the world, most shareholders vote by proxy. Proxy material is often legalistic and difficult to understand, and many shareholders do not bother to vote at all. Only rarely does a dissident shareholder group succeed in taking control of a publicly held company from a management that is attempting to maintain its position.

Institutional shareholders. Since the end of World War II, institutions have had an increasingly important influence on the behavior of the U.S. equity markets. These institutions include entities such as corporate pension funds, public retirement funds, charitable foundations, and educational endowment funds with assets that have grown very rapidly in recent years. Further, most institutions have placed increased emphasis on common stocks in their portfolios. Prior to World War II, such institutions invested primarily in fixed-income securities. Common stock investment was left to individual investors. Today, the emphasis on common stocks by institutions has grown to the point where it is common for even a conservative institution to have two-thirds of its assets in common stocks, with the remainder in bonds or other fixed-income securities. More than half of the common stocks of U.S. publicly owned companies are still held by individuals, but the institutional share is increasing rapidly.

ATTRACTIVE FEATURES

Because of the inherent qualities of common stock and the depth and diversity of the market, there are a number of unique advantages available to the individual or institutional investor in common stocks.

Current Income

While there is no guarantee as to the return from a particular company, historical data suggest that, in general, common stocks provide dependable and consistent performance in the income area. (Detailed performance data are provided in article on Historical Returns on Principal Types of Investments, elsewhere in this volume.)

Hedge Against Inflation

Over the past thirty years, in periods of both low and high inflation, common stock dividends have always increased at a level greater than the rate of inflation. Further, common stock dividends have been remarkably resistant to periods of recession. In the aggregate, dividends have shown only two very small year-to-year declines during the past three decades.

Liquidity. Unlike some kinds of investments, common stocks in the most depressed market can quickly be converted to cash.

Adaptability to investor needs. The great number of listed issues and the wide availability of counsel specializing in common stocks gives the individual or institutional investor maximum flexibility in tailoring holdings to meet particular requirements.

POTENTIAL RISKS

Fluctuation in Capital Performance

Even though common stock values have kept pace with inflation over an extended period of years, there have been intervals of five to ten years in which they have not. Because common stock prices are subject to emotional forces and classic fear-and-greed thinking, they can also be significantly overvalued at times. Common stocks typically experience a period of perhaps five or ten years in which they produce substantial excess returns, only to be followed by a similar period of disappointing results.

Although the dividend performance of a common stock can be projected with a fair degree of confidence subject to moderate error, a projection of future capital performance is subject to great error because of market volatility and because capital gain is extremely dependent on the entry price. The purchaser of a particular common stock in March might have a drastically different three-year capital performance than would the purchaser of the same stock just three months later in June. This is one reason that the investor with a continuous flow of new capital will often achieve a better result. He is able to select a superior company and then get an average purchase price over a period of time. By definition, with a constant dollar flow, more shares will be acquired when the price is low than when it is high.

Identifying Risk

Risk is an elusive concept to deal with since it is very difficult to identify and define. From the investor's standpoint, one of the important determinants of the amount of risk that is acceptable in an investment portfolio is a function of the investor's ability to generate new capital in the future to make up for possible investment losses. The investor who has no present or prospective earning power or income stream that could be used to offset capital losses should pursue a strongly risk-averse investment program. However, he should be aware that the common stock arena is littered with the remains of disastrous investment programs that were designed by investors who thought they were avoiding major risks. To the unwary and inexperienced, risk, like beauty, can be much in the eye of the beholder. Only a decade or two ago it would have been unthinkable to anticipate that Penn Central or W.T. Grant would go bankrupt, or that Chrysler or International Harvester could get into financial difficulties that would threaten their existences. Yet these events have happened.

A company's vulnerability and exposure to adverse future developments probably can be placed into two risk categories: the first is financial risk; the second is business risk.

Financial risk. Financial risk relates primarily to the strength of a company's balance sheet and its access to the capital markets. The first point to examine is the relationship of a company's current assets to its current liabilities, which is a measure of working capital. The second is the relationship of a company's long-term debt obligations to its equity capital base and to its current and prospective earnings stream. Generally, there is a direct relationship between financial strength and size. A large company normally has been in business for many years and has had an opportunity to build up a strong balance sheet. A smaller one is often in a growth phase in which the financial demands of expansion are straining the company's capital resources. Further, a large company that runs into unexpected financial difficulties has much better access to capital markets to solve its short-term problems than does a small one. However, even very large companies can also get into insoluble financial difficulties, as did the Penn Central Railroad.

Business risk. Business risk is normally more difficult to analyze and to appraise than financial risk.

Technological change. Most business risk is associated with competition, particularly new competition, as buttons were severely affected by the invention of the zipper, and the makers of vacuum tubes were distressed by the invention of the semiconductor. A key form of protection against business risk arising from technological change and new competition is diversification. Companies such as General Electric or Minnesota Mining, which make an extremely broad array of products to serve a variety of customers across many different marketplaces, have very limited vulnerability to technological change. No new competitor's product is likely to affect more than a small part of their total profitability. In contrast, a company such as Champion Spark Plug or Tampax finds itself in a decidedly different position.

Demographic change. However, not all serious new competition comes from technological change. Business risk can arise from sociological changes or demographic changes, for example. The fact that American eating habits have changed radically, so that in certain areas of the country over one-half of meals are consumed outside the home, has created difficult problems for some manufacturers of traditional food products.

Competitive forces. Other competitive forces can be the result of a very successful new marketing campaign that can move a consumer product from an also-ran to the position of a dominant brand name. One important determinant of business risk is the degree to which the company's product or service has a consumer franchise. Wrigley's gum or Campbell's soup could be subject to adverse sociological changes over time, but they represent two of the strongest consumer franchises. In contrast, no manufacturer of sheet steel, fir housing studs, or chlorine has any kind of consumer franchise. These companies may have some customer loyalty because of dependability of supply or quick delivery time, but for the most part their customers will switch to another supplier if they can get steel, lumber, or chlorine at a lower price.

Cyclicality. Another form of basic business risk is that of sensitivity to changes in the general level of business activity, or, a company's cyclicality. The consumption of electricity or food and tobacco products is rarely affected by a decline in overall corporate profits or a drop in consumer disposable income. On the other hand, the purchases of machine tools, structural steel, and luxury automobiles can decline radically during a serious depression. The manufacturers of these products may see their earnings vanish and even experience operating losses.

"Low-risk" common stock. It seems clear from the foregoing that even if an investor can determine to his satisfaction what risk tolerance should be set, there is still the very difficult problem of appraising the level of risk that exists in any given common stock that may be considered for purchase. However, it follows from the previous discussion that a reasonable, although imperfect, definition of a low-risk common stock is one that is the stock of a large company with a strong balance sheet that has been in existence many years, producing a broad variety of essential goods or services that are sold in markets throughout the world, and can be readily identified and differentiated so that it has a strong consumer franchise.

It should be noted, however, that even if an investor finds a common stock that fills all these requirements, he still cannot be sure how long the low-risk investment will continue to maintain these characteristics. The most important method of reducing portfolio risk for the individual investor is the same one that a company uses in reducing business risk — diversification. With a portfolio of the common stocks of twenty or thirty sound companies in a variety of industries that meet most of the low-risk requirements outlined above, the investor probably has achieved close to the minimum possible risk from investing in common stock.

APPROACHES TO COMMON STOCK EVALUATION

There are a great many ways in which individual investors approach the development of a discipline in order to arrive at a timely and accurate common stock evaluation — or, in other words, to make rewarding buy and sell decisions. Such approaches appear to be almost limitless in their variety; however, they fall into two broad categories: the fundamental and the technical.

Fundamental Approach

The fundamental approach is a traditional one. It requires understanding of the present and future operations of the particular company under scrutiny, the industry of which that company is part, and the overall economy of the country or countries that make up the company's particular market.

Technical Approach

This approach focuses on the market price action of the company's securities. It assumes that there are enough fundamentalists studying the outlook for the company itself that their conclusions will be reflected in the market price of the security. If the security's market price behavior reveals what the fundamental researchers have found out, the investor does not need to do the research himself.

Those who follow the technical school of evaluation, in turn, probably fall into the two broad categories following:

Chartists. The first group might be called chartists in that they believe in the likelihood that cycles occur over and over again, and that a chart of past price behavior can aid in predicting future price behavior. Chartists believe in ideas such as resistance points and overhead supply levels, which assume that buyers or sellers will rush into the market when stocks reach price levels that have marked low points or high points in a prior period.

Price-volume analysis. The other school of technical analysis relates more to the relationship between market price changes and the level of trading activity. These analysts believe that a price advance in a stock on high volume means something quite different from a price advance on low volume, and vice versa. They attempt to develop relationships between upside volume and downside volume or interpretations of the advance-decline ratio that will contribute to profitable investment decisions. The primary difference between these two technical approaches is that the chartist usually focuses on individual common stocks or on industry groups, while the price-volume investigator more often tries to derive conclusions about the future behavior of the market as a whole.

TAX CONSEQUENCES

Gains and losses on common stock holdings are subject to ordinary income rates for securities held for less than one year and capital gains rates for securities held for one year or longer. The annual dividend exclusion is $100 for an individual and up to $200 for a joint return. There is an 85 percent dividend exclusion for corporations; that is, only 15 percent of the dividends received by a corporation from a domestic corporation are subject to tax. Exceptions apply in the case of nonprofit entities including universities, labor unions, and pension funds, all of which are exempt from income taxes.

REPRESENTATIVE TYPES OF INVESTORS

As discussed in *Common Stock Ownership* in this article, investors in common stocks include an extremely wide variety of individuals and institutions. Determining the kinds of common stocks appropriate for a particular investor requires a thoughtful examination of a number of variables.

Tax Requirements

The first of these is the investor's tax situation. The investor may be an individual with substantial earned and investment income, in which case much of any short-term capital gains, interest, or dividend income will be taken away in taxes; or the investor may be a charitable foundation or corporate pension fund for which all interest, dividends, and capital gains are tax-exempt. The potential impact of taxation on returns is an important influence on selecting the appropriate security.

Needs and Goals

The second important variable is the investor's particular needs and goals. Some individual or institutional investors need all the income that can be generated from their portfolios to support existing activities or programs. Other investors will be adding substantial new capital to their portfolios in a program aimed at accumulating a pool of capital large enough to meet some requirement in the distant future.

IMPORTANT FACTORS IN BUYING AND SELLING

Designing a common stock investment program aimed at minimizing current income and maximizing long-term capital growth is the most difficult challenge an investor faces. There is no orderly or precise way in which the market translates gains in earnings per share or in book value into gains in market price. For several years, the market may virtually ignore a stock or a group of stocks whose earnings and book values are increasing rapidly, only suddenly to catch up in a period of six months when the stocks are discovered by the investment community. Often, the best way to achieve capital appreciation is to look for a rapidly increasing dividend stream from a growing company whose earning power and cash flow are beginning to permit accelerating dividends, even though dividends may begin from a very small base.

Selecting an Investment Professional

The selection of a broker or investment counselor depends on the answers to such questions as these: Does the investor want to determine the securities to be purchased and sold based on his own knowledge and research work, or on those of a broker or an independent investment counselor? Does the investor want to register the securities in his own name and collect dividends and stockholder material directly, or would a custodial account, with a broker or at a bank, be preferable?

Broker services. The range of services offered by brokerage firms vary substantially from one organization to another. Some firms offer a very broad range of resources, while some attempt to concentrate in a few areas. Some large national firms provide broad product lines and advice in areas ranging from tax shelters to oil-drilling syndications to real estate partnerships to marketable securities, including both common stocks and fixed-income issues. Other firms choose to concentrate in a particular region of the country and on a narrower line of investment alternatives. In addition, there is a new group of discount brokers that has developed in recent years who aim to service the investor who wants only efficient execution, not advice. The discount broker does not normally engage in equity research, fixed-income research, or investment banking, but concentrates on executing transactions. Commissions are normally 30 to 50 percent below those charged by traditional, full-service investment firms. However, it is usually true that the full-service firm will be competitive in a particular situation. If the customer points out that a discount broker would execute a transaction at a smaller commission, the full-service firm usually will move to meet the competition.

Broker limitations. Many stockbrokers are experienced investors who can be of great help in constructing a sound investment program. Unfortunately, however, the broker's sole source of compensation typically is commissions on buy and sell transactions. Since, in many cases, the best investment advice is to do nothing, the broker-adviser has a basic conflict of interest. Furthermore, some brokerage transactions carry higher commissions than do others, again making it difficult for the broker to be even-handed.

Investment counselors. The investor who does not want to take the responsibility for doing research and making investment decisions may wish to retain an investment counselor for the management of a securities portfolio.

In the past ten years or so, there has been substantial growth in the number of investment counseling firms in the country. There are several large, national organizations such as Scudder, Stevens & Clark, and Loomis-Sayles, which have offices in most major cities. In addition, there are normally many independent local investment counseling firms in major cities. Today, even most medium-sized cities have at least several investment counselors who have been in existence for several years or more.

Investment counselor limitations. Investment counselors operate for a flat professional fee, which is determined by the value of the assets under management. The fee is usually from 0.5 to 1.0 percent. However, the small investor faces the problem that in recent years, most investment counselors have substantially increased the size of the minimum account they will manage. Most established investment counsel firms are reluctant to manage portfolios with a total value of less than $500,000. Many have minimums of $1 million or more. When an investor employs an investment counselor, it is probably advantageous to be an important client to that firm. Therefore, the small investor is faced with a problem of obtaining adequate attention when employing a professional investment adviser.

Doing without professional help. In the matter of common stock selection, many investors are very successful in identifying profitable common stock commitments without professional help. However, these people are usually successful by investing in managements or products of which they have a personal knowledge and are therefore in a position to compete with full-time professionals. In other words, doctors are apt to be successful investors in pharmaceutical companies or hospital supply companies. This approach usually does not permit adequate diversification; nonetheless it is often successful.

Measuring Investment Results

Prior to 1960, most investors were likely to measure the success of their programs in absolute terms — that is, the dollar value of the income received and of the appreciation in market value. The developing importance of institutions created more professional administrators and, with them, a search for more sophisticated tools with which to measure investment results. As a result, the success or failure of a common stock portfolio investment program, particularly those of institutional funds, is determined by the relative performance either compared to the results of equivalent funds in terms of size and objectives or compared to some index of common stock prices. These indexes of comparative performance are usually broad-based indexes such as the Standard & Poor's *500 Stock Index* or the New York Stock Exchange Index.

In addition to the shift from absolute to relative measures of investment results, the growth of professionally managed institutional common stock portfolios has also produced an attempt to evaluate an investment program over shorter intervals of time. Today the results of most large institutional portfolios are calculated monthly, or even more often, in an effort to detect at a very early stage the development of a trend in either a positive or a negative direction.

Mutual Funds

One solution to the investment management problems of the smaller common stock investor is to secure professional management through the use of a mutual fund. There are currently over 600 different mutual funds available to the individual investor. These funds serve an almost unlimited variety of objectives, so that a combination of several funds will permit any investor to tailor a program aimed specifically at his particular requirements. Each mutual fund has an offering prospectus that sets forth the objectives of the fund, describes the investment organization that will be managing the portfolio, and sets forth in detail the historical investment results of the fund. The use of mutual fund portfolios allows the investor to focus on the important major decisions as to the types of common stocks needed to attain his goals and yet leave the selection of individual securities to full-time professional managers. In addition, there are many mutual fund management companies. Some are subsidiaries of financial institutions, such as insurance companies and brokerage firms, while others are independent. (See article on Mutual Funds, elsewhere in this volume.)

CUSTODIAL CARE

There is no clear-cut consensus as to how large an investor or what type of investor should appoint a bank trust department or some similar corporate fiduciary to act as custodian for his securities portfolio.

Bank Custodial Account

A bank custodial account provides complete services in the mechanics of supervising a securities portfolio, such as collecting bond coupons and dividends when due, handling stock splits and stock dividends, dividend re-investment plans, tenders of securities for repurchase offers, and mergers; it also maintains thorough, easily understandable records of the transactions to aid in the preparation of tax returns. Most important of all, perhaps, is that this kind of institution gives the investor a maximum degree of assurance that his securities are safe and secure.

Brokerage Firm Custody

The investor whose securities are left in custody at an NYSE member firm also receives a complete record to facilitate the preparation of tax returns. However, in this latter case, the security is less certain. If the investor signs a margin agreement with the broker, the securities can be pledged by the broker as collateral for loans to the brokerage firm.

Insurance. As an offset to this risk, an agency of the federal government provides a substantial amount of insurance to the investor in the same way that the Federal Deposit Insurance Corporation provides insurance to bank depositors. In a number of failures of brokerage firms in recent years, investors have been protected against any losses through actions of the SEC and other federal agencies. The only negative impact experienced by the customers of brokerage firms that have failed has been a delay of several months in recovering the securities in custody of the firm in question. So far, however, the degree of protection has not been tested by any extensive and widespread number of problems within the brokerage community.

Disadvantages of Professional Custodial Care

Use of a corporate fiduciary or a brokerage firm may to some extent prevent the investor from being a currently informed and active shareholder. Securities in custody are registered either in a nominee name of a corporate fiduciary or in a street name with a brokerage firm. As a result of this nominee registration, communications to the shareholder are sent to the custodian first and then forwarded to the investor at a later date. This process involves some delay; in many instances, the material is of limited value to the investor by the time it arrives. Information contained in quarterly or annual reports or special announcements has already been known to the general community for some time. In the case of proxy material on which the shareholder has the opportunity to vote, it may be too late for that vote to be received by the company in time for the counting of the ballots because the material must be returned through the same custodian or broker from which it has been received.

Activity Test

The manner in which an investor may choose to handle the mechanics of managing a securities portfolio may depend in large measure on how active that investor intends to be. The term "active" relates both to the amount of activity that an investor anticipates in his portfolio and to the degree to which the investor wishes to participate in voting on issues proposed by management and other shareholders. The investor who is seeking short-term gains by frequently buying and selling stocks will find that registering the securities in his name and having the securities delivered to him for personal custody will create a considerable degree of inconvenience. In most cases, the actual stock certificates in the investor's name will not be delivered for a security purchased for a period of three, four, or five weeks.

The active investor with frequent transactions should consider some form of custody arrangement with either a bank or a broker. For the investor who plans to hold securities over a longer term, the only disadvantage of having them registered in his own name and holding them in a safe-deposit box is the need to keep a record of transactions and dividend and interest receipts.

GLOSSARY

broker— One who buys and sells stocks and other securities on commission for a client's account; may also provide investment management and related services.

capital gain— The excess of selling over purchase price realized upon sale of a security.

charting— Establishing a basis for buy-sell decisions through graphic analysis of a security's past price performance.

custodial account— A portfolio whose records, paperwork, and physical safekeeping are the responsibility of a bank or other agency.

margin— The percentage of purchase price of a security required of a customer who buys on broker's credit.

over-the-counter— The market made by investment firms who buy and sell stocks not listed on an exchange.

par value— The dollar value assigned to a share of stock by the issuer at time of issue.

price earnings ratio— Market price per share divided by net earnings per share in the preceding year.

prospectus— The formal description of a new issue of securities as required by the Securities Act of 1933.

proxy— Authorization to vote on behalf of a shareholder at a corporate shareholder's meeting.

stock index— A composite historical record of market prices of a selected group of stocks.

working capital— Current assets less current liabilities.

yield— Dividend and interest payments made to security holders.

LEADING BROKERS

This list is highly selective and includes a number of firms with offices throughout the United States. The Yellow Pages in many localities lists the names of nearby brokers.

A.G. Becker, Inc.

Bache Halsey Stuart Shields, Inc.

Bear Stearns & Co.

Brown Brothers Harriman & Co.

Dean Witter Reynolds, Inc.

Donaldson Lufkin & Jenrette, Inc.

E.F. Hutton & Co., Inc.

First Boston Corp.

Goldman Sachs & Co.

Josephthal & Co.

Kidder Peabody & Co., Inc.

Lehman Brothers Kuhn Loeb, Inc.

Loeb Rhoades Hornblower & Co.

Merrill Lynch Pierce Fenner & Smith, Inc.

Morgan Stanley & Co.

Paine Webber Jackson & Curtis, Inc.

Shearson Hayden Stone, Inc.

Smith Barney Harris Upham & Co., Inc.

SUGGESTED READING

Fabozzi, F.J., and Herskoff, R.A. "Effect of the Decision to List on a Stock's Systematic Risk." *Review of Business and Economic Research* 14:77-82, Spring 1979

Haugen, R.A. "Do Common Stock Quality Ratings Predict Risk?" *Financial Analysts Journal* 35:68-71, March 1979

"How to Play Against the Experts and Win." *Forbes* 124:122, November 26, 1979

Modigliani, F., and Cohn, R.A. "Inflation, Rational Valuation and the Market." *Financial Analysts Journal* 25:24-44, March 1979

"Rationale for Leveraging in Stocks." *Fortune* 101:306, May 5, 1980

Ruland, W. "Management Forecasts, Stock Prices, and Public Policy." *Review of Business and Economic Research* 14:16-29, Winter 1978-1979

Schlarbaum, G.G., et al. "Common-Stock-Portfolio Performance Record of Individual Investors: 1964-70." *Journal of Finance* 33:429-41, May 1978

Studness, C.M. "Market in Utility Securities." *Public Utilities* 105:36, May 22, 1980

Travel, M.K. "Can Pension Funds Beat the Market?" *Pension World* 16:37-40, Fall 1980

Winthrop, G.F. "Buying Discount Stock With Dividends." *Fortune* 98:193, October 1978

Common Stock—New Issues

Peter A. Bernard *

BASIC CHARACTERISTICS

Like any common stock, a new issue gives the owner an equity participation in the issuing company. New issues represent an important investment market for individual shareholders, investment professionals, and financial institutions. While few, if any, investors would want to limit themselves exclusively to them, well-chosen new issues do have a potential role to play in the portfolios of investors who can afford the risks.

Seasoned and Unseasoned Issues

Some new issues are seasoned, that is, issued by companies (such as Hospital Corporation of America, Commonwealth Edison Company, or any of thousands of others) with shares already traded on the open market. Other issues are unseasoned, involving initial public offerings by corporations with stock that has not previously been available to the public. This article focuses primarily on the second category: initial public offerings.

Special Qualities

Despite their basic similarities to existing issues of stock, new issues do have a character all their own.

The most fundamental investment trait of new issues is their tendency toward high risks and, therefore, potentially large rewards — and potentially large losses when prices turn down. Or, looked at another way, new issues are generally marked by high price volatility. Another trait is that new issues are often less liquid than established securities — a matter of particular concern to institutional investors. The investor also faces a number of other specific considerations when buying new issues, including the availability of new issues at initial offering prices, whether disclosure is adequate to make informed investment choices, and the need to understand new issues market cycles.

Dimensions of the Market

Unseasoned new issues of common stock do not represent an especially large marketplace. In years when stock prices are weak and investor demand for new

* Peter A. Bernard is Executive Vice-President and head of the Investment Banking and Trading Group at Bache Halsey Stuart Shields Inc., New York.

issues are small, fewer than half a dozen corporations may go public. Even in the most active years, a few hundred corporations might do so, with the combined value of their initial public offerings approaching $4 to $5 billion — a value equivalent to less than 2 percent of annual trading volume on the New York Stock Exchange.

Nonetheless, initial offerings, because of their risks and their potentially large rewards when market conditions are favorable, attract much greater investor interest than dollar volume alone might indicate.

Sources of New Issues

Initial public offerings are generally primary offerings, made by young, expanding corporations that need capital to finance their continued growth. A new issue can also arise because some of the owners of a privately held company decide to sell shares — a secondary offering that raises money for the owners. Or, an initial public offering may involve a combination primary/secondary issue.

Although the overwhelming majority of initial offerings are made by smaller companies, occasionally they are made by large, established corporations that have simply remained privately owned over the years, such as Ford Motor Company's initial public offering in 1956 in which the Ford Foundation sold 10.2 million Ford Motor shares.

Specific advantages to the company of going public include

- Broadened access to capital markets;
- Heightened prestige and public visibility;
- Establishment of a clear market value for the company's shares; and
- Ability to attract and retain employees by offering stock options and stock-purchase plans.

Economic benefits to issuer. Small companies are the wellspring of new technologies and provide the vast majority of new jobs. By supplying capital for these companies, initial public offerings play a vital role in our nation's economic growth.

Data General Corporation, founded in 1968, is a classic example. A pioneer in the development of minicomputers, Data General went public with a $3.5 million offering of stock one year after its founding. Exciting as the minicomputer concept seemed at that time, investors were taking a chance that Data General could make the concept work and succeed in a challenging marketplace.

And succeed it has. By 1980, just twelve years after the company got started in a small storefront office west of Boston, Data General's annual sales totaled more than $650 million, and the company provided jobs for nearly 15,000 employees. This growth would not have been possible without the core capital provided by the company's initial public offering.

As the company has prospered, so have its shareholders. According to *Fortune* magazine, Data General shareholders earned a 25 percent compound annual return on their investment in the ten years through 1980, one of the best investment returns in American industry.[1]

How an Underwriting Works

In buying new issues, it is important that an investor understand the underwriting process through which new issues are brought to market, since this process affects the pros and cons of new issues as well as their availability to investors.

The underwriting syndicate. Typically, the transaction is arranged between the issuing company and an underwriting syndicate. The underwriting group negotiates the stock price with the issuer, purchases the securities, and assumes all financial risk of being able to resell the securities to investors.

Stabilizing bids. In the days immediately following the offering, the underwriters may attempt to minimize any price decline for the stock — a potential plus for investors. This is done through stabilizing bids. In a successful underwriting, investor demand for the stock is equal to or greater than supply. But if demand falls short of supply, investors may sense this and begin selling their shares to cut their potential losses. This selling could quickly drive the price lower, and the underwriting group might suffer a severe financial loss.

To protect against this possibility, SEC rules permit the managing underwriter to maintain a stabilizing bid for the stock at a price equal to or below the offering price. As a result, buyers can generally resell their shares at or near the original offering price even if the offering is going poorly. However, once the syndicate disbands — generally within a few days after the offering — the stock becomes freely traded on the open market and its price is left to find its own free-market level based on supply and demand.

Allocations to investors. The allocation of shares to various members of an underwriting group has a major impact on the availability of new issues to investors. As a practical matter, the most attractive new issues may simply be unavailable to smaller investors at the initial offering price.

How a syndicate allocates stock. Formation of an underwriting syndicate is the responsibility of the managing underwriter, which generally asks a number of firms to join the syndicate in order to spread the financial risks of the underwriting and achieve broad distribution for the stock. Each firm is allocated a specific number of shares, based on such factors as the firm's size, distribution capabilities, and any special relationship with the issuing company. In a 500,000 share offering, for example, the managing underwriter might retain more than

---

[1] "The Fortune Directory of the Largest U.S. Industrial Corporations." *Fortune.* May 4, 1981, page 340.

100,000 shares, while the smallest participants in the syndicate might each be allocated 1,000 shares or less.

For a hot new issue — one for which investor demand exceeds supply by a wide margin — it becomes very difficult for the average investor to acquire shares at the initial offering price. A firm with an allocation of, say, 10,000 shares must, in turn, distribute those shares among its branch offices, which must then allocate them to prospective buyers. Through this filtering-down process, a smaller branch might end up receiving as few as 100 to 200 shares — even though the branch's customers may be seeking thousands more.

Best-efforts offerings. Some new issues are marketed on a best-efforts basis. Rather than purchasing the entire issue, the investment bankers agree to sell as many shares as they can. Best-efforts offerings are usually very speculative, as indicated by the unwillingness of the investment bankers to put their own capital at risk. If an issue is being marketed on a best-efforts basis, the fact is noted prominently in the prospectus.

ATTRACTIVE FEATURES

Potential for High Returns

As the Data General example suggests, the main reason investors purchase initial public offerings is in hopes of making a large profit. Getting in on the ground floor of any new company is bound to entail great risk, as well as the potential for sizable rewards.

An early study. One study examined the relative performances of fifty-three new issues marketed between December 1963 and June 1965.[2] Price comparisons were made for three time periods: from the offering date to the first Friday following the offering; from the offering to the fourth Friday following the offering; and from the offering to the first Friday one year after the offering. Initial public offerings in this study turned in an average performance well ahead of both the Dow-Jones industrial average and two over-the-counter indices. (See Table 1 on page 172.)

Initial offerings in a declining market. However, because this study concentrated on a period of generally rising stock prices, one of the authors decided to conduct a second study during a period of generally declining prices.[3] Thus, he examined the performance of sixty-two new issues marketed just prior to the 1966 market decline. (See Table 2 on page 172.)

---

[2] Reilly, Frank K., and Hatfield, Kenneth, "Investor Experience with New Stock Issues." *Financial Analysts Journal.* Sept.-Oct. 1969, pages 73-80.

[3] Reilly, Frank K., *Performance of New Stock Issues During a Declining Stock Market, Working Paper No. 33.* University of Kansas, School of Business, July 1970.

TABLE 1. Relative Price Performance for New Issues During a Rising Stock Market

	Friday after offering	*Fourth Friday after offering*	*Year after offering*
Average percentage change in all new issues	+9.9	+8.7	+43.7
Average percentage change in the National Quotation Bureau OTC Industrial Average	+0.3	+0.9	+23.1
Average percentage change in the Dow-Jones Industrial Average	+0.3	+0.5	+ 6.8
Average percentage change in randomly selected OTC stocks	+0.9	+2.2	+32.5

TABLE 2. Relative Price Performance for New Issues During a Declining Stock Market

	Friday after offering	*Fourth Friday after offering*	*Year after offering*
Average percentage change in all new issues	+10.2	+12.8	+20.4
Average percentage change in the National Quotation Bureau OTC Industrial Average	+ 0.3	+ 3.2	+ 3.1
Average percentage change in the Dow-Jones Industrial Average	+ 0.3	+ 2.1	−11.9
Average percentage change in randomly selected OTC stocks	+ 1.1	+ 4.5	− 3.9

SOURCE: Author's data.

TABLE 3. Relative Price Performance for New Issues Purchased at Post-Offering Prices

	Friday after offering to year after offering		*Fourth Friday after offering to year after offering*	
	Rising market	*Declining market*	*Rising market*	*Declining market*
Average percentage change in all new issues	+29.8	+ 6.3	+31.3	+ 4.9
Average percentage change in the National Quotation Bureau OTC Industrial Average	+22.7	+ 2.7	+22.0	− 0.1
Average percentage change in the Dow Jones Industrial Average	+ 6.6	−12.2	+ 6.3	−13.7
Average percentage change in randomly selected OTC stocks	+31.3	− 5.7	+29.4	− 7.4

SOURCE: Author's data.

Once again, new issues outperformed, on average, both the Dow-Jones industrial average and two other market indices.

However, there have been other periods when new issues prices have fallen precipitously, such as that following the 1969-1970 stock market sell-off and, to a lesser degree, the 1981 market decline.

Post-Offering Performance

New issues can also be an attractive, although still risky, investment if bought at post-offering prices. One study [4] in this area extends the two studies referred to previously. In this additional study, the authors made two assumptions: that each new issue was purchased on the first Friday following the actual offering and held until one year after the offering, and, alternatively, that each was purchased on the fourth Friday following the offering and also held until a year after the offering. The results are shown in Table 3.

[4] Reilly & Hatfield, note 2 *supra;* Reilly, note 3 *supra.*

New issue performance at post-offering prices was moderately better than other market indices almost across the board.

How post-offering prices fluctuate. For the patient investor, many new issues actually become available at or below the initial price in the weeks following the offering. A May 1981 survey of eighty-two new issues found that fifty-one, or nearly two-thirds, traded at or below the offering price in the after-market.[5] Investors who acquired all fifty-one issues in the after-market at the best possible prices would have achieved an average appreciation of about 125 percent over two and a half years — nearly equal to the 130 percent average gain on all eighty-two issues purchased in the initial offerings.

Long-Term Capital Appreciation

There is a tendency to view new issues as short-term trading vehicles that generate big profits only for those investors lucky enough to get a piece of the initial action. And, in fact, following that strategy is a perfectly valid approach for those traders who have access to initial offerings and can afford high risks.

But the evidence suggests another valid approach. Well-chosen new issues often turn out to be very good vehicles for long-term capital appreciation, whether acquired at the initial price or in the post-offering market.

"Net" Price

Another advantage to investors is that new issues are generally free of brokerage commissions. The broker is compensated by receiving part of the selling spread — the difference between the price the underwriters pay the issuing company and the price at which they resell to investors. There are no add-on commissions, as are generally charged when an investor purchases existing securities on the open market.

POTENTIAL RISKS

Untried Companies

The stocks themselves tend to be speculative, sometimes involving young companies with little or no financial record on which to judge investment potential. Although some companies (such as Data General) thrive after going public, others languish or go bankrupt.

Market Timing

Market cycles. The new issues market tends to move through cycles of unpredictable duration. Each cycle might begin quietly with a few issues per year,

---

[5] "After-Market Buying Produces Plus 125% Profit." *New Issues.* May 29, 1981, page 1.

then build and finally erupt into a great outpouring of new issues at ever higher prices, frequently followed by collapse.

Particularly at the height of the cycle, some new issues may carry price-earnings ratios (P/E) of 20, 30, or more — even though well-established equities may be available at ratios of five- to ten-times earnings. Does it really make sense to gamble on an unseasoned new issue at a very high P/E? Investors must decide for themselves, based on their investment objectives, willingness to take risks, and perceptions of each new issue's specific investment merits.

Overall equities environment. Market timing also relates to the overall market environment. If stock prices in general decline, chances are that prices for recently offered new issues will fall as well. The new issues market does not function in a vacuum. Price movements are closely related to conditions in the total equities marketplace. Therefore, before investing heavily in new issues, an investor should have some basis for being bullish about the overall market outlook.

Fads. The new issues market is also prone to fads. A highly successful offering by one company in a particular industry may spawn imitators, including start-up companies that have questionable business purposes. If the offerings of these companies are successful, promoters may soon create companies with only remote involvement in the field in question and then take these companies public. Inevitably, there is a shake-out, as the weaker and more ill-conceived ventures go bankrupt or are absorbed by other companies.

Speculators who are nimble enough to get out before the fad runs its course can sometimes make large profits. But this is a very risky game for the average investor.

Liquidity

Post-offering liquidity depends on a number of variables, including

Float. It is generally believed that a minimum initial offering of at least 300,000 shares, at a minimum initial price of $8 to $10 a share, is necessary to support an active post-offering market. Investors should view smaller offerings with some caution. Liquidity also relates to the types and number of owners of the shares and is particularly enhanced by large numbers of individual shareholders.

Post-offering market. Leading underwriting firms with large positions in a new issue are likely to make markets in the shares once the offering is completed — out of commitment to both the issuing company and customers who bought the shares. However, without active market-making, the stock could become an orphan, with erratic price movements and low liquidity. Investors who want to minimize their risks should consider the reputations of the leading underwriters before buying.

Listing. Some new issues qualify for listing on the New York or American Stock Exchange. If the company does plan to apply for listing, that fact is usually noted in the prospectus. Though listing can help liquidity, the after-market support of the lead underwriters remains the critical variable that generally counts most.

TAX CONSEQUENCES

There are no special tax advantages in buying new issues, other than the favorable tax treatment of long-term capital gains and the limited dividend income exclusion available on common stocks in general.

REPRESENTATIVE TYPES OF INVESTORS

Investors in initial public offerings fit into two basic categories — those who speculate primarily for short-term gains, and those who invest for long-term capital appreciation. Each strategy mandates a very different approach.

Speculators

For speculators, new issues are a marketplace of opportunity requiring, above all, an ability to pick the right time to buy. Speculation is a difficult game for the average investor, since it involves very high risks and necessitates enough trading volume to gain allocations of new issues at initial offering prices. For those traders who are able to get in at initial prices, the profits can be sizable — assuming that a trader also has a knack for getting out before prices fall (which they can sometimes do precipitously, especially if a new issues cycle has run its course).

Long-Term Investors

The long-term investor faces a very different task: He or she must be able to sort through all the initial offerings and pick those companies with the most solid business and financial prospects.

For the long-term investor, getting in at initial prices is not especially urgent. But this investor does need patience to avoid chasing after stocks that move to enormous initial price premiums. Very often, such stocks eventually settle back to more realistic buying levels.

The long-term investor must also have the fortitude to ride out temporary price swings; short-term price movements in the new issues market can be extremely volatile. And it is best to acquire a diversified portfolio of new issues, since the risks of any single new issue are bound to be fairly high.

In evaluating underwriters, the long-term investor will be less concerned with those firms that currently have the hot hand, and more attuned to those firms that have consistently adhered to quality offerings, regardless of fads.

IMPORTANT FACTORS IN BUYING AND SELLING

How Investors Get New Issues

It is probably unrealistic for the small, inactive investor to expect to obtain hot new issues at initial offering prices. However, for the more substantial investor, one strategy might be to concentrate all brokerage business with a single office of a leading new issues underwriter. When demand for a new issue exceeds supply, members of the underwriting syndicate typically give first preference to buyers who are active customers.

To improve their chances of receiving the most attractive offerings, some traders go so far as to buy all new issues, reaping big profits from the winners while immediately selling the mediocre performers back into the managing underwriter's stabilizing bid. However, this strategy can sometimes backfire by creating more enemies than friends among new issues underwriters.

Buying at Post-Offering Prices

For investors who do not have access to new issues at initial offering prices, another possibility is to buy selected issues in the open market shortly after the initial offering. The question is purely one of price — whether new issues are still bargains once the initial offering has been completed.

Disclosure

Buyers of new issues must make the effort to obtain all the facts they need to make informed investment choices.

The prospectus. A prospectus is the basic disclosure document for new issues. Prepared by the company, the prospectus describes the corporation's business and its financial results, the securities being offered, and other relevant data.

Red herring. A preliminary prospectus, or red herring, available to investors before the offering can help investors evaluate such questions as the following:

- What business is the company in? Obvious as it may seem, a basic — and often overlooked — test of any new issue is whether the company holds a significant market position in an attractive, growing industry.
- Is the company essentially in a start-up mode, or is it an established organization with a proven record of rising profits? The former indicates high risks for investors; the latter suggests lower risks.
- How does the company plan to use the money from the offering? The most favorable answer is to expand the business. Investors should be wary if insiders plan to sell most of their stock. While there could be legitimate reasons for such sales, they could also indicate that insiders are not especially optimistic about the company's future.

- Which investment banking firms belong to the underwriting syndicate? Are they reputable firms with a history of sponsoring successful new issues? Some firms — national firms as well as top regional investment banking houses — do a consistently superior job in bringing out attractive, quality offerings. A serious new-issues investor must, therefore, monitor underwriter performance — not just the performance of individual offerings per se — as a key element in picking the best investment opportunities.

However, the prospectus has limitations as a disclosure document. In most cases there is little, if any, discussion of the company's future prospects. Earnings projections, although a basic decision-making tool for investors, are not disclosed.

The registration statement. The prospectus is Part I of a broader document, a registration statement that the issuing company must file with the SEC. Part II of the registration statement contains additional data, including supplemental financial tables. Few individual investors look at Part II, or even seem to know it exists. On the other hand, security analysts and institutional investors often find that additional facts in Part II help make an informed choice.

SEC review. Before an actual offering can be made, the prospectus is reviewed by the SEC for adequacy of disclosure and compliance with applicable laws (particularly the Securities Act of 1933).

The SEC can insist on additional disclosures in the prospectus or changes in information or language. But it has no authority to judge the investment merits of an offering.

GLOSSARY

best-efforts offering— An offering in which the investment bankers act as the issuing company's agents, selling as many shares as possible but (unlike a firm commitment underwriting) not agreeing to buy the entire offering.

blue sky laws— Regulations of each state governing securities offerings in the state.

hot issue— An initial public offering that is in heavy investor demand. The market price, it is expected, will immediately rise to a premium.

initial public offering— A company's first public sale of common stock.

intrastate offering— A new issue sold within a single state and, therefore, exempt from registration with the federal SEC. The company must be incorporated in the state where it makes the offering and must do a significant portion of its business there, and all buyers of the issue must reside within that state.

primary offering— An offering that raises money for the issuing corporation, not for company shareholders. (See *secondary offering.*)

prospectus— The official offering circular that must, by law, be given to buyers of a new issue.

red herring— A preliminary prospectus.

registration statement— A disclosure statement filed with the SEC preparatory to a corporate offering of securities to the public. The registration statement includes the prospectus plus other business and financial data.

secondary offering— An issue of securities being marketed by company shareholders, such as the company's founders or senior executives. None of the money goes to the company itself.

Securities Act of 1933— The primary federal law governing new issues. Essentially, it requires that a registration statement, with full disclosure of relevant facts, be filed with the SEC before a new issue can be marketed to the public.

selling group— An extension of the underwriting syndicate. Securities firms in the selling group agree to market part of an issue for a fee based on the actual number of shares sold.

spread— The difference between the public offering price of a new issue and the proceeds to the issuing company or to selling shareholders; the underwriting commission.

stabilizing bid— A standing market bid, made by the managing underwriter at a price equal to or just below the offering price. The purpose is to forestall any price decline that might undercut the offering.

syndicate— An ad hoc group of underwriters and selling group members who band together for a specific offering to distribute the securities being sold to the public.

underwriter— The middleman between a company issuing securities and the investment public. Sometimes referred to as an investment banker. The usual practice is for one or more underwriters to buy a new issue of securities outright from the corporation, and to assume all financial risk of being able to resell the securities to investors. This practice guarantees the issuing corporation the full amount of capital it is seeking. Public offerings are only one among a variety of financial services underwriters provide to corporations.

SUGGESTED READING

A number of periodicals provide information on new issues trends and offerings. Here is a sampling:

Going Public: The IPO Reporter. Published by Howard & Co., Philadelphia, Pa. Weekly; a loose-leaf service providing reports profiling companies going public.

The Market Chronicle. Published by William B. Dana Co., New York, N.Y. Weekly; lists new issues in SEC registration, preparatory for public offering.

New Issues. Published by Institute for Econometric Research, Fort Lauderdale, Fla. Monthly; an advisory service recommending specific new issues for investment.

Over-the-Counter Newsletter. Published by Review Publishing Corp., Jenkintown, Pa. Biweekly; monitors the over-the-counter market, including initial offerings.

Over-the-Counter Review. Published by Review Publishing Corp., Jenkintown, Pa. Monthly; contains a report on new offerings.

Convertible Securities

Bancroft G. Davis *

BASIC CHARACTERISTICS

Convertible securities consist of debt instruments (bonds or debentures) or preferred stock of a corporation that may be exchanged for a specified number of shares of the common stock of the same corporation at a specified price as defined by the corporation upon the issuance of the security. Convertible debt possesses all the characteristics of straight debt of the corporation with regard to the payment of principal and interest, while convertible preferred stock possesses all the characteristics of straight preferred stock for preference in the payment of dividends. Both have a higher claim than common stockholders on the assets of the corporation upon liquidation or reorganization.

Convertible debt and convertible preferred stock both have unlimited potential for price appreciation based on the performance of the corporation's common stock, and have limited downside risk when the common stock price declines because their value stabilizes when their yields equal that of the other long-term debt or nonconvertible preferred stock of the corporation. In periods of sharply rising interest rates, their value tends to decline only to the point of their conversion value, while in periods of declining interest rates, their value tends to be enhanced when their yields are compared with those available on similar newly issued securities. Convertible preferred stocks generally rank junior to the company's convertible debt and have a lesser preference in bankruptcy or reorganization. However, convertible preferred shares, by and large, sell at yields and conversion premiums similar to those of debentures because of the favorable tax treatment of dividends given to corporate holders of the shares.

Types of Convertible Securities

In addition to straight convertible debt or preferred stock of a corporation, there are also several types of less well-known investments that provide some or all of the characteristics of standard convertible issues. These include

- Debentures or preferred stocks convertible into the common stock of another company, usually issued when the corporation has acquired a large block of shares of another company in an acquisition or open-market purchase;
- Cash-plus convertibles, which require the additional payment of cash in order to exercise the conversion privilege (see example in Figure 1 on page 181);

* The late Bancroft G. Davis was Chairman of the Bancroft Convertible Fund, Inc., New York.

- Discount convertibles, which are priced below stated par value to enhance their yield for fixed-income investors, but which have higher conversion premiums;
- Debentures with rights or warrants to purchase common shares attached, in order to make the security more attractive to the investor and reduce the corporation's borrowing costs;
- Synthetic or fabricated convertibles occasionally issued by a company in the form of a debenture with warrants attached, which permit the warrant holder to use either cash or the debentures at par in exercising the right to obtain the common stock;
- Unit convertibles, which are sometimes offered, as the result of a merger, by the surviving company to the stockholders of the merged company, and can be exchanged for common and/or preferred stock; and
- Christmas tree offerings, which generally refer to offerings by new companies seeking to raise capital. These may include various combinations of common stock, straight debt, convertible securities, and stock rights or stock warrants.

Major Factors in Analyzing Convertible Securities

In recent years, there has been an explosion of convertible securities offerings becausc the issuers felt that the interest burden arising from raising new capital by straight debt was too high and that it was unattractive to sell common at what seemed to be historically low prices. This influx of new convertible issues has led to a wider selection of better quality issues than have been available in the past. However, before investing in convertible securities, certain factors must be considered to determine whether the investment is attractive. These are the attrac-

> A typical cash-plus convertible is the Rio Grande $.80 preferred A. This is convertible into one-half share of common or full share upon payment of an additional $20. This example shows how this leverage worked in the investors' behalf in 1980.
>
> The common was selling at $40 and the preferred at $20. An investor could buy the preferred at $20, add $20 of his own, and obtain a share of the common worth $40. However, if the common should go to $60, a 50 percent rise, the preferred would jump from $20 to $40 in order to maintain the $20 differential, for a rise of 100 percent.
>
> The Rio Grande common stock crossed $40 and continued on to $61, which succeeded in setting off a rise in the preferred from $20 to over $44.
>
> There are not too many cash-plus convertibles available in the market today, and in many cases (such as the Northern Indiana Public Service 4.25s of 1992), the common is selling at too low a price to justify buying the convertible. When the common is rising sharply it can be a most rewarding investment.

FIG. 1. Example of Leverage Benefits in a Cash-Plus Convertible

tiveness of the underlying common stock, the conversion premium, the yield on the security, the break-even time for the investment, and the investment value.

Attractiveness of the Common. Before making an investment in a convertible security, the average investor should be convinced that it is an issue whose common stock he would like to own, using subjective standards.

Conversion Premium. The conversion premium, which is the difference between the market price of the convertible and its value in common stock if converted, should not be too high. The following example shows the method by which one can calculate the conversion premium. Assume that a convertible debenture is selling at $800 and is convertible into thirty shares of common stock at $25 a share. The conversion premium would equal the market price ($800) minus the conversion value (30 shares × $25 per share, or $750) or $50 per debenture. As a percentage of the market value of the debenture, the $50 represents a premium of 6.6 percent paid by the holder for the right to convert the debenture to common stock sometime in the future.

While it is usually true that the lower the premium, the more attractive the convertible, investors should not take too arbitrary a view on what numerical figure is too high because this judgment will depend on the conversion price, the current price, and the past performance of the stock. For example, the convertible issues of Pan American World are often actively traded at premiums that in some cases exceed 100 percent. With the common selling at $3 (down from $40), the premium could be substantially reduced in a relatively short period of buoyant market trading.

On the other hand, the 13 percent premium at which the U.S. Steel debentures were issued in 1976 could be considered high if one ascertained that the conversion price ($62.75) would have been an all-time high for the common.

Yield. To be attractive, the yield on a convertible must be at least as high as the yield on other convertible issues of the same or similar issuer — all other things being equal. It should also carry a considerable premium over the yield on the common, particularly if the company has a consistent record of dividend increases. If the common pays a minimal dividend, or no dividend at all, a yield lower than normal is acceptable. This explains the popularity of the high technology convertibles, such as the recent Wang Laboratory issues.

Yield carries with it another important factor: It is one of the three determinants of break-even time.

Break-even time. Break-even time is the mathematical relationship among the yield on the convertible, the yield on the common stock, and the conversion value. It gives the investor an idea of the time it will take to pay back the conversion premium through the superior yield of the convertible. In addition; it is an important factor to be considered given the length of time an investor wishes to hold an investment in convertible securities. For the short-term investor, a break-even time of two years or less is preferable. For the long-term investor, break-even times of up to ten years are not unusual. Break-even times for convertible investments are not fixed over the life of a security, but vary with the price of the underlying common stock, the current dividend on the stock, and the price of the convertible.

The following examples illustrate three methods of calculating break-even time. The first is a simple analysis that gives the investor an approximate break-even time. The second and third analyses arrive at more precise break-even times, using, respectively, a new convertible issue selling at par ($1,000), and a convertible debenture selling at a discount.

Example 1. Ampex Corp. 5.5 Percent Convertible Debentures Due 1994

Recent price of common	$28
Times: Conversion rate	×2.772
Conversion value	$77
Recent price of bond	$81
Differential	$4
Yield on bond	6.7%
Yield on common	2.7%
Differential	4.0%

$4 ÷ 4 = 1 year break-even time

Example 2. Cash Flow Method: New Issue at Par

Given:

Norton Company, 9½ percent — November 1, 2005 at 100
(Convertible at $45.25 into 17.85 common shares)

Norton Company common $1.80 annual dividend at current price of 45¼

Basic calculations:

Market value of bond	$1,000.00
Less: Conversion value (45¼ × 17.85)	807.71
Premium over conversion value	$192.29
Yearly income from bond	$95.00
Less: Yearly income from common ($1.80 × 17.85)	32.13
Yearly income advantage of convertible	$62.87

$$\text{Payback period}^{*} = \frac{\text{Premium over conversion value}}{\text{Yearly income advantage}} = \frac{192.29}{62.87} = 3.05 \text{ years}$$

Example 3. Cash-Flow Method: Discount Bond

Given:

K-Mart Inc. 6 percent — July 15, 1999 at 70
(Convertible at 35½ into 28.17 common shares)

K-Mart common $0.92 annual dividend at current price of 19¼

Basic calculations:

Market value of bond	$700.00
Less: Conversion value (19¼ × 28.17)	542.27
Premium over conversion value	$157.73
Yearly income from bond	$60.00
Less: Yearly income from common ($0.92 × 28.17)	25.92
Yearly income advantage of convertible	$34.08

$$\text{Payback period}^{*} = \frac{\text{Premium over conversion value}}{\text{Yearly income advantage}} = \frac{157.73}{34.08} = 4.63 \text{ years}$$

Investment value. The investment value is the estimate of the price at which the straight debt of the same or a similar issue would sell if there were no conversion feature. Ideally, in selecting convertibles, one should hunt for a combination of the lowest possible premium over conversion value and the lowest possible premium over investment value. In so doing, however, one must determine whether these factors indicate the poor financial condition of the corporation rather than the intrinsic value of the investment.

Less important factors. Other factors should also be considered before an investment in convertible securities is made, including the following.

Liquidity. Basically, this is not a great problem in today's markets because of the growing interest in convertibles.

A possible exception is the case of odd-lot debentures. Most sell decisions

* Identical to break-even time.

arise when the market action of the underlying stock has been either very strong or very weak. In the first case, the conversion premium probably has disappeared and it is easy to convert and sell the common. If the company is beset with severe problems and the convertibles fall far below par, there is a surprisingly good junk bond market. For example, when Cenco Instruments had problems in 1977, there was a very active market in the convertibles at around 50 cents on the dollar.

Call provisions and sinking funds. It is basically unsound to purchase a convertible selling at any sizable premium when it is also well over the call price. Assuming a call price of $105 and a conversion value of $115, purchasing a convertible at $125 runs the risk of call and the immediate loss of 10 points.

Conversely, if the convertible is selling at $75 and has a near-term maturity at a call price of $100, an investor can wait out the call and take 25 points in capital gains. However, if the company has been or must shortly start buying for its sinking fund, its purchases act as a nice price floor in even the worst of markets. Often the company starts buying in anticipation of the commencement of a sinking fund if the price is well below call.

A delay in the conversion privilege or future changes in conversion ratio. An example of delay in the conversion privilege was a new issue, NuCorp Energy 19.75 to 10 percent Delayed Convertible Debenture, due 2001. The coupon is 19.75 percent through November 30, 1982, and 10 percent thereafter. Starting December 1, 1982, the debenture is convertible into common stock at a price not less than $14 nor more than $35.

Banks, it should be noted, are prohibited from purchasing a convertible where there is a delay in the conversion privilege.

Yield as a factor in forcing conversion. This occurs when one purchases a convertible that has a small yield advantage over the common dividend. When the common yield exceeds that of the convertible by some number of basis points, the investor probably would want to either convert or sell. This is quite common when dividends tend to be increased far more often than they are reduced.

ATTRACTIVE FEATURES

Commonly Recognized Factors

Limiting risk — maximizing appreciation. The advantage of purchasing a convertible security over buying straight debt or straight equity of a corporation is that an investor is purchasing a call on the common stock of the corporation at a yield much higher than the current dividend yield on the common stock. Although the investor accepts a yield lower than that available on a straight debt issue, he has the possibility of making significant capital gains through the appreciation of the underlying common stock. If the investor is not absolutely sure that the common stock price will rise, or whether interest rates will rise or fall, purchasing a convertible security makes it possible to hedge the risk without sacrificing too much opportunity for capital gain or safety. However, as already stated, convertibles increase in value at a rate equal to the common stock once parity with the conversion price has been reached, taking into account the number of shares of common into which the preferred or debenture is convertible and the market price. For example, the Union Pacific Corporation's 4¾ debentures, maturing in 1999, originally issued at par ($100), were selling at $485 in the spring of 1981.

Likelihood of consistent performance. In terms of past performance as an investment vehicle, convertible issues have been remarkably consistent. Over an extended period of time, they have provided an excellent vehicle for sharing in the generally rising trend of stock prices. At the same time, an investor knows, based on the soundness of the issuing company, that the principal would be repaid at the maturity of the debt issue, or he would have a superior call on the assets of the corporation in a reorganization or bankruptcy should the company encounter financial difficulties.

The double floor on the downside. Convertible securities rarely sink below either of two distinct floors — their investment value or conversion parity. In sharply declining markets, as the conversion value of the convertible becomes diminished, the price decline of the convertible comes to a halt at or near the investment value, the point where the yield equals that of the straight debt securities of the same or similar issues. In periods of sharply rising interest rates, when the investment value is no longer a factor, the convertible never sinks more than a point or so below its conversion value.

Relatively Unexplored Areas of Attractiveness

The Eurobond market. Perhaps the least explored area in convertibles is the Eurobond market. When the interest equalization tax became effective in 1963, a separate market developed for new issues of domestic companies marketed abroad. The European market is quite different from ours in that a large majority of Eurodollar bonds have been placed in the trust departments of major European banks. Foreign trust officers primarily use bond valuation standards for making investment decisions, and for this reason it is quite possible to uncover very attractive issues with extremely low premiums.

Another factor is that the European banks tend to emphasize companies that have wide international reputations and allow lesser-known names to be traded at bargain prices. For this reason, alert investors could have purchased Eurobonds of a highly regarded domestic company, Masco, as low as $82 in the late summer of 1979. The bonds were then selling at a discount from conversion value, with a much higher yield than the common, and were due in January 1988.

It is increasingly difficult to discover such gems in the Eurobond market, but it may continue to be a source of profit as long as foreign sellers are dominated by bank-oriented policies.

Other opportunities in convertibles. Other opportunities open to investors are

- Selling covered calls — A continuous source of capital gains can come from selling covered calls against a convertible position.
- Using convertibles in hedging — With the rapid growth of the options market, this technique has now become a fine art.
- Investing in convertible funds — For the small investor, there are a number of investment companies specializing in convertibles, thus making it possible to achieve diversification and avoid the problems of odd-lot trading.
- Tender offers to refinance discount bonds — Recent high interest rates have caused many convertibles issued several years ago to sink well below par. When this occurs, the issuing company can reduce the book debt-equity ratio by issuing a much smaller number of high yield debentures in exchange for the outstanding issue. For the company, this not only reduces total debt but results in net income during the year the exchange is made. For the debenture holders, the offer has to be attractive enough to induce a tender, which is normally 15 to 20 percent over market value.

POTENTIAL RISKS

Unexpected troubles in the company's business can, of course, depreciate the convertible holder's investment. However, this is a problem no different from that which occurs in making any other debt or equity investment. A typical example is the recent case of Itel, a major issuer of convertible securities. This highly successful company derived a large percentage of its revenues from computer and freight car leasing. However, major changes in both industries occurred when IBM changed its pricing policies and many of the major railroads decided to build and lease their own freight cars. Certainly, ample storm warnings were given before the company got into more serious trouble.

Missing a Call

When convertibles are called, the conversion value of the common stock almost always far exceeds the call price. Allowing the call to expire costs the debenture holder a large percentage of the profits. No matter how diligent the company is, or how widely spread the notice of the call, this invariably happens to a few investors.

Other Caveats

Overlooking changes in conversion ratio. Changes in conversion ratio are not apt to be very dramatic, but they should be checked from time to time in one of the services, such as Value Line or RHM. (See *Suggested Reading* in this article.)

Buying at excessive premium over call. As a standard rule, one should never pay anything but a very modest premium if the convertible is selling considerably over call price. Even though the company has allowed its bonds to trade well over call price for quite some time, this is still no reason to be lulled into a false sense of security.

Lack of dilution privilege. If one buys a debenture convertible into twenty shares of common selling at $50 and the common is split two for one, in almost every case the debenture is now convertible into forty shares of the new common stock. This is provided for in the indenture covering the convertible issue. But when a company pays, for example, a one percent stock dividend each quarter, in most cases this is not covered by the dilution language. This has been a source of minor irritation to the debenture holders of such companies as Georgia Pacific, which used to pay a one percent quarterly dividend.

Of more importance is a spin-off of a valuable property or a block of stock that is not covered by the dilution language in the indenture. For example, American General Insurance spun off its holdings in the Texas Bank of Commerce in June 1978, and their convertible preferred had no compensatory rise in conversion ratio.

TAX CONSEQUENCES

The tax factors in the case of convertibles are no different than those of other debt or equity investments. The debenture holder pays taxes on interest payments received at ordinary income rates. The convertible preferred holder pays taxes on dividends at ordinary income rates but can exclude up to $100 in dividends ($200 in the case of a joint return) from personal income taxes.

Any gain resulting from the sale of a convertible security is treated as a capital transaction and taxed at capital gains rates. Losses on sale or exchange can be offset against capital gains or deducted against ordinary income in amounts up to $3,000 per year, with any amounts thereover carried forward into successive years until the loss is fully deducted.

The corporate holder can claim a deduction for up to 85 percent of any corporate dividends earned.

Holders of a Fund Specializing in Convertible Securities

All convertible funds have a mixture of debentures and preferred stocks and, therefore, their distributions contain a similar mixture of dividends and interest. Fund distributions are commonly called dividends and as such are available for exclusion by the individual in their entirety.

This is not true for the corporation that might own shares in the fund. It is allowed the corporate deduction for dividends only to the extent that the fund distributions actually consist of dividends received. An allocation of such percentages is readily available at the fund's office if it does not appear in the quarterly reports.

Securities Received on Mergers

The tax consequences of a merger and other reorganizations are generally spelled out in the proxy material. Some are constructed to be tax-free exchanges and others are not.

Switching Out of Convertible Securities

At times, the holder may switch from one convertible into another of the same issuer or convert into the common. As a general rule, no gain or loss is recognized on a conversion, but it is recognized in a tender offer exchange. (See *Attractive Features* in this article.)

However, in converting Eurobond securities another factor is involved. In many instances, the Eurobond issue is an obligation of a subsidiary, so that the conversion creates a taxable event. Such Eurobond issues generally have the word "international" or "financial" listed after the name of the company.

Covered Calls

If the investor sells covered calls on the common when the convertible is owned, the same general rule applies as when the common is owned. If the call is unexercised, the profits are short-term capital gains. If the call is exercised, the amount of the call is subtracted from the original purchase price of the convertible to ascertain the amount of profit or loss.

REPRESENTATIVE TYPES OF INVESTORS

Tax-Exempt Institutions

Ten years ago, there were very few pension funds that set aside a percentage of their money to be invested solely in convertibles and managed by specialists in that field. This has been changing rapidly due to the growing popularity of convertibles.

In prior years, convertibles found their way into pension portfolios by the back door; that is, through debt managers trying to help their performance by adding an equity kicker, or equity managers trying to increase their yield. A number of investment advisers, particularly Trust Company of the West, have been successful in persuading pension fund managers that convertible securities should be treated separately.

Banks and Insurance Companies

Banks and insurance companies traditionally have been the major market for convertibles because of the attractive features listed earlier.

Individuals

Convertibles have probably been less popular with individuals than institutions for several reasons:

- Since the basic unit for a debenture is $1,000, it is difficult for the truly small investor to obtain proper diversification.
- On buying and selling odd lots of less then 100 bonds, markets are less active and the spread is apt to be larger than normal.
- The two reasons above do not apply to preferred stocks. However, it may be stated as a general rule that the average account executive is not an expert in convertibles and, therefore, finds it easier to recommend the underlying common to his clients.

The solution to this problem would seem to be to invest in bank-pooled funds or investment companies that specialize in convertibles.

IMPORTANT FACTORS IN BUYING AND SELLING

Round-Lot Trading

Convertible preferreds can be purchased or sold through any good brokerage house. When buying or selling debentures in lots less than 100, the same problems exist as in trading in any bond. For this reason, this article shall not go into such technical matters as the nine-bond rule or cabinet bonds. All that the individual investor need know is that the odd-lot market is inactive and the spreads can be large, so patience is required.

When buying and selling round lots, trading is a fairly simple matter. Even though many convertible debentures are listed on the New York Stock Exchange, most of the trading is done over-the-counter. The principal markets used to be made by the block arbitrage houses, but now a whole variety of major houses have active convertible trading desks. These include Goldman Sachs, Salomon Brothers, Morgan Stanley, Merrill Lynch, Wertheim, Drexel Burnham Lambert, and many others.

Less Active Issues

For less actively traded convertible debentures that are not listed on the New York Stock Exchange, houses such as Wechsler & Krumholz and Murphy, Durieu & Neddell can be most helpful.

Junk Bonds

There is an active market in convertibles selling at a deep discount from parity, the so-called junk bond market. The houses active in this field vary from year to year.

Eurobonds

Eurobonds are most effectively sold through houses that have either a London office or strong European connections, such as First Boston with Credit Suisse. Kidder Peabody, Merrill Lynch, and Jesup & Lamont are also very active in this field. It can also be quite effective to use the services of a domestic trader who has considerable expertise in the European markets and who is willing to get up at 4 o'clock in the morning, when these markets open.

Large Block Sales

In selling out of a large block of debentures that are selling at or near parity, often the best method is to offer the entire position to an arbitraguer, who will compute the accrued interest and give the investor a net price that includes the commission. If satisfactory, he shorts the common, converts the debentures when received, and delivers them against the common. (See article on Arbitrage, elsewhere in this volume.)

If the investor wishes to retain part of his interest, it is relatively easy to ask the transfer agent to make the necessary conversion, while at the same time making short exempt sales of part of his position against the box. An example of short exempt sales against the box would be selling short common stock for which one owns the convertible equivalent, where the transaction is exempt from the plus-tick rule.

Commissions

On purchases and sales of preferred stocks, there are normal stock exchange commissions, including whatever discount can be negotiated. On bonds, the commission is generally $2.50 per bond, but round lots are frequently traded net. This means that if the bonds are quoted 90 bid — 91 asked, the investment dealer may find a willing buyer and willing seller at both prices and take his commission out of the spread.

GLOSSARY

break-even time — The time it takes to recoup the conversion premium from additional yield.

cash-plus convertible — A bond or preferred that requires the addition of cash to exercise the conversion right.

christmas tree offering — A complex original issue involving three or more units.

conversion rate or ratio — The number of shares of common into which a bond or preferred is convertible.

conversion value — The market price of the common multiplied by the conversion rate.

convertible — A bond or preferred stock convertible into common.

dilution privilege— The right to a change in the conversion ratio to reflect changes in capitalization or distribution of assets.

Eurobond— Bonds payable in dollars, but issued in Europe and not available to U.S. investors on the original underwriting.

fabricated convertible— A debenture with warrants attached that permits the warrant holder to use either cash or the debenture in exercising his conversion right.

investment value— The supposed value of the bond or preferred stock if it had no conversion feature.

parity— The point at which the market price of the convertible equals the conversion value.

payback period— The time it takes to recoup the conversion premium from additional yield.

premium— The amount by which the market price of the bond or preferred exceeds the conversion value.

short against the box— Establishing a short position in a stock in which the investor already has a long position (used for tax purposes).

spread— The difference between the broker's buying and selling price of a security; the brokerage commission.

synthetic convertible— A debenture with warrants attached that permits the warrant holder to use either cash or the debenture in exercising the conversion right.

unit convertible— A convertible that may be exchanged for more than one issue of the same company.

SUGGESTED READING

Primary Sources

These are of great value, and the leaders in the field are the *Value Line Convertible Survey* and the *RHM Convertible Survey.* Another publication, *Lipper Convertible Analysis Report,* is available to institutional investors (only in return for commission business, so-called soft dollar).

Addresses of the above publications are as follows:

Lipper Convertible Analysis Report
74 Trinity Place
New York, New York

RHM Convertible Survey
417 Northern Boulevard
Great Neck, New York 11201

Value Line Convertible Survey
Arnold, Bernhard & Co., Inc., 711 Third Avenue
New York, N.Y. 10017

Brokers' Publications

Far more brokerage houses cover convertibles in periodic publications, and cover them far more thoroughly than they did ten years ago. Leaders in monitored recommendation lists are E.F. Hutton and Merrill Lynch and, to a lesser extent, Shearson and Paine Webber. Thomson McKinnon has entered the field, and special mention should also be given to Stephens & Co. of Little Rock, Arkansas.

Many houses have unmonitored lists that can be used for factual information, including Morgan Stanley, Goldman Sachs, Bear Stearns, and Lehman Brothers Kuhn Loeb (for recent issues).

Eurobonds

In the Eurobond field, by far the most inclusive list is put out by the International Association of Bond Dealers, Zurich. This, however, is not available to the general public. The *RHM Convertible Survey* and Kidder Peabody have less inclusive Eurobond lists.

Corporate Bonds

*Irving D. Friedman, Esq.**

BASIC CHARACTERISTICS

Corporate bonds are the contractual obligations of a corporation to pay a fixed amount of money at a specified date, called the "maturity date," with interest, usually paid at semiannual intervals, until the bonds are paid. A bondholder's rights, and the corporation's obligations, are found in the bond and in a related contract called an "indenture."

A corporate bond is often considered a corporate note. The two terms are synonymous. However, the term "note" describes a short-term obligation, usually one that matures in ten years or less from the date it is issued, while the word "bond" more correctly describes a long-term obligation. Sometimes the corporate obligation is called a "debenture," which is a special type of note or a bond that is unsecured. It is usually guaranteed by the general creditworthiness of the issuer.

A corporation may also borrow money by issuing and selling bonds convertible into its own stock. (For a discussion of convertible bonds, see article on Convertible Securities, elsewhere in this volume.)

A secured bond or note is one that is backed by collateral of real or personal property. If the collateral is real estate, the bond is called a "mortgage bond." If it is personal property, the obligation is called a "secured note" or a "secured bond." An equipment trust bond or certificate is one that is secured by a pledge of specific property, such as one or more locomotives, box cars, or trucks.

The secured bonds of a corporation are ranked according to seniority. For example, there may be first mortgage bonds, second mortgage bonds, and subordinated bonds. The seniority of a secured bond becomes important when the company's business fortunes become so bad that default and insolvency occur. Obligations of greater seniority receive better treatment in insolvency proceedings than obligations of lesser seniority.

Although corporations issue bonds of millions of dollars, the bonds are sold to the public in denominations of as little as $1,000. The usual minimum denomination in which bonds are now issued and sold is $5,000. On the New York Stock Exchange, the unit of trading is one bond of $1,000 denomination. The expression "fifty bonds" thus refers to fifty $1,000 bonds.

---

* Irving D. Friedman is a registered representative with Muller & Co., Inc., and Managing Attorney for the New York law firm of Ballon, Stoll & Itzler.

Interest on Bonds

Bonds usually pay interest at a fixed rate, set when they are issued, on fixed dates until the bond matures unless the bond is paid before maturity. For example, a 12 percent bond (of $1,000 denomination) pays interest of $120 a year, payable in semiannual installments of $60 on January 1 and July 1 of each year. Normally, bond interest is paid semiannually; however, some bonds pay the interest quarterly, and some annually.

Income bonds. Income bonds are a type of bond on which the issuing corporation is not required to pay bond interest if it does not have sufficient income to pay it. The omitted interest is either lost to the bondholder for that interest period, or becomes cumulative, depending on the bond. If the interest becomes cumulative, the issuing corporation is obligated to pay it in the future if its income available for the payment of interest justifies or requires it. The formula for computing the corporation's income available for the payment of income bond interest, and whether or not such interest is cumulative, is found in the bond and the bond indenture.

Floating-interest-rate bonds. In certain bonds, interest is computed on the basis of a floating interest rate. The bond contract in such cases provides that the interest rate be adjusted, usually every six months, to the prevailing interest rate in the marketplace. Many floating-interest-rate bonds provide that the interest rate for the following six months be adjusted by adding either one-half or one percentage point to the rate the U. S. Treasury then pays on its three-month bills. The basis for the rate-fixing is stated in the bond and the bond indenture.

Examples. Some issues of Alabama Bancorporation, Chase Manhattan Corporation, Chemical New York Corporation, Citicorp, Continental Illinois Corporation, and Manufacturers Hanover Corporation are floating-rate bonds.

A 1981 issue of $100 million in floating-rate bonds, maturing in forty years, was made by Tucson Electric Power, a publicly owned Arizona utility. The interest rate on these forty-year bonds is to be changed monthly at plus or minus 10 percent of an index of high grade, thirty-day paper of similar issues.

Zero coupon bonds. An innovation in the issuance of corporate bonds is the zero coupon or zero interest bond. Zero coupon bonds do not pay any annual interest. Instead, the return to the investor is the difference between the low original purchase price and the redemption value of 100 at maturity.

An example is the zero coupon debenture issue of Continental Illinois Corporation, due November 1, 1989. These debentures were originally issued at a price equal to 33.246 percent of the principal amount of the debentures at maturity. This deeply discounted price of $332.46 for a $1,000 debenture represents a yield to maturity of 14.25 percent, computed on a semiannual basis.

Prepayment of Bonds

Virtually all bonds have a fixed maturity date (although a few are perpetual). However, the corporate borrower may want to pay its bonds before maturity, to get out of debt, to borrow money at a lower interest rate, or to get rid of restrictions that the bond contract puts on its operations. Some bonds are noncallable, and thus cannot be prepaid. Many bond contracts, however, include a prepayment provision.

Call price. The call price of a bond is the amount required for prepayment of a bond, often at a premium above face value. The corporation may, for example, be required to pay a premium of 10 percent, that is, 110 percent or $1,100 for each $1,000 bond. Some bonds provide for prepayment without premium, that is, for a call price equal to the face value of the bond.

Other bonds are noncallable for a certain period of time after they are issued, such as five or ten years; thereafter, they are callable at premiums that decline according to a fixed schedule.

Sinking fund requirements. In addition to the prepayment provisions, the bond may contain a sinking fund requirement. This means that the company must redeem a specified number of its bonds each year before maturity, in order to reduce its debt. This provision has advantages and corresponding disadvantages for the bondholder. The chief advantage is that the bondholders may get their principal paid back earlier than the maturity date. The main disadvantage is that if the bond is a good one with a good interest rate, they may not want to be paid.

When bonds are to be prepaid, either by call for payment or by sinking fund requirements, the bondholders are notified by the corporation by mail or newspaper advertisements, or both. After a call for payment is effective and complete, the bondholder must take the money, because interest on such bonds ceases on the specified prepayment date.

Value of Bonds

The value of a bond depends on two factors. One is the financial strength of the issuer; bonds of a strong, rich, and successful corporation are a better investment than bonds of a weak company. The other is the fixed interest rate. For example, if a bond carries a fixed interest rate of 6 percent, and interest rates rise, say, to 18 percent, the 6 percent bond will decline in value until its price returns a competitive rate of something near 18 percent.

An example is the highly rated American Telephone and Telegraph 3⅞ bonds, due 1990. This rate is far less than the 1981 interest rate on comparable bonds, which is about 18 percent. On October 2, 1981 these bonds were selling at about $500 each, or 50 cents on the dollar for each $1,000 bond. Thus, an investor who bought these bonds at their original price of $1,000 for a $1,000 debenture suffered a 50 percent loss of market value.

The investor or speculator who purchases bonds at a discount and holds them to maturity will receive a yield at maturity that is higher than the fixed interest rate. The difference between cost and the matured value of the bond is a capital gain. It is not necessary to wait until maturity of the bond to realize a capital gain from a bond purchased at a discount. The bond can be sold in the marketplace, at the then prevailing price, at any time.

Reduction of Risk

The only way to avoid such major losses of principal of bonds because of an increase in interest rates is not to buy them. No one can forecast the future of interest rates with certainty. However, if the investor buys a bond at the current price of about $500 for a $1,000 debenture, and interest rates decline sharply, he will enjoy an appreciation in the value of the bond. It should be noted, however, that a decline in interest rates makes it likely that the corporate obligor will prepay the bond with money it can borrow at a lower rate if the provisions of the bond contract so provide.

One investor solution to violent fluctuations in the value of bonds due to interest rate changes is the purchase of floating-rate bonds.

The other risk in corporate bond investments is the loss of financial strength of the corporation. There is no sure way to prevent such a loss, because a successful corporation can turn into a failure. A case in point is Chrysler Corporation, which was recently on the brink of bankruptcy. Another example is International Harvester Company, a formerly prosperous corporation whose bonds are now selling as low as 35, or $350 for a $1,000 bond. The serious financial problems of this corporation, plus the general increase in interest rates since the bonds were issued, have caused the bondholders to suffer a 65 percent market value loss.

One way to reduce such potential losses is to favor the bonds of financially strong electric companies, telephone companies, and banks, which are generally among the most stable types of corporations. Another way to reduce risk is by diversifying. The investor can do this by investing in a bond fund, such as the Drexel Bond-Debenture Trading Fund, which is listed on the New York Stock Exchange. The advantage of investing in such a fund is that the investor gets expert management as well as diversification of his bond investments. The disadvantage of owning stock in a bond investment company, rather than the actual bonds, is that management expenses reduce income to the investor.

Variety of Corporate Bonds

Bonds are issued by corporations doing business in all areas of human activity. The basic categories of bonds are industrials, public utilities, transportation, and finance. There are shipping company bonds, railroad bonds, airplane bonds (both manufacturing and transportation), entertainment company bonds, insurance company bonds, oil company bonds, paper company bonds, and even gambling company bonds.

ATTRACTIVE FEATURES

Current Return

One advantage of a corporate bond investment is that the bond pays a fixed amount of interest; for example, a 15 percent bond will pay $150 a year on each $1,000 bond. The issuing corporation cannot reduce the interest rate unless it files a petition under the Bankruptcy Code. Thus, the bondholder is entitled to the payment of interest even in bad times.

Seniority

Interest on a corporate bond must be paid before any dividends can be paid or distributed on the common or preferred stocks of a corporation. Furthermore, interest on a corporate bond is payable ahead of federal, state, and city corporation income taxes. These are important priorities. Short of bankruptcy, a bondholder cannot be deprived of the principal and interest on the bond without his written consent. The Trust Indenture Act of 1939 provides that no bond indenture issued under that law shall restrict an individual bondholder's right to the prompt payment of the principal and interest.

Capital Gains Potential

If a bondholder buys a bond at a discount from the face amount of $1,000, and sells it or redeems it at maturity for a profit, the profit is taxed at capital gains rates, subject to the required holding period. The bondholder who buys corporate bonds at a discount knows that a $1,000 bond will not be worth more than $1,000 unless interest rates decline. Therefore, a bond bought for $500, $600, or $800 should be sold at a profit when the price approaches its $1,000 face value.

Safety of Principal

The principal value of the bond will fluctuate with interest rate changes, with safety of principal depending on the financial strength of the corporation. To protect against loss of principal caused by interest rate fluctuations, the investor should buy short-term bonds or floating-rate bonds. To protect against loss of principal caused by a possible bankruptcy of the corporate obligor, the investor should favor the highest rated bonds of utilities and banks, and should also diversify.

Also, to reduce the risk of fluctuations in the prices and values of bonds that occur because of market forces, it is recommended that the bond investor maintain a presence in all maturity sectors of the market. Maturities should be spaced out among short-term, medium-term, and long-term. This diversification in maturity dates is as valuable as diversification of issuing corporations.

POTENTIAL RISKS

Market Volatility

As mentioned earlier, the risk of loss from fluctuating interest rates is a very great one. Although the income and principal on a bond may be safe because the obligor is a creditworthy corporation, the market value of the bond can be diminished by a general increase in interest rates. In 1981, for example, a 4 percent bond went down from $1,000 to as little as $300 because interest rates went up to about 18 percent.

Risk of loss due to increases in interest rates can be minimized by buying short-term bonds; no matter how low the interest rate is, the bondholder will get his money back at an early maturity. The bondholder can then re-invest the money at the then prevailing rate. Bonds maturing in less than two years are recommended to reduce this type of loss.

Not a hedge against inflation. Since they provide for the payment of the interest and principal at future dates, fixed-interest corporate bonds are not a hedge against inflation. In a period of inflation, the money from the interest and matured principal will buy less.

Corporate reverses. Changes in the affairs of the corporate borrower are another source of market volatility. For example, the bonds of Chrysler Corporation and International Harvester were hurt twice: once by the general increase in interest rates, and again by losses in their operations. The president of Chrysler Corporation complained in 1981 that his corporation was suffering because the current high interest rates made it difficult for potential automobile buyers to buy cars with borrowed money. To reduce the risk of loss because of an adverse turn in the corporation's business affairs, the bond investor should buy highly rated bonds. Standard & Poor's rates bonds from AAA for the highest down to D for the lowest. This is an excellent guide, although the investor should keep in mind that corporations and their ratings constantly change. Successful corporations can suffer a drop in profits, lose money, and go bankrupt just as poor corporations can become rich.

To reduce losses, it is recommended that bonds of major utilities and banks be favored. New York Telephone Company bonds and bonds of J.P. Morgan & Company are outstanding examples of financial strength. The prudent investor will favor bonds of corporations that have enough net working capital and profits to pay the interest and principal on their bonds even if business becomes bad; it is also wise to diversify by buying bonds in more than one company.

Fixed Current Return

The fixed return on a fixed-interest bond is a disadvantage (as well as an advantage, as mentioned above). Whereas a stockholder has the possibility of a dividend increase, the bondholder cannot get an interest increase. Exceptions are floating-interest bonds and the rare cases where an indenture is renegotiated by the company. There have been recent situations in which a corporation has asked its bondholders to release it from rigid indenture requirements, such as the maintenance of high collateral or working capital. In exchange, the corporate debtors are willing to compensate the bondholders by increasing the interest rate on the bonds.

Imperfect Liquidity

Although bonds are readily marketable, they are not as marketable as active stocks. Bonds enjoy a good market on the New York Stock Exchange, on the American Stock Exchange, and in the unlisted market. However, it is not unusual for a bond to sell at 70 ($700) with the bond quoted in the post-sale market at 65 bid ($650) and offered at 75 ($750).

Inactive bonds, of course, are more difficult to buy and sell than active ones. It is better to buy an active, marketable, high-grade bond, unless the inactive one gives a much higher yield or a price advantage, or both.

In buying or selling bonds on the New York and American Stock Exchanges, the unit of trading is one bond of $1,000 denomination. This is a very big advantage to the small investor, whose one or two bond order will get the same treatment on the floor of the Exchange as a big order for 500 bonds.

TAX CONSEQUENCES

There are no special tax advantages attached to the ownership of corporate bonds. The profits and losses on the purchases and sales of bonds are taxed at capital gains rates, depending on how long they are held. Bonds held for more than one year are taxed at the long-term capital gains rate, which allows the exclusion of 60 percent of the gain from taxation at ordinary rates.

There are limits on the offset of capital losses against ordinary income. Individuals and corporations may carry forward unused capital losses; corporations must first carry them back. Investors who repurchase bonds on which they realized losses should be mindful of wash sale rules.

While the individual or corporate investor pays regular income taxes on bond interest received, nonprofit institutions, such as labor unions and universities, which are exempt from income taxes in general, do not pay income taxes on bond interest.

In 1981, as a possible tax-saving inducement, some corporate bonds were originally issued well below face value. For example, the deeply discounted 5½ percent debentures of General Electric Credit Corporation were originally sold at $379.24 for each $1,000 bond, a discount of 62 percent. They yielded 15.8 percent to maturity in 2001. These debentures are rated AA by Moody's. Another example is the deep-discount debenture offered by Valero Energy Corporation in 1981. Its 16¼ percent debentures were sold at 82.15 percent of par to yield 19.875

to maturity in 2001. This issue is rated B by Moody's and BBB− by Standard & Poor's.

The purchase of such bonds gives the bondholder a potential capital gain play if interest rates should decline. However, since the interest on deep-discount bonds must be amortized, they are especially suitable for purchase by tax-exempt organizations and funds.

REPRESENTATIVE TYPES OF INVESTORS

There is no single type of investor who buys corporate bonds. Some investors buy them to get higher interest than is available from banks or from U.S. government bonds. Other investors buy bonds that sell at a discount to get the high return plus a capital gain potential. Many investors buy corporate bonds simply to get a return on their money.

Some investors like the idea of a fixed rate of return and a fixed maturity date. Investors also buy bonds because of the superior rights bondholders have over stockholders, and because interest is payable before income taxes.

IMPORTANT FACTORS IN BUYING AND SELLING

Selecting a Broker or a Dealer

All members of the New York Stock Exchange, American Stock Exchange, or National Association of Securities Dealers offer the services required to buy and sell bonds. The major difference among them is what they will charge for their services.

Substantial investors in corporate bonds should go to the big houses, which do a wholesale bond business. Such establishments are Asiel & Company; Bache Halsey Stuart Shields, Inc.; Bear Stearns & Company; Dillon Read & Company, Incorporated; E.F. Hutton; First Boston Corporation; Goldman Sachs; Lehman Brothers Kuhn Loeb; Mabon, Nugent & Company; Merrill Lynch Pierce Fenner & Smith; Morgan Stanley & Company; and Salomon Brothers. Although these firms are headquartered in New York, most of them have networks of regional branch offices in the major cities of the United States.

Some other big bond houses are A.G. Becker Incorporated, of Chicago; J.C. Bradford & Company, of Nashville; Johnson, Lane, Space, Smith & Company, Incorporated, of Atlanta; Edward D. Jones & Company, of St. Louis; Piper Jaffray & Hopwood Incorporated, of Minneapolis; and Rauscher, Pierce, Refsnes, Incorporated, of Dallas.

A complete list of security dealers can be found in a Standard & Poor's publication called *Security Dealers of North America.* This book is available in almost every brokerage office.

The big city banks such as Bank of New York, Chase Manhattan, Continental Illinois National Bank & Trust Company, Manufacturers Hanover Trust

Company, and Morgan Guaranty Trust Company also have corporate bond departments that will service the bond investor.

Commissions

The commission to buy and sell bonds is subject to mutual agreement and negotiation between the customer and the broker. Some brokers charge $2.50 a bond; others charge $5.00, $7.50, $10.00, or $20.00, and many have a minimum charge of $30.00. The bond purchaser should shop around to get the lowest commission charge available.

The most economical time to buy bonds is when they are originally issued. On a new issue the customer pays nothing in commissions. The selling expense is absorbed by the corporation selling the bonds, or the underwriter, or both.

Markets

The market for listed bonds is the exchange on which they are listed. Big blocks of bonds, including the listed bonds, are also traded in the over-the-counter bond market. The over-the-counter market consists of brokers and dealers who buy and sell securities among themselves without using the facilities of an exchange.

Certain bond dealers specialize in securities that are not listed or not well known. Some of these dealers are Cutter Dixon & Company; Kaufman, Alsberg & Company; and Wechsler & Krumholz, all of New York City.

Judging Quality

The easiest way to judge the quality of a bond is to use the Standard & Poor's rating, which is contained in their *Bond Guide:*

AAA — Highest rating
AA — Next to highest rating
A — Below AA
BBB — Adequate
BB, B, CCC, CC — Speculative
C — Income bonds not paying interest
D — Bonds in default

Moody's Investors Service has a similar rating system. If no rating is available, the bond investor should examine the corporation's balance sheet and income statements. The higher the coverage of interest and other fixed charges, the better the bond is; the higher the net working capital, the better the bond is.

For example, if a corporation's interest and fixed charges amount to $1 million a year, and the corporation has earned in each of the ten previous years $5 million to cover this charge, it has a record of earning its interest five times over, which is very good coverage. If the corporation has a total debt of $1 million, and its net working capital has been $5 million dollars or more for the previous ten years, then its net working capital is five times its debt, which is very good.

Using Professional Advisers and Appraisers

The use of professional advisers and appraisers is not necessary. One can get excellent professional advice at a cost of $89 a year by subscribing to Standard & Poor's *Bond Guide.* Their ratings are as good an appraisal as one can get from any other professional. Some brokers even give these *Bond Guides* free to their customers.

Appraisers are not needed because bond prices are adequately quoted in the *New York Times* and the *Wall Street Journal.* The bond market prices are the best appraisals of all; and they can be obtained for the price of a newspaper or a telephone call to a bond broker or dealer.

CUSTODIAL CARE

Physical Safety Precautions

Most bonds issued now come in registered form. They are issued in the name and address of the owner. Checks for the interest are mailed by the corporation directly to the bondholder.

It is recommended that when bonds are bought and paid for, the broker be instructed to transfer and ship the bonds to the bondholder. The bonds should then be placed in the bondholder's safe-deposit box.

Some bondholders prefer to leave their bonds with their broker for convenience, but this procedure is not recommended. When bonds are left with the broker, the bondholder assumes the risk of the broker's insolvency. Although brokers' customers' accounts are insured by the Securities Investors Protection Corporation and private insurance companies for up to $500,000 (and more in some cases), insolvency of a broker creates problems of confusion and delay, which may cause losses to the bondholder.

In the recent financial collapse of John Muir & Company, customers experienced delay in getting their securities because they were pledged as collateral for bank loans made by the broker. Aside from the possibility of bankruptcy, when bonds are left with a broker they are usually registered in the broker's name or in the name of a nominee. In such a case, the interest payments are mailed by the corporation to the broker or the broker's nominee. The broker, in turn, credits the interest to the customer's account, and then remits the interest check to the bondholder. All this requires processing and delay, so that an interest payment due on the first of a month may not reach the bondholder until the tenth. Brokerage house bookkeeping volume may delay payment to the bondholder of interest and principal.

If the account is inactive, the broker may impose a service charge for taking care of the bonds. The broker may also have a lien on bonds in its possession for any money the customer owes on other business transactions.

Some bonds are issued in bearer form, with coupons attached for payment of interest. Such bearer bonds should also be sent by the broker to the customer as soon as they are paid for.

Ownership of such bonds can pass by delivery, the same way currency does. Therefore, they should be put in the bondholder's safe-deposit box and a record should be made of the interest payment dates. When the interest is payable, the interest coupons for that date should be detached from the bond and deposited in the bondholder's bank account.

Income-Collection Procedures

Income collection on registered bonds is easy. The bondholder gets a check in the mail for the interest.

With the bearer bonds, the interest coupons should be detached on the due date and deposited in the bondholder's bank account.

Professional Custodial Care

A bank will open a custodial account for a bondholder if the account is large enough to interest the bank. It may be worthwhile for a bondholder with substantial holdings to hire a bank to take care of the bonds, collect the interest, remit it, and send a monthly and annual report for tax and recordkeeping purposes. The custodial bank will also monitor for redemption notices, tender offers, exchange offers, extension plans, and reorganization plans affecting the bonds. It will notify the bondholder when action is required to be taken. The ordinary registered bondholder does not need all this service, because all important notices will be mailed. Such notices are also published in the financial pages of leading newspapers in major cities.

A holder of bearer bonds should watch published financial notices for a possible call for payment of the bonds, since nothing will be mailed because the corporation has no record of his name and address. Many holders of bearer bonds learn for the first time that their bonds were called for payment when they deposit an interest coupon for payment, and have it returned because the bond had been previously called and paid. This results in a delay in payment and a loss of interest.

GLOSSARY

bond— A paper or document that sets forth the provisions for the payment of interest and principal. The term "a bond" refers to a bond of $1,000 denomination.

call price— The price the corporation is required to pay if it wants to pay the bond before maturity. If the call price is above $1,000, the excess is called a "premium."

debenture— An unsecured note or bond. The difference between a debenture and an unsecured bond is just a matter of nomenclature, like a dollar and a buck.

deep-discount bond— A bond originally issued by the corporate obligor at a price much lower than its face value because the interest rate it pays is below prevailing interest rates. A corporation will sell a $1,000 bond for $500 or $600 because it agrees to pay only 6 or 7 percent when normal interest rates are much higher, say 15 to 18 percent. A deep-discount bond can also be created by market forces. A $1,000 bond, originally issued and marketed for $1,000, can become a deep-discount bond if interest rates soar after it is issued.

floating-rate bond— A bond on which the interest rate is adjusted, usually every six months, for the subsequent six months, according to a formula based on the then prevailing interest rates. The prime rate, federal funds rate, commercial paper rate, and Treasury bill rates are the standards usually used.

income bond— A bond on which interest is payable only if the obligor corporation earns enough income to pay it.

indenture— A contract between the corporate obligor and a trustee, called the "indenture trustee," that itemizes in detail all of the obligations of the debtor corporation under the terms of the bond issue. This includes the remedies the indenture trustee and the bondholders have to enforce their rights in the event the debtor defaults.

interest— The money the borrowing corporation contracts to pay to the bondholder.

point— $10 for each $1,000 bond. If a bond's market price fluctuates 3 points it has gone up or down $30. If it fluctuates half a point, it has gone up or down $5 for each $1,000 bond.

redemption— The act of the obligor to pay all the interest and principal due on its bonds on or before the maturity date.

secured bond— A bond that is secured by the pledge of personal property as collateral security for the payment of the bond. Where real estate is the collateral security for a bond, it is called a "mortgage bond."

sinking fund requirement— A stipulation in the bond that obligates the corporation owing the money to pay a certain number of bonds, at specified dates, before the maturity date.

spread— The difference between the bid and asked prices when the bond is quoted. If a bond is quoted 93 bid, 94 offered, the spread is the difference between 93 and 94, which is a point, or $10 on a $1,000 bond.

yield— The percentage return the bond pays.

zero coupon bond— A bond that pays no interest during the life of the bond. The principal of the bond, when it is paid at maturity, includes the payment of interest.

LEADING DEALERS

The leading bond brokers and dealers would make a very long list. A selection follows.

Allen & Co., New York, N.Y.

Bache Halsey Stuart Shields, Inc., New York, N.Y.

Bear Stearns & Co., New York, N.Y.

Blyth Eastman Paine Webber, New York, N.Y.

Lehman Brothers Kuhn Loeb, New York, N.Y.
Merrill Lynch Pierce Fenner & Smith, Inc., New York, N.Y.
Morgan Stanley & Co., New York, N.Y.
Salomon Brothers, New York, N.Y.
Shearson Loeb Rhoades & Hornblower, Inc. New York, N.Y.

Although these firms are located in New York, they are not limited to that city. They are national and international. All have extensive wire systems and branch offices.

To buy or sell bonds, it is not necessary to go to these leading broker-dealers. Any broker who is a member of the New York Stock Exchange can put a bond order for one bond or more on the floor of the Exchange. American Stock Exchange brokers can do the same on their Exchange. Non-member brokers can execute orders in unlisted bonds, and can give their listed bond orders to a member firm to be executed on the Exchange.

SUGGESTED READING

The *Wall Street Journal* and the *New York Times* have excellent news sections about bonds. The *Wall Street Journal* features news of credit markets, financing business, money rates, and corporate debt offerings. Both papers list bond quotations for the New York Stock Exchange, the American Stock Exchange, the Pacific Stock Exchange, and the Philadelphia Stock Exchange.

For unlisted corporate prices, the Bond Section of the National Daily Quotation Service is available; however, for most bonds, this service lists only the names and telephone numbers of the brokers, rather than the prices. Since most bond dealers will not give a quotation on the telephone to an unknown individual caller, a better way to obtain a quotation on an unlisted bond is to ask one's own broker to get it.

Standard & Poor's *Bond Guide* is an excellent reference work, which gives a summary bond information for individual companies. For more complete bond information, consult Standard & Poor's *Corporation Records,* a reference service that is readily available in most brokerage offices.

A classic textbook on bond values is *Security Analysis* by Graham, Dodd, and Cottle, New York: McGraw-Hill, 4th ed., 1962.

Folk Art and Americana

*William C. Ketchum, Jr.**

BASIC CHARACTERISTICS

Folk art and Americana are distinct fields and each differs not only from the other but also from what is generally thought of as fine art or high-style furnishings.

Folk Art

The term "folk art" has been defined to include the work of individuals who are unschooled in or choose not to follow the tenets of what is generally considered academic painting and sculpture, that is, a sense of perspective, traditional color mixing, and proportion. Such artists may be referred to as naïve, primitive, or folk, but they should not be thought of as non-commercial, for many did and do earn all or part of their living by painting or sculpting. The work discussed here spans the period from the seventeenth century to the present.

An expanding genre. The above definition may be readily applied to what is commonly thought of as art — paintings and pieces of sculpture created by an individual. However, over the past decade interest in the field has outgrown the availability of collectable objects, and the definition has come to encompass objects such as carousel figures and factory-made weather vanes, which were assembled by several individuals working in a shop and which certainly were not thought of by their creators as art in any sense. These later inclusions have led to conflicts among those who consider themselves authorities in the field. Collectors, however, are unconcerned, as they continue to acquire those objects that are inherently appealing and are deemed to have investment potential.

Americana

The term "Americana" encompasses a more nebulous field and one characterized by craft, rather than art, tradition. The generally recognized categories include

Textiles, such as quilts, samplers, and hooked rugs;
Ceramics, specifically redware, stoneware, and Rockingham;
Simple glass objects;

* William C. Ketchum, Jr., is an author, lecturer, and consultant in the field of folk art and Americana in New York.

Furniture made by country cabinetmakers;
Metalwares, such as iron, tin, brass, and copper; and
Woodenware and basketry.

In each category the objects produced are characterized by a simple, folk-oriented quality as opposed to the sophisticated forms being produced at the same time by craftspeople in Europe and in the larger cities of the United States. Thus, high-style American furniture includes distinct styles such as Queen Anne and Chippendale, which are modeled on European prototypes and follow certain rules as to materials and proportions. Country furniture produced at the same time, such as the increasingly popular Shaker type, differs substantially in both form and materials used.

JUDGING VALUE

As with other collectibles, the value of folk art and Americana is determined by supply and demand. Moreover, since the objects themselves, unlike precious metals, gemstones, or realty, seldom have any intrinsic monetary worth, their value is largely determined by popular taste and fads, which may change greatly over a period of time.

Folk Art

Prior to the collecting boom that followed World War II, prices in the field of folk art were generally modest and were determined largely by the reputation of the individual painter or sculptor as established through inclusion in museum or private collections or in the relatively few books that dealt with the field.

Current value structures. At present, folk art values are highly variable and subject to substantial manipulation. On the one hand, examples within the traditional definition (i.e., nineteenth century works and even weather vanes and ship's figureheads) often are sold at auction, and the auction prices (particularly those realized at major galleries such as Sotheby Parke Bernet) set the standard for the field. On the other hand, twentieth-century folk art is seldom offered at auction, and prices may vary greatly. Museum exhibitions, the appearance of a book about a given artist, a massive advertising campaign by a major dealer — any or all may lead to a run on and subsequent rise in the value of works by a given artist. Thus, a collector or dealer may amass a group of works by one or more painters, arrange to lend them to museums for exhibition, write a book on them, and then sell the collection. Such artificial inflation of the market may or may not prove permanent.

Americana

Prices in this field reflect a combination of the previously discussed factors. Museum exhibitions, books in the field, and dealer publicity all will affect prices, but the ultimate determinant, of course, usually will be what the pieces in question bring at auction.

INVESTMENT CATEGORIES

Both folk art and Americana contain a variety of subcategories, some of which appear at present to offer better investment opportunities than others do. Moreover, certain areas have remained relatively stable over a period of time while others have fluctuated sharply.

Folk Art

Oil paintings. Oils, whether portraits or landscapes, remain the most sought-after of folk paintings. Examples by artists such as Edward Hicks, creator of the well-known *Peaceable Kingdom* series, will bring prices in six figures, while there are several dozen nineteenth-century portraitists whose paintings command prices in the $20,000 to $50,000 range. Unattributed works also may bring high prices if they incorporate appealing elements such as bold colors, recognizable background localities, or quaint accessories such as pets, children's toys, and period furnishings. However, the safest investments in this area seem to be paintings that may be attributed to a recognized and appreciated artist.

Watercolors. As in the world of academic art, folk watercolors generally are less desirable and command lower prices than oils do. There are exceptions, though, most notably the brightly colored late-eighteenth/early-nineteenth-century Fraktur paintings of Pennsylvania; these often will sell in the five-figure range. On the whole, however, watercolors remain somewhat underpriced even where executed by a well-known artist. The area that seems most promising at present is that of theorems and memorial pictures, both of which usually are of anonymous origin. These have been increasing in value at a steady rate and offer an appealing investment opportunity.

Miscellaneous graphics. There are many nineteenth-century pastels on the market, as well as calligraphic drawings, sandpaper paintings, and architectural renderings, that are in either pencil or watercolors. Pastels usually are a bad investment. They simply will not sell at any meaningful price level and have shown little advance over the past decade. Calligraphy, on the other hand, continues to enjoy a resurgence in interest and, like architectural drawings, offers an area of investment for the individual of modest means. Good examples often may be purchased for a few hundred dollars. In these areas, one should look for signed works by artists who are known.

Sculpture. Pure sculpture, as opposed to sculptural objects such as weather vanes and carousel figures, is relatively uncommon in the folk field. Demand is strong, and carvings, be they of Lincoln or Washington or a farmer's daughter, will bring prices in the thousands. Most works, however, are unsigned and are judged on their own merits.

Hottest items in the current folk sculpture market are objects that were never thought of as art by their creators — weather vanes, shop figures, carousel figures, and ship's figureheads.

Weather vanes. These are of two types, those that were made in factories from patterns and, therefore, exist in duplicated form, and those one-of-a-kind examples that were created by individuals for their own use. The former represents a safe, if not spectacular, investment. They are traded on the market often enough to allow for established prices and are readily salable. The top of the line are unusual forms such as railroad locomotives and early airplanes, which are currently undergoing sharp price escalation; more common types, such as horses and eagles, are not moving as quickly. More speculative are the hand-crafted wood or iron weather vanes made by the individual user. Fine examples can bring prices well above $20,000, but the discovery of sophisticated fakes has led to caution on the part of many potential buyers. One should not purchase such pieces without a guarantee of authenticity.

Ship's figureheads. Currently in short supply, these will command prices in the five-figure area when a specimen comes on the market. Long recognized as an important form of folk sculpture, most are the work of several persons rather than a single artisan. These pieces are a safe investment. Most examples date prior to 1870; reproductions are rare and usually easily detected.

Carousel figures. Recent additions to the world of folk sculpture, most of these date from the late nineteenth or early twentieth century. Many can be identified by the marks of manufacturers, such as Longg, Stillman, or Parker carnival supply, and these represent good buys, as do unusual forms such as elephants, rabbits, frogs, and the like. Horses are popular, but they are common and overpriced. The wise buyer will seek out examples made from only four or five large units rather than the later figures, which are made from many small blocks glued together. European examples are coming into the market, and these may be confused with American figures, although the former tends to look more elaborate and exotic.

Trade figures and signs. Most popular and highest priced is the well-known cigar-store Indian. Good, authenticated specimens will bring $15,000 or more. Not more than 2,000 such pieces are believed to exist, and the market is tight. Well-made reproductions are encountered frequently, and buyers should be knowledgeable or have the benefit of expert advice. Trade figures in other forms also may be encountered — jockeys, mariners, and bakers are but a few of the available types. These, too, bring high prices, particularly at auction, but many being traded are of European origin. The buyer should proceed with care.

Decoys. A unique American contribution to the world of folk carving, these generally small figures may bring very high prices. Tiny shore birds have sold for over $10,000. Price determination here is generally related to the maker. Examples by well-known carvers such as Elmer Crowell or the Ward brothers will go for more than $1,000, while unidentified decoys may bring but a few dollars. Unusual types — swans, mergansers, shore birds — always sell at a premium.

Twentieth-century painting and sculpture. This area is extremely fluid at present and offers great opportunities for speculative profits as well as substantial risks. The work of some artists, such as Fasanella and Jakobsen, has increased in value ten times over in the past few years. The work of other painters and sculptors has not moved forward nearly so rapidly. Current values seem to be largely tied to effective dealer publicity; and, as previously mentioned, few of the twentieth-century folk artists have been exposed to the test of the auction market. Investors in this field should confine themselves to individuals whose work has a strong track record, including exposure in books and museum exhibitions.

Americana

Quilts and other textiles. The quilt market continues to be vigorous after a full decade of activity. Strong colors and geometric shapes — particularly as seen in Amish quilts — are the key to top prices; age is of considerably less importance. Good quality appliqué quilts also are increasing in value, often into the realm of five figures. Pastel examples from the 1930s and Victorian crazy quilts remain well underpriced; and the latter presents a particularly appealing area for stockpiling against future demand. The price of needlework samplers has increased sharply in recent years, primarily due to important museum exhibitions and a major auction. However, only those samplers with good pictorial qualities seem destined for substantial appreciation, and the presence of many European examples presents problems. The latter look much like native examples, although they often may be distinguished by the presence of non-American symbols such as the lion or a crown, or by use of a foreign language. Needlework pictures are also appreciating in cost, while woven coverlets seem underpriced for their age and quality. Geometric forms seem an especially good buy here.

Ceramics. American red earthenware of good quality continues to advance, with sgraffito plates bringing as much as $25,000. Collectors must, however, be aware of reproductions in this field. Stoneware prices declined after a surge in the early 1970s; and, while examples with superior decoration will still bring prices in the thousands, run-of-the-mill crocks and jugs are not to be thought of as investments.

Furniture. Along with quilts, this is the area of greatest and fastest appreciation in the field of Americana. Furnishings made by the Shaker sect in the nineteenth century and furniture in original grained or sponged decoration will readily reach the four- to five-figure level. However, many pieces, including the popular and expensive Pennsylvania dower chests, have been repainted, and it is extremely important to deal only with those who can stand behind their merchandise. Also, the market for Shaker pieces has leveled off recently, and it may well have reached its limit, something that does not seem to be the case with the painted examples.

Woodenware and basketry. Most woodenware should be purchased for the pleasure it provides rather than with any hope of long-term gain. However, painted and decorated examples border on folk art and will sell for thousands of dollars; these are the things to seek out. A similar situation exists in the basketry field. Most pieces are ordinary, but major price increases are on the so-called Nantucket baskets, which may earn as much as $3,000 for a set of four or five, and also on Shaker baskets. The latter are a risky investment since, unless documented as having come from a Shaker community, they really cannot be accurately attributed.

Metalwares. This is not really an area for serious investment, as interest is confined to a limited number of collectors. Best buys include decorated tinware (tole) and wrought iron signed by such documented makers as Peter Derr, as well as early cast-iron firebacks and stove plates.

ATTRACTIVE FEATURES

Unlike debt and equity securities, folk art and Americana are intrinsically valuable as embodiments of American history, both artistic and cultural. They are, moreover, legitimate investment media.

Aesthetic Rewards

The owner of an early oil painting of George Washington or a fine, handmade quilt takes pride in the possession of a piece of American social history and becomes in a real sense a guardian of that past. Morever, the charm and personality of a rare piece is, for some people, a good deal more satisfying than possession of a gold bar or share of stock.

Hedge Against Inflation

Many antiques and art objects not only have kept ahead of inflation over the past decade, but have increased in value far more than traditional forms of investment. Given the growing interest in Americana, this favorable prospect probably will continue.

Relative Liquidity

While not as easily salable as stocks, quality folk art and Americana can usually be turned into cash within six months (often less) via the auction market. As long as auction market activity remains robust, collectors need have little fear of finding their assets frozen.

POTENTIAL RISKS

Market Volatility

The demand for folk art and Americana, like other kinds of collectibles, is subject to changes in public taste. Increased interest in a new field, such as Art Deco, can draw money away from another field, such as Victoriana. The elements of speculation and market manipulation increase this risk.

Devaluation in a Recession

Along with other investments, experience has shown that in times of depression many luxury or non-essential items will decline in value. However, traditional collectibles such as fine paintings, silver, and jewelry will decline more slowly than will those objects that have most recently attracted the collector's eye. While there is no great amount of hard evidence on the matter yet, one must assume that folk art and Americana pieces would decline in a recession, since they are relatively new additions to the collectibles world.

Fakery and Reproduction

From folk art ship paintings to Shaker boxes, Americana is being reproduced, often with an intent to deceive. If this situation is unchecked, it is likely to have an eventual effect on the stability of the market. Already, the presence of many fakes has scared off some scrimshaw investors and collectors. Serious and knowledgeable investors will, no doubt, remain active; but if large numbers of buyers abandon the field out of fear of deception, it could have a serious effect on values.

TAX CONSEQUENCES

Under federal tax law, profit from the sale of collectibles held by an individual for more than one year is taxable at the capital gains rate rather than as ordinary income. Under certain conditions, collectibles can be exchanged for others of equal or greater value in a tax-free transaction. As with other types of investments, it is also possible to realize a tax deduction on donating folk art or Americana, whose market value has appreciated, to a qualified organization. (See article on Tax Considerations for Collector-Investors, elsewhere in this volume.) For specific guidance in these matters, investors are urged to consult with a professional tax adviser.

REPRESENTATIVE TYPES OF INVESTORS

Investors in folk art and Americana have been individuals for the most part. However, within the past five years, corporations have begun to buy, recognizing that purchases not only represent good long-term investments but also generate favorable publicity and may create substantial goodwill. Paintings, for example, may be exhibited or loaned to museums, thus casting the corporate owner in a favorable light.

IMPORTANT FACTORS IN BUYING AND SELLING

Unless experienced and knowledgeable, the investor in folk art and Americana should buy only from a reputable dealer who can advise and direct acquisitions. Would-be purchasers of scrimshaw or other folk art composed in part or totally of whalebone or tortoiseshell should be aware of current laws governing the sale and holding of such objects, as they affect interstate commerce. Generally, the law applies only to new pieces but, due to some confusion, it has been applied to antiques as well. When in doubt, a statement as to age should be obtained from the seller.

Auctions

Buying at auction offers a wide range of choices and the opportunity to purchase at or below retail. However, buyers and sellers should be familiar with the operation of auctions, the commissions charged, legal liabilities of the parties, and the nature of the objects they are buying.

Dealers

Most antiques are purchased from professional dealers, who should be chosen for their expertise, reputation in the community, and wide selection of quality objects.

Private Sales

Buying from private individuals often can prove most profitable. However, it presumes considerable knowledge of the field on the part of the investor.

CUSTODIAL CARE

All purchases should be recorded in detail and insured. Details relating to the care and preservation of specific items vary substantially, and the collector-investor should consult museum personnel, dealers, or other experts in the field to ascertain the best manner in which to maintain his or her collection. In most cases, individual items should be photographed from several angles in order to obtain a photographic record for insurance purposes.

GLOSSARY

calligraphic drawing— Ink or pencil sketch done in flowing lines on paper. Sometimes highlighted in pastels.

coverlet, woven— Wool and/or cotton bed-covering, made on a loom, in a geometric or floral pattern.

decoy— Carved wooden bird, usually a duck, designed to lure game birds within shooting range.

dower chest— Usually a painted lift-top chest with one or more lower drawers. Most are dated around 1800.

fireback— Decorated cast-iron sheet placed at the back of a fireplace to protect the bricks from excessive heat.

fraktur— Pennsylvania German watercolor often signed and dated and brightly colored. Most are small.

grain painting— Decorative technique for furniture painting that attempts to duplicate wood grain.

hooked rug— Generally small rug made by hooking strips of cloth through a piece of burlap.

memorial picture— Watercolor or textile picture dedicated to a deceased relative and usually featuring a tomb and several mourners.

quilt— Textile produced by stitching three layers of material together. Most are pieced or appliquéd.

redware— Earthenware that turns red after firing.

Rockingham— Earthenware with yellow body covered with a mottled brown and yellow glaze.

scrimshaw— Small ivory objects with engraved patterns into which ink has been rubbed.

sgraffito— A style of scratch decoration applied to ceramics.

ship's figurehead— Carved figure, often of a woman, that was attached to the bow of a nineteenth-century ship.

sponge decoration— Decorative technique employed on furniture involving the dabbing of color onto the surface with a sponge or cloth.

stove plate— Decorated cast-iron sheet used in the construction of early American stoves.

stoneware— Earthenware that turns blue-gray when fired and is typically decorated in blue.

theorem— A form of folk art, usually a representation of a bowl of fruit or flowers, that is created with the use of stencils.

tole— Tin that has been painted, usually with floral decorations.

trade figure— Carved wooden figure, such as a cigar-store Indian, that was placed outside a shop to attract customers.

woodenware— Small, carved wooden objects such as boxes, rolling pins, and chopping or serving bowls.

SELECTED DEALERS

All of Us Americans Folk Art, Bethesda, Md.
Marna Anderson Gallery, New York, N.Y.
Hammer & Hammer, Chicago, Ill.
Jay Johnson America's Folk Heritage Gallery, New York, N.Y.
Just Us, Tucson, Ariz.
Ceril Lisbon, San Francisco, Cal.
Nathan Liverant, Colchester, Conn.
Made in America, New York, N.Y.
Newcomer/Westreich, Washington, D.C.
Norma and William Wangel, Potomac, Md.

SUGGESTED READING

Periodicals

Antique Monthly. Published by Boone Publications, Tuscaloosa, Ala.
The Clarion. Published by the Museum of American Folk Art, New York, N.Y.
The Magazine Antiques. Published by Straight Enterprises, New York, N.Y.
The Newtown Bee. Published by The Bee Publishing Company, Newtown, Conn.

Reference Books

Folk Art

Andrews, Joyce, ed. *How to Know American Folk Art.* New York: E.P. Dutton, 1977.

Bishop, Robert. *American Folk Painting.* New York: E.P. Dutton, 1979.

Christensen, Erwin O. *Early American Wood Carving.* New York: Dover Publications, Inc., 1952.

Fried, Frederick. *Artists in Wood.* New York: Clarkson N. Potter, 1970.

Lipman, Jean, and Winchester, Alice. *Primitive Painters in America, 1750-1950.* New York: Dodd, Mead & Co., 1950. Rep. Freeport: Books for Libraries Press, 1971.

Starr, George Ross, Jr. *Decoys of the Atlantic Flyway.* New York: Winchester Press, 1974.

Americana

Bishop, Robert, and Safford, Carleton. *America's Quilts and Coverlets.* New York: Weathervane Books, 1974.

Bolton, Ethel, and Coe, Eva. *American Samplers.* New York: Dover Publications Inc., 1973.

Guilland, Harold F. *Early American Folk Pottery.* Philadelphia: Chilton Book Co., 1971.

Ketchum, William C., Jr. *American Basketry and Woodenware.* New York: Macmillan Publishing Co., 1974.

———. *The Catalog of American Antiques.* New York: Rutledge/Mayflower, 1977-1980.

Perry, Evan. *Collecting Antique Metalware.* New York: Doubleday & Co., 1974.

Williams, Lionel P. *Country Furniture of Early America.* New York: A.S. Barnes, 1963.

Foreign Bank Deposits

Thomas M. Campfield *

BASIC CHARACTERISTICS

In considering the bank deposits market overseas, the investor will find that eurocurrency deposits are most attractive. The eurocurrency market is unhampered by regulations and restrictions, and since reserves are not required to be kept by the banks involved, interest rates are often nominally higher that they are in the domestic markets.

The eurocurrency market functions in many different currencies, the largest component of which is U.S. dollars. Before considering such deposits, one very important fact should be noted. The Federal Reserve Bank currently discourages U.S. residents from placing domestic source U.S. dollars on deposit in banks or bank branches located outside the United States. While no formal regulations or prohibitions have been introduced as of early 1982, the posture of the Federal Reserve has discouraged most institutions from actively seeking such deposits from U.S. residents.

Background

What exactly is a eurocurrency? A eurocurrency is any monetary unit that is owned by a nonresident of the country whose currency is involved. Thus, when a U.S. traveler buys pound sterling notes for a vacation in England, that money technically becomes eurosterling. On a much larger scale, when the oil-producing countries demand U.S. dollars in payment for petroleum, those dollars become eurodollars at the moment those countries assume ownership. When a country such as Kuwait deposits those U.S. dollars with an English bank in London, the transaction becomes a eurodollar deposit. The basic element that distinguishes a domestic U.S. dollar from a eurodollar is its ownership. When U.S. dollars come into the possession of a non-U.S. resident, they automatically become eurodollars.

Origins of the eurocurrency market. The eurocurrency market did not have an official opening date but rather was a result of developments following World War II. With the rebuilding of Europe, financed to a large extent by the United States with U.S. dollars, a large amount of dollars came into the hands of nonresidents of the United States. In addition, the onset of the Cold War in the 1950s discouraged eastern bloc countries, especially the Soviet Union, from keep-

* Thomas M. Campfield is a Vice-President at Manufacturers Hanover Trust Company, New York.

ing their holdings of U.S. dollars in American banks. From these roots came the first eurodollars and eurodollar deposits. Foreign banks found they could engage in a profitable business by first accepting deposits from those who held U.S. dollars and did not wish to leave them with banks in the United States, and then re-lending those dollars to others who needed them.

Size of the market. No one knows the exact size of the euromarket, since no one agency or government has complete control over it. It has been estimated to be slightly more than $1 trillion, but since a single deposit can change hands from bank to bank with no reserves required, a single deposit of $1 million can quickly appear as a deposit on the books of five different banks. For example, Bank A, having accepted a deposit from a customer, may find no immediate use for the funds and so lends them to Bank B. Bank B then re-lends the money the following day to Bank C, having correctly estimated that interest rates would rise, and makes a profit on the transaction. Bank C finds that it needs only one-half the amount for internal purposes and lends the remainder to Bank D, which lends the money to a client. The initial deposit has now been recorded on the books of several banks before it completes the route from depositor to borrower.

Location of operations. The eurocurrency market has no physical location. Instead, it consists of banks, brokers, and customers who are connected by telephone, telex, and special dedicated communication lines. London traditionally has been the heart of the eurocurrency market, where some 300 banks are licensed to accept deposits. Other major financial centers where eurocurrency deposits are traded include Hong Kong, Singapore, Bahrain, Luxembourg, and Nassau in the Bahamas. The development of these locations as centers for eurocurrency trading has been in a large part attributable to their banking regulations and lack of restrictions on eurocurrency operations. However, at the end of 1981, American banks won the right, after decades of effort, to participate directly in the eurodollar market, and it is expected that New York will quickly become a major center for the market.

Volume of deposits. The size of eurocurrency deposits can vary considerably, but most are in multiples of $1 million or a foreign equivalent thereof. For smaller amounts and for a good customer, a bank will usually be willing to quote an interest rate, but it may vary by as much as one to 2 percent below the current market rate for larger deposits. For individuals, most banks are willing to accept deposits in comparatively small amounts ($10,000 or more), based on some business relationship with the individuals. Here, again, the rate will be below the current market rate.

Since the various expenses attached to the processing of a deposit — such as sending confirmations, telex, and telephone communications; passing debits and credits — are virtually the same regardless of the size of a deposit, it is understandable that banks do not encourage deposits of small amounts.

ATTRACTIVE FEATURES

Rates and Deposit Periods

The rate of interest paid on a eurodeposit can vary from hour to hour but generally reflects the interest rate structure of the country whose currency is involved, with proper adjustments for such factors as local reserve requirements.

Since it is often possible for a bank to participate in both its domestic market and the euromarket, the rate of interest paid in the euromarket (where no reserve requirements exist) would not differ radically from the effective rate of interest paid domestically for deposits (where reserve requirements must be met). However, a bank or bank branch located in London will pay a somewhat higher rate of interest for a eurodeutschemark deposit than the rate paid by a bank in Germany, which must keep reserves against deposits.

Deposits can vary in term from very short periods of one day (or overnight, as it is called) to one week, one month, six months, or a year. A term of more than one year is possible, but it is not as common as the periods of one year and less. The most often-quoted time periods for deposits are one week and one, two, three, six, and twelve months. (Representative deposit rates to March 1982 are shown in Table 1.)

TABLE 1. Month-End Deposit Rates

Three-Month Eurodeposits, 9/81 to 3/82

	Interest Rate		
Date	*U.S. Dollar*	*Deutschemark*	*Pound Sterling*
9/81	18.15%	12.25%	16.80%
10/81	15.35	11.40	16.25
11/81	12.40	10.70	15.00
12/81	13.80	10.60	15.65
1/82	15.35	10.25	14.70
2/82	15.15	10.15	14.10
3/82	15.40	9.12	13.50

Range — Three-Month Eurodeposits, 9/81 to 3/82

	Low	*High*
U.S. Dollar	12.40%	18.15%
Deutschemark	9.12	12.25
Pound Sterling	13.50	16.80

SOURCE: Manufacturers Hanover Trust Company

Variety of Currencies

Deposits can be made in any freely convertible currency, the most common ones being the U.S. dollar, West German deutschemark, Swiss franc, English pound, and Japanese yen. Other less-often-traded currencies are the French franc, Dutch guilder, and Belgian franc.

Liquidity

Investing in eurocurrency deposits usually yields a higher rate of interest to the investor than a domestic deposit will, because of the absence of reserve requirements. With such a large market, investors usually encounter no difficulty in placing deposits; even breaking a deposit before maturity is not unheard of, although the practice is obviously frowned upon. In those cases where it is permitted, the depositor pays any penalty cost necessary for the institution to replace the deposit for the remaining time frame.

POTENTIAL RISKS

The placing of deposits in the eurocurrency market is not a completely risk-free investment. Basically, three types of risk should be considered.

Variability in Exchange Rates

If a U.S.-dollar-based depositor were to take U.S. dollars and convert them to some other currency, deutschemarks for example, in order to have a deutschemark deposit, the depositor must also be aware of the foreign exchange risk involved in such a move. In fact, whenever an investor changes from one base currency into another, a foreign exchange risk is involved. An example will serve to show the implications.

Let us assume that a three-month eurodollar deposit earns 12 percent and a three-month eurodeutschemark deposit earns 18 percent. If an investor had $1 million to place on deposit, a higher rate of return could be earned if those dollars were converted to deutschemarks (DMs). If the exchange rate were 2.50 DM/$, the million dollars would generate DM 2,500,000 and would earn 18 percent for three months (e.g., ninety-two days), yielding a total of DM 2,615,000 on the maturity date. The question now is: At what rate of exchange will these deutschemarks be converted back into U.S. dollars? Three possible situations could occur.

(1) The exchange rate is the same as at the time of conversion, that is, DM 2.50/U.S.$, thus generating U.S.$ 1,046,000 or an 18 percent return in U.S. dollar terms.

(2) The exchange rate is lower, for example, DM 2.60/U.S.$, thus generating U.S.$ 1,005,769.20 or a yield of 2.2572 percent in U.S. dollar terms.

(3) The exchange rate is higher, for example, DM 2.40/U.S.$, thus generating U.S.$ 1,089,583.30 or a yield of 35.0543 percent in U.S. dollar terms.

While possibilities (1) and (3) are acceptable (indeed, (3) is the best of all), if a decrease in the value of the deutschemark relative to the U.S. dollar should occur, all benefits of a higher interest rate yield and more have been lost. While it is possible to eliminate this risk, the cost of covering the risk negates the increased interest rate return. Remaining in one's home or base currency is, therefore, the most conservative and riskless approach.

Individual Bank Risk

When an investor places a deposit with a bank, he or she is basically assuming that the bank will continue in business and that it will repay the deposit to the investor on the maturity date. If for some reason the bank should fail or have its doors closed by its central bank, it is possible that the bank will not be able to repay the deposit. No insurance coverage for eurocurrency deposits exists that is comparable to the Federal Deposit Insurance Corporation for domestic U.S. deposits up to $100,000. The depositor would become one of many investors holding claims on the remaining assets of the bank. Even though recent history shows such events do occur, as with the Herstatt Bank in Germany in 1974 and the Franklin National Bank in the United States in 1975, little risk is usually involved with the large, well-managed international banks.

System Risk

The system risk is more difficult to quantify and analyze than the two types examined above. The interbank deposit market for eurocurrencies consists of banks in the major cities listed previously. These institutions place and accept deposits with one another, and the interlocking relationships that develop are extensive. In transacting business, each bank has a limit on the total amount it will place on deposit with any given bank. Despite this limit, the number of banks in the market and the volume of deposits in the marketplace create a situation whereby hundreds of banks are interrelated and interdependent.

Let us assume that a bank involved in this system failed. If a depositor had no direct relationship with that bank, no immediate problem would arise. The failure of that bank does, however, affect other banks in the eurocurrency market to which the failed bank has obligations. If the amounts are substantial and are not repaid on a timely basis, the solvent banks must obtain funds elsewhere to repay their own obligations. Thus, the pyramid builds. An extreme liquidity crisis could take place for the currency involved, and the marketplace could have difficulty functioning. As a result, a depositor might see a disrupted marketplace and encounter problems in having deposits repaid.

This scenario, while possible, is certainly an extreme case and it is reasonable to assume that the authorities in the country of the bank involved would take measures to minimize the consequences. In addition, other central banks could participate, and a takeover or merger with a larger bank would most likely occur to alleviate the problem.

TAX CONSEQUENCES

The tax considerations involved in placing deposits with the eurocurrency market are dependent on the residence of the depositor. Many companies have chosen to establish offshore subsidiaries in countries with very low or no taxes, such as the Bahamas or Cayman Islands. In this way, the income usually is not subject to taxation until the funds are actually remitted to the company's home country, depending on the particular tax laws of the home country.

In many countries, a withholding tax on all interest payments to nonresidents is deducted by the paying bank before payment is made. This has limited the development of the eurocurrency markets in many countries. Those financial centers listed previously have become prominent to a great extent because they have no withholding tax requirements. Japan, on the other hand, levies withholding taxes on interest paid to nonresidents. Thus, Tokyo is not a major eurocurrency marketplace.

MARKET PARTICIPANTS

The major participants in the eurocurrency market range from governments and government institutions to banks, corporations, and individuals. By far the largest users of the market are the oil-producing countries with vast holdings of foreign currencies, particularly U.S. dollars. These countries have traditionally used London as the center for depositing their excess funds, and that tradition continues today. As part of the diversification of their portfolios, these deposits cover the full range of time periods and usually involve several different currencies.

Corporations have used the eurocurrency market as both depositors and borrowers of funds. Because of the large pool of funds available, many companies have chosen to borrow in this market, with the borrowing rate fixed at some percentage above the lending bank's cost of funds, the London Interbank Offered Rate, (LIBOR). At the same time, companies find the ease of transaction and the lack of restrictions and regulations an enticement for placing excess funds on deposit in this market.

MECHANICS OF DEPOSITING

Given the posture of the Federal Reserve Bank with regard to involvement by U.S. corporations in the eurocurrency market, most deposits in the eurocurrency market are placed by companies located outside the United States. The mechanics of placing a deposit are relatively simple. Once a business relationship has been established between a customer and a bank, only a telephone or telex call to the bank's dealing room is needed to ascertain the current interest rate being paid. If the rate is acceptable to the customer, then the deposit is agreed upon. The customer is responsible for transferring the funds to the bank and the account designated by the bank accepting the deposit. For example, if U.S. dollars are placed on deposit with Swiss Bank Corporation, London, then the instructions to the company placing the deposit might read as follows: "Pay U.S. dollars to Manufacturers Hanover Trust Company, New York, for the account of Swiss Bank Corporation, London." In addition, both the bank and the customer will send each other a confirmation of the deposit, detailing such factors as the currency amount, rate, and term.

Virtually every major international bank operates in the eurocurrency market. With over 300 banks represented in London alone, there is no lack of choice for the depositor looking to place funds.

GLOSSARY

breaking deposit— Withdrawal of funds prior to maturity date, generally subject to a penalty charge.

broker— Intermediary who arranges a financial transaction for a commission.

convertible currency— A currency that can be freely exchanged for another.

eurocurrency— Currency (not necessarily of European denomination) that is owned by a nonresident of the country of issue.

eurodeposit— A deposit in a eurocurrency.

euromarket— The market in which eurocurrencies are placed on deposit or are lent to other banks, institutions, governments, or corporations.

exchange rate— The conversion rate used when changing from one currency to another.

London interbank offered rate (LIBOR) — The rate at which a eurocurrency deposit is offered to prime London banks. When LIBOR is used as a reference rate in a loan agreement, it is tied to a particular applicable time (e.g., 11 A.M. London time).

SUGGESTED READING

Euromoney. Published by Euromoney Publications, Ltd., London, England. Monthly.

Financial Times. Published by Bracken House, London, England. Weekly.

Institutional Investor (international edition). Published by Institutional Investor Systems, Inc., New York, N.Y. Monthly.

Foreign Equities

Nancy J. Kyle *

BASIC CHARACTERISTICS

In recent years, individuals have been attracted by both the generous financial returns on foreign equities and the excitement of owning shares of exotic companies in faraway places. Foreign equities for the U.S. investor consist of the shares of companies incorporated and listed on overseas stock exchanges that generally are not subsidiaries of U.S. corporations.

Foreign equity markets are capitalized at about $1 trillion, compared with a capitalization of $1.4 trillion for the U.S. and Canadian markets. European equity markets are currently capitalized at about $500 billion, with the United Kingdom having the largest by far, despite its smaller gross national product than France or Germany. In the Far East, Japan has the largest equity market, with a capitalization of above $400 billion; smaller markets thrive in Australia, Hong Kong, and Singapore.

These overseas stock markets have taken on greater importance than ever because of the lessening dominance of U.S. business and finance in worldwide economic affairs. In many instances, particularly over the last decade, the growth of foreign economies has far outstripped that of the United States. Other nations' equity markets naturally have grown at a pace commensurate with their general economic expansion. For example, yearly growth of Japan's gross national product (GNP) has averaged 5 percent since 1970, while the U.S. GNP growth rate has been just 3 percent over the same time span. This difference is reflected in the changing positions of the U.S. and Japanese equity markets: Their respective shares of total worldwide equity market value shifted from 61 percent (U.S.) and 11 percent (Japan) in 1975 to 53 percent (U.S.) and 16 percent (Japan) in 1981.

ATTRACTIVE FEATURES

Higher Potential Rewards

An investment in foreign equities creates the opportunity for an American investor to diversify his portfolio on an international basis — over an increasingly interdependent world economic spectrum. This means taking advantage of different growth rates in various national economies, and limiting risk exposure

* Nancy J. Kyle is a Vice-President of Morgan Guaranty Trust Company, New York.

through insulation of the portfolio from localized economic problems in any one country — including the investor's. The result, in many instances, has been a higher rate of return than might have been possible with a portfolio limited to U.S. equities. As shown in Figure 1 below, most foreign equity markets outperformed the United States in total rate of return in both local currency and U.S. dollars during 1970-1979.

Less Variable Returns

It also appears likely that an investor's portfolio is less vulnerable to variability in returns if it is diversified among foreign equities and industry groups. A study by the Morgan Guaranty Trust Company shows that the Capital International world index, as compiled by Capital International S.A. of Geneva, has been 13 percent less variable than Capital International's U.S. index over the last twenty years. These phenomena, taken together, indicate that the potential exists to create international portfolios with both higher rates of return and lower variability of return. (See Tables 1 and 2 on pages 227 and 228, respectively for an illustration.)

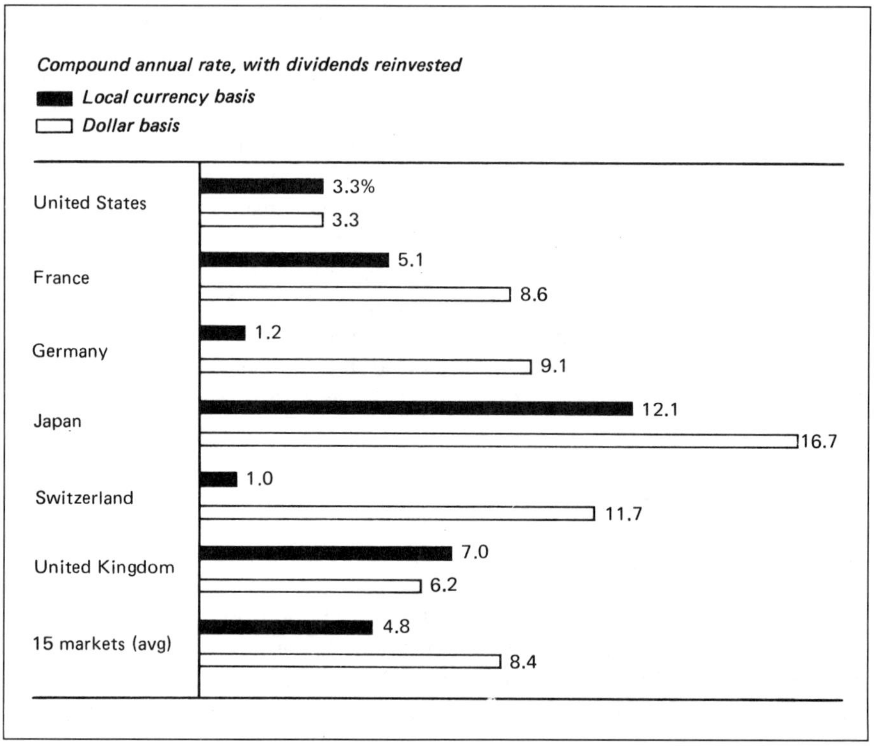

FIG. 1. Total Rate of Return on Foreign Equities 1970-79
SOURCE: Capital International S.A., Geneva

TABLE 1. Correlation of Equity Rates of Returns by Country and Industry 1975-79

Return, excluding dividends, dollar basis

Country	*Coefficient of correlation with U.S.*
Canada	.63
France	.43
Germany	.27
Japan	.32
Spain	.18
Switzerland	.43
United Kingdom	.44
15 markets (avg)	.37

U.S. industry group	*Coefficient of correlation with S&P stock index*
Chemical	.76
Drug	.70
Gold	.16
Office equipment	.80
Oil	.69
Retail stores	.65
Telephone	.61
15 industries (avg)	.65

SOURCE: Capital International S.A., Geneva

Currency-Exchange Impact

Moreover, the higher the degree of economic integration between any two countries, the more the rates of return on their stock markets are apt to move together. Skeptics will argue that foreign investment returns are mainly a result of currency gains, as the dollar declined against most other foreign currencies in the 1970s. Other studies show, however, that changes in each of the world's equity markets are almost entirely uncorrelated with changes in their dollar-exchange rates, as illustrated in Table 3 on page 229.

Thus, market valuations and currency valuations should be regarded as separate considerations when international equity-investment decisions are made. Indeed, analysis of the total dollar returns of Morgan Guaranty Trust Company's international equities fund shows that its relatively better performance, against the Capital International index for non-U.S. stock markets (EAFE Index), results less from currency factors than from the direction and magnitude of stock market movements.

TABLE 2. Correlation Coefficients: Foreign Equity Markets With United States

	Monthly data				
Local currencies	*1960-79*	*1960-64*	*1965-69*	*1970-74*	*1975-79*
Australia	.40	.00	.30	.57	.36
Austria	.13	.38	(.17)	.06	.13
Belgium	.50	.46	.55	.44	.55
Canada	.75	.79	.31	.79	.63
Denmark	.16	.03	(.04)	.21	.32
France	.36	.44	.13	.40	.41
Germany	.31	.48	.16	.30	.27
Italy	.22	.30	.13	.15	.28
Japan	.22	.05	.13	.27	.48
Netherlands	.58	.69	.69	.41	.58
Norway	.29	.36	.05	.34	.34
Spain	.14	.08	(.11)	.28	.21
Sweden	.34	.34	.33	.40	.30
Switzerland	.50	.53	.45	.53	.49
United Kingdom	.42	.35	.27	.50	.47
Average of 15	.35	.35	.25	.38	.39
U.S. dollars					
Australia	.41	.00	.30	.59	.36
Austria	.15	.38	(.17)	.12	.14
Belgium	.45	.45	.57	.41	.48
Canada	.74	.80	.82	.78	.63
Denmark	.19	.02	(.03)	.26	.34
France	.35	.44	.09	.37	.43
Germany	.33	.49	.21	.33	.27
Italy	.21	.29	.13	.18	.21
Japan	.22	.05	.13	.31	.32
Netherlands	.57	.69	.69	.44	.57
Norway	.30	.36	.05	.34	.39
Spain	.12	.08	(.10)	.26	.18
Sweden	.35	.33	.34	.39	.34
Switzerland	.48	.53	.45	.49	.43
United Kingdom	.40	.35	.25	.49	.44
Average of 15	.35	.35	.25	.38	.37

SOURCE: Capital International S.A., Geneva

TABLE 3. Correlation: Stock Prices and Currency Exchange-Rates in Foreign Countries

	Coefficient of correlation between equity price index and price of local currency in terms of U.S. dollars		
	1960-79	*1970-79*	*1975-79*
Canada	.16	.16	.27
France	.09	.14	.19
Germany	.00	.01	−.01
Japan	.00	−.01	.07
Spain	.18	.22	.29
Switzerland	−.12	−.15	−.12
United Kingdom	.09	.12	.13
15 markets (avg)	.03	.04	.05

SOURCE: Capital International S.A., Geneva

Still, foreign-exchange-rate movements can provide opportunities for higher returns, particularly for the institution or money manager with a good track record in currency forecasting. Conversely, it remains possible through poor stock selection for an internationally diversified portfolio to realize either a lower rate of return or a higher variability of return, or both. Here, as elsewhere, there can be no guarantees affecting the performance of freely traded equities.

Inflation Hedge

Owning foreign stocks gives the U.S. investor an opportunity to hedge against domestic inflation by participating in rapidly growing economies abroad — not only through diversification in a larger universe of assets but also through concentration among industries with growth prospects currently much brighter than may be the case with their American counterparts. The mining industry provides an outstanding example: While American investment opportunities diminish as a merger/takeover wave sweeps through the industry here, they literally abound in other countries, particularly Australia, where publicly traded mining companies continue to offer some of the few remaining vehicles for investor participation in commodity cycles anywhere in the world.

Other examples involve gold, shipping, and real estate investments. And there are any number of additional special situations, such as the Japanese supermarket and fast-food sectors, considerably less mature than their aging U.S. counterparts, with attractive growth potential that the American companies already have left behind.

Since the three sources of return from foreign shares are (1) capital gains in local currency, (2) dividends in local currency, and (3) currency gains or losses, they may, of course, provide that hedge against inflation only when the dollar is declining in relation to the currency in which they are denominated. This was precisely the case in the 1970s, when the dollar declined relatively while U.S. inflation accelerated. Securities denominated in other currencies at that time provided a way to protect the purchasing power of dollar-denominated assets.

POTENTIAL RISKS

Currency Losses

Just as a U.S. investor in foreign shares may gain from a weakening dollar, he or she may sustain a loss when selling foreign shares and reconverting to dollars — if the dollar has appreciated relative to the currency in which that stock is denominated. The risk can be reduced by hedging in the forward markets. This allows the currency risk to be separated from the inherent market risk.

For example, an investor might purchase shares of a British exporting company, whose sales would benefit from a declining exchange rate of sterling against the dollar. At the same time, to minimize the potential loss in equity value (since the shares are denominated in sterling), the U.K. currency would be sold at the one-year forward rate, thereby locking in a specific exchange rate of sterling against the dollar. At the end of the year, the actual sale proceeds of the shares may differ from the amount of sterling sold forward — so some of the foreign-exchange transaction may have to be done at spot prices. Continued holding of a fully hedged position can be expensive. (See article on Futures — Financial, elsewhere in this volume.)

Transactional Losses

Each foreign stock market has, to some extent, its own way of doing business, so that at the very least an American needs on-the-scene expertise to steer clear of pitfalls peculiar to a given territory. On the whole, the larger exchanges attracting most U.S. capital abroad have greatly improved their technical and mechanical procedures in recent years, to the point that many compare favorably with Wall Street and, on occasion, can be even more efficient than the U.S. model — although foreign trading and custodial costs, as will be seen, are generally higher.

But trading in foreign securities is hardly without risk, as the 1974 collapse of Germany's Herstatt Bank made abundantly clear. Herstatt Bank was an active trader in foreign exchange markets and had entered into a number of Deutschemark-U.S. dollar transactions with U.K. and U.S. institutions. On that particular day in 1974, Herstatt Bank had entered into a transaction to deliver U.S. dollars in the United States against the Deutschemarks that were delivered, in

Germany, by U.S. and U.K. institutions (banks). The Deutschemarks were delivered in Germany but, because of the time lag between the United States and Germany, the Herstatt never delivered the dollars in the United States. Instead, it was closed down by the Bundesbank (the central bank of Germany) due to overextension of the Herstatt. Therefore, before Herstatt had the opportunity to meet its obligation in New York during New York banking hours, it had been forced to close its doors. Many of these losses to other banks were never recovered. The moral of the story is that anything short of a simultaneous transaction, where both parties are meeting their obligations at the same time, is subject to risk.

A reputable institution or broker reduces the risk of a fraudulent transaction by dealing with only a limited list of well-run and well-capitalized foreign banks and brokers. (The Herstatt, for example, was not well capitalized.) Moreover, all the major stock markets have legal provisions similar to those in the United States, which allow a transaction to be dissolved if either party fails to deliver a security or make payment. Temporary delays in settlement, however — on both the cash side and the securities side — remain not uncommon.

Political Factors

Adding to the discomfort level of investors in foreign stocks is the political risk inherent in doing business abroad. The spectrum ranges from how effectively a government promotes private enterprise all the way to the extreme of sudden expropriation of assets. The attitudes of government and workers towards productivity, wage levels, medical and insurance benefits, and each other all have an impact on equity values. To illustrate, in Japan the close cooperation among government, business, and labor has been a factor helping to build a strong auto industry whose products have achieved a dominant position in world markets — and whose equities, as a result, are highly prized.

Possible tax changes and the treatment of profits are equally important. For example, Hong Kong provides an attractive environment for locally registered companies by taxing profits at 17 percent and by not taxing investors at all. The aforementioned Australian experience very clearly shows the impact of government policies on shareholders' wealth. Although endowed with rich resources of oil, gas, and other raw materials, the share prices of Australian mining companies were not participating in the 1973-1976 commodity price boom because the Labour government then in power discouraged foreign investment by severely taxing corporate profits. After the election of a Conservative party administration in 1976, which immediately reduced taxes, the country has seen record inflows of capital from abroad and a sharply rising stock market.

Confiscation Threats

Of greatest concern to international investors is a situation where locally owned assets are left untouched while those held by foreigners are confiscated or devalued. The 1980 change in Ottawa's petroleum industry policy is widely expected to force many U.S. oil companies to divest themselves of Canadian holdings at distress prices. (At the other extreme is a scenario in which foreign investors are prohibited from selling their shares or, if sold, the proceeds are denied convertibility into foreign currency.)

Most countries whose stock markets are attracting U.S. investors are, as it happens, politically stable Western-style democracies. Most also have citizens and companies with substantial investments in U.S. markets — subject, at least implicitly, to the restraints imposed by reciprocity. But anything can happen in an era that features both multinationalism in business and fired-up nationalism in public affairs. To minimize the risk of unexpected losses that shifts in the political winds can suddenly create, careful and continuous monitoring of foreign governmental policies is essential to the management of an international equities portfolio.

Liquidity Limitations

Illiquidity is yet another common risk in international trading. With the exception of the Japanese, Canadian, and British stock markets, turnover on foreign exchanges is not substantial. Furthermore, the turnover of a particular stock is no more related to its share capitalization than the turnover of a particular stock market is to that market's capitalization. For example, the French company Peugeot-Citroën is now Europe's largest and the third largest automobile maker in the world, but daily activity in its shares over the last year was about 2 percent of the share turnover in General Motors.

The low turnover in foreign stocks does not necessarily indicate a low level of sophistication or maturity in those markets. Germany provides a case in point. The number of listed companies on the eight German stock exchanges, having declined some 17 percent in just the past ten years, is less than 500. Moreover, trading volume of $15 billion a year (compared with $375 billion on the New York Stock Exchange alone) is almost miniscule relative to the size of Germany's huge and highly developed economy. The reason is not naïveté but ingrained national tradition. Historically, German industry draws its capital from retained profits and bank loans rather than through equity financing. Moreover, something over 50 percent of all German equities are held as virtually permanent investments by companies, banks, and government agencies. Whatever the reasons, though, the result is that many key German corporations have stock that is not only unlisted but unquoted, hence, not readily marketable.

A long-standing relationship with reputable local brokers may help to protect against possible illiquidity, and the individual investor new to foreign markets is well advised to search out an established institutional entrée before plunging in. Being a prime institutional customer to major foreign brokers does not guarantee the best prices in a thin market, but it does demand attention from them and allows the institution to select the right broker for each transaction.

TAX CONSEQUENCES

Withholding Taxes on Dividends

No U.S. governmental restraints on foreign equity investments have existed since the expiration, in 1974, of the interest equalization tax and related controls. However, foreign governments (except Hong Kong) withhold a tax on the dividends received by nonresident shareholders. In most countries, some of this tax can be reclaimed through the application of U.S. treaties. And a U.S. taxpayer can offset this withholding tax to some extent by filing IRS Form 1116 with the 1040. The effective withholding tax currently applicable to a stock portfolio owned by a U.S. investor, and invested in most of the major stock markets, runs to about 15 percent on average.

A qualified U.S. pension trust benefits not only from the general provisions of double taxation agreements with foreign countries but also, in a few instances, by means of exemptions from foreign taxes that have been granted to pension and charitable trusts. Where withholding taxes are levied, there is a wide range of procedures for claiming refunds or for applying to have payments made under the concessionary rates of tax specified in the relevant double taxation agreement. Handling of these reclaims and applications is usually done by the custodian.

Capital Gains Tax

Generally, there is no capital gains tax imposed by any foreign government on securities sold by a U.S. investor. However, a U.S. citizen must, of course, include foreign capital gains when filing his or her federal income tax return; the same rate applies as for domestic capital gains.

REPRESENTATIVE TYPES OF INVESTORS

The serious long-term investor, whether individual or institutional, will find foreign equities an interesting alternative to many domestic securities. While limited liquidity and changing conversion rates present problems, these investments demonstrably have the potential to decrease the portfolio's variability of return and increase its overall rate of return.

IMPORTANT FACTORS IN BUYING AND SELLING

Transaction Costs

Trading expenses include brokerage commissions and, in some foreign markets, turnover or local stock-transfer taxes. While Table 4 on page 234 does not reflect precise extracts from regular commission scales, it shows best estimates of the cost likely to be incurred when dealing on stock exchanges for a reasonably substantial portfolio. The figures shown include fiscal charges such as stock transfer taxes.

It is often possible to reduce quite substantially the effective transaction expense by purchasing American Depositary Receipts, discussed below, or by trading directly with off-floor net market makers. In the latter case, trades are not normally subject to brokerage commissions as such, and approximately 0.5 percent (e.g., $100 bid, $100.50 asked) is a fair indication of the spread between bid and asked prices. Because most, if not all, of the securities in an international portfolio will be non-U.S.-dollar-denominated, there are added costs of foreign-exchange dealing.

The overall rate of transaction expense will depend on both the portfolio mix and its activity rate. As a very broad indication, the one-way expense in a characteristically diversified portfolio might be 0.9 percent for stocks on either the buy or sell side. Comparable numbers for a wholly U.S.-invested portfolio might be 0.6 percent. Overseas expenses, therefore, run about 30 basis points higher than those in the United States. (Note: Double commissions may be charged by a U.K. or continental bank to buy equity securities outside its national market. Additionally, stamp, duty, or government transfer taxes may be incurred.)

American Depositary Receipts

In addition to the direct purchase of shares overseas or from among the small number of foreign shares listed on the New York and American Stock Exchanges, investors can buy American Depositary Receipts (ADRs). ADRs remove many

TABLE 4. Transaction and Custody Costs: $10 Million International Portfolio

	Approximate Cost in Basis Points	
Country	*Transactional*	*Custodial*
Japan	80	12
Germany	60	10
United Kingdom	120	10
France	95	10
Australia	140	10
Netherlands	50	10
Switzerland	70	10
Others	110	12
Weighted foreign average	90	10
Comparable U.S.	60	6

SOURCE: Morgan Guaranty Trust Company of New York

of the more formidable custodial and trading inconveniences that go with owning foreign equities. An ADR is a negotiable receipt issued by an American depositary in lieu of the underlying shares it holds in custody overseas. (Morgan Guaranty Trust Company is the principal issuer of ADRs.) Normally, they are issued only for shares that are traded on recognized foreign securities exchanges, and an ADR may represent one share or, as is often the case with Japanese ADRs, many shares.

ADRs are traded and transferred in exactly the same way as U.S. stock certificates. If the holder of an ADR wishes, the underlying shares can be obtained in the United States by surrendering the ADR for cancelation and requesting shipment of the stock. A 0.5 percent fee is charged by the depositary for this cancelation. ADRs are traded on the New York and American Stock Exchanges and on the Over-the-Counter market.

Dividends on ADRs. An ADR holder automatically receives his or her dividend in U.S. dollars — a service for which the depositary deducts $0.01 per depositary share. Under the tax conventions between the United States and other countries, an ADR holder may claim, for federal income tax purposes, certain credits for foreign withholding taxes on dividends. Rights offerings, stock splits, and stock dividends are monitored by the U.S. depositary, which then notifies the ADR holder of such corporate actions.

ADR subscription rights. A rights issue by a foreign company that has complied with the requirements of the U.S. Securities Act of 1933 can be taken up by the ADR holder. If a foreign company has not so complied, which is more often the case, the rights are sold, and the dollar proceeds forwarded by check to the ADR holder. A list of companies for which ADRs are issued is available from any U.S. stock exchange, the National Association of Securities Dealers, or any ADR custodian bank.

Use of Investment Professionals

Brokerage firms with foreign expertise. Many American brokers have expanded their in-house capability to research as well as trade in foreign equities. In some cases, the U.S. broker trades directly as an associate member of an overseas stock exchange. More often, the orders are placed with a local foreign broker on a particular stock exchange. Some brokers prefer to deal only for institutional clients. (See *Brokerage Firms in the United States With Foreign Expertise* in this article for a directory of leading U.S. and foreign brokers with at least one office in the United States. Many foreign banks located in the United States also distribute information about foreign securities.)

International investment managers. U.S. investors' growing interest in foreign equities has led to a sharp increase in the number of international portfolio managers vying for American clientele. Although London remains the base for most leading managers specializing in this area, other cities around the world —

New York, Boston, Chicago, San Francisco, Geneva, Paris, Zurich, Hong Kong, and Tokyo — also are being chosen as headquarters for international management operations. Their services vary in terms of investment style, performance results, risk levels, active/passive management, research-capability depth, and cost. (See *International Investment Managers* in this article.)

CUSTODIAL CARE

Administration

The time lag between a trade and settlement can be so short that it would be impossible to meet settlement deadlines if foreign securities were held in the United States, even in New York. For example, the settlement period for Hong Kong shares is twenty-four hours. Income collection from a distance can also be complicated; coupons on bearer securities must be clipped and mailed to local paying agents. Accordingly, while an unsophisticated investor might believe that the risks inherent in owning foreign stocks can be reduced by keeping the certificates at home, the disadvantages outweigh any apparent gains. Indeed, the cost of insuring and then physically moving the securities back to their base market for sale is usually a sufficient deterrent. Foreign stocks should be kept in the country in which they are purchased.

Loss Protection

The major markets in Europe — Germany, France, Switzerland, Belgium, and the Netherlands — all have computerized central clearing systems. These stock markets also operate under laws that ensure that trade settlements will not expose one party to a loss if the other fails during the settlement process. Even where centralized clearing has not yet been introduced, notably in Britain and the Far East, that protection is fairly well organized. And while many foreign banks do not carry custodial insurance — unlike American banks, which regard it as a routine precaution — investors will find that their U.S. custodian's insurance policy, in fact, covers its overseas agencies where the custody should be maintained.

Custody Costs

Many institutions do not quote separate custodial fees. Instead, the charge may be lumped in with investment-management transaction commissions, underwriting concessions, or even the spreads on other banking business. The aggregate cost of these foreign custodial services, which average between 10 and 12 basis points for a large institutional client, are shown in Table 4 on page 234. Individual investors, it should be noted, often pay more. Custody costs are also a function of activity in the portfolio, just as they are in U.S. equity investing.

GLOSSARY

ADR subscription rights— Stock purchase rights issued by a foreign company. Such rights may or may not be exercisable by the U.S. investor; if not, the rights are sold with dollar proceeds payable to the investor.

American depositary receipt— A negotiable receipt issued by an American depositary institution in lieu of underlying shares of a foreign company held in custody overseas.

basis point— Commission pricing broken down into one hundredths. One hundred basis points equals one percent.

capital gain— The excess of selling over purchase price realized upon sale of a security.

coefficient of correlation— The correlation of performance between two investments, measured as a percentage of 1.0.

hedging— Trading in the forward markets in opposite directions with similar or related securities.

par value— The dollar value assigned to a share of stock by the issuer at time of issue.

price earnings ratio— Market price per share divided by net earnings per share in the preceding year.

stock index— A composite historical record of market prices of a selected group of stocks.

variable return— The suboptimal earnings from a portfolio over time because of limited breadth of holdings.

yield— The total of dividend and interest payments.

BROKERAGE FIRMS IN THE UNITED STATES WITH FOREIGN EXPERTISE

A.B.D. Securities Corp., New York, N.Y.

A.C. Goode Co., Inc., New York, N.Y.

A.E. Ames & Co., Inc., New York, N.Y.

Bache Halsey Stuart Shields Inc., New York, N.Y.

Bear Stearns & Co., New York, N.Y.; San Francisco, Cal.

B.H.F. Securities Inc., New York, N.Y.

Arnhold S. Bleichroeder Inc., New York, N.Y.

Carr Sebag (America Ltd.), New York, N.Y.

Carl Marks & Co., Inc., New York, N.Y.

Cazenove Inc., New York, N.Y.; San Francisco, Cal.

Daiwa Securities America Inc., New York, N.Y.

Dominion Securities Corp., New York, N.Y.

Drexel Burnham Lambert Inc., New York, N.Y.

Grieveson, Grant International Ltd., Boston, Mass.

Lehman Brothers Kuhn Loeb Inc., New York, N.Y.

Merrill Lynch Pierce Fenner & Smith, New York, N.Y.

Nikko Securities Co. Ltd., New York, N.Y.

Nomura Securities International Inc., New York, N.Y.

Oppenheimer & Co., Inc., New York, N.Y.

Richardson Securities Inc., New York, N.Y.

Rowe & Pitman Inc., Boston, Mass.; San Francisco, Cal.

Salomon Brothers, New York, N.Y.

Shearson Loeb Rhodes Inc., New York, N.Y.

Smith Barney Harris Upham & Co., Inc., New York, N.Y.

Vickers da Costa Securities Inc., New York, N.Y.

J.B. Were & Co., Inc., New York, N.Y.

Wood Gundy & Co., Inc., New York, N.Y.

INTERNATIONAL INVESTMENT MANAGERS

Aetna Warburg Investment Management International Ltd., Hartford, Conn.; London, England

Alliance Capital Management Corp., New York, N.Y.; London, England

American National Bank & Trust Co. of Chicago, Chicago, Ill.

Bank of America, San Francisco, Cal.; London, England

Banque Scandinave en Suisse, Chicago, Ill.; Geneva, Switzerland

Bankers Trust Co., New York, N.Y.; London, England

Baring International Research & Management Ltd., Boston, Mass.; London, England

Batterymarch Financial Management Corp., Boston, Mass.

Brown Brothers Harriman & Co., New York, N.Y.

Capital Guardian Trust Co., Los Angeles, Cal.

Chase Investors Management Corp., New York, N.Y.

Chemical Bank, New York, N.Y.; London, England

Citibank N.A., New York, N.Y.; London, England

Continental Illinois International Investment Corp., Chicago, Ill.; London, England

Fidelity International Investment Management Inc., Boston, Mass.

Fiduciary Trust Co. of New York, New York, N.Y.

First Chicago Asset Management Corp., Chicago, Ill.; London, England

The First National Bank of Boston/Old Colony Trust, Boston, Mass.

G.T. Capital Management, San Francisco, Cal.; London, England

Ivory & Sime International Inc., Chatham, N.J.

Kemper-Murray Johnstone International, Inc., Chicago, Ill.

Kleinwort Benson International Investment Ltd., New York, N.Y.; London, England

Lazard Freres & Co., New York, N.Y.

Lombard Odier International Portfolio Management Ltd., New York, N.Y.; London, England

Loomis, Sayles & Co., Inc., Boston, Mass.

Mellon Pictet International Ltd., Pittsburgh, Pa.; London, England

Morgan Grenfell Investment Services Ltd., New York, N.Y.; London, England

Morgan Guaranty Trust Company of New York, New York, N.Y.; London, England

Pierson Capital Management B.V., Amsterdam, Holland

PM Portfolio Management GMBH, New York, N.Y.; Munich, W. Germany

The Putnam Advisory Co., Boston, Mass.

Rothschild International Asset Management, New York, N.Y.; London, England

Rowe Price-Fleming International Inc., Baltimore, Md.

Schroder Munchmeyer, Hengst Management GMBH, Frankfurt, W. Germany

Scudder, Stevens & Clark, New York, N.Y.

State Street Bank & Trust, Boston, Mass.

Thorndike, Doran Paine & Lewis, Boston, Mass.

Wells Fargo Investment Advisors, San Francisco, Cal.

Worldwide Investment Management (Division of Drexel Burnham Lambert Investment Advisors), New York, N.Y.

SUGGESTED READING

Periodicals

Euromoney. Published by Euromoney Publications, Ltd., London, England. Monthly.

Financial Times. Published by Bracken House, London, England. Weekly.

International Investor (international edition). Published by Institutional Investor Systems, Inc., New York, N.Y. Monthly.

South East Asian Review. Published by South East Asian Studies, Gaya, India. Semiannually.

Articles

Bergstrom, Gary L. "A New Route to Higher Returns and Lower Risks." *Journal of Portfolio Management,* Fall 1975.

Lessard, Donald R. "World, Country and Industry Relationships in Equity Returns: Implications for Risk Reduction Through International Diversification." *Financial Analysts Journal,* Jan. 1976.

Solnik, Bruno H. "Why Not Diversify Internationally Rather Than Domestically?" *Financial Analysts Journal,* July-August 1974.

Reference Books

Elton, E., and Gruber, M. *International Capital Markets.* North Holland: Elsevier, 1976.

Esslem, Rainer. *The Complete Book of International Investing: How to Buy Foreign Securities and Who's on the International Investment Scene.* New York: McGraw Hill, 1977.

Sharpe, William F. *Investments,* Ch. 20. New York: Prentice-Hall, 1981.

Foreign Fixed Income Investments

Rhodri Thomas *

BASIC CHARACTERISTICS

Foreign fixed income investments may be classified as:

- Eurobonds;
- Non-dollar-denominated domestic securities; and
- U.S. dollar issues for foreign borrowers in the U.S. market.

The markets for these securities provide the investor with the means to diversify his or her portfolio in terms of both credit and currency. Thereby the investor seeks to maximize the expected return for a given level of risk. Differences in the expected return result from two factors — currency movements and interest rate movements.

Thus, the return on a Deutschemark bond will consist of the currency appreciation or depreciation of the Deutschemark versus the U.S. dollar over some defined investment horizon, the stream of coupon payments on the bond, and the capital appreciation or depreciation of the bond's principal amount caused by interest rate movements. The investor's decision regarding non-dollar-denominated securities will be determined by his or her expectations about both currencies and interest rates.

Although most countries withhold tax at a basic rate on interest payments made to foreign holders of their domestic-market securities, there are many debt instruments to which this does not apply, as will be pointed out in connection with specific instruments. This tax is normally withheld by the custodian bank when the bank makes the interest payment to the foreign holder. The amount withheld depends on the tax laws of the individual country and the tax treaty between that country and the country of residence of the holder of the securities.

ATTRACTIVENESS AND POTENTIAL RISKS

The principal determinants of risk in foreign income securities are:

- Volatility;
- Sovereign risk; and
- Credit risk.

* Rhodri Thomas is a Vice-President of the First Boston Corporation, New York.

The volatility of foreign bonds relative to U.S. domestic bonds may serve to either increase or decrease the total risk level of the portfolio. But if there is a historically low correlation of returns on foreign bonds versus domestic bonds, the inclusion of foreign bonds in a U.S. domestic portfolio should serve to reduce risk (as measured by volatility).

On the other hand, sovereign risk, or the risk of governments refusing to honor their debts or blocking payments of interest and principal to foreign debtors, cannot be quantified. Since World War II there have been no instances of such action on the part of a major industrialized nation.

Finally, credit risk for foreign investments has an added dimension in that the investor must evaluate both country risk in the case of sovereign borrowers and credit risk in the case of non-U.S. corporations. The latter may not be an easy task since accounting procedures and the availability of reliable and comparable figures may vary widely from country to country.

EUROBONDS

Eurobonds are international bonds issued in markets outside the domestic market of the issuer. Interest payments on Eurobonds are free of any withholding tax.

The main difference between a Eurobond (such as a Eurodollar bond) and a foreign bond is that while the Eurobond is underwritten by an international syndicate of banks and sold to international investors, a foreign bond is underwritten by a largely domestic syndicate and sold to both domestic and foreign investors. In the case of Yankee bonds (issues for certain types of foreign borrowers in the U.S. market), it is necessary to register the issues with the SEC, which points up the essentially domestic nature of the security. Because Eurobond issues are not registered with the SEC, they may not be offered or sold to U.S. domestic investors until they have become seasoned, that is, until ninety days from the time that the bonds have been fully distributed to the final buyers.

The Eurobond Market

The Eurobond market owes its origin to the attempts in the 1960s by the U.S. authorities to reduce capital outflows during a time of dollar weakness. The imposition in 1964, retroactive to June 1963, of interest equalization tax on purchases of foreign securities by U.S. nationals and residents caused foreign borrowers to seek new sources of funds. The Voluntary Foreign Credit Restraint Program and the U.S. Office of Foreign Direct Investment restrictions prevented U.S. corporations from funding their overseas operations through direct investments. This resulted in those corporations raising money through Eurobond issues. The market gradually grew from a volume of new issues of $164 million in 1963 to $24 billion in 1980. With the inclusion of foreign domestic-market bonds, the total amount of new issues floated from 1963 to 1980 was $208 billion.[1]

The largest percentage of issues raised has been in U.S. dollars, accounting for some 70 percent of all Eurobond issues over the years. In 1980, Eurodollar issues totaled $16.4 billion, Deutschemark (DM) issues $3.6 billion, Euroguilder issues $1 billion, Euro-Canadian dollar issues $279 million, and there were $2.5 billion of Euroissues in other currencies. Foreign bond issues outside the United States totaled $4.8 billion in DM, $7.6 billion in Swiss francs, $259 million in guilders, $1 billion in yen, and $7.8 billion in other currencies.

Although institutional investors are drawn to the domestic bond markets in foreign currencies, individuals tend to favor Eurobonds when they seek currency diversification for fixed income portfolios. The main attractions of Eurobonds are the wide choice of issues and maturities, the absence of any withholding tax, and the good liquidity for smaller orders.

The major borrowers in the market are sovereign governments, government agencies, international institutions such as the International Bank for Reconstruction and Development and the European Investment Bank, and international banks and corporations.

Apart from the Eurodollar market, there are Eurobond markets for the following currencies: Canadian dollar, Deutschemark, guilder, sterling, and yen. In addition there are Eurobonds in French francs, Kuwaiti dinar, Luxembourg franc, Norwegian kronor, Hong Kong dollar, Australian dollar, and Bahraini dollar.

Composite currency units. There are also issues in composite currency units, the most prominent of which are special drawing rights (SDRs) and European Units of Account (EUAs).

Most currencies offer only fixed-rate obligations, but there is a large market in Eurodollar floating-rate notes (FRNs). FRNs are interest-bearing securities, the coupon of which is reset on a regular basis in relation to the Eurodollar deposit rates. The majority of FRNs are set every six months at a spread of one-eighth to one-quarter over the London interbank offered rate (LIBOR). The market for FRNs has grown in popularity in recent years because of the wide gyrations in interest rates. Because coupons of FRNs are constantly being refixed in line with short-term money rates, the prices at which they trade are generally within 1 or 2 points of their issue prices. The majority of borrowers are international banks, and maturities range from two to twenty years.

Composite units such as SDRs and EUAs provide investors with securities that limit the influence of currency changes on the value of instruments. The value of the EUA is determined in reference to the parities in the European Monetary System (EMS). The EMS, a system operated by the countries of the European Economic Community (EEC) seeks to limit currency movements within the EEC bloc. SDRs were established by the International Monetary Fund as

[1] Morgan Guaranty Trust Company

an international reserve asset to supplement the traditional reserve assets, such as gold and individual currencies, of central banks. Originally the sum of eighteen different currencies, the SDR was simplified in 1980 to include only the following currencies: U.S. dollar (42 percent), Deutschemark (19 percent), sterling (13 percent), French franc (13 percent), and yen (13 percent).

Although these composite units have protected investors from some of the volatility of return caused by currency movements, they do not protect them from changes in interest rates. Because the EUA only includes EMS currencies, the movements of those currencies in relation to the U.S. dollar or other currencies outside the EMS bloc can either benefit or hurt the holder of EUAs.

NON-DOLLAR-DENOMINATED SECURITIES

Outside of the United States, the major markets for fixed income securities are in Canada, Germany, the Netherlands, Switzerland, the United Kingdom, and Japan. Most of these countries have markets for foreign bonds and Eurobonds; the markets vary in size and importance depending on the extent to which there is demand from international investors for the particular currency and the extent to which the country involved is willing to allow its currency to play the role of a reserve asset.

Canada

The Canadian market has the closest ties to the U.S. market and, thus, its structure is rather familiar to the U.S. investor. Canadian dollar bonds are generally free from withholding tax. The main longer-dated securities are government of Canada bonds, provincial government bonds, and corporate bonds. The principal money market instruments are Treasury bills, commercial paper, banker's acceptances, and bearer deposit notes. Of these short-dated securities, only Treasury bills are free of withholding tax.

Canadian government bonds. As of the end of June 1981, $40 billion of Canadian government bonds were outstanding with coupons varying from as low as 3 percent to as high as 18 percent. Maturities range from one to twenty-five years. A common practice in Canada is the issuance of government bonds with an initial intermediate maturity, extendable to a longer date at the holder's option.

Government bonds provide the major vehicle for foreign institutional investors, since they have the most liquid market and there is no withholding tax on interest. Canadian government bonds are not listed on any stock exchange and are traded over the counter.

Provincial and municipal government bonds. Of these bonds, $72 billion were outstanding at the end of June 1981. Maturities are generally up to thirty years, but intermediate maturities have become more popular in recent years.

Corporate bonds. The Canadian corporate bond market has some $32 billion outstanding with both Canadian corporations and banks as the major issuers. Maturities are generally in the twenty-five-year range.

Treasury bills. The Canadian Treasury bill market consists of three-month, six-month, and one-year maturities. Every Thursday the three-month and six-month bills are auctioned by competitive tender through the Bank of Canada. Some Can.$ 22 billion of Treasury bills are currently outstanding. Trading size is normally for Can.$ 250,000, although much larger amounts are quite readily bought and sold.

Other Canadian money market instruments. The other money market instruments are commercial paper, banker's acceptances, and bearer deposit notes. On the earnings of all these instruments, Canadian tax is withheld at a basic rate of 25 percent, reduced to 15 percent for investors from certain countries (depending on provisions of the tax treaty between Canada and that country).

Commercial paper is issued by Canadian corporations and banks and Canadian subsidiaries of foreign corporations. Canadian banker's acceptances are similar to U.S. banker's acceptances, but they are accepted by the eleven Canadian chartered banks. The largest of these in terms of deposits are Royal Bank of Canada, Canadian Imperial Bank of Commerce, Bank of Montreal, Bank of Nova Scotia, and Toronto-Dominion Bank. These chartered banks are the only institutions authorized to issue bearer deposit notes, which are similar to certificates of deposit in the U.S. market. Maturity on these instruments generally extend to one year and minimum denomination is Can.$ 100,000. Banker's acceptances and bearer deposit notes are issued on a discount basis, while commercial paper may be either a discount or an interest-bearing security.

Canadian market making and settlement procedures. Chartered banks and investment dealers are the issuing agents and/or market makers for money market instruments. Settlement is normally on the trade date or the next day. A Canadian bank normally acts as custodian, but it is possible to make deliveries to non-Canadian institutions.

Investors in Canadian securities. Although the dominant investors in Canada are Canadian domestic institutions, international investors are becoming more important. U.S. institutions historically have been the largest foreign buyers of Canadian debt, but the market is increasingly attracting investments by both official institutions (such as central banks) and other institutions and individuals from Europe and the Middle and Far East. U.S. institutions are actively involved in switching between the U.S. and Canadian markets to take advantage of both currency and yield-spread opportunities. Other investors, especially non-official institutions and individuals, find the Canadian market attractive because, unlike U.S. domestic bonds, there is no Canadian withholding tax and yields are usually higher than they are on U.S. instruments. The relationship between the Canadian and U.S. currency is not subject to the wide swings that may occur in other currency blocs. Some European investors cannot buy the Canadian government bonds because they are not listed on any stock exchange, but for Japanese institutional investors this is an advantage because unlisted bonds do not have to be marked to the market in portfolio evaluations.

Euro-Canadian Dollar bonds. The Euro-Canadian dollar bond market originated in 1975, when the Canadian tax law was changed to allow Canadian corporations to pay interest to nonresidents free from withholding tax on bonds of five years' maturity and longer.

The total amount of bonds outstanding is Can.$ 35 billion. Most issues have been floated by Canadian corporations and banks. Maturities are mostly in the five- to seven-year range, although some issues have ten- and fifteen-year maturities. Issue size is normally Can.$ 20–50 million.

The market for Euro-Canadian dollar bonds has been somewhat sporadic and new issue volume peaked in 1976 when Can.$ 1,400 million was issued. New issue volume revived somewhat in 1981 but the amount remains well below the 1976 level.

The secondary market for Euro-Canadian dollar bonds is somewhat limited, with only some six major market makers. Dealer spreads tend to be between 1 and 2 points from bid to offer and the size of dealing normally Can.$ 100,000–250,000.

Germany

There are three main categories of German fixed-interest obligations: German domestic bonds, international Deutschemark bonds, and *Schuldscheindarlehen* (loan agreements). Money market instruments do not exist, as the *Bundesbank* (central bank) has resisted the creation of such securities.

German domestic bonds. The domestic bond market essentially consists only of the obligations of the government (*Bund*), the Federal Railway (*Bundesbahn*), and the Post Office (*Bundespost*). These three issuers rank equally in the eyes of investors and have more than DM 126 billion oustanding. Coupons range from a low of 5 percent to a high of 10.75 percent. Maturities are generally from one year to twelve years and new issues are generally in the five- to twelve-year range.

These *Bundbahnpost* issues, as they are commonly called, are subject to German withholding tax at a basic rate of 25 percent, although double taxation agreements cause this to be reduced to much lower levels for most investors from Western countries. Tax is withheld not only on coupon payments, as is the case for most countries, but also on accrued interest, and investors must file an application with the German authorities to reclaim this tax.

International Deutschemark bonds. The market for International DM bonds is second in size in the Euromarket after the Eurodollar bond market. Germany has both foreign and EuroDM bonds, but the only difference between the two is that foreign bonds are underwritten by a purely domestic syndicate. All International DM bonds, of which some DM 78 billion were outstanding at the end of June 1981, are free from German withholding tax. The issuance of International DM bonds is regulated by the Capital Markets Subcommittee, which is made up of representatives of the six major German banks under the auspices of the *Bundesbank.* The Subcommittee determines the volume of new issues to be offered each month in line with the ability of the market to absorb such issues.

Maturities range from five to fifteen years and issue size is typically DM 100 million with an upper range of DM 250 million.

Schuldscheindarlehen. *Schuldscheindarlehen* or *Schuldscheine* are loan agreements in the form of a promissory letter issued by the borrower. The letter provides that the loan may be assigned in whole or part to other lenders. Issues are generally in the five- to ten-year maturity range and are free from German withholding tax. The main borrowers are the government, post office, and railways, other German official institutions, and the *landesbanken* (the state banks). Transfer of title can only be made by means of a separate written assignment. Terms of most *Schuldscheine* restrict the number of participants in the loan, and the size and transferability of the participations.

Primary and secondary markets. New issues of government bonds are underwritten by a syndicate of some eighty German institutions led by the *Bundesbank.*

Some international issues are done as private placements. The main difference between these and public issues is a smaller underwriting syndicate and the lack of listing on a German stock exchange. *Schuldscheine* are generally sold by one bank, which then assigns participations to other banks.

Secondary market transactions in DM bonds mostly take place on the various German stock exchanges, of which there are eight, with Frankfurt and Düsseldorf the most important. Over-the-counter trading also takes place, particularly between German banks and foreign institutions. The normal trading size in government bonds is DM 1 million, with dealer spreads of one-eighth to one-half, depending on maturity. Larger trades of DM 5 to 10 million are quite commonplace in governments.

The liquidity in International DM bonds is, however, relatively less, with DM 250,000 to DM 500,000 the normal trading unit and dealer spreads of one-half point. Larger amounts are quite common in the more active recent issues, but secondary-market activity tends to be sporadic. Currency considerations dominate the international DM market with few sellers and many buyers when the DM is strong and the opposite when the DM is weak. The number of market makers in International DM bonds is very small.

The secondary market for *Schuldscheine* is somewhat restricted because of the limitation on the assignment of participations. Sizable amounts are usually only available in new issues, and investors normally are forced to resell to the bank or dealer from whom they bought the *Schuldscheine.* Compensation for this lack of liquidity is the generally higher yields available on *Schuldscheine.*

Settlement is normally via a book-entry system through the German *kassenverein* for government and International DM bonds. International DM bonds, however, can be delivered into the two international clearing systems, Euroclear Clearance Systems Limited (Euroclear) and *Centrale de Livraison de Valeurs Mobilières* (CEDEL). A German bank will normally hold a copy of the *Schuldscheine* and the letter of assignment in custody for the investor.

Netherlands

The Dutch bond market is closely tied to the German bond market because of the strong trading relationship between the countries and their membership in the EMS. The main fixed-interest obligations of interest to international investors are: government bonds; issues of the Bank voor Nederlandsche Gemeenten (BNG), which is the Central Bank for Dutch Municipalities; foreign bonds; and Euroguilder notes.

Dutch government bonds. Dutch government bonds provide an attractive alternative to German bonds for foreign investors because of their good marketability and the lack of any Dutch withholding tax. Some fl 34 billion were outstanding at the end of June 1981. Coupons range from 3 to 12.75 percent and maturities are in the ten- to twenty-five-year range.

BNG bonds. Some fl 10.7 billion of bonds of the BNG were outstanding at the end of June 1981. Although the Dutch government does not guarantee the issues, it is the majority owner of the BNG, which re-lends the proceeds of the issues to Dutch local municipalities. Like government bonds, maturities are in the ten- to twenty-five-year range.

Foreign bonds. The market for foreign bonds is much smaller than that for domestic bonds and only some fl 3 billion are oustanding. Maturity is generally in the ten- to fifteen-year range, although some longer-dated issues do exist.

Euroguilder notes. Both Dutch and foreign borrowers may issue Euroguilder notes via a so-called semiprivate placement. The notes are placed through financial institutions without an underwriting syndicate, a stock exchange listing, or a prospectus. Approximately fl 3.9 billion were outstanding at the end of 1981.

Dutch primary and secondary markets. Government bonds are issued via a tender, whereby coupon and maturity is announced by the BNG and investors are invited to submit bids. Upon receipt of these bids, the government decides on the amount to be issued and the issue price. All bids above the issue price are accepted in full and bids at the issue price are accepted only in part.

BNG bonds are issued via a selling group of Dutch banks. Foreign bonds are underwritten by a syndicate of Dutch and foreign banks, with a Dutch bank as the lead underwriter; Euroguilder notes, as noted earlier, are not underwritten.

Transactions in government bonds, BNG bonds, and foreign bonds, which are all listed on the Amsterdam Stock Exchange, are carried out on the Exchange. Dealings between Dutch banks and foreign investors may be done over the counter. The normal dealing size in government bonds is fl 500,000 but larger amounts are quite readily transacted. BNG bonds trade in similar amounts, although larger amounts are less easily done. Foreign bonds and Euroguilder notes have much more limited marketability. Dealer spreads between bid and offer range from 0.6 point for government bonds and 1 to 2 points for Euroguilder notes.

Settlement is usually via a Dutch bank, but all Dutch bonds are eligible for delivery into Euroclear.

Switzerland

The Swiss bond market is closely regulated by the Swiss National Bank, and by contrast to most bond markets, it has no Eurosecurities. Although Swiss bond yields have been low compared with other bond markets, total return in Swiss securities has been high over the past decade because of the strong appreciation of the Swiss franc (SF) in relation to other currencies.

The main fixed-interest obligations of interest to international investors are: government bonds; foreign bonds; and foreign notes.

Swiss government bonds. Some SF 6.9 billion of government bonds were outstanding as of the end of June 1981. Coupons range from 2.75 to 7.75 percent and maturities from one to fifteen years. Most new issues are issued in the eight- to fifteen-year range. Withholding tax is levied at a basic rate of 35 percent, but this rate is lower for some countries via double taxation agreements. Application must be made to the Swiss authorities for a refund on the amount withheld.

Foreign bonds. The major issuers of foreign bonds are similar to those who issue in other foreign bond markets; there is no Swiss withholding tax on these bonds. Maturity is normally eight to fifteen years and issue size is SF 50-200 million. At the end of June 1981, some SF 24.4 billion of foreign bonds were outstanding.

Foreign notes. Foreign notes are private placements for foreign borrowers, and there were some SF 52.6 billion outstanding at the end of June 1981. Maturities are three to eight years and issue size SF 20 to SF 150 million. There is no Swiss withholding tax.

Swiss primary and secondary markets. Swiss government bonds are issued through a tender method similar to the Dutch system.

Swiss franc foreign bonds are issued through syndicates of Swiss banks and each issue must be specifically authorized by the Swiss National Bank. The Bank announces a new-issue calendar every three months with details on the number and size of issues. Most trading of Swiss franc bonds takes place on one of the Swiss stock exchanges; Zurich, Geneva, and Basel are the most prominent. Over-the-counter trading also may take place, particularly if a foreign investor is involved. The liquidity of foreign bonds is somewhat restricted and normal dealing size is SF 100,000 to SF 250,000.

Foreign notes are placed through a single Swiss bank or a syndicate with a maximum of ten banks. There is less restriction on the volume of these notes, although any issue of greater than SF 3 million must be authorized by the Central Bank. Secondary market trades in foreign notes take place on a negotiated basis and there is no official quoted secondary-market price. Thus investors normally can only resell to the bank from which they originally bought the notes.

United Kingdom

The bond market of the United Kingdom rivals that of the United States in terms of both liquidity and sophistication. Despite Britain's economic difficulties over the past two decades, the bond and money markets have continued to provide investors with a wide variety of securities with active secondary markets. The main instruments of interest to foreign investors are:

- Gilt-edged stocks, as government bonds are called;
- Treasury bills;
- Sterling certificates of deposit;
- Sterling bank bills; and
- Eurosterling bonds.

There is no withholding tax on any money market instrument. This, combined with the active secondary market, proves attractive to international investors. Settlement procedures are fairly straightforward, with the securities normally held at a London bank.

Gilt-edged stocks. The U.K. Treasury has issued bonds under a variety of names, such as Treasury, Exchequer, Redemption, Funding, Transport, Gas, Consols, Conversion, and War Loan. Most of the recent issues are for Treasury and Exchequer bonds. Regardless of the name, all issues are treated by investors as homogeneous in terms of quality.

With the exception of War Loan bonds, all issues are subject to U.K. withholding tax at a basic rate of 30 percent. Some issues, however, are issued on special terms, which provide interest to be paid in full to those investors who have filed forms with the U.K. authorities showing they are nonresidents of the United Kingdom. War Loan bonds, which are perpetual, are totally free from withholding tax. On the special-term issues, investors must apply to have interest paid in full on each issue held.

Issues of under five years maturity are traded on a net basis plus accrued interest; issues of longer than five years are traded on a net basis, and the price of the bond will reflect the value of accrued interest implicit in the bond. Some £66.75 billion of gilt-edged bonds were outstanding at the end of June 1981. Gilts range in maturity from three to thirty-nine years and coupons vary from 3 to 15.50 percent.

New issues are sold via a tender system organized by the Bank of England. The Bank specifies a minimum tender price and the amount to be offered. Any amount not taken up by investors is sold on a tap basis (see *Glossary* at the end of this article) in the period following the initial offering. All issues are traded on the London Stock Exchange by jobbers who have the sole right to maintain a secondary market in the issues. The Bank frequently offers partly paid issues, whereby investors only have to put up a part of the full price when the issue is first tendered for. The rest of the money is then due on specified future dates.

Some variable-rate issues are also available with coupons that reset every six months in relation to Treasury bills. Recently, the U.K. Treasury has also issued bonds, the coupons and principals of which are tied to the rate of inflation.

The secondary market in gilts is quite structured in that orders must be placed via U.K. stockbrokers, who then transmit the orders to the jobbers. Brokers charge commissions that are fixed by the London Stock Exchange and are based on a sliding scale depending on the size of the order. The market provides excellent liquidity for orders of all sizes and it is quite possible to deal in £5 to £10 million without affecting the market price. Jobbers' spreads for £1 million are normally three-thirty-seconds to one-eighth point for short-dated bonds and three-sixteenths to one-quarter point for longer maturities.

Treasury bills. Treasury bills, with some £1.2 billion now outstanding, are issued only in ninety-one-day maturities. A tender is held each Friday and only discount houses, brokers, and banks in London may buy directly from the Bank of England. The secondary market in Treasury bills is maintained by the discount houses, whose dealing spreads are one-sixteenth to one-eighth point.

Sterling certificates of deposit. Sterling certificates of deposit may only be issued by recognized banks and licensed deposit takers, which are officially recognized by the Bank of England. Maturities range from three months to five years, and some £4 billion are outstanding. An active secondary market is maintained by the discount houses with spreads similar to those of Treasury bills.

Sterling bank bills. A sterling bank bill is a bill of exchange that has been accepted by a bank, and thus is very similar to U.S. banker's acceptances. Bank bills, of which £6.5 billion are outstanding, are issued by commercial borrowers and accepted by banks. These banks may be eligible or ineligible, and only bills of eligible banks may be rediscounted at the Bank of England. Maturities are mostly three to six months. The discount houses maintain secondary markets with dealer spreads of one-sixteenth to one-eighth.

Eurosterling bonds. In the last decade, a market has developed for Eurosterling bonds that is in line with that of the other Euromarkets. These instruments may be attractive for those nonresident investors who do not wish to file a form with the U.K. authorities in order to have interest paid in full on coupons. Some £800 million are currently outstanding.

New issues are underwritten via an international syndicate of banks, and issue size in the £15 to £50 million range. Maturities are generally five to fifteen years. Compared with gilts, the secondary market is very restricted, with the normal trade some £50,000 and spreads of three-quarters to one point between bid and offer. Both U.K. jobbers and international banks maintain secondary markets, and settlement is normally via Euroclear or CEDEL.

Foreign bonds were recently permitted to be issued in the United Kingdom. This fledgling market, similar to the Yankee bond market, is known as the Bulldog market.

Japan

The Japanese fixed-interest market, in terms of amount outstanding, ranks second in the world to the U.S. bond market. The main instruments of interest to foreign investors are:

- Government bonds;
- Government agency bonds;
- Bank debentures;
- *Gensaki;*
- Yen certificates of deposit;
- Samurai bonds; and
- Euroyen bonds.

Japanese government bonds. Government bonds are issued in both discount form, for issues of up to five-year maturity, and coupon form. The Ministry of Finance sets the terms of new issues, which are underwritten by a fixed syndicate of banks, including city banks, long-term credit banks, regional banks, securities houses, credit associations, life insurance companies, and other insurance companies. At the end of March 1981 approximately ¥67 trillion were outstanding on government bonds. Maturities are two, three, four, and ten years and coupons vary from 6.10 to 8.5 percent.

Government agency bonds. The main issuers of government agency bonds are public corporations wholly owned by the Japanese government. These include Nippon Telephone and Telegraph (NTT), Japan National Railways, the Japan Highway Corporation, and Finance Corporation for Local Enterprise. Some 90 percent of these issues are government guaranteed and the most important single class of these issues is NTT subscriber bonds. New telephone subscribers are required to buy these bonds. The amount outstanding at the end of June 1981 was ¥6.1 trillion. A majority of government agency bonds are privately placed.

Withholding tax on both government bonds and government agency bonds is at a basic rate of 20 percent, but this is reduced to 10 percent for U.S. investors.

A very active secondary market exists for both government and government agency bonds since each government issue has some ¥1 to 2 trillion outstanding. Dealing size in the secondary market is in the ¥1 to ¥10 billion range for governments and ¥1 to 2 billion for agencies. Dealer spreads are normally one-quarter point in governments and one point in agencies.

Bank debentures. Only a limited number of banks are authorized to issue bank debentures. These are the Industrial Bank of Japan, the Long-Term Credit Bank, the Nippon Credit Bank, the Bank of Tokyo, the Norinchukin Bank, and the Shoko Chukin Bank. Debentures are issued monthly on a tap basis under the auspices of the Ministry of Finance. Maturity is three or five years in coupon form and one year in discount form. Some ¥2.6 trillion was outstanding at the end of June 1981.

New issues are placed directly by the issuing banks and secondary markets are maintained by the Japanese securities houses. Dealing size ranges from ¥100 million to ¥10 billion with dealer spreads of one-quarter point. Withholding tax is the same as it is for governments and agencies (20 percent basic rate, reduced to 10 percent for U.S. investors).

Gensaki. The main money market instrument in Japan is the *gensaki,* which is a repurchase agreement involving either coupon or discount bonds. A typical *gensaki* transaction would involve the purchase by an investor of bonds from a securities firm with an agreement to sell them back after a specified time period. Maximum maturity for *gensaki* is one year and most transactions are out to about thirty days. No withholding tax is applicable unless a coupon payment occurs during the *gensaki* period.

Yen certificates of deposit. Although Yen certificates of deposit (CDs) were first issued as recently as 1979, a large market has developed. Some ¥2.5 trillion was outstanding at end March 1981, and the major issuers are the city banks, long-term credit banks, regional and trust banks, and Japanese branches of foreign banks.

The amount of CDs a bank may issue is regulated by the Ministry of Finance. Maturity is normally three to six months. The minimum issue size is ¥500 million, and a secondary market is maintained by both the issuing bank and other dealers. Withholding tax applied is the same as it is on government bonds.

Samurai bonds. The issues of foreign borrowers on the Japanese domestic bond market are known as Samurai bonds. Comparable to the Yankee bond, the first Samurai bond was floated in 1970. The volume of new issues is regulated by the Ministry of Finance, which operates a queue system for borrowers. Interest payments are free from withholding tax.

Some ¥2 billion was outstanding at end March 1981. Issues normally of five to fifteen years' maturity and ¥15 to 50 billion in size are underwritten by a syndicate of Japanese and international banks, led by one of the Japanese securities houses. The secondary market is somewhat limited because of the small size of the issues. Dealer spreads are usually 1.5 to 2 points and trading size is ¥50 billion.

Euroyen bonds. Only some ¥125 billion of Euroyen bonds is outstanding. Maturities are in the seven- to ten-year range and issue size is ¥10 to 25 billion. New issues are underwritten by an international syndicate of banks, led by one of the Japanese securities houses. There is no Japanese withholding tax. Secondary-market liquidity is somewhat limited as in the case of Samurai bonds.

Japanese yield calculation. Unlike all other Eurobond and domestic bond markets, where yields to maturity are calculated in the same way as they are on U.S. domestic bonds, yields to maturity on Japanese bonds are calculated and trading takes place on a non-compounding basis.

The following formula may be used:

$$Y = \frac{C + \frac{(1000 - P)}{n}}{P} \times 100$$

where Y = Yield
C = Coupon
P = Market price of the bond
and n = Number of years to maturity

Because of the Japanese convention of looking at yields on a non-compounding or simple-interest basis, the Japanese yield curve may differ quite widely from yield curves in other currencies. This may provide some opportunities for the international investor, who will normally assess bonds on a compounding basis.

Settlement of Yen domestic bonds takes place in Tokyo, with Japanese banks and securities houses acting as custodians. Samurai bonds may be cleared through Euroclear, although most bonds tend to be held in Tokyo. Euroyen bonds are eligible for both Euroclear and CEDEL.

Index-Linked Foreign Obligations

In an attempt to protect their investments from the debilitating effect of inflation, some investors have been attracted to index-linked investments. Only a limited number of such instruments are available to most investors. The United

Kingdom's index-linked bonds, which are tied to the Retail Price Index, have now been made available to non-U.K. institutions. The main index-linked vehicles that have been bought by international investors are Mexican Petrobonds, which are tied to the price of Mexican crude oil, and gold-backed French bonds.

Petrobonds, issued by National Financiera S.A., the Mexican government's development bank, are a series of trusts with assets that constitute rights to acquire specific numbers of barrels of crude oil. Each issue of Petrobonds has an original maturity of three years, a 12.6 percent coupon, is denominated in Mexican pesos, and entitles the holder at maturity to a certain number of barrels of oil per pesos 1,000 nominal amount. The coupon is subject to a 21 percent withholding tax to give the investor a net coupon of 10 percent. The market price of Petrobonds fluctuates principally in relation to the price of Mexican crude oil.

Two issues with value tied to gold are available on the French bond market. The 7 percent government bond due in 1988 has both capital and interest linked to the price of gold bullion, while the 4.5 percent government bond has its value linked to the price of the napoleon, a French gold coin.

U.S. DOLLAR ISSUES FOR FOREIGN BORROWERS IN THE U.S. MARKET

A variety of foreign borrowers raise money in the U.S. capital markets. These include (1) international agencies, such as the International Bank for Reconstruction and Development, Inter-American Development Bank, and Asian Development Bank; (2) Canadian borrowers such as the Government of Canada and the Canadian Provinces; and (3) other sovereign governments, government agencies, and European institutions.

During the period of 1963-1974, the United States levied an interest equalization tax (IET) on purchases by U.S. nationals of foreign securities. International agencies of which the United States is a member and Canadian borrowers were exempt from the IET, but this tax effectively closed the U.S. market to other foreign borrowers. In 1974, the IET was reduced to zero and the market for other international borrowers, the so-called Yankee bond market, was developed. These issues for foreign borrowers provide U.S. investors with credit diversification and alternative high-grade securities, since most of these issues have been rated triple-A by the two leading U.S. rating agencies. These issues are not subject to U.S. withholding tax and thus are attractive to non-U.S. investors.

TAX CONSEQUENCES

The tax position of the U.S. investor in foreign fixed income investments will not differ from his or her tax position on a similar security in the U.S. domestic market.

What is peculiar to the foreign markets, however, is the withholding tax treatment by the various foreign governments. These tax aspects, which have been previously discussed in the section on the various instruments, may be summarized as follows:

Eurobonds and foreign bonds are free from withholding tax.

Domestic fixed-interest instruments in non-dollar currencies are generally subject to a withholding tax at a basic rate, which is then reduced to a smaller amount or to zero. This reduction, which depends on the double-taxation treaty between that country and the United States, will be accomplished through a claim for refund made by the investor to the foreign country's authorities. The final tax imposed by the foreign country is reduced to zero for U.S. investors in all instances except for Japan with 10 percent on domestic instruments, Canada with 15 percent on money market instruments other than Treasury bills, and Switzerland with 5 percent on government bonds.

In order for Eurobonds issued by U.S. corporations to be free from U.S. withholding tax, it is normally necessary for the Eurobond issue to be floated by a foreign subsidiary of the U.S. corporation. Thus, many U.S. corporations use Netherlands Antilles corporations as their issuing vehicles. Unless a U.S. corporation derives less than 20 percent of its gross income from U.S. sources, its interest payments to foreign holders of its obligations are subject to U.S. withholding tax. The use of a foreign finance subsidiary as the issuing vehicle for the bonds, which are then guaranteed by the parent company, is normally sufficient to avoid any withholding tax problem.

REPRESENTATIVE TYPES OF INVESTORS

The major source of institutional capital for Eurobonds are central banks, pension funds of multinational corporations, international insurance companies, and international banks for both portfolio and trust assets. U.S. domestic institutions hold relatively few Eurobonds because of the seasoning rule and the perceived lack of liquidity. The offshore captive insurance subsidiaries of U.S. corporations, largely based in Bermuda, are also a prominent force in the market. The Eurobond markets also attract significant amounts of money from individuals whose accounts are managed by international banks and brokerage houses. As far as this retail end of the market is concerned, Switzerland is the major source of capital, with other European centers such as Belgium, Luxembourg, and the United Kingdom also playing an important part. The Middle and Far East have been growing in significance in the past decade as a source of both institutional and individual money.

The markets for non-dollar-denominated domestic instruments are largely dominated by the domestic institutions in the individual countries. Foreign official entities such as central banks, however, do play an active role in the world's main financial markets. As a result of the huge transfer of wealth to the OPEC countries, these investors have become very significant in the domestic capital markets surveyed. U.S. domestic institutions and individuals traditionally have not bought large amounts of non-dollar-denominated securities. However, the weakness of the dollar in the past decade has caused an increasing number of U.S. investors to turn their attention to the opportunities of currency diversification. An inhibiting factor has been the relatively poor secondary-market liquidity in many countries. In general, U.S. institutions can find the kind of liquidity they are used to in the U.S. market only in the U.K. gilt-edged market and, to some extent, the Japanese and Canadian government bond markets. The German and Dutch government bond markets can offer good liquidity at certain times but not with the consistency of the other markets.

IMPORTANT FACTORS IN BUYING AND SELLING

The somewhat complicated legal aspects of investment in foreign fixed income securities are paramount in any discussion regarding their purchase.

With the exception of Yankee bonds, the securities under discussion have not been registered with the SEC under provisions of the Securities Act of 1933. For new issues of Eurobonds, underwriters are required to agree not to offer or sell the bonds in the United States or to U.S. persons until ninety days after the bonds are deemed to have been distributed to the final buyer. In order to ensure that bonds are not being sold in the United States, the certificates of indebtedness are issued initially in a temporary global form and may only be exchanged for definitive securities after a minimum of ninety days from the time the bonds are all sold. Many investment banks take the position that the so-called seasoning period should be at least nine months or a year. These banks will generally not sell any Eurobonds to U.S. investors before nine months have elapsed unless the investor signs a nondistribution letter. This letter basically states that the investor understands that the securities have not been registered with the SEC and that he or she agrees not to resell them to unsophisticated U.S. persons.

With regard to the sale of new issues in other currencies to U.S. investors, most U.S. broker-dealers adopt the same attitude towards seasoning as they do towards Eurobonds. Foreign banks and brokers, however, do appear free to approach U.S. investors with new issues in other currencies.

Money Managers

The main firms offering money management services for multicurrency fixed-interest investment are the leading U.S. commercial banks and trust banks, and some U.S. investment banks and money managers. Foreign money managers, such as the U.K. merchant banks and German, French, Belgian, and Dutch commercial banks, are leading factors in providing money management services to institutional investors. Swiss banks have traditionally specialized in offering services to individuals. The fees charged by these managers may be a percentage of the amount under management or on a transaction-by-transaction basis.

CUSTODIAL CARE

For most Eurobond instruments, the simplest way to settle securities is through one of the two leading international clearing systems, Euroclear and CEDEL.

Euroclear and CEDEL, based in Brussels and Luxembourg, respectively, effect the delivery and payment functions for securities by means of bookkeeping entries between participants of the system.

Euroclear is owned by a number of the leading banks involved in the Eurobond markets and is operated by the Morgan Guaranty Trust Company of New York through its branches in major financial centers. CEDEL, which is sponsored by a number of European banks, also operates through an international network of banks.

Both systems are fungible depository systems, in which specific securities are not attributable to specific participants by use of certificate numbers. Rather, when a participant buys a security, he or she retains title to a given nominal amount of an issue but has no claim to specific securities identified by serial numbers.

The systems are designed so that deliveries can also be made from Euroclear to CEDEL, and vice versa, or to institutions outside of the systems.

For domestic securities, the custodial arrangements normally would be made via a local bank. Local laws vary widely between countries, but most systems are quite similar to those operating within the United States.

GLOSSARY

captive insurance company— A subsidiary of a U.S. corporation set up to provide insurance services mainly to its parent company.

composite currency unit— A numeraire, or benchmark, related to a group of currencies designed to limit the impact of currency movements on values of securities.

domestic bond— An issue for a domestic borrower in a domestic market.

EMS— European Monetary System, which fixes currency relationships within the European Economic Community.

foreign bond— An issue for a foreign borrower in a domestic market.

global certificate— A temporary certificate representing a whole issue, designed to prevent the sale of new issues to certain investors during the initial offering period.

IET— Interest equalization tax, imposed by the United States on purchases by U.S. persons and residents of foreign securities.

jobber— A market maker on the London Stock Exchange.

kassenverein— The German central clearance system.

LIBOR— London Interbank Offered Rate, which leading banks charge each other for Eurodollar deposits of maturities ranging from overnight to five years.

mark to market— The valuation of outstanding securities at the current market price.

over-the-counter— Dealings away from a stock exchange.

partly paid issue— An issue where the buyer only has to pay a part of total price when the bond is initially purchased. A practice in the U.K. gilt-edged market.

queue system— A line of borrowers waiting to access a market. A practice for foreign bonds in certain currencies.

seasoning— The period between the initial offering of an issue of securities that are not registered with the SEC and the time it may be offered to U.S. investors; normally 90 to 360 days.

tap— A method of making new issues available on the basis of the demand in the marketplace.

universal bank— An international bank that is involved in all aspects of commercial banking and securities business.

Yankee bond— An issue for a foreign borrower (excluding international organizations of which the United States is a member, and Canadian borrowers) in the U.S. domestic market.

TRADE ORGANIZATION

Association of International Bond Dealers, Zurich, Switzerland

LEADING DEALERS

The leading dealers in the Eurobond markets tend to be the same as the leading money managers, since the international markets are dominated by universal banks, which underwrite and trade securities and offer money management services. For the U.S. investor, it would probably be simplest to contact one of the leading U.S. investment banks. In the various domestic bond markets, the leading local commercial banks or brokerage firms would provide the best services. However, some U.S. investment banks may offer a capability in certain of the non-dollar markets. The following is a partial listing of foreign dealers in Eurobonds:

Belgium

Dewaay, Sebille, Servais & Co.
Kredietbank N.V.

France

Banque de l'Union Europienne
Banque Nationale de Paris
Credit Commercial de France

Germany/Austria

Creditanstalt Bankverein
Deutsche Bank AG
Westdeutsche Landesbank Gironzentrale

Italy

Banca Commerciale Italiana
Banco di Roma
Credito Italiano

Luxembourg

Banque Generale du Luxembourg S.A.

Netherlands

Algemene Bank Nederland N.V.
Bank Morgan Labouchere & Co. N.V.
Bank van der Hoop Offers N.V.
F. van Lanschot Bankiers N.V.

Nederlandse Credietbank N.V.

Norway/Sweden/Finland

Bank of Helsinki Ltd. (Helsingfors Aktiebank)
Bergen Bank
Den Norske Creditbank
Kansallis-Osake-Pankki
Kjobenhavns Handelsbank
Privatbanken Aktieselskab
Skandinaviska Enskilda Banken
Skopbank
Union Bank of Finland
Union Bank of Norway Ltd.

Switzerland

Credit Suisse/Swiss Credit Bank
Swiss Bank Corporation
Union Bank of Switzerland

United Kingdom

Akroyd & Smithers Limited
Bache Halsey Stuart Shields Inc.
Bank of America International Ltd.
Blyth Eastman Paine Webber International Ltd.
Chase Manhattan Ltd.
Chemical Bank International Ltd.
Citicorp International Bank Limited
Credit Suisse First Boston Ltd.
Daiwa Europe Ltd.
Dean Witter Reynolds Overseas Ltd.
Dominion Securities Limited
Robert Fleming & Co. Ltd.
Goldman Sachs International Corp.
IBJ International Limited
Kidder Peabody Securities, Limited
Kuhn Loeb Lehman Brothers International
Lloyds Bank International Ltd.
London & Continental Bankers Ltd.
McLeod Young Weir International Ltd.
Merrill Lynch Pierce Fenner & Smith (Brokers and Dealers) Ltd.
Midland Doherty Ltd.
Morgan Stanley International
Nomura International Ltd.
Nordic Bank Ltd.
Orion Royal Bank Ltd.
Pinchin Denny & Co.
Ross & Partners (Securities) Ltd.
Salomon Brothers International Limited
Samuel Montagu & Co. Ltd.
Smith Barney Harris Upham & Co. Inc.
Vickers Da Costa Ltd.
S.G. Warburg & Co. Ltd.
Wood Gundy Limited

United States

Arnhold S. Bleichroeder, Inc.
Lehman Brothers Kuhn Loeb & Co. Inc.
Merrill Lynch Pierce Fenner & Smith, Inc.
Salomon Brothers
Atlantic Capital Corporation

Middle East

Arab Banking Corporation
National Bank of Abu Dhabi

SUGGESTED READING

Periodicals and Newspapers

The Economist. Published by Economist Newspaper, Ltd., London. Weekly.
Euromoney. Published by Euromoney Publications, Ltd., London. Monthly.

The Financial Times of London.

The International Herald Tribune. (Paris.)

Institutional Investor. (International Edition). Published by Institutional Investor Systems, Inc., New York. Monthly.

Articles

Adam, N. "AIBD Meeting: The Challenge to the Primary Market." *Euromoney* May 1980, pages 13-14.

Boland, J.C. "Hedge Against the Dollar: Savvy Investors Opt for Bonds Payable in Foreign Exchange." *Barrons* 59:9-10, July 9, 1979.

Cohen, J.N. "Measuring Performance in the Eurobond Market." *Banker* 129 supp.:6-8, May 1979.

Field, P., and James, L. "Coming Revolution in Investment Banking." *Euromoney* March 1980, pages 7-9.

Quinn, B.S. "International Bond Market for the U.S. Investor." *Columbia Journal of World Business* 14:85-90, Fall 1979.

Starr, D.W. "Opportunities for U.S. Corporate Borrowers in the International Bond Markets." *Financial Executive* 47:50, June 1979.

"U.S. Corporate Rush for Eurodollar Bonds." *Business Week* April 30, 1979, page 78.

Reference Books

Dobbs-Higginson, M.S. *Investment Manual for Fixed Income Securities in the International and Major Domestic Capital Markets.* London: Credit Suisse First Boston Limited, 1980.

Esslen, Rainer. *The Complete Book of International Investing.* New York: McGraw-Hill, 1977.

Hanna, Jeffrey D., and Campbell, John Y. *International Bond Manual.* New York: Salomon Brothers, 1981.

Lomax, David F., and Gutman, P.T.G. *The Euromarkets and International Financial Policies.* New York: Halsted Press, 1981.

Futures—Agricultural Commodities

*Anne E. Peck**

BASIC CHARACTERISTICS

Background

Active futures markets exist for virtually all major domestically produced agricultural commodities, several agricultural products, and selected imported commodities. The domestic commodities include corn, wheat, soybean, cotton, potatoes, live cattle, and live hogs. The agricultural products include soybean oil, soybean meal, frozen pork bellies, and frozen concentrated orange juice. Imported commodities include coffee, sugar, and cocoa. Though not strictly agricultural, two wood products — lumber and plywood — also have active futures markets.

Price determination. For most of these commodities, futures markets are the primary points for price determination with actual cash as well as with forward transactions priced relative to futures prices. The fundamental determinants of futures prices are the supplies available and the demand for the specific commodities. Thus, factors important in determining prices (and expected price changes) include domestic production, imports and/or exports, domestic use, and stockholdings. Estimates of these numbers are regularly provided by the U.S. Department of Agriculture. These estimates provide a baseline for commodity brokerage firms' analyses and are typically included in commodity newsletters. Much additional analysis is also done by commodity firms, examining the assumptions lying behind the projections and analyzing supplementary data.

Nature of futures contracts. Agricultural commodity futures markets are among the oldest commodity futures markets. In fact, the institution of futures trading originated in agricultural markets — a logical outgrowth of the extensive forward trading that accompanied the marketing of products that were produced only once during the year (harvest), were storable, and were used continuously during the year. Futures contracts are standardized forward contracts. The standards or contract specifications are fixed by the exchange on which the particular future trades. Specifications include quantity (e.g., 5,000 bushels of corn), quality (No. 2 yellow corn), form of delivery (in approved elevator storage), and location (Chicago). Often, contract specifications also include provisions for differences from these standards in the actual delivery of the commodity, normally with fixed

* Anne E. Peck is an Associate Professor at the Food Research Institute, Stanford University.

premiums or discounts for the difference. In addition, futures contracts are traded only for specified delivery months during the year (December, March, May, July, and September in the corn market).

Futures contracts may be bought and sold only on regulated commodity exchanges. All orders are executed by open outcry — buyers and sellers meeting to determine price. Once an order is executed, a buyer has found a seller, and price has been agreed upon, the exchange (technically the clearinghouse of the exchange) becomes a third party to the transaction. Rather than having an obligation to each other, both the buyer and seller now have separate obligations to the exchange. For example, the buyer of a March soybean futures contract has an obligation to the exchange to accept delivery of soybeans according to the predetermined contract specifications in March, and the seller has an obligation to deliver soybeans to the exchange in March. Since the obligations of both buyer and seller are with the exchange, they do not have to find the person with whom the original transaction was made. Rather, someone who has bought futures must simply sell a like amount (a transaction called "offset") to become even in the records of the clearinghouse and out of the market. The clearinghouse's third-party role in all futures contracts thus facilitates market entry and exit and increases market liquidity.

Futures vs. forward markets. Though the institution of futures markets emerged from forward markets, it should not be viewed as replacing forward markets. Standardization of contract specifications encourages a more liquid market, which facilitates price discovery. However, standardization discourages actual delivery, as it cannot accommodate the specific requirements of individual users as to amounts, location, or timing. Deliveries on futures contracts in agricultural commodities remain low, averaging less than one percent of contracts traded. Delivery provisions are an important feature of futures contracts because they imply that prices on these markets must reflect underlying supply of and demand for the specific commodities. Rarely will the outside investor become involved in delivery. In fact, most brokerage firms will encourage their clients to offset any open positions in a futures option that is approaching delivery. The position — buying or selling — then may be reestablished in a more distant future. Forward markets continue to be important in the marketing of agricultural products since contracts can be tailored to individual user's requirements. Prices for forward contracts are normally determined by reference to those for the standardized contracts, the futures prices.

Futures margins. Both the buyer and seller of a futures contract are required to post a performance bond (margin money) with the exchange. Margins are posted directly, with the clearinghouse of the exchange by clearing-member traders, or indirectly, with brokerage firms or clearing-member traders, by all other traders. Minimum levels of initial margins are established (and can be changed) by the exchanges. Margins required of traders by brokerage houses vary among firms and some of the margin may be held in Treasury securities. It is important to realize that margins on futures positions are not down payments against a future position. The only contractual obligation a futures position entails is to do something (make or take delivery) in the future. No ownership of actual commodity has been transferred. Margins are therefore performance bonds.

To ensure contract performance, the clearinghouse not only requires both parties to post margins but also marks all positions to the closing prices of the market daily. Suppose an investor buys one contract of corn at $4.00 per bushel, the closing price. By the close of trade the next day, corn prices have increased to $4.10. After the close, the clearinghouse will transfer to his margin account (through a broker) $500 (5,000 bushels × $0.10/bushel). This $500 will have come from the margin account of a trader who had sold one contract. The monies are transferred daily, even though the actual position remains open. If prices continue up the next day, more money will be transferred into the account. If they decline, money will be removed. If initial margin monies are depleted sufficiently in an individual's account, he will be required to deposit more money to prevent his position from being closed out.

Profile of agricultural futures markets. Table 1 (on page 264) provides a comparative view of size and price volatility of the major agricultural futures markets. It presents information commonly reported with the summary of a day's trading activity in such sources as the *Wall Street Journal.* First, for each commodity the principal exchange is designated. For each agricultural commodity, there is normally one principal exchange where the majority of futures trading in that commodity takes place. There are two exceptions: The most obvious exception in the table is wheat, which is more or less actively traded on three exchanges, although the Chicago Board of Trade (CBT) market clearly dominates. In fact, each wheat market is different in that a different variety of wheat is being traded on each exchange. All three markets have survived because they provide a pricing vehicle for specific groups of users. The less obvious exception is those commodities traded on the Mid-America Commodity Exchange (MACE) in smaller-sized contracts. For example, the standard CBT contract for corn is 5,000 bushels; the MACE contract is 1,000 bushels. Only rarely would an individual choose to trade minicontracts in preference to the standard contracts on the principal exchanges because they tend to be a much less liquid market.

The second column in Table 1 indicates the amount of the commodity represented in a single futures contract. The grains and soybeans are uniform contracts of 5,000 bushels; otherwise contract size tends to reflect an amount commonly used in commercial trade for that commodity.

The next four columns show the units in which prices are quoted and the trading range of prices during 1981. Contract high and low prices are shown for the indicated maturity for a contract that traded nearly the entire year. As these data make clear, agricultural commodity prices are characteristically volatile, with high prices during a year often representing more than twice the year's low prices. Lest this be interpreted as a buy-and-hold recommendation, note that the sequence of market high and low has not been indicated.

TABLE 1. Agricultural Commodity Futures Markets

	Principal Exchange(s)[1]	Contract Size	Price Range During 1981: Future	Unit	High	Low	Volume of Trading in 1981 (1,000 contracts)	Open Interest on Dec. 31, 1981 (1,000 contracts)
Grains and oilseeds:								
Corn[2]	CBT	5,000 bushels	Dec.	¢/bu.	$ 396.25	$ 236.00	10,675	126
Wheat[2]	CBT	5,000 bushels	Dec.	¢/bu.	569.00	362.00	4,512	63
	KCBT	5,000 bushels	Dec.	¢/bu.			1,182	27
	MGE	5,000 bushels	Dec.	¢/bu.			358	6
Soybeans[2]	CBT	5,000 bushels	Nov.	¢/bu.	900.00	625.00	10,490	85
Soybean oil	CBT	60,000 pounds	Dec.	¢/lb.	29.73	18.50	3,047	48
Soybean meal	CBT	100 tons	Dec.	$/ton	259.00	181.00	3,040	39
Livestock products:								
Live cattle[2]	CME	40,000 pounds	Dec.	¢/lb.	75.85	57.55	4,282	51
Feeder cattle	CME	42,000 pounds	Nov.	¢/lb.	77.05	61.90	621	9
Live hogs[2]	CME	30,000 pounds	Dec.	¢/lb.	61.75	37.95	2,258	18
Pork bellies	CME	38,000 pounds	Feb.	¢/lb.	74.75	53.75	1,998	14
Foods and fibers:								
Potatoes	NYME	50,000 pounds	Nov.	¢/lb.	9.07	6.41	237	3
Coffee	CSCE	37,500 pounds	Dec.	¢/lb.	165.50	82.00	515	10
Sugar	CSCE	112,000 pounds	Jan.	¢/lb.	37.80	11.00	2,470	72
Cocoa	CSCE	10 metric tons	Dec.	$/ton	2,595.00	1,538.00	563	14
Orange juice	Citrus	15,000 pounds	Jan.	¢/lb.	164.85	91.50	387	8
Cotton	NYCE	50,000 pounds	Dec.	¢/lb.	86.10	60.30	1,415	29
Wood products:								
Lumber	CME	130,000 board feet	Jan.	$/1,000 bd.ft.	245.00	136.10	636	9
Plywood	CBT	76,032 square feet	Nov.	$/1,000 sq.ft.	237.00	156.50	1,415	4

SOURCE: Futures Industry Association; *Wall Street Journal*

[1] The exchanges are the Chicago Board of Trade (CBT), Kansas City Board of Trade (KCBT), Minneapolis Grain Exchange (MGE), Chicago Mercantile Exchange (CME), New York Mercantile Exchange (NYME), Coffee, Sugar and Cocoa Exchange (CSCE), New York Cotton Exchange (NYCE), and the Citrus Associates of the New York Cotton Exchange (Citrus).

[2] Also traded on the Mid-America Commodity Exchange in smaller size contracts.

The remaining data in Table 1 are the two most often used indicators of market size — open interest and volume of trading — both in thousands of contracts. The open interest is the number of buy or sell contracts outstanding on a specific date (here, the last trading day in 1981). Since every buyer must have found a seller to have entered the market, positions on only one side of the market are counted in these measures of activity. Volume of trading is the number of contracts that have been traded (again, on only one side of the market), either on a specific day or during a specific period. The latter is used here and the volume numbers are totals for the year.

Variety of Investments

There are several alternative ways for an individual to participate in agricultural commodity futures markets, including trading one's own account, participating in some type of managed-account program, or investing in a commodity market mutual fund. The differences among the alternatives involve the degree to which the individual controls his own positions and, to a lesser extent, the number of commodities that the individual is likely to be trading. In addition, the alternatives differ in the extent to which they should be considered as investments. Strictly speaking, trading commodity futures is not considered investing; professional futures traders consider themselves speculators in commodity prices, not investors in commodities. The closer an outsider comes to trading his own account, the more he should consider himself a speculator in commodity prices.

Trading one's own account. The difference between speculation and investment is perhaps only one of degree — indeed, at least one major textbook on investments[1] includes a chapter on commodity futures — but there are several unique features of futures that should be kept in mind. First, future positions are marked to the market every day. All losses (gains) are paid (received) at the end of each day (and occasionally, in fast markets, during the day). Second, ownership of the commodity only changes hands if delivery is made or received, not when the futures position is initiated. Third, a futures contract cannot be held longer than the amount of time remaining until the delivery month. The position can be maintained by closing the position in the current month and reestablishing the position in a more distant future; but there can be significant costs in this transaction, depending upon the relationship of prices among the future maturities. If, for example, an individual had bought one contract of May wheat and May was approaching, he could sell one May wheat and buy one contract of a more distant maturity, such as September. The cost, or change in value of the position, would depend on the price of the September contract relative to the May contract. Finally, the empirical evidence indicates that individual futures positions are not

[1] Sharpe, William, *Investments*. New York: Prentice-Hall, 1981.

held for very long periods of time on average. In the grains and oilseeds, average holding periods are no more than three to five days.[2] Thus, an individual desiring to trade for his own account should be prepared to devote significant time to learning the fundamentals of the commodities involved and then to actively managing the positions.

Managed-account participation. A second way to trade agricultural futures is to establish some type of a managed-account program with a specific commodities broker or firm. These relationships are called discretionary or managed accounts and involve giving the broker power to trade the account. There is no clear distinction between discretionary and managed accounts. The former are usually smaller, trading in only one or two commodities and, while the account is with a specific individual, he is likely to be using the firm's trading advice rather than making his own trading decisions. Managed accounts, on the other hand, usually require a larger initial deposit, will trade in a larger number of commodities, and the broker will likely be making trading decisions based on his own analysis. In addition, it is quite common for a managed-account broker to participate in the profits of the account and not simply the commissions generated by the trading.

Commodity mutual funds. A third way to trade agricultural futures is to participate in a commodity futures mutual fund, and these are much more like traditional investments. Commodity mutual funds must be registered with both the SEC and the Commodity Futures Trading Commission (CFTC). Minimum investments range from $1,000 to $10,000, with $5,000 being common. They are self-liquidating — that is, when net assets fall below a specified level (e.g., 60 percent of the initial assets), all positions are closed and the fund is liquidated.

Characteristically, a mutual fund holds positions in a wide range of commodity futures. Some are limited to agricultural commodities; others will include the precious metals and financial instrument futures as well. The positions are relatively actively traded and may be long or short in buying or selling specific commodities. They provide the individual with a convenient way to hold a portfolio of commodity positions and not simply to trade one or two commodities.

ATTRACTIVE FEATURES

Low Margins

The initial margin deposited with a broker, which permits one to buy or sell a futures contract, is normally quite low, ranging between 5 and 10 percent of the value of the contract. For example, a recent initial margin for a contract of

[2] The average holding period is a ratio, calculated by dividing the open interest by the volume of trading, using daily data. This measure is also called the "turnover," since it shows how many days' trading could turn over ownership of the open interest.

soybeans was $1,500. With beans trading at $6.50, a contract of beans was worth $32,500, or more than twenty times the value of the margin.

Minimum margin levels for all traders are established by the exchange or its clearinghouse. Brokerage firms differ in the margins they require of their customers. In addition, some firms may permit some portion of the margin monies to be held in short-term Treasury bills. Since a margin is a performance bond and not a partial payment on the contract, both buyers and sellers of futures contracts are required to post margin monies in order to trade.

Liquidity

Futures markets for the agricultural commodities are generally very actively traded markets. Prices determined there are taken to reflect the fundamental values of the commodities. Liquidity also means that orders to buy and sell are executed at prices very close to current quotations. Formal bid-asked spreads are not quoted, but in normal circumstances this spread is no more than one tick above and below the last quotation, where a tick is the minimum price change. In all the grain markets, for example, a tick is one-quarter of one cent. Thus, the potential price effects of a specific transaction are very small.

Market Regulation

Commodity futures markets are regulated both by the exchanges on which they trade and by an independent regulatory agency, the CFTC. The markets are monitored quite closely for signs of unusual behavior and potential manipulations. All traders with large positions (currently defined as 1 million bushels in the grains, for example) must report their trading directly to the CFTC. All individuals dealing in or advising about commodity futures positions are required to be registered with the CFTC. Brokerage firms are subject to audit of customer's funds (margin monies must be kept in a segregated account) and of the financial condition of the firms (firms must meet minimum exchange and/or CFTC designated financial requirements).

In addition, the CFTC has adopted industry-wide customer protection rules, including the requirement that brokers provide risk disclosure statements, monthly profit and loss statements, and margin statements to customers. Brokers cannot trade for an individual's account unless specific permission has been given. Finally, the CFTC has established reparations procedures where customer complaints against a commodity broker may be heard and adjudicated in an orderly manner.

Advantages for Stocks and Bond Portfolios

Few individuals or firms not directly linked to agriculture — growing, marketing, processing, industrial users, exporters, and the like — will have interest in agricultural commodity futures markets. However, evidence is beginning to accumulate that suggests that agricultural commodity futures may prove useful in diversifying the risks of stocks and/or bond portfolios. Zvi Bodie, who has done much of the basic correlation analysis, found that the value of an unweighted portfolio of long commodity futures positions tends to rise sharply during periods of unanticipated inflation while other assets, including stocks and bonds, do poorly.[3] Additionally, futures provide a means of significantly expanding efficient portfolio frontiers, creating higher returns for any level of acceptable risks. (See article on Portfolio Management, elsewhere in this volume.)

Thus, while speculating in corn or soybean futures is not likely to be a prudent investment, participation in a commodity fund may serve a useful purpose.

Tax Advantage

Net gains on all speculative commodity futures trading are taxed at a maximum rate of 32 percent. (See *Tax Consequences* in this article.)

POTENTIAL RISKS

Marking to the Market and Low Margins

Commodity futures positions are marked to the market daily. At the close of trading each day, the clearinghouse of the exchange calculates the gains and losses on all open positions and transfers those gains or losses into and out of all margin accounts. Thus, profits on an open position, which are in excess of minimum margin requirements, may be removed from a margin account before the position is closed if the individual trader so desires. On the negative side, losses on open futures positions are deducted daily and, if the remaining margin declines to roughly half its initial level, the individual will be required to add funds (maintenance margin) to his account. If these funds are not forthcoming, the position will be closed. With relatively volatile prices and low initial margins, margin calls can be frequent.

Price Volatility

Futures prices for agricultural commodities are very volatile compared with those of other investments. Expectations about potential supplies and demands domestically, but especially internationally, can change quickly, leading to rapid and dramatic price adjustments. In addition, there are both long-term and short-term government policies that influence the pricing of agricultural commodities

---

[3] See Bodie, Zvi, "An Innovation for Stable Real Retirement Income." *Journal of Portfolio Management,* Fall 1980, pages 5-13; and Bodie, Zvi and Rosansky, V., "Risk and Return in Commodity Futures." *Financial Analysts Journal,* May-June 1980, pages 27-39. Bodie's futures portfolio included copper, silver, and platinum in addition to agricultural and wood product futures positions.

and these may change remarkably quickly. Grain reserve programs, export embargoes, and international commodity agreements are principal examples of important governmental influences on prices that have been changed frequently in recent years. Absolute price volatility combined with low margin requirements significantly magnifies fluctuations in returns when these are measured as percentages of the initial investment.

Price Limits

Futures prices are permitted to change by a maximum amount each day. These limits, set with respect to the previous day's closing price, are established so as not to restrain normal daily price fluctuations. However, as significant new information emerges (information that would cause prices to rise or fall beyond these limits), futures prices will remain locked at the limit price until the next day. So-called lock-limit markets can occur for several successive days, during which period there is no trading.

On the positive side, limiting the maximum daily price change enables the exchange to keep margin levels low. Also, the price limits help to keep market participants from overreacting to new information. When markets close at a limit, suggesting prices would have changed more, traders have nearly twenty-four hours to assess the significance of the new information and perhaps seek additional verification. Thus, price limits help to create a more orderly market.

On the negative side, however, price limits mean that a trader can get caught in a losing position — forced to meet margin calls and unable to trade out of the position.

Vulnerability to Regulatory Change

In most circumstances, exchange and federal regulation of futures markets is to the benefit of the public trader. Traders should be aware, however, that the CFTC has broad emergency powers to alter the rules as well as to cease trading in a specific maturity or commodity altogether any time it is deemed necessary. Exchanges, with CFTC oversight, have similar authority. The most frequent changes in the rules — and the ones of which potential traders should be aware — pertain to margins and price limits. Either or both may be changed overnight. Thus, even though a specific position might have been profitable, if margin levels are changed abruptly, an individual could find it necessary to deposit more margin money.

Hazards of Commodities Speculating

Numerous studies have shown that small, nonprofessional speculators lose money, on average, speculating in agricultural commodity futures. There are, of course, many exceptions to the average. The average does underscore the need to carefully examine a broker's or fund's trading record over a period of years.

TAX CONSEQUENCES

Taxation of speculative gains and losses from commodity futures positions changed fundamentally with the Economic Recovery Tax Act of 1981.[4]

First, all positions open at the end of the tax year will be treated as if they had been closed on the last day of the year; that is, all open positions are marked to the market at the last day's settlement price. Profits or losses from these positions are added to those from positions closed during the year.

Second, net gains on all speculative transactions are treated as though they were 40 percent short-term capital gains and 60 percent long-term capital gains. Thus, with a maximum marginal tax rate of 50 percent and a 20 percent capital gains rate, the maximum rate applied to speculative gains from futures positions is 32 percent.

Finally, if there are net futures trading losses, these may be applied against other capital gains. If there are still net losses, there are provisions in the Act to carry these losses forward into the following tax year.

REPRESENTATIVE TYPES OF INVESTORS

Participants in commodity futures markets are generally catagorized as either hedgers or speculators. The distinction reflects a fundamental difference in the initial position of the participant. Hedgers are those whose business involves them in the underlying cash commodity. In agricultural commodities, the commercial firms include producers, merchants, processors, storers, exporters, and the like. Speculators have no such commercial interests in the underlying commodity.

Commercial Firms

Commercial firms use commodity futures to earn a return to their primary cash market activity, to provide a substitute transaction for an intended cash market transaction, and to reduce the risks of commodity price fluctuations. A particular hedging decision may have elements of all three motives. A common example of hedging in agricultural markets uses an elevator operator who is storing cash grain. In the absence of futures markets, the elevator's return from grain storage is simply the difference between the purchase price and the price at which the grain is later sold. The elevator's returns are fundamentally speculative, since time must elapse between the two transactions. With futures markets, the elevator operator can, on the same day as he purchases cash grain, sell an equivalent amount of futures contracts and know with reasonable certainty what the return to storage will be. When the cash grain is sold, the futures positions

---

[4] Gains and losses from hedging transactions — futures trading done as an integral part of a business — continue to be treated as ordinary income and are not marked to the market at year's end.

are bought back in and the actual profits calculated. These will depend upon the relationship between the cash and the futures price when the hedge was lifted. This relationship, called the "basis," is generally much more predictable than are price changes over time. Thus, in this simple hedge, the futures transaction enabled the elevator to earn a predictable return to storage. The initial futures transaction could be viewed as a substitute for an intended, later cash transaction and the risks of commodity storage have been significantly reduced.

Hedging positions comprise significant percentages of total open futures positions in all futures markets. In the grain and oilseed markets, hedgers have regularly accounted for more than 70 percent of the open interest in recent years. In livestock products, the percentage has been smaller, near 30 percent. As important as commercial use is, however, it is unlikely that an outside investor would fall into the hedging category in any of the agricultural futures markets.

Speculators

Speculators in commodity futures markets are classified as one of three distinct kinds of traders: floor traders, spreaders, and position traders. As speculators, these traders have no other commercial interest in the commodity. Their profits come solely from their futures trading. Although outside investors will most likely be position traders, the functions and type of trading of each are described below.

Floor traders. Floor traders are members of the exchanges, trading on the floor of the exchange. They trade in large volume during the trading session but rarely carry a position overnight. Floor traders, also called "scalpers," are the market makers. They have been described as always ready to buy or sell at a tick below or above the price of the last transaction.[5] Unlike stock market specialists, they are independent traders and are not assigned specific commodities to trade, nor do they hold a deck of outside orders to be executed at various prices. Income from their trading depends entirely on how skillfully they make a market, that is, how skillfully they accommodate the flow of orders into the market during the day.

Spread traders. Unlike scalpers, spread traders and position traders hold open positions at the end of day, endeavoring to profit from somewhat longer-term changes in price levels or price relationships. Spread traders focus on the latter. Basically, a spread trader will maintain offsetting positions in different maturities of the same commodity or in similar maturities of related commodities. For example, he could be long December corn and short March corn on the

---

[5] See Working, H. "Price Effects of Scalping and Day Trading," pages 181-194, in *Readings in Futures Markets — Vol. I: Selected Writings of Holbrook Working,* ed. Anne E. Peck. Chicago Board of Trade, 1977.

expectation that the December option will gain relative to the March option. Well-known intermarket spreads include positions in Chicago versus Kansas City or Minneapolis wheat, or positions in soybeans versus the soybean products (meal and oil).

Position traders. The third type of speculator, the position trader, is the trader of most interest here. Position traders are sometimes further distinguished according to the kinds of analyses they use to anticipate price changes. Fundamental analysis examines the determinants of supply and demand. Technical analysis, on the other hand, focuses on discerning patterns in past price changes, ignoring fundamental factors. Both methods are used extensively, most often together rather than exclusively one or the other.

IMPORTANT FACTORS IN BUYING AND SELLING

Selecting a Broker

Within the constraints of the kind of trading an individual wishes to do — his own account, a managed account, or a commodity mutual fund — he has a wide choice among types of brokers and brokerage firms. Discount firms usually have lower commissions and require minimal margins but they usually do not provide trading advice. Among the regular brokerage houses are commodities-only houses and so-called full-service houses. Commissions and margin levels (particularly as to in what form the margin will be held) are negotiable but will be fairly uniform among these firms. They will also normally provide in-house analysis and trading recommendations for major commodities. The individual should seek information on the performance of the firm's trading recommendations over at least three years.

Brokers specializing in managed accounts may be available within the larger brokerage firms or they can be completely independent of a firm. Again, previous performance should be investigated carefully. A number of individuals who manage futures accounts belong to a group that provides a regular performance report. (See *Adviser Evaluations* in this article.) Managed accounts will vary as to size and percentage of profits going to the manager.

Commodity mutual funds are also available. Again, the most important information will be past performance. Secondary considerations include management fees and the level of losses at which the fund will liquidate.

Adviser Evaluations

Managed Accounts Reports, in Columbia, Maryland collects and publishes monthly performance information from their member account managers. In addition, they run several seminars at various locations during the year on the subject of choosing an account manager.

Jay Klopfenstein (Norwood Securities, Inc., Chicago, Illinois) collects and reports information on commodity mutual funds. A monthly summary of his information on the major funds is available in *Commodities Magazine.*

GLOSSARY [6]

cash (commodity or market) — Pertaining to a commodity as distinguished from *futures contracts* based upon the physical commodity; the commodity as acquired through a cash market.

charting (or technical analysis) — The use of graphs and charts in analysis of market behavior, so as to plot trends of price movements, average movements of price, volume, and open interest, in the hope that such graphs and charts will help one to anticipate and profit from price trends. Contrast with *fundamental analysis.*

clearinghouse — An agency connected with a commodity exchange through which all futures contracts are reconciled, settled, guaranteed, and, later, either offset or fulfilled, through delivery of the commodity and through which financial settlement is made. It may be a fully chartered separate corporation, rather than a division of the exchange itself.

Commodity Futures Trading Commission (CFTC) — A federal regulatory agency charged and empowered under the Commodity Futures Trading Commission Act of 1974 with regulation of futures trading in all commodities. The CFTC is comprised of five commissioners, one of whom is designated as chairman, all appointed by the President subject to Senate confirmation, and is independent of all cabinet departments.

cover — To offset a previous futures transaction with an equal and opposite transaction. Short-covering is a purchase of futures contracts to cover an earlier sale of an equal number of the same delivery month; liquidation is the sale of futures contracts to offset the obligation to take delivery of an equal number of futures contracts of the same delivery month purchased earlier.

discretionary account — An arrangement by which the holder of the account gives written power of attorney to another, often his broker, to make buying and selling decisions without notification to the holder; often referred to as a managed account or controlled account.

forward contract — A cash market transaction in which two parties agree to the purchase and sale of a commodity at some future time under such conditions as the two agree. In contrast to *futures contracts,* the terms of forward contracts are not standardized; a forward contract is not transferable and usually can be canceled only with the consent of the other party, which often must be obtained for consideration and under penalty; and forward contracts are not traded in federally designated contract markets.

fundamental analysis — An approach to market behavior that stresses the study of underlying factors of supply and demand in the commodity, in the belief that such analysis will enable one to profit from being able to anticipate price trends. Contrast with *charting.*

futures contract — An agreement to make or take delivery of a standardized amount of

[6] *Commodity Trading Manual.* Chicago Board of Trade, 1977.

a commodity, of standardized minimum quality grades, during a specific month under terms and conditions established by the federally designated contract market upon which trading is conducted, at a price established in the trading pit.

hedging— The initiation of a position in a futures market that is intended as a temporary substitute for the sale or purchase of the actual commodity; the sale of futures contracts in anticipation of future sales of cash commodities as a protection against possible price declines, or the purchase of futures contracts in anticipation of future purchases of cash commodities as a protection against the possibility of increasing costs.

long— As a noun, one who has bought futures contracts and has not yet offset that position. As a verb (going long), the action of taking a position in which one has bought futures contracts (or the cash commodity) without taking the offsetting action. For example, if an investor had no position and bought five contracts, he would be a long. However, if his previous position was one of having sold five contracts (i.e., being short five), and he then bought five contracts to offset that position, the second action would not be referred to as going long because his position when the second action was concluded would be zero.

margin— An amount of money deposited by both buyers and sellers of futures contracts to ensure performance of the terms of the contract (the delivery or taking of delivery of the commodity or the cancelation of the position by a subsequent offsetting trade). Margin in commodities is not a payment of equity or down payment on the commodity itself but, rather, is a performance bond or security deposit.

margin call— A call from a clearinghouse to a clearing member, or from a brokerage firm to a customer, to bring margin deposits up to a required minimum level.

offset— The liquidation of a purchase of futures, or the covering of a short sale of futures contracts, through the purchase of an equal number of contracts of the same delivery month. Either action transfers the obligation to make or take delivery of the actual commodity to another principal.

open interest— The total number of futures contracts of a given commodity that have not yet been offset by opposite futures transactions nor fulfilled by delivery of the commodity; the total number of open transactions. Each open transaction has a buyer and a seller, but for calculation of open interest, only one side of the contract is counted.

original margin— Term applied to the initial deposit of margin money required of clearing-member firms by clearinghouse rules, or to the initial margin deposit required of customers by exchange regulations.

price limits— The maximum price advance or decline from the previous day's settlement price permitted for a contract in one trading session by the rules of the exchange.

short— As a noun, one who has sold futures contracts and has not yet offset that position. As a verb, the action of taking a position in which one has sold futures contracts (or made a forward contract for sale of the cash commodity) without taking the offsetting action. For example, if an investor had no position and sold five contracts, the action would be shorting the futures, and he would then be a short. However, if his previous position was one of having bought five contracts (i.e., being long five), and he then sold five contracts to offset that position, the second action would not be referred to as shorting, because his position when the second action was concluded would be zero.

speculator— In an economic sense, one who attempts to anticipate commodity price changes and to profit through the sale and purchase, or purchase and sale, of commodity futures contracts or of the physical commodity.

spreading— The purchase of one futures contract and sale of another, in the expectation that the price relationships between the two will change so that a subsequent offsetting sale and purchase will yield a net profit.

technical analysis— An approach to analysis of futures markets and future trends of commodity prices that examines the technical factors of market activity. Technical analysts normally examine patterns of price change, rates of change, and changes in volume of trading and open interest, often by charting, in the hope of being able to predict and profit from future trends.

TRADE ORGANIZATIONS

The CFTC has given approval to the formation of an industry-wide self-regulatory organization of all commodity futures merchants, advisers, and the like. To be called the National Futures Association (NFA), it will be similar to the National Association of Securities Dealers in that it will establish and enforce minimum standards for brokers and advisers to maintain. As of early 1982 the NFA has received approval of its charter, but has not yet started operations.

DIRECTORY OF LEADING DEALERS

Complete Commodity Directory, CFD, Oak Brook, Ill.

SUGGESTED READING

Periodical

Commodities Magazine. Published by Norwood Securities, Inc., Chicago, Ill. Monthly.

Reference Books

Chicago Board of Trade. *Commodity Trading Manual.* 1977.

Jiler, Harry, editor. *Guide to Commodity Price Forecasting.* New York: Commodity Research Bureau, 1967.

Gold, Gerald. *Modern Commodity Futures Trading.* 7th revised edition. New York: Commodity Research Bureau, 1975.

Gould, Bruce G. *The Dow Jones-Irwin Guide to Commodity Trading.* Revised edition. Homewood: Dow Jones-Irwin, 1981.

Hieronymus, T.A. *Economics of Futures Trading for Commercial and Personal Profits.* New York: Commodity Research Bureau, 1971.

Futures—Financial

*Thomas C. Coleman and Jeanne Cairns Sinquefield**

BASIC CHARACTERISTICS

Description and Definition

The term "financial futures," or "interest rate futures," describes future contracts based on financial instruments the price of which fluctuates with changes in interest rates. As with all futures contracts, financial futures represent a firm commitment to buy or sell a specific commodity or financial instrument during a specified month at a price established through open outcry in a central regulated marketplace.

Futures vs. cash contracts. Futures contracts are standardized. Unlike transactions in the cash market where coupon rate, maturity, issuer, price, quantity, and other information must be explicitly stated, buying or selling a futures contract is limited to one variable — price. Thus, futures contracts allow ease of quotation and trading. The contract terms themselves are subject to constant review and are revised as necessary to reflect changes in the marketplace.

Importance of delivery terms. The delivery process has a significant effect on the price at which futures contracts trade. The market trades with the knowledge that delivery can occur at contract maturity. However, few contracts — less than 3 percent of contracts traded — are settled by the buyer's receiving and the seller's making delivery of the actual instrument on which the contract is based. Depending upon the delivery specifications for a particular contract, the price may move differently from that of another contract that, on the surface, looks very similar. Almost all financial instrument futures contracts have a range of deliverable issues; the choice of which issue is actually delivered remains with the seller. The market tends to trade the issue that is cheapest for the seller to deliver. Thus, anyone participating in the financial futures market should have an understanding of the delivery procedure and its ramifications even though he may never take delivery.

For example, the Chicago Board of Trade (CBT) Treasury bond futures contract allows delivery of all Treasury bonds with fifteen or more years to maturity, or to call if callable. Currently, there are fifteen different Treasury

* Thomas C. Coleman is Vice-President and Director, and Jeanne Cairns Sinquefield is a Manager in the Department of Economic Analysis and Planning at the Chicago Board of Trade.

bonds with fifteen or more years to maturity or call. In a typical delivery month, five or six different bonds have been delivered.

Interest rate protection — a useful new commodity. Financial futures are based on the principle that interest rates — the cost of credit — can be viewed in the same way as the price of other commodities, and that certain kinds of institutions need a means of protecting themselves from volatile interest rates. Just as futures in soybeans or silver do, financial futures such as Treasury bond or Government National Mortgage Association (GNMA) futures represent a viable market for transferring the risk of price volatility.

Those who buy and sell on the financial futures markets can be classified as either hedgers, who want to minimize risk, or speculators, who are willing and able to assume risk.

Hedgers. Hedging is the initiation of a position in the futures market, intended as a temporary substitute for the sale or purchase of the actual commodity or financial instrument in the cash market. Hedging occurs when a money manager takes a position in the futures market equal and opposite to his cash market position. The objective is risk management.

Those who plan to make investments at a future date can protect themselves from falling interest rates by hedging through the purchase of futures. If the cash market price rises (yield declines), any increased expense will be counterbalanced, or offset, by an equivalent gain when the futures contracts are subsequently sold at a profit. (See the Treasury Bond hedging example in Figure 1 on page 278.)

Portfolio managers, bond dealers, and others who hold fixed income securities (such as bonds and notes) can protect their holdings from rising interest rates by hedging through the sale of futures. Since cash and futures markets tend to move in parallel, any loss caused by a declining cash market price will be offset by the gain received when futures contracts previously sold at high prices are offset at lower prices.

Speculators. Attitude toward risk separates the hedger from the speculator. The hedger uses the futures market as a means of protection against unpredictable and potentially damaging price changes. The speculator uses the futures market to assume price risk in pursuit of profit opportunity.

Speculators either buy or sell futures contracts, depending on their opinion about future price movement. A speculator will buy a contract when his forecast suggests an increase in price (decrease in interest rates), expecting later to make an offsetting sale at a higher price — and at a profit. A speculator will sell a contract when his forecast suggests a decrease in price (increase in interest rates), expecting later to make an offsetting purchase at a lower price — and at a profit.

Both speculators and hedgers are necessary for efficient functioning of the futures markets. Speculative buyers and sellers help to provide liquidity, allowing hedgers to buy and sell in large volume at minimum cost.

Types of Financial Futures Contracts

Few financial innovations have attracted as much attention in as short a time as financial futures have. The first interest rate futures contract, GNMA Collateralized Depositary Receipt (CDR) futures, was introduced in 1975 at the CBT. In their first full year of trading, GNMA futures contracts equivalent to $15 billion were traded at the CBT.

As of early 1982, financial futures contracts were offered in Treasury bonds

Background. On June 1, a pension fund manager is holding $1 million of 11.75 percent Treasury bonds due 2005-10. He plans to sell the bonds in September and is concerned that their value will decline if interest rates rise. The current market price for an 11.75 percent bond is 117-23 ($117\frac{23}{32}$) with a yield of 9.89 percent.

Objective. To protect his portfolio against a possible interest rate increase, he hedges his position in the financial futures market. Since he is long in the cash market, he hedges by going short — or selling — in the futures market. The variety of deliverable Treasury bond coupons and maturities is related by means of a conversion factor to the nominal 8 percent CBT coupon. Therefore, use of the appropriate conversion factor is the shorthand method for adjusting hedge amounts. For this particular period, a ratio of 1.4 bond futures contracts (corresponding to the 11.75 percent bond's CBT conversion factor of 1.3957) would have resulted in a more effective hedge. Therefore the fund manager sells fourteen September bond futures contracts ($100,000 per contract) at their current price of 83-06.

Outcome. By September 1, rising interest rates have reduced the price of 11.75 percent bonds to 104-12 (yielding 11.24 percent) and the price of September bond futures to 74-09.

Cash Market	Futures Market
June 1:	*June 1:*
Holds $1 million 11¾ percent bonds priced at 117-23.	Sells fourteen September bond futures contracts at 83-06
Market value: $1,177,187.50	Market value: $1,164,625.00
September 1:	*September 1:*
Sells $1 million 11¾ percent bonds at 104-12.	Buys fourteen September bond futures contracts at 74.09.
Market value: $1,043,750.00	Market value: $1,039,937.50
Loss: $133,437.50	Gain: $124,687.50

Result. The manager's weighted futures position offsets 93.4 percent of the cash market loss in the fund's 11.75 percent bonds.

FIG. 1. Illustrative Futures Transaction — Weighted Short Hedge

(T-bonds), ninety-day and one-year Treasury bills (T-bills), two-year and four-year Treasury notes (T-notes), three-month domestic certificates of deposit, currencies, GNMA, three-month Eurodollars, and Value Line Average Stock Indexes. Contracts pending government approval by the Commodity Futures Trading Commission (CFTC) included six- to ten-year T-notes (approved September 1981), six-month T-bills, twenty-five-year corporate bonds, and other stock index futures such as Standard & Poor's 500, and New York Stock Exchange Index.

A pilot program for options on futures was approved by the CFTC in 1981. Approval of specific contracts and trading should begin sometime in 1982. The exchanges each may trade one contract. Contracts submitted include options on T-bond futures, gold futures, domestic CD futures, ninety-day T-bill futures, and platinum futures.

The most successful financial futures contracts have been the GNMA-CDR and T-bond contracts offered by the CBT and the ninety-day T-bill contract offered by the Chicago Mercantile Exchange. The CBT's T-bond contract is currently the most actively traded futures contract in the United States and in the world; T-bills rank fifth, and GNMA-CDRs rank thirteenth. Table 1 on page 280 presents a history of the volume and open interest of these contracts. Other exchanges offering financial futures contracts in the United States are the Commodity Exchange Inc. and the New York Futures Exchange, both in New York, and the Mid-America Commodity Exchange, in Chicago.

ATTRACTIVE FEATURES

The basic economic functions of financial futures contracts are hedging and price discovery. Investors can use these markets for risk transfer or for profit opportunity. Attractive characteristics of these markets include leverage, contract integrity, and liquidity.

Leverage

Because margin requirements are relatively low for commodities, a trader can benefit from the price movement of a contract for a fraction of its full value. This feature, called "leverage," offers speculators the opportunity for returns that are relatively large compared with the amount of margin money they have committed. The speculator can benefit substantially from a small change in the value of a contract. Under adverse conditions, however, such leverage can lead to losses in excess of the margin committed. Low margins also make it economical and practical for hedgers to use futures markets to transfer risk. For example, the initial speculative margin on the CBT $100,000 T-bond futures contract is $2,000.

Understanding margins. While stock markets and futures markets both have margin requirements, there is a significant difference in the nature and purpose

TABLE 1. Historical Volume and Open Interest for Three Selected Financial Futures Contracts 1975-1981

	GNMA-CDR (CBT)[1]		*T-Bonds (CBT)*[2]		*T-Bills (IMM)*[3]	
Year	*Volume*	*Open Interest*	*Volume*	*Open Interest*	*Volume*	*Open Interest*
1975	20,125	1,325	N/A	N/A	N/A	N/A
1976	128,537	5,182	N/A	N/A	110,223	3,343
1977	422,421	20,719	32,101	2,864	321,703	17,194
1978	953,161	62,722	555,350	41,246	768,980	59,208
1979	1,371,078	88,982	2,059,594	90,676	1,930,482	36,495
1980	2,326,292	115,161	6,489,555	243,614	3,338,773	42,903
1981	2,292,882	77,246	13,907,988	221,680	5,631,290	30,069

[1] GNMA began trading on the Chicago Board of Trade on 10/20/75.
[2] T-bonds began trading on the Chicago Board of Trade on 8/22/77.
[3] T-bills began trading on the International Money Market 1/6/76.

SOURCE: Chicago Board of Trade

of these payments in the two markets. In the stock market, margin is a down payment on a loan to purchase securities, and an actual transfer of property rights occurs. The balance on the sale is financed with the borrowed funds.

In contrast, margins in futures markets act as a performance bond. Margin is placed on deposit by both parties to the transaction; it provides the funds that ensure contract performance and financial integrity.

Contract Integrity

In futures markets — unlike forward markets where parties to a transaction deal only with each other — all transactions are ultimately between clearing members and the clearinghouse. In this manner, the clearinghouse becomes a party to every trade; in effect, it becomes the buyer to every seller and the seller to every buyer. For those trading futures, this enhances market performance in several critical ways. It eliminates concern over the credit rating of the party on the other side of the transaction; it frees the original trading partners from delivery or offset from each other; and it provides maximum flexibility in deciding when and how to close out a position.

Clearinghouse responsibilities. Between the close of one day's business and the next day's market opening, the clearinghouse matches that day's trades, settles gains and losses on all transactions, monitors margin calls on all open positions, and matches those buyers and sellers who intend to make or take delivery.

Unlike the responsibility of the clearinghouse of a stock exchange or a bank, the responsibility of the clearinghouse of a futures exchange does not end with reconciling and clearing the traders' transactions. By interposing itself as a party to every trade, it also guarantees financial performance from clearing member to clearing member. Any transaction of a futures exchange must be made through a member of that exchange. Any member who trades futures and is not a member of the clearinghouse must clear and settle his trades through a clearing member.

Source of guarantee. The guarantee of contract integrity comes primarily from the daily margins on deposit, as well as from the clearing members. The members of the clearinghouse — individuals and firms that are also members of the exchange — provide the financial integrity that guarantees performance on every contract traded at the exchange. Since the formation of the Board of Trade Clearing Corporation in 1925, there has never been a financial loss due to default on a CBT futures contract.

Liquidity

Several factors make for a successful futures market. Among them is a strong interaction between the cash and the futures markets, with high levels of liquidity that make it possible for participants to enter and exit from their positions with ease. Currently, there are three very successful financial futures contracts: T-bonds, GNMA-CDRs, and T-bills. By the end of 1981, for example, trading volume in T-bonds averaged 55,600 contracts per day, representing roughly $5.6 billion of face value in government securities daily, while open interest totaled more than 221,000 contracts. Open interest is the total of outstanding futures positions, one side only, at the end of trading.

POTENTIAL RISKS

Like other financial markets, financial futures markets entail market or price risk. For a hedger, this price risk can be reduced to basis risk, where basis is the difference between the cash price and the futures price. Unlike most other financial markets, futures market gains and losses are settled on a daily basis. Investors must meet any daily margin calls or their futures positions are closed out.

Market or Price Risk

Interest rate volatility has become a major factor in our economic life. For the performance-minded trader, speculating in the financial futures market offers the possibility of attractive returns. Before entering into any speculative trades in financial futures, however, traders should carefully assess their financial capacity to withstand risk. Experienced speculators recommend that only a small proportion of an individual's capital should be risked on a single trade. Also, traders should limit their open positions to as many as they can adequately follow, while keeping some capital in reserve for additional opportunities or margin requirements. Because market conditions can and do change rapidly, it is essential that traders maintain flexibility.

Basis Risk

Cash and futures prices tend to move in the same direction, in a roughly parallel pattern. The arithmetic difference between them (the cash price minus the futures price) is called the "basis." Changes in the basis tend to be more stable than either cash or futures price movements. Understanding basis relationships is the key to placing and lifting effective hedges.

Prices for cash and futures move in parallel because both are influenced by the same economic conditions, the possibility of delivery exists in the futures market, and market participants engage in cash/futures arbitrage.

Basis can be positive or negative, depending on whether the cash price is higher or lower than the futures price. In financial instruments, contract prices for delivery in distant futures months usually have been priced lower than those for nearby futures months, and prices for financial futures normally have been lower than cash prices, reflecting a positive cost of carry. The term "cost of carry" refers to the net financial costs (coupon income minus financing costs, i.e., short-term interest rates). Cost of carry can be represented by a positive or negative number.

Effect of changes in basis. Changes in the basis can influence the final result of a hedging transaction. Whether the basis strengthens or weakens has an influence on the hedge's overall profit or loss. The basis strengthens, or becomes more positive, when futures prices decline faster than cash prices, or when cash prices rise faster than futures prices. (A short hedge always benefits from a strengthening basis.) Conversely, the basis weakens, or becomes more negative, when futures prices increase faster than cash prices, or when cash prices fall faster than futures prices. (A long hedge always benefits from a weakening basis.)

For example, in the weighted short hedge illustrated in Figure 1 on page 278, the manager's loss was not completely offset because the basis weakened during his hedge — from 34-17 (117-23 minus 83-06) on June 1 to 30-03 (104-12 minus 74-09) on September 1 — causing some loss in effectiveness.

Margin Calls

Because either buyer or seller could lose money on a subsequent offsetting trade, both sides post margin. As the price changes, each side's account is marked to the market — debited or credited to reflect the most recent settlement price. When the account falls below a prescribed maintenance level, additional margin must be deposited to maintain the position. Additional margin can also be called for when the price volatility of a commodity warrants it.

Margin calls that are not met will result in an investor's futures position being closed out. Therefore, sufficient funds should be available to meet margin calls if investors want to maintain their futures positions. The closing of futures positions will result in a hedger moving from a hedged to an unhedged position. If prices then move in the opposite direction, losses for hedgers could result from both their futures positions and their cash positions.

TAX CONSEQUENCES [1]

The following section discusses the basic features of tax legislation as of the fall of 1981 as it affects futures trading. In many areas, however, the new tax language is ambiguous and will have to be resolved by IRS regulation and rulings. Specific applications of the Economic Recovery Tax Act of 1981 should be discussed with the taxpayer's personal tax adviser.

Mark to Market for Futures

Tax legislation enacted in 1981 requires that all futures positions on U.S. exchanges be marked to market upon the closing of every transaction and at the taxpayer's year end. This means that all realized and unrealized appreciation and depreciation in value occurring during a taxable year will be taken into account

[1] This section is based, with permission, on a paper entitled "House-Senate Tax Conference Agreement on Straddles" prepared by Fred Hickman, 1981.

for tax purposes. It will no longer be possible to realize losses while deferring gains. The mark-to-market rule applies to outright positions as well as to straddles, in which investors buy one futures contract and sell another.

Tax rate for mark to market. All capital gains and losses on futures contracts are to be treated as 60 percent long term, 40 percent short term. This formula translates into a maximum blended tax rate of 32 percent.

Cash and Carry

A taxpayer must capitalize interest and other carrying costs allocable to property that is part of a straddle. Therefore, such costs have to be added to the basis of physicals held as part of a cash-and-carry transaction, to be recovered only through a reduction in the capital gain (or increase in the capital loss) upon disposition of the physical.

Commercial Hedges

Broad rules exempt identified inventory and commercial hedges from the mark-to-market rules for futures, the straddle rules for off-exchange transactions, and the capitalization rule for cash-and-carry transactions. Positions covered by this exemption must produce ordinary income or loss.

REPRESENTATIVE TYPES OF INVESTORS

Futures markets can be used for both risk transference and profit opportunity. Many types of institutions use financial futures to reduce their exposure to interest rate risks. They include banks, bond dealers, pension funds, investment bankers, money managers, savings and loan associations, portfolio managers, financial executives, trust funds, insurance companies, mortgage bankers, corporate treasurers, and state and local governments. Those using financial futures for profit opportunity include arbitrageurs and speculators.

IMPORTANT FACTORS IN BUYING AND SELLING

Futures exchanges are regulated by the CFTC. All new futures contracts must receive prior approval from the CFTC, as must certain changes in rules and regulations. Only members of the exchanges who are subject to the rules and regulations of the exchanges and of the CFTC may execute trades on the floor of the exchange. Members can be either commission brokers, who execute trades for nonmember customers and for other members, or locals, who trade for themselves.

Commission firms, or brokerage firms, are the link between the broker and the customer. Such firms range in size from international investment firms, which are active in both commodities and securities markets, to one-person operations. These firms employ registered commodity representatives (RCRs), also known as account executives, to handle customer accounts. Both the commission firm and the RCR must be registered with the CFTC. RCRs serve their customers by placing orders, handling margin money, providing basic accounting records, and counseling customers on their trading programs.

TRADING PROCEDURES AND CUSTODY

As mentioned earlier, all futures transactions are guaranteed by the clearinghouses of futures exchanges. Margins provide the funds that ensure contract performance and financial integrity. Throughout the trading session, traders turn over endorsed orders for their completed trades to their clearing firms, which are members of the clearinghouse. The clearinghouse settles the account of each member firm at the end of each trading day, precisely matching each day's purchases and sales, and collecting all losses and paying all profits. As a party to every trade, the clearinghouse guarantees the opposite side of the transaction on the exchange while the position remains open. However, it does not guarantee that every entity possessing a federal license to handle customer money will properly and fully safeguard customer funds.

All financial futures contracts, with one exception, allow for delivery of the actual physical commodity. For example, the T-bond contract delivery procedure results in wire transfers of actual U.S. Treasury bonds. The exception is the GNMA-CDR futures contract. In this contract, a CDR backed by actual GNMAs is delivered. At the holder's option, the receipt can be surrendered to obtain the underlying GNMAs, redelivered on the futures market, or sold. The GNMAs that back the CDR are held at an approved depositary. Only approved originators can generate such receipts through the depositaries; they are also responsible for maintaining sufficient equivalent principal balances of GNMAs.

GLOSSARY

cash market— A market in which transactions for the immediate sale and purchase of the physical commodity or financial instruments are made under terms agreeable to both buyer and seller.

contract month— The month in which a futures contract may be fulfilled by making or taking delivery. Most interest rate futures contracts are liquidated prior to the contract month.

cross hedge— Hedging a cash market risk in one financial instrument by initiating a position in a futures contract for a different but related instrument. A cross hedge is based on the premise that while the two instruments are not the same, their price movements correlate.

daily price limit— The maximum advance or decline from the previous day's settlement permitted for a contract in one trading session. This limit is set by the exchange.

forward contract— An agreement to buy or sell goods at a set price and date. Those who use forward contracts expect to make or take physical delivery of the merchandise or financial instrument. Each contract is tailored specifically to the needs of buyer and seller. Trading is generally done by phone in a decentralized marketplace.

futures contract— Firm commitment to make or take delivery of a standardized quantity and quality of commodity or financial instrument during a specified month in the future under terms designated at the exchange where the contract is traded.

long hedge— The purchase of a futures contract or contracts in anticipation of actual purchases in the cash market. Often used to lock in a cost (favorable yield).

margin— Money deposited by both buyers and sellers of futures contracts to ensure performance of the terms of the contract (making or taking delivery). Margin in the futures market is not a down payment on equity; it is a performance bond or security deposit for an executory contract.

mark to market— The debits and credits assigned to each account after the close of every trading session. Each day all market losses are collected and all gains disbursed.

open interest— The contracts that have not yet been offset by opposite transactions in the futures market or fulfilled by delivery. Although each transaction has a buyer and a seller, the calculation of open interest reflects only one side of every trade.

physical— The underlying physical commodity in a futures transaction.

short hedge— The sale of a futures contract or contracts to eliminate or reduce the possible decline in the value of an asset.

spreading— Taking opposite positions in two futures contracts with the objective of profiting through changes in relative price relationships.

volume— The number of transactions occurring on any given day.

TRADE ORGANIZATIONS

The American Association of Commodity Traders, Concord, N.H.

Financial Futures Society, Northwestern University, Evanston, Ill.

Futures Industry Association Inc., Washington, D.C.

International Financial Futures Association, Chicago, Ill.

National Association of Futures Trading Advisors, Chicago, Ill.

DIRECTORY OF LEADING DEALERS

Complete Commodity Futures Directory, CFFD, Oak Brook, Ill.

SUGGESTED READING

Periodicals

American Banker. Published by American Banker, Inc., New York, N.Y. Daily.

Commodities. Published by Commodities Magazine Inc., Cedar Falls, Iowa. Monthly.

Financial Analyst Journal. Published by Financial Analyst Federation, New York, N.Y. Monthly.

Institutional Investor. Published by Institutional Investor Inc., New York, N.Y. Monthly.

Journal of the Futures Markets. Published by John Wiley & Sons, New York, N.Y. Quarterly.

Pensions and Investment Age. Published by Crain Communications, Inc., Chicago, Ill. Biweekly.

Reference Books

Arthur Andersen & Co. *Interest Rate Futures Contracts — Accounting and Control Techniques for Banks.* Chicago: Chicago Board of Trade and Chicago Mercantile Exchange, 1980.

Chicago Board of Trade. *An Introduction to Financial Futures.* Chicago, 1980.

———. *A Pension Fund Managers Guide to Financial Futures.* Chicago, 1982 (in press).

———. *Financial Instruments Markets: Cash & Futures Relationships.* Chicago, 1980.

Hieronymous, Thomas A. *Economics of Futures Trading.* New York: Commodities Research Bureau, 1977.

Powers, Mark J., and Vogel, David J. *Inside the Financial Futures Markets.* New York: John Wiley & Sons, 1981.

Schwarz, Edward W. *How to Use Interest Rate Futures.* Homewood: Dow Jones-Irwin, 1979.

Stigum, Marcia, and Mann, John. *Money Market Calculations: Yields, Break-evens, and Arbitrage.* Homewood: Dow Jones-Irwin, 1981.

Weberman, Ben. *Interest Rate Futures: Profits and Pitfalls.* New York: Ben Weberman, 1980.

Note: Care has been taken in the preparation of this article but there is no warranty or representation expressed or implied by the Chicago Board of Trade or its member firms as to the accuracy or completeness of the material herein. The opinions expressed in this article should not be considered a recommendation or endorsement by the Chicago Board of Trade.

Futures—Metals *

Thomas C. Coleman and June M. Butler **

BASIC CHARACTERISTICS

Futures were originally developed in the middle 1800s, in grains, as a means to find protection from the risk of price changes. Price volatility is characteristic of many basic commodities, including metals, and through the years futures have been developed for many non-agricultural commodities, including such metals as gold, silver, platinum, palladium, tin, copper, aluminum, nickel, and zinc.

A metal futures contract is a firm commitment to make or accept delivery of a certain quantity and quality of a metal during a designated month in the future at a price determined through open bidding in a central exchange. A person can buy or sell a contract for any of the designated delivery months currently being traded on an exchange. For example, a person buying a December gold contract at $414 per troy ounce is obligated to accept delivery of 100 troy ounces of gold during the month of December at a price of $414 per troy ounce. Buying a contract is referred to as "taking a long position" and selling a contract is termed "taking a short position."

Futures Contracts

Futures markets are different from other markets. Unlike transactions in cash markets, where contracts are designed to meet the individual needs of the contracting parties, futures contracts are based on standardized terms. The contract size, quality, and delivery requirements are fixed and explicitly stated. The only thing that is not stated in the contract is price, which is determined in the marketplace.

All transactions — including those orders from the public — are executed in a central location via an open outcry competitive auction. This provides an informational advantage. Every bid by a buyer is known to every seller, and every offer by a seller is known to every buyer. Everyone knows the price at that moment. Since the market participants are in the same location (the trading pit), this competition should result in a better price — a narrower bid-ask spread — than may occur in a decentralized market in which many prices can be in effect at any given moment.

Delivery terms directly affect futures prices. Although very few contracts are

* See also article on Metals — Gold, Silver and Platinum, elsewhere in this volume.

** Thomas C. Coleman is Vice-President and Director, and June M. Butler is an advisory economist in the Department of Economic Analysis and Planning at the Chicago Board of Trade.

settled by delivery of the commodity upon which the contract is based, this is always a possibility. At any time before the month the contract matures, the buyer or seller may close out his obligation through an equal but offsetting trade in the same delivery month. The difference between the price at which the trade is initiated and the price at which it is offset, less transaction costs, is profit. For example, the purchase of a December silver contract resulting in a long position may be liquidated by selling a December contract (for the same year) any time before the calendar month of December. This is different from a forward contract where delivery is intended. Although the vast majority of contracts are settled by offset, the fact that sellers and buyers have the option of making the offset or taking delivery of the metal is an important and, indeed, essential facet of futures trading. The possibility that delivery can take place assures that future prices will be related to the actual cash value of the commodity.

Since a futures price is just that — a price for future delivery — buyers and sellers must take into account the cost of storage and other expenses such as financing costs and insurance. These expenses are usually lumped together and called "carrying charges." In consideration of carrying charges, metal prices for future delivery are normally higher than prices for immediate delivery. There is an exception in times of shortage when buyers in urgent need of a product immediately may be willing to pay a higher price.

Metals Futures Exchanges

During 1981 metal futures trading accounted for 17.3 percent of the total futures contracts traded in the United States. Metals trading began in the United States in 1933 when trading in silver futures began on the Commodity Exchange Inc. Trading was suspended in 1934 because of the Silver Purchase Act, which authorized the Treasury to purchase silver until the price rose to $1.2929 or until the value of the U.S. silver stock equaled one-third of the value of U.S. gold stock. The Treasury's price for newly mined silver was much higher than the prevailing market price and users were forced to purchase silver abroad. Silver futures trading resumed in 1963 and now takes place on three U.S. exchanges: the Chicago Board of Trade, Commodity Exchange, and Mid-America Commodity Exchange.

The New York Mercantile Exchange began trading platinum in 1956 and palladium in 1968. Gold futures began trading in the United States on December 31, 1974, when it became legal for Americans to own gold. It is traded at the Commodity Exchange Inc. of New York, the International Monetary Market of the Chicago Mercantile Exchange, the Chicago Board of Trade, and the Mid-America Commodity Exchange. Abroad, gold is traded on the Hong Kong Commodity Exchange, the Gold Exchange of Singapore, the Sydney Futures Exchange, the Tokyo Gold Exchange, and the Winnipeg Commodity Exchange.

Copper and zinc are the only base metal futures contracts that are traded in the United States; both are traded at the Commodity Exchange of New York.

Aluminum, copper, nickel, silver, tin, and zinc are traded on the London Metals Exchange.

In late 1981, there were four gold coins futures contracts awaiting approval from the Commodity Futures Trading Commission (CFTC). A pilot program for options on futures was approved by the CFTC in 1981. Approval of specific contracts and trading should occur in 1982, with each exchange allowed to trade one option contract. In the spring of 1982 the CFTC was considering options on gold and platinum futures.

Futures Markets

A futures market is a public marketplace where members may place direct orders and nonmembers may place orders through members. Hedgers use the futures markets to protect themselves against unfavorable price swings; speculators buy or sell in the hopes of making a profit.

Hedgers. The basic principle underlying hedging is that cash market prices and futures prices tend to move in a predictable relation to each other and generally tend to move higher or lower in an approximately parallel fashion.

A firm that would be hurt by declining price, perhaps because it owns a large inventory of silver, takes a position in the futures market that enables it to benefit from declining prices — by selling a silver futures contract that can be bought back later at a lower price. If silver prices decline, the gain in the futures market roughly equals the decline in the market value of the silver inventory. Cash prices and futures prices tend to move up and down together in response to varying market conditions, although they do not fluctuate by precisely equal amounts.

Often a refiner-fabricator will hold inventories of silver in many forms: wire, bars, sheet, powders, foil, and so forth. The refiner's cost is established at the time of purchase. His objective is to further fabricate the silver and sell the products at prices that will cover the costs of purchase, of storing and protecting the silver, and of fabrication, plus a reasonable profit. The use of silver futures makes it possible for the refiner to establish a price at which he will sell silver in the future, to protect the value of his inventory.

Illustrative example. Assume that on March 20 a refiner-fabricator has purchased 6,000 ounces of silver at $13.16 per troy ounce. He faces the risk that silver prices will decline before he is able to turn over his inventory. His business is highly competitive and the products he sells must be priced close to prevailing cash market prices at the time of sale.

On March 20, when the refiner purchases 6,000 ounces of silver at $13.16/ounce, he finds that the August futures contract is trading at $14.13/ounce. He instructs his broker to sell six August 1,000-ounce futures at the market. Later the order is confirmed, filled at $14.13/ounce.

During the interim period, the price of silver weakens because of high interest rates and a decrease in the rate of inflation. On July 2, the refiner is requested to quote a price on a sale involving the 6,000 ounces of silver acquired in March. The current price is $8.40/ounce and the August futures is trading for $8.48/ounce. He quotes a firm price of $8.60/ounce to the customer and informs the broker to lift his hedge at $8.48. The refiner sells the silver at $4.56 per ounce less than he paid for it, a loss of $27,360 on an inventory of 6,000 ounces. However, because cash and futures prices have both declined, the hedge protected him from the loss, as shown below.

Cash	Futures
March 20: Buy 6,000 ounces of silver at $13.16 per troy ounce	*March 20:* Sell six August 1,000-ounce silver at $14.13 per troy ounce
July 2: Sell 6,000 ounces of silver at $8.60 per troy ounce	*July 2:* Buy six August silver at $8.48 per troy ounce
Loss: $4.56 per troy ounce	Gain: $5.65 per troy ounce

Net result: $1.09/troy ounce profit

Speculators. The speculator's trades reflect his judgment about future price movement. He will buy a contract in anticipation of a price increase, expecting to profit with an offsetting sale at a higher price. Conversely, he sells in expectation of a price decrease, intending to make a later purchase at a lower price and resulting profit.

The presence in the market of both speculators and hedgers helps to assure efficiency, with speculators providing liquidity and permitting hedgers to trade in large volume at minimum cost.

ATTRACTIVE FEATURES

Leverage, contract integrity, and liquidity are some of the attractive characteristics of metal futures.

Leverage

Relatively little capital — usually 5 to 15 percent of the total value of the contract — gives the trader the benefit of the price movement on the full contract. This leverage permits speculators to receive possible returns that are large compared with the amount of margin money committed.

For example, an investor may decide to purchase 100 ounces of gold for June delivery at $450 per troy ounce. If he deposits with a commodity broker a minimum of $2,500 (margin) to assure his performance under the contract, a purchase is made for his account. A 5 percent increase in the price of gold (to $472.50) per contract means a profit of 90 percent on the investor's deposit. The same profit can be realized if the trader has sold short and the price decreases by 5 percent. This ability to invest in metals without tying up the total value of the metal means that the investor has the flexibility to put the rest of his money to use elsewhere. Of course, if the price moves adversely, the leverage will work against the trader, long or short, and may lead to losses in excess of the margin committed. Low margins also make it economical and practical for hedgers to use futures markets to transfer risk.

Futures vs. equity margins. Certain important distinctions should be noted between the functions of margins in the stock markets and the futures markets. In the case of equities purchases, the buyer is in effect making a down payment on the purchase; in the case of futures, the buyer's margin serves as a sort of performance bond. Paid by both parties to the transaction, the futures margin helps to ensure that the buyer will buy and the seller will sell at the contract price.

Contract Integrity

The integrity of a futures market hinges on the integrity of the contracts. The contract terms themselves are subject to constant review and are revised as necessary to reflect changes in the marketplace.

Role of the clearinghouse. The futures exchange clearinghouse provides clearing services and assures the financial integrity of all futures contracts. The clearinghouse becomes the contractual party to each transaction, that is, the buyer to every seller and the seller to every buyer. By severing the direct relationship between the original buyer and seller, the system eliminates counter-party risk (the risk of default by a particular buyer or seller with whom the contract was made) and provides a way to offset transactions. This gives maximum flexibility to market participants in deciding when and how to close out a position. This system differs from the cash market where if unanticipated circumstances prevent one of the parties from fulfilling part of the contract, that party must liquidate the contract with the original trading partner.

Between the close of one day's business and the next day's market opening, the clearinghouse matches that day's trades, settles gains and losses on all transactions, monitors margin calls on all open positions, and matches those buyers and sellers who intend to make or take delivery.

The clearing process is as follows: Clearing members give the clearinghouse information for clearing such as the commodity, the quantity, the delivery month, and the identity of the buyer and seller. The clearinghouse then matches all purchases to the corresponding sale. Each clearing member receives a listing of its own and customer positions and an amount to pay to or to collect from the clearinghouse for each commodity and delivery month. The pay and collect amounts are combined and the difference is indicated. The clearing member pays or collects this amount.

The clearinghouse of the futures exchange, in addition to reconciling and clearing transactions, makes itself a party to every trade. It settles gains and losses directly with its clearing members — individuals and firms — and these in turn settle with any members of the exchange who are not clearing members. Thus, there is a guarantee of performance on each contract traded.

Liquidity

The strong interaction between the cash and the futures markets and the high levels of liquidity provided make it possible for participants to enter and exit from their positions with ease. Currently, there are very popular futures contracts in gold, silver, and copper. By the end of 1981, for example, trading volume in gold on all exchanges was over 50,000 contracts per day, while open interest totaled more than 200,000 contracts. Open interest is the total number of futures contracts of a given commodity that have not yet been offset by opposite futures transactions nor fulfilled by delivery of the commodity or the total number of open transactions. Each open transaction has a buyer and a seller, but for calculation of open interest, only one side of the contract is counted.

POTENTIAL RISKS

Metal futures markets entail market or price risk for speculators, basis risk for hedgers, and cash-flow risks for all market participants.

Price Risk

Metal prices are volatile and thus futures offer the possibility of attractive returns. Speculators should assess their financial capability to withstand the price risk before entering into any speculative futures trades. Experienced speculators recommend that only a small proportion of an individual's capital should be risked on a single trade. It is important not to make more open commitments than can be carefully followed, and the investor should maintain the financial flexibility to meet new opportunities or margin requirements.

Quite often, profitability is not dependent on being right or wrong on the long-term direction of price, but on developing a trading system to maximize profits and minimize losses.

Success in speculating can be enhanced by the appropriate use of stop-loss orders. These are used to limit losses or to protect profits. Their protection is approximate because neither a stop order to buy nor a stop order to sell guarantees that the position will be liquidated precisely at the stop price. If the stop orders are placed too close to the current market price, they may be activated quickly in a volatile market. Then the position may be liquidated on what may be only a temporary trend.

Basis Risk

For a hedger, this price risk is reduced to basis risk. The fundamental assumption of hedging is that futures prices and cash prices tend to move in the same direction or in a predictable pattern. It is because of this tandem movement that an equal or opposite position in the futures market can be considered a hedge on a given position in the cash market. The difference between the cash price and the futures price is called "basis." The risk of basis change is less than the risk of change in cash price. Basis can be positive or negative depending upon whether the cash price is higher or lower than the futures price.

When the basis becomes increasingly more positive (or less and less negative), it is strengthened. This happens when futures prices decline more than cash prices or when cash prices rise more than futures prices. A short hedge always benefits from a strengthened basis.

In the previous example of a short hedge in silver, the hedge was placed when the cash price was $13.16 per troy ounce and the futures price was $14.13 per troy ounce, a basis of −$0.97. When the hedge was lifted, the cash price was $8.60 per troy ounce and the futures price was $8.48, a basis of +$0.12. The futures price fell more than the cash price (the futures price fell by $5.65 and the cash price by $4.56) and thus the basis was strengthened. This meant that the refiner's gain on the futures exceeded the loss on the cash transaction. If the cash price had declined more than the futures price, the hedge would not have covered the entire loss on the cash transaction and the refiner would have experienced a cut in profits. However, in the example even this imperfect hedge would have been preferable to not hedging at all. Prices moving in opposite directions could result in losses for hedgers, from both their futures positions and their cash positions. Prior to hedging, it must be determined whether the market price risk is greater than the basis risk.

Cash-Flow Risk

Either party to the futures transaction can lose on a later offsetting trade; hence the requirement that both sides post margin. All participants in futures face the risk of margin calls. As the price changes, each side's account is marked to the market, debited or credited to reflect the most recent settlement price when the account falls below a prescribed maintenance level. Additional margin may also be called for when the price volatility of a commodity increases. Meeting margin calls can affect cash flow.

If a call for more margin is not met, this will result in the closing out of an investor's futures position. Therefore, sufficient funds should be available to meet margin calls if investors want to maintain their futures position. However, just as margin calls for additional funds are made to an investor when prices move against his position, the investor may call on his broker for a withdrawal against the account when the price moves in his favor.

TAX CONSEQUENCES [1]

The language of the Economic Recovery Tax Act of 1981 is ambiguous and will have to be resolved by IRS regulation and rulings. Specific applications of

[1] This section is based, with permission, on a paper entitled "House-Senate Tax Conference Agreement on Straddles," prepared by Fred Hickman, 1981.

the new Act to futures trading should be discussed with the taxpayer's personal tax adviser.

Mark-to-Market Treatment

The tax legislation enacted in 1981 required that all futures positions on U.S. exchanges be marked to market upon the closing of every transaction and at the taxpayer's year end. This means that all realized and unrealized appreciation and depreciation in value occurring during a taxable year will be taken into account for tax purposes. It will no longer be possible to realize losses while deferring gains. The mark-to-market rule applies to outright positions as well as to straddles, where an investor buys one futures contract and sells another.

Tax Rate for Mark-to-Market

All capital gains and losses on futures contracts will be treated as 60 percent long term, 40 percent short term. This formula translates into a maximum blended tax rate of 32 percent.

Cash and Carry

A taxpayer will have to capitalize interest and other carrying costs allocable to property that is a part of a straddle. Therefore, such costs will have to be added to the basis of physicals held as part of a cash-and-carry transaction to be recovered only through a reduction in the capital gain (or increase in the capital loss) upon disposition of the physical.

Commercial Hedges

Broad rules will exempt identified inventory and commercial hedges from the mark-to-market rules for futures, the straddle rules for off-exchange transactions, and the capitalization rule for cash-and-carry transactions. Positions covered by this exemption will have to produce ordinary income or loss.

REPRESENTATIVE TYPES OF INVESTORS

Futures markets are used for risk transference and profit opportunity. Hedgers using metal futures to reduce their exposure to price risks include producers, smelters-refiners, fabricators, distributors, chemical firms, importers-exporters, electroplators, jewelry manufacturers, and pharmaceuticals firms. Those using metal futures for profit opportunity include speculators and arbitrageurs.

IMPORTANT FACTORS IN BUYING AND SELLING

Futures exchanges are regulated by the CFTC. All new futures contracts must receive prior approval from the CFTC, as must certain changes in rules and regulations. Only members of an exchange who are subject to the rules and regulations of the exchange and the CFTC may execute trades on the floor of the exchange. Members can be either commission brokers, who execute trades for nonmember customers and for other members, or locals, who trade for themselves.

Commission and Brokerage Firms

Most commission and brokerage firms employ registered commodity representatives (RCRs) who handle client accounts. Both the commission firm and the RCR must be registered with the CFTC. RCRs serve their customers by placing orders, handling margin money, providing basic accounting records, and counseling customers on their trading programs.

Each exchange sets minimum margin requirements. The brokerage firms determine how much margin each customer should deposit. For example, a customer wanting to sell a gold futures contract (i.e., 100 troy ounces of gold) may have an initial margin of $2,500 and a maintenance margin of $1,000 per contract.

Price Determination

Throughout history, precious metals have been considered a store of value, and many were used to give value to paper currencies. Although the metals have been demonetized, they are still held as stores of value to enable their holders to protect and preserve purchasing power. Investors purchase precious metals because of an expectation of substantial price appreciation or as insurance to preserve real asset value. Over the years many industrial uses for precious metals have developed.

The expectations concerning whether or not a metal is overvalued, the cost and availability of funds to finance holdings, rates of return on money market assets, and political and economic events all influence the investment demand for metals. When trading metal futures, speculators must consider the supply, the industrial demand, as well as the investment demand to hold metal.

CUSTODIAL CARE

Futures do not carry the problems of handling and storing the actual metal. The market offers enough liquidity so that the speculator can make an offsetting purchase or sale and need never take or make delivery of the actual metal.

However, delivery can occur at the option of the seller during the delivery month. Delivery is usually made by receipts that are issued by authorized depositaries or warehouses. These receipts are negotiable bearer documents and are readily acceptable as collateral. Receipt holders must pay storage fees to the issuing depositary.

There are quality assurances that the metals meet the contract specification.

For precious metal futures, the metal must come from an approved source and be brought to the depositary by bonded carrier. If the holder wishes to take the metal out of depositary (to a non-approved source, e.g., his home), he must realize that metal cannot be placed back in the depositary without assaying, or possibly obtaining other certification.

GLOSSARY

basis— The difference between a cash price and the price of a particular futures contract.

cash market— A market in which transactions for the immediate sale and purchase of the physical commodity are made under terms agreeable to both buyer and seller.

contract month— The month in which a futures contract may be fulfilled by making or taking delivery. Most interest rate futures contracts are liquidated prior to the contract month.

cross hedge— Hedging a cash market risk in one commodity by initiating a position in a futures contract for a different but related instrument. A cross hedge is based on the premise that while the two instruments are not the same, their price movements correlate.

daily price limit— The maximum advance or decline from the previous day's settlement permitted for a contract in one trading session. This limit is set by the exchange.

forward contract— An agreement to buy or sell goods at a set price and date. Those who use forward contracts expect to make or take physical delivery of the commodity. Each contract is tailored specifically to the needs of buyer and seller. Trading is generally done by phone in a decentralized marketplace.

futures contract — Firm commitment to make or take delivery of a standardized quantity and quality of commodity during a specified month in the future under terms designated at the exchange where the contract is traded.

long hedge— The purchase of a futures contract or contracts in anticipation of actual purchases in the cash market. Often used to lock in a cost.

margin— Money deposited by both buyers and sellers of futures contracts to ensure performance of the terms of the contract (making or taking delivery). Margin in the futures market is not a down payment on equity — it is a performance bond or security deposit for an executory contract.

market order— Order in which the customer states how many contracts of a given delivery option he wishes to buy or sell. The price is not specified. Market orders are used when the customer wants the order placed as soon as possible at the best possible price.

mark to market— The debits and credits assigned to each account after the close of every trading session. All market losses are collected and all gains disbursed each day.

open interest— The contracts that have not yet been offset by opposite transactions in the futures market or fulfilled by delivery. Although each transaction has a buyer and a seller, the calculation of open interest reflects only one side of every trade.

physical— The underlying physical commodity in a futures transaction.

short hedge— The sale of a futures contract or contracts to eliminate or reduce the possible decline in the value of an asset.

spreading— Taking opposite positions in two futures contracts with the objective of profiting through changes in relative price relationships.

stop order— This order becomes a market order when a given price level is reached. A stop order to buy becomes a market order when the commodity sells (or is bid) at or above the specified price. A stop order to sell becomes a market order when the commodity sells (or is offered) at or below the stop price.

volume— The number of transactions occurring on any given day.

TRADE ORGANIZATIONS

The American Association of Commodity Traders, Concord, N.H.

The Futures Industry Association, Washington, D.C.

The Gold Institute, Washington, D.C.

International Precious Metals Institute, Brooklyn, N.Y.

National Association of Futures Trading Advisors, Chicago, Ill.

Silver Institute, Inc., Washington, D.C.

Silver Users Association, Washington, D.C.

DIRECTORY OF LEADING DEALERS

Complete Commodity Futures Directory. CCFD, Oak Brook, Ill.

SUGGESTED READING

Periodicals

American Metal Market. Published by Fairchild Publications, New York, N.Y. Daily.

Commodities. Published by Commodities Magazine, Cedar Falls, Iowa. Monthly.

The Gold News. Published by the Gold Institute, Washington, D.C. Monthly.

Journal of the Futures Markets. Published by John Wiley and Sons, New York, N.Y. Quarterly.

Metals Week. Published by McGraw-Hill, New York, N.Y. Weekly.

Mineral Industry Series. Published by the Department of the Interior, Washington, D.C. Monthly. (Gold, silver, copper, and platinum.)

Minerals Yearbook. Published by the U.S. Government Printing Office, Washington, D.C. Annual.

Mining Annual Review. Published by the Mining Journal, London, England. Annually.

The Silver Institute Letter. Published by the Silver Institute, Washington, D.C. Monthly.

Reference Books

American Bureau of Metal Statistics, Inc. *Non-Ferrous Metal Data.* New York, 1981.

Chicago Board of Trade. *Trading in Gold Futures.* Chicago, 1979, revised 1980.

Hieronymous, Thomas A. *Economics of Futures Trading.* New York: Commodities Research Bureau, 1977.

Note: Care has been taken in the preparation of this article but there is no warranty or representation expressed or implied by the Chicago Board of Trade or its member firms as to the accuracy or completeness of the material herein. The opinions expressed in this article should not be considered a recommendation or endorsement by the Chicago Board of Trade.

Gemstones

*Benjamin Zucker**

BASIC CHARACTERISTICS

Emeralds, rubies, sapphires, and diamonds are among the oldest economic investment vehicles. Kings, noblemen, Renaissance princesses, twentieth-century political refugees, and harried Middle Eastern tycoons all have found gems to be a source of real wealth and a hedge against future political and economic uncertainties.

Diamonds and colored stones (rubies, sapphires, and emeralds) are very much a specialist's domain. Generally, standards of value are fully appreciated only by experienced personnel at fine retail stores, dealers, cutters, and an occasional connoisseur-collector. The value of the colored stones depends primarily on the purity of color. In diamonds, the value depends on the whiteness of the stone and the purity of crystallization. Helping the investor today is an ever-improving certification system as well as an increased opportunity to view precious stones in museums, shops, and auction rooms.

A key factor, therefore, is for the purchaser to understand the determinants of quality. Precious stones will vary enormously in price, depending on how close they are to gem color and purity.

ATTRACTIVE FEATURES

Precious stones primarily offer the owner something of beauty. Historically, they have been purchased by the wealthy and have given psychic and aesthetic pleasure to the owner. In the Middle Ages, people believed that gems made one healthier; during the Renaissance, they were invested with spiritual importance; and in the nineteenth century, gems often commemorated either a birth or a death in the family. It is perhaps characteristic of our times that in the twentieth century gems have been regarded as amulets against inflation. In a certain sense, gems probably have been all of these things. In literature, treasure and gems have always been synonymous. This parallelism makes one believe that over the short

* Benjamin Zucker is Chairman, Precious Stones Company, New York. Portions of this article are based on information in *How to Buy and Sell Gems* by Benjamin Zucker (New York: Times Books, 1979), and several articles on connoisseurship in rubies, sapphires, emeralds, and white diamonds, by Benjamin Zucker in *The Connoisseur* in 1979.

term, and probably the long term as well, gems will always be of great value throughout the world.

POTENTIAL RISKS

Lack of Current Cash Return

Colored stones and diamonds offer no income and are unusually susceptible to changing market conditions. Diamonds are far more liquid than colored stones, but they are far less rare. As a hedge, a small amount of one's assets might be placed in a diversified portfolio of ruby, sapphire, emerald, and diamond. For example, a portfolio of gems might include: a fine 1-carat D-Flawless diamond (approximately $20,000); a fine 1- to 2-carat gem Colombian emerald, of good color but not flawless ($25,000 per carat); a 1-carat Kashmir sapphire or a 2-carat gem Burmese sapphire ($20,000); and a 1-carat Burmese ruby or a 2-carat superfine Thai ruby, relatively free of inclusions ($20,000). By balancing a portfolio among diamond, ruby, sapphire and emerald, a collector guards against substantial capital losses.

Market Volatility

Demand for gems over time is unpredictable and subject to many influences. Auction sales records for rubies, sapphires, and emeralds indicates the market volatility despite the general upward movement in the past ten years.

Further, there is always a chance that somewhere, someone will discover a new mine for ruby, sapphire, or emerald, which will consequently depress prices. This would not be as serious for diamonds because of the stabilizing effect of the De Beers organization. De Beers Consolidated Mines, Ltd. reduces its supply offering markedly in times of slow diamond business, and when the market becomes hot it raises the price of its offerings.

Illiquidity

The big difficulty in precious stone investment, aside from the expertise needed in deciding what is, in fact, gem quality, is the relative illiquidity of stones. On the one hand, auction houses such as Sotheby's and Christie's now sell almost $200 million annually in jewelry throughout the world. The auction house channel enables a private individual to sell jewelry at an open auction for a fee of roughly 10 percent. Similarly, fine retail stores as well as important dealers, who are always on the lookout for gem-quality ruby, sapphire, emerald, and diamond, have made precious stones much more liquid than they were several years ago. On the other hand, there is a significant difference between buying a gem and reselling it. Precious stones should not be regarded as a business for the investor. Rather, they should be considered long-term holdings — a hedge against the decline of paper money and against unfavorable political or social conditions.

TAX CONSEQUENCES

Under current tax law, profit from the sale of gemstones held for more than one year is taxable at the capital gains rate rather than as ordinary income. Gemstones can be exchanged for others of equal or greater value in a tax-free transaction under certain conditions. (See article on Tax Considerations for Collector-Investors, elsewhere in this volume.) For specific guidance in these matters, investors are urged to consult a professional tax adviser.

REPRESENTATIVE TYPES OF INVESTORS

Wealthy people have been buying gems for thousands of years. With the tax advantages of IRAs and Keogh Plans no longer applicable to gems under the Economic Recovery Tax Act of 1981, it is expected that persons of substantial means who buy stones as a hedge against economic or political instability will continue to comprise the principal investors.

JUDGING QUALITY

Diamonds

Diamonds are distributed into the market in a very orderly fashion. De Beers Consolidated Mines, Ltd. sells approximately $1.5 billion annually of rough diamond, of which about $1.2 billion can be cut into faceted diamonds. Most of this $1.2 billion (at least 90 percent) is for jewelry stones, not investment stones. Investment stones are gem-quality diamonds of the highest caliber. Color, clarity, cutting proportions, and carat weight determine a diamond's quality, and the diamond certificate will summarize the nature of these characteristics.

Color. Color is the most important parameter. If a diamond has one atom of nitrogen in 100,000, the stone will have a slightly yellowish color. During the 1950s the Gemological Institute of America (GIA) developed a system for grading diamonds. Until then diamonds had been termed "River" if they were of high color (very white). River diamonds were alluvial, as opposed to diamonds found in situ (in land). The second and third degrees of whiteness were termed "Top Wesselton" and "Wesselton," respectively, as the Wesselton Mine tended to yield diamonds with a very faint yellow tinge. Lower grades were Top Crystal, Crystal, and, finally, Cape stones. The latter were noticeably yellowish. The GIA set up a system in which the perfectly white stones are called "D color," the next, "less white E color," and so on, until the color Z. A J-color stone is yellow to the eye. By splitting the River grade into two colors, D and E, and the Top Wesselton into two colors, F and G, a more precise standard of separation was set. At first, the more traditional diamond dealers fought this system. The term "River" had lasted seventy years. Everyone was used to it, and D and E seemed an unnecessary separation.

The GIA procedure determines a diamond's color by placing the stone in a light box, an instrument with artificial, filtered, non-fluorescent, indirect light in it. This light is calibrated to exactly match northern light (also known as Low Country light). Before the invention of the light box, diamond dealers could sort diamonds and make value judgments based only on northern light on a reasonably clear day. The light that diamond dealers consider true northern light is the light in Antwerp, Belgium and in Holland, where many of the fine diamond connoisseurs originally came from. By duplicating this Low Country light, the GIA has enabled diamond sorting to continue under any conditions.

The diamond to be graded is placed in the light box, in a table-down (flat top of stone down) position. Inside the box, dormant like resting soldiers, are perhaps six or seven pregraded diamonds. If a diamond appears whiter than the F color but not as white as the E color, the diamond is said to be F. Diamond dealers throughout the world have sample stones that have been pregraded. Upon being offered a cut diamond, they will match the stone against their own master set and determine the color of the diamond in question. Such an analysis cannot be done with precision if the diamond is already set in a mounting. In a yellow-gold mounting, for example, flashes of color from the prongs will make the diamond seem slightly yellowish and reduce its apparent color grade. Similarly, if the diamond is set in platinum, color distortion will also occur. On important stones, therefore, where a critical judgment is essential, the diamond should be taken out of the mounting and graded. As prongs can be bent fairly easily by a skilled setter and then bent back to accommodate the stone again, it is much safer to remove the stone than to judge it in its mounting when making a significant grading decision.

Judging a diamond's color is an art for the connoisseur and takes many years of practice. Even so, the GIA has found that it is best to have two or three opinions before issuing a certificate. A D-color diamond is like a piece of ice in a glass of water sitting on a gem dealer's table in Bombay on a bright, sunny day. It has a transparency and whiteness that are incredibly pure. It is so rare that no more than one out of 1,000 diamonds would possess that white shade. White as that is, however, the old Golconda Mine (India) stones were whiter still. Place a Golconda diamond from an old jewelry piece alongside a modern, recently cut D-color diamond, and the purity of the Golconda stone will become evident. The term "blue-white" refers to the phenomenon of very white stones sometimes fluorescing in the sunlight and thus looking blue-white. Because the term was so overused by zealous salespeople over the last century, it is currently in disfavor. Even J, K, and L are yellowish (not quite yellow), and can be considered very beautiful. Fancy yellow or "canary" diamonds are those stones that have a rich yellow, not the off-yellow of J through Z stones. The GIA will label the deeply yellow stones not by letter but by the term "fancy" or "intense" yellow. These are colored diamonds, much more costly than off-yellow stones.

Clarity. Clarity is the second parameter of value in diamond grading and connoisseurship. Here, too, the GIA perfected a method of separating flawless stones from imperfect ones. The diamond is examined with ten-power magnification for internal flaws, fractures, inclusions, carbon spots, and so on. If the stone is flawless under 10X, it is so graded on the report. If it has flaws, depending on the proximity of the flaws to the center of the stone and their seriousness, the stone can be graded as follows:

Flawless. This grade indicates complete absence of internal or external flaws or faults of any description when graded under 10X binocular magnification.

Internally flawless. An internally flawless stone shows a complete absence of internal flaws or faults but has minor identifying surface characteristics such as growth lines, small naturals, or extra facets.

VVS 1-2 (very, very slightly included). This has minute inclusions such as a feather or pinpoint that are seen with difficulty even by the trained eye under 10X.

VS (very slightly included). This grade indicates small inclusions that affect neither appearance nor durability and cannot be seen with the unaided eye.

SI (slightly included). This stone has fairly obvious inclusions under 10X magnification, with the lower end of this grade containing stones in which flaws may be visible to the unaided eye when observed through the back of the stone but not in a face-up position.

Imperfect. Flaws in this stone can be seen with the unaided eye and are serious enough to lower the durability of the stone.

Judging inclusions requires more experience than judging color does. Just as a D-color is exceptionally rare, so too is a flawless diamond, one in perhaps 800 to 1,000 stones. The inclusions of a VVS stone and a VS stone cannot be seen without a jeweler's loupe. It is only when diamonds have an SI or Imperfect rating that the inclusions block the passage of light so that, in fact, optically, the diamond is of less aesthetic interest. It is duller and less brilliant. Fine retail stores, which traditionally have been the avenue for purchasing important diamonds, generally offer an accompanying gemological certificate describing a diamond.

Cut. Perfection of cut is the third parameter of quality. Marcel Tolkowsky, a mathematician, established the proper proportions for achieving maximum brilliance in a round diamond. If his proportions are used, diamonds will indeed be most brilliant and dispersive. Proportions, however, tend to go out the window in the face of Pythagorean round numbers. An average person in Des Moines generally will want a 1-carat diamond and not a 0.94-carat diamond. The cutter will therefore sacrifice ideal proportions and swindle the table, or make the pavilion (bottom) of the diamond unnecessarily deep so as to keep the total weight of the stone over a carat. All too often, a stone that should be cut into a 1.75-carat diamond is swindled into a 2-carat size. That the stone is slightly less brilliant will not be appreciated. On resale, however, the stone will be valued at Tolkowsky recut size. It should be noted that the retail price per carat of a diamond increases proportionally with increases in its weight. A 2-carat diamond is worth more than twice the amount of a 1-carat stone because of its much greater rarity.

Certificate. A diamond certificate will summarize these parameters of quality. First noted are the shape and cut of the diamond. Ninety percent of diamonds tend to be cut in the round brilliant fashion, although pear shapes, marquise shapes, and emerald cuts are used when the shape of the rough dictates. A thin, longish diamond rough crystal, for example, generally would be faceted into an emerald cut. Fashioning the rough into a round shape would result in too great a weight loss. The certificate goes on to state measurements in millimeters as well as the exact weight of the stone. It then notes the proportions and finish and, finally, the all-important clarity and color grades.

Today, diamond certificates enjoy international acceptance. A diamond dealer in New York can telephone his counterpart in Hong Kong and offer a stone of E color, VVSI clarity, in a round brilliant cut, 1.24 carats, for $8,000 per carat, as part of a wholesale series, and the Hong Kong merchant will be able to visualize almost precisely the diamond being offered. The GIA has set up, in effect, an Esperanto language of diamonds, usable for all gemologists and dealers throughout the world.

Colored Stones: Rubies, Sapphires, and Emeralds

Colored stones do not have the organized strength of a central selling organization standing behind their prices. Colored stones are, however, about fifty times as rare as diamonds. It is more difficult to identify color differences in these stones because rubies have many more shades of red, sapphires many more shades of blue, and emeralds many more shades of green than the various yellow tints in white diamonds.

Rubies. The color of a ruby and of many other precious stones is a critical factor in determining their origin and market value. Ruby (red corundum) comes about when chromium mixes with aluminum oxide. The varying degrees of chromium determine a ruby's shade. The percentage of chromium in rubies can differ by an infinitesimally small degree among mining sites in Ceylon, Burma, Thailand, Cambodia, Afghanistan, and, more recently, Kenya. The varying degrees, however, can make all the difference between a stone's being worth $5,000 or $3,000. Over the past few years, Thai rubies have shown a greater increase in value than Burmese rubies.

One of the talents marking the colored-stones expert is the ability to remember shades of red within rubies and to keep that memory clear and accurate over many years. Because of the great extent to which diamonds have been standardized by the GIA, color memory is no longer as important for a diamond dealer, who simply can say, "In the early 1970s I sold a 3.22-carat round D-Flawless stone for $12,500 a carat," for example. The color and clarity grades serve to recall the exact stone for the dealer.

But the expert in colored stones must remember, for example, the balance among the blue, violet, and orange shadings within the red ruby. The investor, likewise, must know the different shades of red that indicate a ruby's origin. A reputable dealer can give advice — always a good idea, even for those who have trained their eyes — but it is important that the investor have a grasp of the essential differences. The following chart, listing the characteristic colors of rubies, may help.

Burmese ruby. This has the finest shade. It is full-bodied red with a touch of orange in it, at the very center of the red spectrum, called "pigeon's blood" or "Burmese red." A blackish, bluish-red stone or one with too strong a hint of pink is of lesser quality.

Ceylon ruby. A Ceylon ruby has a more pink variety of red, called "Ceylon red" in gem dealer shorthand.

Siamese ruby. A Siamese ruby has a slightly violet shade of red called "Siamese red," and is often very brilliant.

African ruby. An African ruby has a somewhat brownish shade of red.

Unfortunately, color differentiation is not always simple. One can sometimes see a Burmese stone that is pink or a fine Ceylon ruby that has a deep red color.

Gem dealers and buyers do not always agree about a stone's origin. A dealer might say, "Here is a nice 3-carat Burmese ruby," and the buyer might immediately protest, "That's not Burmese; that's Ceylonese. Can't you see all the pink in the stone?" And because there has been no precise method of measuring the shades of colored gems, this argument and its variations often lead to zesty disputes.

A fascinating aspect of determining whether a ruby is pink or red always has been that the color is dependent on the light in which it is seen; it will look different in a shop window along Fifth Avenue, in a room with an overhead incandescent light, in an outdoor Indian market, in the overcast, natural northern light of Antwerp, or in an Amsterdam gem office. One of the gem dealer's distinctive talents must be to mentally add or subtract portions of the color and brilliance that he sees in order to make allowances for these differences.

On a June afternoon in Bombay, the light is so overpoweringly bright that a ruby will take on a brilliant, magnificently deep, red color. (Perhaps gems are so highly prized in India because the sun reveals all their inherent beauty.) In natural New York City daylight, the same ruby will appear to be a considerably darker shade of red and will look less brilliant than it would in Bombay. The high degree of pollution over New York City and its position farther from the equator than Bombay account for the differences. But Amsterdam daylight is even grayer than New York daylight. And finally, under an indoor incandescent light, a ruby will look more brilliant and will sparkle more, but the color might change enough to make the ruby look a bit more purple.

There are two possible solutions to the problem. Socrates said that if a man is wise enough, he can sit in his own home, in his own chair, and wait, and the whole world of knowledge will stream to his doorstep. At the very top of the gem profession today are people who sit at their desks and examine each stone offered them under their own, never-varying lighting conditions. By standardizing the light, they have greatly reduced their chances of unpleasant surprises in their gem purchases.

Alternatively, a gem dealer may pursue a more adventurous route, buying under any light but examining the stone in as many lights as possible within one environment. For example, a gem dealer in Bombay, on that sunny afternoon, might hold the ruby at the window and look at the stone, then examine it in the shade, then take it indoors and inspect it under artificial light. In general, the dealer would try to play with the ruby at different times of the day — when the sun was more intense, and then less bright — in order to achieve a balanced idea of how the stone really looks.

Internal world of rubies. Inclusions are one of the most fascinating distinguishing characteristics of a gem. They are the tiny growth markings within the colored stone or diamond. Gems take many millions of years to grow, and if there are any unusual occurrences during this long, slow period — for example, if spinel crystals are suddenly interjected into a ruby — the resulting ruby crystal, under magnification, will show a tiny spinel crystal. The layperson who sees such a ruby will assume that this is simply a flaw or a darkish spot within the stone.

Within Burmese rubies or sapphires, one can find elongated, crisscrossing needles of foreign material called "rutile." This rutile is so densely intertwined that if the stone is tilted at a certain angle, the markings, called "silk," sometimes can be seen with the naked eye. If these needles extend virtually through the whole stone, it is a silk that is characteristic of Ceylon rubies or sapphires.

The silk in rubies helps one determine whether a stone is from Burma or Ceylon, but there are a host of other inclusions that will divulge a ruby's Thai or African origin. Both Thai and African rubies are created under conditions of enormous geologic pressure. Consequently, when these stones are examined under a microscope, parallel lines, called "stress lines" or "twinning lines," often can be seen. The material has been subjected to so much pressure that the crystal has actually spun around repeatedly on its axis while growing.

How to value a ruby. The primary consideration in determining the value of a ruby is the depth of the stone's redness. A 1-carat ruby can vary between $100 and $15,000 a carat, depending on the shade of red. Each stone differs in its internal landscape (the amount of chromium, the number and length of inclusions) and this can affect redness. The red color is generally not spread uniformly throughout the stone, but is more intense in one section. Rubies are never without inclusions (i.e., flawless).

As with other commodities, supply and demand affect the price. Very few ruby mines have been discovered in the last 3,000 years. Aside from the ones uncovered recently in Kenya, there have been no ruby mines of any consequence found in the last generation.

The supply of rubies, which has always been limited, is becoming even smaller. It follows that the larger the ruby, the more valuable it will be (provided it is relatively free of inclusions and color deficiencies). Fine rubies over 5 carats are considered extremely rare.

Sapphires. Sapphire, with its magnificent blue color, has always been central to the human spiritual and aesthetic sense. Marco Polo journeyed from Constantinople through Samarkand, across the Gobi Desert into Cathay with sapphires as his calling cards. The stones he presented to the Khan, as well as his charm as a storyteller, earned him the post of merchant-ambassador in the court of the Khan.

Ceylon, the country that was Marco Polo's chief source of sapphires (and rubies), continues to be the principal source of sapphires today.

How to value sapphires. What was the quality that Marco Polo and other gem dealers were looking for in sapphires? Basically, it was the same quality for which their merchant counterparts look today: purity of blue color. Sapphire is aluminum oxide (Al_2O_3) with tiny additional traces of titanium and iron oxide, which create the blue color. Sapphire is in the corundum family. If chromium, titanium, and iron oxide mix, a purple sapphire results. Iron oxide mixed with aluminum oxide only produces a yellow sapphire. Although sapphire comes in yellow, orange, purple, and green, as well as blue, it is the blue shade that historically has been most sought-after. Marco Polo was searching for the pure, perfect, and platonic blue, a blue without any admixture of gray, green, violet, or black. In Ceylon, however, the majority of sapphires have in them an overtone of gray.

For purity of blue, the Burmese mines were a godsend. There, a deep shade of blue — a royal blue — occasionally was present in a sapphire. Burmese sapphires are sought-after by gem connoisseurs. Typically, a connoisseur will take a Burmese stone and lay it alongside other sapphires to compare nuances of the shade of blue. More important than the size of the stone is the presence of secondary colors. The Ceylon blue at its finest has a cornflower cast to it. This is a lively, lighter shade of blue than Burmese blue, which at its finest tends to be more royal.

Until the fifteenth century, it was almost impossible to facet (cut with flat edges) a sapphire. Consequently, sapphires were cut by hand in cabochon (rounded top) form. After faceting techniques were improved in the fifteenth and sixteenth centuries, Ceylon stones were appreciated even more. The inherent brilliance and life of a Ceylon sapphire was all the more impressive when flat edges were placed on the crystal rough. What the Ceylon stone lacked in color, it more than made up for in fire.

Ceylon and Burma, however, still do not produce the finest quality sapphire. Pride of place goes to a remote corner of the northwestern Himalayas, Kashmir, India. In 1862 a rock slide on the high slopes of the Zanskar range of mountains exposed sapphire-bearing rock. For about fifty years, some extraordinary gems were mined. The blue in the Kashmir sapphire became legendary — an intense, rich blue that did not change in sunlight or artificial light. (Burmese or Ceylon stones tend to lose or bleed color slightly in artificial light.)

The color of Kashmir sapphires is so beautiful that the term "Kashmir" has been applied to Ceylon or Burmese stones if they have this top shade of blue. Kashmir sapphires are also somewhat sleepy in appearance because of internal inclusions. Notwithstanding this, the shade of Kashmir color often makes other sapphire blues appear greenish or grayish when the stones are placed side by side.

In the 1930s a new source of sapphire was discovered outside of Bangkok, Thailand. Although they often have very good luster, these sapphires, after cutting, tend to be blackish or greenish. Large quantities of sapphires in the rough form are coming from Queensland, Australia and going to gem cutters in Bangkok, where they are mixed in with the Thai material.

In recent years the Sri Lanka State Gem Corporation has been set up to standardize the gem industry in Sri Lanka (Ceylon). The corporation's very able staff tests all stones shipped from that country for genuineness.

Cutting. Moslem cutters remain in Ceylon as part of a thousand-year-old tradition of faceting sapphires. Unlike diamond, in which the color is uniformly spread throughout the crystal, sapphire rough poses a great intellectual challenge to the cutter. Color is often in one corner of the crystal or more concentrated in one part of the crystal than in other parts. The Ceylon cutter also must cope with the fact that in all sapphires, there are two shades of color — blue and violet — depending upon the direction of the optic axis of the crystal rough. The cutter must orient the stone so that the blue color reflects through the top, or table, of the stone. Typically, a sapphire viewed through the side, or girdle, will look slightly violet or purplish-violet. In addition to orienting the stone correctly, the section of rough bearing the most intense color should be faceted so that that color is reflected through the table of the stone, upwards toward the eye.

Internal world of sapphires. In a Ceylon sapphire one can see the remnants of the crystallization pattern, a diary of the gem's millions of years of growth. It is common to find a microscopic zircon inclusion surrounded by a brilliant halo of light. Often, one also can see a liquid lake with round edges that looks like a feather. A sapphire from Burma, on the other hand, has within it densely woven, crisscrossing rutile needles that are different in character from rutile needles in a Ceylon sapphire. Finally, a Kashmir sapphire will have long bands of color in a parallel form. Thus, while a gem expert might say that a particular gem sapphire has a Kashmir color, under a microscope, one can in fact tell exactly where that stone crystallized.

Internal inclusions are not only beautiful but are key factors in separating synthetic from genuine stones. Nature expresses itself in straight lines in gemstones. The presence of crisscrossing rutile needles or zircon crystals, for example, is an indisputable sign of genuineness. Curved lines, on the other hand, are a sign that the sapphire has been created artificially.

Emeralds. Emeralds rarely have a rich green color or a brilliant interior. Those that do are extraordinary to the eye. An emerald is a complex combination of beryllium-aluminum silicate. When tiny traces of chromium combine in nature with the beryl, the resulting mineral is green and is termed an emerald. Beryl can be other colors such as purplish red (morganite) or blue (aquamarine). Aluminum silicate itself is quite rare. The juxtaposition of chromium with it, however, occurs in few places — hence, the great rarity of emeralds.

Sources. Slight differences in the amount of chromium will alter radically the depth of green in an emerald. Within its green shade are worlds of difference. The finest green, which comes from the Muzo Mine in Colombia, is called "old mine" green. It is a deep, intense, velvety, almost blackish shade of green. When the Spanish conquistador, Gonzalo Jiménez de Quesada, uncovered the site of the Chivor Mine, the Spaniards reasoned that there should be more emerald mines nearby. In 1567 they discovered Muzo, after great toil and effort. The Muzo site is torrid, jungle-like, and inaccessible. One hardly can breathe the air. Each section of the mine had to be cleared by hand because any explosives would have destroyed the fragile emerald crystals. The result, however, was breathtakingly deep green gem emerald crystals. The emeralds that were wrested greedily from the earth were sent all over the world by the Spaniards.

The second finest shade of green emerald is to be found in the Chivor Mine. This shade tends to have more blue than the Muzo shade does. To a novice, the Chivor blue-green stones appear, at first sight, to have more warmth and fire. The Muzo stones often look overly dark, with a hint of yellow in them. Although connoisseurs occasionally will prefer Chivor's bluish green to Muzo's generally yellowish green, all are unanimous in hailing the Colombian emerald as the finest in the world.

After exploiting the Chivor and Muzo mines for several years, the Spaniards were unable to wrest important stones from the ground. Both mines were abandoned and forgotten until the late nineteenth and early twentieth centuries. Muzo was rediscovered in 1895 and Chivor was reopened in the early 1920s. Old mine emeralds are those stones that came from Colombia before the seventeenth century and were shipped throughout the world. More recent emeralds from Colombia cannot compare in depth of color to these.

Russia, India, and Africa also have been the sites of emerald mines. A seam of emeralds was discovered in the Ural Mountains of Russia in 1832. The early 1800s saw quite a few jewelry pieces with Russian emeralds, which, while somewhat light in color, were relatively free from inclusions. These Russian mines have stopped yielding the purer emeralds; the material today is very opaque and generally uninteresting. In 1945, emerald mines were discovered near Ajmer, in northwestern India, but their output was disappointing.

The great hope for an abundant and top-quality emerald supply has been Africa. In 1955, prospectors in Rhodesia looking for lithium stumbled upon a fabulous emerald find. Because the base camp for the prospectors had been Sandawana, the emeralds were termed "Sandawana" emeralds. The size of the stones tended to be well under a carat. The color was a less intense shade of green than Colombian stones. Because of their brilliance, however, these stones were greatly sought-after by jewelry makers. Small Rhodesian emeralds went into bracelets, pins, and cluster rings. The emeralds had tremendous life and were reasonably priced.

Within twenty years of mining, however, Sandawana output fell considerably. Because the stones were small, Sandawana emeralds never took over the premier position in the emerald world.

Stones from a second African source, Zambia, started to appear on the market in the mid-1970s. Slightly blackish in overtone and often highly included, they, too, were sought-after for the commercial end of the emerald field. Because the green shade lacked the crispness of Colombian emeralds and the inclusions prevented light from traveling through the stone as much as it did within Colombian material, Zambian emeralds (often cut in Israel) also do not compete seriously with the South American material. A few Zambian stones are indeed very fine, however, and may be considered gem quality.

Brazil is another important emerald source. Brazilian stones tend to lack the peppery inclusions common to African emeralds. The material, however, is very opaque. Brazilian lapidaries are very skilled and are able to cut the material so that a Brazilian emerald is often very well proportioned and, at first glance, quite attractive. The presence of many open veins often found in Brazilian crystals is a problem, however. The emerald is sometimes oiled through these veins to improve its color. The tremendous bargains that one may obtain from a street gem merchant in Rio de Janeiro often lose their color as the oil evaporates over the years. Colombian material, having fewer surface scratches, does not pose such a problem.

Other locations for emerald are not commercially important. Isolated emeralds can be found in North Carolina, Austria, and Norway, but these have been uniformly of medium and poor quality. For gem emerald, one must turn to Colombia.

Internal world of emeralds. Aside from their color-shade differences, Colombian emeralds can be further subdivided on the basis of their inclusions. It is possible to know, with the aid of a microscope, from which mine — Muzo, Chivor, Cosquez, or Gachalá — an emerald comes. The noted Swiss gemologist, Dr. Eduard Gubelin, in his landmark study, *The Internal World of Gemstones,* points out that aside from the yellow shade of green common to most Muzo emeralds, the presence of a yellow-brown inclusion (a parasite) definitely indicates a Muzo original. Peering into a Muzo stone under the microscope or with a jeweler's loupe, one often can see a pool of swirling color, deep yellow-green, with tiny squares of calcite swimming alongside the yellow-brown crystals of parasite. French jewelers call this organic effect *jardin.* People expecting to find a flawless emerald are always disappointed. Aside from their bluish cast of color, Chivor Mine stones often reveal, under a microscope, a brilliantly lit, golden-faceted ball of pyrite crystal. Occasionally, a Muzo stone will have a pyrite crystal, but pyrite is usually suggestive of Chivor origin. Colombian emeralds generally will have a three-phase inclusion. This is a peculiar jagged island containing a circle that is a gas bubble and a square that is a solid inclusion. Upon seeing such an inclusion, one can be certain that the emerald indeed grew up in the hot climate of Colombia. These inclusions also indicate that the emerald is genuine.

Synthetic emeralds. Vast numbers of synthetically grown emeralds abound on the market. Gilson and Chatham are two of the processes used to simulate emeralds. Under magnification, such emeralds often reveal veil-like and wispy inclusions, occasional gas bubbles, and jagged tubes. Color is not a good means of separating synthetic from genuine emeralds because something close to the subtle green shade sometimes will show up in a simulated emerald. However, typically, synthetics tend to be much freer from inclusions than their genuine counterparts are.

Newcomers to the world of emeralds are always curious about the effect of the great numbers of synthetic emeralds on the value of genuine ones. How can a genuine emerald be so highly valued when an often purer and larger synthetic stone is sold for a fraction of the price? First, after a lengthy education, one is able to notice metallic nuances in the color of synthetic emeralds. One can see a manufactured look in the color of such stones. Second, stones can be readily submitted to a local gemological laboratory where, for a fairly minimal fee, the lab will issue a certificate attesting to their genuineness. Thus, although synthetic emeralds have been on the market for at least forty years, the price differences between them and their genuine counterparts have increased markedly. At auction, 10-carat emeralds have fetched over $50,000 per carat, while a synthetic will often sell for only hundreds of dollars for the entire stone.

PRICING GEMSTONES

Colored Stones

It is rather difficult to state exactly what should be the price for a superb ruby, sapphire, or emerald, as each stone has an individual personality and is slightly different from other stones. The price increase in the past years has been considerable, however. A stone should be held for a long period (at least five years) and past increases in prices do not guarantee future increases.

Rubies. In May 1969 in Geneva, a 3.25-carat specimen ruby was sold at auction for $46,000 per carat. A similar group of three specimen rubies, of 4-carat size, fetched $18,000 per carat at the Geraldine Rockefeller Dodge sale at Parke Bernet Galleries (October 1975). On November 10, 1977, a superb 7.80-carat ruby, which was tremendously lively and came with an expertise by Gubelin stating that it was Burmese, sold for $40,000 per carat. In 1981, among wholesale dealers, rubies have changed hands for prices considerably in excess of $100,000 per carat. A 4.12-carat Burmese ruby was sold in Geneva for the record price of over $100,000 per carat. Naturally, this price was exceptional, but it shows how much the finest gem can fetch.

Sapphires. In May 1970 in Geneva, Christie's auctioned a superb 48-carat sapphire for $1,300 a carat. A similar quality stone, a fabulous 28-carat sapphire, fetched $6,100 per carat in May 1975. At the Geraldine Rockefeller Dodge sale, a 40-carat magnificent sapphire was auctioned for $7,500 per carat. In April 1978, a superb Kashmir cabochon sapphire, cut in the old-fashioned, pointed sugarloaf style, sold for $15,000 per carat. And in April 1981, a 9.5-carat gem Kashmir sapphire fetched $30,000 per carat at Sotheby Parke Bernet in New York. At present there seems to be an ever-decreasing supply of fine gem sapphires available for purchase.

Emeralds. At the Enid Haupt sale in 1972 in New York, a beautiful 34-carat emerald sold for $10,000 per carat. Such a stone, if it were to come on the market today, would sell easily for four times that price, which is more than six times its price in 1968, when it sold for $6,000 per carat. At Christie's in Geneva in 1979, a 12-carat emerald sold for $48,000 per carat.

Diamonds. Diamond prices also have been volatile but generally upward. Unlike colored stones, however, diamonds experienced price weaknesses in 1980. Because of high interest rates, demand fell off for diamonds, even in the extraordinary D-Flawless category, causing prices to decline. At one point in 1980, a D-Flawless round stone sold for $65,000 per carat, whereas in 1982 prices sank below $20,000 per carat. Remember that minute differences in diamond, one step down in color from a D to an E, for example, will lower the price from $20,000 to $16,000 per carat. Two steps down in color will represent a further decrease to $10,000 per carat. The closer a purchaser can get to a D color and a flawless stone, the less volatility and risk he faces. (See Tables 1 and 2, on pages 314 and 315 respectively, for more details on diamond prices.)

CUSTODIAL CARE

All diamonds should be submitted to the Gemological Institute of America, in New York City, where they can be described and certified. The GIA's rating

TABLE 1. Wholesale History of Diamond Prices

(These prices are for internally and externally flawless diamonds of D color, in a round brilliant cut diamond.)

	Weight in Carats	*Value per Carat*	*Total for Diamond*
1968	3	$ 3,000	$ 9,000
1970	3	4,000	12,000
1972	3	5,000	15,000
1974	3	11,000	33,000
1976	3	14,000	42,000
1978	3	18,000	54,000
1979	3	50,000	150,000
1981	3	55,000	165,000
1982	3	21,000	63,000
1968	2	2,000	4,000
1970	2	3,000	6,000
1972	2	3,500	7,000
1974	2	8,000	16,000
1976	2	11,000	22,000
1978	2	15,000	30,000
1979	2	44,000	88,000
1981	2	52,000	104,000
1982	2	20,000	40,000
1968	1	1,400	1,400
1970	1	1,500	1,500
1972	1	1,900	1,900
1974	1	5,000	5,000
1976	1	6,500	6,500
1978	1	10,000	10,000
1979	1	41,000	41,000
1981	1	35,000	35,000
1982	1	18,000	18,000

SOURCE: Author's data.

of a diamond, as to color and clarity, is respected throughout the world. Moreover, their certificate will enable a purchaser both to insure accurately and to have a clear idea of the value of his diamond.

The American Gemological Laboratories (AGL), in New York City, also offers certificates on precious stones and diamonds. The AGL has developed a color grading and analysis system for colored stones that is meeting with increasing favor.

TABLE 2. Medium Quality Diamond Prices — Slightly Flawed

(VS, I-J Color)

	Weight in Carats	*Value per Carat*	*Total for Diamond*
1968	3	$1,000	$ 3,000
1970	3	1,250	3,750
1972	3	1,500	4,500
1974	3	2,700	8,100
1976	3	3,000	9,000
1979	3	6,000	18,000
1981	3	6,200	18,600
1982	3	4,500	13,500
1968	2	950	1,900
1970	2	1,150	2,300
1972	2	1,400	2,800
1974	2	2,300	4,600
1976	2	2,500	5,000
1979	2	5,500	11,000
1981	2	6,000	12,000
1982	2	4,000	8,000
1968	1	550	550
1970	1	700	700
1972	1	900	900
1974	1	1,400	1,400
1976	1	1,500	1,500
1979	1	4,000	4,000
1981	1	4,500	4,500
1982	1	3,000	3,000

Once people buy precious stones, the writer believes they should place them into settings and wear them on important occasions. The mounting should not account for more than 10 percent of the value of the entire jewelry piece (gems included).

Jewelry can be insured under a floater policy that describes each piece clearly. Again, the need for accurate certification is apparent.

GLOSSARY

alluvial deposit— Debris and gems carried by a river; found along a riverbank.

brilliance— The return of white light to the eye; the sparkle of a precious stone.

carat— One-fifth of a gram; unit of weight.

corundum— The mineral aluminum oxide, otherwise known as ruby and sapphire. Red corundum is ruby. All other shades (blue, green, yellow, pink, and colorless) are sapphire.

De Beers syndicate— The so-called diamond syndicate.

diamond— Carbon arranged in an isometric way.

dispersion— The splitting of white light into various colors. When a diamond is turned, one can see the play of colors because of this optical phenomenon.

emerald— A transparent green stone (in the beryl family) that gets its color from chromium.

gemstone— It has beauty, rarity, and portability.

GIA— The Gemological Institute of America, a nonprofit, educational institute.

inclusion— The internal landscape of a gem.

kimberlite— The veins containing diamonds.

melee— Tiny precious stones less than 0.5-carat size. The bulk of diamonds and colored stones are of melee size.

reflection— The return of light to the eye after it passes through the gemstone.

refraction— The bending of light within a stone.

River diamond— An alluvial diamond of great whiteness.

rough— Uncut gem material; cut and faceted rough is a gem.

ruby— Corundum that is red.

rutile— Titanium oxide, a mineral that often occurs as an inclusion within sapphire and ruby.

sapphire— Corundum that is blue or any color other than red.

sight— The parcel containing rough stones sent ten times a year to 250 diamond dealers.

silk— 1. Inclusions of rutile that are interwoven and look like silk. 2. The trade term for rutile arranged in a crisscross pattern.

spinel— A gem, often red or blue, that can resemble a ruby.

synthetic stones— Having the same physical and chemical proportions as gems but artificial and of limited commercial value.

table— The flat top of a cut stone.

TRADE ORGANIZATION

The American Gem Society, headquartered in Los Angeles, California, is an association of fine retail stores. It stresses gemological knowledge and a high degree of corporate responsibility. The society can give the name of a reputable and knowledgeable jewelry store in a particular area. Sotheby Parke Bernet, in New York City, operates a fine auction house that can value and appraise jewelry. Similarly, Christie's, also in New York City, is a very fine auction house. It too can make appraisals and offer fine jewelry on an almost monthly basis.

The most important factor in buying jewelry is the selection of a seller who both knows gem quality and will take the time to explain why a particular jewel is of gem quality. The fact that American Gem Society members and the auction houses have generally been in business for generations lends extra credence to the weight and importance of their advice.

LEADING DEALERS IN PRECIOUS STONES

Samuel Beizer & Associates, New York, N.Y.
Carimati Jewelers, Inc., New York, N.Y.
Fred's, Beverly Hills, Cal.
Godshaux, New Orleans, La.
Kazanjian Bros., Inc., Los Angeles, Cal.
Neiman Marcus, Bal Harbour, Fla.
Neiman Marcus, Dallas, Tex.
Precious Stones Co., New York, N.Y.
Jules Schubot Jewelers, Troy, Mich.
H. Stern Jewelers, Inc., New York, N.Y.
VanCleef & Arpels, Inc., New York, N.Y.
Harry Winston, Inc., New York, N.Y.

SUGGESTED READING

Popular Magazines and Gemological Studies

Gems & Gemology. Published by the Gemological Institute of America. Quarterly; containing many articles, of a technical nature, on gems.

Jewelers Circular Keystone. Published by Chilton. Monthly; readable, business oriented review of events within the U.S. jewelry industry.

*Jeweler/*Lapidary Business. Published by ULW, Inc. Monthly; for rock hounds and lapidary enthusiasts.

Newsletters

Gem Market Reporter. Published by Kurt Arens, Phoenix, Ariz.

Gemstone Price Report. Published by David Federman, New York, N.Y.

PreciouStones Newsletter. Published by Bernard D. Cirlin, Thousand Oaks, Cal.

Because of the rapidly changing nature of the gem world, these three newsletters are highly recommended for their up-to-date information.

Reference Books

Background Studies

The following books cover the history of jewelry from earliest times to the present day.

Gregorietti, Guido. *Jewelry Through the Ages.* New York: McGraw-Hill, 1970. Translated from Italian, this book is illustrated sumptuously and presents an extensive history of gem cutting and the use of precious stones as jewelry. It is also a marvelously documented study of the major pieces of jewelry found in the principal museums and collections throughout the world.

Heiniger, E., and Heiniger, J. *The Great Book of Jewels.* Greenwich: New York Graphic Soc'y, 1974. This book is a study of the stones themselves and presents the gemological data on precious stones. Because of the size of the illustrations and the care taken in presenting them, it is a most remarkable study of the principal gems of the world.

Hughes, Graham. *The Art of Jewelry.* New York: Viking Press, 1972. This book contains excellent chapters that give detailed descriptions of how gold and silver are crafted.

Gemological Texts

Anderson, B.W. *Gem Testing.* London: Butterworth, Ltd., 1971. This book is an excellent, standard British work.

Gubelin, E.J. *The Internal World of Gemstones.* Zurich: ABC Edition, 1974. This is a technical, standard text on gem inclusions, that is, what can be learned from the inclusions within a gemstone. An extraordinarily beautiful book.

Liddicoat, R.T., Jr. *Handbook of Gem Identification.* Los Angeles: Gemological Institute of America, 1969. A major study of the methods of testing colored stones and diamonds, this book is considered the standard text of the GIA.

Webster, R. *Gems — Their Sources, Descriptions and Identification.* New York: Anchor Books, 1970. Another respected study.

Investment Studies

Moyersoen, J.S. *Investing in Diamonds.* New York: Wolf Publications, 1980. An excellent review of the investment world of diamonds.

Zucker, Benjamin. *How to Buy and Sell Gems: Everyone's Guide to Rubies, Sapphires, Emeralds and Diamonds.* New York: Times Books, 1979. This book was reprinted and updated from the 1976 study. It has color photos as well as price charts and extended descriptions of gems. It is also available from Precious Stones Co., New York, N.Y.

Museum Collection Studies

Desautels, Paul. *The Mineral Kingdom.* New York: Grosset & Dunlap, 1974.

———. *Gems in the Smithsonian Museum.* Washington, D.C.: Smithsonian Institution Press, 1972. Both of these are exciting texts. The former contains information on minerals as well as on precious gems.

Meen, V.B., and Tushingham, A.D. *The Crown Jewels of Iran.* Toronto: University of Toronto, 1968. This book is a landmark study of the difficulties the authors encountered in examining the fabulous Iranian collection, as well as a detailed study, with color illustrations, of the splendors of the collection. An extraordinary book.

Index Funds

Evan Schulman *

BASIC CHARACTERISTICS

The investment objective of an index fund is to provide results that correspond to the performance of common stocks in aggregate, as represented by a particular index. To do this, index funds allocate their monies in a fashion similar to the weights used to construct that market index. They do not try to select securities that will outperform, nor do they try to time the market — that is, to purchase securities when the market is low and raise cash when it is high. Index fund managers save their clients' money by avoiding expenses — the research, brokerage, tax, custodial, and accounting costs involved in trying to beat the market. As long as the market index copied is broadly based and weighted by the market value of each company's total outstanding shares, and the costs of entry, exit, and management of the fund are low, then index funds are a highly prudent investment for trustees.

Making use of index funds rather than individually managed portfolios or mutual funds is much like prescribing or purchasing generic rather than brand-name drugs. The result in both cases is clearly a cost savings to the purchaser and, in the case of index funds, protection from a disproportionate or an incomplete mixture of the ingredients. (See *Performance* in this article.) The only caveat to the above is that for individual trustees, as opposed to the corporate trustees, the number of suppliers of this product are few and the product is currently available in only one variety for one medium — equities.[1] Since in most cases the cost of buying, selling, and custodial care are all included in the supplier's fee, the following discussion will concentrate on the rationale for the statements made above.

Prices vs. Values

Competitive markets ensure that security prices will approximate security values. Neoclassical economists define a "perfectly competitive market" as one that has a large number of both buyers and sellers in a central location dealing with perfect knowledge in a homogeneous product. It is further stipulated that no barriers to entry exist. Applying this definition to the stock market requires qualification of only the perfect-knowledge assumption. Rather than having per-

* Evan Schulman is Senior Vice-President of Batterymarch Financial Management, Boston.

[1] Jennison Associates in Boston, Northern Trust in Chicago, and Wells Fargo in San Francisco manage passive bond portfolios. These are buy-and-hold strategies that are not linked to any one specific index and that are not mutual or commingled funds available to the public.

fect knowledge of General Motors, Acme Auto Supply, Exxon, Parker Drilling, etc., it is assumed that all investors have the same time horizon and agree on the outlook for the various companies over that time period.

While models should not be accepted or rejected on the descriptive merits of their assumptions, the above set is a fair description of the mechanics of the American securities markets, with one exception — the assumption of identical outlooks over the same time period. However, it may be easier to accept this assumption if it is restated as follows: When dealing with the future, we are all equally ignorant. The other assumptions appear quite appropriate. For America's largest companies, which represent the bulk of its equity wealth, there are centralized stock markets with many buyers and sellers operating at the same time. The product is homogeneous — a 100-share certificate of Kodak entitles the owner to precisely the same rights as any other 100-share certificate of Kodak. Also, the barriers to entry for participation (not to be brokers, but to be participants) are low. A 100-share round lot of Kodak currently costs some $6,500 plus approximately one percent in commissions. If this appears steep (one may not want all of one's eggs in one basket), the use of investment clubs or mutual funds brings market participation within the reach of almost everyone.

Given these assumptions, it is possible to prove that security prices will be such as to equalize returns among securities of the same risk class. (See *Glossary* in this article for the definition of "risk.")

In the bond market, for example, one would expect the bonds of similar utility companies with the same maturity and coupon and the same quality rating to sell at the same price. If this were not so, security analysts and brokers would advise their clients to sell the higher-priced bond in order to purchase the cheaper one. These transactions would push prices toward equilibrium. Calculating stock values is more difficult than calculating those of bonds, of course, because analysts must deal with dividend and other flows that change through time and, it is to be hoped, are of indefinite maturity. Yet about 15,000 members of the Financial Analysts Federation are striving to perform such calculations, and the chance that they may have overlooked some information on a particular firm or industry is highly unlikely. Further, the costs involved in an independent evaluation would most probably not be offset by gains achieved through an evaluation of what is publicly available information.

Indexes

Perhaps the two best known U.S. market indexes are the Standard & Poor's Composite Index (S&P 500) and the Dow-Jones Industrial Average. The Dow-Jones index has not been used as a vehicle for fiduciary funds. It consists of only thirty stocks, it is not broadly representative, and, rather than being weighted by the shares outstanding, the thirty stocks are weighted by their price.

The S&P 500. The S&P 500 has been utilized as the model for virtually all the U.S. index funds. It is weighted by shares outstanding. Its 500 securities present a representative slice of corporate America, and its historical record has made it a fast rabbit on the performance track. Critics have pointed out that it does have imperfections, however. In the first place, judgment is used in selecting the firms and industries to be represented in the index. A committee of five employees of the Standard & Poor's Corporation (a division of McGraw-Hill) selects those securities. It does not religiously follow a buy-and-hold strategy. To maintain the magical number of 500, it removes firms that merge, declare bankruptcy, or lose investment favor, and it adds firms with favorable historical records.[2]

The result is that this Index sometimes reflects the investment fads of the time while sacrificing diversification. In the early 1970s, the Index had approximately a 40 percent representation in those growth stocks that were institutional favorites. By November 1980, the S&P 500 had some 30 to 40 percent of its weight in energy and energy-related stocks. An exposure of 40 percent of a portfolio to any one investment theme is of questionable prudence and, within the pension fund industry, attempts are being made to create extended indexes for buy-and-hold strategies with as many as 5,000 securities involved.

Regardless of the criticism leveled at the S&P 500, one should remember that a weighted market portfolio of 500 securities represents a more diversified portfolio than most other fiduciary alternatives do. Such a vehicle is the only index product available to individual trustees at this time.

Current indexing methods. The index funds industry now has approximately $15 billion under the administration of about twenty managers, with another ten banks and one no-load mutual fund offering the service. It is possible to discern four schools or methods of portfolio construction, called the "full," the "sample," the "institutional," and the "tilt" models.

Full method. The full model uses virtually all the stocks in the S&P 500 in order to ensure close tracking. Practitioners of this approach include several major banks, and they tend to emphasize precise tracking (excluding costs) in their sales literature. About five stocks are not purchased for reasons of prudence.

Sample method. The sample method builds portfolios that resemble the S&P 500. This is accomplished by investing in the index's largest 150 to 200 stocks with most of the funds and investing the remainder so as to obtain the same industry weightings as the index. The portfolios produced by the sample method have characteristics that closely parallel the full index. This approach trades precise tracking for reduced custodial and transaction costs and was designed to accommodate accounts with frequent cash flows.

Institutional method. The institutional approach was designed to take advantage of the sample method's cost savings while incorporating a cross-sectional representation of institutional holdings to obtain above-average liquidity. To achieve this, investments are limited to approximately the top 250 companies

---

[2] Standard & Poor's has capitalized on this flexibility in index design. For an annual fee of $800, they will telephone changes in the Index the very day they are made, but after the market has closed.

ranked by market capitalization. A portfolio generated by this method looks like one that would be obtained by merging the holdings of several different institutional account managers, and thus represents a diversified core portfolio of typical institutional equities. Firms using this technique point to cost savings and improved investment quality as significant advantages. As in the sample strategy, the attractions of lower operating costs and a liquid portfolio do have an offset in terms of less accurate short-term tracking, should such tracking be a requirement.

Tilt method. The tilt product has evolved as clients better understand the construction of the S&P 500 and their own needs. For instance, tax-exempt investors such as pension funds and endowments may well be able to generate a better long-run return by tilting the portfolio towards higher yield and not competing with taxable investors for growth stocks. Other biases or tilts are those that would push the portfolio's risk away from the corporate sponsor's own business risks.

Index matching. Index matching should be viewed as a set of techniques, not as an end in itself. The techniques developed for efficiently and mechanically implementing a specific investment strategy at low cost can be applied to other potentially attractive strategies, such as international diversification and stock universes other than the S&P 500. Indeed, these passive techniques are now being used to structure diversified foreign equity accounts and extended domestic portfolios for large institutional clients.

ATTRACTIVE FEATURES

As pointed out in the discussion of *Basic Characteristics,* index funds combine the important advantages of broad diversification (within the equities spectrum) and the cost saving that follows from absence of research, commission, and related trading expenses.

POTENTIAL RISKS

The following discussion will assume that the price of the larger, frequently traded stocks represents their value, given all currently available public information.

Specific Risk

Fundamental to the following is recognition of the fact that society and its institutions do not reward individuals for taking risks that can be avoided. Walking on the road rather than on the sidewalk does not result in an increased salary, nor does it earn a stipend from any group that could possibly have an interest in roads or sidewalks. Indeed, if an insurance company were aware of this aberration, it would raise the policyholder's premiums. Other interested groups would also ask for sanctions. Certainly life expectancy and, hence, expected earnings, would be reduced. Taking needless risks is an activity that will not only go unrewarded, it may negatively affect wealth and income.

This also holds true for the security markets. If only one security is purchased, even though it was priced appropriately at the moment of purchase (a result of the competitive securities market discussed above), all wealth or financial well-being will be tied to the fortunes of the issuing firm. Such a relationship can be sometimes good, sometimes bad. Over time, the returns will be more volatile (fluctuate more) than those of well-diversified portfolios. As in the walking example, taking risks that can be easily avoided (by using the sidewalk or diversifying the portfolio) will impose costs on the individual. This cost becomes apparent should the investor need to liquidate that holding when the issuing firm is experiencing hard times. The holding will then have to be liquidated at a depressed value because of extraneous or non-investment reasons.

Systematic Risk

It is inherently reasonable that the effect of specific or individual company risk can be reduced to virtually zero in a portfolio by including a large number of stocks. However, all risk cannot be eliminated that way. The market itself moves up and down and, if a portfolio of stocks is well diversified, exposure to this market risk (or systematic risk) certainly will be present. Individual stocks have differing exposures to this element of market risk. The twofold question for trustees is: How much exposure to this risk is acceptable, and what is the best way to construct portfolios that avoid it?

Prices change in the market so that the market clears. In other words, at any time when the markets are open, all of the securities are voluntarily held by someone at current prices. Willing sellers and buyers may be present in a large number of securities, but they are separated by the bid-ask spread; otherwise, a transaction would occur. If prices serve both functions, that is, if they are indicators of nominal value and allocators of security holdings, then the market portfolio becomes a most meaningful benchmark. Indeed, it represents the collective wisdom of all investors.

If a client requires a portfolio of less risk than the market, the trustee can sell off the riskier holdings of the market portfolio and purchase more of that set of securities that have less risk than (i.e., less exposure to) the market. Utilities are a good example of securities that have less market risk, as their earnings and dividends are relatively stable. However, by exchanging securities with higher market risk for utility stocks, an undiversified portfolio will result. Such a portfolio is certainly vulnerable to, among other things, changes in energy prices and to the rate increase lag that is characteristic of regulatory bodies in an inflationary period.

The process of exchanging market or systematic risk for individual company or industry-specific risk is an unhappy trade-off because, as stated earlier, the bearing of specific risk will not be rewarded. A more feasible solution is to maintain the diversification of the market portfolio by investing a portion of the client's monies in an index fund. The rest of the account can be placed in government short-term debt, which is default-free in money terms, Treasury bills, or, if the client's tax bracket so warrants, in a money market account that invests solely in a diversified portfolio of short-term, high-quality municipal obligations. (See article on Portfolio Management, elsewhere in this volume.)

The power of this argument can be demonstrated with the case of a trustee who feels that a higher-than-market risk is appropriate for his client. The trustee can purchase a set of risky or aggressive stocks and discover that when the market rises the client's portfolio will do better than the market, and when the market falls the portfolio will do worse. Compared to the market benchmark, the client will have an undiversified portfolio because it will lack exposure to the securities of large, stable companies that have a market exposure equal to or less than the benchmark. This lack of diversification will cost the client, as outlined above. It should be obvious that it would be more appropriate for the trustee to borrow in order to purchase a market fund with leverage, thus achieving the required risk-reward exposure. Again, the client's wealth will move up and down faster than the market, but the portfolio will do so without suffering the added variations and costs due to inadequate diversification.

The prohibition against borrowing is recognized, and few if any trustees would consider a portfolio that is more aggressive than the market to be appropriate for their client. To the extent that the trustees did purchase a portfolio composed of aggressive securities, they would find that, on the whole, the firms in that portfolio would have above-average debt ratios. Whether trustees borrow or invest in companies in which managements borrow appears to be a moot point. The diversification argument is clear.

Aside from suggesting that few if any trust beneficiaries should be exposed to greater-than-market risk, the argument for index funds has little to say about the appropriate position between a market risk and a no-risk portfolio. What is clear are the tools that should be used to position the client.

PERFORMANCE

Over any five- to ten-year period some 50 to 75 percent of actively managed portfolios underperform the S&P 500. Of those that do beat the index in one such period, few repeat that feat in the subsequent period. The implication of this line of argument is that one should not place much faith in the historical record of any portfolio manager's funds when determining whether that manager's services are appropriate for a specific client. Perhaps this can be best understood in terms of sampling. Portfolio managers with 30 to 50 or even 100 holdings are really just taking samples of a market that consists of 5,000 firms. Since it is very difficult to get a representation of the market with so few selections, the range of results generated by any investment process or department will be large and, hence, if prices really do reflect all available information, it will be difficult to determine whether or not perceived differences in results are due to luck or skill. By just picking sets of thirty or so securities at random as portfolios, it is possible to generate distributions of returns that look very similar to the distributions of returns actually achieved by portfolio managers over any particular time period. This finding is consistent with the theoretical discussion above, which implied that one way to have results that differ from the market is to have portfolios that are undiversified. In fact, most portfolio managers do just that.

Effects of Diversification

What one would expect, based on theory, is that the longer the time period involved, the fewer the account managers who would succeed in beating the market. This is so because portfolio returns will suffer from: (1) the cumulative effects of management fees and the transaction costs required to keep the portfolio in line with perceived value, and (2) the fact that return over the long run (the compound return) is a function of the arithmetic average of annual returns less a portion of the variance around that average. (Thus for a given average return, the more the variability of the series, the less the compound return.) This theoretical prediction is indeed borne out by the data in Table 1, below.

TABLE 1. Banks and Insurance Companies Pooled Equity Funds Annualized Returns Data*

Years	*S&P 500*	*First Quartile*	*Median*	*Spread*	*S&P Less Median*
1	−5.0	3.3	−1.8	5.1	−3.2
2	12.3	15.2	12.7	2.5	−.4
3	14.4	17.1	14.6	2.5	−.2
4	12.4	14.5	12.6	1.9	−.2
5	8.2	10.5	8.6	1.9	−.4
6	10.7	12.1	10.1	2.0	0.6
7	14.1	14.7	12.5	2.2	1.6
8	8.0	9.1	7.1	2.0	0.9
9	5.2	5.4	3.7	1.7	1.5
10	6.5	6.4	5.0	1.4	1.5

*For periods ending 12/31/81.

SOURCE: Crain Publications Piper Survey

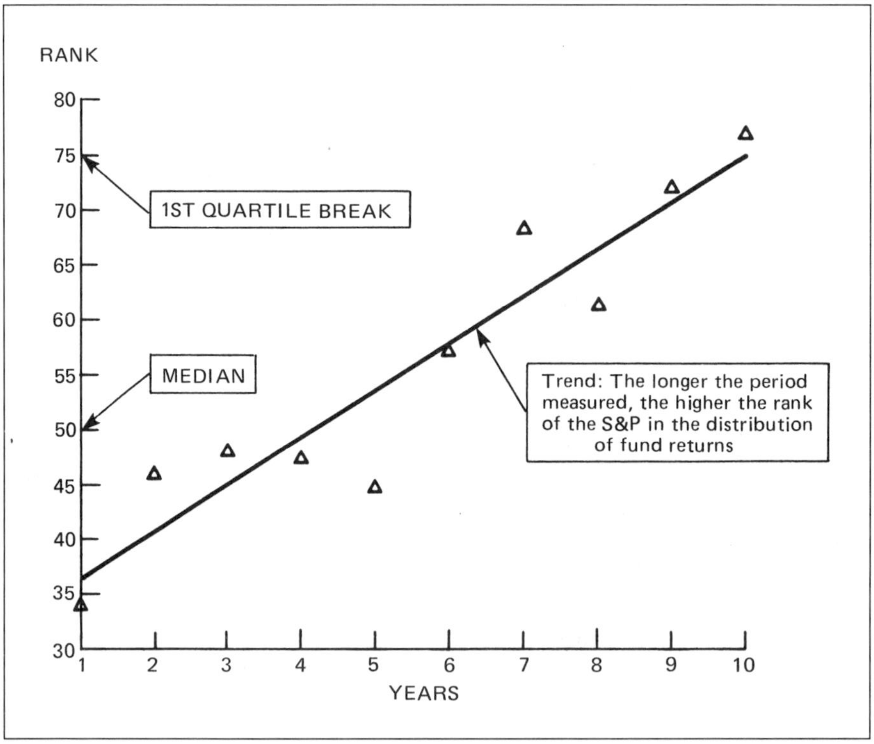

FIG. 1. Relationship of the S&P 500 to the Distribution of Fund Returns to 12/31/81

Within limits, the longer the period, the further up the distribution of returns the S&P rises (S&P 500 being a proxy for the market). Figure 1 above confirms that impression.

It remains true that because an index account remains fully diversified, it will not be the best performing account over any particular period measured. Some managers will build portfolios that outperform, just as some managers have in the past. But which managers? An examination of the evidence indicates that a trustee's chance of picking a winner is about one out of four. It is questionable that such a bet is a prudent fiduciary investment.

REGULATION AND THE LAW

The law, as represented by court decisions, has changed radically over the years and now supports index funds as prudent investments. From the British court decisions in the 1700s, which held that only investments in government bonds would leave the trustee free from liability (a reaction to the South Sea

Bubble of 1720), to the U.S. court decisions in the 1960s, holding that trustees may invest their clients' assets in common stock mutual funds, is a significant journey in both time and concept. A readable summary of this evolution can be found in Langbein and Posner (see *Suggested Reading* in this article), who argue that the thrust of the law has always been concerned with speculation. They note that, to the extent that securities were being selected for the portfolio by the trustee on a one-by-one basis, the courts could properly evaluate them on a one-by-one basis as being prudent or not. However, the acceptance of equity mutual funds as fiduciary investments ushered in the age of investment products or vehicles. Here, the individual components of the fund or vehicle shrink in both legal and investment importance as portfolio design becomes significant. In this new era the portfolio becomes the relevant security.

Pension Funds

This radical change in concept has been carried through to government regulation under the Employee Retirement Income Security Act of 1974 (ERISA). This law requires pension funds to be administered in a manner similar to the prudent man rule of traditional trust law, and then virtually invites pension funds to invest in mutual funds.[3] Further, the U.S. Department of Labor's regulations for implementing the law sets forth the following basic factors that a fiduciary generally should consider in evaluating the role that an investment or investment course of action plays in the plan's investment portfolio:

> "(i) the composition of the portfolio with regard to diversification;
>
> "(ii) the liquidity and current return of the portfolio relative to the anticipated cash flow requirement of the plan; and
>
> "(iii) the projected return of the portfolio relative to the funding objectives of the plan."

The regulation makes it clear that under ERISA the relative riskiness of a specific investment or investment course of action does not render such investment or investment course of action either per se prudent or per se imprudent.

TAX CONSEQUENCES

Capital Gains

Capital gains are not taxable until appreciated securities are sold and the gains distributed to the shareholders. Due to the buy-and-hold strategy of index

---

[3] ERISA Section 401(b)(1).

funds, the turnover of assets should be low, barring heavy redemptions in a mutual fund. This action thus defers capital gains taxes until the liquidation of holdings.

Dividends

Dividends are subject to tax as income. In order to qualify as regulated investment companies under the federal tax laws and thus avoid the double taxation of shareholder dividends, mutual funds must distribute at least 90 percent of their taxable income to their shareholders. These dividends are taxable in the hands of the beneficial owner as income whether accepted in cash or re-invested in the funds' shares. In the case of index funds based on American securities, this income qualifies for the limited dividend exclusion provision. The beneficial owner of these shares, however, may be subject to state and local taxes on the income and/or capital gains distributions.

REPRESENTATIVE TYPES OF INVESTORS

Index funds were originally designed for large pools of money such as pension or endowment accounts. These accounts would and should be able to take advantage of the promised economies of scale. For this reason, and since these pools of money are readily subject to scrutiny concerning sufficient and appropriate diversification, index funds are appropriate investments for individual estates and trusts. Finally, the individual investor is also a candidate to participate in an indexed mutual fund. A survey of the individual shareholders of Vanguard's First Index Fund, as reported in an advertisement for that fund, indicated that relative to shareholders in sixteen other Vanguard funds, the Index Fund investors had the highest percentage of postgraduate degrees, the highest percentage of persons in professional occupations, and the highest percentage of persons under age 55.

COSTS AND FEES

Cost Comparisons of Index and Mutual Funds

Vanguard's First Index Investment Trust estimates its annual operating expenses to be three-tenths of one percent of the fund's assets. In addition, a $6 annual account charge is made, and brokerage costs absorb another 0.04 percent of assets. Total operating expenses will thus amount to 0.3 to 0.4 percent of a client's holdings. Large, managed mutual funds tend to generate fees and expenses at the 0.6 to 0.8 percent level, or two to three times those of the index vehicle.[4] Index funds offer investment management at half-price.

---

[4] Lipper, *Director's Analytical Data.* New York: Lipper Analytical Distributors, Inc. This service

TABLE 2. Leading Equity Indexers

Management Firm	*Location*	*Mid-Year 1981 Size (Millions)*	*Indexing Method*
American National Bank and Trust Co. of Chicago	Chicago	$3,500	Sample
Bankers Trust Co.	New York	3,200	Sample
Batterymarch Financial Management	Boston	2,000*	Full, Tilt
First Index Trust (Vanguard Group)	Valley Forge, Pa.	100	Full
Harris Trust and Savings Bank	Chicago	700**	Full
State Street Bank and Trust Company	Boston	950*	Full, Tilt
Wells Fargo Bank	San Francisco	4,500	Full, Tilt, Extended

* Includes internationally indexed monies
** Includes two market timing accounts

Typical Expenses of Maintaining an Index Fund

For pension accounts that wish to index, total costs should be in the order of 0.1 to 0.3 percent. Again, as in the mutual fund case, these costs are a half or less of the normal charges incurred by separate pension or endowment accounts.

The cost of managing a separate index fund varies within the field. As an example, Batterymarch recently offered to manage index accounts for a fee of one-tenth of one percent with a maximum fee of $100,000 when the client had $100 million or more in assets subject to the index strategy. The client was responsible for custodial and brokerage charges, but these tended to be nominal.

INDEX SERVICES

Approximately thirty banks, one investment adviser, and one mutual fund offer indexing services. The investment adviser manages only separate accounts

reports that the average expense ratio in the most recent year was 0.63 percent for mutual funds in excess of $250 million. Brokerage would add another 0.1 to 0.3 percent to this ratio. For funds under $25 million, the expense ratio averaged 1.26 percent, again with brokerage expenses to be added.

and has an account-size minimum of $10 million. The banks all offer commingled accounts, usually with relatively low minimums. However, most of these commingled funds have been designed for ERISA accounts, and it may not be possible to use them for individuals, estates, or personal trusts. If such funds are available for trusts, the client must be a trust client of the bank. Finally, the First Index Fund of the Vanguard Group is available to all as a no-load indexed mutual fund. Table 2 on page 329 provides a partial list of those who have amassed significant index funds over the years. However, the investor should check with his bank as to the availability of indexing for his needs.

GLOSSARY

fiduciary— A person who exercises any discretionary authority or gives advice concerning the management, investment, or disposition of assets of a pension plan subject to the provisions of ERISA. See ERISA definitions Section (3)(21)(A).

growth stocks— Securities whose dividends (if they exist at all) represent only a nominal yield on current market price. The return on these securities needed to attract investors must therefore be in expected price appreciation.

index— A measure of a basket of items at a point in time. Properly constructed, an index should be useful in measuring the central tendency of movement of these items over time.

index fund— An investment vehicle designed to closely follow the movements of a stock market index.

institutional client— A customer of an investment adviser for whom a board of trustees acts in the interest of many beneficial owners (e.g., pension or endowment funds).

investment performance— The total return generated by a portfolio of securities over a period of time including dividends, interest payments, plus all realized and unrealized gains and losses compared to the market value of the account at the beginning of the period adjusted for cash contributions.

market value— The number of shares outstanding (market) or held (portfolio) multiplied by the price of the security.

mutual fund— A commingled account investing in marketable securities. The fund's shares, which represent ownership of the underlying securities, are available to the public either directly or through a stock broker.

passive investment— A buy-and-hold strategy for investing funds. Such a strategy does not respond to new information as it arises for either securities owned or those not owned.

risk— A measure of the fluctuations in the price of securities rather than risk of bankruptcy. While such a measure includes upward movements as well as drops in price, it has simple mathematical properties, and tests indicate that it behaves in much the same manner as a measure that just looks at price declines. Critics point out that if an investor's time horizon is truly long term, then it is terminal wealth that is important, not the path over time taken to achieve it.

tracking— Measurement of how closely an account moves with a given market index.

SUGGESTED READING

Periodicals

An asterisk (*) indicates the more technical publications.

Financial Analysts Journal. Published by the Financial Analysts Federation, New York, N.Y. Bimonthly.

Institutional Investor. Published by Institutional Investor Systems, New York, N.Y. Monthly.

**Journal of Business.* Published by the University of Chicago Press, Chicago, Ill. Quarterly.

**Journal of Finance.* Published at 100 Trinity Place, New York, N.Y. Quarterly.

**Journal of Finance and Quantitative Analysis.* Published by the University of Washington, Seattle, Wash. Quarterly.

The Journal of Portfolio Management. Published by Institutional Investor Systems, New York, N.Y. Quarterly.

Articles

Armstrong, J. Scott. "The Seer-Sucker Theory: The Value of Experts in Forecasting." *Technology Review,* M.I.T. June/July 1980, pages 19–24.

Brealey, Richard A. *An Introduction to Risk and Return From Common Stocks.* Cambridge: M.I.T. Press, 1969.

Cuneo, Larry J. and Wagner, Wayne H. "Reducing the Cost of Stock Trading." *Financial Analysts Journal,* Nov./Dec. 1975, pages 35–44.

Ehrbar, A. F. "Index Funds — An Idea Whose Time Is Coming." *Fortune.* June 1976, pages 145–154.

Ellis, Charles D. "The Loser's Game." *Financial Analysts Journal.* July/August 1975, pages 3–8.

Fama, Eugene F. "Efficient Capital Markets: A Review of Theory and Empirical Work." *Journal of Finance.* May 1970, pages 383–414.

Fisher, Lawrence, and Lorie, James H. "Rates of Return on Investments in Common Stocks: The Year-by-Year Record, 1926-65." *The Journal of Business of the University of Chicago.* Vol. 41, No. 3., July 1968, pages 291–316.

Ibbotson, Roger G., and Sinquefield, Rex A. "Stocks, Bonds, Bills, and Inflation: Year-by-Year Historical Returns (1926-1974)." *The Journal of Business of the University of Chicago.* Vol. 49, No. 1, January 1976, pages 11–47.

Langbein, John H., and Posner, Richard A. "Market Funds and Trust-Investment Law." *ABF Research Journal.* Dec. 1975.

Lorie, James H., and Hamilton, Mary T. *The Stock Market. Theories and Evidence.* Homewood: Richard D. Irwin, Inc., 1973.

Samuelson, P.A. "Challenge to Judgment." *The Journal of Portfolio Management.* Vol. 1, No. 1, Fall 1974, pages 17–19.

Williamson, J. Peter. "Measurement and Forecasting of Mutual Fund Performance: Choosing an Investment Strategy." *Financial Analysts Journal.* Nov./Dec. 1972, pages 78–91.

Leasing Ventures

Frank P. Slattery, Jr. *

BASIC CHARACTERISTICS

When the Economic Recovery Tax Act of 1981 was passed, the business press carried stories to the effect that up to one out of every three dollars for capital expenditures during the next several years would be the subject of a leveraged lease. This anticipated the entrance of many new investors into the leasing market as lessors. With $40 billion of equipment expected to be financed each year, both corporate and individual investors must appear in large numbers. Leasing ventures, in other words, are expected to become an increasingly important investment medium.

Leasing can be a profitable venture for both the lessor and the lessee. A lessor is one who owns property and leases it to another (the lessee). The lessee is therefore the user of the property.

The lessor may be an individual, a group of individuals operating as a trust or a partnership, a corporation (either public or private), or a combination of individuals and corporations operating as a partnership or a trust. The lessor enters into the equipment leasing transaction to obtain the tax and financial benefits of ownership of both during the lease term period and after the end of the lease term. The lessor may realize residual value at the end of the base lease term if the lessee purchases the equipment for its fair market value, or returns it so that it may be disposed of elsewhere. The lessee, on the other hand, acquires the right to use the property during most of its useful life, and has a deduction on federal income taxes for the rentals paid to the lessor.

Types of Leases

There are several types of lease transactions. By far the most common is the leveraged lease. A leveraged lease is a lease of property for a substantial part of the useful life of the property, in which a portion of the property's acquisition cost is raised from borrowed funds. The rents paid by the lessee to the lessor go to amortize the lessor's borrowing. A second type of lease is the straight lease transaction, in which the owner and the user enter into a non-leveraged, two-party transaction. This type of lease is particularly popular in fields that experience rapid technological advances. The lessor is often the manufacturer of the

* Frank P. Slattery, Jr. is President of Lease Financing Corporation, Radnor, Pa.

product. The third common type of lease is a sale-leaseback. The lessor buys the equipment from the lessee and then leases it back to the lessee. A sale-leaseback may be either a leveraged or a straight lease transaction. The chief advantage to the lessee is that such a transaction can raise significant amounts of cash, probably more than if the lessee mortgaged the property.

All the foregoing leases are generally, although not always, net leases. In a net lease, the lessee is responsible for all expenses associated with the maintenance of the equipment, the payment of taxes, insurance, and other costs generally associated with personal property. The lessee also must keep the equipment in good condition, excluding reasonable wear and tear. The lessor, on the other hand, is considered the owner of the equipment for tax purposes, and thus is entitled to the depreciation expense of ownership, the interest expense for the acquisition of equipment if the equipment has been mortgaged, and, if available, investment tax credit.

Tax-Oriented Benefits

The lessee may deduct the entire rent payment as an ordinary expense, but may not depreciate the equipment. However, the lessee may benefit from the lessor's investment tax credit as either a pass-through of such credit from the lessor or a correspondingly lower lease rate. The lessor must treat the lease payments as rent, reporting the payments as ordinary income in the year in which they are received or, in some cases, when constructively received. The lessor is entitled to depreciate the equipment over its useful life. If the equipment is new, the lessor is entitled to the investment tax credit, or, it may, at its option, pass the tax credit through to the account of the lessee.

Most benefits of equipment leasing are tax oriented. The one exception to this is the residual value in the equipment when the equipment is no longer subject to lease. Receipts from residual values are taxed as ordinary income to the owner when realized.

The annual leasing market has been in excess of $20 billion per year. Most of the multimillion-dollar transactions are done by corporate lessors. This is because the amount of investment required is large, and under current tax law individual investors may not take advantage of an investment tax credit in a net lease situation, except under certain restricted circumstances that are described below. Because the leveraged lease and other leases are primarily creatures of the tax law, taxes become one of the most important considerations in entering into a transaction. A lessor would not enter into a leasing situation unless it could take advantage of depreciation, interest expense, and, perhaps, tax credit. In order to value these tax benefits effectively, the taxpayer must remain a taxpayer during the term of the lease. Use of the investment tax credit by a lessor is, in effect, a forgiveness of tax. Use of interest expense and depreciation is a tax deferral or timing device only. Since the receipt of residual value is taxed to the lessor as ordinary income, some of the benefit that is available in capital transactions is not available in this type of investment. (See *Tax Benefits and Other Attractive Features* in this article.)

Residual Value

Inflation has caused the cost of most items of equipment to appreciate considerably over the past twenty years. An investor purchasing a piece of equipment that will be subject to a net lease for an extended term of years often finds that the residual value of the equipment has increased significantly during the period for which it was owned. Consequently, when the equipment is disposed of at the end of the lease term for its then fair market value, the return to the investor far exceeds the return originally contemplated. Of course, an investor contemplating such a transaction today will have to consider whether inflation will continue during the term of the lease in such a way as to provide this type of windfall benefit.

TYPES OF LEASING INVESTMENTS

Straight Leases

In a straight leasing situation, a lessor may choose to purchase the asset from the vendor by providing 100 percent of cost from its own funds. Or, in the case of industries marked by rapid technological change, a manufacturer may decide to lease rather than sell its product. Since it is uncommon for an investor to provide all funds for the acquisition of large items of equipment, unless the lessor is the manufacturer of the equipment, this type of leasing transaction will not be considered here in any detail.

If the anticipated reward is to lease equipment on a money-over-money basis, the lessor will attempt to mark up its money above the rate at which it borrows. The obvious pitfall is that if the lessor must borrow money on a floating-rate basis and lend out in effect by writing fixed-rate lease rentals, then, in a period of volatile interest rates, a lessor may find its portfolio under water. However, floating-rate leases are becoming more common. In this structure, the additional cost or decrease in cost for funding is passed on for the benefit or obligation of the lessee.

Typically, a lessor in a money-over-money leasing transaction will not factor all of the benefits of ownership, such as tax benefits, into its price. A lessor in this situation may decide to lease the item of equipment to the lessee for a short period of time with an idea of remarketing the equipment at the end of the lease term. This is an operating lease (see further discussion below) and one that does not have the normal characteristics of a full-payout lease. The lessor must be in a position, through its own efforts or the efforts of a third party, to remarket the equipment to a second user and perhaps to subsequent users after that. Obviously, this is a riskier situation than one in which the lessee contracts to use the equipment throughout most of its useful life.

Leveraged Leases

Often, corporate investors use leveraged leasing to lease equipment having a purchase price of $5 million or more. Bank leasing companies are among the most common investors of this type. Today, however, many industrial corporations as well as other finance-related companies have leasing subsidiaries that engage in leveraged leasing of major items of equipment. Almost all types of personal property have been leased during the past decade, including such large capital items as aluminum smelter plants, ocean-going tankers, and large aircraft. The individual investor typically cannot deal in transactions of such magnitude. However, a number of pools of investors have been or are being formed to take advantage of ownership of larger items. Depending upon the amount of leverage available by borrowing, such capital pools are able to acquire relatively expensive equipment.

Many of the so-called full-payout leases for transportation equipment and other long-lived equipment may have lease terms of as much as twenty to twenty-five years. A cost in excess of $50 million for this equipment is not uncommon. The lessor is almost always a large corporation or a group of corporations. Most of the leases undertaken on a leveraged basis are full-payout leases, which pay out at least the financing and utilize up to 80 percent of the asset's useful life. Today, however, an increasingly large number of transactions are based on an operating lease.

Operating Leases

An "operating lease" is defined under Statement on Financial Accounting Standards (SFAS) No. 13 of the Financial Accounting Standards Board as one that is not a capital lease. A capital lease is one that has been referred to above generally as a full-payout lease. The basic definition of an "operating lease," therefore, is one in which the lease term is equal to less than 75 percent of the estimated economic life of the leased property, or in which the present value of the lease rental is less than 90 percent of the fair value of the leased property, excluding any investment tax credit available to the lessor. The criteria for determining whether a lease is a capital or an operating lease are quite clearly spelled out in SFAS No. 13. Each is accounted for quite differently from the other. In the case of a corporate entity, the accounting may be very important indeed.

Only in an operating lease can a non-corporate taxpayer take advantage of the investment tax credit. Hence, a number of the limited partnerships being formed today provide that the equipment will be leased to the first user for 50 percent or less of its useful estimated life. Tax credits are then retained for the account of the lessor. Bank-related types of lessors are precluded, for the main part, by regulatory considerations, from entering into a short-term operating lease. No such prohibition, however, affects large corporate entities, although it is rare today to find many involved in short-term operating leases except in the computer mainframe and peripheral area, or where the corporation is the manufacturer of the equipment.

MEASURING INVESTMENT RETURNS

A uniform type of analysis must be undertaken in order to understand a leasing transaction from an investor's standpoint. Typically, in a leveraged leasing situation, a before-tax analysis will indicate a negative yield to the investor. In a straight-leasing transaction, often referred to as a money-over-money transaction, a before-tax analysis will indicate a positive return to the investor.

Straight Lease

In the straight-leasing transaction, a present value analysis is undertaken of the cash flows from the transaction, the residual, and the tax benefits. In that type of situation, it is relatively easy to determine the actual yield to the investor. It is nothing more than a compendium of the present value of the cash flows and the immediately available tax benefit arising from the investment tax credit and the potential for tax benefit from the accelerated depreciation.

Leveraged Lease

Today, in leveraged leasing, there are two popular types of analysis available, the multiple investment sinking fund (MISS) method and the single investment sinking fund (SISS) method. Both methods attempt to measure the return to the investor throughout the term of the investment. The SISS method provides for the payment of any taxes through the operation of a sinking fund. In the MISS method, payment of taxes is accomplished partly by a sinking fund and partly by direct payments from the lessor. According to the MISS method, the assumed rate of earnings is the same as the yield rate. The yield found by the SISS is always less than or equal to the MISS yield. In both types of analysis, the cash flow from the transaction to the lessor (i.e., the cash not necessary to pay a lender) is relatively small.

Yield rate and sinking fund rate. Leveraged leasing typically uses one rate, referred to as the yield rate, for the investment stage, and a second rate for the sinking fund stage. The yield period is usually a relatively short portion of the total lease term during which the investment is returned to the lessor together with the yield on the original investment. The original investment typically will be between 10 and 45 percent of the acquisition cost of the equipment. The return to the lessor is the projected cash flow from the investment and the tax payments saved. When the lessor has recovered its investment and the yield, additional after-tax flows are available to the lessor. This surplus of cash flow, which the lessor will receive before tax payments are required, is often referred to as the sinking fund. The surplus earns at the sinking fund rate. Such earnings are compounded back into the sinking fund. Later on, when the depreciation of the equipment has been reduced because of the accelerated method of depreciation, and the cash flow becomes negative due to the necessity for payment of taxes, the payments will be made from the sinking fund until its balance is reduced to zero.[1]

Effects of MISS and SISS. In both types of analysis, the sinking fund balance and the investment balance will be zero at the end of the lease term. Under the SISS method, the net cash flow consists of an investment followed by positive cash flow until the investment is repaid and the yield has been received. All tax payments must be provided through the operation of the sinking fund.

In the MISS method, payment of taxes is accomplished partly by the funds accumulated in the sinking fund and partly by direct payment (investment) from the lessor. Therefore, it is the timing of the use of sinking fund and investment that differs, as well as the different rates ascribed to investment (yield) and sinking fund rates (which will always be less than the yield rate).

In either case, it is essential that the lessor earn at the sinking fund rate chosen in order to earn its desired yield on the transaction. Hence, the more conservative the investor, the greater the reason for utilizing the SISS method and a relatively conservative sinking fund earning rate. Typically, the sinking fund investment rate should equate to 3.5 to 5 percent after tax, although current rates could justify a higher rate.

Book earnings for corporate entities in a leasing transaction are governed by SFAS No. 13. In a leveraged lease, the lessor's earnings are recognized over the same period as yield. An estimated residual value may be utilized, but no earnings from the sinking fund may be recognized. Hence, the accounting for a leveraged lease is in conformity with economic analysis.

Structure of borrowed funds. The economics of the leveraged lease will be determined by the structure of the borrowed funds. Smaller transactions tend to provide for the straight mortgage amortization of debt, which is equal payments made on a periodic basis; the larger portion of each installment is used for interest payments at the commencement of the lease and for principal at the end. However, in many larger, more complicated transactions, debt service decreases as the lease progresses. In such cases, significant cash becomes available to the lessor when tax payments become due.

This latter type of sophisticated debt structuring is typically utilized, however, only in the largest leveraged leases, where almost certainly the lessor is a large corporate entity or group of corporate entities. One of the reasons for this

[1] This is a hypothetical analysis tool, since the build-up of the sinking fund occurs on paper only. The sinking fund is reduced to zero at the time that all the tax payments have been made. There may be several investment stages and several sinking fund stages, depending on the transaction.

is that in order to structure the debt in this manner a much larger equity investment as a percentage of cost is required in order to pay off the debt sufficiently by the time payments are due. The major advantage is that the lease becomes self-supporting in the sense that the lessor need not enter into any form of cash-flow planning to provide for future tax liability.

Residual Value

One critical area in the economics of leasing is the determination of the residual value. At the end of the net lease term the asset typically will have value. In an economic analysis, a conservative lessor will usually choose a value less than the anticipated residual value. Of course, if the residual value assumed in the analysis is not available at the end of the lease term, the analysis and, consequently, the yield to the lessor will be lower than assumed. If a high residual value is assumed by the lessor, a larger yield will result. Hence, an investor must be certain that the residual value assumed for the equipment at the end of the lease term is both realistic and conservative.

It should be noted that lessees may now negotiate with corporate lessors for a prearranged purchase price of the assets at the end of the lease. This may cause residual valuations to fade from a transaction. On the one hand, this will result in certain parties agreeing to lease where they have never done so, while, on the other hand, precluding certain lessors from continuing in the business. Those lessors currently involved in leasing large assets who have made a great deal of money from sudden windfalls arising from fair market value residuals may choose to remove themselves from the leveraged leasing market. Since the safe-harbor rules (see *Safe-Harbor Provisions* in this article) do not apply to individuals and noncorporate investors, it is entirely possible that fair market value residuals will be involved in smaller (less than $3 million) transactions as well as some large transactions (i.e., where assets are used outside the United States) in cases of industrial revenue bond financing and other areas excluded from the Economic Recovery Tax Act of 1981.

TAX BENEFITS AND OTHER ATTRACTIVE FEATURES

Depreciation and Income Sheltering

Both corporate and individual investors who own equipment are entitled to depreciation expense as well as interest expense for monies borrowed. The depreciation is usually on an accelerated basis for tax purposes and, particularly in a leveraged leasing situation, the borrowed funds are nonrecourse to the borrower. This means that the owner of the equipment borrows the money on the strength of the credit of the lessee without the lender having a direct claim against the lessor. The net result is that, for tax purposes, the owner of the equipment has a write-off during the early years of the lease, which shelters other income of the owner; however, the owner has no obligation to repay the balance of the funds borrowed except from rental payments from the leased equipment.

The obligations of the lessee under the lease are hell-or-high-water obligations under which the lessee, under all circumstances, must continue to make payments. Consequently, an assignment of the lease to a financing institution creates chattel paper, which is a piece of collateral based on the credit of the lessee. This allows the owner to borrow most of the money needed to acquire the equipment on a nonrecourse basis to the owner-borrower.

Accelerated write-off. Under the Economic Recovery Tax Act of 1981 (the 1981 Act), equipment purchased after January 1, 1981 must be written off under one of the methods prescribed by the Accelerated Cost Recovery System (ACRS). The ACRS replaces the previously used depreciation methods and generally reduces the period of time over which equipment may be written off. The rules apply to both new and used tangible property used in a trade or business or held for the production of income. Special anti-churning rules are designed to prevent property acquired prior to January 1, 1981 from being covered by ACRS.

Some property — specifically, certain public utilities property, railroad tank cars, and residential property — is written off over a ten-year period; certain public utility property with a current asset depreciation range (ADR) class life exceeding twenty-five years may be written off over fifteen years. Most equipment must be written off over five years. Under ACRS, salvage value is ignored. For assets acquired after December 31, 1985, the recovery is on an even more accelerated basis. There are provisions under which equipment can be written off over a longer period on a straight-line method, but such provisions would be rarely used in leasing.

In the first year of the equipment lease, significant amounts of depreciation are available as a charge against other taxable income of the lessor. Additionally, the interest paid to the lender will be expensed in the year in which the interest is due and paid. The tax write-off for the first and beginning years of a lease, therefore, is typically greater than the ordinary income ascribed to the rental paid by the lessee. In effect, a deferral of taxes is available to the investor.

Transferability of Tax Benefits

Prior to 1981, Revenue Rulings 75-21 and 75-28 established the ground rules for leveraged leasing of equipment. The two rulings were commonly referred to as the guidelines. The 1981 Act, although utilizing the device of a lease, allows certain corporate entities to buy and sell tax benefits without the other trappings of a leveraged lease. The 1981 Act provides that the minimum investment may be reduced to 10 percent of equipment cost. The old guidelines provided that the asset's remaining useful life at the end of the lease must cover at least one year or 20 percent of the estimated useful life. However, the law now provides that the term of the lease cannot exceed a period equal to 150 percent of the life of the properties under the former ADR system or 90 percent of the useful life of the asset.

The old guidelines provided that the lessor must be able to show that the transaction was entered into for economic profit, whereas the 1981 Act provides that the tax benefits of ownership are motive enough for a true lease. Under the old IRS guidelines, the lessee was only allowed to purchase the equipment at its fair market value at the end of the lease term, or lease it for the then fair rental value. In fact, the lessor did not have a right to enter into a contract for any other party to purchase the asset at the commencement of the lease term. Under the 1981 Act, the lessee has the option to purchase the asset at a fixed price, whether the price is one dollar or whether more than fair market value. Also under the 1981 Act, the lessee or a related party may provide the financing or guaranteed financing for the transaction, whereas under the old guidelines that could not be done.

Under the 1981 Act, tax benefits are transferred from a party who cannot use them, such as the lessee in the transportation industry, to a lessor who can, such as a bank or industrial corporation. A leveraged lease is used for this purpose. The lease may have all the criteria of a conditional sale agreement or other type of financing. However, as long as the parties intend it to be a lease, and as long as the lessor is treated as the owner and the lessee as the user, the IRS cannot attack the transaction. This is a drastic and significant change in the federal tax law in respect to corporations. It eliminates all risk of the lease being upset so long as the minimum criteria defined above are met.

Minimal Investment

Interestingly, since there is a 10 percent investment tax credit and since the corporate lessor need only put up 10 percent at risk, in effect the lessor may be entering into the transaction without any significant investment. Whether the markets will develop in such a way that an investor can in fact enter into a transaction with an investment as low as 10 percent remains to be seen.

For publicly held corporations and financial institutions, the current SFAS No. 13 accounting for a leveraged lease by a lessor would, in most cases, show a pre-tax loss if a transaction were leveraged to the maximum (i.e., 90 percent) debt. As of this writing, the Financial Accounting Standards Board has issued an exposure draft for the sale of tax benefits. A final standard with some expected changes is likely to be published in 1982.

Investment Tax Credit

If the investment tax credit, which is currently equal to 10 percent of original cost, is retained by the lessor, then the tax credit is available in the year in which the equipment is accepted for lease. Instead of a deferral, this in effect is a forgiveness of tax for the lessor. Under the 1981 Act, retention of ownership for a five-year period for most equipment results in full vesting of the tax credit.

An individual may not retain the investment tax credit for his own account under current law where the equipment is subject to a net lease, unless the lease is an operating lease for a period of less than half of the estimated useful life of the equipment. Additionally, the lessor's business-expense deductions, other than rental payments and reimbursed expenses related to the property, must be more than 15 percent of the rental income from the property for the first year of the lease. The limitation applies to partnership and tax option corporations as well. In addition, under the 1981 Act, the individual lessor must be at risk for 20 percent of the equipment cost and remain at risk pro rata until full vesting occurs at the end of the five-year period.

The one other circumstance under which an individual or noncorporate lessor is eligible for the investment tax credit is where the leased property has been manufactured or produced by the lessor. Of course, the only equipment for which a tax credit is available is property that is new when the owner purchases it and that is "Section 38 property," defined as new, tangible personal property.

Additional investment tax credits are available, such as the business energy investment credit. This applies to certain pieces of energy property, such as solar or wind energy property, recycling equipment, and shale oil equipment.

Tax credit limitations. There are certain limits on the investment credit that a taxpayer may utilize for a given taxable year. For a corporation, credits may be applied up to 100 percent for the first $25,000 of taxable income and 90 percent for all income thereafter in tax years ending in 1982. Lessors and their tax advisers must be aware of the very complicated rules relating to Section 38 property, which depend on the type of equipment and the uses to which it will be put. For example, certain uses of equipment, such as use by a savings institution or a not-for-profit user, do not qualify for investment tax credits. Since tax considerations are extremely important in any investment in a leveraged lease, the taxpayer ought to be represented by competent tax advisers.

The equity investor, whether corporate or individual, may elect to pass the tax credit through to the user of the property. In effect, the lessee is treated as the owner of the property for investment tax credit purposes. The lessee, therefore, becomes liable for the possible recapture of investment credit if the asset should be disposed of prior to the end of the vesting term, or in the event of other disposition of the property, such as destruction of the equipment.

Equipment leased outside the United States. One special note relates to equipment that is leased for use outside of the United States. The rentals constitute foreign source income under Sections 861 through 864 of the Internal Revenue Code. Any loss generated by the transaction is a foreign source loss. This point is more relevant to corporate investors than to individuals, who typically do not have foreign source income. Additionally, under the 1981 Act, some of the ACRS provisions are not applicable for equipment leased outside the United

States, and tax credits are not available for property predominantly used outside the United States except in certain narrow areas.

Tax Liability Indemnification

Since tax benefits are so important in a leveraged leasing situation, it is quite common for the lessee to indemnify the tax treatment of the investment tax credit and ACRS claimed by the lessor. It is rare for such a tax indemnification to be found in a straight lease. The rationale for the indemnity in the leveraged lease is that since the taxes play such an important part in the transaction, somehow the lessor ought to be assured that the tax consequences envisioned will indeed occur.

Safe-Harbor Provisions

Under the 1981 Act, certain safe-harbor rules are available for corporate lessors. A safe-harbor lease is one that is characterized as a lease for purposes of allowing ACRS deductions and investment tax credit to a nominal lessor. In order to qualify, all parties must characterize the arrangement as a lease and agree to treat the lessor as the owner. The designated lessor must be a corporation, other than a Subchapter S corporation, or a personal holding company. At all times during the term of the lease, the lessor must be at risk for not less than 10 percent of the adjusted basis of the property, and the lease term, including all extensions, cannot exceed the greater of 90 percent of the useful life of the property or 150 percent of the property's current ADR class life. The leased property must be new Section 38 property, to be placed in service after January 1, 1981, and leased within three months after being placed in service. Alternatively, a sale-leaseback transaction may occur within three months after the lessee places the chattel in service. Certain transitional rules are in effect for equipment that was placed in service prior to August 13, 1981. No safe-harbor rule applies where the owner of the equipment is an individual, a group of individuals, or a partnership of individuals.

Under a safe-harbor rule bargain purchase prices, or one dollar purchase options, may be a part of the transaction. The practical result is that the lessor no longer receives the benefit of residual values in equipment; nor, on the other hand, must the lessor take a risk in the value of the equipment.

Residual Profits

In addition to the tax benefits outside of safe-harbor elections, opportunities to own personal property utilizing leverage make significant economic sense to lessors. So long as the lease of the property is for something less than its full economic useful life, there must be residual value in the equipment for the benefit of the lessor. Those benefits may be far distant but, depending upon the type of equipment involved and the inflation rate during the lease term, there may be a very large residual value as a percentage of original cost.

It is not uncommon for railroad rolling stock leases to have an original term of from fifteen to eighteen years. The same is true for large aircraft transactions. At the end of the lease term, such assets often have an economic value equal to 20 to 80 percent of original equipment cost. This produces significant future profits and cash for the owner. Of course, if the asset still can be profitably employed in the lessee's business, the lessee may be willing to continue the lease for its then fair rental value or may desire to purchase the equipment for its then fair market value.

In the past, large, corporate lessors have received large residuals and hence have shown significant profits in the years in which major leases terminate. Many of the aircraft that were leased to the major airlines during the 1950s and 1960s now have been purchased for their then fair market value by the airlines. In many cases, large banks acted as lessors; they found that the residual value of the equipment was in the neighborhood of 50 percent of the original cost. However, true leases now may be written by corporate lessors pursuant to the safe-harbor rules when a lessee can purchase equipment for as little as one dollar at the end of the lease term. Significant transactions have been consummated under the 1981 Act. It does seem likely, however, that there will be significant impetus on corporate taxpayers that have large operating loss carryforward or investment tax credit carryforward to convert such benefit into immediately realizable cash. From the standpoint of the seller, it is very cheap capital indeed.

As of early 1982, several bills have been introduced in both houses of Congress to repeal the safe-harbor leasing portions of the 1981 Act. Additionally, various Congressional representatives have spoken out against the provisions of the 1981 Act.

On a more modest basis, individuals acting as lessors on leveraged-leasing transactions have found that their returns were magnified greatly by virtue of inflation driving up the then fair market value of the equipment over the lease term. Transactions that were placed on the books for ten years in the early 1970s often bring 20 to 50 percent residual values in the early 1980s. This results in large profits for the lessor.

Inflation Hedge

It often makes sense for lessors to defer payment of taxes as long as possible. By owning a series of equipment leases, an individual or corporation can defer the payment of taxes for a significant period of time on the theory that inflation will cheapen the dollars that are required to pay taxes. The residual value of the equipment, which is growing during the lease term, will provide significant amounts of cash at the end of it. Both of these factors suggest that funds should be sheltered in a series of leveraged or unleveraged leases.

Typically, there are cash flows available to an equity investor in excess of the cash required to service debt. Indeed, this cash flow may be tax-sheltered during the early years of a lease by virtue of depreciation and interest expense available to the owner of the equipment. The credit of the lessee and its ability to continue to make payments to the lender that has provided the borrowed money and to allow the transaction to go forward become of primary importance.

RISKS AND TYPES OF INVESTORS

Leasing ventures offer important investment opportunities as well as certain hazards to a range of institutions and individuals.

Corporations

Banks. Corporate banks, operating through their holding companies or bank-owned leasing subsidiaries, have dominated the market for leveraged leasing of big ticket items for the past decade. Large organizations have been built up and have flourished on a nationwide basis. Much of the dollar volume of leasing is done by the top twenty banks in the country, although more and more well-run, aggressive regional banks have entered the leasing market. Since the banks provide services to many of the lessees in the United States, they tend to have a competitive advantage in bidding leasing business. The appetite of commercial banks for such ventures, however, is limited by their tax base, which has been reduced over the years through a combination of leasing and other tax-exempt devices. Based on federal regulation, however, banks have not been a force in the operating lease market.

More and more, banks have used syndication, whereby the bidding bank takes a portion of the transaction for its own account and sells the balance of the equity portion to correspondent banks. There is no reason to expect that the volume of bank leasing will decline significantly in the next several years. The one uncertainty, as of early 1982, is the effect of the 1981 Act. In the past, banks have relied heavily on large fair-market-value residuals for part of their economic benefit. If these are not available, the banks may be less interested in the market.

Large industrial corporations. A second major group of corporate investors is the large industrial companies. General Electric Credit Corporation is perhaps the largest leveraged leasing arm of a major industrial corporation. More and more large companies are looking at leveraged leasing and, for that matter, operating leasing, as ways in which to further their business aims. In some cases, the corporate investors in this field have relied on transactions brought to them by third-party syndicators; in others, they have developed their own leasing arms. It is likely that industrial investors will play an increasing role in the 1980s, especially in the leasing of large ticket items of equipment. The 1981 Act provides incentive for industrial corporate lessors to buy tax benefits in the leasing market. A profitable industrial corporation should prefer to buy tax deferral and forgiveness rather than pay the full federal tax rate.

Small corporations. The third type of corporate investor that has been prominent in the past is the smaller, private corporation. However, this province is almost the exclusive preserve of the syndicator leasing company. Most small corporate investors will purchase one or more transactions a year. By building a portfolio of investments in various leasing transactions, the successful corporate lessor will ultimately benefit from both tax deferral and significant residual participation. Under the Revenue Act of 1978, however, in certain circumstances, the privately held company may have to take more risk to enjoy the benefits of depreciation and tax credit. The company must have more recourse financing than a publicly held company.

If more than 50 percent of the stock is owned by fewer than three individuals, it is necessary for the corporate investor to go at risk in order to obtain sufficient basis in the transaction. Hence, a significant part of the debt financing is recourse to the investor. If the credit is good, this may not present a problem. In addition, there are tax preferences payable by the corporate entity for accelerated depreciation deduction. However, the preference is at a 15 percent rate, far below that of the top corporate rate of federal tax of 46 percent. Of course, if the corporation is taxed at a lower level, as are many small corporate entities, the preference tax of 15 percent may be burdensome. It is likely that small corporate entities will continue to act as lessors during the 1980s.

Individuals

The term "individuals" includes, for purposes of this discussion, not only individuals, but partnerships of individuals, trusts of individuals, Subchapter S corporations, often referred to as tax option companies, and joint tenancies.

Limited partnerships. The most visible type of individual involvement in a leasing transaction is the public or private partnership transaction offered by a number of the major Wall Street firms. In such a transaction, an individual purchases an interest in a partnership, becoming a limited partner. The leases may be either full-payout leveraged leases, short-term operating leases, or a combination of both. If the lease is a properly structured operating lease, the individual may avail himself of tax credits as well as tax deferrals. Of course, the limited partner's recovery of an investment is dependent upon the general partner's ability to continue to lease the chattel at a rental rate at least sufficient to recover the investment, together with the financing and the cost of financing.

As in all limited-partnership transactions, the major deterrent to the transaction is that fairly significant fees are paid to the promoter and other parties associated with the transaction. In addition, the taxation of partnerships is governed by a highly complex set of rules. For the average investor, it is very difficult to understand any particular limited partnership offering. Also, in most cases, those offerings are subject to events that cannot be foreseen at the commencement of the lease term. Nonetheless, the Wall Street firms are having unusual success in selling this type of investment to individuals. Since there can be both tax benefits and economic advantage to the individuals entering into such partnerships, it is likely that this type of vehicle, particularly that relating to operating leases, will increase during the 1980s.

Equity investors. The second type of participation by an individual is one in which a syndicator leasing company originates a transaction and sells the equity portion to an individual or to several individuals as either general partners or tenants in common. Individual investors have been using this device for the last twenty years. However, each of the tax acts of the 1970s has cut down on the benefits available to equity investors.

Restrictions on individual investors. The Revenue Act of 1971 denied investment tax credit to individual investors except in specific instances. The general rule was that investment tax credit was not available to individuals unless the lease was a short-term operating lease. The Tax Reform Act of 1969 provided that certain tax preferences were established. The most important of these was that the excess of depreciation from accelerated depreciation over straight-line depreciation in the net lease was subject to a 15 percent minimum tax. A tax preference could not be sheltered; additional restrictions were added by various tax reform bills.

Individuals are limited by certain formulas on the amount of interest expense that can be taken on their personal returns. The general rule is that interest expense in excess of interest income plus certain additional sums may not be taken, although the excess expense can be carried forward by the individual taxpayer. The 1976 Tax Reform Act provided that individuals must go at risk in the financing of a lease up to an amount equal to the cumulative losses that are available under a leasing transaction. The 1981 Act increased the amount of tax preferences by virtue of expanding the formula for computation of tax preference. In addition, under the 1981 Act, for the first time, an individual availing himself of tax credit for an operating lease has to be at risk for at least 20 percent of the cost of the asset for the five-year period until tax credit vests. Also, if tax credit is to be part of the transaction, whether retained by the lessor or passed through to the lessee, it is absolutely essential that the equipment be new, qualified Section 38 property. The owner-lessor has to rely on its own expert to make a determination if this is the case.

Substantial funds at risk. Since there are no safe-harbor rules for individuals, it is necessary that the individual have a substantial amount of funds invested in the transaction as equity, and further, that he remain at risk during the term of the lease. In other words, the transaction must meet all the requirements of a true lease. The lessor must have his own funds at risk or borrow such funds on a recourse basis equal to the cumulative amount of tax loss available under the lease in its early years. Additional IRS guidelines under Revenue Procedure 75-21, at least in most of its material aspects, ought to be met to shield an individual investor safely. Although this Procedure is not to be used in audit but only for ruling purposes, and since rulings are not available to individuals, it can be argued that the terms of this Revenue Procedure do not apply to individuals. Nonetheless, in a series of cases during the past several years, the IRS has used these ruling guidelines as the basis for an attack on leases where the equipment was owned by individuals. This is so even though the guidelines are not applicable to individuals, since the IRS will not give advance rulings where individuals act as lessors.

At the very least, an individual investor must have a material equity investment at risk in the transaction and a profit motive exclusive of the tax benefits in entering into the deal. In addition, at the end of the lease term, it is critical that there be no bargain or rental option available for the user of the equipment.

All of these rules are highly technical and require that an individual consult with a sophisticated, knowledgeable tax expert who is familiar with the individual's current tax position. However, even with the deterrent built in by several tax reform acts, individuals still become involved in a significant number of transactions, particularly for assets having a value of $3 million or less. In the past several years, boxcar leasing, barge leasing, and other types of transportation equipment leasing on a short-term operating basis have been dominated by individual investors. The ultimate return to the investor, however, requires that the asset be successfully re-leased two or three times in the future.

Tax lien. In the event that a group of individuals acquires ownership of the equipment, through either a partnership or some other type of entity such as joint tenancy, there is always the problem that one of the individuals might become subject to a tax lien. This might cause an interception of rents to the partnership or the other lessor. This problem, however, affects the senior lending institution more than any other party, since it could cause an interruption of debt payment. However, a properly protected senior lender should run no risk in this area if the transaction is a true lease. From the lessee's standpoint, it will have fulfilled all of its requirements should it make the payment even if there is an interception of the rental payment by the taxing authorities.

Need for sophistication. Because of the variety of ways in which a lease can be evaluated, any individual wishing to participate in a leasing transaction should discuss it with his financial adviser. The financial adviser should be particularly sophisticated in tax law and the benefits and risks involved in leasing ventures. In addition, an individual must anticipate the tax bracket he expects to be in during the next several years when entering into the venture. Obviously, the higher the tax bracket, the better the after-tax yield on any leasing transaction. An individual also ought to determine that, indeed, the interest expense, which will be an investment interest expense, can be used by him currently. Current tax law prohibits the expensing of interest that is not offset by investment income and other items.

Finally, an individual must be well advised in the ultimate valuation of the type of equipment to be purchased. It is imperative that the investor or his adviser obtain an appraisal of both the short-term and long-term value of the equipment. Since the individual often must factor some residual value in order to obtain a positive yield on the transaction, one of the major risks is that the equipment will not have the requisite value at the end of the lease term. This can result in a reduced or even negative yield. It is not uncommon for unscrupulous promoters to indicate that a certain item will have a certain value when in fact such an item historically has never had such value. More importantly, there are variations among types of equipment; for example, one type of corporate jet aircraft may be very valuable in ten years, whereas another may be virtually worthless because it is no longer fuel-efficient.

Economically sound transaction. In evaluating a transaction, an individual must be certain that the economics of the transaction make sense. Only then should the tax attributes be examined. The economic issues to be faced are the residual value of the equipment, the underlying credit of the lessee, and, equally important, the expertise and reliability of the general partner if one is involved. The promoter, too, ought to be closely scrutinized. Other transactions in which the promoter or general partner has been involved should be examined to determine that in fact the results of such other ventures have been as advertised.

Wraparound mortgage. Often a leasing company, in selling a transaction to an individual, will either become the lessee or in some manner be directly involved in the transaction. This can be a warning signal to the investor. For example, in any instance in which a so-called wraparound mortgage is employed, the investor should beware. Computer leasing transactions are particularly subject to this type of arrangement. For example, an individual leases a computer to a leasing company for a long period of time, such as nine or ten years. The leasing company leases the computer to a third-party user for a considerably shorter period of time. In such an arrangement, the tax benefits will appear seductively attractive. Unfortunately, the useful economic life of the computer in all probability will not begin to approach the life assumed under the original lease. The cash flow from the rentals and the residual value assumed will be unrealistic.

Asset markup. Another trap for the unwary is a situation in which the asset is marked up significantly over the price charged by the vendor. Particularly in the case of corporate aircraft, this abuse has crept into the leasing business. In such instances, it is common to indicate that the world value, or the U.S. value, for the aircraft has appreciated during the year from the time it was ordered until the time it was delivered. The added value is paid or credited to the lessee or the promoter and the original contracted cost is passed on to the vendor. The lessor often assumes that the IRS will allow the increased basis for the transaction, and an appraisal is produced by the promoter that indicates that in fact the asset has appreciated to cover the amount to be paid to the lessee. In many cases, the appraisal is written by a one-person firm that has a habit of writing several appraisals and then disappearing. In every case, it is incumbent on the investor to determine that the value being paid for the asset in the first instance is in fact fair market value, equivalent to prices being paid for similar assets. Unless properly documented, the IRS might deny basis in the marked-up portion of the asset.

Repurchase by leasing company. A third type of transaction to be wary of is one in which the leasing company agrees to purchase back the asset at a certain time for a specific price. In this case, the lessor must determine whether the leasing company has the funds with which to purchase the asset. In particular, the lessor ought to determine that the leasing company has not agreed to do the same thing with many other investors. If it has, and if the value of the asset plunges and each of the owners decides to return the asset to the leasing company, the leasing company may not be able to buy the asset. In addition, there are certain tax risks where puts of equipment to related or unrelated persons are involved. A variation on this is the situation in which the leasing company gives the same right to a lessee to return the equipment to it. If that occurs, then the owner may find itself in the position of attempting to obtain money from the leasing company, which does not have the ability to pay it. Of course, if the original underlying lease is a full-payout, hell-or-high-water lease, this cannot be the case. Most leases are written on this full-payout basis.

Deferral. Often, a portion of the investment may be deferred. This tends to increase the yield to the investor, since more funds are borrowed. The problem, however, is that ultimately the funds must come up and the investor remains liable to pay them. This is just a gimmick employed by promoters to make the yield appear higher. In fact, on a true economic analysis, this is of little value.

IMPORTANT FACTORS IN ENTERING A LEASE TRANSACTION

Need for Expert Advisers

The most obvious and essential requirement for a corporate or individual investor in acquiring a leasing transaction is that the investor have a sophisticated adviser who can analyze the transaction. This person may be a tax lawyer, a tax accountant, or an experienced investment adviser.

Many of the Wall Street investment firms currently sponsor and sell leasing programs. It is best to have an adviser who has no direct monetary or other interest in the transaction. In this respect, a professional tax adviser is invaluable. However, a tax adviser may not be able to determine the economics of a transaction.

Examination of Basic Assumption

The basic assumption presented in the transaction must be examined first. If any of the basic assumptions are not realistic, then the entire transaction makes no sense from either an economic or a tax standpoint. For example, if the residual value of equipment assumed cannot be obtained reasonably at the end of the lease term, the transaction is not economically sound.

IRS Requirements

In order to escape the odious cost of an audit and perhaps litigation, the investor must be sure that a transaction meets current IRS requirements. Many leasing transactions have been attacked by the IRS as being, for example, financing transactions and not leases. Because of the numerous precedents, it is relatively easy for one who knows the case law and has been involved in similar transactions to determine whether the necessary margin of legitimacy is implicit in the transaction. A private corporation or an individual entering into a leasing transaction without expert advice may pay for the lack of it several years later.

Type of Equipment

The lease term should not be for more than 80 percent of the useful life of the equipment, except in the case of safe-harbor transactions for corporations. Additionally, the equipment should have significant residual value at the end of the lease term. It would be helpful for an investor to discuss the particular type of equipment to be leased with an appraiser or one familiar with such equipment. For example, hospital and computer equipment often become obsolete in a relatively short period, due to rapid technological changes.

Sinking Fund Analysis

Since a transaction is looked at as though the latter portion of the transaction (i.e., after the tax loss period) assumes an earning rate, this should be realistic. Typically, the after-tax earnings rate on the sinking fund should be between 3.5 and 5 percent. Because of the high rate of inflation and high interest rates prevailing today, many transactions are now presented with a 7.5 or 10 percent after-tax re-investment rate. This becomes valid only if one can determine that rates will remain exceedingly high for the balance of the lease transaction. A conservative approach would be to use a re-investment rate not in excess of 5 percent per annum.

Tax Preferences

A transaction can result in tax preferences if the accelerated depreciation exceeds straight-line depreciation. Since in most cases that will be the case, this must be taken into consideration in analysis. Under the 1981 Act, the preference on leased personal property for individuals is calculated as though the straight-line recovery period is eight years for the five-year recovery deduction for most equipment. This results in more tax preference than would have existed under the old law. If the investor is subject to an alternative minimum tax, or will be utilizing averaging conventions under the tax law, then this must be taken into consideration for the analysis of the transaction. Most transactions assume a 50 percent taxpayer. If the individual or the corporate entity is not to be taxed at that high rate, then the economics and the after-tax analysis may fluctuate dramatically. A transaction that makes sense for a 50 percent taxpayer may make no sense whatsoever for a 30 percent taxpayer.

Syndicators

Most transactions that will be purchased by individuals or private corporations originate with syndicators. A syndicator is one who originates transactions for third-party investors. Some have a first-rate reputation, while others are fly-by-night firms that operate in the twilight zone of the tax law. The quality of the lease syndicate becomes of paramount importance. More often than not, money center banks and good regional banks that are involved in the leasing industry can provide the names of reputable syndicators. In addition, tax professionals often have had experience with a variety of lease syndicators and can provide expert advice to potential investors.

Fees and administration. The fees to be paid to a syndicator and/or adviser in a transaction normally are amortized over the life of the lease transaction. Fees ought not to be so substantial as to impair the economics of a transaction.

It is important that the syndicator be available to provide administrative services. Although the lessee's payments pay off senior financing and provide cash flow to the investor, there are administrative requirements to be met. For example, if there are multiple items under the lease, there may be casualty losses in which equipment is destroyed. The lessee is generally responsible for payment of a lump sum for destruction of equipment at any particular time during the lease. Such funds are adequate to pay off remaining senior financing and return the investment with the after-tax yield to the owner. However, someone must do the accounting for the transaction and oversee proper disposition of the funds. For this reason, it makes sense to keep the syndicator involved in the transaction from start to finish.

The equipment must be disposed of at the end of the lease term. Typically, an equity investor has neither the skill nor the expertise to negotiate the highest price for the equipment disposition, with either the current lessee or third parties. Hence, it is not uncommon for a syndicator to charge a deferred-origination fee or a disposition-of-equipment fee at the end of the lease term in order to make its services available. This is often money well spent for the equity investor.

Since the investor must assimilate the transaction into its own tax return, someone must determine the tax aspects of the transaction with respect to the investor's position. Often, the syndicator makes this service available. Working with the individual's tax advisers, the syndicator provides the necessary information on a year-to-year basis. Although this information can be estimated with accuracy at the commencement of the lease term, this estimate is dependent upon there being no future changes in the tax law, destruction of items of equipment during the lease term, or early termination of the lease by the lessee. Particularly with items such as railroad cars, other transportation equipment, and widely dispersed equipment, there may in fact be significant changes in the collateral during the lease term.

Property Identification

It is important to the lessor that equipment be properly marked and identified so that, at the end of the lease term, it can be easily recognized by the owner. Normally, plaques or other identification are applied to equipment. More often than not, this notes the security interest in the equipment to the senior lender in the transaction. However, a lessor ought to have this equipment further marked and identified to the extent that it is the property of the investor. In this manner, there can be no dispute at the end of the lease term. Although a transaction is often looked at by an investor as a tax deal, the value of the residual becomes exceedingly important to the investor as the realization of this residual approaches. When coupled with inflation, residuals today have often become a bonanza or windfall to the equity investor.

Credit Standing of Lessee

Assuming that a leveraged lease or a straight lease is documented properly and that the tax incidents of ownership are as anticipated, one area that is still of some concern to the owner of the equipment — or, for that matter, the lender who provides the funds to finance the purchase — is credit. Since the financing institution is looking to an assignment of the lease and a flow of rentals from the lessee to pay down the borrowed debt, and since it has no further recourse over to the lessor, it is clear that if the lessee is unable to make rental payments, the bank debt will not be paid.

This may result in a foreclosure by the institutional lender, which has a first secured lien on the equipment. The foreclosure results in the forgiveness of debt to the lessor, which had borrowed the funds on a nonrecourse basis. Unfortunately, this may provide for a recapture of prior utilized benefits of ownership such as the investment tax credit or accelerated depreciation. In addition, under the Bankruptcy Act in effect as of early 1982, under certain circumstances there may be difficulties in repossessing equipment that is subject to a lease. Such difficulty may hinge on whether a lessor is indeed an owner or whether the equipment is deemed to be owned, for purposes of the bankruptcy statute, by the lessee.

GLOSSARY

capital lease — A lease in which all the benefits and risks of ownership are substantially transferred to the lessee; usually, lease term is for at least 75 percent of the useful economic life of the property; often includes an option to purchase; accounting and tax treatment differ from those for an operating lease; also called full payout lease.

full-payout lease— See *capital lease.*

lessee— An individual, corporation, or other entity that leases equipment or other property from another in order to obtain its use.

lessor— An individual, corporation, or other entity that owns equipment or other property and leases it to another.

leveraged lease— A lease for a substantial part of the useful life of the property, in which a portion of the property's acquisition cost is raised from borrowed funds.

money-over-money transaction— A straight (nonleveraged) leasing transaction.

net lease— A lease in which the lessee is responsible for maintenance and other costs of ownership of the equipment, including taxes, while the lessor is entitled to the tax benefits of ownership.

operating lease— A lease in which the expenses of ownership are substantially the responsibility of the lessor; usually, lease term is for only a portion of the useful economic life of the property; accounting and tax treatment differ from those for a capital lease.

residual value— Value of the equipment at the end of the lease term.

sale/leaseback— A leasing transaction in which one party buys the equipment from another and then leases it back to the second party (the lessee).

sinking fund— An assumed surplus cash flow to the lessor after recovery of principal and yield on the original investment.

straight lease— A two-party, nonleveraged leasing transaction.

LEADING INVESTMENT FIRMS WITH LEASING PROGRAMS

Bache Halsey Stuart Shields, Inc., New York, N.Y.

Merrill Lynch Pierce Fenner & Smith, Inc., New York, N.Y.

Oppenheimer & Co., Inc., New York, N.Y.

Shearson/American Express, New York, N.Y.

Smith Barney Harris Upham & Co., Incorporated, New York, N.Y.

SUGGESTED READING

Leasing is very tax-oriented, and as the tax laws change, so do the basic ground rules underlying leasing. A careful reading of current periodicals in the accounting, business, and tax areas is essential to keep abreast of the latest developments.

Barron's. Published by Dow Jones & Company, New York, N.Y. Weekly.

Business Week. Published by McGraw-Hill, Inc., New York, N.Y. Weekly.

Financial Executive. Published by Financial Executives Institute, New York, N.Y. Monthly.

Forbes. Published by Forbes, Inc., New York, N.Y. Biweekly.

Fortune. Published by Time, Inc., New York, N.Y. Biweekly.

Harvard Business Review. Published by Harvard University, Graduate School of Business Administration, Boston, Mass. Bimonthly.

Institutional Investor. Published by Institutional Investor Systems, Inc., New York, N.Y. Monthly.

Management Accounting. Published by National Association of Accountants, New York, N.Y. Monthly.

Real Estate Review. Published by Warren, Gorham & Lamont, Boston, Mass. Quarterly.

Wall Street Journal. Daily, Monday through Friday.

Life Insurance Investments —Annuities

Robert S. Rubinstein *

BASIC CHARACTERISTICS

Definition

Literally speaking, the word "annuity" means a series of payments made at regular intervals (annually, monthly, or quarterly) over a defined period (e.g., for a number of years, for life, or in perpetuity). It has been said that the concept of the annuity is life insurance in reverse. Life insurance represents a risk-pooling arrangement whereby many individuals contribute so that substantial funds may be paid on behalf of those who die in any given year. The life annuity contract also embodies a pooling arrangement. However, in the case of the annuity, those who live long benefit at the expense of those who die early. While life insurance protects the purchaser against dying too soon, annuities protect against living too long — that is, the hazard of outliving one's income.

Although differing in function, life insurance and annuities have certain characteristics in common. Both are insurance arrangements involving risk pooling. Both deal with probabilities of survival. Importantly, in the case of whole life insurance and most deferred annuities, both include an investment element and provide significant cash surrender values in addition to protection against a major hazard.

All annuities can be characterized as either immediate annuities or deferred annuities.

Immediate Annuities

An immediate annuity contract provides for a single-sum payment, or premium, to be made to the insurance company. In return, the company agrees to make to the annuitant (or contract owner, if different) a periodic series of payments beginning within a year of the commencement date of the contract. A life annuity provides for payments to be made as long as one or more persons are alive. A life annuity can also contain a minimum payment period. For example, a life-ten-year-certain annuity provides for periodic payments during the lifetime of one or

* Robert S. Rubinstein is an actuary with The Equitable Life Assurance Society of the United States, New York.

more individuals, and guarantees that a minimum of ten years' payments will be made either to the annuitant(s) or to a named beneficiary if the annuitant is deceased.

Deferred Annuities

A deferred annuity contract can be broken into two main parts: provisions applicable to the accumulation period and provisions governing settlements. Unlike an immediate annuity, which is intended only to produce a given income from a certain sum of money, a deferred annuity is a vehicle intended to accumulate funds and also to achieve an income at retirement or some other later date.

The typical contract will provide for either a single payment or a series of payments. If a series of payments is contemplated under the contract, the owner usually has discretion over the amount and timing within certain prescribed limits. Such a contract is said to be flexible premium-paying.

During the accumulation period the premiums, less any applicable charges (described below), are invested in a manner described in the contract. A fixed deferred annuity provides for investment in the company's general account. A variable deferred annuity provides for investment in one or more variable annuity funds, known as separate accounts.

Settlement options. When a deferred annuity contract matures, the holder generally is entitled to select from several settlement options, including single-sum immediate cash payout, life annuity, or annuity certain (not depending on the annuitant's survival). If the contractholder elects annuitization, for example, the account balance, less any applicable state premium taxes, would be applied to purchase a life annuity or annuity certain at current settlement rates. Since the insurance company has usually recovered its sales expenses by this time, the current rates are often more favorable than rates applicable to new money used to purchase an immediate annuity. In addition, the contract will stipulate a set of minimum guaranteed settlement rates. These rates are based on conservative interest assumptions; therefore, they presently provide less income than do the current rates. It should be noted that it is the existence of these guarantees that causes the contract to be classified by the IRS, SEC, and other regulatory bodies as an annuity. For example, an individual may invest in a mutual fund directly, without an annuity wrapper, or open up an individual retirement account (IRA) or Keogh account (HR-10) with a bank. Due to the absence of any annuity rate guarantees, and indeed any provision for annuitizing whatsoever, these alternative investments should not be confused with the annuity contract. While other financial institutions offer many of the same investment features during the accumulation period, only the insurance company can offer a life annuity income option.

Tax qualification. Many annuities are purchased under special tax-favored arrangements that have been authorized by Congress. These annuities are termed tax-qualified. These tax-favored arrangements include corporate pension, profit-sharing and thrift plans, individual retirement annuities, HR-10 plans, tax-sheltered annuities, and certain public employee deferred compensation plans. Annuities not purchased under one of the tax-favored arrangements are referred to as non-tax-qualified. Non-tax-qualified annuities also contain significant tax advantages.

Primary Determinants of Value

If an immediate guaranteed lifetime income is desired, it is a simple matter to compare the annuity income offered by the XYZ Company to that of other companies and select the company that pays the highest amount. In addition, the investor should compute the percentage of the purchase price (return) paid out each year and compare this to the yield currently obtainable on other conservative investments. In doing this, the investor should require a significantly higher return on the annuity than on a long-term investment since, unlike other investments, the investor cannot recover his principal. Also, the investor should consider his health, need for inflation protection, and personal tax situation.

In the case of a deferred annuity, a comparison even among other like annuities can be extremely complicated due to variations in expense charges, interest guarantees, investment flexibility, and so on. The following are the important factors to consider when choosing among competing deferred annuities and when comparing deferred annuities to other investments such as bank certificates of deposit and mutual funds.

Sales and administrative charges. A variety of charges exist, and many products have several types of charges.

Front-end load. This is a percentage charge that is deducted from each payment before the payment is credited to the holder's account. In the 1960s, many annuity contracts had loads of 15 percent and higher. In the 1970s, as competition increased, front-end loads were reduced below 10 percent. Today, those companies that do have front-end loads generally either have level loads in the 5 percent range, or higher early-year loads that grade down rapidly as the aggregate contributions increase. Perhaps an average of 75 percent of such charges are used to pay the agent's commission and other sales-related expenses, with the remainder for administrative expenses. The commission paid to the selling agent can be as high as 10 percent or more of the first years' payments, and grade down to as low as 1 to 3 percent in renewal years.

Contingent withdrawal or surrender charge. In the last two or three years, there has been a tremendous number of new annuities on the market that do not have front-end loads, except perhaps for premium taxes (described below). Instead, a contingent withdrawal, or surrender, charge is levied for some or all withdrawals. Companies that are licensed in New York State, for example, are limited by law to a charge equal to 7 percent of the accumulated contract value. The typical no-front-end-load single-premium annuity contains charges that grade down rapidly, such as 7 percent in year one, 6 percent in year two, etc., down to no charge in year eight. However, some companies levy a permanent surrender charge, which is not waived except upon annuitization, that is, unless the holder converts the accumulated value into a life annuity or an annuity certain.

Periodic payment annuity surrender charges do not grade down nearly as quickly, since the company is continually incurring additional sales and administrative expenses when each new payment is made. The SEC has effectively limited aggregate variable annuity surrender charges to 9 percent of payments (excluding account appreciation). Many companies have even lesser charges. Nationwide's Spectrum policy, for example, has a 5 percent surrender charge, which may not exceed 5 percent of payments made during the last ninety-six months. Thus, a holder who left payments in for eight years would thereafter never incur a surrender charge with regard to these payments.

Many companies offer the right to withdraw up to 10 percent of the annuity's value without charge, either immediately or after a set number of years. This feature can be used to withdraw funds for an emergency or for a child's education, for example. (See *Potential Risks* and *Tax Consequences* in this article.)

The surrender charge assists the insurer to recover unamortized acquisition expense. In the case of fixed annuities, it also helps protect the insurer from having to liquidate large amounts of investments below amortized value in order to pay contractholders who surrender during periods when other new investments are yielding more than the annuity. Such a situation is referred to as financial disintermediation. The surrender charge serves both to deter surrenders and to reimburse the insurer for a portion of the resultant loss.

Annual administrative charges. Many single-payment fixed annuities do not have any explicit charges other than those stated above. However, some single-payment and most periodic-payment annuities contain an administrative charge. The typical charge is from $15 to $30 per year, up to an annual maximum of 2 percent of account value. The charge usually is made whether or not premiums are paid in a given year. Some companies have a smaller annual charge along with a per-payment processing fee of up to one dollar.

Premium taxes. About 20 percent of the states impose a premium tax upon the insurer, ranging from 0.20 to 2.35 percent, with respect to payments under some or all types of annuity contracts. Companies differ in the manner in which they pass along this expense to the contractholder. Some companies do not have a direct tax charge, but absorb this expense in their general pricing. Other companies do charge for the tax, either as the payments are remitted or upon annuitization (but not if a partial or full cash surrender is made).

Asset charge-interest holdback. Under variable contracts (and some fixed contracts), the insurer deducts a daily charge from the unit value (i.e., price) of the account in order to cover investment expenses and mortality and expense guarantees. This charge typically equates to an annual charge of 1 to 1.75 percent. In other words, if the account's investment performance were such that a 10 percent investment gain (net realized and unrealized capital gains and losses after any charges for federal income taxes) were realized for a year, a company with a 1.5 percent asset charge would pass on an 8.5 percent gain to the contractholder.

In comparing the asset charges of a contract that utilizes an insurance company separate account with one that invests in an outside mutual fund, the investor should add the mutual fund's underlying asset charge to the charge levied by the insurance company. For example, one company's contract specifies an asset charge of only 1.3 percent, but when this is added to the charges of the underlying mutual funds, the total charge is as high as 2.24 percent. It is this total charge upon which the investor should focus.

Underwriters of fixed annuities finance the investment expenses and the cost of providing mortality and expense guarantees through the difference between the interest rate earned and the rate credited to the contract. The amount of interest held back is generally not stipulated in the contract, nor is such an amount set in advance. However, the insurance laws of the vast majority of states require companies to credit interest in an equitable manner. For example, a company must be able to demonstrate that it is not favoring new business over existing business. Companies utilizing the investment year (or new money) method of allocating investment income may, however, credit higher rates to new contractholders than to existing holders if the expectation is for a higher rate of investment return on assets underlying the new contracts than for those underlying the old.

In comparing the charges of competing annuities, the prospective annuitant should evaluate his intentions regarding the purpose and future use of the annuity. Does he intend to use the contract as a long-term retirement vehicle? If so, it may be worthwhile to select a contract with a relatively higher early surrender charge, if the contract appears favorable in other respects. Is there a need to draw on the account value within a few years? Then a contract free-corridor provision, permitting free withdrawals up to a certain percentage of the premium(s) or account value, is an important feature.

Interest rate. Along with the contract charges, the interest rate credited on payments allocated to the fixed account is of utmost importance to the buyer, particularly if the fixed account is the only investment option available under the contract. The relative importance of the interest assumption is even greater than many investors expect, due to the nature of compounding. For example, an individual investing a level amount annually over a twenty-year period and earning an effective annual rate of 10 percent would achieve an account value that is 5.8 percent higher than if the effective rate were 9.5 percent. In other words, 0.5 percent additional interest each year is equivalent to a 5.8 percent load after twenty years. Generally, differences in interest rates paid far outweigh differences in load or surrender charges as a factor in determining final retirement account values over a period of years.

In addition to the amount of interest currently credited to new contracts, the investor should also consider the duration of the current interest guarantee. This usually ranges anywhere from none to around five years, with one year being very common. There also may or may not be significant later-year guarantees.

Portfolio vs. new-money basis. Another consideration is whether the company credits interest on a portfolio or new-money basis. On the portfolio basis, every like contractholder, regardless of the contract issue date, receives the same interest rate. Under the new-money method, different rates are usually credited to different pockets of monies, depending on when they were contributed. One company, for example, currently credits 12 percent on contributions remitted after December 31, 1978 and 9 percent on contributions remitted earlier. Under a modified new-money method that at least one company utilizes, each contractholder receives a single rate, but this rate may differ among contractholders depending on the issue class to which the contract belongs. Companies that utilize a new-money approach are usually better able to increase rates on existing contracts when new-money rates increase than are companies that utilize a portfolio approach. However, the converse is also true: Companies on a new-money basis are more likely to lower rates on existing contracts when new-money rates decrease. Hence, an investor who believes future interest rates will increase or who wishes to obtain protection against future interest rate increases even at the risk of sharp sudden declines might prefer a company that uses a new-money basis. An investor who seeks to receive a more stable interest rate over time might prefer a company utilizing a portfolio approach.

It may be helpful for the investor to know the historical rates credited on existing classes of business. For example, a prospective purchaser of a single-premium deferred annuity that offers a yearly renewable one-year interest guarantee should inquire as to the recent renewal rates of contracts issued one or more years ago.

Investment policy. The investment policy of the fixed account is also of concern to the investor. The contract, itself, may state merely that the assets are invested in the company's general account, but the selling agent may be able to provide the purchaser with a statement of the company's investment policy. Investments generally consist of good-quality (BAA quality or higher) publicly traded bonds, direct placements, and perhaps mortgages. Short-term money market instruments are also used. Traditionally, the companies have invested in issues that mature in fifteen years or more. Since only a small fraction of these investments were repaid each year, companies were unable to pass along the full benefit of higher new-money rates where such rates existed. Since 1979, rapid fluctuations of yields on fixed investments have resulted in many companies shortening their maturities. When companies do choose to invest long-term, they are increasingly turning to inflation-adaptive instruments that provide for periodic renegotiation of the interest rate. While these companies cannot usually afford to offer significant long-term interest guarantees, they do have the ability to adjust rates fairly often, either up or down. This provides the purchaser with some protection against future rampant interest rate rises.

Finally, the prospective annuitant who is not interested in short-term or long-term rate guarantees, but whose chief objective is to receive a return reflective of current short-term rates with minimal risk of loss of principal, can invest in a variable annuity with a money market account.

Investment flexibility. The investor should consider the range of investment opportunities available under the contract. Fixed contracts offer only one account, while one variable annuity has as many as nine. Any restrictions regarding transferability of past accumulations and changing future payment allocations between accounts should also be considered. Many contracts have no restrictions whatsoever.

Investment performance. In the case of variable annuities, investors should examine the prior investment performance coupled with the investment objectives of the account. This information can be obtained from the prospectus or annual statement of the separate account.

Settlement rates. Since the investor under a deferred annuity may wish to annuitize at a later time, he should consider both the range of settlements offered and the quality of the current and guaranteed rates (as compared with those offered by other companies) before selecting an annuity. The current settlement rates, although not contained in the contract, largely influence the amount of income the annuitant will be able to purchase at retirement. Settlement rates vary greatly, and a product's attractiveness in the accumulation phase is often not indicative of the quality of its settlement options.

Company's Best rating. A highly respected independent company, A.M. Best Company, publishes *Best's Insurance Reports: Life — Health,* which assigns a letter rating to all life insurance companies, ranging from C (fair) to A+ (excellent). This rating indicates Best's opinion of the long-term ability of the company to discharge its responsibilities to contractholders. Two of the criteria used are particularly important to annuity contractholders: net resources adequate to absorb unusual shocks, and soundness of investments.

Types of Life Insurance Annuities

The annuity, as defined earlier, encompasses a wide range of products. The following is a description of each major type:

Fixed immediate annuity. As mentioned earlier, this is an arrangement whereby the company, in return for a single premium, agrees to pay the annuitant (who is usually the owner) a specific number of dollars each month, quarter, or year, for life. The simplest form is the straight life annuity, under which the income ceases with the last regular payment prior to the annuitant's death.

Refund annuity. This provides that should the annuitant die before total payments have equaled or exceeded the premium, the difference shall be payable to the beneficiary named in the contract. The cash refund annuity provides for this payment in a single sum, whereas the installment refund annuity provides for a continuation of the annuity's periodic payments until the premium has been recovered.

Period certain annuity. This provides that should the annuitant die before the stated period (e.g., ten years from the date of issue), the payments will be payable to the beneficiary until the period has elapsed. The beneficiary may also choose to receive the commuted value of the remaining payments (based on the commutation interest rate contained in the contract) in lieu of a stream of payments.

Joint and survivor annuity. This provides for payments during the joint lifetime of two annuitants and during the lifetime of the survivor. The buyer can elect that a lower income be payable to the survivor rather than to the joint annuitants. For example, a contract could provide for payment to the survivor equal to 50 percent of the initial payment.

Payments under all types of annuities, except for the joint and survivor, are usually level. However, a few companies sell fixed annuities with increasing payments.

Rates for these various annuities differ depending on the amount of risk the insurance company is asked to assume. Therefore, the amount of income that can be obtained from a fixed premium is, for example, higher for a straight life annuity than for a refund annuity, and higher for a male than for a female of the same age (due to the female's longer life expectancy). One company's sample rates are shown in Table 1 on page 363.

Variable immediate annuity. The discussion above applies to this product also, except that here the company agrees to pay the annuitant a set number of annuity units, not dollars. The dollar value of an annuity unit is linked to the investment performance of a separate account, which is usually invested in common stocks. The initial amount of income is based on the insurer's mortality and expense assumptions and an assumed interest rate mandated by state law. This rate is 5 percent for most states. Subsequent payments increase if the account's unit value increases at an annual rate higher than 5 percent and, otherwise, decrease. For example, if the unit value grows at a 9 percent annual rate, the payments increase at about a 4 percent annual rate. Thus, unlike the case of a fixed immediate annuity, the purchaser bears all of the investment risk. However,

TABLE 1. Typical Annuity Rate Structure — 1981

Type of Annuity	*Age*	*Single Premium Per $10 of Monthly Income*	
		Males	*Females*
Straight life	75	$706	$784
Straight life	80	609	665
Installment refund	75	780	832
Straight life — joint and survivor (100 percent of initial income paid to survivor)	75 Male 72 Female	$924	

as in the case of a fixed immediate annuity, the company bears the mortality and expense risk.

Variable immediate annuities have not been well received since they were introduced in the 1960s. One reason is that the initial payment is much lower than that of a fixed annuity (which might be based on an assumed long-term invested earnings rate of 12 percent or more today). Also, although this product offers potential for future increases in payments, many annuitants dislike receiving payments that fluctuate greatly from month to month, depending upon the investment performance of the separate account. Many individuals who will accept variable accumulations before retirement will not accept variable payouts after retirement. This is because most annuitants prefer to receive predictable amounts of regular income and are usually unwilling to assume much risk over a time period as short as the life expectancy remaining at retirement.

Annuity certain. Under this type of annuity, the purchaser pays a single premium to the company and, in turn, receives a regular fixed payment (principal and interest) for a specified number of years. No life contingencies are involved. Since New York licensed companies are not permitted to sell this annuity except in specialized situations (such as the funding of state lottery prizes), many companies do not offer this product.

Fixed deferred annuity. Under this contract a relatively low rate of interest (e.g., 4 percent) is typically guaranteed throughout the accumulation period; the company periodically credits additional interest based on either its past or projected investment experience with respect to the underlying assets. In recent years, companies have begun to guarantee initial interest rates that are significantly higher than the long-term guaranteed rate. For example, a contract might guarantee 12 percent for the first policy year and provide for a declaration of a new rate before each subsequent policy year, but specify that such new rate shall never be less than the minimum guarantee of 4 percent.

Variable deferred annuity. Under this contract, the premiums are invested in one or more separate accounts. Unlike a life insurance company's general account, which is required by state laws to be invested primarily in bonds and mortgages, separate accounts are generally invested in common stocks. Separate accounts can also be invested in other instruments, such as long-term bonds, money market instruments, and real estate. The accumulated value of the contract changes daily to reflect the market value of these underlying funds and the deductions and charges that are described in the prospectus. There is no minimum investment guarantee (except, perhaps, upon death of the annuitant); hence, account values can fluctuate widely.

The traditional variable deferred annuity, first widely marketed in the early 1970s, utilized one or two (rarely more) separate accounts managed by the insurance company. An important variation of the traditional product is the investment wraparound annuity. In one type of arrangement, the purchaser of an insurer's variable annuity can choose among several of the various mutual funds managed by an investment management company that is otherwise unaffiliated with the insurance company. Merrill Lynch, Dreyfus, and Putnam are among the firms that have recently affiliated with insurance companies to offer such a product. This second generation variable annuity permits the insurance company to offer a much wider range of investment alternatives than it could economically offer if it had to set up its own separate accounts. As a result, variable annuities offering as many as eight mutual fund separate accounts are now being offered.

Some variable annuities include a fixed account that is contained in the insurer's general account. Under this combination annuity, the insurer declares one or more rates of interest applicable to the fixed account monies and the insurer bears the risk of capital loss with respect to this account.

In another variation, an insurance company enters into agreements with participating federally insured savings and loan associations to sell annuity certificates to existing and new depositors of the associations. Thus, the annuity can be wrapped around a certificate of deposit, for example. (Note: As described in *Tax Consequences* in this article, the tax status of several types of wraparound annuities have been attacked by the Treasury Department.)

Group deferred annuity. Under this contract, the purchaser pays the insurer a single premium on behalf of each annuitant that purchases life income benefits that are scheduled to commence at later dates, usually at the annuitants' scheduled retirements. Such contracts usually do not have cash surrender values before retirement although, if an annuitant dies before retirement, the contract may specify that the premium, with or without interest, will be refunded. After the income commences, the contract functions as an individual immediate annuity with respect to the annuitant. Such annuities are typically purchased to fund accrued benefits for participants of a terminating pension plan. The rates will be partially based on the insurer's expectation of the participants' mortality experience.

Group deposit administration (DA) contract. The DA contract is used to provide unallocated funding (i.e., pre-retirement funds are not allocated to individual participants) for company pension plans that provide predetermined retirement benefits (defined benefit plans). Contributions are generally allocated to the insurance company's general account and are credited with a guaranteed amount of interest (e.g., 5 percent) plus additional interest, included in the annually declared dividend, which is determined by the investment year (new-money) method. The insurance company also guarantees a set of annuity settlement rates for accumulations that derive from contributions received during an initial period, such as five years. (The guaranteed rates are periodically re-established thereafter.) The insurance company's current rates apply if they produce a higher income. In addition to investment experience, expenses and post-retirement mortality rate experience, to the extent that they are more favorable than was assumed by the insurer in pricing, are gradually passed through to the plan trustee in the form of dividends.

With a group DA contract, unlike an individual fixed deferred annuity, a market value adjustment is charged if the purchaser withdraws funds prematurely when the book value of the contract's reserves exceeds market value (such as when new interest rates are higher than the average rate earned on the account). In addition to general account funding, companies also offer funding through separate accounts, in which diverse pension plan clients share ratably in a fund's performance or, for very large cases ($10 million or more of assets), individually managed accounts.

Annual administrative charges grade down with the size of the fund (as a percentage of the fund), with a typical contractual annual minimum of $2,000. For example, the fee could be 0.50 percent of the first $2 million of mean funds grading down to 0.04 percent of the portion of mean funds that exceed $50 million. Additional fees are charged for certain services the insurer performs, such as keeping individual employee records, processing withdrawals, processing retirements, and paying retirement benefits.

Immediate participation guarantee (IPG) contracts. Many pension plan administrators, particularly the larger ones (such as $100,000 or more in annual premiums), are not interested in complete insurance company guarantees followed by gradual participation through dividends. Instead, they prefer immediate full participation with only residual guarantees. Under the IPG contract, as long as the unallocated (i.e., pre-retirement) funds are maintained at a certain level (e.g., not less than 10 percent of those allocated to retired lives) the total funds, including those allocated to retired lives, will be credited with the full investment results, charged with the full expenses incurred, and charged or credited with the post-retirement mortality results actually experienced.

In another variation, sometimes referred to as a direct experience DA contract, the insurer provides full guarantees with respect to the retired lives only.

ATTRACTIVE FEATURES

Lifetime Income Option

The annuity is the only vehicle that can offer the investor a guaranteed lifetime income, either immediately or at some future date.

Investment Flexibility

Some variable annuities, particularly those that allocate contributions to one or more mutual funds or separate accounts, offer an uncommon degree of investment flexibility. Contributions may be allocated in any way among many accounts, and past accumulations may be transferred among accounts without charge or tax consequences. While invested monies often may be transferred between various no-load mutual funds without charge, the annuity vehicle is unique in permitting inter-account transfers without the owner incurring current income tax on the gain (i.e., the excess of the accumulated amount over the amount invested). For example, if an annuitant contributed $10,000 to a common stock account, and with appreciation this had grown to $15,000, the $15,000 could be transferred to another account within the annuity, such as a fixed-interest account, without the $5,000 gain being subject to current income tax. However, if the same $10,000 had been invested in a common stock mutual fund, appreciated to $15,000, and the shares were sold and transferred to, say, a bank CD, the gain would be subject to tax for the year of transfer. Although many contracts are extremely flexible, the annuitant should note any restrictions that a particular contract imposes on transferability between accounts.

The IRS permits tax-free exchanges of one annuity contract for another. This enables an annuitant to take advantage of another company's product should, for example, its interest rate be higher than it is under the current product.

Tax Deferral of Income

Deferred annuities defer current taxes on investment earnings, which compound tax-deferred until actually withdrawn or received as income. This is an extremely attractive feature that, for the man-in-the-street (non-qualified) market, is unique to the annuity. (For further discussion, see *Tax Consequences* in this article.)

Investment, Mortality, and Expense Guarantees

Interest. As noted earlier, the current trend is away from long-term interest guarantees on deferred annuities. However, many products still offer significant guarantees that often apply to future as well as current contributions. Insurance companies are alone in offering interest guarantees with respect to future contributions.

Money-back guarantee. Many no-front-end-load annuity contracts guarantee that the company will return the full premium to the owner upon termination. Thus, an individual has the option of switching out of a fixed annuity to another vehicle a month or two after issue, only forfeiting interest earned to that date.

Minimum death benefit. Many deferred variable annuities specify that upon death of the annuitant the beneficiary will receive an amount equal to either the total contributions less withdrawals or the account value, whichever is greater. In other words, in the event of the annuitant's death, the company bears the risk of account depreciation.

Expense guarantee. Under individual contracts, expense loadings, termination charges, administrative charges, and asset charges are usually guaranteed for the contract's lifetime. Thus, the insurer bears the risk that the administrative and investment expenses will exceed the amounts anticipated at issue. The insurer often includes a risk charge in the asset charge to cover this.

Annuity rate guarantee/betterment of rates provision. Most individual deferred contracts contain lifetime fixed annuity rate guarantees that can be significant if interest rates ever drop to the levels that existed before the 1970s, or if mortality improves significantly. The contracts state that current declared rates, as modified by the company from time to time, will apply should those be more favorable than the guaranteed rates.

POTENTIAL RISKS

Through selection of the particular contract, the buyer has considerable discretion regarding the amount of risk to assume. The company's rates, of course, reflect the amount of risk it is being asked to assume. Over the years, there has been a trend away from traditional insurance company guarantees to fewer and weaker guarantees. The payoff to the consumer is a less expensive product with the potential for higher yields if the insurer's experience should prove favorable. The following risks are assumed in varying degrees by the buyer and the company, depending on the product selected:

Possible Principal Risk — Market Volatility

Although fixed deferred annuities are considered to be one of the safest investment vehicles around, variable annuities involve market risks comparable to those inherent in mutual fund investments. The investment policies of the separate accounts (stated in the prospectus) should be examined closely. The amount of capital risk to which the investor is exposed can be either virtually none, as in a money market fund; or some, as in a fixed income bond fund; or considerable, as in a high-growth stock fund. The historical account unit values shown in the prospectus can serve as a barometer of past volatility.

Income Variability

As discussed previously, many companies have moved away from offering high, long-term interest guarantees and have changed to shorter-term and/or inflation-adaptive investment strategies. While such companies offer little income protection if market interest rates should decline markedly, they may offer more inflationary protection than the traditional products do.

A feature found in many single-premium contracts, known as a bailout provision, can help cushion a buyer's fear that the company will keep future rates significantly below market levels. This provision states that should the current declared rate ever fall below a contractual minimum, which is often within 1 and 2 percent of the initial rate, the contract can be surrendered without charge.

Liquidity Problems

A buyer of an immediate annuity sacrifices all liquidity, since the contract does not have any cash surrender values. A buyer of a deferred annuity should be aware that, while he generally can liquidate the contract for its cash value at any time, there may be significant contractual penalties for doing so.[1] Even if the contract does not stipulate early withdrawal penalties, it may have significant front-end charges that render it a poor investment if surrendered in the first few years.

Possible Tax Exposure

As discussed below, tax deferral on the investment income earned under the contract is a major consideration in purchasing a deferred annuity. However, the Treasury Department has already ruled that owners of annuities that provide for the allocation of contributions to either an individually managed fund (Rev. Rul. 77-85) or a savings and loan CD (Rev. Rul. 80-278) are not able to defer tax on

---

[1] Under certain tax-qualified plans such as individual retirement annuities and HR-10 plans, there are also substantial penalties imposed by the IRS for premature distributions before age 59½. Also, New York State requires companies licensed in that state to reserve the right in their contracts to withhold payments of fixed annuity cash values for up to six months in order to protect the company from having to take substantial capital losses during periods of extremely heavy surrenders. Companies almost never invoke this right, however.

the underlying securities' dividend and interest income. In addition, under Revenue Ruling 81-225, the annuitant was treated as the owner of the underlying investment vehicle if the shares of the fund(s) under an annuity contract were also sold directly to the general public without the annuity wrapper. The owner of the annuity would thus be taxed as a mutual fund owner. However, this ruling, as clarified by Revenue Ruling 82-54, maintains the tax status of fixed and variable annuities, in which the annuitant is unable to directly participate in the underlying investments without purchasing the annuity.

TAX CONSEQUENCES

Annuitants and individuals contemplating the purchase of an annuity should be aware of the tax ramifications related to the various types of products. The investor who uses the annuity vehicle shrewdly can obtain significant tax advantages, some of which are not available with respect to any other type of investment. The rules governing the income taxation of amounts received under annuity contracts are contained in Section 72 of the Internal Revenue Code.

As of early 1982, the Treasury Department was planning to recommend changes in the Code that would limit the tax advantages of non-tax-qualified annuities.

Deferred Annuities

Tax deferral — non-tax-qualified contracts. The major tax advantage of a non-tax-qualified deferred annuity contract during the accumulation period is that the contractholder avoids the payment of federal, state, and local income taxes on the earnings credited to the contract until they are withdrawn, presumably at retirement when the holder will generally be in a lower tax bracket. Moreover, earnings are not considered to be withdrawn during the accumulation period until the aggregate withdrawals from the contract since its inception exceed the original cost basis, which generally equals the aggregate premiums paid for the contract (so-called capital withdrawal privilege).

The advantage to the contractholder is twofold. First, by timing the withdrawals of the contract earnings to occur during a period when his marginal tax rate is less than the marginal rate in effect at the time the earnings were accrued, the percentage tax bite can be lessened. In other words, the investor can determine the best time to pay tax on the earnings. Second, money that normally would be paid in taxes is automatically re-invested, producing additional tax-deferred earnings thereon.

Table 2 on page 370 provides an example of an investment with and without a tax deferral of earnings; this is valid in comparing an investment in which all income is currently taxed as ordinary income (such as a savings account or money market fund) with an annuity. However, investors who compare investments that are intended to produce significant net long-term capital gains with an annuity

TABLE 2. Effect of Tax Deferral on $10,000 Lump-Sum Annuity Investment

Without Tax Deferral	*With Tax Deferral**
$10,000 investment (50 percent tax bracket)	$10,000 investment
Earnings: 10 percent/year, before tax, compounded annually; 5 percent/year after tax	Earnings: 10 percent/year, compounded annually
$16,289 cash value in ten years at 5 percent interest (after tax)	$25,937 account value in ten years (before taxes)
	$17,968 cash after 50 percent tax on earnings
	$21,953 cash after 25 percent tax on earnings
$26,533 cash value in 20 years (after taxes)	$67,275 account value in twenty years (before taxes)
	$38,638 cash after 50 percent tax on earnings
	$52,956 cash after 25 percent tax on earnings

*Assumes no front-end load or withdrawal charge applies. Also, excludes effects of any annual administrative or asset charges. The investor should carefully consider the impact of any applicable charges contained in the annuity contract.

should take note of the favorable capital gains treatment accorded these investments. This treatment is not available with respect to an annuity. For example, consider a common stock mutual fund. If the fund were to grow at, say, a 10 percent annual rate, perhaps 3 percent would be due to dividends and 7 percent to net long-term capital gains. Since only 40 percent of the net long-term gain is taxed by the IRS, an investor in a 50 percent marginal tax bracket would realize about 7.1 percent $[(3\% \times 0.50) + (7\% \times 0.40 \times 0.50) + (7\% \times 0.60)]$ after tax, as compared with the 5 percent return used in Table 2. If the investment were made instead in a variable annuity common stock account earning the same 10 percent, income taxes would be deferred but the entire gain eventually would be subject to ordinary income tax at withdrawal. (Also, note that the annuity asset charges probably would exceed the mutual fund charges. Therefore, a variable annuity separate account would produce a lower pre-tax yield than would an identically managed mutual fund).

An example of the capital withdrawal privilege is as follows: An investor purchases a $10,000 no-front-end-load single-premium deferred annuity that provides for free annual withdrawals of up to 10 percent of the single premium. The annuity earns 10 percent per year. The investor withdraws $1,000 for each of ten years, which is also the amount of interest earned annually. After ten years, the investor has withdrawn $10,000 of earnings, and is left with the full $10,000 principal amount, but has not yet paid any tax on the annuity earnings. Future withdrawals would be fully taxable. However, perhaps the investor would be retired and in a lower tax bracket or, for example, choose not to make any further withdrawals. In the latter case, the beneficiary would eventually incur the tax based on his tax bracket.

When an annuity is paid out, a constant pro rata portion of each payment is considered to be taxable earnings. The rules pertaining to immediate annuity taxation (as described later) would apply except that the investment in the contract would equal the original cost basis less any amounts withdrawn that were not included in taxable income. For example, if a $15,000 contract were purchased, and $5,000 had been withdrawn earlier, the $5,000 would not have been taxable. When the annuity payment period begins, the investment in the contract would be $15,000 − $5,000 = $10,000 regardless of the contract's value at that time.

Tax deferral — tax-qualified contract. Holders of this contract not only enjoy the benefit of tax-deferral on contractual earnings as described above for non-tax-qualified contracts, but, in addition, forgo current income taxation on the contributions. Withdrawals, however, are fully taxable when taken [2] — either as a lump sum or in the form of annuity payments. Table 3 on page 372 illustrates the tax benefit that might be experienced by a public-school teacher who contributed $100 per month to a tax-sheltered annuity.

Note that the amount of money accumulated under this contract would greatly exceed the amount accumulated in a non-tax-sheltered investment even if the same yield were earned and the tax bracket did not change.

Taxation of death benefit under non-tax-qualified contract. If the annuitant dies before his deferred annuity contract matures, any contract earnings that have not been previously withdrawn are taxed as ordinary income to the beneficiary. However, the beneficiary will not be fully taxed on those earnings in the year of death if he elects, within sixty days after the annuitant's death, to apply the death benefit under a life income or annuity certain option. In that case, the periodic payments will be taxable to the beneficiary under the regular immediate annuity rules, based on the decedent's investment in the contract and the beneficiary's expected return. The entire value of the annuity is includable in the gross estate for estate tax purposes.

Taxation of death benefit under tax-qualified contract. Generally, the entire death benefit is taxable to the beneficiary as ordinary income and is also subject to estate taxes. However, in several of the tax-qualified markets, a more favorable tax treatment is available. Two examples follow:

---

[2] Usually, distributions are taxed as ordinary income. However, a favorable ten-year-averaging method may be elected by HR-10 and pension plan participants in certain instances.

- In the case of an individual retirement annuity, proceeds paid to a named beneficiary as an annuity in substantially equal installments over at least three years are free from federal estate tax (and are taxed as ordinary income as received).
- Distributions from an HR-10 plan to a named beneficiary may be free from federal estate tax if the beneficiary does not elect to use the special ten-year-averaging method for the calculation of federal income taxes. (If ten-year averaging is used, estate taxes would apply; however, ten-year averaging would result in significantly lower income taxes on the distribution than under ordinary income taxation rules.)

Tax penalties for early withdrawals. In order to discourage use of an IRA or HR-10 plan for purposes other than to provide retirement income, the IRS imposes a 10 percent penalty tax on distributions prior to age 59½ (except for death or disability) to IRA participants and owner-employees under HR-10 plans. For both types of annuitants, income payments must start in the year the annuitant attains age 70½.

Non-qualified variable annuity double-taxation problem. A serious tax pitfall of the non-tax-qualified variable annuity is that both the insurance company and the contractholder incur a tax with respect to realized net long-term capital gains in the separate accounts and in the mutual funds used in wraparound annuities. The insurer pays a tax of about 28 percent, which is reflected in the

TABLE 3. Effect of Tax Deferral on $100 Monthly Annuity Investment

Without Tax Shelter		*With Tax Shelter**	
$100	earnings	$100	earnings
35	tax (based on 35% bracket)	0	tax
$ 65	invested	$100	invested
Earnings:	10 percent/year, compounded annually	Earnings:	10 percent/year, compounded annually
Less tax:	3.5 percent	Less Tax:	0 percent
Earnings:	6.5 percent after tax	Earnings:	10 percent after tax
$31,176 cash value in twenty years (after taxes)		$71,826 account value in twenty years (before taxes)	
		$46,687 cash after 35 percent tax	
		$50,278 cash after 30 percent tax	
		$53,870 cash after 25 percent tax	

*Assumes that no front-end load or withdrawal charge applies. Also, excludes effects of any annual administrative or asset charges. The investor should carefully consider the impact of any applicable charges contained in the annuity contract.

account's unit value, and the holder is subject to ordinary income taxation when the earnings are withdrawn. (This double taxation phenomenon does not apply to net long-term capital gains under tax-qualified contracts.) As a result, non-tax-qualified variable annuities that emphasize common stock investments are of limited appeal unless the policy of the separate account management is to avoid taking long-term capital gains.

Tax-free exchange of annuity contracts. Contractholders should take advantage of Internal Revenue Code Section 1035(a) when desiring to transfer the cash value of one annuity contract for another contract to obtain, for example, a higher yield. This Section provides for a tax-free exchange of one annuity contract for another as long as the contracts are payable to the same person or persons. Where contracts of different insurers are used, the holder must assign the existing contract in exchange for the new one, rather than simply surrender the existing contract and allocate the proceeds to the new contract.

Immediate Annuities

A pro rata share of each payment received under an immediate annuity (or an annuity settlement under a deferred annuity) is considered to be interest and is thus subject to ordinary income taxation. This contrasts with the non-qualified deferred annuity, in which distributions are received tax-free until the premiums have been recovered. The percentage of each payment that is deemed to be principal is called the exclusion ratio; it is obtained by dividing the expected return by the contract's cost basis (generally, the premium cost in the case of a non-qualified immediate annuity). The expected return of a life annuity is generally equal to the annual payment times the annuitant's life expectancy in years, based on IRS tables; for an annuity certain, it is simply the total amount of guaranteed payments. For example, if a 70-year-old male purchased a straight life annuity with $50,000 of after-tax dollars and received an income of $6,600 per year, his exclusion ratio would be 62.6 percent, obtained as follows:

$$\begin{aligned}&\text{Premium} \div (\text{annual income} \times \text{life expectancy})\\&= 50{,}000 \div (6{,}600 \times 12.1)\\&= 50{,}000 \div 79{,}860\\&= 62.6\%\end{aligned}$$

Thus, if the annuitant were in a 20 percent marginal tax bracket, his tax would only be 7.48 percent of each payment (20% × 37.4%, where 37.4% = 100% − 62.6%.)

Investors in their seventies and eighties who are considering whether to purchase a life annuity or an interest-bearing investment, such as a taxable CD, should consider the relative tax effects of the two investments, noting that 100 percent of the interest earned under a CD (other than an All-Savers, which pays a much lower rate than a taxable CD) is taxable. Of course, the investor should also note that the full principal is left intact under a CD but entirely lost under an immediate annuity, except for any refund feature that may allow for recovery of a portion of the principal upon the annuitant's death.

Payments under immediate annuities purchased with pre-tax dollars, such as qualified annuities bought under pension plans, are fully taxable. When a deferred annuity contract begins to pay out a regular income, an exclusion ratio applies only to the portion of the premiums that represents after-tax dollars. For example, assume an annuity purchased with a $10,000 premium had grown in value to $15,000 and no prior withdrawals had been made. If the $15,000 were applied towards a life income option, the exclusion ratio would be two-thirds of the ratio calculated according to the method previously described.

REPRESENTATIVE TYPES OF INVESTORS

Investors fall into two broad categories: purchasers of non-tax-qualified contracts and purchasers of tax-qualified contracts.

Non-Tax-Qualified Contracts

The typical purchaser of a deferred annuity is an individual, usually age 45 or older, who has a need for a tax-deferred accumulation vehicle that will be used to supplement his pension and Social Security income at retirement. Many purchasers are in high marginal tax brackets (40 percent and up) and thus have a particularly strong need to defer taxes on investment earnings.

The typical purchaser of an immediate annuity is an individual in the 65- to 90-year range who desires a guaranteed lifetime income. Such an investor is not concerned with preserving his principal in the event of death. Due to the safe high-yield investments available today, many investors are not finding this an attractive contract until they are into their seventies and thus are able to receive an income of 15 to 20 percent of the principal.

Other types of buyers include casualty insurance companies, which purchase annuities to fund long-term claim settlements due to accidents that (for example) result in permanent disability; and charitable and other nonprofit institutions that issue, in return for gifts, immediate life annuities on the lives of donors.

Tax-Qualified Contracts

These are purchased either to fund retirement benefits or to defer income to a later date when the individual presumably would be in a lower tax bracket. A number of different individuals and groups are eligible to purchase tax-qualified annuities.

Pension, thrift, and profit-sharing plans. Larger plans (typically, those with an annual premium of $25,000 or more) can fund their plans through a group deposit administration contract or a group immediate participation guarantee contract. Smaller plans can utilize specially designed small-group contracts or individual annuity contracts.

Tax-sheltered annuity (TSA). A provision of Section 403(b) of the Internal Revenue Code allows employees of educational institutions and certain other nonprofit organizations to exclude a portion of their salary from current taxation through the purchase of an annuity contract. The maximum amount that can be contributed is generally 20 percent of includable compensation (total compensation less the employee's TSA compensation), multiplied by the number of years of service with the employer, less total contributions made in prior years by the employer into a TSA or qualified pension plan on the employee's behalf. This amount is also subject to the general limitations for defined contribution qualified plans described in Section 415 of the Code. In addition, more liberal maximum contribution rules, described in Section 403(b) of the Code, are available with respect to TSAs purchased by employees of educational institutions, hospitals, and home health-service agencies.

Individual retirement annuity (IRA). All individuals who have earned income can contribute up to $2,000 (or the amount of earned income, if less) during a taxable year. If there is a non-employed spouse, an additional amount can be contributed on the spouse's behalf as long as the total contributions for both spouses do not exceed $2,250 and no more than $2,000 is contributed on behalf of either spouse.

Simplified employee pension (SEP). The 1978 Revenue Act allows employers to establish SEPs, under which employers can make contributions toward their employees' retirement income without becoming involved in more complex retirement plans. Under a SEP, the employer makes contributions directly to IRAs established on the employees' behalf. The maximum employer contribution on behalf of each employee is the lesser of $15,000 or 15 percent of the employee's total annual compensation. The employee can also make the regular IRA contribution described in the preceding paragraph, either to the SEP plan, if it permits this, or to a separate IRA.

Keogh or HR-10 plan. Self-employed individuals and partnerships that actively operate an unincorporated business are eligible to adopt Keogh or HR-10 plans. Generally, all full-time employees who have worked 1,000 hours during the last twelve months and who have completed at least two years of service with the employer must be included. The maximum annual contribution is the lesser of $15,000 or 15 percent of each participant's total annual compensation.

Public employee deferred compensation plan (PEDC). The 1978 Revenue Act provides for PEDC plans on a tax-qualified basis. Employees and independent contractors performing services for a qualified employer may voluntarily elect to defer a portion of their compensation, by way of a salary reduction agreement, to some later date. Qualified employers may be a state, including political subdivisions or agencies of a state, or tax-exempt rural electric cooperatives as defined under Section 501(c)(12) of the Internal Revenue Code, as well as their affiliates (Section 501(c)(6) organizations). With the exception of a catch-up rule, the normal maximum limitation is 25 percent of income not to exceed $7,500.

Rollover IRA. Under the conditions and limitations of the Internal Revenue Code, a person receiving a cash lump-sum distribution from a tax-qualified retirement plan, a distribution from an IRA or individual retirement account (i.e., an IRA funded through a bank), or the spouse of an employee receiving a lump-sum death benefit from the employee's tax-qualified retirement plan may purchase a rollover IRA with all or part of the monies in order to further defer taxes on the distribution. The contract must be purchased within sixty days after the distribution is made. Generally, a lump-sum distribution is a payment of all amounts in the person's account that were received in a distribution that occurred during one of the individual's tax years (generally a calendar year), that became payable as a result of separation of service (except in the case of a self-employed individual), attainment of age 59½, disability (only in the case of a self-employed individual), or termination of the plan or, in the case of a stock bonus or profit-sharing plan, complete discontinuance of contributions under the plan.

For example, consider a 45-year-old male who has terminated service with the XYZ Corporation and has a vested benefit of $50,000 under the corporation's pension plan. Assume he has the right to take a cash settlement. If he needs $10,000 now (which would be subject to ordinary income tax), he could invest the $40,000 balance in a rollover IRA and defer taxes until it is withdrawn. However, the normal IRA restrictions would apply. Hence, withdrawals before age 59½ would be subject to the 10 percent penalty tax (in addition to ordinary taxation) and distribution would have to commence by age 70½. (See article on Retirement Income — Individual Retirement Plans, elsewhere in this volume.)

Corporate trustee annuity. This is purchased by trustees of corporate pension plans on behalf of terminating employees or upon plan termination. Unlike the rollover IRA, there are no restrictions or penalty taxes on withdrawals.

IMPORTANT FACTORS IN BUYING

On the market today are large numbers of annuity products with a variety of charges, interest rates, investment alternatives, and other features. The reader has already been given a survey of features offered and their relative importance. A discussion of how to get into the market follows. (Note: A list of selected companies is included here. A potential buyer generally cannot purchase from the company directly, but most companies will assign an agent or broker to the client if requested. The buyer should consult *Best's Retirement Income Guide* for comprehensive surveys of available individual annuity products.)

Comparison of the Individual Deferred Annuity and Alternative Investments

As mentioned throughout this article, the investor who is contemplating purchasing an annuity should also examine alternative investments, such as bank CDs, money market funds, common stock mutual funds, and individual common stocks and bonds. The investor in the non-tax-qualified market has a full range of alternative products available, while investors in tax-qualified markets have a more limited selection of products from which to choose. In comparing the annuity to alternative investments, the investor should determine whether the additional benefits provided by the annuity contract (e.g., personalized service from an agent, investment and mortality guarantees, unusual investment flexibility) are worth the charges that the annuity imposes (e.g., front-end loads, termination charges, premium taxes in some states, annual administrative fees, asset charges). For example, in comparing a non-tax-qualified, no-front-end-load wraparound mutual fund annuity with a direct investment in one or more mutual funds, the investor should determine if the asset charges levied by the insurance company (over and above the mutual fund charges) and the early withdrawal charge are worth the benefits derived from such annuity features as tax deferral, investment flexibility, guaranteed settlement rates, and the minimum death benefit.

IRAs and Keogh (HR-10) Plan vs. Bank CD

A common example is the individual who wishes to invest in an IRA or HR-10 plan and is faced with the choice of funding through either an annuity offered by an insurance company or a bank CD. Unlike annuities, bank CDs do not contain loads, withdrawal charges (except before the CD's expiration date, which is generally one-and-a-half or two-and-a-half years), or annual administrative fees. However, the annuity offers a wide range of features not offered by the bank.

For instance, an annuity offers the option of obtaining, at a later date, an income for the investor that cannot be outlived. Note that although the purchaser of a bank IRA eventually could use all or a portion of the account's value to purchase a life income from an insurance company, he would not have the benefit of a minimum rate guarantee nor the opportunity to purchase life income at rates more favorable than those available to brand new purchasers.

Many annuities offer one or more investment accounts in addition to an interest-bearing account. Many annuities provide significant interest guarantees with respect to future payments, while a CD only guarantees interest on the current payment.

Furthermore, most periodic-payment annuities accept very low payments, such as $20, and credit the contractual interest rate from the date of receipt. Banks, on the other hand, often require substantial minimum payments ($500 and up) in order to earn their highest rates.

Withdrawal charges under no-front-end-load annuities are generally stiffer than those of CDs, which waive all charges at the expiry date of the interest guarantee. However, CD withdrawal penalties before the expiry date (which involve significant interest forfeitures) are often comparable to those of the annuities. In addition, the investor who requires a relatively small amount of emergency cash may be able to avoid a withdrawal charge under an annuity contract that contains a free corridor, but could not avoid a penalty under a CD (except at the expiry date).

Finally, the purchaser of an annuity receives the personal services of an agent or broker, often including an individualized projection (based on the purchaser's actual age, sex, and contribution level) of account growth and retirement income under a range of settlement options. The agent or broker, through his training and experience, is often able to furnish quality advice in such areas as tax and estate planning. While assistance can also be obtained from a designated individual at the local bank branch office, that individual may not be equipped or have the time to offer the range of services offered by an agent or broker.

Channels of Distribution

Career agents. These are licensed selling agents who generally sell products offered by one company only, although at times they will place business in another company if that company's rate is much better or if the desired product is not offered by their own company. The career agents' job is to service as well as to sell the company's products. As servicers, they are often able to obtain the company's prompt attention to a customer's problem due to the traditionally strong relationship between career agent and company.

Insurance brokers. These are licensed salespersons who market products offered by several companies. Such brokers are often better able to shop around for a superior rate than are career agents.

Stock brokerage houses. As part of a drive to provide total financial services to their clients, several brokerage houses have recently begun to market insurance company products, including annuities.

Sales representatives. Unlike agents and brokers, who are compensated virtually entirely on a commission basis, these individuals are salaried (often with some incentive compensation). Like career agents, they work solely for a single company.

Individual Immediate Annuities

These are primarily marketed through career agents and insurance brokers. The buyer should shop around, since rates vary widely. Note that competitiveness of a company's deferred annuity or insurance products is often not indicative of the competitiveness of its immediate annuity rates. Commissions are in the 2 to 3 percent range.

The following is a list of some of the major underwriters of individual immediate annuities. Most of these companies write in both non-tax-qualified and in tax-qualified markets and are licensed to sell in the majority of states.

Bankers Life Company, Des Moines, Iowa
Connecticut General Life Insurance, Hartford, Conn.
Crown Life Insurance Company, Toronto, Ontario, Canada
Equitable Life Assurance Society of the United States, New York, N.Y.
Great West Life Assurance Company, Winnipeg, MB, Canada
John Hancock Mutual Life Insurance, Boston, Mass.
Lincoln National Life Insurance Company, Fort Wayne, Ind.
Manufacturers Life Insurance Company, Toronto, Ontario, Canada
Metropolitan Life Insurance Company, New York, N.Y.
New England Mutual Life, Boston, Mass.
Phoenix Mutual Life Insurance Company, Hartford, Conn.
Prudential Insurance Company, Newark, N.J.
Traveler's Insurance Company, Hartford, Conn.

Individual Single-Premium Deferred Annuities

These are heavily marketed by career agents, insurance brokers, and stock brokers; advertisements for these products appear daily in major financial news publications, such as the *New York Times* financial pages and the *Wall Street Journal.* Commissions range from 2 to 5 percent of the premium. Products are extremely competitive.

Listed below is a selection of major underwriters. Most companies write in both qualified and non-qualified markets and are licensed to sell in most states.

Anchor National Life Insurance Company, Phoenix, Ariz.
Bankers National Life Insurance Company, Parsippany, N.J.
Capitol Life Insurance Company, Denver, Colo.
Charter Security Life Insurance Company, Jacksonville, Fla.
Charter Security Life Insurance Company of New York, New York, N.Y.
Equitable Variable Life Insurance Company, New York, N.Y.
Executive Life Insurance Company, Beverly Hills, Cal.
Great American Life Insurance Company, Los Angeles, Cal.
Great-West Life Assurance Company, Winnipeg, MB, Canada
Investors Life Insurance Company of North America, Philadelphia, Pa.
John Alden Life Insurance Company, Coral Gables, Fla.
Kemper Investors Life Insurance Company, Chicago, Ill.

Manufacturers Life Insurance Company, Toronto, Ontario, Canada
Metropolitan Life Insurance Company, New York, N.Y.
North America Life and Casualty, Minneapolis, Minn.
Presidential Life Insurance Company, Nyack, N.Y.

Individual Periodic-Payment Deferred Annuities

Most of this business is sold through career agents, although insurance brokers are also active. (Stockholders are not active in this business.) Since the periodic-payment market is not as competitive as the single-payment market (particularly for non-tax-qualified business), an investor who has enough funds to meet the single-payment minimum (e.g., $5,000) may do better to purchase such a product and invest ongoing payments in a periodic-payment annuity. Commissions vary considerably, from 3 to 12 percent of first-year payments and from 1 to 5 percent of renewal-year payments. Some of the leading companies actively selling this product are listed below. Most of these companies write in both non-tax-qualified and tax-qualified markets and are licensed to sell in the majority of states.

Aetna Life and Annuity Company, Hartford, Conn.
Equitable Life Assurance Society of the United States, New York, N.Y.
Great-West Life Assurance Company, Winnipeg, Canada
Hartford Life Insurance Company, Hartford, Conn.
Lincoln National Life Insurance Company, Fort Wayne, Ind.
Metropolitan Life Insurance Company, New York, N.Y.
Nationwide Life Insurance Company, Columbus, Ohio
Prudential Insurance Company, Newark, N.J.
Teachers Insurance and Annuity Association (tax-sheltered annuities only), New York, N.Y.
Travelers Insurance Company, Hartford, Conn.
Union Mutual Life Insurance Company, Portland, Maine
Variable Annuity Life Insurance Company, Houston, Tex.
Washington National Insurance Company, Evanston, Ill.

Group Annuities

Insurance companies generally market large group products through salaried company representatives who are trained pension consultants. Smaller group products are often marketed by company agents.

A few of the companies active in this business are Aetna Life and Annuity Company, Connecticut General Life Insurance, The Equitable Life Assurance Society of the United States, Metropolitan Life Insurance Company, and Prudential Insurance Company.

GLOSSARY

accumulation period— The period under a deferred annuity contract from (i) the date the annuity is purchased until (ii) the annuitant's retirement date, the date the annuity contract is surrendered for its cash value, or the annuitant's death, whichever occurs first.

asset charge— An annual percentage charge that is deducted daily from the assets of a separate account and is reflected in the account's unit value.

bailout provision— A provision, often found in single-premium deferred annuity contracts, that enables the owner to surrender the contract without charge if the current interest rate offered drops below a specified rate set in the contract.

deferred annuity— An annuity that provides for both an accumulation period and a retirement (income-paying) period.

fixed deferred annuity— A deferred annuity that guarantees a minimum accumulation interest rate and provides for dividends or excess interest.

fixed immediate annuity— An annuity that begins to pay, generally within one year of purchase, a regular income for life.

front-end load— A percentage charge that the insurer deducts from an annuity payment to offset sales and administrative expenses.

general account— The account to which the insurer allocates assets to fund fixed annuities. Investments consist primarily of bonds, notes, and mortgages.

non-tax-qualified annuities— A "man-in-the-street" annuity that is not purchased under a special tax-favored program. Income accumulates on a tax-deferred basis, but annuity contributions are not tax-deductible to the annuitant.

separate account— A separate investment account to which the insurer allocates assets to fund variable annuities. The investment experience of such an account is kept separate from the insurer's other assets.

settlement options— Life income, fixed period payment, interest-bearing or other options available at the retirement date to the annuitant under a deferred annuity.

tax-qualified annuity— An annuity purchased under a special tax-favored arrangement. Income accumulates on a tax-deferred basis and contributions are not included in the annuitant's current income.

variable deferred annuity— A deferred annuity that provides for investment of contributions in one or more separate accounts.

variable immediate annuity— An income-paying annuity providing for regular payments varying in dollar amount depending on the investment experience of a separate account.

SUGGESTED READING

The following is a list of selected publications that contain information of interest to potential buyers of annuities.

Articles and Publications

Campbell, Paul A. *The Variable Annuity.* Hartford: Connecticut General Life Insurance Company, 1969.
This publication contains a comprehensive discussion of the variable annuity; it covers history, inflation responsiveness, technical design, and government regulation.

Hopkins, James M., and Blackman, Dennis. "Individual Retirement Arrangements — Planning and Problems." *TAXES — The Tax Magazine,* March 1978, pages 149–153.
This article compares the tax-planning opportunities and problem areas of an IRA with those of available alternative investments, and includes a discussion of the restrictions placed on IRAs by federal legislation and the possible effects of tax penalties.

Medical College of Georgia. *Tax-Sheltered Annuities: A Comparative Analysis.* Augusta, 1980.

Morehart, Thomas B. "Evaluating the Tax-Sheltered Annuity vs. The Taxed Investment." *CLU Journal,* Jan. 1979, pages 23-30.
The two publications above discuss tax-sheltered annuity products — what they are, how various products compare with each other, and advantages and disadvantages as compared to a fully taxed investment.

Reference Books and Annuals

Best's Retirement Income Guide. Published by A. M. Best Company, Oldwick, N.J.
A comprehensive survey, updated and published semiannually, of the three basic types of individual annuity plans: single-premium deferred annuities, flexible-premium retirement annuities, and single-premium immediate annuities. The emphasis within the Guide is to provide a comparison of these contracts offered by the approximately eighty-five contributing life insurance companies.

Best's Settlement Options Manual. Published by A. M. Best Company, Oldwick, N.J.
An annual publication giving complete rates and procedures used by most of the larger insurance companies upon settlement of life insurance or annuity proceeds under the various options.

Note: Two statistical studies by A.M. Best, released annually, rank the leading life insurance companies on amounts of prior year's business for individual and group annuity premiums, and major benefits paid, respectively. These studies are published in *Best's Insurance Management Report* and *Best's Review.*

Tax Facts. Published by National Underwriter Company, Cincinnati, Ohio.
An annual publication that reflects selected pertinent legislation, regulations, rulings, and court decisions affecting life, health, estate, business, and annuity plans.

Insurance Contracts Profiles. Published by Evaluation Associates, Inc., Westport, Conn.
This publication surveys group deposit administration contracts, immediate participation guarantee contracts, and other types of unallocated group funding contracts, and contains comparative information regarding fund charges, investment alternatives, and contractual features. Published annually.

Life Insurance Investments —Guaranteed Interest Contracts

*Gordon J. Munro**

BASIC CHARACTERISTICS

Guaranteed interest contracts (generally referred to as "GICs") are custom-designed, fixed-dollar funding arrangements offered by many life insurance companies to large, tax-qualified corporate pension and profit-sharing funds and to tax-exempt foundations and government plans. Although a GIC is similar in many ways to an unmarketable bond, the contract that evidences the arrangement is not considered a security. It is a group annuity contract, subject to regulation by the various state insurance departments, and as such is currently exempted from regulation by the SEC. Because it is a group annuity contract, it will contain ancillary features that are not generally available with any of the traditional investment vehicles. Among these is the option to purchase, at predetermined rates, pension benefits guaranteed for life. In addition, the insurance company can usually make available a variety of administrative services, such as participant recordkeeping or payment of retired life benefits, if these services are required.

The essential function of a GIC, however, is to provide guarantees of principal, interest, and expense charges for a specified period on funds deposited with the insurance company. Such deposits may be made in a single sum or on a recurring schedule. Interest is usually at a fixed rate but sometimes is offered on a minimum-floor basis with higher rates credited if earned by the insurance company. Expenses may be billed separately or withdrawn directly from the accumulation of deposits. At the end of the period of guaranteed accumulation, the funds held by the insurance company will be paid out, without any market-value adjustment, either in a single sum or in installments over a period of years with interest credited at the guaranteed rate on the declining balance. This very general statement should not obscure the fact that these arrangements are custom-designed and, hence, the variations that may be built in are virtually endless.

TYPES OF GICS

The design of a GIC is dictated by the needs of the plan it will serve. Some features may present a problem or risk of loss to the insurance company and

* Gordon J. Munro is a Vice-President in the pension department of New York Life Insurance Company.

hence may be difficult to obtain without some hedging or special device established for the protection of the insurance company. What a prospective GIC purchaser will look for in a contract varies greatly depending on whether the plan being funded is a defined benefit plan or a defined contribution plan.

GICs for Defined Benefit Plans

A defined benefit pension plan is one in which the plan document specifies a formula by which the amount of pension payable to a participant upon retirement is determined. The employer's objective is to provide the promised benefit as economically as possible, subject to the fiduciary and other constraints of the Employee Retirement Income Security Act of 1974 (ERISA). A superior investment result reduces the employer's cost; it does not increase the benefit payable to participants. The decision to purchase a GIC, to deposit or withdraw funds under it, or to terminate the contract is made by a single entity. This may be the plan's investment manager, a board of trustees, or the employer, acting perhaps on the guidance of a third-party consultant.

For defined benefit plans, therefore, the key factors in the design of a GIC are its ability to accommodate the projected cash-flow requirements of the plan and the level (and duration) of the interest guarantee net of all expenses.

GICs for Defined Contribution Plans

A defined contribution plan is one in which the plan document stipulates a formula that determines the amount of contribution to be made by the employer each year for the benefit of each participant. The amount actually collected by a participant is the accumulated value of his vested account. A superior investment result increases the benefits payable to participants but, for all practical purposes, has no effect on the employer's cost. Usually, all decisions to deposit funds in or withdraw them from a GIC issued to such a plan are decisions made by the participants themselves, not by the employer, the trustees, or the investment manager. Such decisions are, of course, subject to whatever restrictions may be contained in the plan.

The usual structure of these plans is to provide the participant with a limited number of investment options — typically, an equity fund, a fixed-dollar investment option, and possibly other funds with specialized investment objectives. A participant may always change an election with regard to future contributions and, typically, may opt once a year to transfer existing funds from one form of repository to another; often, however, there are restrictions on which funds may be transferred where. Finally, some of these plans permit participants (or their beneficiaries) to withdraw vested accumulations in whole or in part on retirement, death, disability, or termination of employment; for hardship or after a fixed period of years; and may permit participants to borrow against their accounts.

For defined contribution plans, therefore, a GIC that is to serve as the repository for fixed-dollar funds must be designed to provide participants with (1) an easily understood, fully guaranteed account and (2) maximum flexibility to move funds in and out without penalty or market-value adjustment. The precise level of interest guaranteed is secondary. A single insurance company will normally be designated, after competitive bidding, to receive all the funds placed under the plan's fixed-dollar election in one plan year, with renewed competitive bidding for each succeeding year's fixed-dollar contributions. In this situation, participants with balances under the plan's fixed-dollar election will have interest credited to these balances at the average rate of return on all the in-force GICs, not at the rate being earned by the individual GICs in which the participants' contributions are actually deposited.

Comparison with alternative investment options. The principal alternative investment options for the funds to which GICs are sold are the following:

Certificates of deposit (CDs). These give an interest yield that may be higher than GICs, for example, when an inverted yield curve exists. Like GICs, they have a fixed maturity date with substantial penalties for early withdrawal. CDs are short- to medium-term and may pay out interest periodically. They also have a limited Federal Deposit Insurance Corporation (FDIC) protection.

Money market funds. These currently give high yields, but there are no guarantees of principal or interest. They have the advantage, compared to GICs, of substantial liquidity.

Deep discount bonds. These offer yields to maturity for a tax-exempt purchaser comparable in level to those available from GICs, and for at least as long a period. They are effectively free from the risk of premature call; and the zero coupon variety, under which no interest is payable prior to maturity, eliminates all re-investment risk prior to maturity. However, they lack the custom-designed flexibility of GICs, particularly in setting the term to maturity and the payout option at maturity. They are not adaptable to the participant withdrawal options of defined contribution plans, and, of course, they are subject to the same risk of default as any other bond portfolio.

Immunized bond portfolios. These provide a measure of protection against fluctuating interest returns and can be arranged to give yields similar to GICs. The effective period of immunization, however, is limited to about eight years and the portfolio requires constant managing. The value of the portfolio must be carried at market, whereas a GIC is carried at book under current IRS regulations.

Equities. These are the antitheses of GICs. They offer a low current yield, give no guarantees of any kind, and have to be sold at market value to realize cash. However, they offer the possibility of capital growth.

ATTRACTIVE FEATURES

General

GICs can be responsive to many investment problems faced by the trustees of pension or profit-sharing funds. They lock in current interest levels not only on the principal but also on the re-investment of interest. This, coupled with the fact that the entire accumulating amount may be carried at book value, provides a very desirable measure of stability and predictability in the operation of the fund. GICs can thus be used to maintain fixed income return in a falling interest market, to hedge aggregate market portfolio performance, to accumulate cash for specific future needs, and to control future cash flow.

Matching Cash Flow

For defined benefit plans, in the optimum arrangement, projected positive inflow of funds would be channeled into a GIC contract constructed to release these funds back to the plan at a time and in a manner designed to match a projected outflow of funds. Any such projections of cash flow are, of course, subject to a good deal of uncertainty. However, within reasonable limits of practicability, a GIC contract can be designed to accommodate projected cash flow, a flexibility that is not available under conventional investment vehicles and that greatly facilitates financial planning. A word of caution, however: If the projected need for cash in future years is underestimated (as might happen, for example, if the impact of inflation is not given adequate recognition), the amount paid out by the GIC under its terms will not meet actual cash-flow requirements and supplementary funding will be necessary.

Shedding the Investment Risk

In defined benefit plans that are large enough to absorb the mortality risk inherent in providing pensions to their participants, many of the trustees are adopting a variation of GIC that retains the mortality risk with the fund while transferring the investment risk to the insurance company. The plan's own enrolled actuary develops a schedule of anticipated monthly payments to participants over the next thirty-five or forty years. A GIC contract that undertakes to make those scheduled payments to the plan trustee is then purchased for a single premium.

This can lead to a significant freeing-up of funds, since the single sum currently called for under a GIC normally would be less than the amount that would be set aside by the enrolled actuary in his valuation of plan benefits. This, in turn, can make it possible to improve plan benefits without additional outlay or, alternatively, to reduce the outlay needed to provide the present level of plan benefits.

Note again, however, that the GIC will pay out only what it promises. If the schedule of payments proves to have been underestimated for any reason, the amounts received from the GIC will be correspondingly inadequate.

Flexibility in Duration of Guarantees

The duration of GICs ranges generally from a minimum of one year to a maximum of ten for single-sum payout, but may be up to forty years for a regular schedule of disbursements. The most recent trend has been for funds to seek shorter rather than longer periods, since investment managers have learned the object lesson of those funds that only a few years ago locked in 9 percent for twenty years.

Guaranteed Interest on Recurring Contributions

A single-sum deposit is common under a GIC, in part because trustees prefer to deal with net investable cash one year at a time. However, a fund that projects a recurring excess of cash inflow over outgo may very well wish to enter into a contract that will accept regular, periodic contributions, locking in minimum levels of interest rates on future deposits.

Known Return on Employee Elections

When a GIC is issued to handle the fixed-dollar elections under a defined contribution plan, the rate that will apply for the guaranteed period to all such elections made in the ensuing plan year usually will be declared in advance. This greatly facilitates the participants' choice of elections and the plan administrator's task in explaining them.

Diversification of Investments

ERISA requires plan fiduciaries to diversify the investments of a plan so as to minimize the risk of large losses unless there are circumstances in which it is clearly prudent not to do so. It is now well settled that a plan may be invested wholly in an annuity contract, such as a GIC, without violating the diversification rules, since the insurance company's assets are invested in a diversified manner.

Option to Receive Single-Sum Payment

GICs issued to fund the fixed-dollar elections under defined contribution plans typically provide that at the end of the guaranteed accumulation period, the total funds will be paid out at book value in equal, annual installments over a period (usually five years). This is designed to minimize any re-investment problem for the plan administrator or trustee. However, the GIC sometimes provides that if, at the end of the accumulation period the insurance company that issued the GIC is offering a guarantee of interest on new contracts of this type lower than the rate at which the accumulation has actually been made, the trustee may have the option of receiving payment of the accumulated amount in a single sum without market value adjustment.

Retrieving Past Mistakes

A few years ago, many GICs were issued for long terms (sometimes up to twenty years) at guaranteed rates of interest that are very low by current standards. These contracts can be terminated, but the funds recovered will be reduced by a very substantial market value adjustment.

If the GIC in question was issued to handle the fixed-dollar elections under a defined contribution plan, any market value adjustment resulting from termination of the contract will, of course, be reflected as a pro rata capital loss in all the participants' fixed-dollar accounts. Participants will be understandably dissatisfied with their returns.

A modified GIC has been developed to retrieve this situation. This form of GIC will accept the reduced amount of cash transferable, after market value adjustment, from a terminated GIC contract, but will credit the fund with the full book value amount that had accumulated under the prior contract before the market value adjustment. Participants in a defined contribution plan may continue to exercise their withdrawal and transfer rights without market value adjustment, and hence the individual account balances need not be reduced. The difference between cash received by the insurer and the amount credited under the GIC is made up, over a period of years, by crediting a rate of interest to the book value funds that is lower than that being earned on cash funds. At the end of this period, the market value of the transferred funds will have been restored to book value and they can then be re-invested at the rates available at that time. If this type of GIC is discontinued before the difference between cash received and book value credited has been fully recovered, any outstanding balance and any other termination charges that may apply at that time are debited by the insurer.

This is an ingenious solution to a difficult problem, but it should be approached with caution and be subject to expert analysis. Depending on the rates of interest involved, the extent of the market value adjustment applied, and the future course of interest rates, it is quite possible for a fund to be worse off under this arrangement than it would have been had it either continued under the original contract or had bitten the bullet by accepting the market value adjustment and then negotiating a new, straightforward GIC on current terms.

Capital Gain GICs

The typical GIC provides guarantees of principal and interest at the cost of forgoing the chance of any capital gains that might have been enjoyed had the purchaser bought marketable bonds. However, a version of GIC is available under which interest is guaranteed for only one year with the proviso that if the interest credited after that year is at a lower rate, the purchaser has the option of cashing out the GIC at the higher of book or market. Strictly speaking, there is no market value for a GIC, but an approximation is developed by accumulating the deposit(s) under the GIC to maturity date at the guaranteed rate and discounting that amount back at the yield given by a specified bond index. This appears to restore the possibility of participating in capital gains if interest rates should fall. However, this result may be more apparent than real, since the insurance company controls the interest rate that triggers the option.

LIMITATIONS

Recurring Contributions

A GIC that will accept recurring contributions over a period of years is not available from all life insurance companies. Typically, there are maximum and minimum limits on the amount of future contributions that will be accepted under the initial guarantee. If the initial contribution is very much larger than projected annual contributions, (e.g., ten times as large), some insurance companies will regard the effect of these future contributions as de minimus, and simply specify a maximum dollar level. However, if the level of projected contributions is significant, more elaborate formulas are adopted. Two alternative approaches that are in common use are:

(1) Each annual contribution is limited, for example, to not less than 75 percent nor more than 125 percent of the initial dollar amount contributed; or

(2) In years after the first, the contribution to the GIC is limited to the same percentage of that year's total contribution to the funding of the plan (plus or minus a small amount) as the first year's GIC contribution was to the first year's total funding.

When an insurance company extends guarantees to future contributions, predictability of cash flow is very important to it. Hence, future contributions often must be paid within thirty days of a due date. Furthermore, not only may the insurer refuse to accept contributions exceeding the specified maximum, but a payment of less than the minimum may invoke substantial penalties.

Withdrawal Options Under Defined Contribution Plans

Withdrawals from a GIC without market value adjustment are allowed only during the accumulation period when they are a result of the exercise of the withdrawal and transfer options of the participants in a defined contribution plan. During the same period, employer-originated withdrawals usually are not permitted at all, but may be allowed under limited circumstances with a market value adjustment. Once the payout phase has started, however, no withdrawals are permitted other than the contractual repayments of the accumulated funds.

Withdrawal of vested benefits without market value adjustment by participants (or their beneficiaries) on retirement, death, disability, or termination of employment is susceptible to statistical treatment and will be allowed for automatically in the pricing of the GIC. Prior to the passage of the Economic

Recovery Tax Act of 1981, options to withdraw benefits for other reasons were usually subject, under the terms of the plan, to some form of penalty designed to avoid a determination of constructive receipt by the IRS. However, with the elimination of the concept of constructive receipt by the 1981 Act, such penalties may well become a thing of the past. They will be retained, if at all, only to limit the traffic on the fund and hence to simplify the administration. Whether or not such penalties exist, how onerous they are, and how vigorously they are policed by the plan administrator are important considerations affecting the degree of permanence of such deposits and the terms that an insurance company is willing to offer.

The option that causes a prospective issuer of a GIC the greatest concern, and that will affect the terms it will offer — or even its willingness to bid at all — is the option allowing participants in a defined contribution plan to transfer funds between the GIC contract and other investment options. The insurance company will look closely at the nature of the other investment options to judge whether or not any of them may create a significant risk of a concerted withdrawal of GIC funds by the participants. A competing fund that is invested exclusively in equities normally would not be a matter of concern, since the considerations that would induce a participant to invest in equities on the one hand or in a GIC on the other are totally diverse. If, however, one of the competing investment outlets were, say, a money market fund, rising short-term rates could lead to the wholesale withdrawal of GIC funds.

The insurance company may simply refuse to issue a GIC to a plan that has an unacceptable competing fund. However, if it does agree to issue a GIC, it will undoubtedly insist on certain safeguards, of which the following are typical:

(1) Both the plan document and the GIC may prohibit transfers from the GIC to such of the other funding outlets as would create unacceptable investment selection. In this case, the insurer will also closely examine the plan transfer provisions to ensure that the prohibited transfer cannot be achieved by an indirect route.

(2) The GIC may provide that if a competing fund is added to the plan later, transfers from the GIC to that new fund may be prohibited, or the GIC itself may be terminated.

(3) In the typical situation, where more than one insurance company GIC has been or will be issued covering contributions of different years, each issuer of a GIC will require:
   - A prohibition against transfers between the GICs, and
   - A contractual provision requiring fixed-dollar withdrawals to be made pro rata from all such GICs.

(4) The insurance company may require that the transfer option in the plan be exercisable by a participant only once in each plan year, perhaps on the anniversary of the individual's participation, rather than optionally or on a single, fixed date within the year.

These kinds of plan and contractual provisions emphasize the negotiated nature of a GIC. The prospective issuer always has the right to bid as requested, to offer an alternative, or to decline to quote.

Recapture Provisions

If the risk involved in issuing a proposed GIC appears to the insurance company to be too great to accept in its entirety, it may offer a contract with the right to recapture experience losses through future guarantees. These provisions are most often found in connection with GICs issued to defined contribution plans where a new interest crediting rate is declared each year.

Premature Termination of a GIC

An insurance company is able to offer guaranteed interest rates and payments at book value because it writes a volume of such business large enough to arrange its own portfolio of investments with repayments scheduled so that sufficient liquid funds will be available when a GIC contract calls for a disbursement. Predictability of cash flow is very important in this context. If a GIC contractholder should wish to terminate a contract and receive payment prior to the date established in that contract, a cash-flow problem for the insurer can result. For this reason, insurance companies take particular care in writing the discontinuance provisions of their contracts, protecting themselves from the possibly adverse effect of a premature withdrawal. In evaluating such contracts, therefore, special attention needs to be paid to the discontinuance terms.

The usual termination calculation, which is designed to approximate a market value, accrues the GIC funds at the guaranteed rate of interest to the end of the guaranteed accumulation period and then discounts this sum back to the date of payment at some (higher) rate of interest, representing currently available interest levels. A published bond yield, such as Salomon Brothers' BBB (long-term) industrials, often is used to define the current interest rate for this purpose. If the current interest rate used in this calculation should be less than the guaranteed rate, payment normally will be made at book value, not at the higher theoretical market value.

It is most desirable that the termination provisions spell out in detail how such a discontinuance calculation will be made and the specific bond index or other measure that will be used to compute the market value adjustment.

TAX CONSEQUENCES

Since GICs are generally available only to tax-exempt funds, federal income tax is not a consideration for the buyer. In a few states, if the option to purchase paid-up annuities is exercised, a state premium tax would be incurred on the amount applied to purchase the annuity. This tax (if any) would be added to the guaranteed purchase rates.

IMPORTANT FACTORS IN BUYING

The leading life insurance companies compete vigorously in the GIC market, and it is most important for a fund to obtain competitive bids, quite apart from the requirement to do so that seems implicit in ERISA. However, the complexity and inherent difficulty of matching the needs of a fund to the product available virtually demand that the fund receive expert, professional guidance in developing specifications, analyzing and evaluating the various responses, and negotiating the best available offer. A partial list of consultants in this field is given at the end of this article.

The offers that will be made on a given set of specifications vary significantly not only from insurance company to insurance company, but also from one time to another for any one insurance company, because each company must respond to changing financial conditions, both current and anticipated, and to its own internal requirements. It is quite normal for an insurance company to be extremely active and competitive in this market one month and totally disinterested the following month. The risks and financial strains incurred by life insurance companies in writing this type of business can be significant; therefore, most will place internal limits on how much will be accepted during any period of time. It would seem a logical corollary for the purchaser to be satisfied about the surplus strength of the insurer chosen to write GIC business. Information regarding the amount of surplus carried and its relationship to total company liabilities can be readily obtained from the insurance company's most recent annual statement.

Under conditions of financial volatility, a purchaser normally will have to accept a bid and pay over funds within not more than fifteen days of the bid being made — and periods as short as three days are not unknown. It is essential, therefore, for a GIC purchaser to be ready to move before soliciting bids. This particularly includes having the necessary assets in readily available funds.

In conclusion, there is currently intense competition for pension fund monies among banks, investment managers, and insurance companies. The battle is being waged with, among others, CDs, money market funds, original issue deep discount zero coupon bonds, immunized bond portfolios, and GICs. This last is the result of some very creative thinking on the part of the major life insurance companies, a creative process that is still unfolding. The best advice to a prospective purchaser of a GIC is expressed in the old shopping adage, "If you don't see it, ask for it."

GLOSSARY

book value — The arithmetic sum of deposits made and interest added, less any amounts withdrawn, all without regard to the market value of the underlying assets.

constructive receipt — The doctrine advanced by the IRS that funds in a tax-qualified plan, which could be obtained by a participant at any time on request without substantial restriction, are constructively received by the participant and, therefore, subject to income tax, even though such funds are not actually withdrawn from the plan. This doctrine was abolished by the Economic Recovery Tax Act of 1981.

enrolled actuary— An individual who, having satisfied certain educational and experience requirements, has been enrolled by the Joint Board for the Enrollment of Actuaries, established by ERISA, as qualified to perform the actuarial valuations for defined benefit pension plans and authorized to sign Schedule B of Form 5500 regarding the solvency of such plans.

ERISA— The Employee Retirement Income Security Act of 1974. This Act established minimum funding standards for defined benefit pension plans, set tough fiduciary standards for those having responsibility for the running of such plans, prohibited particular transactions, and required a large number of plan provisions designed to protect the pension rights of plan participants. It also established the Pension Benefit Guaranty Corporation (PBGC) to insure accrued pension rights in the event of plan termination.

fixed dollar— A term indicating that fluctuations in market value will not be reflected in the value of a fund or benefit. However the fixed-dollar account of a GIC will reflect any reduction in market value in the event of premature withdrawal of the funds.

funding arrangement— Any contractual arrangement entered into by a life insurance company to accept and accumulate monies contributed in connection with a pension or profit-sharing plan.

inverted yield curve— In so-called normal conditions, the longer the period to maturity of a bond or other debt instrument, the higher the yield, reflecting increased reward to the lender for increased risk. When unusual financial conditions result in short-term rates exceeding long-term rates as, for example, during most of 1981, the resulting pattern of interest rates is referred to as an inverted yield curve.

market value adjustment— When funds are withdrawn from a GIC fixed-dollar account before the contractual maturity date, the amount payable may be reduced to reflect any drop in the value of the underlying assets. Such reduction, which may be calculated in a variety of ways, is referred to as a market value adjustment.

mortality risk— In calculating the amount of money to set aside to provide pensions to retired lives, the actuary will discount for mortality; that is, he will assume that the mortality of participants in the plan follows some appropriate mortality table and, as each participant is assumed to die, the funds set aside for his become available to provide pensions to the survivors. If participants live longer, on the average, than was assumed, additional funds (which may be substantial) will be needed. The larger the number of lives, the more likely that mortality will follow closely the assumptions made by the actuary and, hence, the smaller the risk of having to find additional funds. The smaller the number of lives, the greater the risk, and the more need to have this risk underwritten by a life insurance company.

tax-qualified plan— A pension or profit-sharing plan that meets the requirements of Internal Revenue Code Section 401. Contributions made by the employer are tax deductible to it and are not taxable to the employee during the accumulation period. Investment returns on the fund are also exempt from income tax during the accumulation period. Under the Economic Recovery Tax Act of 1981, employees who make qualified voluntary contributions to tax-qualified plans may also deduct up to $2,000 of such contributions each year from their taxable income.

vested benefit— A benefit that has become nonforfeitable to the individual under the provisions of a pension or profit-sharing plan.

PARTIAL LIST OF CONSULTANTS

Alexander & Alexander, New York, N.Y.

George B. Buck, New York, N.Y.

A.S. Hansen Inc., Lake Bluff, Ill.

Hewitt Associates, Lincolnshire, Ill.

Fred S. James & Co., Glen Ridge, N.J.

Kass Germain & Co., Shaker Heights, Ohio

Kwasha Lipton Inc., Englewood Cliffs, N.J.

William M. Mercer Inc., New York, N.Y.

Milliman & Robertson Inc., Seattle, Wash.

Martin E. Segal Co., New York, N.Y.

The Wyatt Co., Washington, D.C.

Locations are given for the main U.S. office of each consultant. However, many of these firms maintain offices in other locations across the country.

SUGGESTED READING

Burroughs, Eugene. "Spectrum of Investments — 1980." Proceedings of the 1980 Annual Education Conference of the International Foundation of Employee Benefit Plans: Brookfield: International Foundation of Employee Benefit Plans, 1981.

Derven, R. "Getting a Handle on the Guarantee in GICs." *Pension World* 20, March 1980.

Freelund, Daniel E. "What Points You Should Consider When Negotiating a Guaranteed Investment Contract for Your Company's Retirement Plan." Pensions & Profit Sharing. Englewood Cliffs: Prentice-Hall Inc., 1980.

Lincoln, S.A. "In Pursuit of Customized GICs." *Pension World* 25, October 1980.

Life Insurance Investments —Separate Accounts

*Frank H. David**

BASIC CHARACTERISTICS

Until 1962, every U.S. life insurance company had a single portfolio of investments that was used for all of its business, ranging from individual life insurance policies to group annuity contracts. This all-purpose portfolio, consisting mostly of bonds and mortgage loans, is now referred to as the general account. During the 1950s, interest began to develop in segregated portfolios for use under specially designed contracts, primarily for pension plans and individual annuities. After many difficult legal problems had been overcome, the first of these separate accounts came into being in 1962. The initial portfolio emphasis was on investments in common stocks, because the insurance statutes in most states impose stringent limits on the portion of a company's general account that can be held in equities. By and large, that emphasis on growth-oriented investments still characterizes separate accounts.

A separate account of an insurance company is a portfolio of investments the results of which are segregated from the results of all other investments of the company. While the term "separate account" is now in general use, similar terms sometimes appear in state law, and "segregated asset account" is the term used in Section 801(g) of the Internal Revenue Code (the Code). A "separate account" is defined in the Securities Act of 1933 (Section 2(14)) as "an account . . . under which income, gains and losses, whether or not realized, from assets allocated to such account, are, in accordance with the applicable contract, credited to or charged against such account without regard to other income gains, or losses, of the insurance company."

Management

Separate accounts are generally established by resolution of the insurance company's board of directors. Most are operated on a pooled basis, but in some circumstances an account may also be established for a single customer. The investments of each account are selected in accordance with the investment policy

*Frank H. David is Vice-President and Associate Actuary of The Prudential Insurance Company of America, Florham Park, N.J.

Portions of this article have been adapted with permission from a chapter contributed by Meyer Melnikoff to *Investment Activities of Life Insurance Companies*, © 1977 by the S.S. Huebner Foundation for Insurance Education.

established specifically for it. Usually, a separate account's portfolio will consist largely of one kind of investment — common stocks, for example. The insurance company's obligations under separate-account contracts generally vary with the investment performance of each account. A few companies, however, also have set up separate accounts for contracts that provide guarantees of both principal and interest.

Administration

The assets of separate accounts, where the company's obligations vary with investment performance, are carried at market value. Participations in such accounts are expressed in terms of units. The value of a unit reflects the investment results of the account, including both income and realized and unrealized capital gains and losses. Deposits to and withdrawals from a pooled separate account can occur only on a day for which unit value has been determined. How frequently this is done varies with the type of investment and will be discussed in a later section.

Growth of Separate Accounts

Separate-account business has been growing rapidly. At the end of 1980, separate-account investments of U.S. life insurance companies totaled $35.8 billion — fully ten times the level just eleven years earlier. Of this total, roughly 50 percent was in common stocks, 35 percent in bonds, 9 percent in real estate, and the balance in other types of investments. Moreover, this $35.8 billion represented about 7.5 percent of the total assets of U.S. life insurance companies, compared with less than 2 percent at the end of 1969. For some insurance companies, more than 15 percent of total assets is held in separate accounts.

TYPES OF SEPARATE ACCOUNTS

Most separate accounts are operated on an open-end basis, although at least one large company manages closed-end accounts for privately placed debt securities and development real estate. The following description classifies open-end accounts according to the kind of contract under which they operate.

Group Contracts for Qualified Plans

Almost 90 percent of separate-account assets is held in accounts used only for group contracts, of the type drawn up for pension, profit-sharing, and savings plans that are qualified under Section 401 of the Code. Separate accounts limited to such plans are substantially exempt from SEC regulation and represent a significant part of the pension business of most large life insurance companies. A typical group-pension contract may provide for the use of several separate accounts, as well as the company's general account. The separate accounts may be pooled or single-customer accounts. For most companies, the bulk of group-pension separate-account assets is held in pooled accounts, classified according to investment policy.

Pooled common stock accounts. This is the most common type of account. Many companies have several pooled common stock accounts, each with different investment objectives (e.g., conservative, aggressive, special situations). Market value of the assets is obtained from publicly quoted stock prices. Unit values are usually determined daily.

Pooled publicly traded bond accounts. Both actively managed and passively managed accounts are available. Active bond management generally is based on anticipation of interest rate changes. Swapping techniques are also used. For example, it is sometimes possible to sell a bond and with the proceeds purchase a similar bond (of the same quality and period until maturity) with a slightly higher yield to maturity. Passive management often will concentrate on high-coupon-rate sinking fund bonds with good call protection to enhance long-term performance with relatively high returns from investment income. Passively managed portfolios also tend to be invested across the maturity spectrum, with diversified sector and investment-grade quality representation. Market values of these investments may not be readily obtainable, because bond trading on the exchanges is relatively light. One alternative is to use the values computed by firms such as Telstat and Merrill Lynch, which offer such valuations as a regular business service. Since market values are more difficult to obtain than they are for common stocks, unit values here are generally determined on a weekly or monthly basis.

Pooled private-placement bond accounts. Several major companies offer pooled accounts invested in privately placed debt securities. Their objective is to obtain a more favorable yield (for comparable quality) than can be earned on publicly traded bonds. Higher yields are available as compensation to investors for the lack of marketability of private placements, and for the fact that issuers borrowing privately often are not as well known as those that borrow publicly. Such issuers are willing to pay premiums to avoid the expense and time of SEC registration, and to get more flexible terms than are generally available on a public debt issue.

Market values of privately placed bonds cannot be established by public trading. Accordingly, the insurance company establishes the current market value of each private-placement debt security through a process of (1) rating the current quality of each issue, (2) establishing a set of current yield curves to maturity for issues of different quality and duration, and (3) discounting, at an appropriate interest rate, the interest and principal payments due. Occasionally, these separate accounts acquire privately placed bonds with equity participation features, such as convertibility or detachable warrants. Special procedures must then be established for placing a market value on, say, warrants to buy unregistered common stock. In view of the complexity, unit values may be determined only at monthly intervals — or even less frequently.

Pooled real estate accounts. The first separate account of a U.S. life insurance company for real estate equity (as opposed to mortgages) was Prudential's Property Investment Separate Account (PRISA), established in 1970. Since then, in response to the growing demand by pension plans for real estate investments, several other leading companies have established similar accounts. They hold equity positions in income-producing properties, such as office and industrial buildings, shopping centers, hotels, motels, and apartment houses. However, since the availability of property for acquisition varies considerably with economic conditions, these companies may control the flow of funds into such accounts by reserving the right to limit or decline new contributions. (To a lesser extent, they may also do this for other types of accounts.)

Market values of the equity investments held in these accounts are based on real estate appraisals by the company's own staff of experts or by independent appraisers. Several methods are used: (1) *current cost of reproducing* a property, less deterioration and obsolescence; (2) *capitalization* of the property's net *earning power;* and (3) recent sales prices for *comparable properties* in the market. Since the appraisal process is time-consuming and costly, unit values here are typically determined only at quarterly intervals.

Pooled mortgage-loan accounts. A few companies have separate accounts invested in mortgage loans on income-producing property. To hedge against inflation, there is growing emphasis on loans with participation features — that is, a share in the income stream generated by the mortgaged properties, or in the properties' market value appreciation. Loans may also be made with interest rates subject to renegotiation at specified intervals. As with privately placed bonds, current market values or mortgage loans must be established by complex, special procedures involving the determination of an appropriate interest rate. Unit values usually are determined quarterly.

Pooled short-term investment accounts. These are invested primarily in certificates of deposit, commercial paper, and Treasury bills. They can serve as a repository for funds awaiting investment in other accounts or as an attractive investment in their own right during periods of high interest rates. Unit values usually are determined daily by accruing the interest on the assets and disregarding changes in market value that are minimal because of the short maturities.

Mixed pooled accounts. Among several other types of pooled-account arrangements, three might be noted here: (1) a portfolio holding both stocks and bonds, with the company given the authority to vary the percentage distribution between them at its discretion; (2) an account investing in both publicly traded and privately placed bonds; and (3) one that holds both mortgages and real estate equities.

Single-customer accounts. Single-customer separate accounts are of two basic types. They may exist solely for the purpose of liquidating an existing portfolio or they may be ongoing accounts receiving new funds and making new investments.

Liquidation accounts. A liquidation account is set up when a pension plan that has been using another funding arrangement (such as a trust managed by an investment counselor) decides to shift the management of its assets to an insurance company. To facilitate liquidation of the existing portfolio, these assets are transferred in kind into the new separate account. The insurance company now is given authority to sell out the portfolio, allocating all investment income and sales proceeds to other investment accounts — either on a predetermined basis or at the discretion of the insurance company.

Ongoing single-customer accounts. These are usually invested in stocks, publicly traded bonds, or both. They may begin with a transfer of assets from another funding agency (see above) and they are used for a variety of reasons. For example, legal restrictions, as in the case of a public-employee retirement system, may forbid the commingling of the assets with those of any other pension plan. Mobility also may be the determinant, as when a large pension plan wants to be in a position to shift its portfolio from the insurance company to another investment manager on short notice. A third reason may be a plan's special investment policy requirements, when these have characteristics that differ from those of the accounts used by other clients of the insurance company.

Group Contracts for Non-Qualified Plans

Several companies have established common stock separate accounts for funding tax-sheltered annuities, satisfying the requirements of Section 403(b) of the Code,[1] under group annuity contracts. The life insurance company tax law gives such contracts the same exemption from taxes as applies to qualified plans, and they are treated similarly under state insurance laws. However, the federal securities laws draw a major distinction between separate accounts used only for qualified plans and separate accounts used for tax-sheltered annuities. The latter are fully subject to these laws. Although the account is part of the insurance company, it must be registered with the SEC as an investment company. The insurance company serves as investment manager and carries out all other functions related to the sale and administration of contracts using the account. Similar accounts have been established to invest in publicly traded bonds or short-term securities. In general, participants may transfer the value of their accumulations among a company's stock, bond, and short-term securities accounts without incurring expense or tax charges.

---

[1] Section 403(b) provides for tax-deferred pensions for employees of public educational institutions and of certain nonprofit educational, charitable, and religious organizations.

Individual Contracts

An insurance company that issues individual contracts for plans qualified under Section 401 of the Code may use any of the separate accounts available to qualified group contract plans. But, in most cases, individual contracts are used only for fairly small pension plans, which require a high degree of liquidity. This means, in effect, that only common stocks, publicly traded bonds, and short-term investments are suitable vehicles. Individual contracts take the form of deferred annuity contracts, that is, contracts under which funds accumulate to provide an annuity with payments beginning at a future date. There is, however, no requirement that the funds actually be used to provide an annuity; participants may take them in a lump sum instead.

Most companies interested in offering individual contracts based on separate accounts do not limit their markets to plans qualified under Section 401 of the Code. They also offer individual contracts issued to tax-sheltered annuity plans established under Code Section 403(b), individual retirement accounts (IRAs) established under Code Section 408, public-employee deferred compensation plans established under Code Section 457, and individuals on a non-tax-exempt basis. (Because of their favorable tax status, the term "qualified" is sometimes used to refer to those in the first three categories, as well as to plans qualified under Code Section 401.) Such separate accounts require full compliance with the federal securities laws.

Other Uses for Separate Accounts

Variable annuities. Retirement plans use separate accounts chiefly for the purpose of accumulating funds that are to be paid out as benefits upon retirement. Separate accounts, however, also may be used to pay benefits in the form of variable annuities. Under a fixed annuity, the amount of monthly payments is fixed on the annuity commencement date. Under a variable annuity, in contrast, the amount of each payment is linked to the investment results of the portfolio supporting the annuity. A variable annuity is expressed in units rather than dollars, and dollar payments vary with the annuity unit value.

When calculating the amount of annuity that can be provided by a given purchase price, insurance companies make an assumption as to the future rate of investment return that will be earned on the funds held in their portfolios. For a variable annuity, this rate is called the "assumed investment result." If actual results exceed the assumed result, annuity payments will increase. Conversely, if actual results fall short of these assumptions, the payments will decrease.

Variable annuities linked to a common stock portfolio were first offered by the College Retirement Equities Fund, established in 1952 as a sister organization of the Teachers Insurance and Annuity Association. In the 1960s, several insurance companies began to market variable annuities reflecting the investment results of separate accounts invested in common stocks. It was hoped that there would be reasonably good correlation between variable annuity payments and the cost of living. Subsequent experience, however, did not bear out this hope. Though variable annuities have increased faster than the cost of living in some periods, at other times common stock prices actually declined while the cost of living was rising. Because of this, sales of variable annuities have remained insignificant.

Variable annuities may be based on a portfolio other than common stocks. In practice, however, this has rarely been done.

Variable life insurance. A few companies also have established separate accounts to back variable life insurance policies. Under these policies, amounts of insurance and cash values vary with the investment results of the separate account, but there is a guaranteed minimum death benefit.

SEPARATE ACCOUNT MANAGEMENT FEES

Group Contracts for Qualified Plans

The investment management fees charged by insurance companies vary with the nature of the assets of the separate account. For common stock and bond accounts, some large companies charge a fee at the annual rate of 0.25 percent of assets. For real estate accounts, a fee of approximately one percent is typical. It is common practice to scale down the fee as the amount of the client's interest in a separate account increases; for example, the fee may be 0.25 percent of the first $20 million and 0.125 percent of the excess. The scaling down may be based on the client's aggregate interest in all or several of the separate accounts in which he or she participates. In addition to the investment management fee, companies charge for administrative services to the pension plan. A typical charge is 0.40 to 0.50 percent of the first $1-2 million, gradually scaled down to 0.10 percent or less of amounts over $25 million. The charge may be more or less, depending on the services provided.

Other Contracts

The investment management fees under individual contracts are generally close to the fees charged by mutual funds, or approximately 0.50 percent. The fee is often reduced on the portion of the fund exceeding, say, $100 million. In addition, companies make a charge for the mortality and expense guarantees provided under individual contracts; this is usually at an annual rate of approximately one percent of assets, but varies considerably among companies. Such a charge is also made under group contracts issued for tax-sheltered annuity plans under Section 403(b) of the Code, which provide guarantees for individual participants. Under both individual contracts and this type of group contract, an annual administration charge of approximately $25 to $30 per individual is also made.

ATTRACTIVE FEATURES

Professional Management and Diversification

Separate accounts enable investors to take advantage of management by the insurance company's professional investment staff. Moreover, investors get the benefit of diversification of assets. Separate accounts offer diversification both by type of investment (common stocks, bonds, etc.) and by particular investment within each type.

Access to Special Investments

Through separate accounts, pension plans can gain access to types of investments not otherwise available to them. Perhaps the most notable example of this is real estate, which is becoming increasingly popular with pension plans as a hedge against inflation. It is not practical for most plans, even large ones, to invest directly in real estate. Insurance companies, though, have invested in real estate for many years, and have built expert organizations that enable them to make attractive investments for their real estate separate accounts. Private placements and mortgage loans are other areas where insurance companies have special experience and facilities.

Automatic Re-Investment

The income and realized gains of a separate account operated on an open-end basis are automatically re-invested. If, however, an investor prefers to receive cash, he can do so by liquidating an equivalent number of units.

POTENTIAL RISKS

Market Volatility

As noted, the unit values of a pooled separate account, in addition to reflecting investment income, vary with the market value of the assets of the account. Thus, the risk of investing in a separate account, as measured by market volatility, is the same as the risk involved in investing in the respective assets directly.

Loss of Liquidity

Contractual provisions regarding liquidity depend on the assets in which a separate account is invested. Separate accounts invested in illiquid assets (private placement loans, mortgage loans, real estate) do not guarantee liquidity. There is no secondary market where this type of asset can be readily sold. If a company were forced to sell real estate to raise cash, the sale might have to be made at a depressed price, to the detriment of the remaining participants. For these reasons, participants in this type of account may withdraw funds only to the extent cash is available, either from investment income or from new deposits.

Companies may impose some limitations even on withdrawals from common stock and publicly traded bond funds in order to avoid forced sales. Such limitations, however, do not apply to separate accounts registered under the Investment Company Act of 1940, which requires that requests for withdrawals must be met within seven days. The portfolio of a separate account established for a single customer may be transferred in kind to another funding agency, avoiding the need to sell assets. Some companies are also willing to make transfers in kind from a pooled account for clients that hold a substantial portion of the account.

TAX CONSEQUENCES

Federal Income Taxes

Separate accounts are taxed as part of the life insurance company of which they are a part. The effect of this is that no federal income tax is payable on the investment income or capital gains credited to contracts issued to plans qualified under Code Section 401, tax-sheltered annuity plans under Code Section 403(b), individual retirement accounts under Code Section 408, and public-employee retirement or deferred compensation plans. Similarly, under the provisions of the Code applicable to life insurance companies, no income tax is payable on the investment income credited to separate-account contracts issued to plans that are not in these categories.[2] The insurance company is, however, taxed on long-term capital gains with respect to assets held for such contracts. Accordingly, the amounts credited to them are reduced by provision for capital gains taxes.

Individuals are taxed in accordance with the applicable provisions of the Code when they receive benefits from the plans or annuity contracts that cover them (except to the extent that benefits represent amounts that have been previously taxed). This means that tax on investment earnings under deferred annuity contracts is deferred until earnings are paid to the annuitant. However, in Revenue Ruling 81-225, issued in September 1981, the IRS denied deferral to certain wraparound annuities. The IRS contended that the contractholder rather than the insurance company owned the mutual fund shares and that, therefore, the contractholder is not entitled to annuity tax treatment.

State Taxes

States generally impose a premium tax on life insurance company contracts. Such tax may be payable when an annuity is purchased for an individual. In about half of the states, however, there is no premium tax on any annuity contracts. In many additional states, annuity contracts issued in connection with plans under Section 401, 403(b), 408, or 457 of the Code are exempt from premium tax. State

---

[2] One company has a separate account under which income and capital gains on accumulating funds are passed through to the participants, so that taxation is the same as for a mutual fund.

income taxes on amounts paid to an individual under an annuity contract vary widely and depend on the laws of the specific state.

IMPORTANT FACTORS IN BUYING

Federal Securities Acts

Interests in separate accounts are considered securities for the purpose of regulation under the federal securities laws — the Securities Act of 1933, the Securities Exchange Act of 1934, and the Investment Company Act of 1940. However, accounts used only by qualified pension, profit-sharing, or savings plans that meet the requirements of Code Section 401 have been granted statutory exemptions from most provisions of these acts. Such accounts are exempt from registration under the 1940 Act, and contracts providing for participation in them are exempt from registration under the 1933 Act. Since 1980, these exemptions have also been available to accounts used by plans of public employee retirement systems (but not public employee deferred-compensation plans) if they meet certain requirements of Code Section 401. The exemption from the 1933 Act means that no prospectus is required. (This exemption is not available to Keogh (HR-10) plans of self-employed persons.)

Separate accounts that do not meet these conditions are subject to all requirements of the federal securities laws. Sales of contracts providing for participation in such accounts may be made only with a prospectus and only by registered securities representatives. The separate account itself must be registered with the SEC as an investment company, in accordance with the 1940 Act. This law requires, among other things, that the separate account have its own board of directors, a majority of whom must be not otherwise affiliated with the insurance company. (Table 1 on page 405 summarizes the status of separate accounts under the federal securities laws.)

State Laws and Regulations

Insurance companies are subject to state laws and regulations. Accordingly, a new separate account must be approved by the insurance department of the company's home state. Some states (New York, for one) require companies to file and maintain a plan of operation for separate-account business. In addition, the contract forms providing for participation in the separate account must be approved in all states in which the company intends to use them.

In most state separate-account laws, the qualitative limitations applicable to insurance company investments for the general account are applied unchanged. But most of the quantitative restrictions on particular forms of investment (e.g., the requirement that not more than 10 percent of assets may be invested in common stocks) have been removed. Some quantitative limits still apply. In New

TABLE 1. Applicability to Separate Accounts of Federal Securities Laws

	Account Interests Exempt from Securities Laws?		
User of Separate Account	*1933 Act*	*1934 Act*	*1940 Act*
Plans qualified under Section 401 of Internal Revenue Code, except plans of self-employed persons (HR-10 plans); certain public employee retirement systems	Essentially Yes		Yes
HR-10 plans	No	No	Yes
Tax-sheltered annuities; public employee deferred compensation plans; tax-favored Individual Retirement Accounts; other individual contracts	No	No	No

Jersey, for example, no more than 8 percent of the outstanding voting stock of any corporation may be held in all of a company's investment accounts — except for any shares on which voting rights are passed along to contractholders.[3] Furthermore, there may be a limit (e.g., 10 percent) on the portion of any account's market value that can be invested in the securities of any single corporation.

Other rules. There also may be dividend or earnings tests that must be met by each common stock acquired. Certain state laws have "basket" clauses under which a portion of an account may be placed in investments that otherwise would not be eligible for the account. Some separate accounts, such as single-customer separate accounts or pooled accounts in which participation is limited to specified types of contracts, may be free of all qualitative and quantitative restrictions — except the limit on an issuer's voting rights held by the company.

GLOSSARY

actively managed account— A separate account the portfolio securities of which are continually bought and sold in accordance with the manager's judgment.

[3] New Jersey Insurance Laws, Sections 17B:20-2 and 17B:28-9.

basket— The portion of the assets of a separate account that state law permits to be invested without regard to otherwise applicable restrictions (e.g., 10 percent in New York).

closed-end account— A separate account in which interests may be acquired only during a limited period. The account is invested in securities or properties acquired at the end of this period and distributes investment income and principal as received.

group contract— A contract issued to a trustee or an employer for the benefit of participants in a plan.

individual contract— A contract covering only one person.

open-end account— A separate account in which interests may be acquired at any time and are redeemable by the insurance company.

passively managed account— A separate account managed by application of a formula or set of rules governing the composition of the portfolio.

wraparound annuity— An annuity issued by an insurance company but funded through another investment medium, for example, a mutual fund.

TRADE ORGANIZATION

The American Council of Life Insurance, Washington, D.C.

SUGGESTED READING

Periodicals

Life Insurance Fact Book. Published by the American Council of Life Insurance, Washington, D.C. Annually.

Pension and Investment Age. Published by Crain Communications, Inc., Chicago, Ill. Biweekly.

Pension Facts. Published by the American Council of Life Insurance, Washington, D.C. Annually.

Real Estate Profiles. Published by Evaluation Associates, Westport, Conn. Quarterly.

Reference Books

Cummins, J. David, ed. *Investment Activities of Life Insurance Companies.* Homewood: Richard D. Irwin, Inc., 1977.

McGill, Dan M. *Fundamentals of Private Pensions.* 4th edition. Homewood: Richard D. Irwin, Inc., 1979.

Note: Life insurance companies publish annual and quarterly reports on their pooled separate accounts.

Metals—Gold, Silver, Platinum

*James E. Sinclair**

BASIC CHARACTERISTICS

For most of recorded history, gold has served as a metaphor for excellence and desirability. For Old Testament kings, it was a royal treasure; for Pharaohs, the price of admission to heaven from their gilded tombs. The Golden Fleece lured the mythical Jason to dangerous adventures, and the golden touch destroyed Midas. A chest of private gold was the hard-won prize for a company of English gentlemen in Stevenson's *Treasure Island* and for the hero of Poe's *The Gold Bug.*

Gold has not lost its appeal. Developments of the last decade, in fact, have done much to restore its glitter as a medium for serious modern investors. Inflation, the growing scarcity of low-cost energy, and political upheaval in the Third World all have served to place a special premium on tangible investments and to establish gold, silver, and, to some extent, platinum as worthy components of well-planned portfolios, along with stocks, bonds, and real estate.

The precious metals concentrate a great deal of value in small weight and volume. All are bought and sold as industrial materials, used in the manufacture of jewelry, held in bullion form for investment, and in the form of futures contracts for hedging and speculation. Gold and silver traditionally have been part of the world monetary systems, and even platinum found its way into official coinage for a few years in Czarist Russia.

Most of the gold that was ever mined is still traceable. Of an estimated 80,000 tons of mined gold believed to exist, about half is under control of central banks and international financial organizations. The remainder is in private hands in the form of bullion, coins, jewelry, and industrial products.

Because the prices of gold and the other precious metals tend to rise when stocks and bonds are shaky and cash is an eroding asset, metal-related investments can be a stabilizing element in a diversified portfolio. Recognizing this, managers of pension funds and trust officers managing substantial private accounts are increasingly willing to recommend and broker the purchase of gold and, to some extent, the other precious metals.

Gold responds less to the normal market factors of basic producer supply and consumer demand than it does to political and psychological forces in the marketplace. The price of gold is a sensitive barometer of world anxiety, rising

* James E. Sinclair is General Partner of Sinclair Group Companies, New York.

in times of tension and fear, declining in times of relative tranquility. To a degree, silver and platinum respond to the same forces.

Determinants of Value — A Historical Perspective

The character of all the markets in precious metals underwent major changes in the 1970s. This was due in part to an oil-fired inflation that rocked the economies of the world, undercutting the currencies of the oil-consuming nations, to the benefit of the oil producers. It was also due to the arrival of a major market force — the American investor — who had been legally forbidden to buy gold for investment or speculation for forty years, and rarely thought of silver and platinum.

Unlike the residents of Europe, Asia, and the Middle East, Americans, during most of their history, were not particularly enamored of gold. The settlers from Northern Europe who populated the continent in the eighteenth and early nineteenth centuries came not for gold but for land, freedom, and stability. Gold was for wedding rings and ornaments, for coinage and circulation. Gold drew adventurers to California and, later, to Alaska, but neither the Californian nor the Alaskan gold rush greatly touched the lives of the great mass of American farmers, factory workers, and ordinary citizens.

The federal government hoarded gold in its vaults to support its currency and to settle foreign debts, but for the average saver, gold held little attraction as an investment. When the dollar was a symbol of solidity and retained most of its purchasing power from one decade to the next, gold — which yielded no income — was a less attractive holding than land, a business, or interest-bearing securities.

But in an odd turnabout, the very solidity of the dollar became a problem in 1934, in the depths of the Great Depression. A money supply that had actually shrunk contributed to a stagnant economy, falling prices, and terrifying unemployment. Seeking ways to achieve reflation, President Franklin D. Roosevelt decreed an increase in the official price of gold from $20.67 an ounce to $35.00 an ounce. To head off private profiteering on the new rate, he put a legal ban on the private ownership of gold for investment or speculation. Roosevelt drew some criticism for inflating the dollar, which, of course, was his intention, but suprisingly little for banning the ownership of gold. Few Americans were greatly affected by the ban and most had far more important things to worry about than the price of gold.

Forty years later, the world had changed profoundly. By 1974, the U.S. government had ceased to guarantee its currency in terms of gold. The official price of gold had risen to $42.22 an ounce, but this was a legal fiction in a world in which the free market price, no longer controlled by the U.S. Treasury, had soared to far higher levels. Legislation to end the ban on private ownership of gold by U.S. citizens became effective December 31, 1974.

Around the world, eager gold traders awaited the new gold rush that they were sure would develop once Americans were free to buy bullion. In anticipation of the opening of the vast new market, buyers bid up the price of gold to $197.50 an ounce on December 30, 1974, only to find that American investors were supremely indifferent. Purchases were minuscule. As the American reaction became clear to professional gold traders, the price of gold went into a long decline, drifting down to a low of $101.50 an ounce late in 1976.

Investors around the world gradually began to realize that the oil crisis of 1973 and 1974 had changed the economic world in profound and irreversible ways. As the price of oil heated up inflation all around the globe, investors began to realize that precious metals offered an alternative to wavering stocks and tumbling bonds. After touching its 1976 low, gold began to appreciate as new waves of buyers entered the market. Many of them were American, operating through the new futures markets in New York and Chicago.

In a world in which instant communications can spread alarm with the speed of light, several factors came together to create a textbook condition for a bull market in gold. American buyers had finally entered the market in strength. Buying increased from the newly affluent oil-producing countries of the Middle East. Demand increased in Europe, especially for gold jewelry.

Late in 1979, the seizure of the American Embassy and its staff in Tehran raised the threat of a major confrontation in the Middle East. At the same time, a decline of oil production in Iran put new upward pressure on world oil prices. Shortly afterward, Moslem militants in Mecca seized the Grand Mosque, posing a threat to the stability of Saudi Arabia, the world's leading oil exporter. These events, coming together, set off new waves of anxiety worldwide and triggered widespread panic-buying of gold as a hedge against the disasters that seemed to be developing.

For a different set of reasons, the price of silver also was surging upward, as was the price of platinum. In January 1980, the price of gold peaked at $887.50, and silver at $52 an ounce; in March, platinum peaked at $1,085 an ounce. These prices were unrealistic even for a panicky market, and soon after reaching their peaks, prices broke for all three metals under weight of profit-taking and an easing of the extraordinary conditions that had prompted the buying.

TYPES OF PRECIOUS METAL INVESTMENTS

The range of possible investments in precious metals is remarkably varied, from the very conservative to the highly speculative. Ownership of metals, particularly gold, offers an equity in a commodity of intrinsic value rather than in an arbitrary number of units of currency. In a world in which inflation has become an alarming fact of life, the ownership of a tangible commodity that has been historically in demand offers a hedge against inflation and some prospect of real capital growth if purchases are timed well.

While the market prices of all the precious metals have fluctuated wildly since 1974, a longer perspective suggests that, over the very long period, ownership of metallic gold has been a surprisingly safe and stable form of investment. One ounce of gold would purchase a well-made man's suit in the eighteenth, nineteenth, and much of the twentieth century. Two hundred ounces of gold would buy a substantial family home at almost any time in the last 200 years except during part of the period when gold was artificially pegged at $35 an ounce. Twenty-five ounces of gold would pay for a Model-T Ford in 1927, or a Cadillac Seville in 1980.

The writer is a proprietor of a New York firm that specializes in investments in precious metals and foreign currencies. For some years, the firm has recommended investments in precious metals, particularly in gold, as a component of almost every private investor's portfolio. These metal-related investments, the company feels, may range from 10 percent to 25 percent of a portfolio, varying with the owner's need for income and the degree of risk that is reasonably acceptable.

Gold

Establishing gold prices. Since price is so basic in discussing any investment, it may be useful to mention how gold prices are established. Basically, there are three mechanisms: the Zurich interbank price, the London fixing, and the spot or near-due-delivery contract price on the New York and Chicago futures exchanges.

Soon after the banking day begins in Zurich, the prices at which early trades have been made are published and publicized worldwide. A little later in the European morning and again in the afternoon, representatives of five merchant banks gather in London, in the offices of N.M. Rothschild, to determine a price at which demand is balanced against supply. Thus, for a moment twice a day, London gold is as close to an authentic price as the market can offer. At about the time of the London afternoon fixing, trading in futures contracts, including the contract for next delivery (spot) opens in the Commodity Exchange, Inc. (Comex) in New York and in the International Monetary Market in Chicago (IMM). After the business day ends in Europe, the Comex and IMM quotations are the key prices for traders all around the world to consider. In the middle of the North American night (the early hours of the European morning), trading is conducted in Hong Kong. Although the Hong Kong market has not yet achieved the stature of the European or North American markets, it is growing in importance. The ease of satellite communications makes it as accessible to the trader as New York, Chicago, or London. (See Figure 1 on page 411 for the record of London gold prices from 1973 to September 1981.)

Gold bullion. The most obvious, but not necessarily the most attractive, form of gold investment is the purchase of bullion, cast in bars or ingots. Bullion is bought outright and held for the long term. It may be held in a depositary either in the United States or in a foreign banking center such as London or Zurich.

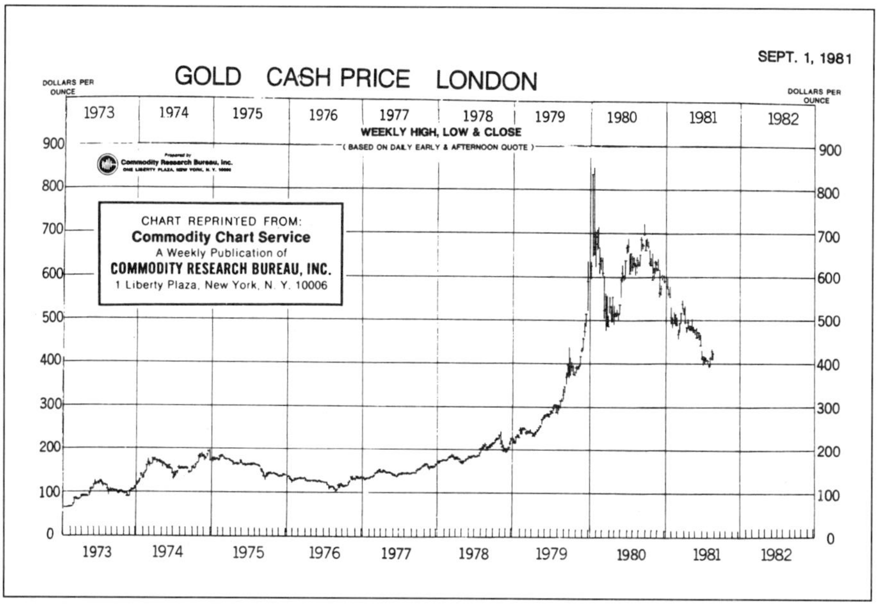

FIG. 1. London Gold Prices 1973–1981
SOURCE: Commodity Research Bureau

The bars should be left in a bonded warehouse or bank vault, partly for security, partly to avoid the cost of a new assay, which many dealers require when purchasing or repurchasing bullion held in private hands. Storage and insurance costs are not excessive relative to the value of the gold.

Bullion coins. Many investors prefer to buy units of gold smaller than bars or ingots. These investors are attracted to such bullion coins as the South African Krugerrand and the Canadian Maple Leaf, which contain exactly one troy ounce of pure gold each. Bullion coins are marketed at a small premium above the value of their gold content. There are active markets for these coins, with reasonable spreads between dealer bids and offers. Typically, a dealer will be prepared to sell one-ounce bullion coins at 5 to 7 percent above the day's market price for gold, and repurchase them at 2.5 percent above spot.

The Krugerrand is also available in fractional sizes of one-half, one-quarter, and one-tenth ounce. A number of other foreign coins such as the Mexican 50-peso, the Austrian 100-corona, the Hungarian 100-korona, and the British sovereign are valued primarily for their gold content and are commonly bought and sold by dealers. Each year for five years beginning in 1980, the U.S. Treasury plans to market an issue of one-ounce and half-ounce gold medallions, each honoring a prominent American (Grant Wood and Marian Anderson were the first individuals so honored). But marketing procedures are cumbersome, requiring a purchaser to pay for the medallions several weeks in advance of delivery, and sales of the first issue were slow. The gold medallions eventually may acquire some premium numismatic value above their gold content.

Jewelry. In the United States, gold jewelry is not commonly bought or sold solely as an investment. In India and the Middle East, however, high-carat gold is frequently fabricated into jewelry and sold by weight at prices based on the day's gold fixing in London. Residents of these regions, as well as tourists, often find such jewelry a convenient form of investment for modest amounts of gold in items with value that closely reflects the bullion value of gold. Such high-carat, low-markup jewelry often becomes part of a family's basic savings or a dowry in areas where families rarely have access to the variety of investments available in the West.

Gold mining stocks. While investment in gold objects has the common disadvantage of yielding no current return, shares in gold mining companies frequently do pay dividends, some quite generous by market standards. Professional market advisers distinguish between shares in North American companies and those in South Africa on a variety of counts. Companies in the United States and Canada enjoy a climate of political stability, but the small size and relatively low grade of their deposits and their production costs tend to limit the profits that can be earned. Even so, the shares of North American gold mining companies frequently respond quite sensitively to the price of gold. In fact, because of leverage, the price of these shares may rise or fall more dramatically than the price of gold itself.

Gold mining companies in South Africa, the world's major producer of gold, typically work deposits of a size and value unknown elsewhere in the world. One South African mine, Vaal Reefs, is the world's largest, producing more gold than the total U.S. production. South African gold shares in 1980 were among the world's most profitable equity investments from the standpoint of total return.

South African mining companies treat their mines as depleting assets. This means that they pay out most of their profits as they operate, rather than set up cash reserves as the ore body diminishes. Thus, when a mine is worked out, the only value remaining is the salvage value of the equipment. Even regarding dividends as a partial return of capital, the South African mines traditionally pay high returns. Against this factor, however, any investor must weigh the risk that South Africa's social problems and political tensions may at some time erupt, at unknown cost to the industry and its foreign investors. However, numbers of American investors have accepted this risk, and South African government sources estimate that in 1980 Americans owned 23.2 percent of all issued shares of South African gold.

Investment participation in South African mining companies is represented not directly by common stock but by depository receipts; these entitle the holder to receive dividends but not to participate in the company's policy-making decisions. By South African law, full participating ownership is restricted to residents of South Africa.

Since both depository receipts and dividends are expressed in South African rands, their value in other currencies varies with the exchange rate on the rand, which has been strong in recent years as mining and general industrial development have flourished in South Africa.

Gold-based mutual funds. With the growth of popular interest in gold and gold mining stocks, several mutual funds have been created to offer shareholders interest in a portfolio of gold-related investments. The first and largest of these funds, the New York-based International Investors, early in 1981 had about 50 percent of its portfolio invested in South African mining stocks, 10 percent in United States gold mines, and 10 percent in Canadian mines. The balance of its investment portfolio was in other foreign gold mining stocks and in cash. For the ten-year period ending December 31, 1980, International Investors compiled one of the best records for capital gains of all U.S. mutual funds, although the value of its shares declined with the sell-off of gold in early 1981.

Among the other gold-related mutual funds are Research Capital, United Services Fund, Gold Conda, and Gold Fund.

Gold futures. This once small and obscure form of gold trading has expanded to such a degree that the spot price of gold on the major futures exchanges is read, along with the Zurich price and the London gold-fixing, as one of the authentic market indicators of gold's value.

Futures contracts are a distinctively North American form of trading, developed in the nineteenth century to faciliate the marketing of farm products. A futures contract is simply an agreement for a buyer to buy and a seller to sell a fixed amount of a commodity on an agreed date in the future, at an agreed price. The contract can be used by buyer or seller to fix a price at which the commodity will be traded in the future, rather than leaving himself at the mercy of market fluctuations. A farmer growing wheat may sell a crop in advance of the harvest and be assured of receiving a known price, no matter what happens to the spot or cash market, as the season advances. A processor of grains also may use the futures market to obtain supplies at a known price.

The world's first gold futures contracts were offered in 1972 in Winnipeg, a major Canadian center for farm commodity trading. As long as American citizens were barred from buying or selling gold, the potential of the Winnipeg market was limited. The real turning point for gold futures, as for many other forms of gold investment, was December 31, 1974, the day when the Roosevelt ban on private investment in gold was lifted. On that day, five American commodity exchanges opened trading in gold futures. Since then, two exchanges, New York's Comex and Chicago's IMM, have come to account for 95 percent of all gold futures trading in the United States, with Comex handling about three times the trading volume of IMM in 1980.

The standard futures contract on the Comex and the IMM calls for delivery of 100 troy ounces of gold on a settlement date out as far as twenty-one months in the future for IMM and out to thirty months for Comex. In practice, fewer than one percent of these contracts result in actual delivery of gold; this means that trading in futures is largely conducted for purposes of hedging or arbitrage, and for technique trading. (See article on Futures — Metals, elsewhere in this volume.)

Hedging. Hedging is a practice followed by businesses that deal in physical gold, as in the manufacture of jewelry or in commercial operations in bullion. A bullion dealer with a large inventory of gold awaiting sale to commercial users may choose to be protected from inventory losses by selling futures contracts in roughly the amount of his inventory. If the price of gold goes down, the dealer will lose money on the inventory but show a profit on short sales, buying back contracts before maturity at a price lower than that of the original sale. If the market moves in the opposite direction, the dealer will lose money on short sales but enjoy an appreciated value for the inventory. The dealer's real objective is not to make a speculative profit, but to be protected against loss.

A commercial consumer of gold, such as a manufacturer of jewelry who must constantly buy physical bullion as a raw material, may also use the futures market to assure stability of costs. Rather than tying up substantial amounts of capital in an inventory of bullion, he may choose to buy contracts for future delivery of gold. Rather than paying in full for the metal, the manufacturer puts up a margin that may be as low as 5 percent of the value of the contract. As the time comes for purchase of physical bullion for his manufacturing needs, he buys at the market price. If the price of gold has risen, the manufacturer suffers increased cost, but makes an offsetting profit on his futures long purchases. Like the bullion dealer described above, the manufacturer has effectively hedged the market risk at modest cost in margin and brokerage fees.

While hedging is the theoretical purpose for which futures markets function, in fact, a great deal of the trading volume in all futures markets is speculative. Traders who have no interest in making or accepting delivery of the commodities traded often buy and sell contracts in hope of turning a profit — a perfectly legal and respectable objective. In effect, speculators seeking a profit accept risks that hedgers avoid. Both hedgers and speculators are necessary if a futures market is to remain liquid and valid, with buyers active in falling markets, sellers in rising markets.

Arbitrage. Speculators use a number of trading techniques in the hope of limiting their risks or of turning modest profits at modest risk. Among the most common is arbitrage, in which a commodity is bought and sold simultaneously in different markets, to take advantage of fleeting price differentials that may prevail for only a matter of minutes. As an example, the purchase of a contract in physical gold in London might be offset by the sale of a futures contract on the Comex or the IMM at a moment when the London price is lower than the New York spot price.

Because arbitrageurs are constantly alert to momentary price differentials in different markets and act quickly to bring them back into line, the price of physical gold in London and the price for spot delivery months in the U.S. markets are rarely far apart. This spot price of gold is the base and the pivot from which the market establishes a price for future delivery months. In the normal trading pattern, the prices for future delivery rise in steps from the spot price, a pattern called a "contango." The price differential between spot and future months is largely a function of interest rates, which establish the theoretical cost of buying at spot prices and holding bullion for future delivery. When interest rates are high, the gradients are steep; with lower interest rates, the gradients flatten out.

Changing patterns in price from near to distant delivery months open the way for a trader to make profits by spreading, a technique in which contracts are simultaneously bought and sold for different delivery dates. For example, if interest rates were on the upswing in January, a trader might reasonably assume that the difference in cost between a near delivery and a more distant delivery would increase. In this case, he might sell a contract for June delivery and buy one for December delivery. The values for both contracts would rise or fall in response to fluctuations in the price of spot gold, but the more distant delivery price would rise higher or fall lower if interest rates rose as expected, widening the differential to favor later delivery months.

Increasing use of these market techniques by professional traders has led to a steady increase in the volume of trading in U.S. gold futures since the markets opened in 1974. Trading volume grew from less than 900,000 contracts bought and sold in all five U.S. futures markets in 1975 — the first full year of trading — to 11 million contracts in 1980. In the early years of U.S. futures trading, U.S. prices largely followed trends established in Zurich and London. In later years, the U.S. prices have tended to establish trends that were followed the next day in Europe.

Silver

In any grouping of precious metals, silver invariably ranks as gold's junior partner: less rare, less valuable, the second prize in any contest in which gold is the symbol of top achievement. Enormous quantities of silver are used in film manufacturing, the largest industry for silver consumption, and in electrical and electronic products. Silver is classified as a strategic material by the U.S. government because of its applications in defense industries, and is held in the national strategic stockpile. Although traders and technicians compulsively follow the changing ratios in the prices of silver and gold, no one can confidently use past performance as a guide to future price relationships between the metals. Silver must be taken on its own terms. On the other hand, silver responds to many of the same market forces that move gold: inflation (real and expected), interest rates, and political tensions. In recent years, its price has swung even more erratically than that of gold.

It is an oddity of the silver market that each year the world consumes more silver than it produces from mines. The deficit is met by the melting of silver from above-ground stocks that are held largely in private hands in the form of coins, jewelry, decorative objects, and ingots; large quantities are also recovered through industrial recycling processes. Handy and Harman, a leading firm of silver dealers, estimates that silver consumption by the non-communist world totaled 355.9 million ounces in 1980, while mine production from non-communist nations totaled only 255 million ounces. The difference of 100.9 million ounces was met by industrial salvage plus the melting of coins and other silver objects.

Consumption of silver for industrial purposes and coinage in the non-communist world actually fell by 20 percent after 1979; a business recession and the high price of silver led to substitution in some industrial processes. It is interesting that even when silver was trading at historically high prices, investors worldwide absorbed an estimated 122.6 million ounces of bullion for the expansion of private holdings. This was the equivalent of 48 percent of all the newly mined silver produced in the non-communist world.

The Hunt crisis. In the world of silver, the names of Nelson Bunker Hunt and his brother, William Herbert Hunt, have come to have special significance. Heirs to a large Texas oil fortune, the brothers began to accumulate silver in 1973 in the form of coins, bullion, futures contracts, and options. By January 1, 1980, the Hunt holdings in bullion and contracts were estimated at 192 million ounces, leading to concern among officials of the Comex and Chicago Board of Trade that the Hunts might corner the market, making it impossible for sellers of futures contracts to meet their obligations to deliver. The exchanges revised their rules in a way that encouraged selling and made it difficult for new buyers to enter the market. The price of silver plummeted, causing the Hunts to suffer enormous losses on their futures contracts, but they managed to avoid major liquidation of their holdings in physical silver.

Since then, the threat of massive sales by the Hunts has had a depressing effect on the silver market; so has the decision by the U.S. government to sell off large quantities of silver from its strategic stockpile. During much of 1981, silver traded at less than one-fifth of the peak price of $52 an ounce it reached in January 1980.

For the private investor, some of the forms in which silver may be bought and held are as follows:

Silver bars or ingots. Much of the world's professional trade in silver is transacted through the purchase and sale of bars of .999 purity weighing 1,000 ounces, plus or minus small tolerances. The standard contract on the London Metal Exchange is for 10,000 ounces, and on the Comex and Chicago Board of

Trade futures markets, for 5,000 ounces. But anyone buying physical silver in amounts under 10,000 ounces is likely to have to pay a premium of 5 to 8 percent on standard 1,000-ounce bars and a higher premium for smaller bars. In addition, many states levy a sales tax on bullion actually delivered. Furthermore, as in the case of gold, silver held outside an authorized warehouse or bank vault may have to be assayed and weighed at the seller's expense when it is resold into professional trade channels. For all these reasons, as well as the difficulty of safely storing large amounts of metal, ownership of silver bars has its drawbacks in cost and convenience, unless the owner is willing to leave the bullion safely stored and accept warehouse receipts as evidence of ownership.

Bags of silver coins. Bags containing silver coins with a face value of $1,000 are commonly marketed at prices that rise or fall with the daily spot quotations for silver. The coins are standard U.S. issue, dating from 1896 to 1964, a period when such coins consisted of 90 percent silver. Because a bag of coins weighs about 65 pounds and thus is difficult to move and store, most buyers prefer to leave their coins in the hands of a dealer, paying a small annual charge for storage and insurance.

The coins in the bags are, for the most part, circulated and have little or no numismatic value; their worth is based entirely on their silver content. Like other forms of physical metal, they of course pay no yield; but as a speculation on a rising price for silver, they offer a relatively popular investment medium.

Silver forward contracts. Silver contracts for forward delivery are traded every business day on the London Metal Exchange. The standard contract is for 10,000 ounces of silver .999 fine. While delivery can be set for any business day, there are two common contracts. One is for spot delivery two days after the sale. The other is three months forward, in which delivery is made and payment accepted three months from the date of sale, or on the first business day thereafter if the prompt date falls on a holiday or weekend. Delivery is normally completed by handing over a warehouse receipt for the silver sold. A buyer or seller awaiting a prompt date may choose to offset a contract by selling if he has previously bought, or buying if he has previously sold. The British practice, unlike that of the U.S. futures markets, is to complete sale by actual delivery of the metal in the form of a warehouse receipt. London is primarily a market in physical metal.

Silver futures contracts. On the Comex and Chicago Board of Trade (CBT), the world's leading silver futures exchanges, the standard contract is for 5,000 ounces of silver .999 fine, for delivery on standard dates out as far as twenty-two months in the future for Comex, thirty months for CBT. In contrast to the British practice, American traders in futures almost always settle their contracts by making offsetting arrangements in advance of the delivery date. As with gold, futures contracts are mainly a device for hedging and speculation rather than for trading in physical silver.

As in gold futures, the prices for distant silver contracts almost always rise in steps from the spot month, the gradients varying with prevailing and anticipated interest rates. The contracts may be used by dealers and industrial consumers of silver to hedge and by speculators in the hope of turning a profit. A variety of trading techniques may be used as in the gold market to arbitrage between different markets and to put on spreads by buying and selling equivalent contracts for different delivery dates. Because margin requirements are relatively low under normal conditions, a trader can use leverage to control a great deal of silver. This opens up the possibility of large profits or equally dramatic losses on substantial market moves. Silver futures prices in New York from 1967 to September 1981 are charted in Figure 2 on page 419. (See article on Futures – Metals, elsewhere in this volume.)

Silver options. A small number of dealers in physical silver have met the stringent requirements of the Commodity Futures Trading Commission (CFTC) to offer options on physical silver. The options are of two kinds: puts and calls. The buyer of a call pays the silver dealer a premium in return for the privilege of buying 1,000 ounces of silver at an agreed striking price within an agreed period of time. If the price of silver rises, the holder of the option may either exercise the call, or resell the contract to the issuer, since the issuers make two-way markets in the contracts.

The buyer of a put pays a premium in exchange for the right to sell 1,000 ounces of silver at an agreed price within the period of the contract. If the price of silver goes down, the buyer profits by reselling the contract or putting the physical silver at a price above the current market. The purchaser of an option can lose the amount of the premium if he fails to exercise the option, but that is the extent of the loss, since he has bought a privilege rather than an obligation.

The CFTC is studying a proposal to allow trading in puts and calls on futures contracts, but there is no assurance that the contract will actually be developed and offered to the trading public.

Silver shares. A number of corporations listed on the New York Stock Exchange are major silver producers; their shares tend to rise and fall with the price of silver. Others, such as Asarco, are primarily base metal producers; these recover silver as a byproduct of their other mining operations. In addition, the Spokane Stock Exchange lists many small regional companies, many of them representing more hopes than confirmed production, and with shares selling for less than one dollar.

Platinum

Platinum and its related metals (rhodium, iridium, osmium, palladium, and ruthenium) are often grouped with gold and silver as precious metals. All the precious metals are traded by the troy ounce, all bear relatively elevated prices, and all share some market characteristics. As a group, precious metals tend to respond to psychological factors far more acutely than do industrial metals.

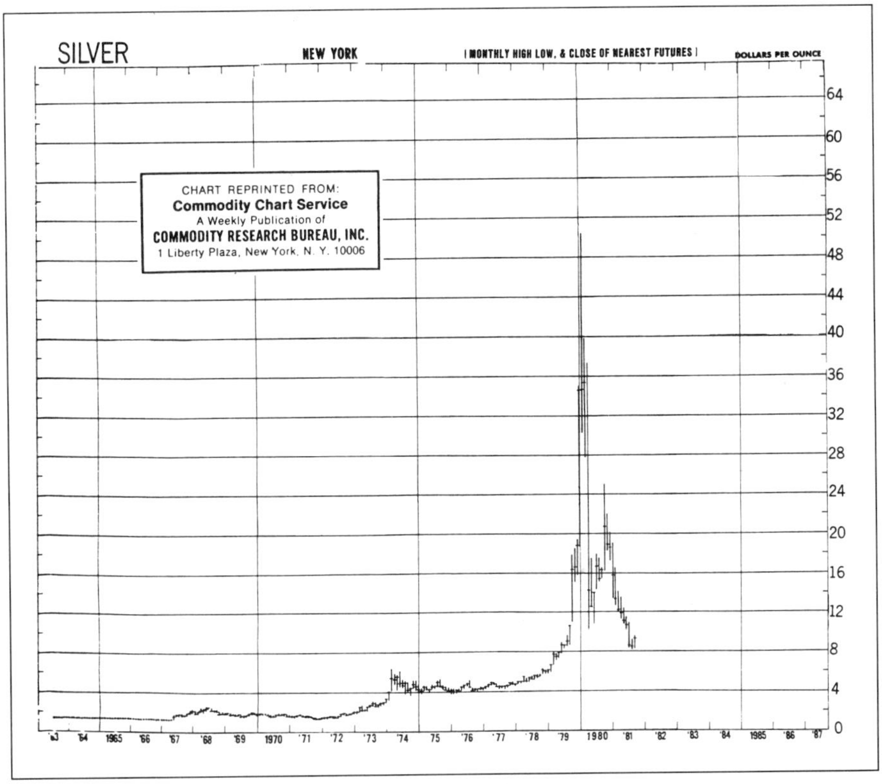

FIG. 2. New York Silver Futures Prices 1967–1981
SOURCE: Commodity Research Bureau

Gold's price has little to do with its real utility as an industrial material and much more to do with the world's anxieties, fears of inflation, and the action of central bankers adding to or liquidating national stocks of gold. Silver reacts to some degree to the same psychological forces, but also to market influences stemming from its industrial uses. Platinum is essentially an industrial raw material that has some market characteristics of a precious metal.

Platinum is the rarest of the major precious metals. The U.S. Bureau of Mines estimates total 1981 world production of the platinum metals at 6.78 million ounces, as compared to a total world production in gold of 39.2 million ounces and, in silver, of 375.5 million ounces.

The major markets for physical platinum are located in London and New York. In the United States, there are three distinct prices for the metal. The producer price is the cash price paid under long-term contracts to suppliers by industrial consumers. The dealer price is the cash price quoted by metal merchants on a day-to-day basis. The futures price is the price established by trading on the New York Mercantile Exchange (NYMEX), where futures contracts in units of fifty troy ounces are traded for delivery in the months of January, April, July, and October. Platinum futures prices in New York for the period of 1957 to 1981 (with interruptions) are shown in Figure 3 below. (See articles on Futures — Metals and Strategic and Critical Materials, elsewhere in this volume.)

The world gets most of its platinum group metals, as it does a whole range of critical and strategic metals, from South Africa and the Soviet Union. South Africa has expanded its production in recent years, selling its output freely on the world markets. This expansion, coupled with the Soviet Union's disposition to withhold its supplies, has made South Africa the dominant supplier of platinum metals to the non-communist world.

Together, Japan and the United States account for some 80 percent of world consumption of platinum. The United States recovers a small amount of platinum

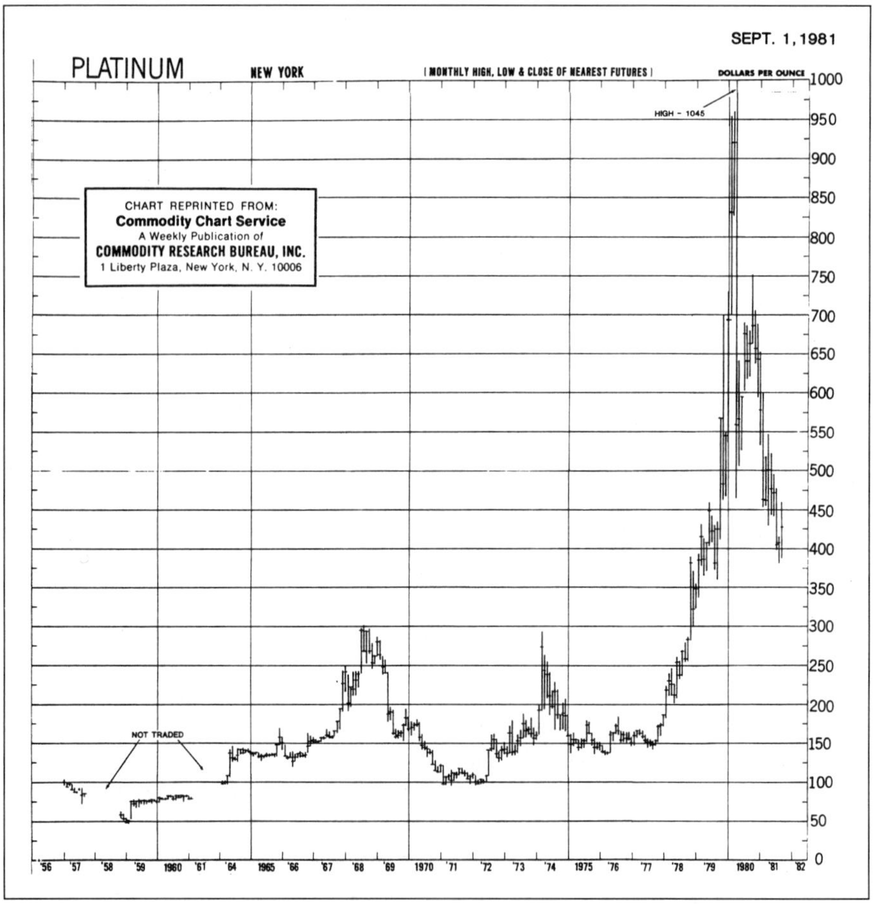

FIG. 3. New York Platinum Futures Prices 1957–1981
SOURCE: Commodity Research Bureau

as a byproduct of copper mining and from industrial recycling, but depends on imports to meet 87 percent of its needs in platinum metals. Japan, the other major consumer of platinum, is also heavily dependent on imports.

World industrial use of platinum peaked in 1979, then eased as recession slowed the U.S. economy. By long-term market patterns, the peak in consumption should have been followed shortly by declining prices, but in fact, the market shifted its emphasis and for a few months treated platinum less as an industrial raw material than as a precious metal. Platinum, gold, and silver all touched new price peaks in the first quarter of 1980, platinum cresting at $1,085 an ounce on the spot contract on the NYMEX on March 5, 1980.

Afterwards, all three of the precious metals experienced sharp price reactions. Platinum entered a long, irregular decline that took it to the range of $450 an ounce in the early months of 1981.

Price relationship with gold. Market followers carefully track the price relationship between gold and platinum. In fact, the two metals often move along roughly parallel tracks, with first one and then the other assuming a higher price. During much of the 1970s, platinum commanded a higher price than did gold; at its peak in March 1980, platinum was traded at more than $400 an ounce higher than gold. But platinum, resuming its more normal behavior as an industrial raw material, reacted to a slowdown in world industrial production, and in early 1981 was trading below gold.

As the world economy lifts from the 1980-1981 recession, demand for platinum seems likely to increase, and this will be a positive occurrence for platinum. Since there is no large, above-ground stock of platinum ingots in existence, prices tend to respond quickly to changing market conditions.

Physical platinum. The metal is cast in plates and ingots, usually stamped with the name of the processor. An investor may buy and take possession of the physical platinum, accepting the same disadvantages present in owning gold and silver ingots: the problem of storing and insuring the metal, and the cost of an assay upon resale.

Platinum futures. An investor with strong convictions about the direction in which platinum's price will move may buy or sell contracts for future delivery of fifty ounces of platinum through the NYMEX. Another technique is to build spreads, platinum against gold. For example, an investor who feels that platinum is underpriced in relation to gold may buy two contracts for platinum on NYMEX and sell one 100-ounce contract for gold on Comex or CBT. Because the market for platinum is much smaller and less liquid than that for gold, the investor would be well advised to make sure to get his platinum contract in place first at a reasonable price, and only then place his gold commitment.

Platinum stocks. While some American and Canadian mining companies produce small amounts of platinum as a byproduct of base-metal operations, the two primary producers of platinum in the non-communist world are Impala Platinum Holdings Ltd. and Rustenburg Platinum Holdings. Ltd., both in South Africa. Both stocks ordinarily sell at modest price-earnings ratios and pay relatively generous dividends. Non-South African residents may participate in these companies through ownership of depository receipts rather than voting stock.

ATTRACTIVE FEATURES

Hedge Against Inflation

The primary attraction of precious metal investments is the protection they provide against inflation. Gold, in particular, tends to retain purchasing power over very long periods of time, ranging into centuries. This is true to a lesser degree for silver. Because platinum has been recognized as a medium for investment for only a few decades, its track record as a shield against inflation is not as clear. It seems likely that an extremely useful metal such as platinum, produced in small quantities by a costly extractive process principally in two countries (one of them the Soviet Union) should sustain value over a long period of time.

Flight Capital

While the concept of accumulating precious metals to serve as flight capital is pleasantly remote from the planning of most U.S. residents, it is a very realistic consideration elsewhere in the world. When Vietnamese of Chinese extraction found themselves a persecuted minority after the Communist conquest of South Vietnam, many were able to use their accumulated savings in gold to purchase documents, bribe officials, make an escape, and re-establish themselves in other countries.

In the Middle East, the Iranian revolution of 1979, followed by the rise of Islamic revolutionary movements in conservative Arab states around the Persian Gulf, touched off waves of alarm among the wealthy and influential leaders of the region. Some wealthy Arabs responded to the growing unrest by placing their gold assets in banks in Zurich and London. The wave of gold buying so generated was almost surely the driving force behind the rise of gold above $850 an ounce in January 1980. These Arab purchases were just as truly flight capital as were those of the Vietnamese refugees, although the Arabs' flight, had it occurred, would have taken place in private jets rather than in leaky boats in the South China Sea.

Long-Term Appreciation and Aesthetic Appeal

While the pleasure of holding a gold ingot in a safe-deposit vault is scarcely the same as the satisfaction of hanging a Vermeer or a choice Picasso in one's living room, the forms of investment have a good deal in common. The chances are very good that both gold and well-selected art will appreciate in value over the long term.

Rare coins. For those interested in both the security of precious metals and the aesthetics of lovely objects, the collection of rare coins offers an appealing enterprise. Rare coins in both gold and silver have shown substantial capital appreciation in recent years, and a certain number of individuals who entered the field as investors have remained to enjoy it as collectors. Sotheby Parke Bernet, among other top-of-the-line auction houses, has re-entered the field of numismatics, holding regular auctions of prized coins and medals in New York. Some choice coins, such as the St. Gaudens high-relief double eagle of 1907, qualify as authentic art objects as well as tangible investments, a pleasure to own and enjoy. (See article on Coins, elsewhere in this volume.)

POTENTIAL RISKS

Lack of Current Return

There are two obvious disadvantages in owning physical metals. One is that for a fairly substantial investment, there is no current return in the form of dividends, interest, or rent. Thus investors forgo the returns that they would have received had they chosen another form of investment.

Market Volatility

The second disadvantage is the risk that the price of the metal will fall rather than rise subjecting the investor to a loss should he be forced to sell. The potential for loss in the short term is very real: Ask those who entered the silver market at $40 an ounce during the Hunt surge of 1980, or bought gold with the Arabs at $800 during the same time. Those who purchased metal outright for cash surely had second thoughts as prices plunged after the first-quarter peaks of 1980. The resolute among them may yet recoup their investments over the long haul; less fortunate were those who bought futures contracts only to see the markets plunge after the splurge was over.

Limited Liquidity of Platinum

Liquidity is rarely a problem with gold and silver; the markets are worldwide, and both metals are highly tradable almost anywhere. For platinum, however, the story is different. Platinum is produced in far smaller quantities than gold and silver are, and the investor market, as distinguished from the industrial market, is relatively thin. Only one U.S. commodity exchange trades platinum futures; at any time, the number of contracts outstanding is far less than the number of gold and silver contracts. Useful as it is for industry, platinum has not caught on as an investment medium to the extent that gold and silver have.

Government Regulation

Any investor in precious metals must be aware of the possibility of changes in the laws and regulations that govern the ownership of his assets. American investors have not forgotten the long prohibition on ownership of gold. While U.S. law has never banned the ownership of silver, the melting of silver coins was prohibited for a time in the 1960s. If such a law were re-enacted, it could have a disastrous effect on the market for bags of silver coins.

Since both silver and platinum are classified by the U.S. government as strategic materials — essential for national defense — it is not inconceivable that in an emergency the government could nationalize private holdings of these metals. Presumably, the owners would be compensated at some fair market value, but in the absence of precedent, it is difficult to know just what legal steps would be taken.

In an effort to avoid such regulations, some investors make it a point to store their precious metals in Europe. There is, however, no guarantee of safety even in such havens of laissez-faire capitalism as Switzerland. In France, the import and export of gold are closely regulated by the state, and other governments could enact similar laws if they judged it in their national interest to do so.

Such risks are difficult to evaluate. What the private investor can do is evaluate the risks and try to hedge against as many as possible. In the real world, the risk-free investment remains as elusive as the free lunch.

TAX CONSEQUENCES

Precious metals are capital assets, and profits are taxed as long-term or short-term gains under the prevailing rules of the IRS and state taxing authorities. Under current rules, profits on assets held for a year and a day are taxed at lower, long-term rates. An exception is made for commodity contracts, which become long-term after six months.

REPRESENTATIVE TYPES OF INVESTORS

Investors in precious metals range from the very conservative to the intensely speculative. Those concerned mainly with the preservation of capital and purchasing power may choose to purchase small amounts of gold, silver, or bullion coins over a long period of time, using the dollar-averaging technique to stabilize the cost of purchases. While there is no assurance of turning a short-term profit, precedent suggests that, over a longer term, the value of gold and gold coins, silver and silver coins, and platinum should increase at least as rapidly as the cost-of-living indices do, offering some protection against the ravages of inflation.

Investors more accustomed to dealing in common stocks may choose to invest in dividend-paying shares in gold- and silver-producing companies in North America or gold producers in South Africa. These shares, being leveraged, tend to rise more swiftly and fall more abruptly than the price of bullion does, but most also spin off some dividend income while they are held.

The most speculative form of metal trading is in the sale and purchase of highly leveraged futures contracts. For a small margin, a purchaser may gain control of a contract for 50 ounces of platinum, 100 ounces of gold, or 5,000 ounces of silver, and as many contracts as nerve and resources permit. Clearly, this form of trading, with its potential for large and sudden gains and losses, is not for the average investor, but for the affluent trader who can accept the substantial risks involved.

IMPORTANT FACTORS IN BUYING AND SELLING

Some banks, currency dealers, and brokerage firms offer facilities for the purchase of small amounts of gold, silver, or bullion coins (coins valued mainly for their gold or silver content) for customers who wish to build up accounts, averaging costs over a period of time. Among institutions offering such plans are Citibank and Republic National Bank in New York, First National Bank of Chicago, and the brokerage firm of Merrill Lynch. Deak-Perera, the bullion and currency dealer, offers plans for the purchase of gold, silver, and platinum. In most plans, the institution will provide storage and maintenance until the customer is either ready to resell the metal or coins or to take delivery.

One practice that is not recommended is the purchase of small wafers of gold or silver, because of the high premium charged by the fabricators and retailers and the state sales taxes levied on such purchases. The overhead costs make this a costly and inefficient way to accumulate precious metals.

An investor contemplating the purchase of bullion or coins should check a number of institutions and their plans to decide which appeals to his needs. Brokerage fees and service charges are generally competitive but do vary.

For an investor dealing in the futures market, it is important to do business with a broker who has access to the overseas markets in Zurich, London, and Hong Kong. Participation in these markets extends the trading day beyond the five hours or so that the New York and Chicago markets are open, and provides an opportunity to act on market developments as early as 5 A.M. New York time for markets in Europe, and as late as 2 A.M. New York time for trades in Hong Kong.

In the case of numismatic coins, a viable and growing branch of the larger precious metals market, the services of a qualified dealer are especially important, because the value of coins is greatly influenced by their physical condition, a matter for expert judgment. (See further discussion in article on Coins, elsewhere in this volume.)

CUSTODIAL CARE

Coins, small ingots, or other objects purchased for investment may be stored in a personal safe-deposit box. If the value of such objects is substantial, however, the investor should check carefully into the rules of bailment that regulate the liability of the institution owning the storage facility in case of fire or theft. Sometimes the institution's legal liability is minimal; in this case, the owner should take out special insurance to guard against risk of loss.

If an investor buys larger amounts of gold, such as 100-ounce or 400-ounce bars, or 1,000-ounce silver bars, he will be well advised to leave the bullion in safe storage, bonded and insured, and accept a warehouse receipt as legal evidence of ownership. Warehouse receipts are normally negotiable instruments, and the bullion can be legally transferred by transfer of the warehouse receipt.

The owner who insists upon taking physical possession of the bullion may do so, of course, but must then arrange for secure storage of the metal and should insure it as well. Very few private homes have truly secure storage areas, and a 1,000-ounce ingot of silver does not fit easily into most bank safe-deposit boxes. In any case, when the owner is ready to dispose of the bullion, if it has been stored outside standard warehouse facilities, the buyer will almost certainly insist upon cutting the bar, running an assay at the seller's expense to test for the fineness of the metal. An assay of a gold or silver ingot will cost about $50 at an independent laboratory. The test for platinum is more complicated and costs about $100.

GLOSSARY

actual— The physical commodity (e.g., gold, silver, platinum) as opposed to forward or futures contracts.

ADR— American Depository Receipt, a document issued by an American bank in lieu of a stock certificate for shares in a foreign corporation. The purpose of issuing ADRs is to simplify the physical handling of securities in foreign issues.

assay— A test to determine the quantity of gold, silver, or other metal in an object or an ore sample.

bullion— Gold or silver in bars or ingots. The term is not usually applied to platinum.

commodity— In general, a raw material, either agricultural or mineral. The term has come to refer to materials bought and sold through the medium of futures exchanges, and has been extended in usage to include such financial instruments as government bonds and Treasury bills.

fineness— The purity of gold, silver, or platinum as a percentage of total gross weight. Thus, when gold is described as .995 fine, 99.5 percent of the weight is pure gold.

futures contract— An agreement, usually entered into through a commodity exchange, under which a buyer agrees to buy and a seller agrees to sell a fixed amount of a commodity at an agreed price for delivery on a set date. The contract may be terminated prior to maturity by negotiating an offsetting contract through the same exchange.

hedge— A transaction designed to counter or offset a prospective loss in another transaction.

long— The position of a futures contract buyer whose purchase obliges him to complete the purchase of a commodity unless the contract is liquidated by an offsetting sale; also, the holder of a long position in the market. (See *short.*)

margin— A cash sum that must be deposited with a broker for each contract as a guarantee of fulfillment of a futures contract; sometimes called a "security deposit."

premium— The difference between a coin's market value and the value of the metallic content of the coin.

security deposit— A cash sum that must be deposited with a broker to guarantee fulfillment of a futures contract. (See *margin.*)

short— The market position of a futures contract seller whose sale obliges him to deliver the commodity unless the contract is liquidated by the execution of an offsetting purchase; also the holder of a short position in the market. (See *long.*)

spread— A market position that is simultaneously long and short equivalent amounts of the same or related commodities. In some markets the term "straddle" is used synonymously.

troy ounce— The standard measure of weight for precious metals, equal to one-twelfth of a pound.

SUGGESTED READING

Periodicals

Because the market in precious metals is so closely attuned to general economic and political conditions, no one can hope to gain much insight in this field without also understanding the background of world geopolitical developments. Attentive reading of newspapers and newsmagazines and attention to the major television news programs is essential.

In addition to Public Broadcasting's *Wall Street Week* and the major business periodicals, *American Metal Market* should be followed by serious metals investors. It is published by Fairchild Publications of New York, and provides more specialized background on mining and metals. For a perspective from London, a major world trading center for metals, *Financial Times* is excellent.

The U.S. Bureau of Mines' annual *Mineral Commodities Summaries* provides basic statistical data on production and consumption of the major and minor metals, including gold, silver, and platinum. Consolidated Gold Fields Ltd., the multinational mining company, publishes an annual review of gold, with statistics and charts that are among the most authoritative available. For statistics and background on silver, one of the best sources is the annual review of markets published by Handy and Harman, the bullion dealers.

Reference Books

Books on gold and silver have appeared in considerable numbers in recent years; any good public or business library will list them. Many are written from somewhat arbitrary viewpoints, and the reader will want to sample several rather than accept any one as a sole guide. A selection of useful sources follows:

Dines, James. *The Invisible Crash.* New York: Random House, 1961, 1972.

Hoppe, Donald J. *How to Invest in Gold Stocks and Avoid the Pitfalls.* Westport: Arlington House, 1972.

Mayer, Martin. *The Bankers.* New York: Weybright and Talley, 1974.

Sarnoff, Paul. *Silver Bulls.* Westport: Arlington House, 1980.

Sinclair, James, and Schultz, Harry D. *How You Can Profit from Gold.* Westport: Arlington House, 1980.

Money Market Funds

Howard Stein *

BASIC CHARACTERISTICS

Definition and Description

A money market fund is a no-load, open-end mutual fund that invests in money market instruments. Such a fund makes a continuous offering of new shares as investors make new commitments. As a result, there is no limit on the number of shares that can be issued or on the number of shareholders. In addition, the open-end mutual fund stands ready to redeem shares at the net asset value as determined at the close of trading each day. The purpose of the open-end mutual fund is to pool the assets of many small investors and provide professional management to purchase and sell securities in a diversified portfolio. The management company that provides the professional investment service receives a fee for its service. Some mutual funds, known as load funds, have a commission charge that is paid at the time of purchase of the shares of the fund. An increasing number of other funds make no commission charge for purchase or redemption of shares and are known as no-load funds. All mutual funds are regulated by the SEC with authority primarily focused in the Investment Company Act of 1940.

Historical Overview

Since their inception, mutual funds have been increasingly diverse in their range of investments. In the early years, mutual funds were generally balanced funds or wholly equity funds. The balanced fund invested assets in different proportions of bonds, preferred stocks, and common stocks, and its major purpose was to emphasize safety of principal while adding an ingredient of growth through the holding of common stock. The purpose of those funds wholly committed to equity was to achieve somewhat more aggressive appreciation potential, with an element of safety imparted by commitment in better-quality issues. It was not too long before mutual funds generally became more aggressive in seeking capital gain and increased tremendously in popularity. During the 1950s and 1960s the mutual funds became even more specialized and more diverse in sector specialization and aggressive efforts of growth.

Money market funds evolved out of this background, making their first significant appearance in 1974. They arrived on the scene during the turmoil of

* Howard Stein is Chairman, President, and Chief Executive of The Dreyfus Corporation, New York.

the oil embargo of 1973 and the ensuing inflation, with consumer prices up almost 8.5 percent. During 1973, interest rates rose sharply and the prime rate reached 10 percent accompanied by three-month Treasury bills at 7.4 percent and good-quality corporate bonds at 8 percent. In 1974, however, the money market funds were clearly accepted by the investing public. While only $3 million were recorded in sales in 1973, the sales in 1974 rose sharply to $2.3 billion. In that same period, redemptions amounted to $566 million, leaving a net sales figure of $1.7 billion. Growth in the money market funds then subsided somewhat; assets were at a level of $3.4 billion at the end of 1976 compared with $3.6 billion at the end of 1975.

In 1977, growth continued but at a rather moderate rate, with money market fund assets totaling $3.9 billion at the end of 1977. An explosion began when the assets of money market funds rose to a level of $10.8 billion by the end of 1978. The pace accelerated in 1979; when the year ended, the assets of money market funds totaled $45.2 billion. This reflected sales of $111.8 billion and redemptions of $78.3 billion. The dimension of the growth of the money market fund is revealed also by the existence, at the end of 1979, of seventy-six active money market funds compared with fifteen active money market funds at the end of 1974.

The surge of interest continued throughout 1981 and into the early months of 1982. At the close of December 1980, total net assets held by ninety-six money market funds totaled about $74.5 billion, as compared with total net assets of about $45.2 billion held by seventy-six money market funds as of the end of December 1979. By the end of December 1981, total net assets equaled $181.9 billion held by 159 money market funds. As of the end of February 1982, total assets held by 175 money market funds equaled $186.2 billion.

TYPES OF FUNDS

Money market funds are attractive to a diverse group, ranging from large, sophisticated, professional institutional investors to small, unsophisticated investors who perhaps have never owned a security of any type before. All investors are seeking to maximize their return on available funds, but the institutional investor is likely to have more diverse reasons for considering and investing in a money market fund.

The universe of money market funds, like Gaul, is divided into three parts: institutional funds, general-purpose funds run by stockbrokers, and general-purpose funds run by mutual funds.

Institutional Funds

These funds limit their shareholders to institutions such as bank trust departments and corporations, and generally require an initial investment of $50,000 to $100,000, although subsequent investments may be as low as $100. Other provisions and features of the money market fund adapted to institutions are the same, except that there are procedures for multiple accounts managed or administered by banks and other financial institutions. Institutional investors of this type find the money market fund of particular value as a repository for their cash reserves. Such cash reserves may be enlarged or reduced in accordance with the needs of the portfolios the investors are managing. For the institutional investor, the liquidity of the money market fund is particularly appealing because it provides flexibility in cash flow. Further, because the fund maintains a constant price, the risk of capital loss that could occur in a wrenching of the market in the short term is reduced to the minimum. The ability of the institutional investor to purchase directly the kind of instrument held by the money market fund tends to heighten the sensitivity of such funds to their yield relative to the yields offered by various money market instruments in the market. Thus, when yields on Treasury bills, for example, exceed the yield offered by the money market fund, institutions are more likely to take cash funds out of the money market fund to purchase such Treasury bills directly.

Broker-Run Funds

The general-purpose funds that are run as part of the service offered by brokers and are under their control are virtually identical in all respects to the third category — funds generally run by mutual fund complexes. The principal difference between them is that the broker-run funds are usually repositories for the free cash balances of the brokerage firm's customers. The funds may be used by individuals or institutions under the same provisions. The money market fund is a valuable adjunct to the brokerage firm as a marketing tool because its customers tend to be somewhat closer to commitment in an equity investment should stock market conditions so warrant.

Funds Managed by Mutual Funds

Funds directly managed by mutual fund management companies were the first of the three major groups to appear; the institutional specialization and broker-run funds emerged later, albeit fairly quickly. Consistent with the background of the open-end mutual fund, these money market funds were directed toward enabling the smaller investor to participate in the higher yields offered by large certificates of deposit and similar instruments. In addition, the money market fund offered by the mutual fund complex allows the small investor to transfer funds without charge to other no-load funds managed by that complex. Thus, the investor is offered a broadened scope of possible participation in a wide range of investments.

ATTRACTIVE FEATURES

The underlying appeal of the money market fund is that it offers to the small investor the opportunity to receive the higher yields offered to the large, institutional-type investor while enjoying maximum liquidity.

Liquidity

Because there is no sales charge for either purchase or redemption of shares, investors have the flexibility to determine the maturity dates of their investments. There is no need to worry about maturity or rollover at maturity. Additionally, the funds are available without cost whenever they are needed.

Low Minimum Investment

Generally, as little as $1,000 can be invested through a broker or dealer, or $2,500 directly. As little as $100 can be added to the holdings and there is no limit on the total size of the account. The net asset value per share is determined as of close of trading on the New York Stock Exchange on days on which the Exchange is open for business. The computation of net asset value is made by dividing the value of the net assets (value of assets less liabilities) by the total number of shares outstanding. Expenses and fees of the money market funds, including the management fee, are accrued daily and taken into account for purposes of calculating the net asset value. The SEC has exempted money market funds from certain provisions of the Investment Company Act of 1940 pertaining to some standards of maturity length and quality of portfolio investment. On the basis of this exemption, money market funds using the principle of amortized cost maintain a constant net asset value of $1.00 per share. There is, however, no absolute assurance that the exemptions will always be in effect nor that variations in market value could not cause the constant net asset value to fall below $1.00 per share, albeit by only a fraction.

Interest and redemption. All net investment income is distributed on a daily basis with dividends declared and paid each day the fund is open for business. Thus, interest is compounded daily. In addition, the investor can withdraw funds from the money market fund (redeem shares owned) in one of three ways:

(1) Regular redemption procedure — Instructions are sent by mail with a signature guarantee from a commercial bank.

(2) Telephone-expedited redemption privilege — If elected by the investor, instructions to redeem shares can be given by telephone. The use of this privilege means the investor has authorized the fund to act on telephone and written redemption instruction from any person representing himself as the investor and believed to be genuine. The proceeds of redemption under this procedure are transferred by Federal Reserve wire only to a commercial bank specified by the investor on the initial application forms.

(3) Check-redemption privilege — The investor writes specially prepared checks that are drawn on the fund. The checks may be made payable to the order of any person, in an amount of $500 or more, although some money market funds will permit as little as $250. Payment to cover the check is made by redeeming a sufficient number of shares in the investor's account to cover the amount of the check. After clearance, the check is returned to the investor. Interest is earned in the account until the check clears.

High Yields

Investment in money market funds provides the smaller investor with access to the highest yields available in the short-term market to large investors, such as institutions. This is of particular value in inflationary periods, when investors seek means by which they can best preserve purchasing power. The short-term sector is most responsive to the pressures of inflation reflected in higher interest rates; by that action the short-term sector, which is the focal point of the money market fund, offers this most sensitive reaction to factors that offset inflation. Further, the liquidity offered to investors in a money market fund, with the privilege of redemption or investment without charge, enables them to move funds quickly to the area of greatest appeal.

Automatic Withdrawal

As a means of receiving distribution from a money market fund, often there is also a provision for automatic withdrawal of a specified dollar amount (usually $50 or more) on either a monthly or quarterly basis. Such withdrawal payments reflect proceeds from the redemption of the shares held in the money market fund and do not refer to the yield. Obviously, if the payments under such a program are in excess of re-invested dividends and distribution, holdings of shares will be reduced and may ultimately be depleted.

Retirement Plans

Shares of money market funds may be purchased in conjunction with a Keogh plan or individual retirement plan. The basis of such purchases and accruals obviously would have to be in accord with rules acceptable to the IRS.

POTENTIAL RISKS

Income and Principal

As far as principal is concerned, the risks are minimal. Although money market funds are not insured, the instruments held in the portfolio provide a high degree of safety through inherent high quality. Such holdings are represented by Treasury bills, offered weekly by the U.S. government, with initial maturities of ninety days and with longer maturities of twenty-six weeks also available; commercial paper issued by the largest corporate entities of the highest quality rating, and with maturities not exceeding nine months; negotiable bank certificates of deposit issued by a selected group of the largest and soundest banks in the United States, of the highest quality and with maturities not exceeding nine months. In addition, many money market funds deal in repurchase agreements, which are of very short maturity and collateralized by U.S. government securities. The net effect and quality of the short maturities is to reduce risks to the very minimal level. The choice of instrument and maturity is keyed to the condition that money market funds cannot buy any instrument with a maturity greater than one year.

Market Volatility

The short maturities and the high-quality standard of the instrument held serves to keep market volatility of the portfolio to a minimum. Further, the size of the markets of these instruments is very large and marked by very active trading, creating a circumstance of maximized liquidity.

Regulatory Constraints

As noted earlier, money market funds fall under the regulatory jurisdiction of the SEC, with the primary element of authority derived from the Investment Company Act of 1940. The nature of the actions of the SEC includes such factors as: investment policies must be set, disclosed, and observed, and any significant change approved by shareholders; independent directors are elected to protect shareholder interests, so there is shareholder approval of directors and auditors; with respect to pricing and valuation, rules are set that extend to procedures of sale and redemption of shares; requirements are set for custodial procedure as well as levels of fidelity insurance that must be maintained; and the staff of the SEC can and does inspect the books and records and receives copies of reports that are sent to shareholders periodically. This broad umbrella of regulation further adds to the procedures already set into place by the funds themselves to assure the highest degree of safety possible.

TAX CONSEQUENCES

There are no elements of capital gain or deferred returns involved in the purchase of shares in money market funds. The dividends received are taxable as current income under present tax law, or tax-exempt in the case of a tax-exempt money market fund.

As far as the individual is concerned, the dividends received from a money market fund are fully taxable for federal, state, and local purposes, subject, of course, to the tax exclusion of $100 for individuals and $200 on a joint return for interest and dividends received. This reflects the fact that the portfolio consists of taxable securities. If the investor borrows to buy shares in a money market fund, interest on the loan is fully deductible. In the case of corporations, the investor should check state laws, as they vary across the country. Some states treat dividends more favorably than they do interest. For example, both New York and New Jersey allow corporations a deduction of 50 percent of dividends received.

In a tax-exempt money market fund, as the name denotes, the dividend received is exempt from federal taxes. In most states the shareholder can take advantage of state laws that exempt the holder from state and local taxes as well.

This would apply only to those securities held in the portfolio issued by the state in which the investor resides. In New York, for instance, the state has informally taken the position that an exempt interest dividend reported by a resident is exempt from New York State tax to the same extent as its ratio of interest from New York State bonds is to total income of the portfolio. In the case of corporations subject to New York State taxation, for example, the state has informally ruled that the exempt interest dividend should be treated as a dividend and thus be subject to a 50 percent dividend exclusion. The balance, together with other investment income based upon average stock allocation percentage, is to be allocated to New York State. The stock allocation percentages of the exempt fund will normally be zero.

Nonresident aliens have an additional advantage with respect to the tax-exempt money market fund. No withholding tax is imposed on the dividends received, as opposed to other income that is subject to the withholding tax. The only income that could be subjected to withholding would be short-term capital gain, which is treated as ordinary income. Considering the factor of the constant net asset value of one dollar, such a gain would not be expected to occur. Just as the calculation is designed to restrict declines, it will inhibit gains.

REPRESENTATIVE TYPES OF INVESTORS

Individual Holdings

Funds deposited by smaller investors remain the core of the money market funds offered by the mutual funds. As holders of money market fund shares, these investors are a major factor in their operation. According to a survey by the Investment Company Institute (ICI), the association of mutual funds, as of April 1, 1981, the total dollar value of individual holdings of money market funds was estimated at $68.8 billion. By comparison, the total holdings of institutional shareholders were estimated at about $43.4 billion. The ICI survey indicated that an average-sized account for an individual equaled slightly over $13,000. Recognizing that a substantial number of individual shareholders had more than one money market fund account, the analysts converted the total number of individual accounts to a household basis. The result showed that an estimated 4 million households, or about 5 to 6 percent of all households, owned money market funds. The average dollar value of those money market fund holdings was slightly over $17,000.

This survey also indicated the following: (1) the median family income of investors was $29,795; (2) nearly 75 percent of these investors were married males; (3) the median age of purchasers was 54, and about 32 percent of all purchasers were 60 years of age or more; and (4) over 50 percent of all holders regarded money market funds as part of a longer-term savings program, with about 20 percent using the money market fund to achieve interest income and liquidity while awaiting improvements and stability in stock and bond markets.

Institutional Shareholders

As of April 1, 1981, institutional shareholders' holdings represented about 39 percent of all money market fund assets, equal to about $44 billion and about 19 percent of all accounts. The average-sized institutional holding was about $86,000. Accounts of fiduciaries, with 54 percent of all institutional holdings, represented the largest single type of institutional owner of money market funds. Business corporations were the second largest institutional holders, with 24 percent of institutional holdings.

IMPORTANT FACTORS IN BUYING AND SELLING

No Broker or Seller

It is apparent from the discussion thus far that the question of selection of a broker or salesperson per se does not arise. The investor deals directly with the money market fund and no sales or commission charges are paid for either investment or redemption. This also means that the investor need not be concerned with dealer spread, the difference between the dealer's quoted bid and asked price. The investor merely fills out the application form that comes with the prospectus, attaches a check in the proper amount, and mails them to the address indicated. Acknowledgment of receipt from the money market fund follows shortly, and is accompanied by a confirmation indicating that the investment has been made and the number of shares involved. In addition, the investor is given an account number that should be used in any communication with the money market fund.

Evaluating the Portfolio

Portfolio mix. The holdings of money market funds are generally confined to the highest rating in any type of security purchased. Obviously, the holdings of U.S. Treasury bills or any other U.S. Treasury security would represent the highest quality available. In the case of commercial paper, negotiable certificates of deposit, and banker's acceptances, purchases are usually representative of the highest ratings in their class. Therefore, it is not necessarily quality per se that becomes an important investment criterion. The mix of these instruments in the portfolio and the length of the maturities become a more meaningful focus of evaluation. Certain variations of yield may be exploited by increasing commitment in one instrument as opposed to another, thereby gaining or losing slight yield differentials. Thus, the investor would want to know the makeup of the portfolio to determine the approach of the portfolio manager.

Maturity structure. Examination of the portfolio with regard to its maturity structure indicates how the portfolio manager predicts the outlook for interest rates. Recognizing that maturities cannot exceed one year, a money market fund rarely extends its average maturities to anywhere close to that length. Indeed, the experience gained thus far indicates that it is fairly unusual to be out as far as seventy-five days. Before most money market funds adopted the principle of constant net asset value, a number of money market funds had average maturities out around 100 days or slightly more. The price fluctuations that resulted were not unduly disturbing to the more sophisticated investor but obviously were of some discomfort to the smaller investor. With the advent of constant net asset value, the trend toward shorter maturities began to develop. This trend evolved also as a result of the increased volatility in the longer-term market as inflation rates rose. As rates went up and prices declined, many investors fled the longer-term sector and sought short-term investments. Money market fund managers were encouraged to shorten their maturities in order to take advantage of the highest yields. Average maturities came down to at least forty to forty-five days, and an even shorter range of twenty days or less became quite common.

The investor obviously can and should select a money market fund with a portfolio manager who shares his perception of the direction of interest rates. A structure of average maturities of twenty days or less indicates that the money market fund manager is anticipating that short-term rates will be rising in the near term and is placing the money market fund in the best position to gain from such a development. When the average maturity schedule is around thirty-five days or more, possibly as much as forty-five days, the money market fund manager is contemplating a decline in short-term rates. The longer maturity schedule is designed to lock in as high a rate as available for as long a period as possible. The effect of these strategies is that, broadly, yields offered by money market funds tend to lag behind a rise in short-term rates, although eventually they do catch up. Similarly, during a decline in short-term rates, yields offered by money market funds tend to be higher than the declining rate for a period of time. Again, as the portfolio turns over, the higher rate offered generally comes into line with the market rates.

CUSTODIAL CARE

Certain other factors must be considered that relate to the handling of the physical evidence of ownership. Periodically, the money market fund will send to the investor a statement setting forth the total number of shares owned and a recording of any transactions that may have taken place during the period. This number reflects the total number of shares owned at the beginning of the quarter plus the number of shares acquired from dividends paid daily into the account for that period. Because dividends are declared and paid each day, interest is in effect compounded daily, an advantage not generally available to savings certificates issued by banks that compound on a less frequent basis.

Virtually all investors leave their shares with the money market fund, with a bank acting as custodian. An investor may request a certificate and hold it in his possession with no effect on the payment of dividends. However, the check redemption privilege then cannot be obtained, nor can the investor take advantage of telephone-expedited redemption privileges. To have access to both of these privileges, the shares must be left with the money market fund.

Most assuredly, statements of the condition of the account should be retained for tax purposes. The final statement for the year, which is available usually four to six weeks after the close of the year, carries information relative to Form 1099, which must be prepared for tax purposes. This information shows dividends received for the year and notes that portion that is exempt under the tax exclusion law. Information provided to corporations states the portion of yield that qualifies for the 85 percent dividend exclusion.

GLOSSARY

bank wire— Used to notify a bank that is part of a computer-based system that it will be the recipient of an action such as the transmission of funds belonging to a customer of the bank.

banker's acceptance— An instrument whereby a draft or bill of exchange involved in a commercial transaction has been accepted by the banking institution that means, in effect, it is guaranteeing payment of the bill.

basis price— Term describing the technique of pricing broken down into 100ths, which is given as a yield to maturity or annual rate of return. One hundred basis points equal one percent.

bid— The price that a potential buyer is willing to pay for a security.

cash management bill— When U.S. Treasury balances are drawn down and cash is needed for a very short period of time, these bills of very short maturity may be issued.

certificate of deposit— An instrument developed and used by banks to attract funds that are essentially time deposits with a set maturity, and are negotiable in large denominations.

commercial paper— Issued by large corporations of recognized credit standing, these are really promissory notes that are unsecured and have a fixed maturity that does not exceed 270 days.

debt security— Representing a borrowing by the issuer, which can take many forms, usually reflective of maturity and presence or absence of collateral.

EuroCD — The term CD refers to a certificate of deposit issued by a bank, and a EuroCD merely indicates that it has been issued by a foreign branch of a U.S. bank or a foreign bank domiciled outside the United States. In almost all cases, EuroCDs are issued in London.

money market— A professional term that has come into vogue, referring to the market dealing in purchase and sales of debt instruments of short-term maturities. These include Treasury bills, banker's acceptance, and commercial paper.

money market fund — An open-end mutual fund that trades only in various money market instruments, passing along the interest received to the investor.

municipal notes — A financing technique, employed by municipalities, of issuing short-term notes to raise funds in anticipation of funds to be received from tax receipts, issuance of a bond, or other sources of revenue.

offer — The price that a potential seller is asking for a security.

prospectus — Material that must be given to a prospective investor to be studied and read before purchase, which details significant data with regard to the company, as required by regulations of the SEC with which the prospectus is filed. The SEC must authorize release of this material; it does not express approval or disapproval of the offering but only that required standards of information have been met.

repurchase agreement — Usually called a repo, such agreements are collateralized by U.S. government securities. In effect, the seller agrees to repurchase the securities at a set price on a set date that is often overnight or very short-term. It is often entered into by money market funds to take advantage of high short-term yields.

Treasury bill — Issued by the U.S. Treasury for financing purposes, Treasury bills have short-term maturities of thirteen weeks, twenty-six weeks, and one year, and are issued in a discount form.

MAJOR GENERAL-PURPOSE MONEY MARKET FUNDS

Cash Reserve Management Trust, New York, N.Y.

Daily Cash Accumulation Fund, Denver, Colo.

Dreyfus Liquid Assets, New York, N.Y.

InterCapital Liquid Assets Fund, New York, N.Y.

Merrill Lynch Ready Assets Trust, New York, N.Y.

Money Mart Assets, New York, N.Y.

Paine Webber Cash Fund, New York, N.Y.

Shearson Daily Dividend, New York, N.Y.

Temporary Investment Fund, New York, N.Y.

Trust for Short-Term U. S. Government Securities, Pittsburgh, Pa.

SUGGESTED READING

Andreder, S.S. "Liquidity Plus Return Adds Up to a Fresh Surge in Money Market Funds." *Barrons* 58:4-5, June 5, 1978.

Eisenberg, R. "Money Market Funds Go Tax-Free." *Money* 8:101-2, Nov. 1979.

Kalogeras, C. "Money Market Funds." *Baylor Business Studies* 7:17-34, Aug., Sept., Oct. 1980.

Morley, Jr., J.E. "Cash Management — Working for Extra 1% of 2%." *Management Accounting* 60:1722, Oct. 1978.

Rundle, R. "Taking a Chance on Money Market Funds Not All That Risky." *Business Insurance* 15:3, May 25, 1981.

"What You Should Know About Money Market Funds." *Financial World* 150:25-6, Apr. 1, 1981.

Wunch, M. "Money Market Funds Lure More Companies." *Industry Week* 204:83, Mar. 3, 1980.

Mortgage-Backed Securities

Kathy August and John Holmgren *

BASIC CHARACTERISTICS

Mortgage-backed securities are income securities that are backed by government agencies and by the assets or the future earnings of mortgage lending institutions, such as thrift institutions, mortgage banks, and commercial banks. These securities fall into two general categories: pass-through certificates, in which an investor's income stream is provided by mortgage-loan payments that are passed through to the investor; and mortgage-backed bonds, in which coupon payments are made out of an institution's overall asset earnings, which primarily come from mortgage loans. Mortgage-backed securities were introduced by the Government National Mortgage Association (GNMA, or Ginnie Mae), a U.S. government agency. At the present time, various types of mortgage-backed securities are issued by state and local agencies and by private financial institutions.

Mortgage-backed securities emerged in the late 1960s and early 1970s as a means of improving the cash flow of mortgage-lending institutions and of bringing investment funds into the real estate market. The need for these securities arose from the regional and national mortgage credit gap, in which demand for mortgage credit outstripped the ability of traditional sources to supply funds; this gap occurred first on a regional basis and then developed into a nationwide shortfall of housing funds.

Mortgage-backed securities started with Ginnie Maes, still the largest volume mortgage security. These securities are backed by Federal Housing Authority/Veterans Administration (FHA/VA) insured mortgages and are guaranteed by the Government National Mortgage Association. Ginnie Maes are pass-through securities, which means that monthly payments and loan prepayments are passed through to investors as they are received by the loan servicer. Pass-through securities backed by conventional (non-government-insured) mortgage loans are offered by the Federal Home Loan Mortgage Corporation (FHLMC or Freddie Mac, a privately managed affiliate of the Federal Home Loan Bank Board), the Federal National Mortgage Association (FNMA or Fannie Mae, a private corporation) and by a number of lending institutions and private conduit firms.

---

* Kathy August and John Holmgren are Vice-President–Treasurer, and Research Analyst, respectively, at PMI Mortgage Insurance Co., San Francisco.

In addition to pass-through securities, there are several mortgage-backed debt instruments. Fannie Mae debentures are bonds used by the FNMA, a private corporation affiliated with the U.S. government, to raise capital with which to buy mortgage loans from mortgage-lending institutions. Mortgage-backed bonds are issued by lending institutions to raise funds for mortgage lending. Tax-exempt mortgage revenue bonds are issued by state and local housing authorities to raise funds that are used to provide subsidized interest rate mortgage loans.

Mortgage-backed securities vary in cash flow, return, and risk. In general, pass-through securities provide a monthly, uneven payment stream. Ratings on pass-throughs are usually AA for privately issued securities; government pass-throughs carry no rating, since they are considered virtually risk-free. Mortgage-backed bonds are much like AAA corporate bonds in risk and cash flow. Interest payments are made semiannually, with the face value paid at maturity or when called. The ratings on private pass-throughs and bonds differ due to the nature of the guarantees provided on each; AA securities carry private mortgage insurance while AAA securities are backed by cash funds, AAA letters of credit, or over-collateralization.

Investors should evaluate mortgage-backed securities in terms of cash-flow characteristics, risk guarantee provided for each level of return, and comparison of risk/return with other available alternatives. Historically, mortgage securities have compared favorably in return with other investments of similar risk. They are also a means of providing additional portfolio diversification, since they are backed by real estate investments. While any fixed-income investor should consider mortgage securities, one must distinguish among pass-through securities (most appropriate for tax-exempt investors, such as pension, profit-sharing, and trust funds), mortgage-backed bonds (FNMA debentures and private institution bonds, suitable for AAA bond investors), and mortgage-revenue bonds (for investors who are looking for tax-exempt income).

Mortgage-backed securities are expected to gain increased prominence in the 1980s, as privately issued pass-throughs are used more frequently to bring funds into the mortgage finance industry. Continued active governmental involvement in mortgage securities will also contribute to the vigorous growth of this type of security.

TYPES OF MORTGAGE-BACKED SECURITIES

Mortgage-backed securities are issued by federal, state, and local governmental agencies and by a number of private mortgage lending institutions, such as thrift institutions, mortgage bankers, commercial banks, mortgage brokerage firms, and mortgage insurance companies. Some securities are issued by private lenders but guaranteed by government agencies; the most important of these are the Ginnie Mae securities, described below. (See Table 1 on pages 444–5 for a summary of the most important forms of mortgage-backed securities.)

Ginnie Mae Pass-Through Securities

The first, and still the biggest, type of mortgage-backed security is the Ginnie Mae. Ginnie Mae securities were first issued in 1970 following the creation of GNMA within the Department of Housing and Urban Development in 1968. Ginnie Maes are backed by pools of FHA/VA-insured mortgages. These mortgages are originated and packaged into securities by mortgage lenders; the securities are then guaranteed by GNMA.

Ginnie Maes have the following characteristics:

- They offer the highest yields of all government-guaranteed securities. Because of this guarantee, yields are somewhat lower than the yields on comparable privately issued securities. However, the yield generally exceeds that of Treasury bonds, often by as much as 200 basis points with no added risk.
- Investor cash-flow is guaranteed, since GNMA guarantees that interest and principal payments will be advanced to the investor whether or not payments have been received by the lender-servicer. Payments are delayed for forty-five days, so the investor is paid forty-five days after the payment is due to the lender.
- There is an active secondary market for Ginnie Maes, so they are highly liquid.
- Sale of Ginnie Mae securities constitutes a sale of loan assets for the lending institution that issues Ginnie Maes.

Mortgage banking institutions are the primary originators of FHA/VA mortgages, most of which are used to form Ginnie Mae securities. Ginnie Mae pools are homogenous in that all mortgages bear the same interest rate and maturity. The minimum GNMA issue size is $1 million, although some special project notes have minimum sizes of $500,000. An issue may exceed those levels by up to 10 percent without GNMA approval. In 1981, $14.3 billion of Ginnie Mae securities were issued. Since their inception in 1970, $130.4 billion of securities have been issued. The minimum denomination on a Ginnie Mae security is $25,000.

Freddie Mac Participation Certificates

Ginnie Mae paved the way for another important form of mortgage-backed security, the FHLMC Participation Certificate (PC). The FHLMC is owned by the twelve members of the Federal Home Loan Bank Board System. Its purpose is to provide a more vigorous secondary market for conventional mortgage loans (those that are not government-guaranteed). Freddie Mac issues two types of securities: the PC and the Guaranteed Mortgage Certificate (GMC).

PCs operate in much the same way as Ginnie Mae securities, since timely payment of interest is guaranteed. Principal payments are not guaranteed to be

TABLE 1. Types of Mortgage-Backed Securities

	Ginnie Mae	*Freddie Mac PC*	*Freddie Mac GMC*	*FNMA CMBS*
Payment Stream	Monthly; guaranteed 15-day delay. Periodic prepayments.	Monthly; guaranteed 44-day delay. Periodic prepayments.	Semi-annually; annual principal payments.	Monthly; guaranteed 25-day delay. Periodic prepayments.
Underlying Asset	FHA/VA mortgages	Conventional mortgages	Conventional mortgages	Conventional mortgages
Guarantee	Full faith and credit of U.S. Treasury	Freddie Mac net worth; private mortgage insurance on mortgages with LTV over 80	Freddie Mac net worth; private mortgage insurance on mortgages with LTV over 80	Fannie Mae net worth; private mortgage insurance on mortgages with LTV over 80
Liquidity/Secondary Market	Active market due to high volume of issue, risk-free status	Active market due to high volume of issue, low risk status	Less active due to lower issue volume	Unknown at this time
First Issued	1970	1971	1971	1981
Rating/Risk Equivalent	Government security; no rating required	Considered nearly equivalent to a government security; no rating	Same as Freddie Mac PC	Same as Freddie Mac PC

Legend: PC: participation certificate; GMC: guaranteed mortgage certificate;
CMBS: conventional-mortgage-backed security; LTV: loan-to-value ratio
SOURCE: PMI Mortgage Insurance Co.

paid on time, but ultimate payment is guaranteed; in actual experience, there has been little problem with late principal payments. The major difference is that the mortgage payment is guaranteed against foreclosure losses by Freddie Mac, a privately managed institution, and not by the U.S. government, as are Ginnie Maes. This, and the fact that the individual mortgages in the Freddie Mac pools are insured by private mortgage-insurance companies instead of by government agencies, explains why Freddie Mac PCs offer a higher yield than Ginnie Maes — typically 15 to 40 basis points more.

Freddie Mac GMCs are much like bonds in that payments are made semi-annually. Principal is paid annually; principal payments are made according to a schedule specified at the time of issue. This schedule may be altered depending on prepayment experience, although GMCs are not pass-through securities, but general obligations, collateralized with mortgage pools in much the same way as

Institution PC	*Conduit PC*	*Mortgage-Backed Bond*	*Mortgage Revenue Bond*
Monthly; intended 25-day delay. Periodic prepayments.	Monthly; intended 25-day delay. Periodic prepayments.	Semi-annually; principal at maturity or sale.	Semi-annually; principal at maturity or sale. Tax exempt.
Conventional mortgages	Conventional mortgages	General assets	Conventional mortgages; some FHA/VA
Private mortgage pool insurance on pool; private mortgage insurance on mortgages with LTV over 80; subordinated position backed by cash fund or letter of credit in lieu of pool insurance	Private mortgage insurance on pool; private mortgage insurance on mortgages with LTV over 80	Overcollateralized by 150-200% with mortgage portfolio	Private mortgage insurance on pool; private mortgage insurance on mortgages with LTV over 80
Less active due to smaller issue size	Same as Institution PC	Same as Institution PC	Same as Institution PC
1977	1979	1975	1978
AA when private pool insurance guarantee provided; AAA when subordinated position guarantee; similar to AA corporate	Same as Institution PC	AAA due to continuous maintenance of overcollateralized position	AA due to private mortgage insurance guarantee

mortgage-backed bonds. These payment characteristics are designed to reduce re-investment risk associated with monthly payments and thus to make GMCs attractive to institutional investors. While the purpose of GMCs was to attract investment funds from outside the housing finance industry during times of credit stringency, they are available to investors at all times in order to maintain the visibility and marketability of these securities.

In 1981, Freddie Mac issued $1.1 billion of PCs; $20.9 billion have been issued since its inception in 1971. Since 1971, $3 billion of GMCs have been issued. None have been issued since 1979 because Freddie Mac was reevaluating the profitability of these securities. PCs are sold in denominations of $100,000, $200,000, $500,000, $1 million, and $5 million. Denominations on GMCs are $100,000, $500,000, and $1 million.

Freddie Mac acquires mortgages for its PCs and GMCs in a weekly auction process. In the competitive auction, lenders offer a group of mortgages to Freddie Mac at a certain yield, which is determined by the lender based on the contract rate on the mortgages offered. Freddie Mac then accepts the most competitive bids, although it limits the volume of mortgages that may be purchased from a single lender in any one week. In the noncompetitive auction, lenders offer a group of mortgages but submit no yield bid; the yield is determined by the average competitive bid as established in the competitive auction. The risk of the noncompetitive auction is that loans may have to be sold at a lower price than desired by the lender; on the other hand, the price may be higher than it would be if the lender had submitted a competitive bid.

Until recently, Freddie Mac could not purchase loans that exceeded a legal limit of $107,000. Congress amended this rule so that this value may be changed annually in line with the Federal Home Loan Bank Board's index of home purchase prices.

Major differences between Freddie Mac PCs and Ginnie Maes. The principal distinctions between the FHLMC PCs and GNMA pass-throughs may be summarized as follows:

- Ginnie Maes are guaranteed by the full faith and credit of the U.S. government; Freddie Mac PCs are guaranteed by the capital structure of FHLMC. Freddie Mac yields are higher for this reason.
- There is a forty-five-day payment delay with Ginnie Maes; the Freddie Mac PC delay is seventy-five days.
- Service payments with Ginnie Maes are made to investors directly by the loan servicer; payments on Freddie Mac PCs come from Freddie Mac.

Fannie Mae Securities

FNMA was a government agency until 1968, when it became a private corporation. Fannie Mae entered the mortgage-backed security market in December 1981 with its first offering of securities backed by conventional mortgages. In the first four months of operation, $2.8 billion of FNMA securities were issued to lenders; of this amount, $251 million were sold to the public. This program operates in much the same fashion as GNMA. However, unlike GNMA, FNMA is the issuer as well as guarantor of the securities; with Ginnie Maes, lenders are issuers and GNMA is the guarantor.

Fannie Mae also sells general obligation debentures. First offered in 1956, Fannie Mae debentures are designed to raise cash that is used to purchase government-backed and conventional mortgages. Fannie Mae performs this function as a means of improving the secondary market for mortgages. As with other debentures, interest is paid semiannually. Debentures may be purchased in a minimum denomination of $10,000, with $5,000 increments thereafter. In 1980, $11 billion in debentures were sold. Fannie Mae is no longer a government agency; its securities are therefore not U.S. government-guaranteed, but are considered nearly so due to their U.S. government agency affiliation.

Fannie Mae also sells short-term discount notes in denominations ranging from $5,000 to $1 million. In 1980, $17.6 billion of these notes were sold. Fannie Mae debentures and discount notes enjoy no preferences as to each other as far as guarantees are concerned. (For further discussion of Fannie Mae securities, see article on U.S. Government Bonds, Notes, and Agency Securities, elsewhere in this volume.)

Private Mortgage Pass-Through Securities

In addition to the U.S. government agency or agency-affiliate-backed securities described above, there are a number of mortgage-backed securities that are guaranteed by private financial institutions. These securities, which are backed by conventional mortgage loans and/or other assets, are issued in the form of state or local revenue bonds, financial institution PCs, private conduit PCs, and mortgaged-backed bonds.

Lending institution PCs. Privately issued mortgage-backed PCs were authorized for use in 1977. They are issued in three forms: (1) bank or thrift institution PCs, (2) private conduit firm PCs, and (3) subordinated position PCs. In the case of a bank or thrift institution PC, an institution packages mortgages from its portfolio into a mortgage pool and then issues PCs that are backed by this pool. PCs are only issued by large institutions when they are publicly offered, since the costs associated with issuance of PCs are high; an institution must have high loan production to package a pool that is big enough to produce sufficient income to cover those costs. An issue would have to be at least $25 million in size to justify the administrative costs involved. Smaller institutions are able to issue private placement PCs, since the lower costs reduce the economic issue size to about $10 million. As will be discussed later, smaller institutions also have the option of utilizing a private conduit to issue PCs.

PCs that are issued directly through lending institutions have the following characteristics:

- The mortgages composing the pool are usually located in the geographical area of the lending institution, which means that most homes would be located within one state. This geographical concentration adds an element of risk to these pools, since a natural disaster that occurs in only one part of the country would have a potentially serious effect on a large portion of the pool mortgages; this would tend to be less true of pools with wider geographical diversification, such as Freddie Mac and private conduit pools (to be discussed below), which are composed of mortgages from all parts of the country.
- Unlike government PCs, timely payment is intended, but not guaranteed by the PC issuer. Typically, however, issuers are able to comply with their non-binding deadline of a fifty-five-day payment delay (versus forty-five for Ginnie Mae and seventy-five for Freddie Mac).
- Like Freddie Mac pools, private issuer pools are composed of a variety of mortgage types, including varying interest rates, loan sizes, and home types (although most are single-family dwellings). The number of loans in a private pool is normally less

than it is in a government pool, because of the higher loan amounts and smaller total issue size. The minimum number of loans is about 100, primarily because of Standard & Poor's rating requirements.

- The guarantees on the mortgages backing the PCs are provided by private mortgage-insurance companies, rather than by government agencies. The guarantee differences are as follows: Ginnie Mae pool mortgages are insured by FHA/VA; the pools are also guaranteed by GNMA against losses through foreclosure, disaster, etc. Freddie Mac and Fannie Mae pool mortgages are insured by private mortgage insurance if their loan-to-value (LTV) ratio (loan amount divided by sales price of home) exceeds 80 percent; the pools are covered against additional losses by the resources of Freddie Mac and Fannie Mae, privately managed corporations that are associated with government agencies. Private issue pool mortgages are insured by private mortgage-insurance companies when the LTV exceeds 80 percent; in addition, there is a private mortgage-insurance policy on the mortgage pool to cover losses not covered by the policies on individual mortgages. Losses on loans that are below 80 percent LTV are rare, since it is unlikely that costs of foreclosure will exceed 20 percent of the home sales price. There is also less risk of foreclosure on these loans, since the borrower has substantial equity that he is more likely to protect. Loans that are insured to below 80 percent LTV are also considered unlikely to generate losses that exceed this insurance coverage; there is rarely a need to resort to the added level of protection provided by pool insurance. Private mortgage insurance is discussed later in this article (see *Second Mortgage-Backed Securities* below).

The first direct PC issue was made by the Bank of America in 1977. This pool carried a coupon rate of 8.375 percent (26 basis points above the GNMA rate) and was $150 million in size. Direct PCs are usually purchased in denominations of $25,000 minimum with $5,000 increments.

Conduit firm PCs. Many lending institutions do not originate enough loans, or do not have the administrative capacity, to issue PCs on their own. For this reason, there are private conduit firms that purchase loans from lending institutions and issue PCs backed by these mortgages. The conduit then serves as the master servicer on the mortgage pool, ensuring that the mortgages are serviced efficiently by lending institutions. Private conduit pool PCs are similar in all respects to direct placement PCs, except for the following differences:

- Conduit firms may or may not limit their loan purchases to any geographical area, so that private conduit pools are often geographically diversified to much the same degree as are FNMA and FHLMC pools.
- Because the conduit firms purchase the loans from mortgage lenders, they require that the lender retain a servicing fee of 25 basis points (0.25 percent of the loan pool balance). As with the GNMA service fee requirement, it is designed to ensure that servicing income is sufficiently large that other mortgage servicers would be willing to perform this function should the original lender be unable to continue servicing its loans for whatever reason.

Private issuers of PCs face a number of obstacles that limit their ability to compete with government securities, particularly the Freddie Mac PC, in issuing PCs. First, contract rates on private pool mortgages all must exceed the overall rate on the pool, so that if the lowest contract rate is 15 percent, for example, the pool rate cannot be above 15 percent. The purpose of this restriction, induced by rating agency requirements, is to ensure that the mortgages in the pool will always provide enough cash flow to pay the pool coupon interest rate, even if the higher yielding mortgages in the pool pay off sooner. This restriction places fairly strict limits on the number of loans in a loan portfolio that can be used in a pool, since many loans may have been originated at rates that are far below current market interest rates.

The second limit on private pool formation is the reluctance of lenders to accept losses on the sale of loans to a conduit firm. This can happen when the mortgage contract rate is below the rate at which a pool must be issued in order to be competitive with market interest rates. When a lender sells a loan at a rate that is below the loan's book value, it must take this loss on its books, which results in a decline in the net worth of the lending institution. Lending institutions must comply with net worth requirements in order to remain solvent.

Finally, since Freddie Mac offers a quasi-governmental guarantee (which enables it to avoid SEC registration and rating requirements) and operates at such a high volume level, its costs are much lower, due to economies of scale in the servicing and administration of the PCs, as well as the lower yields that it can offer because of its guarantee and the somewhat greater liquidity of its PCs. Fannie Mae will probably achieve similar economies in its PC program.

Conduit and direct placement PCs can use a wider variety of loans in the loan pools, and therefore can offer higher yields. Freddie Mac limits its loan purchases to loans that are $98,500 or less (although it now has authority to raise this limit) and loans that have an LTV (loan-to-value ratio) of 95 or less, and it limits purchases to $5 million per servicer per week. Institutions and conduit firms can use higher-risk, higher-yield mortgages and require mortgage insurance coverage on these mortgages to reduce risk.

The first private conduit publicly offered PC was issued in 1979 by PMI Mortgage Corporation. It was a $27 million issue with a yield of 10.34 percent (105 basis points above the comparable Ginnie Mae security) and carried an AA Standard & Poor's rating. (Yields and ratings are further discussed in *Attractive Features* in this article.)

Subordinated-position PCs. The subordinated-position PC is similar in all respects to the direct-placement PC described above except that the mortgage pool guarantee is provided not by private mortgage insurance but by the issuing institution itself in the form of a principal payment set-aside fund normally amounting to 7 percent of the face amount of the pool or a letter of credit equal to 7 percent of the pool value. The fund is invested in highly liquid short-term securities so that the money is always available to pay loss claims on the pool of mortgages. By providing a guarantee in this form, an institution gains two advantages: the cost of maintaining this fund may be less than the cost of mortgage pool insurance, and the cash backing is often sufficient to justify a Standard & Poor's rating of AAA, which increases marketability of the PC and reduces the yield that must be offered on the security.

Mortgage-Backed Bonds

Another type of mortgage-backed security is the mortgage-backed bond (MBB). These are of two varieties: taxable bonds that are issued by lending institutions, and tax-exempt revenue bonds that are issued by state and local housing authorities to finance home construction.

Taxable mortgage-backed bonds. Taxable mortgage-backed bonds are general-obligation debts of issuing institutions. As such, the sale of an MBB does not constitute a sale of assets, as is the case with participation certificates. Instead, the debt of a mortgage-lending institution is collateralized by a pool of mortgages that has a market value far in excess of the amount of the debt (this mortgage pool is not owned by the debtors, but is held by a trustee that represents them). First authorized by the Federal Home Loan Bank Board in 1975, the first MBB issue was by California Federal Savings and Loan in 1975. It carried a face value of $50 million, an AAA rating, and a 9.125 percent coupon rate. It was collateralized at a level of 175 percent and consisted entirely of FHA/VA mortgages.

MBBs are required to maintain collateralization at a level that is well in excess of the face value of the issue. The minimum maintenance level is about 125 percent. To qualify for a Standard & Poor's rating of AAA, however, levels must be maintained in the 150-200 percent range. MBBs operate much like corporate bonds: Interest is paid semiannually, and the principal amount is paid either at maturity or in annual payments, much the way a sinking fund on a corporate bond issue operates.

The advantages of MBBs to issuers are that they can be issued at relatively low yields because of their AAA rating, and they can be collateralized by low-coupon loans that are not salable due to the tremendous book-value loss that would result from sale. With an MBB these low yielding loans can be put to profitable use. Furthermore, a long-term bond can be issued at a fixed interest rate; this enables a lending institution to match the terms of its assets and liabilities so that it can largely insulate itself from fluctuations in short-term interest rates that can cause interest payments on savings deposits to rise above the yield on the institution's loan portfolio.

Tax-exempt mortgage-backed bonds. Mortgage-backed securities are also issued by state and local authorities via public bond issues that are designed to raise funds for housing construction. Proceeds of bond issues are loaned to home buyers at below-market interest rates; this has the effect of stimulating the housing industry in the area and makes housing more affordable for the recipients of the low-interest mortgages.

Mortgage revenue bonds carry a maturity of five to thirty years but usually contain a call provision, so the longer maturity bonds will seldom last their full term. The cash-flow characteristics are just like bonds, with interest paid semi-annually and the principal balance paid at maturity. Interest payments on mortgage revenue bonds are tax-exempt; any capital gains arising from discount purchase are fully taxable. Mortgage revenue bonds were first issued in 1978 by the City of Baltimore. That was an A-rated, $12 million issue with a coupon rate of 6.40 percent. Interest grew rapidly so that a volume of $14 billion was recorded in 1980.

The growth in mortgage revenue bond use aroused congressional concern that the Treasury was suffering a significant loss of tax revenue. This led to the passage of the Mortgage Bond Subsidy Act of 1980. This Act placed caps on the issuance of mortgage revenue bonds and made the terms of issue more restrictive. Among other things, the Act requires that bond proceeds be used to lend to first-time home buyers only and limits the value of the homes that may be purchased; these two restrictions are designed to ensure that the funds be used to benefit people in need rather than simply to provide a subsidized mortgage for people who are financially able to obtain a mortgage through normal procedures. Because of the Mortgage Bond Subsidy Act, the future volume and nature of mortgage revenue bonds are uncertain. However, they are still being issued in many states. If no legislative changes are made, mortgage revenue bonds will no longer be issued after 1983.

In terms of guarantees, mortgage revenue bond mortgage pools are similar to direct-placement private conduit pools. Individual mortgages are insured by private mortgage insurance if their LTV ratio is greater than 80 percent; in some issues, mortgages are insured to 75 percent of their LTV. In addition, a pool insurance policy covers losses that are not covered by the insurance on the individual mortgages.

The rating on most mortgage revenue bond issues is AA by Standard & Poor's. This reflects the fact that the guarantee against losses is provided by mortgage insurance companies, which are AA rated, and because the mortgage properties are located in a limited geographical area, making the pool more susceptible to severe losses in the event of a natural disaster. Mortgage revenue bonds are not general obligations of the issuer.

Mortgage revenue bond issue size varies widely depending on the demand for housing finance funds in the area. Issues may range from less than $1 million to over $500 million.

Second Mortgage-Backed Securities

Pass-through securities backed by second mortgage loans are another form of mortgage-backed security that is expected to be significant in the near future. The first second mortgage-backed pass-through security was a private issue by Granite Financial Corporation in 1980. This $1 million issue was purchased by a profit-sharing plan; the interest rate on the pool was 15.42 percent. (Government pass-throughs were yielding around 11.50 percent at that time.) Insurance on the mortgages in this pool was provided by PMI Mortgage Insurance Company. Second mortgages, or trust deeds, typically have a much shorter maturity than do first mortgage loans, usually three to six years; as with first mortgages, they often pay off prior to maturity. The guarantee on second mortgage pools is also provided by private mortgage insurance. Risk is determined by the combined LTV ratio (balance of first mortgage + second mortgage loan divided by home value). Higher LTV loans are insured.

State-Guaranteed Pass-Through Securities

Ginnie Mae-type pass-throughs that are guaranteed by state governments rather than the federal government are another new type of mortgage-backed security. In order to improve the flow of funds into the housing industry within states, many states are introducing mortgage securities that are designed for sale to state pension funds. The motivation for this movement is to give these funds a means of making a positive contribution to the economic well-being of the state in which the fund's participants live and work. While actual issues of state mortgage-backed bonds or pass-through securities have been few, it appears that these issues will be designed to raise funds to provide below-market interest rate mortgage loans to certain groups of state residents; thus, they will resemble mortgage revenue bonds, except that income will not be tax-exempt and some issues may be pass-through securities rather than bonds.

The administration of these issues will resemble the Ginnie Mae process since securities will be issued and serviced by lending institutions, but the guarantee will more closely resemble Freddie Mac PCs; mortgage pools will carry individual and pool private mortgage insurance, with an additional guarantee against loss provided by the state agency. The first state mortgage security was in North Carolina in early 1981; this mortgage bond issue was issued by the state housing corporation, the North Carolina Mortgage Investment Corporation. This $53 million issue was AA-rated by Standard & Poor's and carried a coupon of 12.30 percent.

ATTRACTIVE FEATURES

Return

In general, mortgage-backed security returns compare favorably with those available on other securities of similar risk. In a recent study of security returns during the period 1974-1980 by Michael Waldman and Steven P. Baum of Salomon Brothers, their Mortgage Index (composed of Ginnie Mae, Freddie Mac PC, and conventional pass-through returns) was found to outperform indexes of corporate bonds and Treasury securities during the same period. The main reasons for the return advantages, according to the study, were the shorter maturities of the mortgage-backed securities (in a period of general rising interest rates) and their higher yields (partially due to prepayments of pass-throughs purchased at a discount). They conclude that the yield advantage of mortgage securities is greatest in periods of rising rates.

The higher yields on mortgage pass-through securities are produced primarily by their more frequent payment stream (monthly versus semiannually), which produces a corporate equivalent yield discussed below and the yield kicker provided by prepayments. As with a bond, when a PC is purchased at a discount, its yield is increased by payment of its face value prior to maturity. This produces a yield kicker because the capital gain (due to the discounted price) is realized sooner. While both of these features are advantages from a yield point of view, they do impose re-investment responsibilities on the investor. In addition, the yield advantage attributed to prepayments is based on the security's conforming with the FHA twelve-year average-life assumption, as discussed below; if this experience does not continue in the future, some narrowing of yield spreads should occur.

Determination of yield. When the yield on a mortgage-backed pass-through security is quoted, it is quoted on a corporate equivalent, FHA average expected-life basis. The corporate equivalence refers to the fact that payments are made monthly rather than semiannually, so that re-investment opportunities are greater, making the equivalent yield on a pass-through security somewhat greater. For example, the corporate equivalent yield on a 15 percent mortgage-backed pass-through is approximately 15.5 percent. The average expected life refers to the expected prepayment of the mortgages in the pool. FHA mortgages on single-family dwellings typically prepay within approximately twelve years (on an original contract term of thirty years). FHA average life differs, however, for different housing types, loan terms, and mortgage interest rates. Ideally, an investor will obtain prepayment data for several GNMA pools and buy out of the pool that offers the most attractive prepayment-yield properties. Prepayment data may also be available for other seasoned pools, such as private issue securities.

As with other income securities, a pass-through that is purchased at a discount will generate a higher yield when it is paid off sooner; the opposite is true when the security is purchased at premium. For example, a $100 11.75 percent coupon pass-through that is purchased at a price of $93 would yield 12.62 percent if held to maturity (thirty years). If, as expected, the security prepays in twelve years, the yield increases to 12.79 percent.

There are also yield differences based on the payment pass-through delays for each of the three basic types of pass-through. For example, a mortgage pool that bears a coupon interest rate of 11 percent (and is purchased at par) will yield 10.93 percent on a Ginnie Mae pool (forty-five-day payment delay), 10.89 percent on a privately issued PC (fifty-five-day delay), and 10.79 percent on a Freddie

Mac PC (seventy-five-day delay). These yield differences reflect the cost of the lost interest on those payments that could have been re-invested sooner had they been received as quickly as they were received by the lender.

The greater the payment delay, the larger are the discounts at which these three pass-through securities sell. Some observers question whether it is accurate to continue to use the FHA assumption of a twelve-year life on mortgages for yield quotations. They note that increasing mortgage interest rates in recent years have led to increased use of assumable mortgages that extend the life of mortgages that bear contract rates that are below current mortgage interest rates. On the other hand, there are also efforts being made by mortgage lenders to enforce due-on-sale provisions in mortgage contracts; these efforts are designed to force home buyers to take out a new mortgage loan when they buy rather than to assume the existing loan. It is unclear at this time how these two conflicting trends will affect the FHA twelve-year average-life assumption. However, because FHA/VA mortgages are assumable by law, there is a greater chance that Ginnie Mae PCs will have lives that extend beyond twelve years, since these securities are backed exclusively by FHA/VA mortgages. Finally, for pools that are backed by mortgages with maturities other than thirty years, or on non-single-family dwelling property types, average life will usually vary from the traditional twelve-year assumption.

There may also be yield differences based on the geographical location of the mortgage pool. Since demand for mortgage credit is greater in the Sun Belt states, for example, than in the Midwest, mortgage interest rates also tend to be higher in those states. This makes it possible for mortgage pass-through security issuers in the Sun Belt to offer higher coupon rates than those offered by Midwestern pools.

Cash-Flow Characteristics

The cash-flow characteristics of mortgage-backed securities differ from those of other types of securities. With mortgage-backed pass-through securities, payments of principal and interest are made to investors as they are received (or before they are received if timely payment is provided). These payments are designed to be level, as they contain a decreasing interest portion and an increasing principal portion. Since mortgages mature at different times, depending on when a mortgage is refinanced or paid off by the borrower, an investor's payment stream may be uneven as the investor's portion of principal prepayments are passed through when received. Early payments of loans are often subject to prepayment penalties, which are also passed through to the investor.

This uneven cash-flow characteristic is not true of mortgage-backed bonds, which follow the same practices as corporate bonds, although they usually have a call provision so that prepayment is often made with these securities also.

In 1979, Ginnie Mae issuers began issuing securities backed by FHA/VA graduated payment mortgages (FHA 245s). These mortgages offer borrowers lower monthly payments in the early years of the mortgage. This type of mortgage is designed for first-time home buyers whose income is expected to increase rapidly but who cannot afford the regular monthly payments at the outset of the mortgage. Because of the graduated payment feature, loan payments do not cover interest and principal payments in the first five years of the mortgage. The payment shortfall is therefore added to the principal balance, so that the loan balance actually increases in the first five years. This is called negative amortization.

Ginnie Maes backed by graduated payment mortgages have somewhat different cash-flow characteristics in that payments are lower in the beginning but increase later because (1) after the graduation period, payments rise to a level that is higher than the comparable level payment mortgage, and (2) as a result of the higher principal balance (due to negative amortization), prepayment amounts are higher.

With the advent of many alternative mortgage instruments, most of which contain interest rate adjustment features, many cash-flow patterns will emerge in future pass-through securities. This innovation in the pass-through market will give investors the opportunity to select payment streams that match their cash-flow preferences.

Liquidity

Another attractive characteristic of mortgage-backed securities is their liquidity. Like most other financial investments, mortgage-backed securities are bought and sold through investment banking companies (brokers). Price and yield quotations on Ginnie Mae and Freddie Mac securities are readily obtained in the financial pages of the newspaper, in just the same way that one would look up a stock or bond price.

Because of the volume of government PC issues and their government guarantee, they are the most liquid of all the mortgage-backed securities. Direct-issue PCs and private-conduit PCs are somewhat less numerous and therefore less visible than the government securities. The larger the issuing institution, the more active a secondary market is likely to exist for the mortgage-backed security issued by that institution. If, as expected, the volume of privately issued PCs increases, the secondary market for these securities should increase and their liquidity should be enhanced.

Liquidity is also influenced by the ratings given to different types of securities. Government securities carry no ratings, since they are backed by the U.S. Treasury and are therefore considered virtually risk-free. Freddie Mac and Fannie Mae PCs are not government guaranteed, but are considered to be nearly the equivalent of Ginnie Mae securities in the marketplace — they typically trade only 15 to 40 basis points in yield above Ginnie Maes. Most mortgage-backed bonds and subordinated position pass-through securities are given AAA ratings because they are guaranteed by cash funds that are maintained to prevent investor losses, or by letters of credit of large financial institutions that issue AAA debt.

Private pass-through securities issued by institutions or by conduit firms normally have an AA rating. This is because their guarantee against investor loss is provided by private mortgage insurance companies, whose debt obligations carry an AA rating since these companies are not considered to have the financial strength of major financial institutions. Mortgage revenue bond issues also carry AA ratings, for the most part, for this same reason — they are insured by private mortgage insurance companies rather than by the U.S. government or by major financial-center institutions.

Diversification

Mortgage-backed securities enable an investor to diversify his portfolio in two ways. First, because mortgage-backed securities are real estate investments, an investor who seeks an alternative to money market and corporate bond income securities may consider mortgage-backed securities as a means of giving more depth to this portion of his portfolio. The real estate option is also important from the standpoint of ERISA regulations affecting pension fund managers; it is another means of ensuring a prudent level of investor protection through diversification.

Second, mortgage-backed securities contribute to portfolio diversification via the geographical dispersion of many mortgage pools. Freddie Mac and private-conduit PCs collect their underlying mortgages nationwide. Ginnie Maes, Fannie Mae PCs, direct-placement PCs, mortgage revenue bonds, and private mortgage-backed bonds are more likely to be located in a specific geographic area within a county or state. For investors who wish to invest in specific areas, however, such as union pension funds, or who wish to support the economy of a given area, the ability to localize may be regarded as a benefit rather than a drawback.

POTENTIAL RISKS

The risk associated with any financial investment may be defined as "the probability that the expected return on that investment will not be realized by the investor for some reason." In evaluating investment risk, the inventor must consider the quality of the underlying asset, the guarantee, if any, that the expected income stream will be forthcoming, and the possibility of any capital depreciation due to increasing interest rates.

The factors that contribute to the stability of the mortgage loans that compose mortgage security pools may be summarized as follows. First, loan underwriting procedures are designed to weed out unsuitable loan applicants or those who are perceived as being unlikely to fulfill their financial obligations. Second, since a mortgage most often represents a family's financial commitment to its place of residence, there is less chance that this commitment will be abandoned in times of financial distress.

Finally, all mortgage-backed securities are backed by some guarantee that the investor will suffer no losses should mortgage loan defaults occur. The guarantee on Ginnie Mae securities is the strongest, because these securities are backed by the full faith and credit of the U.S. Treasury. Thus, an investor could only lose money on a Ginnie Mae in the unlikely event that the U.S. government was unable to pay its obligations.

Freddie Mac and Fannie Mae PCs are guaranteed by a combination of private mortgage insurance on the higher-risk mortgages in the pools and Freddie Mac/Fannie Mae's guarantee against loss on any pool losses not covered by this insurance. While this guarantee is not equivalent to a U.S. government guarantee (since the FHLMC/FNMA are only affiliated with U.S. government agencies), it is nearly perceived as such in the marketplace; yields on Freddie Mac PCs are typically only 15 to 40 basis points above Ginnie Mae yields, while Fannie Mae PCs are expected to trade in a similar range.

Most direct placement pass-through securities and mortgage revenue bonds are guaranteed by a combination of private mortgage insurance on higher-risk mortgages in the pools, a private mortgage insurance pool policy on losses not covered by the individual mortgage insurance coverage, and special hazard insurance for losses not covered by the other guarantees. This level of coverage earns Standard & Poor's rating of AA, since private mortgage insurers are considered to be in the second tier of financial stability of U.S. financial institutions.

Subordinated position direct placement pass-through securities are backed by a cash fund (or letter of credit) — usually 7 percent of the pool value — that is used to pay pool losses. The existence of a guarantee in cash or near-cash form is sufficient to earn an AAA Standard & Poor's rating.

Finally, mortgage-backed bonds are general obligations of the issuer, and therefore do not represent an ownership interest in a pool of mortgages, but they are collateralized by a pool of mortgages having a market value up to twice the face amount of the pool. Because of this over-collateralization, the bond's value is considered well protected against loss. These securities normally carry an AAA Standard & Poor's rating.

Mortgage-backed securities backed by fixed-rate mortgages are like any other fixed income security in that their prices fluctuate with movements of market interest rates. Thus, while the income stream and ultimate payment of outstanding principal balance may be guaranteed, the market value of the security at a given point in time may be more or less than the original purchase value. Investors should bear this in mind when buying any fixed income security, including mortgage-backed securities, particularly when the possibility exists that the investor will have to sell the security on short notice, regardless of current market value.

TAX CONSEQUENCES

As with other types of fixed income securities, the income from mortgage-backed securities is reportable as ordinary income. Gains on resale are recognized as capital gains except in the case of securities purchased as new issues at discount greater than 2 percent. Such gains are taxabie as ordinary income. Because the payment stream is irregular (due to periodic loan prepayments), annual income to be derived from a mortgage pass-through security cannot be precisely anticipated. This is not true of the two forms of mortgage-backed bonds (private and public mortgage revenue bonds); their income stream is fixed. Mortgage revenue bond interest income is tax-exempt.

Because of the uneven cash flow of mortgage pass-through securities, the most likely investor in this mortgage security would be a tax-exempt investor, such as pension, profit-sharing, trust funds, life insurance companies, and, occasionally, casualty companies, depending on their profit picture. Mortgage-backed bonds could appeal to any bond investor, with tax-exempt mortgage revenue bonds being of special interest to high-tax-bracket investors.

Pass-through securities also may be of interest to investors who are not currently in a tax-paying position but who expect to pay taxes in the future, since these securities pay a higher proportion of interest in early years and more principal in later years. Interest payments are taxed as ordinary income; tax treatment of principal payments varies depending on the tax status of the investor and on the discount, if any, in the purchase price of the security. For many investors, principal payments are considered nontaxable repayments of the original investment.

Pass-through securities of any type are of special interest to thrift institutions, since they qualify as mortgage loan assets for thrift tax and regulatory purposes. This feature enables thrift institutions to use the secondary market more effectively to bridge the regional mortgage credit gap.

REPRESENTATIVE TYPES OF INVESTORS

Generally, mortgage-backed securities are most likely to appeal to three sets of investors. Mortgage pass-through securities would appeal primarily to not-fully-taxable institutions or persons due to their cash flow, quality, and return characteristics; one would compare yields available on AA corporate bonds to pass-through security returns to get an idea of investment returns in the same risk class. Mortgage-backed bonds would be most appropriate for investors who would normally invest in AAA corporate bonds, since cash flow and risk are equivalent. Finally, mortgage revenue bonds would appeal to investors in high tax brackets, since income is tax-exempt on these bonds; cash flow and risk are equivalent to AA-rated tax-exempt securities.

IMPORTANT FACTORS IN BUYING AND SELLING

Mortgage-backed securities of all types are bought and sold through investment banking firms. Taxable securities would normally be sold through the fixed income department, while tax-exempt mortgage revenue bonds would be sold through the municipal bond department. Investors should consult their brokers or investment advisers for current information on mortgage security performance and other characteristics.

An investor who is considering investment in a mortgage-backed security should evaluate these investment vehicles using three basic criteria: servicing characteristics, risk/return trade-offs, and loss guarantees.

Servicing Characteristics

First, an investor must choose among level, semiannual payments (provided by mortgage bonds), monthly payments with a timely payment guarantee (Ginnie Mae, Freddie Mac, and Fannie Mae PCs), and monthly payments with an intention to make timely payments (direct and conduit PCs). If one is depending heavily on a monthly income stream, the Ginnie Mae, Freddie Mac, or Fannie Mae PC may be the best alternative.

Risk/Return Trade-Off

While Ginnie Maes provide the lowest risk level (and promptest payment), they also trade at a lower yield than other mortgage securities. Freddie Mac and Fannie Mae PCs provide the second highest level of safety (and also provide a timely payment guarantee), so they trade at a somewhat higher yield — from 15 to 40 basis points over Ginnie Maes. Various private issues trade at higher yields but are also considered to be more risky since they are not government guaranteed.

Guarantee Against Loss

The risk associated with the return on each form of mortgage-backed security is in turn determined by the guarantee against loss. The quality of this guarantee is the basis for mortgage security ratings. Ginnie Mae, Freddie Mac, and Fannie Mae securities have no ratings, but are equivalent to U.S. government securities. Subordinated position PCs and mortgage-backed bonds are AAA-rated, since they are backed by a cash fund or AAA institution letter of credit (in the case of PCs) or are over-collateralized by 150 to 200 percent of the issue value, an asset backing that is considered to make the issue of highest quality.

Private pass-through securities and mortgage revenue bonds carry Standard

& Poor's AA ratings since they are guaranteed by private mortgage insurance coverage. These companies are considered to provide somewhat less financial strength than the highest-level guarantees.

GLOSSARY

corporate equivalent yield— The yield that equates the payment stream on a monthly payment mortgage pass-through security with a semiannual payment corporate bond. Monthly payments produce a higher yield, since they can be re-invested in income-producing assets sooner.

Fannie Mae (FNMA)— Federal National Mortgage Association. Formerly a U.S. government agency and now a private corporation, Fannie Mae improves the secondary market for home mortgages by purchasing them from mortgage lenders.

Fannie Mae debenture— Debt obligations issued by the FNMA to raise funds to finance home mortgage purchases.

Federal Home Loan Bank Board (FHLBB)— A government agency that regulates the thrift industry.

Federal Home Loan Mortgage Corporation (FHLMC or Freddie Mac)— A privately managed corporation that is affiliated with the FHLBB; it purchases conventional (non-government-insured) mortgage loans and issues participation certificates (PCs) that are backed by these mortgage loans.

FHA experience or assumed life— The time in years in which a pool of mortgages is expected to prepay, based on data collected on mortgages insured by the Federal Housing Authority. The current average FHA assumed life is twelve years for thirty-year mortgages on single-family homes.

FHA/VA insurance— Federal Housing Authority insurance covers losses for 100 percent of the value of the mortgage loan. Veterans Administration insurance covers only the top 60 percent of the loan amount, up to $25,000. Mortgages covered by FHA/VA insurance are used to back Ginnie Mae securities.

Freddie Mac guaranteed mortgage certificate (GMC)— A general-obligation security issued by the FHLMC that resembles a Freddie Mac PC, except that interest payments are made semiannually instead of monthly; principal payments are made annually.

Freddie Mac participation certificate (PC)— A mortgage pass-through security issued by the FHLMC that represents an undivided interest in a pool of conventional mortgages owned by FHLMC.

full faith and credit— The guarantee provided to investors in U.S. government securities that their investment will be covered against loss with the financial resources of the U.S. Treasury. This guarantee makes government securities essentially risk-free. Ginnie Mae securities are the only mortgage securities that carry this guarantee.

Ginnie Mae (GNMA)— Government National Mortgage Association. A U.S. government agency within the U.S. Department of Housing and Urban Development; it guarantees securities that are backed by U.S.-government-insured loans.

Ginnie Mae participation certificate (PC)— A U.S.-government-guaranteed mortgage security that is backed by FHA/VA insured home mortgages.

loan-to-value ratio (LTV)— The ratio of a mortgage loan amount to the sales price of the home, this ratio is a common measure of mortgage risk. A high LTV indicates that the home buyer paid a low down payment on his loan. LTVs of 80 percent or less are considered low risk.

mortgage-backed bond— A general-obligation debt of a mortgage lending institution, these bonds are over-collateralized by pools of mortgages and pay interest semiannually, like corporate bonds.

mortgage revenue bond— Debt obligations of state or local housing authorities that are used to raise funds to extend mortgage loans at subsidized interest rates. Income from these bonds is tax-exempt.

mortgage securities— Any security that is backed by mortgage loans. These take the form of bonds or pass-through securities.

participation certificate— A form of mortgage-backed security that represents an undivided interest in a pool of mortgages held by a conduit firm, agency, or institution.

pass-through security— A mortgage-backed security in which mortgage payments are passed through the mortgage lender to the investor in that mortgage.

pool insurance— A private mortgage insurance guarantee against investor losses on securities that are backed by mortgage pools. Pool insurance provides coverage of losses that are not paid by insurance policies on individual mortgages in the pool. Most pool coverage is 5 to 10 percent of the pool face amount.

prepayments— Mortgage loans that are paid off by the borrower prior to the stated term of the loan contract.

private mortgage insurance— Guarantees against mortgage loan losses (due to foreclosure) that are provided by private mortgage insurance companies. Unlike government mortgage insurance, private insurance covers only the risk portion of the loan amount, or the top 25 percent of the mortgage amount.

rating agencies— Security rating agencies assign security risk ratings based on their assessment of the capability of the security issuer to pay its obligations. Standard & Poor's ratings range from AAA (for high-quality, low-risk securities) to B. Mortgage-backed securities are either risk-free (no rating required, government-guaranteed) or carry AAA or AA ratings to date.

special hazard insurance— On privately insured mortgage pools, a form of insurance coverage that pays losses arising from unusual events not covered by private mortgage insurance or private mortgage pool insurance.

SUGGESTED READING

There are few up-to-date publications available on mortgage-backed securities. The best are available from mortgage-banking firms. A partial list of such publications appears below.

Published by the First Boston Corporation, New York:

Fixed Income Glossary. 1981. A general glossary containing definitions of many of the mortgage market terms used by dealers, investors, and mortgage bankers.

Inside Pass-Through Securities. 1978. Deals with what pass-through cash-flows look like and how to measure yields and average lives more accurately.

Mortgage-Related Securities. 1979. A reference of all types of mortgage securities (pass-throughs and mortgage-backed bonds), detailing such information as number and size of issuers, payment procedures, yield assumptions, guarantees, distribution of holders, legal and tax status, etc.

Mortgage-Related Securities Review and Comment. Monthly. This is an ongoing newsletter dealing with market strategies and topics of interest in the mortgage market.

Pass-Through Securities — Portfolio Manager's Handbook. 1981. This contains often-used information plus up-to-date yield tables for all types of pass-throughs.

Prepayment Consistency. 1980. This questions the validity of the fast-pay concept of pass-throughs and shows how to predict future prepayments and yields more accurately.

Published by Salomon Brothers, New York:

Average Life of Mortgage Related Instruments. 1977.

Cash Flow Characteristics of Mortgage Securities. 1980.

Combining Construction Loans and Mortgage Securities. 1980.

A Constructive View of GNMAs. 1979.

The GNMA-GPM Security — Its Yield and Trading Characteristics. 1979.

GNMA Pass Throughs and FHA Experience. 1973.

The Historical Performance of Mortgage Securities: 1972-1980. 1980.

Introducing the Salomon Brothers Total Rate-of-Return Index for Mortgage Pass Through Securities. 1979.

Investment Characteristics of Shared Appreciation Mortgages. 1981.

The Value of GNMA Discounts. 1980.

Motion Pictures

*David Nochimson, Esq.**

BASIC CHARACTERISTICS

Historical Background

From its rudimentary beginnings at the turn of the century, the motion picture industry has grown at an extraordinary rate. By 1946, in the United States alone, 3 billion tickets were sold annually, producing gross box-office receipts of $1.6 billion. Without any real competition for the leisure dollar, Hollywood was turning out an average of 400 pictures per year for the world market. The film industry during these years was dominated by nine companies (MGM, Columbia, Paramount, Twentieth Century Fox, United Artists, Universal, Warner, Walt Disney, and RKO), which were integrated production-distribution-exhibition companies known as "the studios" or "the majors." The studios were dominated by a handful of autocratic and, in some cases, charismatic studio heads whose members included Louis B. Mayer, Jack Warner, and Harry Cohn; their combined judgments determined the motion picture fare for the entire world.

The stranglehold of the majors on the production, marketing, and exhibition of feature films led to the Department of Justice-imposed consent decree in 1950, pursuant to which the majors were required to divest themselves of their American theater holdings. To compound the impact of the consent decree, the studios were losing large portions of the public to the new, free visual entertainment medium — television. The results were nearly fatal. As a direct consequence of the huge drop in audience and income, Hollywood production operations went through a drastic shake-up. Several companies retired from the scene, studio executive staffs were cut to the bone, production departments were mothballed, and large areas of studio real estate were sold off.

As a consequence of this restructuring, the studio heads, whose numbers were severely depleted by death and retirement during this period, lost control of the industry. The important actors, directors, writers, and producers, freed from long-term studio employment agreements, formed their own production companies, created and developed their own material, assembled the casts and directors, and sought from the studio only its funds to finance their films and its marketing organization to distribute them. This shift from studio production to independent production, utilizing studio financing and distribution facilities,

* David Nochimson is a member of the Los Angeles law firm of Mitchell, Silberberg & Knupp.

became and remains today the basic way in which feature films are financed, produced, and distributed.

Current Industry Trends

New growth. As the novelty of free television entertainment began to wear off in the early 1960s, audiences that had forsaken the theaters began to return, and U.S. box-office receipts grew slowly but steadily until 1975, when they reached $2.1 billion. Aided by a series of blockbuster films, box-office receipts rose to over $2.8 billion in 1979. (See Table 1 below for 1966-1980 theater industry statistics.)

This growth and income also reflected impressive changes and the fundamental economics of the marketplace for feature films, including the following:

- Box-office prices from 1973 to 1980 rose faster than the rate of inflation.
- New theater construction, accelerating a trend that began in the late 1960s, contributed to a total number of theaters in 1980 of 16,965, which was approximately the same number that existed in 1946 and that far exceeded the approximately

TABLE 1. U.S. Motion Picture Theater Industry Statistics

	Number of Films Released	*Box Office Gross*		*Average Price Per Ticket*		*Number of Admissions*	
		$ Mils.	*% Chg.*	*Amt.*	*% Chg.*	*Mils.*	*% Chg.*
Average (1966–1980)			7.0%		6.7%		0.3%
1980	N.A.	$2,748.5	(2.6)	$2.691	6.9	1,021.5	(8.9)
1979	248	2,821.3	6.3	2.517	7.4	1,120.9	(0.6)
1978	203	2,653	11.8	2.343	5.1	1,128.2	6.1
1977	226	2,372	16.5	2.23	4.7	1,063	11.1
1976	174	2,036	(3.7)	2.13	3.9	957	(7.4)
1975	176	2,115	10.8	2.05	8.5	1,033	2.2
1974	238	1,909	25.3	1.89	7.4	1,011	16.9
1973	219	1,524	(3.7)	1.76	3.5	865	(7.4)
1972	296	1,583	17.3	1.70	3.0	934	13.9
1971	256	1,350	(5.5)	1.65	6.5	820	(11.0)
1970	236	1,429	10.4	1.55	9.2	921	1.0
1969	235	1,294	0.9	1.42	8.4	912	(6.8)
1968	235	1,282	15.5	1.31	9.2	979	5.6
1967	N.A.	1,110	4.0	1.20	10.1	927	(4.9)
1966	N.A.	1,067	N.A.	1.09	N.A.	975	N.A.
1946	N.A.	1,692	N.A.	N.A.	N.A.	4,067	N.A.

N.A.—Not available

SOURCE: Motion Picture Association of America, National Association of Theatre Owners

11,000 theaters in use in 1963. One factor in this growth was the increasing use of multiplexing (using several motion picture screens in a single building or complex), which in turn was aided by a change in union rules that permitted a single projectionist to handle the projection of more than one picture in the same building.

- While the number of English-language films released continued to drop (from 279 in 1972 to 248 in 1979), revenue earning potentials of pictures released increased dramatically during the 1970s.
- Films played for longer periods in theaters and were reissued to substantially repeat business.
- The decrease in supply and increase in demand for films has resulted in the higher percentage of gross box-office dollars being paid by exhibitors to distributors. Exhibitors were being forced to compete more aggressively in bidding for an increasingly scarce product, resulting in higher film rental terms.
- The attempt to develop meaningful centers for the production and international distribution of indigenous theatrical motion pictures in England, Italy, France, Germany, and Mexico collapsed, leaving the worldwide theatrical motion picture industry almost totally dependent on American films.

Ultimately however, two factors have played and are continuing to play the major role in the resurgent economic strength of the industry. The first is the growth and entrenchment of the practice among the majors of requiring guarantees as a condition to renting their films to exhibitors. Second, sequential markets for films after their theatrical release are major sources of income today, a fact that has dramatically reduced the downside risk historically accompanied by investing in motion picture production.

New markets. New markets for motion pictures include the following:

- U.S. prime-time network television;
- Local non-network television and all foreign television, referred to generically as television syndication;
- The pay-television market;
- The non-theatrical market such as airlines, ships at sea, offshore oil rigs, colleges, hospitals, libraries, construction camps, and defense installations; and
- Videocassettes and videodiscs.

The motion picture industry accounted for total revenues (at the distributor-studio level) of nearly $2.8 billion in 1980 and revenues are estimated to exceed $2.9 billion in 1981. Another $175 million in gross revenues was taken in by the non-majors.

Pay television. Pay television in particular has experienced extraordinary growth since its introduction in the early 1970s. (See Table 2 on page 466 for growth figures from 1978 to 1981.) In a report published in 1976, Arthur D. Little, Incorporated, developed certain projections for the pay-cable industry. It estimated that the number of pay subscribers would be 3.4 million in 1980 and 5.7 million in 1985. These projections were vastly understated.

The potential profitability of pay television is far greater than that of commercial television because, instead of underwriting programs by advertising revenues (at pennies per viewer), revenues from pay television are based on a per-subscriber charge.

The studios doubled their previous year's income from pay television in 1980, showing receipts of $150 million. It is expected that the figure could approach $225 million in 1981. Although a meaningful area of revenue, the jury is still out on the issue of how competitive the theatrical and pay-television markets are, and it is yet to be determined whether in the long term pay television will add more than it will subtract from theatrical revenue.

Videocassettes and videodiscs. Videodiscs and videocassette sales have also shown dramatic growth. Videocassette sales were between $125 million and $150 million in 1980, out of which $20 million to $25 million was retained by the majors. Videodisc revenue was more modest and royalties (as opposed to advances) are expected to be $7 million to $8 million in 1981. It should be noted that there is an increasing trend toward rentals as opposed to sales, which may have a profound effect on the home video market.

Subsidiary rights. In addition to the income from pay television, television syndication, and home video, the revenues that may be obtained from the exploitation of subsidiary rights in the literary materials upon which a picture is based

TABLE 2. Estimated Total Rentals by Source for Feature Films*

($ Millions)

	1978	*1979*	*1980*	*1981*
Domestic theatrical	$1,216	$1,125	$1,200	$1,250
Foreign theatrical	750	775	765	750
Pay television	35	75	155	255
Network television	260	300	350	340
Domestic syndication	110	125	125	120
Foreign syndication	85	100	115	135
Cassette	1	10	22	50
Disc	-	1	16	8
Airline, hotel, other	28	30	30	30
	$2,485	$2,541	$2,778	$2,938

*Estimated gross rentals from all markets for the feature films released by eight principal companies.

SOURCE: Wertheim & Co., Inc.

are of growing importance. Subsidiary rights include theatrical sequels and remakes, television series rights, publishing rights, merchandising exploitation of characters, the marketing of phonograph records and tapes utilizing the soundtrack of a film, and music publishing income.

Until 1970, the amount of income derived from the exploitation of a theatrical motion picture in these sequential markets and from exploiting the subsidiary rights was relatively insubstantial, rarely amounting in the aggregate to more than 20 percent of the production cost of a picture. In the last decade, the rate of growth in these areas has been even more dramatic than the growth in theatrical exhibition income. Indeed, it is generally accepted that the extraordinary interest expressed by outside investors and lenders in the motion picture industry has been prompted by the substantially reduced downside risk in theatrical film investment resulting from the high income potential from these sources.

Short-term trends. A report by Wertheim and Company, Incorporated, published in 1980 and updated in 1981,[1] concluded that the motion picture business was entering a period (estimated to last two to three years) of declining profits due to two factors — the quality of earnings and, more importantly, the escalation, at an alarming rate, of production and marketing costs (illustrated in Table 3 on page 468). The following statistics seem to bear out Wertheim's analysis:

- Box-office revenues failed to advance in 1980, declining 2.6 percent, despite a 6.7 percent increase in average ticket prices. It should be noted, however, that while admissions dropped 2.6 percent, domestic theatrical film rentals rose 6.6 percent, indicating an increase in the share of box-office income retained by distributors.
- Domestic film rentals rose an estimated 6.6 percent, while foreign rentals declined one percent.
- The negative cost of the average film released by a major studio increased 11 percent to $9.4 million.
- The number of films released by the majors rose to 143, including reissues, from 126 in 1979.
- Earnings for the film and television divisions of the major entertainment companies declined 25 percent during 1980.

Film Distribution and Exploitation

Typically, a film is produced either by an independent production company or by a major. In the case of a film financed by a major, the studio-distributor retains worldwide control over all rights and will take a distribution fee depending on the media and territory, thereafter recouping all its distribution expenses and finally recovering its production costs plus overhead plus interest. The balance is referred to as net profits and is shared with certain creative elements (stars,

---

[1] Londoner, David, *The Motion Picture Industry.* New York: Wertheim & Co., Inc., 1980; and Londoner, David, and Blum, Francine S., *Take 2 — A Second Look at the Profit Picture of the Movie Business.* New York: Wertheim & Co., Inc., 1981.

TABLE 3. Operating Income Before Taxes of Film and Television Divisions

Studio (Fiscal Year)	1978	1979	1980	% Change 1980/1979
	($ Millions)			
Columbia (6/30)	$80.1	$59.0	$59.5	+1%
Disney (9/30)	54.1	40.2	48.6	+21
MGM (8/31)	39.0	59.8	35.7	−40
Paramount (7/31)	40.0E	85.0E	76.0E	−11
Twentieth Century Fox	91.1	67.2	55.2	−18
United Artists	58.2	48.0	20.1	−58
Universal (MCA)	159.8	174.3	133.9	−23
Warner	79.9	117.6	60.8	−48
Total	$602.2	$651.1	$489.8	−25%

SOURCE: Wertheim & Co., Inc. E=Estimated

directors, individual producers, etc.). In the case of an independent production company, funds for the production of the film are, in whole or in part, raised independently of the studio; as a result, the independent has a greater opportunity to drive a harder bargain with the distributor and, in addition, to withhold certain rights from the theatrical distributor. For example, an independent may give U.S. and Canadian theatrical rights to a major, reserving the right to make the network and pay-television sale itself, turning over foreign theatrical sales to a sales agent on a territory-by-territory basis, and giving television syndication rights to an independent syndication company.

The independent producer also has a better opportunity to obtain a gross or adjusted gross as opposed to a net deal from a distributor. Instead of the distributor recouping a full distribution fee and all expenses before remitting any monies to the independent producer, at negotiated levels of revenues the producer will get a varying percentage of the revenues received by the distributor.

Break-even rule. As a rule of thumb (which seems to be more an exception than a rule), a film must generate gross film rentals (as opposed to box-office receipts) of approximately three times its production cost to reach break-even. Depending on the cost of the film, its advertising budget, and whether there are so-called gross participants (superstars who participate from the first dollar of film rental), the break-even point can be at a higher multiple.

Distributor-exhibitor-producer exploitation. There are three levels in the U.S. theatrical exploitation of motion pictures: the distributor, the exhibitor, and the producer. As noted above, with studio-financed pictures, the producer is also the distributor. Typically, a film is first distributed to motion picture theaters and the exhibitor (or theater owner) collects box-office receipts. The theater owner receives a share of box-office receipts as negotiated with the distributor, which typically ranges from 10 to 75 percent but averages 55 percent. When the theater owner retains a lower percentage of box-office receipts, he usually recovers the negotiated charge to cover overhead and, in addition, is able to deduct the cost of advertising he is advanced. The balance is remitted to the distributor and is called "film rental," from which the distributor must cover its distribution expenses such as advertising and prints. From film rentals, the distributor will typically deduct a distribution fee (ranging from 30 to 35 percent) and thereafter recoups its distribution expenses. If the distributor has not financed the picture, it will remit the balance to the independent producer, but if the distributor is also the financier, it will recoup its production costs plus interest and overhead plus a share of the profits.

Foreign theatrical distribution takes two forms: Films may be licensed by the producer on a territory-by-territory basis with foreign distributors, in which case the producer will receive an advance against a percentage of receipts (after recoupment by the distributors of their fees and expenses) or, in the alternative, the film can be licensed on a fixed fee or outright sale basis where the producer receives a fixed license fee but not participation of revenues of the film. If the studio or U.S. theatrical distribution controls foreign theatrical rights, it will customarily charge 40 to 50 percent of the film rentals as its distribution fee for foreign theatrical distribution.

In the television markets, films are licensed by producers to pay television and free television (network and syndication) directly or through a distributor (often by the distributor who has the theatrical distribution rights). If licensed through a third-party distributor, the distribution fee charged by the distributor will range from 25 to 40 percent of the license fee.

Production and Marketing of Television Films

Although the focus of this article is on theatrical motion pictures, some attention should be given to an alternative pattern of motion picture production, namely, film production for initial exhibition on television. The network license fees for theatrical motion pictures have escalated over the past five years, but the prices paid by advertisers have not been elastic enough for the networks to pass on all of their costs. As a result, the networks are relying more on film made directly for television. The lower cost, the ability to control the time of release, and the general popularity (an average of a 28 to 30 rating and an excess of 30 share) point to a further emphasis on "Movies of the Week."

A two-hour motion picture for television, as opposed to a television series or mini-series, requires little risk (although the rewards, too, are commensurately limited). Little money will be committed without first submitting the proposed project to the network and, if the network approves the material, it will underwrite the cost of the script and perhaps defer some of the producer's overhead cost. When the teleplay is completed, it will be budgeted and submitted to the network and, if the network approves the project, it will negotiate a license fee with the production company, typically covering two network runs of the film. Current network license fees range from $1.75 million to over $2 million (plus so-called cast breakage to cover the additional cost for major television stars). Following the network telecast, the producer, who owns the film, will be able to license the film for television syndication, pay television, and the ancillary markets. If the film has special attributes (such as an actor well known in the foreign theatrical market), the film can be sold to and exploited by local foreign theatrical distributors before being sold to television stations in the market (and concurrently with the U.S. network run).

The production of a "Movie of the Week" can be done by either the television arm of a major studio, a major independent production company, or an individual producer. Because the network will require producers who are not well established to furnish evidence of financial responsibility (since the producer is responsible for costs in excess of the network license fee), such producers must make arrangements in the form of a co-venture with an umbrella company (a studio or major independent). It should be noted that the network license fee often may not cover the entire production cost, so it is important to arrange for deficit financing, which can be done through an umbrella company or by pre-selling syndication rights. The attractive characteristics of producing "Movies of the Week" include the following:

- The essentially limited nature of the front-end risk, since except for general overhead, the only investment is in the acquisition of rights in the underlying material, which may be passed along to the network.
- On occasion, the network license fee may exceed the production costs of the film.
- After deducting distribution fees and residuals, there may be an opportunity for foreign theatrical income.
- Worldwide syndication income has grown at an attractive rate (although as of early 1982, this market has softened) and it is possible to gross from $500,000 to $600,000, which, after deducting distribution fees and residuals, will leave net income of $250,000 to $300,000.
- Due to the fact that under the Internal Revenue Code the network cannot get the benefit of the investment tax credit, the producer who is responsible for any deficit is entitled to the entire investment tax credit.

Types of Motion Picture Investments

Investments in motion pictures take a variety of forms, including the following:

Development or seed capital investments. The active production of a motion picture is preceded by a development process in which literary material is acquired and/or developed by a producer, a director is assigned to the project, proposed casting is determined, and a budget is formulated. Development costs are relatively modest compared to the production itself but can be nevertheless substantial depending on the nature of the project. For example, an option on underlying literary material (a novel) can cost from $5,000 to $50,000 (although the option for a blockbuster novel may cost $100,000 to $250,000), the preparation of a screenplay from $50,000 to $250,000, the supervisory services of a director or producer from $10,000 to $50,000, plus miscellaneous costs for budgeting, travel and expenses, etc.

Investments in production. After the project has been developed, the screenplay is in finalized form, and the budget is approved, actual production occurs. The average cost of a studio feature motion picture today is $9.4 million, although low-budget pictures can cost from $500,000 to $2 million.

Investments in completed films. Investments in completed films take one or both of the following forms: copyright acquisition, which is the acquisition of the copyright on the completed motion picture after it has been produced; or a distribution expense fund, wherein, instead of or in addition to the copyright acquisition, an investor may advance funds to underwrite the distribution or marketing costs of a motion picture, such as prints and media advertising.

The types of investments referred to above may take the form of a single-picture investment or cover multiple pictures.

Investments in a publicly traded motion picture company. An investor also has the opportunity to make an equity or debt investment in an existing public company that produces and/or distributes motion pictures. Some of the companies are exclusively involved in the motion picture production business and distribution (MGM-UA), others are diversified entertainment entities (Warner Communications, Inc., Columbia Pictures, MCA), and Gulf & Western (which owns Paramount Pictures) is a major diversified conglomerate.

Structure of Investments

The investment in a development, production, or completed film deal can take several forms, depending upon the number and nature of the investors and the securities and tax aspects.

General partnership. The investor may elect to form a partnership with the producer.

Limited partnership. This is the most common form of motion picture investment, where the investor is a limited partner who does not participate in the management and control of the project. (See article on Real Estate Limited Partnerships, elsewhere in this volume, for a discussion of the legal and financial aspects of this method of investment and participation.)

Corporation. Except in the public company context, an investment in capital stock of a motion picture company is rarely used. In certain situations, the Subchapter S corporation may be employed, but this may pose special tax problems.

Types of Deals

In the prototypical motion picture investment (which is not unique to this industry), the money recoups first and money and talent each receive 50 percent of the profits. Therefore, the investor would recoup his investment, pro rata with the other investors, out of the first receipts [2] of the film; thereafter the investor would receive 50 percent of the profits, and the talent (producer, director, cast, etc.) would receive the remaining 50 percent of the profits. There are many variations on this theme, each with its own special characteristics.

ATTRACTIVE FEATURES

Disproportionate Return on Successful Projects

One of the major benefits of a motion picture investment is directly related to its greatest risk, namely, the highly speculative nature of the investment. The reward for a successful motion picture investment can be quite disproportionate to the investment. A motion picture, unlike a manufactured item, does not have a fixed production markup for each item sold and therefore, once its cost has been recouped, all income after marketing expenses is pure profit. It must be noted, of course, that the blockbuster picture is not commonplace, but an investor who chooses the right project (which may be more accidental than planned) will reap the reward of making back many times his investment. The blockbuster mentality that permeates the industry can be dangerous and misleading; one cannot predict which film will be the next *Star Wars.*

Tax Benefits

Depending on the structure of the investment, such tax benefits as the investment tax credit and depreciation deductions are available. These and other deductions may result in leveraged write-offs and considerable tax-shelter benefits.

Intangible Benefits

There is a certain psychological benefit associated with motion picture investment. The glamour of being associated with a film production certainly has intangible rewards irrespective of its economic benefits.

---

[2] It should be noted that first receipts are not box-office receipts or even film rental. It customarily means the first receipts received by the production entity from a third-party distributor, after deduction by the distributor of distribution fees and expenses.

Modest Fixed Costs

Unlike other investments, the motion picture industry requires no significant investment in plant or equipment. It is basically a service business. Personnel can be hired on a project basis and a film can be marketed through existing distribution organizations.

Sequential Marketing

A motion picture has the potential of generating significant revenues long after its initial release by way of reissues, remakes, sequels, and exploitation in new markets.

Contra-Cyclical Nature of the Business

There are many indications that the motion picture industry is contracyclical and may even prosper during periods of economic recession. For example, in 1974 and 1975, the poorest years for the economy since the 1940s due to the Arab oil embargo, movie attendance rose 17 percent. In contrast, in 1976, a boom year for the economy, box-office receipts declined nearly 4 percent. However, the decline in attendance (by 9 percent) in 1980 runs counter to this theory.

Rapid Return on Investment

The theatrical release of a film takes a small amount of time (three to nine months); thereafter, if the film is successful, the return on capital can be accomplished quite quickly. This is especially likely in a completed film acquisition; development and production deals involve a period of time when the investment funds are not producing revenues.

POTENTIAL RISKS

The film business, perceived by the public as glamorous, exciting, and lucrative, must be viewed by the investor as a business and as such must be considered highly speculative. There are greater chances for substantial losses than for meteoric profits.

High Production and Marketing Costs

The cost of producing a motion picture has increased substantially due to such factors as inflation, high union payments, higher talent payments, and higher media costs. Accordingly, the revenues that must be generated to break even become even greater. The average cost of a studio film was $5.5 million in 1978, jumped to $8.5 million in 1979, and was $9.4 million in 1980. The average cost of a studio film in 1981 is estimated at $10.5 million. Advertising costs are on the increase as well, increasing 20 percent a year in recent years. In 1980, the average studio film required nearly $6.5 million of advertising for its domestic release.

Over-budget costs. There is the general risk of the production of a motion picture going over budget. One way of dealing with this risk is to ensure that there is a reputable completion bond (or guarantee) on the picture pursuant to which a third-party guarantor will cover over-budget costs. However, completion guarantors charge a premium equal to 6 percent of the budget, which can add significantly to the cost of the film.

Project Inadequacy

Producers can miscalculate the ability of any particular motion picture to attract audiences due to a lack of interest in the subject matter or a creative failure in execution. It is the nature of the motion picture business that with any film, even starting with an excellent screenplay and excellent talent, there is no assurance of the quality or commercial profitability of the end product. Furthermore, there is no assurance that the film will sufficiently meet public taste so that, at the time of release, it will be able to compete with rival films.

Maldistribution

Theatrical performance of motion pictures is dependent on the time at which they are released. If a film does not enjoy a good distribution window, it may fail at the box office despite its quality. The best times to release a film are in the summer, at Christmas, and at Easter; the best months, in descending order, are June, April, July, August, December, and May. Release is often timed to coincide with the school vacation periods, since 80 percent of the theatrical box office is represented by the 12-to-25 age group.

Lack of Salvage Value

As opposed to tangible assets, motion pictures are worth nothing if they are not shown. If the market does not respond to the product there is no residual or salvage value.

No Public Market

With the exception of the investment of public motion picture companies, there is seldom any public market for the investment in motion pictures.

Risk Reduction Strategy

The risks referred to above can be reduced in a number of ways: investing in more than a single film; making sure that distribution is guaranteed, preferably by a major distribution company; and investing in a completed motion picture rather than in a preproduction (development) deal or a production deal. Acquisition of films in preproduction stages involves significantly greater risks because production can be delayed or abandoned due to labor disputes, death or disability of a cast member, or budget overruns.

TAX CONSEQUENCES

The following discussion is limited to a general overview of a complex subject: the tax consequences of motion picture limited partnerships, which is the customary form used in motion picture investments. Investments in the capital stock of motion picture public companies offer no special tax features.

At-Risk Limitation

Section 465 of the Internal Revenue Code limits taxpayers (other than corporations that are neither Subchapter S corporations, personal holding companies, nor certain closely held corporations) engaged in any activity (with certain exceptions not relevant here) from deducting in any taxable year losses in excess of the amount that the taxpayer is deemed to have at risk at the close of the year. In the case of a limited partnership, this at-risk limitation is applied at the partner rather than the partnership level. A partner will generally be considered at risk under Code Section 465(b) to the extent of (1) cash and adjusted basis of the property contributed; (2) amounts borrowed for use in the activity to the extent the partner is personally liable for its repayment; and (3) the fair market value of property (other than property used in the activity) pledged as security for the borrowed funds. A partner will not be deemed at risk with respect to amounts protected against loss through nonrecourse financing, guarantees, stop loss agreements, or similar arrangements, and amounts borrowed from any person who has an interest (other than as a creditor) in the activity or has a relationship to the partner specified in Section 267(b) of the Code.

The at-risk provisions limit the amount of the loss that may be deducted. This amount fluctuates depending upon the losses sustained, income earned but not distributed, cash distributions, and additional amounts placed at risk. As a result of the at-risk limitation, the limited partnership programs, which in the past offered highly leveraged write-offs resulting from nonrecourse debt, have been curtailed.

Deductible Expenses

In any limited partnership offering, the deductible nature of certain expenses must be scrutinized. This may include the following expenses:

General partner fees. Under Code Section 707(a), payments made by the partnership to the general partner for services rendered or capital furnished may be deductible by the partnership if they are made to the general partner other than in his capacity as a partner, but only if they are reasonable in amount and are ordinary and necessary in trade or business expenses under Code Section 162(a).

Organization and syndication expenses. Under Code Section 709(b), expenses paid or incurred in connection with the organization of a partnership must be capitalized and amortized at the election of the partnership over a period of not less than sixty months. Syndication expenses, on the other hand, may not be deducted currently or amortized.

Depreciation

The customary method for depreciating motion pictures is the income forecast method, under which depreciation is computed by multiplying the capitalized cost of the film by a fraction, the numerator of which is the receipts of the film for the applicable taxable year and the denominator of which is the estimated total receipts of the film over its useful life. Under the Economic Recovery Tax Act of 1981, depreciation of motion pictures can be based on the income forecast method or, assuming that films are categorized as tangible property (a position that the IRS has historically opposed), on a five-year basis. In the latter case, the depreciation for the first year would be 15 percent of the basis of the film (regardless of whether the film was placed in service on the first day or last day of the year), for the second year, 22 percent, and for the last three years, 21 percent. Under the 1981 tax law, the taxpayer could also elect to use straight-line depreciation over either twelve or twenty-five years.

Advertising and Print Costs

Expenditures for advertising are deductible as ordinary and necessary business expenses under Code Section 162, even though such expenditures produce benefits extending beyond the taxable year, if such expenditures do not create or enhance a distinct asset or property interest of the taxpayer. There may be two problems with the deductibility of the expenses for the partnership. First, if the partnership pays these expenses to a distributor who in turn pays the actual advertising invoices, there may be a problem of the timing of the deductions. Second, the IRS, under Section 195, may argue that advertising costs constitute preopening expenses of a new business as distinguished from deductible ordinary and necessary expenses of carrying on an existing business and, therefore, they must be capitalized and amortized. Finally, the IRS may argue that the deductibility of advertising costs in the year paid constitutes a distortion of income and, as a result, under Section 446(b) of the Code, may be deducted only as recouped from income produced by the film.

Film prints, on the other hand, must be capitalized and amortized, but the period over which the prints are amortized may be questioned. The IRS may argue that print costs will only be deducted on an income forecast basis under Section 280 of the Code.

Investment Tax Credit

Section 48(k) of the Code sets forth rules governing the availability of the investment tax credit for motion pictures. A credit is allowable only if the film is new property that is a qualified film and only to the extent the taxpayer has an ownership interest in the film. A "qualified film" is defined by the Code as "any motion picture film or video tape created primarily for use as public entertainment or for educational purposes," but "does not include any film or tape, the market of which is primarily topical or is otherwise essentially transitory in nature." A taxpayer's ownership interest is determined on the basis of his proportional share of any loss that may be incurred with respect to the production costs of such film. Code Section 48(k)(2) provides that, normally, the investment tax credit will be 6.67 percent of the qualified U.S. production costs (although the credit may be 10 percent under specified circumstances). "Qualified U.S. production costs" are defined as "(1) direct production costs allocable to the United States and (2) that if 80 percent or more of the direct production costs is allocable to the United States, all other production costs other than direct production costs allocable outside the United States."

There may be two alternative methods available for calculating investment credits. First, the taxpayer can elect the so-called 90 percent method under Code Section 48(k)(3). Second, assuming a taxpayer is depreciating the film under the principles set forth in the 1981 tax legislation, he can claim investment credit based on the principles applicable to property generally covered by such legislation. In the case of either of these alternative methods, both the rules for calculating the amount of the credit and the rules regarding potential recapture of that credit are changed.

REPRESENTATIVE TYPES OF INVESTORS

Representative investors in the motion picture industry are customarily film industry laymen who have been successful in their own businesses. Some investors choose to bear the entire financial obligation, while others choose to group together, spreading the risk in limited partnerships.

IMPORTANT FACTORS IN BUYING

Motion picture limited partnership offerings fall into two distinct categories, those that are predominantly structured to maximize tax-shelter benefits and those that are basically equity deals emphasizing the return on investment with the tax benefits having secondary, if any, impact. Investors should carefully review the investment to make sure it is structured to meet their particular investment objectives. Investing in motion pictures is not for the faint of heart, and most motion picture investment opportunities are not penny stock situations. They require substantial minimal investments (usually in excess of $25,000 and often in minimum units of $150,000) and, as noted above, the risks are substantial.

In the case of limited partnership investments, it is important to analyze the prospectus or private placement memorandum carefully and to have the advice of a good accountant and attorney, as well as an industry consultant if possible. The motion picture industry is closely knit and is centered largely in one city: Los

Angeles. It is therefore possible to determine quickly the reliability and qualifications of the promoters and the filmmakers. Specific areas of concern should include the following:

Up-Front Commissions and Fees

Broker-dealers usually charge from 8 percent to 10 percent of the sales price as a commission. Promoters' fees and organizational fees should be carefully scrutinized, along with the percentage of the sales price that is allocated to the actual acquisition or production of the film and/or marketing distribution expenses.

Distribution Guarantee

Is distribution guaranteed and, if so, is it by a major distributor? One of the greatest disappointments, and one that occurs all too frequently, is for a film to be completed but go begging for a distributor.

Completion Guarantee

If it is a production deal, how has the producer provided for the completion of the film, and is there a reputable completion guarantor? In addition, is there any over-call right, whereby the general partner can require that the limited partners put up additional funds in the case of cost overruns? If there is no over-call right, how will cost overruns be satisfied, and is the general partner willing to step into the breach?

Investor Recoupment Position

Is the investor in first position with respect to the recoupment of his investment and what, if any, fees and other compensation are payable to the promoter-producer prior to recoupment?

Investor Profit Position

What share of the profits go to the investors? As noted earlier, investors customarily receive 50 percent of the profits of a motion picture.

Tax Opinions

Is there tax opinion from reputable counsel as to the tax effects of the transaction, and how heavily is the opinion qualified?

Projections

Are there economic projections? If so, who prepared them (the promoters or an outside accounting firm)? They should be carefully reviewed to make sure the assumptions underlying the projections are reliable.

Judging Film Quality

This is a most difficult factor in deciding upon a motion picture investment. Filmmaking is both an art and a business. Artistic achievement may not always result in economic reward; conversely, a mediocre film (from a critical point of view) can reap a veritable harvest at the box office. Decisions as to what film to make and how to make it are highly subjective, involving a collective process among various creative elements. It is difficult enough to determine, after a film has been made, whether the marketplace will give it a good reception. It is significantly more difficult to predict its success when it is still on the drawing board. Filmmaking has certain similarities to wildcatting in the oil business, and professional advisers are useful in trying to cope with the decision as to whether or not a project makes sense. As with any investment, a key factor is the proven track record of the producer and his creative team.

Selecting a Broker or Dealer

Several of the motion picture private placements are marketed through major investment houses. Merrill Lynch; Kidder Peabody; Bache Halsey Stuart; A.G. Becker; Drexel Burnham Lambert; and E.F. Hutton, to name a few, have been involved in recent offerings. Other investments are marketed without the use of broker-dealers by the producer alone.

MANAGING THE INVESTMENT

Motion picture investors seldom manage their own investments, and therefore careful evaluation of the film professionals involved is essential. The fees paid to the producer and promoter should be evaluated to make sure they are consistent with these individuals' prior deals as well as competitive within the industry. Again, a professional consultant is advisable in such matters. In a production deal, investors will rely exclusively on the producer to ensure that the picture is made within the budget and in accordance with the screenplay, and to see that it is properly exploited and marketed. Those entrusted with the management of the investment should be experienced, and an investor should carefully check out the producer's track record as well as the past performance of the promoters.

GLOSSARY

break-even rule— The rule of thumb that a film must generate gross film rentals equivalent to three to four times its production costs.

completed film investment— The outlay required for acquiring copyright to a produced film and/or distribution and marketing expenses.

development investments— The funds required to cover literary acquisition and other preproduction costs up to the beginning of production.

film rental— The share of box-office receipts paid by the theater owner to the distributor.

general partnership— Form of organization in which the investor forms a partnership with the producer.

independent production company— A company that raises funds independently of the studio. Typically, it negotiates distribution terms on a more favorable basis than if the studio financed the picture.

limited partnership— The arrangement whereby the investor (limited partner) participates in profits but not in management or control of the project.

negative cost— All costs incurred in producing a motion picture project up to the point of distribution.

production investment— An investment in the cost of producing a motion picture as it is being made.

studio— The integrated production-distribution-exhibition company dominated the film industry until the 1950's; today it distributes the motion pictures it finances or those financed by independent producers.

subsidiary rights— Ancillary film rights such as theatrical sequels, T.V. series rights, publishing rights, recording rights, and merchandising rights, etc.

television syndication— The market of local non-network T.V. stations and all foreign stations.

SUGGESTED READING

Periodicals

Boxoffice. Published by Associated Publications, Inc., Kansas City, Mo. Weekly.

The Hollywood Reporter. Published by H.R. Industries, Los Angeles, Cal. Daily.

The Independent Film Journal. Published by Robert Sunshine, New York, N.Y. Monthly.

Variety. Published by Syd Silverman, Los Angeles, Cal. Daily.

Variety. Published by Syd Silverman, New York, N.Y. Weekly.

Reference Books

Baumgarten, Paul A., and Farber, Donald C. *Producing, Financing and Distributing Film.* New York: Drama Book Specialists, 1973.

Blivan, William A., and Squire, Jason E., eds. *The Movie Business: American Film Industry Practice.* New York: Hastings House, 1972.

Kopple, Robert C., and Stiglitz, Bruce M. *Taxation of the Motion Picture Industry.* Washington, D.C.: Tax Management, 1978.

Motion Picture Almanac. New York: Quigley Publishing Co. Annual.

Television Almanac. New York: Quigley Publishing Co. Annual.

Municipal Securities

Burtt R. Ehrlich and Douglas R. Albert *

BASIC CHARACTERISTICS

Not all bonds are created equal. The debt obligations of corporate entities and the federal government are different from those of state and local governments in one very important way: Interest income earned on corporate and federal bonds is taxable, while interest on municipal securities is exempt from all federal income taxes and, frequently, from state and local taxes levied within the state of issuance. The judicial precedent that granted federal income tax exemption dates back to 1803 and the U.S. Supreme Court case of *Marbury v. Madison.* Subsequent court rulings reinforced the legitimacy of tax exemption in a series of cases that upheld the principle of reciprocal immunity. The extent to which the federal government is prevented from interfering in the affairs of state governments has been tested in the courts and found to include the areas of taxation.

The allure of tax-free income is clear from the perspective of the investor, but this feature also conveys enormous benefits to the issuer. When they turn to the capital markets to raise funds, municipal governments have a distinct advantage over corporate debt issuers: Tax exemption enables municipal borrowers to issue securities at interest rates substantially lower than those on comparable taxable bonds. Tax exemption, therefore, serves as a type of subsidy to state and local governments. In providing an increasing amount of goods and services to an expanding population, the municipal securities market has experienced dramatic growth since the imposition of the federal income tax in 1913. In that year, state and local borrowings were only $5.5 billion. By 1981, the value of municipal government bonds outstanding was in excess of $356 billion.

Municipal securities provide funding for the diverse financial needs of state and local governments and their agencies. These securities, like corporate bonds, are fixed income debt obligations. Their maturities vary depending upon the underlying capital requirement of the issuer.

Description and Composition of Municipal Borrowings

Municipal notes, which may have maturities ranging from one month to three years but generally mature in one year, are used for construction-lending and cash-flow purposes. Municipal bonds, in contrast, have maturities ranging from one year to thirty years, and serve to finance long-term capital projects.

* Burtt R. Ehrlich and Douglas R. Albert are President and Associate Municipal Note Trader, respectively, at Ehrlich-Bober & Co., Inc., New York.

Similar to long-term corporate obligations, municipal bonds return to the investor a stream of semiannual interest payments (coupons) and a repayment of principal in the full face amount of the issue upon maturity. Municipal notes, however, are generally redeemed in one of two ways: Interest-bearing notes return the principal plus an interest payment at maturity, while discount notes carry an implicit interest payment since they sell below par and are redeemed at face value. The use of discount notes has declined substantially in recent years. Municipal notes with maturities beyond one year usually provide coupon payments similar to those associated with municipal bonds.

The financing needs of state and local governments and their agencies expanded enormously during the 1970s. This growth may be attributed to both the enormous number of housing projects that municipal governments sought to finance and the increased costs incurred in developing such projects as nuclear power plants. In 1972 municipal borrowings were $49 billion but had expanded to over $85 billion by 1981. Over this period, new issues increased at a total rate of 52.9 percent. It should be remembered, however, that the economy was beset with high rates of inflation throughout the 1970s. This was an important force in driving up the size and cost of municipal borrowings.

The composition of municipal borrowings also changed dramatically during the 1970s. Construction projects increasingly came to be financed through short-term note issues. In 1966, for instance, new municipal notes totaled only $6.5 billion. By 1981, they had grown to over $37 billion. Within the area of long-term financings, revenue bonds — used to finance a specific facility and repaid from revenues subsequently earned by that facility — grew at a faster rate than general obligation bonds. The fact that revenue bonds may be issued without having to pass a voter referendum accounts for their increased use. Representing 38.4 percent of new bonds issued in 1972, revenue bonds expanded to 74 percent of new long-term financings by 1981. In contrast to the nearly $40 billion in new corporate debt issues in 1980, the value of new securities issued by municipal borrowers approximated $85 billion. Figure 1 on page 483 illustrates the relative growth of general obligation and revenue bonds throughout the 1970s.

Types of Municipal Securities

In addition to being classified with respect to their maturities, municipal securities may be further characterized by the purpose for which they have been issued and by the sources of income that provide for their repayment.

General obligation securities. These are backed by the full faith, credit, and taxing powers of the municipal borrower. In a sense, they may be considered senior municipal debentures because they place a lien on municipal revenues. That is, general obligations securities attach a legal claim to the unencumbered revenues received by a municipal government. These typically include tax receipts plus federal and state aid. General obligation notes fulfill short-term borrowing needs of state and local governments, while general obligation bonds raise funds

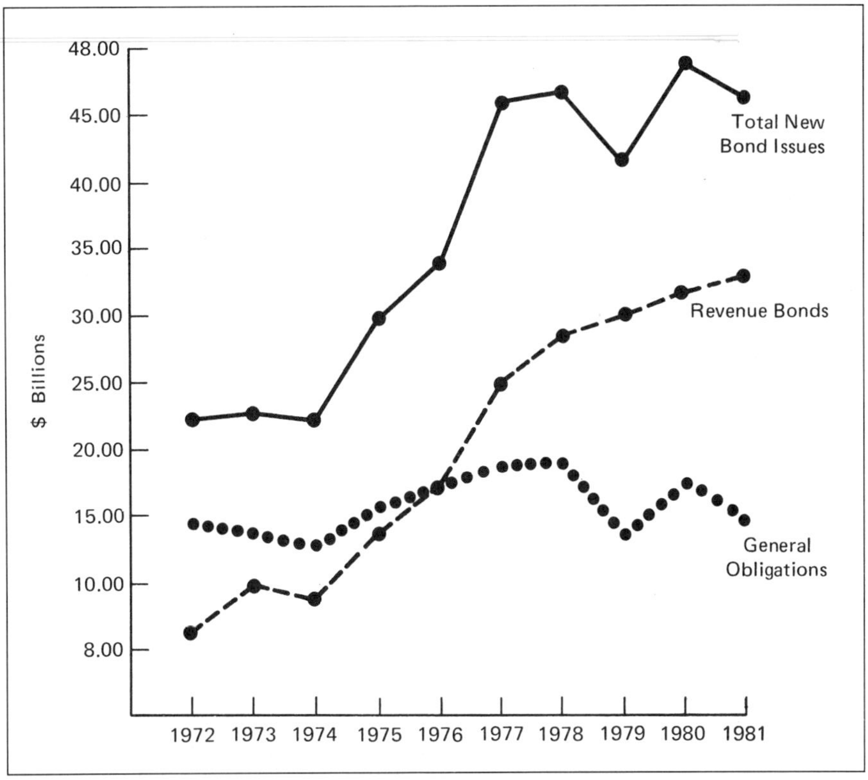

FIG. 1. New Bond Issues 1972–1980 — Revenue vs. General Obligation Bonds

SOURCE: Adapted from *The Bond Buyer's 1980 Municipal Finance Statistics,* "A Decade of Municipal Financing," and Public Securities Association: *1981 Statistical Yearbook of Municipal Financing*

for municipal capital improvements. Facilities built with these long-term issues serve the entire community, and include schools, municipal buildings, streets, and highways.

Municipal revenues raised through tax levies differ, between state and local governments, as to sources. State governments generally call on sales and income taxes for the repayment of borrowed funds. Local governments rely primarily on property tax receipts to meet interest and principal payments. General obligations of local governments, therefore, tend to assume price and risk characteristics that reflect the value of property and the municipalities' ability to levy property taxes. Securities issued by communities that experience rising property values, for instance, are deemed less risky than are those issued by communities in which property values remain constant or are declining. Similarly, securities issued by municipalities with limited taxing powers are perceived by investors to be less marketable than are issues of a municipality that possesses greater taxing flexibility.

Importance of taxing powers. How a municipality's taxing powers may affect the security of its issues is best exemplified by the recent taxpayer revolts in both California and Massachusetts. One of the effects of the 1978 passage of Proposition 13 in California, which put a ceiling of one percent of fully assessed property values on property taxes, was a significant reduction in the general obligation borrowings of local governments in that state. In November 1980, the voters of Massachusetts supported a measure to limit their property taxes by passing Proposition 2½. This limits the property tax that local governments may impose to 2.5 percent of fully assessed values.

The ramifications experienced in the market for the general obligations of cities and towns in Massachusetts were more serious than those for California municipalities after passage of Proposition 13. When the latter was approved, California enjoyed a budget surplus. The presence of these funds and their potential transferability to faltering municipalities placated investors who feared a loss of liquidity and marketability. Actually, Proposition 13 provided special measures that assured the repayment of outstanding issues. In Massachusetts, however, no such provisions were associated with Proposition 2½. As a result, no municipality in Massachusetts issued a general obligation bond in the last two months of 1980, and the yield levels on outstanding issues rose substantially, relative to the market, as their prices plunged.

As electorates throughout the nation confront the issue of limiting government's power in levying the property tax, it will become increasingly important to evaluate both the way local units finance their operations and the nature of the financial relationship that exists between a state and its local governments.

Revenue bonds. In contrast to general obligations, revenue bonds provide funding for the construction of specific municipal projects. For instance, toll-roads, bridges, and water and sewer projects are among the facilities that municipal governments would finance through a revenue bond. These projects attempt to tax only the component of the general public that uses the facility. Revenue bond borrowings are repaid from the income (user fees) generated by these facilities. Because revenue bonds are not included in the general indebtedness of a municipality, they have provided state and local governments with a powerful instrument with which to raise funds. In 1981, of the $48 billion in new long-term bond issues that came to market, almost 74 percent were revenue bonds. (See Figure 1 on page 483.) In 1969, revenue bonds accounted for less than 25 percent of new municipal issues. If traditional sources of tax revenues become uncertain, the use of revenue bonds can be expected to play an even larger role in municipal financings.

Revenue bond issues include several distinct types of borrowings that should be differentiated by the intended use of the funds.

Housing revenue bonds. These bonds are generally issued by a housing agency created by a state or local government to finance the construction of single-family or multi-family residential units. The proceeds raised by the bond issue may be loaned to a developer or directly to a home buyer. It is not uncommon for the housing agency to turn over the funds to a lending institution for administration of the project.

Public utility bonds. These bonds serve to finance the building of sewer and water projects as well as public power facilities. How these services are delivered to the public varies by how much the public utility participates in the ownership of its facility. Hence, different systems assume different risk characteristics and each issue must be analyzed carefully. In general, the bond proceeds are repaid from the fees charged to users of the system.

Hospital revenue bonds. Hospital revenue bonds fund construction of new hospitals and renovations in existing ones. They are sometimes used to purchase expensive hospital equipment. In general, they are repaid from hospital revenues.

Industrial development bonds. Industrial development bonds are a class of revenue bonds issued to finance construction of such projects as factories, sports stadiums, and industrial parks. Once construction is completed on behalf of the government unit, the facility is leased to a private corporation, whose lease payments provide the revenue to repay the borrowed funds. Generally, the tax-exempt status of interest on municipal securities benefits the investor and the issuing state or local government. Here, the benefit that normally accrues to the issuer in effect is transferred to a private corporation. Pollution control revenue bonds, for example, are a type of industrial development bond through which environmental equipment is purchased by the government unit and leased to a corporation. Since the lease payments provide the security on these bonds, the corporate entity represents the underlying credit risk.

Hybrid bonds. Hybrid bonds combine characteristics of both general obligation bonds and revenue bonds. For instance, a revenue bond may be issued to finance the construction of a new state highway. The primary revenue source that secures the issue is the income earned through the collection of user tolls. The bond may be further secured, however, by the proceeds raised through a fuel tax. These hybrid issues are also referred to as "double-barreled bonds." The purposes for which state and local governments issued bonds of all types through the decade of the 1970s are shown, relative to one another, in Table 1 on page 486.

Municipal notes. Essentially short-term financings, these notes are issued for cash-flow and construction-loan purposes. Frequently, state and local governments find themselves with a temporary cash shortage or deficit caused by timing differences in the expenditure and receipt of funds. For example, a city may need to purchase new fire-fighting equipment, but finds the money not readily available; officials may then decide to borrow the necessary funds through an issue of short-term municipal notes. The equipment is then purchased and the debt repaid from tax revenues received later in the year. Similarly, a local government may wish to begin the construction of a parking facility at a heavily congested

TABLE 1. Relative Percentages of State and Municipal Bonds Sold, by Financing Purpose

	Est. 1981	*1980*	*1979*	*1978*	*1977*	*1976*	*1975*	*1974*	*1973*	*1972*	*1971*
School	10%	10.1%	11.7%	13.5%	11.4%	15.3%	15.2%	21.6%	21.0%	23.3%	23.5%
Water and sewer	6	7.5	8.8	9.7	9.9	9.7	8.4	9.3	10.0	12.3	14.8
Highway, bridge, and tunnel	7	2.4	2.2	4.1	3.0	4.6	3.7	4.3	6.3	9.1	11.2
Gas and electric	13	10.3	11.2	13.0	12.8	13.2	7.4	6.7	6.8	—	—
Hospital	11	7.5	8.3	6.8	10.5	8.1	6.7	5.7	—	—	—
State and municipal housing finance	12	30.3	28.5	—	—	—	—	—	—	—	—
Industrial	7	3.2	3.2	1.3	1.0	1.1	1.8	1.5	1.1	2.1	0.9
Pollution control	10	6.2	6.8	7.5	8.6	7.9	8.6	9.5	9.1	—	—
Public housing authority	—	—	—	—	—	—	—	2.0	4.5	4.2	4.1
Other	24	22.5	19.3	44.1	42.8	40.1	48.2	39.4	41.2	49.0	45.5
Total	100.0%	100.0%	100.0%	100.0%	100.0%	100.0%	100.0%	100.0%	100.0%	100.0%	100.0%

SOURCE: Adapted from *The Bond Buyer's 1980 Municipal Finance Statistics*, "A Decade of Municipal Financing" and Public Securities Association: *1981 Statistical Yearbook of Municipal Financing*

railroad station. The project may be started by issuing a note to raise construction funds. The local government anticipates repayment of the note with proceeds from a later bond sale that ultimately will provide long-term funding for the project.

Although these short-term issues are usually redeemed at maturity, it is not uncommon for them to be rolled over in a manner similar to that used by the U.S. Treasury in refinancing its outstanding debt. However, while the Treasury may refinance its debt continuously, there are mandatory redemption periods for municipal issues. The number of times a municipal government may roll over its debt varies from state to state; usually the limit is a time period of, at most, seven years.

There are four basic types of municipal notes, with many common features.

Bond anticipation notes (BANs). These notes provide interim financing for projects that ultimately are to be funded with a long-term bond. Because the notes are paid down from proceeds of the bond issue, they often may be secured only by the municipality's long-term borrowing capability. In many communities, therefore, BANs are also a general obligation, secured on a parity with outstanding general obligation bonds.

Tax anticipation notes (TANs). These notes are general obligations of the community, utilized to fulfill interim financing needs, and are secured by projected tax receipts plus any other unencumbered revenue of the community.

Revenue anticipation notes (RANs). These, too, are general obligation notes to fund current operations. They are paid down from municipal revenues other than taxes, especially federal and state aid.

Project notes. Housing authorities use these to provide construction funds for urban-renewal and redevelopment projects. They are secured by the full faith and credit of the federal government, and in fact are sold at bimonthly auctions conducted by the U.S. Department of Housing and Urban Development on behalf of local authorities. Because of their backing, these issues are equal in security to U.S. government notes, although they may not be as readily marketable.

ATTRACTIVE FEATURES

In general, investors are attracted to municipal securities for two basic reasons: tax-free interest income and relative safety of both principal and income. As with any fixed-income obligation, a decline in interest rates will increase the price of outstanding issues, and any capital gain that may be realized thereby is not exempt from federal and state capital gains taxes. An investor even may choose to hold municipals for potential capital gain; but if the intent is to defer earnings beyond the investor's peak income years, it probably would be wiser to purchase a long-dated maturity bond for its higher ultimate yield.

Tax-Free Income

The willingness of investors to supply funds to municipal governments is directly related to their respective income tax rates. The benefits of tax exemption increase for taxpayers in progressively higher tax brackets. Households and institutions that earn substantial taxable income, therefore, are the more prominent investors in municipal securities. Yields are proportionately less than pre-tax yields on comparable corporate securities, but this difference is almost entirely due to the tax-exempt feature of municipal securities. Table 2 on page 489 provides a comparison between yields on municipal securities and their equivalent taxable yields for various federal income tax brackets.

The yield that an investor in municipal securities can expect to earn over the life of the bond may be calculated in a number of ways, most commonly by the current yield and the yield to maturity.

Current yield. This approach offers a rough approximation of the more precise yield-to-maturity calculations. The current yield is simply the interest payment divided by the purchase price. For example, a bond bought at 80 ($800 per $1,000 face value) with a 7 percent annual coupon ($70 per year) would have a current yield of 8.75 percent; that is:

$$\frac{\$70}{\$800} = 8.75\%$$

Yield to maturity. A more sophisticated approach, the yield to maturity, adjusts the coupon payments for the timing of their receipt. That is, it allows for the fact that interest payments received earlier in the life of the bond are worth relatively more than identical payments received later. In the above example, if the issue were a ten-year bond, the investor would adjust the $70 annual interest payments according to when they will be received. The general formula:

$$P = \sum_{n=1}^{t} \left(\frac{C}{(1+k)^1} + \frac{C}{(1+k)^2} + \frac{C}{(1+k)^3} + \dots + \frac{C}{(1+k)^n} + \frac{R}{(1+k)^t} \right)$$

where:

P is the price of the bond
C is the annual coupon payment
k is the yield to maturity
R is the principal repayment amount
n is the number of periods to maturity
t is the number of periods to repayment

$$800 = \left(\frac{70}{(1+k)^1} + \frac{70}{(1+k)^2} + \frac{70}{(1+k)^3} + \dots + \frac{70}{(1+k)^9} + \frac{1000}{(1+k)^{10}} \right)$$

Therefore, k = 10.3 percent. Embodied within this yield-to-maturity formu-

TABLE 2. Tax Exempt/Taxable Yield Equivalents—1982 Tax Year

(Individual income brackets–thousands of dollars)

Single Return ($000)		**$18.2 to $23.5**		**$23.5 to $28.8**		**$28.8 to $34.1**	**$34.1 to $41.5**		**over $41.5**
Joint Return ($000)	**$24.6 to $29.9**		**$29.9 to $35.2**		**$35.2 to $45.8**		**$45.8 to $60.0**	**$60.0 to $85.6**	**over $85.6**
% Tax Bracket	**29%**	**31%**	**33%**	**35%**	**39%**	**40%**	**44%**	**49%**	**50%**
Tax Exempt Yields (%) 6.0	8.5	8.7	9.0	9.2	9.8	10.0	10.7	11.8	12.0
7.0	9.9	10.1	10.4	10.8	11.5	11.7	12.5	13.7	14.0
7.5	10.6	10.9	11.2	11.5	12.3	12.5	13.4	14.7	15.0
8.0	11.3	11.6	11.9	12.3	13.1	13.3	14.3	15.7	16.0
8.5	12.0	12.3	12.7	13.1	13.9	14.2	15.2	16.7	17.0
9.0	12.7	13.0	13.4	13.8	14.8	15.0	16.1	17.6	18.0
9.5	13.4	13.8	14.2	14.6	15.6	15.8	17.0	18.6	19.0
10.0	14.1	14.5	14.9	15.4	16.4	16.7	17.9	19.6	20.0
10.5	14.8	15.2	15.7	16.2	17.2	17.5	18.8	20.6	21.0
11.0	15.5	15.9	16.4	16.9	18.0	18.3	19.6	21.6	22.0
11.5	16.2	16.7	17.2	17.7	18.9	19.2	20.5	22.5	23.0
12.0	16.9	17.4	17.9	18.5	19.7	20.0	21.4	23.5	24.0
12.5	17.6	18.1	18.7	19.2	20.5	20.8	22.3	24.5	25.0
13.0	18.3	18.8	19.4	20.0	21.3	21.7	23.2	25.5	26.0
13.5	19.0	19.6	20.1	20.8	22.1	22.5	24.1	26.5	27.0
14.0	19.7	20.3	20.9	21.5	23.0	23.3	25.0	27.5	28.0
14.5	20.4	21.0	21.6	22.3	23.8	24.2	25.9	28.4	29.0
15.0	21.1	21.7	22.4	23.1	24.6	25.0	26.8	29.4	30.0
16.0	22.5	23.2	23.9	24.6	26.2	26.7	28.6	31.4	32.0

1982 Tax Year

lation, however, is the implicit assumption that coupon payments can be reinvested at the coupon rate.

Relative Safety

Municipal security offerings are being protected essentially by the viability of a taxpayer-supported public body. To bolster this relative safety, each new issue is accompanied by documentation that attests to the validity of the liability of the issuing entity, explains the specific features of the issue and the intended use of the borrowed funds, provides financial information relating to the economic health of the issuer, and, most importantly, sets forth the terms of the loan and the schedule of repayments. This information is offered in detail within the Official Statement. Representative samples of the title pages of two different official statements are shown in Figures 2 and 3 on pages 491 and 492, respectively.

Much of the salient information an investor must know before purchasing the security can be acquired by reading the title page. At the top appears confirmation that the issue is exempt from federal income taxes (and, in these cases, state and city income taxes as well). The size of the issue is prominently displayed above the name of the borrowing authority, or issuer. Beneath the issuer's name is a brief description of the type of security. The New York City issue is a general obligation bond while the New York State issue is a tax-and-revenue anticipation note (TRAN). As general obligation securities, both issues are secured by all unencumbered revenues of the respective borrowers.

Both underwritings were conducted by a group of municipal dealers and banks (the syndicate), the names of which appear at the bottom of the page. Typically, in offers the size of these, not all syndicate participants will be named on the title page; rather, just those of the manager and co-managers will appear. The relative share of the issue allocated to each participant is indicated by its positioning, in descending order. Anyone interested in purchasing these issues could have contacted any of the designated firms.

Repayment schedule. Each security began to accrue as of the stated delivery date: May 28, 1981 for the state notes and April 15, 1981 for the city bonds. The amounts due on specific dates (maturities) were to be paid at stipulated rates of interest, and each issue was priced to the investor to provide the yields prescribed. All of this information is presented in the repayment schedule. Beneath the repayment schedule is further information pertaining to the legal firm that served as bond counsel and confirmation that the loans are legal liabilities of the issuing entities.

There are two types of repayment schedules, conforming to the length of municipal financing involved. In one, the term issue, the debt obligation is retired at a single stated maturity. In the other and more common form, the serial issue, a portion of the outstanding issue is repaid annually or semiannually to final maturity.

Term issues. Term issues are usually associated with the retirement of revenue bond borrowings. Because the flow of income generated by revenue-producing facilities is subject to uncertainty, it is difficult to project the amount of borrowings that can be paid down from these revenues in future years. Consequently, revenue bonds typically provide a sinking fund into which revenues are placed for the ultimate repayment of the entire issue upon a single maturity.

Serial issues. Serial issues, on the other hand, usually connote general obligation bonds. This form of repayment was originally tailored to suit the needs of

NEW ISSUE

In the opinion of Bond Counsel, interest on the Bonds will be exempt under existing law from Federal income taxes and from New York State and New York City personal income taxes.

$75,000,000
The City of New York
General Obligation Bonds

Dated April 15, 1981 — Due October 15, as shown below

Principal is payable as set forth in the table below and interest is payable semi-annually, beginning October 15, 1981 and on each April 15 and October 15 thereafter. The Bonds will be issued as bearer bonds, with coupons attached, in the denomination of $5,000 each, or as fully registered bonds in the denomination of $5,000 each, or any integral multiple thereof, in either case fully interchangeable. The Bonds are subject to redemption prior to maturity as described herein. Principal of and interest on the Bonds are payable at Manufacturers Hanover Trust Company, Corporate Trust Division, 40 Wall Street, New York, New York, the Paying Agent.

Principal	Maturity	Interest Rate	Price	Principal	Maturity	Interest Rate	Price
$3,160,000	1982	7.90%	100%	$4,740,000	1992	10.90%	100%
3,160,000	1983	8.30	100	4,740,000	1993	11.10	100
3,160,000	1984	8.60	100	4,740,000	1994	11.20	100
3,160,000	1985	8.90	100	4,740,000	1995	11.30	100
3,160,000	1986	9.20	100	4,740,000	1996	11.40	100
3,160,000	1987	9.60	100	4,740,000	1997	11.40	100
3,160,000	1988	9.90	100	4,740,000	1998	11½	100
3,160,000	1989	10.20	100	4,740,000	1999	11½	100
3,160,000	1990	10½	100	4,740,000	2000	11½	100
3,900,000	1991	10¾	100				

(Interest accrued from April 15, 1981, if any, to be added.)

The Bonds are offered subject to prior sale, when, as and if issued by the City and accepted by the Underwriters, subject to the approval of the legality of the Bonds by Rogers & Wells, New York, New York, Bond Counsel to the City, and subject to certain other conditions. Certain legal matters in connection with the preparation of this Official Statement will be passed upon for the City by Lord, Day & Lord, New York, New York. Certain legal matters will be passed upon for the Underwriters by Brown, Wood, Ivey, Mitchell & Petty, New York, New York. It is expected that the Bonds will be available for delivery in New York, New York, on or about April 15, 1981.

Merrill Lynch White Weld Capital Markets Group
Merrill Lynch, Pierce, Fenner & Smith Incorporated

Goldman, Sachs & Co.

Bache Halsey Stuart Shields
Incorporated

Bank of America NT & SA

Bear, Stearns & Co.

Blyth Eastman Paine Webber
Incorporated

The Chase Manhattan Bank, N.A.

Chemical Bank

Continental Bank
Continental Illinois National Bank and Trust Company of Chicago

Ehrlich-Bober & Co., Inc.

First Chicago
The First National Bank of Chicago

E. F. Hutton & Company Inc.

Morgan Guaranty Trust Company of New York

L. F. Rothschild, Unterberg, Towbin

Salomon Brothers

Security Pacific National Bank

Shearson Loeb Rhoades Inc.

Smith Barney, Harris Upham & Co.
Incorporated

March 25, 1981

FIG. 2. Sample Title Page from Official Statement — Municipal

Rated: Moody's-MIG-1
(See "Rating")

NEW ISSUE | OFFICIAL STATEMENT

Interest on the Notes will be exempt from Federal, New York State and New York City personal income taxes under existing statutes, regulations and court decisions. See Exhibit I.

$3,050,000,000

STATE OF NEW YORK

1981 TAX AND REVENUE ANTICIPATION NOTES

The Notes will be in bearer form and, subject to availability, in the denominations of $5,000 and $500,000. Principal and interest will be payable on the date due at the principal corporate trust office of The Chase Manhattan Bank, N.A., New York, New York. The Notes will be dated May 28, 1981, and will not be subject to redemption prior to maturity. Notes of $500,000 denomination will be exchangeable for Notes of $5,000 denomination.

Amount	Due	Rate	Yield
$ 200,000,000	September 30, 1981	9.10%	8.00%
750,000,000	December 31, 1981	9.15	8.70
200,000,000	January 29, 1982	9.20	8.75
1,900,000,000	March 31, 1982	9.20	8.75

(Interest accrued from May 28, 1981 to be added.)

The Notes will be general obligations of the State of New York (the "State"), and the full faith and credit of the State will be pledged to their payment.

The Notes will be legal investments for State-chartered banks and trust companies, insurance companies, fiduciaries and investment companies and may be accepted by the State Comptroller, the State Superintendent of Insurance and the State Superintendent of Banks when the deposit of obligations is required by law.

The Notes will be offered when, as and if issued by the State and received by the underwriters and subject to the receipt of an opinion of the Attorney General of the State that the Notes are valid and binding obligations of the State. See Exhibit I. Certain legal matters will be passed upon for the underwriters by their counsel, Dewey, Ballantine, Bushby, Palmer & Wood. The Notes, in definitive form, will be available for delivery on or about May 28, 1981 in New York, New York.

Merrill Lynch White Weld Capital Markets Group
Merrill Lynch, Pierce, Fenner & Smith Incorporated

Citibank, N.A.

Salomon Brothers

The Chase Manhattan Bank, N.A.

Morgan Guaranty Trust Company of New York

Chemical Bank

Bank of America NT & SA

Bankers Trust Company

Continental Bank
(Continental Illinois National Bank and Trust Company of Chicago)

The First Boston Corporation

Manufacturers Hanover Trust Company

Goldman, Sachs & Co.

Ehrlich-Bober & Co., Inc.

State Bank of Albany

W. H. Morton & Co.
(Div. of American Express Co.)

Dated: May 20, 1981

FIG. 3. Sample Title Page from Official Statement — State

commercial banks, which prefer to receive step-wise repayments of their loans to municipal borrowers. The banks' reasons are to maintain liquidity and the flexibility to move into the commercial loan market and to match more easily the maturities of their assets and liabilities.

POTENTIAL RISKS

Given its constitutional rights to print and coin money, there is no fear that the federal government will default on its borrowings; U.S. Treasury securities therefore are accepted by investors as risk-free assets. The bonds and notes of state and local governments — with regard to their ability to meet interest payments and principal repayments — are generally considered to rank second only to Treasury obligations. What this means, of course, is that municipals cannot be regarded as absolutely risk-free. The risk factors fall, essentially, into three categories: erosion of principal value, potential for default, and regulatory pitfalls. (It should also be noted that there may be market limitations for a particular issue, as described in *Important Factors in Buying and Selling* in this article.)

Erosion of Principal Value

The risk of erosion in principal value is not unique to municipal securities. Rather, it is common to all fixed-income debt obligations. Although municipalities are extremely unlikely to suffer the debacle of bankruptcy, to which any corporate security is exposed, they are not inflation-proof. They cannot protect against the potential depreciation of principal value caused by unanticipated increases in interest rates.

Risk of Default

Municipal securities that either fail to make interest and principal payments or delay these payments are considered to be in default. This situation might arise for a number of reasons. Actual collection of tax receipts may be significantly lower than had been anticipated, or underlying income-generating facilities might not produce the projected revenues. Though both extensive and relatively safe, the income sources of municipal governments are associated with some degree of risk and uncertainty.

It follows that the ability to meet debt-repayment schedules without undue strain varies widely among municipal borrowers. However, for an individual investor to become familiar with the financial, demographic, and managerial strengths of all issuing entities would present an impossible task. Consequently, rating agencies such as Moody's and Standard & Poor's are engaged by the state or municipality or by the public borrowing authority to grade their creditworthiness. (Fitch's Investor Service is a smaller rating agency specializing in the area of hospital issues.) By carefully evaluating a community's strength according to a number of different factors, the rating agencies convey to investors a sense of the municipality's ability to meet interest and principal payments (i.e., how much risk is present) and, in so doing, markedly affect the rate of interest that that community must offer investors in order to market its debt.

Rating general obligations. The rating agency begins its analysis by examining the sources of funds from which debt issues can be repaid. Thus, with regard to general obligation securities, a thorough understanding of the strength of the issuer's tax base is developed and a forecast made of how it may change over time. The agency further evaluates the community and its economic assets. A highly diversified economy is preferable to one in which local employment is concentrated in a single major corporation or industry or in relatively few businesses. The community in which population is stable or growing steadily is stronger than one in which population is declining. The proportion of working-age residents to those under 18 and over 65 is another vital determinant. The current debt and potential debt capacity of the community are important considerations in judging the ability both to service outstanding debt and to take on additional obligations. Finally, the rating agency interviews municipal leaders personally and reviews their track record in order to evaluate managerial effectiveness and their general competence as financial controllers.

Rating revenue bonds. Analysis of the quality of revenue bonds is similar to that for general obligations; but, of course, the income sources that underlie revenue bonds require specific cash-flow evaluation. Both major rating agencies employ analysts with expertise in particular project-financing areas, to facilitate evaluation and maintain continuity from one issue to the next. As with general obligations, credit risk is graded according to historical economic performance, the ability to control finances and collect revenues, and the borrowing entity's managerial competence. Table 3 on page 495 provides a description of the ratings assigned to municipal bonds by Standard & Poor's (S&P) and Moody's. Table 4 on page 496 describes the ratings assigned to municipal notes by Moody's.

Insurance protection. A recent market innovation is the insurance-backed municipal bond. The Municipal Bond Insurance Association and the American Municipal Bond Assurance Company will insure the interest and principal payments on tax-exempt issues. Although Moody's continues to rate variously the credit risk of the issuing entity, Standard & Poor's gives bonds that carry this insurance feature an automatic AAA, presuming that the issue would have achieved at least a BBB on its own standing. From the perspective of the municipal borrower, the decision regarding insurance comes down to whether the reduction in interest costs, arising from the enhanced credit rating, will exceed the cost premiums on the insurance itself.

Legal recourse. To assure that a municipal security represents a legal and binding liability of the issuer, all new issues must be verified with regard to the

TABLE 3. Municipal Bond Ratings

Description of Ratings	*S & P*[1]	*Moody's*[2]
Capacity to pay interest and repay principal is extremely strong.	AAA	Aaa
Very strong capacity to pay interest and repay principal and differ from highest-rated issue only to a small degree.	AA	Aa
Strong capacity to pay interest and repay principal, although they are somewhat more susceptible to the adverse effects of changes in circumstances and economic conditions than bonds in higher-rated categories.	A	A
Adequate capacity to pay interest and repay principal; while they normally exhibit adequate protection parameters, adverse economic conditions or changing circumstances are more likely to lead a weakened capacity to pay interest and repay principal for bonds in this category than for bonds in higher-rated categories.	BBB	Baa
Ability to pay interest and repay principal deemed speculative.	BB	Ba
Speculative in nature—low grade.	B	B
More speculative than higher-rated bonds—poor grade.	CCC	Caa
Highest speculative grade.	CC	Ca
Lowest-rated class of bonds. May be paying no interest or extremely poor prospect of reaching investment status.	C	C

[1] Standard & Poor's may add a plus (+) or minus (−) on grades AA through BB to indicate relative strength within these categories.

[2] Moody's adds the number one (1) to the grades A and Baa to indicate greater strength within these categories.

SOURCE: Moody's Investor Service and Standard & Poor's Corporation

TABLE 4. Municipal Note Ratings

Description of Rating	*Moody's Grade*
Loans bearing this designation are of the best quality, enjoying strong protection from established cash flows of funds for their servicing or from established and broad-based access to the market for refinancing, or both.	MIG 1
Loans bearing this designation are of high quality with margins of protection ample though not as large as in the preceding group.	MIG 2
Loans bearing this designation are of favorable quality, with all security elements accounted for but lacking the undeniable strength of the preceding grades. Market access for refinancing, in particular, is likely to be less well established.	MIG 3
Loans bearing this designation are of adequate quality, carrying specific risk but having protection commonly regarded as required of an investment security and not distinctly or predominantly speculative.	MIG 4

SOURCE: Moody's Investor Service

legality of the debt obligations and the tax-exempt status affecting interest payments. This practice grew out of the general panic of the 1870s and the number of municipal issues that did default during that period. Investors found that they had no legal recourse. To restore investor faith in these obligations, municipalities thereafter engaged legal counsel to attest to the validity of the claim on municipal revenues. As municipal securities proliferated through the 1960s and 1970s, the responsibilities of legal counsel expanded. Today, the legal opinion is rendered by an outside bond counsel — usually a legal firm specializing in this area — and must accompany all issues when delivered to investors.

Pitfalls of Regulation

Historically, the federal government has been reluctant to assume regulatory authority over the municipal securities industry. In adhering to the concept of reciprocal immunity, the separation of state and federal powers had, until 1975, provided the industry with virtual freedom from the SEC. The Securities Act of 1933 and the Securities Exchange Act of 1934 were primarily concerned with bringing order and integrity to the markets in which flagrant abuses appeared to be rampant. Although a number of municipal securities did go into default during the Depression, the SEC considered the borrowings of state and local governments to be rather small and, in general, relatively free from default risk.

Self-regulatory limits. In the early 1970s, however, the sale of municipal securities in both Florida and Tennessee were marred by accusations of unethical behavior on the part of certain broker-dealer firms. Then in 1975, New York City's temporary default on some maturing notes prompted an evaluation of the regulatory environment surrounding the entire municipal securities industry. Following congressional review, in 1975 the SEC set up the Municipal Securities Rulemaking Board (MSRB). Acting as a self-regulating authority composed of representatives from broker-dealer firms, banks, and the public, the MSRB was charged with setting forth administrative, definitional, and general procedural rules for the industry.

The MSRB remains an independent body, requiring only SEC approval of its membership, and specifies areas of mandatory rulemaking. The areas to which its regulatory authority extend include monitoring underwriter and dealer registration fees, defining market participants, and promulgating rules for such procedures as recordkeeping and clearing. But, whereas underwriters and broker-dealer firms must register corporate new-issue securities with the SEC before bringing them to market, municipal securities do not have to be registered. The issuance of municipals, accordingly, is far less regulated than the marketing of corporates.

Accounting practices. With regard to state and local government financial reporting, neither the SEC nor the MSRB may authorize or enforce supervisory review, disclosure procedures, or standard accounting practices. However, without uniform reporting requirements, the users of municipal financial information have not been well-served. To accommodate them, private organizations (e.g., the American Institute of Certified Public Accountants and the National Committee on Government Accounting) are working with municipal governments, broker-dealer firms, and investor groups to develop a uniform accounting system for state and municipal reports.

TAX CONSEQUENCES

Income Tax Exemption

The most important characteristic of municipal securities to the investor is their special tax feature, specifically, exemption of interest payments from federal income taxes. That benefit increases with higher tax brackets. For instance, a 9 percent tax-exempt yield to the investor in a 32 percent marginal tax bracket is equivalent to a 13.24 percent yield on a taxable issue. The same tax-exempt yield would be equivalent to an 18 percent taxable yield to an investor in the 50 percent bracket. In the inflationary 1970s, as wages and salaries increased, taxpayers were pushed into progressively higher brackets; inflation was described, indeed, as a hidden tax on real income. Growth in the demand for municipal securities over this period is attributable largely to the phenomenon of bracket creep.

The IRS, however, disallows interest deductions on money that is borrowed by individual investors expressly for purchasing tax-exempts. If this were not the case, a double tax benefit would result. The taxpayer could deduct from the federal income taxes the interest expense on indebtedness while earning tax-free income. Similarly, the potential for corporations to use borrowings to purchase tax-exempts motivated the IRS to restrict to 2 percent the total value of assets invested in municipals for those corporations with debt on their balance sheet.

State and local taxes. Municipal securities are usually exempt from state and local taxes within the issuing state as well. But they are often subject to state taxes outside the state of issuance. The significance of the federal tax-exempt feature is greatest to the investor whose income from municipals is also exempt from all state and local taxes. (When determining the equivalent taxable yield for any municipal security, however, it must be borne in mind that state and local taxes constitute federal income tax deductions.)

Equivalent taxable yields. The mechanism most widely used to determine a municipal security's equivalent taxable yield is the following:

$$\frac{\text{Tax-Exempt Yield}}{1 - \text{Marginal Tax Bracket}} = \text{Equivalent Taxable Yield}$$

For example, to calculate the equivalent taxable yield on an 8 percent tax-exempt for the investor in a 50 percent marginal tax bracket:

$$\frac{8\%}{1 - .50} = \frac{8\%}{.50} = 16.0$$

Thus an 8 percent tax-free yield is equivalent to a 16 percent taxable yield. For representative equivalent taxable yields, see Table 2 on page 489.

Capital Gains Treatment

Any capital gain that accrues on municipal securities is not exempt from federal income taxes, with one exception. The gain realized on securities purchased in the secondary market at a discount, and held to maturity or sold at a profit before final redemption, is subject to all capital gains taxes. But the capital gains tax does not apply to securities originally issued at a discount; that discount is considered an implicit interest payment.

Similarly, a deductible capital loss is incurred if securities are sold below their purchase price. But the rule does not apply to issues purchased at a premium and held to maturity. Instead, the premium is amortized on a straight-line basis over the life of the bond, and at final maturity the amortized basis is equivalent to the principal repayment. For issues purchased at a premium and sold before maturity, a capital loss may be incurred if the sale price is less than the amortized basis. For example, a bond purchased at $1,100 with a twenty-year maturity would normally be amortized at $5 per year. At maturity, the basis would equal the principal repayment of $1,000. After ten years, the adjusted basis would be $1,050. If the issue is sold at $1,020 after ten years, a taxable loss of $30 would be sustained.

REPRESENTATIVE TYPES OF INVESTORS

Municipal securities hold the strongest attraction for individuals in relatively high income tax brackets, as well as for certain taxpaying institutions. Since pension funds pay no income taxes, they are not investors in the municipals market. Neither (because they are subject to low tax rates) are savings (thrift) institutions and life insurance companies among the substantial buyers of tax-exempts. The primary suppliers of funds to state and local government borrowers are the commercial banks, fire and casualty insurance companies, corporate treasuries, and high-bracket individual investors. Because these investment groups require significant and secure after-tax interest income, tax-exempt bonds and notes are usually favored for their portfolios.

Cyclical Patterns

Historically, the aggressiveness with which these groups have pursued municipal securities has been cyclical.

Commercial banks. When the demand for credit is strong, commercial banks tend to sell off parts of their municipal portfolios and channel these funds into the more profitable commercial loan market. In contrast, when loan demand is weak, these institutions are heavy lenders to the municipal market. In addition to commercial loans, there are alternative investments that banks consider that strongly influence their decision to hold municipal securities. In the early 1970s, for instance, through leasing, real estate, and other types of creative financings, banks found new ways to shelter their earnings. These were not very profitable times for commercial banks and these financing opportunities seemed to provide higher after-tax yields than municipal securities. By 1977, however, commercial banks had substantially rebuilt their portfolios of tax-exempts.

Fire and casualty insurers. When underwriting business is strong at the fire and casualty insurance companies, they are extremely active buyers in the municipal area. When business is slack and underwriting losses are anticipated, however, the expectation of narrow profits encourages these firms to enter the higher-yielding corporate market.

Growth of Individual Investors

Individuals assumed an increasingly active role in the municipal securities market throughout the 1970s. With nominal incomes rising rapidly throughout the decade, households sought to reduce their overall taxable incomes by investing heavily in municipals. By 1981, they held 24 percent of outstanding municipal securities. In that year, commercial banks held 42 percent of all outstanding issues and fire and casualty insurance companies held 26 percent. The remaining 8 percent of outstanding issues was held by other financial intermediaries and non-financial corporate businesses. Table 5 below indicates the major holders of municipal securities and their relative importance.

IMPORTANT FACTORS IN BUYING AND SELLING

Primary Market

When a state or local government or agency must borrow funds, it turns to the capital markets. But rather than selling new issues directly to the ultimate holders of municipal securities, municipal borrowers typically engage the services of one or more financial institutions that act as a conduit through which private

TABLE 5. Relative Importance of Major Holders of State and Local Government Debt

	Commercial Banks	*Fire & Casualty Insurance Cos.*	*Individuals (Households)*	*All Others**
1981 (Est.)	42.0%	26.0%	24.0%	8.0%
1980	46.5	25.6	19.3	8.6
1979	44.4	24.7	21.8	9.1
1978	43.3	21.4	25.7	9.6
1977	43.5	18.8	27.9	9.8
1976	44.3	16.2	29.5	10.0
1975	46.0	14.9	30.4	8.7
1974	48.7	14.8	29.8	6.7
1973	50.0	14.9	28.1	7.0
1972	51.0	14.0	27.4	7.6
1971	51.0	12.6	28.4	8.0

*Includes: Non-financial corporations, mutual savings banks, savings and loan associations, pension funds, life insurance companies, brokers and dealers.

SOURCE: *The Bond Buyer's 1980 Municipal Finance Statistics,* "A Decade of Municipal Financing" and Public Securities Association: *Fundamentals of Municipal Bonds*

funds are made available to the borrowing entity. The process that includes the functions of pricing and structuring the loan, and of selling the issue to the public, is referred to as underwriting. The source of funds for such new offerings is known as the primary market. Issues come into this market through either negotiated or competitive underwritings. Negotiated underwritings are usually more expensive than their competitively bid counterparts, but they require more work for the underwriter. In many states, municipal borrowers are instructed by law to conduct competitive underwritings for general obligation issues. Revenue bond issues, on the other hand, are usually sold on a negotiated basis. In 1981, of the $48 billion in new long-term bond offerings, 59 percent were conducted through negotiated underwritings.

Negotiated underwritings. These involve the selection of an underwriter or syndicate by the municipal borrower, and are common when the size of the issue is large and distribution capabilities important, or when a new type of security must be carefully explained to potential investors. Usually, the government unit will ask certain prospective underwriters to submit proposals. From an evaluation of both the cost of their plans and the managerial and distributive strength of the participating firms, a single underwriter or syndicate is chosen.

Competitive underwritings. Competitively bid offerings require prospective underwriters or syndicates to submit their proposals to the municipal borrower in a sealed envelope. Once the sealed bids are reviewed by the issuing entity, the bond is sold to the group that offers the lowest interest costs to the government unit.

General underwriting procedures. While the mechanics that precede the final bid proposal by an underwriting syndicate are often complicated, the procedure itself has become largely routine. Underwriters are made aware of municipal borrowing needs through solicitations for bid proposals, which appear in a variety of trade publications, most notably the *Daily Bond Buyer.* Frequently, the municipality extends invitations to bid on an issue directly to municipal dealers. The larger municipal-dealer firms usually assume the responsibility of managing the syndicate and earn managing fees for their efforts. Depending upon the size of the issue, some deals may be co-managed by two or more dealers.

Generally, a manager tries to reassemble the same syndicate with which it has participated on previous issues. This patronage is extremely important, since a strong allegiance between the firms facilitates development of final bid proposals. Through a series of meetings conducted by the manager, the syndicate participants discuss the rate they intend to submit. Once the bid is in, the syndicate participants are bound by contract (the legal syndicate letter) to the provisions relating to the reoffering price and the percentage of the issue to be sold by each participant. Competing syndicates are ethically bound to develop their bids in the strictest privacy — with the reputation of each firm's name at stake.

Secondary Market

The buying and selling of older or seasoned issues, after completion of the underwriting and up until final maturity, is known as the secondary market. In this nationwide over-the-counter market, broker and dealer firms maintain close relationships with each other through telephone communication. Although most individual investors purchase and hold municipal notes until maturity, institutional portfolio managers tend to trade their longer maturities actively to capitalize on changes in interest rates and to time the realization of taxable gains and losses. As a result of this active trading — particularly in the larger and better-known municipals — the securities provide liquidity and marketability to a significant degree for their investors. *The Blue List,* a daily bulletin published by Standard & Poor's, lists those securities that dealer firms are willing to sell each day. On any given day, *The Blue List* will contain municipal bond offerings having a total par value of perhaps $1 billion, as well as industrial development bonds, obligations of some federal agencies, and municipal notes with a total par value exceeding $750 million.

Market limitations. Although the trading of municipals in the secondary market may be extensive, the activity in any particular issue may be quite small. As a result, unlike the price listings for corporate stocks and bonds, which appear in a variety of daily and weekly business publications, there are no comparable postings of municipal security prices. Investors in municipals will find that they must engage the services of a municipal securities dealer to obtain such ongoing price and yield information. But the great number of banks and dealer firms that underwrite and sell municipal securities demands investor caution. A dealer's strength in a number of areas should first be evaluated.

Choosing a dealer. To begin, the dealer should be capable of making a market in any security in which the investor is interested. This ability derives from a broad client base and a reputation position vis-à-vis the industry. The maintenance of a competitive market is an important consideration to any municipal securities buyer. Making competitive bids and maintaining spreads suggest that the dealer is extremely market-sensitive. In this way, the investor can be assured that liquidity and marketability are available for most municipal securities.

In addition, the investor should have confidence in a dealer's ability to understand thoroughly the credit risk represented by the issuing entity. (See *Potential Risks* in this article.) A municipality's rating from Moody's or Standard & Poor's should be augmented with independent analysis conducted by the dealer. Prior to New York City's default on a note issue of 1975, to illustrate, both rating agencies had given the city an A rating. If a dealer has reservations about the creditworthiness of a particular community, despite widespread feelings to the contrary, the dealer should convey that information to the customer. The dealer must also understand each customer's needs in order to judge the amount of risk to which each is willing to be exposed. Dealers that underwrite bad credit risks in hopes of earning wider spreads are firms of which newcomers to the municipals market should beware. But when a dealer meets all the positive criteria, an investor can reasonably anticipate a satisfying relationship.

CUSTODIAL CARE

Repayment procedures differ depending upon whether the issue is a coupon bond or a registered bond, and this difference is significant. Registered bonds require the bearer's name to be recorded on the books of the municipality. It is difficult to effect inter-party transfers of these bonds since title exchange requires the bearer to indorse the issue. Although registered bonds provide safety to the owner, they are unwieldy and not easily pledged in collateralized transactions. Since the security thus loses much of its marketability, registration should be discouraged. Coupon bonds, in contrast, are physically delivered to the bearer and, while more susceptible to theft, they are much more marketable and easily pledged.

The registered-bond owner receives semiannual or annual interest payments via check on prescribed dates over the life of the bond. Coupon bonds may be registered with respect to interest or principal or both. If, for example, the interest is registered, payments are sent directly to the registered owner in the form of a check. The payment procedure usually entails the separation and retention of the coupons by the borrower. On interest payment dates, the borrower mails a check to the registered owner. If the bond is sold prior to its maturity, the new owner must be registered with the municipal borrower.

If interest and principal are not registered, the bonds are considered in bearer form and ownership extends to whoever is in possession of the security. Payment of interest on bearer bonds requires the holder to clip coupons from the bond on payment dates, and redeem them at particular paying agent banks specified by the borrower. (Paying agency banks typically include a regional bank in the area of the municipal borrower and a co-paying agency bank in New York City.)

Municipal-note owners generally take physical possession of the security and redeem the note at designated banks upon maturity, receiving both interest payment and principal repayment.

RECENT DEVELOPMENTS IN MUNICIPAL FINANCING

The long period of increasingly high interest rates has directly affected the market for municipals in a number of ways. With short-term rates at historically high levels, investors appear averse to holding long-term bonds, preferring instead to purchase securities at the shorter end of the maturity scale. While the requirement that any general obligation issue be approved by a voter referendum effectively limits municipal borrowers' innovations to the revenue-bond-type of financing, several new methods have developed with which to raise funds in the capital markets.

Tax-Exempt Commercial Paper

In the early 1970s, tax-exempt commercial paper was introduced to the market. This consists of short-term unsecured promissory notes of a state or local government or its agencies, usually backed by a bank line or letter of credit. Issued in bearer form, tax-exempt paper is sold at a discount from par and redeemed at full face value. From the perspective of the issuer, it allows the raising of funds more quickly and at lower cost than do municipal note issues. Furthermore, it provides the borrower with the flexibility to roll over the issue continuously. From the investor's standpoint, commercial paper offers greater liquidity, since most issues mature in fifteen to ninety days. Although not all states permit this method of raising funds, if high interest rates persist it can be expected to account for an ever-increasing share of the market for new municipal securities.

Put Options

To attract investors back to the bond market, some municipal borrowers have experimented with attaching a put option feature to their bond offerings. Thereby, the borrower pays the underwriter (typically a bank) a flat fee against the eventuality that investors may sell the bond at par before its maturity. For instance, a twenty-year bond may provide a put option to be exercised after five years. That is, at the end of five years, the investor may choose to sell the issue back to the bank at par value, presumably because interest rates have moved up and the principal can be re-invested in higher-rate offerings. After five years, moreover, the issue is regarded as a series of successive one-year notes. The investor is willing to accept a lower yield for the privilege of redeeming the bond before final maturity. The bank usually charges a fee equal to 2 percent of the total issue. For a bond with a five-year put option, the market would compare its return to other five-year offerings. In essence, then, the put option is a mechanism to enhance long-term financings in an otherwise sagging bond market.

Variable-Rate Issues

The advent of variable-rate issues is another device to enhance the attractiveness of long-term bonds. Variable rates depart from typical long-term issues to the extent that the interest rate is not fixed but tied — for example, to the ninety-day Treasury-bill rate or the prime lending rate. That is, the bond's interest rate is tied to, say, the average prime rate over a designated period as charged by a pre-selected money-center bank. An investor does not purchase a variable-rate bond for speculative reasons since they generally trade at or around par.

Enhanced Security Issues

In an effort to reduce their financing cost, tax-exempt borrowers often attempt to gain higher credit ratings on their issues. For example, dormitory authorities that need to borrow construction funds may pledge part of the university's endowment fund to enhance the security of the bond issue. Similarly, a municipal borrower may obtain a bank letter of credit to provide further collateral on a bond offering. The bank would usually charge a flat fee for the potential use of these funds. In both of these circumstances, the greater security enhances the quality of the issue and reduces the overall financing costs to the borrower.

Open- and Closed-End Municipal Bond Funds

Over the last two decades, legislative changes in many states have cleared the way for the creation of tax-exempt municipal bond funds, both closed- and open-ended. These changes have been enacted primarily to make the market for municipal securities more accessible to individuals. As a result, a variety of funds have emerged to meet a wide array of investor needs.

Fixed-unit investment trusts. Instituted in 1961, fixed-unit investment trusts have come to play an increasingly dominant role in the demand for municipal securities. The trust is simply an investment company that assembles a fixed portfolio of municipals, shares that are then sold to the general public. Because these shares are typically denominated in $1,000 to $5,000 blocks, they have become a viable investment alternative that may be likened to a closed-end fund for municipal bonds. Once the fund is created, only under very special circumstances may the shares in it be traded or sold. (Sales and trading are generally allowed if the trust's ability to meet interest payments or principal repayment becomes seriously impaired.) Because active trading is restricted, most shareholders incur only a sales charge upon initial investment; there are no yearly management fees. In addition, for some unit investment trusts whose shareholders are solicited by direct mail, there may be no sales charge to buy into the fund.

Fixed-unit trusts are usually organized by an investment firm (the sponsor), which selects the securities that are to be held in the fund's portfolio. Frequently, a fixed-unit investment trust may be tailored for a particular class of investors. Thus, a specialized fund may be set up to hold only municipal securities issued by the same state, making interest income exempt not only from federal taxes but also from state and local taxes. Administration of the fund is usually assigned to a bank (the trustee), whose responsibilities include safeguarding the securities, collecting interest payments and executing any income distributions. Such a trust provides the shareholder with safety, diversification, and liquidity.

- Safety is derived from the investment quality of the bonds held in the portfolio (Standard & Poor's AAA to BBB and Moody's Aaa to Baa).
- Diversification is achieved through the holding of a large number of municipals, typically ten to fifty different securities.

- Liquidity is gained through the assurances given to investors that their shares may be redeemed at any time. If the sponsor chooses not to repurchase the shares, the trustee usually is obligated to do so.

The value of both the outstanding shares and the underlying portfolio will fluctuate with general market conditions. Shares that are sold before their final expiration are retired and not resold to other investors. If all outstanding shares should be retired — or when all securities in the portfolio reach final maturity — the entire principal is distributed to the shareholders of the trust, and it loses its character as a legal investment entity.

Municipal bond mutual funds. In 1976, Congress enacted legislation to facilitate the establishment of open-ended tax-exempt municipal bond funds. Unlike the fixed-unit trusts, open-ended or mutual funds may be actively managed and, when they are, a management fee is usually charged. Some open-end funds are passively managed, however, and simply held until the portfolio reaches final maturity. Open-end funds that are managed actively may be less susceptible than unit trusts to erosion of principal value caused by inflation. In 1976, when these funds first became legal, sales of the shares in them totaled $475.5 million. By year-end 1980, sales of municipal-bond mutual funds had more than trebled, to $1,756.6 million.

GLOSSARY

amortization — Periodic charges to premium bonds that gradually reduce the book value of the debt.

bearer security — A security that extends ownership privileges to the holder. Bearer securities do not require that the owner be registered with the borrower.

bond — An interest-bearing debt obligation that promises to pay the principal on a specified date.

bond anticipation note (BAN) — Short-term borrowings of states and municipalities to obtain interim financing for projects that will be funded long-term through the sale of a bond.

broker — An agent who brings together a buyer and a seller in the exchange of a security in the secondary market. The broker does not assume a position in the security but earns a commission on the trade.

callable bond — A bond that the issuer has the option of repaying prior to its stated maturity date. Repayment is usually made at a specified price above par.

competitive underwritings — A bond sale conducted by prospective underwriters submitting sealed bids.

coupon — The annual rate of interest on the bond's face value or interest payment to be made by the issuer. It also refers to the physical certificate that is often detached from the bond and presented for collection of interest payments.

dealer— An agent who assumes a position in a security. The dealer is involved in underwritings and in the buying and selling of securities.

debt service— The amount of income required for annual interest on and principal repayment of borrowed funds.

discount bond— A bond that sells below the face amount or par value.

discount notes— Non-interest-bearing securities that, when issued, sell below par, but are redeemable at full face value upon maturity.

double-barreled bond— A bond that has at least two potential sources of funds for repayment.

equivalent taxable yield— The pre-tax yield on a taxable security that would provide an investor with the same return after taxes as a given tax-exempt security yields.

general obligation bond— A municipal debt issue backed by the full faith, credit, and taxing powers of the borrowing state or locality.

industrial revenue bond— A bond issued by a municipality or public authority to finance the construction of a facility to be leased to a private corporation. They are secured by the private corporation's credit.

municipal securities rulemaking board— An independent, self-regulatory authority established by the SEC in 1975 to promulgate rules for the conduct of brokers, dealers, and banks that participate in the municipal securities market.

negotiated underwritings— A bond sale performed by the municipal issuer, pre-selecting an underwriter or group of underwriters to price and distribute the new issue.

new issue market— The market for original issues or newly issued securities. Also referred to as the primary market.

notes— Debt obligations with maturities of one month to three years, although generally recognized as one-year issues.

over-the-counter market— A securities market created by dealer negotiations rather than the auction system typical of organized exchanges.

par value— The principal amount of a security that is to be repaid at maturity, generally $1,000.

premium bond— A bond that sells above the principal amount or par value.

project notes— Short-term debt obligations issued on behalf of public housing authorities by the U.S. Department of Housing and Urban Development for the purpose of financing housing and urban development projects.

refunding— The process by which a new bond issue is sold to redeem an outstanding issue.

registered bond— A bond whose owner is registered on the books of the borrower.

revenue anticipation note (RAN)— Short-term borrowings of state and local governments in anticipation of future receipt of revenues.

seasoned issue— An issue that has been sold and trades actively in the secondary market.

serial bond— A bond issue in which a portion of the debt obligation matures annually or semiannually until final maturity.

spread— 1. Difference between bid and asked prices on a security. 2. Difference between yields on or prices of two securities of differing maturities. 3. In underwriting, difference between price realized by the issuer and price paid by the investor.

tax anticipation note (TAN)— Short-term borrowing of states and municipalities to finance current operations. TANs are repaid out of anticipated tax revenues.

term bonds— A bond issue in which the debt obligation is repaid on a single date.

trading market— The market for buying and selling issued bonds.

yield— The annual rate of return on an investment.

DEALERS

Like corporate securities, municipals are widely available in securities brokerage firms where qualified personnel are prepared to discuss specific issues in light of individual requirements.

SUGGESTED READING

Periodicals

Forbes, R.W., and Frankle, A.W. "Tax-Exempt Revenue Bonds: Are Ratings a Proxy for Credit Quality?" *Review of Business and Economic Research* 14:68-77, Winter 1978-1979.

Guild, G.A. "U.S.-Backed Municipal Bonds." *Financial World* 148:70, Aug. 15, 1979.

Joehnk, M.D., and Kidwell, D.S. "Comparative Costs of Competitive and Negotiated Underwritings in the State and Local Bond Market." *Journal of Finance* 34:725-731, June 1979.

Morner, A.L. "Case For Buying Municipals." *Fortune* 100:135, Dec. 3, 1979.

"Ranking the Municipal Underwriters." *Institutional Investor* 14:133-134, March 1980.

Reference Books

Darst, David M. *The Complete Bond Book.* New York: McGraw-Hill, 1981.

Lamb, Robert, and Rappaport, Stephen P. *Municipal Bonds.* New York: McGraw-Hill, 1980.

The Public Securities Association. *Fundamentals of Municipal Bonds.* New York, 1980.

Stigum, Marcia. *The Money Market: Myth, Reality and Practice.* Homewood: Dow Jones-Irwin, 1978.

Van Horne, James C. *Function and Analysis of Capital Market Rates.* Englewood Cliffs: Prentice-Hall, 1970.

Mutual Funds

*John C. Bogle**

BASIC CHARACTERISTICS

Mutual funds in the United States have enjoyed a remarkable resurgence in asset growth in recent years, following a period of consolidation during most of the 1970s. Total assets of mutual funds, which had risen from $17 billion at year-end 1960 to $60 billion at year-end 1972, were just $56 billion at year-end 1978. Assets then more than trebled, to $240 billion at year-end 1981. This increase clearly reflects the growing numbers of individual and institutional investors that have found that mutual funds can help them solve their financial problems.

To be sure, the lion's share of recent asset growth represents the growth of money market funds in 1979, 1980, and 1981. These funds invest in short-term instruments and pay a market rate of interest that has often exceeded 15 percent. The use of money market funds by investors will be discussed in this article only in conjunction with conventional mutual funds. (See article on Money Market Funds, elsewhere in this volume.)

Mutual funds are a type of investment company of which there are two basic types:

• Open-end funds. Open-end companies issue and redeem shares daily at a price representing the underlying net asset value of the shares. This article is primarily concerned with the open-end companies (excluding money market funds) that are generally known as mutual funds.

• Closed-end funds. Closed-end companies have a fixed number of shares outstanding. Shares change hands at an auction market price that may be more or less than their underlying value. Closed-end funds are basically the investment equivalent of open-end (mutual) funds, and are discussed in detail in a separate article.

Background

For the first twenty-five years of the post-World War II era, mutual funds were probably the fastest growing major financial institution in the United States. Assets were just over $1 billion at the end of 1945, $8 billion at the end of 1955, $35 billion at the end of 1965, and $60 billion at the stock market peak in 1972. Investors then began to withdraw their assets from the mutual funds by redeem-

* John C. Bogle is President of the Vanguard Group of Investment Companies, Valley Forge, Pennsylvania.

ing more shares than they purchased, and the funds suffered an outflow of capital each year thereafter, with the sole exception of 1977. In 1980, however, this trend was reversed, capital inflow was resumed, and fund assets again reached the $60 billion mark in the spring of 1981. The initial asset surge, the subsequent decline, and the recent resurgence hold an important message for today's investor, and a brief review of this history is in order.

Factors affecting original growth. The steady and substantial growth of mutual funds from 1945 to 1972 was based on four essential factors. First, this period was one in which common stocks surged upward, with the Dow-Jones industrial average rising from a level of 150 to over 1,000. Second, since nearly all mutual funds then invested largely in common stocks, they enjoyed an enviable record of investment return. Third, the funds provided an increasing range of services (dividend re-investment plans, monthly purchase plans, etc.) that made them convenient and useful for investors. Fourth, stock brokerage firms from coast to coast became the principal marketing arm of the industry, recognizing that their clients (especially investors of modest means) could own a share in America on a sound and convenient basis, and that their sales representatives could earn substantial commissions on the growing fund volume.

A decline in the 1970s. A number of key events brought this growth to a sudden halt. First, the great post-war bull market ended. The Dow-Jones average declined from a high of 1,052 in 1973 to a low of 578 in 1974. While it then snapped sharply back, its level of just around the 1,000 mark in mid-1981 was about at the 1973 level, and not much higher than the 1966 peak of 995, a fifteen-year period during which common stocks — the investment that promised great profit — had gone nowhere. Second, during the late 1960s and early 1970s, the mutual fund industry became more and more competitive regarding performance, and speculative funds were formed by the hundreds, abandoning the industry's traditional, conservative investment approach. When the market plunged, these funds led the way downward. Third, while the mutual fund industry had been progressive in its marketing of new services, it had been slow in developing new products beyond the equity arena. When the equity plunge came, the industry had little on which to fall back. Finally, disappointed by the performance of the new speculative funds, and with clients who had hoped for large gains but instead had suffered large losses, the brokerage firms virtually abandoned their marketing efforts.

An upsurge in popularity. But why, then, the renaissance of mutual funds as the decade of the 1980s begins? First, time healed some of the wounds the stock market had sustained in 1973-1974, and investors, so accustomed to making their investment decisions by looking in a rearview mirror, saw a better climate, one in which most of the water had been squeezed out of equities. Stocks were again fairly valued in relationship to fundamental factors such as earnings, dividends, and book values.

For example, in the heady days before the 1973-1974 bear market, stocks were selling at prices about nineteen times the annual corporate earnings, on average. At the beginning of 1981, stocks were much more reasonably priced, at about nine times earnings.

Second, common stock mutual funds (with many of the speculative funds departed from the scene) had provided excellent records of growth in the market rise and, over even longer periods, had provided results that were distinguished relative to the results achieved by other investment advisers (such as bank trust departments, insurance companies, and investment counsel firms) and — although concrete data are not available — relative to what investors achieved on their own. Third, the industry at last diversified its product line, developing income funds, corporate bond funds, and municipal bond funds to go along with the traditional equity funds. (The development of money market funds dwarfed these other new funds, and is the best example of the industry's capacity for innovation.) Fourth, a new marketing channel arose to replace the lost volume from stock brokers: no-load funds were offered, without sales commissions, to investors who sought them out, rather than requiring the assistance of a salesman. As the United States entered an era of consumerism, the idea caught on that many individual investors, well-educated, self-motivated and often wealthy, could decide how to meet their own investment needs. Institutional investors such as pension funds — cost conscious, possessing substantial analytic ability, and seeking the optimum rate of return — also began to make large purchases of fund shares.

This brief history of mutual funds in the United States is presented for two reasons: to aid the investor's understanding of the sections that follow, describing fund characteristics and attributes, past investment results, and considerations in selecting a fund; and to place the future in the context of the past, remembering Santayana's admonition that "Those who cannot remember the past are condemned to repeat it."

Types of Mutual Funds

Mutual funds come in an extraordinary variety, with a wide diversity of investment objectives and policies. While it is not possible to precisely catalogue funds into a series of common categories — there will always be exceptions — the principal groups are listed below.

Stock funds. Stock funds invest primarily in common stocks. Within this category are: (1) growth-and-income funds, placing relatively equal weight on capital growth and dividend income; (2) growth funds, primarily seeking capital growth, with income incidental; (3) aggressive growth funds, investing in smaller or riskier stocks, seeking maximum capital gains; and (4) income funds, selecting high-yielding common stock for maximum income, with growth a secondary goal.

Bond funds. Bond funds obviously emphasize bonds. The principal types are (1) U.S. government bond funds, owning only issues with federal government guarantees; (2) investment-grade corporate bond funds, emphasizing top-rated corporate bonds in order to offer higher yields with limited credit risk; and (3) high-yield bond funds, which own lower quality corporate bonds, with greater credit risk, in order to maximize income.

Balanced funds. Balanced funds combine bonds and stocks to make a complete investment program that will conserve capital, pay reasonable income, and provide some capital appreciation. Balanced funds include (1) traditional balanced funds, which are typically composed of about one-third bonds and two-thirds stocks; and (2) income balanced funds, which aim to pay generous income by emphasizing bonds when interest rates are high relative to dividend yields, reversing the emphasis when this relationship is reversed.

Municipal bond funds. Municipal bond funds are a completely separate category of bond fund, providing tax-free income to investors. The principal types are: (1) short-term, in substance, a tax-free money market fund; (2) long-term, taking greater price risk by owning high-grade bonds with long maturities, and seeking higher income; (3) intermediate-term, falling between the first two types; and (4) high-yield, comprising lower grade long-term bonds for maximum income.

Tax-managed funds. Tax-managed funds concentrate on utility stocks and are structured to minimize taxes by re-investing income rather than paying dividends. Shareholders, therefore, pay no current tax, but qualify for long-term capital gain treatment if their holdings appreciate, provided that they hold their shares for at least a year and a day.

Specialized funds. Specialized funds include (1) gold-based funds, investing in the stocks of gold-mining companies, which generally parallel gold prices, and (2) international funds, purchasing the securities of companies in other nations, sometimes along with U.S. investments.

Diversity of Objectives

This diversity of objectives obviously makes it possible for almost any investor to select a fund — or a combination of funds — to meet his investment goals. Table 1 on page 513 provides summary data for each fund category, including performance records for the five-year period, 1976-1980. "Performance" is defined in terms of total return, which takes into account the change in a fund's net asset value, adjusted for income dividends and capital gains distributions.

To put the following table in perspective, three things should be kept in mind. First, the five-year period in which total return was measured was a strong period for the stock market. Smaller companies enjoyed larger gains than blue chips, and bond prices declined sharply. Second, income yield is a function both

TABLE 1. Major Categories of Investment Companies

	No. of Funds	*Asset 1/1/81 ($ Billions)*	*Five-Year Total Return 1976–1980*	*Current Yield 1/1/81*
Stock Funds				
Aggressive growth	80	$ 7.9	+224%	1.8%
Growth	112	17.8	+146	2.8
Growth/income	59	15.9	+113	3.7
Income	13	0.7	+94	5.5
Total	264	$42.3		
Bond Funds				
U.S. government	10	$0.2	+15	9.6
Investment grade	28	3.0	+28	11.0
High yield	12	1.7	+59	12.1
Total	50	$4.9		
Balanced Funds				
Traditional	20	$3.3	+72	5.7
Income	48	5.1	+70	8.6
Total	68	$8.4		
Municipal Bond Funds				
Short-term	13	$2.2	NA	*5.6
Intermediate	2	0.1	NA	*7.8
Long-term	39	2.6	NA	*9.1
High-yield	5	0.4	NA	*9.6
Total	59	$5.3		
Specialized Stock Funds				
Gold	4	$0.6	+352	6.1
International	6	0.7	+135	2.0
Total	10	$1.3		
Totals	451	$62.2		

*Tax-free
NA—not available. Municipal bond funds were formed only after a change in the tax laws in mid-1976.

SOURCE: Prepared by Vanguard Statistical Services Department, using data from Wiesenberger Investment Companies Services, *Management Results,* December 1980

of a fund's dividends and its net asset value. Dividends from stock funds have grown over time; dividends from bond funds have remained stable. Finally, of course, no mutual fund can assure similar returns in the future.

Table 2 below shows investment company performance over a longer period of time, divided among three sets of market conditions, each, curiously, covering six years: (1) the great bull market of 1963-1968, (2) the generally bearish market of 1969-1974, and (3) the ensuing recovery of 1975-1980. The first and last of these periods will provide some idea of the rewards available through equity mutual funds (few other types have as extended a history), using three types of funds: (1) aggressive growth funds (the riskiest group); (2) growth funds (generally riskier than average); and (3) growth-and-income funds (carrying a market, or businessman's risk).

This table makes it clear that mutual funds — and even equity funds — may be sharply differentiated under various market conditions. In the first bull market, the riskier the fund the larger the gain; in the bear market, the riskier the fund (as one might expect), the larger the loss; and, in the later bull market, aggressive growth funds again led the way, with growth funds outperforming growth-and-income funds by only a modest amount, despite the greater risk involved.

It should be emphasized that equity funds should not be picked by throwing darts, for there are significant differences in quality, cost, risk, and managment competence. In particular, investors should carefully choose the broad objective group that best matches their own investment goals, picking from the aggressive

TABLE 2. Cumulative Performance of Equity Funds—1963–1980

12/31/62 = 100%

	Aggressive Growth		*Growth*		*Growth and Income*	
	Total Return	*Annual Return*	*Total Return*	*Annual Return*	*Total Return*	*Annual Return*
Total period	+686%	+12.1%	+418%	+9.6%	+367%	+8.9%
Market rise 1963-1968	+263	+24.0	+153	+16.7	+120	+14.0
Market decline 1969-1974	−50	−11.0	−36	−7.1	−24	−4.5
Market rise 1975-1980	+332	+27.6	+218	+21.3	+180	+18.7

SOURCE: Prepared by Vanguard Statistical Services Department, using data from various editions of Wiesenberger Investment Companies Services, *Investment Companies*

growth, growth, or growth-and-income categories. Funds with greater emphasis on growth have exhibited higher rates of return, but the aggressive fund should be selected only by those investors who have the heart and stomach to ride out not only the inevitable swings in the stock market, but the sharp magnification of these swings by the aggressive funds.

Organization of Mutual Funds

Most mutual funds are organized, sponsored, distributed, managed, and administered by an external management company. (The Vanguard Group is believed to be the sole exception to this rule.) Although a fund normally has a board of directors, a majority of whom are independent of the management company, the company controls the fund. The management company markets the fund, creates new funds, and assumes responsibility for providing a family of funds with a diversity of objectives. Under these circumstances, the fund may be viewed as the product of the company. If the investor is dissatisfied with the performance or management of the fund, he may "vote with his feet" by cashing in an investment. This will be an expensive decision for an investment of short duration when a sales charge has been paid, but essentially a cost-free decision if a no-load fund is involved.

A family of funds. A typical fund organization comprises a family of funds with a variety of objectives. For example, a fund family may include a growth stock fund, an income stock fund, a corporate bond fund, a municipal bond fund, and a money market fund. Each fund is normally a separate corporation or trust, although today there is increasing use of the series fund, a single corporation with a series of completely independent portfolios (e.g., a municipal bond fund with a long-term portfolio and a short-term portfolio). While virtually no functional distinction exists between these two forms of corporate organization, the growth of the series fund probably indicates both a means of improved response to the needs of those investors who are willing to take the responsibility of selecting the appropriate fund for their individual needs (via a single prospectus that presents multiple options) and a way to take advantage of substantial economies of scale and resulting cost savings, especially in marketing activities.

Operating expenses. A wide range of costs is involved in the operations of individual funds. Normally, the largest portion of operating expenses (sometimes 100 percent of such expenses) is the advisory fee or management fee paid by the fund to the adviser. In addition, the fund usually pays all of its own expenses, including shareholder statements, custodial and audit fees, taxes, etc. The total of these costs is the fund's expense ratio (annual expenses as a percentage of fund assets). A low expense ratio is an important, if often overlooked, factor in adding to the long-run investment results of equity funds and to the current yield of bond and money market funds. There are surprisingly wide variations in expense ratios, which appear to be partly related to fund objectives (stock fund ratios are higher) and to fund asset size (large fund ratios are lower). (See Table 3 below.)

Clearly, other things being equal, the investor should seek out funds with low expense ratios, or at least avoid funds with high ratios. However, other things are rarely equal, and the expense ratio is but one factor the investor should consider.

Industry regulation. All mutual funds are organized and operate under the Investment Company Act of 1940. Administered by the Securities and Exchange Commission (SEC), the Act requires disclosure in a variety of areas, including advisory contracts, sales charges, composition of the board of directors, capital structure, and insider transactions. The stringent regulation of the industry by the SEC over a period of more than forty years has been an important contribution to the fact that few marginal operators entered the industry, and that major scandal has been virtually unknown. Nonetheless, investors should be aware that the SEC's regulatory purview does not extend to the oversight of fund investment objectives and portfolio management.

ATTRACTIVE FEATURES

The concept of mutual funds is really quite simple: Many investors seeking similar goals combine their resources so as to diversify over a large number of

TABLE 3. Expense Ratios for Categories of Mutual Funds

	Average Expense Ratios		
Fund Objective	*Highest 10%*	*Lowest 10%*	*All Funds*
Stock funds	1.65%	0.47%	1.02%
Bond funds	1.60	0.52	0.96
Municipal bond funds	1.37	0.44	0.79
Money market funds	1.08	0.39	0.68
Size of Fund			
Less than $50 million	1.71%	0.54%	1.13%
$50-250 million	1.24	0.50	0.83
More than $250 million	0.97	0.36	0.63

Note: Sample excludes funds with expense ratios of 2 percent or more.

SOURCE: Prepared by Vanguard Statistical Services Department, using data from Wiesenberger Investment Companies Services, *Mutual Funds Panorama,* December 31, 1980

TABLE 4. Cumulative Rate of Return (1965=100)

Year	*Bank Equity Accounts*	*Insurance Company Equity Accounts*	*Equity Mutual Funds*
1966	92.7	91.5	95.1
1967	112.4	114.0	126.0
1968	124.6	128.4	146.9
1969	117.5	117.1	127.4
1970	114.9	114.2	125.2
1971	135.7	134.5	148.0
1972	156.1	152.6	168.0
1973	124.7	118.9	135.1
1974	94.4	91.0	102.8
1975	119.8	118.9	135.7
1976	141.6	140.4	170.1
1977	132.8	132.1	171.8
1978	141.2	141.2	190.4
1979	166.3	167.8	242.6
1980	214.7	220.1	322.1

SOURCE: A.S. Hansen, Inc. Results of growth funds and growth-and-income funds have been combined to provide equity mutual fund data, since no comparable division exists in the bank and insurance equity account data

securities (thus reducing risk) and to obtain professional investment management that they could not employ individually (thus enhancing the possibility of reward). This concept is hardly of recent vintage. The first known ancestor of today's mutual fund was the Société Génèrale de Belgique, formed in 1822. Indeed, more than a century ago, in 1875, an English barrister named Arthur Scratchley gave a particularly good description (albeit in somewhat turgid prose) of the purposes of a mutual fund:

> Whether a man has a large sum or a small sum to invest . . . if he subscribes to a general fund, which (assisted by the advise of persons of experience in such matters) would divide its purchases carefully among a selected variety of investments — each member would derive greater benefit with much security from loss by the distribution of the risk over a large average.[1]

Performance Results

One reason for the spreading acceptance of mutual funds by larger investors — individual and institutional alike — is the growing perception that mutual

[1] Scratchley, Arthur. *On Average Investment Trusts.* London: Shaw & Sons, 1875.

TABLE 5. Annual Rate of Return

Year	*Bank Equity Funds*	*Insurance Equity Funds*	*Equity Mutual Funds*
1966	−7.3%	−8.5%	−4.9%
1967	+21.2	+24.6	+32.5
1968	+10.9	+12.6	+16.6
1969	−5.7	−8.8	−13.3
1970	−2.2	−2.5	−1.7
1971	+18.1	+17.8	+18.2
1972	+15.0	+13.5	+13.5
1973	−20.1	−22.1	−19.6
1974	−24.3	−23.5	−23.9
1975	+26.9	+30.7	+32.0
1976	+18.2	+18.1	+25.4
1977	−6.2	−5.9	+1.0
1978	+6.3	+6.9	+10.8
1979	+17.8	+18.8	+27.4
1980	+29.1	+31.2	+32.8
Compounded annual rate of return	+5.23%	+5.40%	+8.11%

SOURCE: A.S. Hansen, Inc. *Annual Hansen Investment Performance Survey,* various years

funds have provided returns generally superior to those achieved by other investment advisers, notably trust companies, investment counsel firms, and insurance companies.

Numerous studies have been made in recent years on performance of mutual funds. The overwhelming weight of evidence indicates that mutual funds in fact have provided investment results superior to those achieved by other types of institutional investors. Table 4 on page 517 and table 5 above show the results of a study, prepared annually by A.S. Hansen, Incorporated, an independent Chicago actuarial and consulting firm that has been providing performance data for pooled equity accounts managed by banks and insurance companies since 1968. Table 4 shows the cumulative results of these equity accounts as compared to equity mutual funds over the past fifteen years.

To be sure, cumulative data is not complete without the inclusion of annual data. It is always possible that one or two individual years may have had an inordinately strong effect, or that performance is heavily influenced by good results in rising markets (or poor results in declining markets), thus suggesting riskier investment policies. In examining these data, the consistent superiority of mutual funds is clear.

It is evident that the mutual funds outpaced both the bank and insurance funds in every year but one (1972) in which the stock market rose. Mutual funds provided somewhat better results in 1977, when bank and insurance funds declined but mutual funds rose; about the same results in the severe 1973-1974 decline; and rather worse results in the 1969-1970 bear market. It would appear that mutual funds achieved a portion of their excess returns in 1967-1968 by assuming greater risk, but significant risk differentials were not evident either before or since then.

Statistical evidence, then, shows that mutual funds have in the past not only been competitive equity vehicles, but surprisingly superior ones. Precise quantification that gives reasons for this is not available, but some investment studies and subjective impressions may be worth setting forth.

Spectrum of investments. Mutual funds are more likely than banks to have a wide spectrum of investments beyond the giant blue chip companies. A study of 1977 data,[2] for example, indicated that banks had 36 percent of assets invested in the largest twenty-five stocks in the Standard & Poor's 500 Composite Stock Price Index, compared to 42 percent in the Index itself. Mutual funds, however, had only 19 percent of assets in these holdings. Mutual funds are more diversified than bank funds. Banks had 64 percent of assets in their 100 largest holdings, mutual funds just 45 percent.

Fund size. On average, mutual funds are much larger than bank-pooled funds. For example, at the end of 1980, the average bank-pooled common stock fund had $82 million in assets, as opposed to $160 million for the average stock mutual fund. Thus, they can command the full-time attention of a dedicated portfolio management group, rather than being one of a large number of accounts under management.

Well-defined objectives. Mutual funds usually seek specific objectives (e.g., growth or a combination of growth and income) and adhere closely to them. Bank and insurance funds, on the other hand, have more open charters, and may be whipsawed by shifting their objectives and policies at inopportune times.

Aside from their fine record of performance, mutual funds offer a number of other important advantages for investors.

Risk Spreading

Diversification is almost universally acclaimed by investment advisers and academic researchers, who have found there is virtually no value added by holding only a limited number of stocks; that is, investors who do not (or cannot)

---

[2] Bogle, John C., and Twardowski, Jan M. "Institutional Investment Performance Compared." *Financial Analysts Journal,* Jan.-Feb. 1980.

hold a broadly diversified portfolio are taking a risk that is not offset by a higher reward potential. Fund diversification usually means owning a relatively large number of stocks (50 to 100 or more) issued by a wide range of industries, or by companies with different investment characteristics (e.g., a growth fund may own seasoned growth stocks, cyclical growth stocks, and emerging growth stocks), or even owning stocks of corporations in different nations. The table below shows the relationship between diversification and investment risk, defined as the relative variability of annual returns of a stock portfolio.

Number of Stocks	*Risk Ratio*
1	6.56
2	3.77
4	2.38
10	1.55
50	1.10
100	1.04
500	1.00

Note that the variability of return, or risk, associated with holding just one stock is over *six times* as great as the risk of a 100-stock portfolio typical of a mutual fund. Yet, a study of 1971 tax returns showed that 51 percent of households listing dividends owned just one or two dividend-paying stocks, and that 89 percent held nine or fewer stocks.[3] Given the fact that the typical American investor is diversified among only a few stocks, the fund obviously fills a critical need.

Diversification is also important in bond portfolios. A corporate bond fund will own the debt securities of many different companies in a variety of industries; a municipal bond fund will own the debt securities of many different governmental bodies, such as cities, states, school districts, etc., in different parts of the country. In either case, a significant reduction of the risk in holding any one bond results with no commensurate sacrifice in yield.

Skilled Management

Management is a characteristic common among most mutual funds. The idea that a trained, skillful, professional management organization can successfully select a stock portfolio and change it as conditions change, is hardly counterintuitive. Nonetheless, despite the inordinately high degree of professionalism manifested by mutual fund investment advisers as a group, the ability to outpace the performance of stocks in general (or, in the case of bond funds, bonds in general) is remarkably difficult to come by. The records of hundreds of mutual

---

[3] Blume, Marshall E., and Friend, Irwin. *The Changing Role of the Individual Investor.* New York: John Wiley & Sons, 1976.

funds support this conclusion. Some are outstanding, some are more or less average, and some are distinctly poor. The performance range is large, even among funds sharing similar investment policies and characteristics. Table 6 below shows the differences among equity funds in various categories over the past decade.

The reason for this dispersion of management results lies largely in three areas, which are as follows:

(1) Despite comparable investment objectives within each of the three categories, policies may differ — and often substantially so — and thus, in various types of markets, some funds will certainly surpass others. For instance, some long-term growth funds emphasize seasoned growth stocks, while others tend to own stock of smaller, less well-known companies. Similarly, some growth-and-income funds hold cyclical stocks (General Motors, U.S. Steel) or income stocks (American Telephone & Telegraph), while others take a different tack altogether, perhaps choosing out-of-favor stocks with low price-to-earnings ratios.

(2) Some markets favor stocks in one industry versus another; for example, energy stocks led the market upward in 1980 — but they fell sharply in 1981.

(3) Management competence in fact differs; when all explanations have come and gone, some fund advisers simply do better than others. It may be luck, or it may be skill, and the challenge to the mutual fund investor is to evaluate the past by giving appropriate weight to the fund's relative return numbers (e.g., what rate of total return has been earned by the fund, compared to similar funds, and to the stock market averages in general), but not getting carried away with picking the best in retrospect, a recipe for investment disaster. (See *Important Factors in Buying and Selling* in this article for a discussion of the fund selection process.)

Investor Convenience

Simplicity is an important, if often overlooked, characteristic of mutual funds. While a shareholder often owns 50 to 100 or more individual securities through a mutual fund investment, the investment program is pooled, and he need not be concerned with the bookkeeping, tax records, and sheer flow of paper

TABLE 6. Ten-Year Total Return on Types of Equity Funds

	No. of Funds	*Average*	*Highest 10%*	*Lowest 10%*	*Range*
Aggressive growth funds	74	+218%	+541%	+44%	497%
Long-term growth funds	104	+150	+332	+34	298
Growth-and-income funds	53	+145	+335	+62	272

SOURCE: Prepared by Vanguard Statistical Services Department, using data from Wiesenberger Investment Companies Service, *Management Results,* December 31, 1980

associated with owning a diversified portfolio of many individual issues. Instead, he owns a single investment — admittedly one whose success or failure depends on the net accomplishment of its stock or bond portfolio — making it easy for the investor to judge the performance of his investment program. The mutual fund represents a conveniently packaged investment program, offering the advantages of diversification and professional investment counseling, with management, custodial, and administrative services provided at remarkably low costs.

Service

A key element in the success of the funds is service (one might call it marketing). It is simple to purchase shares, either directly from no-load funds, through sales representatives from brokerage firms, or from direct sales forces of financial behemoths. Examples of no-load fund groups are T. Rowe Price and Vanguard; brokerage firms include Merrill Lynch and everybody else, and direct sales firms are exemplified by the giant Investors Diversified Services or Waddell & Reed. In each case, the investor's purchase of fund shares — whether with an initial front-end charge ranging from 8.5 percent down to one percent or less (depending on size of purchase), or without such costs (no-load funds impose no commission charges) — buys a diversified, managed investment program. Further, the fund handles all of the income collection and bookkeeping, and distributes the net income (after fund expenses) to shareholders, who may receive these dividends either in cash or in additional shares of the fund through a dividend re-investment program.

Mutual fund shares are easy to purchase. They are also easy to redeem on demand, directly by contacting the fund, or through a broker or salesperson. Plans for adding regular monthly investments to the fund are available, along with plans for receiving regular monthly withdrawal checks, the former for investors accumulating assets in their earning years, the latter for investors who require income in their retirement years. An annual statement showing complete tax information is provided. Tax-deferred retirement plans established under Keogh programs or under the Individual Retirement Act have been an important part of the industry's growth, and may well become even more important as federal tax policy seeks to encourage individuals to invest rather than spend.

In recent years, the exchange privilege has found increasing interest on the part of investors, as the single funds of yesterday have blossomed into the fund families of today with a variety of funds, usually five to twenty or more. Investors may exchange their shares from one fund in the family to another, usually without commissions — another valuable service. For example, an investor might accumulate money in a stock fund during his accumulation years, and exchange to an income fund in the same fund family on retirement. Or an investor might exchange from a growth fund to a money market fund to protect his assets when he expects stock market declines, and reverse the process in anticipation of stock market rises. The exchange privilege, then, offers a new dimension of investment flexibility to the fund investor.

TABLE 7. Likely Response of Funds in a Falling Market

	10% Decline	*20% Decline*	*30% Decline*	*40% Decline*
Aggressive growth fund	−12.5%	−25.0%	−38.5%	−50.0%
Growth funds	−11.0	−22.0	−33.0	−44.0
Growth-and-income funds	−9.5	−19.0	−28.5	−38.0
Balanced funds	−6.5	−13.0	−19.5	−26.0

POTENTIAL RISKS

Risk is well defined in the question: How much can I lose? Investors must consider how much risk they are willing to assume. While this factor can never be precise, Table 7 above (based on the writer's past experience) may be of some value.

The investor should focus on the risk associated with his entire investment program rather than with its various components. Just as risk can be reduced by forming a portfolio of stocks that move to some degree independently, creating a portfolio of mutual funds — with either differing investment objectives or differing investment policies — will serve to reduce the volatility or risk of the overall investment portfolio. Thus, even an extremely conservative investor may reasonably hold a small commitment in an aggressive fund, given judicious holdings in more conservative stock funds, as well as bond and money market funds.

TAX CONSEQUENCES

The tax impact of fund payments should also be considered. Mutual fund dividends are normally taxed — like all corporate dividends — at rates from 0 percent up to 50 percent, depending on the investor's tax bracket, and are generally considered to be dividend income even though their source (in a bond fund) may be interest. The income from municipal bond funds, however, is in a special category under federal tax law, and investors pay no federal tax although the income may be subject to state and local taxes. Long-term capital gains distributions are eligible for a 60 percent exclusion from income, so that a tax is paid (at ordinary income-tax rates) on 40 percent of the gain. Thus, the effective tax rate on long-term capital gains distributions would be 8 percent for an investor in the 20 percent tax bracket, 16 percent in the 40 percent bracket, and 20 percent in the 50 percent bracket. The same treatment (a 60 percent exclusion) is accorded long-term gains resulting from redeeming a fund's shares at a price higher than that of the original purchase.

Because of the variety of funds available, their low cost, and investors' convenience, as well as the ability to exchange between funds with different objectives within one fund family, mutual funds are ideal vehicles for investors eligible to take advantage of the tax and retirement planning benefits of Keogh (HR-10) plans and individual retirement accounts (IRAs). While Keoghs are available only to self-employed individuals and their employees, the Economic Recovery Tax Act of 1981 makes IRAs available to any individual with earned income beginning in 1982. Both types of plans offer a tax deduction for contributions made to the plan (up to the lesser of 15 percent of earned income or $15,000 annually for a Keogh plan; the lesser of 100 percent of earned income or $20,000 for an IRA). Moreover, both plans permit the investor to defer taxes on income dividends and capital gains until withdrawals begin at retirement, so that the investment compounds at the higher, before-tax rate.

REPRESENTATIVE TYPES OF INVESTORS

Originally considered as an investment principally for the average individual, mutual funds today are owned by an extraordinarily wide range of investors — large as well as small, institutional as well as individual. Table 8 below shows the broad range of mutual fund ownership at year-end 1980. The profile of mutual fund shareholders is hardly a static one. For example, in recent years the mutual fund industry has attracted growing investments from institutional investors not heretofore considered to be prime prospects for mutual fund investment, as shown in Table 9 on page 525.

The recent increases in institutional use of mutual funds are impressive.

TABLE 8. Types of Mutual Fund Shareholders

	No. of Accounts (Thousands)	*Value of Accounts (Millions)*
Individuals	5,841	$42,648
Institutional		
Pension and profit-sharing plans	222	$ 2,932
Trust accounts	730	6,690
Business corporations	36	1,507
Financial institutions	13	1,093
Keogh/IRA plans	333	4,207
Other institutional	53	1,236
Total institutions	1,388	$17,665
Total industry	7,229	$60,313

Note: Data excludes money market funds.

SOURCE: Investment Company Institute, *Mutual Fund Fact Book,* 1981

TABLE 9. Institutional Accounts

Year	*Assets (Millions)*	*% Total*
1966	$ 3,984	11.4%
1970	6,174	13.0
1976	10,720	22.5
1980	17,665	29.3

Note: Data excludes money market funds.

SOURCE: Investment Company Institute, *Mutual Fund Fact Book,* 1981

Some perspective is added, however, by considering the growing — but still quite limited — extent of pension fund investments in mutual funds. Pension plan investments in such funds more than doubled between 1978 and 1980, rising from $1.4 billion to $2.9 billion. Nevertheless, this total represents a miniscule portion of total pension fund assets, which amount to more than $300 billion.

IMPORTANT FACTORS IN BUYING AND SELLING

Purchasing Shares

Fund shares may be purchased from a stockbroker, from a fund salesperson, or directly from the fund. In each case the purchase price is directly related to the fund's current net asset value per share (the market value of its assets, less liabilities, divided by the number of shares outstanding). Here ends the similarity between the three purchasing approaches, however. For funds distributed by stockbrokers, a maximum sales commission of just under 9 percent is added, as the broker is compensated for providing a fund evaluation and review service and recommending a specific fund. (This commission is usually described as 8.5 percent of the amount invested (including the commission). It is scaled down for larger purchases, such as 7.5 percent on $10,000 to $25,000, 6 percent on $25,000 to $50,000, and so on, down to perhaps as little as one-half of one percent on single purchases over $10 million.)

For funds distributed directly by fund sales representatives, a comparable sales commission is added, although here the salesperson — who normally offers only the funds from the family he represents — is compensated for a financial planning service, usually including both life insurance and mutual funds. For funds whose shares are purchased directly from the fund itself, there is no sales commission. (Commissions are often referred to as sales loads; hence, the designation of such funds as no-load funds.) The investor does his own evaluation, makes his own decision, handles his own transaction, and avoids the payment of a substantial commission.

Redeeming Shares

Just as the baseball manager is described as hired to be fired, so a mutual fund share is bought to be sold, sooner or later, as the investor's objectives are reached. To take an obvious example, the accumulation of fund shares for a child's college education must be sold in order to pay tuition bills, room and board, etc. Fund shares are normally sold by tendering them back to the fund for redemption at the current net asset value. This liquidation is normally handled simply and expeditiously, for the liquidity of mutual funds is one of their important advantages.

Of course, other reasons exist for fund redemptions. The need for cash (to build a house, purchase other investments, etc.) is one. Dissatisfaction with the fund's management, policies, or performance is another. Until recent years, two other reasons were significant: a change in the investor's investment objective (e.g., seeking retirement income after the accumulation phase); and an investor's preference for liquidity versus risk (e.g., redeeming a stock fund and putting the proceeds in a savings account, perhaps in order to lock in profits or to implement a view that stocks are overpriced). However, the growth of families of funds with a broad range of objectives is gradually converting redemptions to exchanges, wherein the shareholder in the two previous examples, respectively, might switch from a growth fund to an income fund, or from a stock fund to a money market fund (perhaps reversing the process should stock prices decline materially). In neither case would there normally be any additional commission cost.

Mutual Fund Distributions

There are two common types of mutual fund distributions: income dividends and capital gain distributions.

Income dividends. Income dividends represent the interest and/or dividends earned by the fund's portfolio, less the fund's expenses. Such dividends tend to be regular and relatively stable, although the dividends paid by most equity-oriented funds have grown rather consistently in the past. In fact, common stock dividends have been an excellent hedge against inflation in the past half-century, as Figure 1 on page 527 shows.

Capital gains distributions. Capital gains distributions are generally just as erratic as income dividends are stable. They arise during years in which the fund realizes profits in excess of losses on the sale of portfolio securities, and may be either short term (one year or less) or long term (more than one year) depending on the fund's holding period. It is an improper strategy for a fund to try to equalize capital gain distributions (paying a similar amount each year, good or

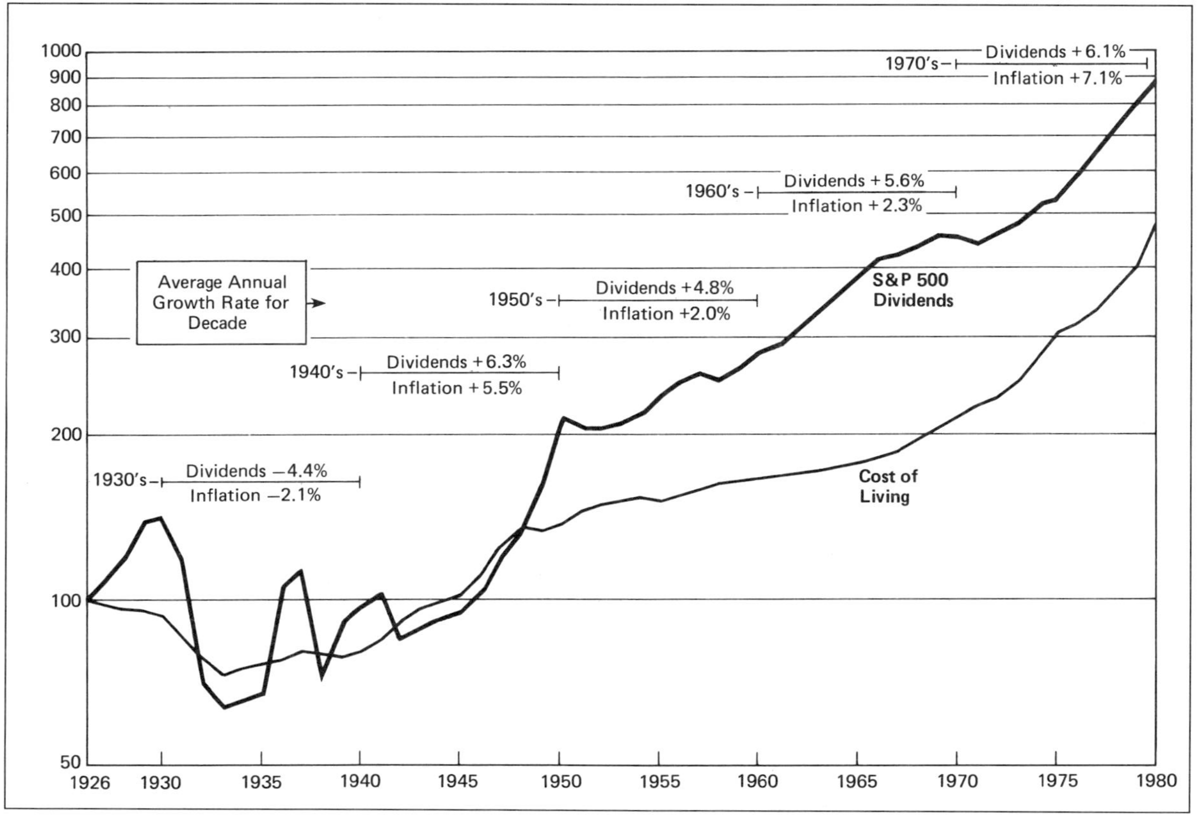

FIG. 1. Inflation and Dividends
SOURCE: Bogle, John C. "Strategies for an Inflationary Era." *Mutual Funds Forum*, Apr. 1981

bad), in part because it may impair investment results (e.g., selling winners, holding losers) and also may mislead fund shareholders in projecting the payments into the future, which is simply not proper.

Income Re-Investment

Both income dividends and capital gains distributions normally may be used to purchase additional shares in the fund at no cost (although some funds charge an additional sales commission on these purchases). Such dividend re-investment programs are very convenient, with the shareholder receiving a statement from the fund on each payment date, showing the number of full and fractional shares acquired. Re-investment of capital gains is preferred by nearly all fund investors (90 percent), since taking them in cash is viewed as a withdrawal of capital from the fund. About 60 percent of fund investors also re-invest dividend income, suggesting that this group of investors is in the accumulation phase of their investment program, rather than in the retirement phase.

Dividend yields (as shown in Table 1 on page 513) vary greatly by fund objective. More often than not, high yields are currently associated with more conservative funds (i.e., bond funds), that normally do not offer substantial capital growth potential. Low yields generally are associated with growth-oriented funds, which have greater prospects for capital appreciation and involve greater risk to the investor's principal. Given this difference, it is hardly surprising that many bond funds pay dividends on a monthly basis, most growth-and-income funds pay quarterly, and most growth funds pay annually.

Performance Measurement

It is essential that the measurement of mutual fund performance be done on a total-return basis, taking into account not only the change in asset value, but also all dividends and distributions, as if they were re-invested in additional shares. This process puts all types of investments on a common measurement standard, expressed as a compound annual rate of return. Thus:

Initial purchase price	$10,000
Sale price ten years later (including re-invested dividends)	25,000
Total gain	$15,000
Annual rate of return	+9.6%

It requires only a moment's reflection to see the soundness of this concept of compound annual rate of return. Compare, for example, a bond fund paying dividends of 12 percent per year (assuming principal value unchanged), with a growth fund paying 2 percent per year, but with its asset value growing at the annual rate of 10 percent over ten years. (See Table 10 on page 529.)

Note that, on a compound interest basis (i.e., assuming dividends are re-invested), both investments have the same rate of return — namely, 12 percent.

TABLE 10. Comparison of Bond and Equity Fund

	Bond Fund		Stock Fund	
	Simple Interest	*Compound Interest*	*Simple Interest*	*Compound Interest*
Initial investment	$10,000	$10,000	$10,000	$10,000
Final value	10,000	10,000	25,937	27,549
Dividends paid	12,000	21,059	2,000	3,510
Final value (including dividends)	$22,000	$31,059	$27,937	$31,059
Annual rate of return	8.2%	12.0%	10.8%	12.0%

However, the simple-interest computations result in misleadingly lower annual returns, because they ignore the time value of the dividends paid during the holding period.

Selecting a Fund — Individuals

There are a number of considerations that should enter into the selection of a mutual fund by an individual investor. Among the more important factors are the following:

Personal objectives. As mutual funds usually seek specific investment objectives, a prerequisite for successful fund selection is that the investor's objectives are compatible with those of the fund chosen. Thus, an individual seeking current income without risk to principal will likely select a money market fund; a bond fund would be chosen by an individual seeking stable income; and a growth equity fund would likely be selected for the purpose of obtaining capital appreciation. Of course, this does not suggest that a single fund will necessarily fulfill all of an investor's objectives. Clearly, a retired investor with a lump sum to invest will want a combination of funds — perhaps including a stock fund for inflation hedging, a bond fund for durable income, and a money market fund for safety of principal.

Fund size and investment policies. Normally, it is best to avoid very small and new funds and fund families, unless the investor is satisfied with the resources available and the probity of the fund's management. Huge size, on the other hand, may serve to limit an equity fund's ability to differentiate itself from the stock market in general.

The fund's prospectus should be examined carefully to see what its objectives are and the policies through which it proposes to achieve them. Its policies should appear reasonable and sound. Also, it is wise to examine the fund's latest shareholder report, to learn about the adviser's investment approach and to find out about the specific portfolio under consideration. What type of stock portfolio is being purchased — a collection of blue chips or stocks of small, less well-known companies? What is the average quality of the bond fund — is the portfolio's high yield explained by an emphasis on lower quality bonds? In other words, the investor must know what he is buying.

Costs. The investor should determine what it will cost to own the fund, including the initial sales charge (if any), and the operating expenses (the annual expense ratio). Other things being equal (although they seldom are), these two costs should be minimized.

Fund performance record. Of course, the fund's record of past investment returns is a very important factor in the fund selection process. It is listed last in these criteria, however, for several reasons. First, the investor should consider his own goals, the fund's objectives and policies, the cost of investing, and the amount of risk he is willing to assume before getting down to the brass tacks of evaluating the performance of comparable funds. Second, there is no conclusive evidence that the past record of relative performance provides reliable criteria for judging future performance. And third, given the investing-in-a-rearview-mirror syndrome noted earlier, excessive reliance on past performance can be diametrically opposed to sound decision-making (e.g., buying agressive growth funds after they have achieved their best results and, often, just before they go into a decline).

For example, the top five performing equity mutual funds provided an average total return of +402 percent in the strong stock markets of 1963-1968, compared with a return of +99 percent for Standard & Poor's 500 Index. However, in the next six-year period, 1969-1974 — a difficult period for the stock markets — these five funds declined on average by 60 percent, compared to the loss of 19 percent suffered by the Index. Clearly then, selecting funds on their superior past records provides no guarantee of excellent results in the future.

Timing. Once the investor has selected a fund or group of funds, the next question involves when to invest. If the investor is going to invest regularly, the time to begin is now. Individuals investing a large lump sum, however, should not be in a hurry to invest but should consider spreading the purchase over a year or more on a quarterly basis, perhaps by starting with the entire investment in a money market fund and periodically exchanging into an equity fund within the same family. Such a program of dollar averaging is an effective way to reduce the risk of investing.

What about using mutual funds for market-timing? Why not switch from money market funds to stock funds at market lows, and reverse the process at market highs? Why not emphasize aggressive funds in ebullient markets, and conservative funds in trading markets? Sad to say, this sound theory rarely, if ever, works consistently in practice. The available evidence suggests, indeed, that market-timing advice is utterly worthless. Thus, it should be far more rewarding, over time, for investors to let their objectives and risk tolerance set their asset mix among various types of funds, changing this mix, not as markets fluctuate, but only as their objectives change.

Selecting a Fund — Institutions

For institutions of moderate size (say, up to $5 million in assets), the basic factors in fund selection are not unlike those for individuals. However, endowment funds, some pension funds, foundations, and corporations, often have a fixed pool of assets in which capital additions are relatively modest or even extremely rare. Such institutions normally have an equity position in the 30 to 70 percent range (with the remainder in bonds or cash reserves). Once this policy on risk tolerance is set by the trustees, it should be changed only as fundamental market and economic conditions change, and certainly it should be subject to the dollar averaging approach set forth in the preceding paragraph. However, changes in investments on a like-for-like basis may be made without delay; for example, moving from a separately managed portfolio of common stocks to an equity mutual fund. Here the primary considerations might be the expectation of superior performance from a particular fund, the possibility of participating in a specialized portfolio (such as emerging growth stock or international equities), and lower costs.

For corporate thrift plans, Keogh and IRA plans, and Section 403(b) plans,[4] there is another special consideration. These are usually dollar-averaging plans, and therefore can utilize an equity-oriented approach without excessive risk. Over extended periods of time, equities have produced the highest returns of any type of investment (such as real estate, bonds, Treasury bills, etc.) insulated against excessive risk by the regular addition of investment dollars. Here, the variety of mutual funds available, their administrative capabilities, shareholder accounting, financial controls, daily valuation, and regular reports to investors offer an exceptional level of convenience and service.

For moderate-sized to large corporate pension accounts of, say, $5 million or more, the use of mutual funds is growing steadily, albeit from modest levels. Part of the reason for this acceptance is fund performance results, part is fund accounting controls and fund service, part is the emergence of no-load funds as a major component of the industry, and part, in fact, is a gradual breaking down of the old shibboleth that mutual funds are appropriate only for the small investor. Some corporations use a selected list of carefully chosen equity funds; others retain separate account equity management for most of their assets, but may use specific equity funds with investment policies that are often differentiated from those presented by most other institutional advisers.

For example, the largest single mutual fund holding is believed to be $90 million, owned by a corporate pension fund that wants this portion of its $500

---

[4] Basically, Section 403(b) plans are those that qualify for tax deductions and accumulate income on a tax-deferred basis, frequently available to teachers and administrators of schools and colleges.

million of assets in a fund that seeks out companies (usually those with low price-to-earnings ratios) deemed overlooked by other institutional investors and undervalued in the marketplace. Since mutual funds normally express their objectives and policies with considerable specificity (as compared to most banks and investment counselors), and have demonstrated their ability to provide impressive investment results, the use of mutual funds by pension plans seems destined to increase.

GLOSSARY

capital gains distribution — A distribution representing a fund's net realized capital gains (either short- or long-term). Importantly, the shareholder is taxed for capital gains distributions based on the fund's holding period, not its own.

closed-end fund — Investment company characterized by having a fixed number of shares outstanding. Unlike a mutual fund, the closed-end fund does not redeem or buy back its shares at net asset value; rather, shares are bought and sold at market-determined prices.

diversified investment company — An investment company that meets certain standards of diversification under the Investment Company Act of 1940; primarily, that in regard to 75 percent of its assets, it has not invested more than 5 percent of its total assets in any one company, and owns no more than 10 percent of the voting securities of any single company.

dividend — A distribution of the fund's net investment income (i.e., income net of expenses). Dividends may be paid daily, monthly, quarterly, semiannually or annually, depending primarily on the role of income in the fund's investment objectives.

dollar averaging — Purchasing mutual fund shares regularly in constant dollar amounts. Results in an average cost per share lower than the average price at which purchases are made, because fewer shares are purchased when prices are high and more are purchased when prices are low.

exchange privilege — An option offered by most mutual fund complexes allowing the sale of shares in one fund and the use of the proceeds for purchase of shares in another fund within the same fund family, usually for a nominal charge.

expense ratio — Total annual expenses of the fund divided by average net assets.

hedge fund — A specialized and speculative mutual fund seeking maximum capital appreciation. Such a fund may generally borrow money to purchase stocks, and may also sell securities short in pursuit of its objectives.

individual retirement account (IRA) — A retirement plan originally for individuals who were neither self-employed nor covered by a qualified pension plan, offering special tax benefits (tax-deferred status and deductibility of contributions). Under the Economic Recovery Tax Act of 1981, IRAs were made available to any individual with earned income, beginning January 1, 1982. Also, on ending participation in a qualified pension plan, an individual may roll over the assets tax-free into an IRA. An individual qualified to establish an IRA may use a mutual fund as the chosen investment vehicle.

investment adviser— The organization employed by a mutual fund to invest the fund's assets. Usually the investment adviser also sponsors the fund, distributes its shares, and provides many of the necessary administrative services.

Keogh account— Offers self-employed individuals and their employees benefits similar to those of an IRA.

mutual fund— An open-end investment company, which is distinguished from a closed-end investment company by the fact that shares may be redeemed at net asset value, rather than at a market-determined value, as is the case with closed-end funds.

net asset value per share— The per-share value of the assets — securities, cash, and accrued earnings — in an investment company's portfolio, net of liabilities such as accrued expenses. Represents the share price at which shares of open-end companies are redeemed.

non-diversified investment company— An investment company with fewer investment restrictions than a diversified investment company, permitting, for example, investments in a single industry or in a group of related industries.

transfer agent— The organization that maintains shareholder records and processes shareholder transactions. The fund's transfer agent may be a bank or part of the mutual fund organization itself.

unit investment trust— A type of investment company that holds a fixed portfolio of securities — most commonly consisting of long-term municipal bonds — usually sold through brokerage houses with a sales commission.

MAJOR MUTUAL FUND COMPLEXES

	Year-End 1980	
	*Assets * (Millions)*	*No. of Funds**
American General	$1,592	11
American Funds	4,380	14
Dreyfus	3,181	7
Fidelity	3,844	17
Investors Diversified Services	5,367	11
Lord Abbett	1,991	4
Massachusetts Financial Services	2,877	8
Putnam	3,613	14
T. Rowe Price	3,335	6
The Vanguard Group	2,544	19

* Excluding money market funds

TRADE ORGANIZATIONS

Investment Company Institute, Washington, D.C.

No-Load Mutual Fund Association, Valley Forge, Pa.

SUGGESTED READING

Periodicals

Annuity & Closed-End Survey. Published by Lipper Analytical Distributors, New York, N.Y. Monthly.

Management Results. Published by Wiesenberger Investment Companies Services, New York, N.Y. Quarterly.

Mutual Fund Performance Analysis. Published by Lipper Analytical Distributors, New York, N.Y. Weekly.

Portfolio Analysis Report on Fixed Income Funds. Published by Lipper Analytical Distributors, New York, N.Y. Quarterly.

Risk-Adjusted Mutual Fund Performance Review. Published by Computer Directions Advisors, Silver Springs, Md. Monthly.

Reference Books

Investment Company Institute. *Mutual Fund Fact Book.* Washington, D.C., various years.

Wiesenberger Investment Companies Services. *Investment Companies.* New York, various years.

Oil and Gas

Eugene G. Martin *

BASIC CHARACTERISTICS

Oil and gas programs have fast become one of the most popular tax shelters and investment media on the market today. Public involvement in these programs hit a record $1.8 billion in 1980, an impressive 72 percent increase over the record-setting 1979 figure of $1.1 billion.[1]

This enthusiasm for oil has been spurred in part by an eighteen-fold jump in the price of crude oil from around $2 per barrel in 1973 to a post-Arab-embargo price of about $35 per barrel in 1981. In the past decade, it is estimated that the world market value of proven oil and gas reserves in the United States has leaped more than $1,000 billion. This appreciated value, combined with recent decontrols on the price of domestically produced crude oil, has resulted in additional profits for the industry of some $2 billion for 1981 alone.[2] It is no wonder then that in spite of the present ample supply of oil, the industry was expected to spend another $30 billion in 1981 on exploration and drilling.[3]

Energy Stocks

The simplest way to participate in the oil and gas industry is through the purchase of energy stocks, which make up about 18 percent of the Standard & Poor's 500 Composite Stock Index. The major advantage of this investment strategy is its liquidity. Energy stocks are easily traded in exchanges throughout the country. Any amount can be purchased and the timing of both purchases and sales is at the discretion of the investor. The risks involved are not much different from those of any other stock. Unfortunately, energy stocks do not directly reflect the jump in oil and gas prices and are subject to the pricing vagaries of the stock market as a whole. Consequently, they do not rate high as long-term hedges against inflation. For the upper-income investor, however, the greatest disadvantage of these stocks is that they offer no tax shelter.

Oil and Gas Programs

A more direct participation in this booming industry can be accomplished through what is known as "oil and gas programs" or "drilling funds." These are

* Eugene G. Martin is Vice-President, National Investment Services, Milwaukee.

1 *The RPI Survey: A Report on the Oil and Gas Program Industry.* Resource Programs, Inc., New York, 1981 (hereinafter cited as *The RPI Survey*).

2 Lohr, Steve. "The Great Oil Rush," *New York Times* Magazine, Aug. 30, 1981, page 23.

3 *Pensions & Investments Age,* April 13, 1981, page 3.

not the same as mutual funds, although the two share some common characteristics. Both are investment pools run by professional managers. In both there is a pass-through of profits and losses to investors and both are diversified in their holdings. Mutual funds, however, buy and sell the securities of businesses over which they have little control and provide a certain liquidity for their members.

The purpose of oil and gas programs, on the other hand, is to explore or drill for oil, or purchase producing oil wells. This is not a passive investment but a principal interest in a closed-end business. These programs are normally joint ventures or limited partnerships offered for a given number of months and then closed off from further trade. Therefore, each program is a distinct operating business. Their size can vary from $1 million up to $300 million and minimal investments for individuals are usually $5,000 to $10,000.

The public offerings of oil and gas programs are regulated by the SEC as well as by the individual states in which the offerings are sold. Private placements involve much larger amounts of money, are unregulated by the SEC, and are normally purchased by wealthy individuals, insurance companies, and institutional investors such as pension funds.

Institutional investors are quickly becoming a source of capital as important to oil and gas exploration as to the taxable market. Their participation is a recent development, however, and exact figures are hard to come by. However, in one six-month period in 1981, $500 million of institutional money was committed to domestic oil and gas exploration in one form or another, compared to virtually no involvement two years earlier.[4] With public oil and gas programs at the $1.8 billion mark in 1980, it is likely that institutional involvement in this market will soon exceed the funding provided by individual investors.

As members of a limited partnership, each participant in the program receives a pro rata share of the profits, losses, and assets of the enterprise. Unlike a corporation, a partnership pays no income tax of its own. If the undertaking is successful and substantial oil reserves are discovered, developed, or acquired, the investors should benefit substantially. The real advantage of these programs to individuals or corporations, however, is their ability to provide tax shelters. Investors who drill for oil and gas normally can deduct from 70 percent to 90 percent of the cost of their investment in the first two years of a well-run program. (See *Tax Consequences* in this article.)

Organizers of oil and gas programs. Oil and gas programs are put together and offered to investors either by independent oil companies or by oil investment managers.

Oil companies. The oil companies have their own staffs of supervisory engineers, geologists, and technicians, although they may hire outside contractors to do the actual drilling. Some people feel that oil company management provides

---

[4] Anderson, Truman E., Jr. *Oil Program Investments.* Tulsa: Petroleum Publishing Co., 1972, page 30.

a higher level of industry expertise, better supervision over wells, and reduced overhead and fees. If the company has been successful in its drilling of wells, it can also show investors an impressive track record of past experience. However, if the company has only had experience in one geographic location, and little exposure to other prospects, its chances for success may be limited.

Oil investment managers. Oil investment managers normally do not maintain their own geologists, landsmen, or engineers. Rather, they acquire prospects and enter partnerships with operators in various geographical areas and rely on the operators' technical staffs. Some investors feel that oil investment managers, who choose prospects from a broad range of geographical areas, can provide greater diversification and improved chances of success. The ability to enter into contracts with local exploration offices also provides oil investment managers with a flexibility that may not be available to oil companies with their own staffs. Oil investment managers are also less likely to run into conflicts of interest since they are merely managers of funds and do not directly participate in the oil business as oil companies do.

Types of programs. Both management approaches play major roles in oil and gas investing and both can offer the five types of oil programs available today. They are exploratory, development, balanced, income-producing, and royalty programs.

Exploratory programs. An exploratory program is one whose goal is to discover new petroleum reserves. Exploration normally takes place in untested areas not part of known commercial reservoirs or deposits. Consequently, the success rate for exploratory drilling is not high. One or two prospects may result from ten drillings. And only one in forty may be an economic success. Obviously, then, the more test wells the program puts into the ground, the higher the chances of success.

Since an exploratory or wildcat well must be developed after discovery, additional capital and time are necessary before any cash flow is seen. This is not an investment for someone interested in an immediate return on capital. A purely exploratory program is a high risk/high reward venture. Consequently, it is recommended for only the upper-bracket taxpayer who is comfortable with risk. An investor in a 50 percent tax bracket, for example, could save $5,000 on a $10,000 oil and gas program. An investor in the 30 percent bracket would only save $3,000. If the program were a complete loss, the higher bracket investor would lose only $5,000 while the fellow investor in the 30 percent bracket would lose $7,000.

The bulk of capital raised in oil and gas programs registered with the SEC is directed toward exploratory drilling. In 1980, 44 percent of all oil and gas investments went for exploration.[5]

---

[5] *The RPI Survey,* page 1.

Development programs. These programs set up wells near existing oil reserves in areas where production is already underway. Naturally, the chances of success in development programs are higher than they are in exploratory ones. On average, about 70 percent of developed programs end up with productive wells. Since the drilling takes place in a proven area, these programs must pay higher prices for their leases and usually drill on a smaller prospect or block of acreage than exploratory programs will. Since the chances of finding oil are greater with these programs than with exploratory programs, investors can expect a quicker return on their investment. They will probably hit a greater percentage of productive wells, and the wells will be located in developed areas where pipelines for transporting the oil are in place, thus reducing the costs and perhaps eliminating the need for additional money from investors.

In short, development programs have a higher success ratio but their return on capital is often proportionately less than exploratory programs. Consequently, they are good investments for people who want tax shelters and less risk than wildcat drilling involves. Investors in development programs can usually get an earlier and more favorable cash surrender on their interest than owners of exploratory programs, whose involvement is longer term. Development programs accounted for 27 percent of the capital raised in 1980 for public direct participation oil ventures.[6]

Balanced programs. These investments include both exploratory and development wells in similar proportions in one program. They try to combine the advantages of higher yields produced by successful exploratory wells with the early cash flow and lower risk of development wells. It should be kept in mind, however, that few programs can be classified either all exploratory or all development. Even programs that title themselves as development might follow a drilling policy in which 80 percent of their capital goes into development prospects and the balance goes toward drilling exploratory wells.

The difference between one kind of program and the next is a matter of degree. Each oil and gas program will set out in its prospectus, under the title of "Proposed Activities," exactly what its drilling policy is and the mix of wells it expects to drill.

In 1980 almost as much capital was raised for balanced programs involving exploratory and development drilling as was raised for development alone — 20 percent of all registered oil and gas investments.[7]

Income programs. These investments are unlike either exploratory or development programs in that they purchase producing properties rather than develop drilling sites themselves. The risks inherent in income programs are considerably less than in the other kinds of oil and gas investments. Income programs also do

---

6 *Id.*
7 *Id.*

not offer the same tax advantages as the others. Most of their tax write-offs come from the depletion of their oil reserves rather than from developmental drilling costs.

The principal advantage of these programs is their income stream over the life of the oil well, which is normally ten years, or the gas well, which may last fifteen years. As the oil or gas is removed from the well, the income to investors decreases until the well is abandoned as nonproductive. Because these programs produce income with less risk, they appeal to a broader market of investors, and not just to taxpayers in the 50 percent bracket.

Royalty programs. A fifth type of oil and gas investment is a royalty program. The first fund offered to the public that was designed to invest in landowner royalties was introduced in late 1979, so the concept is relatively new. The growth and success have been rapid, however, since a royalty fund is attractive to both the institutional and the individual investor. Some royalty funds can be assembled to offer wide diversification and lower risks than drilling funds with potential returns that equal or exceed the more aggressive programs.

A royalty interest is a percentage of future production retained by the landowner when his land is leased for oil and gas production. The royalty interest bears no part of the cost, risk, or expense of drilling or producing the wells. It is a gross interest in oil and gas revenues.

Currently, Callon Petroleum Company has the largest pool of capital of any company that invests exclusively in royalties.

ATTRACTIVE FEATURES

Oil and gas exploration offers a number of attractive characteristics to both the taxable and tax-exempt investor. For the taxable investor — who in 1980 provided the largest source of funds for oil and gas programs — the primary attractiveness is its ability to shelter taxes. This tends to enhance returns by lowering the risks.

For the larger institutional investor, the attraction lies in the inflation-hedged returns, which potentially outpace competing investment returns. The larger commitments made by institutions also allow a reduction in selling and administrative expense, broader diversification, and, in some cases, a trade-off of potential tax benefits for improved risk or return characteristics. Other attractive features include favorable cash flow, the relatively small amount of money required for a minimum investment, and the diversification it provides.

Tax Shelters

Tax law changes in the mid- and late 1970s closed the door to numerous popular tax shelters. In particular, they limited the amount of deductions that could be taken to only the amount of money the investor has at risk, with only a few exceptions.

Oil and gas investment deductions, however, remained intact and now provide one of the best ways to shelter income. Most oil and gas programs are set up as limited partnerships so that the tax advantages can be passed on pro rata to the investors.

Intangible drilling cost deductions. The most significant tax shelter is the intangible drilling cost deduction. It is allowed in exploratory and development programs, but is not available in other, less risky programs, including income and royalty programs where investors do not share in intangible costs associated with drilling a well.

Intangible drilling costs are those that cannot be capitalized, including fuel, labor, and drilling rig costs. They include the cost to the operators of drilling or development work done by contractors, and in general apply to expenditures for drilling and developing items that do not have a salvage value. Also included are all costs associated with dry holes. Thus, if the program is unsuccessful, as much as 100 percent of the investment can be deducted. Obviously this limits the risk to a taxable investor.

The intangible drilling costs are usually incurred in the first twelve to twenty-four months of a program. The write-offs typically are in the neighborhood of 85 percent of the cost of the investment in the first year. For this reason they make excellent investments for gifting. After taking the write-off in the first two years, at which time cash payments often begin, the investor can gift the investment to a family member in a lower income tax bracket. After the first two years of a program, the liquidation value of the investment is still relatively low and a gift of such an investment can come under the annual gift limitation, which was raised in 1981 from $3,000 to $10,000 per year per person.

Depletion allowance. In a successful drilling program another tax advantage that can be enjoyed is the depletion allowance, which permits oil and gas income to be reduced by a certain amount before taxes are calculated. The effect of the allowance is to reduce the amount of taxes paid by the investor.

Cost depletion. The cost depletion method permits the capitalized costs of a property to be recovered over its productive life. Cost depletion with respect to a particular property for a taxable year is computed by dividing the adjusted cost basis of the property by the total units (barrels of oil and thousand cubic feet of gas) expected to be recoverable therefrom and then multiplying the resulting quotient by the number of units sold during the taxable year. Cost depletion cannot exceed the basis of the property involved.

Percentage depletion. The percentage depletion method is based on a statutory allowance equal to a percentage of the gross income from production of a property. The allowance may not exceed 50 percent of the taxable income from the property. Percentage depletion for a given year is further limited to a maximum of 65 percent of the taxpayer's taxable income for the year, computed without regard to the percentage depletion deduction and without regard to losses occurring in subsequent years and carried back to the taxable year. If percentage depletion exceeds this limitation, the excess is disallowed as a deduction for the current taxable year, but may be carried over by the participant and deducted as a depletion deduction, subject to the same 65 percent limit, in the succeeding taxable year and subsequent years until used. Unlike cost depletion, percentage depletion is not limited to the basis of the property involved, but continues to be allowable as a deduction each year, even after all costs have been recovered. The allowable percentage depletion rate is currently 20 percent, but will be reduced to 18 percent in 1982, 16 percent in 1983, and 15 percent in 1984 and thereafter.

An example of the percentage depletion allowance and its tax effect can be seen in an oil and gas well that produces, say, $100 worth of income. The depletion allowance is 20 percent of gross revenues, or $20. If charges against the investor for raising and marketing the oil amount to $50, the investor's net return is $50 (gross revenue minus the charges). Of that amount, the depletion allowance ($20) is tax-free. The investor ends up paying taxes on $30, which is taxed at his income bracket. At the 50 percent income tax bracket, that would be $15, versus the $25 without the depletion allowance, or an effective tax rate of only 30 percent.

The depletion allowance is similar to depreciation and is a recognition of the declining value of the well as production drops and eventually reaches zero.

High Returns

One of the main reasons many investors embrace oil and gas programs is the potential for high returns. Over the past decade oil and gas program returns have actually outpaced the inflation rate. Indeed, energy costs have been on the leading edge of inflation.

Successful exploratory programs offer the highest returns available, but they are the most risky. In addition, sister wells are usually drilled next to successful exploratory wells, and investors can put more money into those wells with a fairly high chance of good return. A successful exploratory program can return as much as ten times the original investment.

Development wells generally have a much lower payout than exploratory wells, usually not more than twice the original investment. These wells tend to succeed 65 percent to 85 percent of the time, however. Income programs offer even lower returns but have higher chances of being successful. Royalty funds have combined the relative certainty of developmental royalties with those of the high risk/high return exploratory wells. The record to date suggests very high total estimated returns.

In order to lower their risks, most drilling programs offer combinations of exploratory and development wells. An example of successful combination programs are some of those offered by Energy Management Corporation in Denver, Colorado. The programs combine low- and high-risk exploratory drilling with development drilling. Its Omicron partnership, started in the early 1970s, paid cash distributions to its participants totaling $15,032 per $10,000 investment through July 1980.

The total estimated return (which includes future net revenues projected from proven returns) is $41,908 per $10,000 investment. Even more successful is the 1973-A partnership, which had cash distributions of $14,538 per $10,000 investment through July 1980 and has a projected total return of $59,577 per $10,000 invested.

The Petro-Lewis Oil Income Programs provide a good example of income program returns. While not as high as the successful exploratory programs, they offer consistent returns at good rates. All three partnerships formed in late 1970 (70-1, 70-2, and 70-3) returned over $44,000 per each $10,000 investment as of March 31, 1981.

Similarly, all 1980 partnerships (1 through 10) had first-quarter 1981 cash distributions of $300 per $10,000 invested; the first three programs, formed in early 1980, each had cash distributions of $1,110 per $10,000 invested over the four quarters ending March 31, 1981.

In the area of royalties, the Callon 1979 Royalty Fund invested 45 percent of the funds raised to buy tested royalties and 55 percent to purchase higher risk exploratory royalties. The total estimated future return, based on a 1981 engineering report, is expected to be $106,000 per $10,000 investment.

Of course, not all oil and gas partnerships are successful, and returns, obviously, are influenced by changing world markets. (For a discussion of how to appraise such a venture, see *Important Factors in Buying* in this article.)

Investment Vehicle Benefits

The different vehicles for oil and gas investments have different features that make them attractive to various taxpayers. As stated before, the major attractions in exploratory and development programs are the tax shelters available and the possibility of very high rates of return, whereas income programs provide more consistent return rates at lower risk.

Royalty programs also have attractive features. The payments on oil and gas royalties have priority over all others as revenue from the production and sale of the oil and gas is generated. The royalty interest bears no expense or risk in any of the exploration, drilling, completion, or operating costs. In addition, the investor is not called on for any assessments. Royalties themselves can be bought on all kinds of properties and offer one of the only ways for the investor to share directly in the success of the major oil companies' exploration efforts in the more difficult, but prolific, deep new gas prospects. Royalty programs generally invest some portion in proven properties, reducing risk and creating positive cash flow early in the life of the program.

Programs involving gas exploration and production also have a number of attractive characteristics. The windfall profits tax does not apply to natural gas.

In addition, the new gas finds have frequently been in the deeper zones of oil finds where pipeline and other facilities already exist, reducing the development costs. All categories of natural gas are in the process of being deregulated.

Attractions for Tax-Exempt Investors

Tax-exempt investors — notably pension funds — seek oil and gas participations, first, for returns. Returns are high by any standard of history in the conventional securities markets. The second reason is the cash-flow characteristic that complements pension planning. Cash is returned to the investor at regular intervals, usually starting in the first year and stretching, perhaps, into the fiftieth year after the initial investment. A third reason is the inflation-hedge characteristic that the extended payout provides. In later years, if inflation has accelerated, the price the investor receives for gas is going to reflect this price trend. Since energy has been on the leading edge of inflation, any general price increase through the years will be directly reflected in future cash flows.

POTENTIAL RISKS

Oil and gas exploration investments are highly speculative and involve a large number of risks that investors should consider before investing. These are not just limited to drilling risks, but could include problems relating to liquidity and assessment calls as well as management, regulatory, and legal considerations.

Oil and Gas Drilling Risks

The most publicized risks among oil and gas programs are those associated with dry holes and low-production wells. This can mean a substantial investment loss — up to 100 percent, in fact — in a drilling program.

The prospectuses for exploration and development programs all have detailed explanations in their sections dealing with risk. Most say substantially the same thing. The 1981 Damson Development Drilling Program prospectus provides a good example. It states:

> Exploration and drilling for oil and gas involve a high degree of risk. Upon completion of a well there can be no assurance that the well will produce oil or gas in commercial quantities or that it will continue to produce for an appreciable period of time. There can be no assurance that investors will recover any part of their Capital Investment.

Further risks in drilling include unusual or unexpected formations, pressures, downhole fires, blowouts, or other conditions that may either delay or prevent completion of a well. Most operators further warn that these conditions may result in substantial losses and possible liability to third parties. These risks may not be covered by insurance, because it is either unavailable or considered impractical due to high premium costs. If these costs are incurred in most partnerships, the funds available for exploration and development are reduced accordingly.

Income Program Risks

Income programs have few of these risks. They do, however, have some risks associated with oil and gas production. Producing oil and gas properties are purchased for the programs on the basis of geologic and engineering data. In addition, the operators make certain assumptions when they purchase properties regarding the future price of the oil and gas and the future development and production costs of the well. To the extent that these estimates and assumptions are incorrect, returns will be lower.

Royalty Program Risks

In royalty programs, the partnership does not bear any costs associated with drilling or production, but an investment in a royalty will be affected if the drilling does not result in a commercial oil or gas reserve. The royalty may also be affected if natural hazards (such as blowouts) occur, to the extent that oil and gas reserves are diminished and income is delayed.

Return Risk

The riskier oil and gas programs — the exploratory and development programs — have widely varying success rates. Some will produce returns many times the original investment while others may lose almost the entire investment. This risk can be evidenced by taking a look at some of the programs sponsored by Energy Management Corp., cited earlier.

The Delta partnership, formed in 1972 for exploratory and development drilling, made cash distributions of $5,464 to participants for each $10,000 invested through July 1980. Future net revenues from proven reserves are estimated at $136 per each $10,000 investment, for a total estimated return of $5,600. Of the total wells drilled, 50 percent were productive. The 1973-B partnership made cash distributions to participants of $1,423 per $10,000 investment through July 1980. Future net revenues are estimated at $544 per $10,000 investment for a total estimated return of $1,967 per $10,000 investment. The program had 38 percent of its total wells drilled turn into productive wells.

Typically, the industry handles return risk by diversification across a sufficiently large number of prospects to average into the high returns available. Clearly, large institutions are more able to commit the investment funds required for a variety of programs than individuals are, yet both should commit sufficient investment dollars to diversify as widely as is practical.

Liquidity Risk

Investments in all types of oil and gas programs are essentially illiquid. The typical oil well generally produces for about ten years and profits to investors, if any, are received only as the well pays out. A problem could arise if an investor needed cash quickly.

There is only a small market for the sale of limited partnership units. Also, any accumulated losses on the investment are not transferable for tax purposes to the purchaser, and so the resale value is very low compared to the future revenues the program should be generating for the original investor.

Cash redemptions. Most programs try in some way to reduce this liquidity risk. Many do this by providing cash redemptions. Essentially, the operator agrees to buy back investment units for an amount based on the company's valuation of that unit. Cash redemptions generally are not available, however, until several years into the program. In addition, the manager could run into a problem if there are too many redemptions. Unlike a mutual fund, redemptions cannot be paid by selling off assets.

Conversion into stocks. A conversion of the investment units to common stock is another method some programs use to increase liquidity. This alleviates the manager's problem of coming up with needed cash for redemptions. However, this too occurs only after several years into the program. And the market for the common stock of a former partnership will likely be very thin. Finally, such a conversion does not allow the tax-free flow-through of any remaining tax shelter from the investment.

Management and Performance Risk

Management risk is one of the more serious problems in oil and gas investments. The people responsible for managing a program and overseeing its prospects are the key to its success or complete failure. Conflict of interest and self-dealing can and do arise in these programs. These situations are not necessarily illegal or detrimental to the program, but the SEC requires that these problems be detailed in program prospectuses and that investors be aware of them. Despite detailed disclosures of possible conflict of interest and self-dealing in program prospectuses, it is still difficult to determine if these possibilities pose real dangers to a program.

Conflict of interest. The type of program that is most susceptible to a conflict of interest is one that is managed by an oil company. The company is acting as an agent for the investor in the program, but at the same time it may be selling services to the program.

In addition, the company's geological staff will be evaluating properties in an attempt to generate oil and gas prospects. The staff may be doing this for both the company and the program. The conflict lies in determining into which portfolio the prospect will be placed — the oil company's or the program's.

Self-dealing. Self-dealing can occur if the operating company has an affiliate or is itself providing services to the program. The operator then is acting as both buyer and seller. Operators that supervise a series of different programs will encounter conflict when they must decide which properties are going to go into the various programs.

Managerial performance. Accurately measuring the past performance of managers is another investor problem, in spite of the reporting requirements of the SEC and the various states. Most programs will provide statistics regarding previous performance, but comparing these is difficult because not enough information is provided regarding the underlying values of the program.

For example, in exploratory programs, operators can drill wells on properties having a wide range of risk. A step-out well, or a well drilled near a proven well but in an unproven area, is still an exploratory well but is far less risky than one drilled far away from any proven areas. An exploratory program drilling a large number of step-out wells will have a higher success ratio — and a lower risk — than one drilling in unproven properties located away from proven areas. The two programs are both exploratory and both are drilling in the same geological area, but may have unreported differences in the risks involved, which account for their different success ratios.

Assessments Risk

Although assessments are generally a good sign, most investors do not like them and therefore they are classed as risks. An assessment is made to provide funds to develop discoveries that are made using the funds from the original investment. If the drilling has been very successful, the operator will need a sizable amount of cash up front to develop the wells. This cannot be financed through the cash flow of the well.

These new costs are not predictable, so some programs will provide for assessments in which each investor must put more money into the program. The amount callable can be either limited or unlimited, according to the program's prospectus.

Regulatory Risks

The energy industry is highly political and new regulatory legislation affecting this area is being continuously enacted. Most of the regulatory risk involves the pricing of oil and gas and could affect oil and gas investments.

President Reagan decontrolled the price of crude oil and refined petroleum products in early 1981. These had been subject to the allocation and price controls adopted in the Emergency Petroleum Allocation Act of 1973.

Natural gas prices are being deregulated more slowly under the Natural Gas Policy Act of 1978. By 1985, the Act provides for the deregulation of newly discovered natural gas. High-cost natural gas was decontrolled effective November 1, 1979. In addition, federal controls were imposed on intrastate gas marketing for the first time.

Natural gas production is regulated by the Federal Energy Regulatory Commission (FERC), which is part of the Department of Energy. The FERC has control over the transportation and marketing of natural gas and can change the selling price of gas.

The U.S. government has the power to increase or decrease the amount of imported oil, which directly affects oil and gas prices in the United States. It can also pass laws and regulations regarding pollution controls and the conservation of oil and gas that would affect the prices of these commodities.

ERISA Considerations

Employee benefit plans are subject to the Employee Retirement Income Security Act of 1974 (ERISA), and have certain requirements for investments in oil and gas programs.

Some programs will make tax-exempt institutions liable for unrelated business income tax. (See *Tax Consequences* in this article.) Also, proposed regulations by the Department of Labor may affect investments by employee benefit funds in limited partnerships. The proposals state that if an employee benefit plan invests in a pooled investment vehicle, the assets of the plan include not only its direct ownership in the investment vehicle but, in addition, the assets of the pooled vehicle.

This may cause some program investments to be considered "prohibited transactions" as defined under ERISA. In addition, the fiduciary standards stated in ERISA would, under those circumstances, apply not only to the persons controlling the employee benefit plan investments, but also to those controlling the investments made by the pooled vehicle — in the case of oil and gas investments, the operator. Certain exemptions are provided for in the proposed regulations, those for investment vehicles registered under the Investment Company Act of 1940 or the Securities Exchange Act of 1934. Some of the recent oil and gas participations sold to ERISA clients have ignored the proposed plan-asset regulations and others were constructed so as to avoid a potential conflict. The interpretation of these rules, however, is uncertain at this time and should be thoroughly discussed with legal counsel, investment adviser, managing partner, and selling broker.

TAX CONSEQUENCES

It is impractical and imprudent to attempt here a detailed explanation of all the tax consequences involved in oil and gas partnerships. Major changes in applicable federal tax laws were made by the Tax Reform Act of 1976, the Revenue Act of 1978, and, most recently, the Economic Recovery Tax Act of

1981. These laws affect businesses, individuals, estates, and the tax shelters themselves. Many more changes will take effect annually at least through 1984.

For example, tax brackets will be broadened each year through 1984. To remain in the 49 percent tax bracket in 1981, a taxpayer must not earn over $60,000. In 1982, that figure will increase to $85,000 and finally, in 1984, the 50 percent tax bracket begins at $162,001. This will significantly decrease the population of taxpayers in the 50 percent bracket.

Since exploratory and development programs traditionally have been recommended only to upper-bracket taxpayers, the profile of these investors could change considerably in the next few years. New financial structures for oil and gas programs or further changes in the tax laws could result.

With these many variables in mind, this section will outline only the most significant tax considerations. Since oil and gas programs are not appropriate for all investors, it is advisable to consult an accountant, tax attorney, broker, or even oil and gas specialist before launching into a program.

Tax Benefits and Caveats for Exploration-Development Investors

Without a doubt, the tax benefits involved in exploratory and development oil programs are their most attractive characteristics. Oil and gas drilling offers taxpayers the benefit of immediate deduction of intangible drilling and development costs, a tax-free depletion allowance, and the depreciation and amortization of capital assets. In addition, certain expenses are also deductible, such as management fees and overhead costs. It should be kept in mind, however, that several of these tax benefits have a reverse side that could cost the taxpayer money in the future.

For example, a taxpayer must be careful of depreciation and amortization deductions and investment tax credits. While these will effectively lower an investor's tax liability, they could return to haunt him in the form of higher taxes later on. If a partnership sells property on which depreciation has been claimed by investors, the gain attributable to the depreciation will be treated as ordinary income and not as capital gain. Similarly, the sale or abandonment of property on which an investment tax credit has been claimed could result in a tax equal to the amount of the previously claimed credit.

Along these same lines, tax preference items are anything but preferred by taxpayers. In essence, they are special tax benefits on which the IRS taxes the investor. In other words, an investor can enjoy the deductions, but he is going to pay for them. The tax preference items are subject to a 15 percent additional tax when they exceed the exemption allowed.

Tax preference items include certain intangible drilling costs, certain development costs, preference depletion, amortization, and accelerated depreciation on leased personal property. The tax is equal to roughly 15 percent of the taxpayer's preference items for that year to the extent they exceed the greater of $10,000 ($5,000 for a spouse filing a separate return) or one-half of the taxpayer's regular federal income tax. For example, a taxpayer with $20,000 in intangible drilling costs and a regular tax liability of $15,000 would pay a minimum tax of $1,500 on his preference items, as shown below:

Tax preference income	$20,000
Less: The greater of $10,000 or half the tax liability (½ × $15,000 = $7,500)	10,000
	$10,000
Multiplied by: Minimum tax rate	× 0.15
Tax preference tax	$ 1,500

The drilling program investor also should remember that intangible drilling costs are deductible only in the year in which they are incurred, and a drilling year may not be the same as a calendar year. For example, if a taxpayer purchases a $10,000 drilling program in October, hoping to shelter 85 percent of his investment through the intangible drilling costs of the first program year, he may be sorely disappointed. In fact, the taxpayer may only be able to deduct 20 percent of his investment that calendar year and the remaining 65 percent will apply to drilling that takes place between January and September of the next year. That program's drilling year is October to September, not January to December.

Therefore, oil programs should be purchased as early as possible in the calendar year if the taxpayer is interested in maximum deductions for that tax year. This is particularly true if the taxpayer knows he will be receiving a large, one-time payment of money from a bonus or the sale of a capital asset. He might even consider borrowing the money for the program if the bonus is not to be received until the end of the year.

The intangible deductions the taxpayer will receive should far outweigh even today's high interest costs. Also, a 50-percent-bracket taxpayer borrowing at 15 percent is really borrowing at a net effective rate of only 7.5 percent, since net investment interest is largely deductible.

Windfall Profits Tax

Few pieces of tax legislation have prompted the heated debates that the windfall profits tax has. Formally known as the Crude Oil Windfall Profits Tax Act of 1980, it imposes an excise tax on domestic crude oil produced after February 29, 1980. Many experts in the field claim that this tax will not significantly reduce the advantages of oil and gas programs for the limited partners.

As a result of the legislation, oil is classified as Tier I, II, or III, depending on when it was removed from the well and the kind and amount of oil per day the well produces. A base price is attributed to each tier ranging from $12.81 to $16.35. The windfall profits tax is applied against the difference between the price an investor receives for the oil and the applicable base price adjusted for certain state taxes and inflation. Most limited partners qualify as independent producers and pay a lower tax rate for Tier I and Tier II oil than do the larger majors, normally oil companies or producers of more than 1,000 barrels per day.

The oil tax will reduce profits depending on the kind of property the program owns. It is estimated that for wells producing prior to January 1, 1979, the Windfall Profits Tax will reduce after-tax profits about 29 percent. This figure drops down to 15 percent for properties producing after the beginning of 1979.

Although this legislation does reduce profits somewhat, it was followed by price decontrols that mitigate these losses by greatly increasing after-tax profits per barrel of oil. And so, even with the tax, oil and gas program returns are expected to remain strong.

Sale of a Partnership Interest

If an investor is in an upper-income bracket and is interested in tax shelters rather than income, he may want to dispose of his oil and gas program after exhausting most of its deductions during the first two years or so of the program. Of course, the taxpayer can gift this to a lower-income member of the family, as was explained earlier. However, if this is not possible or practical and the program is sold back to the general partners, the investor probably will be entitled to long-term capital gains tax consideration.

The taxpayer must remember to take into account the adjusted basis in this asset. Let's say an investor with a $10,000 program enjoyed deductions of 80 percent — or $8,000 — over two years. If the program is sold for $7,000, he does not realize a loss of $3,000 — the difference between the purchase price and the selling price. Rather, the taxpayer pays capital gains tax on $5,000, the difference between $7,000, the selling price, and $2,000, which is the adjusted basis.

By deducting $8,000 from the original $10,000 investment, the investor claims to the IRS that the program is worth only $2,000, and that is his basis. If the asset is sold, he pays tax on the difference between the adjusted basis and the selling price.

Once a year, the oil program managers usually offer the limited partners the opportunity to sell out. The partnership must be careful not to allow too much turnover in ownership, since this could jeopardize the program's tax classification as a limited partnership and may instead turn the program into an association taxable as a corporation. Usually a general partner will limit the number of transfers per year to 10 percent or 20 percent of the outstanding units, a figure substantially below the prohibited figure set by the IRS.

Other Taxes

In addition to federal income taxes, partnership interests also may be subject to state income, gift, inheritance, and estate taxes.

Certain kinds of oil and gas investments may subject tax-exempt institutions to taxation. Tax-exempt organizations that participate directly in business ventures through limited partnerships may be generating "unrelated business income" as defined by the IRS. In such cases, those organizations will have to pay unrelated business income taxes on revenues received from the investment.

REPRESENTATIVE TYPES OF INVESTORS

In the public oil and gas programs, the upper-bracket taxpayer is unquestionably the most significant investor. Of the oil and gas funds raised in public programs in 1980, fully 75 percent were earmarked for exploratory drilling, development drilling, or balanced exploratory and development drilling programs. In these programs, tax considerations are key components and only those individuals in a 50 percent income tax bracket or higher should be involved.

High-Income Individuals

Investors in drilling programs are generally well to do. Most oil and gas programs have minimum investment requirements of at least $5,000, and many investment counselors recommend investing in two or three programs to diversify and minimize risk. In addition, many programs have high net worth requirements. For example, the Stone Oil Corporation 1981-II Ltd. drilling program has a minimum subscription of $25,750. It is also limited to persons with a net worth of not less than $225,000 (excluding home, furnishings, and automobiles) or to persons with a net worth of not less than $60,000 (excluding home, furnishings, and automobiles) and taxable income for the previous year of $60,000 or more.

These investments can be used by taxpaying individuals in a variety of different fashions. If an investor is expecting to receive a large amount of money in a given year, the programs provide a good tax shelter. They can also be purchased by a high-income investor just prior to retirement. The large write-offs can be taken in the years the individual is still working and making a large income. Income generated from the investment, if any, would be received several years later, when the individual is in a lower tax bracket. Obviously, someone who is about to retire would not invest in such a speculative area without having a significant amount of other, more conservative, investments.

These investments also are used by high-tax-bracket individuals who wish to gift their assets to a benefactor. The write-offs are used by the original investor in the first several years and the asset can then be transferred — preferably to a lower-income individual.

Lower-Income Individuals

Investors in the less risky income programs are looking for consistent cash flow from their programs. This income is also partially sheltered. Lower-tax-bracket individuals invest in these programs, which include individual retirement accounts (IRAs), Keogh plans, and pension plans. Income programs also have re-investment provisions allowing investors — particularly those with IRAs and

Keogh plans — to build their asset bases for future retirement income. And the fairly consistent rate of return enables pension plans to do benefit-cost projections.

Corporations

Corporations also are starting to enter the oil and gas arena through private placements, although their number is still small. The investment is used as a hedge against future energy costs that the company may be forced to incur as energy prices escalate.

Insurance Companies

Insurance companies also are investing in oil and gas exploration, largely through private placements. Insurance companies have the available capital to invest in such placements for relatively long periods of time and, in addition, can take advantage of some of the tax-shelter aspects. The attraction is the inflation-hedged return. Firms active in this area include Prudential, Aetna, Equitable, Allstate, and Northwestern Mutual Life.

Tax-Exempt Institutions

Tax-exempt institutions are starting to invest in oil and gas for similar reasons. These investments also have been largely through private placements and, most recently, have been in the form of royalty interests. Traditionally very conservative, pension funds appear to favor this relatively passive approach to oil and gas investing; in addition, the royalty interests appear to provide the best legal arrangements in light of ERISA requirements. Another indirect participation enjoyed by pension funds has been debt offerings with equity kicker features.

An advantage of the private placement is that the deals can be structured specifically for the pension funds involved in the deal because of the large amounts of capital the funds are able to put up. Pension funds also have invested smaller amounts in some public offerings, a few of which have been set up primarily for institutions.

A representative sampling of major pension funds that have invested in oil and gas deals includes the pension funds of Hughes Aircraft, General Electric, DuPont, Beatrice Foods, Eastern Airlines, AT&T, IBM, and Atlantic Richfield. Investment amounts are as great as $10 million, and many have been for less than $1 million.

IMPORTANT FACTORS IN BUYING

Not all oil and gas programs are successful. The bewildering number of oil and gas drilling programs may look much the same to the inexperienced investor. Nothing is further from the truth. Even the good programs can have a bad year and, without doubt, there are poor programs. It is always advisable to make this kind of investment through a reputable financial intermediary. In addition, the following broadly applicable guidelines may be useful. Note that some of the information needed may only be available verbally pursuant to current securities regulations.

Past Performance

The most important information the potential investor can get is how the drilling company has done in the past. Past performance is measured in terms of net future revenues from proven oil and gas reserves in relation to limited partner capital contribution. Net future revenues are the estimated sale value of oil and gas discovered less estimated operating costs and borrowings. The limited partner's capital contribution is the original investment plus any assessments. Essentially, a desirable return is an average of twice the limited partner investment in net future revenues (undiscounted) as an average over the preceding three to five years. Even more desirable is about 1.4 times the investment in net future revenues discounted at a rate of about 10 percent.

The investor should be sure, in making comparisons, to use only proven reserves, not what are called "probable" or "possible reserves." He should notice what price escalation formulas are used; the most trustworthy figures are those provided by an independent reserve engineering firm.

The past performance information provided in a prospectus, such as the so-called success ratios and the cash distribution tables, can be meaningless or very hard to interpret. A better success ratio does not necessarily mean a better economic result. The success ratio is the percentage of all wells drilled that are completed as producers. Drilling should be successful 90 percent of the time in the Appalachian Basin (Ohio, West Virginia), but perhaps only 30 to 40 percent of the time in Louisiana. Why, then, drill in Louisiana? The answer is more prolific reserves, potentially more dollars back per dollar spent.

The cash distribution tables show the cash actually paid out to the investor. This too can be deceptive. Some types of wells pay out (or produce) over 50 percent of all that they will ever pay out in the first two years of their productive lives and do not produce any significant revenues after the first four or five years. Other types of wells produce a lower percentage of the total early on, but produce over a twelve- to fifteen-year life.

Front-End Costs

Another factor to consider is how much of the investor's capital contribution goes into the ground. The rule of thumb is 87.5 percent. This applies to oil and gas drilling or leasing costs, as opposed to management fees, general and administrative overhead, brokerage commissions, and offering costs. An investor who is asked to pay more front-end bills can seriously dilute the chance for a good investment.

Importance of Expert Advice

The most important step that a potential investor should make is to seek the help of an expert in determining whether an investment in oil and gas is prudent, based on the investor's particular financial condition.

An outside adviser can provide both taxable investors and tax-exempt institutions with the expertise needed to determine the appropriateness of such an investment and to evaluate the different kinds of programs available. For the taxable investor, it is advisable to have an accountant or tax adviser review the investor's tax situation and the effect the potential investment will have on it.

For further advice on the different kinds of programs, a reputable stock broker can provide a wealth of research information. For tax-exempt institutions, a number of firms provide advice on oil and gas investing. (See *Companies Offering Programs and Investment Placement Advisers* in this article.)

A good adviser should provide an investor with the following:

- Help in determining the risk tolerances the investor can live with;
- Help in determining if the investment will assist the investor in achieving particular financial objectives and needs;
- Help in evaluating alternative investments and setting up a suitable asset mix for the investor's portfolio;
- Help in determining which of the numerous oil and gas programs available would be best for the particular investor;
- Research on many of the programs to help eliminate the questionable ones;
- Help in evaluating the tax implications of a chosen investment for the taxable investor; and
- Assistance in structuring a private placement suited to the needs of the large institutional investor.

Judging the Particular Program

There are numerous oil and gas programs on the market at any given time. Evaluating them properly is difficult and time-consuming.

Management record. One of the most important features in an oil and gas investment is management, and this is one of the most difficult areas on which to find information. Brokers and investment advisers can provide some help in this area. Familiarity with management — either through previous investments or through the experience of others — is also a plus in judging programs. Some background information on the general partners is also provided in program prospectuses.

Financial structure. Investment consultants strongly recommend that investors study the financial structure of the program. The general partner should be sharing in some of the program costs. How those costs are divided among the general and limited partners is also important, particularly in drilling programs. Limited partners should pay the intangible costs so as to benefit from the tax write-offs. At the same time, revenues should provide the general partner with some incentive fee. This probably will mean that the general partner will receive a proportionally larger percentage of the revenues than that to which the general partner's capital contribution would entitle him. A typical agreement would give the general partners a 40 percent share of the revenues based on a 15 percent contribution of capital.

Obviously, it is better for the investor if the general partners' profit is based on the success of the program and not simply on the successful selling of the program. Also, management fees and sales commissions among the various programs should be compared.

Other considerations. Investors should check to see if the program will be incurring any indebtedness. If so, there should be limitations on the amount.

The size of the oil and gas program should be substantial to provide enough capital for proper diversification. Programs probably should be investing in a fair number of wells (at least twenty-five) in a number of different locations.

Investors also should be aware of the conflict-of-interest potential in the different programs, and the possibility of future assessments. If the program will be making such changes, they should be limited in size. In addition, the consequences of not paying the assessment should be examined.

Redemptions are important because they provide the investment with at least a small amount of liquidity. Some programs may provide for redemptions earlier than others. Transferability of the units is also important, since programs often have limitations on this.

For investors interested in a program for its cash flow, a prospectus should indicate when revenues can be expected.

MANAGING THE INVESTMENT

Investments in oil and gas programs should be treated with the same kind of care given to any security. The investor should make sure that the program's general partner provides detailed, audited annual reports on the financial status of the partnership, including fees and commissions paid to the general partner. Generally, unaudited reports on the partnership activities are provided quarterly.

General partners also provide the limited partners with necessary tax reporting information on the program. At the end of the calendar year the general partner files tax information on the partnership with the IRS and sends each limited partner a schedule indicating his share of the deductions and tax credits, if any.

GLOSSARY

appraisal drilling— Drilling performed in the vicinity of a discovery well for the purpose of evaluating the extent and importance of the find.

blowout— A violent and sudden escape of mud, oil, and gas from a well that is being drilled, followed by an uncontrolled flow from the well.

bottom out— To reach the total depth of the well.

capital assets— Assets that are purchased for purposes of investment and are not for sale; require no management duties. An example is a royalty if it is held for investment purposes.

capital expenditure— Expenditures that are nondeductible; items in the oil industry of this nature include geophysical and geological costs and well equipment.

commercial well— A well capable of production in quantities sufficient to pay out in a reasonable time and to produce a profit.

completed well— A well in which drilling and completion operations have been finished.

completion costs— The costs associated with completing a well.

confirmation well— A well that is drilled in order to prove a production zone discovered by an exploratory well.

developed acreage— The number of acres assignable to productive wells.

development well— A well drilled in an area that is proven productive in an oil and gas reservoir.

discovery well— An exploratory well that has found a new and untapped petroleum deposit.

engineering appraisal— An appraisal of the proven and probable reserves in a region; it includes a future net income estimate and is conducted by an independent petroleum engineer.

exploratory well— A well that is drilled for the purpose of either discovering a new reservoir of oil and gas or extending the limits of a pool. The subcategories of exploratory wells are: wildcat wells, drilled in unproven areas; step-out or field extension wells, drilled in an unproven area but near a proven area to extend the proven limits; and deep test wells, drilled in a proven field but to deeper zones that are unproven.

fee— The ownership of land; the title to the land is held by the fee owner.

formation— Sedimentary rock beds distinct in character and forming an identifiable geologic unit.

independent producer— In general, an oil company that is relatively small and unintegrated, producing oil but having no pipeline system or refinery.

intangible drilling costs— Expenditures incurred in drilling a well on items that do not have salvage value, such as labor, fuel, repairs, and hauling, which are allowed as tax deductions.

mullet— An industry term referring to a sucker who knows nothing about the oil business but who puts money into the drilling of an oil well.

operating costs— Costs incurred from completed wells in the producing and marketing of oil and gas.

reserves— The estimated amount of recoverable oil or gas in a pool; subcategories include: proven developed reserves, proven reserves that are estimated to be recoverable from existing wells; probable reserves, potential productive new reserves in proven fields; and possible reserves, speculative reserves that can be proven only by more drilling.

royalty— A percentage share in the oil and gas revenues produced from a property.

stripper well— A well that is producing less than ten barrels a day and is in the final stages of producing oil and gas.

undeveloped acreage— Acreage that has not been drilled or completed to produce commercial wells; undeveloped acreage can contain both proven and unproven reserves.

working interest— The interest that bears the costs of drilling and operating a property in the production of oil and gas properties.

TRADE ORGANIZATIONS

American Association of Petroleum Landmen, Fort Worth, Tex.

American Petroleum Institute, Washington, D.C.

Gas Research Institute, Chicago, Ill.

Independent Petroleum Association of America, Washington, D.C.

International Association of Drilling Contractors, Houston, Tex.

International Association of Oil Well Drilling Contractors, Houston, Tex.

International Oil Scouts Association, Austin, Tex.

Mid-Continent Oil and Gas Association, Tulsa, Okla.

National Petroleum Council, Washington, D.C.

National Petroleum Refiners Association, Washington, D.C.

Petroleum Equipment Institute, Tulsa, Okla.

Petroleum Marketing Education Foundation, Columbia, S.C.

Society of Exploration Geophysicists, Tulsa, Okla.

Texas Independent Producers and Royalty Owners Association, Austin, Tex.

COMPANIES OFFERING PROGRAMS AND INSTITUTIONAL PLACEMENT ADVISERS

Below is a sampling of the companies offering oil and gas programs and the amounts they raised in 1981.

Apache Corp., Minneapolis, Minn. — $70,000,000 (drilling)

Callon Petroleum Co., Natchez, Miss. — $15,000,000 (drilling)/$71,000,000 (royalty)

Can-Am Drilling Programs Inc., Ft. Worth, Tex. — $74,000 (drilling)

C&K Petroleum Inc., Houston, Tex. — $17,587,500 (drilling)

Damson Oil Corp., New York, N.Y. — $192,000,000 (income fund)/$17,000,000 (drilling)

Energy Management Corp., Denver, Colo. — $49,500,000 (drilling)

ENI Exploration Co., Seattle, Wash. — $62,645,000 (drilling)

Petro-Lewis Inc., Denver, Colo. — $499,000 (income fund)

Stone Oil Corp., Lafeyette, La. — $46,100,000 (drilling)

Woods Petroleum Corp., Oklahoma City, Okla. — $50,000,000 (drilling)

Investment Bankers

MacDonald & Co., Cleveland, Ohio

Mason Street Securities, Milwaukee, Wis. (a subsidiary of National Investment Services)

Moseley Associates, Boston, Mass.

Investment Advisers

Bank of America Investment Management Co. (BAIMCO), San Francisco, Cal.

The Boston Co., Boston, Mass.

Chase Investor Management Corp., New York, N.Y.

National Investment Services of America, Milwaukee, Wis.

SUGGESTED READING

Periodicals

Institutional Investor. Published by Institutional Investor Systems, Inc., New York, N.Y. Monthly financial magazine covering institutional investments.

Oil and Gas Journal. Published by Petroleum Publishing Co., Tulsa, Okla. Weekly newspaper covering news of the American oil producers.

Pensions & Investment Age. Published by Crain Communications, Inc., Chicago, Ill. Biweekly newspaper for the tax-exempt investor.

Platt's Oilgram News Service. Published by McGraw-Hill Inc., New York, N.Y. Daily newsletter giving all oil news and the prices of main petroleum products.

Reference Books

Adelman, M.A. *The World Petroleum Market.* Chicago: Johns Hopkins, 1977.

American Petroleum Institute. *Basic Petroleum Data Book.* Tulsa, 1978.

Chevalier, Jean-Marie. *The New Oil Stakes.* London: Allen Lane, 1973.

Dam, Kenneth W. *Oil Resources: Who Gets What How?* Chicago: University of Chicago Press, 1976.

Griffin, James M., et al. *Energy Economics & Policy.* New York: Academic Press, 1979.

Johnson, William A., et al. *Competition in the Oil Industry.* Washington, D.C.: Energy Policy Research Project, 1976.

Lattes, Robert, ed. *Energy: The Countdown.* London: Pergamon Press, 1979.

McDonald, Stephen L. *Petroleum Conservation in the U.S.: An Economic Analysis.* Washington, D.C.: Johns Hopkins Press, 1971.

McQuown, Judith H. *Tax Shelters That Work For Everyone.* New York: McGraw-Hill, 1979.

O'Connor, Harvey. *The Empire of Oil.* New York: Monthly Review Press, 1963.

Stanger, Robert A. *Tax Shelters in the 80s.* Fair Haven: Robert A. Stanger & Co., 1980.

Options—Puts and Calls

*Myron S. Scholes**

BASIC CHARACTERISTICS

Definitions

A call option is the right to buy an asset — for example, 100 shares of common stock — at a fixed price, on or before a date in the future. A put option is the right to sell the asset to another investor. The fixed price of the option is called its "striking price" or its "exercise price"; the date of expiration of the contract is called its "maturity date" or its "expiration date"; the asset itself is called the "underlying security." The sellers of options are known as option writers and the buyers of options are known as option buyers. The price of an option is called the "option premium."

Similarity to Other Securities

Since 1973, call options and, more recently, put options have been trading on organized secondary markets. Investors have become familiar with the characteristics of these contracts, which are relatively simple contracts with set maturity dates and exercise prices. They may be unaware, however, that other commonly traded securities are first cousins to options. Warrants, executive stock options, and even the common stock and bonds of a corporation are examples of securities that are closely related to put and call options.

The common stock of a corporation with bonds in its capital structure is an option because the shareholders have the right to buy back the assets of the firm from the bondholders by paying off the face amount of the debt (its fixed price) at the maturity of the bond (the expiration date of the contract). Since many financial instruments have characteristics similar to those of put and call options, a detailed knowledge of put and call options may be helpful in understanding these other contracts, and vice versa.

Market History

Put and call options are traded on the Chicago Board Options Exchange (CBOE), the American Stock Exchange (AMEX), the Philadelphia Stock Exchange (PHLX), and the Pacific Stock Exchange (PSE). For many years prior to the formation of the CBOE in 1973, options were traded over the counter. This

* Myron S. Scholes is the Edward Eagle Brown Professor of Banking and Finance at the Graduate School of Business, University of Chicago.

method of trading had numerous disadvantages. For example, transaction costs were high, secondary trading was limited, option contracts were not standardized, investors had to look directly to the writer for fulfillment of the contract, and option prices were seldom published, and therefore hard to find. With the formation of the CBOE, many of these problems were overcome. As a result, investor interest and trading volume exploded. Indeed, listed options are particularly attractive to investors who want a low-cost contract that is guaranteed and standardized, with an active secondary market.

Market Procedures

Preset dates. The options traded on the exchanges expire in preset months. On any particular exchange and at any one time, options on an underlying security expire in each of three given expiration months. A listed option on an underlying security trades in one of three expiration month cycles: January, April, July, October; February, May, August, November; or March, June, September, December. Even though there are four months in a cycle, only three maturity months trade because exchange rules allow listing of a new option contract only if it expires in nine months or less. With this rule, in November the CBOE can only trade options on IBM that expire in January, April, and July, but by the end of January, the CBOE can trade options on IBM that expire in April, July, and October. Technically, the options expire on the Saturday following the third Friday in the expiration month. This means that on any trading day, including that Friday afternoon, option buyers may instruct their brokers to exercise their options through the clearing corporation, the guarantor, on the next working day, including that Saturday morning. Prior to expiration, investors holding long positions (option buyers) can sell their holdings and investors with short positions (option writers) can liquidate their commitments at any time that markets are open for trading, including the third Friday of the expiration month.

Striking price. The striking price of an option must be a whole number that is a multiple of five. The striking prices are set at $5 intervals for stocks trading below $100 and at $10 intervals for stocks trading above $100. When an old contract month ends, two new contracts are introduced on the underlying security. These new contracts, which expire in the new trading month of the series, have striking prices set to bracket the price of the underlying security. For example, if the stock were trading at $52, the new options would be traded with striking prices set at $50 and $55. If the price of the underlying stock changed by more than $5 ($10 for a stock selling at a price over $100), new options with different striking prices would be introduced. On exchange-traded options, the standard contract is for 100 shares of the underlying stock. Stock split or stock dividend adjustments, however, may cause striking prices to be changed to odd numbers, and odd lots of shares to be used. For example, the adjustment for a 10 percent stock dividend would be to give the buyer the right to buy 110 shares of stock at 90 percent of the striking price. The introduction of new contract strike prices is limited by various regulations of the exchanges and of the Securities and Exchange Commission (SEC).

How an Option Differs From Similar Investments

Buyers exercise their options only if it is in their economic interest to do so. Unlike investors in other securities, investors in call options do not have to buy the shares, and investors in put options do not have to sell the shares of the underlying common stocks on which they hold these options. On expiration of the contract, call options are exercised only if the price of the underlying stock is above the striking price; put options are exercised only if the price of the underlying stock is below the striking price. Buyers of options may find it in their interest to exercise prior to the expiration of the contract.

An option contract is similar to an insurance policy. The asset being insured is the underlying common stock. Investors insure against possible loss in return on the holdings of common stock by buying put options on their stock; a put option with the same exercise price as the current stock price insures against a decline in the stock price for the term of the put option. Loss, like a fully deductible insurance policy, is limited to the premium paid for the put option; on a fall in price the investor puts the stock to the put seller, the insurer, and receives the exercise price in return. Naturally, if the stock increases in price, the put is not exercised; the insurance is not used. This article will show how a call option also provides insurance and how a call option is related to a put option. (See *Use as Investment Insurance* in this article.) As an insurance policy on a home insures against the loss from a fire, holding put options on common stock insures against the loss from a drop in the price of the stock. Using options, investors can sell off part of the risk — insure part of the risk of common stock investments. The sellers of options, like insurers generally, expect that the option premiums will cover the costs of the insurance they sell to the buyers of the options. If actuarially fair, neither the buyer nor the seller expects to earn an above-normal rate of return at the expense of the other side of the trade.

Although options are similar to insurance contracts, options have been confused with futures contracts and with forward contracts. The confusion arises because the terms are similar. Several concepts used in the marketing of futures contracts were adopted by the CBOE for use in the trading of options. Buyers of futures contracts for July wheat have bought the July wheat, although they will not take delivery until July. The buyer of a forward contract for delivery of an asset in July — such as a house — has bought the asset. The futures contract is marked to market, settled for cash each day, whereas the forward contract will change in value with changes in the value of the asset. Buyers of options for July IBM, in contrast, have not bought IBM, but only the right to buy IBM at a fixed price.

Margin on futures, held by the clearing corporation, and margin on forwards, held by an agent in escrow, may be a small fraction of the value of the underlying asset. Margin assures that buyers and sellers fulfill their obligation in settling the contracts. The value of an option contract is a small fraction of the value of the underlying stock; for example, July call options on IBM would be priced at about 10 percent of the price of IBM, with the striking price the same as the market price and with six months to expiration. This small premium has been compared to the margin of the futures contract.

Percentage changes in the prices of an option are greater than the percentage changes in the prices of the underlying common stock; percentage changes in the margin account of a futures contract are greater than the percentage changes in the price of the underlying commodity. Some consider the two instruments to be substitutes because the percentage movements are leveraged and appear similar; both instruments are ways to buy leverage in the market.

Another point of comparison is open interest. In the futures market, the open interest (the number of contracts on which buyers can request delivery) is greater than zero; however, the net number of futures contracts is always zero; for every buyer of a futures contract there is a seller on the opposite side of the futures contract. The clearing corporation keeps the book; therefore, a buyer is not matched with a particular seller. In the options market, the open interest is the number of contracts that can be exercised in that month; the net open interest is zero. The options market has its own clearing corporation.

Since buyers match sellers and no new money is raised by corporations, these contracts have been compared to side bets and to gambling, contracts without an economic purpose. Futures and options both have economic purposes; they help investors with portfolio planning, thereby facilitating the functioning of the primary and secondary markets in the commodities or securities.

Short positions, spreading, hedging, and covering positions also occur in both markets. Moreover, the two markets share similar concepts: the clearing corporation as guarantor of the obligations to deliver on exercise of an option; the expiration month cycle with common expiration months; competing market makers on the floor of the exchange (only on the CBOE); the use of floor brokers; and common trading locations. While the terms and concepts may overlap, futures are different from options.

Primary Determinants of Value

Value at maturity. At the expiration of the option contract, its value is easy to determine. The call price will be zero if the stock price is below the exercise price. Otherwise, the call price will be the difference between the stock price and the exercise price. The put price will be zero if the stock price is above the exercise price. Otherwise, the put price will be the difference between the exercise price and the stock price. A call option is in the money if the stock price is above the exercise price; a put option is in the money if the stock price is below the exercise price.

Value before maturity. To price an option prior to maturity is more difficult. With the development of the Black-Scholes model, a theoretical model to price options, it has become easier to explain the determinants of the value of an option prior to maturity. A caveat at the outset, however, by way of an analogy, is worthwhile. Using the principles of optics in playing billiards, it is possible, in theory, to play billiards and never miss a shot. A computer can be programmed to determine trajectories and to beat the average player. The better players, however, would nearly always win. The computer program could never see the shots or combinations of shots as seen by the good players; asking them to describe their strategy would be to no avail — they just saw them.

The good eyes of the option market, whether those of buyers or of sellers, influence prices, moving them quickly to new equilibrium values. Competition to make profits in the option market prevents prices from deviating systematically or far from equilibrium values. Option maturity dates are too close to prevent arbitrageurs from trying to take advantage of any deviations from equilibrium values.

Option pricing models. In a paper published in 1973, Black and Scholes developed a theoretical valuation model for pricing options. In the same year, Merton published a paper in which he refined and extended the Black-Scholes model. Many other empirical and theoretical papers have added to the understanding of the pricing of option contracts. It must be noted, however, that any option pricing model is derived from a set of assumptions, and that the parameters of the models are estimated and thus may be subject to error. Past data alone may not be sufficient to estimate the inputs of the pricing model. Market traders may use additional information to estimate option prices; therefore, limiting estimates to past data only handicaps any user of a pricing model.

Current price of underlying security. The price of an option depends strongly on the current price of the underlying security. The greater the current price of the underlying stock relative to the striking price, the greater the value of a call option and the less the value of a put option. The price of an option would never be greater than the price of the underlying security; investors would not pay more for an option with a positive striking price than they would pay to buy the security outright.

The value of an option would never be less than its exercise value, that is, the value at the expiration of the contract. Prior to maturity, if the striking price is $50 and the stock price is $55, the price of the call option must be at least $5; otherwise, investors would buy the option, exercise, and sell the stock, thereby making a sure profit. Since everyone would want to do this, the price of the option would never be less than $5.

As reported in the financial press, violations in pricing relations may seem to exist. These violations, however, may arise because the press reports the last traded price of the options and the stock; the prices may be recorded at different times during the day; most likely, they would not be the prices at which investors could transact the following trading day.

Interest rates. Percentage premiums on call options increase with increases in short-term rates of interest. For a given price of the underlying stock, the higher the rate of interest on default-free government bonds with the same maturity as the option, the lower is the present value of the striking price that would be paid for the underlying stock. The striking price, however, is paid only if the option is exercised. As a result, the effects of changes in the rate of interest on the value of an option depend upon the probability of exercise; the greater the probability of exercise, the greater the effect of a change in the rate of interest. Increasing the rate of interest is the same as reducing the striking price — both increase the price of the call option. Since a put option is more valuable if the striking price is high relative to the price of the underlying stock, higher interest rates reduce the value of a put option.

Volatility of returns. The volatility of the return on the underlying security influences the value of an option. Volatility is the total variability of the returns on the underlying common stock, including the variability caused by market-wide influences (the beta risk of modern portfolio theory), the variability caused by industry-wide influences, and any additional variability caused by factors specific to that security. When a call option is exercised, the holder does not ask what caused the price of the underlying security to rise above the striking price — market or specific volatility. Option buyers select which options to exercise, a selectivity that is not available when investing in a portfolio of securities. With a portfolio, good luck with some securities tends to balance bad luck with other securities. Risks specific to an individual security are diversified away. An option writer, however, cannot diversify away the specific risks of writing an option on an underlying security by writing options on many securities because option buyers are not forced to exercise each and every option. The more volatile an underlying security, the greater the price movements of the security either up or down. The buyer gains on the upside and limits loss on the downside; therefore, the more volatile an underlying stock, the more valuable an option on that stock. The same holds true for a put: The more uncertain the outcome, the more valuable is the option. In other words, investors would pay a larger percentage premium for an option ensuring against the risk of a decline in the price of a more volatile underlying security than that of a less volatile one.

Time to maturity. Time to maturity is another important determinant of the value of an option contract. Time can not have negative value if the investor can exercise at any time up to the maturity of the contract. In general, the longer the time to maturity of a call option, the greater the value of the contract. Time works to increase volatility, by allowing more time for the underlying security to experience wider price fluctuations. Time also works to reduce the present value of the exercise price: Increasing the time period is similar to increasing the interest rate. For a put option, the effects of time can be ambiguous. Although the value of a put option is increased by greater volatility, it is reduced by a lower striking price.

Anticipated dividends. The dividends expected to be paid on the underlying security prior to the maturity of the option are another important determinant of value. The holders of listed options do not receive the rights to any cash dividends. With stock splits and stock dividends, adjustments are made to the striking price and to the number of shares under contract, but this is not so with cash dividends. On an ex-dividend date, the price of the underlying security will fall by approximately the amount of the cash dividend. A call option on a high-dividend-yielding security, such as American Telephone & Telegraph, is not as valuable as a call option on an underlying security with exactly the same terms and market characteristics except for the payment of dividends. Losing dividends has approximately the same effect on the value of a call option as does reducing the price of the underlying security by an amount equal to the present value of these lost dividends. Reducing the stock price relative to the striking price reduces the value of a call option by making it less likely that the option will be exercised. On the other hand, reducing the stock price increases the value of a put option. A put option on a dividend-paying security is more valuable than a put option on a non-dividend-paying security.

To summarize, the greater the stock price to striking price ratio, the greater the percentage call premium, the lower the percentage put premium. Listed call options on longer-term options almost always sell at a higher price than near-term options in the same series. For the same maturity and for the same stock price to striking price ratio, options on more volatile stocks have greater percentage premiums. Given the other factors, the higher the level of interest rates, the greater the percentage call premiums, the lower the percentage put premiums. Dividends act to reduce the prices of call options and increase the prices of put options.

Other factors influencing value. Although the factors discussed above are the primary determinants of the value of options, other factors — some basic and some institutional — have been suggested and may influence the price of an option. The expected rate of return on the underlying security, for instance, does not affect directly the value of an option; however, higher expected rates of return on the underlying security influence the price of the underlying security, and this price in turn is used to value an option.

Institutional rules, such as tax laws, margin requirements, and transaction costs, may also be a factor in the pricing of options. Even with these rules, investors do price options and other assets, however difficult it is to quantify their effects, if any, on market pricing. Prices in the market may be set as if no one individual were subject to these institutional restrictions. The investors, who set prices in the market, may profit by buying or selling options until prices are the same as those that would have been set without these institutional rules.

For example, investors using options to obtain leverage may find that the prices of options were the same with margin rules and borrowing costs as they were without them. Transaction costs may be significant in managing an option portfolio. With transaction costs, however, option prices may still be efficient. Even when differential transaction costs between options and other equivalent investments may affect values, competing market makers and brokerage houses, buying and selling options at close to zero marginal transaction costs, bring the prices of option contracts extremely close to the prices of the option contracts that would prevail in the absence of transaction costs.

ATTRACTIVE FEATURES

Reduction of Risk in Investment Portfolios

The attractive characteristics of options become evident when options are combined with other securities. Combining options with other securities transforms the returns and risks of an option into the returns and risks of an investment strategy: options combined with other investments to produce patterns of returns for a portfolio of investments. There are several important ways to limit the risk of investing in securities. Diversification is one of the main ways to limit the risk of holding securities. The larger the number of assets held in a portfolio, the smaller will be an investor's exposure to the risks of any one of the securities within the portfolio; the risk of the portfolio approaches the risk of the market portfolio. Another approach to limiting the risk of holding securities is to invest a percentage of the assets in bonds. By holding a larger fraction of the portfolio in bonds or money market funds, the investor unlevers the portfolio. The percentage changes in the value of the total portfolio will be less than the percentage changes in the value of the risky securities.

With options, investors can limit risk by insuring against adverse changes in the prices of their holdings of securities, or against adverse changes in the value of a portfolio of assets. Options provide patterns of returns that cannot be duplicated at reasonable cost by combining securities in various ways to try to produce the same result.

Increased Efficiency of Securities Market

Options trading has made the market for securities more efficient. In an efficient market, the prices of securities adjust quickly to changes in the economic prospects of the firm and the economy. Investors who want to adjust their holdings of securities have the protection of a competitive market; they expect neither to buy nor to sell at too high or too low a price. When equilibrium values of a security change, its price should be allowed to move immediately to the new equilibrium value. If not, investors trading in the interim will lose money to more knowledgeable investors.

Increased Liquidity of Secondary Market

One impediment to the operation of a well-functioning securities market is the limited ability of specialists and other market makers to buy or to sell large blocks of stock because of limited capital and the strictures on market makers obtaining participations in the block by outside investors. Market makers can reduce the risk of their holdings by selling options: The buyers of options assume some of the risk; they participate in the trade. This increases the liquidity of the secondary market for securities by providing the market maker with some depth needed to make better trading markets. Option trading may reduce the price variability in the secondary market and may allow investors to obtain better execution prices on their trades.

Lower Costs of Short-Selling

Many investors evaluate the prospects of firms and act on these evaluations. This process is one way in which security prices reflect the value of information. Although investors acting on information profit from this trading, the profits are not large given the costs of the trade and of gathering the information. Moreover, other investors discover the same information at about the same time; therefore, competition forces the price to the new equilibrium value. Unfortunately, it is more difficult to act on unfavorable information than on favorable information; investors must abide by the short-selling rules of the various exchanges. Short-selling rules impose costs on investors. Investors must wait for an increase in the price of the stock before making a short sale, and they do not earn full interest on the proceeds of short sales. Selling call options is one method of doing what amounts to borrowing shares for short sales without these costs.

Use as Investment Insurance

Put options as insurance. A put option is like a term insurance policy in which the term or maturity is the length of time between the purchase of the put and its expiration date; the item being insured is the value of the underlying stock. The face value of the policy, or the maximum claim that is paid in the event that the underlying stock becomes worthless, is equal to the number of shares specified in the contract times the exercise price. For partial losses, the amount received is equal to the number of shares times the difference between the exercise price and the market price of the underlying security at the time that the put is exercised.

Moreover, depending upon the relation between the striking price and the price of the underlying stock when the put is purchased, the put option will have features quite similar to an insurance policy with a deductible amount. If investors own 100 shares of stock with a market value of $100 per share, and if they buy a put with a striking price of $100, they insure totally against any decline in the price of the stock during the life of the option. If, however, investors buy instead a put on the stock with an exercise price of $90 per share, they are not insured against the first 10 point decline (i.e., the first $1,000 in losses), although they are covered against any additional losses resulting from a decline below $90; therefore, the put has a $1,000 deductible. It is even possible to buy the insurance with a negative deductible: The investor purchases a put option with an exercise price of $110, thereby insuring against the event that the stock price does not appreciate by at least 10 percent. Unlike traditional insurance, however, the investor can buy the insurance without owning the asset.

Call options as insurance. Call options are also akin to insurance policies. Consider the following investment strategy: (1) Buy one share of a non-dividend-paying security; (2) take out a term discount loan promising to pay $E, the striking price, at the maturity of the option, T months in the future. The loan, if prepaid, is prepayable at face value; (3) buy a put option on one share of the stock with a striking price of $E and an expiration date T months in the future. If, at the end of T months, the stock were selling for $S per share, the value of the position would be as follows. If S were less than E, the put would be exercised, the stock delivered, for $E. The face amount of the loan, $E, however, must be repaid. The net value of the position is zero. On the other hand, if S were greater than E, the put would expire, the stock would be sold for $S, and the loan repaid from the sale of the stock. The net value of the position would be $(S – E). In abbreviated form, the payoff to the net value of the position is the $MAX [0, S – E].

Suppose the investment strategy consisted of buying a call option on one share of the stock with an exercise price of $E and an expiration date T months in the future. If, at the end of T months, the stock were selling for $S per share, with S less than E, the call would expire unexercised; the value of the position would be zero. If S, however, were larger than E, the call would be exercised, paying $E for the stock, selling the stock for $S; the value of the position would be $(S – E). In abbreviated form, the payoff to the net position is the $MAX [0, S – E].

Since the payoffs to both strategies are the same for every possible price of the underlying security at the maturity of the contracts, the two are functionally equivalent: Call options are equivalent to a long position in the underlying security levered by a term loan with a face value of $E plus an insurance policy against declines in the stock price below $E per share. While the leverage component of a call option is its most commonly known characteristic, the insurance characteristic distinguishes call-option strategies from simple stock strategies such as buying stocks on margin.

For two call options with the same maturity, the one with the higher striking price will have more leverage; also, it will have a larger insurance component. A call option on a volatile stock is more valuable than a call option on one that is less volatile; the source of this greater value is the insurance component.

Conversion strategies. Strictly speaking, this exact relation holds for put and call options that can be exercised at maturity only. With the right to exercise early, puts have greater value than implied by the above parity theorem. Many brokers use these relations to convert puts into calls and to convert calls into puts. To convert puts into calls, they buy the security, while selling a call option and buying a put option. To convert calls into puts, they sell the underlying security short, while buying a call option and selling a put option. These positions have low risk and will earn a return close to the short-term rate of interest.

Analyzing returns. The procedure of analyzing the payoffs on a strategy at the end can be used to analyze the functional characteristics of various option strategies. The naked option-writing strategy is simply a short sale of a call option. The characteristics of this strategy are equivalent to: (1) selling the stock short; (2) lending money on a term basis; and (3) insuring the buyer against declines in the stock below the exercise price. If the naked strategy is combined with buying 100 shares of the underlying security, the strategy is called a "fully covered option-writing strategy," a strategy used by many pension fund managers. The stock purchase offsets the implicit short sale of shares associated with the naked strategy; therefore, a fully covered writing strategy is functionally equivalent to lending money on a term basis and to issuing an insurance policy against declines in the stock below the exercise price. Moreover, as the fully covered writing strategy is applied to options with higher striking prices to stock price ratios, the insurance component becomes a larger component of the investment. On the other hand, if the options written in a fully covered strategy have striking prices well below the stock price, the essential characteristic of the strategy is to lend money with a small amount of insurance.

Consider investors who choose the option strategy of buying a call option and investing in low-risk, fixed income securities such as money market instruments. Depending on the amount allocated to the fixed income securities, the strategy will be functionally equivalent to a long position in the stock plus an insurance policy against declines in the stock; the strategy is similar to insuring a stock by buying put options on the stock. A strategy of buying call options and bonds can make option buying into a more and more conservative investment by buying more and more bonds relative to options.

Buying call options and bonds is similar to buying put options on stock, a conservative investment strategy. Writing call options against a stock investment is similar to selling insurance and to lending money, investing in bonds. Although this does not seem as conservative as buying options and bonds, the fully covered strategy is thought to be more conservative. Investors, however, should realize what they are doing when they use the fully covered strategy; namely, that they are doing something akin to selling a put option naked and escrowing the exercise payment in bonds. If the stock goes down, the investor will have the put premium and interest to offset part of the loss on the stock; if the stock goes up, the investor will have the put premium plus interest only. By using fully covered writing strategies, investors are selling insurance on securities.

POTENTIAL RISKS

Exaggerated Effect of Market Swings

To understand the risks of buying and selling options, it helps to consider why an option differs from the underlying common stock. An investor can acquire leverage by buying an option. Although the change in the price of the option will always be less than the change in the price of the underlying security, the percentage changes in the price of the option will always be greater than the percentage changes in the price of the underlying security. If the exercise price of an option was $100 when the stock price was $125, the option could not sell for less than $25; for example, it might sell for $26 a share. If the stock price were to decline by 10 percent at expiration of the contract, a 100 share investment in the stock would fall from $12,500 to $11,250; a 100 share option contract would fall from $2,600 to $1,250, a 50 percent decline. Holding one option was five times riskier than holding the common stock.

The differences between the risk of the option and the risk of the underlying security change dramatically with changes in the ratio of the price of the underlying security to the striking price of the option. If the price of the underlying security were far below the striking price, investors would view the probability of an exercise as being low; small changes in the price of the underlying security would cause small changes in the price of the option. If the price of the underlying security, however, were above the striking price, the probability of an exercise would be greater; a change in the price of the underlying security would cause larger changes in the price of the option — less than the change in the price of the underlying security but greater than the change in the price of the option when there was less probability of an exercise. When the price of the underlying security was $125, a $1 change in its price would cause about a $1 change in the price of the option, about a 3.8 percent change in its price (1/26). Assume, however, that at $80, the option to buy the underlying security at $100, would be priced at about $1; a $1 change in the price of the underlying security might cause a $.05 change in the price of the option, about a 5 percent price change. The dollar change in the price of the option will always be less than the dollar change in the price of the underlying security. The percentage change in the price of the option will always be greater than the percentage change in the price of the underlying security.

Since options are riskier to hold than the underlying common stock, option buyers never hold only call options as their entire portfolios; option sellers never sell only call options. Although the buyers of call options expect a positive rate of return (the expected terminal value of an option is much greater than its present value) the risk of holding only a portfolio of call options is so great that an investor could go bankrupt; all the options could expire worthless. Put options are riskier than the underlying common stock. Buying put options, however, is a short sale; investors expect that the put will lose value. Since they expect that the price of the underlying stock will increase, they must expect that the price of the put will decrease; the put becomes less valuable as the stock price increases. The writers of call options expect a negative risk premium; the writers of put options expect a positive risk premium, the premium of return over the rate of interest. The entire return from holding an option comes from changes in the price of the option.

The prices of options are very sensitive to changes in market prices. If the market is a boom, the prices of call options explode. If the market is a bust, the prices of call options fizzle. Since options are a leveraged instrument, their prices are sensitive to any changes in the prices of underlying securities.

TAX CONSEQUENCES

Call Options

Call option contracts are considered to be capital assets for tax purposes. The buyer of an option will have a short-term capital gain or loss if the option is sold in the market, and a short-term capital loss if the option expires worthless. The gain or loss is computed as the sale price minus the purchase price reduced by the brokerage fees. Since options expire in less than a year, all gains and losses are short term. If a call is exercised, the cost of the call — the premium plus brokerage fees — is added to the exercise price to form the new basis in the stock. Since the holding period of the stock starts with the exercise of the option, capital gains or losses on the underlying security may be long term (more than a year) or short term (less than a year).

The writer of a call option will have a short-term capital gain or loss on the call option itself. If the option expires unexercised, gain will be short term. The holding period of an underlying security, however, is not affected by the sale of a call option. On exercise of the option, the sale price of the stock is increased by the amount of the call premium received when the option was written initially.

Put Options

Buying put options is considered to be a short sale; all gains and losses on a put option are short term regardless of whether the stock is put to the writer of the option. The put option affects the holding period of the underlying security for determining whether the stock was held for more or less than a year in computing gains.

Use in Adjusting Tax Positions

Tax rules by their nature are complex. Buyers and writers should consult the books or their tax representatives before trading in options. Options, however, can be used to change tax liabilities. The Economic Recovery Tax Act of 1981 provided that the maximum tax rate for 1982 and beyond would be 50 percent, a 20 percentage point reduction from the maximum tax rate of 70 percent in 1981. Those with 1981 gains that could be taxed at 70 percent could have reduced their tax bills to, at most, 50 percent by selling an option on a security and buying an option on the same security with different striking prices or maturity dates.

For tax purposes, an option is not considered to be identical to the security; an option is not considered to be identical to another option if the maturity date or the exercise price differs. If options bought and sold in 1981 expired in 1982, an investor could take the loss in 1981 and the gain in 1982 regardless of which way the prices moved. The 1981 Act provided that tax rates would be reduced each year through 1984. Investors can use these strategies to move gains into a year with lower taxes. Loss deduction, however, is limited to net gains plus $3,000 on a joint return. More sophisticated arrangements were worked out: Investors became the partners of broker-dealers in options. These dealers trade in options as a business; thereby, all gains and losses that are part of their market-making function are ordinary income and loss, not subject to the limitation on the deduction of loss. It is obvious that loss was taken in 1981, and gain in 1982. This is a relatively inexpensive way to reduce taxes permanently.

Taxable investors do incur potential extra tax costs by trading in options. If securities are bought and held, unrealized gain is not subject to tax. If securities are sold long term, capital gains taxes are limited to 20 percent. Options, if traded, are subject to short-term capital gains and loss tax — a maximum rate for 1982 of 50 percent.

Risk Insurance in Retirement Investments

If investors want to insure stock investments against price declines, it may be more efficient to insure stocks within a pension fund, a Keogh plan, or an individual retirement account. Within these accounts, the holding period of an asset does not matter; all income to investors is taxed as earned income, but only when withdrawn from the accounts. Buying options within these accounts benefits investors. Automatically, they maintain a balanced program, buying insurance on stock investments as they buy insurance on cars. This prevents a common error in many investment programs, that of switching between bonds and stocks in anticipation of market moves or when the market has moved already.

Timing the market by switching between bonds and stocks increases risk for little, if any, extra return. In contrast, the strategy of using call options and bonds (puts and stock) is a perfect timer of movements in the market. Investors participate in up movements in the market and avoid the down movements. A major advantage of these strategies is that they change the patterns of returns on investments; the new patterns discipline investors to stay in the market and to maintain a constant level of risk for their holdings of assets. For long-term investments such as pension accounts, keeping risk constant is the best strategy; for a given level of expected return, it has the minimum risk.

REPRESENTATIVE TYPES OF INVESTORS

Individuals

Individuals buy and write options for many reasons. Options may be used to adjust tax liabilities; they defer gain until next year, they convert short-term to long-term capital gain, and they convert ordinary income into long-term gain (broker-dealers). Options may be used to buy or sell shares of an underlying common stock, which may be less costly than buying or selling stock, including short-selling, outright. Some investors, trading on information, use the options market to obtain leverage. Other investors write options, sell insurance to other investors, and pick up extra income on their investments. Options may be used by investors who like to gamble. They may also be used to insure against market declines. Indeed, investors use options in a variety of investment strategies. As a result, trading in listed options has exploded and, in a relatively short period of years, options have become an established financial instrument.

Institutional Investors

While individual investors have participated in the options market since the CBOE first traded listed options in 1973, institutional investors have not participated in proportion to their share of investment dollars. Many argue that when options are traded on other instruments, such as government bonds or GNMA mortgage contracts, institutional investors will buy and sell options for their own accounts and for the accounts of their pension clients. Examples of the many uses of these bond options are legion, especially in recent years, in which investors observed extreme volatility in bond prices. An often-cited example is the use of options by insurance companies or savings and loan associations to hedge against the fluctuations in the value of their holdings of bonds and mortgages by buying put options on these instruments. Although the option exchanges trade options on common stocks only, they have petitioned the SEC to allow them to expand into options on bonds and mortgages. These petitions are in the courts. Other exchanges, now trading futures contracts on bonds and on mortgages, have petitioned also; however, not to the SEC but to the Commodity Futures Trading Commission (CFTC) — their underlying asset is the futures contract on bonds or on mortgages. The trading of options on financial instruments and on futures contracts representing financial instruments were to begin in 1982.

Pension Funds

Fully covered strategy. In a limited way, pension fund managers do use option contracts in their investment programs. Most programs are geared to the writing of options — the fully covered strategy. With the fully covered option-writing strategy, pension fund managers sell options against underlying common stock held in their pension portfolios. This strategy is popular not because it is thought of as the writing of insurance on common stock, but because it appears to produce extra income, the premium, and to reduce the risk of holding common stock. The worst application of the fully covered writing strategy is to assume that the pension fund will never sell the underlying common stock; therefore, the premium is extra income, or the premium income cushions declines in the price of the stock, or the premium income covers small advances in the price of the stock. As with writing insurance generally, the pension fund participates in down markets and gives up the gains in up markets. Big up-market movements are lost; the stock that was never to be sold is sold by being called away at the exercise price; although, in reality, the in-the-money call option is repurchased at a loss. The fully covered strategy and variations on this strategy produce patterns of returns resulting in more income, usually balanced with an occasional big loss when compared to holding the underlying stock outright.

The reduction in risk of a fully covered strategy arises from the nature of the option contract. If, at the time the call option was written, a change in the price of the underlying common stock of $1 results in a change in the price of the option of $0.60, writing an option is as if sixty shares of the underlying common stock were sold, a $100 gain on the 100 shares of stock is offset by a $60 loss on writing the option contract. The riskiness of the position changes over the life of the option; as the price of the stock changes, the offset changes. For a deep out-of-the-money call option, the offset is virtually 0 percent; for the deep in-the-money call option contract, the offset is virtually 100 percent — changes in the underlying common stock are offset completely by the short position in the option. The total premium includes a premium for this risk, the insurance premium, and the total premium includes a premium for the time value of the option, lending the exercise price money to the buyer of the calls.

The option managers mentioned frequently as being option writers are Chase Investors; Loomis Sayles; Balch, Hardy & Scheinman; and Analytic Investment Management.

Other strategies. Several pension fund managers buy call options and balance the risk of holding a long position in call options by holding short-term instruments such as Treasury bills or certificates of deposit. This strategy insures against price declines in the underlying common stock. Several managers are buying put options against stock held in a portfolio, a strategy that is functionally equivalent to buying calls and short-term instruments. The patterns of returns on these strategies are such that, in most time periods, the pension fund produces a lesser return than one with an uninsured portfolio; occasionally, its return exceeds that of an uninsured portfolio. If prices of securities shoot up, the uninsured portfolio outperforms the insured portfolio; if prices drop, the insured portfolio outperforms the uninsured portfolio. For small movements in the market, the net benefits are not as clear; in this market, some securities may shoot up in price while others may fall in price. Naturally, the insurance is used selectively, distinguishing the overall portfolio from each security within it.

The effects of intra-portfolio dispersion (the relative price movements of securities within a portfolio) can best be illustrated by the example of two securities, each priced at $100, each with a striking price of $100, and each with a six-month call option selling at $10. Six months later, one security is up 20 percent at $120, the other security is down 20 percent at $80. The portfolio, assuming no dividends on either security and an initial investment of $10,000 in each security, is unchanged, a zero rate of return over the six-month period. Alternatively, buying an option contract on each security at the start of the six-month period for a total investment of $2,000 also results in a dollar return of $2,000 at the end of the six-month period — the one in-the-money option is sold for $2,000, the other remains unexercised.

Although the portfolio was unchanged, investors are better off with the insured portfolio strategy because, in addition to their options, they have an additional $18,000 earning interest in the bond market over the six-month period. A rate of return on a portfolio of approximately zero does not imply that all call options, in a calls and bonds strategy, expire unexercised; some options are exercised even in quiet market periods. The Travelers Investment Management Company is the company most frequently mentioned as using the buy calls and bonds strategy; their option portfolios perform as predicted by the theory.

IMPORTANT FACTORS IN BUYING AND SELLING

Trading Through Brokers

To buy and to write options traded on an exchange, investors must use a broker. Naturally, the leading retail brokerage houses handle option accounts. Several of the discount brokerage houses also handle option trades. A buyer acquires an option by making an opening purchase transaction and cancels an option by making a closing purchase transaction. Writers are willing to be on the other side of an opening purchase transaction. In either case, brokers send an order to their firms' booth on the floor of the exchange; then, a floor broker trades it at a designated location, called a "post," trading with any of a number of other traders including another floor broker, a market maker, a board broker, or an order book official. Although the other floor brokers represent other writers or other buyers, and the market makers may trade for their own accounts, the board brokers and order book officials are exchange representatives trading not for themselves but for public customers.

Position Limits

On the CBOE, two of these traders agree on a price. Trades that are matched later in the day are reported to the clearing corporation the next business day. The option is issued after a clearing member, usually a broker, pays for it. The contract is settled in one business day. A customer cannot hold more than 2,000 contracts on the same underlying security. These position limits, however, are flexible if both calls and puts are held; an investor could buy up to 2,000 call options and, in addition, buy up to 2,000 put options on the same underlying security. The investor, however, could not buy 2,000 calls and sell 2,000 puts on the same underlying security; position limits prevent investors from receiving a positive return on more than 2,000 contracts on a change in the price of the underlying security.

Types of Orders

As with trading in common shares, investors place market or limit orders. A market order is an order to buy or to write an option at the best price at the time the order reaches the floor of the exchange. Floor traders handle these orders. By contrast, a limit order to buy or to sell an option specifies a price or better once the order reaches the floor. Board brokers handle these orders. Some traders use spread orders or straddle orders if they are simultaneously buying options and selling other options within a series. They may limit their order to trading at a set spread or better.

Exercising the Option

Investors exercise options by instructing their brokers to exercise; the broker notifies the clearing corporation, which randomly selects a writer of the option to deliver the shares through an exercise notice. The notice requires that the writer deliver the shares in return for the exercise price money in five business days, the exercise settlement date.

Transaction Costs

Trading costs include bid-ask spreads and brokerage fees. The liquidity of the market is such that competition keeps the bid-ask spreads and brokerage fees relatively low when compared to stocks; however, options are traded frequently relative to stocks, since options have a maximum maturity date of nine months. Investors should expect to incur higher transaction costs trading in options than in common stocks. On the other hand, with negotiated commissions, institutional investors pay for the services of the brokerage house; therefore, it is difficult to assign a commission or cost to a particular trade.

GLOSSARY

actuarial value— Value of a contract computed using the probabilities and payoffs on an outcome.

AMEX— American Stock Exchange.

arbitrage— Buying an asset and selling another asset to make a sure profit.

Black-Scholes— Pricing model for options used by practitioners.

call option— Right to buy a security for a fixed price on or before a given date.

CBOE— Chicago Board Options Exchange; first options exchange formed in 1973.

clearing corporation— Guarantor and maker of all option contracts.

clearing margin— Money deposited by a clearing member with the clearing corporation.

clearing member— Broker allowed to deliver contracts to the clearing corporation.

exchange— Place to trade standardized contracts with set terms and conditions.

exercise value— Value of the option if it was to be exercised.

expiration cycle— Three-month trading cycle for a listed option.

expiration date— Last day on which the option can be exercised.

fully covered— Writing an option on stock held by the writer.

futures contract— Buying an asset today for delivery in the future.

hedging— Reducing risk by selling an asset similar to the one held.

insurance contract— Protects against a contingent event such as a fire.

interest rate— Rate subtracted from the reciprocal of the price of a pure discount government Treasury bill.

in-the-money call— Stock price is above the striking price of the option.

in-the-money put— Stock price is below the striking price of the option.

leverage— Borrowing money to buy an asset.

limit order— An order not to buy or not to sell unless possible at a set price or better.

listed call option— Right to buy 100 shares from clearing corporation in a set month and for a set price.

listed put option— Right to sell 100 shares to clearing corporation in a set month and for a set price.

market maker— An exchange member trading on its own account on the floor of the exchange.

market order— An order to trade at the current market price of the option.

naked option— Writing an option to deliver a security that is not owned.

open interest—Number of contracts held by option buyers on a security.

option buyer— One who has the right to exercise the option.

option writer— Person who sells the right of exercise to the buyer of the option.

out-of-the-money— For a call option, the stock price is below the striking price; for a put option, the stock price is above the striking price.

premium— Price paid for the option to the writer by the buyer.

put option— Right to sell a security for a fixed price on or before a given date.

spreading— Buying a call option and writing a call option on the same security but with a different expiration date or striking price.

striking price— Price at which the option can be exercised.

time value— Value of the option attributable to the discount loan.

underlying security— Common stock on which the option holder has the right to exercise the option.

volatility— A measure of the dispersion of the percentage price fluctuations in the price of the underlying security.

LEADING DEALERS

Goldman Sachs & Co., New York, N.Y.

Merrill Lynch & Co., New York, N.Y.

Morgan Stanley & Co., Inc., New York, N.Y.

Salomon Bros. Inc., New York, N.Y.

SUGGESTED READING

The CBOE and the AMEX have information centers. By writing to each exchange, it is possible to obtain many information booklets describing trading procedures and the use of options.

Black, Fischer. "Fact and Fantasy in the Use of Options." *Financial Analysts Journal* 31:36-41, 61-72, July-August 1975.

——— and Scholes, Myron. "The Pricing of Options and Corporate Liabilities." *Journal of Political Economy* 81:399-417, May-June 1973.

———. "The Valuation of Option Contracts and a Test of Market Efficiency." *Journal of Finance.* 27:399-417, May 1972

Cox, John; Stephen, Ross; Rubinstein, Mark. "Option Pricing: A Simplified Approach." *Journal of Financial Economics* 7:229-263, 1979.

Galai, D. "Tests of Market Efficiency of the Chicago Board Options Exchange." *Journal of Business* April 1977, pages 183-194.

Merton, R.C. "Theory of Rational Option Pricing." *Bell Journal of Economics and Management Science* Spring 1973, pages 141-183.

———. "The Relationship Between Put and Call Option Prices: Comment." *Journal of Finance* 28:183-194, March 1973.

———, Scholes, M., Gladstein, M. "The Returns and Risk of Alternative Put Option Portfolio Investment Strategies." *Journal of Business* 55:1, 1982.

———. "The Returns and Risk of Alternative Call Option Portfolio Investment Strategies." *Journal of Business* 51:183-242, 1978.

Smith, C.W. "Option Pricing: a Review." *Journal of Financial Economics* 3:3-51, Jan.-March 1976.

Options—Warrants

*Allan E. Young**

BASIC CHARACTERISTICS

Description

Warrants are a form of security that derive their value as the result of their interrelationship with a related common stock. While a warrant holder does not have the same rights as a common stockholder (such as a claim on earnings and assets; the right to vote for corporate board members, changes in the corporate charter, bylaws, or other corporate matters such as certain resolutions; and the right to receive dividends when declared and paid), a warrant holder has the ability to obtain these rights by converting the warrant into common stock.

Conversion option. By owning a warrant, an investor has the option of converting his security into common stock (usually on a one-for-one basis) by paying the issuing company a specified sum. However, in the vast preponderance of cases, the warrant holder must make this request for conversion of his security into common stock before a specified expiration date.

Exercise Price. The amount paid to convert a warrant into common stock, or the exercise price, is usually above the market price of the common stock at the time of the issuance of the warrant. The exercise price frequently changes at stated times during the life of a warrant. Most warrants are protected from dilution of value arising from stock dividends and stock splits and may, in unusual cases, be protected from abnormally large cash dividends as well.

Expiration date. A European warrant can be exercised only on its expiration date; however, American warrants can be exercised at any time during the length of their lives. The vast preponderance of warrants have finite lives, which are specified in their terms of issue. There are some warrants, however, such as those issued by Alleghany Corporation, Atlas Corporation, and Tri-Continental Corporation, which have an indefinite length of life and are known as perpetual warrants. Some warrants (sometimes called "CD warrants") give their holders the option to purchase common stock either with the payment of cash (as with other warrants) or with the surrender, at par, of a stipulated amount of the company's debentures. If these debentures can be acquired by a warrant holder

* Allan E. Young is Professor of Finance in the School of Management at Syracuse University.

at a discount from their par value, the effective exercise price of the warrant is thereby reduced by an equal percentage.

Since 1919, because they were considered highly speculative instruments, warrants were not listed on the New York Stock Exchange. Thus, trading in these securities took place on the American Stock Exchange, the regional stock exchanges, and in the over-the-counter market. However, in 1970, American Telephone and Telegraph Company (AT&T) issued a warrant as part of a bond offering. This issue became a landmark offering in many respects, particularly because it led to the eventual listing of the warrant on the New York Stock Exchange. In subsequent years, a number of additional warrants have been listed on the New York Stock Exchange and, as of the fall of 1981, a total of ten such listings could be found.

The AT&T warrant gave its holder the right to exchange this security for common stock on a one-for-one basis with the payment to the company of $52. However, warrant holders were to have this right only until May 15, 1975. After that date, when the exercise right of the warrant was to expire, the security would be worthless. For about a year prior to the expiration of its warrant, there was some speculation that AT&T might extend its life. On the one hand, by securing exercise of the warrant, the company could, in effect, obtain equity financing. On the other hand, since its common stock was selling below the $52 level, it seemed that the company could extend the life of the warrant and thus make it more likely that its common stock would reach $52 before expiration. The common stock did, in fact, increase to just about $52 in the last few days of the life of the warrant. Relatively few warrants were exercised (slightly more than 10 percent of the number originally issued) and the company did not attempt to extend the expiration date so as to increase the number of warrants exercised. Nevertheless, companies have been known to extend the lives of their expiring warrants in spite of the damage this caused to those who were short the warrants and the legal ambiguities of the procedure. (To the author's knowledge, the procedure of extending the life of expiring warrants has never been legally tested.)

Other Securities — Similarities and Differences

Call Option. The security most similar to a warrant is a call option. The holder of a call option also has the right to convert his security into common stock with the payment of a specified sum. Additionally, as in the case of a warrant, this conversion right on the part of the owner of a call option must be exercised within a specified period of time (by the expiration date) or the right will lapse and the security will become worthless. An exercise of the conversion right of both call options and warrants will only occur if the common stock price rises above the exercise price (in the case of call options, this is normally referred to as the striking price) sometime before the expiration date of the security.

However, call options and warrants differ in a number of important respects:

Time period. Calls are normally written for rather brief time periods. Periods of three months and six months are common, and few are as long as a year. On the other hand, recent warrants have been issued with expiration dates as long as five to ten years away.

Issuing party. Calls are issued (the more common term in the case of options is written) by an investor, individual, or institution. Warrants are issued as a financing mechanism by a corporation seeking funds. Thus if and when either security is exercised (converted into common stock), the party receiving payment is different. In the case of exercise of a call option, the holder pays the writer of the option (who is also an investor) an amount equal to the striking price and receives his common stock from this party. Alternatively, upon exercising his conversion right, the holder of a warrant pays the exercise price to the issuing company and is given common stock in return by the firm.

Convertible bonds and preferred stock. The conversion feature of a warrant makes it comparable to convertible bonds and convertible preferred stock. However, unlike these latter securities, the holders of warrants receive no current income, as the issuing firm pays warrant holders neither interest — as in the case of convertible bonds — nor dividends — as in the case of convertible preferred stock.

Stock rights. Finally, warrants are similar to stock rights, which also give the holder the opportunity to purchase common stock with cash and surrender of the instrument. However, stock rights are issued by corporations with expiration dates far shorter than those of warrants.

Basic Determinants of Value

The primary determinants of the value of a warrant are similar to those of a call option because of the similarity, as noted above, between these two securities.

Relationship between exercise price and market price. One of the most significant factors in determining value is the relationship between the exercise price of the warrant and the current market price of the related common stock. Obviously, the value of a warrant will be far greater if the current market price of the related common stock is far in excess of the exercise price of the warrant than if the exercise price is considerably above the current market price of the common stock. In effect, since a warrant can be exercised at any time prior to expiration, when the price of the common stock is in excess of the exercise price of the warrant, the value of the warrant can never be less than the difference between these two prices. (This, of course, ignores transaction costs.) For example, if a warrant is exercisable at $30 (the investor submits $30 and the warrant to the issuing firm in order to receive a share of its common stock), and the current market price of the common stock is $40, the value of the warrant cannot be less than $10. Should the price of such a warrant fall below $10, traders would buy this warrant, sell short the common stock for $40, convert the warrant into common stock to cover their short position by paying the issuing firm $30, and make a sure profit.

However, the value of a warrant that is about to expire (after expiration, the value of all warrants is zero under any circumstance) will be zero if the exercise price of the warrant is above the current market price of the common stock. For example, if the warrant discussed above is about to expire and the current market price of the common stock is $30 or less, the value of the warrant must be zero, since the common stock can be bought more cheaply without the warrant. As discussed below, however, certain warrant hedging strategies require that warrants be sold short — a position that is often covered by purchases of warrants on their expiration date even if their exercise price is below the market price of the common stock. Transactions such as these give such warrants a small trading value on their expiration date.

Time remaining before expiration. Another important determinant of value is the period of time before expiration of the conversion right of the warrant. Warrants have a speculative appeal in that the owner of the warrant may profit if the price of the underlying common stock rises before the conversion right of the warrant expires. When a warrant is about to expire, its speculative appeal is zero. Therefore, other things being equal, warrants with a greater amount of time before expiration will have a greater value than warrants with less time before expiration.

Degree of leverage. Since warrants normally trade at prices far lower than the price of the underlying common stock, and since the price of the common stock is an important determinant of the price of the warrant, greater percentage returns can be achieved from favorable movements in the price of the warrant than from similar movements in the common stock. The extent of this leverage difference between a warrant and its related common stock is determined by the relative prices of the two securities. The greater the price of the common stock relative to the price of the warrant, the greater the degree of leverage from purchase of the warrant as opposed to the common stock. And since warrants are rather speculative instruments and the potential for leverage enhances their speculative appeal, other things being equal, the greater the degree of the leverage in a warrant relative to its common stock, the greater the value of the warrant.

Volatility of the common stock. As mentioned above, warrants are largely speculative instruments and derive a good part of their value from the speculative potential of a rise in the price of the common stock. Other things being equal, the warrants that relate to volatile stocks with a greater potential for larger favorable price movements can be expected to have a greater value than the warrants of stable stocks because they have a greater speculative appeal.

A related concern is the degree of speculative interest in the general stock market at any particular point in time. Since warrants are largely speculative instruments, their appeal is enhanced by a greater speculative fervor on the part of investors in general.

Other considerations. Two final considerations are the time value of funds to investors and the extent of the dividend paid on the common stock. As the time value of funds to investors increases, the price of the warrant falls, making it increasingly more attractive relative to the common stock. Further, the greater the dividend paid on the common stock, the relatively less attractive the warrant vis-à-vis the common stock.

In sum, then, the value of a warrant is determined by the period of time before expiration and the relationship between the market price of the underlying common stock and the exercise price of the warrant. The value of warrants that are about to expire is determined by the extent to which the market price of the common stock exceeds the exercise price of the warrant. However, for warrants that still have time before expiration, the extent of this time period and the relationship between the market price of the common stock and the exercise price of the warrant are of primary relevance in determining the value of the warrant. Also of consideration is the degree of leverage in the warrant relative to the underlying common stock, the degree of volatility of the common stock, the degree of speculative interest in securities in general, the time value of funds to investors, and the dividend paid on the common stock. In no case, however, can the value of a warrant ever be greater than the price of its underlying common stock.

ATTRACTIVE FEATURES

Leverage

One of the primary advantages of the use of warrants is the leverage they offer over the purchase of common stocks. As mentioned above, warrants normally sell for prices far lower than their related common stocks. Further, as long as a common stock is selling above the exercise price of the warrant, a given dollar increase in the price of the common stock must bring about at least an equal dollar increase in the price of the warrant. If, for example, a warrant is exercisable at $30 and the related common stock is selling for $40, arbitrage will assure that the warrant will not sell for less than $10. Further, if the common stock increases by $10 to $50, arbitrage also assures that the warrant will increase by at least $10 to $20; a 25 percent increase in the price of the common stock will bring about a 100 percent increase in the price of the warrant. With warrants selling at prices lower than the related common stock and offering at least equal dollar increases (when the common stock is selling above the exercise price of the warrant), the warrant holder has a potentially greater return for a given dollar investment than does the common stockholder. A greater percentage return to the warrant holder implies a leverage advantage over the common stockholder. Even warrants whose common stock is selling below their exercise price have a leverage advantage over the common stock. The normally low price of such warrants offers great percentage returns should the common stock move favorably.

Thus, if a common stock goes up, its warrant will go up faster on a percentage basis; the leverage thereby provided can turn a few hundred dollars invested in warrants into a call on many thousands of dollars worth of common stock. This leverage factor inherent in warrants is valuable and frequently results in a warrant selling at a considerable premium above its minimum value. In cases where the warrant is about to expire or where the common stock is greatly in excess of the exercise price, the warrant will sell at little or no premium, since there is either little time or little leverage left. However, when there is an extensive time before expiration or the common stock is much below the exercise price, the premium can be considerable. Further, as the premium on a warrant is a measure of the speculative value attached to the instrument, warrant premiums tend to decline in bear markets and rise in market rallies.

Warrant premiums. Since warrants selling at greater premiums are encumbered with a greater downside risk in the event of a market fall, it is appropriate at this point to define the premium on a warrant more precisely.

Warrant premiums are expressed as a percent of the common stock price and are defined as the excess cost of a share of common stock acquired through exercise of a warrant as opposed to a direct purchase of the common stock in the market. In percentage terms, the premium on a warrant is best expressed by subtracting from the warrant price the excess of the common stock price less the exercise price, and dividing the result by the price of the common stock. For example, if the price of a common stock is $25, and its related warrant, which carries an exercise price of $20, is selling for $8, the premium is 12 percent.

$$\frac{8 - (25-20)}{25} = 12\%$$

Thus, common stock purchased through purchase and exercise of the warrant costs 12 percent more than common stock purchased directly in the stock market.

However, should the common stock fall below the exercise price of the warrant, the premium on the warrant would likely rise considerably. If, in the above example, the common stock were to fall to $10 and the warrant sold at $2, the premium would be 120 percent.

$$\frac{2 - (10-20)}{10} = 120\%$$

In this instance, the common stock purchased by an investor through purchase and exercise of the warrants costs 120 percent more than the market price of the stock. Or, stated differently, the common stock in this case must advance by 120 percent in order for the intrinsic worth of the warrant to be equal to its market price.

Use of Warrants in Hedging

Hedging strategies employing warrants can be a fruitful investment technique for certain categories of investors. (For an expanded discussion of certain warrant hedging strategies, see *Hedging With Warrants* in this article.)

POTENTIAL RISKS

Risk of Total Loss

One of the major disadvantages of a long position in warrants is that a warrant to purchase shares of common stock will be worthless on the expiration date if the exercise price of the warrant is above the market price of the common stock. Holders of such warrants will then incur a total loss (in other words, they will lose an amount equal to their entire investment).

No Current Income

For investors who desire a current return, the absence of either interest or dividends from the ownership of warrants can represent a considerable disadvantage. Although warrants may be exchanged ultimately for common stocks (which may pay dividends), payment must be made for the common stock at the exercise price before dividends can be received.

Greater Volatility Than Common Stock

Another important disadvantage of warrants is that they are normally far more volatile than their related common stocks. This greater volatility stems from a number of sources, including the following:

- The dividends on a security normally fluctuate far less than the price of the security and constitute the more stable segment of total return. (The total return equals the price change plus the dividends received.) Since warrants pay no current income, all of the total return on the instrument is made up of price changes.
- Warrants have an expiration date at which time, unless converted, they will be worthless to their holders. Not only does the loss of value, in itself, produce volatility, but the inexorable movement to this condition as time passes further diminishes the warrant's stability.
- While warrants have a leverage advantage over common stock, the presence of greater leverage for a security works in both directions and makes it more volatile and, in turn, more risky.

Removal of Conversion Rights

A final disadvantage to the ownership of warrants is the risk that the right to convert the warrant into common stock will be removed prior to its normal expiration date. This situation has occurred, for example, when the firm issuing the warrant is acquired by another company.

Warrant agreements (complex legal documents setting forth a warrant's terms and the conditions under which these terms may be altered) frequently indicate that, in the event of a liquidation, dissolution, or winding up of the affairs of the issuing corporation, the right to purchase its stock contained in the warrant will cease to exist. Certain companies, prior to their acquisition by other firms, have interpreted their acquisition as tantamount to a liquidation for purposes of determining the rights of their warrant holders. Under this interpretation of the warrant agreement, all warrants that were not converted into common stock were extinguished. Warrant holders in this situation do have the option to convert to common stock with the payment of the exercise price. However, in the case of an impending acquisition, this option must be exercised immediately and is worthless if the exercise price is above the market price of the common stock. Thus, although warrant holders must be notified of an impending extinguishment of their conversion rights, they may suddenly find their security without value.

TAX CONSEQUENCES

There are no real differences between the taxation of investments in common stocks and/or call options and the taxation of warrant holdings. However, because of the unique properties of warrants, certain tax consequences of an investment in warrants should be explained.

As mentioned above, warrants pay no current income (dividends or interest); therefore all returns from warrants are capital transactions and are short- or long-term depending on the length of the holding period. A gain or loss is calculated by comparing the purchase and sale prices of the warrant.

Further, it should be noted, one of the hedging strategies analyzed later in the article requires selling warrants short. And, as in the case of common stock, short positions normally give rise to gains or losses that are short-term regardless of the period of time for which such positions are maintained.

The exercise of a warrant is not a taxable transaction; however, the worthless expiration of a warrant results in a capital loss that is long- or short-term, depending upon the holding period.

Finally, when a warrant is exercised and converted into common stock by the payment of a given sum, that sum, plus the original purchase price of the warrant, becomes the basis for computing any gain or loss on the subsequent sale of that common stock. The time period used to determine whether the transaction is long- or short-term depends upon when the warrant was exercised. If the time from the exercise of the warrant to the final disposition of the common stock is sufficient to qualify for long-term treatment, then the transaction is viewed as long-term for tax purposes.

REPRESENTATIVE TYPES OF INVESTORS

Institutional Investors

Warrants are attractive to institutional investors, such as certain investment companies and hedge funds, that are seeking large returns and are able to assume considerable risk. The leverage warrants offer vis-à-vis common stock may make warrants particularly appropriate to these investors.

Warrants are not recommended, on the other hand, for institutional investors, such as college endowment funds or income-oriented investment companies that require current income. For these investors, the lack of either interest or dividend income accruing to the holders of warrants makes them inappropriate investment vehicles. Moreover, some institutions are prohibited from taking short positions and thus are unable to avail themselves of the kind of hedge transactions that involve short positions. Their own charters and state laws prevent certain institutional investors from holding warrants and, for them, the instrument is therefore per se inappropriate.

Individual Investors

Individuals, like institutional investors, who are highly averse to risk and/or who desire current income will find the holding of warrants inconsistent with their investment goals. However, warrants may be very attractive to those speculative individual investors who seek substantial percentage returns and who are willing to assume considerable risk in order to do so. Such individuals would normally be in high income-tax brackets and in a position to withstand the total loss that sometimes occurs if the market price of the underlying common stock does not exceed the exercise price prior to the warrant's expiration date.

Investors Who Benefit From Hedging

Although warrants are highly speculative when held as a long position, the use of such instruments in hedge transactions can, as shown below, often result in a highly conservative transaction. Thus, unlike the simple holding of warrants, the employment of the security in certain hedging strategies may be inappropriate for risk-taking speculative individual and institutional investors seeking high returns, but highly valuable for most categories of conservative risk-averse investors seeking current income and secure returns. Certain warrant hedging reduces risk and increases the likelihood of a moderate to considerable return. By the same token, it may reduce the probability of loss while at the same time limiting the maximum level of returns.

HEDGING WITH WARRANTS

Procedures of Warrant Hedging

A hedge is a transaction in which one is able to limit one's losses. In warrant hedging the limiting of losses is in terms of the market price of the underlying common stock. In one type of warrant hedge, the investor is assured of avoiding a loss (or of making a profit) as long as the market price of the common stock remains within specified boundaries until the expiration of the warrant. In another variety of warrant hedge, a profit will result at expiration of the warrant as long as the common stock has moved beyond another set of boundaries, either on the upside or the downside.

One might employ a warrant hedge with any security that is convertible into common stock, such as convertible bonds or convertible preferred stock. However, for simplicity, this article is concerned only with hedge transactions that relate a warrant to its underlying common stock.

Warrant hedging vs. reverse warrant hedging. The procedures for the two types of warrant-hedging transactions discussed here are fairly simple. Briefly stated, for the first kind of warrant hedge, sometimes referred to as a reverse warrant hedge, the investor simply sells a warrant short and establishes a long position in the underlying common stock. The second type, referred to simply as a warrant hedge, requires precisely the opposite procedure, buying warrants and selling the underlying common stock short. By employing the reverse warrant hedge, the investor collects dividends on his long position and profits from all upward movements in the price of the common stock. Of course, he also incurs a reduction in profits from all downward movements in the price of the common stock. Additionally, downward movements in the price of the warrant increase his returns, while upward movements in the price of the warrant reduce returns. The opposite procedure (shorting the stock and buying the warrants), of course, produces precisely the opposite results.

Advantages and Disadvantages of Hedging Procedures

As was indicated earlier, while taking a long position in warrants constitutes a rather risky endeavor (offering the possibility of both total loss on the commitment and substantial percentage returns), using warrants in a hedging or reverse-hedging strategy represents just the opposite kind of investment situation. By hedging or reverse hedging with warrants, an investor can limit (in some cases rather rigidly) his chance of loss and/or his dollar exposure. But in so doing, the investor may also have to place limits on potential gain or the price boundaries under which a gain will occur. In this sense, warrant hedging or reverse warrant hedging represents a conservative investment strategy. However, the historical returns from reverse warrant hedging have not only exceeded those on the Standard and Poor's 500 Composite Stock Index, but have also proven more favorable than a simple buy-and-hold strategy for the common stocks that underlie most of the warrants in question.[1]

As demonstrated below, utilizing a warrant hedge (buying the warrant and selling the common stock short) limits the maximum dollar loss that can occur. However, in such a transaction, gains do not occur unless a considerable movement has taken place in the price of the common stock. Alternatively, in the case of a reverse warrant hedge (shorting the warrants and buying the common stock), the opposite will prevail; a gain will result unless the common stock incurs a substantial movement in either direction. Additionally, the potential gain, at least theoretically, on a warrant hedge is unlimited. However, for a reverse warrant hedge the maximum gain is limited. Thus, at least for reverse warrant hedging, the investor need not accurately predict the movements of the securities that comprise his portfolio in order to profit. An investor can find a reverse warrant hedge quite profitable even if the price of the common stock that underlies the warrant remains roughly unchanged over the life of the hedge transaction. The common stock can even move moderately in an unfavorable direction and still provide the investor with a considerable return. Only if a substantial movement in the price of the common stock occurs can a loss result from a reverse-warrant-hedge strategy.

Illustration of warrant-hedging strategies. The following numerical examples illustrate the two warrant-hedging strategies. By relating a warrant, such as the AT&T warrant mentioned earlier, to its underlying common stock, one sees not only what the prospective rates of return might have been for various price movements, but also what the actual rate of return would have turned out to be for investors utilizing these strategies and employing the hedge ratio shown. (The hedge ratio refers to the number of warrants sold short for each share of common stock purchased (a reverse warrant hedge) and/or the number of warrants purchased for each share of common stock sold short (a warrant hedge).)[2]

On May 15, 1972, the AT&T warrant was selling for approximately $7 (fractions have been eliminated for simplicity of computation). At that time, AT&T's common stock was selling for about $42. The warrant was exercisable at $52 and was to expire in three years on May 15, 1975. To be determined are the rates of return that would have resulted from various terminal prices for the common stock (on May 15, 1975) and a hedge ratio of, say, 2:1 (two warrants sold short for each common share purchased for a reverse warrant hedge and two warrants purchased for each share of common stock sold short for a warrant hedge). It is assumed that transaction costs are 1.5 percent on each of the buy and sell sides. Finally, for the reverse warrant hedge, a full cash payment for the common stock will adequately margin the short sale of the warrants. For simplici-

---

[1] See Kim, Moon K., and Young, Allan E. "Rewards and Risks From Warrant Hedging." *The Journal of Portfolio Management.* Summer 1980, pages 65-68.

[2] For the determination of the optimal hedge ratio, see Kim and Young, *ibid.*

ty, it is also assumed that for the warrant hedge, Treasury bills already in an investor's portfolio are used to satisfy any margin requirements beyond a full cash purchase of the warrants. For each hedge strategy, a rate of return can now be calculated based on the assumption of no more cash required than that needed for a full cash purchase of the long position.

If a reverse warrant hedge were undertaken and if the common stock stood at the original purchase price of $42 on the expiration date of the warrant, neither a gain nor a loss would have resulted from the long position. However, the warrants would have expired worthless, resulting in a gain of $14 ($7 × 2) and the investor would have received dividends that averaged somewhat in excess of $3 a year over the three-year period of May 15, 1972 to May 15, 1975. Alternatively, if a warrant hedge were employed, the warrants would have expired worthless, resulting in a loss of $14 ($7 × 2). Neither a gain nor a loss would have resulted from the short position in the common stock. However, dividends of $3 per share of short position would have to be paid. Assuming a 1,000 share position in the stock (either long or short), the rate of return can be approximated as follows:

FROM A REVERSE WARRANT HEDGE		*FROM A WARRANT HEDGE*	
On the Common Stock		*On the Common Stock*	
Buy for	$42,000	Buy (cover) for	$42,000
Sell for	$42,000	Sell short for	$42,000
Gain or (loss)	0		0
On the Warrants		*On the Warrants*	
Buy (cover) for (As mentioned above, practically speaking, warrants would sell for a small fraction)	$ 0	Buy for	$14,000
Sell short for	14,000	Sell for	0
Gain or (loss)	$14,000	Gain or (loss)	($14,000)
Dividends	9,000	Dividends	(9,000)
Transaction costs ([$42,000 + $42,000 + $14,000] × 0.015)	(1,140)	Transaction costs ([$42,000 + $42,000 + $14,000] × 0.015)	(1,470)
Net Gain or (loss)	$21,530	Net Gain or (loss)	($24,470)
Rate of return over three years or total dollar (loss) if negative ($21,530 ÷ $42,000)	51.3%	Rate of return over three years or total dollar (loss) if negative	($24,470)
Approximate rate of return annualized for one year (51.3% ÷ 3)	17.1%		

On the reverse warrant hedge, 17.1 percent represents a rather handsome rate of return in a situation where the common stock in question moves neither favorably nor unfavorably. However, a rather considerable loss resulted from the warrant hedge.

Now, one might ask, How far down can the stock go before a loss occurs for the reverse warrant hedge or a profit results from the warrant hedge? The answer is, to approximately $20 for a reverse warrant hedge and $18 for a warrant hedge, as illustrated below:

FROM A REVERSE WARRANT HEDGE		*FROM A WARRANT HEDGE*	
On the Common Stock		*On the Common Stock*	
Buy for	$42,000	Buy (cover) for	$18,000
Sell for	20,000	Sell short for	42,000
Gain or (loss)	($22,000)	Gain or (loss)	$24,000
On the Warrants		*On the Warrants*	
Buy (cover) for	$ 0	Buy for	$14,000
Sell short for	14,000	Sell for	0
Gain or (loss)	$14,000	Gain or (loss)	($14,000)
Dividends	9,000	Dividends	(9,000)
Transaction costs ([$42,000 + $20,000 + $14,000] × 0.015)	(1,140)	Transaction costs ([$42,000 + $18,000 + $14,000] × 0.015)	(1,110)
Net gain or (loss)	($140)	Net gain or (loss)	($110)

After consideration of dividends, therefore, a profit results from a reverse warrant hedge when the terminal price for AT&T's common stock is between $42 and $20. However, a profit does not begin to occur for a warrant hedge until the price goes below $18. But what about movements on the upside for the common stock? When will a loss result from an upward movement in the price of the security for a reverse warrant hedge and a profit occur for a warrant hedge? As shown below, a loss will occur for a reverse warrant hedge if the price of the common stock goes above $82 on the expiration date of the warrant. Only when the price of the common stock rises above $88 can a profit result from a warrant hedge.

FROM A REVERSE WARRANT HEDGE		*FROM A WARRANT HEDGE*	
On the Common Stock		*On the Common Stock*	
Buy for	$42,000	Buy (cover) for	$88,000
Sell for	82,000	Sell short for	42,000
Gain or (loss)	$40,000	Gain or (loss)	($46,000)

On the Warrants

Buy (cover) for ([$82 − $52] × 2,000)	$60,000
Sell short for	14,000
Gain or (loss)	($46,000)
Dividends	9,000
Transaction costs [($42,000 + $82,000 + $60,000 + $14,000) × 0.015]	(2,970)
Net gain or (loss)	$30

On the Warrants

Buy for	$14,000
Sell for ([$88 − $52] × 2,000)	72,000
Gain or (loss)	$58,000
	(9,000)
Transaction costs [($88,000 + $42,000 + $14,000 + $72,000) × 0.015]	(3,240)
Net gain or (loss)	($240)

For all prices between $42 and $82, therefore, a profit must result from the reverse-warrant-hedge strategy; thus, there is a band of profitability of from $20 to $82 from such a strategy. Any terminal price for the common stock within this range must result in a profit. It might be noted that, on a historical basis, this is a rather broad band of profitability for the common stock in question. The common stock of AT&T had remained well within this range for a rather considerable period of time prior to May 15, 1972, and the chances of it continuing to do so for the period in question had to be considered highly likely. However, a profit could only result from a warrant hedge if the common stock would go either below $18 or above $88 within the period in question, a rather unlikely outcome.

One might also ask about the maximum rate of return one might have earned on a reverse warrant hedge, and the actual historical rate of return that resulted from such an undertaking. Fortuitously for those who undertook this strategy at the time in question, the answer is one and the same: in each case, $52. This is computed as follows:

On the Common Stock

Buy for	$42,000
Sell for	52,000
Gain or (loss)	$10,000

On the Warrants

Buy (cover) for	$ 0
Sell short for	14,000
Gain or (loss)	$14,000
Dividends	9,000
Transaction costs ([$42,000 + $52,000 + $14,000] × 0.015)	(1,620)
Net Gain or (loss)	$31,380

Rate of return over three years

$$= \frac{\text{Net Gain or (loss)}}{\text{Amount Invested}}$$

$$= \frac{\$31{,}380}{\$42{,}000} = 74.7\%$$

Approximate rate of return annualized for one year (74.7% ÷ 3)	24.9%

It might be noted that $52 represents the maximum loss from the warrant-hedge strategy, as demonstrated below:

On the Common Stock

Buy (cover) for	$52,000
Sell short for	42,000
Gain or (loss)	($10,000)

On the Warrants

Buy (cover) for	$14,000
Sell for	0
Gain or (loss)	($14,000)
Dividends	($ 9,000)
Transaction costs ([$52,000 + $42,000 + $14,000] × 0.015)	($ 1,620)
Total dollar (loss)	($34,620)

Dangers and Pitfalls

The principal danger involved in reverse warrant hedging is not the risk of loss resulting from the common stock moving beyond the bounds of profitability. Such boundaries can often be made broad enough (as in the above example) that the chance of the common stock moving beyond those limits is quite small.

Risk of a buy-in: reverse warrant hedging. Rather, the principal danger in a reverse warrant hedge is that the investor may not be able to retain a short position in the warrants until the expiration date. Short positions can only be maintained as long as the security in question can be borrowed. If the broker handling the transaction finds himself unable to continue to borrow the warrants, he may have to buy them in and close out the short position prior to the expiration date. In this event, of course, the investor need not incur a loss on the entire reverse warrant hedge, but it is harder to predict the pricing relationship between the warrant and the common stock prior to the expiration date than it is on the expiration date.

To increase the likelihood that the short position can be maintained until the expiration date, the investor should maintain a good relationship with his broker and secure the broker's assurances that a buy-in will be unlikely. He can also decrease the chance of a buy-in by choosing a reverse warrant hedge in a security whose short interest is relatively small in relation to the number of warrants outstanding and the floating supply of such warrants.

On a reverse warrant hedge, there is a band of profitability with a maximum at the exercise price of the warrant. Returns are then scaled downward towards the bounds of profitability in such a manner as resembles a triangle. On the other hand, for warrant hedging undertaken when the common stock is below the exercise price of the warrant, the maximum loss occurs when the common stock rises, on the expiration date, to the exercise price of the warrant.

Risk of a buy-in: warrant hedge. The above discussion is also relevant to the danger of a buy-in of common stock in a warrant hedge. A warrant hedge will only be profitable if the common stock moves considerably in either direction from the exercise price of the warrant. Such a movement may take some time to develop. However, if the common stock is bought in before this movement can occur, a hedge that is potentially profitable may not prove to be so. Nevertheless, as there are normally more common shares than warrants outstanding, a buy-in of common stock in the face of a warrant hedge is less likely to occur than a buy-in of warrants.

Risk of warrant extension. Another danger involved in reverse warrant hedging is that the corporation might extend the life of warrants that have been sold short. Aside from maintaining the position longer than had been originally contemplated, the reverse warrant hedger can lose through extension of the life of the warrant as the result of its likely increase in value. (As stated above, reverse warrant hedging requires a short position in warrants and their increase in value is detrimental to the reverse warrant hedger.)

One obvious precaution that the investor can take to mitigate the effects of a warrant extension is to cover the short position as expiration is about to take place, rather than waiting to see if the company extends the life of the warrants. The investor should also try to ascertain, at the time the hedge is originally contemplated, whether a particular warrant is likely to be extended. A company's practices in the past with respect to its expiring warrants might be of assistance in this respect. Also, a company that wants its stockholders to purchase its new equity issues would not wish to alienate them and/or possibly violate their preemptive rights by extending the life of its warrants. Finally, reverse warrant-hedgers should avoid employing their strategy with respect to real estate investment trusts and other stock groups that frequently extend their warrants.

As was evident from the AT&T illustrations, reverse warrant hedging generally is the better strategy when the common stock has a relatively high dividend yield and the investor expects only moderate movements in either direction from the security. Alternatively, a warrant hedge is the more appropriate strategy when the yield on the common stock is relatively low and considerable movements in either direction are anticipated for the common stock.

Limited Use of Reverse Warrant Hedging

The reasons that reverse warrant hedging are not employed more generally can only be speculated upon. (More frequent use of the strategy by investors would reduce some of its profitability.) However, it would seem as though the limits in some cases to institutional short sales and their dealing in warrants would account for some of the lack of the use of reverse warrant hedging. Further, the fact that there is an absolute limit to the returns that can be earned may inhibit some speculative investors desirous of achieving very high returns. (Alternatively, for warrant hedging there is no limit to returns, at least on the upside.) Most reverse warrant hedges are best employed over a period three to four years prior to the expiration date until the expiration date; some investors may not wish to maintain a position for this long a period.

GLOSSARY

exercise price— The amount of money that must be given by the holder of a warrant (along with the warrant itself) to the issuing corporation in order to exchange the warrant for common stock.

expiration date— The date at which the right to convert the warrant into common stock ceases. A warrant may be exercised (converted into common stock through the payment of the exercise price) at any time prior to the expiration date.

hedge— A means of limiting one's losses. Hedging with securities is normally accomplished by trading in opposite directions with similar or related securities (i.e., buying one while selling the other short).

hedge ratio— The relationship between the number of warrants sold short (or purchased) and the number of shares of common stock purchased (or sold short) in a reverse warrant hedge (or a warrant hedge).

optimal hedge ratio— That hedge ratio which maximizes the probability of obtaining returns on a warrant hedge or reverse warrant hedge, which is in excess of a required rate of return or a rate stipulated by the investor.

perpetual warrant— A warrant with an infinite life and, thus, no expiration date.

reverse warrant hedging— Buying warrants and selling the underlying common stock short.

warrant— A security issued by a corporation, which gives its holder the right to purchase shares of the issuing corporation's common stock at a stipulated price.

warrant agreements— Rather complex legal documents setting forth a warrant's terms and the conditions under which these terms may be altered.

warrant hedging— Operating on opposite sides of the market between a warrant and its related common stock (i.e., buying the warrant while selling the common stock short).

warrant premium — The excess of the cost of a share of common stock acquired through purchase and exercise of a warrant, as opposed to a direct purchase of the common stock in the market. This is usually expressed in terms of a percent of the current market price of the common stock. The warrant premium is found by subtracting the excess of the common stock price from the warrant price, less the exercise price, and dividing the result by the price of the common stock. (See *Warrant Premiums* in this article for examples of this calculation.)

SUGGESTED READING

Ayres, H. F. "Risk Aversion in the Warrant Markets." *Industrial Management Review,* Fall 1963, pages 45-53.

Bierman, Harold, Jr. "The Cost of Warrants." *Journal of Financial and Quantitative Analysis,* June 1973, pages 499-504.

Chen, Andrew H. Y. *A Dynamic Programming Approach to the Valuation of Warrants,* Unpublished Ph.D. Dissertation, Graduate School of Business Administration, University of California, Berkeley, 1969.

———. "A Model of Warrant Pricing in a Dynamic Market." *Journal of Finance,* Dec. 1970, pages 1041-1059.

Hayes, Samuel L., III, and Reiling, Henry B. "Sophisticated Financing Tool: The Warrant." *The Harvard Business Review,* Jan.-Feb. 1969, pages 137-150.

Hilliard, Jimmy E., and Leitch, Robert A. "Analysis of the Warrant Hedge in a Stable Paretian Market." *Journal of Financial and Quantitative Analysis,* March 1977, pages 85-103.

Kassouf, S. T. "Warrant Price Behavior — 1945 to 1964." *Financial Analysts Journal,* Jan.-Feb. 1968, pages 123-126.

Kim, Moon, and Young, Allan. "Rewards and Risks From Warrant Hedging." *The Journal of Portfolio Management,* Summer 1980, pages 65-68.

Leabo, Dick A., and Rogalski, Richard J. "Warrant Price Movements and the Efficient Market Hypothesis." *Journal of Finance,* March 1975, pages 163-177.

Madrick, Jeffrey. "Inside Wall Street: Safety First With a Very Cheap Warrant." *Business Week,* Feb. 9, 1976, page 75.

Miller, Jerry D. "Effects of Longevity on Values of Stock Purchase Warrants." *Financial Analysts Journal,* Nov.-Dec. 1971, pages 78-85.

Pease, Fred. "The Warrant — Its Powers and Its Hazards." *Financial Analysts Journal,* Jan.-Feb. 1963, pages 25-32.

Rogalski, Richard J. "Trading in Warrants by Mechanical Systems." *Journal of Finance,* March 1977, pages 87-101.

Samuelson, Paul A. "Rational Theory of Warrant Pricing." *Industrial Management Review,* Spring 1965, pages 13-39.

——— and Merton, Robert C. "A Complete Model of Warrant Pricing That Maximizes Utility." *Industrial Management Review,* Winter 1969, pages 17-46.

Schwartz, William. "The Advantage Warrants Have — Leverage Prospects." *The Commercial and Financial Chronicle,* March 5, 1970, pages 18-20.

Shelton, J.P. "The Relation of the Price of a Warrant to the Price of its Associated Stock." *Financial Analysts Journal,* May-June 1967, pages 143-151; July-Aug. 1967, pages 88-99.

Sprenkle, C.M. "Warrant Prices as Indicators of Expectations and Preferences." *Yale Economic Essays,* Vol. 1, No. 2, 1961, pages 178-231.

Stanton, Thomas C., and Maxwell, Philip H. "Warrants: A Cost of Capital Perspective." *Financial Executive,* Sept. 1980, pages 27-31.

Stone, Bernell K. "Warrant Betas and the Effect of Warrant Financing on Systematic Risk." Cornell University Working Paper. 1980

———. "Warrant Financing." *Journal of Financial and Quantitative Analysis,* March 1976, pages 143-153.

Turov, Daniel. "Beyond Maturity: More Companies Are Extending the Life of Their Warrants." *Barron's,* July 22, 1974, pages 11-12.

———. "Dividend Paying Stocks and Their Warrants." *Financial Analysts Journal,* March-April 1973, pages 76-78.

———. "Trampled Rights: Warrant-Holders Have Become an Oppressed Minority." *Barron's,* March 19, 1973, pages 11, 25.

Van Horne, James C. "Warrant Valuation In Relation to Volatility and Opportunity Costs." *Industrial Management Review,* Spring 1969, pages 19-32.

Yeasting, Kenneth. "CD Warrants." *Financial Analysts Journal,* March-April 1970, pages 44-47.

Paintings

*J. Patrick Cooney**

BASIC CHARACTERISTICS

Although paintings, broadly speaking, encompass works of art executed in oils, watercolors, charcoal, ink, and other media, the term as used in this article refers to oil paintings, since oils are by far of the greatest importance in the investment context. In the discussion that follows, paintings are dealt with in six major categories: Old Master, nineteenth-century, impressionist and postimpressionist, modern, contemporary, and American.

The purchase and sale of paintings dominate the art market overall in terms of both dollar value and publicity. No other category of art attracts the international interest or the multimillion-dollar prices achieved by paintings. In fact, for many, paintings are synonymous with art. The market for paintings covers a broad range of periods as well as nationalities, ranging from Greek icons painted on panels to contemporary oil-stained canvases.

The value of a work of art is in a large part subjective. Unlike many other instruments, art does not provide cash dividends; it is certainly not a substitute for money. Rather, the value of a painting is established by what viewers, buyers, sellers, and owners think that value is. Unlike paper money, shares, or coins, art is not related to a means of production, to the ability of a government to honor its obligations, or to skills organized to deliver a service. Works of art can be created for a number of purposes. In some cases, they have magical qualities, as in religious pictures or artifacts. In other cases, they are commemorative, such as portraits and paintings of battle scenes. In still other cases, works of art are designed to be useful, as with furniture, silver, or many of the decorative arts. Ironically, the value of a work of art increases when it is no longer being used for the purpose for which it was created. For example, collectors during the early twentieth century paid enormous prices to coax portraits of English gentlemen from their ancestral halls. Similarly, Meissen teacups that once were in daily use become priceless when sitting in a museum showcase. It could be argued that objects become more highly valued when they cease to be what their creators made and become something special — a work of art.

Determinants of Value

Various factors, some of them elusive, contribute to the market value of paintings. The following, although difficult to measure in dollar terms, are the principal determinants.

* J. Patrick Cooney is Assistant Vice-President, Fine Arts Management Service, Citibank, New York.

Quality. There are a number of characteristics that affect the price of any work. Quality is undoubtedly the most important of these; it is also the most difficult to define, as it is based upon connoisseurship, a consensus of scholarly opinions and taste. Certainly no one today would question that Rembrandt's *Self Portrait* at The Frick Collection in New York is a work of supreme quality. However, this opinion has not always been held. During the eighteenth century, works by Rembrandt were not as highly prized as those of some of his contemporaries.

Authorship. Works by established, respected artists command higher prices than those by unknown artists. Clearly, a signed work by Gauguin will sell for more than even a high-quality work by one of his unknown contemporaries.

Authenticity. It is essential that the work being purchased is by the artist to whom it is attributed. With works by modern artists, this can usually be checked with galleries or scholars; however, with Old Master paintings, questions often arise and debates between scholars are frequent. If there is any doubt, the investor should check with several authorities.

Provenance. Provenance is the history of ownership of a painting, which becomes especially important in the case of an unsigned work. It includes where the painting has been exhibited in the past, which also can affect the price. A work of art that has been in a royal collection or that of a distinguished collector frequently commands a higher price than a similar work without such a history.

Market demand. The existence of a number of collectors willing to pay high prices for what they want is essential to establish and stimulate an active market. The investor who buys a work with the intent of selling it should be sure there will be a market. Impressionist pictures are prized throughout the world. German baroque paintings, on the other hand, are sought-after only by a handful of specialized connoisseurs.

Rarity. Prices continue to rise as high-quality works become less frequently available. However, in certain areas, rarity does not necessarily indicate value. A plentiful supply of a certain type of work can stimulate interest in the market and make collectors very competitive. On the other hand, a unique work may appeal only to a certain limited group of collectors and therefore may not command the highest price. Premium prices can be expected where supply is just below the market demand.

Condition. Collectors, investors, and institutions continue to seek works of art in pristine condition. Even slight damage may severely affect the value of a painting, particularly when similar works are available on the market.

Price Guides and Indexes

Price lists. A number of aids are available to help the investor track the price of works of art. In almost all categories of art objects, it is usually accepted that the prices achieved at public auctions are the best general indicator of overall market trends. In June 1960, *Fortune* magazine stated "it is safe generalization that public auctions set basic price trends, and a dealer, while listening to hearsay of private transactions, takes prices reached through open bidding as the main basis for evaluating his own stock." A growing number of price guides are published on an annual basis. Following each public sale at the major auction houses, price lists are made available. Of the many lists of prices achieved at auction, *The Year's Art,* started in 1880, is probably the oldest and *The Annual Art Sales Index* by Richard Hislop is the best known. However, these publications present merely the raw facts of the prices fetched by works of art. They do not provide reliable analysis of the changes in prices or trends.

Indexes. Since November 1980, Sotheby's has published a weekly art index presented in *Barron's.* This index is a highly sophisticated attempt to quantify the art and antiques market. It offers a statistical look at what has happened in twelve important areas in the overall market, and provides a single aggregate figure intended to show how the market as a whole has performed. In each category, the index is based on a generic sampling that is representative of the types of objects that come on the market fairly frequently. Sampling specifically avoids the kind of blockbusters that come up only rarely and make their way onto the front pages of the *New York Times* by virtue of having reached seven-figure prices. The sampling of items is reevaluated following each major sale, or approximately ten to fifteen times a year. Although Sotheby's index is constructed as accurately as possible, it cannot pretend to be as accurate as a stock market index. However, it is a good general guide to the movements of the art market.

ATTRACTIVE FEATURES

Art is not always a good investment, any more than any other vehicle is. However, art certainly can be regarded as a durable asset.

Independence of Money Economy

As Gerald Reitlinger has pointed out in *The Economics of Taste,* Vol. III, "The slump of 1968-69 produced a paradox which threatened to become an orthodoxy. It is that works of art go up in proportion as capital values, profits, and dividends decline, that as substitutes for money, works of art are not liable to the same erosions as money itself."

Long-Term Appreciation

In case after case, particular pieces of art have provided investors with substantial increases in value. However, art must be looked at as a long-term investment, with minimum holdings between five and ten years. Works of art cannot be quickly resold with sizable appreciation. The costs of moving an item in and out of the market are considerable. Not only are there high fees incurred in transactions, but works of art are adversely affected by appearing too frequently on the market. When a work of art is sold more than once within a short period, it is often considered burned.

Psychic Income

For most, the unrivaled benefit of investing in works of art is an intangible one: the pleasure of ownership. The profound psychological and aesthetic enjoyment provided by works of art has stimulated many of the best financial investments.

POTENTIAL RISKS

Limited Appreciation for Overall Market

The art market overall has moved in steady, consistent trends. Contrary to the impression one receives from newspaper headlines, the art market as a whole has shown only a gradual increase in prices over the past twenty years. Although there are specific examples of individual works returning 30 and 40 percent a year, for the past ten years the average painting has performed in a steady and much less spectacular fashion.

Low Liquidity

The art market is not as liquid as many other investment media. Liquidity to a large extent depends upon market conditions. To sell a work of art at auction will take a minimum of several months for cataloguing and publication of information. Following the sale, thirty days must be allowed for payment to be made. Private sales often can be arranged more quickly; however, this depends upon the desirability of the material being offered.

Risk of Fraud

As paintings become increasingly expensive, the proliferation of forgeries becomes a greater consideration. The best protection against fakes is to know the market and to seek expert advice. Certain dealers and auction houses will guarantee items they sell, but these guarantees are limited and vary widely.

Import and Export Regulations

Before investing in any work of art, the investor should make sure that the item being purchased has free and clear title and can be exported from the country in which it is purchased. It is not infrequent for a foreign government to prohibit the exportation of national treasure (i.e., works of art that it seeks to maintain as part of its national heritage).

Changes in Fashion

The value of works of art to a certain extent depends upon taste. In contemporary art, in particular, there is a great risk that today's master will be tomorrow's forgotten painter.

OLD MASTER PAINTINGS

Definition

"Old Master paintings" are defined as European paintings created up to, but not including, the nineteenth century.

Marketplace

Auction houses. London traditionally has been the largest center for the sale of Old Master pictures. Sotheby Parke Bernet and Christie's, the two largest auction houses, started in London, although both are now international operations. However, in recent years a substantial percentage of the Old Master market has shifted to New York, where a third auction house, Phillips, is making a bid for a share of the market.

Dealers. Dealers play a very strong role in the Old Master market. Although the largest number of paintings may pass through the hands of the auction houses, dealers probably sell the more important Old Masters. A dealer will often guarantee a selling price, either through outright purchase or by contract. It is not unusual for a dealer to guarantee anonymity to a seller or buyer. This can be of great importance in delicate situations and is not as easily achieved in the auction world.

Private sector. The private sector of the market traditionally has been thought to be dominated by European buyers, but North and South Americans also provide a strong market. During the 1981 season, European buying, especially German, was curtailed by the strengthening of the U.S. dollar. Obviously, foreign exchange fluctuations tend to discourage buying by holders of devalued currencies.

Important Factors in the Old Master Market

Stability. Old Master pictures are traditionally known for their stability. One reason for this is that museums have been the major purchasers of high-quality, important Old Masters. Established collections will pay to enhance or round out a collection. New museums, such as the Kimbell Art Museum and the J. Paul Getty Museum, reportedly push up the price of Old Masters in building new collections.

Quality and reputation. Quality is a vital factor in the Old Master market as well as most other painting markets. High-quality works sell under all conditions, while lesser-quality pieces are not sold. The inclusion of a painting in a show, catalogue, or scholarly work strengthens its reputation.

Attribution. Attribution is very important; a painting by the hand of the master is much more valuable than a school picture. A portrait believed to have been painted by Sir Peter Paul Rubens was bought for $100,000 in 1901 by J.P. Morgan. In 1935, it was sold to the Metropolitan Museum of Art for over twice that sum. Scholarship, however, has shown the picture to be by the School of Rubens, and the picture was recently sold at auction for only $22,000.

Subject matter. Subject matter often affects the salability of a picture. Portraits, popular earlier in this century, are not collected today except by institutions. Landscapes and flower pictures are now sought-after, although Dutch Old Master pictures, which had been selling for $100,000 to $200,000 for flower subjects and $200,000 to $300,000 for landscapes, did not sell well during 1981.

Supply. The supply of first-quality Old Master pictures is very small. Virtually no important Old Masters sold at auction during the 1977-1978 season, and only two sold at auction during the 1978-1979 season: Dirk Bout's *Resurrection* for $3.74 million to the Norton Simon Museum in California, and *Samson and Delilah* by Sir Peter Paul Rubens for $5.4 million to the National Gallery in London.

In the past few years, auctions have made headlines with spectacular prices for Old Master paintings. Rembrandt's *Aristotle Contemplating the Bust of Homer* sold to the Metropolitan Museum of Art for $2.3 million in November 1961. Velasquez' *Portrait of Juan de Pareja* sold to the same institution for $5,544,000 in November 1970. Table 1 on page 604 provides bought/sold prices on selected Old Masters auctioned at Sotheby's in 1979 and 1980. The percentage distribution of sales at Sotheby Parke Bernet (New York) in terms of dollar values during the 1979-1980 season is illustrated in Figure 1 on page 605.

Private sales, the exact price of which are unpublished and circulate only by rumor, may be substantial deals. Albrecht Aldorfer's *Christ Taking Leave of His Mother* was reportedly sold to the National Gallery in London for over $5 million in one of several deals in which Christie's acted as agent instead of as auctioneer. The National Gallery in Washington, D.C. spent in the area of $6 million for Leonardo da Vinci's *Genevra di Benci.* Other private sales include the Louvre's purchase of the portrait of *Sigismondo Malatesta* by Piero della Francesca and Lorenzo Lotto's *Madonna, Child and San Rocco,* purchased by the National Gallery of Canada for $2.15 million.

TABLE 1. Recent Sotheby's London Sales of Old Master Paintings

Detail	*Purchase Date*	*Purchase Price*	*Sale Date*	*Sale Price*	*Annual Growth Rate*
The Madonna, Eusebio da San Giorgio	6-12-68	£ 450	7-16-80	£ 1,600	11.1%
Still Life, J.B.S. Chardin	6-12-68	4,000	7-16-80	8,500	6.5
Christ and the Adulteress, De Mura,	6-12-68	2,500	4-16-80	3,000	1.5
St. Joseph and the Infant Christ, Guido Reni	6-12-68	600	4-16-80	3,800	16.6
Venice: Piazzetta Seen From the South East, Luca Carlevaris	3-26-69	12,000	7-16-80	38,000	11.0
Venice: Piazzetta Seen From the North, Luca Carlevaris	3-26-69	15,000	7-16-80	40,000	9.3
An Arctic Scene: Dutch Whalers off Greenland, Abraham Storck	3-26-69	1,600	12-12-79	18,000	27.4
Raphael's Dream, Breughel the Elder & Hans Rottenhammer	6-25-69	5,200	12-12-79	40,000	22.6
Portico and Courtyard of a Venetian Palace, Francesco Guardi,	6-25-69	13,650	12-12-79	50,000	15.5
Cascade at Tivoli, Claude-Joseph Vernet	7-12-72	6,500	12-12-79	36,000	27.7
Italian Landscape with Waterfall and *Italian Landscape with Castle* (pair), Hendrick van Lint	12-10-75	9,500	12-12-79	11,000	3.7
The Wings of a Triptych: The Annunciation with 4 Saints, Alvaro Portoghese	1-22-76	8,900	12-12-79	14,000	16.3
A Coastal Scene, Ludolf Bakhuizen	8-12-76	8,600	7-16-80	15,000	21.9
A Wooded Landscape with Latona and the Lycian Peasants Kerstiaen de Keuninck	2-7-79	1,700	12-13-79	4,500	164.7

SOURCE: Sotheby's of London

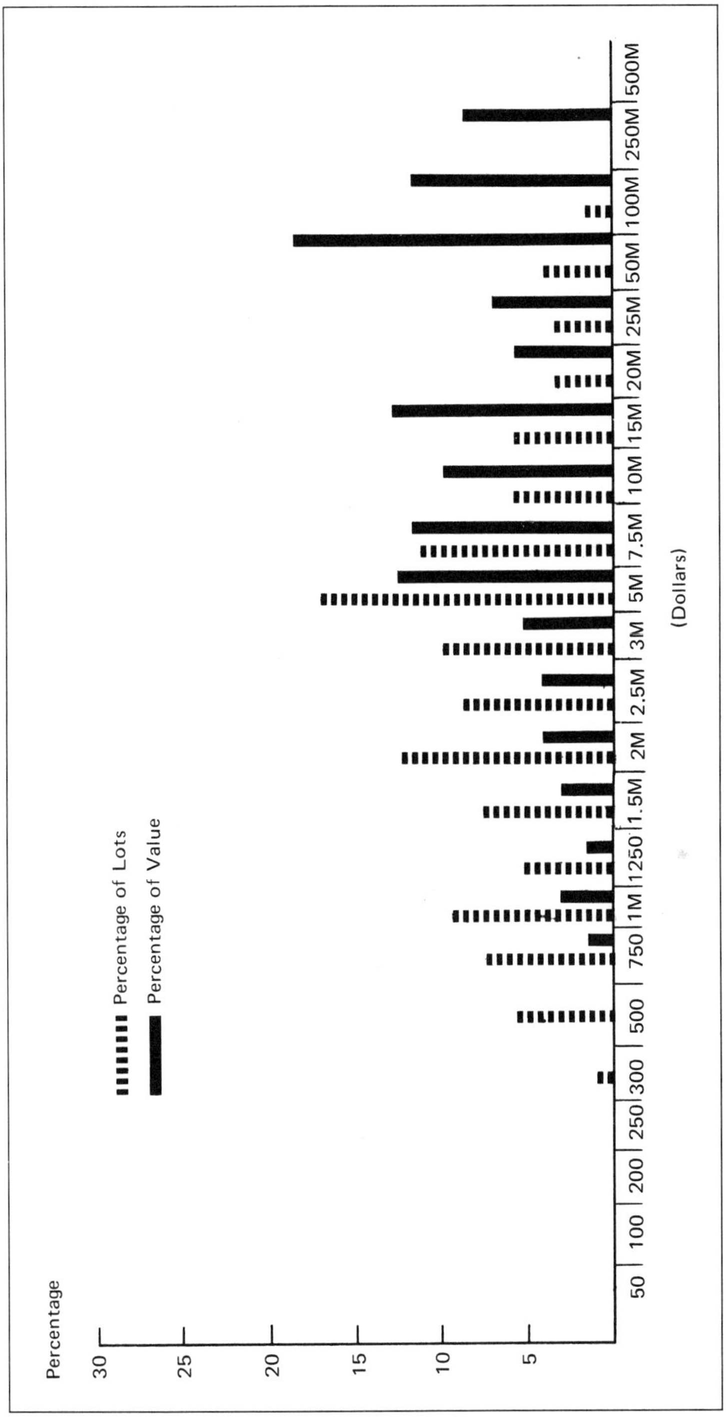

FIG. 1. Distribution of Old Master Paintings Sold at Sotheby Parke Bernet New York During the 1979–1980 Season
SOURCE: Sotheby Parke Bernet, New York

NINETEENTH-CENTURY PAINTINGS

Definition

This category includes all nineteenth-century paintings exclusive of the impressionist and American paintings.

Marketplace

Nineteenth-century paintings are widely sold in Europe and in the United States. In the nineteenth century, American millionaires went to Europe and bought paintings right off the walls of the salons to hang in their homes. Therefore, large numbers of nineteenth-century European paintings are now in the United States. The demand for these paintings took a decided downward turn about the time of World War I. Many paintings came off the walls and into storage and are only now being rediscovered. The major buyers of the nineteenth-century paintings today are Europeans themselves; national pride helps motivate the sale of many of these paintings. German, Dutch, and Belgian collectors dominate the world market, while the English and French find paintings within their own borders. Sentimental subjects are very popular, and recognizable scenes bring heavy competition in the country involved.

A current sub-group consists of rich buyers from the Middle East who are looking for Middle Eastern subjects, a popular theme during the nineteenth century. Collectors are so anxious to get works that they often fly to sales in American cities — New York, Boston, Philadelphia, San Francisco, and New Orleans — to buy particular paintings. Seventy percent of buyers at auction are European.

In addition, many dealers have set up businesses just to handle nineteenth-century European paintings and to cater to the European market coming to the United States to buy. Small but growing interest is seen in U.S. museums, some of which are anxious to build collections while prices are still affordable. Dealers often show interest in artists whose work is given a major show in the United States, since the reputation and therefore the prices of an artist's work are often rehabilitated by a major show in a museum or reputable gallery.

Value of Nineteenth-Century Paintings

The price range for nineteenth-century paintings is between $10,000 and $100,000 or more. Recognized painters bring, as one would expect, the highest prices. Jean Francois Millet's *Peasant Grafting a Tree* sold for $350,000 at a Sotheby's New York sale in 1976. A private sale of six paintings and three oil sketches by Adolphe Wilheim Bouguereau realized $500,000. Sir Lawrence Alma-Tadema's *Caracalla and Geta Bear Fight in the Colosseum, 203 A.D.,* was discovered in India and sold in London for $316,000. As the more popular artists' work becomes more expensive and less available, experts feel that the work of lesser nineteenth-century artists will jump in price.

IMPRESSIONIST AND POSTIMPRESSIONIST PAINTINGS

Definitions

The works of the French artists known as Impressionists attracted wide attention during the 1874-1886 period, when they were shown together at various exhibits. The Postimpressionists, whose work began about the same time and continued to the end of the century, repudiated the impressionists through emphasis on form and structure.

Marketplace and Value

Impressionism has long been one of the most prestigious areas of art collecting. Works by the great impressionist and postimpressionist painters are prized by collectors all over the world. Europeans, North and South Americans, and Japanese are all actively bidding for these paintings. Ever since the London Goldschmidt auction sale in 1958, when impressionist works first brought auction prices that rivaled the amounts paid for the most important Old Masters, French impressionist and postimpressionist paintings have been the money center of the art market. Fine impressionist pictures are truly the blue chips of the art world.

Although many of the impressionist and postimpressionist painters were unknown in their own lifetimes (Van Gogh sold only one painting during his entire life), by the turn of the century there was already a thriving market for these artists' work. In 1912, Dégas's *Danseurs à la barre* sold to the Louvre for $102,270. Renoir's *Les Cantoniers* sold to Duncan Phillips for $200,000 in 1923. During the early part of this century, great European and American private collections of impressionist and postimpressionist paintings were formed. Most of these collections were subsequently given to museums, providing the foundations of the great public collections now to be seen in Europe and America.

The major market for impressionist pictures is now among private individuals. Only rarely do institutions buy, and usually it is to fill a gap in a collection. One notable exception in the United States was the Kimbell Art Museum of Fort Worth's purchase of Cézanne's *Peasant in a Blue Blouse* for $3.9 million at the Henry Ford II sale in 1980. Japanese museums are also building collections.

During the 1979-1980 season at Sotheby's New York, 312 impressionist paintings sold for $34,451,000, at an average price of $110,000. Meanwhile, Sotheby's sale in London brought in £13 million sterling or approximately $30 million. Over 50 percent of impressionist paintings sold for $50,000 or less. Almost 75 percent sold for $100,000 or less, while 90 percent sold for $250,000 or less. An analysis of the important dispersal of the Paulette Goddard Remarque collection in November 1979 showed a mixed international market with strong European interest: 51 percent of buyers were foreign, 49 percent were American; 59 percent were private buyers, 40 percent were dealers, and 1 percent represented an institutional buyer. American buyers were from Connecticut, New York,

California, Colorado, Pennsylvania, Michigan, Chicago, Maryland, and Vermont. Foreign buyers were from Germany, France, England, Switzerland, Mexico, and Japan.

Important Factors in the Market

Unlike the Old Master market in which attributions change frequently, new discoveries are made, and restoration and condition problems are numerous, the impressionist and postimpressionist market is relatively uncomplicated. Most attributions to an artist are firm, although a large number of convincing fakes plague this market as well as the modern market. Discoveries are rare, since most artists have been well catalogued and investigated. It is unlikely that large numbers of important pictures have disappeared in old family homes and are waiting to be discovered. Condition problems, ever-present with Old Masters, are not as frequent, since impressionist and postimpressionist paintings are so much newer. This market is particularly attractive to a wide range of buyers; thanks to easy recognition of a painter's work, a Renoir always looks like a Renoir, with pleasant subject matter, landscapes and cityscapes, still lifes, and nudes.

Although the impressionist and postimpressionist market can be described as stable and blue chip, large monetary gains are not certain on all paintings. The best-quality works will fetch high, often staggering, prices while lesser-quality works by the known masters will go unsold. High-quality works, even those that may have been in the marketplace recently, will gain in price.

When works of art sell for high prices at auction, the prices for similar works are driven up at private galleries. Although high prices have existed for impressionist and postimpressionist work sold privately, public sales of major collections certainly increase values in the private sector. The sales performance of certain impressionist paintings at 1980 sales in New York and London is demonstrated in Tables 2 and 3 on pages 609 and 610, respectively.

MODERN PAINTINGS

Definition

"Modern paintings" have been defined as pictures created between 1900 and 1945. The modern market, comprising a relatively few years of artistic production when compared to the Old Master or the American painting markets, is nevertheless complex.

Marketplace

The modern market did not really gain million-dollar status until 1979, when Matisse's *Le Jeune Marin I* brought $1.5 million at auction. Until the 1960s,

TABLE 2. Impressionist and Modern Paintings Sold at Sotheby's and Christie's in New York, May 1980

Item	*Year of Purchase*	*Purchase Price*	*Sale Price*	*Annual Growth Rate*
Peasant in a Blue Blouse, Cézanne	1959	$ 406,000	$3,900,000	10.7%
Nude Study, Dégas	1962	197,700	660,000	6.9
Tahitian Women Under the Palms, Gauguin	1960	38,000	1,800,000	15.6
Argenteuil, Monet	1948	8,500	570,000	14.0
Fog Near Dieppe, Monet	1949	1,500	120,000	15.8
Saltimbanque Seated With Arms Crossed, Picasso	1972	1,400,000	3,000,000	10.2
The Garden, Renoir	1957	200,000	1,200,000	8.1
Young Girl With a Hat, Renoir	1959	6,000	52,500	11.2
Woman Seated In a Garden, Toulouse-Lautrec	1965	105,000	800,000	14.5
The Garden of the Poet, Arles, Van Gogh	1958	372,000	5,200,000	12.7
Portrait of Adeline Ravoux, Van Gogh	1966	435,000	1,800,000	10.7

SOURCE: Sotheby's of London

TABLE 3. Impressionist and Modern Paintings Sold at Sotheby's London, July 1-2, 1980

Item	*Date of Purchase*	*Purchase Price*	*Sale Price*	*Annual Growth Rate*
Vase d'Anemone, Renoir	1972	£32,000	£ 54,000	6.7%
Nature Morte au Givier, Boudin	1969	£3,800	16,200	13.8
Dieppe: Place Nationale un Jour de Marche, Boudin	1950	FR215,000	9,300	13.1
Environs d'Antibes, Boudin	1967	£6,000	8,000	2.2
Venus et l'Amour, Renoir	1969	£9,379	28,000	10.4
La Tougues à Deauville, Boudin	1962	£7,200	19,000	5.5
La Sortie du Bain, Dégas	1968	$72,500	75,000	7.7
Nature Morte: Bouilloire, Pot-au-lait, Sucrier et Sept Pommes, Cézanne	1973	$620,000	480,000	9.8
Les Deux Soeurs Legendaires, Toulouse-Lautrec	1974	£16,000	26,000	8.1
Monsieur Paul Viaud, Taussat, Arcachon, Toulouse-Lautrec	1974	£205,000	230,000	1.9
Nu à la Fenêtre Ouverte, Pablo Picasso	1968	$47,500	32,000	4.0
Les Aieux du Pecheur, Picasso	1971	£52,000	136,000	11.0
Vase de Trefles et Verre, Braque	1968	$40,000	42,000	7.8

SOURCE: Sotheby's of London

modern pictures could be bought relatively inexpensively while the impressionist and postimpressionist market had already skyrocketed.

Investment interest in some modern artists is international. Picasso, Matisse, and Leger are actively sought out throughout the world. German Expressionist paintings, works by Wassily Kandinsky, Emil Nolde, Franz Marc, and Ernst Ludwig Kirchner, rose in price in 1980, but the market remains mostly European, although recent shows in U.S. museums have sparked interest in the U.S. market.

The surrealist market was strong in the early 1970s but was damaged by a recession in the mid-1970s, regaining strength in the November 1979 sale of the collection of William N. Copley, in which sixty-four paintings fetched $6.4 million. Man Ray's *A l'Heure de l'Observatoire: les Amoureux* brought $750,000. Americans still do not seem to be as avid purchasers of surrealist paintings as the Europeans.

Picasso. The most famous and also the most prolific artist in the modern period was Pablo Picasso. The Picasso market itself is complex. The artist lived an unusually long life and produced tirelessly during his entire lifetime. Although Picasso's masterpieces are in great demand, the flood of second-level Picasso paintings and his enormous print production make the market less than a sure buy. The Analytic Cubist period (1910-1912) and the later Rose, African, Blue, and Neoclassical periods are the most popular. Picasso's *Saltimbanque Seated with Arms Crossed,* 1923, sold for $3 million at the May 1980 sale at Sotheby Parke Bernet, making it the second most expensive modern painting ever sold at auction. His self-portrait entitled *Yo* was the most expensive, at $5.3 million. However, many Picasso works can be expected to bring below $100,000.

Current values. During the 1979-1980 season at Sotheby's, over 50 percent of modern paintings sold for $3,000 or less, approximately 75 percent sold for $7,500 or less, and about 90 percent sold for $20,000 or less. The average selling price of modern paintings was approximately $7,800. On the other hand, individual works by modern masters may bring prices far above the average. In the London Sotheby's sale of April 1, 1981, Edvard Munch's *Two People* sold for $1,569,750.

Fakes

Like the impressionist and postimpressionist market, the modern market is hampered with the spectre of fakes. Modigliani, Leger, and Rodin have all suffered from the existence of a large number of fakes, causing buyers to look elsewhere when not absolutely sure of authenticity. Experts among dealers, auction houses, and museums are generally highly cooperative and always should be consulted in any case of doubtful authenticity.

CONTEMPORARY PAINTINGS

Definition and Marketplace

Contemporary art is usually understood to mean art produced after World War II. Although regional interest in local artists both in the United States and Europe surely exists to a certain extent, New York is indisputably the center of the contemporary art scene. The major activity in sales takes place in galleries. The major buyers of contemporary art are Americans, with the Swiss, Italians, and Germans providing the major impetus from Europe.

The contemporary market got its start in the late 1950s with the work of Jackson Pollock and other Abstract Expressionists capturing the imagination of buyers. Although Pollock's work could be bought in the early 1950s for only hundreds of dollars, by the end of the decade his *Autumn Rhythm* had sold for $30,000, his *Blue Poles* recently sold to the Australian National Gallery for a reported $2 million, and his *Lavender Mist* sold to the National Gallery in Washington, D.C. for a reported price in excess of $2 million.

Contemporary pictures reached the $1 million mark when Jasper Johns' *Three Flags* was sold privately for that figure to New York's Whitney Museum of American Art; it is believed to be the highest price ever paid for a work of art by a living artist. Other Jasper Johns works have sold well; for example, his *Double Maps* sold at auction in 1973 for $240,000. Works can sell for higher prices at auction than at the private galleries. However, it is certainly the art galleries that are giving the young and lesser-known contemporary artists their starts.

AMERICAN PAINTINGS

Definition

This category includes all paintings produced in the United States up to World War II. Post-World War II works are considered contemporary. The most important schools are colonial portraiture, early American folk art, the Hudson River school, Luminism, American barbizon, American nineteenth-century academic paintings, (including genre painting and history painting), Western art, American Impressionism, the Ashcan school, the Stieglitz group, the American Modernists, Regionalism, the American scene, WTA, and American abstract artists. Some, such as Western art, are thriving markets in themselves.

Marketplace

The overwhelming majority of buyers of American art, as one would expect, are Americans, both museums and private individuals. In the past few years, an increasing number of Europeans have become interested in American art. New York must be considered the center of the American art market, with a large number of galleries and three large auction houses, Sotheby Parke Bernet, Christie's, and Phillips. However, thriving galleries exist in most cities on both coasts as well as the Midwest and South, where regional schools are of particular importance.

The biggest monetary gains, rediscovery, and critical acclaim have been the area of nineteenth and early-twentieth-century American paintings. Long neglected and forgotten, and often stored in attics and basements, these paintings have come under scrutiny from art historians and dealers and have found enormous acceptance and enthusiasm from an ever-growing number of museum-goers and private collectors. Although large prices, perhaps in excess of $1 million may have been realized by dealers in recent years, the million-dollar mark was not reached in public auction until the 1980 sale of Frederic Edwin Church's *Icebergs,* found in an English home for boys and sold at Sotheby Parke Bernet for $2.5 million. The high price of Church's masterpiece has pushed prices higher in all categories of fine-quality American paintings.

As recently as 1978, the highest price ever paid at auction for an American painting was $320,000 for James Peale's *Washington and His Generals at Yorktown.* The June 1978 sale of George Caleb Bingham's 1848 *The Jolly Flatboat Men* at Sotheby's, Los Angeles, marks the beginning of the auction boom in American art. The piece was sold for $980,000 to New York's Hirschl and Adler Gallery and was later sold to the New Terra Museum of American Art in Evanston, Illinois for over $1 million. Other important auction landmarks include Winslow Homer's *Signal of Distress* for $1.7 million, William Merritt Chase's *Gravesend Bay,* a pastel, for $820,000, and William Tyler Ranney's *A Sleigh Ride* for $680,000. A Ranney had never sold at auction before for more than $50,000.

The sales performance of American paintings sold at Sotheby's, New York, is shown in Table 4 on page 614 for the years 1979-1980. Distribution of sales by dollar value is shown in Figure 2 on page 616.

TAX CONSEQUENCES

Under federal tax law, profit from the sale of a painting held by an individual for more than one year is taxable at the capital gains rate rather than as ordinary income. Under certain conditions, paintings can be exchanged for others of equal or greater value in a tax-free transaction. As with other types of investments, it is also possible to realize a tax deduction on donating a painting whose market value has appreciated to a qualified organization. Separate rules apply to those who are recognized as investors by the IRS. (See article on Tax Considerations for Collector-Investors elsewhere in this volume.) For complete guidance in these matters, readers are urged to consult a professional tax adviser.

TABLE 4. American Paintings Sold at Sotheby's New York, 1979-1980

Item	*Date of Purchase*	*Purchase Price*		*Latest Price*	*Compound Growth Rate*
The Plains Country West Texas, Thomas Hart Benton	1961	$ 2,500	(1979)	$ 11,000	8.6%
On The Swing, John George Brown	1966	1,100	(1980)	43,000	30.1
The Sidewalk Dance, John George Brown	1914	730	(1980)	105,000	7.8
Street Musician, John George Brown	1938	100	(1980)	15,000	12.8
The Parade, Charles Burchfield	1972	15,000	(1979)	40,000	15.0
Centerport Series, Arthur G. Dove	1973	2,700	(1979)	3,500	4.0
The Beach at Cohasset, Sanford Robinson Gifford	1968	2,200	(1980)	47,500	29.2
Sea Widow Summer #2, Mardsen Hartley	1944	1,500	(1980)	42,000	9.7
Still Life with Calla, Mardsen Hartley	1974	2,000	(1980)	7,500	23.5
Hutchison House, Easthampton, Childe Hassam	1971	21,000	(1979)	38,000	7.2
Wild Swans Sacred to Apollo, Childe Hassam	1954	800	(1980)	11,000	10.5
Reading the News, Edward Lawson Henry	1973	2,094	(1980)	21,000	44.6
The Girl I Left Behind Me, Eastman Johnson	1907	60	(1980)	120,000	11.0
View of New York Harbor, N. Jorgensen	1971	3,250	(1980)	10,000	13.8
Autumn, John La Farge	1948	125	(1979)	40,000	20.0

Item	Date of Purchase	Purchase Price		Latest Price	Compound Growth Rate
In My Garden, Ernest Lawson	1956	$ 300	(1979)	$24,000	20.3%
October Flowers, George Luks	1951	225	(1980)	25,000	18.0
A Snake Pursuing a Crow Horse Stealer, Alfred Jacob Miller	1966	1,800	(1979)	20,000	19.6
The Hay Cart, Maurice Prendergast	1939	375	(1980)	26,000	11.1
Still Life with Two Roses, Hovsep Pushman	1952	700	(1979)	6,000	8.1
Still Life with Magnolia Flower, Hovsep Pushman	1948	625	(1979)	3,250	5.4
Snipe, Percival Rosseau	1976	6,750	(1980)	9,500	9.6
Mountain Goat, Carl Rungius	1968	3,200	(1980)	21,000	16.1
Bighorn Sheep, Carl Rungius	1968	1,800	(1980)	15,000	18.3
A Frigate Off Greenrock, Robert Salmon	1972	9,000	(1980)	27,000	3.4
Saturday Night—Ringling Hotel, Sarasota Florida, Everett Shinn	1977	23,000	(1979)	60,000	46.5
The Tightrope Walker, Everett Shinn	1959	2,750	(1980)	40,000	14.0
Subway Platform, Raphael Soyer	1965	4,750	(1980)	15,000	7.8
Duck and Ducklings, Arthur Tait	1947	550	(1980)	17,000	10.9
Hard Fare, Arthur Tait	1947	225	(1980)	18,000	14.1
The Practical Idealist, Grant Wood	1973	9,000	(1979)	14,000	7.8
The Sentimental Yearner, Grant Wood	1973	10,000	(1979)	22,000	14.4

SOURCE: Sotheby's of London

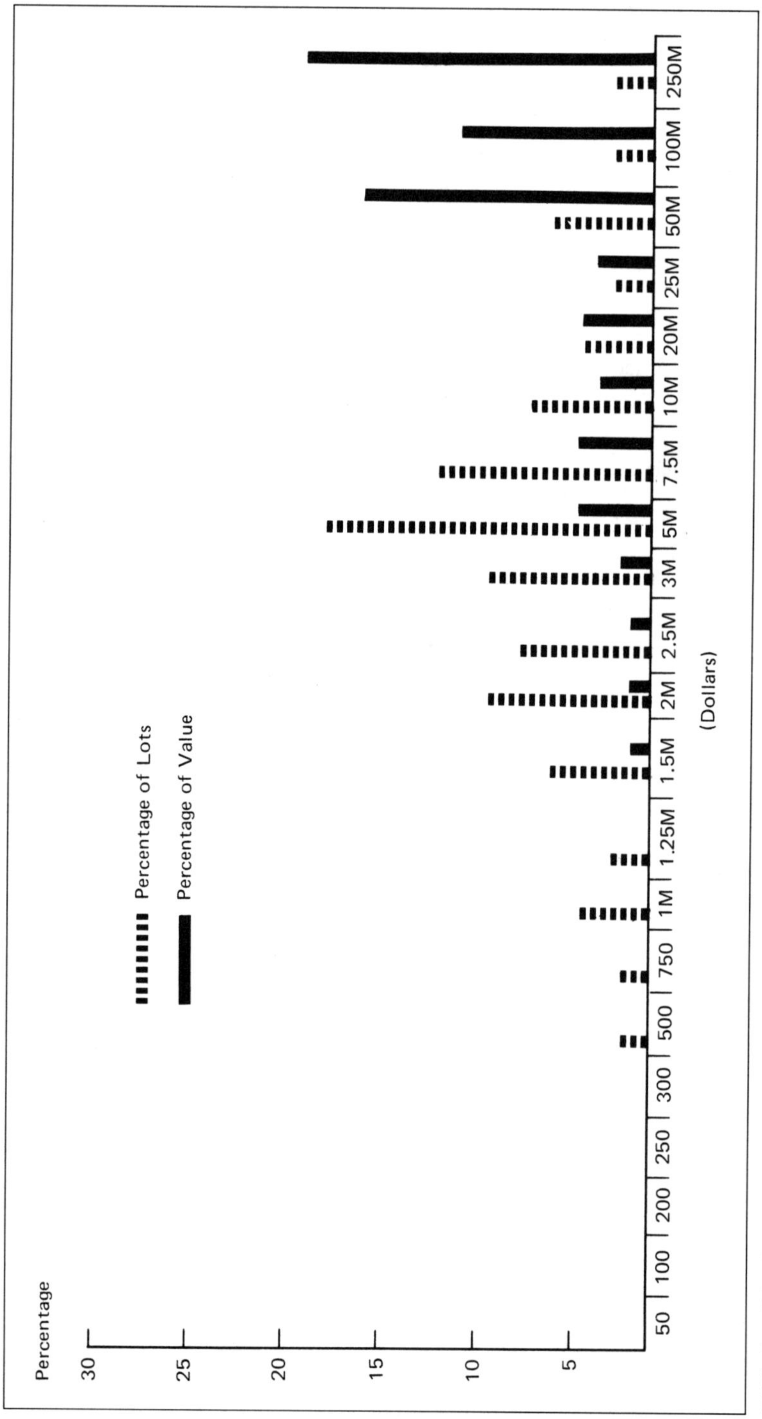

FIG. 2. Distribution of American Paintings Sold at Sotheby's New York During 1979–1980
SOURCE: Sotheby's of London

REPRESENTATIVE TYPE OF INVESTORS

Dealers

The market for paintings remains dominated by dealers, the professional art market investors. As astute businesspeople, they must watch the market closely and buy with an eye to marketability.

Private Collectors

The second major force in the market consists of private collectors, those with a passion for acquisition who reach for the best and acquire the most desirable. It is the individual collector in most cases who is willing to pay the highest price for an object.

Institutions

Universities and museums continue to play a role in the market. However, they are increasingly dependent upon the generosity of private collectors and corporations.

IMPORTANT FACTORS IN BUYING AND SELLING

Acquiring Information

The uninitiated buyer should find out what he really likes, and then become educated in that area. As in every investment area, knowledge is the key to success. There is no substitute for one's own expertise. Information on art is readily available from museums, art libraries, auction houses, and major dealers.

Books on collecting, auctions, and art history will give the investor an essential introduction to the market. For practical information on how the market functions, dealers and specialists at local auction houses can be consulted. Auction houses regularly have exhibitions of items a week before they are sold. The in-house specialists are happy to show prospective buyers these items and explain, for example, why one item is expected to bring a higher price than similar items in the sale. Similarly, dealers will readily talk about the items in their galleries. When beginning to buy, an investor should buy one or two objects of personal interest and live with them to see how he enjoys them after a few months. Perhaps it would be wise to start with smaller, less expensive items. An investor should start making acquisitions slowly while becoming familiar with the business.

Combining Taste and Investment Value

If personal inclination attracts an investor to well-known artists and art movements that command top prices, he may have to look for other less expensive collecting areas with greater potential for price appreciation. For example, someone whose favorites are the French Impressionists might look for the works of some lesser-known American Impressionists that are still considered underpriced by many experts. Another alternative is to look to the drawings and sketches by the artists he admires most.

Specializing Within the Field

Specializing, even within the general area of his interests, an investor's knowledge will increase dramatically. After having focused his attention, an investor will be able to spot good buys. When dealers know of an investor's specific interest, they will call him when they have exceptional pieces.

Moreover, specializing can make a collection more valuable. The total value of the items in a unified collection is greater than the sum of the prices of the individual paintings. Also, when selling, the knowledge that the piece has come from a well-known collection may increase the price.

Selecting Quality

An investor should buy the very best affordable and always look for quality. Selection is vital. It is the quality pieces that will show the most appreciation in value. Even during recessions, higher-quality works usually maintain their value because they attract the wealthier, more recession-proof buyers. Auction experts, in fact, have recently noted the existence of a two-tiered art market: Museum-quality work continues to be in demand regardless of fluctuations in the economy, while the market for lesser-quality work attracts little interest in times of low prosperity.

Inspecting the Work

Before buying, an investor should be sure to get full information about the condition and history of the specific work. Knowing the broad price levels for similar works is not enough. Close inspection is especially important for works of art being sold at auction. Descriptions of condition in the catalogue are not detailed. Certain damages, even tears and improper restoration, may not be immediately apparent, but they can make a big difference in the price.

Appearance is not everything. It is not unusual for a painting actually to have lost value because it has been restored. The quality of the restoration is extremely important. At the same time, slight damage can give the investor an opportunity to buy a painting by a major master at a lower price. If the condition problems are minor and do not affect important areas of the painting, a buyer may actually be able to purchase advantageously. Sophisticated buyers often prefer to purchase a painting uncleaned to be sure any restoration is done properly.

Working With Experts

It is a good idea for an investor to get involved personally with museum curators, art experts, and scholars who specialize in the area in which he is interested. These experts will give information and advice if the investor is serious about collecting. Even the most modest catalogue that has a text by a respected scholar can bring a collection to the attention of other experts in the field. It can have a real impact, especially if the catalogue is one of the few documents on the artist or school.

BUYING AND SELLING COSTS

Auction House Commissions

All works of art bought and sold at auction bear a commission payable to the auctioneer. In the case of major auction houses in London, Paris, and New York, this includes commission by both the buyer and the seller. These commissions change from time to time. In the 1930s, auctioneers in London charged a commission of only 7.5 percent to vendors of pictures. There was no buyers' commission. In New York, commissions are currently 10 percent for both the buyer and the seller. In London, commissions vary from house to house.

Value-Added Tax and Sales Tax

In London, there is also a value-added tax (VAT) of 15 percent on the auction commission; thus a buyer bidding £100,000 at a Sotheby's London auction would pay the following:

Hammer price (bid price)	£ 100,000
Buyer's premium	10,000
Value-added tax (15%)	1,500
Total purchase price	£ 111,500

Therefore, immediately upon purchasing a work of art, the buyer must pay 11.5 percent in addition to the hammer price.

In New York, although there is no VAT, a sales tax is levied on all works of art delivered to the purchaser in New York City. An example of this would be as follows:

Hammer price (bid price)	$100,000
Buyers' premium	10,000
New York City sales tax	9,075
Total purchase price	$119,075

Thus, a buyer receiving delivery of a work of art in New York pays an additional premium of 19.1 percent on the bid price.

Insurance

An investment in fine art should be covered against loss or damage through carelessness, fire, or theft. Expenses involved in insuring a work of art can be extremely high at times. Costs vary according to the location. Reliable, objective evaluation or appraisal is necessary in setting the value for insurance purposes. These evaluations in themselves may cost the owner one or 2 percent of the total value of the painting.

CUSTODIAL CARE

A collection must be maintained properly. This costs money, but condition is an important part of the value. Paintings or water colors that are damaged by direct sunlight decrease in value. Room humidity and temperature should be maintained at an even level. A work of art must be handled carefully. A collection should be regularly appraised by an expert to ascertain its value for insurance purposes.

If restoration is necessary, the collector should consult a nearby museum for recommendations. Many museums have professional conservators on their staff. The American Institute of Conservation, in Washington, D.C. can also recommend conservators. Museums should also be consulted about framers.

GLOSSARY

attribution — An educated assignment by an authority of the authorship of a work of art.

auction — Public sale where highest recognized bidder is purchaser.

bid — The amount offered for a painting being sold at auction.

buyers' commission — Fee charged to purchaser on top of the hammer price. At Sotheby's and Christie's in New York, a standard 10 percent is always charged.

buy-in — Item at auction that does not reach the pre-established reserved price.

consignment — Item given to auction house or dealer for sale. Auction houses usually charge a 10 percent sales commission, plus fees for insurance, storage, and for catalogue illustration. Dealers negotiate fees usually between 20 and 25 percent.

contemporary painting — American art produced after World War II.

hammer price — The accepted bid price for a lot. The buyers' commission is added on to this price.

impressionist painting — A school of painting that started in France during the 1860s, of which the best known artists were Monet, Renoir, Manet, Pissaro, and Dégas. The Postimpressionists, Cezanne, Van Gogh, and Gauguin, are often included in sales with the Impressionists.

lot — An item, or group of items sold together, at an auction.

modern painting — Painting from the postimpressionist period to 1945.

nineteenth-century painting — European and American painting from 1800 to 1900.

old master painting— European painting to the nineteenth century.

order bid— A bid placed in writing before an auction. The bid is executed on a client's behalf by the auction house.

presale estimate— Range of prices set as an expert's best guess as to what a lot will bring at auction. These ranges are published by the auction house prior to the sale.

provenance— A record of the previous private collections, museums, artists, and dealers who have owned an object.

reserve— An amount set by the seller below which he will not sell the consigned material. The auction house will bid on the owner's behalf up to the reserve price.

sellers' premium— Fee charged consigner by the auction house for arranging the sale. Usually this is a 10 percent charge; however, on major items the percentage can be negotiated.

LEADING NEW YORK GALLERIES

A.A.A. (Associated American Artists), New York, N.Y.

ACA, New York, N.Y.

Acquavella Inc., New York, N.Y.

Blum Helman, New York

Blumka, New York, N.Y.

Alexander Brooke Inc., New York, N.Y.

Leo Castelli, New York, N.Y.

Christie's (Christie, Manson & Woods U.S.A. Ltd.), New York, N.Y.

Richard L. Feigen & Co., New York, N.Y.

Frumkin Gallery, New York, N.Y.

Gimpel & Weitzenhoffer Ltd. (Peter Gimpel & A. Max Weitzenhoffer, Jr.), New York, N.Y.

Stephen Hahn, New York, N.Y.

Hammer Galleries, New York, N.Y.

Hirsch & Adler Galleries Inc., New York, N.Y.

Kennedy Galleries (L. A. Fleischman, R. Wunderlich), New York, N.Y.

M. Knoedler & Co., Inc., New York, N.Y.

Marlborough Gallery Inc., New York, N.Y.

Pierre Matisse, New York, N.Y.

Stanley Moss & Co., Inc., New York, N.Y.

Newhouse Galleries Inc., New York, N.Y.

Perls Galleries (Klaus G. Perls), New York, N.Y.

Plaza Art Galleries, Inc. (W.H., E.P. & W.E. O'Reilly), New York, N.Y.

Paul Rosenberg & Co., New York, N.Y.

Rosenberg & Stiebel Inc. (Eric Stiebel), New York, N.Y.

William H. Schab Gallery Inc., New York, N.Y.

Shepherd Gallery, New York, N.Y.

Sotheby Parke Bernet Inc., New York, N.Y.

Sotheby's of London, New York, N.Y.

E.V. Thaw, New York, N.Y.

Wildenstein, New York, N.Y.

Zabriskie, New York, N.Y.

SUGGESTED READING

Magazines

Apollo. Published by Bracken House, London, England. Monthly.

Art and Auction. Published by Auction Guild, New York, N.Y. Monthly.

Art in America. Published by Whitney Communications Corp., New York, N.Y. Monthly.

Artnews. Published by Artnews, New York, N.Y. Monthly.

Connoisseur. Published by The Hearst Corporation, New York. Monthly.

The Magazine Antiques. Published by Straight Enterprises, New York, N.Y. Monthly.

Portfolio. Published by Grosvenor Publications, Inc., New York, N.Y. Bimonthly.

Newsletters

The Art/Antiques Investment Report. Published by Wall Street Reports Publishing Corp., New York, N.Y. Biweekly.

The Art Newsletter. Published by Artnews, New York, N.Y. Biweekly.

The Gray Letter. Published by Boone, Inc., Tuscaloosa, Ala. Weekly.

The International Art Market. Published by Art in America, Inc., New York, N.Y. Monthly.

Reference Books

Butler, John. *Art As Investment.* (Special Report No. 74, The Economist Intelligence Unit Ltd.) London: Spencer House, 1979.

Gordon, Martin. *Gordon's Print Price Annual.* New York: Martin Gordon, Inc., annual.

Hislop, Richard. *The Annual Art Sales Index.* Surrey (England): Art Sales Index Ltd., annual.

Mayer, E. *International Auction Records.* New York: Editions Publisol, annual.

Reitlinger, Gerald. *The Economics of Taste.* Volumes I to III. London: Barrie & Jenkins, 1970.

Period Furniture

*Paul A. Kunkel**

BASIC CHARACTERISTICS

Period furniture, like other forms of collectable art, has seen a historic rise in value during the 1970s. The concept of collecting art and antiques as a serious investment has had far fewer supporters in America than it has in Europe, where precious objects have traditionally held their value in periods of economic unrest. However, more than a decade of inflation has affected most conventional forms of investing, combined with widely publicized prices for everything in the art market from Picassos to ceramic thimbles. Even the most conservative financial analysts now consider certain forms of art and antique objects as valuable additions to an overall portfolio of assets. The unique quality of fine furniture, combined with its proven potential for long-term capital gains (when intelligently selected, acquired, and sold), is attracting many people to invest in American, English, or French period furniture.

Principal Areas of Furniture Collecting

Collecting and investing in period furniture is generally limited to four major fields: American furniture, English furniture, French and Continental furniture, and furniture of the nineteenth century. (See Table 1 on pages 624 and 625 for the principal periods, makers, and designers of American, English, and French furniture.)

American furniture. While American furniture designs were largely influenced by English and Continental fashion in the eighteenth century, few people today see American Queen Anne and Chippendale furniture as provincial copies of London prototypes. Serious collecting begins with early eighteenth century pieces, since furniture was scarce in America before 1700.

American furniture follows a consistent progression through the eighteenth century from the baroque William and Mary style, through Queen Anne, rococo Chippendale, and neoclassical Hepplewhite and Sheraton styles, with many beautiful examples surviving in public and private collections. The various centers of American cabinetmaking — Boston, Newport, New York, Philadelphia, and Baltimore — each had its own recognizable character. Of the various regional styles, the austere Massachusetts Queen Anne, the innovative Goddard-Townsend school of Newport furniture, and the eccentric curvilinear American rococo

* Paul A. Kunkel is Associate Editor of *Art & Auction,* New York.

TABLE 1. Principal Style Periods, Makers, and Designers

	American		*English*		*French*		
1600							**1600**
			Tudor		Louis XIII (1610-1643)		
	The Pilgrim Century			Stalker and Parker			
			William & Mary (1688-1702)	Coxed & Woster	Louis XIV (1643-1715)	Charles-André Boulle	
1700							**1700**
						Nicolas Petit	
	William and Mary	Itinerant craftsmen	Queen Anne (1702-1713)		Régence (1700-1735)		
	Queen Anne		George I (1714-1730)	Giles Grendy William Kent Benjamin Goodison		Charles Cressent Roger vanderCruse 'RVLC' Bernard van Riesenburgh 'BVRB'	
	Chippendale	Jonathan Brooks Thomas Affleck Goddard-Townsend Group Benjamin Randolph William Savery	George II (1730-1760)	William Linnell Thomas Johnson Thomas Chippendale William Vile Robert Manwaring	Louis XV (1735-1765)	J.B. Tilliard Pierre Roussel Joseph Baumhauer J.F. Leleu Jacques Dubois Pierre Migeon J.F. Oeben J. H. Riesener	
	Adam-Hepplewhite-Sheraton	The Adam Family Eliphet Chapin	George III (1760-1810)	John Cobb William Hallett Ince & Mayhew			

Adam-Hepplewhite-Sheraton	Samuel McIntire John Elliott	George III (1760-1810)	John Linnell Pierre Langlois Robert Adam George Hepplewhite	Louis XVI (1765-1790)	C.C. Saunier Charles Topino Martin Carlin
	Benjamin Frothingham John & Thomas Seymour			Directoire	Georges Jacob Adam Weisweiler
1800			Thomas Sheraton		Pierre Gouthiere **1800**
Federal			George Smith Thomas Shearer	Empire (1799-1815)	Bernard Molitar
	Duncan Phyfe C.H. Lannuier	Regency (1811-1820)	John McLean C.H. Tatum Robert Gillow Henry Holland Thomas Hope		Jacob Desmaiter
Empire		George IV (1820-1830)	A.W.N. Pugin	Louis-Phillippe (1830-1848)	
Revival Furniture	Thomas Brooks Alexander Roux			Second Empire	
Victorian	John Henry Belter Charles Baudoinne J & J Meeks	Victorian (1837-1901)		Napoleon III (1852-1872)	Michel-Victor Cruchet H.M.A. Jacquemart L.A.A.Beurdeley C.G. Diehl
	Herter Brothers		Charles L. Eastlake		Henri Dasson
		Arts & Crafts	William Morris A.H. Mackmurdo Charles Godwin		Michael Thonet Francois Lincke
Arts & Crafts	Gustav Stickley L. & J.G. Stickley Elbert Hubbard		Charles Rennie Mackintosh		
1900					**1900**
		Edwardian (1901-1910)		Art Nouveau	Emile Gallé Louis Majorelle Jean Dunand
	Frank Lloyd Wright		Eileen Gray	Art Deco	

found in Philadelphia, Chippendale furniture is the most seriously collected today.

Some staggering prices have resulted. In November 1980, for example, $360,000 was paid by New York dealer Harold Sack of Israel Sack, Inc., for a Goddard-Townsend school block- and shell-carved mahogany chest of drawers made circa 1760. The first piece of American furniture to reach $500,000 at auction will probably be a classic piece of Philadelphia Chippendale or Newport furniture.

American Federal (neoclassical) and Empire (Napoleonic style) furniture are widely available and somewhat less expensive than fine eighteenth-century pieces, but even here the price gap is closing. For example, in April 1981 a pair of Empire rosewood and gilt card tables by C.H. Lannuier of New York fetched $185,000 from a New York private collector.

Collecting interest in nineteenth-century American furniture has been sporadic, but intense speculation in the rococo revival pieces made by John Henry Belter has caused prices of these items to soar. As expected, this demand has created a suction effect that has improved prices for pieces of lesser quality. It has yet to be seen whether such pieces will be able to hold their value.

Vernacular forms achieved great refinement in the nineteenth century, producing two styles of furniture that are highly collectable today — that made by the Shaker religious sect and that made by craftsmen of the American Arts & Crafts Movement, particularly the Craftsman Workshops of Gustav Strickley, Elbert Hubbard's Roycroft Workshops, and the early work of Frank Lloyd Wright.

English furniture. Although an enormous amount of material survives from the seventeenth century, collectors by tradition have been most interested in English furniture dating from 1700 to about 1830 — from the date of Queen Anne's ascendency to the throne, through the Georgian period, to the end of the Regency and the dawn of the Victorian era. Most of England's greatest furniture was produced during this Golden Age. All phases of eighteenth- and early nineteenth-century English furniture are seriously collected today. Since 1978, astronomical prices have been realized for all kinds of walnut, mahogany, and painted furniture. Generally speaking, prices for eighteenth-century English furniture have at least doubled from 1970 to 1980, with prices for the most outstanding pieces increasing by as much as three times.

English Victorian furniture holds less interest for collectors than nineteenth-century French or American pieces do, with the possible exception of so-called gothick furniture designed by the visionary eccentric A.W.N. Pugin.

The late nineteenth-century antidote to Victorian absurdity was born in England, chiefly in the work of William Morris, whose Arts & Crafts Movement resurrected the English vernacular tradition. Competition in this area is particularly hot for what is called "artist's furniture." For example, in 1979 an ebonized secretaire designed by Charles Rennie Mackintosh fetched £80,000 ($176,000) at

Sotheby's Belgravia auction room in London. The same cabinet changed hands for £10 in 1933.

French and Continental furniture. The best French furniture is generally considered the finest ever made, and naturally has always commanded a high price. Even during the nineteenth century, when countless reproductions of classic French eighteenth-century pieces were available, an eighteenth-century French commode realized £12,000 at the Duke of Hamilton's sale in 1882 — a price that was far higher than was being paid for all but the very greatest paintings.

There has been consistent interest in all phases of formal French furniture — from Louis XIV baroque classicism, through the rococo styles of the Régence and and Louis XV, to the resurgence of neoclassical in the arts of Louis XVI — and at the same time a genuine scarcity of investment-quality pieces. Prices for pieces of all kinds range from $2,000 and $3,000 to as much as $50,000 and $70,000 for a piece of real distinction. Hundreds of thousands of dollars can change hands for a piece of great rarity, but so few of such pieces remain in private hands today that the chance of acquiring an outstanding piece of French furniture is remote.

Nineteenth-century furniture. Within the past five years, nineteenth-century furniture, primarily French, has gained considerable recognition in the marketplace. In 1970, when good nineteenth-century pieces could be had for a few hundred dollars, one could hardly find a respectable dealer in this area. With some of these same pieces now fetching thousands or tens of thousands of dollars, dealers in nineteenth-century furniture can be found at the best addresses in New York, London, and Paris. Auctioneers in New York and London now offer huge specialized sales of Victorian decorative art.

In Europe, the nineteenth century was an era of eclecticism and historical revival in furniture. Gothic, Renaissance, Egyptian, Oriental, Louis XV, Louis XVI, and even the English Chippendale style all had a period of revival in French furniture. Empress Eugenie spawned the industry of creating precise duplicates of eighteenth-century masterpieces — most of a quality that is extremely poor when compared with the originals.

A significant percentage of nineteenth-century furniture seen in the market is simply second-rate, and while prices have risen considerably since 1977 when Sotheby Parke Bernet held their first Victorian International sale, the field is long overdue for a reevaluation and prices may yet see a correction.

Determining Value

The same criteria exist for judging the value of period furniture whether a collector's interest leans toward American, English, or French antiques. Very simply, they are quality, condition, relative rarity, and historical importance. Applying these concepts to prospective purchases is not an easy task. Generally, at least one of these criteria will be lacking in nearly every piece available at any particular time. Such objects should be either acquired for a reasonable price or avoided altogether.

Quality. Quality is the best key to value in furniture, and learning to recognize fine quality is the essence of furniture collecting. Indeed, it is more important to develop a good comparative sense of quality in furniture than it is to have a historian's knowledge of style periods and makers' names. Craftsmen's labels, ownership by persons of historical importance, and family histories, while interesting to help document a piece of furniture, are all of secondary importance to its construction, proportion, ornamentation, and condition. Since very few period pieces have a proven history, a legitimate bill or maker's label naturally adds to the price of a piece of antique furniture. However, it says nothing for its quality or aesthetic merit. The history of collecting recounts many examples of foolish buyers paying too much for mediocre pieces bearing impressive labels.

Proportion. Assessing quality in furniture is primarily a visual process. We have all seen so-called connoisseurs, when first approaching a piece of furniture, immediately remove a drawer and scrutinize the dovetails. This is precisely the wrong way to approach fine furniture. Proportions are always the first thing to notice when assessing a piece of furniture. The rightness of the height versus the length versus the depth becomes obvious when fine furniture is compared with the mediocre. The manner in which a chair back is designed and executed, the subtle graduation of drawers (when drawers near the top are shallower than the lower drawers), the manner in which the top of a Pembroke table relates to its base — all of these relationships are of singular importance when judging furniture.

Detail. Moving beyond proportions, quality can also be judged from the care with which the carver or cabinetmaker executed structural and ornamental details. The color and figuration of the wood is also significant. The absence of original hardware on an eighteenth-century piece is common in English and American furniture, but sufficient reason to dismiss a piece if it happens to be French. Constantly comparing the quality of furniture in the marketplace with classic examples in museums or public collections will eventually enable the collector to recognize the better examples.

Condition. The quality and value of a piece of period furniture are directly related to its state of preservation. A piece that has been neglected or over-restored is far less desirable than a similar piece in pristine condition. The most common flaws in condition result from damage, neglect, and improper restoration. Reputable dealers rarely offer pieces in less than fine condition, so the most expedient way for the neophyte to judge condition is to visit dealers on a regular basis; pieces in inferior condition then become immediately apparent.

Rarity and historical significance. Rarity in the furniture market is that magical quality that can make an astonishing difference in the value of a piece of furniture. Of course, the finest examples of nearly every period and school of furniture making are rare by the fact of their survival. But rarity in the furniture market denotes an object's unique quality that makes it desirable for nearly every collector in the field. Following are three examples of period furniture that belong in this exalted category. The first two pieces are the only examples of their kind. The third example is both rare and historically significant.

Examples of outstanding period furniture. Each of the following three examples of fine period furniture has passed through the market within the past two years and realized a price that was consistent with values at the time it was sold.

Chippendale walnut wing armchair with its original companion slipper chair (Figure 1). Both were made in Rhode Island, probably Newport, circa 1750, and are outstanding in boldness of design and strength of construction. The carving of the plain cabriole legs, webbed claw-and-ball feet, and block- and ring-carved stretchers is very fine and subtle. To the writer's knowledge, they are the only wing and slipper chairs to have survived together and intact. Unfortunately, they

FIG. 1. Chippendale Walnut Wing Armchair With Its Original Companion Slipper Chair

SOURCE: Sotheby Parke Bernet

do not have the original upholstered covering, but that would be almost too much to ask for.

Widely illustrated, the chairs were once handled by the venerable New York firm of Israel Sack, Inc. Sold at Sotheby Parke Bernet from the collection of Cornelius Moore of Newport in October 1971, the chairs fetched $20,500 when sold as separate lots. Fortunately, they remained together and were offered at auction once again by Sotheby Parke Bernet in May 1981, from the collection of John and Marjorie Schorsch. After very heated bidding, Connecticut dealer John Walton paid $80,000 (estimated pre-auction value $60,000–$90,000) for the pair, nearly four times the price they had commanded ten years before.

George II burl walnut pier-desk and bookcase (Figure 2). This is a rare example of the kind of English writing desk that was placed in the narrow pier between two windows, hence the name. Made circa 1735, it is probably the earliest bow-fronted pier-desk in existence. Over 80 inches tall, the desk measures only 25½ inches wide and 19 inches deep, making it appear almost diminutive. From any angle or distance, it is superbly proportioned, having a slightly low waist, an expansive upper section, and a gracefully compact undercabinet. The unusually tall feet give it an undeniably graceful appearance. Its details are superb as well. Fluted pilasters (flattened columns) on either side of the mirror are finished with Corinthian capitals. Its upper and lower fitted interiors are very fine, and the brass hardware appears to be original. The fragile walnut veneer is nearly all original, and its color and figuration are both fine. In short, it is outstanding in every way.

Offered at Christie's in London in 1939, the pier-desk actually failed to sell at $2,438. As part of the Marjorie Wiggin Prescott collection at Christie's in New York, it fetched $105,000 from the London firm of Phillips & Harris (estimated pre-auction price $50,000–$75,000).

Early neoclassical Louis XVI ormolu-mounted painted satinwood commode (Figure 3). This rather severe-looking piece was made in Paris, circa 1770, by the German-born cabinetmaker Joseph Baumhauer. The commode is stamped "JOSEPH" three times. Made of somewhat darkened satinwood with vernis martin painted decoration in the style of the Flemish still-life artist J.B. Monnoyer, the commode was beautifully mounted with ormolu framing the decorated panels, and heavy ormolu legs, each formed as a tapering fluted column with acanthus leaf capitals. It is doubtful whether the veined marble top is original. Nevertheless, its extraordinarily original design and obvious quality places it in the uppermost rank of early Louis XVI furniture.

Extensive research uncovered that Joseph made this commode as part of a large commission for Nicolas Beaujon (1718-1786), the French counselor of state. (Beaujon's vast collection included the famous Boucher panels painted for Madame de Pompadour; they are now in the Frick Collection, New York.) Only a handful of pieces from this suite are known to exist today: a vernis martin satinwood bureau-secretaire at Waddesdon Manor, Buckinghamshire; a similarly

FIG. 2. A Fine and Rare George II Burl Walnut Small Pier-Desk and Bookcase, circa 1735

SOURCE: Christie's, N.Y.

FIG. 3. Early Neoclassical Vernis Martin, Bois Satine, and Ormolu-Mounted Commode, circa 1770
SOURCE: Christie's, N.Y.

decorated armoire in a Paris private collection; and a pair of similarly decorated commodes at Mentmore, the English country estate of the Earl of Rosebury.

On April 10, 1980, the Paris-New York firm of Didier Aaron paid $240,000 for the Joseph commode at Christie's in New York (estimated pre-auction price $300,000). It was immediately sent to Paris and sold at a significant profit.

ATTRACTIVE FEATURES

The principal investment motive for collecting any form of art or antiques is interim- or long-term capital gains, defined in the art market as holding pieces for at least four or five years. It goes without saying that for the individual who loves fine things, the pleasure of building a fine collection may overshadow thoughts of potential profit upon resale. Selling is one of the last things collectors wish to contemplate. But the investor in period furniture should realize that he is in the rare position of having his cake as well as eating it. Consciousness of the upward trend of prices for the finest period pieces should directly influence a collector's selection and disposition.

Inflation has certainly played some part in the recent price movement of antique furniture, but its effect is small compared with the general resurgence of interest in fine things, and the growing awareness that, as competition to acquire art and antiques increases and supplies begin to dwindle, prices of period furniture will rise. (See Table 2 on page 634 for auction records for 1980 and 1981 showing price appreciation of various pieces of American, English, and French furniture.)

POTENTIAL RISKS

Misrepresentation

The risk of buying mediocre or fake furniture is always a possibility. For example, while misrepresentation exists in varying degrees in nearly all fields of art and antiques, the French furniture market is notorious for spawning questionable merchandise. Because French furniture is so valuable, this particular market is a very dangerous place for any but the most knowledgeable collector. With the price of an eighteenth-century commode ranging from $5,000 to $100,000 or more today, there is every incentive for the unscrupulous to improve the marketability of an existing piece.

The prudent investor should avoid such an obvious problem through self-education, seeking competent, professional advice, and exercising full recourse should a dispute arise after a purchase.

Illiquidity

The market for fine period furniture has been so durable in recent years that it is difficult to visualize a significant downturn in activity, unless caused by purely external factors. While art and antiques are not nearly as flexible as other investments in terms of liquidity, it is a situation that all collectors readily accept. Waiting six months to a year to place an object in an appropriate auction, or keeping it on consignment with a dealer for several months, is the price an investor should accept in order to command a high markup on his investment. Investors requiring immediate access to their capital should not, as a rule, invest in art and antiques.

Deterioration

Damage can be perpetuated on antique furniture by well-meaning owners, as well as by accident or sheer neglect. Proper maintenance is required to minimize the risk of deterioration that will affect the value of the investment. (See *Custodial Care* in this article.)

TAX CONSEQUENCES

Under federal tax law, profit from the sale of a piece of furniture held by an individual for more than one year is taxable at the capital gains rate rather than as ordinary income. Under certain conditions, it can be exchanged for

TABLE 2. Recent Auction Records for Important Pieces of Period Furniture

English Furniture

Item	*Previous Sale*	*Previous Price*	*Sale*	*Price*	*Appreciation (Compounded Annually)*
Pair of George II gray-painted and parcel-gilt pier mirrors, circa 1735	Christie's Northwick Park, Gloucestershire, 1964	$4,760	Christie's, N.Y., 1981, lot 199	$135,000	22.78%, p.a.
Fine George III mahogany window seat, probably by Thomas Chippendale, circa 1760	Christie's, Harewood House, Yorkshire, 1976	3,312	Christie's, N.Y., 1981, lot 290	11,000	28.75
William and Mary green japanned dressing-glass-on-stand, circa 1700	Christie's, London, 1968	2,535	Christie's, N.Y., 1981, lot 350	26,000	19.61
George III ormolu-mounted mahogany tambour writing table, circa 1775	Sotheby's, London, 1974	27,500	Christie's, N.Y., 1981, lot 353	85,000	18.96
Fine pair of William and Mary black japanned card tables, circa 1700	Christie's, London, 1967	4,704	Christie's, N.Y., 1981, lot 351	60,000	20.58
Important suite of George II needlepoint upholstered carved mahogany seat furniture, circa 1755	Christie's, London, 1964	17,052	Sotheby's, N.Y., 1981, lot 71	340,000	19.89

Item	Previous Sale	Previous Price	Sale	Price	Appreciation (Compounded Annually)
Pair of fine George III giltwood settees, designed by Robert Adam, circa 1780	Christie's, London, 1956	$2,600	Christie's, N.Y., 1981, lot 214	$68,000	14.03%, p.a.
French Furniture					
Fine Louis XV ormolu-mounted kingwood parquetry bureau plat, signed J.-M. Chevallier, circa 1750	Sotheby's, London, 1971	20,000	Sotheby's, N.Y., 1981, lot 170	180,000	40.0
Pair of Louis XV giltwood open armchairs, circa 1750	Christie's, Ravenscliff, 1978	7,000	Sotheby's, N.Y., 1981, lot 178	14,000	39.9
Louis XV ormolu-mounted tulipwood parquetry bureau plat, circa 1750	Sotheby's, N.Y., 1978	14,000	Sotheby's, N.Y., 1981, lot 181	41,000	80.3
Louis XV ormolu-mounted parquetry small table, stamped "R.V.L.C.," circa 1755	Sotheby's, N.Y., 1978	21,000	Sotheby's, Monte Carlo, 1981, lot 83	52,000	35.3
Late Louis XV ormolu-mounted marquetry commode, stamped G. Kemp, circa 1755	Sotheby's, Mentmore, 1977	27,000	Sotheby's, Monte Carlo, 1981, lot 84	40,000	7.3

(Table continued)

TABLE 2. Recent Auction Records for Important Pieces of Period Furniture — *Cont'd*

Item	*Previous Sale*	*Previous Price*	*Sale*	*Price*	*Appreciation (Compounded Annually)*
Louis XVI marquetry commode, stamped E. Levasseur, JME, circa 1770	Sotheby's, Monte Carlo, 1979	$72,000	Sotheby's, Monte Carlo, 1981, lot 91	$76,000	3.0%p.a.
Louis XVI bureau plat and cartonnier, attributed to Joseph Baumhauer, circa 1770	Sotheby's, London, 1974	450,000	Sotheby's, Monte Carlo, 1981, lot 144	909,000	10.8
American Furniture*					
Chippendale block-and-shell-carved mahogany knee-hole desk, attributed to Edmund Townsend, circa 1770	Sotheby's, N.Y., Oct. 21, 1972	120,000	Sotheby's, Pokety Farms, Md., 1980	250,000	9.6%
Chippendale carved mahogany bonnet-top chest-on-chest, circa 1770	Parke-Bernet Galleries, N.Y., 1971	6,250	Sotheby's, N.Y., 1980, lot 760	15,000	11.0

*Valid price comparisons can only be made on identical or nearly-identical items. Since fine pieces of American furniture rarely pass through the market twice in a decade, there are few examples to cite for the purposes of this study.

p.a. = per annum

SOURCE: *Art & Auction* Magazine, 1981

another piece of equal or greater value in a tax-free transaction. As with other types of investments, it is also possible to realize a tax deduction on donating a particular piece whose market value has appreciated to a qualified organization. Separate rules apply to those who are recognized as investors by the IRS. (See article on Tax Considerations for Collector-Investors, elsewhere in this volume.) For complete guidance in these matters, readers are urged to consult a professional tax adviser.

REPRESENTATIVE TYPES OF INVESTORS

As a group, private dealers constitute a potent force in the market, buying for their own account as well as for private clients. At auctions of English and French furniture, dealers can literally dominate the proceedings, but this should not suggest that period furniture does not draw a wide audience. Innumerable corporate, institutional, and private collectors continue to form fine collections of antique furniture for pleasure as well as investment.

IMPORTANT FACTORS IN BUYING AND SELLING

Becoming Acquainted With the Field

Two paths exist for the serious collector-investor who wants to acquire great pieces of antique furniture as an investment: Seek out the best (and often very expensive) professional advice available or become as knowledgeable as possible through self-education. Exploring the first alternative will naturally lead the reader to one or more of the dealers mentioned toward the end of this article. The second method is advisable whether or not one seeks professional guidance. Unsurprisingly, art is like every other type of investment in at least one respect: Knowledge is power. Doubtless at least some knowledge about art and antiques will keep the collector-investor on the proper path and out of the hands of a growing number of charlatans that have entered the field. More importantly, without at least a budding appreciation of fine objects, there is little sense or reason (financial or otherwise) to collect period furniture or any other form of art.

For the collector wishing to learn more about antique furniture, there are dozens of excellent books to read and several excellent public collections to visit and study. But no experience will prove as valuable as actually going to dealers' galleries, auction exhibitions (remember to keep track of the post-sale results), and antique shows to examine and price furniture that is on the market. Should an investor discover collector's blood flowing through his veins, the time spent in these activities will become pure pleasure. Such is the reason that more than a few collectors have given way to temptation, resigned their other professions, and become respected and highly successful dealers.

Brokers and Dealers

The principal distinction collectors and investors must make is that between the private trade (dealers) and the auction market. The concept of wholesale versus retail has become somewhat blurred in the furniture market recently. Although dealers sometimes mark up as much as 300 percent to allow for the hefty commissions that decorators demand on the retail side of the transaction, there is no denying that recent prices at auction for the very best pieces are nearly as high as those the dealers themselves charge.

Aggressive competition from the British firms Sotheby Parke Bernet and Christie, Manson & Woods in the area of fine furniture has partially eclipsed the role of the dealer by attracting important consignments from museums and private collections. For many collectors, this situation is at best only a mixed blessing. Paying large sums for furniture at auction is risky, since auctioneers are traditionally loathe to make good on errors of description or condition on the things they sell. Establishing close relationships with prominent dealers or consultants who have been in the business at least ten years is an excellent way to minimize the risk of making a costly mistake at auction. A 5 percent commission for such advice is a small price to pay in the long run.

CUSTODIAL CARE

All antique furniture bears the signs of age, but proper maintenance can minimize the risk of deterioration affecting the investment value of the pieces.

Environmental Control

Environmental control should be the collector's first concern. All furniture should be kept in a constant atmosphere or one that changes only very gradually. The relative humidity should be between 40 and 60 percent, and the temperature around 70 degrees, as anything higher than 80 degrees is detrimental to antique furniture. Once the climatic conditions for which the piece was designed are achieved, the materials of which nearly all furniture is made — wood and glue — will retain their properties and the piece will live quite happily. It is important to avoid any abrupt changes, to which veneered furniture is more sensitive than solid-wood furniture.

All furniture is at its most sensitive during the change of seasons in spring and autumn; at these times, extra care is called for. The atmosphere should be sufficiently humidified all year round, even in summer, either by active means such as humidifiers or by placing a vase of flowers or potted plants nearby. Another good method is to place a large, saturated sponge in a plastic container under the piece of furniture or (better still) inside a drawer, when there is sufficient empty space.

Even modest amounts of sunlight every day can adversely affect stained or patinated wood over a long period of time. While it is impractical to remove furniture from indirect light, direct sunlight must be avoided at all costs.

Moving and Storage

There are many sensible precautions one can take to preserve a piece of furniture. When an object is moved, it should be lifted rather than dragged along the floor. Marble tops are best removed first and carried on edge rather than flat. Loading should be kept within reasonable limits and all doors should be kept closed and locked to prevent warping. It is also a good idea to secure console tables that cling to the wall by means of a metal bracket, designed to take the weight of either the back rail of the table or the marble above.

Veneered furniture requires scrupulous attention to maintain its integrity. A piece of veneer that starts to lift should be held in place provisionally with paper tape and reglued at the earliest possible moment. Flat, horizontal surfaces of Boulle marquetry should be covered with a pane of glass to prevent the intricate brass and tortoiseshell network from becoming dislodged.

Cleaning and Polishing

Proper upkeep minimizes the danger of undermining an investment through excessive cleaning and waxing.

Wood is a living thing; maintaining the integrity of wood requires a certain respect. When dusting, care should be taken not to catch and lift pieces of veneers in the duster. Wood furniture should be polished once every few years with a natural resin varnish, which allows the wood to breathe. Wood furniture should not be waxed more than once a year, preferably in the spring or autumn, using as little beeswax as possible to do the job, while buffing off all excess wax with a clean, dry cotton cloth. Furniture should never be cleaned with linseed oil; alcohol, too, can easily damage polished and waxed finishes.

One should not wax painted, gilded, or lacquered furniture. Dusting with a perfectly dry cloth should be all that is required. Anything more complicated must be handled by a professional.

DEALERS AND AUCTIONEERS

Collector-investors of period furniture will by necessity become acquainted with the leading dealers and auctioneers who specialize in furniture and decorative art. It is important to visit as many dealers, antique shows, and auctions as time permits in order to guage differences in quality and price.

Leading Dealers of American Furniture

Philip Bradley Co., Downingtown, Pa.

Benjamin Ginsburg, New York, N.Y.

Bernard & Dean S. Levy, New York, N.Y.

Israel Sack, Inc. (Harold and Albert Sack), New York, N.Y.
H. & R. Sandor, Inc., New Hope, Pa.
David Stockwell, Inc., Wilmington, Del.
John Walton, Inc., Jewett City, Conn.

Leading Dealers of English Furniture

U.S. Dealers

Arthur Ackermann & Son, Ltd. (Charles Saltner), New York, N.Y.
Alfred Bullard, Inc. (William Bertolet), Philadelphia, Pa.
Thomas Devenish & Co., Inc., New York, N.Y.
Malcolm Franklin, Inc. (Paul Franklin), Chicago, Ill.
James Hansen, Santa Barbara, Cal.
Glen Randall, Inc., Alexandria, Va.
John F. Smith, New York, N.Y.
Stair & Co., Inc., New York, N.Y.
Vernay & Jussel, Inc. (Christian Jussel), New York, N.Y.
Wellington Antiques, Ltd. (Neil Sellin), New York, N.Y.

British Dealers

Asprey & Co., Ltd., London
H. Blairman & Sons, Ltd. (George J. Levy), London
Richard Courtney, Ltd., London
Hotspur, Ltd. (Robin Kern), London
Jeremy, London
Mallett & Son, Ltd., London
Mallett at Bourdon House, London
Partridge (Fine Art), Ltd., London
Pelham Galleries (Henry W. Rubin), London
Phillips & Harris, London
Spink & Son, Ltd., London
Stair & Co., Ltd., London
Trevor (Michael Trevor Venis), London

Leading Dealers of French and Continental Furniture

U.S. Dealers

Didier Aaron, Inc. (Hervé Aaron), New York, N.Y.
A La Vielle Russie, Inc. (Peter & Paul Schaeffer), New York, N.Y.
The Antique Porcelain Co., The Antique Company of New York, Inc. (Rotraut Beiny), New York, N.Y.
Dalva Brothers, Inc. (David & Leon Dalva), New York, N.Y.
Rosenberg & Steibel, Inc. (Gerald Steibel), New York, N.Y.

European Dealers

H. & G. Calvet, Paris, France

Fabre et Fils, Paris, France

Jacques Kugel, Paris, France

Etienne Levy, S.A., Paris, France

Partridge (Fine Art), Ltd., London, England

Jacques Perrin, Paris, France

William Redford, London, England

Auction Houses

Vast quantities of period furniture are bought and sold at auction around the world. In fact, auction houses remain a principal source of supply for many dealers. The collector-investor who neglects to attend auctions on a regular basis is missing the opportunity to buy fine pieces at prices that are often lower than those found in the private trade. Following is a select list of auctioneers who routinely handle fine period furniture. For a more complete list of auctioneers and sales of art and antiques worldwide, consult the monthly magazine *Art & Auction.*

U.S. Houses

Richard A. Bourne Co., Inc., Hyannis, Mass. Particularly for American furniture.

Butterfield & Butterfield, San Francisco, Cal. Offers furniture of all periods, but is particularly strong in nineteenth-century Continental and Oriental furniture.

Christie, Manson & Woods, Ltd., New York, N.Y. American furniture, English, French, and Continental furniture up to 1830, Arts and Crafts, Art Nouveau, and Art Deco.

Christie's East, New York, N.Y. Nineteenth-century furniture, and pieces of lesser quality.

William Doyle Galleries, New York, N.Y. Particularly strong in nineteenth-century French and Continental furniture.

Samuel T. Freeman, Philadelphia, Pa. Particularly for English and American furniture.

Morton's Auction Exchange, New Orleans, La. Particularly for nineteenth-century American and European furniture.

Robert W. Skinner, Bolton, Mass. and Boston, Mass. Particularly for American furniture.

C. G. Sloan & Co., Washington, D.C. Furniture of all periods.

Sotheby Parke Bernet, Inc., New York, N.Y. They regularly offer every imaginable kind of furniture, but are particularly strong in American and nineteenth-century furniture.

British Houses

W. & F.C. Bonham & Sons, Ltd., London. English, French, and Continental furniture.

Christie, Manson & Woods, Ltd., London. English, French, and Continental furniture.

Christie's South Kensington, London. Nineteenth- and twentieth-century furniture.

Phillips, Blenstock House, London. English, French, and Continental furniture.

Sotheby Parke Bernet, Inc., London. English, French, and Continental furniture to 1830.

Sotheby's Belgravia, London. Nineteenth- and twentieth-century furniture.

French Houses

Auctions in Paris are held at the Hôtel Drouot. During the auction season, Drouot is a beehive of activity. For a complete list of auctioneers and sales held at Drouot, consult the weekly *Gazette de l'Hôtel,* available on Paris newsstands or by subscription. The most active Drouot auctioneers of period furniture are:

Ader Picard Tajan, Paris

Boisgirard de Heeckeren, Paris

Cornette de Saint Cyr, Paris

Monaco. Fine French and Continental, Art Nouveau, and Art Deco furniture are periodically offered in Monte Carlo at Sotheby Parke Bernet, Monaco, S.A.

PUBLIC COLLECTIONS OF PERIOD FURNITURE

Visiting important museums and public collections of period furniture and decorative arts will add immeasurably to the collector-investor's understanding and recognition of fine quality. Though nearly all public collections forbid visitors to touch or otherwise examine their finest pieces during public hours, arrangements can sometimes be made through application to the appropriate curator. Most are quite willing to share their love for the things they themselves have collected, and they take every opportunity to cultivate a potential benefactor.

American Furniture. All of the most important collections in this field are in America, as one would expect. Winterthur, the American Wing of the Metropolitan Museum of Art, and the Karolik Collection of the Boston Museum of Fine Art should be seen by every collector of American furniture.

Albany Institute of History & Art, Albany, N.Y.

The American Wing, Metropolitan Museum of Art, New York, N.Y.

Bayou Bend Collection, Houston, Tex.

Boston Museum of Fine Art, Boston, Mass.

Colonial Williamsburg, Va.

Connecticut Historical Society, Hartford, Conn.

[Old] Deerfield, Deerfield, Conn.

The Francis Henry du Pont Winterthur Museum, Wilmington, Del.

Henry Ford Museum, Dearborn, Mich.

Museum of the City of New York, N.Y.

New York Historical Society, N.Y.

The Philadelphia Museum of Art, Pa.

Yale University Art Gallery, New Haven, Conn.

English Furniture. The most important encyclopedic collection of English furniture is at London's Victoria & Albert Museum. Much English furniture has survived in the eighteenth-century homes for which they were commissioned. Buckingham Palace collection (open only at brief times during the year) and Harewood House (a Chippendale house) are particularly important in this regard. The Irwin Untermeyer collection at the Metropolitan Museum of Art is the finest public collection in the United States.

Boston Museum of Fine Art, Mass.
Harewood House, Yorkshire, England
Metropolitan Museum of Art, New York, N.Y.
Philadelphia Museum of Art, Pa.
The Royal Collection, Buckingham Palace, London, England
Victoria & Albert Museum, London, England

French Furniture. While the Getty Museum and the Metropolitan Museum of Art have many fine pieces of French furniture, the most important collection in this field is at the Louvre in Paris. The Rothschild collection at Waddesdon Manor, the Jones collection at the Victoria & Albert Museum, and the Wallace collection in London are three outstanding English collections.

The J. Paul Getty Museum, Malibu, Cal.
Metropolitan Museum of Art, New York, N.Y.
Musée des Arts Decoratifs, the Louvre, Paris, France
Victoria & Albert Museum, London, England
Waddesdon Manor (near Aylesbury), Buckinghamshire, England
The Wallace Collection, London, England

GLOSSARY

auction house— An establishment where pieces are sold to the highest bidder, usually for a commission charged to both buyer and seller. The auction catalogue is a useful indicator of the range of prices associated with various pieces.

broker— An agent who specializes in buying and selling pieces for a commission, for the account of a collector.

cabriole— The style of forming an "S" shape in leg of a chair, table, or other piece of furniture, beginning with an outward curve and descending in a reverse curve to the foot.

dealer— A buyer and seller of antiques who maintains an inventory, and stands ready to offer advice to clients.

marquetry— A mosaic created through the use of small pieces of wood or other material to form a pattern in wood veneer. Geometrical patterns in marquetry are usually called parquetry.

ormulu— Base metal (usually bronze) finished to resemble gold.

pier piece— A piece of furniture designed to be put between two doors or windows; hence the term "pier mirror," "pier table," etc.

pilaster— A vertical projection on the face of a piece, simulating a classical column, often carved or fluted.

SUGGESTED READING

General

Cescinsky, Herbert. *The Gentle Art of Faking Furniture.* New York: Dover, 1967.

Hayward, Helena. *World Furniture.* New York: McGraw-Hill Co., 1965.

Hinckley, F. Lewis. *A Directory of Antique Furniture.* New York: Bonanza, 1953.

———. *Directory of the Historic Cabinet Woods.* New York: Crown, 1960.

American Furniture

The Collection of Francis P. Garvin, New York: American Art Association, Anderson Galleries, Inc., 1931.

Collection of Israel Sack. New York: American Art Association, Anderson Galleries, 1929.

Colonial Furniture, the Superb Collection of the Late Howard Reifsnyder. New York: American Art Association, American Art Galleries, 1929.

The Garbisch Collection, Volume 4: Important American Furniture and Related Decorative Arts. (Sale held at Pokety Farms, Cambridge, Maryland.) Sotheby Parke Bernet, Inc., 1980.

Girl Scouts Loan Exhibition Catalogue. New York, 1929.

Hornor, William Macpherson. *Blue Book of Philadelphia Furniture, William Penn to George Washington.* Philadelphia, 1935; revised edition, Washington, D.C.: Highland House, 1977.

Iverson, Marion Day. *The American Chair, 1630-1890.* New York: Hastings House, 1957.

Montgomery, Charles F. *American Furniture, The Federal Period.* New York: Henry Francis du Pont Winterthur Museum, 1978.

One Hundred Important American Antiques, Collection of Israel Sack. New York: American Art Association, Anderson Galleries, 1936.

Randall, Richard H., Jr. *American Furniture in the Museum of Fine Art.* Boston: Museum of Fine Art, 1965.

Sack, Albert. *Fine Points of Furniture, Early American.* New York: Crown, 1950.

English Furniture

Catalogue of a Collection of English Furniture, Barometers, and Clocks formed by a Gentleman residing in New York. [Arthur Leidesdorf.] London: Sotheby & Co., 1974.

Coleridge, Anthony. *The Chippendale Period in English Furniture.* London: Faber, 1966.

Edwards, Ralph. *Georgian Furniture,* 2nd ed. London: Victoria & Albert Museum, 1958.

——— and Jourdain, Margaret. *Georgian Cabinet-makers, circa 1700-1800.* London: Country Life, 1955.

Gilbert, Christopher. *The Life and Work of Thomas Chippendale.* New York: Rizzoli, 1978.

Hackenbroch, Yvonne. *English Furniture With Some Furniture of Other Countries in the Irwin Untermeyer Collection.* London: Thames, 1958; New York: Metropolitan Museum of Art, 1958.

Heal, Sir Ambrose. *London Furniture Makers From the Restoration to the Victorian Era.* London: Dover, 1953.

Jourdain, Margaret. *Regency Furniture, 1795-1820.* Second edition, London: Faber, 1948. Revised edition by Ralph Fastnedge, 1963.

——— and Rose, F. *English Furniture, The Georgian Period, 1750-1830.* London: Faber, 1953.

Joy, Edward, T. *English Furniture, 1800-1851.* London: Sotheby Parke Bernet, Inc. 1978.

Macquoid, Percy, and Edwards, Ralph. *The Dictionary of English Furniture,* 3 vols., 2nd ed. revised by Ralph Edwards, London: Country Life, 1960.

Musgrave, Clifford. *Regency Furniture.* London: Faber, 1961.

The Prescott Collection, Volume II: Objects of Art, Important English and Continental Furniture. New York: Christie, Manson & Woods, Ltd., 1981.

The Walter P. Chrysler Collection of English Furniture, Decorative Objects, Paintings, and Rugs, 2 vols. New York: Parke Bernet Galleries, Inc., 1960.

French Furniture

Brunhammer, Yvonne, and de Fayet, Monique. *Meubles et Ensembles Epoques Régence et Louis XV. Meubles et Ensembles Epoque Louis XVI. Meubles et Ensembles Epoques Directoire et Empire,* 4 vols. Paris, 1965.

Connaissance des Arts. *Grands Artisans d'Autrefois: Les Ebenistes du XVIII Siècle Francais.* Paris, 1963.

Highly Important French Furniture, Decorations, Porcelain, Works of Art, and Gold Boxes From the Collection of Henry Ford II. New York: Sotheby Parke Bernet, Inc., 1978.

Magnifique Ensemble de Meubles et Objets d'Art Francais, Collection Monsieur Akram Ojjeh. [Formerly the collection of Georges Wildenstein.] Monte Carlo: Sotheby Parke Bernet, Monaco, S.A., 1979.

Watson, F.J.B. *Furniture.* [Catalogue of the Wallace Collection.] London, 1956.

———. *The Wrightsman Collection: Furniture.* New York: Metropolitan Museum of Art, 1965-1973.

Photographs

*Daniel Wolf**

BASIC CHARACTERISTICS

In the past several years, photography has become an important area of interest for serious investors. What follows is meant not as an exhaustive discussion but as an outline for the prospective collector. Photography's single most salient characteristic — which is perhaps the most disturbing for new investors — is the theoretical potential for the limitless reproduction of an image. It must be stressed that this potential is purely theoretical. In fact, the primary determinants of value for photographs are similar to those for the other graphic arts: the ability and reputation of the artist, the content of the image, the physical condition of the print, its relative scarcity, the date of the print, and whether it was made by the artist or produced under his supervision or issued posthumously. Finally, there are the unpredictable elements of trends and fashion within the market.

VARIETY OF INVESTMENTS

The closest equivalent to a blue chip security would be a signed vintage print of a famous image by an acknowledged master in excellent condition. Such material is very scarce, always highly sought-after, and virtually certain to increase in value. The term "vintage print" means a print made by the photographer at or about the time the picture was taken. It is a shorthand description, used mainly to differentiate between the older and newer versions of the same image. For example, a print made by Edward Weston of one of his famous nudes or still-lifes will probably cost several thousand dollars, while a modern print made by his son from the same negative costs only one-tenth as much. This is true even though the two might be superficially indistinguishable.

The equivalent to growth stocks consists of lesser images by famous artists or work by artists whose reputation is solid but not yet at the superstar level. Examples of the latter are aerial landscapes by William Garnett, portraits by Berenice Abbott or August Sander, or scenes of American life by Robert Frank. Another growth area is commercial photography, such as fashion or advertising, exemplified by the work of people like Baron de Meyer, Cecil Beaton, and Martin Munkacsi.

The most volatile part of the market is new work by contemporary artists. As with any highly speculative investment, risks and returns are equally great,

* Daniel Wolf is Chairman of Daniel Wolf Gallery, New York.

and almost the only criterion is the expertise (or boldness) of the individual collector.

ATTRACTIVE FEATURES

Low Cost

One feature that makes photography an especially attractive investment is that it is still quite inexpensive compared to the other fine arts. At a time when prime paintings regularly sell for hundreds of thousands of dollars, blue chip photographs (as described above) are available for a few thousand dollars. The most expensive single photograph sold at auction, as of this writing, has been a unique daguerreotype by Southworth and Hawes that went for $36,000 — a modest sum for an extraordinarily important piece. As material of this quality becomes scarcer, prices are sure to rise, but it is still possible for a new investor to acquire excellent material without major expenditure.

High Yield

Careful buying can yield a return on investment that can only be described as spectacular. The best known case is probably that of Ansel Adams, whose *Moonrise, Hernandez, N.M.* rose from $500 to over $15,000 in little over three years. Although the increases were not usually as dramatic, most other sections of the market have showed similar gains. It is true that the surge has slowed somewhat, partly because of general economic conditions, partly — and paradoxically — because of increasing sophistication on the part of collectors. Nonetheless, there remains a great deal of material that is still quite undervalued and offers the opportunity for sizeable profits.

Intangible Benefits

The non-quantifiable pleasure of owning and living with a beautiful object is another benefit of investing in photography. Photographs exist in a huge range of styles, techniques, and genres, each of which carries its own particular aesthetic charge. There is more than enough variety for every taste. While it is possible to buy purely for investment, it is safer and, in the long run, much more rewarding to acquire only what one can expect to enjoy.

POTENTIAL RISKS

The drawbacks involved in investing in photography are the same as those for the art market as a whole. The photographs have to be properly cared for and insured against hazards such as fire and theft. They generate no income until they are actually sold, so that the investor must be prepared to defer gains, sometimes for a period of several years if he wants maximum profit. Liquidity is a problem, although not as great as is sometimes supposed. Pressure for a quick sale, of course, can be expected to decrease profits. Above all, the investor must try to avoid faddish or copycat buying. The best material is protected from sudden devaluation, but changing tastes inevitably affect the market. The growth of the market itself provides protection against drastic fluctuations.

TAX CONSEQUENCES

Under federal tax law, profit from the sale of a photograph held by an individual for more than one year is taxable at the capital gains rate rather than as ordinary income. Under certain conditions, photographs can be exchanged for others of equal or greater value in a tax-free transaction. As with other types of investments, it is also possible to realize a tax deduction on donating a piece whose market value has appreciated to a qualified organization. Separate rules apply to those who are recognized as investors by the IRS. (See article on Tax Considerations for Collector-Investors elsewhere in this volume.) For complete guidance in these matters, readers are urged to consult a professional tax adviser.

REPRESENTATIVE TYPES OF INVESTORS

At one time, serious interest in photography was restricted to a small group of enthusiasts and a few institutions such as the Museum of Modern Art in New York. Now, however, the number of collectors has expanded to include most of the major museums, numerous colleges and universities, and many more individuals. Some dealers have established buying plans, on the model of mutual funds, in which investors pool their resources to purchase photographs. Members of such groups also have the opportunity to buy at favorable rates from the common holdings.

IMPORTANT FACTORS IN BUYING AND SELLING

Most buying and selling is done through dealers or at auction; the main difference between the two is in the level of price and the level of service. There are advantages and disadvantages to both methods. The major auction houses in New York regularly hold large sales in fall and spring. Before the sales, the material is put on display so that the buyers can examine it first-hand. The chief advantages to buying at auction are that there is usually a very broad range of material and that prices tend to be lower, sometimes much lower, than at commercial galleries. On the other hand, since the auction houses cannot provide detailed advice on purchasing, the prospective buyer must be fairly knowledgeable about the field. In addition, the auction houses require immediate payment (typically the successful bid plus a premium of 10 percent). The item cannot be exchanged and can be returned only if there is proof of misrepresentation. Dealers' prices are full retail, and the selection is more limited. Dealers do, however, offer more individual attention. Among the services that dealers provide are advice on purchasing, putting together portfolios of photographs for investment, appraisal for insurance purposes, and, usually, some provision for extended payment and exchange.

Investors wishing to sell their photographs also have the choice of going to an auction house or to a dealer. At the auction house, the seller consults with the appropriate specialist to set a reserve price, the lowest bid at which the piece will sell. If the piece reaches its reserve, the seller then receives the amount of the highest bid, less a 10 percent premium and whatever fees the house may charge for catalogue illustration, insurance, and other miscellaneous expenses. If the piece does not reach its reserve, it is returned to the consigner and there is no charge. If the investor decides to sell through a dealer, it is most likely that the dealer will take the picture on consignment rather than buy it outright. There are two possibilities for the seller: He can either specify a fixed price for the piece or agree to take a percentage of the selling price that the dealer gets. In the latter instance, the dealer's commission can be anywhere between 10 and 40 percent, with 25 to 30 percent the average.

The advantages of selling at auction are that the houses charge a relatively low commission and that, as auctions increase in popularity, there are steadily larger numbers of prospective buyers. However, if the piece does not sell, the investor has to wait until the next season for another auction. The principal advantage of selling through a dealer is that there is no time limit; the dealer can hold the material until it finds a buyer. The dealer's higher commission may be at least partially offset by a higher selling price.

CUSTODIAL CARE

Like all collectibles, photographs must be properly cared for if they are to retain their investment value. Principally, photographs should be protected from long exposure to intense light, and they should be displayed and stored in an environment that is free from chemical contaminants. The chemically stable products that are used, such as mat board and storage cases, should be labeled "archival" or "acid-free." Such materials are available at most large art-supply stores or at professional framers. Small collections do not require any special custodial care beyond these precautions.

Photographs should be insured for their replacement value. Most insurance companies offer fine-arts coverage as an adjunct to their regular homeowners' policies. The owner must provide a signed appraisal from a dealer; the rate for the policy is then determined as a percentage of the appraised value of the entire collection. For a collection worth $50,000, for example, the average annual cost of insurance would be around $125.

GLOSSARY

auction house— A marketplace providing a wide range of material on pre-auction display, with the advantage of generally lower prices. Advice to investors is usually not available, however.

daguerreotype— Early photographic process in which the image is produced on silver plate or silver-covered copper plate.

dealer— A buyer and seller of photographs who offers individual advice to clients in assembling photograph portfolios, generally at higher prices than available in auction houses.

vintage print— A print made by the photographer at the time the picture was taken.

TRADE ORGANIZATION

Association of International Photography Art Dealers, Inc., New York, N.Y. Founded in 1979, with seventy-five members in the United States, Canada, and Europe. Directory of leading dealers is available on request.

SALES CATALOGUES

Christie's East, New York, N.Y.

Sotheby Parke Bernet, New York, N.Y.

SUGGESTED READING

Periodicals

American Photographer. Published by Image Nation Co., New York, N.Y. Monthly.

Modern Photography. Published by ABC Leisure Magazines, Inc., New York, N.Y. Monthly.

The *New York Times* Sunday "Arts and Leisure" Section (Section 2).

Popular Photography. Published by Ziff-Davis Publishing Co., New York, N.Y. Monthly.

The *Village Voice* photography reviews. New York, N.Y. Weekly.

Reference Books

Blodgett, Richard. *Photographs: A Collector's Guide.* New York: Ballantine Books, 1979.

Newhall, Beaumont. *The History of Photography: From 1839 to the Present Day.* New York: Museum of Modern Art, 1964.

Szarkowski, John. *Looking at Photographs: One Hundred Pictures From the Collection of the Museum of Modern Art.* New York: Museum of Modern Art, 1973.

Witkin, Leon D., and London, Barbara. *The Photograph Collector's Guide.* New York: New York Graphic Society, 1979.

Porcelain

*Michele Beiny and Rotraut Beiny**

BASIC CHARACTERISTICS

Porcelain collecting is a pursuit with a long history; for more than 1,000 years porcelain has been esteemed in China, where it was first made, and for 500 years it has been cherished and collected in the West.

Kinds of Porcelain

The four major categories of porcelain are the following:

Hard-paste (true) porcelain. For true porcelain, two special ingredients are required: kaolin, or china clay, which produces a hard white material when fired at a high temperature; and petuntse, or china stone, which supplies the unique translucency. The mixture forms the paste, and the shaped ware is fired in a kiln at a very high temperature, between 1,300 and 1,400 degrees Celsius to produce a white, vitrified, translucent material. Many things can go wrong during the firing; forms can shrink, crack, sag, or collapse, or a series of fine cracks, called "crazing," can develop.

Porcelain that has been fired but not glazed is known as "biscuit," or "bisque." It resembles white marble and has often been used to imitate sculpture. Usually, porcelain is glazed. Glaze is a thin coating of a glassy compound that fuses with the porcelain on firing to form an extremely hard surface. Various colored glazes are produced by the oxides of different metals. Glaze that is crackled has a pattern of small cracks that originate in the firing, either accidentally or intentionally, for effect, the latter being peculiarly Chinese.

Painted decoration can be applied before glazing; this is called "underglaze decoration." Only colors that can withstand the high firing temperatures, such as cobalt blue and copper red, can be used for this purpose. A wide palette of enamel colors can be applied over the glaze. Such colors are fired on at a lower temperature, so that signs of wear sometimes become evident.

Early porcelain. This category includes not only "true porcelain" as defined in Europe, which must be white and translucent when fired, but also fine, hard, dusky, and gray materials fired to such a vitrified state that they emit a musical

* Michele Beiny and Rotraut Beiny are Vice-President and President, respectively, of The Antique Porcelain Company of New York, Inc.

note when struck, as made in China in the T'ang and Sung Dynasties (618-1279). This resonance was the principal test of early Chinese porcelain.

Soft-paste (artificial) porcelain. This is not readily distinguishable by eye from hard paste, but it shows a granular surface when chipped. Also, the glaze does not appear to be one with the body as in true porcelain. The recipe varies. One of several glassy substances, called "frit," is mixed with white clay and water to form a paste. This is fired at about 1,000 degrees Celsius to produce a biscuit. A lead oxide glaze is sprayed over the piece and overglaze decoration applied. Kiln losses are heavy. Soft paste is a less useful ware than true porcelain; it is inclined to craze, and it chips, stains, and scratches more easily than hard paste does. But the beauty and softness of the material as well as the ability of the painted decoration to sink into the glaze have made soft paste irresistibly alluring to the collector. Soft-paste porcelain was used by the early French factories and by most eighteenth-century English ones, but it has rarely been used since the early nineteenth century.

Bone china. This has been the standard English porcelain since the early nineteenth century, the formula being credited to Josiah Spode II. Burned animal bones are added to the basic hard paste, making it more durable than most porcelain.

HISTORY

The history of porcelain manufacture in the Far East is distinct from that of Europe; however, they have had considerable reciprocal influence. The following brief summary deals with the most salient features of each and the most collectible ware from the main factories.

Early Porcelain of the Far East

Chinese porcelain is categorized first by dynastic periods, then by type of ware. The dynasties of greatest interest to the porcelain collector are as follows:

T'ang	618-906 A.D.
Sung	960-1279
Northern Sung	960-1127
Southern Sung	1127-1279
Yuan	1280-1368
Ming	1368-1644
Ch'ing	1644-1912

It is generally believed that the first true porcelain was made under the T'ang dynasty, which is better known for its earthenware.

Under the Sung dynasty, extremely fine porcelains with outstanding monochrome glazes were produced by hundreds of kilns in northern and southern

China. *Kuan yao,* the imperial ware made specially for the emperor's court, is today considered one of the high points of Chinese art. Decoration, incised or moulded, is subtle and understated; motifs include floral designs, fish, ducks, and human figures. Among the best known Sung wares is *ying ch'ing,* which has a glaze tinged with a very pale, shadowy blue. The haunting color celadon, varying from delicate green to gray-blue, gave its name to objects glazed in that color. White porcelain is covered with an ivory glaze, imparting an orange translucency to the body; the decoration is carved or incised. Sung wares have always fetched very high prices.

Contemporary with the Sung dynasty, the Koryo period in Korea (918-1400) saw the production of superb celadons. Korean ceramics of this period, typically decorated under the glaze with cranes, waterfowl, and willow trees, have long been collected in the West.

During the Yuan period, true hand-paste porcelain was produced. A noteworthy development was the use of underglaze painting, especially in cobalt blue; this was to evolve into China's famous blue-and-white decoration. It was during the reign of Kublai Khan (1216-1294), founder of the dynasty, that Marco Polo visited China, which was to be an event of enormous cultural importance to Europe.

Ming wares were the first Chinese porcelains introduced into Europe in quantity, and are therefore the most widely familiar. They are noted for the rich palette of polychrome enamels on glazed porcelain; blue-and-white decoration also flourished. The painting has echoes of the noble Chinese art of calligraphy. Many pieces were monumental in size, four feet or more. Porcelain with a fine-grained body covered with a thick white glaze, called "blanc de chine" was first made at Tehua in the Fukien province in the late Ming period.

Oriental Porcelain in Europe

By the fifteenth century, several European monarchs had some Chinese porcelain in their treasuries. The Chinese did not want European interlopers to learn much about China; in particular, they jealously guarded the lucrative secret of porcelain-making until the mid-nineteenth century. They were, however, willing to trade in porcelain with the Portuguese and later with the Dutch East India Company. Huge amounts of porcelain were imported into an insatiable Europe from the sixteenth through the eighteenth centuries.

Japanese porcelain. The Dutch, who sought new sources of porcelain for importation into Europe, were responsible for the production of porcelain in Japan, already known for its pottery. The Japanese were eager to trade, and soon began to turn out porcelains based on Chinese and Korean models to satisfy European tastes. Kaolin was discovered at Arita in 1616; the earliest decoration in polychrome enamels is associated with a celebrated family of Japanese potters, of whom the most famous is Sakaida Kakiemon. He gave his name to an elegantly asymmetrical style of decoration that had the greatest influence on many eighteenth-century European factories. European Kakiemon-style wares are among the most collectable today. Imari ware has also been much admired and imitated in the West to the present day. It is prized for its colorful and amusing decorations. In the late seventeenth century, striking porcelain was manufactured at Kutani, with a nineteenth-century revival: the most sought-after wares are those decorated in gold on a coral red ground. Other Japanese porcelains collected today are Nabeshima (made after 1675), decorated in underglaze blue and enamels, and Hirado (made from 1712), with underglaze blue or relief decoration.

Chinese export ware. Generally speaking, porcelains sent to Europe from China, Japan, and Korea before the late seventeenth century were decorated in the prevailing tastes of those countries. But after that, much Oriental porcelain was made expressly for export to the West, often catering to Western taste. The development of these wares was primarily an eighteenth-century phenomenon, known as "Chinese export" or "China trade" porcelain. The porcelains began to show a Western influence. Many were made to special order. Some were decorated with Western signs, symbols, and coats of arms; some pieces, such as wigstands, were designed specifically for Occidental needs. Large dinner services were ordered by both Europeans and Americans. The periods of K'ang-hsi (1662-1722), Yung Cheng (1723-35), and Ch'ien Lung (1736-95) saw many changes, however. The blue and white gradually gave way to an explosion of color, as seen in famille verte and famille rose decoration. Export wares produced from the nineteenth century on are not of great interest to the collector.

Early European Porcelain

Throughout the eighteenth century, Oriental porcelains continued to be imported into Europe in vast quantities. This "Chinamania" was beginning to ruin whole families and, in some cases, countries, because of the enormous expenditures devoted to this luxury. Indeed, China was called the "bleeding bowl of Saxony" by one dismayed minister. Efforts to make porcelain in Europe were redoubled. Europe was well aware that domestic porcelain manufacture would be an excellent source of revenue.

German porcelain. The greatest collector of porcelain in European history was Augustus II, Elector of Saxony and King of Poland (1670-1733). He bought Oriental porcelain in massive quantities, and even traded an entire regiment of dragoons to the King of Prussia for a collection of 117 pieces of Chinese porcelain. He was determined to have his own factory producing porcelain as good as the Chinese wares. On January 15, 1708, the combined efforts of the physicist and philosopher, von Tschirnhaus, and a young alchemist, Johann Friedrich Boettger, produced the first piece of true hard-paste porcelain made in Europe. In January 1710, Augustus opened the Meissen factory by official decree.

The body of Meissen porcelain was equal in quality to the Chinese, and very soon the decoration and modeling were to surpass it. A series of master decorators, including Herold Loewenfick, Hauer, and Heintze, and of master modelers, especially Kirchner and Kaendler, with his assistants Reinicke and Eberlein, managed to create a new, totally European style of decorative art. Their artistic accomplishment in the first half of the eighteenth century made porcelain one of the clearest expressions of the Baroque and then the rococo art in Europe.

Kaendler was a modeler of genius who worked at the Meissen factory from 1731 to 1775. He probably created over 1,000 different figures and groups. His animals and birds are worthy of particular mention. So, too, were his vivacious figures, which often formed sets that were very much to the eighteenth century taste: the Four Seasons, the Four Continents, the Italian Comedy figures, peasants, street vendors, nationals, and crinoline groups depicting court life. Religious subjects were the topic of some of his greatest works.

Count von Bruhl became director of the factory in 1733 on the death of Augustus, and from then until the beginning of the Seven-Year War in 1756, Meissen enjoyed its greatest period. Magnificent tablewares and huge dinner services, such as the famous Swan Service, were in fashion.

The European courts were a ready market, with their taste for grandiose table decoration — large porcelain centerpieces, every imaginable type of tableware and vessel, and porcelain figures to replace those decorations which had previously been made of sugar and wax. Special importance was attached to the utensils used in the aristocratic pursuits of drinking tea, coffee, and chocolate. The Meissen collector can also choose from a whole range of small, highly decorative objects, such as needle cases, snuff boxes, scent bottles, cane handles, patch boxes, and pipe bowls.

Meissen at its height produced a wealth of enamel colors and an enormous variety of original painted decoration, all of excellent quality. The earliest decorations from 1715-1719 were usually straightforward copies of the Chinese; later, this developed into Chinoiserie, the Europeans' naïve and charming idea of what Chinese life ought to be. Harbor scenes were a great favorite, as were the European landscapes. Kakiemon designs took on a European interpretation, especially the *indianische Blumen* (Oriental flowers), followed later by *deutsche Blumen* (naturalistic flowers). Pieces were often painted with an overall background color. As the rococo set in, a taste for pastoral and Watteau scenes emerged.

By 1756, the great days of Meissen had passed. The jealously guarded secret of the manufacture of hard paste managed to leak out by various devious means; defectors from Meissen were bribed, kidnapped, and coerced into revealing what they knew. Rulers in central Europe were intent on having their own factories; it was almost a necessity of the princely state. The end of Meissen's monopoly of the European market paved the way, during the second half of the eighteenth century, for the emergence of many factories in the German-speaking world. Their products are for the most part of very high quality, although in some cases they are primarily of interest to the more specialized collectors. At first they were influenced mainly by Meissen; their artists worked in the rococo and later in the neoclassical style. Each factory produced both tablewares and figures in its own distinctive forms, colors, and decorative subject matter, although there was some overlap. Continuity was increased by the curious phenomenon of the eighteenth-century wandering workman: artists and modelers were in the habit of moving around Europe from one factory to another during their working life.

Half a dozen of these factories are the most important from the collector's point of view. Vienna (1719-1864), especially the early du Paquier period (1719-1744), was among the most noteworthy. This was the only German factory besides Meissen to use Chinoiserie decoration frequently. Furstenberg (1747-today); Hoechst (1750-1798); Nymphenburg (1753-today) boasted a modeler, Bustelli, who rivalled Kaendler in the excellence of his figures; Frankenthal (1755-1800) specialized in a great variety of figures and groups; Ludwigsburg (1758-1824); and Berlin (1761-today) were all of great importance. There were many other factories, such as Fulda and Kelsterbach, that produced wares of extremely high quality and originality, although examples are now rare.

Other factories of note in Northern Europe were St. Petersburg, Zurich, and Copenhagen.

Italian Porcelain

In Italy, several factories started up in the eighteenth century, of which the most important in today's market are Cozzi, Vezzi, Doccia, and especially Capodimonte (1743-1759). The soft-paste porcelain made at Capodimonte, in the Kingdom of Naples, is today considered the finest Italian production, especially the figures modeled by Giuseppe Gricci. When King Charles IV of Naples became King Charles III of Spain in 1759 and moved to Madrid, his beloved factory followed him. Known as Buen Retiro, it remained in production until 1808. There are no longer many examples of Capodimonte on the market today.

French Porcelain

Soft-paste porcelain is a true reflection of eighteenth-century French taste, as epitomized in the production of the well-known Sèvres factory. Before this factory opened, there were a few others producing wares of great charm and delicacy, in a style totally distinct from that of the German factories. Soft-paste wares have a creamy, warm texture, and the softer coloring is most appealing to the eye.

St. Cloud (1677-1766) was the first French factory with any significant output and success. It specialized in making figures and many small objects for domestic use such as covered jars, potpourri vases, pastille burners, and snuff boxes. Its wares were often undecorated, relying on moulded decoration. Chinoiserie was very popular. Chantilly (1725-1800) was established by Louis-Henri de Bourbon, Prince of Condé. The style of the wares was very restrained; strong colors were seldom used, and by far the most popular decorations were Kakiemon designs, still the most sought-after by collectors. Figures of Orientals were popular. Mennecy (1734-1785) is especially known for its distinctive, delicate pink and blue enamel colors, which were used to decorate a wide variety of tablewares, vases, and figures. Their style of decoration was more European than Oriental, and the paste was a beautiful creamy white. Tournai (1751-1891) was one of the few major European factories of the eighteenth century to supply utilitarian wares destined for use in middle-class households. The factory was successful and the production large.

Sèvres is considered by many to be the queen of porcelain factories. Originally called Vincennes, it first produced porcelain in 1745. The production of extremely realistic porcelain flowers accounted for about 80 percent of its sales. The flowers were either mounted on wire stems in vases or used as ornaments on other objects, often from other factories. In 1753, Louis XV took charge of the factory, thanks to the encouragement of his mistress, Madame de Pompadour, a great patroness of the arts. After 1756, the factory was known as Sèvres. Restrictions were placed on the production of porcelain at the other French factories, and these soon went out of business. Louis XV obliged his courtiers to purchase heavily. Production was very ornate, elegant, and refined to suit the highly sophisticated taste of a frivolous aristrocracy whose life centered around the palace of Versailles. Many dinner and tea services were made, as well as flowerpots, large potpourri vases, covered bowls on stands, and elaborate clocks, often mounted on ormolu. Sèvres is celebrated for its ground colors, such as bleu céleste, dark royal blue, rose pompadour, and apple green. Gilding was richly tooled and applied. Favorite decorations included birds and flowers, putti, paintings inspired by Watteau and Boucher, marine scenes, and emblems. From the second half of the eighteenth century onward, Sèvres took over Meissen's position as the leading porcelain factory in Europe and greatly influenced the production of other European competitors from then on. It became the major supplier of dinner services and decorative vases to all the royalty and nobility in Europe.

English Porcelain

No princely sponsorship was bestowed on the English factories, which operated as private enterprises. Precise historical data and records are not readily available in many cases. All but three factories produced soft paste in the eighteenth century. English porcelain, like French, has a very distinct style and flavor.

Chelsea (circa 1745-1770) is classified by its marks, the Raised Anchor (1749-1752) and Red Anchor (1752-1758) periods being generally considered the finest. Silver shapes greatly influenced the form of the wares. The factory was very fond of Kakiemon designs, as well as botanical decoration, which attained a peak unrivaled by any other factory. Freshness and charm characterized the early English factories. Tureens and dishes in the form of vegetables and animals were popular. Chelsea's excellent modeling also produced some very fine figures and birds. During the final Gold Anchor period (1758-1770), Chelsea adopted the more formal Sèvres style with rich decoration, striking ground color, and much gilding. The factory excelled at toys, and is particularly famous for its many delightful scent bottles.

Bow (circa 1744-1776) was the busiest factory in eighteenth-century England, noted for its primitive charm. The most valued products include brightly painted and somewhat crudely modeled figures and animals, as well as tablewares decorated with Oriental designs or botanical motifs.

Derby (circa 1750-today) concentrated on figures in its early days, often copying Meissen originals; tablewares were decorated with flowers, birds, insects, and butterflies. In 1770 it acquired the Chelsea factory, and in 1776, Bow. Called "Chelsea-Derby" from then on, it increased its production of tablewares.

Worcester (1751-today) was successful from the start, its most important period from the collector's point of view being from 1751-1783, called "Dr. Wall" or "First Period." It made many useful wares, especially sauceboats, jugs, baskets, leaf dishes, and mugs. Hardly any figures were produced. Worcester is noted for its decoration; its chinoiseries, transfer printing, extraordinary ground colors and scale ground colors that were overlaid to look like fish scales, and flamboyantly exotic birds and foliage.

Another factory of note was Longton Hall (1750-1760), producing charming botanical wares in a distinctive yellowish green, crudely modeled but colorful figures, and decorations by an unidentified artist called the "Castle Painter." Caughley, Liverpool, Lowestoft, Plymouth, Bristol, and New Hall are also noteworthy.

Nineteenth-Century Porcelain

From approximately 1775 to 1850, porcelain styles were strongly affected by neoclassicism, showing Greek, Roman, and Etruscan influences. Vienna, Nymphenburg, and Berlin excelled in this style. The well-known factories of Hutschenreuther and Rosenthal, still operating today, were founded during this period. Royal Copenhagen flourished. Sèvres, which had now adopted hard paste, was very active, producing many large pieces with florid decoration. The Paris and Limoges factories were founded.

In England, porcelain factories flourished, especially those producing large dinner services that are still sought-after today. The colorful Japanese Imari designs and the formal elegance of Sèvres were a great inspiration. Spode, Derby, Worcester, Coalport, New Hall, Minton, and Rockingham are all known for their tablewares. Wedgwood became one of the most successful business enterprises in England.

Some porcelain manufacturers existed in America during this period, but their wares are collected for patriotic rather than aesthetic reasons. Examples are Bonnin and Morris of Philadelphia, Tucker and Hulme, and the United States Pottery Company. Lenox, perhaps the best known, is still commissioned to make state dinner services for the White House.

Twentieth-Century Porcelain

Fresh techniques of manufacture and decoration, such as *pâte-sur-pâte,* were developed from the 1880s on. Art Nouveau influenced porcelain designs, especially at Sèvres. The Scandinavian factories of Rörstand, Royal Copenhagen, and Bing and Gröndahl were great innovators. In the 1920s, Sèvres produced elegant dinner wares in the Art Deco style, which also inspired Meissen and Nymphenburg. Dorothy Doughty and Edward Marshall Boehm are noted for their limited editions of bird sculptures. Royal Copenhagen's Flora Danica service is famous. At Sèvres today, the factory's director, Jean Mathieu, is encouraging contemporary artists and sculptors to express themselves in porcelain, with notable success.

ATTRACTIVE FEATURES

Few kinds of collecting have a grander pedigree than porcelain; today's collector begins against an impressive background. From the start, fine porcelain was enthusiastically sought-after in the Far East and eagerly received by the Europeans, who found it equally irresistible. Their reverence for it often found expression in the custom of complementing objects with silver, gold, gilt, and ormolu mounts. The image of porcelain collecting is both elegant and aristocratic and carries with it a certain refinement of taste and an aura of sophistication.

Aesthetic Appeal

Porcelain's unique properties make it attractive as both useful and collectable ware. A sculpturally malleable material, it can be shaped into useful and decorative forms. The hardness of the body, its hauntingly white surface, its translucency and glitter appeal to the eye and invite decoration. Its high tactility makes it pleasant to handle. It has always lent itself to articles of style, luxury, and charm.

As a result, until recently, porcelain collecting was almost exclusively a pastime of royalty and the aristocracy in China and Europe; this is reflected in the quality of many of the pieces on the market. Nowadays, as porcelain is more widely appreciated and collected, more types are available. Surprisingly large amounts of antique porcelain are still in the hands of private collectors and dealers, and so may eventually come on the market. Trade in antique porcelain is vigorous in the West and in Japan, with specialist auctions from London to New York to Hong Kong. The supply, aside from the rarities, is ample. Scientific aids for its identification and dating are being developed. Helpful scholarly publications appear frequently.

Investment Value

Buying a piece of porcelain is a more personal and pleasurable form of investment than buying stocks or gold bullion. Not many collectors are in it for investment alone. Nevertheless, porcelain has proved to be a fine investment performer. Along with that, eighteenth-century Meissen remains the most desired and highest-priced type of porcelain. In the spring of 1980, a pair of Meissen swans on ormolu, circa 1747, fetched $143,000 at auction in New York; a large Meissen dish from the Empress Elizabeth of Russia's service, circa 1745, was bought in 1968 for $3,840 and sold in 1980 for $15,400; a Meissen figure of a greeting harlequin from the Italian Comedy Series, circa 1740, was bought in 1963 for $8,960 and sold recently for $62,700; early in 1981, a cup and saucer from the famous Swan Service fetched $46,200. In June 1978, at the Von Hirsch sale in London, a large white Meissen parrot, circa 1731, fetched $213,328.

Although some of the appreciations are large, the field is overall a stable one, not subject to the sudden swings of some other collectibles. In some cases, it can be cheaper to buy a nineteenth-century English dinner service than a modern one, while making an investment that will retain its value, where a contemporary service will have little, if any, resale value.

POTENTIAL RISKS

The art market as a whole is always affected by the current general economic situation. When money is scarce in times of recession, the art market suffers. On the other hand, when confidence in money and intangibles is shaken, investment in art becomes more favored. Overall, porcelain has proved to be a good hedge against inflation.

However, the porcelain market may tend to be more chauvinistic than most art markets; the prices fetched by various factories often will be closely related to the economic situation of the countries involved. This may be an advantage as well as a risk for a potential investor. While the Deutschmark and Japanese yen are strong, German and Oriental porcelains will continue to do best. The Americans with their strong dollar, the Australians, and the South Africans are now boosting the prices of English porcelains.

Value can also be affected by a variety of intangible factors: current vogue, the object's provenance, a successful show in a leading museum, publicity, and media coverage in popular magazines. The whims of fashion, an elusive factor, may be difficult to predict. For instance, at present, eighteenth-century French soft-paste porcelain, once very strong, is less popular and does not fetch such high prices as it had in the past. On the other hand, for the investor who also wishes to enjoy the beauty of his possessions, this is the time to acquire some good bargains in that area.

The market may be more volatile in highly specialized areas, rising suddenly if two or more collectors appear on the market competing for the same limited supply of objects. This happened recently in the field of Vienna-du-Paquier-period porcelain (1719-1744), where prices suddenly soared.

Many people worry about liquidity as regards investment in works of art. Of course, an investor cannot expect to liquidate a portfolio of tangibles overnight. But an auction house or dealer will take the piece off a collector's hands and turn his asset into money quite quickly. If a forced sale takes place, the price realized will be by no means the best.

Whatever economic fluctuations occur, the golden rule is to always buy the best and the rarest in a chosen field of interest. Then, as experience has proven, the objects will retain their value and appreciate over time.

TAX CONSEQUENCES

Under federal tax law, profit from the sale of porcelain held by an individual for more than one year is taxable at the capital gains rate rather than as ordinary income. Under certain conditions, objects of porcelain can be exchanged for others of equal or greater value in a tax-free transaction. As with other types of investments, it is also possible to realize a tax deduction on donating a porcelain piece whose market value has appreciated to a qualified organization. Separate rules apply to those who are recognized as investors by the IRS. (See article on Tax Considerations for Collector-Investors, elsewhere in this volume.) For complete guidance in these matters, readers are urged to consult a professional tax adviser.

IMPORTANT FACTORS IN BUYING AND SELLING

Dealers and Auction Houses

A collector has a choice of operating through a dealer or an auction house. The latter is an important marketplace, and following auction results is one of the essential means of gauging current market prices and trends. But there are disadvantages for a private collector working through the auction houses. In their conditions of sale, auction houses refuse to accept responsibility for the statements in their catalogues, which are merely statements of opinion. They will not guarantee the genuineness, date, attribution, provenance, or condition of any piece they sell. Proven deliberate forgeries can only be returned within seven days of their sale.

In addition, many people, both buyers and sellers, dislike the publicity of an auction. In the art world, privacy and anonymity are highly valued; this element is lost at auction, where the identity of purchasers and sellers, as well as the prices paid, become public knowledge. If unsold, for whatever reason, an object becomes tainted in some way. Newspapers report the record prices fetched at auction, but tend to ignore those lots that do not reach their estimates. It is always considered more prestigious to acquire a piece that has not been offered to the world at large; therefore, on the whole, the best prices are obtained privately. The exception will be in the case of the occasional highly publicized and important object, especially as private individuals are more prone to get carried away, driving prices sky high; a dealer, who is far more aware of market value, will know when to stop bidding.

Alternatively, it is possible for a seller to be unlucky; his piece may be included in a poorly attended or a non-specialized sale where the price will be unnaturally low. An object invariably suffers if, unsold the first time, it is subsequently re-offered for sale. Again, it is possible for an object to be wrongly catalogued for auction, as the auction house has to deal with the thousands of pieces that pass through its hands. Attention to any particular object or person may be lacking. Finally, both buyer and seller must bear in mind the 10 percent minimum commission that an auction house will charge each of them on every transaction.

For several reasons, a reputable dealer is an invaluable adviser to the collector. Obviously, a knowledgeable collector can seek bargains in antique stores or take some risks by following the auction market. On the other hand, a reputable dealer has the advantage of many years' experience. He will guarantee the genuineness and condition of the pieces he sells. And a collector can be sure that a dealer will be willing to spend time with him, since the dealer is interested in establishing an ongoing relationship. He will often take great pride in the collection he is helping to form. A dealer's expertise is an invaluable barometer for many crucial factors: authenticity, quality, condition, price, the importance of the piece, historically or as it relates to other works of the same period.

Authenticity, Quality, and Condition

The eye and hand have to be trained to recognize the various indicators of authenticity, quality, and condition. This comes only with time and experience. Various scientific aids are being developed today to analyze the composition of the paste. Ultraviolet lights are most useful in exposing forgeries, marks that have been tampered with, and repairs that are undetectable to the naked eye, as well as differentiating hard from soft paste. Many collectors own hand-held lights that can be purchased at a relatively low cost.

The feel of the paste, its color as well as the colors used in the decoration, and the resonance of the porcelain when struck will tell an experienced person a great deal about the date, origin, quality, and condition of an object: whether it was decorated later or outside the factory, whether it is soft or hard paste, whether it is a forgery. For instance, a certain stickiness to the touch may indicate to the expert that the object he is handling has been restored.

Pastes vary a great deal in translucency and color. Each factory has its own distinctive traits. For example, a characteristic of Chelsea porcelain is the formation of transparent glassy spots in the paste, clearly visible when a piece is held to the light; early Worcester, which includes soapstone in its body, has a slightly greenish tone and its thin glaze tends to shrink away from the foot.

Marks

Marks on porcelain are a very useful guide to origin and identification. Many porcelains were marked, and comprehensive publications on the subject are available. There is, however, one great caveat: By no means are all originals marked, but almost all forgeries are. Many factories forged the marks of other factories, or forged marks used in earlier periods at their own factory. As a result, most experts emphasize that, in establishing the origin and value of a piece of porcelain, marks are secondary to style and quality. The extreme irregularity of marks should also be noted; lack of uniformity in drawing and spelling is commonplace. In addition, marks of various kinds were added by modelers, gilders, decorators, and dealers. The absence or irregularity of a mark does not, therefore, necessarily detract from the value of a piece.

Forgeries

The problem of forgeries must be considered. As porcelains have always been highly prized, forgers have found their occupation a lucrative one; as early as the sixteenth century, there were potters renowned for their imitations of Sung wares. It was common for factories to sell off stocks of white porcelain that were decorated by the enterprising buyers and often passed off as genuine factory-decorated products. In the nineteenth century, for instance, some lightly decorated Sèvres pieces had their decoration removed with acid and a heavier decoration substituted to bring a higher price. Sèvres imitations were made by Martin Randall at Madeley, England, in the 1820s, as well as at Coalport. In this connection, special mention must be made of the nineteenth-century firm of Edmé Samson et Cie. of Paris, whose fame rests entirely on its excellent imitations. It was founded with the express purpose of making reproductions of ancient works emanating from museums and private collections, specializing in Chinese export, Meissen, and Sèvres. The products of this manufacturer have now become collector's items in their own right.

Finding the Right Market

A dealer's advice is helpful in deciding what to buy and when to buy it, whether to follow an existing fashion or to go against it. The collector who always seeks quality first and foremost cannot go wrong in the long run. The best pieces will always retain their value; in times of economic uncertainty, when money is short, it is the value of the mediocre that will suffer. With that in mind, many collectors choose to collect with a purpose or theme in mind. For instance, they may choose armorial porcelain bearing coats of arms, botanical motifs, wild animals and birds, or ground colors.

CUSTODIAL CARE

Condition

The condition of an item of porcelain is an important consideration. A porcelain object should not be ruled out automatically merely because it has some flaw, such as a chip to a leaf on an elaborate figurine. Some damage or repair is often to be expected in the case of a delicate object that is over 200 years old.

The question of how much the value of an object is affected by a flaw depends on several factors: (1) the type of piece, as a chip out of a plate will affect its value more than damage to a foot or finger in a figure; (2) the rarity or importance of an object; if a piece is very rare or important it will not lose its value simply because it has been broken and repaired; (3) the type of damage involved; there is a world of difference, for instance, between a firing crack that occurred while an object was being made and a crack that happened yesterday, when it was dropped. A broken arm on a figurine is regarded as relatively minor, while a head break is far more serious. If the broken arm has been completely reconstructed out of plaster, however, the value of the piece is seriously affected. There are a variety of possible flaws, such as discoloration, rubbing, crazing, and fritting, whose seriousness can be evaluated only with experience and good advice.

Restoration

The question of how extensive or invisible a repair should be is a controversial issue. On the one hand, some maintain that ceramics are decorative objects and should be restored as completely as possible if any damage is visible to the eye. On the other hand, many insist that, ethically, and for the sake of historical integrity, repairs should be clearly visible, only minimally affecting the work of the original craftsman. If a piece is tampered with too much, it may end up looking fake, especially if some inauthentic addition or reconstruction is undertaken. Very often the extent of a repair must be an emotional and aesthetic personal decision on the part of the owner.

The quality and cost of repair can vary tremendously. With the techniques available today, it is possible to make totally invisible repairs that cannot be detected, even under ultraviolet light. An object intended for use can be repaired with strong epoxies, reinforcing pegs, and clamps. The cost can vary from under $50 to several thousand dollars. Dealers or museums can generally recommend a reputable and suitable restorer.

Day-to-Day Care

The care and preservation of porcelain is a relatively simple matter. There is no need for special humidity or temperature control devices, as in the case of many other collectibles. Porcelain is a strong and durable material, which needs little attention if it is housed in a safe place. It can be dusted with a camel's hair brush or washed in diluted dishwashing liquid with a soft paintbrush. It is best to let the object drip dry, especially if it has many projections and crevices.

GLOSSARY

arcanist— A craftsman who knew the secret of the formula for making true porcelain.
biscuit or bisque— Porcelain that has been fired once but not glazed.

blanc de chine— European name for fine Chinese porcelain with a milky white glaze, popular in Europe from the seventeenth century on, and much imitated by European factories.

bone china— A translucent ware, neither soft- nor hard-paste porcelain, that contains kaolin, petuntse, and bone ash.

celadon— European name given to Oriental stoneware and porcelain glazed in a color that varies from delicate green to gray-blue.

Chinoiserie— A European interpretation and idea of what was characteristic of China and the Chinese taste. During the eighteenth century, Chinoiserie was fashionable in all the decorative arts.

crazing— The formation of a web or mesh of fine cracks over the surface of a glaze.

enamels— Pigments made from metallic oxides and mixed with ground glass to produce a wide variety of colors for overglaze decoration on porcelain. Enamels fuse onto the surface of the glass when fired at relatively low temperatures.

famille— Rose, verte, jaune, and noire porcelain; a classification of Chinese enameled porcelain according to the predominant background color.

glaze— A glassy coating, produced in many colors, and applied to porcelain by immersion or spraying.

hard-paste porcelain— Porcelain made from china clay (kaolin) and china stone (petuntse), fired at a high temperature.

imari— Originally the name of a Japanese porcelain made at Arita and exported through the port of Imari; later indicating heavy decoration in polychrome enamels on European porcelain in the style of the Japanese product.

Italian comedy figures— A series of comic figures derived from the Italian theater, which were produced at many Continental and English factories in the eighteenth century. Among the most famous of these figures are Harlequin, Columbine, and Pantaloon.

kakiemon— Style of porcelain decoration; simple, delicate, and asymmetrical, with large spaces left white.

pâte-sur-pâte— Decoration in low relief and painted using liquid clay, called "slip"; a technique developed at Sèvres circa 1859 and later used in England and Germany.

repairer— A worker in a porcelain factory who assembles pieces made from several molds.

soft paste— Porcelain made by mixing clay and water with a glassy compound called "frit." It is fired at a lower temperature than hard paste is.

TRADE ORGANIZATIONS

The British Antique Dealers Association, London, England

The National Antique and Art Dealers Association of America, Inc., New York, N.Y.

LEADING DEALERS

Adams Antiques, London, England

Armin B. Allen Inc., New York, N.Y.

The Antique Porcelain Company, New York, N.Y.

The Antique Porcelain Company, Ltd., London, England
Bluett & Sons Ltd., London, England
Eskenazi Ltd., London, England
Elinor Gordon, Pa.
Fred B. Nadler Antiques Inc., New York, N.Y.
Nicholas Grindlay, London, England
R. & J. Jones, London, England
Ralph M. Chait Galleries, Inc., New York, N.Y.
James Robinson, New York, N.Y.
Rochelle-Thomas of Palm Beach, Fla.
Rosenberg & Steibel, New York, N.Y.
John Sparks Ltd., London, England
Spink & Son Ltd., London, England
Stair & Co., New York, N.Y.

SUGGESTED READING

Periodicals

Antiques. Published by Straight Enterprises, New York, N.Y. Monthly.

Antiques World. Published by Antiques News Associates, New York, N.Y. Monthly except June, July, and August.

Appollo. Published by Appollo Magazine, London, England. Monthly.

Architectural Digest. Published by Knapp Communications Corp., Los Angeles, Cal. Monthly.

Art & Antiques. Published by Billboard Publications, Inc., New York, N.Y. Bimonthly.

Burlington. Published by Burlington Magazine Publications, Ltd., London, England. Monthly.

The Collector-Investor. Published by Crain Communications, Inc., Chicago, Ill. Monthly except July and August.

Connoisseur. Published by National Magazine Company, Ltd., London, England. Monthly.

Weltkunst. Published by Kunst und Technik Verlagsgesellschaft mbh, Munich, West Germany. Semimonthly.

Reference Books

General

Boger, Louise Ade. *The Dictionary of World Pottery and Porcelain.* New York: Charles Scribner's Sons, 1977.

Hillier, Bevis. *Pottery and Porcelain, 1700-1914: England, Europe, and North America.* New York: Meredith Press, 1968.

Savage, George. *Porcelain Through the Ages,* 2nd ed. Baltimore: Penguin Books, 1963.

British

Godden, Geoffrey A. *British Porcelain: An Illustrated Guide.* New York: Clarkson N. Potter, 1975.

Savage, George. *Eighteenth-Century English Porcelain.* New ed. London: Spring Books, 1964.

Continental

Pauls-Eisenbeiss, Dr. Erika. *German Porcelain of the Eighteenth Century.* Fribourg: Office du Livre, 1972. (Available through The Antique Porcelain Company.)

Savage, George. *Eighteenth-Century German Porcelain.* New York: Macmillan Company, 1958.

———. *Seventeenth- and Eighteenth-Century French Porcelain.* New York: Macmillan Company, 1961.

Syz, Hans. *Catalogue of the Hans Syz Collection.* Washington, D.C.: Smithsonian Institution Press, 1979.

Oriental

Beurdeley, Michel. *Chinese Trade Porcelain.* Translated by Diana Imber. Rutland: Charles E. Tuttle, 1963.

Jenyns, Soame. *Japanese Porcelain.* New York: Frederick A. Praeger, 1965.

Medley, Margaret. *The Chinese Potter: A Practical History of Chinese Ceramics.* New York: Charles Scribner's Sons, 1976.

Valenstein, Suzanne G. *A Handbook of Chinese Ceramics.* New York: Metropolitan Museum of Art, 1975.

Marks

Chaffers, William. *Marks and Monograms on European and Oriental Pottery and Porcelain.* 15th rev. ed. New York: Dover Publications, 1966.

Cushion, J.P., and Honey, W.B. *Handbook of Pottery and Porcelain Marks.* 3rd ed., rev. London: Faber & Faber, 1965.

Preferred Stock

*Charles W. Lard**

BASIC CHARACTERISTICS

Preferred stock, like common stock, legally represents a portion of ownership in a corporation. It is classified on the balance sheet along with the common stock in making up the capital of the company.

Preferred stock has certain advantages over common stock in terms of receiving dividends and obtaining assets at liquidation. A specific dividend must be paid to holders of preferred stock before any dividends can be paid on the common stock. Also, preferred stock almost always takes precedence over common stock in the distribution of assets upon dissolution of a corporation.

Usually, the dividend paid on preferred stock is set at a fixed rate, such as a percentage of the par value of a company's stock. In contrast, the dividend rate on common stock may be changed by the board of directors. Holders of preferred stock normally do not have voting power, as do common stock shareholders.

Under certain conditions, convertible preferred stock can be converted into a certain number of common shares. Nonconvertible preferred stock, however, does not offer this opportunity. Since the value of convertible preferred stock is affected by fluctuations in the value of the common stock, nonconvertible preferred is more stable in value than is convertible. (For further discussion of convertible preferred stock, see article on Convertible Securities, elsewhere in this volume.)

Value of preferred stock is also determined by the ratio of the dividend to the market price and by the quality rating. Also important are the industry sector, the size of the issue, and the call price. The existence of a sinking fund is also important to the value and to increased liquidity. This is because the issuing company is required to repurchase a predetermined amount of the preferred at a certain price at a fixed maturity date.

A Hybrid Security

Nonconvertible, or straight, preferred stock is a hybrid security. It has some of the features of a debt instrument and some of the characteristics of an equity investment. For instance, preferred stock is like a debt instrument in that it has a fixed-rate dividend similar to the fixed interest rate of a bond. But, as with common stock, the holder of preferred stock cannot claim a dividend unless it

* Charles W. Lard is Assistant Treasurer at United Technologies Corporation, Hartford, Conn.

is earned and declared. The bond holder, on the other hand, has a legal claim to both the interest and the principal upon maturity. Preferred stock is like an equity issue in that it has a prior claim on earnings up to the fixed amount of the dividend. However, rarely does it participate in the earnings available to stockholders after the dividend has been paid.

The preferred stock shareholder stands between the bondholder and the common stock shareholder in legal status. Preferred stock stands after bonds but before common stock in terms of claims on the assets of a company at liquidation.

Contractual Features

A wide variety of contractual features is offered by the preferred stock of various companies, as stipulated in corporate charters, bylaws, and stock certificates, or state statutes. These features include participation in profits, redemption clauses, and cumulative dividends. An interesting current development is the floating-rate coupon preferred. These issues feature a coupon rate that is tied to Treasury issues and adjusted at three-month intervals.

In those rare instances where nonconvertible preferred stock is participating, the shareholders receive a stipulated dividend and then share in the earnings or dividends along with the common stock shareholders.

Some types of preferred stock have redemption clauses, which provide that the stock may be called in by the company and redeemed at a certain price. An example of a nonparticipating issue is a seasoned cumulative preferred with a dividend of $3.64. The issue is noncallable before May 1, 1983, at which time the call price is $52.81 on shares the company may decide to redeem at that time. On May 1, 1984 a sinking fund is to be established for 300,000 shares, which must be redeemed at $50 per share. The current price of $30.50 is lower than the sinking fund price or the call price, adding to the attractiveness of the investment.

Most preferred stock is cumulative in that any arrears in dividends from prior years must be paid to preferred stock shareholders before any dividends can be paid on the common stock.

Kinds of Issues

Nonconvertible preferred stock is issued by corporations in most kinds of industries. It can be publicly offered or privately placed. Utility companies — including electric, gas, telephone, and water — represent over half of the issues and an even larger proportion of the dollar value of preferred stock outstanding. Industrial, financial, and insurance companies also offer preferreds, with each industry category offering the investor a wide range of quality and risk in the hands of shareholders from which to choose.

A total of $2.95 billion of nonconvertible preferred stock was offered in 1980, according to a statistical study by Dillon Read & Company. The total value of all public and private nonconvertible preferred stock outstanding at the end of

TABLE 1. New Corporate Security Offerings (Millions of Dollars)

Year	*Total Corporate Issues*	*Total Preferred Stock*	*Preferred Stocks to Total Issue*
1980	$17,889	$3,634	.046%
1979	51,094	3,650	.071
1978	46,616	2,832	.061
1977	51,836	3,916	.076
1976	52,290	2,803	.054
1975	52,539	3,458	.066
1974	37,729	2,254	.060
1973	31,680	3,341	.154
1972	39,705	3,370	.085
1971	45,090	3,670	.081
1970	38,945	1,393	.036
1969	26,744	681	.025
1968	21,966	637	.029
1967	17,385	574	.033
1966	14,782	724	.049

SOURCE: SEC Statistical Review

1980 was estimated at $43 billion by Dillon Read. The average size of a nonconvertible preferred public issue was $35 million to $40 million.

Table 1 above shows the market value of preferred stock issued in relation to the total market value of corporate securities issued. Convertible and nonconvertible preferreds amount to less than 7 percent of the market value of securities issued in recent years.

ATTRACTIVE FEATURES

High Current Yield

The most attractive characteristic of a preferred stock for corporate investors is its high after-tax current yield. In the fall of 1981, the yield on AA (second highest rating) utility preferreds was in excess of 15 percent. A corporation need report only 15 percent of these dividends as income. Thus, a corporation that pays taxes at a rate of somewhat less than 50 percent would realize an after-tax return of somewhat more than 13.875 percent. This yield is higher than that of tax-exempt bonds that yield 10 percent. The lower an investor's tax bracket, the more attractive the after-tax return.

The high-yield preferred is an ideal instrument to own when the inflation rate is low. However, in a highly unstable and inflationary period, the fixed coupon (dividend) and high sensitivity to interest rate changes make this investment a poor hedge against inflation.

The present yield on AA quality preferreds compared with tax-free municipal bonds for the last three years is shown in Table 2 below.

Added Liquidity

The existence of mandatory sinking funds in certain preferred issues reduces the average life. This sinker provides a calculable return that provides a return higher than the current yield. This return would include some guaranteed capital appreciation provided the preferred is selling at a price below the sinking fund repurchase price. Additionally, many preferreds have call prices above the current market price that may be utilized by the issuing company. The sinking fund and call price provisions offer added liquidity relative to common stocks, which do not have these two provisions.

Protection of Income and Principal

The preferred stock features with regard to dividends and distribution of assets on liquidation are attractive relative to common stocks. An investor would purchase preferred rather than common stock for the protection of capital, although he or she does not receive any upside appreciation if the common stock moves higher.

The higher after-tax yield for many corporate holders makes preferreds more attractive than bonds, although the preferred holder has inferior protection against liquidation of the issuer.

TABLE 2. Yields on Preferreds, Municipal, and Corporate Bonds

	New Preferreds		*Municipal Bonds*		*Corporate Bonds*	
	High	*Low*	*High*	*Low*	*High*	*Low*
1981 (5 mo.)	14.25%	12.75%	10.99%	9.76%	15.25%	12.60%
1980	13.75	10.00	10.48	7.48	14.13	9.76
1979	11.00	8.80	7.63	6.34	11.80	8.90

SOURCE: Merrill Lynch Pierce Fenner & Smith, Inc.

POTENTIAL RISKS

Possible Risk to Income

While the holder of preferred stock has preference over the common stock shareholder in the payment of a declared dividend, the company does have the discretionary right to spend the cash available for preferred dividends on other items (excluding common stock dividends) if the board of directors feels it is prudent to do so. If a company foregoes a preferred dividend, it is a sign of financial weakness, and is viewed negatively by the financial markets.

Risk to Principal

Risk to the principal is a function of the liquidation rights of the holder, although the preferred stock shareholder has liquidation preferences on the claim of assets over the common stock shareholder. The rights are generally stipulated in the case of involuntary or voluntary liquidation. In addition, some preferreds have sinking funds to further protect the safety of the principal.

Market Volatility

The market volatility of preferred stock is a function of interest rate changes. This means that the preferred rates as a yield instrument. Since the preferred does not have a stated maturity, the market value fluctuates inversely with the percentage change in the yield. Nonconvertible preferred stock has characteristics comparable to a perpetual bond, except when it has a sinking fund or purchase fund. Thus, if required yield increases from 7.11 percent to 9.48 percent (a 33 percent increase), the price of the preferred would fall by 25 percent.

Different industry sectors have yield-spread relationships that change as investors perceive greater risk. For instance, utility preferreds today have higher yields than industrial preferreds do.

Possible Illiquidity

Liquidity is mainly a function of the size and the quality of the issue. Larger issues have more market makers, and this increases the liquidity. However, large purchases of preferreds by insurance companies, for example, can later produce an imbalance in the market as these companies respond to policyholder redemptions and policy loans during credit crunches with block sales. An individual holder of a small issue may be forced to rely on a thin market.

TAX CONSEQUENCES

An important difference between preferreds and bonds is the 85 percent tax exclusion of dividends received on stocks by corporate owners. Since preferreds do not carry an income tax savings to the paying company, the receiving corpora-

TABLE 3. Investor After-Tax Yield

Investor	*Preferred Gross Yield*	*Dividend Exclusion*	*Tax Rate*	*Net Yield*
Individual	15%	-0-	.50	7.50%
Corporation	15	.85	.50	13.88
Insurance company	15	.85	.25	14.44
Pension fund	15	-0-	-0-	15.00

Note: Tax rate established for hypothetical investor. Dividend exclusion established for corporations by the IRS.

tions can exclude 85 percent of dividend income from their federal taxes. (This exclusion also applies to dividend income from common stocks.) However, individuals do not receive this exclusion. Most states tax dividend income, which would reduce the net yield.

At present, comparable nonconvertible preferreds yield less than bond counterparts. This abnormality of getting less return for greater risk reflects the 85 percent dividend exclusion. Today, there is a shortage of preferreds for income-oriented corporate portfolios because of the demand created by the tax treatment of the dividend. Meanwhile, the preferred is vulnerable to any changes in tax legislation that might reduce this exclusion provision.

The Economic Recovery Tax Act of 1981 permits individual holders of preferred stocks of electric utilities with qualifying dividend reinvestment plans for reinvestment of the preferred dividend into new shares of common stock to be exempt from federal income tax as follows: $750 per individual, or $1,500 for couples filing jointly on an annualized basis.

Of course, nonprofit institutions such as universities and qualified pension funds do not pay taxes and, consequently, do not benefit from the tax shelter now available to corporations. Table 3 above shows how the corporate rate affects the net return on preferreds.

REPRESENTATIVE TYPES OF INVESTORS

The biggest holders of preferred stocks are institutions that can qualify under the 85 percent dividend income exclusion. This category includes corporations and insurance companies. Ideally, institutions that have a low income tax rate and a need for high income invest in preferreds where investors in high brackets might use tax-exempt municipal bonds.

Life and property-casualty insurance companies are big purchasers of preferreds because of the high after-tax return and favorable accounting treatment allowed by the National Association of Insurance Commissioners (NAIC). The NAIC has ruled that all preferreds that have a sinking fund of 2.5 percent per year or that amortize the issue over forty years, starting within ten years of the date of issue, can be carried at cost. The accounting entry at cost allows the insurance company to avoid writedowns in the market value if the interest rates increase, which would cause the yield on new offerings of preferred stock to increase and the market value of existing preferreds to drop. In addition, life insurance companies can carry non-sinking fund preferreds at cost.

Pension funds and universities could use preferreds, but they can obtain higher yields with bonds and at the same time get higher safety in terms of claims on the issuing company's assets.

IMPORTANT FACTORS IN BUYING AND SELLING

Selecting a Broker

In selecting a broker, it is important to consider several factors. The integrity of the organization and its employees is of utmost importance. The more quantifiable factors that should be considered include the number of issues in which the organization is willing to make a market, the amount of capital it is willing to commit, and the number of professional analysts and preferred traders it employs.

Markets

Preferreds are traded in two markets. It is estimated that more than 50 percent of preferred stock outstanding can be traded on the major exchanges. The over-the-counter market handles the remaining trading in preferreds.

Dealer Spread

Historically, the dealer spread is wider in preferreds than in common stocks, since it is not a continuous market. In some over-the-counter issues there may be only one market (broker or dealer). The institutional trades are negotiated on an individual basis. The spread ultimately is determined by the individual issues' characteristics, not by the location of the listing.

Quality

The investor can use any of the standard reference books to judge quality of issues. Moody's and Standard & Poor's have proprietary grading systems. Both systems rate the highest quality AAA and the lowest CC. Several major brokerage firms, including Salomon Brothers, Merrill Lynch Pierce Fenner & Smith and Dillion, Read & Company publish tabulations that also may be useful.

CUSTODIAL CARE

The physical safety precautions for preferreds are the same as for any equity security. Almost all nonconvertible preferreds are registered. Since preferreds are registered, dividends are mailed automatically to the holder of record.

LEADING DEALERS

Like common stocks, preferreds may be purchased from brokerage firms and dealers throughout the country, as listed in classified directories.

GLOSSARY

convertible preferred— Preferred stock that may be converted into a stipulated number of common shares.

cumulative preferred— Feature of preferred stock whereby the dividends not paid in any year will accumulate, and must be paid before dividends can be paid on the common stock of the corporation.

liquidation rights— In a preferred contract, provision for preference above common stock in claims on assets in case of involuntary or voluntary dissolution of the issuing corporation.

participating— Dividends paid in excess of the stipulated amount of the preferred.

redemption provision— Provision according to which the issuer can call and retire all or a portion of the issue, generally at a premium.

sinking fund— A fund established through periodic payments for meeting a specific obligation, such as redemption of stock shares.

straight preferred— Term used to describe nonconvertible preferred stock.

voting rights— Right to vote stock, which may range from full voting to contingent voting based upon specific conditions. For example, holders of preferred stock may have the right to vote as long as accumulated dividends remain unpaid.

SUGGESTED READING

Periodicals

Commerce Clearing House. New York, N.Y. Daily; card system; notification of changes in capital structure of corporations.

Moody's Bond Record. New York, N.Y. Daily; details on features of preferred issues.

Moody's Bond Survey. New York, N.Y. Weekly; highlights on credit analysis.

Moody's Dividend Record. New York, N.Y. Daily; reporting preferred dividend record, payment date, ex-dividend date, and amount of dividend.

Standard & Poor's Daily Dividend Record. New York, N.Y. Reporting preferred dividend record date, payment date, ex-dividend date, and amount of dividend.

Standard & Poor's Fixed Income Investor. New York, N.Y. Weekly; highlights of credit analysis.

Standard & Poor's Monthly Stock Guide/Bond Guide. New York, N.Y. Key financial characteristics of preferred issues.

Articles

Fischer, D.E. and G.A. Wilt, Jr. "Non-convertible Preferred Stock As A Financing Instrument — 1950-1965." *Journal of Finance* 23:611-624, Sept. 1968.

Gardner, D.R. "Sinking Fund Preferred Stocks: An Attractive Alternative." *Best's Review (Property Edition)* 80:22, Oct. 1979.

Roth, M.J.C. "New Look at Preferred Stock Financing." *Public Utilities* 105:26-28, Mar. 27, 1980.

Prints

*Randy Rosen**

BASIC CHARACTERISTICS

At the two leading print auction houses, international sales volume for prints has climbed dramatically in recent years. From worldwide sales of $4.4 million in 1974-1975, Sotheby's print sales vaulted to $19.6 million in 1979-1980. Print volume at Christie's jumped from a mere trickle of $612,000 in 1975 to $6.5 million worldwide in 1979-1980. At the hub of print sales activity, the New York auction sales alone add more startling figures for the 1980-1981 season: Christie's sales ran to $9.784 million while Sotheby's New York volume billed $9.7 million with an $11.6 million total for prints sold in North America as a whole. And this is just the tip of the print iceberg. Below the visible level of auction activity in graphics with international trading interest lie the thousands of good prints produced by first-rank contemporary artists and works from under-collected periods of art sold yearly at the gallery level. Many of these already command prices that would have been unthinkable just five years ago. They form a growing pool of prints that will be fueling auction sales and collection choices for years to come. These indications of a continually expanding secondary market for prints — along with rising prices generally — have attracted collectors with investment goals. The collector-investor is turning to the print market as a hedge against inflation and as an alternative for the preservation and appreciation of capital.

But as much as investors may enjoy discussing works of art in financial terms such as blue chip, growth, and speculative prints, analogies between art and financial instruments, if they apply at all, are extremely superficial. Not all prints appreciate in value. Many never develop resale markets. Individual impressions, even within a single print edition, can bring drastically differing prices. Attempts to bypass the elusive and unmeasurable questions of aesthetic value at the core of art, by focusing on market value alone, ultimately can send the collector off on a chase after names rather than quality. In the last analysis, it is quality that makes the best print investment. How then, does the collector-investor choose prints? He must develop or employ the expertise needed to identify quality. A discerning eye remains essential to collecting, whatever its premise.

What Is an Original Print?

Probably the biggest hurdle in getting started is the ambiguous meaning of the word "print" itself. In the same year that Picasso's print, *La Minotaurachie,*

* Randy Rosen is President of Artists Originals, Corporate Art Advisory Service, New York.

brought $137,500 at auction, thousands of people were receiving a slick mail brochure urging them to invest $250 to become the original owner of a print by Andrew Wyeth. The print was merely a high-priced reproduction of a famous painting by Wyeth. Such ubiquitous use of the word "print" for everything from worthless reproductions to fine, original prints — which can be masterpieces and extremely valuable — is understandably baffling to beginners.

What exactly is an original print? How can an image that exists in multiple examples be original? On the simplest level, the concept is understood most easily by imagining inking a thumb and then pressing it against a piece of paper several times. Which of the fingerprints is the original? All the prints are original prints. Each was taken from the master image, the thumb. A similar relationship exists in printmaking. The artist creates a master image on a stone, metal plate, block, or stencil, from which the original prints are then pulled (printed). The master image functions as the tool for producing prints much as the pencil is the tool for producing drawings.

Beyond this basic concept, the boundaries of the term "original print" still must be defined. Traditional definitions had to become more flexible as innovative contemporary printmakers stretched orthodox uses of the medium by incorporating modern technologies into their work. However, two key elements are essential for a print to qualify as an original:

(1) The artist alone must create the master image for the plate, stone, block, or stencil.
(2) The artist either must be the one who pulls the edition or must personally supervise the master printer who prints it.

An original print is not a reproduction of anything else. It is not a copy of art work originated for a painting, watercolor, or drawing.[1]

An artist's skill as a printmaker is evaluated on the ability to interpret his ideas through the unique characteristics of the print medium. Although some contemporary artists employ techniques such as photography or offset printing, which are normally considered reproductive processes, their prints qualify as original if these techniques represent an intrinsic part of the concept rather than an easy way to produce copies. Originality in applying any techniques becomes a yardstick for establishing a particular print's value in the artist's overall graphic output and in the history of printmaking. One of the most sought-after contemporary American prints is Jasper Johns' color lithograph, *Ale Cans,* produced in an edition of only thirty-one in 1964. The print, measuring 14¼ × 11³⁄₁₆ inches, brought $19,800 at Sotheby Parke Bernet (Los Angeles) in 1980. Five months later, in New York, another impression fetched $24,200 at Christie's.

---

[1] It should be noted here that, as with most rules, there are exceptions: In the case of Old Master prints, hand-executed copies such as the engravings made of Raphael's paintings by Marcantonio Raimondi have achieved a collector status in their own right. Prior to the invention of photography, the copyist's skill in reproducing famous paintings sometimes developed craftsmen with styles of great distinction.

Jasper Johns not only uses reproductive technologies in his work, he also recycles the same subject matter (e.g., ale cans) from paintings to drawings to print after print. What makes these variations original is that each version represents a fresh problem that the artist has set himself to solve in the medium used. Tracing Johns' prices in *Gordon's Print Price Annual,* one sees that Johns' creativity as a printmaker has been identified by collectors. In fact, Johns is one of the few contemporary artists with strong international auction appeal. His prints have headed the general upward move in prices, pushing key works in this category into the five-figure realm. Of the thirty-six Jasper Johns prints auctioned in 1977, only two brought over $3,000. Most sold for under $1,800, with the majority below $1,000. But by 1979, seventy-five Johns prints came up at the major auctions; sixteen sold under $1,000, twenty-four between $1,000 and $2,-000, and seventeen over $3,000. In 1980, Johns' prints broke records for contemporary American graphics sold at auction, reaching the $24,200 at Christie's for *Ale Cans* and $39,600 for a portfolio of ten lithographs. When first published in 1968, individual prints in the portfolio sold for $350; *Ale Cans* sold for about $350 in 1964.

What Determines the Value of an Original Print?

The artist's reputation. Work by artists whose reputations are already established in art history makes the safest investment, although it often carries a premium price tag. Picasso made close to 2,000 prints and not every one is a masterpiece. Knowing what to buy is as vital as knowing whom to buy. Many name artists are not recognized as outstanding printmakers. Alexander Calder's reputation is based on his innovative sculpture. Although he made many prints, Calder never became engrossed enough in the problems of printmaking to produce an important body of graphics.

Quality of the image. The ability to correctly identify quality, to anticipate which prints are likely to become important, to judge whether a particular print is a key example of an artist's work or merely a minor one, or whether an impression is a crisp, bright printing or a weak one, can spell the difference between a strong collection and an inferior one — a difference that may be worth thousands of dollars at resale. This is especially true in the case of Old Master prints, made prior to the modern tradition of retiring and canceling a plate or block after the edition is pulled. Some plates and blocks remained active for centuries, and late, posthumous editions exist. A superb example is Rembrandt's *The Agony in the Garden* (Figure 1 on page 680).

In May 1974, Sotheby Parke Bernet in New York offered several impressions of Rembrandt's etching, *Adoration of the Shepherds.* The following descriptions appear in the catalogue. They are almost identical, but not quite. The difference was worth $5,500. Which seems the better choice to bid on?

Lot 88: (B., Holl. 45; H.273; BB54-1), etching, a very good clear impression of the first state of two, on lightly tanned paper, with 2 to 4mm margins, in good condition.

Lot 89: (B., Holl. 45; H.273; BB54-1), etching, a very good, bright impression of the second state of two (Nowell-Usticke's second state of three, early, before the wear in the dark shading above the cows), printed with slight retroussage at right to enhance the lighting effects, with small margins, in good condition.

Lot 88 is the rarer, first state of the print, executed in the artist's lifetime. It

FIG. 1. Rembrandt van Rijn, *The Agony in the Garden.* Etching and Drypoint, circa 1657.

SOURCE: Sotheby's, New York

fetched $7,500, against $2,000 for Lot 89. A third impression of the print, from a late edition, sold for only $750 in the same sale. In a *New York Times* article entitled "Art: A Nice Quiet Time for Old Master Prints," John Russell remarked on the special astuteness required in buying Old Masters:

> Buying old prints is a tricky business. In an ideal world all prints that had been pulled from the same plate would look the same, and cost the same, and have been equally well looked after. But in practice the plates get worn, and the quality of paper and ink may vary from one pulling to the next. So may the size of the sheet.

Exceptional use of the medium. When a major artist explores the technical aspects of printmaking in a unique way, or produces exceptionally sensitive renderings, such prints become landmarks of quality in printmaking and thus are highly desirable. Rembrandt's hand-wiped etchings, often pulled individually as sold (rather than at a single printing), are considered almost unique works of art. They command prices comparable to major watercolors and drawings. A copy of Rembrandt's *The Three Trees* brought $114,600 at auction in 1980. Likewise, Picasso, at the age of 77, executed a remarkable series of linoleum cuts that changed thinking about that medium. One of the linocuts, *Buste de Femme d'après Cranach le Jeune* sold for about $600 in the 1960s. At the November 13, 1979 Sotheby's print sale in New York, *Buste de Femme d'après Cranach le Jeune* brought $85,000, plus a 10 percent buyer's commission.

Rarity. Rarity is a two-sided coin. Many rare prints appeal only to a small, relatively sophisticated market. This narrows competition to a clutch of cognescenti, such as those who make up much of the Old Master print field. Rarity in other cases can raise a price far beyond the expected level for a print. A rare-proof print (an example pulled before the actual edition and generally existing in very few impressions) of Picasso's *Le Repas Frugal* (see Figure 2 on page 682) brought a staggering $154,000 at auction in 1973. This particular example was rare. It came from the collection of George Bloch, the man who wrote the catalogue raisonné on Picasso's prints, and it was one of a very few brilliant impressions of the image made prior to the time the plate was steel-faced (reinforced) in 1912. But the regular edition impressions, while quite sought-after, do not come anywhere near that figure. (See the record of subsequent auction sale prices in Table 1 on page 683.)

Celebrity prints. Prints that come up frequently at auctions acquire a celebrity status. They recur in museum and gallery exhibitions and in catalogues and books. Such prints tend to attract a broad spectrum of buyers; they develop a strong secondary market appeal that may not exist for fine but rare works. Inexperienced buyers, especially, feel more comfortable bidding on celebrity prints with easily traceable price records. This competition, in turn, feeds upward price movement and demand for the print. Paul Klee's very popular 1923 litho-

FIG. 2. Pablo Picasso, *Le Repas Frugal.* Aquatint, 1904.
SOURCE: Sotheby's, New York

TABLE 1. Prices at Auction for Pablo Picasso's *Le Repas Frugal* (Etching, 1904; printed 1913), 1977–1980

Auction	*Lot*	*Date*	*Price*
1977			
Sotheby's (N.Y.)	271	11/77	$17,000
Sotheby's (Lon.)	157	10/77	13,984
1978			
Christie's (N.Y.)	210	11/78	$29,000
Sotheby's (Lon.)	332	4/78	40,700
Kornfeld & Klipstein	782	6/78	26,239
Christie's (N.Y.)	232A	11/78	22,000
1979			
Sotheby's (N.Y.)	409	11/79	$30,800
Sotheby's (Lon.)	261	11/79	28,524
Kornfeld & Klipstein	975	6/79	30,153
Kornfeld & Klipstein	974	6/79	30,838
Sotheby's (L.A.)	290	9/79	27,500
1980			
Sotheby's (Lon.)	186	5/80	$31,862
Drouot	75	2/80	26,386
Kornfeld & Klipstein	1065	6/80	33,888
Sotheby's (N.Y.)	494	11/80	34,100
Sotheby's (L.A.)	449	2/80	22,000
Christie's (N.Y.)	332	5/80	26,400
Sotheby's (Lon.)	653	11/80	30,244
1981			
Sotheby's (N.Y.)	399	5/81	$34,100
Sotheby's (N.Y.)	304	11/81	34,100
Kornfeld & Klipstein	135	6/81	27,500

graph, *Seiltänzer* (Tightrope Walker) (see Figure 3 on page 685), appears regularly at auction. Table 2 on page 684 indicates that, with the exception of Lot 105, an impression in poor condition, demand has sustained and built a strong following for the work.

Condition of the print. Physical damage, such as trimmed margins, stains, tears, foxing, or discoloration due to overexposure to light, greatly reduces the value of a print. This is especially true with contemporary or modern prints, with which one expects to find examples in perfect condition.

TABLE 2. Prices at Auction for Paul Klee's *Seiltänzer,* 1977—1981

Auction	*Lot*	*Date*	*Price*
Sotheby's (Lon.)	107	10/77	$ 5,632
Sotheby's (L.A.)	151	9/77	7,500
Hauswedell & Nolte	233	5/77	8,500
Sotheby's (N.Y.)	911	11/79	11,833
Hauswedell & Nolte	648	6/79	13,235
Sotheby's (N.Y.)	316	11/80	17,600
Christie's (N.Y.)	105	11/80	5,500
Sotheby's (N.Y.)	306	2/81	11,050

Trends and fashions in collecting. The print market moves in short-term cycles. Short-term supply and demand creates immediate price trends and fluctuations that can reflect either a genuine increase in value or a merely exaggerated, momentary activity in the market for an artist's work. For example, a price jump often occurs prior to a major museum retrospective of an artist's work; this may subside within six months. Sustained long-term trends are more indicative of the schools, artists, and particular prints that warrant investment consideration. It is rare to find price comparisons on a print at convenient intervals. Some prints do not reappear on the market for years. When they do, different impressions may vary greatly in states and conditions. Fashions in buying can be national or regional. But generally trends are dictated by basic changes in taste and in availability of material. As the bulk of major prints are absorbed off the market, or achieve extraordinary prices, more accessible artists and periods move into popularity. Currently, the demand for prints by American artists of the 1920s and 1930s is growing, as Table 3 on page 686 indicates.

Economic changes. Economic turmoil and inflation have traditionally lured investors into art, which has historically weathered financial storms better than the stock market has. The prints that best withstand an economic contraction are top-quality examples by major artists. The prints most severely hit in times of stress are works by lesser known artists, medium-grade works by major artists, and contemporary works. Prints whose prices have been artificially pushed up by unsophisticated investors jumping into the market, buying names rather than quality, suffer when these investors drop out in a crunch.

Auctions of a large body of prints by an artist. When a large body of work by a recognized artist hits the block, the atmosphere of competitiveness and excitement often sets price records for the artist's prints. At Sotheby's print sale in the Spring of 1980, in which seventy-seven prints and drawings by Mary

FIG. 3. Paul Klee, Seiltänzer. Lithograph, 1923.
SOURCE: Courtesy of Carus Gallery, New York

TABLE 3. Prices at Auction for Selected Prints by American Artists

Thomas Hart Benton, *Frankie and Johnnie* (Lithograph, 1936; edition: 100; originally published at $10)

Auction	*Lot*	*Date*	*Price*
Sotheby's (N.Y.)	119	1975	$1,100
Sotheby's (N.Y.)	25	5/79	3,960
Sotheby Parke Bernet (N.Y.)	24	2/79	2,750
Christie's (N.Y.)	202	4/79	3,850
Christie's (N.Y.)	65	3/79	3,740
Sotheby's (N.Y.)	55	6/79	3,960
Sotheby's (N.Y.)	34	11/79	4,180
Christie's (N.Y.)	302	9/80	7,700
Sotheby's (N.Y.)	41	11/80	9,075
Sotheby's (L.A.)	49A	2/81	8,800

Grant Wood, *Approaching Storm* (Lithograph, 1942; originally published at $35 by Associated American Artists)

Sotheby's (L.A.)	330	9/77	$ 675
Christie's (N.Y.)	532	11/79	1,320
Sotheby's (L.A.)	424	9/79	1,650
Sotheby's (N.Y.)	806	11/80	1,870
Sotheby's (N.Y.)	805	11/80	1,870
Sotheby's (N.Y.)	612	6/80	1,760

In 1977, of thirty-two Grant Wood prints recorded in *Gordon's Print Price Annual* as sold at auction sales, thirty sold under $1,000 and two over that amount. By 1980, of thirty-one listings, twenty-five sold between $1,000 and 2,000, and only six under $1,000.

George Bellows, *Dempsey and Firpo* (Lithograph, 1923-1924; Edition: 103; original price unknown)

Sotheby's (N.Y.)	131	5/77	$ 3,700
Martin Gordon	231	5/77	5,000
Sotheby's (N.Y.)	9	5/80	14,300

Martin Lewis, *Spring Night, Greenwich Village* (Drypoint, 1930; edition: 100; sold in 1974 for $45)

Christie's (N.Y.)	349	4/79	$1,100
Christie's (N.Y.)	275	9/79	1,210
Sotheby's (N.Y.)	264	2/80	1,760

Cassatt were auctioned, the sale rung up an amazing $880,050. A single print, *La Toilette* (1891), sold for $72,000 (plus commission). This print, which had a presale estimate of only $28,000, fetched the highest price ever paid for an American print at auction. Many felt that had the print appeared by itself, rather than in the context of the Cassatt sale, its price would have been closer to half that figure.

Publication of a catalogue raisonné of the artist's work and/or a major museum exhibition. Between 1975 and 1978, no less than ten books on Giovanni Battista Piranesi came out commemorating the artist's death, along with numerous publications and exhibitions of the artist's work. This triggered a price rise that is still building momentum.

Variety of Investments Within the Medium

The beginner should specialize in a specific category of collecting interest. Concentration develops in-depth expertise in a period of art, educates a discerning eye for quality, permits the collector to keep current on pricing, and develops the network of sources and collectors from whom prime material and information can be obtained.

For purposes of this article, prints fall into five key collecting groups. They parallel auction and gallery designations.

Old Master prints. These are fifteenth- to eighteenth-century works including those of such masters as Dürer, Rembrandt, Altdorfer, Van Ostaade, and many lesser known artists. Fine prints are still available in this area at moderate prices. Goya's prints (although the artist worked well into the nineteenth century) generally are included with the grouping.

Nineteenth-century prints. This designation usually represents prints by the more academic nineteenth-century artists, such as Tissot and Robbe. It is an area of developing collecting interest.

Modern masters. Artists whose reputations were established as part of the history of Modern Art prior to 1950, such as Matisse, Picasso, Toulouse-Lautrec, Braque, Lissitsky, Klee, Munch, and Kandinsky, are included in this group. It is the most robust collecting category, since the prints of these artists have stood the test of time but are not as rare as those of the Old Masters. Major examples are steeply priced, although fine prints are also available at more moderate prices.

American modern prints. Renewal of interest in American art generally has sparked activity for prints by early twentieth-century Realists such as Winslow Homer, John Sloan, George Bellows, and Edward Hopper, and particularly for prints from the 1920s-1930s era, by such artists as Grant Wood, Thomas Hart Benton, Louis Lozowick, and Martin Lewis.

Contemporary prints. This category includes two types of work: contemporary master prints by artists with established international standing and auction track records, such as Jasper Johns, Frank Stella, and David Hockney; and prints by a group of emerging artists, whose reputations are growing, but who have not yet obtained an international market base for their work or proven staying power.

ATTRACTIVE FEATURES

Shortly after Hitler came to power in the 1930s, a young man from Holland approached the great print collector Lessing Rosenwald and asked if he would like to look at some prints. As the boy unwrapped the plain brown paper package, Rosenwald's eyes widened. Spread before him was the world-famous Aufhaüser collection of fifteenth-century metal cuts and woodcuts. He bought the group, providing Aufhaüser, a German banker, with the funds to begin life anew when he was forced to flee Germany.

As this anecdote demonstrates, good prints are a portable asset with international currency. They are also a physical asset with intrinsic worth and the potential to increase substantially in market value. While all collectors are aware of these pragmatic aspects, and naturally like to see the prints they buy increase in value, such rewards are rarely what hook dedicated collectors of the Rosenwald and Aufhaüser ilk. Just as discovery is at the heart of art, it is at the heart of collecting. Hunting for the best artists and the best prints becomes a catalyst for personal growth, travel, worldwide social and professional contacts, deep friendships with artists, and a genuine involvement in their search to find fresh meanings in reality.

Such non-marketable dividends often seem ephemeral to the newly initiated or to those who prefer to view prints as simply another form of commodity. Yet it is the viewpoint constantly reiterated by the great collectors. Asked to explain why he collected, Morton L. Janklaw put it this way:

> As the passion grows and becomes consuming, the collector becomes aware of his own increasing identification with the artist and with his objectives. While it is only the work of the creative genius which survives, collecting those works in a scholarly and analytical way is a reflection of the unconscious desire to share in his artistic expression in some small way. We seek, in the end, the same kind of spiritual and aesthetic renewal which causes the great artist to constantly launch himself into the unknown.[2]

POTENTIAL RISKS

Frauds and Fakes

Relatively few prints are produced as outright counterfeits. The caveat emptor of the print world is the good reproduction masquerading as an original

---

[2] "Notes on Collecting and Friendship, A Tribute to Jean Dubuffet." *Jean Dubuffet: A Retrospective Glance at Eighty,* page 6.

because someone has added a false signature and, sometimes, edition numbering. Reproductions made by photomechanical processes break up into dots when viewed under magnification. But reproductions also can be made by the hand processes used for originals. During the 1950s, when the groundswell for prints first emerged, several major European artists (Chagall, Miró, Picasso, and Braque among them) sanctioned the production of handmade copies of works they had created in other media, such as watercolors. Professional etchers and lithographers made the copies by hand. The artists later signed and numbered these reproductions. A group of prints by Marc Chagall, referred to as the "Sorlier Chagalls," fall into this category. The images were drawn on the stone, not by Chagall, but by Charles Sorlier from sketches by Chagall, and the prints were later signed by the artist. For a while, people paid substantial sums for the reproductions. But high as the quality of such prints may be, to pay thousands for what amounts to a signature does not make sense. Today such copies are listed as reproductions by reputable galleries and many are designated as *estampes à tirage limité,* bringing at most a few hundred dollars. Properly identified and fairly priced, reproductions are neither fakes nor frauds. However, the disclosure that Salvador Dali's signature was affixed to thousands of blank sheets of paper prior to publication exposed the worst kind of deception. It is all the more unfortunate because the Dali buyer generally is new to the print market and unsophisticated. Most knowledgeable collectors have done their homework and are well aware of the questionable quality of many Dali prints.

Other prints that occasionally fall prey to false signatures are those published in both signed and unsigned versions, or editions of which the artist only signed some of the impressions. Also, posters occasionally have been altered by cutting off the type areas, signing the images, and passing them off as originals. While galleries return money on such frauds, most of these fakes are not destroyed and can slip back into circulation. The buyer's best protection is familiarity with the prints, working with a reputable dealer or adviser, and documenting the print through a catalogue raisonné if one exists. Several states have passed disclosure laws to protect buyers. Such laws require that a dealer disclose and guarantee the accuracy of information on several points, including how the print was made (medium); who published it; when the work was signed; whether it is a reproduction created by the artist or someone else; and size of the edition. States with such laws include New York, California, Hawaii, Illinois, and Maryland. While infractions certainly exist, it should be remembered that the majority of prints are correct.

Problems With Forecasting

Prints by the same artist can vary in quality and price from one edition to another. All Picassos are not great Picassos. Buying "names" is not a good investment strategy. Even within a single edition, one impression in poor condition and another in pristine shape can differ greatly in price. The broad stroke type of forecasting used in stock market price quotations simply is not appropriate for works of art. Even given the consistency of printing quality in most contemporary editions, there is no guarantee that all impressions will be equal in value. If the print has been on the market for a while, the condition of an individual impression and its scarcity will affect the price. However, by identifying an artist's outstanding works, and by recognizing distinctions in the quality of individual impressions, the buyer can exercise a high level of prudence and judgment.

Relative Illiquidity

Stocks produce dividends. Bonds produce interest. Real estate produces rent. Prints produce the daily dividends of living with great art, as well as a capital appreciation potential that can more than justify investment over the long run. But print collecting is a long-term commitment, with three to five years the general minimum period without cash flow. It is, of course, possible to purchase a print just as the artist's market begins to rise, but this is not easy to accomplish or predict.

Important prints that have shown durability over time have a steady and strong resale capacity and usually can be sold in a relatively short time. But prints are not negotiable into cash overnight. Achieving an advantageous price often requires waiting for an advantageous time to sell. The appropriate auction or season may be preceded by a wait of months. Prints by unknown artists, or from periods momentarily out of favor, are harder to resell; they are generally traded privately, if at all. An art history grounding, and a well-trained eye for quality, allows the collector to buy against the grain or invest in emerging talents. This may be one way to build an impressive collection on relatively low initial outlays.

TAX CONSEQUENCES

Under federal tax law, profit from the sale of a print held by an individual for more than one year is taxable at the capital gains rate rather than as ordinary income. Under certain conditions, prints can be exchanged for others of equal or greater value in a tax-free transaction. As with other types of investments, it is also possible to realize a tax deduction upon donating a print whose market value has appreciated to a qualified organization. (See article on Tax Considerations for Collector-Investors elsewhere in this volume.) For specific guidance in these matters, investors are urged to consult a professional tax adviser.

Questionable Tax Shelter

Around 1977, groups of investors became active in using tax-shelter financing to fund print editions. The best publicized of these groups, Jackie Fine Arts, mass-produced prints to feed the demand. Many of these tax-shelter editions were of questionable aesthetic value. This practice underlines the problem created when high-powered marketing people move prints into the market with little knowledge — or concern — for artistic merit. The tax-shelter promoter allocated the value of an edition to the master plate (i.e., stone, stencil, plate, or block) used in producing the prints. As tangible property, the master plate was considered eligible for investment tax credit and accelerated depreciation. The IRS disagreed with the tax-shelter people, and such vehicles currently are under heavy scrutiny by the IRS. Beginning in 1980, the IRS pulled returns for audit based on total positive income rather than on adjusted gross income, in order to ferret out shelters that function primarily as tax dodges.

REPRESENTATIVE TYPES OF INVESTORS

Once considered the poor man's passport into the art world, prints have become the darlings of an expanding international market. The major auction houses reported $42,933,260 in sales in 1980. Dealers, collectors, investors, corporations, museums, libraries, universities, and young people who cannot afford major paintings but want major artists all are in the market for prints.

IMPORTANT FACTORS IN BUYING AND SELLING

Selecting a Dealer

A dealer's daily contacts with the market are an important resource for the collector, both for buying and for self-education. Developing close, working relationships with a few knowledgeable dealers puts years of experience in looking at prints at the novice's fingertips. But dealers, like most people, favor clients who do more than "pick their brains." Dealers will give loyal clients first crack at prime prints and better deals, especially if a client does not bargain when a quoted price is a fair one. Popular wisdom has it that one picks up better buys at auctions than through dealers. Often the reverse is true. In the same year that an impression of Picasso's *Femme au Fauteuil No. 1* brought $25,000 at auction, the writer purchased an equivalent impression for a client at a New York gallery for only $9,500. (See *Leading Galleries and Dealers* in this article for a partial listing of the important dealers nationwide.) To locate reputable local dealers, check with a museum.

Finding the Right Market

Prints are published either by the artist or by a publisher who also wholesales the prints to dealers (and sometimes to collectors, although a collector may not be given a full discount). Some publishers also may have a distributor who wholesales the editions. A new contemporary print selling for $1,000 at publication generally will wholesale anywhere from $500 to $800, depending on the publisher and the drawing power of the stable of artists he publishes. Name artists with strong resale do not require as high a discount to outlets. As a rule of thumb, discounts off retail price on a new edition run between 30 and 50 percent. Edition sizes in contemporary prints normally are between fifty and a hundred impressions. To raise capital for a project, some publishers cover costs on an edition by offering a pre-publication subscription price below the price at publication time. This assures an immediate gain to the buyer willing to commit in advance.

Prices for new contemporary prints stretch from a few hundred to several thousand dollars for well-known artists. A recent etching by David Hockney was released at $6,000; within months, copies were selling for as high as $8,000. Many prints are marketed in such a way that when a new edition is sold out by its initial distributor, remaining impressions in the market are immediately priced higher. Some publisher-distributors stimulate these price rises by creating an initial scarcity on hot prints. They hold back a portion of a new edition. When the first group of prints released are absorbed by the market, further impressions are sold to dealers at higher wholesale levels. Collectors who are highly sophisticated in the market sometimes purchase several impressions of a new print when it is published if they feel it will be important. Like the publisher, they take advantage of the price run-up by selling off most of their impressions, retaining one for their own collection at negligible cost. But even a well received new edition of sixty to a hundred prints can take eighteen months to two years to sell out, so the resale waiting time must be taken into account.

After the initial edition is sold out, prices are controlled by supply and demand in the market. One should "shop" for prices on prints that have been out on the market for a few years or more. Dealers who purchase a print early and cheaply still may have it at a lower markup than will those who acquired the print later on.

Auction houses. With Modern Master or Old Master prints, one can look to auction houses as well as to galleries. Auctions are the vortex of the art market, the place where price records and reputations can be made or undone in a single day. (See *Major Print Auction Houses* in this article.)

Print auction houses issue catalogues for each sale. Those of the major houses are often profusely illustrated and accompanied by estimated prices. Serious collectors should subscribe to, and follow, at least one auction house's catalogues annually, and build a library of auction catalogues for price reference.

Some key terms used in the print auction market are as follows:

Estimate. The estimate is the price a print is estimated to bring at auction. Major auctions list these prices in their catalogues. But estimates can be deceptive. Always use the final knockdown price as a guide in evaluating market value.

Reserve. The reserve is the price set by the owner of the item for sale, below which the auction house is not permitted to sell the print. If the print is bought in (not sold), the owner pays a handling penalty.

Provenance. The provenance of a work of art is its history of ownership. Collectors' marks of previous owners are of special value in Old Master prints, where impressions run from mediocre to brilliant; previous ownership by a major collector becomes a sign of quality.

Buyer's/seller's commissions. The buyer's or seller's commission is the amount paid on the price of a print sold at auction. In the United States it is generally 10 percent for buyer, 10 percent for seller. But check the catalogue. Also, seller's commissions on major works can be negotiated with the auction house.

With the exception of the most prominent artists' work, most contemporary prints, however excellent, do not come up at auction regularly. These works have not yet developed strong secondary international markets, and large quantities of such prints still are available outside the auction sphere.

Appraisals

Most large auction houses offer two types of appraisal: an informal verbal appraisal as to what the print or collection is likely to bring at a sale, and a formal written appraisal for tax or insurance. For insurance purposes, the material should be evaluated at replacement value. The IRS requires appraisals at "fair market value" for both estate taxes and charitable donations. The IRS defines this value as "the price at which the property would change hands between a willing buyer and a willing seller, neither being under any compulsion to sell and both having reasonable knowledge of relevant facts." For appraisal charges, contact the individual auction house's customer-service office. The IRS also recognizes prints appraised by the Art Dealers Association of America, in New York. Up to one-third of the appraisal fee on formal appraisals may be rebated if an item is placed for auction within a year of the auction house's appraisal work for the seller.

Judging Quality

The ability to evaluate quality and value comes with exposure to prints, a knowledge of print history and techniques, and lots and lots of looking. One way to become oriented quickly is to study the auction house catalogues for major print sales. Many of these are profusely illustrated and include pre-auction estimates and documentation. Studying these catalogues and attending pre-auction exhibitions, which are often miniature museum shows in themselves, can speed up a novice's education; it is the quickest way to develop a feel for the various schools of prints and their price movements. But pre-auction estimates never should be relied on. The sale should be attended or the price list should be studied later to see what price the print actually achieved. A blank appears on the list if the print was bought in. When planning to bid on a framed print, an appointment should be made with the print department of the auction house to inspect it out of the frame. Many contemporary prints have not yet reached auction trading status, but are, nonetheless, investment calibre art works. Visiting a few of the more important print galleries before buying will familiarize the novice with the best in current work. Another option is to set up an appointment to study the contemporary work at a major museum print room.

Using Professional Advisers

The advantages of using a professional adviser are multiplied if the collector does not have the time to become immersed in the process of learning the market. An educated eye, crucial to investing in prints, cannot be acquired overnight. While dealers provide invaluable information that should be tapped, they have a vested interest in the artists and periods they represent as well as a need to move inventory. An adviser works objectively for the collector. An adviser's fee may be either part of the retail price of the prints purchased (galleries deduct a portion of their markup) or a retainer based on an annual buying budget. The latter is by far the more professional approach, and generates the kind of sustained working commitment and identification with the client's goals that builds a strong collection.

CUSTODIAL CARE

Collectors can become unwitting accomplices in destroying the value of their own prints through improper conservation and maintenance. Unlike stock certificates, prints require care.

Common disasters — which can halve the resale value of a print — result from improper framing. The margins of a print *never* should be trimmed to fit a frame. Prints always should be backed and matted with acid-free board, specifically four-ply, 100-percent rag board (also called museum board). Be certain it is rag all the way through. Framers have a cheap version that is rag only on the surface. When a mat opening is cut, it exposes the harmful wood pulp core inside the cheap board and exudes chemicals that can damage a print. Tapes that are self-adhering, such as utility or masking tape, stain the paper almost immediately and should be avoided, along with rubber cement and animal glues. If a framer balks at these requirements, a reputable print gallery or museum print room may be able to recommend a qualified framer who will do the job properly.[3]

---

[3] See Rosen, Randy, *Prints: The Facts and Fun of Collecting,* New York: E.P. Dutton, 1978, pages 188-199 for a detailed discussion of conservation and environmental precautions.

Restoration

A print that has been restored is less valuable than an unrestored version of that print. But the degree and success of the restoration must be taken into account. Another consideration is how common it is to find that print in perfect condition in the first place. The price of an Old Master print might be influenced less by restoration than by the price of a modern print. A collector of Old Master prints might prefer a repaired or slightly damaged example over one in perfect condition if the former represented a magnificent bright impression of an important subject, where the pristine version was a weaker, later printing. A modern print, on the other hand, generally is expected to be unrestored.

GLOSSARY

Artists have invented endless variations of the basic printmaking processes, but there are essentially four methods by which prints are made. Since each technique has an extensive vocabulary of its own, this glossary is limited to basic techniques and key terms.

artist's proofs (or épreuves d'artiste)— These are impressions set aside for the artist's use above the basic edition size, generally about 10 percent of the edition. Artist's proofs are indicated by an A.P. or E.A. in place of numbering. B.A.T. (bon à tirer) means good pull, and is the impression selected as the standard of quality for pulling the entire edition. Usually it is given to the master printer. The Hors de Commerce (H.C.) is an impression reserved for the publisher's personal use. Originally, the H.C. was given to critics and friends.

editions and limited editions— The term "edition" refers to the total number of impressions printed. The idea of limiting the size of editions is relatively modern. Almost all contemporary modern prints are limited, with most running between fifty and a hundred examples on the average. The size of an edition is set at the time of the printing.

intaglio process (engravings, drypoints, etchings, aquatints, mezzotints)— The term "intaglio" derives from the Italian *intagliare,* meaning to cut, carve, or engrave. The prefix "in-" is the key to the method. Much as a person might cut a design into sand with a finger and watch the channels fill with water, the intaglio artist cuts or bites the image below the surface of the metal plate, leaving channels that later fill with ink. The artist cuts a design into the plate either by using a direct tool (for drypoints and engravings) or with the help of acids (for etchings, aquatints, and mezzotints) that bite the image down below the surface of the metal. When the plate is inked, a moistened paper is placed over it, and both plate and paper are run through a press at high pressure. The paper is sucked down into the inked channels of the plate, where it picks up the image. Printing pressure produces a plate mark or indentation around all intaglio prints — one sign that they are authentic rather than reproductions.

relief method (woodcuts, linoleum, or linocuts)— Discovered by the Chinese centuries ago, the relief process is the oldest and simplest printing technique. It works on a principle similar to that of the ordinary office rubber stamp in which the raised portion of the stamp (the part containing the letters or numerals) is inked and pressed to paper. In the relief print, much the same occurs. The artist cuts away all portions of the wood or linoleum block except the design. The design remains in relief, raised above the rest of the block surface. This raised design is inked. Paper is placed over it and rubbed, transferring the image to the paper. An artist also can work the procedure negatively by reversing the design emphasis. The design is cut away so the key forms lie below the surface, and will not accept ink. The main images in the final print, therefore, show up as white rather than black areas.

restrikes or reprints— Restrikes are pulled from the original plate after the original edition has been issued, often years after an artist's death. There are legal restrikes and illegal ones. Restrikes are relatively inexpensive and should be identified as such. Image quality is generally poor. Most contemporary plates, stones, blocks, and stencils are either destroyed or "marked" (canceled) once an edition is pulled. One should be particularly careful with prints from before the twentieth century and with those of prolific print artists such as Picasso, Käthe Kollwitz, Marc Chagall, and Georges Braque.

signatures— Most contemporary prints are numbered and signed in pencil. The practice is a relatively modern one and should not be one's only guide to value or authenticity. An unsigned Rembrandt of 1657, *The Agony in the Garden,* measuring only 4¾ × 3¼ inches, was knocked down at auction for $70,000 at Sotheby Parke Bernet in 1973. Important prints from prior to the nineteenth century, and some from well into the twentieth century, were not signed. An artist's signature is most relevant where the edition is known to have been signed. Some artists, such as Pierre Bonnard, signed only portions of their editions. The term "signed in the plate" indicates that the artist signed the image (i.e., stone) prior to its printing. Such signatures become part of the printed image, often reproducing backwards. Since the pencil signature after printing is meant to indicate the artist's approval of the print's quality, a print signed in the plate is essentially unsigned.

states— An artist may develop and alter an image through many phases (states) before pulling the final full edition. These pulls can show radical changes in the artist's idea, and provide one of the most fascinating insights into creativity in all printmaking.

stencil process (silk screens/serigraphs)— The basic premise underlying the stencil method is the same one that makes a simple school alphabet-lettering stencil work; the shape (e.g., the letter A) to be printed appears as an open form in the stencil. The area around it is solid, so that no color can pass through when it is painted over. Color drops through the A opening only, printing on the paper below. Although modern silkscreening is a more complicated procedure, the theory is the same. A piece of mesh (originally, this was silk, hence silkscreening) is stretched taut over a wooden frame. The stencil is applied to this mesh so that positive areas (the image) remain open and areas the artist does not want to paint are blocked out (remain closed). The stencil is inked by pulling color across the full stencil so that paint drops through the open areas onto the paper below, thereby printing the design. Generally, each color in a print requires a separate stencil.

surface or planographic process (lithographs)— Lithography works on the principle that oil and water do not mix. The artist draws an image on the flat surface of a stone or plate with a greasy crayon or ink. The stone is given several baths with chemicals that make the stone more receptive to water where there is no greasy crayon, and chemicals that fix the greasy design so its edges will not smear during inkings. The stone is then dampened with water. When the stone is inked with a greasy colored ink for printing, the ink adheres to the greasy design area, but is repelled by the water-wet portions of the stone. Paper is placed against the inked stone and a heavy press applied. Under pressure, the colored area (the design) transfers to the paper. The artist never cuts into the stone (or plate); the image prints from the flat surface, hence the term "surface process."

LEADING GALLERIES AND DEALERS

Brooke Alexander, Inc., New York, N.Y.
Aldis Browne Fine Arts, Ltd., New York, N.Y.
Associated American Artists, New York, N.Y.
Carus Gallery, New York, N.Y.
Castelli Uptown, New York, N.Y.
Drown Point Press, Oakland, Cal.
Fitch-Febvrel Gallery, New York, N.Y.
Gemini GEL, Los Angeles, Cal.
Getler/Pall, New York, N.Y.
Barbara Gladstone Gallery, New York, N.Y.
Lucien Goldschmidt, Inc., New York, N.Y.
Martin Gordon, Inc., New York, N.Y.
Pasquale Iannetti, Inc., Galleries, San Francisco, Cal.
Bernard Jacobson Ltd., New York, N.Y.
Harcus Krakow Gallery, Boston, Mass.
Margo Leavin Gallery, Los Angeles, Cal.
Multiples/Marian Goodman, New York, N.Y.
Orion Editions, New York, N.Y.
Pace Editions, New York, N.Y.
724 Prints, New York, N.Y.
Tamarind Institute, Abuquerque, N.M.
David Tunick, New York, N.Y.
Tyler Graphics Ltd., Bedford, N.Y.
Van Straaten Gallery, Chicago, Ill.

MAJOR PRINT-AUCTION HOUSES

Christie, Manson & Woods Ltd., London, England
Christie, Manson & Woods International, Inc., New York, N.Y.
Christie's East, New York, N.Y.
Dorotheum, Vienna, Austria
Hauswedell & Nolte, Hamburg, West Germany
Karl und Faber, Munich, West Germany
Kornfeld und Klipstein, Bern, Switzerland
Sotheby Parke Bernet, New York, N.Y.

Sotheby's, London, England
Sotheby's, Los Angeles, Cal.
Sotheby's York, New York, N.Y.

Sources of Market and Price Information

Gordon's Print Price Annual. Published by Martin Gordon, Inc., New York, N.Y. Lists all fine art prints sold at twenty-six major international auction houses annually. Decorative, sporting, and topographical prints are reported, but to a lesser degree. Publication began in 1978. *Gordon's* is a basic price reference for the serious collector.

International Auction Records. Published by Editions Publisol, New York, N.Y. Includes a section on prints, but is not as extensive as *Gordon's.*

The Print Collector's Newsletter. Published by Print Collector's Newsletter, New York, N.Y. Bimonthly; includes articles, a selected listing of newly published editions and books on prints, as well as a listing of galleries and publishers.

World Print Council, San Francisco, Cal. A nonprofit organization providing access to information about printmaking.

SUGGESTED READING

Catalogues raisonnés. One of the best sources of information about prints is a catalogue raisonné. This is the standard reference catalogue on an artist's prints. It provides the most complete compendium available of an individual artist's work. Such a catalogue gives the title of each of the artist's prints known up to the time of the catalogue; publisher and date of the print's publication (if known); technique; number of impressions in the complete edition (if known); size of image area and overall sheet; number of states (alterations in the development of the image; impressions pulled at each stage are differentiated) and any pertinent data known about them; paper used; whether or not the print was signed in pencil, pen, or crayon (and where the signature appears), or whether an estate stamp or monogram was used. If the edition is known to be canceled (i.e., the master plate effaced or marked), this is generally indicated also. Reproductions of the artist's official signatures, estate stamps, and/or monograms are also included, permitting verification of signatures with those on the prints being contemplated.

Seeing a picture printed in a book is never a substitute for seeing a print directly, but browsing through these catalogues raisonnés provides a quick overview of an artist's work and helps in evaluating the overall consistency of the quality, the richness (or poverty) of the artist's creative invention, and the periods or mediums (i.e., etchings or lithographs) best collected. Marc Chagall, at 93, still produces prints. But the artist's deeply felt earlier works, such as *Daphnis and Chlöe,* or the experimental etchings, such as *Equinox (1968),* are more highly prized than recent prints that reflect a more decorative, predictable, and repetitive imagery.

Unfortunately, not every artist has a catalogue raisonné. Few such references exist, for example, on the work of contemporary artists, since it is still in process. In such cases, the best way to get information on prices, quality impressions, and market activity is to check gallery and auction catalogues, or to write to a major museum print room, which will direct the collector to a dealer who specializes in a particular artist's prints. There are also a number of excellent books that give a general introduction to prints.

Basic Books on Prints

Castleman, Riva. *Contemporary Prints.* New York: Viking, 1973. Insights into creative thinking and techniques of major contemporary printmakers through discussion of ninety key works.

Donson, Theodore. *Prints and the Print Market.* New York: Thomas Y. Cromwell Co., 1977. Insiders' handbook; sophisticated look at the market for those with some basic knowledge of the field.

Mayer, Hayatt. *Prints and People.* New York: The Metropolitan Museum of Art, New York Graphic Soc'y, 1971. One of the richest and most fascinating melanges of data and tales about prints, but best read after some exposure to the field.

Rosen, Randy. *Prints: The Facts and Fun of Collecting.* New York: E.P. Dutton, 1978. A basic how-to-go-about-it book for the beginning collector, covering history, techniques, aesthetics, and marketing.

Zigrosser, Carl, and Gaehde, Christa M. *A Guide to the Collecting and Care of Original Prints.* New York: Crown Publishers, Inc., 1965. Basic text on conservation of prints.

Standard References

Following are the standard references on some major artists and schools of interest to the collector. Some of these are catalogues raisonnés. Note that many of these works are not available in English. However, a librarian can often translate essential data needed to authenticate a print.

Bauhaus

Wingler, Hans M. *Graphic Work from the Bauhaus.* Trans. by Gerald Onn. Greenwich: New York Graphic Society, 1969

———. *50 Jahre Bauhaus.* (Exhibition Catalogue) Stuttgart: Württembergischer Kunstverein, 1968.

Max Beckmann

Gallwitz, Klaus. *Max Beckmann: Die Druckgraphik.* Karlsruhe: Ausstellungskatalog, 1962.

Thomas Hart Benton

Fath, Creekmore. *Thomas Hart Benton: A Catalogue Raisonné of the Lithographs.* (Revised Edition), 1979.

Georges Braque

Hofmann, Werner. *Braque: His Graphic Work.* New York: Harry N. Abrams, 1961.

Mourlot, Fernand. *Braque Lithographe.* Monte Carlo, 1963.

Mary Cassatt

Breesking, Adelyn D. *A Catalogue Raisonné, The Graphic Work of Mary Cassatt.* New York: H. Bittner and Co., 1948.

Marc Chagall

Kornfeld, Eberhard W. *Verzeichnis der Kupferstiche, Radierungen und Holzschnitte* [Engravings and Woodcuts] *von Marc Chagall. Werke: 1922-1966.* Bern: Kornfeld und Klipstein, 1970.

Mourlot, Fernand. *Chagall Lithographe,* 4 vols. Monte Carlo, 1973, 1974.

Jim Dine

Galerie Mikro. *The Complete Graphics of James Dine.* Berlin, 1970.

Albrecht Dürer

Knappe, Karl-Adolf, ed. *Dürer, The Complete Engravings, Etchings and Woodcuts.* New York: Harry N. Abrams, 1965.

Meder, Joseph. *Dürer Katalog; ein Handbuch über Albrecht Dürers Stiche, Radierungen, Holzschnitte, deren Zustände, Ausgaben und Wasserzeichen.* Vienna; Gilhofer & Ranschburg, 1932.

Dutch and Flemish Etchings, Engravings, Woodcuts

Hollstein, F.W.H. *Dutch and Flemish Etchings, Engravings and Woodcuts (c.1450-1700),* 19 vols. Amsterdam: M. Hertzberger, 1949-1976.

Francisco Goya

Delteil, Löys. *Le Peintre-Graveur Illustré,* vols. 14-15. Paris: Löys Delteil, 1922.

Harris, Tomás. *Goya: Engravings and Lithographs,* 2 vols. Oxford: Bruno Cassierer, 1964.

Erich Heckel

Dube, Annemarie and Wolf-Dieter. *Erich Heckel: Das Graphische Werk,* 2 vols. New York: Ernest Rathenau, 1967.

David Hockney

Midland Group and the Scottish Arts Council. *David Hockney Prints 1954-77.* Introduction by Andrew Brighton. Edinburgh: Petersburg Press, 1979.

Jasper Johns

Field, Richard. *Jasper Johns: Prints 1970-1977.* Middletown: Wesleyan University Press, 1978.

———. *Jasper Johns: Prints 1960-1970.* (Exhibition Catalogue) Philadelphia: Philadelphia Museum of Art, 1970.

Wassily Kandinsky

Roethel, Hans K. *Kandinsky: Das Graphische Werk.* Köln: M. Dumont, Schauberg, 1970.

Ernst-Ludwig Kirchner

Dube, A. and W.-D. *E.L. Kirchner, Das Graphische Werk.* Munich: Prestel-Verlag, 1967.

Paul Klee

Kornfeld, E.W. *Verzeichnis des Graphischen Werkes von Paul Klee.* Bern: Kornfeld und Klipstein, 1963.

Reginald Marsh

Sasowsky, Norman. *The Prints of Reginald Marsh.* New York: Clarkson N. Potter, Inc., 1976.

Henri Matisse

Katalog Pully. *Henri Matisse: Gravures et Lithographies de 1900-1929.* (Exposition Annuelle de gravures et dessins) Pully, 1970.

Lieberman, William S. *Matisse: Fifty Years of His Graphic Art.* New York: George Braziller, 1956.

Joan Miró

Joan Miró Lithographe, 4 vols. Paris: Maight Editeur, 1930-1969. (Vol. 4 in preparation.)

Benhoura, Margueritte. *Miró: L'oeuvre Graphique.* Introduction by Alexandre Cirici. (Exhibition catalogue) Paris: Musee d'art Moderne de la Ville de Paris, 1974.

Edvard Munch

Schiefler, Gustav. *Verzeichnis des Graphischen Werk Edvard Munch,* 2 vols., 1906 and 1906-1926. Berlin: Euphorion Verlag, 1906, 1927. Reprint. Oslo: J.W. Cappelens Forlag, 1974.

Emil Nolde

Schiefler, Gustav, Mosel, Christel. *Emil Nolde: Das Graphische Werk,* 2 vols. Köln, 1966, 1967.

Pablo Picasso

Bloch, Georges. *Picasso: Catalogue de l'Oeuvre Gravé et Lithographie 1904-1967,* 3 vols. Bern: Kornfeld und Klipstein, 1968, 1966-1969, 1971.

———. *Picasso: 347,* 2 vols. New York: Random House/Maecenas Press, 1970.

Karshan, Donald H. *Picasso Linocuts 1958-1963.* New York: Tudor Publishing Co., 1968.

Rembrandt van Rijn

Hind, A. *A Catalogue of Rembrandt's Etchings Chronologically Arranged and Completely Illustrated,* 2 vols. London: Methuen and Co., 1923.

Georges Rouault

Kornfeld & Klipstein, *Auktionskatalog (Auktion 120).* Bern: Kornfeld und Klipstein, 1966.

James Abbott-McNeill Whistler

Kennedy, Edward G. *The Etched Work of Whistler.* New York: The Grolier Club of the City of New York, 1910.

Note: Print titles in auction catalogues are often followed by a notation such as: (B.587;M134). The abbreviation indicates the standard reference(s) on the artist's work and under what number the particular print is listed in the book. In this example for Picasso's 1949 lithograph, *Femme au Fauteuil No. 1,* the B directs us to number 587 in Georges Bloch's book listed above, and the M 134, to listing 134 in the Mourlot reference above. Such guides are especially important with old master prints where numerous editions may exist, and with prints such as *Femme au Fauteuil* in which different states (variations) were made under the same title.

Real Estate—Commercial and Industrial

*J. Marc Myers**

BASIC CHARACTERISTICS

Commercial and industrial real estate includes office buildings, shopping centers, and warehouses. The office buildings group includes single and multi-story suburban structures and high-rise central city buildings.

The shopping centers group includes strip centers (5,000 to 50,000 square feet) without anchor tenants; community centers (50,000 to 250,000 square feet) normally anchored by at least one grocery and one drug store; specialty centers (50,000 square feet and up) for tenants with similar products, such as a fashion center; and regional malls (up to 2 million square feet) anchored by several major department stores.

Industrial buildings include dock-height rail- and nonrail-served warehouses, grade-level service center buildings, office-showroom facilities, and research and development (R&D) or tech center buildings.

Principal Determinants of Value

The most commonly used approaches to determining value of commercial and industrial real estate are through calculation of capitalized cash flow and the establishment of reproduction costs.

Current capitalized cash flow. In this approach, assume that a property with a net cash flow of $50,000 per year has a market value range of $555,555 to $500,000, determined by capitalizing the cash flow (dividing the cash flow by a market-derived capitalization rate) at a market rate of between 9 and 10 percent. The most common methods used to establish the value of an income property are pre-debt analysis and cash-on-cash analysis. In pre-debt analysis, operating expenses are deducted from gross revenue and the resulting net operating income is capitalized to indicate the value of the real estate. Then the equity is determined by subtracting any outstanding debt on the property. Cash-on-cash analysis is determined similarly to the pre-debt method except that cash flow is capitalized to estimate the net value of the property. The following table compares the two methods, assuming a typical 100,000-square-foot warehouse.

* J. Marc Myers is a Partner in Trammel Crow Company, Dallas.

		Pre-Debt Method		*Cash-on-Cash Method*
Potential gross rent		$220,000		$220,000
Less: Vacancies		11,000		11,000
Property taxes		20,000		20,000
Insurance ($0.03/s.f.)		3,000		3,000
Maintenance ($0.02/s.f.)		2,000		2,000
Management		6,600		6,600
Leasing commission		5,000		5,000
Pre-debt income		$172,400		$172,400
	Capitalize at 10%	$1,724,000	Less: Debt service	120,000
	Less: Mortgage	1,000,000	Cash flow	$ 52,400
	Balance	$ 724,000	Capitalize at 10%	$524,000
Equity value		$ 724,000		$524,000

In this example, the pre-debt method indicates a value of $1,724,000 or $17.24 per square foot, whereas the cash-on-cash method indicates a value of $1,524,000 ($524,000 equity plus $1 million mortgage balance.) The pre-debt method generally indicates a higher value since overall capitalization rates in recent years have been generally lower than the mortgage constant.

The pre-debt method is typically used for financial statements, but the cash-on-cash method is virtually always used for investment purposes. Since fixed mortgages are, as a practical matter, not available for real estate invesment today, the pre-debt method should be used in virtually all circumstances.

The capitalization rate is established by transactions in the market place and varies according to the type of real estate, the location and age of the project, whether single- or multi-tenant creditworthiness of the tenants, design of the project, size of the financial transaction, and the investor's requirement and expectation regarding yield over the investment holding period.

Reproduction costs. Reproduction costs (the total cost to construct a comparable new structure) can be determined by consulting with an architect or contractor with experience in the area of the proposed investment. Purchasing a property at a price below reproduction cost can help assure faster lease-up because of the low competitive advantage and can also result in a larger profit in the event the property is sold or refinanced.

Capitalized cash flow vs. reproduction costs. An investor may be willing to purchase real estate at a yield of only 4 percent if the reproduction cost or the existing rental rates are below market. For example, the typical warehouse used in the pre-debt and cash-on-cash analysis showed a value of approximately $17.24 per square foot during the initial lease terms. Assuming the terms of the leases were three years, the increases in rent will substantially increase the cash flow of the property and the resulting market value. Assuming a 25 percent increase in rents (8 percent per year), the following would be the impact for the same 100,000-square-foot warehouse.

		Pre-Debt Method		*Cash-on-Cash Method*
Gross rent		$275,000		$275,000
Less: Vacancy		13,750		13,750
Property taxes		20,000		20,000
Insurance ($0.03/s.f.)		3,000		3,000
Maintenance ($0.02/s.f.)		2,000		2,000
Management		7,250		7,250
Commission		6,250		6,250
Pre-debt income		$222,750		$222,750
	Capitalize at 10%	$2,227,500	Less: Debt service	120,000
	Value per square foot	$22.27	Cash flow	$102,750
	Increase in value	28%	Increase in cash flow	96%

An investor may decline the purchase of a property where the capitalized value substantially exceeds the project's reproduction cost, because the yield would be reduced substantially in the event of a vacancy. For the investor, the ideal balance is where the capitalized value of the investment approximates the reproduction cost of the real estate.

Kinds of Commercial Real Estate Investment

Purchase 100 percent interest and manage the property. This option may require that the investor build a staff of property managers, leasing agents, and so forth, and is generally not economical unless the investment is substantial, repetitive, and continues over a significant period. Outright purchase of the property generally requires less documentation and gives the investor 100 percent of cash flow and residual value. However, the investor should be cautious about the quality of the construction and staff marketing capabilities and management experience.

Purchase 100 percent and retain management by the seller. Today, most office buildings, warehouses, and shopping centers are constructed by major developers whose leasing and management experience and expertise are generally available to the real estate investor for a fee ranging from 2 to 5 percent of the gross income. For this fee, the developer will provide accounting, property management, and marketing services.

Purchase of 50 percent interest on a joint venture basis. Many investors prefer that the seller develop, manage, and retain an interest in the property, since the seller should have an incentive to make the property perform for the benefit of both the seller and investor. Because the seller's interest is structured as a mortgage, the developer can take advantage of substantial tax benefits.

Joint venture of property to be developed. In this arrangement, the investor contributes the majority of capital required and the developer constructs, leases, and manages the property for the joint venture and shares in the ownership and tax benefits on a pre-determined basis.

Convertible mortgage. The investor advances the majority of the funds as a mortgage convertible to an equity interest in the real estate at a pre-determined future date. This arrangement minimizes documentation and provides the investor an opportunity to determine whether the property performs as expected before converting to an ownership opportunity.

Sale-leaseback. The owner-occupant sells the property to an investor and simultaneously executes a lease on the property on mutually agreeable terms and conditions. This method is most commonly associated with industrial buildings, although there are some opportunities for sale-leasebacks in office buildings. A sale-leaseback may be advantageous to an owner who can use the cash proceeds for expansion of the business or to reduce short-term bank debt. In addition, the owner can take advantage of the capital appreciation of the building, and rental payments to the investor are deductible as an ordinary business expense. For the investor, the sale-leaseback can provide an immediate income-producing asset without a vacancy risk, and lease terms can often be structured at rates and terms better than those available in the general market. In addition, sale-leaseback transactions are done on a net basis, which reduces the investor's management and maintenance responsibilities. The investor should place particular emphasis on the creditworthiness of the tenant and on the nature and marketability of the real estate, and ensure that both the rentals paid by the tenant and the purchase price of the building are consistent with market transactions.

ATTRACTIVE FEATURES

Appreciation

The principal incentive for investing in real estate is potential appreciation that will equal or exceed the inflation rate, thus providing a hedge against inflation during the period in which the property provides a satisfactory cash return on the investment.

During the past decade, office buildings, warehouses, and shopping centers have appreciated in value approximately 10 percent per year compounded annually while generating an average cash return growth rate of approximately 8 percent per year non-compounded.

Table 1 on page 706 indicates the estimated yield on investment of a typical industrial building. Market renewal rates are computed by assuming that market

TABLE 1. Operating Projections for the Period Beginning Jan. 1, 1982

Cost	*1982* $3,000,000	*1983* $3,000,000	*1984* $3,000,000	*1985* $3,000,000	*1986* $3,000,000	*1987* $3,000,000	*1988* $3,000,000	*1989* $3,000,000	*1990* $3,000,000	*1991* $3,000,000	*1992* $3,000,000
Income											
Rents—A Property	$ 97,574	$ 97,574	$ 97,574	$ 97,574	$ 97,574	$ 97,574	$ 97,574	$ 97,574	$ 97,574	$ 97,574	$ 97,574
Rents—B Property	57,024	57,024	62,726	63,867	63,867	63,867	63,867	70,347	71,643	71,643	87,143
Rents—C Property	47,362	47,362	47,362	59,676	59,676	59,676	75,170	75,170	75,170	94,656	94,656
Rents—D Property	16,940	16,940	19,500	21,340	21,340	24,580	26,880	26,880	30,960	33,860	33,860
Rents—E Property	15,720	15,720	17,760	17,760	17,760	22,380	22,380	22,380	28,180	28,180	28,180
Rents—F Property	31,075	31,075	37,523	38,813	38,813	47,590	49,338	49,338	54,829	62,150	62,150
Rents—G Property	26,419	26,419	27,585	33,306	33,306	34,764	41,942	41,942	43,764	52,802	52,802
Rents—H Property	81,700	81,700	81,700	81,700	84,882	120,056	120,056	122,636	151,274	151,274	154,542
Rents—I Property	93,412	93,412	93,412	117,700	117,700	117,700	148,339	148,339	148,339	186,825	186,825
Rents—J Property	70,127	93,420	93,420	111,606	117,709	117,709	140,628	148,351	148,351	177,124	186,840
Less Vacancy	− 10,747	− 11,213	− 11,571	− 12,867	− 13,053	− 14,118	− 15,723	− 16,059	− 17,002	− 19,122	− 19,691
Total Income	$526,606	$549,433	$566,991	$630,475	$639,574	$691,778	$770,451	$786,898	$833,082	$936,966	$964,881
Expense											
Ground Lease	$86,292	$86,292	$86,292	$86,292	$86,292	$86,292	$86,292	$86,292	$86,292	$112,192	$112,192
Management fee	21,064	21,977	22,680	25,219	25,583	27,671	30,818	31,476	33,323	37,479	38,595
Total Expenses	$107,356	$108,269	$108,972	$111,511	$111,875	$113,963	$117,110	$117,768	$119,615	$149,671	$150,787
Net Cash Flow	$419,250	$441,164	$458,019	$518,964	$527,699	$577,815	$653,341	$669,130	$713,467	$787,295	$814,094
Less Depreciation	− 159,000	− 159,000	− 159,000	− 159,000	− 159,000	− 159,000	− 159,000	− 159,000	− 159,000	− 159,000	− 39,000
Taxable Income	$260,250	$282,164	$299,019	$359,964	$368,699	$418,815	$494,341	$510,130	$554,467	$628,295	$775,094
Net Cash Flow	$419,250	$441,164	$458,019	$518,964	$527,699	$577,815	$653,341	$669,130	$713,467	$787,295	$814,094
Yield	13.97%	14.71%	15.27%	17.30%	17.59%	19.26%	21.78%	22.30%	23.78%	26.24%	27.14%

SOURCE: Author's data

rates are increasing by 8 percent, compounded annually. It assumes that "x" percentage of the building is leased under long-term leases with fixed renewal options at less than market rates, that half of the remaining space is leased under five-year leases, and half under three-year leases. The projection assumes that as leases roll over at market rates, rentals increase at the rate of 8 percent compounded annually. This project would generate approximately 22 percent return after six years and the value of the property at that time would be approximately $6.5 million ($653,341 capitalized at 10 percent) versus an initial investment of $3 million.

Cash Return

At 95 percent occupancy, investment real estate should provide a return on total costs of 12 to 13.5 percent upon completion and initial lease-up. Return on total costs for the initial lease term is approximately the same for warehouses, shopping centers, and office buildings. For leveraged projects, the returns on cash invested are increased substantially. For example, if the property described in Table 1 on page 706 was mortgaged for $2,400,000 at a rate of 12 percent, the return on investment increases from 13.97 percent to 15.35 percent during the initial term. Assuming the debt service were fixed for at least ten years, the yield on investment (total costs) during year seven would increase from 21.78 percent on an unleveraged basis to 44.60 percent on a leveraged basis.

Favorable Tax Treatment

Another major benefit of owning real estate is the favorable tax treatment available to the investor-owners. Real estate is the only investment not subject to the at-risk rules. Therefore, a partner as well as an investor-owner can deduct tax losses in excess of actual money invested in addition to the pro rata share of nonrecourse debt. All other investment activities require the investor to be on the hook for each dollar of tax losses deducted.

The Economic Recovery Tax Act of 1981 allows owners of office buildings, warehouses, and shopping centers the option of a fifteen-year straight-line or accelerated (175 percent declining balance) depreciation. (See Table 2 on page 709 and Figure 1 on page 708.) If straight-line depreciation is used, profits from the sale of the property are taxed at a capital gains rate (maximum rate of 20 percent). However, if accelerated depreciation is elected, profit from the sale of the property is taxed as ordinary income to the extent of all depreciation previously deducted. (See Figure 2 on page 712.)

With fixed mortgage debt, office buildings, warehouses, and shopping centers depreciated on a straight-line basis would provide enough taxable losses to shelter cash flow during the first five to seven years of the project in addition to generating excess taxable losses to shelter other income.

The operating projection of an actual building displayed in Table 3 on page 710 indicates a tax loss for income tax purposes of $3,629 in 1982, yet the project

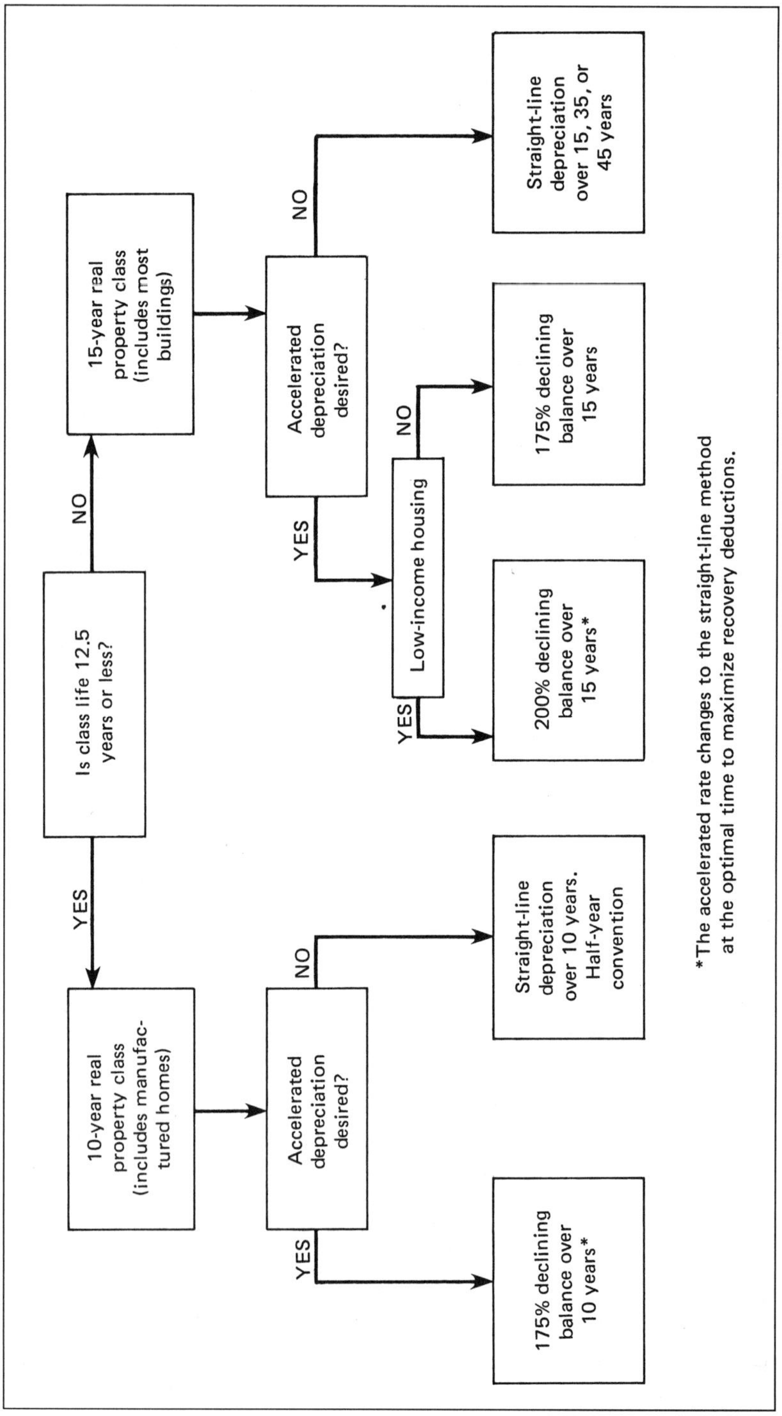

FIG. 1. Recovery Class and Allowable Cost Recovery Methods for Buildings
SOURCE: Texas Real Estate Research Center

TABLE 2. Accelerated Cost Recovery Tables for All Buildings Except Low-Income Housing (Based on calendar year taxpayers)

If the recovery year is:	*The applicable percentage is:**											
	Jan.	*Feb.*	*Mar.*	*Apr.*	*May*	*Jun.*	*Jul.*	*Aug.*	*Sept.*	*Oct.*	*Nov.*	*Dec.*
1	12%	11%	10%	9%	8%	7%	6%	5%	4%	3%	2%	1%
2	10	10	11	11	11	11	11	11	11	11	11	12
3	9	9	9	9	10	10	10	10	10	10	10	10
4	8	8	8	8	8	8	9	9	9	9	9	9
5	7	7	7	7	7	7	7	8	8	8	8	8
6	6	6	6	6	7	7	7	7	7	7	7	7
7	6	6	6	6	6	6	6	6	6	6	6	6
8	6	6	6	6	6	6	5	6	6	6	6	6
9	6	6	6	6	5	6	5	5	5	6	6	6
10	5	6	5	6	5	5	5	5	5	5	6	5
11	5	5	5	5	5	5	5	5	5	5	5	5
12	5	5	5	5	5	5	5	5	5	5	5	5
13	5	5	5	5	5	5	5	5	5	5	5	5
14	5	5	5	5	5	5	5	5	5	5	5	5
15	5	5	5	5	5	5	5	5	5	5	5	5
16	-	-	1	1	2	2	3	3	4	4	4	5

*Use the column for the month in the first year the property is placed in service.

SOURCE: Internal Revenue Service

generates a positive cash flow of $38,221. Accelerated depreciation for the same building would substantially increase the loss for tax purposes without affecting the net cash flow. However, taxable income increases during the life of the project. When carried to year thirteen, for example, this projection results in taxable income that approximates the cash flow from the project, at which time the investor should consider a sale, refinancing, or trade of the property. Since depreciation is the only deduction for nonleveraged property, the tax losses would shelter only approximately 30 percent of the taxable income for industrial projects and approximately 50 percent for office projects.

In addition, investors in real estate can take advantage of investment tax credits for a portion of the improvements ranging from 2 to 5 percent of hard costs on warehouses to 8 to 10 percent on shopping centers and office buildings.

Safety and Preservation of Capital

Safety of capital is the primary reason that many foreign investors have purchased real estate in the United States. In many cases, purchases that generate

TABLE 3. Operating Projections for the Period Beginning Jan. 1, 1981

	1981	*1982*	*1983*	*1984*	*1985*	*1986*	*1987*	*1988*	*1989*	*1990*	*1991*
Estimated Income	$194,105	$194,105	$194,105	$211,731	$211,731	$259,806	$281,981	$281,981	$281,981	$309,273	$376,482
Less Vacancies	–3,882	–3,882	–3,882	–4,235	–4,235	–5,196	–5,639	–5,639	–5,639	–6,185	–7,529
Rental Income	$190,223	$190,223	$190,223	$207,496	$207,496	$254,610	$276,342	$276,342	$276,342	$303,088	$368,953
Expense											
Maintenance	$ 775	$ 814	$ 814	$ 897	$ 942	$ 989	$ 1,039	$ 1,091	$ 1,145	$ 1,202	$ 1,262
Insurance	775	775	775	775	775	775	775	775	775	775	775
Prop. Tax	18,600	18,600	18,600	18,600	18,600	18,600	18,600	18,600	18,600	18,600	18,600
Mgt. Fee	5,707	5,707	5,707	6,255	6,255	7,688	8,290	8,290	8,290	9,039	11,069
Total Expenses	$25,857	$25,896	$25,936	$26,497	$26,542	$28,002	$28,704	$28,756	$28,810	$29,670	$31,706
Debt Service	$126,106	$126,106	$126,106	$126,106	$126,106	$126,106	$126,106	$126,106	$126,106	$126,106	$126,106
Net Cash Flow	38,260	38,221	38,181	54,893	54,848	100,502	121,532	121,480	121,426	147,312	211,141
Depreciation	49,128	49,128	49,128	49,128	49,128	49,128	49,128	45,195	45,195	45,195	45,195
Debt Amortization	6,622	7,278	8,039	8,881	9,811	10,838	11,973	13,227	14,611	16,141	17,830
Taxable Income	$ –4,246	$ –3,629	$ –2,908	$ 14,646	$ 15,531	$ 62,212	$ 84,377	$ 89,512	$ 90,842	$118,258	$183,776

SOURCE: Author's data

current returns as low as 2 percent indicate that the investor has assigned a higher priority to long-term safety in politically stable areas than to favorable short-term yield.

Opportunity to Leverage

It is quite common to borrow 75 percent of a property's cost. Thus, an investor can quadruple the amount of property working for him in terms of appreciation potential and can diversify investment equity into more properties. Generally, interest on the debt is tax deductible and all of the improvements can be depreciated for tax purposes.

Intangible Benefits

Many individuals derive pride and satisfaction from owning something visible and tangible, such as real estate. This is especially true in the case of real estate developers who have conceived, constructed, and leased the property. Developers take obvious pride and a sense of accomplishment in their responsibility for such landmark buildings as New York's Empire State Building, San Francisco's Embarcadaro Center, Atlanta's Peachtree Center, and Dallas' World Trade Center. Investors will often pay a premium for these landmarks, as demonstrated in the bidding war associated with the purchase of the Pan Am building in New York City, and the sale of the General Motors Building, also in New York.

POTENTIAL RISKS

Losses From Vacancies

Real estate is a cyclical industry that responds directly to the expansion or contraction of the general economy. An expanding economy generates higher retail sales, which in turn generates construction of shopping centers, and subsequently creates a demand for more warehouse space. Conversely, declining consumer purchases in a contracting economy often result in higher vacancies for shopping centers, office buildings, and warehouses.

Inasmuch as a slight reduction in property value can lead to a drastic percentage change in value of equity, slight changes in vacancy rates (and/or rental income and operating expenses) can lead to high percentage changes in cash flow. Consequently, investors should be mindful of the break-even point for property that they are considering.

Break-even occupancy (the point of zero cash flow) is approximately 80 percent for office buildings and shopping centers and approximately 75 percent for industrial real estate. Except for participating financing, practically all costs associated with real estate are fixed costs that are relatively unaffected as occupancy levels fluctuate; therefore, 100 percent of the potentially realizable cash flow from real estate results from the final 20 percent of occupancy. In other

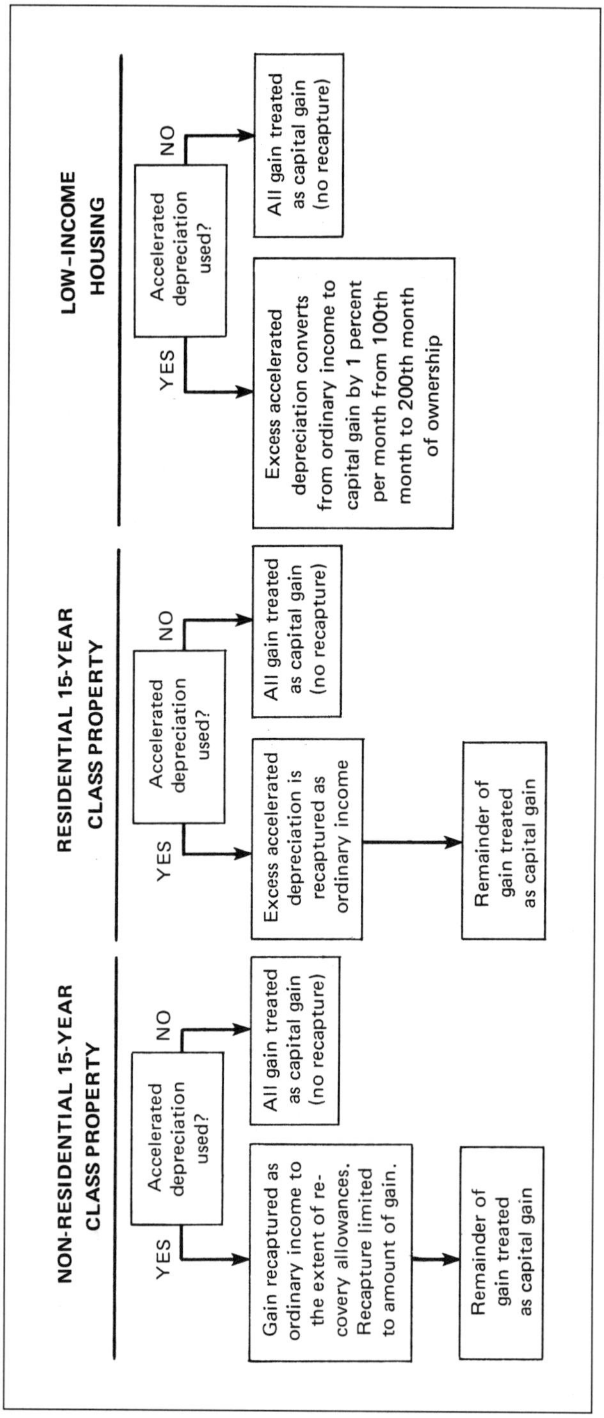

FIG. 2. Depreciation Recapture on Buildings (Disposition After Dec. 31, 1980 for ACRS Property)
SOURCE: Texas Real Estate Research Center

words, a fully leased property is twice as profitable as a property at 90 percent occupancy.

Adverse Trends

A major risk in owning real estate is a basic shift in the character of the neighborhood, city, or state in which the property is located. Property values can be adversely affected by a declining residential neighborhood, a change in the highway system serving the city, or the relocation of a major industry. National demographic trends, such as the migration of people and industry to the Sun Belt, can adversely affect real estate investments in entire geographic regions.

Functional Obsolescence

Office building values and profitability are affected most by functional obsolescence. Their ability to compete in the marketplace can decline as a result of insufficient floor space, inefficient and/or inadequate elevators, inefficient and outdated air conditioning and heating systems, or inadequate parking. Shopping centers can deteriorate as a result of poor management, improper tenant mix, or the loss of a major anchor store. Although warehouses are least affected by functional obsolescence, substantial vacancies can occur in industrial property as a result of low ceiling height, inadequate truck loading-maneuvering area, or inefficient bay spacing, as well as a change in neighborhood demographics.

Illiquidity

Since each real estate parcel must be analyzed separately and appraised as a separate investment, months are often required to convert real estate equity values to cash. During the last half of 1981, investors obtained 18 percent returns on short-term "paper" investments compared to a 10 percent return on investment real estate. Obviously, the growth of money market funds has absorbed some of the capital that would have been invested in real estate. However, as institutional investors have acquired more real estate during the past five years, liquidity for real estate has improved because general guidelines have been established for real estate transactions and institutional investors have brought a higher level of sophistication to the marketplace.

Regulatory Problems

Most regulatory problems associated with real estate apply to the development phase, and include zoning problems, neighborhood objections to shopping centers, height restrictions on office buildings, and difficulty in obtaining building permits. Although these issues arise before a project is constructed, there are additional risks after a project is completed, such as difficulties in obtaining a Certificate of Occupancy for either the initial or subsequent tenants, or in conforming to government-mandated changes such as those required by OSHA or the proposed federal guidelines for energy conservation.

TAX CONSEQUENCES

The tax advantages of commercial and industrial real estate investments are inseparable from their overall attractiveness. (See *Appreciation* and *Favorable Tax Treatment* and accompanying tables in this article.)

REPRESENTATIVE TYPES OF INVESTORS

Until the late 1970s, the majority of real estate was owned by individuals and development companies. Until that time, long-term mortgages were available at fixed interest rates and developers-investors could borrow 80 to 110 percent of the project cost. Equity requirements, if any, were supplied from a combination of internally generated cash, foreign investors and investors oriented to tax shelters. Approximately $15 billion per year was supplied to the real estate market by life insurance companies, savings and loan institutions, and banks. This stable, fixed-rate capital enabled thousands of individual investors and developers to accumulate substantial portfolios of real estate.

U.S. Pension Funds

During the past five years, pension funds have directly invested approximately $10 billion in real estate, representing 2 percent of their total assets. Guidelines issued by Employee Retirement Income Security Act (ERISA) are consistent with the investment of 10 percent of total assets in real estate. It is estimated that by 1990 total U.S. pension fund assets will exceed $1 trillion. More than 90 percent of pension assets invested in real estate are handled indirectly through life and casualty companies, which have the personnel and expertise in underwriting and investing in real estate.

Pension funds expect to receive internal rates of return of between 16 and 17 percent, beginning with an initial cash return of approximately 10 percent, and assuming increases in net income of 8 percent per year compounded and a sale of the real estate asset at the end of the tenth year. The bulk of this money is used to purchase a 100 percent interest in investment real estate with management provided by the developer. The balance of the money is invested in joint ventures with real estate developers.

Foreign Investors and Pension Funds

Foreign pension funds (principally European) have invested approximately $5 billion per year in real estate between 1970 and 1980. These investments were in the form of free and clear purchases in investment real estate as well as the purchase of partial interests. As discussed earlier, many foreign investors invest here because they consider the United States a politically stable location for investment, and U.S. real estate quite competitive compared to most European countries. For example, prime office land in most major European cities would cost in excess of $500 per square foot; the same property could be purchased in most American cities (except New York and San Francisco) in the range of $22 to $300 per square foot. The same discrepancy in price applies to agricultural land as well as to industrial properties and shopping centers.

U.S. Life and Casualty Companies

Until interest rates escalated dramatically in 1979, these institutions were content to make long-term fixed-rate mortgages to the real estate industry. However, as a result of the ensuing debacle in the bond market and the huge withdrawals by individual policy owners, the life and casualty industry had very little cash to loan or invest. As funds become available from premiums and investment income, this group is demanding a participation in the ownership of real estate as a condition to making a loan. This participation in ownership will reduce the potential investment rewards for individuals as well as developers and reflects the national trend toward consolidation of financial institutions and concentration of capital.

IMPORTANT FACTORS IN BUYING AND SELLING

Selecting a Broker or Salesperson

Selling commercial and industrial real estate is a specialty. Even in large cities, there may be only a few dozen specialists in office buildings, shopping centers, or warehouses. Some concentrate further in certain-sized buildings and/or in a certain part of a city or suburb. By specializing, a broker gets to know details about every property and every owner. A prospective purchaser should attempt to find such a specialist, particularly one with a reputation of reliability and trustworthiness. Property owners are good sources of information, as are bankers, lawyers, and other professionals.

Designations, such as CCIM (Certified Commercial Investment Member) and SIR (Society of Industrial Realtors), are also indications of the broker's affiliations and qualifications. These organizations are affiliates of the National Association of Realtors. Many outstanding brokers do not have and never will apply for these designations. Still, an investor who knows nothing about the type of property he plans to buy will face better odds of finding a qualified salesperson if he seeks out one who is designated.

Purchasing the Right Property

Selecting the right property and determining a fair price to offer the seller require careful attention. When buying, it is most important that investors select property that is suitable for their financial needs. Some investors like the idea of level, fixed income. For them, net leased property, with a very strong tenant and long-term lease, is ideal. Other investors want more of an inflation hedge, so lease escalation (according to the Consumer Price Index, for example) is sought, or renegotiated leases based on reappraisals or market rental rates are used. Still other investors in commercial property seek inflation protection through purchasing landmark buildings, especially sound structures or those on a large plot of land in the path of growth.

Determining price. Price is one item that is always negotiable in real estate. Unlike the financial and commodity markets, there are no published quotations. Transactions are private. Often, concessions such as favorable seller-financing obscure the true value of property.

Some property is on the market almost continuously. The owner maintains an asking price of 15 to 25 percent above market value, hoping for an anxious buyer to pay the asking price. In bad times, particularly when financing is difficult to arrange, some property may be on the market for 15 to 25 percent below its value. Real estate is illiquid, and some sellers can become anxious or desperate. A good broker will want repeat business, so he will advise if a proposed price is far from the market. It is perfectly acceptable for a transaction to occur at a price above or below market value, so long as all parties are conscious of the facts. Brokers will carry negotiations between principals until a "meeting of the minds" is reached.

In some markets, space is quoted on a per-square-foot basis; in others, prices are based on capitalized cash flow or net operating income. In negotiating a purchase price, it is a good idea for the buyer to verify forecast income and operating expenses as carefully as possible. It is often possible to review the seller's records, compare forecast income to market norms, and read leases, mortgages, and other documents.

Location. Many investors want to purchase property near their homes (or home offices). It is easier to note property conditions, visit tenants and managers, and so forth. In recent years, however, there has been a fast-growing tendency to invest anywhere that a good deal can be found. Competent management combined with carefully written leases generally obviates the need for owner visits.

The investor must determine what part of the country is most desirable for investment. In recent years the Sun Belt, particularly Florida, Texas, and California, has attracted attention because of population growth. Some other factors include taxes, transportation facilities and access, political climate, labor supply, and competition.

Foreign investors may have certain preferences. Orientals invest heavily in California and Hawaii. German and Dutch investors prefer North Carolina and Virginia because of their investment in manufacturing. Latin American investors are heavily attracted to Florida because of its proximity and the availability of air travel. Some Middle Eastern investors put money in Houston because of its reputation as a center for refining and oil exploration. Canadian investors can be found in the downtown areas of almost all U.S. cities. Domestic investors may have similar biases for specific geographic areas.

Professional Advisers and Appraisals

Appraisals are often sought as assurance that the price is a fair one or that a proposed mortgage loan is comfortably within the property's market value, for insurance purposes, and for other reasons. The best-recognized appraisal designation is MAI (Member of the Appraisal Institute), an affiliate of the National Association of Realtors. The Society of Real Estate Appraisers in Chicago offers two designations for appraisers of income-producing property: SRPA (senior real property appraiser) and SREA (senior real estate appraiser).

The American Society of Counselors offers the CRE (Counselor of Real Estate) designation. These professionals may be helpful in matters beyond appraisal, such as suggesting alternative uses of land and buildings, and performing market studies.

MANAGING THE INVESTMENT

Few investors want the burdens of managing a commercial or industrial property. For a fee, usually in the range of 4 to 7 percent of gross income, professional management can be arranged. A good manager will assure that the property is leased to a good mix of tenants (leasing often calls for an additional fee), rents collected, daily maintenance performed and paid for, repairs done, and adequate insurance kept in force.

Tenant lease agreements determine not only the legal rights and obligations of landlord and tenant, but the services the landlord will provide and what the tenant must do. In a gross lease, the landlord is expected to pay taxes, insurance, utilities, and so on. In a net lease (also qualified as net-net or triple-net), the tenant pays for utilities, taxes, maintenance, and other expenses.

The simplest arrangement is a triple-net lease of a single-tenant building to a tenant such as K-Mart. This is a passive investment whereby the tenant is to do everything and pay all expenses. Such a lease should require the tenant to present annually documents showing that hazard and liability insurance premiums have been paid, and the same for taxes.

In regional malls, leases will vary among tenants. Major or anchor tenants sometimes own their land and buildings themselves or have net leases. Smaller tenants, located in a strip between the anchors, will frequently have gross leases with escalation clauses. The owner's obligations include parking lot and mall maintenance and whatever interior maintenance is described in the lease. There has been a recent trend toward requiring all tenants to pay a pro rata share of maintenance for the common areas.

Office buildings generally require daily cleaning and other maintenance. Owners (or their property managers) must properly manage utility costs and be certain that the building functions properly (elevators and lobby areas, for example, should be maintained in a safe condition).

Generally, management of commercial and industrial buildings is a specialty area. Expert management can be had in most large cities. The designation Certified Property Manager (CPM), which is offered by an affiliate of the National Association of Realtors, is a mark of professional competence.

GLOSSARY

after-tax cash flow— Actual spendable income from an investment after income taxes; net income increased by depreciation and reduced by mortgage principal amortization payments, less income tax payments.

anchor tenant— A major chain or department store that is strategically located in a shopping center so as to generate traffic for the smaller, satellite stores; sometimes called a "magnet store" or "traffic generator."

balloon mortgage— A mortgage for which the stipulated periodic payments do not result in complete amortization of principal at maturity, thus necessitating a final payment much larger than the previous ones.

before-tax cash flow— Actual spendable income from an investment before income taxes; rental income less cash payments for operating expenses and debt service.

capitalization rate— The rate at which a future flow of income is converted into a present value figure; expressed as a percentage.

commercial property— Improved real estate held by its owner for the production of income through leases for commercial or business use; for example, office buildings, retail stores, shopping centers.

debt service coverage ratio— The ratio of annual net operating income from a property to the annual debt service on a mortgage loan on the property; also, debt coverage ratio.

depreciation— The gradual loss or shrinkage of value of property (except land) due to wear and tear and the action of the elements; a tax-deductible expense for investment or business property.

equity— In accounting and finance, net ownership, that is the extent of the owner's right in a property above all claims and liens against it expressed in money value.

equity dividend rate— Before-tax cash flow divided by the initial equity investment.

financial leverage — See *leverage.*

gross rent multiplier— A rule-of-thumb method of appraising the fair market value of real estate by multiplying gross rental income by a factor that varies with the type of property and its location; also, gross multiplier or gross income multiplier.

internal rate of return— The discount rate that will produce a present value of cash inflows equal to that of cash outflows.

leasehold— An estate in realty that arises by virtue of a lease; the right of a lessee to the use and occupancy of real estate.

leverage— A financial term meaning a result that is disproportionate to the amount of equity investment; in real estate, a situation created when the debt service on funds borrowed to acquire the real estate is lower than the free-and-clear return from the real estate (upside leverage) or higher than the free-and-clear return (downside or reverse leverage).

net lease— A lease under which the lessee assumes the responsibility of paying all of the operating expenses of the property so that the rental received by the lessor is entirely net to the lessor; see also *triple-net lease.*

net operating income— The balance remaining after the operating expenses of a property are deducted from the gross rental income or gross receipts received from the property; in contrast to cash flow, net operating income is determined without deduction for debt service on any mortgages.

occupancy rate— The ratio of rented units or space to total rentable units or space in a property; expressed as a percentage.

percentage lease— A lease of commercial property under which the total rental to be paid by the tenant varies according to the business done by the tenant; the rental is usually determined by gross sales, gross revenues, or gross receipts.

pro forma statement— A financial statement for real estate projecting gross income, operating expenses, and net operating income for a future period (usually one year) based upon specified assumptions; literally, according to form.

reappraisal lease— A lease under which the rental is to be reappraised at periodic intervals during the life of the lease; normally used only for long-term leases.

replacement reserve— A fund set aside for making replacements of property; typically, required by a lender of a borrower in cases where owners install on the premises property with a short life expectancy, such as furniture, carpeting, appliances.

triple-net lease— a net lease under which the tenant is responsible for operating expenses, including real estate taxes, and debt service on a mortgage taken out by the landlord, as well as rental paid to the landlord; also, net-net net lease.

variable-rate mortgage— A mortgage that calls for installment payments of varying amounts during its term and may or may not be fully amortized (liquidated) at maturity.

TRADE ORGANIZATIONS

Building Owners and Managers Association, Washington, D.C.

Institute of Real Estate Management, Chicago, Ill.

National Association of Corporate Real Estate Executives (NACORE), Miami, Fla.

Real Estate Securities and Syndication Institute, Chicago, Ill.

Society of Industrial Realtors, Chicago, Ill.

LEADING DEALERS

Ackerman & Co., Atlanta, Ga.

Arthur Rubloff, Chicago, Ill.

Cabot, Cabot & Forbes, Boston, Mass.
Coldwell Banker, Los Angeles, Cal.
Gerald Hines, Houston, Tex.
Helmsley Spear, New York, N.Y.
Henry S. Miller, Dallas, Tex.
John B. Levy & Associates, Richmond, Va.
Questor Associates, San Francisco, Cal.
Trammell Crow, Dallas, Tex.
Vantage, Columbus, Ohio

SUGGESTED READING

Periodicals

The Appraisal Journal. Published by the American Institute of Real Estate Appraisers, National Association of Realtors, Chicago, Ill. Quarterly.

Journal of Property Management. Published by the Institute of Real Estate Management, National Association of Realtors, Chicago, Ill. Bimonthly.

Mortgage and Real Estate Executive's Report. Published by Warren, Gorham & Lamont, Boston, Mass. Biweekly.

National Real Estate Investor. Published by Communication Channels, Inc., Atlanta, Ga. Monthly.

Real Estate Review. Published by Warren, Gorham & Lamont, Boston, Mass. Quarterly.

SIR Reports. Published by the Society of Industrial Realtors, Washington, D.C. Monthly.

Reference Books

Arnold, Alvin. *The Arnold Encyclopedia of Real Estate.* Boston, Mass.: Warren, Gorham & Lamont, 1978.

———. *Real Estate Investor's Deskbook.* Boston, Mass.: Warren, Gorham & Lamont, 1982.

Building Owners and Managers Association International. *Downtown and Suburban Office Building Experience Exchange Report.* Washington, D.C. Annual.

Friedman, Jack P., and Ordway, Nicholas. *Income Property Appraisal and Analysis.* Reston, Virginia: Reston Publishing Co., 1981.

Johnson, Irvin E. *The Instant Mortgage-Equity Technique.* Lexington, Mass.: D.C. Heath & Co., 1972.

Kinnard, William N., and Messner, Stephen D. *Industrial Real Estate.* Washington, D.C.: Society of Industrial Realtors, 1979.

Urban Land Institute. *Dollars and Cents of Shopping Centers.* Washington, D.C. Annual.

Real Estate—Condominiums, Cooperatives, Timesharing

Keith B. Romney *

BASIC CHARACTERISTICS

History and Background

The concept of multiple ownership of a building has been known since at least the time of the Roman Empire. However, although there was some earlier condominium activity in Europe and South America, it was not until the 1920s that the cooperative concept was introduced into the United States. (Condominiums were introduced later, in 1960.) Since then, because of the increasing cost of the single-family residence, there has been a great deal of interest in and development of cooperative and condominium first-homes as well as resort condominiums.

The timeshare aspect of condominiums is a more recent arrival. The term is borrowed from timesharing by users of computer equipment. Resort timesharing was first introduced in Europe in the late 1960s and commenced in the United States in the early 1970s, primarily in response to the inability of recession-plagued developers to market whole condominiums in resort areas. They began to market periods of time to individual purchasers.

Resort timesharing is a hybrid, combining the attributes of being an owner with attributes of being a guest, with all of the attendant hospitality and management functions of a hotel. The management becomes very important to maintain the continuity and quality of the project because owners, many of whom live a long distance from the resort and only buy a few weeks' time, do not have the voice or influence of whole-unit owners, many of whom live on site. Fee timeshares are bought and sold in the same manner as other real estate, but right-to-use timeshares (no fee interest is acquired) can only be used and dealt with as allowed in the documentation, and it is not uncommon to find a prohibition against selling. Some projects have provisions for resales while others, if resales are allowed, let the owners make their own arrangements.

To put condominium and timeshare in perspective, visualize a large tract of land. (1) Divide the land into separate parcels that can be deeded to various individuals. This is fee-simple land ownership. (2) Assume that some or all of these individuals build structures upon their land. This connotes single-building

* Keith B. Romney is Founder of Keith Romney Associates, Condominium and Timesharing Consultants, Salt Lake City, Utah.

ownership. (3) Suppose one individual builds a twenty-unit apartment house. The building is divided so that each apartment owner owns his own unit. It is legally described and separately deeded. (4) Divide these units as to time, and fifty owners are sold one week's usage each.

In this simple example, step 3, which divides the apartment building into individual units, corresponds with the concept of condominium. It is the legal concept whereby an individual unit is described and deeded, and the ownership rests with the individual purchaser. The swimming pool, grounds, hallways, and other facilities are called "common elements," and are owned by all of the individual unit-owners collectively.

Step 4 in the preceding scenario describes timesharing. The timeshare concept requires a consistency of management because most of the owners occupy their units for one week, several weeks, or a relatively short period of time. Therefore, timeshare owners are not present to conduct the affairs of management.

A condominium has many of the characteristics of a single-family residence as an investment, but it is distinguished primarily by the required membership in a homeowners association, involvement with management, and the ownership of common elements that generally have restrictions on their usage. The owner of a single-family residence could probably tear up his back lawn and plant a garden. Because the owner of a condominium is not the sole owner of the back lawn, garden, or grounds, he would need the permission of the homeowners association to make any changes in the common elements.

Cooperatives offer many of the same features as condominiums, but there is a major difference in the ownership form. In a cooperative, a nonprofit corporation owns the land and buildings. The corporation blanket-mortgages the entire property. Shares of stock in the corporation are sold by the developer. The purchase of certain shares allows the stockholder to use a certain dwelling unit in the building. Stockholders are assessed each month for their pro rata share of mortgage payments, taxes, and maintenance. Section 216 of the Internal Revenue Code allows tenant-stockholders to deduct interest and property taxes as well as business depreciation for the portion of the dwelling used in a trade or business.

The chart below summarizes some of the major differences between condominiums and cooperatives.

	Condominium	*Cooperative*
Finance unit individually	Yes	No
Finance entire property	No	Yes
Owners personally liable for mortgage	Yes	No
Make up unpaid taxes on others' units	No	Yes
Make up unpaid principal and interest on others' units	No	Yes
Tax deductions for interest and property taxes	Yes	Yes, if certain provisions are met

Current Standing

Condominiums as well as cooperatives and timeshare units have been inflation-responsive and their popularity has increased substantially since their respective introductions. Inasmuch as they are composed primarily of land and building construction materials, like single-family residences, they have continued to increase in value. The fact that there are some economies achieved in construction of condominiums as compared to single-family residences has in many instances brought dwellings into a more attractive price range. The timeshare has also been inflation-responsive and many persons who have purchased timeshares in resort areas do so to avoid the ever-increasing costs of hotel or resort accommodations. By purchasing a timeshare, they are able to secure tomorrow's vacations at today's cost.

As with single-family residences, condominiums and cooperatives can be found in most price levels. There are entry-level economy condominiums at one end of the spectrum, and luxury high-rise or luxury resort condominiums at the other end. The same holds true for timeshares. There are conversions from small motels up to new construction units in luxury resort surroundings. Condominiums are found in most major cities across the United States and are now spreading to many smaller cities and suburbs. Cooperatives have been quite popular in New York City and its surrounding area, but, in other regions, they have not spread as rapidly as condominiums. Timeshares are found primarily in either destination resort areas or regional resort areas. Recently, timeshared units have begun to appear in some urban locations, such as San Francisco, New Orleans, New York City, and Salt Lake City.

ATTRACTIVE FEATURES

Psychological Benefit of Ownership

The American dream usually includes the ownership of land and property. Condominiums and cooperatives, much like single-family residences, fulfill this dream and give the psychological benefit of ownership. Most people are aware of the many great fortunes that have been founded upon ownership and development of real estate. Americans like to consider themselves a landed class of people and therefore there is a deep desire to own and control property. Condominiums in fee-simple ownership fulfill this desire.

Inflation Hedge

Given the length of time needed to construct a project, high inflation has produced a narrow but lucrative investment opportunity: the investment, or, in some cases, the speculation, on presales. Investors place deposits on cooperatives and condominiums in projects to be constructed and then sell at a profit before the closing on the unit. This practice has been particularly prevalent in the "hot" areas of the early 1980s, such as Hawaii, California, and Florida.

A somewhat similar method of investment based on inflation has been to purchase condominiums in overbuilt or low-demand markets and hold them for resale until demand improves or the excess inventory is reduced.

Timeshare investments have also had significant price increases in their relatively short history. One survey indicated that timeshare investments have been increasing in value at a rate of 26 percent per year. Specific examples of this are the Imperial, in Hawaii, and Laguna Shores, in California. One-week ownership of the "Ohia" unit (a studio unit) in the Imperial increased from $2,900 to $6,300 in the first eighteen months of the project. Likewise, the "Captain" unit in the Laguna Shores project increased from $3,500 to $6,500 in eight months.

Because land and existing buildings have been inflation-responsive and have received much media attention as being good hedges against inflation, there has been a great deal of interest in ownership of property. Condominiums, cooperatives, and timeshares, like single-family residences, have responded to the pressures of inflation and have continued to increase in value.

Capital Gains Treatment

Condominiums and cooperatives, like many other investments that are held for the period of one year, qualify for long-term capital gains. There are investors who purchase them with the intention of selling after one year to qualify for the capital gains treatment. As a simple example, assume the purchase of three condominiums per year with an initial price of $100,000 per condominium, 10 percent down in each case, with a 10 percent inflation rate. Further assume that after the end of the first year, three condominiums will be sold each year and the down payment for the next year's purchase of condominiums will be taken out of the proceeds. For simplicity, assume no real estate commissions. In the first year, the investor will spend $30,000 to purchase $300,000 worth of condominiums. At the end of that year, the $300,000 will have inflated to $330,000, giving the investor a $30,000 profit plus the return of the $30,000 down payment, or a total of $60,000. He now buys three condominiums at the new, inflated price of $110,000, requiring an investment of $33,000. This means the investor has $27,000 left over from the $60,000 proceeds from the sale of the first three condominiums. At the end of the second year, the three condominiums have inflated to $363,000, an increase of $33,000. Taking the profit of $33,000 plus the down payment of $33,000, the investor now has $66,000. His purchase of an additional three condominiums will now cost $121,000 each or $363,000. After subtracting the down payment of $36,300, the investor has $29,700.

This example could go on from year to year, but the point is that if the condominiums were held for a year, these gains will be taxed at the capital gains rate and not at the ordinary income rate. An investor could vary this theme to meet his situation. By purchasing more units initially and holding them longer he can avoid the costs of sale and turnover. An investor who needs little or no income can wait and defer sales until a later time, or take any number of approaches that would enable the condominium to be a good investment vehicle for his portfolio. And, again, all this profit can be taxed at the capital gains rate.

Safety of Principal

One of the primary incentives and motivations for owning real estate is the safety of principal. Real estate traditionally has not been as volatile as some other investment mediums. There have been times when real estate sold slowly, and times when appreciation was modest, but real estate has traditionally provided safety of principal. Condominiums are no exception.

Cash Return (Income)

The cash return on condominium or cooperative ownership generally is less than on other investment mediums. However, many investors feel that this is a small price to pay for the safety of principal and for the appreciation. The return on condominium investment does not flow in on a monthly basis as does the return on a bond or other, similar investments. However, many investors have found that they can provide a periodic income by refinancing their properties. Borrowing money normally is not a taxable event. Therefore, properties can be refinanced and cash withdrawn. Later, upon sale of the condominiums, there will be less cash proceeds and the same amount of tax to be paid.

For simplicity's sake, assume the purchase of a condominium for $50,000 and assume the refinancing of that condominium whereby the investor gets $15,000 of the appreciated value of the property. This will not have any tax consequence at the time the cash is received, but will be deferred to point of sale.

There is, of course, some rental income to be derived from condominium ownership and investment, but, as previously mentioned, this is generally insufficient to provide an adequate return on the monies invested.

POTENTIAL RISKS

Stability of Principal

For many years single-family residences were not considered good investments, but the perception of this has changed greatly in recent years, which have been characterized by high inflation. Many writers now indicate that single-family residences may be the best investments some people ever make. This also can be said of condominiums. Because they have participated in the rate of inflation and because demand for condominiums has kept up with the need for housing, which has been strong (with the exception of areas that have had temporary overbuilding), they have been a good investment. Timeshare has also participated in this phenomenon, although its history is relatively short. Most new industries go through a shake-out period. The prospect of high returns has drawn and will continue to draw many developers into the timeshare field. An industry-wide overdevelopment could result in at least a temporary glut of timeshare offerings. However, to date, developers and purchasers of timeshares have been able to sell them quite readily.

Particularly during the inflationary years of the 1970s, an investment in condominium or timeshare has been and remains an excellent way to protect principal, because these investments have tended to appreciate, at least at the inflation rate.

Market Volatility

The possibility always exists that overbuilding will occur in a particular area, making it temporarily difficult to sell a condominium. Other than that, condominium, cooperative, and timeshare have been and continue to be steady means of protecting principal. These investments do not react to the daily news, rumors of war, overseas crises, or many other of the myriad of factors that cause more volatile investments to change price rapidly. These investments have been steady and represent the American commitment to investment in land and property. Most people agree that land and property ventures are substantial and sound.

Liquidity

In a normal market, condominium, cooperative, and timeshare units would be salable within a reasonable period of time. This period of time usually can be determined by the average length of time it takes to sell similar properties in a particular area. Very often, local real estate boards keep accurate information on this time period and it is available simply by contacting a real estate broker or local real estate board. However, it should be pointed out that in times of recession, economic stagnation, high interest rates, or a general unavailability of financing, condominium and, to a lesser degree, timeshare, may take a longer period of time to sell than would be expected under normal conditions. This is a special consideration for investors in this medium and should be considered in the timing of investment sales so as to prevent having to cut price, and therefore profit, in order to accomplish a sale. In other words, real estate does not have the liquidity of some other investments such as stocks, bonds, gold, etc. There are many who feel that the protection and stability of principal is worth the loss of liquidity and, therefore, many continue to invest in condominiums and cooperatives for this reason.

Source of Income

Traditionally, single-family residences have not been an economically viable investment relative to income. Condominiums and cooperatives share this characteristic. Demand for condominiums is expected to continue to grow, but land costs, building costs, and financing costs are also expected to increase or remain high. This may prevent condominium from being an economical rental for owners. Although subsequent increases in land and building value do not affect coverage of rent, they do affect return on equity and need to be compared with alternative investments in that respect. Long-term, fixed-rate mortgages do not affect rent coverage, but variable-rate mortgages do.

An investor who holds a piece of real estate encounters certain costs, such as debt service, taxes, and expenses. He also must consider what his equity could earn in an alternative investment, and he is entitled to a return on that equity. Generally, obtainable rent will not cover debt service, taxes, expenses, and return on equity. After a period of time, the rental income may cover these costs, but it usually fails to cover if consideration is given to the return on equity as that equity is increased by inflation.

Many condominium owners have found that if the investment is held long enough, and if inflation increases the rents that can be obtained, there is usually a point at which the rental income can carry the debt service and expenses. However, if a true investment approach is used, and the owner's equity is computed based on the inflated value of the condominium, the rental income will not yield the rate of return that would be expected from income-based investments. However, those who invest in condominiums generally are seeking safety of principal and appreciation (most of which has come through inflation) rather than income. In other words, condominium investors seek capital gains rather than cash flow.

Regulatory and Political Risks

The risk factors in purchasing an existing condominium or cooperative are relatively few. One must always consider the possibility that zoning on adjacent property will allow undesirable business, industry, or development. However, the risks of going into a proposed multiple-unit project are much greater because of the government processes through which these projects must pass. There are now environmental considerations as well as zoning considerations in nearly all areas of the country. Certain localities oppose apartment projects and condominium projects routinely. There are other areas that, for political reasons, make it difficult for a multiple-unit project to get the necessary construction permits and approvals.

The trend to convert apartment projects to condominium often is opposed by local government authorities, both regulatory and political, who feel that widespread conversions could substantially reduce the number of available apartments for rentals. Not everyone can afford to purchase a condominium, and government authorities assume responsibility for either providing adequate rentals or making certain that adequate rentals are provided. Partially as a result of rent ceilings and controls, many owners of apartment house rental property are very interested in converting to condominium, because their projects have become uneconomical as apartments.

Therefore, although the risk associated with investing in an individual existing condominium is minimal, particularly if the investor goes through the normal steps of checking out the location, zoning, and property, and reviewing the condominium documents, the risk of investing in proposed projects or conversion projects is much greater due to governmental attitudes and restrictions.

TAX CONSEQUENCES

Ownership of condominiums and qualified cooperatives offers all the tax benefits to the owner-occupant that owning a single-family residence does. The owner-occupant can deduct mortgage interest and property taxes, and the increase in value or appreciation is taxed at capital gains rates if the property is held for more than one year. In addition, those who use a condominium as a principal residence may sell it at a gain. If they purchase another residence that costs at least as much as the amount realized from the sale of their old one, they can defer tax on the gain. Those over age 55 can exclude up to $125,000 of gain from tax, once in a lifetime, if they meet certain qualifications, regardless of whether they buy another residence.

Regarding investor-owner second-home condominiums, the Tax Reform Act of 1976 put a limitation on the ability of the owner to take deductions. The general rule is that the owner cannot deduct business-related expenses that exceed the gross income, and there are time restrictions on the owner's usage. Prior to 1976, the rule of law was whether or not this was a casual income-producing activity, and the test was unclear. The IRS now has made the test very clear, and has thereby reduced the economic ability of an investor to carry a second home or vacation condominium with only an occasional rental.

However, one of the greatest benefits of condominiums as an investment is the ability to obtain profit at the capital gains rate. The sale of a condominium as an investment prior to the one-year time period results in ordinary income. This may be acceptable to nonprofit institutions, but this investment usually should not be undertaken by the average investor unless the holding period can qualify for the capital gains rate.

REPRESENTATIVE TYPES OF INVESTORS

Because of the broad availability of condominiums and cooperatives, as well as the wide selection of types, locations, price ranges, quality, down payment, and so on, they have become an attractive vehicle to almost all classes of investors, with the exception of those seeking income. The majority of investors in condominiums have been individual rather than institutional or corporate investors. However, corporations, universities, and similar institutions have found condominium investment and ownership to be an asset because of both the appreciation in capital gains and the opportunity to use the condominium facility for their own purposes.

IMPORTANT FACTORS IN BUYING AND SELLING

Selection of Broker, Salesperson, or Developer

The investor in condominium should use the same principles in selecting a broker, salesperson, or developer that he would use in selecting a doctor, accountant, or lawyer. While the writer cannot recommend specific brokers, salespersons, or developers, he can recommend that careful attention be given to the reputation for honesty and fair dealing of these people. An investor should check with the Better Business Bureau, the local Board of Realtors or real estate brokers, the local builders' association, and, of course, anyone who is known to be active in the business. Sometimes real estate editors or real estate departments of leading newspapers can provide information on various brokers, salespersons, or developers.

Finding the Market

A good way to find condominiums for sale is to review the newspaper. Very often condominiums are advertised in the classified section and developments are advertised in the real estate section. Home buyers' guides and similar publications that advertise real estate offerings are also helpful.

Using a Real Estate Broker

The decision has to be made as to whether an investor should utilize the services of a broker for marketing. This will depend on the investor's proximity to the site of the condominium, knowledge of real estate, and willingness to get involved in the sales process. Most people find that the commissions a broker charges to handle the sale are well worth the cost. While commissions vary from location to location, in general they are approximately 6 percent of the sales price. Commissions on timeshares are generally higher, averaging 10 to 12 percent of the sales price.

Quality of Investment and Professional Advice

The investor who understands real estate and can judge the quality of construction as well as quality of maintenance may not need the help of a professional appraiser. The Yellow Pages usually lists local appraisers who specialize in housing and are experienced in appraising condominiums or cooperatives. These appraisers also can offer valuable input as to quality of construction, level of maintenance, and other areas of concern to the investor. Fees vary greatly and depend on the appraiser's workload and willingness to take the assignment. Depending upon the length of report and quantity of information desired, they range from approximately $75 for a FHA or VA appraisal up to $400 for a professionally designated or other qualified appraisal.

Sources of Financing

One very important factor in purchasing a condominium is the availability of financing. Most often, investors are seeking leverage. Condominium financing terms, rates, and availability are generally very similar to those for single-family residences, although down payment requirements may be more stringent for investors than for owner-occupants. The leading banks, savings and loan associations, and some credit unions or pension funds are all possible sources. Sometimes individuals willing to finance the condominium can be identified. Also, very frequently, the seller can be persuaded to carry back a portion of the sales price and thus become an important source of financing. There are government programs through the VA and FHA that do provide some financing for condominium. As with any other service, the investor should carefully shop the sources to determine the points, current interest rate, length of loan, and any other factors that may affect the investment.

CUSTODIAL CARE

Physical Maintenance

Exterior maintenance and much of the management of a condominium or cooperative are handled by the homeowners association, thereby relieving the investor of the responsibility for mowing the lawn, painting the exterior, calling a plumber, and many other tasks that the owner of a single-family residence must perform. However, the investor is responsible for the interior of his individual unit and any plumbing, maintenance, or similar expenses incurred or caused by a tenant. Having much of the maintenance taken care of by the homeowners association relieves the investor of some of the burdens of ownership. This can be a definite advantage when compared to a single-family residence or multi-family rentals.

Collecting the Income

As with any other real estate rental, the condominium investor should have written leases with the tenants of the condominium to ensure the rights of the investor to collect rental income and to maintain the condominium in a state of good repair. Many investors utilize the services of banks or savings and loan associations as collection agents, particularly if they live out of the area. This also allows the flexibility to move from an area without disturbing the flow of rental income from a tenant.

Insurance

Although the homeowners association will have insurance coverage and protection for the common areas, it is up to the unit owner or occupant to provide insurance coverage for the interior and for any personal property within the unit. The investor should give consideration to this and have adequate fire insurance. He should also either provide contents coverage for the tenants or make sure the tenants obtain that coverage.

Property Management

In all major cities and communities across the United States, there are real estate firms or companies that specialize in property management. For a fee plus actual expenses incurred, they will undertake to manage condominiums or cooperatives as well as other real estate. If the condominium investment is located in an area some distance from the investor, it may provide greater peace of mind to have a property manager overseeing the investment. Naturally, the property manager will not provide any services without charge. Under the normal arrangement, the manager is paid from 5 to 10 percent of the gross income and is reimbursed for any expenses or extraordinary costs incurred. This fee is for the basic management function of receiving the telephone calls relating to tenant relations and contacting qualified people to do the repair, maintenance, and other work or services required. The services rendered to the property or for the owner are usually billed to the owner in addition to the basic management fee. For example, if the plumbing stops up in a unit, the management company will receive the call from the tenant and call a plumber as part of the basic management fee. The plumber's services for repairing the problem will be billed to the owner as a separate item, in addition to the basic management fee. Very often the costs of owning condominiums some distance away are increased because of the need to make extra trips, telephone calls, and so on. The investor should consider these things when purchasing a condominium for investment.

Status of Homeowners Association

The homeowners association prepares or causes the preparation of a budget of the operating expenses, which are then divided among the various owners and assessed to them as their share of those expenses. One of the things that should be determined by the investor is the status of the homeowners association. Are its assessments current? Is it functioning? Is there dissension or harmony? Does the project look like it has been receiving periodic maintenance? Are the yards, lawns, and shrubbery in good condition? The performance of the homeowners association should be evaluated and considered. In addition, the investor who wishes to become a force in the homeowners association, in order to change attitudes through action and involvement, should realistically evaluate the extent to which this is possible.

GLOSSARY

amenity— A feature of real property that enhances its attractiveness and increases the satisfaction of its occupants or users.

common elements— In a condominium, those portions of the building, land, and amenities owned by the condominium association and used by all the unit owners, who share in the common expenses of their operation and maintenance.

condominium — Individual ownership of units combined with joint ownership of common elements of the condominium building, structure, or development.

condominium owners association — An association of condominium unit owners, empowered to operate the condominium and to maintain the common elements. Where the association is incorporated, it is organized as a not-for-profit corporation.

declaration of condominium — An instrument in the form of a deed, which must be filed in the proper office by the developer or owner(s) of the property. When duly executed it binds the present owner and all future owners of the property.

fee simple absolute— Ownership without time limitation (in perpetuity); the most inclusive type of real estate ownership.

fee simple condominium — A form of real property ownership in which the condominium unit owner is the exclusive owner of his own unit only, and is an owner in common with respect to the land and other common elements of the property.

maintenance costs— Costs assessed on unit owners to provide for the needs of the common elements of the building and development.

timeshared ownership— The exclusive right to occupy a unit in a resort development for a specified period of time each year.

LEADING FRANCHISE BROKERS

Century 21 Real Estate
Electronic Realty Associates (ERA)
Gallery of Homes
International Real Estate Network
Meredith Publishing (Better Homes & Gardens)
Realty World Corporation
Red Carpet Corporation

TRADE ORGANIZATIONS

American Land Development Association, Washington, D.C.
Community Associations Institute, Arlington, Va.
National Association of Homebuilders, Washington, D.C.
National Association of Realtors, Chicago, Ill.
Urban Land Institute, Washington, D.C.

SUGGESTED READING

Periodicals

Multi-Housing News. Published by Gralla Publications, New York, N.Y. Monthly.

NAHB Builder. Published by the National Association of Home Builders, Washington, D.C. Monthly.

Resort Timesharing Law Reporter. Published by Land Development Institute Ltd., Washington, D.C. Monthly.

Resort Timesharing Today. Published by CHB Company, Inc., Los Altos, Cal. Monthly.

Reference Books

Bloch, Stuart M., and Ingersoll, William B., eds. *Timesharing.* Washington, D.C.: Urban Land Institute, 1977.

California Association of Realtors. *How to Manage Condominium Developments.* Los Angeles, 1976.

Dombal, Robert W. *Residential Condominiums: A Guide to Analysis and Appraisal,* Chicago: American Institute of Real Estate Appraisers, 1976.

Institute of Real Estate Management. *The Condominium Community: A Guide for Owners, Boards, and Managers.* Chicago, 1978.

Richard L. Ragatz Associates, Inc. *The Resort Timesharing Industry: A Socio-Economic Impact Analysis of Timesharing.* Volumes I and II. Washington, D.C.: The Resort Timesharing Council of the American Land Development Association, 1980 and 1981.

Rohan, Patrick J., and Reskin, Melvin A. *Condominium Law and Practice.* New York: Matthew Bender Co., 1965 (revised periodically since 1969 by Patrick J. Rohan).

Romney, Keith B. *Condominium Development Guide: Procedures, Analysis, Forms.* Boston: Warren, Gorham & Lamont, 1974 (annual supplements).

Keith Romney Associates. *Timesharing Guide for Buyers and Developers.* Salt Lake City, 1982 (updated periodically).

Wolfe, David B. *Condominium and Homeowners Associations That Work.* Washington, D.C.: Urban Land Institute, 1978.

Real Estate—Farms and Ranches

James E. Hamer and John R. Schumann, Esq. *

BASIC CHARACTERISTICS

The market value of the 2.4 million farms and ranches in the mainland United States (forty-eight states) is estimated to exceed $825 billion (total value of land and buildings).[1] In the year ending March 1, 1981, 18 million of these acres were sold at a total value of $15 billion.[2] Roughly 18 percent of this land was purchased by either absentee investors (not residing in the county of purchase), non-farming corporations, or nonresident aliens (foreign buyers).[3]

Agriculture is this nation's largest business, with nearly $149 billion in sales in 1980 (fifty states), according to the U.S. Department of Agriculture. This huge volume has attracted a highly sophisticated network of producers and investors. To be a successful investor in farm or ranch land, one must buy well, operate efficiently, and sell profitably. This scenario has become increasingly difficult to achieve because of the large percentage of poor farm and ranch investment alternatives appearing in the marketplace.

Primary Determinants of Value

Farm and ranch income. Historically, the average return on the fair market value of farms and ranches in the United States has ranged from 2 to 5 percent (net operating income before taxes divided by market value of the land asset). When land appreciates rapidly, as it did during the early 1970s, this capitalization rate has decreased to as low as one percent. For example, in late 1980 in Illinois, an average farm cost approximately $3,100 per acre. Farm rents in Illinois were averaging about $155 gross income per acre, so an average investment would yield roughly 5 percent (before tax). Farm and ranch investors have traditionally realized more from capital appreciation than from net farm or ranch income.

Inflationary pressure. This has been a major factor in the strong performance of farm and ranch values. Since the early 1930s, agricultural land has been

* James E. Hamer is a Trust Officer with The Northern Trust Company, Chicago; and John R. Schumann is a Vice-President and attorney in the Trust Department of The Northern Trust Company.

1 U.S. Department of Agriculture, Economic Research Service, *Farm Real Estate Market Developments.* CD-86, August, 1981, page 17.

2 *Id.*, page 25.

3 *Id.*, page 29.

an ideal inflationary hedge. During the mid-1970s, land values far exceeded the rate of inflation, as illustrated in Figure 1, below.

Land supply factors. Nearly 3 million acres of agricultural land are lost annually to urban development, highways, rights of way, and so on. Farm and ranch land cannot be manufactured, and the supply side of the land value equation is steadily decreasing.

Land demand factors. An increasing world population is requiring more food products annually. This increased demand has contributed to higher production levels, higher agricultural commodity prices, and increased land values.

Less than 3 percent of the total number of farms and ranches in the United States are sold each year. The competition for this land is led by farmers and ranchers, who use existing acres as collateral to bid at an advantage against nonagrarian competition.

However, farmers, speculator-investors, corporations, investment groups, and foreign buyers are currently maintaining a healthy competition for available farm and ranch land.

Variety of Investments

Before investing in a farm or ranch, potential buyers must determine which type of agricultural enterprise will satisfy their objectives. In choosing from among hundreds of crop and livestock alternatives, geography, economics, or personal preference may emerge as the deciding factor. One may consider irrigat-

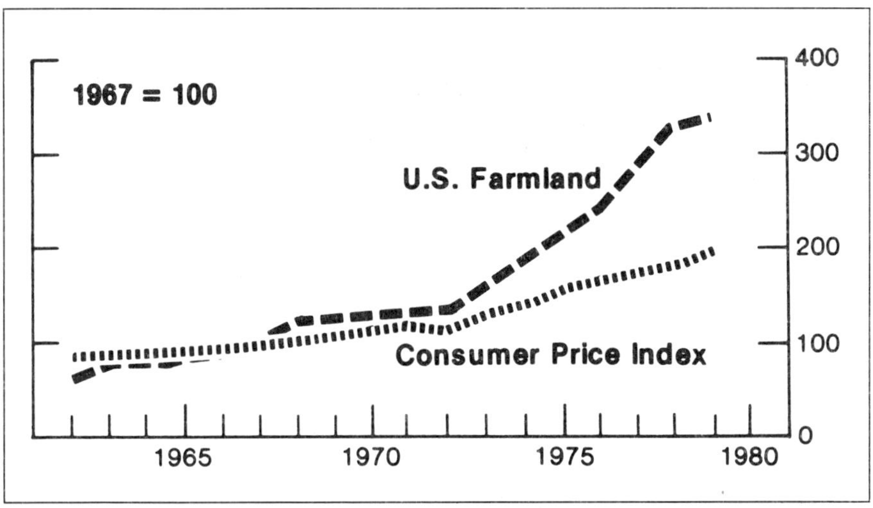

FIG. 1. Farmland as a Hedge Against Inflation
SOURCE: U.S. Department of Agriculture

ed or dry land cultivation, row crop or permanent crop farming, grazing livestock, concentrated livestock, or combinations of crop and livestock. The investor needs to clearly define objectives and compare them to the risk-reward ratio of the alternative enterprises.

Permanent crops. These include perennial fruit- and nut-bearing trees and bushes. With a high risk-reward ratio, these agricultural enterprises require both sophisticated management and large capital input. They are among the most intensive operations in agriculture and are not recommended for the passive investor. Among the most attractive regions for permanent crop investments recently have been:

- Imperial, San Joaquin, Napa, and Salinas Valleys in California (citrus, grapes, kiwi, nectarines, peaches, pears, plums)
- Rio Grande Valley in Texas (citrus, avocados)
- Florida (citrus)
- Arizona (citrus, pecans, grapes)

Livestock or dairy. Extremely large capital requirements make entry into livestock or dairy operations prohibitive. Land investors are best advised to enter livestock operations on a non-participating basis, that is, by renting land and facilities to a livestock operator. This in effect minimizes overall risk exposure and reduces or eliminates operating costs. There are, however, successful livestock share arrangements, and these remain an alternative for the risk-tolerant investor who can sustain both heavy operating costs and volatile cash flow.

Vegetable crops. These farms, selling to the fresh, canned, or packaged vegetable markets, are secular and highly specialized in nature. Production costs are high, volume is relatively low, and intensive management is required. Although production and market risks are high, there is real potential for excellent operating returns. The San Joaquin and Imperial Valleys in California and the Rio Grande Valley and Winter Garden areas in Texas have recently attracted a large number of absentee investors in vegetable farms.

Field crops. Feed grains, grasses, and cotton are typical of these farm or ranch operations. Extremely high in volume with liquid markets, these operations are typical of the Corn Belt, Plains states, and Cotton Belt. They require lower production costs and offer a more consistent return on invested capital than other types of farm and ranch operations. In the Corn Belt states, competition for land among tenant farmers has created a favorable climate for securing good cash-rent or share-crop operators. Top-quality land in this area has increased by over 300 percent since 1972.

The row crop alternative offers the lowest risk and is probably the most amenable to absentee investor ownership.

ATTRACTIVE FEATURES

Hedge Against Inflation

Throughout the world, land has traditionally served as an inflationary hedge. Inflationary pressure was the largest single factor in the tremendous gains in farm and ranch values during the 1970s. During that period, values increased by more than 200 percent across the country, while at the same time consumer prices rose by 100 percent.

Safety of Principal

Given a stable political climate, continuing growth in world demand for food products, and continued inflationary pressure, farm and ranch land will be an attractive investment for preservation of capital.

Current Cash Return

The absentee investor's potential for income is dictated largely by the type of lease arrangement he negotiates with his tenant or resident-operator. The four major lease alternatives are the cash rental, the crop or livestock share, the custom arrangement, and the direct operation.

Cash-rental lease. Under the cash-rental lease, the landowner simply rents his property and facilities at some flat rate, usually on a per-acre fee. This type of lease eliminates most production risk and guarantees a steady cash flow. This lease also requires the least amount of management input by the absentee investor. Variations of this lease include rents payable in some predetermined crop or livestock quantity, regardless of production levels.

Crop or livestock share agreement. Under this arrangement, the landowner accepts his share of income as a percent of crop or livestock production. The landowner is also responsible for participating in a specified portion of production costs. A common crop-share lease in the Midwest is the 50-50 arrangement. Here, the landowner receives half of the crop production and pays for half of the seed, chemical, and fertilizer costs. Share agreements vary according to crop, geographic locale, potential production levels, and community tradition. Under these leases, an owner participates in production risks, but can also benefit from increases in production or market prices.

Custom arrangement. A variation of the direct operation, the custom farm contracts all of its field work individually with one or more custom operators. The landowner accepts all of the production risk and receives all of the farm or ranch receipts.

Direct operation. This is usually limited to a large-scale enterprise. The investor/owner owns all operating equipment and hires the labor necessary for production. Usually a salaried resident-manager assumes operating responsibilities. As in the custom operation, the owner accepts all production risk and receives all farm or ranch income.

Intangible Benefits

The lifestyle associated with agriculture is attractive to many investors. For those with any agrarian spirit, pride of ownership has a very real impact on the value placed upon a farm or ranch. Many investors also cite security as a motivating factor in pursuing an agricultural investment.

POTENTIAL RISKS

Despite impressive appreciation of farm and ranch lands during the past quarter century, land values have at times yielded to economic pressures. During the great depression, for example, land values decreased by nearly 60 percent, and much land was sold as forced liquidations.

The investor must be aware of production risks, rapid fluctuations in commodity prices, and tenant or operator risks that exist in any agricultural enterprise. Political maneuvers such as the Russian grain embargo of 1980 can also drastically affect farm income and ultimately land values.

Income Limitations

The low cash throw-off of 2 to 5 percent on farm and ranch investments is an immediate deterrent to many investors. However, farm and ranch land has provided a safe, consistent, and attractive vehicle for preserving and increasing real dollar wealth. A comparison of stocks to farmland provides a good frame of reference, as Figure 2 on page 739 illustrates.

Liquidity

Farm and ranch land is not a highly liquid holding and should only be considered for long-term investment or speculation.

The propitious timing of a sale is dictated by the farm income situation, commodity prices, competing land prices, and available financing. To avoid an untimely offering, only those investors with staying power should consider including agricultural property in their portfolios.

Special Risk Factors

The investor who is accustomed to the more traditional debt or equity vehicles will find several risk factors unique to agriculture. First, natural phenomena such as floods, drought, disease, and insect pests threaten agricultural production annually. Second, a pricing strategy is replaced by a marketing strategy in agriculture and the market clearing price of commodities is determined

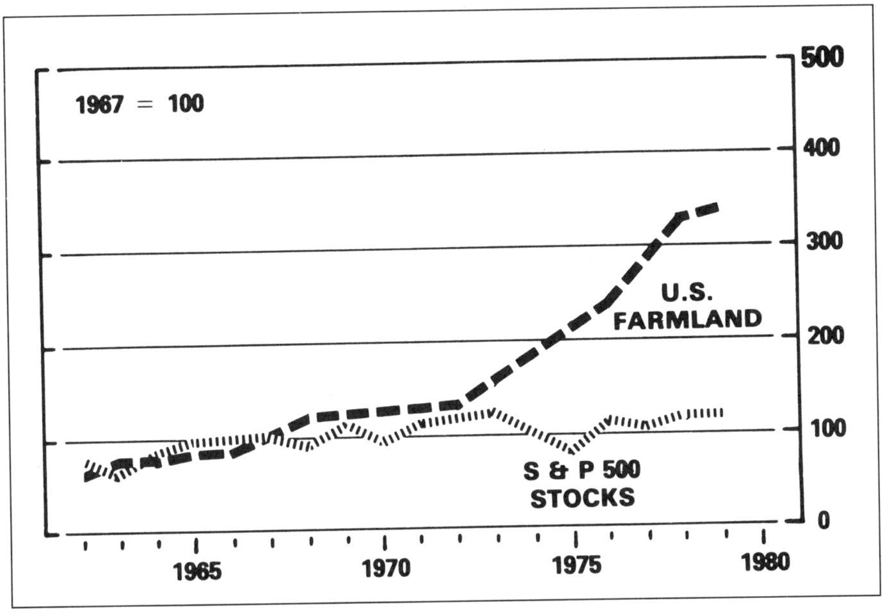

FIG. 2. Farmland Compared With Stocks
SOURCE: U.S. Department of Agriculture

largely by the buyer. Effective marketing of these commodities is an extremely sophisticated process, and usually determines the difference between profit and loss. Third, good management (often the exception rather than the rule in agriculture) is absolutely essential. Locating the highly skilled, capable operator and farm manager is a critical factor for success in farm or ranch investments.

REPRESENTATIVE TYPES OF INVESTORS

The farmer's activity in the market will ultimately dictate the value of farms and ranches. In the year ending March 1, 1981, he accounted for roughly 70 percent of the land purchased.[4] Absentee investors, defined as those living outside of the county in which land is purchased, account for 18 percent of land sales. Absentee investors fall into one of four general categories: the individual, the investment corporation, the limited partnership, and the foreign investor.

TAX CONSEQUENCES

Farms and ranches are, for the most part, very similar to other forms of real estate investments insofar as income taxes are concerned. As with an investment

---

4 U.S. Department of Agriculture, Economic Research Service, *Farm Real Estate Market Developments.* CD-86, August, 1981 page 28.

in an office building or an apartment complex, there are three distinct tax phases or stages in the full-cycle transaction:

(1) Acquisition
(2) Operation
(3) Liquidation

With each phase of the cycle of farm and ranch ownership, there are, however, several tax-related aspects that are unique to involvement in agriculturally oriented enterprises. In this section, the basics of farm acquisition, operation, and liquidation will be briefly discussed, and unusual tax treatments found only in agricultural land investments will be presented in some detail.

Acquisition

Conflict between buyer and seller permeates the entire acquisition process. It is this conflict that comforts the Internal Revenue Service when it reviews transactions between unrelated parties. The crux of the conflict between the buyer and seller is, of course, the allocation of value among assets involved in the transaction. The seller is interested in allocating as much of the total purchase price as possible to assets that will cause generation of neither recapture of investment tax credits nor depreciation, and will not cause recognition of ordinary income. The farm investor is, however, interested in just the opposite. With the exception of some permanent crops (e.g., grapes, fruit, nuts) and livestock properties, the normal ratio of depreciable assets to total investment is quite low, thereby making the allocation issue relatively insignificant when investing in "plain ole' dirt farms."

Timing. Although the Installment Sales Revision Act of 1980 has alleviated some of the timing problems associated with farm acquisition, concerns still exist about bunching of income to the seller. The farm investor will certainly want to immediately acquire items eligible for depreciation or credit to be used to offset other income in the year of acquisition. But if the seller has sold his on-farm grain inventory and realized ordinary income, he will want to delay sale of assets triggering recapture of investment tax credit or depreciation.

Unlike other forms of real estate investment, there are two areas of the acquisition of farm or ranch properties where, generally speaking, there is no inherent conflict between investor-buyer and seller. The first is the purchase of raised production livestock. Unless the seller still carries an excess deduction account, he will not face any recapture problems. The second area (discussed in greater detail in *Liquidation* in this article) involves growing crops bought with the land. Briefly stated, if growing crops are bought with the land, the seller will realize capital gains for the amount allocated to the crop. The investor-buyer receives a basis in the crop equal to the allocated amount, which lowers his taxable income after harvesting and selling the crop. Because of the lack of investor-seller conflict in these two areas, each is very closely scrutinized by the IRS.

Allocation agreement. The above discussion on acquisition of farms assumes there will be an asset allocation agreement, in writing, between buyer-investor and seller noted in the sales contract. There are cases, however, when the parties cannot reach an agreement and each party has to make his own allocation. One approach in determining allocations preferred by the IRS is to first value the land and then attribute the difference between land value and purchase price to the other assets. From an investor's point of view, however, it is usually better to first value non-land assets and then allocate to the land the difference between other asset values and purchase price.

In viewing the acquisition from an asset-by-asset perspective, most tangible items, other than land, traditionally associated with farms and ranches are depreciable. As with investment in other types of real estate, the depreciable lives of assets purchased depend on the type and condition of each asset. In general, those assets eligible for accelerated depreciation (equipment, breeding stock, single-purpose horticultural buildings, special fencing) are also the assets affording investment tax credit to the investor.

Operation

As discussed elsewhere, there are basically four ways an investor can operate a farm or ranch:

(1) Cash-rental lease
(2) Crop or livestock share agreement
(3) Custom arrangement
(4) Direct operation

Importance of risk factor. From an investor's tax perspective, the key difference among all the operating alternatives listed is risk assumed. Cash rental, by definition, shifts all risks associated with the actual business of operating a farm to the lessee/farmer. It is this shift in risk, not present in the other forms of operating a farm or ranch, that is the crux of the tax differences in farming.

If an investor cash-leases his farm, he is precluded from shifting income from one tax year to another. This shifting (growing a crop in one year and, if personal income tax exposure dictates, selling the crop in another year) is available to investors operating property by crop share, custom, or direct labor methods.

Because cash rental of a farm is not the conduct of an active trade or business, there are strong arguments that the investor may be

- Precluded from taking the tax deductions normally associated with land-clearing or soil- and water-conservation expenses. Normally a farm owner may elect to deduct the lesser of $5,000 or 25 percent of taxable farming income for land-clearing expenses. Annual clearing expenses exceeding the limit must be capitalized. In the case of soil- and water-conservation expenses, a farm owner, arguably not cash-leasing a farm, may elect to deduct 25 percent of gross income from farming for expenditures incurred for nondepreciable soil and water conservation. Amounts exceeding the annual ceiling may be indefinitely carried forward.

- Considered a limited entrepreneur for purposes of application of the rules relating to taxation of farm syndicates. If an investor is deemed to be a limited entrepreneur, he must automatically deduct expenses for feed, seed, and fertilizer when the items are used (not bought) and capitalize certain preproductive period expenses for orchards and vineyards.
- Eliminated from any possibility of taking a special estate tax election allowing "materially participating" farmers' estates to value farmland based on its ability to generate income rather than on its fair market value. Although there is a ceiling of $750,000 by 1983 and years following to the amount of valuation reduction afforded to each estate, it is still a significant consideration if an investor's estate meets other qualifying criteria.

Hobby loss rules. Hobby loss rules are relatively unique to farm investors who operate non-horse farmland investments at a loss for two out of five years. Unless they can show that their intent has been to operate the farm or ranch at a profit, farm losses are nondeductible. Intent is always difficult to demonstrate; courts try to ascertain whether the farm was a retreat, whether competent people were hired, and so on.

Mention has already been made of cash-basis accounting, soil- and water-conservation expenses, and land-clearing expenses. These are unique to both farming and ranching. In livestock enterprises, however, one must distinguish between types of operation when analyzing tax alternatives. Simply stated, livestock owned only for resale is taxed at ordinary income rates upon disposition. Livestock bought or raised for breeding and held for requisite periods will be taxed at capital gains rates.

Assuming hobby loss and cash rental are not issues for an investor, operation of a farm or ranch, from a tax perspective, is very similar to any business. The vocabulary and terms of art are, however, different.

Liquidation

When selling a farm or ranch an investor-owner will be bargaining from the opposite side of the asset allocation table discussed earlier. Here, too, the rules of the game are very similar to the sale of other forms of real estate investment. Planning is the key to avoiding the pitfalls associated with recapture of investment tax credit and depreciation and, yes, those land-clearing and soil- and water-conservation expenses.

The sale of land with unharvested crop involves no basic dispute between buyer and seller because their respective tax positions are not adverse, and it is therefore subject to IRS scrutiny. (See *Acquisitions* in this article.) Interestingly enough, however, expenses to produce the crop must be recaptured. This is not true in the sale of other farm assets, such as breeding stock, where production expenses do not have to be recaptured. The recapture provision requires recapture in the year crop production expenses were actually incurred and disallows deductions for items attributable to crop production.

To qualify for this special provision, the land on which the crops are grown must be held for more than one year and be used in a trade or business (precluded by cash rental). In addition,

- The seller can retain no direct or indirect right to reacquire the land on which the crop grows, except for a mortgage.
- The crop must be sold at the same time and to the same purchaser as the land.
- The unharvested crop cannot be on leased land.

Definition of "crop" includes all traditional crops, seasonal as well as permanent, and has been interpreted to include grass grown for sod. Crop is, indeed, broadly defined — but it is clear that something must be growing.

There is no apparent necessity for the sales contract to allocate portions of the sales price to land and crops to qualify. The allocation must be reasonable. The seller's position is that both land and crops receive capital gains treatment unless there have been land-clearing or soil- and water-conservation expenses taken. The buyer, on the other hand, receives a basis in the crop equal to the amount allocated at the time of sale and, to minimize income taxation at the time of crop marketing, seeks a high allocation of the total land transaction. Thus, the allocation of the sales price to unharvested crops is an important consideration for both buyer and seller. In light of this, the popular notion that farm sales should transpire only in dormant production cycles may not have credence.

It is always easy to let the tax tail wag the investment dog. There are many attractive tax reasons to invest in farmland, but the investor should not lose sight of the overall economic viability of a farm or ranch enterprise.

IMPORTANT FACTORS IN BUYING AND SELLING

A potential buyer should have professionals analyze the price, terms of agreement, and quality of a farm or ranch investment. Purchasing a quality farm or ranch is the first and most important of the three steps to a successful farm or ranch investment — buy well, operate efficiently, sell profitably. A good real estate broker, attorney, accountant, and farm consultant can prevent many unforeseen disasters. Most professional land traders use all four when buying or selling.

Selecting a Broker, Dealer, or Salesperson

Choose an agent who specializes exclusively in agricultural properties. Check his credentials and reputation carefully. A good place to do this is with the Farm and Land Institute in Chicago. This affiliate of the National Association of Realtors maintains accreditation standards and can refer members by geographic location. In addition, the American Society of Farm Managers and Rural Appraisers in Denver is an excellent place to seek professional consultation.

Commissions and Fees

Determining a sales commission is, of course, part of the negotiation process. However, most brokers charge 3 to 10 percent of the gross sales price. The seller is responsible for this fee.

An agent-consultant usually represents the buyer and typically requires one to 5 percent of the purchase price. He will usually charge a minimum fee, which varies according to the complexity of the investment.

Judging Quality

This is the most difficult and critical factor in securing a good farm or ranch investment. Soil productivity, water quality and rights, mineral rights, irrigation requirements, conservation factors, physical facilities, markets, transportation, and availability of labor are but a few of the many considerations that must be thoroughly analyzed. There are many more poor farm and ranch investments than good ones. Quality should be judged by a professional consultant.

MANAGING THE INVESTMENT

The same management input that makes any type of business successful also makes a farm or ranch investment work. Planning, organizing, and controlling an agricultural operation in a professional manner is the key to a profitable farm or ranch business. The investor-owner may choose to manage his investment alone, may rely solely upon his tenant or operator, or may hire a farm and ranch management firm to represent him.

Professional Management

The typical absentee investor does not have the time, interest, or expertise to manage the property efficiently. In addition, most tenant farms are not accustomed to preparing the inspection reports, budgets, cash-flow projections, year-end reports, insurance reviews, and other communications required by the absentee investor-owner. Most investors seek professional management services to represent their interests.

Quality farm and ranch management, whether by a qualified operator or an organization, should include at least the following services:

- Negotiation of leases and contracts;
- Three- to five-year development plan;
- Cash-flow projections and production budgets;
- Detailed inspection reports;
- Monthly or quarterly reports;

- Marketing services;
- Budgeting for needed capital improvements;
- Cash management services;
- Rent or income collection;
- Payment of bills; and
- Annual tax summary.

Fees for these services vary from 6 to 12 percent of the owner's share of gross farm or ranch income.

GLOSSARY

acre— A measure of land area equivalent to 43,560 square feet.

cash-rental lease— An arrangement whereby the landowner leases property and facilities at a flat rate, usually a per-acre fee.

crop— All traditional plants grown and harvested for profit and/or subsistence, seasonal as well as permanent, including grass grown for sod.

crop or livestock share agreement— An arrangement where the landowner accepts a share of income as a percentage of crop or livestock production.

custom arrangement— A variation of the *direct operation,* whereby the custom farm contracts all of its field work individually with one or more custom operators.

direct operation— An arrangement whereby the individual-owner owns all operating equipment and hires labor necessary for production.

farmland— Land used for the cultivation of crops or for the maintenance of cows and chickens to produce food products; includes the land upon which the farm buildings stand.

liquidity— The condition of an individual or business wherein a high percentage of the assets can be quickly converted into cash without involving a considerable loss by accepting sacrifice prices.

ranch— Grazing acreage used for the raising of livestock for the production of beef.

LEADING DEALERS IN AGRICULTURAL ACQUISITION SERVICES, BROKERAGE, AND MANAGEMENT

Acquisition Consultation

Continental Bank & Trust Co., Chicago, Ill.

Doane's Agricultural Services, St. Louis, Mo.

Northern Trust Company, Chicago, Ill.

Oppenheimer Industries, Kansas City, Mo.

Farm and Ranch Brokerage Services

In addition, most national and regional real estate brokerage firms maintain farm and ranch specialists at local offices.

Doane/Western Farm Management, Denver, Colo.

Farmers National Company, Omaha, Neb.

Huber Farm Services, Memphis, Tenn.

Oppenheimer Industries, Kansas City, Mo.

Farm and Ranch Management

There are many regional management firms in addition to these national operations. Check with the American Society of Farm Managers and Rural Appraisers in Denver for referrals.

Doane/Western Farm Management, St. Louis, Mo.

Fact's, Inc., Memphis, Tenn.

Farmers National Co., Omaha, Neb.

First National Bank, Oklahoma City, Okla.

Ft. Worth National Bank, Ft. Worth, Tex.

Huber Farm Services, Memphis, Tenn.

Northern Trust Company, Chicago, Ill.

Oppenheimer Industries, Kansas City, Mo.

Plantation Services, Albany, Ga.

Wells Fargo, San Francisco, Cal.

SUGGESTED READING

Periodicals

Agricultural Financial Outlook. U.S. Department of Agriculture, Washington, D.C. Monthly; summarizes agricultural production and farm real estate values.

Agricultural Statistics. U.S. Department of Agriculture, Washington, D.C. Annual.

Agri Finance Magazine. Skokie, Ill. Monthly; deals with farm management problems and frequently publishes articles appropriate for farm and ranch investors.

Doane's Agricultural Report. Doane's Agricultural Services, St. Louis, Mo. Weekly; a concise newsletter with excellent reporting on farm price trends.

Farm and Land Realtor. Farm and Land Institute, Chicago, Ill. Monthly; geared directly toward farm and ranch real estate brokers.

Farmline. U.S. Department of Agriculture, Washington, D.C. Monthly; tracks current government activities, price cost data, and farm and ranch values.

Farm Real Estate Market Developments. U.S. Department of Agriculture, Washington, D.C. Monthly; tracks farm and ranch transfers and land values.

Landowner. Professional Farmers of America, Cedar Rapids, Iowa. Biweekly; a series of short articles on farmland real estate. Geared mainly toward the Midwest, it is valuable both for buyers and sellers.

Progressive Farmer. Progressive Farmer, Inc., Birmingham, Ala. Biweekly; published regionally, it offers many good tips on buying, managing, and selling agricultural land.

Successful Farming. Meredith Corporation, Des Moines, Iowa. Monthly; most appropriate for the owner/operator or farm manager, but frequently prints articles on farm and ranch acquisition and sales.

Reference Books

Coopers & Lybrand. *Tax Planning for Real Estate Transactions.* Chicago: Farm and Land Institute, 1978.

Farm and Land Institute. *Farm and Land Real Estate Manual.* Chicago, 1975.

Jurdt, Dwight W. *Buying or Selling Farms.* St. Louis: Doane's Agricultural Services.

U.S. Government Printing Office. *National Agricultural Lands Study.* Washington, D.C.

Warren, Gorham & Lamont. *Real Estate Review Portfolio No. 22. How To Evaluate an Investment in Agricultural Real Estate.* Boston, 1980 (updated annually).

Real Estate Investment Trusts

John B. Nicholson *

BASIC CHARACTERISTICS

Publicly held real estate investment trusts (REITs) were designed ostensibly to combine the best features of the Wall Street stock market and Main Street's realty markets to produce a liquid investment, traded daily on the stock exchanges, but with all the benefits of otherwise illiquid income-producing real estate. Although the REITs grew tremendously in the early 1970s, several built-in conflicts, discussed later in this article, have hampered their subsequent growth and development.

Passive Investment Requirement

A REIT is often a trust, free from taxation, although it may be a corporation that elects to be taxed as a REIT. Its trustees (or directors) must agree to invest passively in only real estate assets on behalf of shareholders. The portfolio of realty investments — either mortgage loans secured by real estate, or ownership of real estate directly, or ownership of equity in other REITs — must conform to certain rules so as to be qualified for special avoidance of federal income taxation. (See *Qualifying Tax Rules* in this article.)

The portfolio of realty investments is like any other funnel of funds. Some REITs invest only in hotels, others invest only in short-term construction loans. Others specialize in second mortgages that wrap around the existing low-rate mortgage.

Whatever the composition of the portfolio, publicly held REITs, so long as they remain tax qualified, have the following characteristics:

- The individual REIT investor owns a share of a real estate portfolio rather than operating a business. This distinction separates a REIT from a publicly held development company, for instance. Profits can come only from the operation of real estate assets by others through separate management contracts. Some REITs have elaborate procedures so that the investment adviser, often a subsidiary of the REIT's sponsor, is deemed to be separate from the independent property management subsidiary even though there may be common ownership of the entities.
- The REIT investor derives income almost exclusively from the "passive" ownership of realty. Capital gains (or losses) cannot be the primary source of dividends. REITs must be managed so as to justify their recognition in real property. For this reason, some REITs elect to have a non-qualified status, which permits them to

* John B. Nicholson is President of Berryhill Associates, Washington, D.C.

derive dealer profits from selling off condominium units. The requirement for passive ownership also prevents REITs from speculatively owning vacant land for the purpose of reselling it. However, the tax law does permit a REIT to buy raw land on which to build income-producing improvements; at this point, the REIT is deemed to be holding land for the purpose of income production sometime in the future.

Types of Holdings

As a practical matter unrelated to their tax qualification procedures, REITs have tended to buy or build all forms of income-producing real estate, especially the more novel or unusual types in which "creative financing" is involved. Strip shopping centers are a staple for most REITs. The larger centers attract bigger investors, usually, although many REITs own some major shopping centers. Apartments tend not to be favored by most REITs because of the inability to raise rents quickly enough to keep pace with inflation. Mini-warehouses, motels, office buildings, free-standing single-tenant structures, and speculative rental warehouses in industrial areas are often owned by REITs, too. Generally speaking, operating corporations can sell their real estate assets through investment banking sources at a better price than REITs are willing to pay, although one REIT owns a number of Chrysler warehouses.

Qualifying Tax Rules

REITs incur no tax liability while acting as a conduit to pass income through to their stockholders. In order to qualify for conduit treatment under Sections 856 to 860 of the Internal Revenue Code, an organization must declare its intention to be taxed as a REIT and then must fulfill several requirements concerning structure, sources of income, nature of assets, and dividend distribution. Among other obligations the REIT must:

- Pay out more than 90 percent of its taxable income to its shareholders;
- Invest more than 75 percent of its capital in real estate or real estate-related investments;
- Never have more than 30 percent of its income in any one year derived from the sale of real estate held less than four years;
- Always be a passive investor, that is, never derive gains from the sale of property held for sale rather than for investment (There are some minor exceptions to this rule, aimed mostly at allowing the sale of assets acquired through foreclosure on property securing the mortgage loans); and
- Comply with certain organizational strictures designed to keep the REIT from becoming a personal holding company (i.e., there must be more than 100 shareholders, no 5 percent of whom own more than 50 percent of the shares).

Origins and History

The trust form in which many REITs were created, and exist today, reflects the somewhat tortured history of the oldest survivors. In the late 1800s, New

England legislators truncated the company-town movement by requiring that all operating (mill) corporations could own only the realty needed to do business. They were not allowed ownership of realty investments such as employees' houses, etc. Thus, individual investors who sought to own income-producing property through professionally managed companies were forced to adopt the trust vehicle.

These trusts were deemed to be taxable like corporations, and thereby became subject to the federal corporate income tax during the 1930s. However, when the mutual fund lobby won its conduit-type exemption from taxation, just before World War II, the dozen or so REITs in business at that time set their legislative sights to gain similar tax treatment. Throughout the 1950s, the real estate lobby battled back, fearing takeover by the major companies once REITs had won their tax-favored status. Thus, in 1961, after an Eisenhower veto, the survivors won. The tax-favored treatment was limited to trusts — no corporations — and only passive investments were explicitly permitted.

Growth and development. REITs grew slowly as instruments to own income-producing properties. Some of the larger regional real estate brokerage houses found the sponsorship of a REIT a suitable device for unloading income-producing project listings that had not attracted the interest of more established institutional owners. However, any underwritten issue of a new REIT created substantial amounts of money to be invested all at once (not the usual way to buy deals), so managers from the realty world were reluctant to seek huge new offerings.

Two types of trusts evolved that pursued radically different investment philosophies. One type invested in mortgages, the other owned real estate. The cash flow of a mortgage-lending operation provided stark contrast to the rather dowdy dividends of equity ownership, and the difference was not overlooked by Wall Street. That seven- or eight-year record difference was tailor-made for the Wall Street hot-stock specialists.

At the same time, federal rules were amended and the regulatory agencies decided commercial bank holding companies could create advisers to REITs as a financially related activity. Thus, the stage was set for the bank-sponsored REITs to take off, sold on the reputation of the sponsor, with the history of mortgage-lending REITs to support the theory.

The investment banking community had just concluded a period of rapid growth of retail sales forces. Suddenly, with tight money, stocks were not quite attractive. New product was needed to keep active the massive sales force of account executives. The new issues of REITs graced by famous sponsors' names were launched and soon kept retail brokers busy.

An additional factor favoring the rise of REITs was that the real estate world was contracting because of tight money, and REIT money, equity dollars without a fixed rate of return required, could be committed on deals that others were shunning. Investors believed that REITs were counter-cyclical, although in retrospect they were really supercyclical, exacerbating the ups and downs.

Eventually, Wall Street's excessive enthusiasm resulted in equity leveraging. When new equity issues became treacherous because the numbers were catching up with the new REITs, Wall Street invented the dealer-placed commercial paper backed by bank lines of credit to the REITs. Because bankers did not have to provide reserves against standby lines of credit, the placement fees went directly to current earnings for the bankers.

By 1975, the industry had grown from $2 billion to $21 billion in five years.[1] REIT managers had more money than they could invest wisely. Innovative lending techniques flowered. Incentives were based on leverage, so bankers were encouraged to lend more at virtually no cost through providing back-up lines of credit.

Decline and stabilization. The REIT bubble burst quickly as oil price increases and fuel shortages exacerbated the decline. Developers were forced to terminate projects prior to completion and defaulted on their construction loans. Market prices plunged to new depths. The REITs turned to the banks, who were urged to honor their standby lines so that no investor in REIT commercial paper ever lost money by default. But the banks suddenly owned many of the REITs.

At least throughout the latter half of the 1970s, most industry developments centered around the final disposition of those REITs that failed. The stages of unwinding are still being played out. The lure to latecomers is the age-old promise of real estate undervalued assets. (See *Valuation of Assets* in this article.)

For the surviving REITs, life today is more stable, as the survivors work to live down their reputation as high-flying stocks. Their present low profile is partly due to the lessons learned from the REIT experience, but it also reflects that the ownership of real estate, rather than lending to develop it, is not a hot-stock business.

Revised tax law. Partly as an outgrowth of the chaotic REIT history, the Tax Reform Act of 1976 made substantial changes in the eligibility and operational requirements of REITs that had substantive tax consequences for the owners (see *Tax Consequences* in this article), and enhanced the viability of REITs as investment vehicles.

The additional freedom given REITs by the new operating rules increased the number and kinds of activities in which they could partake. But Congress avoided attempting to make any changes aimed at protecting investors: tax laws remained straightforward in motive — to raise taxes rather than to duplicate securities regulation.

---

[1] National Association of Real Estate Investment Trusts. *REIT Fact Book, 1978.* Washington, D.C.

Types of REITS

As the industry grew rapidly in the late 1960s and early 1970s, three basic kinds of REITs emerged — equity REITs, which owned real property primarily; mortgage REITs, which made real estate secured loans, primarily construction and development (C&D) loans; and combination, or hybrid, REITs, doing a little of each.

Today, most of the surviving mortgage REITs hold assets that were usually acquired involuntarily through foreclosure. The few REITs still active in mortgage lending intentionally seek other lenders to take longer-term positions — in contrast to the boom days, when long-term lenders were pursued only after the project was up and running.

Equity REITS. The real-property-owning REITs, mostly Massachusetts business trusts back in the early 1960s, have been formed and run primarily by real estate brokers — users of capital, not lenders.

Most of the equity trusts that survived the early 1970s were guided by trustees that eschewed substantial lending. Two REITs, for instance, capitalized on the growth of the Washington, D.C. area by owning shopping centers and multifamily projects regionally (Federal Realty and Washington REIT) — and suffering the taunts of their peers as they steadfastly avoided borrowing money to lend out in mortgage finance.

Pricing equity trusts remains an enigmatic problem. Usually, stock analysts capitalize the dividend or, more precisely, the periodic distribution of the REIT. Many equity REITs choose to pay out their depreciation (characterizing a portion of their cash-flow return as a return of equity to shareholders, that portion equal to the amount of earnings sheltered by the book depreciation expense). At least one equity trust (General Growth Properties) has found a special stock market niche among investors seeking a tax-free distribution through this process.

Mortgage REITS. There are still many REITs specializing in the active business of making mortgage loans. Considerable skepticism remains in the investment community about mortgage-lending REITs, however, on the part of those burned by the proliferation of mortgage REITs in the boom period.

The mortgage-lending REITs that survive are generally associated with strong sponsors (the life insurance company REITs, or Lomas & Nettleton's REIT), specialize in strong markets (M&T Mortgage Investors or First Continental REIT), or have other attributes that set them apart from the typical C&D REIT of the early 1970s.

There are variations, however, which survive today, thanks to the unregulated nature of the REIT instrument. There is one small REIT that has specialized in making second mortgages on homes. Another specializes in wraparound second mortgages. Several REITs make primarily subordinated land sale-leaseback transactions.

Combination REITS. Few REITs initially intended to offer investors a mix of short-term lending and long-term investing, other than the life-insurance-company-sponsored REITs, which had the capacity to make both loans and investments without having to create two separate staffs. The classic formula was to match the REIT's equity with the ownership of properties, to match short-term borrowings (usually commercial paper backed by bank lines of credit) to the short-term C&D loan portfolio, and to match longer-term debenture issues with long-term mortgage debt. Symmetry in the balance sheet was the goal.

The surviving insurance-company-sponsored REITs (four of the eight remain, sponsored by The Equitable, MONY, Northwestern Mutual, and Mass. Mutual), continue with variations on that theme. Analysts who follow these REITs closely focus on the relationships between the sponsors' portfolio activity and the loans or investments placed into the REIT.

Valuation of Assets

Traditionally, real estate is valued either by comparison (which does not work well for income-producing property), replacement cost (which means little in income-producing property management), or capitalization of income. Capitalization of the future stream of income, while logical, depends upon significant assumptions — future cap rates, sales volumes if there are percentage leases, and (not uncommon) lease concessions that kick in only at later stages of development, a factor not usually publicly known.

Consequently, valuation of a REIT's assets is not ascertained with any specificity. Many REITs must now prepare a present value estimate of assets. The value effectively caps the REIT's share price, is highly dependent upon the assumptions used in arriving at the appraisals, and serves only to stimulate contentious debate about the value of the REIT's management contribution.

The ultimate value of the REIT's assets can be determined only if it is sold. Even then, selling assets from a company that has announced liquidation does not necessarily result in shareholders obtaining full value. (When the buyer knows the seller must sell for all cash, price reflects that knowledge.) The few REITs that have announced liquidation and sold off all assets have paid shareholders much beyond book value, but the prompt turnover by the buyers of the formerly-REIT-held property at nearly double the price suggests shareholders may not have received full value. And especially for undeveloped land, but probably true for most all income-producing property, the future intentions of the developer-owner are as much a part of the value as the real estate itself.

ATTRACTIVE FEATURES

The problems inherent in REITs alluded to earlier (briefly summarized in *Potential Risks* in this article) do not negate some powerful benefits available only through the REIT investment vehicle. The fact that many REITs have survived the major fallout period of the mid-1970s is testimony to the vehicle's staying power. And it is certainly a well-known institution on Wall Street, if not fully appreciated. Especially when compared to other forms of realty ownership, the REIT has several advantageous characteristics, including the following:

Liquidity

Ordinary direct ownership of real estate, or participation in a publicly distributed partnership, implies no legitimate secondary market. (The "underground" resale market for widely held partnership shares cannot be made explicit without jeopardizing the tax status.) However, most REIT shares are traded actively. While most markets are rather thin compared to major industrial stocks, the pricing of most REIT shares reflects market conditions. Most major REITs are traded on either the New York or American Stock Exchange.

Well-Defined Purpose and Yield

In contrast to publicly held real estate development companies (which can mix income from past investments with gains or losses from current active business transactions), REITs always must be passive investors, dependent upon investment income. REIT yields do not depend on the tax status of the investor. In fact, REIT dividends do not qualify for the standard deduction of investment income. Thus, historic trends are often a good indication of future yield, in contrast to the speculative promise of most realty syndications.

Daily Pricing

Many institutional funds require the ability to value their portfolios as of a day certain. REIT shares are the only form of direct realty investment that can be priced daily, without engaging the services of an appraiser. (Whether or not the stock market price accurately reflects the value of the real estate owned by the REIT is a wholly different issue.)

Disclosure

The REITs are the most exposed segment of the income-producing real estate business. Ownership of each project must be made known. Lending policies have become well refined and publicly stated. Accounting procedures have been created solely as a result of the REITs. The role of trustees to shareholders has been clarified and expanded, creating a slightly different role for them in contrast to general partners of publicly held realty partnerships.

POTENTIAL RISKS

Several built-in conflicts and pitfalls have plagued REITs since their inception. Some of the following problems are characteristic of real estate investment in general; others arise as a result of the blending of the stock market with the real estate market.

- Valuation of real estate is, at best, an imprecise art. Book value, current value, liquidation value, or other objectives behind the setting of the value create confusion that may erode investor confidence.
- Lending short-term construction money is the riskiest business known to banking, yet the public was sold REIT shares primarily to finance short-term construction lending.
- REITs, while exempt from income taxation, are promoted not as an income vehicle, but as an asset play, a hedge against inflation.
- Stock market investment in realty is for the long haul, not suited for those of the hot-stock-market mentality.
- Striking a lucrative real estate deal is intensely personal and private, yet the REIT must operate in the goldfish bowl atmosphere of full disclosure under securities laws.
- Professional money managers prefer widely held stocks so they can unload without affecting price. Few REITs are widely held today, because most analysts who have studied the REIT well enough want to build ownership positions for control purposes. Thus, ever-thinner markets have led to a fall-off among institutional analysts following the REITs, which in turn has led to fewer and fewer analysts.

TAX CONSEQUENCES

In general, there are no tax advantages to owning REIT shares. Unlike partnership shares, where artificial (book) losses can flow to the investor's income for shelter, only the REIT itself escapes taxation. And it does so only if it returns all earnings to shareholders. Thus, REIT owners obtain a higher-than-usual dividend (which is not eligible for the deduction of the first $100 in dividend income).

While the tax benefits associated with owning real estate accrue only to the REIT itself, some REIT trustees have adopted a policy of passing along part of the benefit of making cash distributions in excess of stated REIT income. The cash flow sheltered by book expense of depreciation can be paid out as a form of return of capital. Other trusts, however, prefer to retain that cash flow in anticipation of the days when most of the cash-flow payment on amortizing mortgages secured by the REIT-held property is more a return of principal than interest — and thus not subject to the payout requirement of previous quarters. The latter choose not to rely on the ability to refinance assets as a means of perpetuating taxable cash flow.

REPRESENTATIVE TYPES OF INVESTORS

Some of the equity REITs, owning hotels or shopping centers, for example, have demonstrated a stability of dividend growth that attracts long-term, high-income-seeking investors who also look for upside protection from inflation through ownership of real estate. The downside risk of declining income to the trust due to reduced revenues in the shopping center or hotel has not been a problem since inflationary trends have persisted throughout the recent history of equity REITs.

Major foreign interests with significant funds have decided to own American realty, and their Wall Street advisers now have developed major positions in various REITs to satisfy that requirement. Other investors have bought controlling interest in some of the weaker REITs and have used them as conduits to buy into other REITs. One such investor in Mississippi owns a major position in more than a dozen REITs and keeps them, as he says, "on a string, like catfish, ready to up whenever a buyer happens by."

Because the complexities of sophisticated realty investment in income-producing projects are not well understood on Wall Street, REIT stock remains potentially volatile. As often as once a year, retail stockbrokers become excited about some REIT's hidden asset value and a flurry of orders takes place. More than once in the industry, the net outcome from such a flurry has been for the REIT to either liquidate or merge out of the public securities market.

IMPORTANT FACTORS IN BUYING AND SELLING

What to Look for in a REIT

The National Association of Real Estate Investment Trusts (NAREIT) publishes materials designed to assist investors in learning more, generally, about the REIT members of the Association. However, NAREIT has not registered as an investment adviser, and most of its publications reflect its desire not to be characterized as such. NAREIT describes the investment attributes of its members' stocks in its brochure, *What to Look For in a REIT*,[2] in this way:

> *intention to pass through earnings*— trusts or corporations which intend to meet the REIT qualification standards established in the Internal Revenue Code generally state that intention in the annual report, prospectus and SEC filings.
>
> *term of existence*— some REITs are "self-liquidating" or of a specified term; others are intended to exist indefinitely. Either case is generally specified in the annual report and prospectus.
>
> *experienced real estate management*— most REIT financial reports, proxies, prospectuses and SEC filings carry the names and credentials of executive and advisory officers and trustees.

---

[2] National Association of Real Estate Investment Trusts Inc. *What to Look for in a REIT.* Washington, D.C., 1981.

investment orientation— the real estate investment types in which a REIT will concentrate are generally specified in some form in the prospectus. Changes in investment orientation are usually described in the annual or other financial reports.

actual real estate investments— the types and locations of a REIT's investment holdings are usually included in the annual report and SEC filings.

Using REIT Analysts

While the publication of these attributes reflects NAREIT's desire to avoid becoming an investment adviser about the industry, it is being forced to take on this function increasingly because fewer analysts currently are following the industry's stocks. The following analysts, however, are worthy of mention.

Kenneth Campbell (Audit Publications, New York, N.Y.) has followed the REITs ever since he left the editorship of *House & Home* mazagine. Yet, today, he has broadened his services so as to follow all real estate securities.

Michael Oliver and Robert Frank at Alex. Brown and Sons, Baltimore, Maryland, remain the closest followers of the REITs, including several REITs that Alex. Brown helped bring out. Other analyst-brokers-investment bankers currently following at least some of REITs include Henry Wilf at Drexel Burnham Lambert's Philadelphia, Pennsylvania, office, Thomas Kearns (retail sales) and James Donohue (investment banking) at Merrill Lynch in New York (which has its own REIT, Hubbard Real Estate Investments, through its commercial properties division), and Bruce Garrison of the Underwood, Neuhaus firm in Texas.

GLOSSARY

declaration of trust— A document establishing the legal existence of a REIT, analogous to the charter of a corporation. Among other things, it outlines the investment objectives and may also specify restrictions on the trust's financial structure or operation.

equity leverage— The consequence of selling new equity interests in a corporation, real estate investment trust, or other business or investment entity at a premium over the book value of existing equity. As a result of such sale, earnings per share on the existing equity are increased.

equity participation— The right of a lender to a share of gross profit, net profit, or cash flow from a property on which the lender has made a loan, thereby deriving some of the upside benefits without becoming a loan.

equity REIT— A REIT that invests in real estate on a long-term basis, primarily in real property subject to prime tenancies and derives its principal source of income from rents.

hybrid REIT— A REIT that takes equity positions in real estate and also invests in real estate mortgages.

mortgage REIT— A REIT that finances various phases of a real estate venture, including the acquisition and development of the land and the construction and completion of the buildings and other improvements.

real estate investment trust (REIT)— A trust organized to pool capital for the purpose of investing in real estate or in real estate mortgages. The term is also used to refer to trusts or corporations that elect to be taxed as a REIT.

secondary-mortgage market— Transactions mostly between mortgage originators (who wish to sell mortgage loans) and investors (who are willing to buy mortgage loans to hold for income), involving the purchase and sale of existing mortgages by government agencies and by private institutions and investors.

tax qualification— Compliance with requirements of the Internal Revenue Code in order to qualify for special tax treatment.

SUGGESTED READING

Periodicals

Audit Investments. Published by Audit Investment Research, Inc., New York, N.Y. Biweekly.

Real Estate Law Report. Published by Warren, Gorham & Lamont, Boston, Mass. Monthly.

Real Estate Review. Published by Warren, Gorham & Lamont, Boston, Mass. Quarterly.

REIT Industry Investment Review. Published by the National Association of Real Estate Investment Trusts, Inc., Washington, D.C. Monthly; one-page statistical summary.

REITs Monthly. Published by the National Association of Real Estate Investment Trusts, Inc., Washington, D.C. Monthly.

REITs Quarterly. Published by the National Association of Real Estate Investment Trusts, Inc., Washington, D.C. Quarterly.

Articles

Brody, M. "Sounder Ground: Despite Rise in Interest Rates, REITs Continue to Prosper." *Barrons* 59:4-5, May 21, 1979.

Greenebaum, M. "Return of the REITs." *Fortune* 103:111-112, May 18, 1981.

Leventhal, K. "Inflation and REITs Complement Each Other." *Professional Builder* 45:77, March 1980.

———. "Viability of REITs Deserves Reconsideration." *Professional Builder* 44:35, October 1979.

Nicholson, S. "REITs Making Comeback as Property Owners." *Buildings* 73:46, May 1979.

Sullivan, M.J. "Recent Developments in the Tax Treatment of the Real Estate Investments of Employees Trusts." *Taxes* 59:291-299, May 1981.

Weberman, B. "New Breed of REIT. [Lomas & Nettleton Financial.]" *Forbes* 127:319, May 11, 1981.

Reference Books

Arnold, Alvin L., and Smith, Owen T. *Modern Ownership and Investment Forms.* Boston: Warren, Gorham & Lamont, 1978.

Campbell, Kenneth D. *Real Estate Trusts: America's Newest Billionaires.* New York: Audit Investment Research, Inc., 1971.

National Association of Real Estate Investment Trusts, Inc. *REIT Fact Book.* Washington, D.C., 1979 (periodic update).

Practising Law Institute. *Real Estate Securities: Public and Private Course Handbook* (Real Estate Law and Practice Course Handbook Series 1977-78). New York, 1978.

Warren, Gorham & Lamont. *Real Estate Review Portfolios: No. 11, How to Syndicate Real Estate; No. 12, How Securities Laws Affect Real Estate Offerings; No. 13, Real Estate Tax-Shelter Techniques.* Boston, 1977, 1977, 1979, respectively (updated periodically).

Real Estate Limited Partnerships

Jack P. Friedman *

BASIC CHARACTERISTICS

The real estate field is a complex and varied one, demanding considerable expertise and ranging from ventures that require only a few thousand dollars in capital outlay to deals involving many millions of dollars. For many investors, partnerships are the most practical way to participate in this type of investment. Therefore, a partnership may be the best vehicle for many individual investors. Depending upon the type of partnership, the risk, liability, and responsibility for management of the venture may be shared in a number of different ways.

Major emphasis is placed on the limited partnership in this article since this is the practical vehicle for individual investors who are not real estate professionals.

General Partnership

A general partnership is often preferred by a relatively small and intimate group of investors who do not depend on venture capital for their financing and are willing to forgo the limited liability offered by a limited partnership or a corporation, but who want to retain collective control over policy decisions and also provide a measure of liquidity for their estates.

Each partner in a general partnership may bind the partnership by his acts or conduct; each is personally liable for the partnership debts and is entitled to an equal voice in the management of partnership affairs.

In the unusual case of a large general partnership, the partnership agreement usually limits control by the investor-partners to delegating the ultimate decision-making power to the promoter-partner who acts as agent for the investor-partners. Under such an arrangement, the investor-partners usually are given residual control over major decisions, such as whether to modify a lease or mortgage or whether to sell, transfer, or refinance the property that is the basis of the partnership venture.

Limited Partnership

A limited partnership consists of one or more general partners and one or more limited partners. While the general partner or partners manage the affairs

* Jack P. Friedman is head of the Research Division of the Texas Real Estate Research Center, Texas A&M University.

of the partnership and are personally liable for the debts and obligations of the partnership, the limited partners, who are the passive investors, are not personally responsible for the partnership's debts and obligations.

A limited partnership is something of a hybrid between a corporation and a general partnership. It is similar to a corporation in that the exposure of a limited partner, like that of a corporate shareholder, cannot exceed his equity investment. Moreover, his status as a limited partner under the Uniform Limited Partnership Act precludes any right to control or actively participate in the affairs of the organization. The general partners' role and functions, on the other hand, are generally similar to the role and functions of the directors and officers of a corporation.

Just as a corporation must file a certificate of incorporation with the appropriate state agency, a limited partnership, upon formation, must file a certificate of limited partnership with the appropriate state authority.

Real Estate Syndicate

In a real estate syndicate, the real estate professional (the syndicator) finds and purchases a property that he feels has a significant investment potential and sells ownership interests in the property, usually in the form of a limited partnership. The limited partnership allows the syndicator to combine his own expertise in real estate and tax matters with the financial resources of private investors. At the same time, it allows private investors the opportunity to invest in substantial real estate ventures with relatively small capital outlay. Limited partners benefit from limited personal liability on the debts of the venture, a tax-free cash return on part of their investment, and, frequently, tax shelter for their income from other sources as well. As passive investors, they are free from administrative concerns such as recordkeeping and the day-to-day management and operation of the venture, which are the responsibility of the syndicator or general partner.

Public offerings. There are several publicly held limited partnerships and many that are privately placed. Generally, the publicly held limited partnerships raise much more money and have acquired or will acquire a diversified set of properties. Publicly held entities include JMB, Balcor, McNeil Real Estate Fund, American Property Investors, National Property Investors, and Consolidated Capital.

Quite often, however, a real estate broker or developer will syndicate limited partnership interests in a single property, with investment returns based on the performance of that property only.

Publicly held limited partnership interests offered for sale to the public generally promise returns that are considered competitive. Privately placed interests, by nature, are more speculative, with greater variability or risk in returns.

Limited Partnership Participants

General partner. The general partner in a limited partnership manages the partnership affairs, can bind the partnership by his acts and conduct, and can be held personally liable for the partnership obligations. There are certain limitations on the general partner's authority, the most important of which are as follows:

- He may not perform any act in contravention of the limited partnership certificate.
- He may not perform any act that would make it impossible to carry on the ordinary business of the partnership.
- He may not possess partnership property or assign rights in specific partnership property for other than a partnership purpose.
- He may not admit a person into the partnership as a general partner.

However, a general partner may be given authority to perform such acts by written consent of all of the limited partners. In addition, all the limited partners may ratify such an act once performed by a general partner.

Limited partners. All the limited partners stand on an equal footing with each other as to the return on and of their contributions, their right to income, and all other partnership matters, unless there is an agreement providing for priority as to such items. Such priority provisions must be stated in the partnership certificate.

Rights and obligations. Generally, a limited partner can neither bind the partnership by his acts nor be held liable to partnership creditors. However, the limited partner is liable to the partnership for the contributions he has agreed to make to the partnership and for any breach of the partnership agreement for which he is responsible. Also, the limited partner may be held liable to the partnership for a sum equal to the amount he has received plus interest as a return of his capital contribution where necessary to discharge the partnership's liabilities to creditors who extended credit to it or whose claims arose before the contribution was returned to him.

ATTRACTIVE FEATURES

The limited partnership form of real estate ownership combines for investors the advantages of limited legal liability, such as a corporation offers its stockholders, with important tax and other advantages.

Multiple Financial Benefits

Financial benefits from real estate limited partnerships can be significant. Appreciation and cash flow that result from the selection of well located, well constructed, and efficiently managed property can provide generous returns. Inflation tends to boost these returns, and financial leverage to magnify them. The absence of double taxation and the ability to offset nonproject income by artificial tax losses (see *Deductibility of Losses* in this article) serve to minimize an investor's tax bill. The opportunity to derive all these benefits — appreciation, cash flow, and tax savings — without personal liability makes a limited partnership a highly attractive mechanism for investing in real estate.

Deductibility of Losses

Unlike losses that cannot be passed through to stockholders, limited partnership taxable losses (e.g., depreciation) may be deducted by individual partners even though each partner's equity is only a small portion of the total. This result is achieved by the nonrecourse-liability rule. Although a partner, including a limited partner, can deduct losses only to the extent of the basis (cost) of his partnership interest, he may include in his basis his share of those liabilities of the partnership for which no partner is personally liable (nonrecourse liability). At-risk rules that apply to certain investments do not apply to partnerships that are mainly concerned with real estate. Thus, real estate partners may deduct losses in excess of the capital they contribute.

Pooling of Equity Capital

Several investors can pool their equity capital and so acquire larger and higher-priced properties, which generate substantial tax deductions and which usually are not only of better quality but also are more easily financed than lower-priced properties.

POTENTIAL RISKS

Integrity of General Partner

It is extremely important for potential investors to investigate the reputation of the offeror of a limited partnership interest, and to study the terms of the offering with care. (See further caveats under *Important Factors in Buying* in this article.)

Entrepreneurial Risks

There is no assurance that, for a proposed development, there will be no construction delays. Labor strikes, material shortages, and weather conditions are beyond the control of a developer-promoter. Upon completion, it may prove more difficult than anticipated to find suitable tenants. Real estate markets are subject to local economic conditions that change; after a project is fully rented there is no guarantee it will remain occupied. There is no assurance that operating expenses will be as forecast. They may rise unexpectedly because of tax increases or labor costs. Finally, insolvency of the general partner is always a possibility. This could cause termination of the partnership.

Illiquidity

Limited partnership investment units are highly illiquid. There is no organized market for units, so if an investor needs to sell, the price received may be lower than anticipated and the transaction may take much longer to consummate than in the case of most other investments.

Taxation of Limited Partnership as a Corporation

The IRS has the right to examine a limited partnership, and, if it finds that the partnership has a predominance of corporate characteristics, it can treat the partnership as a corporation, thus converting it from a mere conduit for tax purposes into a taxable entity. However, if a real estate limited partnership does not have as its principal purpose the avoidance of taxes, it should qualify to be taxed as a partnership, barring substantial corporate characteristics.

Tax avoidance guidelines. Tax evasion will probably be found to exist where there is virtually no possibility of realizing an economic profit from the investment or venture. However, the mere fact that the investors (the limited partners) actually realize no current cash flow and merely use the taxable losses the property produces is not sufficient to render the partnership a taxable entity and invalidate it as a tax-shelter vehicle. In determining whether a limited partnership was organized for the principal purpose of avoiding or reducing federal taxes the IRS applies the following guidelines:

- All general partners must, in the aggregate, have at least a one percent interest in each material item of partnership taxable income, gain, loss, deduction, or credit.
- The aggregate tax deduction of the limited partners (the investors) during the first two years of the partnership's operations cannot exceed the amount of the equity investment in the partnership.
- No creditor who makes a nonrecourse loan to the partnership may acquire, as a result of making the loan, any direct or indirect interest in the profits, capital, or property of the limited partnership, other than as a secured creditor.

Characteristics that can make a partnership a taxable entity. To qualify as a conduit for the pass-through of taxable gains and losses to its investors, a limited partnership must not show more corporate than partnership characteristics. Corporate characteristics are as follows.

Continuity of life. Continuity of life indicates a corporation and not a partnership. Since a limited partnership can provide that death, insanity, or retirement of a general partner terminates the partnership, continuity of life usually is not present.

Centralized management. A fundamental characteristic of a limited partnership is that the general partner (or partners) manages the partnership while the majority ownership usually lies in the passive investors who are the limited partners. Thus, management is centralized. Consequently, this corporate characteristic is present in a limited partnership.

Limited liability. Corporate shareholders have limited liability. For income tax purposes, limited liability of a general partner is not present and partnership treatment is indicated if the general partner is personally liable for the partnership's nonmortgage debts and also has substantial assets.

Free transferability of interests. There is no free transferability of partnership interests, and partnership treatment is indicated if a limited partner needs the general partner's consent to transfer his partnership interest to a substitute limited partner. A provision requiring the general partner's consent is common in real estate limited partnership agreements. Likewise, there is no free transferability of partnership interests if a partner's right to assign his interest is limited to assigning his share in the profits of the enterprise. Free transferability of partnership interest is also lacking where the transfer of a partner's interest results in the dissolution of the partnership and the formation of a new partnership under state law.

Since many real estate limited partnerships will not show continuity of life, limited liability, and free transferability of partnership interests, partnership treatment (i.e., the pass-through directly to the partners of taxable partnership income, gains, and losses) can be reasonably assured.

TAX CONSEQUENCES — DEMONSTRATION VENTURE

When a promoter organizes a limited partnership and plans to sell interests to investors, he often prepares a descriptive memorandum that provides all relevant information, including pro forma financial projections. A complete package of pro forma financial statements includes

- Required sources and applications of funds;
- A forecast of taxable income and cash flow;
- A partnership allocation of taxable income and cash flow; and
- A rate of return computation on an investment unit.

Tables 1 through 3 on pages 766 through 768 illustrate the first three statements from a particular development for an apartment complex that is to be financed by an FHA mortgage. There is a loan commitment of $2,608,400. Twenty limited partnership units of $20,000 each are to be sold in order to raise $400,000 of equity. The limited partners will own 95 percent of the project. The general partner will manage it and retain a 5 percent ownership share.

As protection for the limited partners, their investment contributions are staggered as follows: one-third payable upon becoming a partner, one-third upon completing construction, and one-third upon attaining a break-even occupancy rate (where cash flow before taxes is zero).

TABLE 1. Fund Requirements and Sources*

REQUIREMENTS

Land:		
Market value of land	$ 188,000	
Landscaping and land improvements	205,150	
		$ 393,150
Appliances, carpets, and specialties		183,350
Cabinets		45,120
Buildings:		
Construction costs	1,683,116	
Architect's fee, design, and supervision	36,000	
Bond premium	2,500	
		1,721,616
Other costs and expenses allocable to land and buildings:		
Builders' and sponsors' profit and risk allowance	400,000	
Builders' general overhead	41,064	
Title and recording expenses	16,600	
		457,664
Total land and building costs		2,800,900
Other costs incurred prior to final mortgage closing		376,500
Total		$3,177,400

SOURCES

Mortgage proceeds	$2,608,400
Capital contributed by limited partners	400,000
Rental income	169,000
Total cash sources	$3,177,400

*This projection is dependent on future events and may be significantly affected by changes in economic and other circumstances.

SOURCE: Author's data.

TABLE 2. Projection of Taxable Income and Cash Flow*

	Year 1	*Year 5*	*Year 10*	*Year 20*
Rent at full occupancy	$ 6,000	$ 387,168	$ 387,168	$ 387,168
Less allowance for vacancies and resident manager's apartment	3,000	38,717	38,717	38,717
Rental income	3,000	348,451	348,451	348,451
Interest earned on funds reserved for replacements		838	3,341	908
Total income	3,000	349,289	351,792	349,359
Expenses:				
FHA mortgage insurance		12,913	12,541	11,217
Interest	18,750	193,769	188,233	168,496
Operating expenses and property taxes	5,750	105,981	105,981	105,981
Amortization of deferred charges	11,814	1,513	1,513	1,513
Depreciation	4,729	156,922	136,604	76,408
Total expenses	41,053	471,098	444,872	363,615
Taxable income (loss)	(38,043)	(121,809)	(93,080)	(14,256)
Add, depreciation and amortization	16,543	158,435	138,117	77,921
Cash flow from operations	(21,500)	36,626	45,037	63,665
Less, additional cash requirements:				
Mortgage principal payments		12,212	17,749	37,486
Replacement reserve		10,719	10,719	10,719
Interest on funds in replacement reserve	- 0 -	838	3,341	908
Total additional cash requirements	- 0 -	23,769	31,809	49,113
Add, funds provided by mortgage proceeds	21,500	- 0 -	- 0 -	- 0 -
Cash flow available for distribution	$ - 0 -	$ 12,857	$ 13,228	$ 14,552

*This project is dependent upon future events and may be significantly affected by changes in economic and other circumstances. Rental rates may be increased with the consent of FHA; cash distributions are limited by the FHA.

SOURCE: Author's data.

TABLE 3. Partners' Shares of Projected Income, Cash Flow, and Cash Generated

	Cash Flow			*Taxable Income (Loss)*			*Cash Generated*
Year	*General Partner 5%*	*Limited Partners 95%*	*Total*	*General Partner 5%*	*Limited Partners 95%*	*Total*	*Limited Partners' Share (50% Bracket)*
1				$ (1,902)	$ (36,141)	$ (38,043)	$ 18,070
2				(10,044)	(190,839)	(200,883)	95,420
3				(9,363)	(177,887)	(187,250)	88,943
4	$ 640	$ 12,158	$ 12,798	(6,829)	(129,752)	(136,581)	77,034
5	643	12,214	12,857	(6,090)	(115,719)	(121,809)	70,073
6	646	12,274	12,920	(5,454)	(103,636)	(109,090)	64,092
7	649	12,340	12,989	(4,994)	(94,889)	(99,883)	59,784
8	653	12,410	13,063	(4,641)	(88,178)	(92,819)	56,499
9	657	12,485	13,142	(4,279)	(81,295)	(85,574)	53,133
10	661	12,567	13,228	(4,654)	(88,426)	(93,080)	56,780
11	666	12,655	13,321	(3,908)	(74,256)	(78,164)	49,783
12	671	12,750	13,421	(3,371)	(64,048)	(67,419)	44,774
13	676	12,852	13,528	(2,916)	(55,401)	(58,317)	40,552
14	682	12,961	13,643	(3,055)	(58,051)	(61,106)	41,986
15	689	13,079	13,768	(2,692)	(51,151)	(53,843)	38,655
16	695	13,208	13,903	(2,267)	(43,079)	(45,346)	34,747
17	703	13,345	14,048	(1,804)	(34,276)	(36,080)	30,483
18	710	13,493	14,203	(1,571)	(29,852)	(31,423)	28,419
19	718	13,653	14,371	(1,173)	(22,292)	(23,465)	24,799
20	728	13,824	14,552	(713)	(13,543)	(14,256)	20,596
21	737	14,011	14,748	(237)	(4,498)	(4,735)	16,260
22	748	14,211	14,959	146	2,774	2,920	12,823
23	759	14,426	15,185	590	11,223	11,813	8,814
24	771	14,658	15,429	1,102	20,930	22,032	4,193
Total	$14,502	$275,574	$290,076	($80,119)	($1,522,282)	($1,602,401)	$1,036,712

The statement of Table 1 on page 766 shows the expected cost of the project (land, building, and overhead interest during construction) and the sources of funds (mortgage, equity, and some rental income).

Table 2 on page 767 shows expected rental income, operating expenses, depreciation, and other matters. From these items, total annual taxable income and cash flow can be projected. Table 2 illustrates this statement for selected years. [1]

The next statement (Table 3 on page 768) indicates the distribution of benefits to the two types of partners based on the assumption that each limited partner can expect to receive an annual cash distribution beginning in the fourth year. Amounts range from $609 to $733 per unit of investment per year, which is just over a 3 percent cash return per $20,000 investment unit. This is quite meager compared to some projects, but not untypical for FHA projects. However, projected tax losses in the early years are substantial and provide the bulk of the return.

Tax losses are caused by accelerated depreciation and high interest requirements in the early years of ownership. These are largely artificial losses because they may be claimed regardless of the true changes in property value. Cash generated (also called after-tax cash flow) is the annual benefit of cash flow plus the value of tax savings from sheltering outside income from taxation.

During the early years of construction and occupancy, the project is expected to generate more than $4,000 of after-tax cash flow per year for each investment unit. As time passes, amounts of cash generated diminish because accelerated depreciation (cost recovery) and interest deductions decline with time. Thus, there will be fewer tax deductions available in later years. If the project is held for more than twenty years, taxable income can be expected. At that juncture, it probably will be desirable to refinance the debt or to sell the property.

This particular projection conservatively estimates that the property will be resold for the unpaid mortgage balance (i.e., no reversion to equity). Yet, because of the large tax losses claimed during ownership, a high tax would be payable at resale. This is because the projected mortgage balance will exceed the investors' adjusted tax basis at resale. After figuring the tax due at resale, all of the variables needed for a rate of return computation are included. That includes the investment required, holding period after-tax income, and resale results, which have been forecast. An after-tax rate of return is included in the projections. There is

---

[1] Construction of this project began in year one, and continued through year two. A few units became available for rent at the end of year one and could be depreciated that year. Rent-up continued through years two and three. Normal operations, with a steady occupancy rate, are expected to begin in year four.

Rent increases are permitted by the FHA to the extent of operating expense and property tax increases. Projections of these amounts were kept constant for simplicity, because they have no effect on the bottom line. Amortization of deferred charges in year one represent the write-off of certain fees paid during construction. Interest earned on funds reserved for replacements varies as those funds are used to purchase new appliances, carpets, and the like.

one further assumption: that money saved to pay taxes due at the end of the holding period can be invested at a 4 percent after-tax rate.

Provided the assumptions prove valid, an investor will earn the equivalent return of a municipal bond that returns a 17.9 percent rate (or a corporate bond that yields 35.8 percent to a 50-percent-bracket taxpayer).

REPRESENTATIVE TYPES OF INVESTORS

Illiquidity and other risk factors described earlier make limited partnership units suitable for relatively few investors. Many offerings suggest that the investor have a minimum net worth of $100,000, minimum annual income of at least $50,000, and be in the 50 percent tax bracket.

Limited partnerships are unique in allowing the pass-through of tax losses, and tax losses are worth more to high-bracket investors than to others. Consequently, most limited partnership interests are marketed to individuals who are in high tax brackets and who expect to continue to be in that situation. Investors include business people, physicians, attorneys, and highly paid executives.

Non-tax-paying entities such as pension funds, universities, and charities get no benefit of losses, so they generally are not suitable investors.

Investors who are willing to accept the risk of a single project can often find a suitable privately placed project. However, search costs may be rather high, as one would want an attorney, CPA, and real estate counselor to review the project and assumptions. Public limited partnership offerings are easier to find through stockbrokers and offer less risk, but seldom offer as high a potential return as does a single-project venture.

IMPORTANT FACTORS IN BUYING

Regulation and Licensing of Dealers

In general, the broker or salesperson who sells a real estate limited partnership interest is subject to regulation under the federal securities laws. Not all real estate transactions involving groups of investors are securities transactions, but the exceptions are narrow and the line between what is and what is not a security is not always clear.

For example, if a broker sells to a group of investors who comes to him as a group, and earns only a sales commission and does not also manage the property, he probably has not sold a security and the transaction is not subject to securities regulations. Even if the broker offers management as an option but the investors do not take him up on the option, he has probably not sold a security. If the investors do accept the offer to manage the property, it begins to be somewhat less certain that the transaction is not a security transaction. If the investors have no practical alternative to accepting the offer to manage, a sale of a security has almost certainly occurred. Lastly, where the broker sells and his management of the property is an essential part of the deal, there is a sale of a security.

Track Record of the Syndicator

The most important protection an investor in a real estate syndication has is the syndicator himself — his reliability, expertise, and skills. For this reason, it is always important for a prospective investor to check out not only the proposition offered, but also the syndicator's track record and reputation.

There are some syndicators who prey on high-tax-bracket individuals who have no expertise in real estate. They attempt to palm off distressed, overpriced, ill-managed properties as a tax shelter. Some of these promoters project the image of a Fortune 500 executive. They are often successful, but this does not necessarily mean success for their investors. Many will earn a huge fee for brokerage only. A 5 percent brokerage fee on the total sales price of a $3 million project is $150,000. That amount may be as much as one-half of the money they raise as equity from limited partners.

Some syndicators will commit to buy the property themselves for, say $3 million, then syndicate it for $4 million. They may take the $1 million increase in the form of a second mortgage or wraparound mortgage. Interest payments they will receive drain the project's potential cash flow. Some others claim excessive management fees and/or retain the right to share excessively in the proceeds from resale. Others will take their money "up front" and disappear, leaving the property without adequate management.

There should be incentive for good management, but there is a line between reasonable and excessive compensaton. Investors should review all documents to determine whether the promoter-general partner seems to be fair or plans to milk the property. However, actions speak louder than words, and it is wise to check for fair treatment with investors in other projects of the promoter. Note that this in itself does not assure a risk-free project.

MANAGING THE INVESTMENT

The promoter-general partner usually is responsible for managing the property or hiring professional management. The voice of limited partners in the daily activities of the business must be limited or the liability status of the limited partners will be jeopardized.

The general partner should provide annual reports and necessary income tax information to the investors. Newsworthy property conditions, such as the bankruptcy of an important tenant or a lawsuit affecting the property, should be immediately conveyed to the limited partners.

Offers to buy the partnership or the property, or to refinance it, should be presented to the investors. Generally, limited partners can vote in these matters.

GLOSSARY

after-tax cash flow— Actual spendable income from an investment after income taxes; net operating income (or loss), reduced by mortgage principal and interest payments, less income tax payments.

artificial tax loss— A loss reported for tax purposes that does not necessarily reflect the true economics of an investment.

equity capital— Funds invested in property or in an enterprise in consideration of receiving a share of future profits but which bear the first risk of any loss. These funds are distinguished from debt capital, which represents funds loaned to the enterprise or to acquire property in which specific interest is to be paid and which represents a claim on the assets that is superior to the claim of the equity capital.

general partnership— A partnership in which all the partners share in the profits and losses of the enterprise and in the management and operation of partnership affairs.

limited partnership— A partnership in which a general partner (or partners) manages the partnership affairs and can bind the partnership, and limited partners are passive investors in the enterprise. They cannot by their acts or conduct bind the partnership, and their liability is limited to the amount of their contribution to the partnership.

nonrecourse loan— A loan in which the lender waives any personal liability by the borrower; in case of default, the lender is limited to foreclosing on the mortgage and acquiring the real estate.

partnership— An association of two or more persons for the purpose of carrying on a business for profit and sharing both profits and losses.

safe-harbor rule— An IRS rule that applies to the taxation of limited partnerships. Under the rule, if a corporate general partner maintains a specified net worth and the venture meets the additional partnership requirements, the IRS will issue an advance ruling treating the venture as a partnership rather than as an association for tax purposes.

securities broker— Any person or entity engaged in the business of effecting transactions in securities for the account of others (as defined by the Securities Exchange Act of 1934).

syndication— An organization through which a real estate professional, who is the syndicator or sponsor, obtains investors who provide the funds required to engage in a real estate enterprise.

TRADE ORGANIZATION

Real Estate Securities and Syndication Institute, 430 N. Michigan Avenue, Chicago, Ill. 60611

COMPANIES OFFERING LIMITED PARTNERSHIP PARTICIPATIONS

The following is a list of companies offering real estate limited partnership interests and the amounts they raised in 1980.*

---

* Questor Real Estate Newsletter, San Francisco

Angeles Corporation, Los Angeles, Calif. — $60,298,000
The Balcor Company, Skokie, Ill. — $137,455,000
Consolidated Capital Corporation, Emeryville, Calif. — $314,702,000
First Capital Investment Corporation, Coral Gables, Fla. — $63,355,000
Fox and Carskadon Corporation, San Francisco, Calif. — $314,433,000
Integrated Resources Inc., New York, N.Y. — $391,067,000
JMB Realty Corporation, Chicago, Ill. — $478,582,000
Robert A. McNeil Corporation, San Mateo, Calif. — $340,071,000
Merrill Lynch Hubbard, New York, N.Y. — $40,300,000
Public Storage Properties Inc., Pasadena, Calif. — $103,245,000
Shearson-Murray Real Estate Funds, Dallas, Tex. — $29,600,000
Smith Barney Real Estate Corporation, New York, N.Y. — $68,812,000
University Group Incorporated, Long Beach, Calif. — $66,962,000
Winthrop Partners, Boston, Mass. — $28,920,000
Paine Webber Properties, Inc., Boston, Mass. — $25,687,000

REAL ESTATE LIMITED PARTNERSHIP UNDERWRITER/DISTRIBUTORS

Dean Witter Reynolds Inc., New York, N.Y.
E.F. Hutton & Company Inc., New York, N.Y.
Merrill Lynch Pierce Fenner & Smith Inc., New York, N.Y.
Oppenheimer & Co., Inc., New York, N.Y.
Paine Webber Jackson & Curtis, Inc., New York, N.Y.
Shearson/American Express, New York, N.Y.
Smith Barney Harris Upham & Co., Inc., New York, N.Y.

SUGGESTED READING

Periodicals

Questor Real Estate Investment Yearbook. Published by Questor & Associates, San Francisco, Cal. Annually.

Questor Real Estate Newsletter. Published by Questor & Associates, San Francisco, Cal. Monthly.

Real Estate Securities Journal. Published by the Real Estate Securities and Syndication Institute, Chicago, Ill. Three times a year.

RESSI Review. Published by the Real Estate Securities and Syndication Institute, Chicago, Ill. Monthly.

Reference Books

Arnold, Alvin L. *Tax Shelters in Real Estate Today.* Boston: Warren, Gorham & Lamont, 1978.

———. *Real Estate Investor's Deskbook.* Boston: Warren, Gorham & Lamont, 1982.

——— and Smith, Owen T. *Modern Ownership and Investment Forms.* Boston: Warren, Gorham & Lamont, 1978.

Coopers & Lybrand. *Tax Planning for Real Estate Transactions.* Chicago: Farm and Land Institute, 1978.

Epley, Donald R., and Millar, James A. *Basic Real Estate Finance and Investments.* New York: John Wiley & Sons, Inc., 1980.

Freshman, Samuel K. *Principles of Real Estate Syndication.* 3rd ed. Beverly Hills: Law and Capital Dynamics, 1980.

Henszey, Ben N., and Friedman, Ronald M. *Real Estate Law.* Boston: Warren, Gorham & Lamont, 1980.

Miller, Daniel. *How To Invest in Real Estate Syndicates.* Homewood: Dow Jones-Irwin Co., 1978.

Pyhrr, Stephen A., and Cooper, James R. *Real Estate Investment: Strategy Analysis Decisions.* Boston: Warren, Gorham & Lamont, 1982.

Roulac, Stephen C. *Real Estate Syndication Digest.* San Francisco: Questor & Associates, 1972.

Warren, Gorham & Lamont. *Real Estate Review Portfolios: No. 11, How to Syndicate Real Estate; No. 12, How Securities Laws Affect Real Estate Offerings; No. 14, How to Choose a Form of Ownership for Real Estate.* Boston, 1977. (Updated periodically.)

Real Estate—Multi-Family Rental

Harris Lawless *

BASIC CHARACTERISTICS

General Description

A multi-family rental is usually described as a building or series of buildings that includes more than four living units that share certain common facilities. Those common facilities may include hallways, entries, heating and air-conditioning facilities, laundry room, and parking lots, as well as amenities, and certain common area facilities provided for the tenants' recreation. Some typical amenities are swimming pools, saunas, club houses, tennis courts, wading pools and children's play areas. A profusion of amenities not only makes the units easier to rent but also justifies higher rents.

Groups of rental units consisting of fewer than four are generally referred to as duplexes, triplexes, or fourplexes and usually have separate entrances. The smaller complexes are usually managed and maintained by the owner who, most likely, will also occupy one of the units. Many people jokingly remark that purchasing a rental unit of four or fewer units is not an investment — the owner bought a job. That is not entirely true, as the units provide the owner with living space at a lower occupancy cost in addition to a certain amount of tax shelter. For the investor in the 1980s, the primary motive is long-term appreciation, as there will probably be little, if any, positive cash flow from the investment.

Some people invest in single-family houses, condominiums, or cooperatives that they intend to rent to others rather than use for personal occupancy. Under current rental levels and interest rates, in most cases the owner will be out of pocket to carry the unit. The investment motive is a certain amount of tax shelter and an appreciation potential. These smaller investments are usually thought to be inflation hedges.

Common Rules of Thumb

Economy of scale. Although every investment is different and must be dealt with individually, as a general rule of thumb the more living units contained in a multi-family rental unit, the better the return to the investor. There are certain fixed or semi-variable costs associated with any complex that, spread over a larger number of units, will result in a better return. Also, the greater the number of units, the more likely it will be that the complex can afford the professional

* Harris Lawless is President of Harris Lawless & Associates, Sausalito, Cal.

management fees necessary to manage the complex efficiently. If the complex is too small, the owner-investor is going to have to invest sweat equity to operate the complex.

For economic efficiency, it is generally agreed that a multi-family complex should have a minimum of fifty units. Anything smaller usually cannot pay professional management fees, which means that the owner will have to be involved in the management. Even that rule of thumb is not completely reliable. In a very high-rent area where apartments rent for $1,000 a month or more, possibly as few as twenty units would be sufficient. In a low-rent area where rents are $200 or so a month, it might be necessary to have a minimum of seventy-five or more units.

Gross multipliers. Economy of scale also affects another commonly used rule of thumb called the "gross multiplier." A gross multiplier is a factor that is used to multiply the anticipated gross annual income from a multi-family complex to arrive at an approximate value. The gross multiplier for a reasonably large complex will usually be between six and eight. The factor will reflect the quality of the complex, the location, and the nature of the tenancy. Assume, for example, that the annual scheduled rentals are $200,000 and the gross multiplier is seven. The approximate value would be $1,400,000. This, of course, is only an approximate value. Every investment must be individually analyzed.

The fewer the number of units, the higher the factor will be. For example, a fourplex usually will sell with a factor of twelve to fourteen. With rents of $250 per unit, the annual gross income would be $12,000. Using a multiplier of thirteen, the approximate value would be $156,000. Since a smaller number of units will usually carry a higher multiplier, an investor pays more for the income stream from the smaller complex.

The reason for the variance in the factor is simply the effect of supply and demand. There are probably millions of people who can afford to invest in a fourplex. There are probably only a few hundred who can invest in a $4 million complex. As a result, the cost for the income stream from the smaller complexes is relatively higher than it is for the income stream from the larger complexes. There is a far larger market for the smaller complexes.

Another reason for the higher relative cost of the income stream from the smaller complex is that the people that buy the smaller units tend to invest on an emotional rather than a rational basis. The investor (and the seller) of the $4 million complex will not get emotionally involved in the purchase and will buy on the basis of a rational analysis of the potential returns. Pride of ownership is a credible emotion but it should not interfere with investment.

The investor must keep in mind that the gross multiplier is only a rule of thumb and not a financial analysis. It is not even uniformly applied. Some investors will apply the multiplier to the total of the scheduled rents (i.e., the amount of rent charged for each apartment on an annual basis) without regard for existing or expected vacancies. Others will apply a 5 or 10 percent vacancy factor before using the multiplier. At best, it is only a very rough estimate of value. It is useful in screening out opportunities that probably would not be appropriate candidates for the detailed financial analysis that should be done.

There are no rules of thumb for valuation of a single-family or condominium rental unit since the income stream does not establish the value. An appraiser would base his value judgment almost entirely on comparable sales of similar units in the same area and on some consideration of the replacement cost. In fact, under current conditions, the income stream probably would not be enough to carry the property financially and hence the equity would have a negative value.

Subsidized Housing Programs

The U.S. Department of Housing and Urban Development (HUD) offers forty-six programs to provide government subsidized housing. It would be impossible to discuss all of them here, but for an investor who is interested and wants to gain a general understanding of the programs, HUD publishes a booklet entitled *Departmental Programs,* which is frequently updated. It can be obtained by writing to the Office of Public Affairs, Department of Housing and Urban Development, Washington, D.C. The booklet also contains the addresses for all the regional and area HUD offices.

Tax Orientation. Generally speaking, most investors in subsidized programs are motivated by very high tax-shelter benefits, with the possible exception of the Section 8 programs. Section 8 is a program that pays the difference between 25 percent of the adjusted income of low-income tenants and the market rents for the multi-family unit. HUD must approve the market rate. This program offers an owner an opportunity to realize cash flow and appreciation as well as tax shelter. In general, however, HUD regulations are so restrictive that little significant cash flow or appreciation can be realized.

Subsidized housing offers a high level of tax shelter for two reasons. First, the IRS is more lenient toward investments in subsidized housing than it is toward conventional multi-family investments. Second, most subsidized housing projects are far more highly leveraged than conventional projects; that is, more of the cost is represented by nonrecourse debt, thereby establishing a larger tax base for deduction purposes.

Under the present-value-of-money concept, to a high-income taxpayer, even a subsidized program that ends up in foreclosure may still be a worthwhile investment. There will be some tax consequences as result of the foreclosure that should be anticipated in advance so that the funds to pay the taxes will be available. Cancellation of debt by the foreclosure process is generally considered income for tax purposes; if accelerated depreciation is used, the accelerated portion will be recovered as regular income and taxed accordingly. Other income will be considered capital gain.

ATTRACTIVE FEATURES

Potential Returns

Figure 1 below represents the four benefits of investing in real estate in general and in multi-family units in particular since all four returns usually will be available.

Cash flow. Cash flow can be described as any cash remaining from operating income after payment of all operating expenses and interest and principal on any debt, and setting aside any funds needed for reserves. Cash flow can be increased over a period of time by raising rents, controlling expenses, and arranging for loan(s) that carry better terms for the borrower. Neglecting to set aside reserves for replacement of material, equipment, and contingencies, although it will increase cash flow, is usually a mistake.

Cash flow in the real estate industry can best be described as feast or famine. At the present time and probably for some time in the future, cash flow is not a significant benefit from multi-family units. As long as interest rates stay at a relatively high level and inflation continues at a relatively high level, cash flow will not be significant. Rents from multi-family units tend to lag behind increases in operating expenses. Currently, the lag among operating expenses, interest, and rental levels is so great that very few new multi-family units are being built except in some very rapid-growth areas that are not, as yet, sensitive to resistance to increasing rents. When interest and expenses do reach a parity with rental levels,

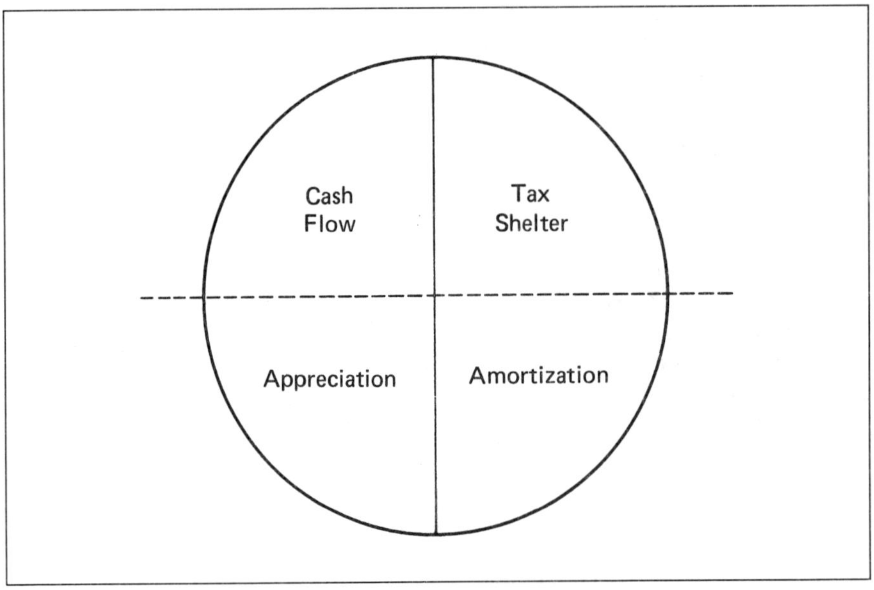

FIG. 1. Potential Returns From Real Estate

it will be financially feasible to develop new complexes. Since it takes up to three years to plan and build a multi-family unit, there will be a period of time when owners of such units will enjoy a handsome cash flow. This will not last indefinitely, however, since the real estate industry periodically overbuilds. Overbuilding creates a high vacancy level, which in turn results in lower rents or lower rent increases. These periods of underbuilding and overbuilding seem to occur in seven- to eight-year cycles.

Tax shelter. Improved real estate can provide what is commonly described as tax shelter. That shelter is the result of the non-cash expense of depreciation of the improved portion of the investment. The bulk of this so-called shelter is deferral of taxes and conversion of all, or a substantial portion of, future taxes on profits to taxation as capital gains rather than ordinary income.

Investment tax credit — limited applicability. In most investments in income-producing real estate, investment tax credit is usually available as a tax shelter. Both the 1976 and 1978 Tax Reform Acts severely restrict the availability of that credit on any property used primarily for long-term lodging. The credit, in effect, does not apply to multi-family units except motels and hotels. However, even with the exclusion, depending on the circumstance, there is usually some tax credit available. For example, coin-operated washing and drying equipment may be considered Section 38 property that would be eligible for the credit. Under some conditions, food or drink vending equipment may be eligible.

The Economic Recovery Tax Act of 1981 allows a five-year depreciation schedule for certain rehabilitation programs involving residential real estate and, in addition, a 25 percent investment tax credit on the rehabilitation costs if the residential property is considered a historic structure.

Effect of sheltering over time. Bearing in mind that most of the tax shelter available from multi-housing units is deferral and conversion of profits from ordinary income rates to capital gains, the tax-shelter umbrella shown in Figure 2 on page 780 illustrates how tax shelter works in a multi-family investment.

The umbrella shelters three things: (1) some overthrow losses that are not otherwise needed and can be applied against income from other sources, such as salaries; (2) the cash flow generated by the property for which the owner does not have to pay taxes; and (3) the principal payments that are made on the mortgage(s).

The amount of shelter available will decrease each year. As a result, this umbrella will begin to close from one side. First, the amount of excess losses that can be applied against other income begins to shrink and will eventually be lost. As the umbrella continues to close, the owner will begin to pay taxes on part of the cash flow and, eventually, on all of it. At that point (which is called the "cross-over point") part of the principal payments will become taxable and will have to be paid from the after-tax cash flow. It is possible, in a relatively short period of time, to reach a point where the after-tax cash flow is not enough to

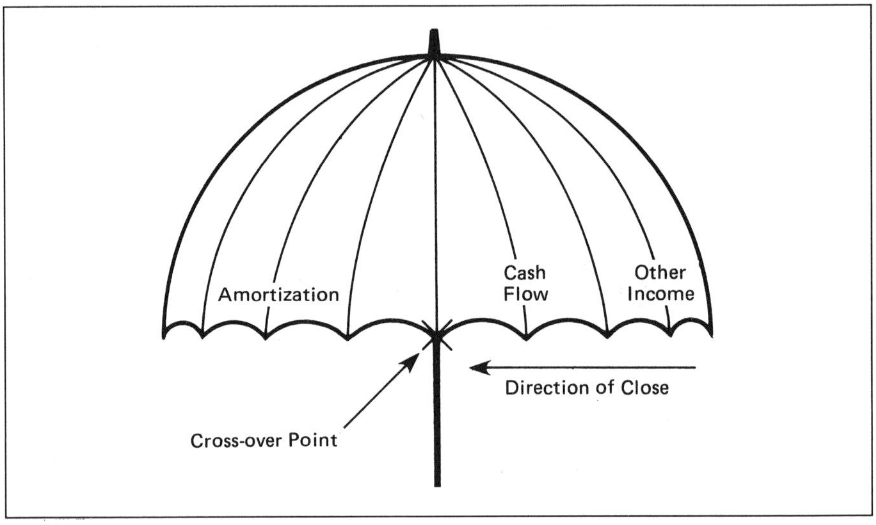

FIG. 2. The Tax-Shelter Umbrella

pay those taxes. The owner is then out of pocket for the privilege of owning a multi-family complex. (Many look on principal payments on mortgage(s) as an involuntary investment.)

The highest level of tax shelter in a multi-family investment usually will be available in one or another of the government-subsidized housing programs that were discussed earlier in this article. In fact, in many government programs, tax shelter is the only benefit that can be expected.

The amount of tax shelter decreases each year because an investor in residential property should always use accelerated depreciation and the shortest lives available for that property. It is true that, on resale of the property, the accelerated portion of the depreciation will be recovered for tax purposes and taxed at regular income rates. However, the investor has had the use of the money, without interest, that otherwise would have been paid in taxes. The present value of that interest-free money is far greater than the present value of tax payments to be made in the future. The portion of the depreciation that represents normal straight-line depreciation will still be eligible for capital gains treatment.

Appreciation. Currently, most investors in conventional multi-family housing (i.e., not government subsidized) are investing for appreciation. Appreciation is any increase in value that may occur as the result of inflation and increasing rents. Many other factors may affect appreciation. A complex located in an area that is improving in residential desirability will appreciate more than one in a deteriorating area. Generally speaking, a quality complex is likely to appreciate. The general economy of the area in which the complex is located also will affect the appreciation rate. Upgrading the property and adding amenities have a direct effect on appreciation, often in excess of the cost to do so.

Amortization. Amortization is the pay-down of the principal amount of the mortgage(s). In effect, it increases the owners' equity in the property. Had that principal not been paid, the owner would have had more cash flow.

Unless it is a long-term investment, amortization generally does not have a significant effect on return. For example, assuming a $1 million self-amortizing 12 percent loan for a term of thirty years, at the end of five years the balance of the loan would still be $977,000, and at the end of ten years $934,000. The higher the rate of interest, the slower the rate of amortization, and conversely, the lower the interest rate, the greater the rate of amortization.

Short-Term vs. Long-Term Benefits

Note that the pie chart of benefits shown earlier (Figure 1 on page 778) has a dotted line through the center of the pie. The two benefits above the dotted line are immediate benefits that can be measured on at least an annual basis. Some refer to the benefits of cash flow and tax shelter as the here-and-now benefits.

The two benefits below the dotted line, appreciation and amortization, are future benefits. Appreciation will not be realized until the property is sold and there will only be appreciation if the property did in fact increase in value. Amortization benefits will only be realized when the property is sold for an amount at least equal to its cost or when it is refinanced at some point in the future. These two returns are sometimes called the "if-and-when returns."

Structuring the purchase for desired benefits. It is possible to structure the purchase of multi-family units to increase one or more of the returns or to remove some of the risk of losing the return. The investor should keep in mind that structuring a purchase to achieve a greater amount or more certainty in one or more of the benefits may decrease the likelihood of receiving the other benefits. The investor who wants to secure a known amount of cash flow on a regular basis might get the seller to lease back the property and/or guarantee a certain cash flow. To assume that risk, the seller will want a higher price for the property. The higher price means that the investor has given up all or part of future appreciation. If the investor obtains an interest-only loan, he will not realize any amortization. If, on the other hand, the investor buys a property with a very high ratio of debt, he increases tax shelter at the expense of cash flow. However, if there is any appreciation, his portion will have increased through the use of leverage.

The investor must be wary of sellers or brokers who represent the long-term returns as short term. For example, they may claim that he will receive a 10 percent cash flow on the funds invested. This is then added to the value of the tax shelter of, say, 4 percent a year, and that debt amortization will average 2 percent a year. By adding those four percentages together, there is an annual return of 21 percent on the investment. Clearly that is not so. The investor must not be misled.

The investor also must be careful to distinguish between short- and long-term benefits when negotiating special terms. The effects of special terms should be analyzed on a present value basis. For example, it might be worthwhile to give up all or part of the long-term appreciation to receive the short-term benefit of the here-and-now cash flow.

Present value and internal rate of return. Most knowledgeable real estate investors agree that the only way to measure return on investment is by a present value computation on a completely after-tax basis. The fact that a substantial part of the return from a multi-family investment is represented by tax shelter makes this method of calculating the return even more useful. In present value analysis, each future period's cash flows are discounted to their present value.

The terms "internal rate of return" (IRR) and "present value" are used interchangeably and most of the time give equivalent answers. Very simply, the concept behind either is that a dollar in hand today is worth a dollar. The promise of a dollar to be delivered at some future date is worth less than a dollar. The difference is the amount that could have been earned with that dollar between now and the delivery date, if it had been invested at current interest rates.

Any investor in apartments should understand and use IRR. Not only is it the truest way to measure an after-tax return, it is also the best way to compare alternative investment opportunities, not just real estate. The investor should be certain, however, to compare all investments on an after-tax basis. A real estate investment that promises an 18 percent after-tax IRR is equivalent to an 18 percent municipal bond, or a 36 percent corporate bond for someone in the 50 percent tax bracket.

Computing present value. While the internal rate of return calculations are rather complex, many accounting firms, real estate offices, banks, and savings and loans associations have access to computer programs that can calculate the returns very quickly. Investors who do not have access to a computer program can compute returns by using tables available for that purpose. A word of caution: The IRR calculations usually assume that the returns will continue to earn or be re-invested at the rate shown. In the case of a very high or low rate this will tend to skew the result. Most computer programs will accommodate a fixed re-investment rate. Such a program is usually called an "adjusted internal rate of return." In fact, many CPA firms use a zero re-investment rate based on the theory that the investor will receive the money and spend it.

POTENTIAL RISKS

Return on Investment

Potential risk in this area is difficult to measure since every property is different and every location is different. Rent control in some communities can have a profound effect on return on investment. The tax bracket of the investor and the purpose of the investment can make a difference. For example, most investors in subsidized housing programs usually invest for the tax shelter the investment will provide. The cash flow remaining after expenses, debt service, and reserves will usually be minimal, if any. Government-subsidized housing programs will provide a minimum of appreciation, if any. In fact, many investors in subsidized housing go into a project with the assumption that there will be a foreclosure after several years. Why would anyone invest in real estate who expected to lose through foreclosure? As discussed earlier, investors do so because of the projected internal rate of return on a completely after-tax basis.

Illiquidity

Another potential risk is the relative illiquidity of the investment. If the investor has a need for cash, it may take several weeks to several months to find a buyer and effect a sale. To obtain cash, the seller might even be forced to sell at a price less than full value. He may obtain junior mortgages on the property at inordinate terms and interest rates to obtain cash.

Overbuilding

There is also the possibility of overbuilding of apartment units. This will create vacancy rates that could lower the value of the property. In times of overbuilding, public acceptance of investment in apartment units wanes, thus lowering the value of the units.

Changes in the Market

The investing public is very fickle. There is a herd instinct in investing. In late 1981, the herd only wanted to invest in apartments in the Sun Belt. As a result, prices of apartments in those areas were bid up to unreasonable levels. Just as in the stock market, the key to success is to buy low and sell high. It is never advisable to buy at the peak of public interest.

Money market conditions can limit a potential resale market size. In 1981, an investor seeking cash flow looked to the money market rather than real estate because the cash return was higher in the money market. The only real estate buyers were those seeking appreciation.

Variations in Income and Operating Expenses

Income and operating expenses vary widely from project to project. A very broad rule of thumb is that the expenses will range from 40 to 60 percent of the gross operating income. The largest variable will usually be real estate taxes and insurance. Many investors fail to recognize that the sale of a property will usually trigger an increase in assessment for tax purposes based on the selling price. They blithely expect future real property tax bills to be the same as those the seller had been paying. A knowledge of the policies of local tax assessors is helpful in making reasonable, accurate estimates of future annual taxes.

The same is true of insurance. The investor always gets a quote from his own agent. While the seller may have some type of discount due to a "master" policy or a very high deductible, the investor may not qualify for a "master" policy or may not want to live with a high deductible.

Income also will vary widely, depending on the location and quality of the multi-housing units and the existence or lack of rent control. Rents will also vary in relationship to the vacancy level of competing units. In past years there has been a tendency for developers to overbuild when rentals reach a profitable level.

TAX CONSEQUENCES

As has been demonstrated, ownership of multi-family rental properties, as with many kinds of real estate, brings substantial tax benefits. (See *Tax Orientation* and *Tax Shelter* in this article.)

REPRESENTATIVE TYPES OF INVESTORS

Investors in multi-family housing represent a very wide spectrum of individuals and entities. Generally speaking, individuals usually invest in the smaller properties, although a few individuals do invest in very large complexes. Most individual investors are involved in a pooled investment with one or more other investors. Some are formally organized as limited partnerships, others as informal general partnerships or as joint tenancies. Subchapter S corporations are not used because of passive income limitations. Apartment rents are considered passive income.

Many of the more active purchasers of larger complexes now are public and private syndications. Again, generally speaking, the average investment in a public syndication will be less than $10,000. In private syndications the individual investment may be well in excess of $50,000.

Many banks and insurance companies have commingled funds that acquire apartments. They usually do not get involved in projects that require less than $3 million or $4 million of equity money, since it does not take much more time to acquire a larger project than a smaller one.

A recent entry into the field of apartment investments consists of pension funds. They usually do so through credible real estate firms or advisers who can also manage the projects.

Some real estate investment trusts also invest in apartment projects, but they usually participate as owners of the land, which is then leased to the owner(s) of the building and other improvements.

Buyers of most subsidized housing projects are either high-income individuals seeking a high level of tax shelter or small private syndications of a number of such individuals.

In terms of total numbers, most smaller multiple-housing units are owned by individuals. How they make the investment is based on their attitude toward the degree of management responsibility they will undertake. Active investors are those who will manage the project in their own name. Passive investors will only do so if someone else is going to manage the day-to-day details. Managing an apartment project is an endless succession of small problems that may not be of interest to the high-capital investor.

IMPORTANT FACTORS IN BUYING AND SELLING

Selecting the Property

It is often said that the key to successful real estate investment is based on three things: location, location, and location. The average multi-family developer or investor does not have complete control over location. Local zoning laws, in most areas, will dictate where a multi-family project can be built. Even so, location should be given careful consideration.

Location. It is important to know whether or not the local area is improving in quality, is static, or is deteriorating. The investor is usually well advised to invest in a community where property is appreciating; the cost per square foot in a neighborhood that is declining will be lower, but the property will probably lose value rather than appreciate.

People who rent multi-family units usually do not have the same degree of mobility as those who own single-family homes. They are more likely to depend on public transportation than to own one or more personal cars. Therefore, the proximity to shopping facilities, schools, industry, and public transportation becomes more important. A multi-family project located near a major hospital can expect that most of the tenants will be employees of that hospital. If the hospital closes there will be an exodus of tenants. The same would be true of a single-purpose industrial plant or office building area.

Physical condition. Before an investment in an apartment project is decided on, a careful physical inspection should be made to ascertain the physical condition. It is important to know whether or not there is deferred maintenance, which will create future higher costs. If the investor does not have the expertise to do so, in most cities of any size there are experts who specialize in making such inspections. The few hundred dollars of cost will be a good investment. If deferred maintenance is found, it can often be used to negotiate a lower price.

In addition to the inspection of the soundness of the basic structure, all mechanical equipment such as furnaces, air conditioning, kitchen appliances, and sprinkler systems should be inspected. Every apartment should be visited to determine the condition of the rugs and drapes, the need for paint, and general cleanliness. The common areas such as hallways, parking lots, and entrances, lighting, landscaping, swimming pools, and saunas should be reviewed. If necessary, experts should be hired in each of these areas.

Appraisal. Unless the investor is able to conduct his own appraisal, an independent appraiser should be hired to make an appraisal. The investor should not rely on an appraisal prepared for the seller. Not only will the independent appraisal be a less biased view of the value, but the independent appraiser can also be helpful in establishing value. Appraisers often can call attention to items that might have been overlooked by a less sophisticated buyer. This might include neighborhood information, comparable rents in the area, physical faults, the condition of the industrial base, and potential competition.

Quality of tenancy. An apartment investor should probably avoid a unit in which there is a high rate of tenant turnover because of dissatisfaction with the facilities or past management. Such dissatisfaction is very difficult to turn around.

The ideal tenants enjoy a relatively high income and are not transient workers. The physical inspection of the occupied units will assist in judging the nature of the tenancy. If the parking lots contain a number of abandoned vehicles or vehicles with flat tires there might be reason to suspect a low-income transient tenancy. A lot full of expensive cars would tell another story.

If possible, the investor should try to talk to some of the tenants, away from the seller, to determine their attitude towards the complex and what they do for a living. Their ages can be important. A group of newlyweds living in studio apartments will have a high turnover rate as babies are born.

Resale

The owner of a multi-family unit must not be so involved in its day-to-day operations as to lose the overall view. This overview should include the current market for multi-family units, availability of mortgage money, the current market for real estate, and the area in which the property is located.

In addition to these basic considerations, other factors must be taken into account, such as:

- Condominium conversions — Owners should be constantly alert to the possibility of converting the units to condominiums, which generate the highest possible price. Conversion, however, requires some capital for improvements and may require paying taxes on the profits as regular income rather than as capital gain.
- Cross-over point — It is also necessary to watch for the cross-over point, that is, the point at which all tax shelter of other income and the cash flow is lost. Tax shelter is an important return from real estate, so this could be a vital consideration in determining the time to sell.
- Improvements — Once the investor decides to sell, he should make certain cosmetic improvements to the property, such as repainting, landscaping work, and parking lot striping.
- Use of a broker — The next decision is whether or not to use a third-party broker. Before making that decision, the property should be offered to adjoining owners. They often want to add to their holdings in a particular area for management efficiency.

If a third-party broker is engaged, he should not be given a long-term exclusive listing. Two months should be the limit. The seller should also ascertain if the property will be placed in a multiple-listing service if one is available in the area. Commissions are negotiable; there is no such thing as a fixed commission rate. The greater the value of the property, the lower the commission rate should be as a percentage of the sales price.

MANAGING THE INVESTMENT

Increasing Income

Over the past several years, rents have lagged far behind the cost of building multi-family units. Simple economics dictate that, eventually, rent levels must increase to reflect costs, and rentals charged for existing units eventually reflect the higher rentals required to make new units profitable.

If a seller tells the investor (the potential buyer) that his multi-family unit is always 100 percent occupied, what he is really saying is that the rents are too low. To obtain the optimum rents, a constant upward pressure on the rent levels must be maintained. Every time a unit is vacated, it should be put back on the market at a higher rent level. If it does not rent in a reasonable time, the rental can always be put back to its original level. In the meantime, the investor has tested the market.

After a number of units have been rented at the higher level, the investor should consider raising the rents for all occupied units. If the units are renting at the current market rate, there is little danger of a massive evacuation by existing tenants.

Controlling Expenses

Some expenses, such as taxes, insurance, and utilities, are considered by many to be relatively fixed. That is only partially true. The property owner can appeal, or can engage a specialist to appeal, the tax assessment. The owner must be able to make a good case based on income or on assessments of comparable units. Real estate tax specialists usually receive a percentage of the tax savings over two or more years.

The owner should shop around for insurance among agents that specialize in his particular type of property, asking for competitive bids. There is no such thing as a fixed rate for fire and casualty insurance. One owner of about $60 million of real estate was able to decrease his annual premiums from $115,000 to $30,000. He obtained a master policy and increased the deductible from $1,000 to $10,000, feeling that the additional risk was well covered by the reduction in premium.

Services are available to review utility bills. Utility companies are not infallible and often will apply rates higher than those allowed. Again, the fee is usually a share of the savings.

For other operational expenses, budgeting is essential. Any deviation from the budget should be studied and fully justified. One of the budgeted expenses will be a vacancy factor. An on-site manager should be asked to make sure that careful records are kept of vacancies. In addition, it is important to make periodic audits of the units that are listed as vacant. This point is particularly critical if many of the tenants pay rent with cash rather than by check.

Reserves

The owner of a multi-family property should plan to keep a certain amount of cash in reserve for (1) necessary replacements and (2) contingencies. Unless the owner is willing to furnish funds from other sources, the reserve should be set up from operating income.

Replacement reserve. Planning the replacement reserve is a mathematical exercise. The owner must calculate when the replacements will be necessary and accumulate the needed funds. For example, carpets normally last about five years, kitchen appliances seven years, roofs fifteen years, etc.

Contingency reserve. This reserve is set up to cover any unexpected event that might occur. The owner of a multi-family property on the West Coast that was slipping downhill used his contingency reserve to shore up the slope to avoid losing his building. Although it would be impossible to provide reserves that cover complete destruction (e.g., damage done by an earthquake), most owners set aside some funds for unexpected expenses.

Reserves need not be unproductive if and when they are unused. They can be invested and earn interest. In the current market, reserves may earn more cash than the real estate itself.

Property Management

Poor management can turn a good property into an investment disaster whereas good management can sometimes turn a marginal investment into a good one. Management of a multi-family property entails responsibility for the ongoing maintenance, renting, re-renting, and general supervision of all ongoing activity. Records must be maintained and goods and services ordered and paid for. Disputes between tenants must be resolved. Data must be provided, and access to the property assured when requested by government agencies. These functions can be accomplished by the owner or through an independent third-party management group. Smaller properties are usually owner-managed, while larger ones are frequently managed by a third-party management group.

Executive management. Executive management sets the general policy of how the property will be operated, establishes budgets, maintains accounting for the operation, handles the money and hires and supervises the on-site manager(s). Advertising and promoting the project will usually be accomplished at this level also.

On-site management. If the owner is not personally managing the property, there will usually be a resident on-site manager. Quite frequently, this will be a husband and wife combination, who share responsibility for cleaning and repainting apartments for new tenants. In addition, traditionally the wife has shown and rented apartments and kept the office records, while the husband has performed or supervised on-site work such as landscape maintenance, plumbing, electrical, and other mechanical repair. If there is a swimming pool, it is common practice to hire a pool service.

The on-site managers should participate in the preparation of and agree to the annual budget. They should also be provided a written policy covering their jobs so that they clearly understand their responsibilities, duties, and limitations. Usually, the on-site managers collect rents and deposit them into a rent depositary account, which is under the owner's control. The managers generally have a small petty cash fund and the right to order goods and services up to a limited amount without the owner's approval.

Usually, the compensation for on-site management consists of a living unit plus a monthly salary. Smaller projects may provide only the living unit. Some incentive arrangement may increase the on-site managers' income if certain occupancy or gross income goals are achieved. The managers' living unit also may serve as the on-site office, but most larger properties have a separate office.

The on-site managers should be reasonably personable and intelligent, as they are often the owner's only contact with tenants. In addition, in some states, anyone who rents out apartments must have some type of real estate license. There is usually a high rate of turnover among on-site managers. Often the job is looked on as an interim occupation or as a stepping stone to a better one.

Third-party management. In some cases, the owner may not have the time to manage a property, even with the help of on-site managers, and must hire a third party. Arrangements for third-party management vary greatly from region to region. For example, in some of the southeastern states, the on-site manager is an employee and on the payroll of the third-party manager. In other areas, the on-site manager may have been hired by the third-party manager but the owner pays the salary directly. In some cases, the third party will handle the money and keep the books, while in others, the owner will perform these functions. It should be clearly understood what the third party's responsibilities include and they should be specified in a contract.

Third-party managers are usually paid a percentage of the gross income. Normally, for multi-family housing, if the owner is paying for the on-site management, the fee will be 4 to 6 percent of the gross income. If the management company is paying the cost of the on-site management, the percentage will be higher.

Leases

The region of the country and the relative value of the project usually determine the nature of the lease. The most common form of lease is the month-to-month lease. Under this arrangement, the tenant need give only thirty days' notice to vacate and the owner needs to give only thirty days' notice to have someone move or to raise rents. The disadvantage of the month-to-month rental is that it leads to higher turnover rates since the tenant can move at any time. A high rate of turnover increases operating expenses because the units must be prepared for new tenants.

In some areas, particularly in larger cities, a longer lease period is used. Properties are often leased for periods of at least one year and as long as five years. Sometimes the lease will provide for cost-of-living increases in the rent and for renewal options at a rental to be negotiated. The latter provision really is not of much value to the tenant and of no or negative value to the owner.

Owners who negotiate longer-term leases should try to avoid granting the tenant the right to sublease the unit. In so doing, the owner loses control over tenant quality and mix.

GLOSSARY

amenity value— The value of the pleasures of the property, such as good neighborhood, schools, parks, playgrounds, etc.

assessed value— Value placed on property for the purpose of computing real property taxes.

balloon payment— The large final payment on a debt.

capital investment return— Ratio of cash down payment to net spendable income the investor earns.

deferred maintenance— Negligent or "put off" care of a property. An excessive form of deterioration.

depreciation— Loss in value due to any cause. Also a tax deduction that allocates the cost of property over its useful life.

exclusive agency listing— An agreement giving a broker the right to a commission if the listed property is sold during the listing period by anyone except the owner.

exclusive right to sell listing— An agreement giving broker the right to a commission if the listed property is sold during the listing period, regardless of who obtains the buyer.

graduated lease— A lease that provides for a varying rental rate, often based upon some future determination, such as a periodic appraisal of the property.

gross income— Total income before deduction of expenses.

lessee— Tenant; a person who receives the right to occupy property by a lease.

mortgage— A document used to make property security for payment of a loan.

net income— Gross annual income less expenses.

partnership— A method of persons joining together for operation of a business for a profit. Tax benefits flow through the partnership to the partners.

rent— Consideration paid for the use and possession of a property.

sinking fund method of depreciation— Setting aside from the income of property an amount that, with accrued interest, will pay for the replacement of improvements when needed.

special assessment tax— Charge against real estate by a public authority to pay the cost of public improvements for the property such as sewers and street lights.

straight-line depreciation— Depreciation spread evenly over the useful life of property.

sublease— A lease given by a lessee.

title insurance— Insurance to protect against certain defects in title.

TRADE ORGANIZATIONS

Apartment Owners and Managers of America (AOMA), Watertown, Conn.

Institute of Real Estate Management (IREM), Chicago, Ill.

LEADING BROKERS

Ackerman & Co., Atlanta, Ga.

Arthur Rubloff, Chicago, Ill.

Cabot, Cabot & Forbes, Boston, Mass.

Coldwell Banker (various cities)

Gerald Hines, Houston, Tex.

Helmsley Spear, New York, N.Y.

John B. Levy & Associates, Richmond, Va.

Henry S. Miller, Dallas, Tex.

Questor Associates, San Francisco, Cal.

Trammell Crow, Dallas, Tex.

Vantage, Columbus, Ohio

SUGGESTED READING

Akerson. *The Internal Rate of Return in Real Estate Investments.* Chicago: American Society of Real Estate Counselors & American Institute of Real Estate Appraisers, 1976.

American Institute of Real Estate Appraisers. *The Appraisal of Real Estate,* 7th ed. Chicago, 1978.

Arnold. *Real Estate Investor's Deskbook.* Boston: Warren, Gorham & Lamont, 1982.

California Association of Realtors. *Apartment Houses . . . How to Invest, How to Sell.* Los Angeles, 1978.

———. *How to Manage an Apartment House.* Los Angeles, 1974.

Case. *Investing in Real Estate.* Englewood Cliffs: Prentice-Hall, 1978.

Glassman. *A Guide to Residential Management,* 3rd ed. Washington, D.C.: National Association of Home Builders, 1978.

———. *Tools for Creative Property Management.* Chicago: Institute of Real Estate Management, 1974.

Heintzelman. *The Complete Handbook of Maintenance Management.* Englewood Cliffs: Prentice-Hall, 1976.

Institute of Financial Education. *Mortgage Lending Principles and Practices,* 3rd ed. Chicago, 1978.

Institute of Real Estate Management. *Income/Expense Analysis: Apartments.* Chicago. Issued annually. (Information is presented by geographic area, types of apartments, size of multi-housing units, and furnished or unfurnished units. Includes model income/expense form.)

Kelley. *Practical Apartment Management.* Chicago: Institute of Real Estate Management, 1976.

Robinson. *Federal Income Taxation of Real Estate,* 3rd ed. Boston: Warren, Gorham & Lamont, 1979 (updated periodically).

Stauss & Lewman. *Ratios and Methodology in Apartment House Valuation.* Chicago: American Institute of Real Estate Appraisers, 1975.

Warren, Gorham & Lamont. *Real Estate Review Portfolio No. 16, Tax Planning for Landlords and Tenants,* and *No. 18, How To Evaluate Apartment Building Investments.* Boston, 1978 (updated annually).

Real Estate—Single-Family Rental

*R. Bruce Ricks**

BASIC CHARACTERISTICS

The single-family owner-occupied residence has long been referred to as the American Dream. While providing shelter and privacy, it has traditionally entitled the owner to important income tax advantages and, upon sale, has often brought a price well in excess of the purchase price. The combination of tax benefits and appreciation has also made the single-family residence attractive to many investors, especially since a house as an investment is also entitled to additional tax advantages.

According to industry sources, the average selling price of existing dwellings increased by 188 percent in the past decade, from $25,700 in 1970 to $74,100 in mid-1980. Overall and regional averages for selected years are shown in Table 1 below. During the same ten-year period, the overall consumer price index rose only 8.59 percent.

While the potential for growth is clear, for some people, the detraction from residential rental investments is the need for most investors to assume the role of landlord, a position carefully avoided by those who wish to remain passive investors.

TABLE 1. Selling Prices of Existing Single-Family Homes for the United States and Each Region
(Not Seasonally Adjusted)

	United States					
Year	*Median*	*Average (Mean)*	*North-east Median*	*North Central Median*	*South Median*	*West Median*
1968	$20,100	$22,300	$21,400	$18,200	$19,000	$22,900
1972	26,700	30,100	29,800	23,900	26,400	28,400
1977	42,900	47,900	44,400	36,700	39,800	57,300
1981	66,400	78,300	63,700	54,300	64,400	96,200

SOURCE: Based on data from National Association of Realtors

* R. Bruce Ricks is a real estate finance and investment counselor in Portola Valley, Cal.

Developments in Housing Finance

Housing finance has undergone major changes in recent years. In the 1920s, home mortgage credit was available only on a short-term basis for a modest portion of the purchase price. Typical terms from a commercial bank were a five-year loan for 50 percent of the purchase price; the borrower expected, but was not promised, a renewal every five years — until the crash and Depression came. In the 1930s, the Federal Housing Administration (FHA) was created to insure lenders against loss and encourage them to make long-term, fully amortizing loans for a high percentage of purchase price. The Federal Home Loan Bank System was created to strengthen savings and loan associations — the specialized housing lenders. Through the joint efforts of governmental and private entities, housing mortgage credit grew more available and liberal.

By 1971-1972, loans were available for 95 percent of purchase price (with FHA or private mortgage insurance) for thirty years at fixed interest rates. These terms were better than those available to most high-quality corporations. Active secondary markets and pooling of mortgages for mortgage-backed securities offerings, standard mortgage instruments, and the use of passbook savings at 5 percent interest to fund mortgages at 7 to 8 percent made housing credit plentiful and cheap. However, this system was based on the use of short-term funds borrowed at low interest rates to provide the money for long-term mortgage lending at rates only some 2 to 3 percentage points (200 to 300 basis points) in yield over the savings rate.

Several credit crunches in the 1970s and early 1980s proved the fallacy of borrowing short and lending long. In 1981 and early 1982, the thrift industry (savings and loan and mutual savings banks) portfolios were full of 7 to 9 percent mortgages with long maturities. Their only sources of funds were the popular certificates of deposits with interest rates tied to Treasury bill rates that floated between 12 and 15 percent.

Alternative mortgage instruments. The untenable position of traditional mortgage lenders resulted in a major redesign of contracts between lender and purchaser. Mortgage arrangements now feature variable interest rates, graduated or balloon payments, sharing of appreciation with lenders, wraparound mortgages, renegotiation of rates every several years, etc.

Lender resistance. Of even more importance was the withdrawal of many lenders from the home mortgage market, preferring to invest their funds in short-term, high-yield paper. Those lenders who offered fixed-term mortgages to home buyers offered them at rates that exceeded the market rates for other long-term investments. (A 16 to 17.5 percent mortgage rate in 1982, when the official prime was 15.5 percent, implied that the local savings institutions were protecting themselves against an inflation rate of 11 to 12 percent throughout the term of the mortgage.)

As of early 1982, many home buyers have been priced out of the market, and sales of single-family houses for investment have slowed noticeably. However, it is still possible to make a profit in the residential rental market for considerably less cash outlay than is required for other forms of real estate investment. Although many popular real estate investment manuals suggest the leveraged purchase of a two- to four-family unit as offering the greatest return, the first-time investor might well choose to start with a single-family dwelling. With a possibly lesser return on investment, it also promises fewer headaches.

ATTRACTIVE FEATURES

Capital Appreciation

Although a rental residence produces low periodic cash flow in times of high mortgage rates, the single-family home has for two decades proved an effective insulator against the erosion of capital by inflation. However, the expectation of property appreciation can be justified only if property values are likely to rise in the general area and if the subject property is well located and well constructed.

Prices of one-family houses rose dramatically during the 1970s, sometimes as much as one percent per month. While it is unlikely that appreciation in the 1980s can continue to exceed inflation substantially, particular markets may see higher appreciation because of local conditions. In regions of growing population, the prices of existing residences may well continue to rise at least as fast as the cost of building new houses.

Tax-Sheltering Benefits

The investor in residential real estate may deduct from his rental income all mortgage interest as well as depreciation on the property. He may further deduct operating costs — repairs, maintenance, heating, and utilities (if they are included in the lease) — and local property taxes. In the early years of an amortized mortgage, the investor is certain to enjoy the benefits of a considerable tax loss that may offset against other income.

Leverage

The initial cash investment for single-family residences is often relatively low, with down payments generally running from 20 to 30 percent of purchase price. In times of easy money, buyers have put down as little as 5 percent. Some creative financing techniques (see further discussion in *Important Factors in Buying and Selling* in this article) provide for the seller's offering a second mortgage that requires little initial cash investment.

Steady Demand

If the investment is wisely made in terms of community and neighborhood, there is usually a steady demand for desirable rental houses. The rental house is the first choice of many corporate transferees. It gives other newcomers who are prospective homeowners the opportunity to get acquainted with the community before assuming the burden and complications of outright ownership.

Investment Advantages Over Multi-Family Units

Single-family houses are often more attractive than multi-family houses since there is less of a threat of rent control. Single residences are usually exempted in most of those municipalities that impose rent controls. Further, individual dwellings are easier to sell than large, multi-unit buildings, and management may be less onerous to the extent that fewer tenants are involved.

POTENTIAL RISKS

Uncertain Market Values

During economic slowdowns, prices may not keep up with inflation. In some areas of the country and in some neighborhoods, prices of residential real estate deteriorate as strong industries decline and towns have difficulty maintaining physical plants and services. The lesson to be learned here is obvious: Location is all important. (This point will be discussed in *Important Factors in Buying and Selling.*)

Limited Cash Flow

The investor in today's market must be sure to have sufficient cash reserves to offset negative cash flows and to make any repairs or replacements that may be necessary. He must also be prepared to meet increases in property taxes and energy costs.

Most important, it is always possible that the investor will find himself without tenants for a month or two, or even longer. There is no forgiveness of carrying charges because of non-occupancy.

Illiquidity

One should not get involved in any kind of real estate investment if he is not in a position to tie up his money for some time — at least four years in the case of residential property. This is not a liquid investment, and if the house must be sold within a year or two, broker's commissions and other transaction costs may well eat up any appreciation in value. Transaction costs, unlike those of marketable securities, are high. Moreover, selling takes time; houses cannot be sold for cash with a telephone call.

Tenant Problems

Destructive or irresponsible tenants are always a risk. Although most leases provide for one month's rent as security, this may prove insufficient to cover damage caused by a destructive tenant. Moreover, the court process for collecting delinquent rent and evicting tenants who violate leases may be time-consuming. The investor must be certain he is emotionally suited to the landlord role; it is essential to maintain a reasonably harmonious but businesslike relationship with tenants.

Over-Investment

There is always the risk of making improvements that cannot be justified in terms of prospective resale price. Houses normally will not sell for a great deal more than surrounding properties that are comparable in major respects. The buyer, therefore, should think carefully before making changes that may not affect the selling price. Any necessary repairs, of course, should always be made promptly.

Managerial Requirements

Managing a rental residence may require concentrated time and labor periodically, particularly in making the property ready for a new tenant. In addition, the prudent owner will visit the property frequently as part of a routine surveillance. Street observation is usually sufficient for this purpose.

TAX CONSEQUENCES — DEMONSTRATION VENTURE

Assume a three-bedroom ranch on a quarter-acre plot that is purchased for \$75,000 on the terms indicated in Figure 1 on page 798. A twenty-five-year mortgage is obtained for \$55,000 at 16 percent interest. The investor's initial equity, therefore, is \$20,000. Monthly principal and interest payments are \$747.39. Of the purchase price, \$15,000 represents the value of the land, which is not depreciable. The remaining \$60,000 represents the value of improvements (buildings), which can be depreciated using a fifteen-year life. Fifteen-year life and straight-line depreciation are elected. (An accelerated method approximating 175 percent declining balance is also allowed for buildings purchased after 1980 under the Economic Recovery Tax Act of 1981. However, the use of accelerated depreciation for residential property triggers tax recapture of excess depreciation at the time of sale. It is therefore assumed in this example that the investor chooses straight-line depreciation.)

The owner is assumed to be in a 40 percent marginal tax bracket for ordinary taxable income, and therefore a 16 percent effective tax bracket on capital gains.

Projected results of operations for five years, culminating in resale, are shown in Table 2 on page 799. It is assumed that the house can be kept fully occupied throughout the year at a rental rate of \$750 per month (\$9,000 for the first year) and that rents will increase by 10 percent per year. Operating expenses including real estate taxes, repairs, insurance, and maintenance are estimated at

Mortgage Information	
Initial mortgage	$55,000
Interest rate	16%
Term	25 years
Periodic payment	$747.39
Annual payment	$8,968.66
Total depreciable assets	$60,000
Land	$15,000
Total debt	$55,000
Initial equity	$20,000
Ordinary income tax rate	40%
Capital gains tax rate	16%
Depreciation information	
Amount depreciable	$60,000
Depreciable life	15 years
Depreciation method	Straight-line
Commission rate on resale	0%
Vacancy rate	0%
Growth rates (compounded annually)	
Property value	10%
Potential gross income	10%
Operating expenses	10%

FIG. 1. Data Summary — Single-Family Ranch Acquired for Rental (Purchase Price: $75,000)

$250 per month, or $3,000 for the first year. These expenses, too, are expected to increase by 10 percent each year. The property value is also assumed to increase by 10 percent annually, compounded. Resale expenses are not considered.

Net operating income ($6,000 for year one) is derived by deducting operating expenses ($3,000) from potential gross income ($9,000). Annual principal and interest requirements for the mortgage are $8,969, leaving a $2,969 negative before-tax cash flow in year one.

The principal payment is not deductible, but depreciation is, so the tax-deductible expenses exceed rental income by $6,787 in year one. That tax loss can shelter the owner's income earned from other sources and save $2,715 in taxes (40 percent of the loss) for year one. This $2,715 tax savings offsets all but $254 of the $2,969 before-tax cash-flow deficit. Thus, the house almost carries itself in year one, and with luck it will appreciate with inflation and housing demand pressures.

In following years, rents are forecast to rise more than operating expenses, so the negative amount of before-tax cash flow decreases. At the same time,

TABLE 2. Five-Year Financial Projections—Single-Family Ranch Rental

	Year 1	*Year 2*	*Year 3*	*Year 4*	*Year 5*
Potential gross income	$9,000	$9,900	$10,890	$11,979	$13,177
Vacancy allowance	0	0	0	0	0
Misc. income	0	0	0	0	0
Less operating expense	3,000	3,300	3,630	3,993	4,392
Net operating income	6,000	6,600	7,260	7,986	8,785
Less interest expense	8,787	8,756	8,719	8,676	6,626
Less principal amortization	182	213	250	293	343
Before-tax cash flow	−2,969	−2,369	−1,709	−983	−184
Less depreciation expense	4,000	4,000	4,000	4,000	4,000
Plus amortization	182	213	250	293	343
Taxable income	−6,787	−6,156	−5,459	−4,690	−3,841
Tax savings (−payment)	2,715	2,462	2,814	1,876	1,536
After-tax cash flow	−254	94	475	893	1,352
Selling price	82,500	90,750	99,825	109,808	120,788
Mortgage balance	54,818	54,606	54,356	54,063	53,720
Adjusted tax basis	71,000	67,000	63,000	59,000	55,000
Total gain	11,500	23,750	36,825	50,808	65,788
Tax on sale	1,840	3,800	5,892	8,129	10,526
After-tax proceeds	25,842	32,344	39,577	47,615	56,542
Int. rate of return on Initial Equity	27.9%	26.7%	25.8%	25.0%	24.3%

projected tax losses diminish each year because of more rental income and less deductible interest. Straight-line cost recovery allows the same depreciation deduction for each year spread over the fifteen-year life used.

The property value, which is presumed to increase by a 10 percent annual rate, is projected to be $120,788 at the end of year five. At that point (year five), the adjusted tax basis (cost minus depreciation) will be $55,000. All of the resulting $65,788 gain upon resale will be taxed at capital gains rates because straight-line cost recovery was used. At a 16 percent capital gains rate, the tax on resale is forecast at $10,526. That amount plus the unpaid mortgage at resale, $53,720, is subtracted from the $120,788 resale price to derive the $56,542 after-tax proceeds. The result, based on these assumptions, is a 24.3 percent after-tax rate of return before transaction costs and any seller financing.

This rate of return is quite competitive in today's market. True, it is based on assumptions, and returns are certainly not guaranteed. A decrease in rental rates, or increase in expenses or vacancies will have a significant effect on the rate of return. So will a reduced resale price. Commissions and other expenses of reselling the property will reduce the rate of return, as will accepting a mortgage upon resale for part of the sales price.

Higher rates of return can be achieved with greater debt (provided terms are favorable), higher appreciation and rental rates, accelerated cost recovery, and reduced operating expenses. Periodic refinancing, instead of a resale, can yield cash to pyramid holdings.

REPRESENTATIVE TYPES OF INVESTORS

A present or former homeowner who has had a satisfactory investment experience with his own house and who is interested in a moderate-risk, low-liquidity investment with better than average growth potential is a logical investor in residential real estate. As stated before, the temperament to deal with sometimes demanding and inconsiderate tenants is probably one of the most important requirements unless one is prepared to sacrifice income for the services of professional management. With professional management, any investor looking for long-term growth may want to consider residential real estate.

IMPORTANT FACTORS IN BUYING AND SELLING

Does the disappearance of 6 to 9 percent mortgages make housing an unattractive investment? Clearly, some spectacular rates of return, which were available in the late 1970s because of high inflation, low levels of housing production, and very attractive fixed-rate mortgage credit, are no longer attainable. But, if inflation persists and new housing starts continue to fall below basic demand for housing needed for new household formation, replacement, and relocation, prices of housing can be expected to continue to rise strongly in areas to which people want to migrate. The investor therefore will have to pay close attention to demographics and supply and demand, as well as to carrying costs.

Where to Buy

In selecting a single-family house, the investor should concentrate on one factor above all — location.

Geographic guidelines. In general, communities with a moderate amount of transient population are preferable to towns with little population turnover. The suburbs of major metropolitan areas are attractive since they are sought out by families transferred from other parts of the country. If one can sense major population shifts before they are too far underway, there are excellent rental prospects in and near the major cities at the center of these migrations.

Neighborhood guidelines. The value of a property is largely determined by houses in the immediately surrounding area. Most neighborhoods are in a state of transition, and it is very important to determine whether a particular neighborhood is in a period of growth, stability, or decline. Judgments can be made on the basis of property maintenance and the types and quality of municipal services.

In lower-income neighborhoods, proximity to public transportation and shopping facilities is important. In upper-income neighborhoods, the availability of desirable schools is particularly important.

Price

The price paid by the investor must be reasonable and fair. It will probably be based on recent sales prices of comparable properties in the general area. There will also be additional factors to consider: costs of repairs and renovation and the prospects for appreciation. Above all, the investor should beware of being carried away by a property that appeals to his particular esthetic values. Location must still remain the primary factor. A beautifully maintained house, advertised as a cream puff, is worth only a slight premium in price since it will not remain in that condition after having been occupied by two or three tenants despite the landlord's reasonable maintenance efforts. If it is in an undesirable neighborhood, the risks escalate.

Financing the Purchase

Double-digit mortgage rates make it necessary for many buyers to turn to creative financing. This usually means persuading an eager seller to take back a short-term (second) mortgage at rates that may run from 60 to 70 percent of market rates. There may be definite advantages to paying a seller's price if one can get a below-market mortgage. It is possible that the mortgage, when due, can be rolled over into a cheaper first mortgage.

Selling the Property

The investor may have to resort to the same devices that made the purchase of the property possible in the first place when it is his turn to sell. The investor must be prepared for the possibility that some profits at the time of resale — and perhaps some down payment — may have to remain invested and that a portion of the equity may convert to a note.

Marketing. It generally pays to develop a working arrangement with local brokers. A professional can easily keep abreast of the market — what is happening in the area, prevailing prices — and has access to serious buyer prospects.

Necessary repairs plus cosmetic renovation — painting, cleaning, and possibly some landscaping — always should be done because the cost will be returned several times over by a higher selling price. However, the investor must think very carefully before making substantial improvements that will over-improve the house in terms of the market prices of other homes in the neighborhood.

A final but important tip: It is well worth the time, effort, and cost to put the interior of the house in immaculate condition, with special attention to the kitchen, baths and all appliances. This factor alone persuades many prospects to close the deal — possibly at a higher rental than they were prepared to pay.

MANAGING THE INVESTMENT

It is very difficult to succeed by oneself as an absentee landlord. The only substitute for personal surveillance is to retain the services of a broker or other person who is willing to manage the property, possibly including the collecting of rents. Few brokerage firms specialize in rental management of individual houses. When the house is in good condition and the tenant has a long-term lease and pays rent promptly, the usual fee (6 percent of rental) is too high; if there are problems with the property or the tenant, it may be too low.

The best course for the strictly passive investor probably is to seek out an individual who owns rental homes in the area and who manages them actively. The agreed-upon fee reflects the manager's expertise in knowing which plumber, electrician, or painter to hire, and how much to pay; it also may include deciding on appropriate rent and explaining it to the tenant, finding a new tenant, or dealing with or evicting a delinquent tenant.

GLOSSARY

alternative mortgage instrument— A mortgage instrument created by varying one or more of the four factors that are held fixed in the usual mortgage: amount of principal, interest rate, periodic or monthly payment of principal and interest, and repayment terms.

amenity value— The value of the pleasures of the property such as good neighborhood, schools, parks, playgrounds, etc.

assessed value— Value placed on property for the purpose of computing real property taxes.

balloon payment— A large final payment on a debt.

basis points— One basis point is one-hundredth of one percent in yield. The difference between a mortgage yielding 10.25 percent and one yielding 10.75 percent is 50 basis points.

closing— In the case of a sale of real estate, the final meeting of the parties at which title passes from the seller to the purchaser and the consideration for the purchase passes from the purchaser to the seller, the final documents are signed and delivered, expenses are prorated, and other closing adjustments are made.

closing costs— The expenses incurred in the consummation of a real estate or mortgage transaction.

deposit receipt— Document by which a prospective purchaser makes an offer to buy and submits a deposit to accompany that offer; also known as agreement of sale and earnest money contract.

due-on-sale clause— A clause in a mortgage permitting the mortgagee to accelerate the mortgage debt (so that it becomes immediately payable) in the event of a sale of the real estate by the borrower.

equity build-up— The increase in value of a property owner's equity as a result of mortgage loan amortization or appreciation in the total value of the property, or both.

exclusive agency listing— An agreement giving a broker the right to a commission if the listed property is sold during the listing period by anyone except the owner.

exclusive right to sell listing— An agreement giving a broker the right to a commission if the listed property is sold during the listing period, regardless of who obtains the buyer.

gross lease— A lease in which the landlord pays operating expenses.

housing starts— The number of residential units of which construction has begun within a specified period of time. Used together with number of construction permits, issued as an indicator of real estate, construction, and mortgage activity and trends.

imputed rent— The fair rental value of owner-occupied or otherwise unrented property.

loan-to-value ratio— The ratio (usually expressed as a percentage) of the mortgage loan(s) to the value of the mortgaged property.

net lease— A lease in which the tenant pays operating expenses.

occupancy value— Fair imputed rent for a property for its occupancy.

private mortgage insurance— Protection to the lender for the riskiest 25 to 30 percent of a loan; if the borrower defaults and foreclosure becomes necessary, the private mortgage-insurance company will pay the lender an amount equal to 25 to 30 percent of the mortgage balance.

renegotiable-rate mortgage (RRM)— automatically renewable three- to five-year loan notes, secured by mortgages of up to thirty years for residential dwellings, providing for renegotiation of the interest rate upon each renewal (similar to rollover mortgage, except that the latter involves both short-term notes and short-term mortgages).

reverse annuity mortgage (RAM)— A form of mortgage that permits a homeowner to draw on the accumulated equity in the home (cash inflows and outflows are in reverse of those associated with a conventional mortgage loan).

shared appreciation mortgage (SAM)— A mortgage plan under which the lender offers the home buyer an interest rate that is, for example, one-third lower than the rate prevailing in the market. In return, the lender receives a third of the appreciation in the value of the property when the property is sold or the mortgage matures.

tax-free sale of residential property by over-55 taxpayer— A taxpayer who is 55 years of age or over at the time of the sale may exclude from gross income up to $125,000 of gain on the sale of a principal residence (Section 121 of the Internal Revenue Code).

wraparound mortgage— A second mortgage that, instead of being wholly independent of the first loan, wraps around it; that is, the borrower pays debt service on the entire wraparound loan to the second mortgage lender, who then pays the first lender its share.

LEADING FRANCHISE BROKERS

Century 21 Real Estate

Electronic Realty Associates (ERA)

Gallery of Homes
International Real Estate Network
Meredith Publishing (Better Homes & Gardens)
Realty World Corporation
Red Carpet Corporation

SUGGESTED READING

Arnold, Alvin L., and Kusnet, Jack. *The Arnold Encyclopedia of Real Estate.* Boston: Warren, Gorham & Lamont, Inc., 1978 (supplemented annually).

———, Wurtzebach, Charles H., and Miles, Mike E. *Modern Real Estate.* Chapters 3, 9, 14, 16, 19. Boston: Warren, Gorham & Lamont, Inc., 1980.

Bloom, George F., and Harrison, Henry S. *Appraising the Single Family Residence.* Chicago: American Institute of Real Estate Appraisers, 1978.

Boykin, James H. *Financing Real Estate.* Lexington: Heath Lexington Books, 1979.

Friedman, Jack P., and Ordway, Nicholas. *Income Property Appraisal and Analysis.* Reston: Reston Publishing Co., 1981.

Levine, Mark L. *Real Estate Fundamentals.* Chapter 16. New York: West Publishing Co., 1976.

Lyons, Paul. *Investing in Residential Real Estate: A Guide to Increasing Your Income and Profit.* Reston: Reston Publishing Co., 1981

Pyhrr, Stephen A., and Cooper, James R. *Real Estate Investment: Strategy Analysis Decisions.* Boston: Warren, Gorham & Lamont, Inc., 1982.

Seldin, Maury, ed., *The Real Estate Handbook.* Chapters 20, 21, 28. Homewood: Dow Jones-Irwin, 1980.

Sumichrast, Michael, and Seldin, Maury. *Housing Markets; The Complete Guide to Analysis and Strategy for Builders, Lenders and Other Investors.* Homewood: Dow Jones-Irwin, 1977.

Unger, Maurice A. *How to Invest in Real Estate.* New York: McGraw-Hill Book Co., 1975.

Vidger, Leonard P. *Borrowing and Lending on Residential Property.* Lexington: Heath Lexington Books, 1981.

Warren, Gorham & Lamont, Inc. *Real Estate Review Portfolios No. 5: Real Estate Financing Techniques; No. 5A: Case Studies in Creative Real Estate Financing.* Boston, 1974, 1979.

Real Estate—Undeveloped Land

Jack P. Friedman and Terrence L. Love *

BASIC CHARACTERISTICS

"Undeveloped land" is defined here as acreage having the potential of being subdivided or developed within fifteen or so years. The land may be currently lying fallow or otherwise not being put to its potential highest and best use. Thus undeveloped (and underdeveloped) land, although perhaps currently being farmed, differs from farms and ranches because of its potential for development. Undeveloped land also differs from small recreational lots, suburban lots, and urban lots, all of which have already been provided with infrastructure and subdivided. Consequently, some of the gains from demographics (people) and site improvements (utilities) have already been realized. It is useful to think of undeveloped (and underdeveloped) land as currently undergoing a use transition period. Development can be expected within the foreseeable future. The purchaser hopes to benefit financially during this transition period by buying at or just above agricultural land prices and selling at a predevelopment price.

Undeveloped land has certain physical characteristics from which flow unique economic and investment attributes. These characteristics include immobility, indestructibility, and nonhomogeneity (no two parcels are identical). Economic attributes include scarcity, modification potential, and location.

Undeveloped land is tangible and immobile, has the ability to satisfy certain human needs, and is scarce in many geographic areas. Therefore, it offers desirable investment characteristics. Value may be enhanced by real appreciation and inflationary gains, by the possibility of receiving periodic income from rents, and by income tax deductions for business expenses, real estate taxes, and interest. Land also offers the opportunity of favorable capital gains tax rates at resale, the ability to magnify gains through financial leverage, and the possible monopoly inherent in a specific location.

Land Speculation in the Early Seventies

In the period between 1969 and 1973, several areas — particularly in the Sun Belt states, and including such major cities as Atlanta, Dallas, Houston, Orlando, and Phoenix — experienced such strong speculator markets that the marketing techniques that were used then are still associated with investment in raw land, despite the fact that some of them are no longer used.

* Jack P. Friedman is Head of the Research Division at the Texas Real Estate Research Center, Texas A&M University. Terrence L. Love is Chairman of Land Development Analysts, Atlanta.

The syndications popular at that time were almost always limited partnerships comprised of a broker-general partner and numerous limited partners who were not knowledgeable in land values or development, but typically sought tax shelter for other income. The bulk of the shelter was achieved through prepaid interest paid to sellers as an inducement to offer attractive purchase-money notes. Prepaid interest is no longer allowed as a tax deduction. A second tax law that has subsequently been revised, affecting installment sales, tended to hold the down payment required by a landowner to less than 30 percent of the purchase price. Many aggressive general partners were able to get their limited partners to borrow cash for the down payment, resulting in purchase with no cash of their own (mortgage-out).

Deductions for interest were the only tax deductions available to these partnerships, but they were sufficient to create an artificial land boom. The "mortgaging out" situation of paying interest only results in what brokers term "one-to-one write-offs"; that is, every dollar paid is deductible. Deduction for prepaid interest has been disallowed in the Tax Reform Act of 1976. However, many partnerships had matured by that time into principal-paying periods and many land investments — perhaps most — were abandoned; this brought a whole new condition of tax setback in that some foreclosures/abandonments can be treated like sales by the IRS with tax due on profits that never occurred.

With raw land speculators quickly pushing prices beyond levels that subdividers could feasibly pay, the only prospective purchasers were other syndicators. Although this market soon collapsed with losses to many participants, many still associate the excitement of that period with raw land investing today.

Cash Returns

Cash returns during ownership of undeveloped land are seldom significant. Some farmable parcels are rented, but seldom does property bring an annual rent of more than 5 percent of its market value. Such rent may pay the taxes, but rarely is there cash flow. The sale of timber, mineral rights, hunting rights, easements, and other partial interests is often helpful in offsetting property tax payments and some of the interest expense. Income tax deductions for property taxes and interest reduce the net carrying costs of undeveloped land.

Factors Affecting Values

Factors that affect the value of undeveloped land fall into four categories. These are physical, economic, governmental, and sociological.

Physical attributes. These include such items as the size, shape, topography, vegetation, soil, and subsoil conditions. The size of a parcel of land must be adequate for development to its highest and best use. Small or awkwardly shaped parcels may be difficult to develop, hence marketability is affected. Topography is important, as not all land is suitable for construction. Some will be lost to flood-prone areas. Adequate drainage is important, because low areas may require costly filling.

Vegetation can be important for some parcels. Wooded residential lots are generally more valuable, although some builders prefer cotton patches. Soil and subsoil conditions affect the type of buildings that can be erected and the construction technique used. Ground water, percolation, and drainage capabilities are important. Soil boring tests can be performed to assess these factors.

Economic factors. Economic factors at work at the national, regional, state, and local levels include employment, economic base, price levels, interest rates, and inflation.

Since the rationale of buying undeveloped land is based on its growth potential, a trend toward growing employment in the local area is an important factor. The economic base consists of industrial activity, wholesale, retail, and service trade, productivity, and sensitivity to influence by outside forces. Strong growth areas with a diversified economic mix are preferred by investors.

Total area income growth and rising per capita or family income is desirable. Investing in land located in a declining income region is unwise unless the land can be acquired at an extremely depressed price.

High interest rates tend to depress the price of non-income-producing land; investors put their money elsewhere. If the high interest rates are a symptom of anticipated high inflation, land prices will rise along with other tangibles. Land buyers should be prepared to ride out the storms created by fluctuating interest rates.

Governmental factors. These include utilities and services available, taxes, building codes, and environmental regulations. Landowners will, of course, want the best services at the lowest cost, and the greatest possible freedom from hindrances to development. Prices for adjacent parcels can vary sharply when the parcels are separated by municipal or school district boundaries.

Utilities (water, sewer, gas, electric, telephone) are essential to development. A land investor should be certain that someday they will be available to the property. Municipal services include fire and police protection, education, refuse collection, and controls such as planning, zoning, and codes. Transportation facilities are generally within the government's purview.

Some local governments have adopted no-growth policies. Although attitudes may change someday, a land investor must have great fortitude to buy undeveloped land in such an area or one where similar attitudes might be implemented.

Sociological factors. Demography and local attitudes and tastes also help determine whether land is a good investment.

Demographics includes the population of an area, natural increases and immigration trends, household and family size, age and sex composition, ethnic background, density, and geographical distribution. Growth in population combined with shrinking household size indicates a growing need for housing units, and therefore a promising potential for development.

Local tastes and attitudes are also important. Preference for high or low density may be indicated by the composition of the population (permanent, transient, or mixed), the climate, and transportation facilities. This may offer hints to the land buyer as to whether to acquire small, close-in tracts or larger tracts that are distant from the central city.

ATTRACTIVE FEATURES

Appreciation Gain on Resale

Appreciation gain realized upon resale is the primary motivating force behind most undeveloped land investments. Two of the main avenues of gain are local growth and inflation.

Local growth. Local growth may be in the form of geographical expansion or population and employment increases. As a city and its suburban areas grow, highways and other transportation arteries are planned and built to accommodate existing and future demand. Utility lines are extended; other public facilities such as parks, schools, and libraries are built in newly developed areas, as are shopping centers, office buildings, and factories. As this development ensues, land that was formerly fallow is put to a higher and better use. Development potential becomes more obvious for land that was once considered too distant from the city. Although appreciation gains generally occur gradually, some changes can cause rapid appreciation. These include the announcement of plans for or the actual completion of roads, utilities, reservoirs, annexation by a city or town, rezoning, speculative interest, and new employment opportunities.

Hedge Against Inflation

Because it is tangible, indestructible, and useful, undeveloped land is considered an excellent hedge against inflation. As the purchasing power of money shrinks, it takes more dollars to buy the same parcel of land. Of course, some have paid more for land than it was worth and were disillusioned later, when they tried to sell but could not realize what they paid, at least not for many years.

Leverage

Leverage, the ability to borrow, can enhance capital gains from land. Some institutional lenders are willing to lend with raw land as collateral; however, in most situations, owners must finance the property that they sell. Down payments typically range from 10 to 40 percent, the balance financed over five to twenty years. Interest rates are sometimes lower than lending institutions are then charging.

With a typical 25 percent down payment at 10 percent interest, a 33 percent property appreciation rate is magnified to a 100 percent rate of return on equity. Such returns can occur in raw land, but rarely with improved properties. However, leverage is a two-edged sword. Unless the property appreciates at a rate above the interest rate paid for borrowed money, the equity will be eroded. Such conditions, leaving little way to achieve a positive return, generally result in abandonment or foreclosure.

Financing from the seller can often be arranged on a nonrecourse basis, which means that the property is the sole collateral for the loan. A 60 to 80 percent loan-to-value ratio is sought. In the event of default, the mortgage holder has no recourse to the personal assets of the debtor. Release provisions, whereby portions of the property are deeded free and clear to the purchaser upon payment of part of the principal owed, are commonly used. They are quite desirable to the buyer who employs leverage. Typically, the less attractive acreage will be released first, generally upon a payment of 25 percent more than the average acreage price.

Safety of Principal

In most cases, land cannot be sold or stolen (exceptions include erosion of beachlands, adverse possession, and political upheavals). Although environmental restrictions occasionally may reduce or otherwise retard value, land is generally solid security. Except in rare instances following speculative binges and the troughs of economic depression, the value of most undeveloped land in the United States has steadily climbed upward.

Intangible Benefits

Land ownership provides intangible benefits for many. Notable among these groups are American farmers and their families, Europeans, and Japanese. For them, land provides safety, security, a feeling of well-being and pride for community involvement. Development of the land offers a sense of artistic and business accomplishment.

POTENTIAL RISKS

Variable Rates of Return

Rates of return from undeveloped land investments will exhibit an extremely wide range of variability. Land investments are unlike Treasury bills, which offer a certain income. Landowners cannot tell their brokers to sell and expect to receive a check next week for market value. Land is subject to many other risks, as described below.

Illiquidity

Land, unlike many other investments, cannot be sold at market value on a moment's notice. It is difficult to parcel out or subdivide land into undivided interests. The selling of the back forty to send a child to college is not always possible. Land may require several months or years on the market for the owner to realize its market value. Impatient or desperate sellers may be forced to sell at a loss, or may fail to sell at all. Investors should be cognizant of this significant drawback and not purchase land unless they have an amount of liquid assets sufficient to meet their needs.

Regulatory and Political Risk

A government agency enforcing environmental regulations can cause expensive development delays, or even prevent full development of the land. The states of Florida and California require Environmental Impact Statements (EISs) for many kinds of development. Regional and local planning councils have become increasingly concerned with the environmental impact of proposed projects. Powers beyond review and recommendation have been awarded some planning commissions within a specified area (e.g., river corridors of 2,000-foot width). When a Federal Housing Administration (FHA) mortgage-insurance project is to be requested on a development proposed for more than 500 homes, the Department of Housing and Urban Development (HUD) will require an EIS to be prepared and made available to specified public agencies, as well as to the public at large.

Rezoning applications, no matter how justified the owner feels they are, may be disapproved by political bodies. In recent times, courts have been hearing complaints from landowner-developers that zoning councils have acted capriciously and arbitrarily. At first the courts declared some land free of zoning, then rezoned other land, and now appear to be remanding cases back to the original zoning body. In some cases they are upholding the zoning boards. These cases, however, may be considered a step forward for the landowner in that for many years the courts refused to hear such cases at all, declaring zoning issues to be the exclusive domain of the zoning boards.

Private ownership is subject to the government's right of eminent domain. Landowners sometimes feel that condemnation awards are insufficient. They have always had the right to contest these awards and have frequently won in court. Juries can go either way, however, and litigation is expensive, with attorney and appraisal fees paid by the landowner. These risks often affect the maximum gain realized. However, they seldom cause substantial losses to careful buyers when they compare actual resale prices to original costs. In fact, for some investors, having land condemned can be highly profitable.

Market Volatility

Markets for undeveloped land are generally local. They are subject to influence at all levels of government and the economy, national, state, and, particularly, local. Stability is the general rule, but wide swings can occur for specific property. Lack of activity often masks volatile prices. In a period of tight money, such as the mid-1970s, transactions may be infrequent and characterized by distress-selling at depressed prices. After a year or two, activity resumes and prices continue to ratchet upward, as they did in the late 1970s.

TAX CONSEQUENCES

The three phases of the life cycle of land as an investment are acquisition, ownership, and resale.

Acquisition

Purchase. The acquisition cost for property purchased serves as the purchaser's initial tax basis in the property. This cost includes both the equity paid and any debt burdens taken on in the purchase. The cost of title insurance, survey costs, legal fees, appraisal, option payments, broker commissions, and most other items paid at closing are included in the initial tax basis. Prorated property taxes and unexpired insurance paid by the purchaser at closing are generally deductible as expenses in the period to which they relate.

Gift. The recipient of a gift takes the donor's basis as his own. In computation of a donee's gain or loss upon resale, the basis is the lower of the donor's basis or fair market value at the time of the gift. Part or all of the federal gift taxes paid can be added to the donee's basis in many situations.

Inheritance. The basis of inherited property is generally its fair market value at the time of the decedent's death or an alternative valuation date, which is ordinarily six months after death. Tax law as to basis of inherited property changed in 1976, but implementation was delayed and the law essentially reversed in 1980. Consequently, unrealized appreciation at death generally skips income taxes.

The basis of property acquired in an exchange is carried over from the property surrendered. (Exchanges are described in *Tax-Deferred Exchange* on page 813.)

Ownership

During the period of ownership of land, deductions are permitted for expenses, including real estate taxes, insurance, and interest. Deductions for investment interest expenses on land are generally limited (except for corporations) to $10,000 plus the taxpayer's net investment income. Unused investment interest expense can be carried over indefinitely.

Capital improvements such as the cost of a new fence or costs to connect to utility lines are generally added to the landowner's tax basis. Deductions for depletion and depreciation, for example, generally reduce the original tax basis. Raw land itself, however, is not depreciable.

Resale

Upon the resale of land that had been held as an investment, capital gain or loss is recognized. The amount realized (sales price less expenses of sale) less the adjusted tax basis (original basis modified by improvements or subtractions) is the amount of capital gain or loss.

If the property has been held for over one year, long-term capital gain rates (maximum of 20 percent) apply, because a maximum of 40 percent of the net gain is included in an individual taxpayer's income, and the highest ordinary income tax bracket is 50 percent. An individual may deduct half of long-term capital losses up to $3,000 against ordinary income each year. Excess losses may be carried over to subsequent years. Individual taxpayers with capital gains may be subject to the alternative minimum tax.

Corporations may use the alternative tax rate for long-term capital gains. They may also be subject to a minimum tax. Corporations may carry capital losses back three years or forward five years to offset such capital losses against previous (or subsequent) capital gains. Corporate carryovers of capital losses are treated as short-term losses.

Installment Sale

Land sellers who finance the land that they sell can use installment sale provisions. This allows them to pay a tax on the gain as they collect the proceeds from the sale. Since October 1980, payments in the year of sale are no longer restricted to 30 percent of the sales price; the full price may be paid in any year. The seller need not elect the installment sale. For contracts entered into after September 1980, the stated rate of interest must be at least 9 percent on the note taken by the seller. The IRS will impute a reasonable rate when lower rates are used.

As an example of an installment sale, suppose the tax basis of land to a seller (non-dealer) is $40,000. The land is sold for $100,000 with $30,000 down and a $70,000 note payable over seven years with equal payments to principal. Interest on the unpaid balance is payable annually at 10 percent. The gross-profit ratio is 60 percent ($60,000 gain divided by a $100,000 contract price). Of the $30,000 cash down payment, 60 percent ($18,000) would be taxable as a capital gain and $12,000 considered a nontaxable return of capital. Of each annual $10,000 principal payment to be received, 60 percent would be a capital gain, the rest a nontaxable return of capital. Interest income is taxable as ordinary income.

When property with an existing mortgage is sold, the contract price is reduced by the amount of the existing debt taken on by the buyer. In the same $100,000 sale, if an existing $25,000 mortgage is taken on by the buyer, the contract price would be $75,000 ($100,000 sales price less $25,000 mortgage). The gross-profit ratio would change to 80 percent ($60,000 gain divided by $75,000 contract price).

To the extent that an existing mortgage taken on by the buyer exceeds the seller's tax basis, the excess is a payment in the year of sale and does not affect the contract price.

Tax-Deferred Exchange

Section 1031 of the Internal Revenue Code states that "no gain or loss shall be recognized if property held for productive use in trade or business or for investment is exchanged solely for property of a like kind to be held either for productive use in trade or business or for investment."

A tax-deferred exchange occurs when property held for productive use or for investment is exchanged for property of a like kind to be held for productive use or for investment.

The provisions of Section 1031 apply to both gains and losses. Further, the section is mandatory if all requirements are met. Consequently, if property is traded and the transaction meets all of the requirements, the taxpayer cannot elect to pay a tax on the gain or to recognize a loss. Alternatively, a taxpayer can sell property to recognize a gain or loss.

The three basic requirements for a tax-deferred exchange are as follows:

(1) There must be an exchange. (A sale and separate purchase will not qualify.)
(2) Both the asset surrendered and the one received in the exchange must be held for productive use in trade or business or as an investment.
(3) The exchange must involve property deemed to be of like kind. (Generally, one form of real estate may be exchanged for another.)

REPRESENTATIVE TYPES OF INVESTORS

Anyone can invest in land: individuals, pension plans, insurance companies, savings and loan associations, partnerships, corporations, developers, and others. The nature of land investments — their illiquidity, the uncertainty of returns, and the likelihood that returns will be deferred — makes the most suitable investors those who can wait for the time it takes for the property to reach desirable fruition and can pay carrying costs (interest, taxes, insurance) with money from sources outside the property. Since most carrying costs are tax-deductible, after-tax costs are least for those in the highest tax brackets.

Patient but persevering investors are best suited. Since returns are deferred, the rewards occur years after the investment. Moreover, an investor should be prepared to upgrade the land's value. Often this requires action and reaction to proposed utility lines, thoroughfare extensions, and zoning changes. It may be possible for an investor to purchase land near his own residence; if not, it is wise to establish a rapport with brokers and attorneys where the site is located. Then, the investor can rapidly learn of pending changes that affect the land use and its value.

Syndications

Although the small investor can purchase the amount of land that suits his own pocketbook, such tracts are seldom among the most desirable. Syndicates (limited partnerships) often serve the best interests of the small investor. Reputable, experienced syndicators often arrange purchases of large tracts with good potential by a group comprised of small investors. Twenty investors who each put up $10,000 cash for the down payment can frequently control a choice $1 million tract. However, syndicates may fail to accomplish their goal due to many causes. These include market downturns, setbacks on other properties experienced by the syndicator, and unwillingness or inability of investors to continue their annual financial commitment to the property. Consequently, investors must be careful in their selection of the syndicator and other investors as well as of the property under consideration. Since most syndications are limited partnerships, the general partner has total control of decisions. (See article on Real Estate Limited Partnerships, elsewhere in this volume.)

Foreign Investors

For various reasons, raw land has become a favored investment of foreign investors. Tens of thousands of acres of farmland and raw land have been quietly acquired by non-American investors in the last five years. These investors have frequently paid cash and have been able to outbid many local investors. Government agencies are monitoring this activity now, though no quotas are known to be in the making nor other federal restrictions being developed. In many areas the new money was most welcome.

Developers

Real estate developers may purchase land three to five years in advance of their needs. In some areas, it takes a minimum of one year to secure the necessary building approvals, but fixing the land cost and excluding competitors for a particular site is more often the motivating force.

Other Investors

Insurance companies and most pension plans are obligated to meet certain actuarially determined commitments. Investing in raw land, because returns are uncertain, is virtually prohibitive except for a small portion of their money. State or federal laws may prohibit large-scale raw land investments.

Some savings and loan associations are partners in real estate developments through their service corporations. They may hold some raw land as a small fraction of their assets, with an eye toward development. Few will invest in land unless it has obvious immediate development potential, although they may make acquisition and development, construction, and permanent home loans.

Industrial and retail corporations sometimes will acquire land prior to needing it for business expansion. The land cost is locked in at an early date and the potentially best site is purchased. However, land purchase in advance of need is often perceived as an inefficient use of corporate capital.

IMPORTANT FACTORS IN BUYING AND SELLING

The most important concerns when buying and selling are selecting a broker, finding the right market, judging the quality of properties, using professional advisers, negotiating the purchase or sales price and terms of sale, and negotiating acceptable terms of financing.

Selecting a Broker

In 1981 there were over 2 million licensed real estate salespersons or brokers in the United States. Of these licensees, about 1 million were active in real estate on a full-time basis. Most full-time brokers concentrate on sales of single-family homes. Consequently, selecting a real estate salesperson at random to help buy or sell a parcel of land suitable for investment is an uncertain proposition.

It is important to find a local person who is knowledgeable about land: its physical, economic, governmental, and social environment. It is crucial that a land salesperson have a reputation for honesty and knowledge. Other professionals such as lawyers, CPAs, and bankers are sometimes able to recommend good land salespeople. Real estate appraisers and developers are also potentially good sources.

Membership in the Farm and Land Institute and/or the Real Estate Securities and Syndications Institute, indicates some commitment to professionalism in the field. Both organizations are affiliates of the National Association of Realtors. Membership also denotes adherence to a code of ethics.

Finding the Right Market

The market for land is imperfect. In a given local area there are generally few buyers and sellers. In contrast to securities or commodities markets, transactions are infrequent and private. Sometimes the only information known with certainty is that the buyer paid $10 and other valuable consideration. This situation provides both hazards and opportunities. Jokes abound about whether the farmer took the city slicker or vice versa.

The investor should approach land buying in a disciplined and systematic manner. One approach is to find the specific site that he wants to own and negotiate with the owner. The other is to select from what is offered on the market. In either case it is prudent to plot known offerings and sales on a map. Consider what is known about each sale. This includes prices and terms, topography, utilities, flood-prone areas, nearby roads, and other special features. Try to ascertain why sale of one site realized more (or less) per land unit (acre, foot) than that of a comparable site. A real estate appraiser can be of great help. When selling, the information will help an investor to price the land intelligently. When buying, he will be able to recognize obvious bargains (there could be desperate sellers) or overpriced parcels (there are smug sellers). Whether buying or selling, it is wise to be patient. Marketing land or making investment tastes known takes time.

Negotiating the Purchase

Real estate owners who want to sell quote an offering price through their brokers. It is known that they will accept that price in cash, but negotiation is customary in real estate. Buyers, generally acting through their broker or the listing broker, will submit an offer at a lower amount and request generous financing terms. The offer may also stipulate certain conditions and subject the property to physical tests and title checks by experts. The owner may reject it with or without a counter-offer. Further negotiations ensue until an agreement is reached. Provided that all conditions to the contract have been met, closing takes place. Money and property change hands.

Professional Advisers

Appraisers, attorneys, planning consultants, brokers, and accountants are the professionals commonly used by land buyers or sellers. Depending upon the complexity of the property and the transactions, others can be helpful. These include farm, ranch, or timber specialists, counselors, mortgage brokers, architects, and engineers.

Those dealing in land should select professionals with care. Some real estate appraisers concentrate in residential or commercial property, and so have little experience with land. Many attorneys are specialists in matters other than real estate and the same is true for most accountants. The property buyer or seller is advised to seek out professionals who have participated in and are knowledgeable about the type of transaction involved.

A farm or ranch acquired by an investor is not the same as idle land. It is a business, and experienced management is needed. Land with timber can be managed to maximize profits or reduce holding costs; planting, harvesting, and maintaining healthy trees is a science.

When land approaches the development stage, architects and engineers may be necessary to plat subdivisions and decide where utility lines and streets should be put. Counselors and marketing experts can be helpful in deciding on suitable improvements, targeting the market, and timing sales. Most projects require mortgage financing, so mortgage bankers or brokers may be called upon to assist.

Packaging

Professional predevelopment work is generally termed "packaging"; it means getting raw land into a market-ready condition. Skilled syndicators plan the ultimate sale of properties as they first acquire them.

The greatest increment of profit occurs with the changing of a land parcel's highest and best use — not necessarily its actual use. A land investor might commission a detailed survey, field-checked topographic study, hydrological analysis, subdivision lot layout, or other land-use plan, zoning approval, water-sewer layout approval, and perhaps soil borings and building permits. The capital gains tax treatment is typically not affected as long as the land is not graded or otherwise physically disturbed.

Broker Commission

Real estate brokers generally work for sellers and are paid by them. Commission rates on land range from 3 to 10 percent. These rates are negotiable, although some brokers will not take less than a certain rate. Some brokers are amenable to deferring a part of their commission when the seller finances part of the sale. For example, the broker may take half of the commission in cash at closing and the other half ratably as the seller collects on the note.

A listing is a contract whereby a broker is engaged by a principal. If a licensed broker finds a ready, willing, and able buyer at the terms of the listing, the broker is entitled to a commission.

There are several types of listings. An open listing gives the owner the option of employing any number of agents. An exclusive listing allows the engaged broker to collect a commission regardless of which broker effects the sale. The exclusive right to sell allows the broker to collect a commission no matter who sells the property. In a net listing (illegal in many jurisdictions), the owner states a minimum acceptable price. The broker's commission is any amount received above the net figure. Though an open and/or net listing may seem to be in the owner's best interest, frequently it is not. Few brokers will work hard to market property under an open listing knowing that other brokers may sell it or that a purchaser might go around all the brokers. The net listing creates a conflict of interests. A seller would like to accept an offer that is $1 above the net figure. But would a broker solicit it? In most situations, exclusives are used. The term of the listing is negotiable. At least three months but less than one year would seem reasonable.

In a growing number of situations, buyers pay brokers for finding suitable land. Compensation arrangements are negotiable. Still, the general rule is that sellers pay the commission.

MANAGING THE INVESTMENT

Physical Inspection

Periodic physical inspections are recommended for landowners. Although the land itself cannot be destroyed, it is subject to forces of nature (e.g., erosion, fires, pests, and flooding) and of people (e.g., waste dumping, encroachments, squatters, and theft of timber or minerals). Periodic inspections, at least annually, should uncover any problems.

Liability Insurance

Liability insurance is recommended to protect against unforeseeable events such as an accidental drowning on the property. Although such events are rare, liability insurance is particularly necessary when the land is being used for recreational purposes.

Other Precautions

Tax payments are mandatory. Tax assessors should be notified of address changes, and the owner should be certain that taxes and other assessments are paid.

Foreign investors should be certain to maintain a relationship with a knowledgeable person in the United States to file necessary documents.

GLOSSARY

acre— A measure of land containing 43,560 square feet.

eminent domain— The power to take (condemn) private property for public use upon payment of a fair compensation.

highest and best use— The legally permitted and otherwise feasible use of the land that will bring the greatest income or value to the land.

internal rate of return— The discount rate that equates the present value of expected cash inflows with expected cash outflows.

land residual process— Method of appraising vacant land.

leverage— Use of others' money to complete an investment transaction.

listing— An agreement to engage a broker to sell or lease.

nonrecourse loan— The lender may claim only the property as collateral; the borrower is not personally liable.

option— A contract providing the right to buy, sell, or lease property for a stated period and under certain specified terms.

parcel— Any area of land contained within one description.

purchase-money mortgage— A loan from the seller to the buyer of property.

raw land— See *unimproved land.*

release provisions— A clause in a mortgage that allows some property to be freed as collateral.

unimproved land— Land in its natural state, undeveloped, with no building or other improvements.

water table— Level of water in the ground.

zoning— Local government control of the use of land.

PROFESSIONAL DESIGNATIONS IN REAL ESTATE

Designation		*Certifying Organization*
Real Estate Sales		
CRB	Certified Residential Broker	Realtors National Marketing Institute, Chicago
CRS	Certified Residential Specialist	Realtors National Marketing Institute, Chicago
GRI	Graduate, Realtors Institute	Graduate Realtors Institute, Chicago, and State Realtors Association
Industrial, Commercial Investment		
CCIM	Certified Commercial Investment Member	Realtors National Marketing Institute, Chicago
CRSS	Certified Real Estate Securities Sponsor	Securities & Syndication Institute, Chicago
SIR	Society, Industrial Realtors	Society of Industrial Realtors, Chicago
Management		
CPM	Certified Property Manager	Institute of Real Estate Management, Chicago
AFM	Accredited Farm Manager	American Society Farm Managers & Rural Appraisers, Denver
AFLM	Accredited Farm and Land Member	Farm & Land Institute, Chicago
Appraisal		
SRA	Senior Residential Appraiser	Society of Real Estate Appraisers, Chicago
SRPA	Senior Real Property Analyst	Society of Real Estate Appraisers, Chicago
SREA	Senior Real Estate Analyst	Society of Real Estate Appraisers, Chicago
RM	Residential Member	American Institute of Real Estate Appraisers, Chicago
MAI	Member Appraisal Institute	
SR/WA	Senior Right of Way Agent	American Right of Way Association, Chicago
ARA	Accredited Rural Appraiser	American Society Farm Managers & Rural Appraisers, Denver
CRA	Certified Review Appraiser	National Association of Review Appraisers, Minneapolis
Assessment		
CAE	Certified Assessment Evaluator	International Association of Assessing Officers, Chicago
AAE	Accredited Assessment Evaluator	International Association of Assessing Officers, Chicago
RES	Residential Evaluation Specialist	International Association of Assessing Officers, Chicago

Counseling

CRE	Counselor, Real Estate	American Society of Real Estate Counselors, Chicago

Financial

CMB	Certified Mortgage Banker	Mortgage Bankers Association, Washington, D.C.

LEADING BROKERS

Adams-Cates Co., Atlanta, Ga.

Baird & Warner, Chicago, Ill.

Grubb & Ellis, San Francisco, Cal.

Henry S. Miller Co., Dallas, Tex.

Julian J. Studley, New York, N.Y.

Sonnenblick-Goldman Realty, Miami, Fla.

Wilhelm Leyendecker Morrison & McCanse, Houston, Tex.

SUGGESTED READING

Periodicals

Appraisal Journal. Published by the American Institute of Real Estate Appraisers, an affiliate of the National Association of Realtors, Chicago, Ill. Quarterly.

Federal Home Loan Bank Board Journal. Published by the Federal Home Loan Bank Board, Washington, D.C. Monthly.

Journal of Real Estate Taxation. Published by Warren, Gorham & Lamont, Boston, Mass. Quarterly.

Land Economics. Published by University of Wisconsin, Madison, Wis. Quarterly.

Mortgage and Real Estate Executives Report. Published by Warren, Gorham & Lamont, Boston, Mass. Monthly.

Real Estate Appraiser and Analyst. Published by the Society of Real Estate Appraisers, Chicago, Ill. Bimonthly.

Real Estate Review. Published by Warren, Gorham & Lamont, Boston, Mass. Quarterly.

Real Estate Today. Published by the National Association of Realtors, Chicago, Ill. Monthly.

Tierra Grande. Published by the Texas Real Estate Research Center, College Station, Tex. Quarterly.

Reference Books

Arnold, Alvin L. *Tax Shelters in Real Estate Today.* Boston: Warren, Gorham & Lamont, 1978.

Benke, William. *All About Land Investment.* New York: McGraw-Hill Book Co., 1976.

Coopers & Lybrand. *Tax Planning for Real Estate Transactions.* Chicago: Farm and Land Institute, 1978.

Friedman, Jack P., and Ordway, Nicholas. *Income Property Appraisal and Analysis.* Reston: Reston Publishing Co., 1981

Hinds, Dudley; Carn, Neil; and Ordway, Nicholas. *Winning at Zoning.* New York: McGraw-Hill Book Co., 1979.

Seldin, Maury. *Land Investment.* Homewood: Dow Jones-Irwin, 1975.

Warren, Gorham & Lamont, Inc. *Real Estate Review Portfolio No. 3, Investing in Raw Land.* Boston, 1974. (updated periodically).

Wendt, Paul F., and Cerf, Alan R. *Real Estate Investment Analysis and Taxation,* 2nd ed. New York: McGraw-Hill Book Co., 1979.

Retirement Income—Individual Retirement Plans

Donald S. Grubbs, Jr., Esq. *

BASIC CHARACTERISTICS

An individual retirement plan is a plan to which an individual can make tax-deductible contributions for personal savings. The amount of contribution is generally limited to $2,000 or to $2,250 for certain married persons, but not more than 100 percent of compensation. The plans are of four different types: individual retirement accounts (IRAs), individual retirement annuities, accounts established by employers or employee associations, and retirement bonds. The term "IRA" is popularly used for all four types of plan. Simplified employee pensions (SEP-IRAs) are IRAs established by employers under rules that allow deductions as large as $15,000.

IRAs may be established by employees or self-employed individuals or may be established for such individuals by employers, unions, or employee associations.

Prior to 1982, an individual could not contribute to an IRA if he were covered under an employer's pension plan. This made about half of all workers ineligible. Use of IRAs is substantially greater by upper-income individuals, reflecting their greater ability to save and their greater interest in tax deductions. A 1981 report of the President's Commission on Pension Policy showed the following information about IRA participation:

Percentage of People Who Are Eligible for and Who Have IRAs by Income Class — 1977

Family Adjusted Gross Income	*Percentage of People Who are Eligible for IRAs*	*Percentage of Eligible People Who Have IRAs*
$ 0 - 5,000	85.0%	0.2%
5,000 - 10,000	70.0	1.3
10,000 - 15,000	60.0	3.3
15,000 - 20,000	45.4	5.5
20,000 - 50,000	24.9	21.7
Over 50,000	28.6	52.4

* Donald S. Grubbs, Jr., is a consulting actuary with George B. Buck Consulting Actuaries, Inc., Washington, D.C.

IRAs may be invested in most kinds of investments. This article describes the requirements for IRAs in taxable years beginning January 1, 1982 or later, based upon the Economic Recovery Tax Act of 1981 enacted August 13, 1981.

IRAs — Legal Requirements

An individual retirement account is a trust created or organized in the United States for the exclusive benefit of an individual, for which the trust agreement meets the following requirements:

- Except for rollover contributions, the trust will accept contributions only if they are in cash and do not exceed $2,000 on behalf of any individual for the taxable year.
- The trustee must be a bank or individual allowed under regulations.
- No trust assets may be invested in life insurance contracts.
- An individual's interest in his account must be nonforfeitable.
- Trust assets may not be commingled with non-IRA property, except in a common trust fund or common investment fund.
- Benefit distributions must be made within certain periods.

Timing of benefit distributions. Benefit distributions must begin no later than the year the individual attains age 70½. The amount of distribution in that year and each year thereafter must be at least equal to the account balance at the beginning of the year divided by the individual's life expectancy or the life expectancy of the individual and his spouse. Based upon regulations, these life expectancies are 12.1 years for a male age 70 and 15.0 years for a female age 70. The combined life expectancy of a husband and wife depends on their particular ages; for example, if both husband and wife are age 70, the combined life expectancy is 18.3 years.

If the individual dies before his entire interest has been distributed, the entire account must be distributed to his beneficiaries within five years or applied to purchase a life annuity for them within that period. An exception occurs if the benefits had commenced before the individual's death and were being paid over the joint life expectancy of the individual and his spouse. In such a case, the payments can continue to be paid over the remainder of the original combined life expectancy if more than 5 years remain. Although not disallowed, distributions before age 59½ are subject to tax penalties. (See *Tax Consequences* in this article.)

Custodial accounts. A custodial account may be used in lieu of a trust if the account is held by a bank or individual allowed under regulations, provided the custodial account otherwise satisfies the requirements for trusts. For tax purposes, such custodial accounts are treated as trusts.

Investments. There is no legal restriction under federal law on the type of assets an individual retirement account may invest in. However, in effect, there is a restriction against investing in collectibles such as art and stamps, since such investments are treated as distributions and included in the individual's gross income. If an IRA is established by an employer under an employee pension plan, it is governed by the fiduciary requirements of the Employee Retirement Income Security Act of 1974 (ERISA). (See article on Retirement Income — Pension Plan Investments, elsewhere in this volume.) The trust laws of the various states may also affect investments, although use of a custodial account may avoid such requirements. (See *Prohibited Transactions* in this article.)

Individual Retirement Annuities

An individual retirement annuity is an annuity contract in which

- The contract is not transferable by the owner.
- The contract provides for flexible premiums.
- The annual premium on behalf of an individual may not exceed $2,000.
- Dividends must be applied to increase benefits or pay premiums, and may not be distributed in cash.
- The entire interest of the owner is nonforfeitable.
- Benefit distributions must be made within the same periods as required for individual retirement accounts.

It is allowable for contracts to provide for waiver of premium on disability. A group annuity contract with individual accounts can be used.

Accounts Established by Employers and Employee Associations

Employers, labor unions, and other employee associations may establish a trust to provide IRAs. Such trusts must satisfy all of the requirements for IRAs. The assets of the trust may be held in a common fund, but there must be separate accounting for the interest of each employee or member. Few, if any, such trusts have been established. Employers have preferred to avoid the additional responsibility and expense, particularly since many alternative forms of IRAs are already available for employees.

Retirement Bonds

A retirement bond is a federal bond issued under the Second Liberty Bond Act that meets the following requirements:

- It pays interest only on redemption.
- It pays no interest if the bond is redeemed within twelve months of issue.
- Interest stops if the registered owner attains age 70½, or five years after death if that is earlier than he would have attained age 70½.

- Except for rollover contributions, contributions on behalf of an individual do not exceed $2,000 for any taxable year.
- It is not transferable.

Retirement bonds for IRAs are distinct from qualified bond purchase plans, which use similar bonds.

TAX CONSEQUENCES

Deduction of Contributions

Individuals are allowed a deduction from gross income for their IRA contributions, regardless of whether or not they itemize deductions. The basic maximum deduction equals the lesser of $2,000 or 100 percent of the individual's compensation. Compensation includes earned income of self-employed individuals. IRA contributions for a year can be made by the due date (including extensions) for the individual's tax return. It is not necessary to establish the IRA before the end of the year.

Contributions for spouses. A married person is allowed a deduction for contributions to an IRA for his spouse, provided they file a joint tax return and the spouse does not work for pay. The maximum deduction equals the lesser of $2,250 or 100 percent of the working spouse's compensation, reduced by the deduction taken for the working spouse's own IRA. The $2,250 can be split between the two IRAs in any manner, except that not more than $2,000 can be contributed to either one.

The two IRAs must be separately owned. A joint trust can hold the accounts of both, but their interests must be separately accounted for. This does not prevent each from naming the other as beneficiary with a right of survivorship.

Restrictions. No deduction is allowed if the individual has attained age 70½ before the close of the taxable year. And no deduction is allowed for a retirement bond if the bond is redeemed within twelve months of issue.

Contribution by employers. If an employer contributes to an IRA for an employee, the entire contribution is included in the employee's gross income, but the employee is allowed to take the appropriate deduction. (See *Simplified Employee Plans* in this article for deductions for SEP-IRAs.)

Rollover Contributions

Distributions from qualified pension and profit-sharing plans are ordinarily taxable when received. But if an individual contributes part or all of a qualifying rollover distribution to an IRA within sixty days of receipt, he is not taxed currently on the amount of the rollover. A qualifying rollover distribution is a lump-sum distribution or a distribution made upon termination or discontinuance of a qualified plan. The maximum amount that may be rolled over may not exceed the fair market value of the cash and property received in the distribution, reduced by the sum of any employee contributions included in the distributions. If the employee receives property other than cash, the property received may either be transferred to an IRA or sold and the proceeds transferred to an IRA. If a participant rolls over only part of a distribution received from a qualified plan, the remainder is taxable as ordinary income.

Rollover contributions are not subject to the $2,000 limitation. Of course, there is no deduction on the rollover, which is a tax-free transfer. Similar rollover rules apply to distributions from tax-deferred annuities. In addition to rollovers from qualified plans, IRA-to-IRA rollovers are allowed tax-free, if the entire amount received from an IRA is rolled over into another IRA within sixty days. Only one such tax-free rollover is allowed in any 365-day period.

Excess Contributions

If an individual makes a contribution to an IRA (other than a rollover contribution) that is larger than can be deducted, a 6 percent excise tax is imposed upon the excess contribution. But if an excess contribution, together with the net income it has earned, is returned to the individual before his tax filing date (including extensions) for the year the excess contribution was paid, there is no excise tax and only the net income paid is taxable income.

The excise tax on excess contributions is assessed not only for the year in which the excess contribution is made, but for each year that it remains in the IRA. To avoid continuing excise taxes, an individual may either withdraw the excess contribution or offset it against IRA contributions that could have been made in future years.

Excess contribution — illustration. For example, assume that John Doe contributes $2,000 to an IRA in 1982, but because of business difficulties his total earned income for 1982 is only $800. Since he is allowed to deduct only $800, he has made an excess contribution of $1,200 for 1982. Unless he withdraws this $1,200 together with the net income it earns by his tax filing date (April 15, 1983, unless extended), he must pay an excise tax of $72 (6 percent of $1,200). Assume John Doe fails to withdraw the $1,200 by his tax filing date; and assume that in 1983 he has only $1,000 of earned income, makes no IRA contribution, and again fails to withdraw his 1982 excess contribution of $1,200. Because John Doe makes no contribution in 1983 while he is entitled to contribute and deduct $1,000, $1,000 of his excess contribution will be treated as contributed in 1983 and John Doe will be entitled to a $1,000 deduction in 1983. However, he will have to pay a 6 percent excise tax in 1983 on the remaining $200 of the excess contribution, unless he withdraws it.

Investment Earnings

An individual retirement account is exempt from taxation. Thus there is no current tax upon investment income received or upon realized and unrealized appreciation of assets, so long as the investment return is retained within the IRA. Similarly, there is no current tax on a retirement bond until the bond is redeemed.

The taxation of individual retirement annuities is more complex. The reserves for such annuities receive favorable tax treatment. For this reason, in determining the rate of net investment income to be credited under the contracts, insurance companies usually make little or no deduction for federal income tax.

Distributions

Except as noted below, all distributions from IRAs are taxable as ordinary income when received by an individual. The individual's basis is zero, so 100 percent of the distribution is included in gross income.

There is no tax upon distribution from an IRA if the entire distribution is rolled over into another IRA within sixty days. However, only one such tax-free rollover is allowed in any 365-day period. In the case of an IRA under which all of the contributions were rollover contributions from a qualified plan, there is no tax upon distribution from the IRA if the entire distribution is rolled over into another qualified plan within sixty days. A similar rule applies to rollovers from and to tax-deferred annuities.

Distributions of excess contributions. There is no tax on the distribution of any excess contribution if the distribution is received by the individual's tax filing date (including extensions) for the year the excess contribution was made, and if the distribution of the excess contribution includes any net income attributable to the excess contribution.

If a distribution of an excess contribution is made from an IRA after the tax filing date for the year of the contribution, the distribution will still be recovered tax-free (to the extent no deduction was previously claimed) if the aggregate contributions did not exceed $2,250 in the year in which the excess contribution was made. If an individual has erroneously made a rollover contribution larger than allowed because he or she received incorrect information from the plan administrator, the excess can be recovered tax-free even if it is larger than $2,250.

Transfer of account upon divorce. A transfer of an individual's ownership interest in an IRA to his spouse, incident to a divorce, is not a taxable transfer. The spouse will pay no tax until distributions are made from the IRA.

Penalty for premature distributions. If a distribution is made from an IRA before the individual for whom the IRA was established attains age 59½, it is a premature distribution, unless the individual is disabled (as defined in the Code). Any premature distribution included in gross income is subject to an additional 10 percent tax.

Penalty for insufficient distributions. IRAs are required to make distributions beginning the year the individual attains age 70½. In any year in which the minimum distribution required exceeds the amount actually distributed, a 50 percent tax is assessed on the excess. The IRS may waive this severe penalty if the shortfall was due to reasonable error and reasonable steps are being taken to remedy it.

"Worst Case" Illustration. Fred Brown, whose salary puts him in the 50 percent tax bracket, changes employers at age 55. He receives a $300,000 distribution from the old employer's profit-sharing plan on June 1, 1982 and rolls it over into an IRA on August 1, 1982. He excludes the distribution from his 1982 gross income as a tax-free rollover. Upon auditing Fred's 1982 return in 1984, the IRS notices that it was sixty-one days between June 1 and August 1, and therefore Fred was not eligible for a tax-free rollover. The IRS recomputes Fred's 1982 tax, including additional income of $298,000 ($300,000 less the regular $2,000 IRA deduction). This increases Fred's 1982 tax by $80,920 (based upon lump-sum distribution treatment), less $1,000 resulting from the effect of his $2,000 deduction for the year. But the extra $298,000 contribution was also an excess contribution in 1982, subjecting Fred to an additional $17,880 excise tax (6 percent of $298,000). In addition, because he failed to withdraw the excess in 1983, there was $296,000 remaining excess contribution ($298,000 less a $2,000 deduction for 1983) for which the 1983 excise tax of 6 percent is $17,760.

Fred needs to withdraw the $296,000 to prevent the continuing annual excise taxes; he also needs the money to pay his back taxes. But he cannot obtain a tax-free withdrawal of the excess contribution because his tax-filing date for 1982 has passed, the 1982 excess exceeds $2,250, and it was not caused by a reporting error of the plan administrator. If he withdraws the $296,000 in 1984 to avoid the annual 6 percent excise taxes, the distribution will be taxed as ordinary income, increasing his 1984 income tax by $148,000. In spite of the fact that Fred has already paid tax on the money once and received no deduction, his case is still subject to the rule that withdrawals from an IRA are taxed as ordinary income and have zero basis. In addition, since Fred is under 59½, distribution of the $296,000 excess contribution in 1984 will be a premature distribution, resulting in an additional 10 percent tax of $29,600.

The total tax liability incurred by Fred's $300,000 profit-sharing distribution is shown below.

1982 income tax on distribution	$ 80,920
1982 excise tax	17,880
1983 excise tax	17,760
1984 income tax on distribution	148,000
1984 tax on premature distribution	29,600
Total additional taxes	$294,160

Less: Savings for IRA deductions for 1982 and 1983	2,000
Net additional taxes	$292,160

Fred could have avoided this disastrous result initially by making his rollover contribution within sixty days, or by withdrawing his excess contribution by his tax filing date for 1982.

Summary of Tax Advantages and Disadvantages of IRAs

The principal tax advantages of IRAs are the deduction of contributions and the tax deferral of investment income. The principal disadvantages of IRAs are the low limits on contributions, restrictions on when money can be withdrawn, and taxation of all distributions as ordinary income.

SIMPLIFIED EMPLOYEE PLANS (SEP-IRAs)

SEP-IRA Objectives

Congress established simplified employee pensions (SEP-IRAs) in order to encourage small employers to establish pensions for their employees. Some small employers have been discouraged from maintaining qualified plans for employees because of the complexity of ERISA and the burdensome nature of its reporting and disclosure requirements. With simpler requirements, Congress felt more small employers would adopt plans, particularly employers who, as owners, could thus set aside more for themselves than allowed under regular IRAs. But to assure that rank and file employees would also receive equitable treatment, it was necessary to require that the SEP-IRAs be nondiscriminatory.

Limits on Contributions and Deductions

A SEP-IRA must prohibit contributions greater than $15,000 per year on behalf of an individual. Employer contributions to a SEP-IRA are included in the employee's gross income, but are deductible by the employee. The largest employer contribution that an employee may deduct in a year is the lesser of $15,000 or 15 percent of compensation. Unlike regular IRAs, SEP-IRAs provide no special allowance for employer contributions on behalf of a spouse.

In addition to any employer contributions, an employee may also make his own contributions and deduct them under the usual IRA rules and limits. Such employee IRA contributions may be made to the same SEP-IRA as employer contributions are, or may be made to a separate regular IRA.

Participation Requirement

If an employer contributes to a SEP-IRA in a given year, contributions must be made for each employee who has attained age 25 and has worked for the employer in at least three of the preceding five years. Exceptions are allowed for employees covered under a collective bargaining agreement that includes an agreement on pensions, and also for certain nonresident aliens.

Non-Discriminatory Contributions

Employer contributions must be a uniform percentage of total compensation up to a stated limit. The limit may not exceed $200,000, and may exceed $100,000 only if employer contributions are at least 7.5 percent of compensation.

Integration with Social Security. In determining whether employer contributions meet these requirements, Social Security taxes paid by the employer may be treated as employer contributions to the SEP-IRA. In the case of a plan including owner-employees (proprietors and 10-percent partners), the entire Social Security tax paid by the owner-employee must be taken into account if the employer Social Security tax for other employees is taken into account.

For example, Dr. Miller is not incorporated. He may contribute to a SEP-IRA 7.5 percent of his self-employment income not exceeding $200,000 (7.5 percent of $200,000 = $15,000) less his Social Security tax, provided he contributes 7.5 percent of pay, less the employer Social Security tax, for all employees age 25 or over who have worked for him during three of the five prior years.

Other Rules

A SEP-IRA allows the employer complete flexibility to determine whether or how much to contribute during any given year, so long as the maximum limits are not exceeded. But it must include a written allocation formula specifying how each contribution is to be allocated.

All contributions must be 100 percent vested in the individual participant's account. The employer cannot restrict an employee's right to withdraw any portion of his account. However, the employee is subject to the tax on premature withdrawals and the funding media can impose penalties for early withdrawal.

SEP-IRAs may be funded through individual retirement accounts or individual retirement annuities, but not through retirement bonds.

IRS Form 5305-SEP

The Internal Revenue Service has published Form 5305-SEP, "Simplified Employee Pension — Individual Retirement Accounts Contribution Agreement." An employer completing this model SEP-IRA agreement form has assurance that his plan complies with IRS requirements. The form should not be submitted to IRS. No advance determination from IRS is needed or possible.

The IRS model SEP-IRA will not meet the needs of all employers. For example, an employer using the form cannot integrate contributions with Social Security taxes. Therefore, some employers will prefer to use an individually designed IRA or an approved prototype IRA of an insurance company, bank, or other institution.

Reporting Requirements

For employers using model Form 5305-SEP, reporting requirements are very simple. The employer must provide each employee with a copy of the form at the time the employee becomes eligible to participate. At the end of each calendar year, the employer must give a written statement of the amount of any employer contribution. If the employer selects, recommends, or otherwise influences the choice of the particular IRA or of the type of IRA, and if the particular IRA restricts withdrawals (e.g., by a penalty for early withdrawal), the employer must provide a clear explanation of the restrictions, including a statement that other IRAs may not have such restrictions.

Reporting requirements for employers that do not use model Form 5305-SEP are much more rigorous. Department of Labor regulations fail to reflect congressional intent that such plans have simplified reporting.

INVESTMENT MEDIA FOR IRAs

There is almost no limit to the kinds of investments that may be used for IRAs, except for collectibles (as of 1982) and insurance contracts. However, the small amount of each IRA, except for rollover IRAs, places a practical restriction on some types of investments. The investment alternatives differ in their rates of investment return, in the existence and nature of guarantees on principal or interest, in liquidity, and in expense charges.

Variety of Investment Objectives

Individuals have differing needs and objectives, and therefore the same form of investment is not suitable for all. For everyone, the goals during the period after withdrawals begin are usually different from the goals during the earlier accumulation period.

For all investors, the objective is to maximize the total investment return within acceptable limits of risk. But individuals differ greatly in the extent they desire or can afford to take the risk of greater market value fluctuation in the pursuit of greater investment return. During a long accumulation period, the individual may be little concerned with year-to-year fluctuation if the long-term prospect of appreciation is good. But many retired persons cannot afford the risk of fluctuation.

For most, the greatest risk is not that the dollar amount of their IRA will fluctuate but that its purchasing power will decline with inflation. Selecting investments to counter inflation over both short periods and long periods is difficult.

During the payout period, an individual who needs to use both capital and income but must avoid outliving his capital should consider some form of annuity. For example, a person may have an individual retirement account invested in mutual funds during the accumulation period, but roll it over into an individual retirement annuity during the payout period.

Savings and Loan and Mutual Savings Bank Media

More than half of all IRA assets are held by savings and loan associations and mutual savings banks. The funding arrangements of federally chartered institutions differ slightly from those of state-chartered ones, and differ from state to state. The two principal investment alternatives offered are certificates of deposit and passbook savings accounts.

The Federal Savings and Loan Insurance Corporation (FSLIC) or Federal Deposit Insurance Corporation (FDIC) guarantee both passbook savings and certificates of deposit in federally chartered savings and loans and mutual savings banks up to $100,000. State agencies usually provide similar guarantees for state-chartered institutions.

Certificates of deposit. Often a single institution will offer two or more alternative forms of certificates of deposit (CDs), differing in duration, interest rates, and other features. CDs have a substantial penalty for early withdrawal, but a minimum return such as 5.5 percent may be guaranteed in any event. Minimum deposits, such as $250 or $500 or more, are required for CDs. Some CDs allow additional deposits to be added after the initial purchase, while others do not. If an additional deposit is made, some banks treat the entire CD, including prior deposits, as a new CD for purposes of determining the period when early withdrawal penalties apply.

Passbook savings accounts. Passbook savings accounts guarantee the right to withdraw the entire principal and interest at any time. Interest rates on such accounts are generally unattractive, usually 5.5 percent in 1981. A passbook savings account may be used for an IRA when the amount is less than the minimum required for a CD.

Commercial Bank Media

Commercial banks are used to fund IRAs in two ways: as the investment medium and as the trustee or custodian for other investments.

Acting as the investment medium, commercial banks fund individual retirement accounts in much the same way as savings and loan associations and mutual savings banks do. Certificates of deposit and savings accounts are the principal vehicles used. Although aggregate statistics are lacking, it appears that commercial banks have made only a small inroad into the IRA market, compared to savings and loan associations.

A bank may serve as a trustee through an individual trust arrangement. The small amount involved in most IRAs, however, usually makes this uneconomical. Some banks serve as trustees for all of the IRAs funded through a particular mutual fund or a particular broker-dealer.

Mutual Funds

Almost the whole range of types of mutual funds, including growth stock funds, income stock funds, balanced funds, and money market funds, are used to fund IRAs. Tax-exempt bond funds are not used for IRAs, since there would be no tax advantage for an IRA, already tax-exempt, to invest in such funds, which have relatively low yields.

Broker-Dealer Plans

Stock brokerage firms arrange for IRA funding, some passively accepting the business and others actively seeking it. Brokers actively seeking the business often have their own approved prototype plans. These plans generally fall into two categories: mutual fund IRAs and self-directed IRAs.

Mutual funds whose investment manager and distributor are affiliated with the broker sometimes may be used. If self-directed investment is chosen, a custodial account is established; the individual directs the investment of his own account. Prototype plans of brokers may limit investments to marketable securities. One major brokerage firm will not allow investments in commodity futures or in precious metals.

Insurance Company Investments

Insurance companies usually fund IRAs with individual flexible premium annuities. A flexible premium annuity allows the policyholder to vary the time and amount of premiums, or to pay no premium at all. If a flexible premium annuity is used as an individual retirement annuity, it must prohibit premiums in excess of $2,000 per year except for rollover contributions.

An expense charge is subtracted from the premium received and the balance is accumulated at an interest rate that is guaranteed for the life of the contract. Interest guarantees vary greatly from company to company. Often there is a high first-year guarantee, with successively lower guaranteed rates applying to more distant years. Most companies actually credit interest higher than the guaranteed rates when their investment earnings substantially exceed the guaranteed rates.

The policyholder may receive his account balance in a lump sum or have it applied to provide a monthly income for life under one of several forms of annuity. Annuity purchase rates are guaranteed in the contract, but more attractive current rates are used when they provide a larger income.

Previously, endowment contracts and level premium annuity contracts were issued for IRAs; some of these are still in force, but amendments to the Internal Revenue Code no longer allow such contracts to be issued for IRAs.

United States Individual Retirement Bonds

United States individual retirement bonds issued for IRAs comply with the statutory requirements previously described. Individual retirement bonds may be purchased in person or by mail from a Federal Reserve Bank or Branch, or from the Bureau of Public Debt, Securities Transaction Branch, Washington, D.C. Remittance must accompany the purchase application Form PD-4345. Bonds are issued at par in $50, $75, $100, and $500 denominations. New bonds issued in August 1981 guaranteed interest of 8 percent compounded semiannually.

Collectibles Excluded

The Economic Recovery Tax Act of 1981 effectively prevents the acquisition of collectibles after 1981. "Collectibles" are defined as any work of art, rug, antique, metal, gem, stamp, coin, alcoholic beverage, or other tangible personal property specified in the regulations. While such investments are not prohibited, they are taxed as distributions to the individual. IRAs may continue to hold collectibles acquired before 1982. As of early 1982, an effort is being made to repeal the restriction on collectibles.

Expense Charges

Expense charges take a variety of forms. There may be a charge deducted from deposits. There may be a direct deduction from investment income, or an indirect deduction because the funding medium credits less than it earns on its investments. There may be brokerage fees for buying and selling investments. There may be a charge on distributions, particularly a penalty for early withdrawal if the deposit is not held for a minimum period. If annuities are purchased at retirement, the purchase price includes an expense charge. There may be a flat dollar fee to establish the IRA and a flat annual fee to administer it.

Utilization of Various Investment Media

The American Council of Life Insurance reports that the amount of assets of IRAs invested with selected financial institutions as of the end of 1979 were as follows:

Institution	*Amount ($Millions)*
Life insurance companies	$2,465
Savings and loan associations	6,100
Mutual savings banks	2,031
Commercial banks	Not available
Mutual funds	453
U.S. retirement bonds	43

A convenient checklist of alternative opportunities for IRA investors is provided in Figure 1 on page 835, which also provides typical yield figures as of

	Typical current yield Percent
30-month bank certificate of deposit	15.9% (compoundable)
IRA/Keogh term bank account	8
Self-directed securities brokerage accounts	Variable
Covered option-writing brokerage account	Variable
Money market fund	17.5
Short-term corporate unit trust (six months)	16
Intermediate corporate unit trust (six to seven years)	14.5
Long-term corporate unit trust (25 years)	16-19
Government bond fund	13.75
Corporate bond fund	14.5
Corporate junk bond fund	16
Income stock fund	8.5
Balanced stock fund	7
Long-term growth fund	4.5
Corporate thrift plan equity account	5
Corporate thrift plan fixed-income account (guaranteed investment contract)	12
Insurance annuity contract	14
Real estate limited partnership	Variable

FIG. 1. A Checklist of IRA Investment Opportunities

SOURCE: *Business Week,* September 14, 1981; reprinted by special permission.

September 14, 1981. Figure 2 on page 836, from the same source, summarizes the disadvantages of particular media for IRA purposes.

SUITABILITY OF IRAs FOR INDIVIDUAL INVESTORS

Every employee who receives compensation and every person who has self-employment income is eligible to invest in an IRA. Any such person who can afford to defer current income until age 59½ or beyond should consider the tax advantages and disadvantages. The current deduction of contributions and deferral of tax on investment income are most favorable. But all distributions will be

Tax-exempt funds and unit trusts	Tax shelter is redundant, and income is taxable as ordinary income at distribution
Investments dependent on capital gains treatment	All proceeds taxable as ordinary income at distribution
Collectibles such as diamonds, coins, rugs	Purchase considered a taxable distribution under the statute
Endowment or other retirement plan involving a life-insurance contract	Prohibited by statute
Investments purchased with the aid of debt, including mortgaged real estate	Debt-financed income is taxable
Six-month bank money market certificates	Minimum purchase $10,000, too large to qualify for IRA. Subject to excess-contribution limitations
Margined stock and bond trading accounts	Subject to debt-financed income rule and excess-contribution rule in case of a margin call
Commodity futures	Subject to same limitations as margin accounts

FIG. 2. IRA Investments to Avoid — and Why
SOURCE: *Business Week,* September 14, 1981; reprinted by special permission.

taxable as ordinary income. This is unfavorable for a person who expects to withdraw an IRA in a lump sum or to receive income during a period when his tax rate is substantially higher than his current tax rate. Thus, IRAs are generally most suitable for a person who expects to withdraw the money in installments during retirement years while in a lower tax bracket.

PROHIBITED TRANSACTIONS

An IRA may not engage in a prohibited transaction with a disqualified person. The general effect is to prevent self-dealing by persons who exercise control over the IRA.

Disqualified Persons

The term "disqualified persons" includes fiduciaries, persons providing services to the IRA, employers, unions, and certain persons related to any of the above by blood, employment, ownership, or otherwise. A fiduciary is any person who exercises authority or control over the plan or its assets or renders investment advice for a fee or other compensation. The individual for whom the IRA is established is ordinarily a fiduciary, since he ordinarily has authority to roll over the IRA into a different funding medium.

Prohibited Transactions Defined

All transactions between the IRA and a disqualified person are prohibited transactions, unless an exemption is granted. This includes the sale, exchange, or leasing of any property, lending money, extending credit, furnishing goods or services, and similar transactions. Such transactions are prohibited even if they are at arm's length for full consideration. For example, an individual could not even sell a listed security to his own IRA for its current market value.

Penalties

If an individual engages in a prohibited transaction with his IRA, the IRA loses its tax-exempt status and the entire assets of the IRA become current taxable income to the individual.

If some other disqualified person, such as the trustee, engages in a prohibited transaction, that disqualified person must pay an excise tax equal to 5 percent of the amount involved. If the 5 percent tax is assessed and the transaction is not corrected within the correction period (generally ninety days after IRS sends a notice), an additional 100 percent tax may be imposed.

GLOSSARY

custodial account— An account held for the benefit of an individual by a bank or individual in lieu of a trust, but meeting the requirements for trusts.

employer-employee association account— A trust to provide IRAs for individual employees, that may be established by employers, labor unions, or other employee associations.

individual retirement account (IRA)— A trust set up for the exclusive benefit of an individual in conformance with federal income tax law. If established by an employer under an employee pension plan, the account is governed by fiduciary requirements of ERISA.

individual retirement annuity— A retirement plan based on an annuity contract providing for a flexible premium, and nontransferable by the owner.

retirement bond— A federal bond used in an individual retirement plan, which pays interest only on redemption and is nontransferable.

rollover contribution— That portion of a lump-sum distribution of a qualified plan, or distribution on termination of a qualified plan, that is contributed to an IRA within sixty days of receipt of the distribution.

simplified employee plan (SEP-IRA)— An employee pension plan for small companies that relieves employers of the burden of meeting ERISA reporting and disclosure requirements.

SUGGESTED READING

Barron's. Published by Dow Jones & Company, Inc., New York, N.Y. Weekly.

Institutional Investor. Published by Institutional Investor, New York, N.Y. Monthly.

Pensions & Investments. Published by Crain Communications, Chicago, Ill. Biweekly.

Pension World. Published by Communication Channels, Inc., Atlanta, Ga. Monthly.

Taxation for Lawyers. Published by Warren, Gorham & Lamont, Inc., Boston, Mass. Bimonthly.

Trusts & Estates. Published by Communications Channels, Inc., Atlanta, Ga. Monthly.

Wall Street Journal. Published by Dow Jones & Company, Inc., New York, N.Y. Daily.

Retirement Income—Pension Plan Investments

Donald S. Grubbs, Jr., Esq. *

BASIC CHARACTERISTICS

A pension plan is not an investment. Rather, it is a program that uses investments to accomplish its goals. There are many definitions of the phrase "pension plan." The Employee Retirement Income Security Act of 1974 (ERISA) defines pension plans extremely broadly as:

> [A]ny plan, fund, or program . . . established or maintained by an employer or by an employee organization, or by both . . . [that]
>
> (A) provides retirement income to employees, or
>
> (B) results in a deferral of income by employees for periods extending to the termination of covered employment or beyond,
>
> regardless of the method of calculating the contributions made to the plan, the method of calculating the benefits under the plan or the method of distributing benefits from the plan.

The ERISA definition applies both to plans that accumulate assets and to unfunded plans that are merely an employer's promise to make future payments. It applies to written plans and unwritten plans, to plans that are qualified under the Internal Revenue Code, and to plans that are not qualified.

Qualified Plans

Plans that meet certain requirements of the Code in order to receive favorable tax treatment are called qualified plans. All qualified plans must be in writing and must be funded. (See *Requirements for Qualification* in this article for a summary of the requirements for qualified plans.) The overwhelming majority of private employers' plans are qualified plans. This article generally discusses only qualified plans, although some statements apply equally to non-qualified plans.

The Code describes several types of qualified plans: pension plans, profit-sharing plans, stock bonus plans, annuity plans, and bond purchase plans. Under the Code, "pension plan" refers to one particular type of qualified plan. Under

* Donald S. Grubbs, Jr., is a consulting actuary with George B. Buck Consulting Actuaries, Inc., Washington, D.C.

ERISA, all qualified plans are called pension plans. This discussion follows ERISA in using the term "pension plan" to refer to all types of plans, including profit-sharing, stock bonus, annuity, and bond purchase plans.

Extent of Pension Plans

Approximately 500,000 qualified plans cover 31 million active workers in private employment. About 6,000 plans of state and local governments cover another 11 million workers. Within the federal government, sixty-eight plans cover about 3 million federal civilian employees. In 1981 pension plan assets of private employer plans totaled about $500 billion, and government employee plans held an additional $300 billion. The number of employees covered by private employer plans ranges from one employee to hundreds of thousands.

TYPES OF PLANS

All pension plans are either defined benefit plans, defined contribution plans, or a combination of the two. Each of these categories can be divided into subcategories, and many variations exist for each type. Investment objectives and legal requirements vary considerably according to the type of plan. The distinction between defined benefit plans and defined contribution plans is particularly important.

The design of pension plans is a very broad topic, and is subject to complex legal requirements. This article endeavors to summarize only those characteristics of plan types that bear upon investment objectives.

Defined Benefit Plans

Definition. A defined benefit plan specifies the amount of benefit that will be paid. For example, a defined benefit plan may provide a pension upon retirement at age 65 equal to one percent of the employee's average pay for his last five years of service, multiplied by total years of service. A monthly pension payable for life is the usual form of benefit, but many defined benefit plans also allow lump-sum distributions.

Funding and costs. The amount of contributions needed to provide the benefits under the plan is not defined. Ultimately, the cost of a defined benefit plan is the sum of the benefits paid plus expenses of administering the plan, reduced by any investment earnings on the plan assets. An actuary determines the estimated amount needed to be set aside currently to provide for the ultimate cost of the plan. Some plans require employee contributions. The employer contributes whatever is needed, in addition to any employee contributions, to finance the plan.

Contributions for all employees usually are combined for investment purposes in a single fund. The fund generally is not allocated among employees. An individual employee has no claim to any part of the plan assets; his only right is to receive the benefits promised by the plan. Individual benefits generally are unaffected by increases or decreases in investment earnings.

The employer's cost is affected by investment experience. If the plan's investment return increases by one dollar, ultimately the employer's cost is reduced by one dollar. Because plan assets are invested over long periods of time, the effect of compound interest is great. In a typical plan, increasing the long-term investment return by one percent will decrease plan costs by about 20 percent. Thus, employers have a strong incentive to maximize the investment return in a defined benefit plan in order to reduce plan costs, and a corresponding incentive to minimize losses.

Most plans have a positive cash flow in almost all years. Usually, it is not necessary to liquidate investments in order to pay benefits. For this reason, defined benefit plans generally are more concerned with long-term investment returns than with short-term fluctuation.

Multiemployer plans. A multiemployer plan is a plan established under a collective bargaining agreement between one or more unions and two or more employers. Almost all multiemployer plans are defined benefit plans. The collective bargaining agreement specifies the amount of employer contributions to the plan (e.g., eighty cents per hour worked). But the collective bargaining agreement usually does not specify the level of benefits to be provided by the plans.

When a multiemployer plan is set up, a joint board of trustees is established, with an equal number of labor and management trustees. Both labor and management trustees must act in the sole interest of participants and beneficiaries. An actuary engaged by the board advises it of the level of benefits that he estimates can be supported by the estimated future contributions. Based upon the actuary's advice, the board establishes the plan and determines the level of benefits to be provided.

The actuary's estimate of the level of benefits that can be supported is based upon various actuarial assumptions, including the rate of future investment return. If the fund earns more than assumed, the excess can be used to increase the level of benefits. If it earns less than assumed, it may be necessary to reduce the promised level of benefits. Thus, participants and plan trustees acting in their behalf have an interest in maximizing the investment return. The investment return ordinarily has no direct effect upon employer costs, which are fixed by the collective bargaining agreement. However, poor investment performance may create greater union demands for employers to increase their level of contributions during the next bargaining period in order to maintain the promised benefit level.

The Multiemployer Pension Plan Amendments Act of 1980 created new liabilities for employers contributing to multiemployer plans. Employers who withdraw from a multiemployer plan are now liable for their share of the excess of the value of vested benefits over the value of plan assets. This gives employers a new interest in maximizing the investment return of such plans and in minimizing negative fluctuations in asset values in order to minimize the potential withdrawal liability.

Other jointly trusteed plans. Sometimes a jointly trusteed plan is established by an agreement between a single employer and a union. Such a plan may have all of the characteristics of a multiemployer plan except that there is only one employer. This type of plan generally has the same investment considerations as a multiemployer plan; however, it is not subject to the Multiemployer Pension Plan Amendments Act.

Mandatory employee contributions. At one time, a large proportion of defined benefit plans required participating employees to contribute. Mandatory employee contributions are not tax-deductible. Because of tax and other considerations, most plans have eliminated these contributions.

In a defined benefit plan with mandatory employee contributions, a withdrawing employee may be entitled to his own contributions with accumulated interest. Because of certain provisions of ERISA, interest is usually credited at 5 percent regardless of the rate of investment earnings of the plan's assets. Thus, the existence of mandatory employee contributions does not introduce any investment considerations.

Voluntary employee contributions. Some defined benefit plans allow employees to make voluntary contributions in order to increase their benefits under the plan. A separate account must be maintained for each employee's voluntary contributions. This account must be credited with its share of the plan's investment income and with realized and unrealized appreciation and depreciation. Voluntary employee contributions introduce investment considerations that are entirely different from those for funding the defined benefits. These considerations are similar to those for defined contribution plans, described below.

In the past, voluntary contributions have not been tax-deductible, and few employees have actually made voluntary contributions even when their plans allowed such contributions. In 1981, however, legislation was enacted allowing employees to make tax-deductible contributions of up to $2,000 annually to an individual retirement account (IRA), or $2,250 for combined IRAs with a nonworking spouse, regardless of whether they are covered under a pension plan. (See article on Individual Retirement Accounts, elsewhere in this volume.) This same legislation allows IRA-type accounts to be established as an adjunct to a pension plan to receive such tax-deductible voluntary contributions. It is too early to know if many plans will allow such accounts, and if so, whether or not many employees will use them. If the employer's plan allows such accounts, the employee can choose between establishing an IRA-type account in a pension plan or establishing a separate IRA. Some employees may prefer to let the employer decide on the investment of their IRA-type account, while others may prefer to choose their own investment medium with a separate IRA. Some employers may not provide the convenience of automatic payroll deductions for separate IRAs. The inclusion of IRA-type accounts in a pension plan obviously increases the work and expense of plan administration and communication.

Variable annuity plans. Some defined benefit plans are variable annuity plans. Under such plans the amount of pension after retirement varies with the investment experience of plan assets. Under some variable annuity plans, units of variable annuity are credited and funded prior to retirement and fluctuate with investment experience before as well as after retirement. Under defined benefit variable annuity plans, as under all defined benefit plans, the amount of annuity first credited is based upon the plan's benefit formula (e.g., one percent of pay for each year's service). But variable annuity plans differ from other defined benefit plans in one respect: Investment performance affects the amount of employee benefits in such plans.

A variable annuity plan has an assumed investment return (AIR), which the employer uses for the purpose of determining its contributions to the plan. If plan assets earn the AIR, they are expected to be sufficient to provide the promised benefits. If the total investment return, including realized and unrealized appreciation and depreciation, exceeds the AIR, the percentage of the excess will increase the amount of annuity. If the return is less than the AIR, the percentage of deficiency will decrease the amount of annuity. The amount of annuity may be adjusted annually or monthly to reflect the investment experience.

Some variable annuity plans are funded with trusts, while others are funded with special variable annuity policies issued by insurance companies. Many variable annuity plans were established in the 1950s and 1960s with the hope or expectation that funds invested in common stocks would keep pace with inflation. Some plans called for investing 100 percent of plan assets in common stocks. Other plans established an investment policy of a balance of fixed and equity investments to lessen extreme fluctuations in annuity payments. With market value declines of the 1970s, many of these plans were amended to eliminate the variable annuity feature. Recently, a number of variable annuity plans have been established using money market investments.

Defined Contribution Plans

A defined contribution plan (also called an "individual account plan") is a plan in which each participant has an individual account to which an amount defined by the plan is allocated each year. The sum of all of the individual account balances ordinarily equals the total assets of the plan. Each participant's account shares in the investment income and in the realized and unrealized appreciation and depreciation of the plan.

When an individual is eligible to receive benefits from the plan, his benefit is whatever his account balance can provide. The account balance may be paid in a lump sum or in installments, or may be applied to purchase an annuity payable throughout the participant's life. Some plans allow a choice between a fixed annuity, with unchanging monthly payments, and a variable annuity, under which monthly payments fluctuate with investment performance.

Effect of investment experience on benefits and costs. The amount of future benefits under a defined contribution plan, unlike those in a defined benefit plan, depends upon the plan's investment return. Because of the effect of compound interest over the long period of an employee's career, the effect of the rate of investment return can be very substantial. An investment of $1000 at the end of every year over a forty-year career will accumulate to $154,762 at 6 percent interest, or $199,635 at 7 percent — about 29 percent more for a one percent change in the annual return. Thus there is a strong incentive to maximize the long-term investment return.

Fluctuation in market values can have an important effect upon the amount of benefits. If a participant becomes eligible for a benefit at a time when the plan's market value is low, this benefit will be lower than it might have been at a different time. This may cause some defined contribution plans to avoid investments with substantial market value fluctuation, in part or all together.

Under a defined contribution plan the investment performance usually has little or no effect upon the employer's cost.

Money purchase pension plans. A money purchase plan is one type of pension plan under the Internal Revenue Code. Because it is classified as a pension plan under the Code, there must be a definite formula for determining employer contributions to the plan (e.g., 5 percent of pay). Contributions cannot be contingent upon employer profits. All qualified pension plans are required to make benefits available in the form of an annuity, although a pension plan may allow participants to elect a lump sum as an alternative. Some money purchase plans allow the payment of lump sums, while others require every employee to apply his account balance to provide an annuity.

Some money purchase plans have invested all plan assets in annuity contracts and other fixed-dollar investments in an effort to protect the benefits from market value fluctuations. Other money purchase plans have endeavored to maximize the long-term investment return, with less attention to the problems of market value fluctuation.

The largest money purchase plan is the plan of the Teachers Insurance Annuity Association and College Retirement Equities Fund (TIAA-CREF). Most participants are college and university employees. TIAA-CREF allows each participant to elect what portion of his contribution is to be deposited in a fixed investment fund to provide a fixed life annuity, and what portion is to be deposited in an equity fund to provide a variable life annuity.

Target benefit plans. A target benefit plan is a money purchase pension plan that has some of the characteristics of a defined benefit plan. Like a defined benefit plan, a target benefit plan has a formula (e.g., one percent of pay multiplied by years of service). The employer is required to contribute to each employee's individual account a level annual amount which, together with interest at a total assumed rate of between 5 and 6 percent, is expected to be sufficient to provide the target benefit. Thus the target benefit plan has defined contributions and individual accounts, like all other defined contribution plans. The amount of benefits is the amount that can be provided by the account balance. Unlike a defined benefit plan, a target benefit plan may miss the target. It may provide more or less than the target benefit, depending on whether the actual investment return is more or less than the 5 to 6 percent assumed.

A target benefit plan is often established in lieu of a defined benefit plan. It has a stated pension objective, a target. To avoid the possibility of missing the target on the low side, some target benefit plans invest in annuity contracts or other fixed-dollar investments that assure that the target at least will be met. Other target benefit plans are more willing to accept investment risk in the attempt to maximize benefits.

Deferred profit-sharing plans. A deferred profit-sharing plan under the Internal Revenue Code is a defined contribution plan in which employer contributions can be made only out of the earnings of the current year or retained earnings of prior years. Some profit-sharing plans specify that the amount of contributions to the plan will be based directly upon the amount of profits (e.g., 25 percent of profits in excess of $1 million). Other profit-sharing plans leave the amount of contribution completely at the employer's discretion each year.

Some profit-sharing plans are established primarily to provide retirement income. Others are established for varying purposes, particularly when the employer also has a defined benefit pension plan to meet retirement income needs. They are often established to give employees incentive to make the business profitable. Almost all profit-sharing plans provide for lump-sum distributions. Some plans also allow the participant to elect to receive his account balance in installments or to have it applied to purchase a life annuity. Where provision of retirement income is not a primary purpose of the plan, the plan sponsor's concern about market value fluctuation may be less than it would be under a money purchase plan.

Particularly when employee profit incentive is the key purpose of the plan, the employer may decide to invest part or all of the profit-sharing plan assets in the employer's own common stock. Then the employees' benefits have a further dependency upon employer profits, perhaps increasing the profit incentive.

Thrift or savings plans. A thrift plan (also called a "savings plan") is a defined contribution plan under which employer contributions are made to match a stated percentage of employee contributions. Most thrift plans are qualified profit-sharing plans under the Code, but some are established as money purchase pension plans.

Under a typical thrift plan, employees may elect to contribute any amount up to 6 percent of pay. The employer agrees to contribute a stated percentage of whatever the individual employee contributes. Usually the matching percentage is 50 or 100 percent, although some plans have matching contributions as low as 25 percent or as high as 200 percent.

Thrift plans are often established, in part at least, to encourage employees to save. Employers usually want to encourage employees to participate in order to meet this objective. In addition, if participation falls below 70 percent of all employees who satisfy the plan's minimum age and service requirements, the plan's tax-qualified status may be in jeopardy. Therefore, employers may want the plan's investments to be attractive in order to encourage participation.

Some employees want to be able to invest in common stocks in the hope that market values will appreciate. Others are more concerned about preservation of principal, preferring guarantees that their investment will not decline in market value. Therefore, many thrift plans maintain two accounts, one for equity investments and one for fixed-dollar investments. This allows each employee to determine what proportion of his contribution is to be deposited in each account. Some plans offer more than two investment alternatives. Most thrift plans allow the election of investments to apply to both employee and employer contributions, although some restrict the election to the employee's own contributions.

Employee contributions. Some defined contribution plans include employee contributions and others do not. In certain plans, all employees are required to participate and to make contributions to the plan. Some employers require employee contributions only if an employee elects to participate. Thrift plans, as noted above, allow employees to elect whether and how much to contribute.

Some plans, unlike thrift plans, allow voluntary employee contributions that are not matched by employer contributions. The Economic Recovery Tax Act of 1981 provides new tax incentives for employees to make voluntary contributions, subject to IRA-type restrictions. (See article on Retirement Income — Individual Retirement Plans, elsewhere in this volume.)

Regardless of whether employee contributions to a defined contribution plan are mandatory or voluntary, employees must share directly in the plan's investment return. In defined benefit plans, on the other hand, mandatory employee contributions generally are credited with 5 percent interest whatever the rate of earnings of the plan's assets.

In defined contribution plans, some employers believe that principal preservation is more important for employee contributions than for employer contributions. Therefore, employee contributions may be invested in fixed-dollar investments with guaranteed principal, while employer contributions are invested in common stocks. Some employers believe that the employee should be entitled to direct the investment of his own contributions, at least among several alternatives. Others have taken the opposite approach, requiring employee contributions to be invested in fixed-dollar investments for safety, but allowing employee choice in the investment of employer contributions.

Qualified bond purchase plans. Internal Revenue Code Section 405 allows employers to establish qualified bond purchase plans. These plans are defined contribution plans and can be designed like either money purchase pension plans or profit-sharing plans.

Employer contributions and any employee contributions must be used to purchase a certain series of federal bonds. If an employer establishes a qualifed bond purchase plan, there is no discretion in the plan's investments. Very few employers have adopted such plans.

Stock bonus plans. A stock bonus plan is similar to a profit-sharing plan, except that the employer contributions are not necessarily dependent upon profits and the benefits are distributable in stock of the employer. Such plans are generally subject to the same requirements as profit-sharing plans.

The employer may contribute stock to the plan or the plan may purchase employer stock in the market. Although distributions from a stock bonus plan must be in stock of the employer, there is no general requirement that all assets of all stock bonus plans must be held in employer stock. Stock bonus plans are usually fully invested in employer stock, except for cash that is temporarily uninvested.

Employee stock ownership plans (ESOPs). An ESOP is a defined contribution plan that is designed primarily to invest in qualifying employer securities and that meets other IRS requirements. It may be a qualified stock bonus plan or a combination of a stock bonus plan and a money purchase pension plan. A qualifying employer security is stock or a marketable obligation, but a Subchapter S corporation may not establish an ESOP, since the stock of a Subchapter S corporation may not be held by a trust.

The laws concerning ESOPs have changed annually in recent years, changing the plans themselves and the terminology applied to them.

A tax credit ESOP is one that meets the requirements of Section 409A of the Code. Employers are entitled to tax credits for contributions to such plans under two distinct and differing sections of the Code. A leveraged ESOP is designed to meet financial objectives of the employer corporation or its key stockholders. Usually, the plan borrows money to purchase employer securities, either directly from the employer or from stockholders. Employer contributions to the plan are used to repay the loan. At times, ESOPs have been used to acquire the stock of a principal owner who dies or retires. They have also been used by corporations to spin off a subsidiary and sell it to their employees.

Combination of Defined Benefit and Defined Contribution Plans

Many employers have both a defined benefit plan and a defined contribution plan. In such cases, the defined contribution plan usually is a thrift plan or a traditional profit-sharing plan. The defined benefit plan usually is intended to meet retirement income needs, while the defined contribution plan primarily serves other purposes. Ordinarily, the investment objectives of each plan are not affected by the existence of the other plan.

Floor plans. A floor plan is a defined benefit plan under which the amount of monthly pension is determined first under a benefit formula, then reduced or offset by the amount of monthly pension that can be provided by a profit-sharing or other defined contribution plan. Floor plans provide a floor of protection, assuring that the combined benefit will never be less than the amount of pension determined under the benefit formula. When a new profit-sharing plan is adopted, it is often expected that this plan by itself will provide adequate pensions for younger employees. But for older employees, there may not be enough time to build up adequate benefits. A floor plan can assure that minimum benefit requirements are met for older workers who will not have time to build up large profit-sharing accounts.

Sometimes the floor plan is expected to benefit most of the members of the profit-sharing plan. In other cases it is expected that the profit-sharing account will more than offset the entire calculated benefit under the floor plan, leaving no benefit to be paid from the floor plan. Unless the profit-sharing account balance is sufficient to provide more than the benefit under the floor plan, the effect of greater or lesser investment earnings of the profit-sharing plan is to decrease or increase both the benefit and the employer's cost under the floor plan. To the extent that this occurs, the employer, and not the employee, really is bearing the investment risk under the profit-sharing plan. This may change the investment objectives of the profit-sharing plan.

Combined target benefit — floor plan. Target benefit plans and floor plans can be combined, and the same benefit formula can be used for both. If the target benefit plan exactly meets its assumed investment objective of 5 or 6 percent, it will exactly hit the target benefit and no benefit will be payable under the floor plan. If the target benefit plan earns more than the assumed rate, the excess increases the amount of benefit provided. If the target benefit plan earns less than the assumed rate, the floor plan picks up the difference. Thus, employees benefit from favorable investment experience while the employer bears the risk of unfavorable experience. This feature makes the combination undesirable to many employers, but attractive to some. The employer, for example, may want to invest the target benefit plan assets in more speculative investments, expecting this to increase the investment return, but may establish the floor plan to assure employees that they will be protected if results are poor. This combination may also alleviate the problem of the target benefit plan's restriction on employer contributions, which occurs because of contribution limits under the Code.

Tax advantages of combinations. In the case of small close corporations, including professional corporations (PCs), the primary objective of establishing a pension plan may be to defer taxable income for the owner rather than actually to provide pensions. Section 415 of the Code limits the amount of benefits that can be provided under defined benefit plans and the amount of contributions that can be provided under defined contribution plans. The combination of a defined benefit plan and a defined contribution plan can provide more tax deferral than either plan can alone. If the owners of the business are generally older than their employees and want to maximize their own tax deferral while minimizing costs for employees, a combination of a target benefit plan and a defined benefit plan (not a floor plan) may be the best way to accomplish those objectives. Projections of benefits and costs under assumed rates of investment return are needed to determine the most effective combination.

Annuity Plans

The Internal Revenue Code defines an annuity plan as a plan, funded with annuities, that would meet the requirements to be a qualified trust except that there is no trust. Annuity plans can be either defined benefit plans or defined contribution plans, and can take almost all of the forms of benefit design discussed above. The only exception is that an annuity plan cannot, of course, be a stock bonus or employee stock ownership plan, since an annuity plan is invested entirely in annuities. An annuity plan may be invested in any of a number of types of group or individual annuity contracts. (See *Insured Funding Media* in this article.)

Tax-deferred annuities. A separate type of plan is a tax-deferred annuity (sometimes called tax-sheltered annuity), established under Section 403(b) of the Code to provide tax-deferred savings for teachers and employees of certain nonprofit organizations.

Keogh (HR-10) Plans for Self-Employed Individuals

Plans established to cover partners or sole proprietors of unincorporated businesses are known as Keogh, or HR-10, plans. Partners and sole proprietors generally are treated as though they were employees, and their earned income is treated as compensation, provided their personal services are a material, income-producing factor in the business. Keogh plans generally are subject not only to all of the requirements of other qualified plans, but to other requirements as well. Thus, Keogh plans are more restrictive than are other plans.

Keogh plans may be either defined benefit or defined contribution plans, and can take most of the forms of corporate plans. Of course, a partnership or proprietorship cannot have a stock bonus or employee stock ownership plan, since it has no stock.

The special restrictions on Keogh plans are generally of three sorts. (Special limitations on deductions are discussed under *Tax Aspects of Pension Plans* in this article.) Special rules apply to all defined benefit plans covering self-employed individuals (proprietors and all partners); and special restrictions apply to plans covering owner-employees.

Restrictions on plans covering owner-employees. An owner-employee is an employee who owns the entire interest in an unincorporated trade or business, or a partner who owns more than a 10 percent interest in the capital or the profits of a partnership. In some large law and accounting firms, no partner owns as much as 10 percent interest, but most partnerships and all sole proprietorships include at least one owner-employee.

Plans covering owner-employees have restrictions on who may serve as trustee. The plan must cover all employees with three or more years of service, and all contributions must be nonforfeitable (vested) at the time they are paid into the plan. In the case of a profit-sharing plan, there must be a definite formula for determining contributions to the plan.

A number of restrictions apply only to owner-employees and not to other employees. An owner-employee may not be included in the plan unless he has consented to be included. Contributions for the owner-employee by the business may not exceed the amounts that may be deducted. Employer contributions may not discriminate in favor of owner-employees, and for this purpose contributions may not be integrated with Social Security taxes if more than one-third of the employer contributions are for owner-employees (as is usually the case). If the plan includes only owner-employees, they may not make employee contributions (i.e., personal contributions, as distinguished from contributions by the business). Special penalties apply if a distribution is made to an owner-employee before age 59½, unless he is disabled.

Defined benefit Keogh plans. A defined benefit plan covering self-employed individuals is subject to the same requirements as other defined benefit plans. In addition, two other restrictions apply.

First, the benefit formula applied on all self-employed individuals is limited to a fixed percentage of each year's compensation not exceeding $100,000. The percentages for sample ages are as follows:

Age When Participation Begins	*Applicable Percentage of Annual Pay*
20	6.5%
30	6.5
40	4.4
50	3.0
60	2.0

The limits on benefits that apply to all defined benefit plans also apply to Keogh plans, and they may produce lower limits than the special Keogh limits above. Second, defined benefit Keogh plans that cover any owner-employee may not provide benefits that are integrated with Social Security.

Subchapter S corporations. The plan of a corporation that elects to be taxed as a partnership under Subchapter S of Chapter 1 of the Code is subject to some of the same restrictions that apply to Keogh plans, if the plan covers any shareholder-employees (i.e., employees owning 5 percent or more of the outstanding stock). Forfeitures of non-vested employees may not benefit shareholder-employees.

The limits on benefits that apply to defined benefit Keogh plans also apply to such Subchapter S corporations. Employer deductions for shareholder-employees are not subject to the limits for self-employed individuals under Keogh plans, but any contribution in excess of these limits are included in the shareholder-employees' gross income. However, none of the special limits that apply to owner-employees and plans that cover owner-employees apply to Subchapter S corporations.

Investments for Keogh plans. As indicated above, Keogh plans are defined contribution plans or defined benefit plans subject to special limitations. These limitations generally have no effect upon investment policy. Therefore, the investment considerations for Keogh plans generally are the same as they are for corporate plans.

TAX CONSEQUENCES

Tax Effects of Qualification

If a plan is qualified under Section 401(a) of the Code, it enjoys several tax advantages.

Employer contributions to a qualified plan are deductible by the employer, up to certain limits, for the year in which they are paid to the plan; but they are not taxable to the employee at the time contributed, even if he has a nonforfeitable interest in the contributions. Investment earnings of the trust are not currently taxable to the trust, the employer, or the employee. Life insurance company reserves attributable to qualified plans are subject to reduced taxation or, in some instances, none at all. The employee generally is taxed on payments received only in the year in which they are received, even if he has an unrestricted right to receive them earlier. An employee who receives benefits in the form of a lump-sum distribution gets favorable tax treatment under capital gains rules, a ten-year forward averaging rule, or a combination of the two rules. If employer stock is distributed to the employee, the employee is not taxed on the unrealized appreciation at the time of distribution.

Investment Implications of Qualification

As an investment for the employee, participation in a qualified plan is quite favorable in terms of tax treatment. If the employee received the employer contribution in cash, he would pay current income tax on it. The employee could then invest the difference, paying tax currently on investment income. It can be shown that the usual effect of the tax-deferred buildup of a qualified plan ultimately is to produce a more favorable after-tax accumulation than individual investment of after-tax income will produce, if the rate of investment return is the same.

Employees who are considering investing their own contributions, even if they do not receive a current deduction for the contributions, will benefit most from the tax deferral on investment income. Thus, the qualified plan is generally a good investment for employees from the tax viewpoint. It is possible, however, that contributions may be paid-in in years when employees are in tax brackets lower than when benefits are received.

From an employer's viewpoint, a pension plan is an expense, just as salaries are an expense. But the employer may be able to prepay its pension expense for future years. In effect, the employer may be investing money currently in a tax-exempt fund to pay for future years' expenses.

The tax-exempt status of the trust affects its investment considerations. It would be foolish to acquire tax-exempt bonds with their lower yields, for example, since tax-exempt income has no special value to a trust that already is tax-exempt.

Similarly, a qualified trust has no tax preference among investment income received, realized gains and losses, and unrealized appreciation. The decision as to whether to invest in low-income growth stocks or higher income securities with little growth potential need not be influenced by tax considerations as it is for individual investors. Similarly, the decision to buy or sell a security with unrealized appreciation or depreciation can be made strictly from investment considerations, since there is no tax effect upon realizing the gain or loss. Unlike an individual investor, a trust that desires to sell a security has no need to wait until the end of a one-year holding period for the purpose of getting capital gains treatment.

Requirements for Qualification

The requirements for obtaining qualification of pension plans are numerous, detailed, and complex. The principal requirements are as follows:

(1) The plan must be funded with a trust, a custodial account, annuities, or retirement bonds.
(2) It must be in writing.
(3) It must be for the exclusive benefit of employees and beneficiaries.
(4) It must not discriminate in favor of officers, shareholders, or highly compensated employees.
(5) Eligibility for participation must satisfy certain age and service rules.
(6) It must meet minimum vesting requirements.
(7) It must meet certain requirements for limiting plan mergers and transfers of assets and liabilities.
(8) Benefits may not be assigned or alienated.

(9) Benefits must commence within stated periods.
(10) The plan must include certain limits on contributions and benefits.
(11) Separate additional rules apply to qualified pension plans, profit-sharing plans, stock bonus plans, ESOPs, annuity plans, Keogh plans, and other specific types of plans.

A plan sponsor may obtain an advance IRS determination of a plan's qualified status. But even if an advance determination letter is received, the IRS may determine upon audit that the plan is not qualified in practice. Such determinations can be both prospective and retrospective.

INVESTMENT OBJECTIVES

Pension plans have the same general objectives as other investors do. But the relative priorities given to liquidity, preservation of principal, investment income, and market value appreciation tend to be different for pension plans than they are for most investors. The need for these elements varies substantially according to the type of plan, and from one plan to another. There is extensive literature on investment objectives. This discussion deals only with the ways that pension plan investment objectives may differ from general investment objectives.

Liquidity

The liquidity requirement is related to the plan's cash flow. Apart from the purchase and sale of assets, the plan receives contributions and investment income and pays benefits. In the large majority of plans, projections will show that the plan's cash flow is positive for many years into the future. In such cases, there is little need for liquidity.

A minor need for liquidity may occur because of the timing of cash flow within a year. Many employers pay their entire annual plan contribution in a single payment, while benefits may be paid throughout the year. The plan may need to retain sufficient liquid assets to pay benefits between the annual contributions.

In a small plan, the termination of a participant entitled to a large benefit may necessitate liquidation of investments. If such events can be predicted, asset liquidity can be planned around the event. To the extent that a plan faces such events and that they cannot be predicted, liquidity may become an important investment objective for a portion of the plan assets.

Security of Principal

Security of principal is a consideration of every investor. But because most defined benefit plans expect a positive cash flow for many years into the future, they can take a long-term view of security. Short-term market value fluctuations usually are of little importance for defined benefit plans.

In defined contribution plans, the benefits paid to withdrawing participants will depend upon the market value of assets at the date of withdrawal. Some defined contribution plans are concerned with preventing loss of principal, which could decrease benefits; others feel comfortable having the benefits vary with market value fluctuations, for better or for worse. Some employers are particularly concerned with preventing loss of principal with respect to the employee's own contributions. Individual employees differ in their desire for security of principal; to accommodate this, some plans allow employees to choose from alternative investments for their funds, while some allow employees to make transfers between funds, particularly where retirement is only a few years away.

Investment Return

Maximizing the total investment return, within acceptable limits of risk, is an objective of every pension plan. Increased investment return will either increase employee benefits or decrease employer costs, depending upon the type of plan.

The investment return that matters generally is not the investment income received, but the total investment return, including investment income and realized and unrealized appreciation and depreciation. As stated earlier, there are no tax reasons for a pension plan to prefer investment income, realized gains, or unrealized appreciation as a form of investment return. The form of investment return does affect the plan's cash flow, but the positive cash flow of most plans usually makes this a very minor consideration.

Plans differ as to the relative importance placed on short-term versus long-term investment return. A defined benefit pension plan is concerned primarily with the long-term investment return; a defined contribution plan, particularly a thrift plan, may be concerned with the short-term return.

For the purpose of funding defined benefit plans, assets are valued at their actuarial value, such as average market value over a period of years. Such methods tend to gradually recognize appreciation and depreciation of market values, while dampening the short-term fluctuations. This reduces the adverse effect of market value fluctuation, enabling the assets of a defined benefit plan to focus more on long-term investment return than on short-term fluctuations.

Risk

Like other investors, pension plans are concerned with investment risk. Some commonly used measurements of risk actually measure fluctuations, both positive and negative. Of course, pension plans only want to limit negative fluctuations. For example, a convertible bond for which the conversion price does not currently affect the market value may have the potential for substantial upward fluctuation but little downward fluctuation from its present value.

For a pension plan, it is the risk of the entire portfolio that matters. The risk associated with individual investments is important only as it relates to the risk of the whole plan. A highly diversified portfolio of fairly high-risk investments may represent less of a risk than does a less diversified portfolio of low-risk securities.

Another question as to how much risk is acceptable is the question of who bears the risk. Employers generally bear the risk in defined benefit plans, and are able to spread any investment losses over long periods of time. Employees bear the risk in defined contribution plans. In some defined contribution plans, employees select the amount of risk they bear by choosing between a guaranteed principal fund and a common stock fund. In such a situation, the two funds will be invested with entirely different risk objectives.

Compliance With ERISA Fiduciary Requirements

General requirements. ERISA has imposed a number of requirements on those who control plan assets, called "fiduciaries." A fiduciary must discharge his duties to the plan solely in the interests of participants and beneficiaries

(A) for the exclusive purpose of providing benefits to participants and beneficiaries and defraying reasonable administrative expenses,
(B) with the care, skill, prudence and diligence of a prudent man,
(C) by diversifying investments to minimize the risk of large losses, and
(D) in accordance with plan documents.

Profit-sharing, stock bonus, thrift, ESOP, and certain money purchase plans are exempt from the diversification requirement to the extent that they invest in qualifying employer real property or qualifying employer securities. The definition of qualifying employer real property was designed to apply to the retail stores of one particular employer, and applies to few, if any, other situations. A qualifying employer security is a security of the employer that is either a stock or a marketable obligation satisfying certain ERISA criteria.

Exemption of qualifying employer securities from the diversification requirement does not exempt them from other fiduciary requirements. In one case, pending as of 1982, participants alleged that investing profit-sharing-plan assets in the employer's stock was imprudent and caused extensive damages.

No plan may acquire or hold any employer security that is not a qualifying employer security, or any employer real property that is not a qualifying employer real property. Defined benefit plans and certain money purchase plans may not acquire qualifying employer securities or qualifying employer real property if they constitute over 10 percent of plan assets; after 1984, they may not hold such investments in excess of 10 percent of plan assets.

If a defined contribution plan allows individual participants to exercise control over their own assets, the fiduciary is not liable for losses resulting from the participants' decisions. Fiduciaries are liable for losses resulting from their own breaches of fiduciary duty and, to a large extent, are liable for breaches by co-fiduciaries. But trustees are not liable for breaches by an investment manager. Fiduciaries may obtain fiduciary liability insurance, and they must be bonded.

Prohibited transactions. ERISA contains very broad prohibitions against transactions between pension plans and parties in interest. Parties in interest include all fiduciaries, persons providing services to the plan, the employer, any union involved, officers, directors, and 10 percent shareholders of any of the above, certain relatives, and others. Prohibited transactions include the sale, exchange, or leasing of property; lending or extending credit; furnishing goods, services, or facilities; and transfer of assets. There are statutory exemptions from the broad prohibited transaction rules, as well as a procedure for obtaining class or individual exemptions. Hundreds of individual and class exemptions have been issued by the Department of Labor. Prohibited transactions are the subject of an automatic excise tax equal to 5 percent of the amount of the transaction; if the transaction is not corrected, an additional 100 percent tax can be assessed.

Investment objectives and fiduciary responsibilities. A major objective of all fiduciaries is to avoid prohibited transactions or fiduciary liability. It is argued that the prohibited transaction rules have prevented plans from taking advantage of good investment opportunities, and that fear of fiduciary liability has caused some trustees to become too cautious to be good investors. But the rules undoubtedly have deterred some improper investments.

Investment Expense

Minimizing unnecessary investment expense has the same effect as increasing the investment return. This affects decisions concerning which investments to acquire and how to acquire and manage them. The objective is to maximize the net investment return after expenses. Some types of investments, such as mortgages, have higher investment expenses than other types do. The real question is whether or not higher investment return offsets higher investment expense.

The fees of trustees, investment managers, and consultants are reviewed by plan sponsors who select them. If a particular trustee, investment manager, or consultant can increase the investment return by even a small amount, the increased return usually will more than pay for the fee. But if an equal return can be obtained with less expense, any additional expense would be a waste of plan assets.

Social Investment

Some forces in organized labor, as well as some endeavoring to support broad public interests, argue that the investment of pension plan assets should serve social purposes as well as the usual investment goals.

Organized labor often sees a connection between jobs for union members and the investment of pension plan assets. For example, it is argued that the union-organized textile industry of the Northeast is losing out to new, lower-cost, non-union textile factories in the South, and that the new factories are financed in part by the investments of pension assets of plans for Northeastern union workers. Unions would prefer that the assets instead be invested in the development of businesses that produce jobs for their members.

Another example is the investment of the pension assets for New York City employees in loans to the city in 1975. The city needed the loans to prevent a bankruptcy that, among other things, would have cost many of the covered workers their jobs. It was argued that the loans were imprudent investments for the pension funds, since the nation's leading banks had refused to extend comparable credit because they perceived the risk as too great.

Some want particular plans to make investments that will directly benefit participants in those plans, such as new housing or a children's day-care center in the area where the particular workers live. Others want pension funds invested in areas they believe serve broad social purposes, such as low-cost housing. Another aspect of social investing is the blacklisting of investments that are considered socially undesirable. These may include companies doing business in South Africa, or companies with an anti-union reputation.

Effects of social investment. Most employers and banks have argued that plan assets should be invested solely in the interests of plan participants and beneficiaries, and that social investment objectives may either increase investment risk or decrease investment return. Blacklisting certain investments has little effect on the investor or on the business being blacklisted. From the viewpoint of the pension fund, many good alternatives for investment are available, so eliminating one alternative does not matter. If the business being blacklisted is actually a good investment, it will have no trouble finding other investors at comparable terms. Positive investments for social purposes, however, may adversely affect a plan if it causes the plan to accept higher risks or lower investment returns than are otherwise available.

Funding Policy

Every employee benefit plan must, as ERISA states, "provide a procedure for establishing and carrying out a funding policy and method consistent with the objectives of the plan." Some have mistakenly assumed that "funding policy" means "investment policy." Legislative history makes it clear that a funding policy is not an investment policy; however, a funding policy is needed in order to establish an investment policy.

The funding policy is the employer's policy regarding how much to contribute to the plan and when to contribute it. Knowledge of the funding policy assists the trustee to project the plan's cash flow, which helps in planning the investment policy, particularly to meet any liquidity needs. In some plans, the employer has no flexibility to vary contributions. In others there may be substantial flexibility to vary contributions from one year to another. In making the decision as to how much to contribute, the employer may compare the rate of investment return being earned by the pension plan with the amount that can be earned by investing more in the business, or with the rate the employer is paying on its indebtedness.

Investment Policy

Investment policy may be established by the plan sponsor, trustee, or investment manager. It may be written or unwritten. Many sponsors, particularly larger plan sponsors, adopt a written investment policy, primarily to describe in what types of assets the plan will invest and how assets will be allocated among the various types. The investment policy provides a framework for selecting insurance companies, trustees, and investment managers, as well as providing guidance when making investments and reviewing investment results.

Statements of investment policy vary from those that state broad, general goals to those that are quite detailed and specific. Investment policies usually are reviewed from time to time and revised as appropriate. Some employers believe that they can reduce their potential fiduciary liability by adopting a suitable investment policy. Others seek to reduce fiduciary liability by delegating investment policy decisions to the insurance company, trustee, or investment manager. If the latter approach is used, it is important that the investment manager be familiar with the investment needs of the particular plan.

TRUSTS AND TRUST INVESTMENTS

Trusts

In most cases, all assets of an employee benefit plan must be held in trust by one or more of the trustees. The principal exception is for plans invested in insurance and annuity contracts and certain other assets held by insurance companies. Qualified bond purchase plans, government plans, and church plans also are exempt from the trust requirement. The establishment and operation of trusts are controlled by state laws and vary somewhat from state to state.

A Keogh plan may use a custodial account in lieu of a trust if the custodian is a bank or a person satisfying IRS requirements. A custodian is responsible for the safekeeping and accounting of plan assets, but not for investments. The principal use of custodians has been for plans fully invested in mutual funds. Sometimes they are used to hold insurance and annuity contracts, although this is not required by law.

Trustees

A bank or trust company usually is named as trustee. Some plans designate an individual or a group of individuals as trustee. Multiemployer plans always have a joint board of trustees consisting of an equal number of union and employer representatives. Where there are individual trustees, they frequently enter a second trust agreement with a bank or trust company to hold and invest the plan assets.

The duties of the trustees are set forth in the trust agreement. These duties generally include responsibility for holding, investing, and accounting for plan assets. The trustee usually is authorized to pay benefits and expenses from the trust upon direction of the plan administrator. In the case of trustees who are individuals, the trust agreement may give the trustees part or all of the responsibility of plan administration.

The trustee is given extremely broad discretion in the investment of plan assets in some trust agreements. In others, the investment is restricted in various manners, including the requirement that the trustee follow instructions of the employer or a designated outside investment manager. Even when it is not required by the trust agreement, the corporate trustee normally consults with the employer and gives serious consideration to any of the employer's investment preferences that do not breach the trustee's fiduciary responsibility. However, the trustee or trustees have exclusive authority and discretion under ERISA to manage and control the assets of the plan, unless the plan expressly provides that the trustee is subject to direction from a named fiduciary, or some authority is delegated to one or more investment managers.

Trust Investments

Trust assets may include almost any type of investment. These various types (e.g., bonds, common stocks, mutual funds) are all discussed in detail elsewhere in this volume.

Commingled funds. Most banks that serve as pension plan trustees maintain one or more commingled trusts, which combine the assets of many qualified plans. These pooled funds operate very much like mutual funds. Most banks maintain a fund for bonds, a fund for common stocks, and, often, a balanced fund. Some banks maintain many specialized pooled funds for income-producing stocks, growth stocks, money market instruments, mortgages, and other types of investments. These pooled funds are used as the investment intermediary for most small plans and for some quite large ones. The pooled funds may provide greater diversity of investment, better investment management, and lower investment expenses than are possible for small plans investing their assets separately. Since the pooled fund as a whole almost always has a positive cash flow, even when some of its individual plans have a negative cash flow, liquidity problems are minimized.

The investment considerations for each pooled trust are similar to those for the investment of a separate pension plan, except that each pooled trust may be restricted to specific classes of investments or to specific investment goals (growth or income). The assets of the individual plan can be invested in the combination of pooled trusts that are expected to accomplish the plan's investment objectives. Individual employers may designate the proportion of plan assets to be invested in each pooled fund, or that decision may be left to the corporate trustee. (See article on Bank-Managed Investment Accounts, elsewhere in this volume.)

Marketable securities. Most trusts limit their investments to securities that are publicly traded in established markets in order to reduce the problems of valuation, investment, and administration, But increasingly, trusts are investing in real estate and other assets that present valuation difficulties.

Distribution of Assets by Type. The market value of trust assets of private noninsured employer pension plans as of December 31, 1980 was documented by the Securities and Exchange Commission (SEC) as shown in Table 1 below.

INSURED FUNDING MEDIA

More than one-third of all private pension plan assets are invested with life insurance companies. Insurance companies fund plans under a wide variety of types of contracts. The contracts may be classified broadly, as either group contracts covering a group of employees or individual contracts for each employee. Contracts also may be classified as either annuity contracts or insurance contracts. Both types may provide annuities after retirement. The distinction is that upon death before retirement, annuity contracts never pay death benefits exceeding the reserve, cash value, or premiums paid, whichever is greatest, while insurance contracts guarantee larger death benefits. Contracts also differ in the extent to which the insurance company guarantees the payment of benefits or the costs to the employer.

TABLE 1. Trust Assets of Private Noninsured Pension Plans

	Market Value (billions)	*Percent of Total*
Cash and deposits	$ 9.3	3.1%
U.S. government securities	26.3	8.8
Corporate and other bonds	60.0	20.2
Preferred stock	1.4	0.5
Common stock	174.4	58.7
Mortgages	3.8	1.3
Other assets	22.0	7.4
Total assets	$ 297.2	100.0%

SOURCE: SEC News Release 81–21 (May 15, 1981)

Group Annuity Contracts

Deposit administration (DA) group annuity contract. Under deposit administration contracts, contributions to the plan for active participants are placed in a deposit fund. The insurance company does not allocate the fund among participants. The fund is credited with interest and charged with expenses. When a participant becomes eligible for a pension, the plan administrator notifies the insurance company, which makes a withdrawal from the deposit fund to purchase an annuity for the participant. If the participant is eligible for a lump-sum distribution, it is paid directly from the deposit fund.

The insurance company guarantees a minimum rate of interest to be credited to the deposit fund and guarantees the level of expense to be charged against the deposit fund. The insurer also guarantees the annuity purchase rates that will be used to purchase annuities and, after annuities have been purchased, it guarantees payment of the promised pensions. It does not guarantee that the deposit fund will be sufficient to purchase the annuities.

The guarantees are conservative in nature. Experience more favorable than that assumed by the guarantees may be reflected in dividends or experience credits, which are added to the deposit fund. The insurance company may provide a full package of consulting, administrative, and actuarial services in connection with the plan, or the functions may be provided by the employer and consultants.

If the contract is discontinued, the employer may have the option of applying the deposit fund account balance to purchase annuities or withdrawing it for transfer to a trust or another insurance company. In case of withdrawal, the insurance company may subtract a surrender charge or a market value adjustment, and may require that the transfer be paid out over several years.

Separate accounts. Insurance companies offering deposit administration contracts generally make available one or more separate accounts for common stock investments to be used in connection with the DA contracts. The separate account is very similar to a mutual fund. The employer may direct that part or all of the contributions to the plan be invested in the separate account. Transfers can be made from the deposit account into the separate account. Any transfers out of the separate account are based upon the current market value.

In addition to separate accounts for common stock, many insurers maintain separate accounts for bonds, mortgages, real estate, and other classes of investment. Some insurers will establish a special separate account for a large individual plan, investing the account to meet its particular investment objectives. (See article on Life Insurance Investments — Separate Accounts, elsewhere in this volume.)

Immediate participation guarantee (IPG) contract. Also known as "pension administration" or "investment-only" contracts, immediate participation guarantee contracts are similar to DA contracts. However, the insurer guarantees to credit its actual rate of investment earnings on its general portfolio rather than a rate stipulated in the contract. The insurer charges the pension fund for an allocation of expenses for the particular contract based upon accounting records, rather than using a stipulated expense charge. Although annuity purchase rates are guaranteed under the contract, usually there are no annuities actually purchased so long as the account balance is more than sufficient to purchase annuities for all those already retired, unless the contract is discontinued. Instead, pension payments are withdrawn from the account monthly as they are paid, just as in a trusteed plan. Some companies use an accounting device that has the appearance of purchasing annuities, but they actually operate the contract as though no annuities had been purchased. In addition, separate accounts are often made a part of IPG contracts, in the same way as they are with DA contracts.

Guaranteed investment contract (GIC). Some employers desire contracts that guarantee the rate of interest to be credited to the deposit account and also guarantee that the full principal can be withdrawn with no surrender charge or adjustment. A guaranteed investment contract offers just such guarantees. The interest guarantee may extend for five to ten years. It is contemplated that the account balance will be paid out at the end of the guarantee period, although the balance may be left on deposit and a new guarantee period established. The GIC may include annuity purchase options, but usually no annuities are purchased. (For a more complete discussion, see article on Life Insurance Investments — Guaranteed Interest Contracts, elsewhere in this volume.)

Group deferred annuity contracts. A deferred annuity contract is one in which the insurance company promises to pay a monthly annuity beginning at a specified future date. Under a group deferred annuity contract the employer pays a premium to the insurer for each participant each year, to purchase the amount of pension earned in that year.

For example, a pension plan may provide a pension at age 65 equal to $10 a month for each year of participation in the plan. Each year the employer would pay a premium to the insurer to purchase a deferred annuity of $10 a month for each participant, to begin when the participant reaches age 65. The amount of premium for each participant depends upon the participant's age and sex. By the time a participant reaches age 65, he will have had a series of deferred annuities purchased each year, so that his entire pension has been purchased and is guaranteed by the insurance company.

The premium rates for deferred annuities may be discounted for mortality before retirement; that is, they may be determined on the assumption that no benefit will be paid if the participant dies before retirement age. In such a case no payment is made upon death before retirement.

Termination of employment before retirement. If the participant terminates employment before retirement and is entitled to a deferred vested pension, the deferred pension that has already been purchased will be paid when the participant reaches retirement age. But if a participant terminates employment before becoming vested, forfeiting his right to the pension already purchased, the insurance company pays a refund equal to its reserve for the forfeited pension. This refund is applied to reduce the employer's next annual premium. Such refunds normally are paid, however, only if the employer provides evidence that the employee was in good health at the date of termination, since the insurer is not liable for any payment upon death and therefore desires to avoid payment upon termination if death is imminent.

Insurance companies usually provide dividends or rate credits reflecting actual experience more favorable than the actuarial assumptions used in determining the premiums.

Group deferred annuities once were the most common form of group annuity contract, but few new contracts have been issued in recent years, except to purchase annuities under terminated plans. Many plans that have changed to other methods of funding still have large amounts of deferred annuities in force, reflecting the benefits funded before the date of change.

Individual Contracts

Many small plans fund each participant's benefit with the purchase of one or more individual annuity or insurance contracts. The premiums for such contracts contain substantially higher margins for expense than do the group contracts, discussed above, in order to meet the higher commissions and higher administrative expense associated with such contracts.

Level premium annuities. As the name implies, the individual level premium annuity contract has level annual premiums. An expense charge is deducted from each premium and the balance is accumulated at interest to obtain the policy's cash value. At retirement, the cash value is converted into a monthly annuity income. If the participant dies before retirement, a death benefit is paid equal to the greater of the cash value or the sum of the premiums paid.

Individual level premium annuities usually are used under defined benefit plans. When an employee first becomes a participant, his projected pension at retirement age is calculated assuming that employment continues at the employee's current salary until that age. A level premium annuity contract is purchased for the level premium amount expected to provide the projected pensions. The premium is paid each year until retirement age. If the participant receives a salary increase the next year, resulting in an increase in his projected pension (above some minimum), a second annuity contract is issued to fund the increase in the projected pension. By retirement age a large number of individual contracts may be in force for each participant.

Retirement income insurance. Retirement income insurance policies are similar to level premium annuities, except that the death benefit generally equals the greater of the cash value or 100 times the projected monthly pension. The death benefit usually exceeds the cash value for two-thirds or more of the policy's duration. Retirement income policies, like level premium annuities, are usually used for defined benefit pension plans.

Flexible premium annuity. A flexible premium annuity contract is similar to a level premium annuity contract, except that the premium may be changed each year. The flexible premium annuity contract may be used to fund defined benefit plans, just like a level premium annuity. But if the participant receives a salary increase that increases his projected pension, the additional projected pension can be funded by increasing the future premiums rather than by issuing another contract. The flexible premium annuity also is used to fund profit-sharing plans and money purchase pension plans.

Split Funded Plans With Ordinary Life Insurance

Many plans, particularly small plans, are funded by a combination of individual ordinary life (whole life) policies and an auxiliary fund. The auxiliary fund, often called a "side fund," may be a trust or an unallocated fund held by the insurance company and credited with interest. Many such funding programs were established to replace individual retirement income policies. The ordinary life policy is usually issued for 100 times the projected pension. At retirement, the policy cash value can be converted into an annuity to provide a monthly pension. But unlike the retirement income policy, the ordinary life policy does not have a cash value large enough to purchase an annuity for the entire pension. Therefore, a transfer is made from the auxiliary fund so that the transfer plus the cash value can purchase the needed annuity. Each year the employer pays the premiums for the insurance and makes deposits to build up the auxiliary fund.

Trusteed profit-sharing plans often allow active participants to direct the trust to purchase an ordinary life insurance policy, in order to provide a death benefit larger than the participant's account balance. Premiums for the policy are deducted from the employer's current contribution for the participant or from the participant's individual account balance.

Group Permanent Insurance

Some insurance companies issue group permanent life insurance contracts. The earliest contracts resembled a collection of individual retirement income contracts. They have almost all of the characteristics of the individual contracts, and are used in the same manner, but a single group contract covers all employees for their initial amount of insurance and for all increases. Because of lower commissions and administrative charges, group permanent insurance costs less than comparable individual policies do. Similarly, insurance companies issue group permanent insurance on the whole life plan, resembling a collection of ordinary life policies. Such contracts can be used instead of the individual policies in funding split-funded plans.

OTHER INVESTMENT MEDIA

Qualified Bond Purchase Plans

Qualified bond purchase plans must be funded by retirement bonds issued under the Second Liberty Bond Act. The bonds provide for payment of interest only upon redemption. They must be purchased in the name of the individual employee and are nontransferable. They may not be redeemed before age 59½, except upon death or disability. They also may be purchased by qualified pension and profit-sharing plans.

Insurance Company Book Reserves

The assets of almost all qualified pension and profit-sharing plans must be held in a trust or custodial account or invested in annuity or insurance contracts issued by a life insurance company. An exception is allowed for plans covering employees and agents of life insurance companies. In such a plan, the insurance company may establish reserves on its books to represent the plan's funding. Another option is to issue group annuity contracts to itself instead, with approximately the same effect. It is possible that the difference in these two approaches may affect the amount of income tax payable by the company.

MANAGING THE INVESTMENT

Investment Management Decisions

After the type of pension plan has been decided on, certain important decisions must be made regarding pension plan investments. The plan sponsor, or a party delegated by the sponsor, must

- Determine investment policy;
- Select the party or parties to perform custodial functions;
- Select the party or parties to provide investment management; and
- Make individual investment decisions.

It is generally desirable that the plan sponsor decide at least the broad direction of investment policy before selecting the parties to perform custodial functions and make investment management decisions, since investment policy is likely to influence the other choices.

Custodial Function

For an insured plan, the insurance company performs the custodial function of holding plan assets. For most trusteed plans, a bank or trust company almost always provides the custodial function. Although it is possible for an individual trustee to provide custodial functions, ERISA's requirements as to fiduciary responsibilities discourage that approach.

Investment Management of Insured Plans

If the plan sponsor chooses an insured approach without the use of separate accounts, the plan's assets are represented by the insurance company's contractual obligation. The insurance company combines the amounts it receives with all of its other assets, to be invested as part of its overall portfolio.

The insurance company also determines the investment of each of its separate accounts. The decision as to which of the insurer's separate accounts a plan should participate in and the proportion of plan assets to be invested in each separate account are investment management decisions that may be either made by the plan sponsor or delegated to the insurance company. Independent investment managers can be used for this function, but they rarely are.

Investment Management of Trusteed Plans

Commingled funds. The investment management of commingled funds is entirely a function of the bank. The choice of which funds to participate in, and the proportion to be invested in each, is an investment policy decision that can be made by the plan sponsor or delegated to the bank. Independent investment managers are rarely used for this purpose.

Mutual funds. Investment in mutual funds is comparable to investment in the commingled funds of banks. The employer or a party delegated by the employer can make the investment management decision as to the funds in which to invest and the extent to invest in each.

Other trusts. The investment management function for trusts that do not use commingled or mutual funds may be performed by the trustee or by one or more independent investment managers.

Selecting Investment Management

The careful determination of investment policy is central to the choice of investment management and should take precedence over all other factors. For example, a decision to invest most plan assets in long-term bonds probably will lead to a different selection of investment management than will a decision to invest entirely in common stocks.

Judging past performance. The past investment performance of managers for funds usually will be compared, by the sponsor, with similar investment objectives. Past performance is not always a good indicator of future performance, but it may be helpful in evaluating the manager's style.

In studying the past performance of an investment manager, there is no consensus on how long a period of time should be examined. A period that is too short may give a misleading picture or show the manager's ability to invest only under certain circumstances, such as a falling market. But a period that is too long may not reflect the manager's current personnel and practices. A five-year period is often used.

Obtaining appropriate information may be difficult. For a manager investing many trusts, complete information may not be available. Any manager investing hundreds of trusts can produce a few with outstanding results, but these may not be representative.

When in doubt, the funds of public record can be used. For insurance companies, one can examine the investment performance of the various separate accounts and the rates of interest credited to group annuity contracts. For a bank, the records of commingled funds can be examined, even if the sponsor contemplates separate management rather than commingled funds. Some investment managers also manage mutual funds, which provide a public record for comparison.

All comparisons must be made with considerable care, to assure that assets with similar investment objectives are being compared. The same period should be used for all managers being compared. If this is not possible, each manager can be compared with an appropriate index for the period about which information is available. Care also must be taken to adjust for difference in accounting methods. Some banks, for example, apply investment income received to increase the unit value; other banks use it to increase the number of units.

Management personnel. The specific personnel of the manager may be considered. Their experience and qualification for investment under the sponsor's investment policy is important. Recent changes in personnel can be vital. An outstanding performance record can be meaningless if the individuals responsible for it are no longer with the manager.

Investment philosophy and methods. The manager's investment philosophies, strategies, and decision-making processes can be studied to determine if they are consistent with the plan's investment policy.

Fees. Investment management fees are an important part of any evaluation. For a small pension plan, the expense of separate investment management may dictate use of an insured approach, commingled funds, or mutual funds.

Pooled funds or separate management. For a particular manager selected, there may be a choice between separate investment management and use of a pooled fund managed by the same manager. If he manages a commingled fund or a mutual fund with investment objectives similar to the pension plan's, is there any reason to believe that the manager will produce better results with a separately managed fund? Unless the pension fund is quite large, it may receive less of the manager's attention and talent than will the mutual or commingled fund. For small plans, diversification is another reason for the pooled approach.

One manager or more than one. Some plans use a single investment manager and others use more than one. Different managers may be selected for different types of investments, since the same managers are not the best for all types. On the other hand, use of more than one manager increases the total management fees, which is a disadvantage, particularly for smaller funds. Some plans divide investments of the same type among two or more managers, perhaps in the hope that competition will spur them to greater effort. The only result of this strategy may be increased management fees.

If more than one manager is selected, the plan sponsor or a party delegated by the sponsor needs to develop guidelines for each, determine the amounts each should invest, and coordinate their work.

Use of consultants. The plan sponsor may engage the services of an independent consultant to assist in establishing its investment policy and in selecting investment management. Consultants work with clients at each stage of the manager selection and coordination process. This includes helping plan sponsors determine what types of managers are appropriate for their situations and investment goals, examining a selection of suitable managers, presenting the leading candidates to the sponsor, participating in the interviewing process leading to the final selection of money managers, and assisting sponsors in developing instructions for each manager to assure implementation of overall investment policy, define expectations for each individual money manager, and make it easier to monitor results.

REVIEWING INVESTMENT RESULTS

Plan sponsors and their consultants may review all aspects of investment results to determine whether investment policy is being followed, whether performance is satisfactory, and whether any changes are advisable in investment policy and management.

Measuring Performance

Measurement of investment return and risk has become a highly sophisticated procedure. Dollar-weighted rates of return are calculated to determine the overall investment results; time-weighted rates of return are used to measure percentage return independent of the volume of assets available for investment during different periods. Some consulting firms provide extensive comparisons with other pension funds that have comparable investment objectives. Risk measurement is an important adjunct to performance measurement, to ascertain whether or not investment policy is being followed and the return is appropriate for the risk.

Evaluating Investment Management

Reviewing investment results can be helpful in eliminating misunderstandings between the plan sponsor and investment managers, and in clarifying investment policy. This process can correct management problems. Review also assists the sponsor in deciding whether to retain existing managers or to seek a change. Results should be reviewed over a period of several years. Except for serious errors or unusual circumstances, the sponsor generally will not replace a manager for poor performance over a short period.

GLOSSARY

annuity plan— A plan funded with annuities, which meets the requirements of a qualified trust, but without a trust.

deferred profit-sharing plan— A defined contribution plan in which employer contributions can be made only from earnings of the current year or from retained earnings.

defined benefit plan— A pension plan that specifies the amount of the retirement benefit.

defined contribution plan— A pension plan in which a specified amount is allocated to each employee's individual account each year.

employee stock ownership plan (ESOP)— A defined contribution plan designed primarily to invest in qualifying employer securities.

Keogh plan— A defined benefit or defined contribution plan for partners or sole proprietors of unincorporated businesses who generally are treated as though they were employees.

money purchase plan— A pension plan with employer contributions determined by a definite formula, independent of profits.

multiemployer plan — A pension plan established under a collective bargaining agreement between one or more unions and two or more employers, usually a defined benefit plan.

pension plan— A defined benefit plan or defined contribution plan, or combination plan, providing for employee retirement income.

qualified bond purchase plan— A defined contribution plan in which joint contributions of employer and employee are used to purchase a certain series federal bonds.

qualified plan— A pension plan that meets the requirements of the Internal Revenue Code in receiving favorable tax treatment.

stock bonus plan— A pension plan in which benefits are distributable in the shares of the employer-company.

Subchapter S corporation— A corporation that elects to be taxed as a partnership under Subchapter S of Chapter 1 of the Internal Revenue Code.

thrift plan— Also known as a savings plan — a defined contribution plan in which employer contributions match a stated percentage of employee contributions.

variable annuity plan— A defined benefit plan in which the amount of pension after retirement varies with the investment experience of plan assets.

SUGGESTED READING

Allen, Everett T., Jr.; Melone, Joseph J.; Rosenbloom, Jerry S. *Pension Planning,* 4th ed. Homewood: Richard D. Irwin, 1981.

Bartell, H. Robert, Jr. and Simpson, Elizabeth T. *Pension Funds of Multiemployer Industrial Groups, Unions, and Nonprofit Organizations.* National Bureau of Economic Research Occasional Paper 105. New York: Columbia University Press, 1968.

Blodgett, Richard. *Conflicts of Interest: Union Pension Fund Asset Management.* New York: Twentieth Century Fund, 1977.

Brooks, John. *Conflicts of Interest: Corporate Pension Fund Asset Management.* New York: Twentieth Century Fund, 1975.

Davey, Patrick J. *Financial Management of Company Pension Plans.* Conference Board Report No. 611. New York: The Conference Board, 1973.

Dietz, Peter O. *Pension Funds: Measuring Investment Performance.* Columbia University, Graduate School of Business Dissertation Series, New York: Macmillian, Free Press, 1966.

Drucker, Peter F. *The Unseen Revolution: How Pension Fund Socialism Came to America.* New York: Harper & Row, 1976.

Federal Reserve Bank of Boston. *Funding Pensions: Issues and Implications for Financial Markets.* Conference Series No. 16. Boston, 1976.

Financial Analysts Research Foundation. *Evolving Concepts of Prudence: The Changing Responsibilities of the Investment Fiduciary in the Age of ERISA.* New York.

Foulkes, Fred K., ed. *Employee Benefits Handbook.* Boston: Warren, Gorham & Lamont, 1982.

Grubbs, Donald S., Jr. *Target Benefit Plans.* Philadelphia: American Law Institute–American Bar Association, 1980.

International Foundation of Employee Benefit Plans. *Investment Peformance of Multiemployer Pension Funds: Measurement and Reporting, Comparision and Evaluation, Implications for Future Policy.* Brookfield, 1976.

Johnson, George E., and Grubbs, Donald S., Jr. *The Variable Annuity,* 2nd ed. Indianapolis: Research & Review Service, 1969.

Livingston, David T. *Investment Practices of Jointly Trusteed Pension Plans.* Research Survey Report No. 2. Brookfield: International Foundation of Employee Benefit Plans, 1975.

Marcus, Bruce W. *The Prudent Man: Making Decisions Under ERISA.* Belleville: ESP Corporation Pensions and Investments, 1978.

McGill, Dan M. *Fundamentals of Private Pensions,* 4th ed. Homewood: Richard D. Irwin, 1979.

President's Commission on Pension Policy. *Coming of Age: Toward National Retirement Income Policy.* Washington, D.C., 1981.

Rugs

Archie Cherkezian *

BASIC CHARACTERISTICS

Historical Background

To the sophisticated collector-investor, Oriental rugs are imbued with a mystique that combines beauty and material value with historical traditions derived from some of the most ancient of the world's surviving cultures. They are produced today by virtually the same methods as those practiced by Eastern weavers 2,000 years ago. They are of infinite variety (no two are exactly alike) but always for essentially utilitarian purposes. Yet whether new or centuries old, Oriental rugs have the potential to appreciate over the long term.

This materialistic trait — unlike that affecting most other collectable media in the universe of art — began to appear in the design of Oriental rugs only in relatively recent times. In the countries where they are woven, rugs originally were used not only to cover bare floors, but as curtains to shield windows or conceal open entrances to rooms, and as shroud-like personal wraps to protect against the desert chill. They were used variously as decorative tapestries, as blessings to feudal lords, and as pillows on which to rest a weary head. They served as saddlebags to carry a family's worldly goods on camel-borne treks across the sands, and as prayer rugs, church aprons, even as a kind of personal "companion" with which an owner chose finally to be buried. In more modern times, rugs gradually have become a symbol of personal wealth.

The pile of a handwoven rug is fashioned by tying knots to vertical threads called the "warp." After tying one line of knots the width of the loom, the weaver passes a weft thread horizontally over the row of knots and tamps it into place. The distance between warp threads determines the weave count or quality of the rug. Rugs are tied with either a Turkish or Persian knot, sometimes misnamed Ghiordes and Senna Knots, respectively. (See Figure 1 on page 872.) The free ends of the knot form the pile. All Caucasian (essentially Eastern European) Oriental rugs are woven with the Turkish knot. A mixture of Persian and Turkish knots will be found in Ionian rugs (from Asia Minor) and those produced elsewhere in the Asian Orient.

A rug that is handwoven in Kansas or California is not, of course, considered an Oriental rug, no matter how well (or richly) it is fashioned. While a particular

* Archie Cherkezian is President of William Cherkezian & Son, Inc., New York, and editor of the monthly trade magazine, *Oriental Rugs.*

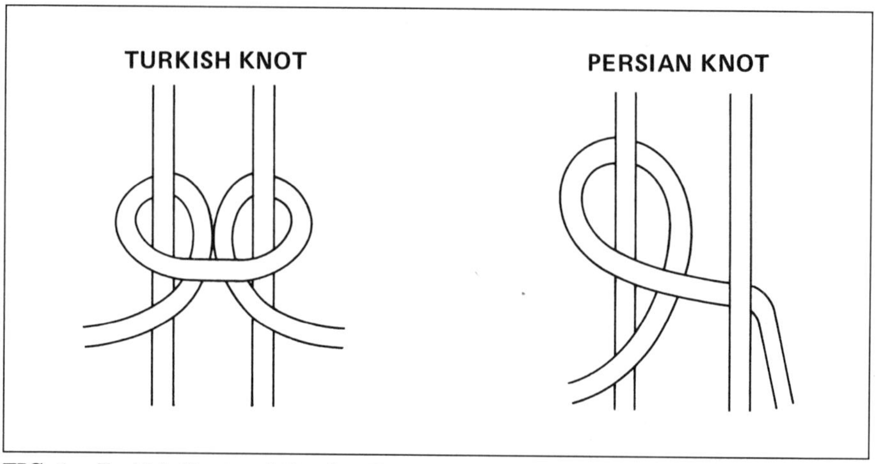

FIG. 1. Turkish Knot and Persian Knot

handwoven piece from a non-Oriental area may have value to some buyers — for example, because it commemorates a specific event — that carpet probably would not have a worldwide market value. Also, a machine-made rug from an Oriental-rug country is not an Oriental rug, even if it has an Oriental design.

Definitions

The Oriental Rug Importers Association (ORIA) defines the term "Oriental rug" as follows: "An *Oriental rug* is handmade of natural fibers, most commonly wool or silk, with a pile woven on a warp and weft, with individual character and design; it is produced only in the Near East, Middle East, Far East, the Balkans and the Caucasus." This definition conforms to standards used by the U.S. Department of Commerce and the U.S. Treasury Department.

The Near East is defined as including most countries of Southwest Asia — specifically Turkey, Lebanon, Egypt, Syria, Jordan, Saudi Arabia, and the smaller sheikdoms of Asia Minor on the Arabian Peninsula — as well as the Balkan States — Greece, Yugoslavia, Romania, Bulgaria, and Albania — which occupy the Balkan Peninsula in Europe. The Middle East is an extensive region consisting of Iraq, Iran, Afganistan, Pakistan, India, Burma, and the Caucasus (that region of European Russia situated between the Black Sea and the Caspian Sea). The Far East includes China, Tibet, Eastern Siberia, Japan, Korea, Cambodia, Laos, Vietnam, and the Malay Archipelago.

All of these nations and regions, at one time or another, have produced handwoven rugs for domestic use or export. The most prolific, traditionally, have been Turkey, Iran, Afghanistan, Pakistan, India, China, and the Caucasus. More recently, Yugoslavia, Romania, and Bulgaria also have become leading world-market suppliers of Oriental rugs.

Handmade rugs are piled textiles that serve as superb coverings for a floor or wall and, with proper selection, constitute a worthwhile investment vehicle as well. Handmade rugs are like fine paintings: they provide aesthetic benefits and simultaneously increase in value, even while being used. Not all handmade rugs are good investments, necessarily, nor is every rug woven by hand automatically an Oriental rug. Machine-made rugs (non-Oriental) are piled textiles used primarily as floor coverings. They are excellent as wall-to-wall broadloom carpeting or as area rugs, but have little, if any, investment value.

PRIMARY DETERMINANTS OF VALUE

Three factors are most important in determining both intrinsic value and appreciation potential for Oriental rugs. The first of these is age. The second factor is quality, relating to both construction materials (silk, wool, and cotton, in that order) and, more importantly, fineness (i.e., density) of weave. The third is place of origin, involving not merely the identity of village, region, or country where a rug was produced, but also the authenticity of that identification. A fourth factor that must be considered in evaluating any rug is its size; in general, the larger it is, the more valuable it is. Showing the sharpest gains in investment value of late are the Oriental rugs of Iran (also called Persian rugs), whether classified as antique, semi-antique or new; the Caucasus (antique and semi-antique); Turkey (antique only); China (antique, semi-antique); and India (all three varieties). Essentially, the balance of this discussion of investment-grade Oriental rugs will focus on these most valuable types.

Age

On world markets, Oriental rugs are classified by age according to relatively strict standards.

Classifications. An antique rug is one that is at least 100 years old; such a rug can be imported into the United States duty-free. Semi-antique rugs generally are twenty to fifty years old and of traditional design. A new rug usually means one recently woven, while a used rug is one that has been in use in a home for twenty years or more. While some degree of wear actually can enhance the worth of a fine rug provided it has been well-maintained, the general experience has been that rugs worn literally to the warp-threads retain little more than sentimental value. Inevitably, the world supply of mint-condition antiques and semi-antiques has diminished; meanwhile, world demand continues to rise, forcing the prices up.

A certain unpredictability adds spice to such exotic markets. In a case still celebrated when American dealers convene socially, one of their number plucked an excellent, semi-antique, 3.6 × 5.2 foot Herez (Iranian) from a New Hope, Pennsylvania trash can in 1956; the rug, being of silk, had evidently been discarded by an unknown person because silk Orientals were out of vogue at the time. A goodly quantity of Caucasian, fine Persian, and old Turkish silks had been sold in the United States from 1895 to 1928. After that period, and up to 1956, Oriental rugs were not purchased in the United States; sales plummeted. This merchandise (1895-1928), much of which remained intact and in good condition in the estates or homes of the wealthy, became available for sale to Europeans after 1956.

Similarly, a prized antique may create headlines in the trade press just by coming to market. At the February 14, 1981 auction conducted by Sotheby Parke Bernet, New York, a fine *Lavar* Kirman (Iranian), 22.4 × 15.2 feet, woven in 1875, was offered for $7,000 to $10,000, and fetched $20,000. Questions of age have become all but academic with regard to the extremely rare antiques and semi-antiques of India and China; those from Iran and the Caucasus crop up more frequently, although a public sale usually remains something of an occasion.

Dating. Appearance of the actual date on a rug — generally woven into the design in such a way as to be more discernible on the back — will add glamour and investor interest (i.e., value). Dated rugs are in great demand around the world. A date is seldom found in Persian or Turkish rugs, but Caucasian rugs are frequently dated. The digits used would probably be Islamic and would appear as follows:

٠	١	٢	٣	۴	۵	۶	٧	٨	٩
0	1	2	3	4	5	6	7	8	9

To calculate the date that corresponds to the Gregorian calendar, divide the number of Islamic years by 33, round off the result, then deduct that figure from the number of Islamic years and add 622. However, a word of caution: Many rugs have woven into their designs dates and signatures (the late Shah of Iran's, for example) that actually pre-date the year of manufacture. An expert should be consulted to authenticate the age of any antique. A newly developed technique of dye analysis is available, capable of throwing light on both the date and location of manufacture.

Quality

No single factor in the market's evaluation of a rug counts for more than quality, which involves both its major material of construction and the fineness of its weave.

Materials. The three major textiles used in Oriental rug-weaving are wool, silk, and cotton. Wool is by far the predominant fiber, accounting for the largest dollar volume of both current annual output and world-market annual sales. But rugs of silk have enjoyed the greatest increase in value over recent decades. Thus, in 1959, a New York dealer sold six semi-antique silk rugs, each approximately 3 × 5 feet, to a dealer in Weisbaden, West Germany, for $275 apiece. Five of the silks were sold during the ensuing ten years at prices ranging from $1,500 to $9,000 each. The last piece hangs in a place of honor in the dealer's shop. Its price tag: $16,000.

As of early 1982, short-term prices dropped on fine small wool and silk pieces because of smuggling from Iran, on some major pieces because of the collapse of the financial base in Iran, and on some new Iranian rugs because of liquidation of holdings by Iranian émigrés.

Fineness. Of all the elements that play a role in the long-term appreciation of Oriental rug values, fineness is the single most important one. This term describes how tightly the rug is woven, by means of a counting of the knots tied off by the weaver during its manufacture. Because that quality affects both the look and feel of a finished rug, as well as its durability, fineness should be the paramount factor in selecting rugs for investment. Indeed, in the parlance of Oriental rug dealers, the term "quality" has come to mean specifically the knot-count measurement — which, as it happens, is determined and expressed differently (owing to tradition) when used to describe the fineness of rugs from different countries.

For Iranian (Persian) rugs, the number of knots in one inch of vertical count (direction of warp) is multiplied by the number of knots in one inch of horizontal count (direction of weft). The product is usually expressed as knots per square inch. Quality-counts for Persian rugs range from 36 to 1,300 knots per square inch. Those for Turkish, Afghan, and Caucasian rugs are determined in the same manner.

In Chinese rugs, quality is determined by the number of knots or threads to the linear foot. Counts range from 70 per line to 240 per line. Indian rug quality is measured by the knots in 36 linear inches. And for Pakistani rugs, it is expressed as a ratio of the horizontal count to double the vertical count: Hence, 9/18 quality means 9 knots per horizontal inch and 18 knots per vertical inch. The range is from 7/14 to 20/20.

But, regardless of origin, fine rugs have been a good hedge against inflation. Best of all have been the finest Persians from Iran, which have increased in value tremendously over the past thirty years. A fine, new 9 × 12 foot Kashan, sold in 1921 for $432, brought $1,296 in 1928, and will fetch about $12,000 today. The increase in price is logical: Fine, new Iranian rugs are in diminishing supply. As Iran marched toward industrialization, the best of its veteran hand weavers left their looms for better paying jobs in other, newer industries. Ever since then, mediocre rugs have been coming on the market.

Place of Origin

Historical factors. The first known Persian carpet — predecessor of everything known today as Oriental rugs — was found in 1945 by Soviet archaeologists in the remote Altai Mountains of Outer Mongolia (i.e., the U.S.S.R. Mongolian People's Republic). It is the twenty-two-century-old Pazyruk Carpet, currently housed in the Hermitage Museum in Leningrad. From its unique, if primitive, techniques flowed rug-weaving developments, first in Persia (Iran), and then throughout the Oriental rug-making universe. Where a rug comes from, as has been noted, affects to greater or lesser degree its value.

Iran. Iran is credited with most of the artistically great creations, including the sixth-century Persian "Spring of Khosrov," usually cited as the most valuable carpet ever made. It is said to have measured 11,300 square feet in area; woven with silk, it was embroidered with gold and silver thread, and further studded with gems. The Persian rug has been the mainstay of the Oriental rug industry in the United States for the past half-century — so much so that the term "Persian rug" is still synonymous with "Oriental rug." From 1930 to 1978, Iranian rugs led both the artistic and investment parades, but very few Iranian rugs are currently being imported into the United States. This is because during the same period, most successful Iranian merchants lost faith in their banks. Savings and checking accounts were translated into piles of rugs in their living rooms. A fine *Nain* was their CD; an old silk Tabriz was even better than the common stock of IBM. So, even before the political strife of the 1980s, export trade to the United States and other world markets had diminished in Iran. Oriental rug stocks were hoarded at home rather than shipped abroad.

India. Indian rugs were produced from the eleventh century until the 1930s. Weaving then stopped until the 1950s. Today, Indian rugs and carpets are in full production and are sold throughout the world, in traditional and modern designs. They have been steadily increasing in wool quality and weave density; today they rival the finest of Persian rugs.

Turkey. Prior to the twentieth century, Turkish rugs were available and in great demand. However, when Kemal Ataturk assumed leadership in Turkey, he initiated a modernization program that did not include weaving. From then until recent years, Turkey produced only a few pieces for domestic consumption.

China. Chinese industry, led by the Nichols factories and others in Tiensin, supplied world markets — particularly an eager American public — until 1949. Then the United States banned trade with Communist China. From that date until the recent trade renewals, used Chinese carpets were bought by dealers at auctions. Today, Chinese carpets are again being imported by the United States in great quantities.

Afghanistan, Turkoman, Baluchistan. Semi-antique rugs from these areas have been in good demand for decades in the United States.

Pakistan. In Pakistan, rug weaving began in 1953, with the first carpets sold in Europe. As production increased and Pakistanis sought new markets, rugs were exported to this country, mainly in Bokhara and Gul designs.

Eastern Europe. Communist bloc production, notably in Yugoslavia, Romania, Albania, and Bulgaria, is primarily of Persian design.

Caucasus. Caucasian rugs of modern design are woven and sold in the Soviet Union, with export to Europe. It is the older (antique and semi-antique) rugs, however, that have captured the fancy of American buyers.

Identification factors. The handwoven Oriental rugs from various countries are identified — and labeled — in different ways. A myriad of potentially confusing names confronts any investor-collector who is new to the market. (See Table 1 on page 878 for names of Oriental rugs.) In order to assess properly the value of an Oriental rug, a professional dealer or collector must be able to identify it with confidence.

Iranian (Persian) rugs are usually named after the province, village, town, or hamlet where they are woven. For example, Kirman rug is one woven in the city of Kirman. Generally, the rugs are knotted from readings by a master singer or woven from individual templates. Nomads weave from memory. Each region is noted for a traditional design that has been handed down from one generation to the next. The designs are often subtly and subconsciously modified by the weaver. A number of different types of rugs may be woven in a particular village; thus, twenty types of Tabriz rugs may be on display at the Tabriz bazaar.

It should be noted that rugs of India are named through an entirely different system than the others. Most Indian rugs are woven in the Varanasi area to specifications of U.S. importers. Importers who are astute entrepreneurs have submitted a weave count, designs, and colors to the supplier in India, and established a line. These lines have been named (e.g., *Super Darbar* and *Sovereign Anatole*); each name identifies the rug and represents a standard of value. Loom owners in India also will weave rugs based on traditional Iranian designs and sell them in the open market.

Chinese rugs are perhaps the easiest of all rugs to identify, with their unique designs, lustrous wool, and deep colors. They are usually sold by line count, such as 80-line or 90-line; thickness of pile, such as ⅜ or ⅝; and the designation open back or closed back. Open back signifies a loose tamping of the pile; closed back means that as each knot is tied, it is pressed into place over the previous row of knots, completely encasing the white weft thread. The entire designation of a Chinese rug might read: 90-line, ⅝, closed back. (This rug would be more expensive than another in which any of those three elements were lower.)

Pakistani rugs are also identified by weave count and design name. A 9/18 *Mori* design single would refer to 162 knots per square inch of a Bokhara design of single thickness. Caucasian rugs are identified by name in a manner similar to Persian rugs.

TABLE 1. Selected Names of Oriental Rugs

Iranian rugs (usually woven in curvilinear designs):		
Birjand	Huseinabad	Khorrassan
Dergazine	Ingillas	Meshat
Genjtepe	Ispahan	Nain
Ghom	Kashan	Sarouk
Hamadan	Kirman	Tabriz
Iranian rugs (usually woven in geometric designs):		
Abadeh	Ferraghan	Serapi
Ahar	Herez	Shiraz
Bijar	Jooshaghan	Simsari
Gorovan	Karaja	Yallemeh
Caucasian rugs:		
Baki	Genja	Shirivan
Capistan	Karabagh	Shousha
Chichi	Kazak	Tscherkess
Daghestan	Kupa	Tiflis
Derbend	Leshian	
Turkish rugs:		
Anatolian	Konieh	Melez
Bergano	Korowan	Rhodian
Ghiordes	Kulah	Sivas
Kirshehr	Ladik	Yuruk
Indian rugs (trademarks):		
Agra	Panir	Super Darbar
Chindia	Rajagra Herez	Teremez
Shangrila	Sovereign Indian Rugs	Zeigler

ATTRACTIVE FEATURES

Appreciation of Investment

The 1960-1980 price increases in home furnishings have played havoc with household budgets. It is not pleasant to put $5,000 to $8,000 into floor coverings and, in a relatively short span of time, have to replace them with new floor coverings. One of the attractive features of the Oriental rug has been its remarkable price resiliency. When prices broke in Iran in 1929, dealers and collectors held on to their inventories and, by 1939, prices started to reaffirm themselves.

Similarly, the consumer who bought Oriental rugs at any time in the last fifty years not only received pleasure and joy from seeing works of art every time he or she walked into a room, but also had the pleasure of realizing an increase in capital when the rug was sold. In 1921, Macy's sold 9 × 12 foot Sarouks for $243. Those same rugs if kept in decent (not mint) condition by the buyers and used for fifty-nine years, would have sold for $3,000 to $5,000 each to a New York dealer.

Worldwide Marketability

Oriental rugs are now an art form that is valued in almost every country in the world. From the time of the Great Depression until 1956, the desire for, and, consequently, the sales of Oriental rugs in the United States were negligible compared with Europe. There were a number of reasons for this lack of appetite for Oriental rugs, among which must be the decorator's interest in other types of floor coverings and the public's complete unawareness of the attractiveness of Oriental rugs, old or new. The entire importation of new Oriental rugs from Iran to the United States in the period of 1950-1958 did not exceed $3 million per year. Iranian imports represented the bulk of handwoven rugs when Indian and Pakistani looms still were in infancy; imports from China were forbidden, and the Balkans had not yet begun to weave.

Post-war reconstruction. As the European countries started to rebuild and prosper (particularly Italy, Germany, and Austria), European dealers surveyed the international art market for products to sell to millions of newly affluent consumers. Turning westward, these overseas dealers found a treasure-house of old Oriental rugs in the United States: *Khilas, Kazaks, Genjas, Capistans,* silks of all weaving areas, and a veritable bonanza of old Iranian and Chinese rugs with which neither the American public nor the American dealer knew what to do.

European dealers descended upon the New York wholesale showrooms, invaded national auction houses, and visited every retail dealer in the country. Finally, they advertised in the local newspapers in forty-eight states to buy old rugs directly from homes. Prices climbed daily. It was no longer a matter of price or profit — only a matter of locating a piece.

Building viable markets. While overseas dealers were buying old U.S. treasures, they also were making our public rug-conscious — largely by word of mouth. The demand for new rugs grew to unprecedented heights and total importations into the United States from all weaving countries totaled $75 million. American demand for new goods was reflected in price rises in Iran. Contributing further to the spiral, the Iranian government initiated a program to locate and replace its national art treasures, in which rugs had priority. Another round of increases was inaugurated with agents around the world searching for old rugs of Iran.

Finally, the oil-producing countries, flush with tremendous incomes, demanded the finest new rugs Iran could produce. A world market was informally, but firmly, established. Today, an Oriental rug can be sold anywhere: in London,

Geneva, Hamburg, Johannesburg, New York, Los Angeles, Milan, Vienna, or Tokyo. If the proper price is paid for the rug, the chances of a loss of capital are minimal, most notably when dealing in Iranian rugs (new or old), and in antique Caucasian or Chinese rugs.

Hedging

Small Oriental rugs have provided a means of moving capital from war zones and countries exiling their citizens. During the recent turmoil in Iran and Lebanon, individuals who were unable to unfreeze bank accounts and transfer their assets to safer havens purchased small, but expensive, Oriental rugs. These were shipped abroad or packed in suitcases to accompany the exiles when they left. Small silk rugs were particularly appropriate, for they were lightweight and readily marketable.

POTENTIAL RISKS

Lack of Income

Rugs, like gold, yield no investment income. The only source of potential profit in rugs bought as investments is through resale at appreciated value.

Potential Oversupply

It is very seldom that an internationally collected art form falls to extremely low prices. Hundreds of thousands of collectors and dealers throughout the world will continue to maintain proper price structures for old rugs, but there is a fear concerning new Iranian rugs. Because the prices of Iranian rugs have increased to a great extent, a large influx of new carpets into world markets may tend to deflate prices until such world markets settle to find their level. As of late 1981, price lists from Teheran did not indicate price reductions in any of the approximately 140 different Iranian weaves.

Misleading Advertising

It is possible, although unusual, to buy a machine-made Oriental-design rug, in the belief that it is an authentic hand made. These rugs are imported from Italy, Germany, and Belgium, among other areas, and some are even made in the United States. The designs are modified forms of traditional Iranian designs and the names of these rugs reflect the design. At present, most of the misleading advertising by department stores has been corrected; however, now and then one will read of a 9 $\times$ 12 foot Sarouk for \$299 and, somewhere at the bottom of the page, find a statement in small letters that all rugs being advertised are machine-made. To verify that a rug is handmade, the nap of the rug along the weft thread should be broken, and the buyer should look for the knots. The appearance of design and color running through to the back of the rug should not be depended upon.

Mislabeling

Occasionally, a dealer will misname a rug, usually due to a lack of knowledge. A *Sparta* — a handwoven Greek rug of little investment value — may be called a *Meshat,* which is a valuable Iranian rug. Unfortunately, many dealers with scant love for rugs have entered the market in recent years. Most of them are not unscrupulous — just uncaring. Caveat emptor.

TAX CONSEQUENCES

As with many intangibles, profit from the sale of a rug held by an individual for more than one year is taxable at the capital gains rate rather than as ordinary income. Under certain conditions, rugs can be exchanged for others of equal or greater value in a tax-free transaction. It is also possible to realize a tax deduction on donating a rug whose market value has appreciated to a qualified organization. Separate rules apply to those who are recognized as investors by the IRS. (See article on Tax Considerations for Collector-Investors, elsewhere in this volume.) For complete guidance in these matters, readers are urged to consult a professional tax adviser.

REPRESENTATIVE TYPES OF INVESTORS

The great majority of Oriental-rug investments are made by individual collectors. In addition, many corporations have purchased Oriental rugs as floor coverings for board rooms and the offices of top executives, choosing them for aesthetic appeal but also with an eye toward prestige and potential appreciation. Moreover, numerous hotels and motels have purchased Oriental rugs in quantity, taking depreciation on the books but, in fact, often realizing a worthwhile appreciation in value. At least one bank in recent years accepted Chinese rugs as collateral on a loan.

IMPORTANT FACTORS IN BUYING AND SELLING

Studying the Market

Before spending any money, there are a number of steps that should be followed by the inexperienced investor:

(1) *Read up on Oriental rugs.* Many books have been written and a few are really great (See *Suggested Reading* in this article.) Read, not to absorb technical knowledge, but to get an idea of the industry's geography: where the weaving countries are located, and where the towns are that have given the glamorous

names to rugs. Start a mental classification system; get a "feel" for the weaving areas.

(2) *Visit department stores and pre-auction exhibitions.* Look at the names of rugs and try to fit the rug into a mental classification. The more exposure, the more experience in seeing rugs, the surer will be the buyer's ultimate grasp of rugs as an investment medium. Rug viewing underscores the truth that a picture is worth a thousand words.

(3) *Know the seller.* Once an idea has been formed about rugs, make friends with a dealer or a knowledgeable department store salesperson. Short of harassment, ask as many questions as necessary.

(4) *Witness actual sales.* Attend auctions after looking over the gallery's exhibitions. Visit department stores on sale days. The buyer will soon start to recognize rugs.

(5) *Specialize.* Whether as collector or investor, make a decision to concentrate on one area — perhaps 4 × 6 foot *Capistans,* or 3 × 5 foot Kashans, or 2 × 3 foot rugs of all types. Studies and discussions will help to analyze that particular market for availability, dealer preference, price structure, and potential rewards.

Recommended Sources

Department stores. When buying Oriental rugs for a home, a major department store is a safe place to buy. Most major department stores have a "return" policy. However, a lot of grief can be saved by taking along both the measurements of the room and the desired color scheme.

Auctions. Seldom should rugs be bought at auction, whether itinerant auctions or standing auctions, without prior examination. The examination should be made with a dealer or broker who will charge a small fee for this service. He or she will put a price range on the rug. It is important that the dulcet tones of the auctioneer do not sway the buyer. Good buys for investors and for consumers can be had at auction when the rugs are truly of estate or home quality.

If ever there has been an itinerant auction whose stock consisted of rugs put up for sale by estates, this writer has yet to see it. The usual practice of the itinerant auctioneer is to obtain a large consignment selection of Oriental rugs from a wholesaler and peddle them from town to town. Obviously, this creates unnecessary risk for the unsophisticated investor. In sharp contrast, standing auctions can be relatively safe and rewarding sources of supply. The buyer should beware of gauging prices by what dealers may be bidding, however. They may be raising prices on their own merchandise. Standing auction houses such as Sotheby Parke Bernet and John Edelmann in New York are responsibly managed, and good purchases can be made there with confidence.

Specialty shops, wholesalers, agents. Most proprietors of specialty shops (new or old) will take the time and have the knowledge to locate the rug that a particular buyer wants. They will show samples of Indian continuity lines and procure the size needed. In addition, they will know who in the country (through the Oriental Rug Importers Association or the Oriental Rug Retailers Association) has the Iranian rug the buyer wants. Professional dealers buy their inventory from wholesalers, but this is not usually a satisfactory situation for consumers or other collector-investors. The wholesaler seldom has the time, facilities, or interest to sell one piece. Unfortunately for the collector, however, there is no middle market for old rugs. So the collector, in the final analysis, must buy rugs where he finds them: wholesale, retail, or at auction.

The serious investor must seek a guide. This can be a broker, dealer, specialty agent, or another collector, but that person must know the world market in old and new rugs from all weaving countries.

CUSTODIAL CARE

Oriental rugs lose their value unless they are properly maintained. Periodic care by professionals is recommended, as it would be for any other valuable property or work of art subject to wear and exposure. Minor repairs, stain removals, and the like sometimes can be done by the owner with guidance from the reputable dealer or auction house at which the rug was purchased.

Wear

To prevent undue wearing in any one area, the carpet should be turned once a year. This ensures even wear and even patination (softening of colors). As the carpet proceeds through the stages of new, used, and, in the fourth generation, antique, it will thus maintain an even pile.

Dry Rot. Dry rot (drying out and brittleness of warp threads) is a fatal illness for rugs and carpets. To prevent dry rot from spillage, make sure water does not overflow or spill onto the carpet and remain for any length of time.

Weekly care, depending on the pollution in the area, consists of vacuuming, using a suction vacuum, but not one of sufficient strength to pull out the individual knots. The owner must be careful not to catch the fringe in the vacuum. If the fringe gets caught and rips off, fringe must be added to that area. A restorer should never be permitted to cut away the original fringe and then sew on domestic fringe. A $10,000 rug could be rendered valueless by such a measure.

Cleaning

Rugs should be cleaned professionally once every five years. Of course the time depends, again, on conditions in a particular area. Moths should be guarded against by frequent inspection of the rug in dark recesses, as under sofas. When calling a professional cleaner make sure he or she is not cleaning Oriental rugs with machine-made rugs.

Insurance and Safety

An Oriental rug is a thing of beauty that may readily be stolen. Take two or three photographs of the rug; note its measurements. If it is stolen, the pictures, which are much like fingerprints, can be circulated.

Pictures, a written description, and evaluations by two recognized appraisers are usually necessary for obtaining insurance. Rugs should be insured as individual pieces, not lumped together under one homeowner's policy.

Where there is a collection of small rugs that needs to be stored, some banks do have vaults large enough for that purpose. Note that the bank will allow only nominal insurance. The rugs must be insured with an outside source, for full value. They should be revalued for insurance every few years and, if stored, examined every six months for moth damage and moth-proofing.

GLOSSARY

abraish— A streak of different shade, which might run the width of a rug.

all-over— A term for a pattern that is repeated all over the field of a carpet without any medallion or other central feature.

bote— Flower design.

dozar— A rug measuring 4 × 7 feet.

fereghan— A small, geometric medallion cornered on four sides by a fish-like pattern.

fringe— The end of the rug containing the warp threads. Many rugs have one end compacted into an apron.

Gul— The abstract form of a flower, usually woven as octagonal medallion.

kelleyi— A long and narrow carpet.

kurk— Top grade of wool.

Persian and Turkish knots— The method of tying the yarn to the warp, the upper parts of which form the pile. The knots have been called "senneh" and "ghiordes" knots, respectively.

pile— The wool surface of the rug, forming the nap.

pushti— A mat measuring approximately 2 × 3 feet.

warp— The foundation threads running top to bottom on which knots are tied.

weft— The foundation threads running from side to side between rows of knots.

zar— Measurement of 36 inches (one yard).

zaronim— A rug measuring 5 × 3.6 feet.

TRADE ORGANIZATIONS

A number of trade and collectors' organizations exist in the United States. These organizations are very selective, accepting for membership only those firms or individuals with the highest credentials of reputation and integrity. They are as follows:

Oriental Rug Importers Association, Inc. — A nonprofit organization consisting of importers of Oriental rugs who have been in the wholesale business for a minimum of three years in the United States. The aim of the organization is to promote the best interests of the Oriental rug industry in the United States and abroad and to raise the standards of the trade.

The Oriental Rug Retailers Association — An association of some of the major retailers of new and old rugs in the United States.

Hadji Baba Club — An organization of Oriental rug collectors dedicated to pursuits of aesthetic and cultural life of the United States through Oriental rugs.

Pittsburgh Rug Society — Consists of individuals (about seventy members) in the Western Pennsylvania region who are interested in Oriental rugs.

Local rug societies have an extremely enthusiastic membership of collectors and frequently feature guest lecturers at their meetings. A few of these organizations are: New York Rug Society; Chicago Rug Society; Oriental Rug & Textile Society of Great Britain; The Oriental Rug Society Inc. of Toronto, Canada; and The Rug Society of Paris.

LEADING DEALERS

Most specialty shops carry old and new rugs from various weaving areas. Department stores usually inventory only new rugs. The following is a list of well-known, established Oriental rug dealers.

Aladdin Co., Greensboro, N.C.

B. Altman Oriental Rug Dep't, New York, N.Y.

Ara Seropian Oriental Rugs, Lancaster, Pa.

Barsamian Bogosian, Memphis, Tenn.

Beckworth Evans, Detroit, Mich.

Beshar's, New York, N.Y.

Votech Blau, New York, N.Y.

L. Boodakian & Co., Boston, Mass.

Breuners Dep't Store, Sacramento, Cal.

Brook Gill & Co., Boston, Mass.

Brookline Oriental Rugs, Boston, Mass.

Davis, Nahigian, Inc., Philadelphia, Pa.

Lou Demanes Interiors, Peoria, Ill.

Dingilian, Inc., Cincinnati, Ohio

Einstein Moomjy, New York, N.Y.

Ellisons, Ft. Worth, Tex.

Frank Eways, Charlottesville, Va.

Galleria International, Baltimore, Md.

The House of Persia, Atlanta, Ga.

Joske's Oriental Rug Dep't, San Antonio, Tex.

The Levant Oriental Rugs, Oakland, Cal.

Lord & Taylor Oriental Rug Dep't., New York, N.Y.

Macy's Oriental Rug Dep't, New York, N.Y.
Richard Markarian, Inc., Cincinnati, Ohio
L.P. Mouradian & Co., Green Bay, Wis.
Parviz Nemati, New York, N.Y.
The Oriental Rug Shop, Memphis, Tenn.
The Persian Rug Co., Springfield, Mo.
Mason Purcell, Charlottesville, Va.
Sanger Harris Oriental Rug Dep't, Dallas, Tex.
Sharian, Inc., Decatur, Ga.
Stark Carpet Company, New York, N.Y.
Sunniland Furniture, Houston, Tex.
Thomas Wright Oriental Rugs, San Antonio, Tex.
Zaven Kish, Memphis, Tenn.

SUGGESTED READING

Periodicals

Hali Magazine. Published by Hali Publications, London, England. Quarterly; a new periodical, it has already gained an international reputation for its scholarly articles and objective dissemination of information.

The Oriental Rug Auction Review. Published by Ron O'Callaghan, Meredith, N.H. Monthly; features rugs sold at auction with descriptions and prices. Also has Oriental rug articles.

Oriental Rug Magazine. Published by the Oriental Rug Importers Association, New York, N.Y. Six issues a year; contains information pertinent mostly to dealers. Sold only to dealers.

Rug News. Published by Trade Data Reports, New York, N.Y. Monthly; contains some news and statistics on Oriental rugs. Concentrates on auction sales.

Sotheby's Fine Oriental Rugs and Carpets Catalogs. Published by Sotheby's, New York, N.Y. Available at sale time, with superb color pictures and descriptions of original rugs.

Journal Articles

Amirian, Lemyel. "The Design of the Pazyryk Rug," *Ararat* Spring 1979, page 2.

Cherkezian, Archie A. "Appreciating Persian Rugs," *Finance* Jan. 1975, pages 52-53.

Dickinson, Ernest. "Rug Importers Thrive," *New York Times* June 6, 1976, page 8.

Harb, Joseph H., M.D. "Oriental Rugs," *The Investing Professional,* vol. 1, no. 9, Oct. 1973, pages 12-16.

"Oriental Carpets: A Flying Start," *New York* April 19, 1972, pages 47-54.

"Oriental Rugs," *Changing Times* May 1977, pages 45-47.

Powell, Jim. "Flying Carpets," *Barron's* Aug. 16, 1976, page 9.

Whitney, Michelle. "Oriental Values for Occidental Floor," *Money* vol. 3, no. 2, Feb. 1974, pages 52-56.

Reference Books

Cherkezian, A. *The Magic Carpet.* New York: Oriental Rug Importers Ass'n, 1955.

Dilley, Arthur Urbane. *Oriental Rugs & Carpets.* Philadelphia: J.B. Lippincott Co., 1959.

Edwards, Cecil A. *The Persian Carpet.* London: Duckworth & Co., 1975.

Eiland, Murray L. *Chinese & Exotic Rugs.* Boston: New York Graphic Soc'y, 1979.

Haack, Herman. *Oriental Rugs.* London: Faber & Faber, Ltd., 1960.

Hackmack, Adolf. *Chinese Carpets & Rugs.* Translated by L. Arnold. Tientsin-Peking, China: Peiyang Press, 1973.

Hawley, Walter A. *Oriental Rugs — Antique & Modern.* New York: Tudor Publishing, 1970.

Izmidlian, Georges. *Oriental Rugs & Carpets Today.* New York: Hippocrene Books, Inc. 1978.

Jacobsen, C.W. *Oriental Rugs.* Rutland, Vermont: Charles E. Tuttle Co., 1962.

Jerrehian, Aram K. Jr., *Oriental Rug Primer.* Philadelphia: Running Press, 1980.

Nemati, Parvis. *Rugs As an Investment.* New York: Agate Press, 1981.

Schurmann, Ulrich. *Oriental Carpets.* London: Geo. Allen & Unwin Ltd., 1979.

Sculpture

Alice Levi Duncan *

BASIC CHARACTERISTICS

Interest in medieval, Renaissance, and baroque sculpture is certainly not recent. The great investor-collectors of the early part of this century, Morgan, Frick, and Kress, to name a few, were avid buyers of bronzes at enormous prices. There are specialized sales of furniture and works of art (including sculpture) from these periods and there are many dealers who handle objects from this category exclusively.

Interest in nineteenth- and twentieth-century European and American sculpture for investment purposes, on the other hand, has evolved recently, along with the current fervor for collecting all fine and decorative arts. Sculpture of this period must be sought out by the investor; it is rarely the subject of specialized sales in the auction houses, and it is not handled exclusively by dealers in New York, London, or Paris. Investment in sculpture is dependent on the knowledge of the buyer and the choice of marketplace. Such an investment can be either a very exciting and beneficial choice or a very secure, but not necessarily profitable, one.

Major Categories of Sculpture for Investment

Three major categories of nineteenth- and twentieth-century sculpture for investment are animalier and academic bronzes, Art Nouveau and Art Deco, and American sculpture. To a lesser extent, medieval, Renaissance, and baroque works of art are still purchased for investment. However, quality sculptures from this early period rarely come on the market, and the number of interested buyers is relatively few.

Bronzes. Because they are of multiple mechanical facture, bronzes are generally classified as decorative arts. It cannot be assumed that two objects made by the same artist in the same medium and depicting the same subject will be priced similarly. Variables such as size, condition, quality and quantity of casting, and authenticity must be considered in determining the value of a bronze. Popular among collectors are animalier bronzes, which depict animals, and academic bronzes cast in a realistic or representational style.

Art Nouveau and Art Deco sculpture. Art Nouveau and Art Deco sculpture has experienced dramatic price increases in the past several years. The Art

* Alice Levi Duncan is Director of Sculpture and Works of Art at Christie's, New York.

Nouveau and Art Deco market has carried that period's sculpture into its recent sweep of public interest and resultant auction records. Works that would not have found their way into the salesroom — either because the artists were not known in this country (as the artistic endeavours were primarily European, particularly French) or because the offering prices did not justify selling them — are now comprising 25 percent of the number of lots offered in a typical Art Nouveau and Art Deco sale. Moreover, the galleries display their more important bronzes of that period, by such artists as Raoul Larche, Agathon Leonard, Gustav Gurschner, Emmanuel Villanis, and even Sarah Bernhardt, with furniture and lamps of the same period.

Art Nouveau and Art Deco sculpture is not collected or bought in a vacuum. The buyer usually has an interest in another aspect of the field (e.g., Tiffany lamps, Marjorelle furniture, Gallé glass) and has turned to sculpture as decoration. It is the least expensive part of a very strong and "pricey" market. The prices range from $1,000 for a bust by Villanis, to $35,000 for a gilt-bronze figure of Loie Fuller by Larche. (For further discussion, see article on Art Nouveau and Art Deco, elsewhere in this volume.)

American Sculpture. The American sculpture market is also very exciting, with enormous collector fervor, rising prices, and the resultant appearance of rare and interesting works of art. Although there are many collectors who buy American sculpture independent of paintings, it is still a field that is tangential to the more expensive and better-known world of paintings. Unlike those who live with Old Master oils or nineteenth-century paintings, the owners of American paintings are usually active and avid collectors of complementary works of art in bronze, marble, plaster, and wood. Even museum classifications and exhibitions accept American sculpture as an equal partner to painting. Because of recent museum exhibitions, monographs, and the influence of the art market, this plastic art is now studied, admired, and collected with a fervor that traditionally has been characteristic of painting connoisseurs.

Unlike the world of paintings, the sculpture market makes no distinction between monumental sculpture that is museum quality and that which is collectable — the only distinction is between what is monumental and what is small scale. Both institutions and individuals are possible purchasers of Hiram Powers marbles, Remington bronzes, or Frishmuth garden fountains. Museums may, however, be more concerned than private collectors with such factors as quality, condition, and provenance, since they must justify their selection of each object by its excellence.

ATTRACTIVE FEATURES

Capital Gains

One benefit of investment in art is the enormous profit that can be gained. For example, a pair of bronze female figures by Agathon Leonard (French, born

1841) fetched the French equivalent of $482 in 1969. A single figure of the pair sold for $3,099 in 1976, and then for $10,000 in 1980. Such increase in price can, of course, be dependent on currency fluctuations or inflation, but the primary cause in this case and in many similar instances is the increase in the number of buyers and the great current interest in this period of collecting. The market is international, with payments in a number of currencies over a period of time, and divided among several parties. Many galleries and dealers also will purchase objects for cash.

Extensive Market

An active trade in sculpture is conducted throughout the world, and the many buyers and sellers have driven up prices for works from numerous periods and geographical origins. Unfortunately, the animalier and academic bronze market has been too stable for too long and, although there are many buyers and a quantity of merchandise, the prices are disappointing.

For those collecting Art Nouveau and Art Deco, the potential market is not limited to those with access to New York salesrooms. Dealers in Paris include fine Art Nouveau sculptures in their inventory, and London, Paris, Geneva, and Monaco offer outstanding sales of this period. The center of selling is developing in the United States, however. This is a result of market trends as well as favorable selling conditions; the U.S. government does not stop the export of any work of art, despite its possible historic or artistic importance.

The market for American sculpture is predominantly an American one. New York traditionally has been the center for both auctions and dealers, but considerable activity takes place in Washington, D.C., California, Texas, and elsewhere in the West. American sculpture can be viewed more often in salesroom catalogues than in galleries, however.

Physical Security

Sculpture requires little care in terms of physical security. It is more difficult to damage or steal than, say, paintings or jewelry, and small bronze sculptures could, indeed, be stolen, but most thieves are less impressed with their appearance than with that of objects made of more precious materials.

In addition, the physical appearance of sculpture changes little over extended periods of time. Those changes that do occur as part of the aging process will often enhance the object's value.

Intangible Benefits

As with all fields of art, sculpture investments are to some extent determined by aesthetic preference. Most collectors expect to enjoy as well as profit from their works of art. In the field of nineteenth- and twentieth-century sculpture, however, such considerations as prestige, interior decoration, and the hobbyist's enthusiasm for a particular subject (i.e., horses) often play a part in investment decisions.

POTENTIAL RISKS

Market Instability and Illiquidity

Although the art market is flexible as to manner and site of sale, including such alternatives as auction, dealers, and private sales, liquidity of capital is a problem. Often it takes several months from time of consignment to payment. Sometimes a market has gone soft at the moment that an investor must sell, and the profits that he has envisioned are wiped out in a short period. Some areas of collecting have been static in value for several years.

TAX CONSEQUENCES

Under federal tax law, profit from the sale of a sculpture held by an individual for more than one year is taxable at the capital gains rate rather than as ordinary income. Under certain conditions, sculptures can be exchanged for others of equal or greater value in a tax-free transaction.

Museum collections in the United States do not have good inventories of Art Nouveau and Art Deco sculpture and, because their purchase funds are usually intended for more "serious" works of art, they are unable to compete with the private buyers to supplement their holdings in a specific area. Therefore, it is possible for an individual to form a representative collection for eventual donation to a museum or university art gallery and to profit from the resultant tax benefits. Separate rules apply to those who are recognized as investors by the IRS. (See article on Tax Considerations for Collector-Investors, elsewhere in this volume.) For complete guidance in these matters, readers are urged to consult a professional tax adviser.

REPRESENTATIVE TYPES OF INVESTORS

The sculpture market is of interest primarily to individual investors; virtually no corporate foundations are buying sculpture other than contemporary works, although many individual collectors do buy under a corporate name. Collectors of different types of sculpture fall into distinct categories.

Nineteenth- and Twentieth-Century Sculpture

Animalier. Most collectors are professionals or business people with an interest in a certain type of animal (e.g., horses) or sport (e.g., hunting or racing).

Academic/salon. Most of the collectors in this field own many bronzes (usually more than thirty), which have been purchased over a number of years with a small capital investment. Typically, they are couples, buy large figures, tend to buy in quantity, and select figures to match their decor (e.g., Victorian furniture).

American. There is an older generation of American sculpture collectors who resemble the buyers of academic bronzes. The new collector-investor, who usually buys on the advice of an agent or dealer, is able to pay higher prices and is interested only in pieces over $25,000.

Medieval, Renaissance, and Baroque Sculpture

The few collectors in this field are not investment-oriented, but are avid students of the period, collecting all books and catalogues as well as the works themselves.

IMPORTANT FACTORS IN BUYING AND SELLING

Auction House vs. Gallery

Collectors faced with the choice of buying through the auction house or the gallery must compare quality, availability, and cost. Dealers have the advantage over the auction house in selection. Because of insurance, storage, shipping, and maintenance, a gallery must mark up the price of an object to a client for a specific price, whereas the auction house can only give a presale estimate with no guarantee of the actual price until after the sale. Often an unsophisticated buyer will assume that he can purchase an object at auction for a fraction of the cost of a similar work in a dealer's shop. He will be bidding on that piece against other private collectors as well as dealers who must protect the asking price for the work in their shops. Certainly a distinct difference exists between wholesale auction prices and retail trade prices, but, with the educating of the private buyer and the rising popularity of the salesroom, the bargains at auction houses, with their enormous catalogue subscriptions, advertising budgets, and publicity, are absorbing too much of the market and they are luring customers from the retail trade. The auction houses respond that, although the trade is necessary, there are too many brokers in each area.

Using an Agent

Another alternative for many serious investors is the agent. These can be either dealers or gallery owners but are usually authorities on the subject who own no stock. The investor will pay the agent a commission on any purchase, whether through auction or dealer, in order to obtain a trusted judgment and protection from publicity. These agents perform the actual bidding and arrange for payment and shipping.

Deciding How to Sell

Sellers as well as buyers of sculpture must choose their marketplace. The auction houses are an increasingly popular choice because they are able to handle a diverse collection (i.e., all categories of sculpture) and because their method is openly competitive with a very public process. As previously stated, auction houses will not make cash payments. The advantage of selecting a dealer or gallery is not only the method of payment but also the speed of the transaction. Dealers will also take goods in consignment, which allows them a percentage of the selling price (quite similar to the auction idea). The most appealing aspect of selling through a gallery or dealer is that a specific price is agreed upon; this eliminates the uncertainty, risk, and speculation of an auction. On the other hand, many collectors feel that, at auction, they can often both obtain higher prices and reap a larger percentage of the profits.

Judging Quality of Nineteenth-Century Bronzes

The major problem in purchasing bronzes lies in the enormous quantity of fakes. It is quite simple to make a *sur-moulage* casting of any object (i.e., make a mold from a bronze). Most new investors have not seen enough period sculpture to be able to judge color of patina, quality of casing, crispness of signature, and method of facture. To them, any cast with a signature, foundry mark, and proof that the material is bronze is authentic. Many investors shy away from bronzes because they cannot tell these differences. The solution is either to buy from a reputable dealer or auction house that guarantees the authenticity of the work or to learn from looking at objects in museum exhibitions, asking experts, and viewing sales exhibits and gallery offerings until the fakes are obvious.

Checking authenticity. The possibility of forgery is a major problem for collectors in this field. When buying an investment bronze, the investor will want to ascertain the answers to the following questions.

- Is the bronze epoxied to a marble base? If so, it is probably fake, as the foundry does not want the buyer to see the casting method or measurements (shrinkage results from *sur-moulage* casting).
- Is the signature crisp, or is there a ghost, as if it were rewritten? This is also a sign of *sur-moulage* casting.
- Is the patina (color) an even color, usually chocolate brown? Good nineteenth-century patinas were multicolored (reddish brown) and were rubbed on, not paint-

ed. If the color comes off with acetone or nail polish remover, or even chips with a touch of a finger, then it is not a nineteenth-century patina.

- Are there pimples and craters on the surface of the bronze, usually towards the bottom? Nineteenth-century casts were smoothed out before they were colored. The recasts do not have the same amount of handwork.
- Do the details, such as fingers and hair, merge with the bronze? Usually, on nineteenth-century casts, the foundry would chase (reinforce with an engraver's tool) certain details to add crispness and individuality to a cast. The recasts have no definition.

Number and comparative quality. Apart from the problem of forgeries, many investors also would like to know how many bronzes were made in an edition and which casting is better. The first question is usually unanswerable, as most foundry records have been lost. The second is one of aesthetic judgment, although certain details, such as shade of patina and amount of chasing, can help determine price.

A new investor in the field should have any bronze examined by an expert, either the auction cataloguers or one of the acknowledged authorities in the field. Museum experts do not have the time to authenticate every object in the market, nor are they allowed to comment on any piece's value, but many people in the trade, as well as scholars, can do so.

Judging Quality of Earlier Sculpture

Sculptures of the fourteenth through the eighteenth century are also judged for quality in terms of authenticity, rarity, and condition. Unlike nineteenth and twentieth-century bronzes, which are usually in original condition, these works of art inevitably show signs of age. However, damage, extent of original color, as well as the quality of the cast very much determine the marketability of a given piece.

External factors such as provenance (history of ownership), exhibitions, literature, and comparison with similar works in museum collections are also important in judging both the quality and the price of a piece. For example, a Paduan sixteenth-century inkwell, which has been shown in several of the major books on the period and was in an extemely well known and highly regarded private collection since 1915, fetched $5,500 in 1980; another inkwell of similar origin but without the extensive literature and provenance brought only $2,000 that same year.

CUSTODIAL CARE

The incidental costs of sculpture ownership can be high. Insurance, warehousing, restoration, appraisals, and shipping are all expensive. As mentioned in *Attractive Features* in this article, however, the sculpture itself requires little maintenance.

GLOSSARY

academic— Traditional and representational as opposed to abstract art.

animalier— The school of French nineteenth-century sculpture that specialized in naturalistic portrayals of animals.

Art Deco— Art produced from World War I until the mid-thirties, characterized by stylization and geometric form.

Art Nouveau— Turn of the century art characterized by exaggerated ornamental detail and a wide range of motifs.

casting— A foundry piece produced by pouring molten metal or a plaster into a mold.

edition— A limited number of castings made from the sculptor's original model.

foundry mark— An identifying inscription, stamp, or seal that can be found on a bronze.

patina— Color that is applied to a bronze (chemically or by brush) or that is acquired through age or use.

sur moulage— A casting made from a casting, not from the artist's original model — usually an unauthorized copy.

TRADE ORGANIZATIONS

Art and Antique Dealers League of America, New York, N.Y.

Art Dealers Association of America, New York, N.Y.

National Antique and Art Dealers Association of America, New York, N.Y.

LEADING DEALERS IN THE UNITED STATES

American Sculpture

J.N. Bartfield Galleries, Inc., New York, N.Y.

Graham Galleries, New York, N.Y.

Kennedy Galleries, New York, N.Y.

James Maroney, New York, N.Y.

Art Nouveau and Art Deco

Lillian Nassau, New York, N.Y.

Macklowe Gallery Ltd., New York, N.Y.

Trent Gallery, New York, N.Y.

Bronzes — Academic and Animalier

Bronzart Antiques, New York, N.Y.

Casal Art, Longmeadow, Mass. (animalier only)

F. Gorevic and Sons, New York, N.Y. (animalier only)

Madison Galleries Ltd., New York, N.Y. (animalier only)

Shepherd Gallery Associates, New York, N.Y.

Universe Antiques, New York, N.Y.

Medieval, Renaissance, and Baroque

Blumka Gallery, New York, N.Y.
Michael Hall Fine Arts, New York, N.Y.
Ed Lubin, New York, N.Y.
Ellen Mitchell, New York, N.Y.

AUCTION HOUSES

Christie's, New York, N.Y.
Christie's, London, England
William Doyle Galleries, New York, N.Y.
Phillips, New York, N.Y.
Phillips, London, England
Sotheby Parke Bernet, New York, N.Y.
Sotheby's, London, England

SUGGESTED READING

Periodicals

Art and Auction. Published by The Auction Guild, New York, N.Y. Ten issues a year; good reporting about auctions and collecting trends.

Connoisseur. Published by National Magazine Company, Ltd., New York, N.Y. Monthly; scholarly articles and brief reviews of exhibitions.

Portfolio. Published by Grosvenor Publications, Inc., New York, N.Y. Bimonthly; articles and reviews.

Reference Books

Broder, P. *Bronzes of the American West.* New York: Abrams, 1974.
Catley, Bryan. *Art Deco and Other Figures.* London: Chancery House Publishing, 1978.
Duncan, J. Alastair. *Art Nouveau Sculpture.* London: Rizzoli, 1978.
Lami, S. *Dictionnaire des Sculpteurs de l'Ecole Francaise.* Reprint, Paris: Kraus, 1970.
Mackay, J. *The Dictionary of Western Sculpture in Bronze.* London: Collector's Club, 1977.

Stamps

*Peter M. Rexford**

BASIC CHARACTERISTICS

In the last fifteen years scarce and rare postage stamps and pieces of postal history have become accepted as a secure and viable investment alternative in a tangible asset. Many individuals and financial planners have recognized the advantage of a diversified investment portfolio that includes rare stamps.

The strength behind the rare-stamp market is due to the buying habits of over 30 million U.S. collectors, a figure higher than that of any other hobby. This strong collector base has convinced many professional investment counselors to invest part of their assets in rare stamps, with notable success. This broad collector base assures them of a consistent demand and high liquidity for quality pieces.

Investment-quality rare stamps can be found within a price range of $50 to $1 million at an auction of rare stamps. Regardless of the amount of money that may be invested, no portfolio of stamps should contain an excessive number of stamps. Generally speaking, it should consist of five to twenty-five stamps and their number, type, and quality should vary with the amount of money that individual wishes to invest and what is currently available on the market.

After deciding how much an individual wants to invest, it would not be unrealistic to invest the entire sum into one very rare issue; however, by diversifying, the investor prepares for the possibility that interest in a particular issue may dwindle, thus assuring that there may be a ready market for his other issues that might continue to appreciate in value. Over the long run, however, the objective is appreciation for the entire portfolio.

A good portfolio of stamps can be put together for as little as $500 and would consist of five to ten excellent quality, early used stamps priced between $50 and $100. This allows some portfolio diversification while retaining the option of adding higher quality material at a later date.

To assemble a portfolio that would include high-quality mint copies of early U.S. issues, an investment of $5,000 to $10,000 would be advisable. The same rule of selective purchases should remain, with a maximum of five to ten items in the portfolio. These stamps would cost between $250 and $1,000 apiece.

A major benefit of purchasing stamps in the $1,000 range is that this is primarily the type of material sold on the major auction markets. (See *Stamp*

* Peter M. Rexford is a Vice-President of the Rare Stamp and Coin Division of Newhard, Cook & Co., Inc., St. Louis.

Auctions in this article.) With a subscription to catalogues and prices-realized lists from a few selected auction houses, the investor will be able to keep a good record of prices that material of this type is bringing on a regular basis.

If the budget of an investor allows an investment in excess of $10,000, then true philatelic rarities can be included in his portfolio. Single stamps and plate blocks [1] costing between $1,000 and $5,000 historically have done very well in appreciating in value. Many of the earlier classic issues in mint condition and nineteenth century material in multiple blocks would be excellent additions. Air-mail plate blocks and some of the rarer proofs have shown very good appreciation also.

For a portfolio valued up to $50,000, anywhere between ten to twenty-five stamps would be best. This allows for each stamp to be one of rarity, in excellent condition. Portfolios with an investment in the area of six figures may contain more stamps or sets but should still be based upon the same guidelines of selective purchasing.

INVESTMENT CRITERIA

In determining the investment quality of a particular stamp, one must consider (1) its attractiveness to collectors; (2) its condition (e.g., centering, color, clarity); and (3) the quantity printed of that issue.

Collector Demand

The U.S. Post Office estimates that there are approximately 30 million stamp collectors in the United States. The supply-demand relationship for a stamp that may be purchased must be gauged from among this huge collection of individuals. Perhaps 10,000 of these individuals might allocate a substantial amount of capital to rare stamps, and, of these, perhaps one-fifth would be interested, for example, in a fine, unused copy of the $5 stamp issued to commemorate the Columbian Exposition of 1893. Of the 27,350 copies of this stamp originally printed, experts estimate that perhaps 50 to 200 copies would still be in unused condition. With the majority of these stamps in the hands of collectors, it is rare that a fine, defect-free copy of this stamp would appear at auction more than ten or twenty times a year. With a potential investment demand for 2,000 of these stamps and a limited supply available, this stamp would be considered a valuable candidate for acquisition under favorable supply-demand conditions. (A group of particularly illustrious stamps is shown in Figure 1 on page 900.)

---

[1] A plate block is the portion of the sheet of stamps that includes the plate printing number in the margin selvedge and a multiple of stamps attached. With earlier issues, along with the plate number, the label of the printing or engraving company may be present. The number of stamps included with the plate number varies with the type of printing and number of colors used on the stamps.

Condition of the Stamp

For the serious collector or investor in rare postage stamps, nothing takes precedence over a stamp's condition in determining its selling price. The examination of a postage stamp has become akin to a science. High-powered microscopes, watermark fluids, ultraviolet lights, and other similar devices are used in determining a stamp's quality. While an investor need not set up a sophisticated laboratory to examine stamps, he should know what to consider in evaluating the investment characteristics of a stamp.

Centering. The centering of the design within the stamp's perforations or borders is one of the easiest key points to consider in judging a stamp's overall quality. It is mainly a matter of visually checking how the design of the stamp is spaced from its edges. Generally speaking, the more evenly the design is centered from the perforations of the stamp, the higher the price it will command. The following rankings of centering range from superb, where the design is equidistant from the edges, to space-filler, a stamp a hobbyist might purchase to fill space in an album.

- Superb — Design is clear of all perforations and borders of stamp are equal.
- Extremely fine — Design is clear of all perforations but not quite perfectly centered.
- Very fine — Design is clear of all perforations but slightly shifted, making borders partially unequal.
- Fine — Design is close to, but clear of, perforations and border may be very small on one or two sides.
- Average — Perforations at one or more points cutting into the design.
- Poor — A significant portion of the stamp's design is missing or affected by perforations in the design.
- Space-filler — Poor perforations. (In addition to being off-center, it will probably have other problems, such as a tear, a corner missing, or extensive thinning of the paper.)

In most cases, a centering rating of very fine or fine would qualify a stamp for an investment portfolio. Often a stamp in very fine condition can be purchased at perhaps 50 percent of the cost of one judged to be superb. Both stamps will have a good possibility for appreciation, but the investor must remember that the base of the stamp market is the collector who is more likely to spend less for a stamp that has a very fine appearance than an exorbitant sum for a perfectly centered one. A stamp graded at less than fine should not be placed into an investment portfolio unless there are known to be few copies of that stamp.

Color, clarity, and freshness. In both the Scott and Harris catalogues, a brief description is included of the ink colors used on each issue. (See *Philatelic Catalogues* in this article.) On the majority of stamps issued after 1935, the exact name

5-cent Benjamin Franklin—
the first regular postage stamp
officially issued by the U.S.
government, July 1, 1847

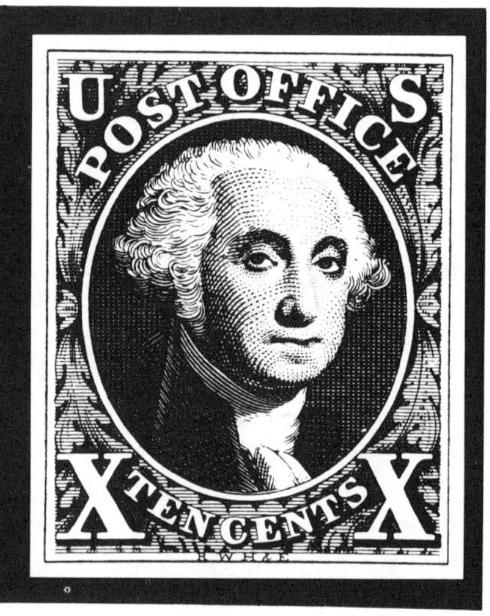

10-cent George Washington—
the second regular postage stamp
officially issued by the U.S.
government, July 1, 1847

90-cent Abraham Lincoln—
highest denomination of
the 1869 pictorial issue,
May 10, 1869

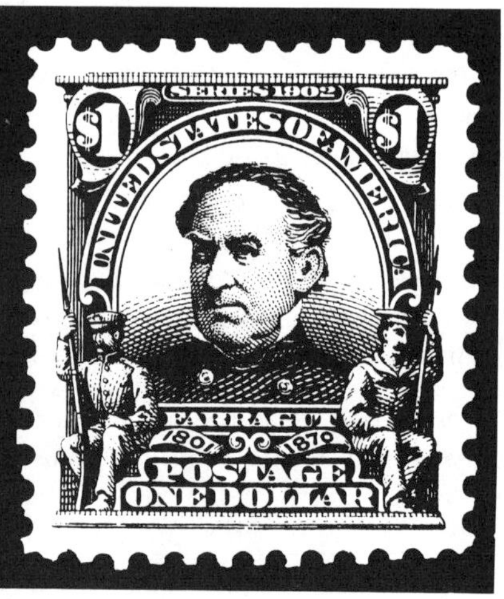

Admiral David G. Farragut
$1.00 denomination of the
1903 regular issue series,
June 5, 1903

FIG. 1. Four Stamps Especially Prized by Collectors

of the color is not absolutely essential to its value. When dealing with stamps from 1847 to the mid-1930s, however, the very slightest color variation can often mean hundreds or thousands of dollars' worth of difference.

The investor should make absolutely certain, when purchasing a stamp whose higher value is due to its color variety, that the stamp is actually the more valuable variety. The best way to accomplish this is to examine the stamp's certificate.[2] If the stamp is not accompanied by a certificate, prior to purchase the buyer should arrange with the seller to secure one that guarantees its authenticity and color variety.

Just as a rare type of color variety can increase dramatically the value of a given stamp, the opposite is true for the condition of the color of a stamp. In other words, if one is purchasing a stamp that is described as dark carmine, that is exactly what it should be. With age and exposure to improper conditions such as excessive sunlight, the color of a stamp can fade dramatically. As a result, although the stamp is completely genuine, its actual color might be light rose or just plain carmine. While this difference generally does not affect the price of the stamp appreciably, it should be kept in mind when looking at a number of similar stamp choices.

The freshness of a stamp is entirely a matter of overall collector preference. A stamp that, when held with stamp tongs, seems to be just as fresh as it was when it was printed, is much more desirable than one that is limp and sags.[3]

Even though the centering of a stamp may be extremely fine or superb, the actual value can be minimal if the perforations surrounding it are not as large as they were when the stamp was originally separated from the sheet. Many times, the perforations around a stamp will wear off from age or be torn off if mishandled. Although seemingly insignificant to the stamp as a whole, this is one of the major reasons that investment stamps should be left in the protective holders in which they are received. Often, the term "nibbed perf" will be used in describing a stamp in an auction catalogue. This means that although some of the single perforation is still attached to the stamp, part is missing. The extent of the nibbed perf must be examined closely, for if the majority of the perforation is missing, its price will be substantially less. Although on rare occasions a stamp with a missing perf may be considered for an investment, it is better to pass it up and look for a better copy.

When purchasing a plate block or multiple combination, it is especially important to hold the stamps horizontally with tongs to ensure that the perforations attaching them are sound and will not separate accidentally. It is not uncommon to see a plate block of stamps listed in an auction catalogue with a description including "minor perf separations." Although only three or four of

---

[2] Certificates that accompany stamps have a scaled photograph attached to them and are notorized if acquired from the American Philatelic Society or Philatelic Foundation.

[3] Stamp tongs are tweezer-like instruments fashioned with tips that handle stamps safely, thus avoiding damage. The tips vary in shape from points to flat pads.

the perforations may have been torn apart, the price realized will still be substantially lower than it would be for a plate block with all of the perforations intact.

Condition of the gum. Undeniably, the condition of a stamp's gum has become one of the most disputed areas for both collectors and investors alike.

Hinged vs. never hinged. In the 1960s, collectors began to pay very careful attention to whether a stamp had ever been hinged, or whether the gum on the back was original. A hinge is a small piece of paper or glassine, with gum on one side, which is folded in half; one half is attached to the stamp, and the other half attached to the collector's album page. The hinge allows the collector to lift up the stamp to read what was printed on the album page underneath, usually the stamp's description or catalogue number. Subsequent removal of the stamp from the album usually would result in some damage to the gum of the stamp or the paper on which it was printed. Until the 1940s, the only way to mount stamps in an album was to hinge them; therefore, never-hinged copies of some issues often command a substantial premium over hinged copies. Very recently, however, the price gap seems to be narrowing slightly. If, at some point, more collectors and investors de-emphasize the importance of gum, a gradual downswing in the never-hinged market is feasible.

Regumming. It is not unusual to find hinged stamps that have been regummed to give them the appearance of never having been hinged. Regumming a stamp is a simple operation and, most often, detectable. To thwart this practice, collectors began to look for hinge-marks on the gum, since the intent of regumming was to remove any trace of a hinge. Soon the regummers became aware of this and lost no time in finding copies that had been heavily hinged, virtually beyond collector appeal, and regummed those copies. Then, to make them appear legitimate, they placed light hinge marks on the regummed copies. The stamps were now in much better condition and still would be purchased by collectors at a premium. When news of this new method of stamp fraud became known, frustration among collectors grew. As a result, the experts responsible for detecting the regumming have a tremendous backlog of material to be examined and judged. (See organizations listed under *Certificates of Authenticity* in this article.)

As a general rule, lightly hinged material definitely should be considered as a solid investment; regummed material never should be considered unless every other facet of the stamp's condition makes the specimen unique. As mentioned earlier, never-hinged rarities will probably always bring premium prices. Equally as important, though, is the high initial price that this material currently demands. With the potential for the hinged/never-hinged gap to begin closing, it would be hard for the investor to be wrong in acquiring lightly hinged stamps at more reasonable prices.

With this buying standard set, it is essential that the investor be able to discern the differences in the degree of severity of a stamp's hinging. Although every stamp is different and judging any point of its condition is relatively subjective, the extent of hinging for any given stamp can be broken down into four categories: (1) never hinged, (2) lightly hinged, (3) hinged, and (4) heavily hinged.

The safest way for the independent investor to guarantee that the gum on a stamp is original is to require that the seller furnish a written commitment or an accompanying certificate.

Reinforcement. When a block of stamps has been transferred from stamp album to stamp album over a period of many years, the perforations may become weak and begin to separate. As a result, collectors often reinforce the intersection of the perforations with a small portion of a hinge. Most reinforcements have been done skillfully and affect the stamp's value only minimally; other reinforcements have been made poorly and may affect the value of all of the stamps in the block. Although it is best to purchase only those multiples that have survived without the need for reinforcement, an investor should consider only those items with little or no hinge reinforcement.

Used vs. mint. Most uninformed investors feel that used stamps do not have the investment potential of mint copies. This is a misconception, for a look through any major auction catalogue will show the vast number of used stamps bringing record-breaking prices. For instance, the world's most valuable stamp, the one-cent British Guiana of 1856 that brought $850,000 at the 1980 "Rarities of the World" sale is a used stamp. Furthermore, since all of the known copies of the 1918 U.S. 24-cent inverted air mail (#C3a) are unused, one that is found used and canceled on an envelope would easily bring at least double the price the mint copies command because it would be unique.[4] This is another example of factors such as collector demand and the quantity issued (or availability) determining stamp prices.

In purchasing used stamps for an investment portfolio, the investor need not be concerned with original gum and hinging since any gum on a used stamp would have been soaked off when removed from the envelope.

Local cancelations. An extremely specialized area of collecting is that of local cancelations. In the early days of the postal system, postmasters often designed their own types of cancelations. Interest in this area has never been greater and new record prices are now being established.

Covers. The market for covers or used envelopes is tremendously active but very specialized. Also referred to as "postal history," covers are most often purchased by collectors of a specific area (first day of issue, singular topic or event, presidential address, etc.). A good-quality stamp on a cover will almost always realize a higher price than if it were not attached.

---

[4] The single known sheet of the 1918 24-cent inverted air mail was purchased by William T. Robey in Washington, D.C. for its face value of $24. In April 1981, a single copy of the stamp sold for $176,000 at auction in New York.

Historical covers and folded letters used prior to the issuance of postage stamps (pre-1845) are avidly sought-after and realize high prices at auction. These are known as "stampless covers."

ATTRACTIVE FEATURES

Collector Base of Millions

As mentioned earlier, the popularity of stamp collecting is international, especially for U.S. issues. This collector base continues to grow at an impressive rate. As more people enter the field of philately, vying for the finite supply of stamps in existence, prices will continue to appreciate.

Relatively High Liquidity

Liquidity for good-quality philatelic material is strong, and there is a ready market of competitive buyers seeking investment material at any time. Because of increased interest in purchasing rare stamps, dealers have been advertising aggressively (the number of advertisements has quadrupled within the past five years) and wholesale prices have increased concomitantly. Auctions frequently allow sellers to achieve optimum prices and are a convenient outlet for selling their merchandise.

Portability

One of the most highly regarded characteristics of a rare-stamp portfolio is the ease of its portability and storage. Great amounts of wealth can be transported in a form that may be virtually undetected from city to city or from country to country. For the value, no other tangible can be stored or transported so conveniently and take up so little space.

POTENTIAL RISKS

Price Distortions

With the vast differences in stamp catalogues and stamp conditions, fair market pricing often becomes distorted, especially for the novice collector or investor. (The fair market price of a rare stamp can be defined as the amount that a buyer is willing to pay.) Both the buyer and seller must have an encyclopedic knowledge of the market to determine a fair price for the very top-grade material. In most cases, the only route for purchasing investment-grade material at competitive prices is the major auction houses. Here, on a monthly basis, the items conforming to every investment category and in every conceivable condition are publicly bought and sold. It is in this market that, once the stamp is properly identified, the true forces of supply and demand prevail.

Volatility

In 1979, the price of a set of three 1930 Graf Zeppelin stamps rocketed in a matter of months from around $4,500 to $11,000 and more. This rapid price rise occurred when an article in a major East Coast newspaper mentioned that the set was scarce, historic, and popular with collectors. It also noted that the set had continually risen in value and might prove to be a lucrative investment for the future.

Panic buying of the Zeppelin sets ensued nationwide. The major purchasers, however, were uninformed buyers who assumed that no matter how high the price, they were making the buy of a lifetime. To make matters worse, the truly uninformed were paying top prices for defective sets that were heavily hinged and had other problems.

When the buying rush began to diminish, and some of these purchasers decided to take an early profit, they found that no one would pay anywhere near the inflated purchase price. Within a year the price plummeted to as low as $2,500; only in 1981 did the price return to a reasonable level of about $4,000. It is important to note, however, that although hundreds of people were caught in the Zeppelin price disaster, there were many warning signs that should have alerted them to the impending danger.

False Scarcity

Anyone from a major dealer to a closet collector can create a false scarcity by mass purchasing of a single issue. Usually, an issue of low printing is selected that formerly had not been widely collected. Purchasing the material may take years, and the individual then must hold onto the purchase until demand for the issue begins. This may take many years, but after it becomes evident that the issue is in short supply, the price begins to rise, depending on what dealers and collectors are willing to pay. The initial purchaser then slowly releases the supply at a very large profit. False scarcities often can be detected in their early stages. The amount of time needed to track them is minimal and can prevent serious financial mistakes.

Physical Alteration

Reperforations. Reperforating the edges of some valuable stamps sometimes is attempted by unscrupulous collectors or dealers because stamps with perforations on all four sides are considered more valuable than stamps appearing at the edge of a sheet with one or two non-perforated edges. Additionally, imperforated stamps that were printed for use in coil vending machines (which perforated the stamps automatically) have been reperforated to resemble rare, higher-value perforated issues. However, careful examination will reveal the vast majority of reperforations.

Camouflaged defects. Stamps that have been mishandled may have defects that have been expertly repaired to deceive a purchaser as to its small faults. A stamp can be rebacked to complete some perforations that may have been torn off or to repair a tear in some small portion of the stamp's margin. A skilled artist might add a few strategic lines to a stamp's design to cover a scuff or, even worse, to make it appear to be a rarer variety.

Faulty copies. An investor should avoid faulty copies of stamps. Their value will never appreciate in the same proportion as that of an extremely fine, sound copy. A natural defect on a stamp would be a design that is too far off center, an easily seen crease in the stamp's paper or gum, or some foreign matter in the gum or paper (larger than the head of a pin) that was processed into the stamp at the time of manufacturing.

A thin in a stamp's paper, which is visible when held to the light or dipped in watermark fluid, also is not acceptable.

TAX CONSEQUENCES

Long-Term Capital Gain

Stamps held for investment purposes have been deemed capital assets by the IRS. If they are held for more than one year, any gain made on their sale is taxed at lower capital gains rates.

Tax-Free Exchange

Stamps qualify under Section 1031 of the Internal Revenue Code as an investment asset suitable for like-kind exchange of property for which no gain or loss will be recognized at the time of the exchange.

This tax deferral gives an investor an opportunity to both consolidate a collection and diversify an investment portfolio with rare stamps. Therefore, an investor who has a collection of 100 stamps in mixed condition passed down to him may sell those stamps and re-invest the capital in a solid rare-stamp portfolio of perhaps five to ten pieces with excellent appreciation potential. (See article on Tax Considerations for Collector-Investors elsewhere in this volume.) For complete guidance in these matters, readers are urged to consult a professional tax adviser.

IMPORTANT FACTORS IN BUYING AND SELLING

Rare-Stamp Brokers

An investor who decides to diversify his or her investment portfolio with rare stamps should acquire them through a qualified rare-stamp broker, who will assist the individual in purchasing a good-quality portfolio with the assurance of full disclosure as to a stamp's value, condition, and potential.

Rare-stamp brokers often offer other services in addition to acquisitions. Some will provide an annual updated valuation of the portfolios. Others may keep a close photographic record of each item to assist the investor in case the stamps are ever lost or stolen. An investor should always obtain instructions for the safe handling, care, and storage of a portfolio.

Investment Services

Investment brokers who work on behalf of the investor emerged as a result of the relatively recent interest in rare-stamp investments and the lack of confidence in the average dealer who sells only from his own inventory. Brokers (sometimes referred to as agents) represent the safest method of purchasing stamps for the investor with a limited knowledge of the rare-stamp market. Most offer a wide range of services to accommodate many different types of investors. A few select agents in the United States are set up to operate strictly on a commission basis, which is usually fixed at 10 percent. Those agents who carry no inventory of stamps are best prepared to service a client by selecting only those items being sold on the open market to individually structure a portfolio suited to the client's needs.

Once the stamp agent or broker is given the investment capital, his goal is to assemble the highest quality portfolio possible, given what is then available on the market. Selecting the issues for the portfolio often may take one or two months, since some stamps may be available only at selected auctions.

Some investment houses will offer to buy back the stamps when the investor decides to sell. Other agents will act as liquidators in the sale. This service can be quite helpful to the investor. In most cases, the agents will charge a commission on the proceeds of the liquidation.

Selecting an agent. When selecting an agent, not only should the investor be certain of the agent's reputation and credibility, but he must also determine whether the agent offers a guarantee regarding a stamp's authenticity. A guarantee that includes the replacement of any item that proves to be either counterfeit or misrepresented is preferable. Often, suppliers will agree to refund the purchase price and pay 10 to 15 percent interest compounded annually if a stamp proves to be different than represented.

Stamp Auctions

For the investor who has done the required background research, investment-grade stamps may be purchased at competitive prices at stamp auctions held at major auction houses. Over 250 auctions are held annually in the United States. The houses each hold up to twenty auctions per year, many specializing in specific areas, including foreign issues. The smaller houses should not be discounted completely as, on occasion, it is possible to find good-quality items at moderate prices, although these houses may not describe the items being offered as fully as the larger houses do.

Bidding by mail. Since the majority of the major auction houses are on the East or West Coasts, bidding by mail is an option for investors to which they are inaccessible. By reviewing the auction catalogue sent to him, the mail bidder is afforded most of the opportunities of the floor bidder.

The specific rules for both floor and mail bidding are printed on the inside of most auction catalogues and should be read carefully by all bidders, as rules do differ from auction to auction. A few weeks after the auction, a list of the prices realized will be mailed to all catalogue subscribers. It is essential that these lists be reviewed and kept, as these are now the prices being paid by dealers, collectors, and investors for the material offered.

Prior to the day of the auction, the house tabulates all of the mail bids and selects the highest and second highest bid for each lot offered. When the lot comes up for sale, the floor bidding begins at one bid increment above the second highest mail bid. For example, on Lot #1, the highest mail bid may be $1,000. If the second highest mail bid is only $500, the bidding will probably start at $550. If no floor bids are received for this lot, the mail bidder of $1,000 will win the lot for $550, even though he was prepared to go to $1,000. This method allows the mail bidders the same benefits as those attending in person.

After the auction, the mail bidder will be notified that he has successfully bid on an item and, upon receipt of the money, the auction house will mail the lot to him. If, after the mail bidder receives the lot, he discovers any defects or inconsistencies in the material that were not mentioned in the auction catalogue's description, the stamp may then be returned on the basis that the condition was misrepresented. Return policies vary from auction to auction so mail bidders are advised to fully understand the conditions of the sale prior to placing bids.

Auction fees. An auction house works strictly on a commission basis, usually 10 percent. However, this commission is added to both sides of the transaction, so most auctions receive from the seller, as well as from the purchaser, a total of 20 percent. This percentage fluctuates for some auctions, and with a few the buyer is not required to pay any commission on a purchase. For the vast majority of the major houses, however, an investor should expect to pay to the house 10 percent over and above the price of the purchase.

Unfortunately, some auction houses may occasionally use shills in the audience to bid up the prices on a number of items. Additionally, the owner of a lot may be able to ascertain its highest mail bid and bid up the price himself once he is on the floor. Although this activity occurs rarely, bidders should be aware of its existence.

Dealers

Dealer integrity. One of the most effective ways for the investor to determine the integrity of a dealership is to check with an acquaintance who has done business with the dealer. A dealer's reputation, good or bad, can spread rapidly by word of mouth, so some discreet checking by the investor could be most profitable.

Furthermore, there is an industry self-regulatory body, the American Stamp Dealers Association (ASDA), that protects the stamp buyer from some of the more unscrupulous dealers. It has established rules and regulations governing the activities of its members and takes whatever action is necessary against a member dealer if a record of impropriety is found.

Since the investor may be considering allocating a large sum of money for a rare-stamp portfolio, an inquiry with the local Better Business Bureau would also be appropriate.

Dealer profit margin. The profit margin for a dealer can range anywhere from 10 to 500 percent. More importantly, the dealer can place his profit anywhere within these percentages and still be dealing very honestly. For example, if a dealer had purchased 100 copies of a stamp in 1970 for $5 apiece and then resold them for $25 each in 1980, the percentage of profit would be great. If the fair market price for those stamps in 1980 was $27, then not only would the customer get a fair deal, but the dealer would still be making 500 percent on the investment. Doing research on a rare-stamp issue and its price is not too difficult and should be a prerequisite to any purchase.

Stamp dealers, large or small, will often have some extremely desirable rare stamps available. For this reason, a local dealer should never be overlooked.

Catalogues. The most effective use of a stamp catalogue is as a reference for background and approximate pricing. Most catalogues will explain their pricing policy dependent on conditions that should be considered. Others list a number of different prices for various types of conditions.

On the whole, more common stamps sell for substantially less than the advertised price in a catalogue. Conversely, rare issues in higher grades may sell for more than the catalogue price. One important consideration in the accuracy of a catalogue's stamp pricing should be whether or not the publishers have a vested interest in the stamp prices. In some instances an order blank can be found at the back of the catalogue. In these instances, the publishers of the catalogue are ready to sell the stamps for the prices published as, in all probability, a high-price safety factor has been figured into the price of the listed stamp to compensate for any major price swings during the year of catalogue distribution.

Certificate of authenticity. As with other tangible investments, a certificate of authenticity is available for rare stamps. The certificate, in addition to verifying or disputing authenticity, will specify any noticeable defects within the stamp itself, such as thins, tears, stain, or condition of the gum. Any investment-quality stamp with an approved certificate from a recognized authority will bring more at auction than will an identical copy that does not have one.

The two organizations that offer the accepted certificates for stamps are the American Philatelic Society (State College, Pa.) and the Philatelic Foundation (New York, N.Y.). One wishing to submit material to them may obtain a mailing form from their offices. There is a minimum charge for their services and an additional fee varies, depending upon the value of the stamp submitted and its authenticity.

CUSTODIAL CARE

Just as portability is a great asset to the collector, it can be an even greater asset to a thief. Unfortunately, it is no longer safe to keep a good stamp collection in the home to be enjoyed. If the collection has any value, it should be stored in a safe-deposit box in a bank vault with a reputable bank or trust company. To go one step further, it would be best to purchase a box located at eye level because bank vaults have been known to have a pipe break and flood. Also, banks monitor the temperature and humidity of their vaults, which helps protect a rare-stamp investment.

GLOSSARY

booklet pane— A small sheet of stamps especially printed and cut to be sold in booklets.

cancelation— A mark placed on a stamp by a postal authority to prevent its reuse.

coils— Stamps issued in rolls for use in affixing or vending machines.

commemorative— A stamp that honors anniversaries, important people, or special events.

cover— The entire wrapping or envelope in which a letter has been sent through the mail.

definitive— A regular issue of a stamp for denominated postal use.

essay— Design submitted for stamp use but not accepted for issuance.

imperforate— Stamps without perforations. Collected in pairs for proof of authenticity.

pen cancel— A cancelation applied to the stamp with pen and ink. Usually of less value than if handstamped.

proof— Trial printing of a stamp made from the original die or plate.

watermark— A design or pattern incorporated into the paper during its manufacture.

STAMP AUCTION HOUSES

This list of auction houses is included strictly as a guide to some of the larger firms. It is in no way complete or a recommendation of any specific auction company.

Auction houses with more than one location are marked with an asterisk (*).

Earl Apfelbaum, Inc., Philadelphia, Pa.

Central Suffolk Auctions, Inc., Farmingville, N.Y.
*Stanley Gibbons International, London, England
*Harmers of New York, Inc., New York, N.Y.
Steve Ivy Philatelic Auctions, Inc., Dallas, Tex.
John W. Kaufman, Inc., Washington, D.C.
Peter Kenedi, Inc., Encino, Cal.
Greg Manning Auctions, Inc., Fairfield, N.J.
Metro Stamp Co., Inc., Middle Village, N.Y.
*Phillips, New York, N.Y.
Scott Auction Galleries, Inc., New York, N.Y.
Robert A. Siegel Auction Galleries, Inc., New York, N.Y.
Simmy's Stamp Co., Inc., Boston, Mass.
*Sotheby Parke Bernet Stamp Auction Co., Inc., Danbury, Conn.
J & H Stolow, Inc., New York, N.Y.
Richard Wolffers, Inc., San Francisco, Cal.

PHILATELIC SOURCES

Trade Association

American Stamp Dealers Association, Lake Success, N.Y.

Philatelic Catalogues

Brookman Price List for Stamps. Published by the Brookman Company, Fairfield, N.J.

Harris Postage Stamp Catalog. Published (semiannually) by H.E. Harris Co., Inc., Boston, Mass.

Scott Specialized Catalog of United States Stamps. Published (annually) by Scott Publishing Co., New York, N.Y.

Rare-Stamp Brokers

Newhard, Cook & Co., Inc., Rare Stamp & Coin Division, St. Louis, Mo.
Stamp Portfolios, Inc., Stamford, Conn.

SUGGESTED READING

Periodicals

The American Philatelist. Published by the American Philatelic Society, Pennsylvania State College, Pa. Monthly.

Linn's Stamp Newspaper. Published by Amos Press, Sidney, Ohio. Weekly.

Scott's Stamp Journal. Published by Scott Publishing Co., New York, N.Y. Monthly.

Stamp Collector. Published by Van Dahl Publications, Inc., Albany, Ore. Weekly.

Stamp Market Update. Published by Scott Publishing Company, New York, N.Y. Quarterly.

Stamp Research Report. Published in Washington, D.C. Monthly.

Stamp Show News and Philatelic Review. Published by West Rock Associates, Larchmont, N.Y. Monthly.

Stamp World. Published by Amos Press, Sidney, Ohio. Monthly.

Reference Books

Armstrong, Martin A. *United States Coil Issues, 1906-1938.* Lawrenceville: Trenton Publishing Co., 1980.

———. *U.S. Definitive Series, 1922-1938.* Lawrenceville: Trenton Publishing Co., 1980.

———. *"Washington-Franklins" 1908-1921.* Lawrenceville: Trenton Publishing Co., 1980.

Herst, Jr., Herman. *The Compleat Philatelist.* Florham Park, N.J.: The Washington Press, 1979.

———. *Nassau Street.* Sunnyvale, Ca.: Western Philatelic Library, 1960.

Johl, Max. *United States Postage Stamps, 1902-1935.* Lawrence, Mass.: Quarterman Publications, 1976.

Luff, John N. *The Postage Stamps of the United States.* Lawrence, Mass.: Quarterman Publications, 1981.

Schmidt, Paul W. *How to Detect Damaged, Altered and Repaired Stamps.* Huntington: Palm Press, 1979.

Wagenheim, Kal. *Paper Gold.* New York: Wyden Books, 1976.

Strategic and Critical Materials

*James E. Sinclair**

BASIC CHARACTERISTICS

Description and Definition

The Federal Emergency Management Agency defines strategic and critical materials as those "that would be needed to supply the military, industrial, and essential civilian needs of the United States during a national emergency, and are not found or produced in the United States in sufficient quantities." Strategic and critical materials are a relatively new medium for private investment. The logic leading a sophisticated and well-capitalized investor to the field is simple and direct: Such metals as cobalt, chromium, manganese, and the platinum group are vital industrial materials, essential for military and civilian use in electronics, telecommunications, aerospace, refining, and other high-technology applications. The United States has no significant domestic sources for any of the big four strategic metals, and it depends on imports for more than 50 percent of its supply of about twenty other vital materials.

Politics and Strategics

The major sources for many of the strategics are in politically fragile areas such as Southern Africa and the Soviet Union. As a result, the United States and its allies are exposed to accidental or planned disruption of their supplies.

Many of these materials are quite costly on a per-ounce or per-kilo scale and their prices are likely to increase through the normal processes of inflation. If supplies are cut off for political or other reasons, prices will increase even faster. Hence, the outlook for price appreciation and capital gain are reasonably promising for the investor who is able to buy the materials outright and hold them for two to four years or longer.

Stockpiles for Security

To assure the U.S. defense industry of adequate supplies of essential materials in time of a national emergency, the government has created a strategic stockpile of sixty-two families of materials (ninety-three separate substances, eighty of which are minerals). Supply goals have been established for each of the materials at levels judged sufficient to meet the nation's essential defense needs

* James E. Sinclair is a General Partner, Sinclair Group Companies, New York.

for a three-year emergency. Yet because successive administrations and congresses failed to provide the funds to create a truly adequate national stockpile, the inventory of materials on hand stands at only about 50 percent of the stockpile's goals. The stockpile was created to enhance national security, not to show a bookkeeping profit. Yet it is significant that raw materials that cost the government $3.5 billion (in the 1950s) rose to a value of $13.7 billion by 1980.

Why have private industries that need strategic materials not built their own stockpiles? Because during the past thirty years most of the materials were available to them through long-term contracts with the producers, and supply interruptions were infrequent. Consuming industries had no need to tie up expensive capital in large stockpiles. Unfortunately, that is no longer the case, and there is increasing risk that supplies of essential minerals may be interrupted for political reasons. In several of the Southern African countries in which mines were developed by European engineers, the quality of management and technical expertise has declined under the post-colonial managements, which are often state-controlled. (See Figure 1 on page 915 for chart of U.S. dependence on foreign sources for twenty-seven strategic minerals and metals.)

The Reagan Administration has shown concern for the problems of mineral dependency and has taken some steps to reduce the nation's vulnerability. Stockpile purchasing has been stepped up, and the Department of the Interior is taking steps to open more of the public lands to mineral exploration and development. While few experts expect to find mineral deposits in the United States as large and rich as those in Southern Africa and the Soviet Union, there are realistic prospects of finding smaller ore bodies that can be developed. These mines are likely to be low-volume, high-cost operations made viable by tax preferences and government purchase contracts. Their net effect will be to assure the United States a minimal supply of strategic metals from domestic sources, and not to lower the United States or world price structure.

Private investors cannot be expected to solve the larger problems of the nation's mineral dependency. That is a task for the government, to be dealt with over a long period of time. But the private investor must be aware of the economic climate and seek to work with the larger economic forces, not against them. The investor can use intelligence and resources to enhance his investment programs.

Types of Investment

Metals. The simplest form of investment in strategic materials is the direct purchase of the metals in the form and degree of purity in which they are commonly traded in commercial markets. Of the metals known as "the big four" — manganese, chromium, cobalt, and the platinum group — all are indispensable industrial materials and not one is produced in significant volume in North America.

Manganese. Manganese is a purifying and hardening agent, essential in the manufacture of steel, imparting strength, hardness, and toughness to the world's

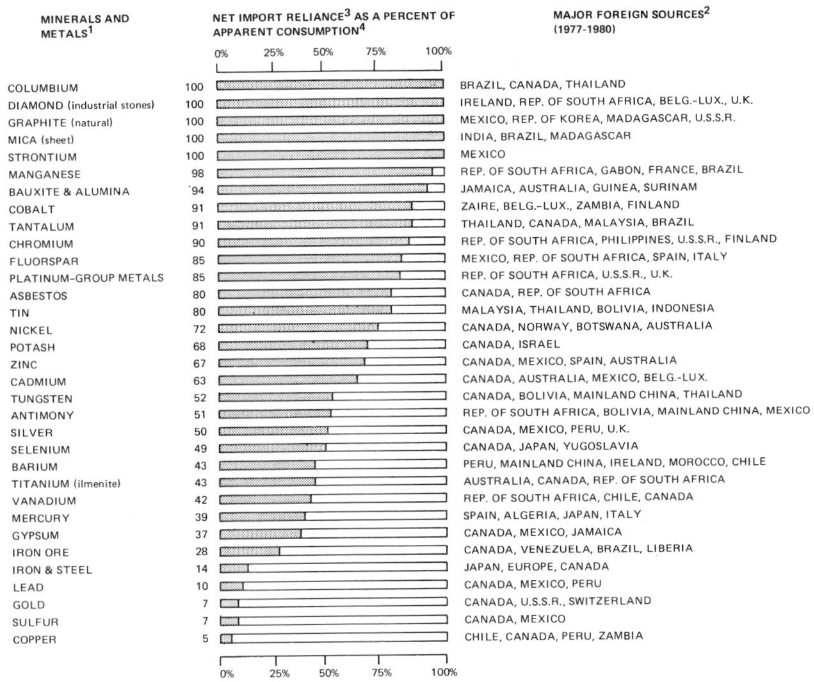

[1]Substantial quantities are imported for rutile, rhenium and zircon. Data withheld to avoid disclosing company proprietary data.
[2]Sources shown are points of shipment to the U.S. and are not necessarily the initial sources of the material.
[3]Net import reliance = Imports-exports + adjustments for government and industry stock changes.
[4]Apparent consumption = U.S. primary + seconday production + net import reliance.

FIG. 1. U.S. Net Import Reliance of Selected Minerals and Metals as a Percent of Consumption in 1981

SOURCE: U.S. Bureau of Mines

most basic industrial metal. The United States imports most of its manganese from Brazil, South Africa, and Gabon. The Soviet Union, once an important source of manganese, is no longer a reliable supplier.

Chromium. Chromium, added to steel, enhances hardness and corrosion resistance; it is an essential component of stainless steel. Most of the world's chromium comes from South Africa and Zimbabwe; the Soviet Union also produces chromium and is a minor supplier to the West.

Cobalt. The demand for cobalt rises with the increased demand for superalloys, metals that retain their shape and strength under the extreme heat of aircraft jet engines and nuclear- and conventional-power generators. More than two-thirds of the world's supply of cobalt comes from a few mines in the CopperBelt of Zaire and Zambia, two African nations plagued by political insecurities. The United States recently added 5.2 million pounds of cobalt to its strategic stockpile.

Platinum. Platinum and its related metals, palladium, rhodium, ruthenium, iridium and osmium, are marked by extreme hardness, durability, and resistance to corrosion. They are used as catalysts in automobile-exhaust devices and in the manufacture of chemicals, glass, explosives, and in oil refining. More than 90 percent of the world's known resources of the platinum group metal are concentrated in South Africa and the Soviet Union.

Other metals. Other metals once known mainly as "laboratory curiosities" are coming into increasing demand as their extraordinary qualities are recognized and put to use. Titanium, strong as steel and much lighter, is in demand for jet engines, airframes, and missiles. Australia is the principal foreign source for the ore used in metal production.

The demand for tantalum, a metal widely used in electronics, is expected to rise by 4.1 percent a year until the year 2000; Canada, Nigeria, Brazil, and Mozambique are suppliers. Gallium and indium, recovered as byproducts in base-metal refining, have important applications in electronics.

Common stocks. Because many of the strategic materials are recovered as by-products of other mining operations, there are only a few companies whose stocks represent principally an investment in strategic materials. Impala Platinum Holdings and Rustenburg Platinum Holdings, both South African producers, are directly and principally involved in platinum mining. In the United States, Hecla and Sunshine Mining are major producers of silver, and Asarco is the largest U.S. producer of silver, although its major operations are in base metals.

For other strategics, South African Manganese and High Veldt Steel and Vanadium are major and profitable producers of manganese and vanadium; Americans may buy American depository receipts (ADRs) in these companies, although the volatile political climate makes South African ventures risky investments. In the United States, Oregon Metallurgical is an investment in the mining of titanium, while Nuclear Metals Incorporated and the Cabot Corporation are processors of strategic metals.

The foregoing discussion does not constitute a recommendation to buy any particular stock; it is presented merely to illustrate the range of possible investments in strategic materials.

Mutual funds. Another form of investment that may open the field of strategic materials to smaller investors is mutual funds, in which relatively modest sums ($5,000 or $10,000) may enable qualified persons to participate in a diversified portfolio of materials.

Among the first of the mutual-fund-type investments in strategic materials to appear was the Strategic Metal Trust, a British fund set up under the laws of the Isle of Man. The minimum investment in this fund is $10,000, and a fee of 5 to 8 percent is added for investments of up to $100,000. The Strategic Metals Corporation Managed Portfolio has been in operation in London since September 1980. Bache Halsey Stuart, a firm active in commodity trading for many years, expects to bring out its fund in 1982. Other funds are in various stages of preparation.

ATTRACTIVE FEATURES

Commodities in Demand

The basic attraction of investments in strategic and critical materials arises from the probability that demand for the materials will increase as supplies are reduced by geopolitical developments in the producing regions. In this analysis, there is a basic distinction between gold and the strategics. If all gold production should cease, the price of the metal would undoubtedly rise, but the world's commerce would continue. Any gold needed for coinage or industrial processes could be supplied with ease from the 80,000 tons of gold now above ground, much of which is locked away in the form of ingots and bars. If cobalt, chromium, manganese, the platinum metals, or any of a score of other strategic materials should suddenly become unavailable, vital industries throughout the world would be paralyzed.

Without manganese and chromium, the production of industrial-quality steel would be impossible. Without cobalt, the world's jet fleets would gradually be grounded and telecommunications would be impaired. Without the platinum-group metals, the petroleum refining and countless other chemical processes, including the manufacture of fertilizer and explosives, would come to a halt. Without titanium, high-performance aircraft and space vehicles could not be built.

Thus, the owners of strategic materials possess real and useful commodities. Prices may fluctuate in the short term, but their long-term direction will be upward. In the writer's judgment, the prospect of price appreciation in some of the strategics in the 1980s compares with the outlook for gold at the beginning of the 1970s.

The germanium surge. As an example of a sudden price increase, consider germanium. In late 1980, the price of germanium began to move up from $700 a kilogram to more than $1,000 a kilogram. Germanium is a relatively rare metal, normally recovered as a byproduct of zinc smelting. It is used in electronic and optical equipment, in the manufacture of optical fibers, and in the night sights of military weapons. Total world production in 1980 was only about 127 tons, so the metal is sensitive to changes in demand.

Two unrelated developments may have prompted the price increase. The Soviet Union, which had been a supplier to the world market, suddenly turned from seller to buyer, possibly to acquire material to outfit its growing fleet of tanks with night sights. Another possibility, never confirmed, suggested that private speculators may have been trying to corner the world market in available germanium. At the old price of $700 a kilogram, the entire world production of germanium might have been worth only about $82 million; therefore, a cornering effort would not be beyond the resources of many market operators. In any case, the market price remained near its new plateau as of early 1982.

Strategic and critical materials bought for investment are paid for in full with cash. Therefore, downside risk is limited. Unlike the futures market, where losses can far exceed the original investment, lack of leverage limits risk.

Intangible Benefits

Investors in strategics also enjoy a certain psychic reward in knowing they are contributing meaningfully to the economic and military security of their nation. Strategic materials would probably be nationalized in the event of a major national emergency, and the investor's holdings would then be put to the useful purpose of national defense.

POTENTIAL RISKS

Price Drops

The most obvious risk of investing in strategic materials is that of price depreciation. Such basic raw materials as manganese, chromium, and antimony are consumed in enormous volume in the normal civilian industrial processes, and are thus subject to the normal market forces of supply and demand. Prices tend to fall during business recessions and rise with business expansion. While the long-term price trends for most of these materials is upward, the possibility certainly exists for loss if purchases are badly timed or sales are made under adverse market conditions.

Transactional Costs

It is clear that investments in strategic materials involve somewhat higher transactional costs than many other investments, which are bought and sold through more liquid markets. Assays, sampling, warehouse services, and insurance are cost items to be taken into account in judging overall investment quality.

Beyond these factors is the obvious one that materials held in inventory yield no income. The investor thus forgoes income that might otherwise have been earned by putting his money into bonds, stocks, or investment real estate.

Fraud

The risk of fraud and sharp dealing is probably higher in strategic metals than in some other commodities, particularly those in which markets are supervised by government authorities. To avoid con artists, an investor should select a competent broker who is familiar with the technical side of the market and is aware, for instance, that a slight difference in the grade or purity of metals may make a substantial difference in value. Cobalt that is 99.6 percent pure will have a distinctly higher market value than metal testing only 99 percent pure.

The growth of markets in strategic materials has attracted some thoroughly reputable financial firms and investment advisers; it has also attracted numerous insubstantial boiler-room operators more adept at telephone salesmanship than at delivery of honest services. The investor's defense is to deal only with brokers who have proven expertise and established reputations, and they in turn should probably deal, at least in London, only with metal traders and dealers known to The Minor Metals Traders Association, London, England, and to the association's secretary, Mr. D.C. Algar.

Illiquidity

Another risk that an investor should understand arises from the nature of the markets in which the metals are traded. While such metals as silver, platinum, copper, lead, and zinc have large liquid markets, others such as titanium, cobalt, manganese, and the more exotic metals are traded dealer to dealer or dealer to client. When the market is inactive or depressed, it may not be easy to find a buyer without sacrificing price.

TAX CONSEQUENCES

Since strategic materials ordinarily will be held for more than one year, most profits when realized will be taxed at low capital gains rates, a maximum of 20 percent under the 1981 tax legislation.

Other tax benefits may develop in the future. Because the accumulation of privately held stockpiles of strategic materials may be judged to be in the national interest, the U.S. government may be amenable to offering tax preferences to encourage private stockpiling. Some of the devices proposed — none of which have yet been legislated — are investment tax credits for private holdings and fast writeoffs for stockpiles held by industrial consumers.

REPRESENTATIVE TYPES OF INVESTORS

Corporations that use gold, silver, platinum, and palladium in their manufacturing processes often hedge their future needs in physical metals through the purchase of futures contracts. Other users of strategic metals for which no futures markets exist also tend to maintain working stockpiles, but they usually regard these holdings as a form of business protection against supply interruption rather than as corporate investments.

Investors in strategic and critical materials are typically individuals whose net worth and incomes are well above average. The writer's firm recommends that investors have a net worth of at least $260,000 in order to put a minimum of $26,000 into a portfolio of strategics. In practice, most investors substantially exceed this minimum. Typically, they are individuals who understand that the case of strategics is made not just on market economics but on the basis of world geopolitical developments. Investors in this field tend to be well-financed, news-conscious risk-takers who are willing to venture into a form of investment that is still foreign to most banks and conservative money management institutions. Investors in strategics may be viewed as individuals hedging against the unpredictable and the unforeseen in a dangerous and unpredictable world.

IMPORTANT FACTORS IN BUYING AND SELLING

Finding the Markets

The markets for most of the critical and strategic materials operate far differently from those of the more commonly traded commodities. A few of the metals that the General Services Administration (GSA) classifies as strategic are commonly traded as precious metals (silver, platinum, palladium) in the form of physical commodities and futures contracts; the same is true for copper and zinc, for which futures markets are maintained at New York's Comex. All of these metals, plus aluminum, lead, nickel, tin, and zinc, are also traded on the London Metal Exchange through the medium of spot and forward contracts. But, for the great majority of the GSA's eighty mineral-based strategic materials, trading is conducted primarily dealer to dealer at a price subject to negotiation, deal by deal. These markets at times are dull and illiquid, and either a buyer or a seller may have only a small number of potential opposite traders with whom to negotiate.

The concept of personal and speculative investment in this field is so new that practices and customs are still being worked out. The arrival of the investor-speculator may, over time, substantially change the character of the markets, adding liquidity and volume to markets that were once the exclusive domain of the professional metals experts.

Purchases of strategic materials are normally paid in full and the materials held for eventual sale for cash. Some of the following general rules may serve to guide and protect the private investor.

How to Buy Strategics

A key factor in buying and selling strategic materials is the choice of a broker who is reputable, well financed, and staffed to do business in London, the world center for trade in strategic materials. The investor will be well advised to check the credentials of any firm that solicits his business.

When an investor places an order for a specified amount (lot) of a strategic material, he will ordinarily, in consultation with a broker, set an upper limit on the price he will pay. When selling it is advisable to set a lower limit on the price he will accept. As a rule, it is not advisable to place either buy or sell orders "at the market," because the market is not yet active and liquid enough to accommodate this kind of trading.

The order ordinarily will be executed in London. Once an acceptable price is agreed upon and a firm order placed, the material will usually be delivered in thirty to ninety days after the trade date. Delivery is customarily completed by transfer of a warehouse receipt, after which the investor is the legal owner of a specific, identifiable lot of the material he purchased, packed in drums, cases, or other appropriate containers.

It is advisable to have the lot inspected, weighed, and assayed by professionals approved by the London Metal Exchange. Warehouse receipts, assay certificates, and other documents may be left in possession of the investor's broker, or the owner may wish to take possession of the documents. Documents left with the broker should be insured, especially the warehouse receipt. The materials themselves also should be insured against theft or destruction by fire and other natural hazards. Ordinarily, storage, insurance, and inspection costs are covered by a monthly charge of about .25 percent of the original cost, or about 3 percent a year.

Investment Strategies

While other investment firms recommend various forms of investment in strategic materials, the writer's firm recommends the purchase of portfolios. The smallest portfolio recommended, representing no more than 10 percent of the buyer's investable funds, is a $26,000 purchase of chromium and manganese. Other portfolios, on an ascending scale but still representing only a minor portion of the investor's total funds, might include:

$40,000 — chromium, manganese, cobalt
$60,000 — chromium, manganese, cobalt, germanium

$70,000 — chromium, manganese, cobalt, germanium, titanium
$120,000 — chromium, manganese, cobalt, germanium, titanium, antimony, rhodium, indium
$160,000 — chromium, manganese, cobalt, germanium, titanium, antimony, rhodium, indium

These portfolios are given only for illustration, and market conditions may change at any time, suggesting other materials and combinations. It is important to diversify as protection against sudden market aberrations of one or more materials.

Investors should try to make purchases when dealers are searching for customers. The ideal time to buy is during a period of quiet trading in the midst of a business slowdown; the time to sell is when expanding business conditions or real or threatened shortages have pushed demand beyond the available supply.

Prices

For most of the widely traded strategic metals that are also standard industrial raw materials, there are two prices to consider: the producer price and the dealer or free market price. The producer price is the price at which a primary producer — a mining concern — has contracted to sell large quantities of metal to a large consumer over a period of time. Normally, this price will not change during the life of the contract. The dealer price is the level at which trades are conducted day to day, which is constantly fluctuating to reflect changing supply and demand. Depending upon the market conditions, the dealer price may be higher or lower than the producer price, but the investor or non-industrial consumer rarely has access to metal at the producer price.

On the other hand, if the buyer in a long-term contract ends up with a surplus of metal when the dealer price is much higher than the producer price, he may choose to sell some of his inventory at a profit on the general market. A decision in this matter must be based on the company's market outlook and strategy rather than on immediate profit opportunity; it would be most shortsighted for a company to sell off its working inventory of a key raw material only to confront a shortage a few weeks or a few months later. As a rule, metals moving from producer to user under long-term contracts never become available on the dealer market. The true market and the true market price for all but the largest industrial consumers and producers are established on the dealer market.

CUSTODIAL CARE

The strategics that are also precious metals — silver and the platinum group — may be purchased in the United States and held for the investor in secure storage by a bank or a metal dealer. But for most of the strategic materials, Rotterdam is the world's principal center for the physical handling and warehousing of the minor metals — the market term encompassing most of the strategics. Pending the development of similar facilities in the United States, it will be advisable to use the available warehouses in Europe, making sure that all purchases are carefully documented. While the investor has the option of leaving the documents with his broker or of taking possession of them himself, in the writer's opinion the investor should accept and hold the basic documents: the brokerage receipts, warehouse receipts, assay and sampling certificates, and insurance policies. Since the warehouse receipts are negotiable, they should be safeguarded as carefully as any other valuable negotiable security.

GLOSSARY

alloy— A substance, usually a metal, combined with one or more other metals to produce a material with characteristics more desirable than those of the original components.

assay— A test to determine the composition and degree of purity of a substance.

catalyst— A substance used to facilitate a reaction between or among other substances without itself being chemically affected.

chromium— A metal used as an alloy to make stainless steel. It is produced mainly in South Africa, Zimbabwe, and the Soviet Union.

cobalt— A tough, lustrous metal used as an alloy to produce steel that retains its strength under extreme heat, as in the hot end of jet engines. Zaire and Zambia are the major world sources of cobalt.

dealer price— The price at which commercial transactions in commodities are currently being made between principals without long-term obligations to each other.

germanium— A scarce metallic element recovered as a byproduct of zinc mining, used in the manufacture of diodes and in optical applications.

indium— A silvery white metal, recovered as a byproduct of zinc ore and used as a component of transistors and in other electronic and electrical applications.

manganese— A gray-white metal used as an alloy in almost all steels of industrial grade. South Africa and the Soviet Union are the major world sources of manganese.

platinum— A hard, lustrous, and very rare metal used in a wide variety of applications as a chemical catalyst and in electronic and electrical applications. Its related metals, some of which substitute for each other, are palladium, iridium, osmium, rhodium, and ruthenium.

producer price— A price for a mineral used as a basis for long-term contracts between suppliers and consuming industries.

titanium— A low-density metal as strong as steel but 45 percent lighter. Widely used in aircraft and aerospace applications.

LEADING BROKERS

Bache Halsey Stuart Metal Co., Inc., New York, N.Y.

Rayner-Harwill, Ltd., London, England

Strategic Metals & Critical Materials, Inc., New York, N.Y.

Strategic Metals, Ltd., Strategic Investments International, Berkeley, Cal.

SUGGESTED READING

U.S. Bureau of Mines publications are standard references for the metal and mining industry worldwide. Among the basic volumes are the *Minerals Yearbook*, published in three volumes, and *Mineral Facts and Problems*, which is updated from time to time. *Mineral Commodity Summaries* is an annual publication that appears early in each calendar year with a statistical summary and basic facts for most traded metals. For each metal, the government provides the name of the bureau's expert on that metal and his office telephone number. These experts are well informed and usually helpful. *Metal Bulletin Handbook*, published by Metal Bulletin, P.L.C., London, England, and *Metal Statistics*, published annually by Fairchild Publications, New York, N.Y., are standard sources for statistical data and some historical background.

The Metals Investor is a very good monthly newsletter published by Common Sense Press Inc. of Costa Mesa, Cal.; so is *Strategic Metals Intelligence*, a product of 21st Century Research, North Bergen, N.J. The Sinclair Securities Company's weekly newsletter, published in New York, N.Y., deals with investments in strategic metals, precious metals, and related fields.

Among the periodicals dealing with strategic materials primarily from the industrial viewpoint rather than from an investment perspective are *Metal Bulletin*, published by Metal Bulletin, P.L.C. (see above), *American Metal Market*, published by New York's Fairchild Publications (see above), and *Metals Week*, published by McGraw Hill, New York, N.Y.

Beyond these specialized publications, investors will want to keep in touch with economic and political developments through the *Wall Street Journal*, *Business Week*, *Fortune*, and the better daily newspapers. *Financial Times* and the *Economist* of London are especially good in covering the European markets, and the *Economist* publishes special supplements that trace political and economic developments in regions of the world. Those on Southern Africa are especially useful to the investor in strategic materials.

Theatrical Productions

Paul H. Epstein, Esq., and Allan M. Shapiro, Esq. *

BASIC CHARACTERISTICS

The legitimate theater represents an unusual investment opportunity in several respects. Financings are handled almost entirely by the principals involved, with no participation by brokers or other securities professionals. The productions to be financed rarely have any operating history and even the artistic form in which they will open to the public (especially musicals) may change drastically from what is envisioned during the period of financing. The investment is highly speculative, balancing a strong likelihood of total loss against a small chance of huge returns. Yet it provides investors with the excitement of a creative adventure, a sense of artistic involvement, and a touch of the thrill of the theater that many investors find far more alluring than tax shelters or high price-earnings ratios.

Unusual Aspects

Over the years, the theater industry has developed traditional methods of doing business. The basic investment terms described below (see *Financing Methods* in this article) — some of which would be extraordinary in other contexts — have long been accepted by both producers and investors to be a fair allocation of risks and rewards. Similarly, the manner in which offerings are made reflects the peculiar nature of the theater industry. New York State, as the center of the American legitimate theater, has recognized the unique nature of these investments by enacting a special statute that governs only theatrical financings.

Broadway productions are by far the major source of investment opportunities in terms both of numbers of shows and of dollars raised. The financing principles involved apply to Off-Broadway presentations as well, although there are likely to be some differences in the terms of the underlying agreements with the playwright and other creative personnel. Most other productions, such as those of regional theaters, are presented on a nonprofit basis and do not seek investment capital. The discussion below deals principally with a Broadway theatrical production.

Initiating a production. A theatrical production usually begins when a producer (who may be one person or corporation, or several acting together) obtains

* Paul H. Epstein is a member of the firm of Proskauer Rose Goetz & Mendelsohn, New York; and Allan M. Shapiro is Associate Counsel, United Artists Corporation, New York.

an option for a license from the playwright to produce specified stage productions of the work. The license expires after the last performance by the last company under the license agreement (subject to a right to re-open the play within a short period). A license for Broadway customarily includes certain additional rights to produce the play on a national tour and in the West End of London (England's equivalent of Broadway).

Financing Methods

In nearly all cases, the option is exercised by presenting at least one paid public performance of the play. To finance that production, the producer seeks money from investors, who customarily become limited partners in a limited partnership of which the producer is the general partner.

An investor who has made a major financial contribution may receive credit as an associate producer, although this billing is given, in most cases, to persons who are limited partners and have no responsibility or rights with respect to the management of the partnership.

The Investment Vehicle

The traditional theatrical limited partnership. Traditionally, the entire financing of a theatrical limited partnership is contributed by the limited partners who receive, collectively, one-half of any partnership net profits, divided in proportion to their respective investments. However, this allocation may vary; the limited partners are sometimes allocated up to 60 percent of the net profits and, at other times, as little as 40 percent. The remaining net profits are divided among the general partners as a group.

Assuming that the limited partners receive the usual 50 percent aggregate share, an investor must provide 2 percent of the capital (entitling him to 2 percent of the limited partners' 50 percent share) in order to receive a one percent participation in total net profits. Each limited partner is liable for a share of partnership losses in proportion to, and up to the amount of, his respective capital contribution. Any partnership liabilities exceeding the limited partners' total contributions are the sole responsibility of the producer-general partner.

At times, the producer uses shares of net profits to compensate persons such as starring actors, directors, general managers, and important financial supporters. While third parties who participate in net profits because of financial support draw only from the general partner's share, creative or artistic participants are often paid off the top, that is, before allocation of the remaining net profits among the partners.

Definition of terms. Generally, the term "net profits" is defined for all limited partnership purposes to be the excess of the partnership's gross receipts over the total of its production expenses, running expenses, and other expenses. While gross receipts include essentially all partnership revenues, as common usage suggests, the other terms have more technical meanings. Production expenses include all costs incurred prior to the official opening of the show. Somewhat surprisingly, operating losses arising from preview or out-of-town try-out performances are also carried as production expenses. Conversely, all costs incurred after opening are carried as running expenses, even if related to capital assets of the production, such as replacement costumes for new performers. (Percentages of gross weekly box-office receipts paid to the playwright, composer, director, theater, and others are included in this category.) The term "other expenses" includes any further costs, such as prosecution and defense of lawsuits, that fit neither of the first two categories.

Distribution of partnership revenues. Capital contributions of the limited partners are returned out of partnership funds after (1) payment of or provision for partnership liabilities and obligations, including weekly running expenses, (2) repayment of any loans, and (3) creation of one or more cash reserves. Normally, the partnership agreement requires funding of a so-called sinking fund of a specified dollar amount before any distribution is made to the limited partners.

The remaining partnership revenues are then distributed among the partners as net profits. When the partnership terminates, any assets remaining after provision for all partnership debts and liabilities are distributed among the limited and general partners in proportion to their respective rights to participate in partnership revenues.

Additional payments to producer. In addition to a share of the net profits, the producer-general partner often receives a fee of a few percentage points of the gross weekly box-office receipts as compensation for services in maintaining the production, such as the handling of cast replacements and advertising. He may also receive a modest weekly cash office charge, commonly a fixed dollar amount, to help defray the overhead and administrative costs. These additional payments reflect the fact that under the usual limited partnership agreement, the producer-general partner is entirely responsible for managing the partnership. He may elect, for example, to abandon or close the production at any time or to arrange for additional companies. Because the limited partner can expect to have no voice in these matters after investing, the integrity and experience of the producer-general partner are investment criteria at least as important as the commercial potential of the script.

Other general partner rights. The limited partnership agreement often gives the producer-general partner the right to demand an involuntary overcall (additional investment) from the limited partners — in some instances, up to 20 percent of their initial investments. In addition, the producer-general partner customarily has the right (rarely, if ever, exercised) to recall any net profits distributed to partners and any capital contributions repaid to the limited partners, if those amounts are required to meet later obligations of the partnership. The producer-general partner may be given discretion to retain as reserves for any proper preproduction or production purposes money otherwise distributable to the partners. Such reserves are most often established to mount additional productions of the play, such as touring or British companies or, in the case of a non-Broadway production, to transfer to Broadway.

Partnership income and assets. The capital of the partnership is the amount contributed by the limited partners, including any involuntary overcall. Most capital contributions are made in cash or, in some cases, by irrevocable letter of credit. On occasion, a limited partner may invest by supplying items required for the production or by assuming liabilities that otherwise would have been borne by the partnership (such as theater deposits or performance bonds posted with unions).

If the production requires more financing, as sometimes happens, the producer-general partner may make or obtain loans or may secure additional limited partners who receive net profits solely from the general partner's share. This additional capital will have a right of repayment equal or superior to that of the original limited partners because, without this infusion of funds, the entire initial investment would be lost.

Basic source of income. The basic source of partnership income is the box-office receipts from one or more companies presenting the play. A successful Broadway production may finance additional companies with its New York profits or with an additional offering, or it may license the rights to another producer for a fee and royalty (the normal arrangement for a London production). The rights of the original limited partners to approve or participate in these further presentations vary according to the particular partnership agreement.

Subsidiary rights. The partnership also may earn income from the so-called subsidiary rights in the play — principally, the rights to produce motion picture and television versions, to license presentations by stock companies and amateur groups, and to record the original cast album of a musical. Less important subsidiary rights include radio versions; second-class touring performances; foreign language productions; condensed, tabloid, and concert tour versions; commercial uses; and grand opera rights. The revenues earned from the exploitation of these rights belong solely to the author, unless and until the partnership's production runs a qualifying number of performances. At that point, the production company generally becomes entitled to receive a share of the revenues the author derives from sales or licenses of those rights entered into during a specified period of time. This right of participation survives the closing of the partnership's production and may continue as a source of revenue — all of which is treated as normal partnership income — for an indefinite period. While this right can prove lucrative, it is likely to have significant value only when the production itself has been successful enough to create public interest in the play.

For most Broadway productions, the right of participation vests upon twenty-one performances in New York (including not more than ten days of previews) or sixty-four performances in and out of New York. Although Off-Broadway requirements are less uniform, the production's participation often begins on the twenty-first performance, including some limited number of previews.

For a Broadway production, the percentage of participation generally diminishes over time. Usually, with respect to contracts entered into during the first ten years from the close of the play, the limited partnership is entitled to receive 40 percent of the playwright's income; during the eleventh and twelfth years, 35 percent; during the thirteenth and fourteenth years, 30 percent; during the fifteenth and sixteenth years, 25 percent; during the seventeenth and eighteenth years, 20 percent; and ceasing thereafter. Again, Off-Broadway provisions are more variable. It is common to have an escalating schedule of participation from 10 to 40 percent, depending on the number of performances and, in any event, ceasing after the tenth year following the close of the play.

Except for any continuing participation in subsidiary rights income, the investment represented by the theatrical production has virtually no value after the end of performances. Because the author rarely grants more than a production license, the production company retains no ownership of the script. Most physical elements, such as sets, costumes and lights, if not rented, are likely to be so highly specialized in design that they have no residual value. Any goodwill or secondary meaning that has become attached to the production becomes worthless unless reflected in the value of the subsidiary rights.

Possibility of total loss. If the production fails totally, the limited partners receive, at best, the return of a small portion of their investment, representing unexpended capital reserves. More commonly, unrecoverable production costs exceed capital contributions, resulting in a total loss to the limited partners and additional losses borne by the producer-general partner. Even a production that enjoys a moderately long run may show little or no profit or may return only a portion of the investors' money. This paradox may result when royalty participants (such as the authors and director) waive or defer all or part of their weekly payments to avoid an operating loss when a production is close to its weekly break-even point. Under such conditions, a show may hover on the verge of operating profitability for more than a year.

Offering and sale. The offering and sale of limited partnership interests are made under whatever provisions of federal and state securities laws are deemed most appropriate to the size and scope of the financing. The offering period customarily expires at the same time as does the producer's option on the play. When contributions have been received for the full production budget (or, in some instances, a smaller alternative production budget), the limited partnership is assigned all of the producer's rights related to the show and begins to function as the production entity. Unless and until that occurs, all funds contributed by the proposed limited partners are held in escrow, to be refunded if the minimum capital is not raised. Preproduction expenses incurred by the producer-general partner are usually reimbursed as a charge against the production budget only at the time full capitalization is reached.

In some instances, an investor will authorize earlier use of all or part of his contribution. (Such funds may be needed to defray preproduction costs, such as theater deposits, advances to creative personnel, or, in some cases, actual rehearsal costs.) In this case, the investor either waives or reserves the right of refund if the financing fails. If his investment has been spent, the investor may be forced to look to the producer's personal assets to enforce a reserved right of refund.

Prior to a formal offering, an investor may advance preliminary funding, often termed "front money," to be used immediately by a producer to pay pre-production expenses, such as the cost of acquiring rights in the play, establishing a production budget, and preparing the offering documents. New York State law permits a producer to receive such investments from no more than four persons. These investors commonly receive up to one percent of the eventual partnership capitalization represented by the amount of their front money; if such an investment is converted to a limited partnership contribution, rather than repaid upon full capitalization, the front-money investor receives a separate proportionate participation as an ordinary limited partner.

An investor who provides front money or who permits his investment to be used prior to the full technical formation of the partnership may risk unlimited liability with respect to expenses incurred prior to the formation of the limited partnership and might be legally classified as a general partner of the partnership until all legal requirements for the formation of the limited partnership have been satisfied. It is possible that such an investor may be held fully liable to creditors, even beyond his investment in the partnership, for all debts incurred during that earlier period. However, such liability has rarely, if ever, been asserted.

An investor rarely has the right to withdraw from the production, even before the full production capital has been raised. Although he may be allowed to assign the right to receive partnership distributions, the investor may not have another party substituted as limited partner, except by operation of law or with the prior written consent of the general partner. Applicable federal and state securities laws often impose additional limitations on transfer of partnership interests. Accordingly, an investment in a theatrical production is nearly always an irrevocable commitment to its success or failure.

ATTRACTIVE FEATURES

Certainly, the chance to earn huge returns entices many investors. Some backers are attracted by the magnitude of the risk involved. For others, the principal appeal is not an economic one, but the intangible benefit of being associated, however indirectly, with the production of an artistic work. There is a group of investors who will help finance what they consider to be important theater, regardless of its commercial potential. Others choose to invest simply because of the opportunity the investment may provide to participate in the glamour and excitement of the traditional Broadway opening-night parties held by some producers, at which backers may meet the stars of the play and share the anxiety of waiting for the reviews.

It is probably fair to say that the majority of investors in theatrical syndications have two common characteristics: First, backing shows gives them a thrill that other investments do not and, second, they are fully prepared to lose whatever amount they invest.

POTENTIAL RISKS

Investing in a theatrical production is a highly speculative undertaking, the results of which cannot be predicted even by skilled and experienced producers. The fact that a major success can sometimes pay a large return on the investment offers many the possibility of sufficient reward to justify the risk. The potential investor for profit is likely to consider the number of performances given and awards won by other shows created by the people who created the production he has under consideration. These are relevant facts, but easily over-emphasized: A production may earn critical acclaim and run for months without accumulating profits and, in any case, prior success with other productions is an uncertain index of the commercial value of a subsequent production.

Ultimately, an investor must evaluate the worth of the play and its commercial appeal, as well as the quality of the production elements and the persons involved. The skill and integrity of the producer are critical considerations. Reviewing the profit and loss history of his previous productions will provide some indication of the producer's ability both to choose productions that will attract an audience and to manage them successfully. This information is contained in the offering circular required by the SEC and the Office of the New York State Attorney General.

Although there are no investment advisers in this field, there are various people connected with the theatrical business (such as general managers, publicists, and lawyers) who can give their opinions as to the chances for the success of a production. Although their artistic opinions probably will vary, these people can be helpful in investigating a producer's business reputation.

By tradition, virtually all theatrical investments are sold directly by producers. As a result, there are no dealers in theatrical syndication interests. Furthermore, because such participations are generally nontransferable without the permission of the general partner, no secondary market exists.

TAX CONSEQUENCES

Generally, theatrical productions are financed solely with equity capital. There is no debt — either recourse or nonrecourse — to leverage the investment.

Although losses incurred by theatrical partnerships are passed through to the investor, they do not generate net cash benefits to the investor. They merely serve to reduce his after-tax cost. In other words, a $100,000 loss will result in an actual out-of-pocket loss of $50,000 to a taxpayer in the 50 percent bracket. On the other hand, income from theatrical productions realized by investors in higher tax brackets will be ordinary income, subject to tax that, at current rates, may be as high as 50 percent. Accordingly, investments in theatrical productions should be viewed as high-risk venture capital transactions, not for any possible tax advantage.

Accounting for theatrical partnerships is made on the basis of the calendar year. Traditionally, production costs are capitalized and are recovered under the cost-recovery method. Under this method, no taxable income is reported until the net income from the operation of the production exceeds the production costs.

Section 280 of the Internal Revenue Code, enacted as part of the Tax Reform Act of 1976, has caused some theatrical accountants to recommend use of the income forecast method to recover production costs. Under this method, production costs must be capitalized and then deducted ratably over the anticipated income-producing life of the production. Thus, for a production that is expected to run longer than the end of its first accounting year, some income may be recognized for tax purposes even before production costs have been fully recovered.

It should be noted also that revenues that represent income taxable to a partner under either accounting method will remain taxable to that partner even if those revenues are held in partnership reserves, rather than distributed.

REPRESENTATIVE TYPES OF INVESTORS

Individual investors, whether attracted by economic or artistic concerns, remain the principal source of production financing. However, various corporate entities in the entertainment industry may be significant investors in certain productions. It has not been uncommon for a motion picture company to contribute a substantial sum towards capitalization of a production in exchange for the right to acquire the motion picture rights for a predetermined price. Because of the unknown value of the play, the predetermined price usually has been lower than the price of rights in a proven success.

Record companies also may invest in musical plays in exchange for the right to record the cast album. With the advent of new television technologies, such as cable television and the numerous satellite-fed pay-television networks, the need for television programming is becoming increasingly important and may generate similar investments by programming services or independent producers for television. The significance of such sources as potential investors is not yet clear.

IMPORTANT FACTORS IN BUYING AND SELLING

Pursuant to provisions of the New York State statute that regulates theatrical syndication financing (the Act), the Attorney General of the State of New York has jurisdiction over any offering of any theatrical syndication interests made in or from the State of New York. The law and the regulations promulgated thereunder by the Attorney General require an offeror to provide detailed disclosure in the form of an offering circular that sets forth all the essential elements of the proposed production and to distribute detailed accounting statements to the investors.

The Act is a unique statute that reflects the actual practices and requirements of the legitimate theater and facilitates investment in theatrical syndications by New York State residents. It provides a system of regulation for these special securities that is separate from the regulation of other securities. However, offerings to and purchases by residents of other states must satisfy their local securities laws as well, and no statute similar to the Act exists in any other jurisdiction. In some states, the laws are interpreted and applied in such a way as to make it impossible, as a practical matter, to offer or sell theatrical syndication interests. The costs and complexities of compliance with such laws — laws that have not been shaped specifically to accommodate the peculiar needs of the theater industry — tend to discourage producers from taking the steps necessary to enable residents of other states to participate in theatrical syndications, no matter how eager to participate such potential investors may be.

The SEC regulates all interstate offerings of securities, including the sale of interests in theatrical syndications. The offering documents for most public offerings must be reviewed by the SEC before they may be used. If, in a particular offering, the total investment sought is less than $1.5 million, the producer may file his documents in accordance with the SEC's Regulation A, which relieves the producer of many of the more detailed disclosure requirements of Form S-1. The New York regional office of the SEC is experienced in the area of investments in theatrical syndications and, in cooperation with the Office of the New York State Attorney General, has compiled a standard form of offering circular that may be used for the offering of limited partnership interests in theatrical syndications. A packet containing this information may be obtained from the New York State Attorney General's Office.

If the offering is to be private (pursuant to Section 4(2) of the Securities Act of 1933, as amended, or Regulation D promulgated thereunder), the SEC form of offering circular need not be followed and the filing of full-disclosure documents with the SEC is unnecessary. Nevertheless, the Act requires a filing with the New York State Attorney General even when an offering relies on Regulation D for a federal exemption; it exempts private offerings from state filing only if the offer is made to fewer than 36 offerees and the producer-general partner complies with a stringent procedure requiring him to file certain documents, including a specified form of signed waiver from each investor.

MONITORING THE PRODUCTION

Generally, the only certificate representing an investor's contribution to a theatrical partnership is a conformed copy of the partnership agreement signed by the general partner and listing the names and percentage interests of each of the limited partners. This document is usually sent to each limited partner after the production is fully financed.

The investor can expect to be advised of the current status of the production by circulars from the producer, as well as by monthly accounting statements once paid performances begin. The financial statements set forth total gross weekly box-office receipts and unrecouped production costs, as well as other relevant information. In addition, the Attorney General of the State of New York requires other accounting reports, both prior to the opening and after the closing of the production. All reports must comply with the Attorney General's regulations for disclosure and accuracy. The office also handles investors' complaints and will investigate suspected malfeasance.

GLOSSARY

front money— Preliminary funding from a small number of investors (under New York State law, not more than four) raised by a producer for a particular production prior to the formal offering and commonly used to pay preproduction expenses.

general partner— In a theatrical limited partnership, a partner (usually a producer) responsible for the management of the partnership and directly liable for its debts in excess of the capital invested by the limited partners.

limited partner— In a theatrical limited partnership, an investor who puts at risk a limited amount of production capital and receives with the other limited partners a share of partnership net profits in proportion to his investment.

net profits— The excess of gross receipts of a theatrical limited partnership over the total of its production expenses, running expenses, and other expenses.

New York Theatrical Financing Act— The New York statute which, together with the regulations promulgated thereunder, governs any offering of interests in a theatrical syndication financing made in or from the State of New York.

other expenses— Expenses incurred for a theatrical production that are not production or running expenses.

producer— An individual or entity who has or shares final executive responsibility for the management of a theatrical production, in many cases including those initially acquiring the production rights from the author and acting as principals in the financing of the production.

production expenses— Expenses incurred for a theatrical production prior to its official opening.

running expenses— Expenses incurred for a theatrical production following its official opening.

subsidiary rights— Rights in a dramatic work other than the license acquired by the production company to present professional stage performances, the most important of which are for motion picture and television productions, presentations by stock companies and amateur groups, and the original cast album of a musical.

theatrical limited partnership— A limited partnership formed for the purpose of financing and presenting a theatrical production on the live stage, used as the traditional financing structure by the theatrical community.

TRADE ORGANIZATIONS

The League of New York Theatres and Producers, Inc., New York, N.Y., is the leading trade organization for theatrical producers. This organization is very active in promoting the theater industry and supporting legislation favorable to the theatrical community.

LEADING PRODUCERS

Because of the large number of producers who are active at any time, any list of producers offered here would be necessarily incomplete. Moreover, even the most active producers have substantial periods between offerings.

The best approach is to contact a producer directly and to request the opportunity to consider participating in the financing of his next production. Although most producers would be receptive to such an inquiry, others prefer to allot participations to known investors who have a serious and continuing interest in their work. Furthermore, the acceptability of an investment from outside New York State will depend upon the offering program and whether the producer deems it desirable to comply with applicable local and state regulations. Active producers can be identified by looking at the credits for shows in performance, or by contacting the League of New York Theatres and Producers. Some producers advertise their offerings publicly in the Sunday "Arts and Leisure" section of the *New York Times* or in the *Wall Street Journal.*

SUGGESTED READING

The most complete source of information on current theatrical productions is the *Theatrical Index. Variety,* an entertainment trade publication that is published daily and weekly, contains useful news also. Sources of more general information include the entertainment pages of the *New York Times,* in particular the Sunday "Arts and Leisure" (second) section. For historical material, the annual volumes of *Theatre World* are invaluable.

U.S. Government Bonds, Notes, Agency Securities

*Bruce E. Paine**

BASIC CHARACTERISTICS

The term "government securities" covers a wide variety of different investment opportunities, each capable of meeting different objectives. However, government securities of all types have the following two characteristics in common:

- All government securities are issued directly by the U.S. government, either through the Treasury Department or through one of the many federal agencies created by various acts of Congress.
- All government securities are debt obligations under which institutions or individuals agree to lend the federal government or its agencies a certain sum of money at a specified rate of interest for a specified period of time. The federal government or its agencies, in return, agrees to make full repayment at the maturity date, and also agrees to pay the lender the predetermined rate of interest for the use of the money.

Every investor is at least partially aware of the extensive money-raising and financing activities of the federal government. Since U.S. government securities are backed by the full faith and credit of the United States, including the ability to tax, the securities carry the highest possible credit rating. These securities thus become the safest type of investment available for guaranteed payment of principal and interest. Also, publicly traded U.S. government securities are highly liquid because of the billions of dollars worth of short- and long-term Treasury securities bought and sold on a normal trading day. Finally, income from U.S. government securities is subject to federal income taxes, but exempt from state and local income taxes.

Market and Yield Differences

Many investors, while aware of these general advantages, are unaware of the market differences between the various issues of the U.S. government and its agencies, and of the different yields that may be available from different Treasury and agency issues. U.S. government securities tend to sell at a relatively higher

* Bruce E. Paine is a corporate Vice-President of Paine Webber Jackson & Curtis, Inc., New York, and Director of its Qualified Benefit Plans Department.

price and yield less than similar short- and long-term investments in two situations:

- During periods of investor concern about the credit safety of other fixed income security investments, investors buy U.S. government securities. As a result, the price of the other securities drops while the price of government securities rises, with a resulting decline in yield on the government securities. With the price differential between government and other securities wider than usual, certain investments in other sectors may offer attractive, higher-than-normal yields.
- In periods when corporations, municipalities, and federal agencies are raising large amounts of capital at the same time as the Treasury is conducting its own open market operations, prices on the corporate, municipal, and federal agency securities may weaken, thus requiring these groups to raise their yields relative to U.S. government obligations, in order to attract investors.

Federal Reserve Board offerings in the public market — open-market operations — are necessary to meet the maturing obligations and redemptions on the U.S. government's outstanding debt. The attraction of U.S. government securities to investors depends not only on safety and liquidity, but also on the relative returns on those issues compared to the returns on other prime-debt issues of corporations, municipalities, and the federal agencies.

The size of the anticipated and the actual budget surplus or deficit greatly influences government borrowing during a given year. If large deficits are anticipated, the Treasury will make heavy demands on the credit and capital market, thus causing interest rates to rise in many situations. The prudent handling of these open-market operations, combined with the Federal Reserve Board's ability to vary member banks' percentage reserve requirements and the interest rate charged to member banks who borrow money from the Federal Reserve System — the discount rate — greatly affects the level and direction of interest rates.

Structure of Federal Debt

The Conference Board, in its series "Cycles in Government Securities — Federal Debt and its Ownership," has analyzed the structure of federal debt by type of security and maturity, as well as the changing patterns of ownership of federal securities, as follows:

> Changes in the structure of the Federal debt by type of security and by maturity distribution reflects the results of the Treasury's management of the public debt. The debt-management problem of the Treasury actually has two stages. First and foremost, the Treasury has to aim for a reasonable distribution of the marketable debt among short, intermediate, and long-term maturities. Second, it has to select a particular strategy designed to retain this proper debt structure. . . .
>
> Any excessive shift of marketable U.S. Government securities toward the short end of the maturity spectrum would force the Treasury into the money-market at fre-

quent intervals for large-scale refunding. It would substantially increase the liquidity, and hence the danger of inflationary pressures in the economy. This situation places additional strains on monetary policy during periods of rapid economic expansion and inflation. The passage of time constantly shortens the maturity of all outstanding issues; therefore, the Treasury has to refund frequently into medium and long-term securities in order to maintain a reasonably balanced debt structure over a period of time. The Treasury, in its timing of the debt lengthening, has two major choices. It can attempt either to minimize the countercyclical impact of its operations or to minimize the interest burden. Because of the cyclical pattern of interest rates, these two basic objectives are likely to be irreconcilable most of the time: a compromise or choice becomes necessary.

TYPES OF U.S. TREASURY AND AGENCY OBLIGATIONS

U.S. Treasury Bills

Treasury bills (T-bills) are short-term obligations of the federal government. T-bills issued weekly are payable within three or six months; T-bills issued monthly are payable in one year. The price paid for T-bills varies from week to week, depending on such factors as prevailing interest rate and the price and yield of competing investment opportunities.

Treasury bills are in book-entry form only. This means the issue are bearer obligations, so whoever presents the maturing bills for payment is normally considered to be the owner. If T-bills change hands or ownership before maturity date, no record of the change of ownership is kept by the federal government.

Because of their extremely short life span, T-bills are marketed on a discounted basis. This means the bills are sold at a price below the face value of the bill, with the difference between the face value and purchase price representing the interest. Interest is considered ordinary income, not capital gain, subject to all federal taxes. However, the interest is exempt from state and local income taxes. (For further discussion, see article on U.S. Treasury bills, elsewhere in this volume.)

Treasury Notes and Bonds

The government borrows billions of dollars by selling notes and bonds. These are IOUs issued by the Treasury Department and backed by the full faith and credit of the U.S. government.

Treasury notes. Treasury notes have an issuance to maturity span of from two to ten years. Notes have the following characteristics:

- They are not discounted issues.
- They are sold at par, or close to par.
- They pay a fixed amount of interest every six months.

- They do not continue to earn interest after they mature.
- Interest rates paid are determined by the auction in which the securities are sold.
- Notes come in either bearer or registered form.

They are issued in denominations of $1,000, $5,000, $10,000, $100,000, and $1 million. Usually, notes with maturities of less than four years are issued in minimum denominations of $5,000, while notes of longer term are available in $1,000 minimum.

Treasury bonds. Treasury bonds are virtually identical to Treasury notes, except that Treasury bonds are issued for a minimum term of ten years. Treasury bonds are available in a wide range of maturities so that investors can make their selection on the basis of future cash needs. The minimum investment is $1,000, and the same denominations are available as for notes.

The yields of Treasury bonds on the open market change along with the yields of other competing bonds. In addition, they are more sensitive to price fluctuations than shorter-term maturities are. Treasury bonds are readily marketable.

Call provisions. A few outstanding Treasury bond issues have call provisions whereby the government may call the issue on any interest payment date during the five years prior to the maturity date. Treasury bonds are the only U.S. Treasury security that allows the government, under the provisions outlined at the time of issuance, to redeem the bonds before the scheduled maturity date.

Federal Agency Securities

Numerous agencies of the federal government also issue securities, some of which are guaranteed by the federal government and some of which are exempt from state and local income taxes. For those not guaranteed by the U.S. government, some form of backing, such as Treasury purchase of securities, is provided.

From time to time, Congress establishes a federal agency to provide credit from the public to certain critical economic sectors. While literally dozens of agency offerings are available, the agencies most commonly involved in the market are those agencies that promote America's agricultural and home-building industries. Some major examples follow:

- Federal Home Loan Bank System lends to the savings and loan associations as well as regulating them.
- Government National Mortgage Association (GNMA) provides money for the nation's mortgage market.
- Banks for Cooperatives make seasonal and term loans to farm cooperatives.
- Federal Farm Credit Bank issues bonds that provide short-term financing for producers of crops and livestock and gives mortgages on farm properties.
- Federal National Mortgage Association (FNMA) provides liquidity in the nation's mortgage market by purchasing mortgages from institutions.

The U.S. government also has interests in various international financial institutions, including the International Bank for Reconstruction and Development (World Bank) and the Export-Import Bank of the United States. These institutions periodically issue notes and bonds in the market. Because of the World Bank's substantial assets and its rights to call on subscribers for additional payments, the bank's bonds are considered high grade. Both principal and interest on issues of the Export-Import Bank are guaranteed fully by the U.S. government.

Federal agencies conduct their borrowing in the open market by issuing notes and bonds. Agency securities bear interest and are issued and redeemed at face value. Federal agencies do not use the auction technique for issuing their securities. Instead, after reviewing the then current market, they determine the best yield at which they can sell a new issue, place the yield and terms on the issue, and sell it through a syndicate of dealers assembled by the federal agency's fiscal agent in New York City. Some agencies also sell short-term discount paper similar to commercial paper. Sales are announced publicly by the agency in advance and are reported in newspaper financial pages.

Agency securities have less liquidity than Treasury securities. Furthermore, they are not backed explicitly by the full faith and credit of the U.S. government (although it is questionable whether the government would allow a default on these obligations). In addition, certain agency issues (e.g., GNMAs and FNMAs) are not exempt from state taxation. To compensate for these disadvantages, agency securities generally have yields somewhat higher than those available on direct Treasury obligations. Thus, they often represent an attractive investment opportunity for individual investors. The dealers who trade government obligations make secondary markets for many of the agency issues and trade them in the same way as they trade U.S. government issues.

See Table 1, pages 953-961, for a complete listing of federal agency and agency-related securities, and their channels of distribution.

Federal Home Loan Banks. The Federal Home Loan Banks (FHLBs) are among the most active agencies in the issuing of securities. Their purpose is to make loans to savings-related institutions, such as savings and loan associations, facing large deposit outflows. FHLB securities are not guaranteed by the U.S. government, but the Secretary of the Treasury may purchase substantial amounts of these securities. They are backed by guaranteed mortgages, cash, and U.S. government securities.

Securities issued by the FHLB include notes with maturities of under one year, discount notes with maturities of 30 to 270 days, and bonds with maturities of one to twenty years. Denominations are \$10,000, \$50,000, \$100,000, and \$1 million. The minimum purchase requirement is \$10,000 (\$100,000 for discount notes). Interest rates for newly purchased securities are posted to reflect current market conditions. Interest accrues on a 30-day month, 360-day year basis.

FHLB securities are subject to federal income taxes, but exempt from state and local income taxes.

Federal National Mortgage Association (FNMA). The FNMA, or Fannie Mae, is a federally chartered, shareholder-owned and privately managed corporation. It raises funds to purchase residential mortgages (mainly FHA, VA, or Farmers Home Administration) from savings and loan institutions, banks, and insurance companies to provide liquidity to the mortgage market in periods of tight credit. Issues are not guaranteed by the U.S. government, but agency obligations are supported by authority to borrow from the Treasury Department.

Fannie Mae securities include guaranteed mortgage pass-through certificates, secondary market notes and debentures, mortgage-backed bonds, capital debentures, and discount notes. The pass-through certificates are based on pools of mortgages originated by local lending institutions. Fannie Mae collects the principal and interest payments, and remits to investors. The Fannie Mae certificate is issued and guaranteed by FNMA. The secondary market notes and debentures are available in bearer form only, in denominations of $10,000, $25,000, $50,000, $100,000, and $500,000, with maturities from three to twenty-five years. Minimum purchase is $10,000. Most issues are noncallable. Although there are also mortgage-backed bonds secured by mortgages, there have been no recent issues, and existing issues are basically illiquid. The issues are in bearer and registered form with a $25,000 minimum purchase. Fannie Mae capital debentures have a $10,000 minimum purchase requirement. Certain issues are convertible to FNMA common stock, which is listed on the New York Stock Exchange. Discount notes have a minimum purchase requirement of $50,000, although they are issued in denominations ranging from $5,000 to $1,000,000. They have a maturity of thirty to 270 days, which can be tailored to the specific needs of the investor. Interest rates on discount notes are similar to, but above, those of T-bills. The interest on other FNMA securities is paid on a 30-day month, 360-day year basis. Fannie Maes are subject to federal, state, and local income taxes.

Other agency securities. The most active agencies include, along with those discussed above, the Federal Home Loan Mortgage Corporation (FHLMC) and the Government National Mortgage Association (GNMA). (For a discussion of Freddie Mac and Ginnie Mae securities, see article on Mortgage-Backed Securities, elsewhere in this volume.)

The Federal Reserve Bank of New York publishes a *Guide to the Securities of Federal Agencies, Government-Sponsored Corporations, and International Institutions,* which provides information on more than thirty agency securities. The *Guide* appears as Table 1 on pages 953-961 (it should be noted that the *Guide* was published before the issue of FNMA pass-throughs began in late 1981).

ATTRACTIVE FEATURES

Marketable government securities have unique strengths that make them highly attractive to investors.

Safety of Principal and Interest

Since government issues are backed by the credit of the U.S. government, which guarantees a full repayment of principal at maturity, government securities represent one of the best credit risks available. Certain federal agency obligations are not backed by the full faith and credit of the U.S. government, but in most of these situations other government agencies, such as the Treasury Department, are empowered to purchase substantial amounts of the securities and/or make loans to these agencies.

Yield

The yield on government securities is competitive with many other investment yields. Long-term government securities (maturing in fifteen or twenty years) often yield nearly as much as quality corporate obligations. Agency obligations may yield even more than other U.S. government securities.

Liquidity

Government securities offer liquidity in the event that they have to be sold before maturity. Government securities are traded actively in the secondary market, so willing buyers can usually be found promptly. Although holders of government securities are exposed to market risk on premature sale, as prices in the secondary market for such securities fluctuate with such factors as interest rate changes, government securities are less vulnerable to price fluctuations than other types of investments are.

Noncallable Issues

Most government securities are not subject to a call provision. This means that the owner is guaranteed a stated amount of interest or "yield" for the entire life of the security, without fear of premature redemption.

Flexibility

Government securities offer investors more flexibility than many other types of investment, with maturities that range from a few days to twenty or more years. This allows individual and corporate investors to manage their cash and investments effectively and to build a portfolio suited to anticipated cash needs.

SPECIAL REASONS TO BUY

There are several principal situations where an investment in government securities could be an attractive choice.

Cash Surplus. It is not uncommon for individuals or families, through sale of property or inheritance, to find themselves with excess cash and no clear idea of what to do with it. Purchase of government securities provides a relatively safe, interest-bearing, short-term solution until a longer range investment decision can be made. The use of government securities for a short period is also a device often used by corporations with temporary cash surpluses.

Provision for Major Expenditures. Government securities are useful in situations where an individual investor can anticipate a future expenditure, such as college tuition. In such a case, government securities can be selected to mature on or about the date that these expenses will be incurred. Thus the cash will be available when needed, but working while not needed.

Retirement planning. There are unlimited ways in which government securities and agency obligation, with their varying maturities and specific characteristics, can be used in retirement planning, both in the investment of the trust fund corpus on a temporary basis, or over a more extended period of time. (See articles on Retirement Income, elsewhere in this volume.)

POTENTIAL RISKS

Even though government securities are virtually free from the risk of the issuer failing to pay the principal in full at maturity, there are at least two potential risks in purchasing government securities:

- Since government securities are fixed commitments, during certain periods in an inflationary economy, they may not be as attractive as appreciation oriented investments.
- In a period of rising interest rates, a bond or note with a fixed interest rate may have to be traded at a discount in the secondary trading market prior to maturity. The amount of discount will normally be related to (1) the disparity between the interest rate stated on the obligation and the prime lending rate, and (2) the years remaining until maturity.

TAX CONSEQUENCES

The interest income from Treasury bonds, notes and most government agency bonds (except the mortgage pools under GNMA or FNMA) is subject to federal income taxes but exempt from state and local income taxes. (GNMA and FNMA obligations are subject to federal, state, and local income taxes.) Government security income is subject to federal and state estate and gift taxes except when "flower bonds" are used.

In judging an investment's yield attractiveness against that of a government security of comparable maturity on which no state and local taxes are due, the following formula should be used:

$$\text{Fully taxable security yield equivalent} = \frac{\text{U.S. government security yield}}{1 - \text{Marginal state plus local tax rate}}$$

Flower Bonds

Flower bonds are a type of bond frequently used in the settlement of estate taxes after death of an investor. The IRS appraises flower bonds at market value in computing the total value of the estate, but appraises them at their full face value for purposes of paying estate taxes. Specific government issues have been designated as flower bonds.

Flower bonds were all issued many years ago at an interest rate that is no longer competitive. As a result, the bonds sell at deep discounts well below par value. When they are used for settling an estate, the government will redeem them at full par value at any time before they mature, provided the money is used to pay federal estate taxes.

The investor must buy flower bonds in the secondary trading market. Quotations for such issues are quoted daily in the financial pages. To qualify for use as flower bonds, the bonds must be purchased by the beneficial owner prior to death; the bonds cannot be purchased and used in this manner after death has taken place.

Note: Prior to buying and using flower bonds, the investor should consult his or her tax attorney or accountant. Under changes in the 1976 Tax Reform Act and recent changes in the Economic Recovery Tax Act of 1981, the estate and gift tax picture has been substantially changed.

REPRESENTATIVE TYPES OF INVESTORS

The market for U.S. government obligations is the largest and most active securities market in the world. On an average trading day, between $6 billion and $10 billion in government securities are traded; $15 billion in trades for one day is not unusual.

Institutional and Governmental Investors

Historically, the chief participants in marketable government securities were commercial banks, state and local governments, savings institutions, insurance companies, and corporations. All of these organizations were governed by investment policies that tended to be cautious and conservative. On the other hand, whenever they moved in or out of the market, they usually traded large, multimillion-dollar blocks of securities.

Individual Investors

In recent years, individual investors have started to participate in the government securities market. Individual investors have found investment opportunities for as little as $1,000 that provide them with some extremely attractive features, including the ultimate in safety of principal; an investment return competitive with, and often better than, the current rate of interest for other investments; and an active market that provides liquidity if the investor has an unexpected need for cash. Today, individual investors own well in excess of $25 billion worth of marketable securities backed by the full faith and credit of the U.S. government.

IMPORTANT FACTORS IN BUYING AND SELLING

Government Securities

As with corporate obligations, government securities are available to the public as issued and in the secondary market.

New issues. Newly issued notes and bonds may be purchased directly through the Federal Reserve Bank or its branches without a fee, or through a commercial bank or securities dealer, which charges a nominal service fee.

New issues can be purchased as they are offered. The only Treasury note or bond offered regularly is a two-year note. The Treasury usually auctions this note monthly: An announcement is made in the middle of the month, and the offer the following week. Quarterly financings usually are announced toward the end of January, April, July, and October; they occur in the first week of February, May, August, and November. Securities offered at these times vary in maturity and denomination. Notes and bonds are also offered periodically as the Treasury raises new funds or redeems maturing issues. Announcements of these auctions appear in the financial sections of major newspapers. In addition, the Federal Reserve Bank of New York maintains a twenty-four-hour information number ((212) 791-7773) for information on scheduled auctions.

Investors who wish to purchase new notes or bonds at the Treasury's auction may submit tenders representing competitive or noncompetitive bids to the Federal Reserve Bank of New York between 9 A.M. and 3 P.M. every business day until the day before the auction and until 1:30 P.M. on the day of the auction (noncompetitive bids must be postmarked by midnight on the day before the auction). A commercial bank or brokerage firm can also submit the bid for the purchaser.

Competitive bid. If bidding is on a yield basis and the purchaser wants to specify the acceptable percentage yield, he submits a competitive bid to two decimal places. Following the auction, the coupon rate is set at the nearest one-eighth of one percent to the average yield of all accepted competitive tenders. The procedure usually produces an average price of par value or less. Investors who submit competitive bids run the risk of bidding a percentage yield below the average yield and, therefore, of paying more than necessary for the securities. Furthermore, if the bid is too high, it may be turned down.

Noncompetitive bid. Most individual investors submit a noncompetitive tender. No yield is specified in a noncompetitive bid. Instead, the investor agrees to accept the average yield and equivalent price determined by the accepted competitive tenders. Noncompetitive bidders normally do not risk rejection of their bid, although the Treasury reserves the right to accept or reject any tender.

Since notes or bonds are sold at the average price of accepted competitive bids, they may be sold at a discount or at a premium.

Occasionally, the Treasury sells additional amounts of the notes and bonds issued earlier at the original offering price and coupon rate with an adjustment made for accrued interest. Such offerings are announced by the Treasury the night of the auction, and can normally be found in the next day's financial section of a large newspaper.

The annual return on a note or bond is equal to the face value of the security times the coupon interest rate on the face of the certificate. The true rate of return, however, reflects the price actually paid for the security, if it is different from the face value.

Procedure for submitting tenders. Before the auction, a letter or tender form with payment must be submitted, specifying the securities desired. The letter or form must include a description of the securities; the face amount desired; whether the investor wants bearer or registered securities (an application for registered securities should include name, Social Security number, and address for interest checks); and delivery instructions (whether securities should be mailed or will be picked up). Payment in full for bonds and notes must accompany the tender.

Tenders should be sent to Government Bond Division, Federal Reserve Bank of New York, New York, N.Y. It is advisable to indicate "Tender for Treasury Notes or Bonds" on the envelope. Payment is acceptable in U.S. currency, a certified personal check, a cashier's check from a bank, or federal funds. (Endorsed checks will not be accepted and U.S. funds only are acceptable.) Treasury securities maturing on or before the issue date of the new notes and bonds are also acceptable. If the note or bond sells at a discount, the difference between the face amount and the discounted price will be mailed to the investor on the issue date, if the amount involved is more than one dollar.

Buyers must specify delivery instructions in the tender or letter. Purchasers of bearer securities taking delivery by mail usually will receive the securities by registered mail within ten days after the delivery date announced by the Treasury. The Treasury pays the postage. Registered securities are normally processed for delivery within four weeks of the issue date. Because of the processing time involved for registered securities, purchasers are urged to take mail delivery.

It should be noted that securities cannot be left at the Federal Reserve Bank. Unclaimed securities will be mailed.

Secondary market. Almost all trading in the secondary market for government securities is done on the over-the-counter market. This market is composed of numerous commercial banks and non-bank dealers who trade with the public and with each other. The primary dealers are the only firms allowed to trade directly with the Federal Reserve Bank when it is acting for the Federal Open Market Committee. Other large banks and brokerage firms that are not primary dealers are also active market makers in government securities.

On transactions over $100,000, no service charge is normally made, but on trades of less than $100,000 a service charge may be made. Broker compensation is derived from markup on the transaction.

Round-lot transactions in government securities normally settle on the next business day following the trade date. Odd-lot transactions usually settle in five business days. Cash trades — same-day settlement — can often be arranged for government securities through banks and brokerage firms.

Quoting government securities. Treasury notes, bonds, and agencies' securities are quoted as a percentage of par value with fractional prices in multiples of 1/32. For example, a bond quoted in the newspaper at 100.20 (100 plus 20/32) is selling at $1006.25. The yield is expressed to the issue's maturity; the current rate of return may be found by dividing the coupon rate by the price. Quotations appear daily in the *Wall Street Journal* and other publications. Bid and asked prices are normally given for round lots. In comparison, T-bills are quoted at a discount rate of return in basis points from par. (See also article on Mortgage-Backed Securities, elsewhere in this volume.)

Agency Securities

Offerings of some federal agencies are no longer available as new issues, but most agency securities are actively traded in the secondary markets.

New issues. Agency issues are offered to investors in three different ways:

Fiscal agent. A fiscal agent is an individual employed on a full-time basis by the agency to monitor developments in the money and capital markets, and to recommend a total size, coupon, and maturity for upcoming agency offerings. The fiscal agent assembles the selling group of banks and securities dealers who distribute the initial offering to the public. The fiscal agent places an offering notice in newspapers about one week before the offering. Investors who wish to buy the issue contact members of the selling group. On the offering date, the selling group members receive the specific offering terms and coupon rate for the security; each selling group member indicates the total amount of its subscription. If the issue is over-subscribed, the fiscal agent allocates the issue among the selling group either on a pro rata basis or based on past performance of the members.

Underwriting syndicate. A syndicate of dealer banks and broker-dealers is formed, headed by one or more managers who organize the selling group and make allocations. The specific terms of the issue may be negotiated in advance of the offering, or the terms may be arrived at on the offering date through a competitive bid between two or more syndicates. Several government agencies offer their short-term discount notes through a permanent group of dealer firms that also maintains the secondary trading market in the notes.

Auction. The auction of agency securities is done directly through the agency (or, in some instances, the Federal Reserve System). Bids are submitted for a specified amount of the issue; the agency selects the highest bids (lowest interest rates). Many agency securities are issued, registered, exchanged, and redeemed at the Federal Reserve Bank of New York. Settlement is normally in federal funds.

Secondary market. The majority of secondary market trading in agency securities is done in the same dealer over-the-counter market as that in which U.S. government securities are traded. Larger agency issues are usually more easily traded in the secondary market than smaller agency issues. The quotation spreads between the bid and asked price are usually wider on all maturities of agency securities than on government securities because government securities are normally more actively traded and therefore more marketable.

REGISTRATION AND CUSTODIAL CARE

Government notes and bonds are available in two forms: registered and bearer.

Registered Notes and Bonds

Registered note and bond certificates bear the owner's name, which is recorded on the Treasury's books. They cannot be sold without the owner's written assignment on the back of the certificate. In addition, a commercial bank, savings bank, savings and loan association, or trust company officer must certify the signature on the assignment and stamp the certificate with the institution's corporate seal or a savings bank validating stamp. This same certification process may also be accomplished through a registered securities broker-dealer.

Interest payments on registered securities are made semiannually, usually by mailing a check to the registered security-holder's listed address. Registration may facilitate safekeeping, but can be bothersome when the security is sold, since it may take a substantial amount of time to re-register the securities. The registration must express the actual ownership. It may not impose any restriction on the owner's authority to dispose of the securities in any manner acceptable under Treasury regulations. Each registration must include a taxpayer identification or social security number in addition to the complete mailing address, including ZIP code.

Examples of registration. Some typical examples of registered note or bond ownership follow.

(1) *One person:*

John A. Doe (123-45-7889).

Mary C. Doe (123-45-6789).

The name of an individual may be preceded by an applicable title, such as Rev., Mrs., Ms., or Dr., or followed by a designation such as M.D., or Jr. In addition, a married woman's given name, rather than the name of her husband, must be used.

(2) *Two or more individuals:*

Mr. John A. Doe (123-45-7889) or Mrs. Mary C. Doe or the survivor, as tenants in common.

Dr. John A. Doe (123-45-7889) or Mrs. Mary C. Doe, Joint Tenants with right of survivorship.

(3) *Minors:*

John R. Jones as natural guardian of Henry M. Jones, a minor (145-00-000).

John R. Jones as custodian for Mary Jones, a minor (123-00-000), under the New York Uniform Gift to Minors Act.

(4) *Trusts:*

John R. Jones, Trustee for benefit of Mary Jones (123-00-000), under Trust dated 1/01/1900.

Any Town Trust Company, Trustee for benefit of Mary Jones (123-45-000) under Retirement Plan dated 1/30/1980.

Treasury notes and bonds may not be registered solely in the name of a minor or individual name of the beneficiary of a trust or other such entity. However, the Social Security number or taxpayer identification of the minor or trust must be indicated on the registration. Information about acceptable registration is available from any bank, trust company, or securities broker-dealer, or from the Federal Reserve Bank, Registration Section, Government Bond Division, New York, N.Y. If the holder of a registered security has not received the semiannual interest check, or wishes to change the mailing address for receiving interest checks, he or she should write to: Bureau of the Public Debt, Department A, Washington, D.C.

Bearer Notes and Bonds

The certificates for bearer notes and bonds do not show the owner's name. These certificates are fully negotiable; whoever possesses them is presumed to be the rightful owner and can sell, transfer, or redeem them at maturity.

Bearer securities have interest coupons attached. These coupons must be detached as they become due and presented at a savings bank, commercial bank, or the Federal Reserve Bank to obtain the semiannual interest payment.

Since bearer bonds are not registered or identified by owner, they must be safeguarded as carefully as cash. Although this form of ownership may require more attention because of the safekeeping considerations, it is the preferable form when the security is to change hands.

Custody and Safekeeping

Bonds, stocks, and certificates always should be stored in a safe place, such as a bank safe-deposit box. Customers of brokerage firms receive custodial services for government securities, usually through major commercial banks.

ALTERNATIVE GOVERNMENT AGENCY INVESTMENTS

The Mutual Fund Alternative

Some persons want to invest in government securities but are either unwilling or unable to forecast interest rate swings or worry about minimum denominations and the details of submitting tenders to the Federal Reserve on time for the Treasury security auctions. Certain mutual funds invest exclusively in the debt instruments of the Treasury and various U.S. government agencies. Funds that invest in government securities permit the investor to own a diversified, professionally managed portfolio of Treasuries and agencies by making an initial investment from $100 to $1,000, depending on the specific fund (a securities brokerage firm can supply a list of these and other funds).

Advantages. Funds such as these are useful to the small investor interested in convenience and diversification.

Disadvantages. First, new purchases of the fund, other than a no-load fund may be subject to a mutual funds sales charge. Second, the investor may not agree with the mix of short-term, long-term, Treasury, and federal agency securities in the fund's portfolio. Finally, if the fund invests a large portion of its assets in long-term securities and interest rates rise, fund shareholders may incur a loss on their investments when they withdraw from the fund.

Futures Contracts

Money market futures contracts were first introduced in 1979. Under these contracts, markets have been created in T-bills, T-notes, and T-bonds for future delivery. The initial futures contract was for three-month T-bills. The basic contract was for $1 million of ninety-day T-bills with quarterly contract maturities. Today there are numerous T-bill futures contracts, which have been particularly useful as a hedge for investors in money market instruments and firms that will be borrowing or lending short-term in the future. The hedging allows the holder to reduce interest rate risk by taking an equal and offsetting position in futures. Also, investors can switch risk from rate level speculation to speculation on spread variation. The area is highly sophisticated, but most brokerage firms with commodity operations are able to advise interested potential clients.

GNMA options and futures contracts are particularly attractive to people connected with the housing, construction, and financing industries. The options also appeal to all investors affected by interest rate fluctuations.

Treasury bond futures are also a useful device to hedge anticipated cash inflow or, in periods of increasing interest rates, to hedge a long position in corporate or government bonds. (See articles on Futures — Financial, and Options — Puts and Calls, elsewhere in this volume.)

GLOSSARY

basis— Number of days in coupon period.

basis price— Price in terms of yield to maturity or annual rate of return.

book value— Value at which debt security is carried on holder's records.

callable security— An issue that may be redeemed before the maturity date according to the terms indicated in the offering.

competitive bid— Bid tendered in Treasury auction by an investor for a specific amount of securities at a specific yield or price.

coupon bond— An issue in bearer form with interest coupons attached. The coupons are clipped as they become due and presented by the holder for payment.

coupon period— Time for which interest rate is paid on bond or note (usually six months).

dealer— An individual or firm in the securities business acting as a principal rather than as an agent. Typically, a dealer buys for his or her own account and sells to his or her customers from inventory. In government securities, certain dealers are specifically recognized by the Federal Reserve Bank. (For list of dealers, see article on U.S. Treasury Bills, elsewhere in this volume.)

discount bond— A bond or note selling below par.

discount securities— Money market instruments issued at a discount and redeemed at maturity for full face value. No other interest is paid.

distribution— Sale at retail of new issues received by dealers from Treasury after auction.

dollar price— Percentage of face value at which a bond is quoted.

dutch auction— Technique used in Treasury auctions by which the lowest price necessary to sell the entire offering becomes the price at which the entire issue is sold.

exempt securities— Securities exempt from registration under the Securities Act of 1933 and the margin requirements of the Securities Exchange Act of 1934. Government and agencies securities are exempt securities.

federal financing bank— A federal institution that makes loans to various credit agencies of funds borrowed from the Federal Reserve Bank.

federal funds— Immediately available funds covered by member deposits with the Federal Reserve Bank.

FHLB— Federal Home Loan Bank — a government agency that regulates and lends to savings and loan associations.

FNMA— Federal National Mortgage Association, a government-affiliated agency; referred to as Fannie Mae.

Freddie Mac— Federal Home Loan Mortgage Corporation or its securities.

flower bonds— Government bonds acceptable at par in payment of estate taxes, provided they are owned by deceased prior to the time of death.

GNMA— Government National Mortgage Association or its securities; referred to as Ginnie Mae.

go-around— Procedure whereby the Federal Reserve Bank solicits bids or offers from its primary dealers to buy or sell securities.

governments— Negotiable U.S. Treasury securities.

hedge— Taking a futures position either equal to or opposite of underlying securities.

investment banker— Firm engaging in origination, underwriting, and distribution of new issues.

market maker— Dealer who quotes and takes positions at the risk of the market in a particular security or group of securities.

mortgage bond— Bond secured by a lien on specific property of the issuer.

negotiated sale— Sale in which terms of offering are determined by discussion between issuer and underwriter.

noncompetitive bid— Bidding for a specific amount of securities at whatever price becomes the average of the accepted competitive bids; used in Treasury auctions.

offer— Price asked by securities seller.

par— Price of 100 percent.

premium— The amount by which an issue exceeds its par value when traded.

principal— Face amount or par value of a debt security.

refunding— Redemption of securities with funds raised through the sale of a new issue.

re-investment rate— Rate at which funds from a maturity or sale can be re-invested.

repurchase agreement— Agreement whereby a holder of securities sells them to an investor with an agreement to repurchase them at a fixed rate on a specific date.

rollover— Re-investment of funds received from a maturing security in a new issue of the same or similar security.

Treasury bill (T-bill)— Discounted note issued for three months, six months, or a year and redeemed at par on maturity.

Treasury bond— U.S. government obligation with maturity over ten years.

Treasury note— U.S. government obligation with maturity up to ten years.

TABLE 1. Guide to the Securities of Federal Agencies, Government-Sponsored Corporations, and International Institutions

In general, these securities are issued under the authority of an act of Congress. Some are backed by the full faith and credit of the United States or by the issuing agency's right to borrow from the Treasury. Some of the issuers lack any formal government backing. Many of the issuing agencies are privately owned; others are wholly governmental.

To facilitate the public sale of their securities, many of these agencies have contracts with a fiscal agent in New York City. When a new offering is to be made, the agent assembles a nationwide selling group of securities dealers and dealer commercial banks, which accepts investor subscriptions on the terms established by the agent. These sales also are announced publicly by the agency and agent in advance and are reported in the newspapers.

For information concerning these securities, individuals should contact the sources listed in the information column. Other sources are dealer commercial banks or securities brokers. Outstanding agency securities may be bought or sold in the open market at any time depending on availability.

Agency or Institution	*Information*	*Distributors*	*Guaranteed*[1]	*Services Provided by Federal Reserve Banks (FRBs)*
ASIAN DEVELOPMENT BANK • Bonds & notes $1,000 minimum Registered[2]	Federal Reserve Bank of New York (FRBNY) Treasury & Agency Issues Division 33 Liberty Street New York, NY 10045 (212) 791-5364	Securities dealers and dealer commercial banks (new and outstanding issues).	No	Only FRBNY issues registered securities, makes interest payments, and redeems.
DISTRICT OF COLUMBIA ARMORY BOARD (D.C. STADIUM) Bonds $1,000 minimum Bearer[3]	District of Columbia Armory Board 2001 East Capital Street Washington, D.C. 20003 (202) 543-6465	Securities dealers and dealer commercial banks (outstanding issues only; new issues no longer being offered).	Yes	Any FRB or Branch can pay coupons and redeem.

(*Table continues*)

TABLE 1. Guide to the Securities of Federal Agencies, Government-Sponsored Corporations, and International Institutions — *Cont'd*

Agency or Institution	*Information*	*Distributors*	*Guaranteed*[1]	*Services Provided by Federal Reserve Banks (FRBs)*
EXPORT-IMPORT BANK OF THE UNITED STATES • Participation certificates and debentures $5,000 minimum Registered,[2] bearer,[3] and book entry[4]	Export-Import Bank of the United States 811 Vermont Ave., N.W. Washington, D.C. 20571 (202) 382-2152	Securities dealers and dealer commercial banks (outstanding issues only, new issues no longer being offered).	Yes	Only FRBNY issues registered securities, FRB of N.Y., Chic., and San Fran. issue and exchange bearer securities. Any FRB or Branch can redeem and pay coupons for bearer securities, and pay final interest and principal for registered securities. Book entry issue, interest, and principal payments handled by any FRB and some Branches.
FARMERS HOME ADMINISTRATION • Bonds $25,000 minimum Registered[2]	Farmers Home Administration 1520 Market Street St. Louis, MO 63103 (314) 425-4406	Securities dealers and dealer commercial banks (outstanding issues only, new issues no longer being offered).	Yes	None
• Insurance contracts No Registered[2]	Federal Reserve Bank of New York (FRBNY) Treasury & Agency Issues Division 33 Liberty Street New York, N.Y. 10045 (212) 791-5364	Securities dealers and dealer commercial banks (outstanding issues only, new issues no longer being offered).	Yes	Only FRBNY issues and transfers registered securities. Pays final interest and principal at maturity.

• Certificates of beneficial ownership $25,000 minimum Registered,[2] bearer,[3] and book entry[4]	Federal Reserve Bank of New York (FRBNY) 33 Liberty Street New York, N.Y. 10045 (212) 791-5364	Securities dealers and dealer commercial banks (outstanding issues only, new issues no longer being offered).	Yes	Only FRBNY issues registered securities. Any FRB or Branch can redeem and pay coupons for bearer securities, and make final interest and principal payments for registered securities. Book entry issue, interest, and principal payments handled by any FRB and some Branches.
FEDERAL FARM CREDIT CONSOLIDATED SYSTEM WIDE SECURITIES • Consolidated Systemwide Bonds $5,000 minimum if original is less than 13 months, Book entry[4] $1,000 minimum if original maturity is 13 months or or more, Book entry[4]	Aubrey K. Johnson, Fiscal Agent 90 William St. New York, N.Y. 10038 (212) 943-2300	Securities dealers and dealer commercial banks (new and outstanding issues).	No	Book entry issue, interest, and principal payments handled by any FRB and some branches.
• Consolidated Systemwide Notes $50,000 minimum Bearer[3]	Aubrey K. Johnson, Fiscal Agent 90 William St. New York, N.Y. 10038 (212) 943-2300	Securities dealers and dealer commercial banks (new and outstanding issues).	No	Any FRB or branch can redeem and pay coupons for bearer securities.

(*Table continues*)

TABLE 1. Guide to the Securities of Federal Agencies, Government-Sponsored Corporations, and International Institutions — *Cont'd*

Agency or Institution	*Information*	*Distributors*	*Guaranteed*[1]	*Services Provided by Federal Reserve Banks (FRBs)*
FEDERAL HOME LOAN BANKS • Bonds and notes $10,000 minimum Book entry[4]	Federal Home Loan Banks Office of Finance 1700 G Street, N.W. Washington, D.C. 20552 (202) 377-6319	Securities dealers and dealer commercial banks (new and outstanding issues).	No	Book entry issue, interest and principal payments made by any FRB and some branches. Coupon payments and redemption of bearer securities by any FRB or branch.
• Discount notes $100,000 minimum Bearer[3]	Federal Home Loan Banks Office of Finance 1700 G Street, N.W. Washington, D.C. 20552 (202) 377-6319	Securities dealers and dealer commercial banks (new and outstanding issues).	No	Only FRBNY issues and redeems.
FEDERAL HOME LOAN MORTGAGE CORPORATION • Mortgage backed bonds $25,000 minimum Registered[2]	Federal Home Loan Mortgage Corporation 1700 G Street, N.W. Washington, D.C. 20006 (202) 789-4700	Securities dealer and dealer commercial banks (outstanding issues only, new issues no longer being offered).	Yes	Only FRBNY issues registered securities. Any FRB or Branch can redeem and pay final interest and principal on registered securities.
• Guaranteed mortgage certificates (GMC) $100,000 minimum Registered[2]	Federal Home Loan Mortgage Corporation 1700 G Street, N.W. Washington, D.C. 20006 (202) 789-4700	Securities dealers and dealer commercial banks (new and outstanding issues).	No	Only FRBNY issues registered securities and pays interest and principal.
• Mortgage participation certificates	Federal Home Loan Mortgage Corporation	Securities dealers and dealer commercial banks (new and	No	None

$100,000 minimum Registered[2]	1700 G Street, N.W. Washington, D.C. 20006 (202) 789-4700	outstanding issues).		
FEDERAL HOUSING ADMINISTRATION • Debentures $50 minimum Registered[2]	Federal Housing Admin. 26 Federal Plaza New York, NY 10007 (212) 264-8503	Securities dealers and dealer commercial banks (new and outstanding issues).	Yes	Any FRB or Branch can pay final interest and principal at maturity.
FEDERAL NATIONAL MORTGAGE ASSOCIATION (FNMA) • Mortgage backed bonds $25,000 minimum Registered,[2] bearer,[3] and book entry[4] •	John Meehan, Acting Fiscal Agent 100 Wall Street Suite 1000 New York, N.Y. 10005 (212) 425-5740	Securities dealers and dealer commercial banks (new and outstanding issues).	Yes	Only FRBNY issues registered and bearer securities. Any FRB or Branch can redeem and make coupon payments on bearer securities, and pay final interest and principal on registered securities. Book entry issue, interest, and principal payments handled by any FRB and some Branches.
• Capital debentures $10,000 minimum Registered[2] and bearer.[3] New issues book entry[4] only as of 1/78	John Meehan, Acting Fiscal Agent 100 Wall Street Suite 1000 New York, N.Y. 10005 (212) 425-5740	Securities dealers and dealer commercial banks (new and outstanding issues).	No	Only FRBNY issues registered and bearer securities. Any FRB or Branch can redeem, make coupon payments and pay final interest and principal for registered securities.
• Secondary-market debentures $10,000 minimum Bearer[3] and book entry.[4] New issues book entry only as of 1/78	John Meehan, Acting Fiscal Agent 100 Wall Street Suite 1000 New York, N.Y. 10005 (212) 425-5740	Securities dealers and dealer commercial banks (new and outstanding issues).	No	Only FRBNY exchanges bearer securities but any FRB or Branch can pay coupons and redeem. Book entry issue, interest, and principal payments handled by any FRB and some Branches.

(Table continues)

TABLE 1. Guide to the Securities of Federal Agencies, Government-Sponsored Corporations, and International Institutions — *Cont'd*

Agency or Institution	*Information*	*Distributors*	*Guaranteed*[1]	*Services Provided by Federal Reserve Banks (FRBs)*
Discount notes $50,000 minimum Bearer[7]	John Meehan, Acting Fiscal Agent 100 Wall Street Suite 1000 New York, N.Y. 10005 (212) 425-5740	Securities dealers and dealer commercial banks (outstanding issues only, new issues no longer being offered).	No	Only FRBNY issues and redeems bearer securities.
GOVERNMENT NATIONAL MORTGAGE ASSOCIATION (GNMA) • Participation certificates $5,000 minimum[6] Registered[2] and bearer[3]	Government National Mortgage Association 451 Seventh St., S.W. Washington, D.C. 20410 (202) 755-5534	Securities dealers and dealer commercial banks (outstanding issues only, new issues no longer being offered).	Yes	Only FRBNY issues registered securities. FRB of N.Y. Chic., and San Fran. issue and exchange bearer securities. Any FRB or Branch can pay coupons and redeem bearer securities and pay final interest and principal on registered securities.
• Mortgage backed securities (pass-through securities) $25,000 minimum Registered[2]	Government National Mortgage Association 451 Seventh St., N.W. Washington, D.C. 20410 (202) 755-5534	Securities dealers and dealer commercial banks (new and outstanding issues).	Yes	None
INTERAMERICAN DEVELOPMENT BANK • Bonds $1,000 minimum	Federal Reserve Bank of New York (FRBNY) Treasury & Agency Issues Division	Securities dealers and dealer commercial banks (new and outstanding issues).	No	Only FRBNY issues, exchanges, transfers, and pays coupons, registered interest, and principal.

Registered[2] and bearer[3]	33 Liberty Street New York, N.Y. 10045 (212) 791-5364			
• Notes $1,000 minimum Registered[2]	Federal Reserve Bank of New York (FRBNY) Treasury & Agency Issues Division 33 Liberty Street New York, N.Y. 10045 (212) 791-5364	Securities dealers and dealer commercial banks (new and outstanding issues).	No	Only FRBNY issues registered securities and pays final interest and principal.
INTERNATIONAL BANK FOR RECONSTRUCTION AND DEVELOPMENT (WORLD BANK) • Bonds and notes $1,000 minimum Registered[2] and bearer[3]	Miss Audrey Lane, Manager Suite 1559 120 Broadway New York, N.Y. 10005 (212) 964-6100 or Federal Reserve Bank of New York (FRBNY) Treasury & Agency Issues Division 33 Liberty Street New York, N.Y. 10045 (212) 791-5364	Securities dealers and dealer commercial banks (new and outstanding issues).	No	Only FRBNY issues registered and bearer securities, transfers and pays coupons, final interest, and principal.
MARITIME ADMINISTRATION • Bonds and notes. No established minimum Bearer[3]	Maritime Administration Office of Ship Financing Guarantees, Rm. 4096 14th & E Streets, N.W. Washington, D.C. 20230 (202) 377-3773	Securities dealers and dealer commercial banks (new and outstanding issues).	Yes	None

(*Table continues*)

TABLE 1. Guide to the Securities of Federal Agencies, Government-Sponsored Corporations, and International Institutions — *Cont'd*

Agency or Institution	*Information*	*Distributors*	*Guaranteed*[1]	*Services Provided by Federal Reserve Banks (FRBs)*
SMALL BUSINESS ADMINISTRATION • Guaranty agreements $10,000 minimum Registered[2]	Small Business Admin. 1441 L Street, N.W. Washington, D.C. 20416 (202) 653-6672	Securities dealers and dealer commercial banks (new and outstanding issues).	Yes	Only FRBNY issues registered securities, pays final interest and principal.
TENNESSEE VALLEY AUTHORITY (TVA) • Debentures $1,000 minimum Registered[2] and bearer[3]	Tennessee Valley Authority Financial Planning Power Building Chattanooga, Tenn. 37401 (615) 755-2813	Securities dealers and dealer commercial banks (outstanding issues only).	No	None
TRUSTEE OF THE PENN CENTRAL TRANSPORTATION COMPANY • Trustee certificates $10,000 minimum Registered[2]	Penn Central Corp. IVB Building 1700 Market Street (215) 972-3000	Securities dealers and dealer commercial banks (new and outstanding issues).	Yes	None
UNITED STATES POSTAL SERVICE • Bonds $10,000 minimum Registered,[2] bearer,[3] and book entry[4]	U.S. Postal Service 475 L'Enfant Plaza, S.W. Washington, D.C. 20260 (202) 245-4878	Securities dealers and dealer commercial banks (new and outstanding issues).	No	Only FRBNY issues registered and bearer securities. Any FRB or Branch can make coupon payments and redeem bearer securities and pay final interest and principal on registered securities. Book entry issue, interest, and principal payments handled by any FRB and some Branches.

WASHINGTON METROPOLITAN AREA TRANSIT AUTHORITY • Bonds $5,000 minimum Registered[2] and bearer[3]	Washington Metropolitan Area Transit Authority 950 South L'Enfant Plaza, S.W. Washington, D.C. 20024 (202) 637-1234	Securities dealers and dealer commercial banks (new and outstanding issues).	Yes	Only FRBNY issues registered and bearer securities. Any FRB or Branch can make coupon payments, redeem bearer securities, and pay final interest and principal on registered securities.

[1] "Yes" means principal and interest fully guaranteed by federal government.

[2] Owner's name is inscribed on the security. Transfer of ownership or redemption must be done through a commercial bank. Periodic interest checks are mailed directly to the owner. Unless otherwise specified, final interest together with principal (face value of the security) are paid at maturity when the security is presented for redemption.

[3] Owner's name does not appear on the security. Possession is all that is needed for transfer of ownership or redemption. Unless otherwise indicated, bearer securities are issued with dated coupons attached. Owner must clip the coupons and submit them on or after each date for payment of interest at a commercial bank or Federal Reserve Bank or Branch as specified.

[4] A record of the issue is maintained on the books of a Federal Reserve Bank or the U.S. Treasury and no physical securities are issued.

[5] Because all new securities are short-term, they are not issued with coupons attached. Any FRB or Branch can redeem the bonds at their maturity and pay the interest at the same time.

[6] Until 12/1/65, minimum denomination was $10,000. From 4/4/66 until 8/12/68, minimum denomination was $5,000. New issues are no longer being offered.

[7] Notes are not issued with coupons attached. They are purchased at less than face value and redeemed at face value at maturity. Your return is the difference between the purchase price and the face value of the note paid at maturity or the price you receive for them if you sell them before maturity. Effective 3/1/79, interest-bearing discount notes are available without coupons. See footnote 5.

SOURCE: Federal Reserve Bank of New York

SUGGESTED READING

Periodicals

Federal Reserve Bulletin. Published by Board of Governors of the Federal Reserve System. Monthly through several districts (New York, Cleveland, and St. Louis Federal Reserve District reports are particularly useful).

Notice of coming offerings is published in the *Wall Street Journal* and other newspapers, and most Federal Reserve Banks and branches have recorded telephone messages giving the schedule. Mail-order forms and instructions are available from any Federal Reserve Bank or branch.

Each of the twelve District Offices of the Federal Reserve can provide free or relatively inexpensive materials describing monetary and fiscal policy formulation, basics on government securities, listings of agency obligations, and other information available through such sources as the annual report of the Federal Reserve districts.

Commercial banks and securities dealers publish regular surveys of the economy and fixed income markets, specific investment ideas, and handbooks, glossaries, and investment kits.

Treasury Bulletin. Published by United States Treasury Department. Monthly.

Reference Books

Darst, David M. *The Complete Bond Book.* New York: McGraw Hill, 1975.

Federal Reserve Bank of New York. *The Treasury and the Money Market.* New York, 1980.

Federal Reserve Bank of New York, Public Information Department. *Federal Reserve Operation in the Money and Government Securities Markets.* New York, 1980.

Federal Reserve Bank of Richmond. *Instruments of the Money Market.* Richmond, 1977.

First Boston Corporation. *Handbook of Securities of the United States Government and Agencies.* New York, 1980.

Levine, Sumner N. *Investment Managers Handbook.* New York: Dow Jones-Irwin, 1980.

Levy, Michael E. *Cycles in Government Securities — Federal Debt and its Ownership.* New York: The Conference Board, 1962.

Paine Webber Jackson & Curtis, Inc. *The Individual Investor's Guide to Government Securities.* New York, 1981.

———. *Q's & A's About GNMA's.* New York, 1981.

Roosa, Robert V. *Federal Reserve Operation in the Money and Government Securities Markets.* New York: Federal Reserve Bank of New York, 1956.

Stigum, Marcia, and Mann, John. *Money Market Calculations: Yields, Break Evens and Arbitrage.* New York: Dow Jones-Irwin, 1981.

Van Horne, James C. *Financial Market Rates and Flows.* New York: Prentice-Hall, 1978.

U.S. Treasury Bills

Jeffrey R. Leeds *

BASIC CHARACTERISTICS

General Description

United States Treasury bills are direct obligations of the United States and, along with U.S. Treasury notes and bonds, comprise the marketable debt of the U.S. government. Bills are issued on a regular schedule with original maturities of three, six, and twelve months, in minimum amounts of $10,000 and multiples of $5,000 above the minimum. In contrast, Treasury notes and bonds have original maturities in excess of one year, and often are sold in minimum denominations of $1,000 or $5,000.

Primary Issuance

Bills are issued regularly by the U.S. Treasury at public auctions. Three-month and six-month bills are auctioned weekly on Mondays. (If a holiday falls on a Monday, the auction is held the previous Friday.) The bills are actually issued, and payment collected, on the following Thursday. Twelve-month bills, called "year bills," are auctioned every four weeks, usually on Wednesdays, with settlement on the Thursday of the following week. All bill auctions are announced nearly a week in advance.

Participation in the auctions takes two forms. Small investors (buying up to $500,000 of bills) may submit a noncompetitive tender. In so doing, the investor agrees to pay the average price determined at the auction and is assured of receiving the entire amount applied for. Alternatively, the investor may submit a competitive tender. In this instance, the investor indicates the amount he or she is willing to purchase at a given price and yield. Depending on the other tenders submitted, the investor may be awarded all, part, or none of the securities bid for.

The auction works as follows: The Treasury announces the bill auction, indicating the date of the auction and the total par amount of securities to be sold. Between the announcement and 1:30 P.M. (Eastern time) on the auction date, competitive and noncompetitive tenders are accepted at the U.S. Treasury and at all Federal Reserve Banks and their branches. After the auction is closed, the total of noncompetitive tenders is subtracted from the size of the issue. The remainder is allocated to the competitive tenders, beginning with the highest price (lowest yield) bid, until the entire amount is sold. The average of the prices

* Jeffrey R. Leeds is a Vice-President of Chemical Bank, New York.

actually paid is then computed, and the noncompetitive tenders are awarded in full at that price. On the day following the auction a summary of the results is published in the financial sections of most newspapers, indicating the volume of tenders received, the high, low, and average prices accepted, the amount of noncompetitive tenders awarded at the average, and the corresponding yields.

Physical Treasury bill securities are no longer issued. Record of ownership is maintained on a book-entry system, with the investor receiving a statement of account rather than a certificate.

Secondary Market

An active secondary market for Treasury bills is part of the overall market for U.S. government securities. It is an over-the-counter market conducted by telephone. Participants include commercial banks, investment banking and brokerage firms, and a small number of specialized government securities trading firms. The nucleus of the market is a group of thirty-six dealers recognized by the Federal Reserve Bank of New York. (See *Thirty-Six Dealers Recognized by the Federal Reserve Bank of New York* in this article.) Smaller banks and brokerage firms have relationships with one or more of these recognized dealers, and small institutional or individual investors may contact any of these firms to obtain quotes or initiate a transaction. Closing quotations for all outstanding Treasury bills — identified by the date of maturity — are found in the financial sections of most newspapers.

Return on Treasury Bills

Treasury bills are discount instruments — that is, while par value is returned at maturity, the purchase price will be less than par by the amount of the discount. The interest or return on the investment, therefore, is equal to the discount and is received at maturity. In contrast, most other money market investments are issued near par and par plus interest is paid at maturity. In the case of Treasury notes and bonds, as well as other fixed income securities with original maturity beyond one year, interest is paid on a regular schedule, usually semiannually, and par value is returned at maturity.

Pricing. The price of a Treasury bill, either at original issue or in the secondary market, is quoted in terms of the annualized discount rate. This annualized discount rate must then be converted to a dollar amount that is paid for the security. The formula for computing the actual price paid for a Treasury bill is as follows:

$$\text{Price} = \text{par} \times \left(1 - \frac{\text{discount rate}}{100} \times \frac{\text{number of days to maturity}}{360}\right)$$

For example, if \$100,000 worth of three-month Treasury bills were to be purchased, either at auction or in the secondary market at a rate of 14.50 percent, the price paid would be computed by evaluating the formula, which comes to $96,334.73.

$$\$96{,}334.73 = \$100{,}000 \times \left(\frac{1 - 14.5\%}{100} \times \frac{91}{360} \right)$$

True rate of return on Treasury bills. Although bills in the secondary market and at auctions are quoted in terms of the annualized discount rate, or discount, the true rate of return, or the yield on the investment, is higher. This is because less than par value is actually invested, and the discount is actually earned on that smaller amount. Thus, to determine the true investment yield of a Treasury bill, the following formula must be evaluated:

$$\text{True Yield} = \frac{\text{Par} - \text{Price}}{\text{Price}} \times \frac{365 \text{ (or 366)}}{\text{days to maturity}}$$

Using the example above, the true yield of a three-month Treasury bill quoted at 14.50 percent discount comes to 15.26 percent.

$$0.1526 = \left(\frac{\$100{,}000 - \$96{,}334.73}{\$96{,}334.73} \times \frac{365}{91} \right)$$

ATTRACTIVE FEATURES

Investment in U.S. Treasury bills offers a number of advantages.

Safety of Principal

Safety from default. Since Treasury bills are the direct obligation of the U.S. Treasury, they are backed by the full faith and credit of the U.S. government. Under no circumstances will par value fail to be returned at maturity.

Safety from market risk. Although Treasury bills are safe from default, changes in interest rates can result in losses of principal. For example, if after purchasing the 14.50 percent bills described above, the discount rate on the three-month bill rose to 14.75 percent, the price, according to the formula, would be $96,271.53. Thus, a capital loss of $63.20 ($96,334.73 – $96,271.53) would be incurred. However, if the investor has a specific investment horizon, use of Treasury bills allows this capital or interest rate risk to be avoided. The frequency with which three-month and six-month bills are issued, and their availability in the secondary market, ensures obtaining a bill that will have a maturity near the investor's investment horizon. By holding the bill to maturity, one can avoid the risk to capital inherent in volatile interest rates. (See *Market Volatility* in this article.)

Liquidity

In terms of average trading volumes, the market in U.S. government securities is the largest securities market in the world. During 1981, an average of $25.0 billion worth of government securities changed hands each day. By comparison, average daily trading volume on the New York Stock Exchange amounted to only $1.5 billion per day. The largest and most active sector of the Treasury securities market is in bills that, in 1981, traded $14.9 billion daily. Typically, trades of $5 million to $10 million can be effected without impact on overall prices, and a round lot is normally considered to be $1 million.

Scale of Investment

Despite the huge size of the bill market, and the round-lot size of $1 million, Treasury bills can be obtained in denominations that are quite small compared to other money market instruments. Bills can be purchased in minimum amounts of $10,000, and in increments of $5,000 above the minimum. In contrast, commercial paper is available in denominations no smaller than $25,000, and the minimum investment in bank-negotiable certificates of deposit is $100,000.

POTENTIAL RISKS

Market Volatility

The recent history of financial markets in general, and short-term markets in particular, has been one of pronounced volatility of yields and prices. As outlined above, changes in short-term interest rates can have a profound effect on the price at which an investment in Treasury bills can be liquidated. Evaluating the formula presented in *Pricing* above, each increase of 25 basis points (hundredths of one percent) results in a price decline, or capital loss, of $63.20 per $100,000 of three-month Treasury bills. For a six-month bill, the increase in the discount costs $126.00. As can be seen, the longer the maturity, the greater the price risk for a given rate change.

During 1980, the average weekly change in the three-month bill discount rate (irrespective of direction of change) was 55 basis points, while for six-month bills it was 48 basis points. Thus, the average weekly price change experienced by investors in three-month and six-month Treasury bills was $139.00 and $222.44, respectively, per $100,000 invested. Of course, if the investor holds the bills to maturity, no capital loss will be incurred. Since Treasury bills with a wide range of specific maturities are available at all times, the possibility of capital loss arises only when liquidation is forced unexpectedly or when the investment horizon and the bill maturity are intentionally mismatched (as described below).

Underperforming Issues

From time to time, certain Treasury bills will tend to underperform the market, by falling in price more than, or rising in price less than bills with similar maturities. This may occur due to technical changes in the relative supply and demand for particular bills. For example, certain bills are eligible for delivery in satisfaction of futures contracts on the International Monetary Market. Alternatively, the Treasury periodically issues cash management bills to assist it in its debt management. These cash management bills may have the same maturity as the regular bills, and thus would add to the floating supply and depress the price relative to other bills. Technical changes in supply and demand of specific bills are not always easy to predict in advance. As a consequence, the holders of the affected bills, if forced to liquidate, may suffer a greater loss of value than if they had owned a very similar bill.

Illiquidity of Specific Issues

Although the Treasury bill market is the most liquid of securities markets because a price can nearly always be found for a significant-sized transaction, a particular bill may only be salable at a discount to the values of other similar issues. Typically, the most actively traded bills are the most recently issued; as bills get older, the frequency of secondary-market trading wanes. Thus, to buy or sell one of the less active issues may require considerable effort on the part of the investor and/or the dealer, and may necessitate paying a somewhat higher purchase price or accepting a lower selling price.

As can be seen, all of the potential market risks cited here involve selling a Treasury bill prior to its maturity. Held to maturity, the U.S. Treasury bill is the closest thing in the world to a risk-free investment.

TAX CONSEQUENCES

Tax treatment of Treasury bill returns is completely straightforward. The return on these discount instruments is the difference between the price paid for the bill and the price received either at maturity or when sold. In either case, the return is considered ordinary income and is taxed as such. Similarly, if yields rise and a Treasury bill is sold at a price below its purchase price, the loss is considered an ordinary income loss, and can offset only ordinary income, not capital gains. The income is considered earned in the period in which the Treasury bills are disposed of.

Income earned on Treasury bills is subject to federal income taxes, as well as federal and state estate and gift taxes. It is not subject to state and local income taxes.

REPRESENTATIVE TYPES OF INVESTORS

The safety and liquidity of U.S. Treasury bills makes them attractive for a wide variety of investors. Table 1 below presents the results of a survey conducted by the Treasury and indicates the wide variety of investors participating in the bill market.

IMPORTANT FACTORS IN BUYING AND SELLING

Buying and selling Treasury bills varies widely in the market, depending on the size of the transaction, the particular investor involved, and the purpose of the purchase or sale. In general, transactions can be divided into two general categories: direct from the Treasury via the regular auction, or from recognized dealers in Treasury securities.

Purchase at Auction

Direct participation in Treasury bill auctions typically is limited to very large, sophisticated investors and to very small, individual investors. For the former, the auction is the ultimate source of the newest and, at least initially, most actively traded Treasury bills. By submitting competitive tenders, the large investor can determine precisely the quantity of bills he or she wishes to own at a particular yield and price. Although the investor is not certain of receiving bills at that particular price, if the bills are sold at those prices, he or she will get them.

The small, individual investor, by submitting a noncompetitive tender, can be assured of receiving his or her required bills at a fair price (the average of the auction determined by professional bidding) without any transactions costs. Moreover, by indicating on the tender, or by filling out a form, the investor can automatically replace maturing bills with the new bills issued on the same day.

A tender can be submitted either by completing a tender form available at

TABLE 1. Ownership of Treasury Bills as of April 30, 1981

	($ Billions)
Commercial banks	9.5
Thrift institutions	1.0
Insurance companies	0.7
Corporations	1.9
State and local governments	5.2
All others	164.3
Total	182.5

SOURCE: U.S. Treasury, *Survey of Ownership*

any Federal Reserve Bank or branch or by letter, delivered in person or by mail to the nearest Federal Reserve Bank or branch or the U.S. Treasury. The letter should include the face amount of bills desired, the maturity (three, six, or twelve months), whether the tender is competitive or noncompetitive (and, if competitive, the price), whether or not re-investment is desired, and the tenderer's name, address, and Social Security and business telephone numbers. Payment in U.S. currency, certified personal check or cashier's check payable to the Federal Reserve Bank, or Treasury securities maturing on or before the issue date must accompany the tender form or the letter. Payment is made in the full face amount.

When the discount is determined at the auction, a check is sent to the tenderer in the amount of the discount. Unless re-investment is specified, the U.S. Treasury automatically will issue and send a check for the face amount at maturity. Change in the re-investment specifications or mailing address can be made up to twenty days prior to maturity by submitting Form PD4633-2, which will be sent after the tender is received and processed.

Transactions With a Dealer

Clearly, participation in an auction limits the investor to the specific maturities being issued and, of course, it is impossible to sell Treasury bills at a Treasury auction. Additionally, it may be simpler to buy through a dealer than to fill out and submit a tender directly to the Treasury.

The market in Treasury securities is organized around a nucleus of primary dealers recognized by the Federal Reserve Bank of New York, which has general oversight responsibility for the market. These dealers report their transactions to the Federal Reserve Bank of New York and most of them are cleared to make transactions with the Federal Reserve's Open Market Account. (See *Thirty-Six Dealers Recognized by the Reserve Bank of New York* in this article.) In addition to this nucleus of primary dealers, most banks and brokerage firms will conduct transactions in government securities for their customers.

The type of interaction with a dealer or dealers will depend on the size and frequency of the investor's transactions. Small volume and infrequent contacts will be handled as odd lots, bought on the bid side and sold at the offered side. Additionally, a transaction fee may be charged. Some dealers may waive or lower the transaction fee for regular customers. For example, large depositors may find lower transaction costs at their bank. In any case, it probably pays to shop around if transactions tend to be frequent.

Large purchases and sales are treated quite differently. Recognized dealers and many other banks and brokerage firms will make markets (provide bids and offerings) and stand ready to buy or sell at those prices. As indicated above, those quotations are made in terms of an annualized discount, and the spread between bids and offerings is from 2 to 4 basis points. For a three-month bill, a four basis point spread between the bid and offer side amounts to $10.11 per $100,000 of bills. On a six-month bill, the spread amounts to $20.22 per $100,000. At any time, different dealers may provide slightly different markets depending on their own circumstances and perceptions of supply and demand. Thus, large and frequent investors may have relationships with several dealers from which they will choose the most attractive price for a particular transaction. In addition to making markets on existing issues, dealers can and will submit either competitive or noncompetitive tenders on behalf of their customers.

GLOSSARY

average price— The average auction price among competitive bids received and accepted.

basis point— A pricing unit equivalent to 1/100 of one percent. Thus, a discount of 30 basis points is three-tenths of one percent.

competitive tender— The investor's bid to purchase at a certain price and yield, without assurance of receiving all or part of the securities bid for.

discount— The amount by which par value is decreased in determining purchase price of the bill.

governments— The full range of negotiable U.S. Treasury securities.

noncompetitive tender— The investor's agreement to pay the average auction price for a Treasury bill, with assurance of receiving the entire amount applied for.

par— Face value of a bill.

primary dealers— Banks and brokerage firms, recognized by the Federal Reserve Bank of New York, that make a secondary market in Treasury securities.

secondary market— Over-the-counter market conducted by telephone for Treasury bills.

true rate of return— The true investment yield determined by applying the discount to the actual purchase price of the security.

THIRTY-SIX DEALERS RECOGNIZED BY THE FEDERAL RESERVE BANK OF NEW YORK

ACLI Government Securities, Inc., Chicago, Ill.

A.G. Becker Inc., New York, N.Y.

Aubrey G. Lanston & Co., Inc., New York, N.Y.

Bache Halsey Stuart Shields Inc., New York, N.Y.

Bank of America N.T. & S.A., San Francisco, Cal.

Bankers Trust Co., New York, N.Y.

Bear Stearns & Co., New York, N.Y.

Briggs Schaedle & Co., Inc., New York, N.Y.

Carroll McEntee & McGinley Inc., New York, N.Y.

Chase Manhattan Bank, N.A., New York, N.Y.

Chemical Bank, New York, N.Y.

Citibank, N.A., New York, N.Y.

Continental Illinois National Bank and Trust Co. of Chicago, Chicago, Ill.

Crocker National Bank, San Francisco, Cal.

Dean Witter Reynolds Inc., New York, N.Y.

Discount Corporation of New York, New York, N.Y.

Donaldson, Lufkin & Jenrette Securities Corp., New York, N.Y.

Drexel Burnham Lambert Government Securities, Inc., New York, N.Y.

First Boston Corp., New York, N.Y.

First Interstate Bank of California, Los Angeles, Cal.

The First National Bank of Chicago, Chicago, Ill.

Goldman Sachs & Co., New York, N.Y.

Harris Trust and Savings Bank, New York, N.Y.

E.F. Hutton & Co., Inc., New York, N.Y.

Kidder Peabody & Co., Inc., New York, N.Y.

Lehman Government Securities Inc., New York, N.Y.

Merrill Lynch Government Securities Inc., New York, N.Y.

Morgan Guaranty Trust Co. of New York, New York, N.Y.

Morgan Stanley & Co., Inc., New York, N.Y.

New York Hanseatic Division, The Securities Groups, New York, N.Y.

The Northern Trust Co., Chicago, Ill.

Paine, Webber Jackson & Curtis Inc., New York, N.Y.

Wm. E. Pollock & Co., Inc., New York, N.Y.

Refco Partners, New York, N.Y.

Salomon Brothers Inc., New York, N.Y.

Smith Barney Harris Upham & Co., Inc., New York, N.Y.

SUGGESTED READING

Periodicals

Federal Reserve Bulletin. Published by the Board of Governors of the Federal Reserve System. Monthly; provides statistics and articles covering money and financial markets.

Treasury Bulletin. Published by the U.S. Treasury Department. Monthly; provides details of Treasury debt outstanding and the official results of all Treasury auctions. Primarily statistical.

Reference Books

Federal Reserve Bank of Richmond. *Instruments of the Money Market.* Richmond, 1977.

First Boston Corporation. *Handbook of Securities of the United States Government and Federal Agencies.* New York, 1980.

Harris Bank. *The U.S. Government Securities Market.* Chicago, 1976.

Stigum, Marcia (in collaboration with John Mann). *Money Market Calculations: Yields, Break-Evens and Arbitrage.* Homewood: Dow Jones-Irwin, 1978.

———. *The Money Market: Myth, Reality and Practice.* Homewood: Dow-Jones Irwin, 1978.

Historical Returns on Principal Types of Investments

*Roger G. Ibbotson, Rex A. Sinquefield, and Laurence B. Siegel**

INTRODUCTION

The twentieth century has seen a remarkable variety of world events — events that have affected capital markets as well as other institutions. The Great Depression, for example, was associated with an 84 percent decline in the value of common stocks, while the long growth era of 1948-1965 showed a thirteenfold gain in the value of stocks with dividends re-invested. Dramatic events have occurred in other markets. In the 1970s, bond markets fell sharply in the face of rising interest and inflation rates while holders of real estate equity found themselves suddenly wealthy. Collectibles and metals also were in vogue and enjoyed high returns in the 1970s; and short-term money market instruments, after underperforming inflation for years, emerged as winners in 1981.

These short- and intermediate-term ups and downs of the various capital markets are interesting to the observer and exciting to the investor. They are, however, only part of the long-term picture. Given a long enough period of study, one can discern the capital market's enduring relationships that are masked by the noise of short-period data.

Perhaps the easiest relationship to observe is that between return and risk. Investors are risk-averse, which means that given two assets that have the same expected return, all other things being equal, investors will buy the less risky one. A corollary of this observation is that investors expect higher returns for taking risk. Although there is no guarantee that these expectations will be realized, the set of common stocks called the Standard & Poor's 500 (the S&P 500; the S&P 90 before March, 1957) outperformed riskless U.S. Treasury bills by an average margin of 5.9 percentage points per year in the period 1926-1981. This extra return (called a "risk premium") may be interpreted as the price paid to investors for bearing the risk of stock ownership.

Scope of Study and Assumptions

This article presents the historical returns on a broad range of assets for long

* Roger G. Ibbotson is Senior Lecturer in Finance and Executive Director of the Center for Research in Security Prices, Graduate School of Business, the University of Chicago; Rex A. Sinquefield is Executive Vice-President and Chief Investment Officer of Dimensional Fund Advisers, Inc., Chicago; and Laurence B. Siegel is Research Division Manager, R.G. Ibbotson & Co., Chicago.

periods of time. For S&P stocks, U.S. government bonds and bills, and inflation, the writers studied 1926-1981. They examined corporate bonds in the United States for 1926-1978, with some aggregate data for 1926-1981. Non-S&P stocks, which include both listed and unlisted issues, were studied for the period 1947-1978; summary data are presented for real estate from this same period. International stocks were studied for 1960-1979 and international bonds for 1975-1980. Also presented is some of the work of writers who examined other asset returns for other time periods.

For most asset categories, the relationship between return and risk is shown by displaying the standard deviation of returns as well as the mean return. Standard deviation is a statistical measure of the volatility of returns. The standard deviation is calculated such that, for a normal or bell-shaped distribution, two-thirds of the observations (returns) fall within (plus or minus) one standard deviation of the mean and 95 percent fall within two standard deviations of the mean. For example, in Table 1 on page 989, the standard deviation of New York Stock Exchange (NYSE) returns is given as 17.73 percent, and the arithmetic mean return, 11.56 percent. These numbers indicate that two-thirds of the outcomes were within 17.73 percentage points (plus or minus) of 11.56 percent, and 95 percent were within two standard deviations (35.46 percentage points) of 11.56 percent. While the standard deviation of returns is not a flawless measure of risk, it is a useful estimate. During most historical periods, higher standard deviations have been associated with higher returns. (See article on Portfolio Management, elsewhere in this volume, for a more detailed discussion of standard deviation.)

In this analysis, the historical risk-return relationship is not used to forecast the future. Such forecasts, however, have been made for stocks and bonds with considerable success. The underlying assumption of these forecasts is that the return paid to investors for taking risk is relatively constant over time and can be deduced from historical results, while the return paid to investors as compensation for inflation varies with the inflation rate. In addition, investors receive a real riskless rate of interest that has varied considerably over short periods but that has averaged zero over the long term. The sum of the inflation return, the real riskless rate of interest, and rate of return compensation for the risk of that asset is the expected return for the asset. An example of the use of this method of forecasting is found in *Stocks, Bonds, Bills, and Inflation.*[1]

There are other factors that influence the return on an investment in equilibrium. These include marketability, taxation, and management costs. Risk itself occurs across different dimensions: economy or beta risk, inflation or interest rate risk, residual or diversifiable risk, and other possible risks. The various assets that are discussed in this article are priced by the market according to the desirability of all their attributes. Thus, expected returns on a wide variety of assets are not determined solely by risk characteristics.

---

[1] Ibbotson, Roger G., and Sinquefield, Rex A. *Stocks, Bonds, Bills, and Inflation: The Past and the Future.* 1982 edition. Charlottesville: Financial Analysts Research Foundation, 1982.

The aggregate market value of an asset category is another characteristic of interest to investors. Investors may want to study aggregate value out of general curiosity or because they want to hold assets in the approximate proportions in which they exist in the market. For example, U.S. government bonds have been falling as a percentage of total investment assets for thirty years. This is surprising in view of the growth of government in that period, but it reflects the great growth of the stock and real estate markets. Summary data on aggregate market values are presented here to highlight trends such as this one.

RETURNS ON A BROAD SPECTRUM OF U.S. ASSETS

Ibbotson and Fall [2] studied the returns on stocks, bonds, and real estate for the period 1947-1978, a thirty-two year period. Figure 1 on page 975 shows the growth (with re-investment of income) of one dollar invested in each of these assets on December 31, 1946. Clearly, common stocks were the big winner over the period, with the dollar growing to $23.30 by the end of 1978. Real estate, which grew to $12.22, was second (although most investors bought levered real estate and had returns even higher than those of the stock market). Fixed income securities — government, municipal, and corporate bonds and preferred stocks — were disappointing performers, all net losers relative to inflation over the period.

The writers formed a market wealth portfolio of the assets shown in Figure 1, consisting of each of the assets represented in proportion to their aggregate market value for each year. The return on the market wealth portfolio is graphed along with the other assets in Figure 1 (market). The aggregate value of each asset category as a percentage of the total for all of the assets is graphed year-by-year in Figure 2 on page 976. From this graph one can see that real estate is the largest component of the market. Common stock increased its proportion of the market over most of the period while the fixed corporate security component (corporate bonds plus preferred stocks) was reduced. The municipal bond component rose during the early part of the period, before leveling off in more recent times. The U.S. government debt has dropped in terms of relative wealth almost throughout the period.

Table 1 on page 989 presents the geometric mean (compound) and arithmetic mean annual return of the components of the market wealth portfolio, along with the standard deviations of returns. This table breaks the broad categories into some of their component parts. One sees that over-the-counter stocks had the best performance of any asset subcategory, with an annual compound return of 12.63 percent. Farmland was a close second, 11.69 percent, with residential housing somewhat lower at 6.88 percent. (Coincidentally, 6.88 percent was also the compound annual return on the whole market wealth portfolio.) Both real estate

---

[2] Ibbotson, Roger G., and Fall, Carol L. "The United States Market Wealth Portfolio." *Journal of Portfolio Management,* Fall 1979, pages 82-92.

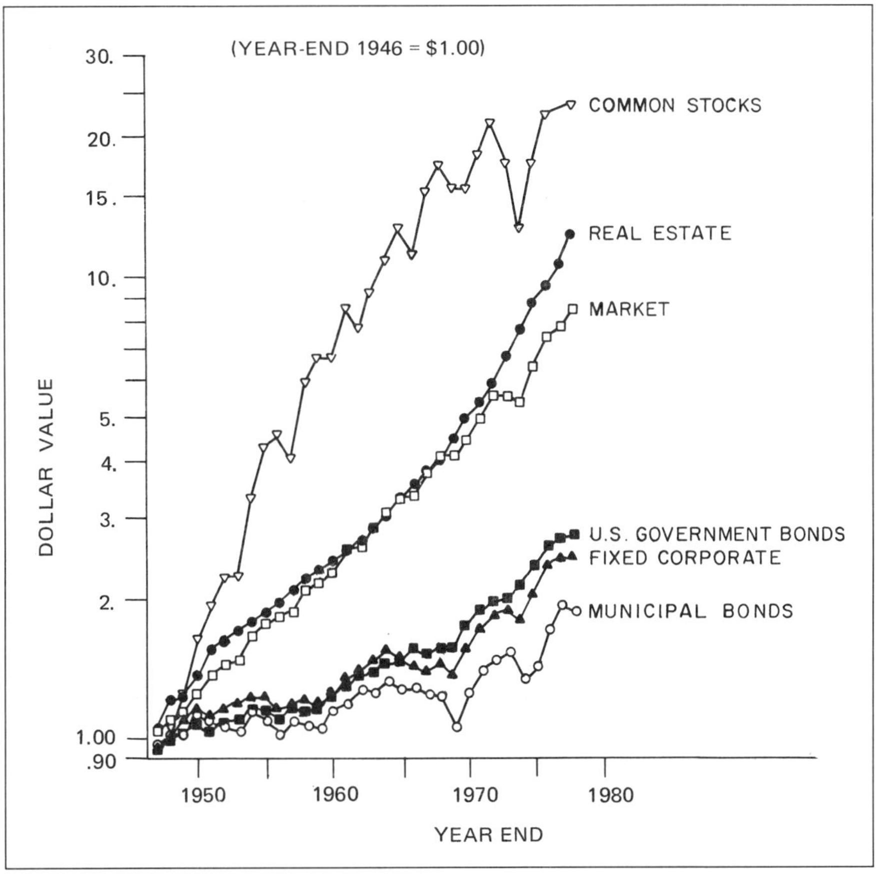

FIG. 1. Cumulative Wealth Indices of Capital Market Security Groups

SOURCE: Ibbotson, Roger G., and Fall, Carol L., "The United States Market Wealth Portfolio." *The Journal of Portfolio Management,* Fall 1979, page 84.

components had relatively low standard deviations of returns, so one might suppose that these assets had high returns and low risk. But real estate price series are often produced using a method that artificially smooths price changes. Thus, while one is justified in concluding that real estate was a very good performer in 1947-1978, one cannot conclude that these particular standard deviations are evidence of low risk in real estate investments.

Real estate has characteristics that distinguish it from stocks and bonds. Real estate, directly held, may not only be hard to sell, but requires management effort by the owner. Thus, buying it has some of the attributes of buying a business rather than investing one's money. Real estate limited partnerships and investment trusts have arisen in response to investors' needs for a management-free investment vehicle in real estate. Some of these instruments preserve the favorable tax characteristics of real estate while others do not. The indices of real estate returns used here represent directly held, nonleveraged real estate.

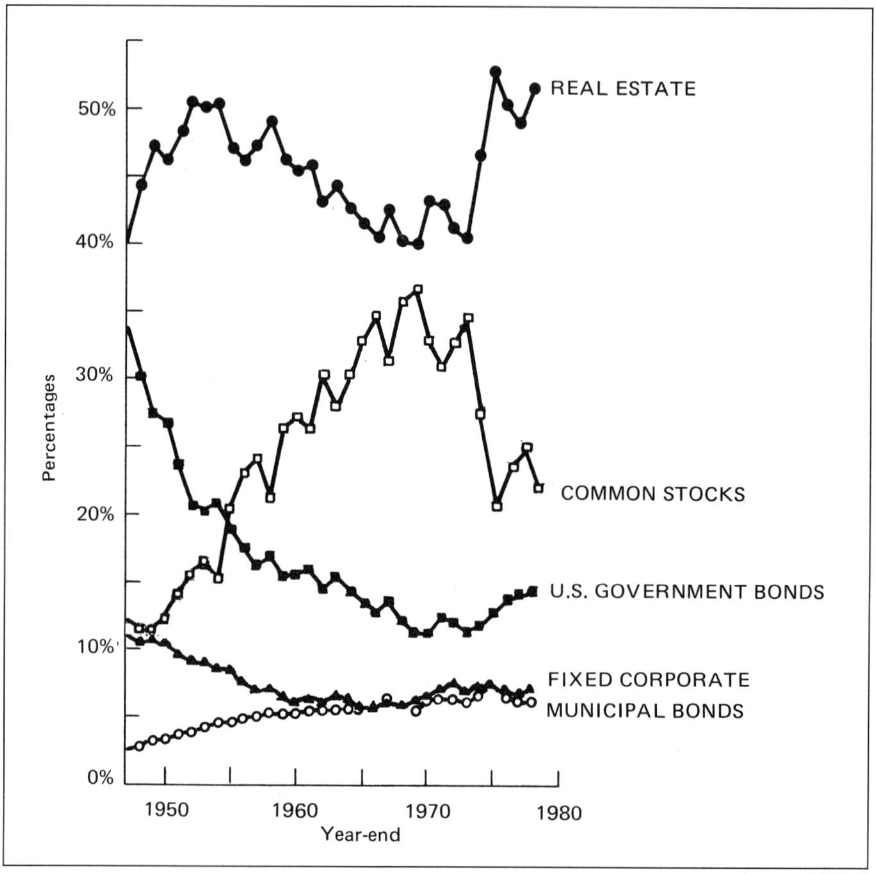

FIG. 2. Value of Capital Market Security Groups as a Percentage of the Total
SOURCE: Ibbotson, Roger G., and Fall, Carol L., "The United States Market Wealth Portfolio." *The Journal of Portfolio Management,* Fall 1979, page 83.

The fixed income securities had uniformly poor returns, with short-term obligations outperforming long-term ones. It is not surprising that municipal bonds did the worst, since they have low yields because of their tax advantages.

The total for each major category is the market-value-weighted sum of the returns of its components. The market return is the market-value-weighted sum of all the component returns.

A FIFTY-SIX-YEAR HISTORY OF STOCKS, BONDS, BILLS, AND INFLATION

As noted earlier, a long-period study can uncover relationships hidden in short-period data. The Ibbotson and Sinquefield book cited earlier covered the fifty-six years from 1926 to 1981, which included many types of events: a major depression, a world war, and various periods of boom and bust and low and high interest rates. Although there is no way of knowing what events will occur in the future, it is reasonable to assume that the historical events of a fifty-six year period are representative of the types of events that will occur. Thus, the relationships derived from this examination of capital market returns may be useful in predicting future returns.

The writers collected capital appreciation and (where relevant) income returns for five asset categories: common stocks, represented by the S&P 500 common stock index; small company stocks, defined as the one-fifth of the stocks on the New York Stock Exchange that rank as the smallest in terms of market value (price per share times number of shares outstanding); U.S. government bonds with approximately twenty years to maturity; long-term corporate bonds; and thirty-day U.S. Treasury bills. In addition, similar data for the general price level (inflation) was collected. While the price level itself cannot be purchased, it represents a market basket of goods and services that can be and serves as a benchmark for asset returns.

Figure 3 on page 978 shows the growth of one dollar invested in four of the above-described assets on December 31, 1925. Stocks were the winner by a very large margin, with small company stocks growing to $597.10 by the end of 1981 with dividends re-invested and S&P 500 stocks growing to $133.62. This phenomenal growth was not without considerable risk. Returns on S&P 500 stocks for individual years varied from plus 54 percent (1933) to minus 43 percent (1931), and short holding periods for stocks variously showed large gains and losses. Total return indices of long-term government bonds, Treasury bills, and inflation all rose by approximately a factor of five during the period.

The graph in Figure 3 can be examined to reveal some specific market facts. The Great Crash of 1929-1932 cut the value of stocks drastically but, with dividends re-invested, the 1929 high was exceeded as soon as 1936 and was passed for the last time in 1943. Likewise, the so-called second great crash of 1973-1974, which was larger than any other decline since the Great Crash, was followed by a recovery that, in 1976, passed the previous peak. The year-by-year common stock returns appear to divide into three periods: the Depression and the first part of World War II, in which returns were poor and highly volatile; the wartime and post-war boom, in which returns were high and stable; and the current period of persistent high inflation rates, 1966-1981, in which returns became more volatile, though not as much as in 1926-1941. The volatility of common stock returns is depicted in the bar chart in Figure 4 on page 979.

Standard & Poor's 500 stock returns were positive in nearly two-thirds of the years (thirty-seven out of fifty-six years). The longest period over which a year-end investor in the S&P 500 (common stocks) total return index would have earned a negative return was the fourteen-year period of 1929-1942. A month-end investor would have earned negative returns for an additional three months, from the beginning of December 1928 through February 1943.

The longest period for which an investor would have earned a negative return in real terms was more recent. It covers seventeen years and seven months,

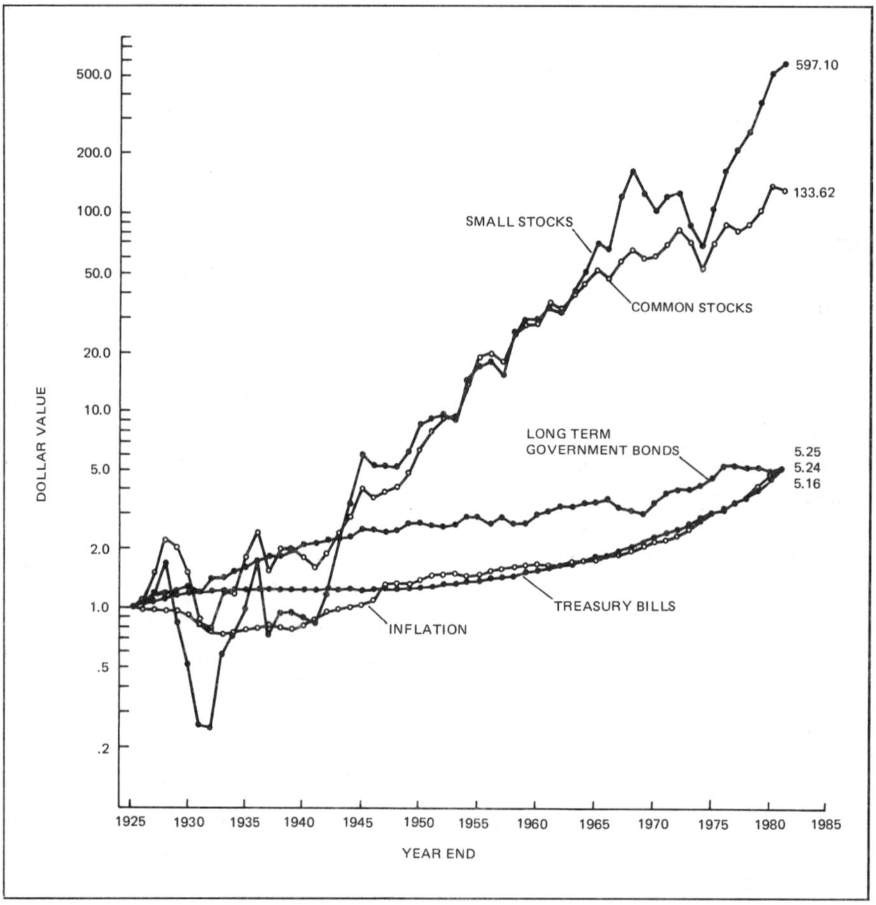

FIG. 3. Wealth Indexes of Investments in U.S. Capital Markets 1926-1981

SOURCE: Ibbotson, Roger G., and Sinquefield, Rex A. *Stocks, Bonds, Bills, and Inflation: The Past and the Future*. 1982 edition. Charlottesville: Financial Analysts Research Foundation, 1982.

from the beginning of June 1964 through the end of December 1981. In nominal terms, the investor would have more than tripled his investment over that same period of time.

Looking at the inflation series in Figure 3, one can see that the first seven years of the study period were deflationary. This is one of the many deflationary times in American and world history; the present-day persistence of high inflation rates is unusual. It comes as a surprise to many that inflation rates (as measured by the Consumer Price Index, or CPI) were negative in forty-seven different months since the end of World War II, and zero in fifty-six more months as of the end of 1981. The last such month was January 1967.

The high inflation rates of 1966-1981 have hurt the bond markets badly. At

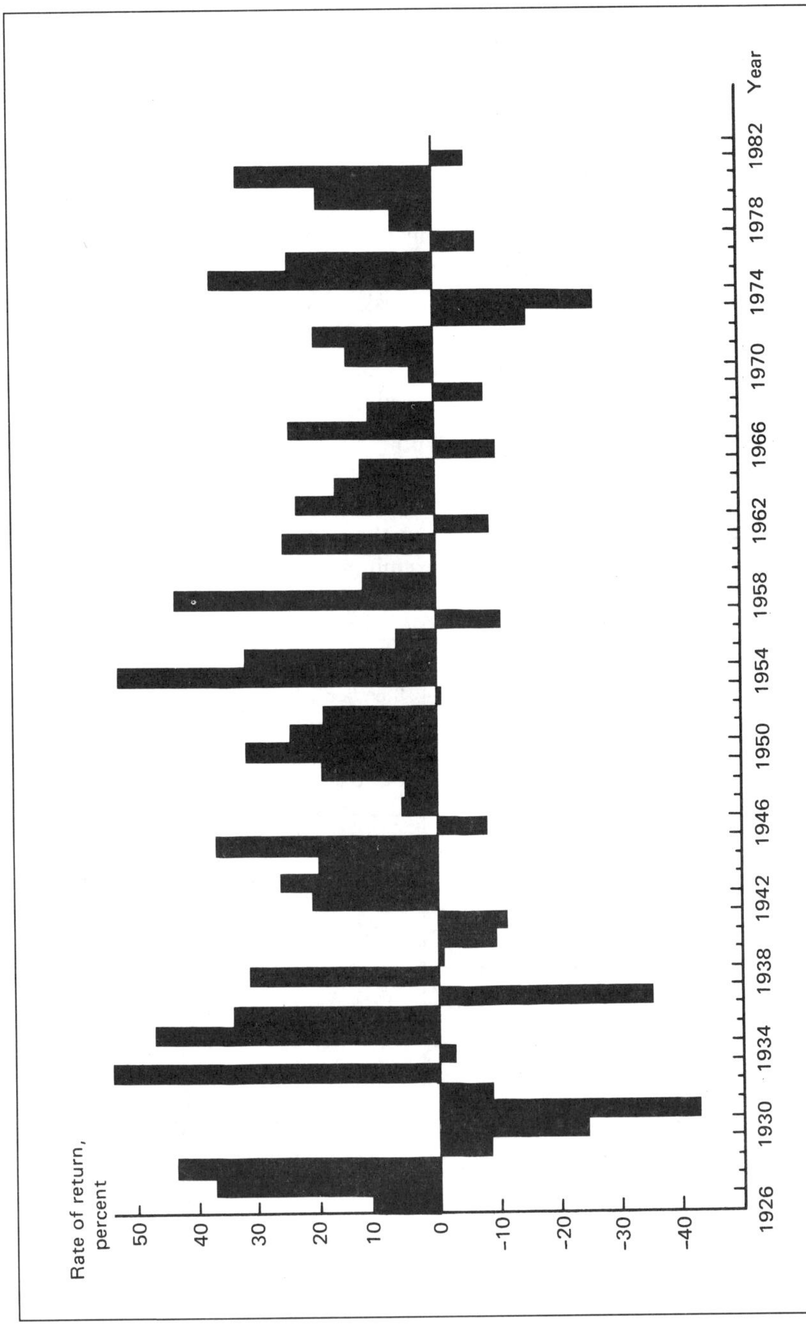

FIG. 4. Common Stocks: Year-by-Year Total Returns 1926–1981

SOURCE: Ibbotson, Roger G., and Sinquefield, Rex A. *Stocks, Bonds, Bills, and Inflation: The Past and the Future*. 1982 edition. Charlottesville: Financial Analysts Research Foundation, 1982.

the end of 1965, a 1925 one-dollar investment in long-term government bonds had grown to \$3.46 (including re-investment of coupons), compared with \$1.78 for the CPI. By the end of 1981, the gap had closed, with long-term government bonds at \$5.16 and the CPI return index at \$5.24. Thus, over the long term, an investment in bonds has not quite kept up with inflation.

Figure 5 below shows the geometric mean (compound annual) and arithmetic mean returns on the asset categories, along with standard deviations. One can see that (in geometric mean terms) common stocks outperformed riskless U.S. Treasury bills by 5.9 percent per year. This may be thought of as the risk premium paid to investors for taking the investment risk of stocks rather than buying riskless securities. From the standard deviations and the distribution histograms, it is clear that stocks are riskier than Treasury bills. (The risk of Treasury bills is in fact overstated by the method used to produce Figure 5; while returns vary from period to period, the return for a given period is known in advance, i.e., it is risk-free.) It is appropriate that common stocks return substantially more than Treasury bills; if they did not, no one would buy stocks.

Bonds, less risky than stocks because of their seniority in a firm's capital structure, do not command as high a risk premium. Long-term corporate bonds

Series	Geometric Mean	Arithmetic Mean	Standard Deviation	Distribution
Common Stocks	9.1%	11.4%	21.9%	
Small Stocks	12.1	18.1	37.3	
Long Term Corporate Bonds	3.6	3.7	5.6	
Long Term Government Bonds	3.0	3.1	5.7	
U.S. Treasury Bills	3.0	3.1	3.1	
Inflation	3.0	3.1	5.1	

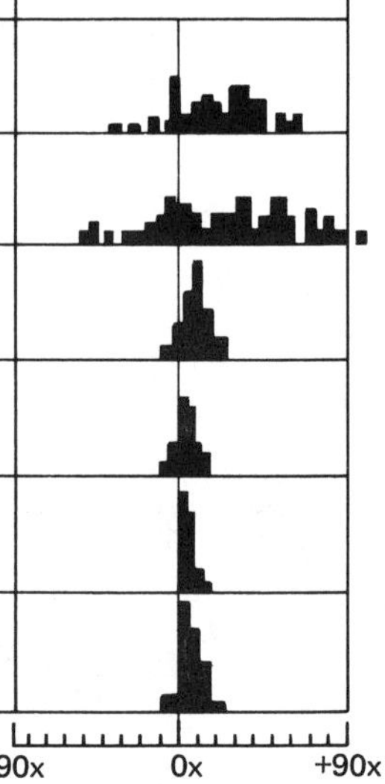

FIG. 5. Basic Series Investment Total Annual Returns 1926-1981

SOURCE: Ibbotson, Roger G., and Sinquefield, Rex A. *Stocks, Bonds, Bills, and Inflation: The Past and the Future*. 1982 edition. Charlottesville: Financial Analysts Research Foundation, 1982.

have outperformed Treasury bills by 0.5 percent per year over the study period. Government bonds, which have almost no possibility of default, have returned a zero increment over Treasury bills. This low number may not be indicative of the future since it reflects the poor performance of bond markets in recent years.

In Table 2 on page 990 are displayed the year-by-year returns on stocks, government and corporate bonds, bills, and inflation presented in summary form earlier. These returns are converted to wealth indices (with year-end 1925 equal to $1.00) and displayed in Table 3 on page 991. The numbers in this table, which show capital appreciation separately for stocks and government bonds, help illustrate the gains from the re-investment of income (dividends and interest). While a one dollar investment in common stocks at year-end 1925 would have grown to over $133 with dividend re-investment, capital appreciation alone (without re-investment) would have raised the value of the investment to only $9.61.

Inflation-adjusted total returns for the abovementioned asset classes are presented year by year in Table 4 on page 992. Wealth indices of these returns are displayed in Table 5 on page 993. The by-now familiar dollar investment in common stocks in 1925 would have grown to $25.13 in 1925 dollars by the end of 1981. This means that the stock portfolio would have had more than twenty-five times as much purchasing power in 1981 as it had in 1925. In contrast, long-term corporate bonds would have had only about one and one-third times their original purchasing power after fifty-six years. Long-term government bonds and Treasury bills both suffered a slight loss in inflation-adjusted terms over the period, although Treasury bills beat inflation by a small margin since the 1950s.

FOCUS ON STOCKS — NYSE, AMEX, OTC, AND INSTITUTIONAL PORTFOLIOS

Large and small stocks have had appreciably different histories. The large blue chip issues that make up the S&P 500 have been laggard performers since 1965, while smaller issues have raced ahead. In fact, as was pointed out in the last section, over long periods of time as well as most subperiods, small stocks outperformed large stocks. Further, according to research by Rolf Banz,[3] the higher betas of small stocks do not fully explain their higher returns. Thus, it frequently would have been preferable to hold small stocks.

Ibbotson and Fall examined the various markets for common stocks. Drawing on those results, the market was divided by exchange listing: NYSE-listed issues (including both S&P 500 and non-S&P 500 stocks), American Stock Exchange-listed (AMEX) issues, and issues traded over the counter (OTC). Annual returns were gathered for 1947-1978 for NYSE and OTC, and for 1963-1978 for AMEX. The year-by-year annual total returns for these series, with dividends

---

[3] Banz, Rolf W. "The Relationship Between Return and Market Value of Common Stocks." *Journal of Financial Economics*, Vol. 9, No. 1, March 1981.

re-invested, appear in Table 6 on page 994. Wealth indices of these returns appear in Table 7 on page 995.

One can see from the data in Table 7 that the wealth index of OTC stocks was twice that of NYSE stocks at the end of the 1947-1978 period. Translated into rates of return, OTC stocks returned 12.6 percent per year compared with NYSE's 10.2 percent. (See Table 1 on page 989.) This relatively small difference in compound annual rates of return produces a large difference in wealth index values after thirty-two years.

The data for AMEX began in 1962, so the wealth index starts with one dollar invested on December 31, 1962. By December 31, 1978, it grew to $3.09, a compound annual return of 6.5 percent. Over the same sixteen-year period, a dollar invested in the NYSE wealth index grew to $2.82 (a compound annual return of 5.9 percent), and a dollar invested in the OTC grew to $3.01 (a compound annual return of 6.3 percent). Thus, AMEX stocks were the best performers of the three groups over this sixteen-year period, a poor period for common stocks by long-term investment standards.

Over both the 1947-1978 and the 1963-1978 periods, AMEX and OTC stocks had higher returns than NYSE stocks did. In general, non-NYSE stocks are smaller issues than NYSE stocks; this is consistent with other findings that small stocks outperform large ones.

While market averages such as the S&P 500, NYSE, and others represent accurately the activity of the stock market in general, they do not indicate how well specific investors fared. Investors generally hold portfolios that are more or less unrepresentative of the whole market, in an attempt to outperform the averages or achieve other investment goals.

Figure 6 on page 983 shows how various classes of institutional investors' portfolios performed over one-, five-, and ten-year holding periods ending December 31, 1980. As one would expect, the dispersion of returns is much less for the ten-year holding period than it is for shorter periods. In 1980 alone, and in 1976-1980, special situations mutual funds had the highest returns, while income mutual funds had the lowest. There is, however, no evidence that one class of institutions performed better than another over the whole ten years. Furthermore, there is no evidence that institutions as a group outperform the market averages in the long run.

FOCUS ON BONDS — AN ANALYSIS OF THE CORPORATE BOND MARKET

The Corporate Bond Market: Structure and Returns, by Roger G. Ibbotson (unpublished), examines the 1926-1978 period. Summary statistics from this study are shown in Table 8 on page 996. The composite portfolio of all corporate bonds achieved a 3.43 percent compound annual return over the period. This was

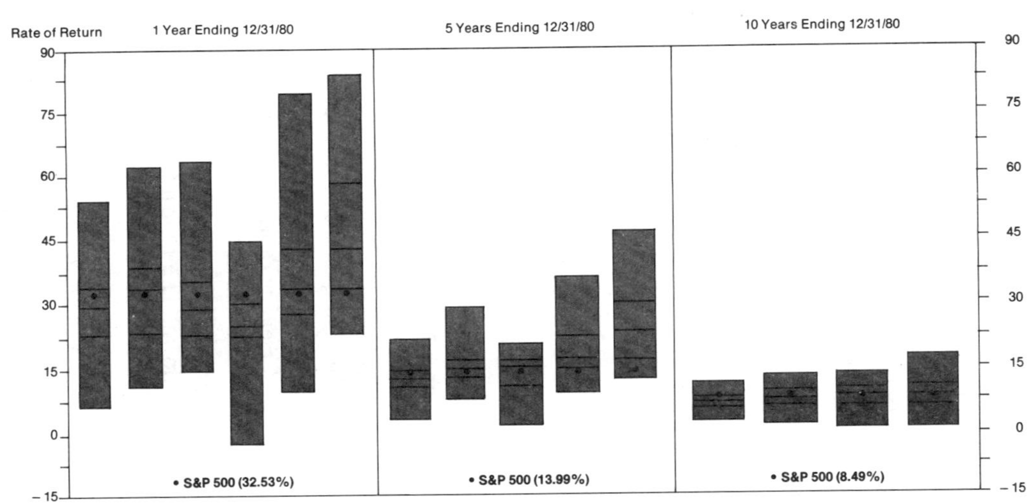

	1 Year Ending 12/31/80						5 Years Ending 12/31/80					10 Years Ending 12/31/80			
	Bank	Insurance Company	Investment Advisors	Income Mutual Funds	Growth Mutual Funds	Special Situations	Bank	Insurance Company	Income Mutual Funds	Growth Mutual Funds	Special Situations	Bank	Insurance Company	Income Mutual Funds	Growth Mutual Funds
High	54.15	62.40	63.56	44.00	78.80	83.80	21.67	28.85	20.94	35.68	46.84	11.46	12.79	13.38	17.76
First Quartile	33.78	38.66	35.17	30.20	42.72	57.91	14.32	16.50	16.80	22.73	29.72	8.03	9.71	10.38	10.73
Median	29.66	33.35	28.74	25.30	33.45	42.50	12.23	14.71	15.36	17.22	24.26	6.68	7.87	8.86	8.80
Third Quartile	23.37	24.02	23.14	22.90	27.87	33.23	10.24	12.25	10.81	14.82	16.95	5.63	6.31	6.57	6.72
Low	5.31	10.89	14.39	– 2.70	9.30	22.96	3.47	7.26	1.48	8.92	12.39	2.19	1.99	0.73	0.89
Average Return	28.89	32.22	30.52	25.86	36.19	45.17	12.34	14.71	14.17	18.91	24.33	6.73	7.99	8.29	8.82
Std. Deviation	9.41	10.74	9.85	8.10	13.44	15.09	3.13	3.86	4.21	6.21	8.26	1.97	2.52	2.89	3.29
No. in Sample	107	41	81	37	70	35	105	40	37	70	31	95	37	37	70

FIG. 6. Institutional Equity Fund Performance

SOURCE: *PMM & Co.'s Survey of Investment Performance*. New York: Peat Marwick Mitchell & Co., 1981, page 11.

far lower than the return earned by stocks and just slightly higher than the inflation rate.

The set of corporate bonds was divided by industry, Moody's Investors Service's rating, and maturity category. In Table 8 one can see that over the whole period industrials had the highest return and transportation issues had the lowest return. A dollar invested at year-end 1925 would have grown to $8.58 by 1978 if invested in industrial bonds, but to only half that much ($4.32) if invested in transportation bonds.

As one would expect, issues rated highest by Moody's had the lowest returns. The difference between Aaa-rated and below-Baa-rated issues is dramatic. A dollar invested in Aaa issues at year-end 1925 would have grown to only $1.45 by 1978, while the same dollar invested in the riskier below-Baa issues would have grown to $12.00. This is a vivid illustration of the principle that investors have been rewarded for taking risk. The writers' estimate of standard deviation for corporate bonds is subject to substantial sampling error (due to small sample size) and should not be used as a measure of risk of these bond categories.

Results are displayed for two maturity categories: 5 to 14.99 years, and 15 years and more to maturity. (The sample for bonds with less than 5 years to maturity was too small to be used.) One can see that intermediate-term bonds (5 to 14.99 years) had a much higher return than long-term bonds. A dollar invested in intermediate-term bonds at year-end 1925 would have grown to $24.12 by 1978, compared with $6.86 for long-term bonds. This differential illustrates the extent to which long-term issues were hurt by rising inflation rates and (consequently) interest rates over the period.

The columns headed *Return in Excess of Yield* in Table 8 show the direction of the market. A negative return in excess of yield means that the attained return was, on average, less than the market-anticipated return (i.e., the yield to maturity). In other words, the bond market went down. The return in excess of yield was negative for the composite portfolio over the period and for all of the components except intermediate-term maturity bonds. The bond market, then, was lower at the end of the period than it was at the beginning. That is, the bond yields rose. A look at the history of this market shows that the price trend was upward (bond yields went down) from 1926 to 1945; then prices fell sharply (and yields rose to unprecedented levels) in more recent years.

THE INTERNATIONAL VIEW — STOCK MARKET RETURNS IN EIGHTEEN COUNTRIES

The U.S. stock market constitutes only about half of the world's common equities. Japan and the countries of Western Europe have important and active markets, and smaller markets are present in still other countries. In the past two decades, foreign stocks were very desirable for a U.S. investor to hold. Over the whole period, the stocks of fifteen out of seventeen foreign countries studied outperformed the U.S. stock market. This was partly because the foreign stock markets did well in their home currencies and partly because foreign currencies appreciated relative to the dollar.

Table 9 on page 997 shows average annual returns for the 1960-1979 period for the United States and seventeen foreign countries. The countries are grouped by continental areas. The Asian and Pacific countries had the highest returns. Japan had the highest compound annual return over the entire period (14.9 percent); a dollar invested in Japanese stocks at year-end 1959 grew to $16.08 in twenty years. Hong Kong and Singapore, for which there are only ten years of data, had compound annual returns of 20.8 percent and 20.0 percent, respectively, for 1970-1979. The Hong Kong return is higher than the highest return that a year-end investor in U.S. stocks could have earned in any ten-year period. (U.S. stocks returned a compound rate of 20.1 percent from the beginning of 1949 to the end of 1958.)

European countries varied widely in their stock market performance. Norway led the group, with a compound annual return of 11.9 percent. Much of this gain was achieved in one year, 1979. Switzerland had the second best performing stock market in Europe (11.2 percent). The other countries of Europe had returns that fell between 6 and 11 percent per year, except for Italy. A dollar invested in Italian stocks actually fell in value over the twenty years of the study, to 92 cents.

The North American region consists of the United States and Canada. Canadian stocks fared somewhat better than U.S. stocks, returning 10.2 percent per year. The United States was the third worst performer of all the countries, with a return of 6.8 percent per year over the twenty-year period.

It should be pointed out that the 1960-1979 period was a relatively poor one for common stocks in the United States. Had a different twenty-year period been chosen, the United States might not have been nearly as bad a place in which to invest in stocks. The writers believe, however, that a span of twenty years is long enough to suggest that there are gains from international diversification in stocks, although they would not necessarily expect such gains to be as great in the future as they were in the decades of the 1960s and 1970s. (See also article on Foreign Equities, elsewhere in this volume.)

THE INTERNATIONAL VIEW — RETURNS ON NON-U.S. BONDS

The idea that diversification across borders is a potentially good policy prompted the writers to look at returns on international bonds as well as stocks. In a study by Ibbotson and Siegel, the international bond market for 1975-1980 was divided into three classes: foreign domestic (the domestic bonds of other countries); foreign crossborder (issued by the residents of one foreign country and denominated in currency of another); and U.S. dollar crossborder (issued by residents of a foreign country in U.S. dollars). A summary of the results of the study is presented in Table 10 on page 998. In this table, the first line entitled "All Foreign Currencies — All Maturities" gives the return for the class of bonds as a whole. One can see that each class outperformed U.S. domestic bonds. The two foreign currency classes also outperformed the U.S. inflation rate.

Each class of bonds was subdivided by currency and by maturity group. The foreign domestics are by far the largest of the three classes. Of the foreign domestics, Japanese bonds were the best performers, providing a compound annual return of 18.2 percent. British government (gilt-edged) bonds were a close second. In the foreign crossborder class, bonds issued in Japanese yen were the best performer — in this case by a substantial margin — due to declining Japanese inflation rates. In the U.S. dollar crossborder class, floating-rate notes (on which the coupon rate is reset periodically according to current interest rates) greatly outperformed the other types of bonds. This was because the floating-rate characteristic of these bonds protected them from the accelerating U.S. dollar inflation of the 1975-1980 period.

The six-year period from the beginning of 1975 to the end of 1980 is not long enough to identify fundamental relationships. In this period, much of the high international bond return came from appreciation of foreign currencies against the U.S. dollar. The writers do not expect that the gain from international diversification in bonds will be consistently as great in the future as it was in 1975-1980. (See article on Foreign Fixed Income Investments, elsewhere in this volume.)

TANGIBLES — ANOTHER SIDE OF INVESTING

In recent years, investors have shown great interest in tangible and/or physically portable assets. This broad asset class includes precious metals and coins, which are fully tangible and portable; other commodities, which are tangible but may not be portable; and collectibles, which have varying characteristics. The class of tangibles also includes real estate, which is part of the set of traditional investment vehicles. Real estate will not be treated in this article.

The main difficulty in investing in tangibles is lack of liquidity. Substantial illiquidity in an asset makes it less desirable, but investors may be compensated for this characteristic by higher returns. Collectibles range from coins, which are fairly easy to sell, to empty beer cans, which are extremely illiquid. Art and antiques, favorite collectible items of recent years, are rather illiquid and suffer from a scarcity of information about them. They do, however, provide nonpecuniary benefits (such as pleasure of ownership), and may be priced at a level that would include this return. If so, only those people who enjoy these items should hold them. One might view these items as hybrids between assets that are acquired for investment purposes and consumption goods that are acquired for pleasure or use. This complicates any discussion of rates of return on these items because the nonpecuniary returns could differ from one person to another on the very same item.

Gold and silver, along with low-premium bullion coins containing one of these metals, are easy to sell quickly at the market price. These metals, however, have been and could be again subject to government price regulation or prohibition on ownership.

Robert S. Salomon of Salomon Brothers has compiled ten-, five-, and one-year compound annual rates of return for various tangible and financial assets for periods ending June 1, 1981. His results are shown in Table 11 on page 1000. For the last ten years, tangible assets have generally outperformed financial assets. (Salomon's returns on financial assets do not agree with the writers' because he used different calculation methods.) This period of study is too short to draw conclusions about the long-term returns on tangibles. In general, however, one would expect tangibles to have a risk-return relationship similar to that of any other investment, after taking into account such factors as illiquidity, tax characteristics, nonpecuniary benefits, and management or storage costs.

Salomon's results show that oil and gold were the best performers over the 1971-1981 period, with compound annual returns of 30.8 percent and 28.0 percent, respectively. Silver had a substantially lower annual return, 21.5 percent. Various collectibles had high returns but the actual returns to most investors probably would be substantially different from those indicated here, with some investors experiencing much greater returns and some much lower returns.

In view of the potential difficulties in determining the returns on illiquid assets and the heterogeneity of the assets within an asset category, the reader should be very cautious in comparing Salomon's data with the writers' capital market results. The writers have little doubt, however, that some tangibles performed much better than stocks and bonds, and outpaced inflation in the ten-year period of Salomon's study.

The writers examined returns on several classes of tangibles in more detail. Table 12 on page 1001 shows returns for several strategic metals over twenty-three-, seventeen-, and six-year holding periods. Returns over the 1958-1981 period ranged from 1.1 percent per year for cadmium to 10.4 percent per year for cobalt. In the 1975-1981 period, which was characterized by high inflation, returns were higher; they ranged from one percent per year for cadmium to 25 percent per year for germanium.

Prices of U.S. coins were studied by *Coin World,* a magazine that constructs price indices of various categories of coins. Compound annual rates of return ranged from 6.4 percent for Lincoln cents (for the holding period from January 19, 1961 to October 7, 1981) to 15.8 percent for $3 gold pieces over approximately the same period.

Price indices of collectable U.S. stamps are maintained by Scott Publishing Company, New York. From 1929 to 1980, the U.S. StampIndex grew at a compound annual rate of 7.7 percent. Compound annual rates of return over subperiods were as follows: 4.6 percent in 1929-1934; 7.1 percent in 1935-1940;

4.3 percent in 1941-1945; 2.1 percent in 1946-1950; 1.3 percent in 1951-1955; 4.5 percent in 1956-1960; 6.2 percent in 1961-1965; 12.1 percent in 1966-1970; 9.9 percent in 1971-1975; and 27.1 percent in 1976-1980. It should be noted that these returns are based on catalogue prices and thus may not reflect realizable returns.[4]

The Sotheby index of art prices rose from 100 in 1975 to 244 in 1981, a compound annual rate of return of 16 percent. Data on sales at Sotheby's have also been used by J. Patrick Cooney, of Citibank (New York), to derive returns for longer periods. Cooney's index of Old Master paintings rose at a 15.4 percent annual rate from 1970 to 1980; impressionist paintings, at a 10.4 percent rate; and modern paintings, at a 13.6 percent rate over the same period. Annual returns on individual paintings quoted by Sotheby's ranged from 1.5 to 46.5 percent (excluding holding periods of less than one year).

One can see, then, that returns on tangibles are highly variable from one asset class to another, from one time period to another, and among individual assets in a class. During periods of high inflation, such as the most recent decade, tangibles as a category have performed relatively well. In other periods, financial assets such as stocks and bonds have often performed better than tangible assets.

CONCLUSIONS

In examining the behavior of most asset categories that investors hold, it is seen that over long periods of time capital at risk in business — common stocks — earns higher returns than less risky assets. Real estate, which is the most widely held tangible asset, also fares well. Bonds have low returns, and short-term money market instruments such as U.S. Treasury bills track inflation.

Over short periods of time, any specific asset class can outperform any other asset class. While it is interesting to compare realized returns on assets over any time period, the writers believe that the most reliable inferences are drawn from results over long periods of time.

Investors should buy and hold assets according to their needs and investment goals, and they should diversify their holdings to include more than one type of asset. An investor should not hold only those assets that went up the most in some past time period. It is very useful, however, for the investor to have access to historical return data in order to understand fundamental risk-return relationships and make intelligent investment decisions.

---

[4] *Stamp Market Update.* November 1979. Published by Scott Publishing Co., New York, N.Y. Returns are calculated from the U.S. StampIndex, which in turn is generated from Scott Catalogue stamp prices. These catalogue prices are Scott's estimate, made in 1979, of the price at which a stamp was likely to be sold in 1980. Thus the returns should not be interpreted as representing realized returns over the holding period.

TABLE 1. U.S. Capital Market Total Annual Returns 1947-1978

	Arithmetic Mean	*Geometric Mean**	*Standard Deviation*
Common Stocks			
NYSE	11.56%	10.16%	17.73%
OTC	14.79	12.63	21.79
Total	11.79	10.34	18.02
Fixed Income Corporate Securities			
Preferred stocks	3.31	2.92	9.20
Long-term corporate bonds	2.42	2.21	6.72
Intermediate corporate bonds	4.00	3.87	5.48
Commercial paper	4.29	4.27	2.37
Total	3.03	2.89	5.53
Real Estate			
Farms	11.88	11.69	6.79
Residential housing	6.93	6.88	3.28
Total	8.19	8.14	3.53
U. S. Government Securities			
U. S. Treasury bills	3.53	3.51	2.11
U. S. Treasury notes	3.73	3.65	3.71
U. S. Treasury bonds	2.56	2.39	6.17
Agencies	4.08	4.01	3.92
Total	3.23	3.17	3.78
Municipal (State & Local) Bonds			
Short-term	2.45	2.44	1.37
Long-term	2.01	1.69	8.20
Total	2.02	1.75	7.62
MARKET TOTAL	6.97%	6.88%	4.65%

*Compound annual rate of return.

SOURCE: Ibbotson, Roger G., and Fall, Carol L. "The United States Market Wealth Portfolio." *The Journal of Portfolio Management,* Fall 1979, page 90.

TABLE 2. Basic Series Year-by-Year Total Returns in Percent 1926-1981

YEAR	S&P 500 COMMON STOCKS	SMALL COMPANY STOCKS	LONG-TERM GOVERNMENT BONDS	LONG-TERM CORPORATE BONDS	U. S. TREASURY BILLS	CONSUMER PRICE INDEX
1926	11.62	0.28	7.77	7.37	3.27	-1.49
1927	37.49	22.09	8.93	7.44	3.12	-2.08
1928	43.61	39.70	0.10	2.84	3.24	-0.97
1929	-8.42	-51.36	3.42	3.27	4.75	0.19
1930	-24.90	-38.14	4.66	7.98	2.41	-6.03
1931	-43.34	-49.75	-5.31	-1.85	1.07	-9.52
1932	-8.19	-5.40	16.84	10.82	0.96	-10.30
1933	53.99	142.90	-0.08	10.38	0.30	0.51
1934	-1.44	24.20	10.02	13.84	0.16	2.03
1935	47.67	40.20	4.98	9.61	0.17	2.99
1936	33.92	64.80	7.51	6.74	0.18	1.21
1937	-35.03	-58.00	0.23	2.75	0.31	3.10
1938	31.12	32.80	5.53	6.13	-0.02	-2.78
1939	-0.41	0.30	5.94	3.97	0.02	-0.48
1940	-9.78	-5.20	6.09	3.39	0.0	0.96
1941	-11.59	-9.00	0.93	2.73	0.06	9.72
1942	20.34	44.50	3.22	2.60	0.27	9.29
1943	25.90	88.40	2.08	2.83	0.35	3.16
1944	19.75	53.70	2.81	4.73	0.33	2.11
1945	36.44	73.60	10.73	4.08	0.33	2.25
1946	-8.07	-11.60	-0.10	1.72	0.35	18.17
1947	5.71	0.90	-2.63	-2.34	0.50	9.01
1948	5.50	-2.10	3.40	4.14	0.81	2.71
1949	18.79	19.70	6.45	3.31	1.10	-1.80
1950	31.71	38.70	0.06	2.12	1.20	5.79
1951	24.02	7.80	-3.94	-2.69	1.49	5.87
1952	18.37	3.00	1.16	3.52	1.66	0.88
1953	-0.99	-6.50	3.63	3.41	1.82	0.62
1954	52.62	60.60	7.19	5.39	0.86	-0.50
1955	31.56	20.40	-1.30	0.48	1.57	0.37
1956	6.56	4.30	-5.59	-6.81	2.46	2.86
1957	-10.78	-14.60	7.45	8.71	3.14	3.02
1958	43.36	64.90	-6.10	-2.22	1.54	1.76
1959	11.95	16.40	-2.26	-0.97	2.95	1.50
1960	0.47	-3.30	13.78	9.07	2.66	1.48
1961	26.89	32.10	0.97	4.82	2.13	0.67
1962	-8.73	-11.90	6.89	7.95	2.73	1.22
1963	22.80	23.60	1.21	2.19	3.12	1.65
1964	16.48	23.50	3.51	4.77	3.54	1.19
1965	12.45	41.80	0.71	-0.46	3.93	1.92
1966	-10.06	-7.00	3.65	0.20	4.76	3.35
1967	23.98	83.60	-9.19	-4.95	4.21	3.04
1968	11.06	36.00	-0.26	2.57	5.21	4.72
1969	-8.50	-25.10	-5.08	-8.09	6.58	6.11
1970	4.01	-17.40	12.10	18.37	6.53	5.49
1971	14.31	16.50	13.23	11.01	4.39	3.36
1972	18.98	4.40	5.68	7.26	3.84	3.41
1973	-14.66	-30.90	-1.11	1.14	6.93	8.80
1974	-26.47	-19.90	4.35	-3.06	8.00	12.20
1975	37.20	52.80	9.19	14.64	5.80	7.01
1976	23.84	57.40	16.75	18.65	5.08	4.81
1977	-7.18	25.40	-0.67	1.71	5.12	6.77
1978	6.56	23.50	-1.16	-0.07	7.18	9.03
1979	18.44	43.50	-1.22	-4.18	10.38	13.31
1980	32.42	39.90	-3.95	-2.62	11.24	12.40
1981	-4.91	13.95	1.85	-0.96	14.71	8.94

TABLE 3. Basic Series Indexes of Year-End Cumulative Wealth 1925-1981 (Year-End 1925 =1.000)

YEAR	S & P 500 COMMON STOCKS		COMPANY STOCKS	LONG-TERM GOVERNMENT BONDS		LONG-TERM CORPORATE BONDS	U. S. TREASURY BILLS	CONSUMER PRICE INDEX
	TOTAL RETURNS	CAPITAL GAIN	TOTAL RETURNS	TOTAL RETURNS	CAPITAL GAIN	TOTAL RETURNS	TOTAL RETURNS	TOTAL RETURNS
1925	1.000	1.000	1.000	1.000	1.000	1.000	1.000	1.000
1926	1.116	1.057	1.003	1.078	1.039	1.074	1.033	0.985
1927	1.535	1.384	1.224	1.174	1.095	1.154	1.065	0.965
1928	2.204	1.908	1.710	1.175	1.061	1.186	1.099	0.955
1929	2.018	1.681	0.832	1.215	1.059	1.225	1.152	0.957
1930	1.516	1.202	0.515	1.272	1.072	1.323	1.179	0.899
1931	0.859	0.636	0.259	1.204	0.981	1.299	1.192	0.814
1932	0.789	0.540	0.245	1.407	1.108	1.439	1.204	0.730
1933	1.214	0.792	0.594	1.406	1.073	1.588	1.207	0.734
1934	1.197	0.745	0.738	1.547	1.146	1.808	1.209	0.749
1935	1.767	1.053	1.035	1.624	1.170	1.982	1.211	0.771
1936	2.367	1.346	1.705	1.746	1.225	2.116	1.213	0.780
1937	1.538	0.827	0.716	1.750	1.194	2.174	1.217	0.804
1938	2.016	1.035	0.951	1.847	1.228	2.307	1.217	0.782
1939	2.008	0.979	0.954	1.957	1.271	2.399	1.217	0.778
1940	1.812	0.829	0.904	2.076	1.319	2.480	1.217	0.786
1941	1.602	0.681	0.823	2.095	1.305	2.548	1.218	0.862
1942	1.927	0.766	1.189	2.162	1.315	2.614	1.221	0.942
1943	2.427	0.915	2.240	2.207	1.310	2.688	1.225	0.972
1944	2.906	1.041	3.443	2.270	1.314	2.815	1.229	0.993
1945	3.965	1.361	5.978	2.513	1.423	2.930	1.233	1.015
1946	3.645	1.199	5.284	2.511	1.392	2.980	1.238	1.199
1947	3.853	1.199	5.332	2.445	1.327	2.911	1.244	1.307
1948	4.065	1.191	5.220	2.528	1.340	3.031	1.254	1.343
1949	4.829	1.313	6.248	2.691	1.395	3.132	1.268	1.318
1950	6.360	1.600	8.666	2.692	1.366	3.198	1.283	1.395
1951	7.888	1.863	9.342	2.586	1.281	3.112	1.302	1.477
1952	9.336	2.082	9.623	2.616	1.262	3.221	1.324	1.490
1953	9.244	1.944	8.997	2.711	1.270	3.331	1.348	1.499
1954	14.108	2.820	14.450	2.906	1.325	3.511	1.360	1.492
1955	18.561	3.564	17.397	2.868	1.271	3.527	1.381	1.497
1956	19.778	3.658	18.145	2.708	1.164	3.287	1.415	1.540
1957	17.646	3.134	15.496	2.910	1.208	3.573	1.459	1.587
1958	25.298	4.327	25.553	2.733	1.097	3.494	1.482	1.615
1959	28.322	4.694	29.744	2.671	1.029	3.460	1.526	1.639
1960	28.455	4.554	28.762	3.039	1.124	3.774	1.566	1.663
1961	36.106	5.607	37.995	3.068	1.092	3.956	1.600	1.674
1962	32.955	4.945	33.474	3.280	1.122	4.270	1.643	1.695
1963	40.469	5.879	41.373	3.319	1.092	4.364	1.695	1.723
1964	47.139	6.642	51.096	3.436	1.084	4.572	1.754	1.743
1965	53.008	7.244	72.454	3.460	1.047	4.552	1.823	1.777
1966	47.674	6.295	67.382	3.586	1.036	4.560	1.910	1.836
1967	59.104	7.560	123.714	3.257	0.895	4.335	1.991	1.892
1968	65.642	8.140	168.251	3.248	0.846	4.446	2.094	1.981
1969	60.059	7.210	126.020	3.083	0.754	4.086	2.232	2.102
1970	62.465	7.222	104.093	3.457	0.791	4.837	2.378	2.218
1971	71.406	8.001	121.268	3.914	0.843	5.370	2.482	2.292
1972	84.956	9.252	126.604	4.136	0.840	5.760	2.577	2.371
1973	72.500	7.645	87.483	4.090	0.775	5.825	2.756	2.579
1974	53.311	5.373	70.074	4.268	0.748	5.647	2.976	2.894
1975	73.144	7.068	107.073	4.661	0.754	6.474	3.149	3.097
1976	90.584	8.422	168.533	5.441	0.815	7.681	3.309	3.246
1977	84.076	7.453	211.340	5.405	0.750	7.813	3.479	3.466
1978	89.592	7.532	261.005	5.342	0.682	7.807	3.728	3.778
1979	106.112	8.459	374.543	5.277	0.615	7.481	4.115	4.281
1980	140.513	10.639	523.985	5.069	0.530	7.285	4.578	4.812
1981	133.615	9.605	597.097	5.162	0.475	7.215	5.251	5.242

TABLE 4. Inflation-Adjusted Year-by-Year Total Returns in Percent 1926-1981

YEAR	INFLATION ADJUSTED S & P 500 COMMON STOCKS	INFLATION ADJUSTED SMALL COMPANY STOCKS	INFLATION ADJUSTED LONG-TERM GOVERNMENT BONDS	INFLATION ADJUSTED LONG-TERM CORPORATE BONDS	INFLATION ADJUSTED U. S. TREASURY BILLS
1926	13.25	1.81	9.37	8.96	4.78
1927	40.08	24.41	11.12	9.63	5.23
1928	45.07	41.29	1.03	3.80	4.22
1929	-8.52	-51.46	3.18	3.04	4.52
1930	-20.09	-34.12	11.27	14.80	8.89
1931	-37.25	-44.38	4.58	8.37	11.59
1932	2.60	5.42	29.99	23.30	12.39
1933	53.25	141.98	-0.71	9.73	-0.37
1934	-3.42	21.81	7.77	11.54	-1.87
1935	43.28	36.14	1.93	6.44	-2.78
1936	32.34	62.79	6.21	5.45	-1.04
1937	-37.02	-59.33	-2.85	-0.39	-2.74
1938	34.82	36.61	8.50	9.12	2.80
1939	0.35	1.57	6.23	4.42	0.45
1940	-10.70	-6.16	5.07	2.40	-0.95
1941	-19.55	-17.23	-8.07	-6.44	-8.90
1942	10.14	32.45	-5.60	-6.18	-8.33
1943	22.22	83.55	-1.09	-0.36	-2.78
1944	17.30	50.57	0.69	2.57	-1.75
1945	33.43	69.96	8.31	1.77	-1.90
1946	-22.91	-26.17	-15.95	-14.39	-15.52
1947	-3.16	-7.47	-10.83	-10.56	-7.93
1948	2.67	-4.65	0.59	1.29	-1.92
1949	20.91	21.91	8.37	5.17	2.93
1950	24.62	31.35	-5.47	-3.51	-4.39
1951	17.23	1.88	-9.33	-8.16	-4.18
1952	17.35	2.13	0.27	2.61	0.76
1953	-1.62	-7.13	2.99	2.77	1.18
1954	53.37	61.38	7.71	5.90	1.36
1955	31.11	20.00	-1.67	0.10	1.19
1956	3.63	1.38	-8.24	-9.44	-0.40
1957	-13.40	-17.08	4.29	5.50	0.11
1958	40.95	62.19	-7.72	-3.91	-0.22
1959	10.30	14.68	-3.71	-2.43	1.43
1960	-1.00	-4.73	12.11	7.47	1.16
1961	26.04	31.18	0.30	4.12	1.44
1962	-9.86	-13.00	5.60	6.65	1.49
1963	20.81	21.56	-0.43	0.54	1.44
1964	15.14	22.10	2.29	3.54	2.32
1965	10.31	39.06	-1.20	-2.35	1.97
1966	-13.03	-10.09	0.27	-3.08	1.36
1967	20.35	78.35	-11.90	-7.79	1.13
1968	6.07	29.92	-4.78	-2.06	0.46
1969	-13.84	-29.51	-10.58	-13.45	0.45
1970	-1.45	-21.88	6.28	12.25	0.98
1971	10.63	12.72	9.55	7.42	0.99
1972	15.09	0.96	2.21	3.73	0.41
1973	-21.77	-36.81	-9.13	-7.06	-1.75
1974	-34.78	-28.93	-7.08	-13.73	-3.78
1975	28.33	43.03	2.05	7.17	-1.14
1976	18.20	50.26	11.43	13.24	0.26
1977	-13.13	17.54	-7.01	-4.77	-1.56
1978	-2.29	13.25	-9.42	-8.41	-1.71
1979	4.55	26.86	-12.95	-15.58	-2.62
1980	17.87	24.40	-14.70	-13.49	-1.05
1981	-12.85	4.53	-6.66	-9.24	5.33

TABLE 5. Inflation-Adjusted Indexes of Year-End Cumulative Wealth 1925-1981 (Year-End 1925 = 1.000)

YEAR	INFLATION ADJUSTED S & P 500 COMMON STOCKS	INFLATION ADJUSTED SMALL COMPANY STOCKS	INFLATION ADJUSTED LONG-TERM GOVERNMENT BONDS	INFLATION ADJUSTED LONG-TERM CORPORATE BONDS	INFLATION ADJUSTED U. S. TREASURY BILLS
1925	1.000	1.000	1.000	1.000	1.000
1926	1.132	1.018	1.094	1.090	1.048
1927	1.586	1.267	1.215	1.195	1.103
1928	2.301	1.790	1.228	1.240	1.149
1929	2.105	0.869	1.267	1.278	1.201
1930	1.682	0.572	1.410	1.467	1.308
1931	1.056	0.318	1.474	1.589	1.459
1932	1.083	0.336	1.916	1.960	1.640
1933	1.660	0.812	1.903	2.150	1.634
1934	1.603	0.989	2.051	2.399	1.604
1935	2.297	1.347	2.090	2.553	1.559
1936	3.040	2.192	2.220	2.692	1.543
1937	1.914	0.891	2.157	2.682	1.501
1938	2.581	1.218	2.340	2.926	1.543
1939	2.590	1.237	2.486	3.056	1.550
1940	2.313	1.161	2.612	3.129	1.535
1941	1.861	0.961	2.401	2.928	1.398
1942	2.049	1.273	2.267	2.747	1.282
1943	2.505	2.336	2.242	2.737	1.246
1944	2.938	3.517	2.257	2.807	1.224
1945	3.920	5.977	2.445	2.857	1.201
1946	3.022	4.413	2.055	2.446	1.015
1947	2.927	4.083	1.832	2.187	0.934
1948	3.005	3.894	1.843	2.216	0.916
1949	3.633	4.747	1.998	2.330	0.943
1950	4.528	6.235	1.888	2.248	0.902
1951	5.308	6.352	1.712	2.065	0.864
1952	6.229	6.487	1.717	2.119	0.871
1953	6.128	6.025	1.768	2.177	0.881
1954	9.398	9.723	1.904	2.306	0.893
1955	12.322	11.667	1.873	2.308	0.903
1956	12.769	11.828	1.718	2.090	0.900
1957	11.058	9.808	1.792	2.205	0.901
1958	15.587	15.908	1.654	2.119	0.899
1959	17.192	18.243	1.592	2.068	0.912
1960	17.020	17.380	1.785	2.222	0.922
1961	21.452	22.799	1.790	2.314	0.936
1962	19.337	19.835	1.891	2.467	0.949
1963	23.361	24.112	1.883	2.481	0.963
1964	26.898	29.440	1.926	2.569	0.985
1965	29.671	40.940	1.903	2.508	1.005
1966	25.805	36.809	1.908	2.431	1.019
1967	31.056	65.649	1.681	2.242	1.030
1968	32.942	85.291	1.600	2.195	1.035
1969	28.382	60.121	1.431	1.900	1.039
1970	27.971	46.967	1.521	2.133	1.050
1971	30.944	52.941	1.666	2.291	1.060
1972	35.614	53.449	1.703	2.377	1.064
1973	27.861	33.775	1.547	2.209	1.046
1974	18.171	24.004	1.438	1.906	1.006
1975	23.318	34.332	1.467	2.042	0.995
1976	27.562	51.588	1.635	2.313	0.997
1977	23.943	60.636	1.521	2.202	0.982
1978	23.395	68.671	1.377	2.017	0.965
1979	24.460	87.115	1.199	1.703	0.940
1980	28.831	108.372	1.023	1.473	0.930
1981	25.126	113.281	0.955	1.337	0.979

TABLE 6. Year-by-Year Total Returns on Capital Market Securities (Percent)

Year	*Common Stocks*			
	NYSE	*AMEX*	*OTC*	*Total*
1947	3.30%	N/A	2.07%	3.20%
1948	2.32	N/A	– 3.04	1.90
1949	20.21	N/A	16.26	19.90
1950	29.95	N/A	29.22	29.90
1951	20.95	N/A	15.72	20.57
1952	13.32	N/A	6.52	12.86
1953	0.37	N/A	3.29	0.55
1954	50.53	N/A	50.40	50.52
1955	25.26	N/A	18.88	24.87
1956	8.62	N/A	15.33	9.00
1957	–10.70	N/A	0.16	–10.79
1958	44.27	N/A	48.34	44.49
1959	12.87	N/A	9.53	12.69
1960	0.60	N/A	0.99	0.62
1961	27.17	N/A	36.28	27.63
1962	– 9.38	N/A	–12.36	– 9.54
1963	21.33	14.75%	24.44	21.05
1964	16.29	15.07	25.87	16.69
1965	13.92	19.47	33.15	15.25
1966	– 8.96	– 5.86	0.90	– 8.20
1967	26.96	56.27	56.38	30.46
1968	12.78	33.18	23.02	14.94
1969	– 9.85	–22.51	1.67	– 9.86
1970	1.40	–16.00	–12.54	– 0.99
1971	15.89	21.60	40.65	18.17
1972	17.92	10.08	34.07	18.98
1973	–16.97	–28.25	–22.88	–18.19
1974	–26.85	–35.43	–38.50	–28.33
1975	37.73	39.56	37.48	37.78
1976	26.27	31.30	15.17	25.59
1977	– 4.89	13.16	14.74	– 2.82
1978	7.40	19.35	14.31	8.47

SOURCE: Ibbotson, Roger G., and Fall, Carol L. "The United States Market Wealth Portfolio." *The Journal of Portfolio Management,* Fall 1979, page 88.

TABLE 7. Cumulative Wealth Indices of Capital Market Securities (Year-end 1946 = 1.000)

Year-End	Common Stocks			
	NYSE	*AMEX**	*OTC*	*Total*
1947	1.033	N/A	1.021	1.032
1948	1.057	N/A	0.990	1.052
1949	1.271	N/A	1.151	1.261
1950	1.651	N/A	1.487	1.638
1951	1.997	N/A	1.721	1.975
1952	2.263	N/A	1.833	2.229
1953	2.271	N/A	1.893	2.241
1954	3.419	N/A	2.847	3.373
1955	4.283	N/A	3.385	4.212
1956	4.652	N/A	3.903	4.591
1957	4.154	N/A	3.429	4.096
1958	5.993	N/A	5.086	5.919
1959	6.765	N/A	5.571	6.670
1960	6.806	N/A	5.626	6.711
1961	8.655	N/A	7.667	8.565
1962	7.843	1.000	6.720	7.748
1963	9.517	1.148	8.362	9.379
1964	11.066	1.320	10.525	10.945
1965	12.607	1.578	14.014	12.614
1966	11.477	1.485	14.140	11.580
1967	14.572	2.321	22.113	15.108
1968	16.434	3.091	27.203	17.365
1969	14.815	2.395	27.657	15.653
1970	15.023	2.012	24.189	15.498
1971	17.410	2.446	34.022	18.315
1972	20.530	2.693	45.613	21.791
1973	17.047	1.932	35.177	17.826
1974	12.470	1.248	21.634	12.776
1975	17.175	1.741	29.742	17.603
1976	21.688	2.286	34.254	22.108
1977	20.628	2.587	39.303	21.484
1978	22.155	3.088	44.927	23.303

* Year-end 1962 = 1.000

SOURCE: Ibbotson, Roger G., and Fall, Carol L. "The United States Market Wealth Portfolio." *The Journal of Portfolio Management*, Fall 1979, page 89.

TABLE 8. Corporate Bond Market 1926-1978 Annual Percentage Returns

	Total Returns			*Return in Excess of Yield*	
Portfolio	*Arithmetic Mean*	*Geometric Mean*	*Standard Deviation* [1]	*Arithmetic Mean*	*Geometric Mean*
Composite	3.68%	3.43%	7.15%	−1.61%	−2.34%
Industry					
Utility	4.10	3.81	6.50	−1.16	−1.66
Industrial	4.36	4.14	6.83	−1.16	−1.35
Financial [2]	3.98	2.80	6.15	−1.82	−1.97
Transportation	3.32	2.80	9.93	−2.99	−3.46
Moody's Rating					
Aaa	1.48%	.70%	11.23%	−2.93	−3.64
Aa	1.46	.95	9.57	−3.10	−3.62
A	3.53	3.25	7.57	−1.57	−1.83
Baa	4.45	4.10	8.46	−1.21	−1.60
Below Baa	5.55	4.80	12.21	−2.94	−3.65
Maturity [3]					
5 to 14.99 years	6.47	6.19	8.11	.57	.28
15+ years	3.93	3.70	7.73	−1.87	−1.93

[1] Standard deviations reflect a small sample size and thus do not exactly reflect the underlying dispersion of returns. [2] Data for financial category is for 1950-1978. [3] Results omitted for 0 to 4.99 years to maturity due to small size.

SOURCE: *Corporate Bond Study 1926-1978.* Chicago: R. G. Ibbotson & Co., 1979, pages 1-13

TABLE 9. International Equity Markets 1960-1979

Country	*Annual Percentage Returns in U. S. Dollars*		
	Arithmetic Mean	*Geometric Mean*	*Standard Deviation*
North America			
United States	8.09%	6.83%	16.11%
Canada	11.60	10.18	17.74
Europe			
Austria	11.43	10.28	16.59
Belgium	11.21	10.38	13.30
Denmark	11.15	9.19	24.81
France	8.61	6.63	21.86
Germany	11.02	9.18	19.91
Italy	1.96	– .45	22.35
Netherlands	10.82	9.16	18.23
Norway	19.14	11.88	49.57
Spain	10.64	8.64	20.29
Sweden	9.13	7.76	16.89
Switzerland	13.48	11.18	23.05
UK	13.47	8.72	33.96
Asia & Pacific			
Japan	18.50	14.90	32.11
Australia	8.47	8.02	20.37
Hong Kong*	37.38	20.79	63.51
Singapore*	34.57	19.98	68.85

*Data are for 1970-1979

SOURCE: *International Equity Study*. Chicago: R.G. Ibbotson & Co., 1980.

TABLE 10. International Bond Returns 1975-1980

	Annual Percentage Returns in U.S. Dollars		
	Arithmetic Mean	*Geometric Mean*	*Standard Deviation*
Foreign Domestic			
All Foreign Currencies			
All maturities	17.17%	16.37%	11.82%
0-4.99 years to maturity	14.73	14.06	10.91
5-9.99 years to maturity	16.37	15.59	11.76
10+ years to maturity	17.34	16.56	14.35
Pounds Sterling			
All maturities	18.64	16.81	17.95
0-4.99 years to maturity	12.69	11.84	12.39
5-9.99 years to maturity	14.72	13.14	16.97
10+ years to maturity	21.97	19.31	21.55
Deutschemarks			
All maturities	13.30	12.29	13.44
0-4.99 years to maturity	12.56	11.63	12.96
5-9.99 years to maturity	13.54	12.35	14.59
Japanese Yen			
All maturities	19.29	18.21	13.70
0-4.99 years to maturity	17.91	16.90	13.33
5-9.99 years to maturity	19.57	18.48	13.77
Dutch Guilders			
All maturities	12.08	11.06	13.63
0-4.99 years to maturity	11.88	11.14	11.60
5-9.99 years to maturity	11.40	10.48	12.94
10+ years to maturity	12.16	11.04	14.23
Foreign Crossborder			
All Foreign Currencies			
All maturities	12.50	11.66	12.28
0-4.99 years to maturity	12.81	11.93	12.56
5-9.99 years to maturity	14.60	13.57	13.46
10+ years to maturity	15.16	13.85	15.19
Deutschemarks			
All maturities	13.59	12.50	13.92
0-4.99 years to maturity	11.93	10.96	13.32
5-9.99 years to maturity	13.65	12.52	14.26
10+ years to maturity	14.05	12.62	16.02
Swiss Francs			
All maturities	17.07	15.52	16.43
0-4.99 years to maturity	13.97	12.82	14.30

	Annual Percentage Returns in U.S. Dollars		
	Arithmetic Mean	*Geometric Mean*	*Standard Deviation*
Foreign Crossborder			
5-9.99 years to maturity	16.00	14.69	15.12
10+ years to maturity	17.31	15.51	17.68
Japanese Yen			
All maturities	19.11	18.05	13.55
0-4.99 years to maturity	18.21	17.21	13.19
5-9.99 years to maturity	19.25	18.20	13.53
10+ years to maturity	18.74	17.65	13.74
Dutch Guilders			
All maturities	12.63	11.62	13.53
Other Currencies			
All maturities	4.53	4.17	8.34
U.S. Dollar Crossborder			
All U.S. Dollar Bonds			
All maturities	8.49	8.33	5.46
0-4.99 years to maturity	7.86	7.77	4.07
5-9.99 years to maturity	6.87	6.68	5.97
10-14.99 years to maturity	8.20	7.84	8.24
15+ years to maturity	7.99	7.49	9.76
Yankee Bonds			
All maturities	6.93	6.67	6.97
0-9.99 years to maturity	7.19	7.07	4.74
10+ years to maturity	6.68	6.20	9.58
0-4.99 years to maturity	6.99	6.89	4.47
5-9.99 years to maturity	5.85	5.61	6.70
10-14.99 years to maturity	9.12	8.62	9.68
15+ years to maturity	6.18	5.68	9.77
Dollar Bonds			
All maturities	8.49	8.32	5.62
0-4.99 years to maturity	8.27	8.18	4.08
5-9.99 years to maturity	7.43	7.24	5.98
10-14.99 years to maturity	7.73	7.40	7.88
15+ years to maturity	8.87	8.33	10.15
Floating-Rate Bonds			
All maturities	15.42	15.40	1.72
U.S. Domestic Bonds (for comparison)			
Lehman Bros, Kuhn Loeb Index			
All maturities	6.35	5.86	9.74
U.S. Inflation Rate			
(for comparison)	8.89	8.85	1.12

TABLE 11. Ten-Year Returns on Selected Investments

	10 Years	*Rank*	*5 Years*	*Rank*	*1 Year*	*Rank*
Oil	30.8%	1	20.9%	5	14.3%	6
Gold	28.0	2	30.7	3	−13.9	14
Oriental Carpets	27.3	3	20.9	6	−0.2	11
U.S. Coins	27.1	4	29.7		−8.0	12
U.S. Stamps	23.5	5	32.9	1	18.0	4
Chinese Ceramics	22.9	6	30.7	2	36.5	1
Silver	21.5	7	20.1		−26.6	16
Rare Books	16.8	8	13.8	11	18.0	5
Old Masters	15.4	9	16.8	9	22.9	3
Farmland	14.6	10	14.8	10	9.7	8
Diamonds	14.5	11	16.9	8	0.0	10
Housing	10.3	12	11.6	12	8.1	9
CPI	8.3	13	9.7	14	10.0	7
Stocks	5.8	14	9.8	13	25.3	2
Foreign Exchange	5.3	15	3.1	15	−17.3	15
Bonds	3.8	16	1.1	16	−9.6	13

All returns are for the period ending June 1, 1981 based on latest available data.
Table prepared by Samuel Liss.

SOURCE: Salomon, Robert S., Jr. "Bonds and Foreign Exchange May Be the Only Bargains Left." *Stock Research Investment Policy.* New York: Salomon Brothers, 1981.

TABLE 12. Returns on Strategic Metals

Metal	*Holding Period*	*Number of Years*	*Compound Annual Rate of Return**
Antimony	1958-1981	23	8.4%
Cadmium	1958-1975	17	1.1
	1975-1981	6	1.0
	1958-1981	23	1.1
Chromium	1958-1975	17	4.4
	1975-1981	6	9.7
	1958-1981	23	5.8
Cobalt	1958-1981	23	10.4
Germanium	1975-1981	6	25.0
Indium**	1975-1981	6	6.6
Manganese	1958-1975	17	2.7
	1975-1981	6	3.1
	1958-1981	23	2.8
Molybdenum	1958-1981	23	2.5
Rhodium	1958-1975	17	7.6
	1975-1981	6	8.5
	1958-1981	23	7.8
Titanium	1975-1981	6	23.8

*Before transaction and storage costs.

**Based on a 1975 producer price and a 1981 free market price; hence, actual return may have been different.

SOURCE: Strategic Metals & Critical Materials Inc.

Portfolio Management

Marshall E. Blume *

OVERVIEW

The primary reason for saving and investing is to provide for future obligations or desires. As an example, a husband and wife may set aside and invest funds to provide for their retirement or their children's education. As another example, a corporation may set up a pension fund to provide for the payments of its future pension obligations.

In addition, some investments, such as housing or collectibles, provide not only potential monetary gains but also services that are of value to an investor. This article will be primarily concerned with the construction of desirable portfolios in terms of the potential monetary gains. Put another way, most of the material in this section was prepared under the assumption that a dollar of return from one asset is just as valuable as a dollar of return from another asset.

Portfolio theory deals with ways of combining assets into portfolios so as to provide for one's future obligations in the best possible way. Any portfolio has associated with it an expected return as well as potential risks of not realizing this expectation. *Rewards and Risks,* in this article, describes the concept and measurement of expected returns and risk. Also in that section is an example that demonstrates that the risk characteristics of a portfolio as a whole can differ substantially from the risk characteristics of any of the component assets. Specifically, it is possible that a portfolio would be of very low risk even though each of the component assets, judged by itself, would be of very high risk.

Currently, it is in vogue to associate principles of portfolio theory with the term "modern portfolio theory" (or MPT), as if there were a substantive difference between portfolio theory of old and of new. In fact, the basic principles of constructing portfolios are not new. What is new is that, following the theoretical contributions of Markowitz in the early fifties, it has been possible to model the process of selecting a portfolio into a very precise mathematical form.

This ability to model mathematically the portfolio selection process has led, at the theoretical level, to a much better understanding of the relationship of expected returns of individual assets to their underlying risks and, at the practical level, to the development of new quantitative techniques for investment analysis. Perhaps the most widely known tool developed from MPT is the beta coefficient for individual assets. Beta coefficients are risk measures for individual assets and

* Marshall E. Blume is Howard Butcher Professor of Finance at the Wharton School, University of Pennsylvania.

are widely available to the investing public, at least for common stocks through such publications as *Value Line.* Beta coefficients measure the relative contribution of different assets to the risk of a well-diversified portfolio. The greater the beta coefficient of an asset, the more the asset will contribute to the overall risk of a well-diversified portfolio.

The basic principles of modern portfolio theory will then be applied to the practical problem of how to allocate one's wealth over the available assets. This article will utilize the portfolio optimization procedures that have been developed by the Rodney L. White Center of Financial Research at the Wharton School. These procedures were developed by a joint effort of the Center and several of its corporate members. This analysis will document the trade-off for optimal portfolios between expected returns and the level of risk assumed by the investor. The factors that should be weighed in determining the specific level of risk one is willing to assume will then be explored.

With an intuitive but fairly thorough discussion of portfolio theory and its implications for optimal investment strategies, there will be a brief examination of what investors actually do. Although many investors' portfolios are constructed in substantial conformity to the precepts of MPT, there are a large number of investors whose portfolios probably expose them to unnecessary or undesirable risks. As is true in many endeavors, theory and practice are not always the same.

REWARDS AND RISKS

As already mentioned, the primary reason for investing is to provide for future obligations or desires over a long period of time. Nonetheless, portfolio theory, or MPT, generally concentrates on results over the short term, such as a year or even a month. Under certain assumptions that are appropriate for many investors, such a concentration on near-term results is warranted. However, for some investors, such as life insurance companies, the investment process is considerably more complicated, and such investors would have to be concerned with more than just short-term results. Investors with a heavy commitment to real estate and perhaps collectibles may face a conceptually similar problem to that faced by life insurance companies. This last type of investor will be examined after the more general material.

Measuring Risk

The usual applications of MPT make the assumption that risk can be measured by volatility over the short term, typically volatility as measured over a one- to twelve-month period. As will be seen, this concentration on the short term is often compatible with a long-term or multi-year investment horizon. The basic reason is that the long term is nothing more than a series of short terms.

However, the specific level of short-term volatility to which an investor will expose himself will be dictated by long-term considerations. Thus, an investor who is saving for retirement and wants to be fairly certain of reaching his goals would generally expose himself to a fairly low level of volatility in the near term. He wants no unpleasant surprises. In contrast, an investor who has little current wealth but wishes to accumulate a large amount of wealth may be willing to take on substantial short-term risks. As we shall see, substantial short-term risks generally imply substantial long-term risks of not meeting one's goals.

A Common Misconception

There is a misconception, which is more frequently espoused in booming markets, that an investor with a long-term horizon should invest in portfolios that have higher short-term expected returns, so-called "growth portfolios," even though such portfolios would entail higher short-term volatility. The logic underlying this misconception is that short-term fluctuations in the value of a portfolio will somehow wash themselves out in the long term. Nothing could be further from the truth. A study of all stocks on the New York Stock Exchange from July 1928 through June 1968 found that the stocks with the greatest increase in value over these forty years were those with moderate risk in the short term, and that both the lowest-risk and highest-risk stocks had lesser increases in value.[1] This result is consistent with expectations for the lowest-risk stocks, but not consistent for the highest-risk stocks.

Besides this empirical evidence, there is a strong theoretical presumption that, if a portfolio with greater expected short-term rates of return has higher short-term volatility, this same portfolio will also have higher long-term volatility. Assume for the moment that this is not the case, so that an investor could be assured of a greater level of wealth in the long term, say, ten to twenty years, by investing in a portfolio of assets with greater short-term volatility as well as greater expected returns. What would happen? Since most investments are made to satisfy long-term obligations or desires, there would be an immediate stampede towards the purchase of those assets with higher short-term volatility, in view of the certainty of greater rewards in the long term. Such purchases presumably would be financed by the sale of assets with lesser short-term volatility. The immediate effect would be to drive up the prices of those assets with the higher short-term volatility, thereby reducing the future expected returns. Similarly, but for the opposite reason, there would be an increase in the future expected returns on those assets with lower short-term volatility. In a well-functioning market, if assets with higher short-term volatility also have greater short-term expected returns, one would expect in the long term greater returns on these assets than on assets with lesser short-term volatility, but there can be no guarantee. The differences between expectations and realizations are sometimes big.

In sum, the long term is nothing more than a series of short terms. If an

---

[1] Blume, Marshall E., and Friend, Irwin. "Risk, Investment Strategy and the Long-Run Rates of Return." *The Review of Economics and Statistics.* Vol. LVI, No. 3, August 1974, pages 259-269.

investor does well in each short-term period, he will necessarily do well in the long term. For instance, consider two bond managers who are each given $10 million to invest. Assume that the first manager judges long-term interest rates to be at their peak and thus commits the entire $10 million to long-term bonds. Assume further that the second manager feels that long-term interest rates will be at their peak in a year and thus commits his money to one-year governments.

If the second manager turns out to be correct, his portfolio will have realized a greater return over the year than the portfolio of the first manager. To be concrete, assume that the portfolio of the second manager, with re-investment of interest, is worth $11.5 million at the end of the year and that of the first manager is worth $10.0 million — a difference of 15 percent. If the second manager at the end of the year were to invest his appreciated portfolio in the same kind of long-term bonds as the first, the subsequent returns of both managers would be similar. For purposes of argument, assume that their subsequent returns were the same. In this case, no matter how many years the two managers are retained, the value of the portfolio of the second manager will always be 15 percent greater than the value of the first manager's portfolio.[2]

Investors With Long-Term Horizons

Despite this argument, it is sometimes felt that bonds for an investor with a long-term horizon are not risky, even while recognizing that the market value of a bond does fluctuate in value over its life. If interest rates were to increase, the market price of a long-term bond would drop but, nonetheless, the price would ultimately increase as the bond approached maturity. In short, a bond has a memory. If its return in the first part of its life is less than expected, the return in the second part of its life will be greater than expected as the market price of the bonds increases to its redemption value.

It might be noted that there is no empirical evidence that stocks have this property of remembering where they have been. The fact that a stock has not performed up to expectations in one year has virtually no bearing on how it will perform in the following year.

This trait of a bond of remembering where its price has been and where its price must go by maturity may be extremely important to a life insurance company, but is probably not very important to most other types of investors. A primary difference between a life insurance company and a typical investor is that the obligations of a life insurance company are denominated in nominal dollars, whereas the typical investor is more concerned with real dollars. In other words, the life insurance company is concerned with the number of dollars available to it and not what these dollars will buy; a typical investor is more interested in what these dollars will buy.

---

[2] It might be noted that the annual compounded rates of return for the two portfolios will approach each other, but the second portfolio manager's annual compounded rate of return will always be sufficiently greater than that of the first, to produce a difference in wealth of 15 percent.

A life insurance company may be able to estimate with a high degree of accuracy the total number of policy holders who will die in a given year and thus the dollar amount of its liability. By buying an appropriate portfolio of bonds, the insurance company can be certain of having this estimated number of dollars at the designated point in the future. In the terminology of the investment world, such portfolios are called "immunized portfolios." Now, a life insurance company may be willing to trade off some degree of immunization in order to obtain a greater expected short-term return; the degree to which a life insurance company will deviate from a fully immunized strategy will hinge upon regulatory considerations, the competitive market for life insurance policies, and the risk tolerance of the company relative to its other goals.

The Nature of the Investors' Liabilities

Thus, the key to the difference between a life insurance company and the more typical investor lies in the nature of the investors' liabilities and goals. Those investors whose liabilities are denominated in terms of nominal dollars will have to concern themselves with more than just short-term volatility and short-term expected returns. Such investors will also have to consider the potential for an asset to remember that it has to have good returns following poor returns.

In contrast, the liabilities of most investors, including most corporations with defined-benefit pension plans, are not denominated in nominal dollars but are more closely tied to real dollars. The certainty of receiving a fixed-dollar amount at some point in the future is not really relevant to these more usual types of investors. By the time the payment would be received, the liability may well have changed. The best way for an investor to discharge such a changing liability is to concentrate on doing the best job possible in each short-term period.

If, however, there were assets available that paid an amount fixed in real terms at some future date, short-term volatility would no longer be an adequate measure of risk to the usual investor whose liabilities are denominated in real dollars. Such assets would provide a hedge if inflation turned out to be greater than anticipated. Are there assets available to the typical investor that would provide such a hedge? Bonds, stocks, and short-term assets are not good hedges if inflation turns out to be greater than anticipated. In fact, bonds behave the opposite of what one would want in a hedge, and the returns on stocks, at least in the United States, have shown little relationship to inflation. If there is any relationship, there is a slight, but almost negligible, negative relationship.

There is some evidence, although skimpy, that private residential real estate has been a hedge against the presumably unanticipated increases in inflation rates from 1953 to 1971, but even so its realized returns have sometimes differed by large amounts from what would be anticipated just due to inflation.[3] In the late 1970s, a period of rapid inflation, private residential real estate in some parts of

---

[3] Fama, Eugene F., and Schwert, G. William. "Asset Returns and Inflation." *Journal of Financial Economics,* Vol. 5, No. 2, Nov. 1977, pages 115-146.

the country had spectacular returns. In view of the diverse returns in differing parts of the country and the 1953-1971 analysis, it is probably safe to conclude that part of the returns on real estate in the late 1970s can be attributed to inflation and part to local conditions. If an investor is considering a substantial commitment to real estate, he would have to take into account not only the short-term expected returns and risks, but also the capability of the portfolio to act as a hedge against realized inflation rates in excess of those expected.

Portfolios

Just as a cocoon transforms a caterpillar into something totally different, a portfolio can transform a set of individual assets into something with characteristics quite different from those of the individual assets. To visualize the potential metamorphosis of a portfolio, commonly called "diversification," consider the following stylized example: Asset A has a 50 percent probability of returning 40 percent on the original investment and a 50 percent probability of losing 10 percent or −10 percent. Thus, on a flip of a coin, the return on Asset A will be either 40 percent or −10 percent. Since roughly half of the time the return on the asset would be 40 percent and the other half of the time the return would be −10 percent, the return expected on average would be 0.5 × 40 percent + 0.5 × −10 percent, or 15 percent. Another asset, Asset B, has coincidentally a 50 percent probability of returning 40 percent and a 50 percent probability of returning −10 percent. The expected return is 15 percent, the same as that of Asset A.

Although most investors probably do not conceive of an asset or a portfolio of assets as a lottery, an investment is actually just that. For a fixed amount of money, an investor buys the right to potential returns, to each of which he could assign a probability. Once one conceives of investments as lotteries, it becomes easier to separate the uncertainty or risk from the expected return. An investment in a government bill has no risk attached to it if one holds it to maturity and is only concerned with nominal dollars. Likewise, an investment in the Pennsylvania State Lottery has very little risk attached to it. The potential return is almost certain −100 percent, which removes most of the uncertainty associated with such an investment. Of course, most investors, given the choice of the State Lottery or the government bill, would choose the bill since it has a greater expected (and, in this case, certain) return.

Now let's form a portfolio of these two assets with an equal amount invested in each. The expected return will be the average of the expected return on each of the two assets or, in this example, 15 percent. The uncertainty of return or volatility will hinge upon the correlation of the returns of the two assets and will be smaller, the smaller the correlation.

Correlation of One

Consider that whenever Asset A has a return of 40 percent, Asset B has a return of 40 percent; and whenever Asset A has a return of −10 percent, Asset

A has a return of −10 percent. In this case, the returns on Asset A and Asset B are said to be perfectly positively correlated; the correlation coefficient is 1.0. In this scenario, the possible outcomes associated with the portfolio of these two assets would be as follows:

	Return		
Probability	*A*	*B*	*Portfolio Return*
50%	40%	40%	40%
50	−10	−10	−10

Notice that the distribution of the returns of the portfolio is identical to the distribution of the returns of either asset. Thus, the expected return would still be 15 percent and the level of volatility unchanged. This example illustrates the general proposition that diversification among assets whose returns are perfectly correlated does not reduce the volatility of the portfolio.

Correlation of Zero

If, however, returns are not perfectly correlated, diversification will generally reduce volatility. Consider, for instance, the case in which there is no relationship between the returns on Asset A and Asset B. Thus, even if the return on Asset A were 40 percent, the probabilities of obtaining either 40 percent or −10 percent on Asset B would still be equal. In this case, the returns on the two assets are said to be uncorrelated; the correlation coefficient is 0.

The possible outcomes with the corresponding probabilities would be as follows:

	Return		
Probability	*A*	*B*	*Portfolio Return*
25%	40%	40%	40%
25	40	−10	15
25	−10	40	15
25	−10	−10	−10

Under the assumed lack of correlation, each of the possible combinations of returns on Assets A and B are equally likely, implying a probability of 25 percent for each combination. The expected return is 15 percent, given as the sum of 0.25 × 40 percent + 0.50 × 15 percent + 0.25 × −10 percent.

A comparison of the case of zero correlation with the prior case of perfect positive correlation discloses that the expected return on the two portfolios is unchanged, indicating that the magnitude of the correlation between the returns on the two assets has no effect upon the portfolio expected return. This property holds for any level of correlation and will be generalized subsequently to the case in which the two assets have different expected returns.

However, the uncertainty or volatility of the portfolio has changed drastically. In the case of perfect positive correlation, the volatility of the portfolio was unchanged from the volatility of the individual assets. In the case of zero correlation, the volatility of the portfolio is less than the volatility of either of the assets alone. There is now only a 25 percent probability of losing 10 percent in contrast to the 50 percent probability for each of the individual assets. Unfortunately, the probability of making 40 percent has also been reduced. In general, diversification, through the formation of a portfolio, reduces the probability of obtaining extreme values — both favorable and unfavorable.

Correlation of Minus One

Finally, consider the case in which, whenever the return on Asset A is 40 percent, the return on Asset B is −10 percent, and whenever the return on Asset A is −10 percent, the return on Asset B is 40 percent. In this case, the returns on Assets A and B are said to be perfectly negatively correlated; the correlation coefficient is −1.0.

The possible outcomes with the corresponding probabilities would be as follows:

Probability	*Return*		*Portfolio Return*
	A	*B*	
50%	40%	−10%	15%
50	−10	40	15

As can be seen, the portfolio has a certain return of 15 percent, which in a trivial sense is also the expected return. The loss on one of the assets is always fully offset by the gain on the other. In this extreme case, diversification has transformed two volatile assets into a risk-free asset.

Although this example is highly stylized, it does contain the essence of how the volatility of a portfolio can be substantially different from the volatility of the component assets. What is happening is that there is an averaging effect — except for the case of perfect positive correlation. A poor return on one asset is not always associated with a poor return on another asset, and, in the case of perfect negative correlation, the poor return on one asset is exactly offset by the favorable return on the other.[4]

[4] As an aside, the case of perfect negative correlation plays a critical role in the Black-Scholes option formula. The basic assumption underlying this formula in the case of calls is that the return on the option in an instantaneous period is perfectly positively correlated with the return on the underlying security in the same period. If the price of the underlying security rises, so will the option.

Standard Deviation

The previous examples illustrated the role of the correlation coefficient in determining the volatility of a portfolio of two assets. Thse examples are highly stylized in that the expected return and volatility of the individual assets were the same. In practice, the equality of these two statistics across assets would be most unusual. The purpose of this section is to examine the more realistic case in which these two characteristics are not identical.

To accomplish this purpose, it is necessary to propose an explicit measure of volatility. Although there are numerous measures of short-term volatility, MPT usually utilizes the standard deviation of return, which is frequently designated by the lowercase Greek letter, σ. Sometimes to refer to a specific portfolio or asset, *A,* for example, the letter is subscripted by *A* as σ_A.

This article will not contain the explicit formulae used in calculating the standard deviation, but it should be noted that many small and inexpensive business calculators contain simple routines to calculate the standard deviation. All one does is enter, for a portfolio or asset, the returns realized over a historical period of time and punch the button for standard deviation. In the case of a portfolio, professional services frequently utilize twenty quarters of quarterly returns for this type of calculation.

An Interpretation

If returns on assets or portfolios are approximately distributed by a normal distribution, the standard deviation has a very useful interpretation. Most people are familiar with a normal distribution, although perhaps not by that name. The bell-shaped curve that educators sometimes use to curve test scores around a C is approximately a normal curve. The number of B grades would be the same as the number of D grades and less than the number of C grades. In turn, the number of A grades would be the same as the number of F grades and less than the number of B or D grades.

Although returns of assets or portfolios are not exactly described by a normal distribution, the approximation is probably good enough to permit an interpretation of the standard deviation within the context of this distribution. The interpretation is as follows: The interval formed by adding and subtracting one standard deviation from the expected return will bracket roughly two-thirds of the possible outcomes. Thus, if the standard deviation were on an annual basis, say 15 percent, and the expected return were 10 percent, one would anticipate that on average

---

Since, in a short position, the sign of the return is the opposite of the return on the long position, Black and Scholes have observed that the correlation, in an instantaneous period of time, between the return from a short position in a call option and the return from a long position in the underlying stock would be -1. They then determine appropriate investment weights for the short position and the long position such that the returns on the short position that are greater than or less than expected are exactly offset by the returns on the long position. Thus, they have created a risk-free asset whose returns must be the same as the risk-free rate to prevent arbitrage. Using this equality, they derive their option pricing formula.

in two out of every three years the actual return would be between −5 percent and 25 percent. A fair bet that the actual return next year would be between −5 percent and 25 percent would have odds of 1 to 2. The odds are 5 to 1 that the return will be in excess of 25 percent and also 5 to 1 that the return will be less than −5 percent. These odds are approximate but are close enough to the mark to be useful in evaluating the uncertainty associated with different possible portfolios.

Bracketing the expected return by two standard deviations results in an interval that will cover approximately 95 percent of the possible outcomes. Thus, there would be a 95 percent chance that the actual return next year will be between −20 percent and 40 percent.

The figures in Table 1 below are annualized standard deviations for well-diversified portfolios of different kinds of common stocks and high-grade corporate bonds. These numbers were estimated over the years 1970 to 1979. To interpret these numbers, consider high-grade corporate bonds with a standard deviation of 6.0 percent. If one expected, say, a return of 15 percent on such bonds, there would be roughly a two-thirds probability that the actual return would fall in the interval 9.0 percent to 21.0 percent, 15 percent plus or minus 6.0.

General Conclusions

There are some general conclusions that can be made about the relationship between the expected return and standard deviation of a portfolio of assets and the expected returns and standard deviations of return of the component assets. If short sales are not permitted, the following two statements are true:

(1) The expected return on a portfolio of assets is the weighted average of the expected returns on the individual assets, where the weights are the proportion of wealth invested in each asset.

(2) The standard deviation of return on a portfolio of assets is equal to or less than the weighted average of the standard deviations of the individual assets, where the weights are the proportion of wealth invested in each asset. The portfolio standard deviation will be strictly less than the weighted average of the individual standard

TABLE 1. Standard Deviations of Annual Returns for Selected Portfolios

Asset	*Standard Deviation*
NYSE common stocks	21.4%
High-grade corporate bonds	6.0%

SOURCE: Rodney L. White Center for Financial Research, Wharton School, University of Pennsylvania

deviations in the usual case in which the correlation between any pair of assets is less than one and non-zero investments are made in each asset.

As an example, if an investor were to place a third of his wealth in a portfolio with an expected return of 15 percent and a standard deviation of 6 percent, and two-thirds of his wealth in a portfolio with an expected return of 21 percent and a standard deviation of 18 percent, the investor's portfolio would have an expected return of 19 percent and a standard deviation of, at most, 14 percent. The expected return of 19 percent is given by the sum of one-third of 15 percent and two-thirds of 21 percent. The maximum standard deviation of 14 percent is given by the sum of one-third of 6 percent and two-thirds of 18 percent. The smaller the correlation coefficient between the two assets or portfolios, the smaller the standard deviation of the portfolio return for fixed levels of investment in each asset.

THE BASIC PRINCIPLES OF PORTFOLIO THEORY

The use of MPT to select an optimal portfolio of assets entails two steps of analysis. The first step is to determine that set of portfolios of risky assets which, for a given risk, maximize the expected return and, for a given expected return, minimize risk. Risky assets are any assets whose returns in the short term are uncertain, such as stocks or long-term bonds. This set of portfolios is called the efficient set of risky assets. The second step is to select one of these risky portfolios to be held in conjunction with an investment in risk-free assets. Risk-free assets are short-term, readily marketable securities of the highest grade. Government bills are one obvious candidate, although some investors might be willing to consider certificates of deposit of the most stable commercial banks, commercial paper of prime grade, or certain, but not all, money market funds as risk-free. In describing these two steps, it will be assumed that the investor is willing to utilize as the measure of risk the standard deviation of annual returns.

The Efficient Set of Risky Assets

To simplify the exposition, consider an investor who has already selected for possible investment a bond portfolio and a stock portfolio, but has not yet determined how much to invest in each. Though highly simplified, this example does parallel the decision process of many investors with substantial assets. In investing its pension fund, a corporation may have interviewed a group of bond managers and a group of stock managers and, based upon these interviews, selected a bond manager and a stock manager without determining exactly how much money each will be given.

Though this procedure is more often followed by larger investors, it is not a bad procedure to be followed by very small investors. Thus, a small investor might select for potential investment a mutual fund specializing in bonds and one specializing in common stocks. If feasible, the investor might select several mutual funds of each type in order to diversify management styles.

Moreover, although the text will use the terms "bond" and "stock funds," these terms are in fact much more general than may appear at first sight. A mortgage participation is really a bond in disguise, while an equity participation is in some ways similar to stock. Thus, the essential characteristics of the two funds to be examined here is that one must be of relatively low risk and the other of relatively high risk, so as to cover assets of all types of risk.

For concreteness, assume that the expected annual return on the bond fund is one percent greater than the rate on risk-free assets, and that the standard deviation of the bond fund is 7 percent. Thus, if risk-free assets were returning, say, 15 percent, the expected return on the bond fund would be 16 percent. Further assume that the expected return on the stock fund is 6 percent greater than the rate on risk-free assets, and that the standard deviation of the stock fund is 21 percent. Though presented as hypothetical, these assumed numbers are close to what has occurred since World War II.

Investing in Bonds and Stocks

The bond fund and the stock fund have been plotted in the expected return-standard deviation space in Figure 1 on page 1014. The stock fund is plotted upwards and to the right of the bond fund, reflecting both its greater expected return and its greater standard deviation.

Now, consider a portfolio consisting of investments in both the bond and the stock fund. Specifically, let 80 percent of the available funds be invested in the bond fund and the remaining 20 percent in the stock fund. As already pointed out, the expected return on the combined portfolio will be a weighted average of the expected return on the bond fund and the expected return on the stock fund. The combined portfolio will have an expected return of 2 percent in excess of the risk-free rate, given as the sum of 0.8 × 1 percent + 0.2 × 6 percent.

The standard deviation of the return on the combined portfolio will depend upon the correlation between the returns on the bond fund and the returns on the stock fund. If the returns are perfectly positively correlated with a correlation of 1.0, the standard deviation of the return on the combined portfolio will be a weighted average of the standard deviation of the component portfolios. The sum of 0.8 × 7 percent + 0.2 × 21 percent = 9.8 percent. The reason the standard deviation is a weighted average is that, with perfect positive correlation, there is no averaging or diversification effect. When one of the portfolios does poorly, the other portfolio also does poorly.

If the correlation between the returns of the two portfolios is less than 1.0, the portfolio return will reflect some averaging or diversification effects. A poor return on one portfolio may be partially offset by a favorable return on the other. The less the correlation, the more likely this averaging effect. Figure 1 contains two examples of correlations less than one. If 80 percent is placed in the bond

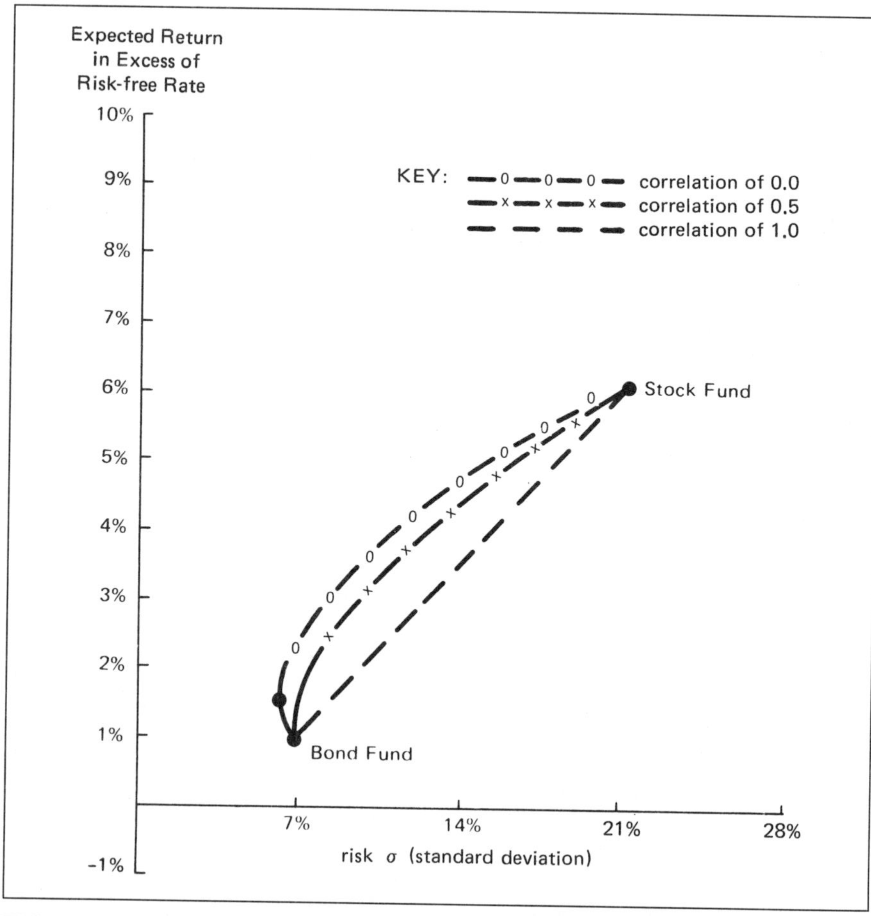

FIG. 1. Bond and Stock Portfolios and Combination Portfolios

portfolio, the expected return will always be 2 percent in excess of the risk-free rate regardless of the correlation.

More generally, if the correlation were 0.5, a positive but weak correlation, an investor who initially had 100 percent invested in bonds and who then began to switch into stocks would first see his expected return increase but at a faster rate than the increase in standard deviation. At some point in this process, the increase in expected return would be at a rate slower than the increase in standard deviation.

If the correlation were zero, an investor, as he decreased his investment in bonds from 100 percent, would initially see the expected return increase while, at the same time, the standard deviation would actually decrease from 7 percent. The averaging or diversification effect is so strong that it overcomes the inherent volatility of the component funds. At some point in this process, the standard deviation of the combined portfolio will increase from the minimum possible value as the volatility of the stock portfolio outweighs the diversification effect.

In this last case, note that an investor would never want to hold just the bond fund. By combining the bond fund with the stock fund, the investor can obtain a greater expected return at the same risk as the bond fund. Thus, if the correlation were zero, the investor would never want to hold a portfolio with 100 percent in bonds and, for the specific values assumed for the expected returns and standard deviations, no investor would hold a portfolio with more than 90 percent in bonds.

"Efficient Portfolio" Defined

Those portfolios of risky assets that no investor would want to hold constitute the inefficient set of portfolios of risky assets. The set of portfolios that some investors may want to hold is termed "the efficient set." Portfolios in the efficient set have the property that, for a given standard deviation, the expected return is maximized and, for a given level of expected return, the standard deviation is minimized.

Frequently, an investor would be considering more than just a single bond fund and a single stock fund as components of his risky portfolio. Figure 2 on page 1016 illustrates this more general case, assuming that no two assets are perfectly correlated. The edges and the shaded area represent every feasible portfolio, but the efficient set would only consist of those portfolios on the heavy line. No investor would want to hold a portfolio off this line.

Although it would generally require a computer to calculate the efficient set except in the simplest cases,[5] the concept of the efficient set has an important implication for money management. An investment adviser, using that term in a broad sense, does not need to know the objectives of his clients in order to construct desirable portfolios of risky assets. Basically, for any given level of risk, he would want to choose a portfolio so as to maximize its expected return. The goals of the client enter into determining which efficient portfolio to hold.

If one thinks about it, this concept of the efficient set underlies the marketing strategy of families of mutual funds or of bank commingled funds. For mutual funds, a family might have a growth fund, a growth-income, an income-growth, and an income fund. The growth fund is presumably the most risky; the growth-income, the next risky; the income-growth, the next risky; and the income, the least risky. The investment adviser would try to obtain the greatest level of expected return for each of these risks. The goals of the client enter in determining which fund or combination of funds he should hold.

Thus, investments do not have to be managed separately to satisfy the goals of an investor. This observation is important for an investor who is debating as

---

[5] Texas Instruments' *Calculator Analysis for Business and Finance* (1977) contains a program, suitable for the MBA calculator, for a problem involving two risky portfolios or assets.

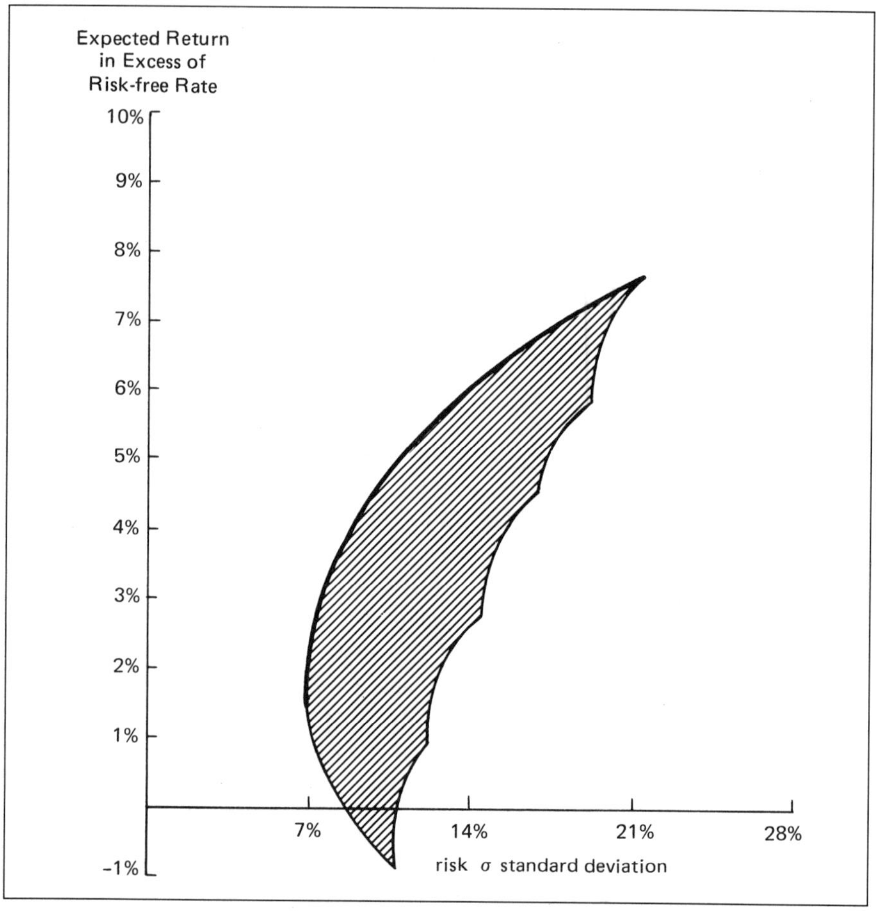

FIG. 2. The Efficient Set of Risky Assets

to whether his funds should be managed in separate accounts or in a mutual fund or in a bank commingled fund. The critical question to ask in solving this problem is: Which approach promises the greatest expected return for a given level of risk?

The Role of the Risk-Free Asset

Investments in a risk-free asset play a central role in MPT. Such investments permit an investor to modify the risk of a risky portfolio to the level of risk with which he is comfortable. Particularly for investors who do not wish to bear a great amount of risk, the judicious use of an investment in the risk-free asset can frequently lead to a substantial increase in expected return with no increase in overall risk. This point will be examined below.

Illustrative Example

Consider Asset A, which above was assumed to have an equal probability of realizing 40 percent or losing 10 percent. An investor might well judge the expected return of 15 percent quite attractive relative to the volatility or uncertainty associated with the investment, but at the same time feel that the risk is too great for his own particular situation.

By placing a portion of the money in Asset A and the remainder in the risk-free asset, the investor could obtain a portfolio with an overall level of risk lower than that of Asset A alone. If the risk-free rate were 10 percent and the investor placed 60 percent of his wealth in Asset A with the remaining 40 percent in the risk-free asset, he would obtain the following possible outcomes, each equally likely:

Probability	*Return A*	*Portfolio Return*
50%	40%	.60(40) + .40(10) = 28%
50%	−10%	.60(−10) + .40(10) = −2%

The expected return will be 13 percent, given by the sum of .50 × 28 percent + .50 × −2 percent. The maximum loss is now 2 percent instead of 10 percent.

Although the range of outcomes is not as satisfactory a measure of risk as the standard deviation for types of investments encountered in real life, it is a reasonable measure for lotteries with two outcomes, each having the same probability. The range of returns for Asset A is 50 percentage points, and the range for the combined portfolio is 30 percentage points.

The expected return of 13 percent is 60 percent of the way from 10 percent to 15 percent, or 10 percent plus 60 percent of the difference between 15 and 10 percent. Likewise, the range of 30 percent is 60 percent of the range of Asset A. If standard deviations were calculated, the standard deviation of the combined portfolio would likewise have been 60 percent of the standard deviation of Asset A. These linear relationships are not an accident and would occur when any risky asset or portfolio is combined with an investment in the risk-free asset. An investment in a risk-free asset in conjunction with an investment in a risky portfolio provides no averaging or diversification effects, only a straightforward risk-reduction effect.

This linear relationship between expected returns and standard deviations is illustrated in Figure 3 on page 1018. The risky asset or portfolio is taken to be the stock fund used in the last section with an assumed expected return in excess of the risk-free rate of 6 percent and a standard deviation of 21 percent. If an investor wanted a portfolio with two-thirds of the volatility of the stock fund, he would invest two-thirds of his assets in the stock fund and one-third in the risk-free asset. The resulting standard deviation would be 14 percent, and the expected return in excess of the risk-free rate would be 4 percent. This portfolio is designated *a* in Figure 3.

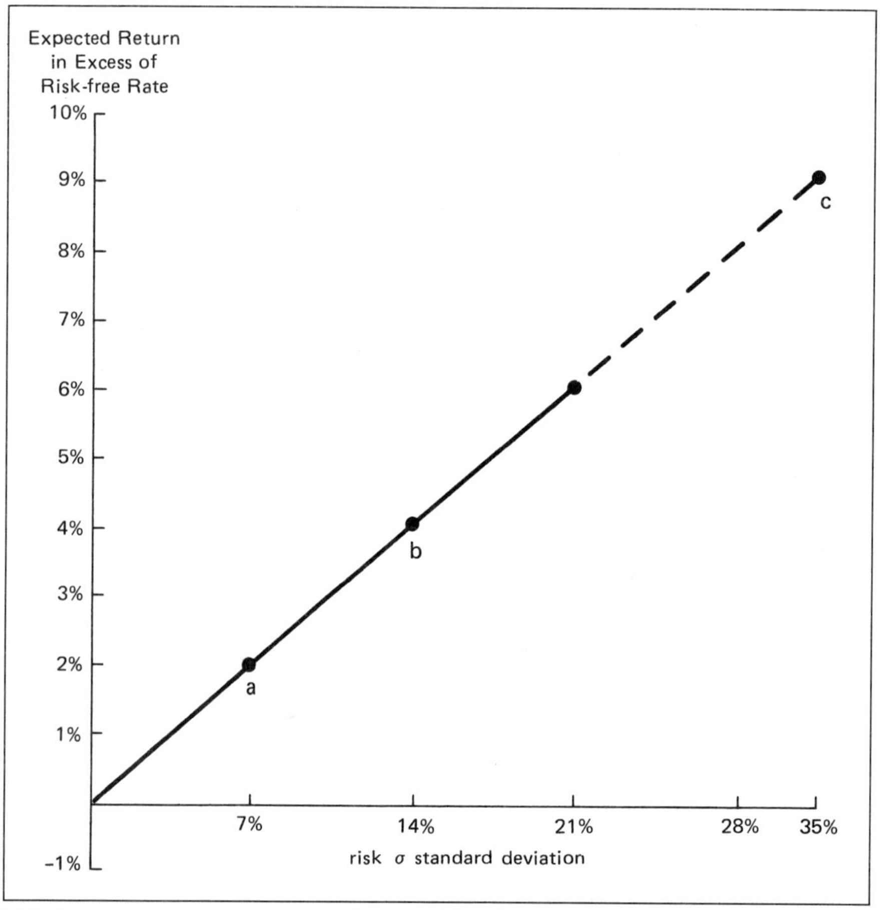

FIG. 3. The Use of the Risk-Free Rate to Alter Risk

If the investor felt that such an expected return was not great enough to justify assuming a standard deviation of 14 percent, he might further reduce the risk of his overall portfolio by placing only a third of the assets in the risky portfolio. Such a portfolio, designated by point *b* in Figure 3, would have a standard deviation of 7 percent and an expected return in excess of the risk-free rate of 2 percent.

Although most institutional investors are usually concerned with reducing the overall risk, some investors increase the risk of their overall portfolios in pursuit of a greater expected return. Individuals who have margin accounts are effectively utilizing a short position in a risk-free asset to lever their risky portfolios. A short position in a risk-free asset is equivalent to borrowing at the risk-free rate. If the borrowing and lending rates were the same, an investor could move a portfolio up the dotted line in Figure 3. At point *c* in Figure 3, the investor's overall portfolio would have a standard deviation of 31.5 percent and an expected return in excess of the risk-free rate of 9 percent. Assuming a net worth of $100, to obtain portfolio *c*, an investor would borrow $50 and, combined with the initial $100, would then invest $150 in the risky portfolio. As long as the realized return of the risky portfolio is greater than the risk-free rate, this leverage would increase his total realized return; but, if the realized return were less, this leverage would decrease his total realized return.

The assumption in Figure 3 is that the risk-free borrowing and lending rates are identical. In fact, the borrowing rate is usually in excess of the lending rate. The effect is to reduce the increase in expected return from leveraging a portfolio. It costs less to borrow at 15 percent than at 18 percent. However, there is no effect upon the standard deviation of the levered portfolio. Thus, the investor with a net worth of $100 who borrowed at, say, 3 percentage points above the risk-free lending rate to finance an investment of $150 in the stock portfolio would have an expected return in excess of the risk-free rate of 7.5 percent and a standard deviation of 31.5 percent. Such a portfolio is indicated by the point *c* in Figure 4 on page 1020. Differences in borrowing and lending rates just introduce a kink in the straight line.

Adjusting the Risk of a Portfolio

Besides merely understanding the geometry of combining a risk-free position with a risky portfolio, the reader should note that by varying the investment in the risk-free asset an investor can obtain any risk level with which he is comfortable regardless of the original risk of the risky portfolio. Thus, a conservative investor who typically doesn't want to assume much risk could invest in a highly speculative venture that he thought to be well managed. By placing a substantial portion of his net worth in risk-free assets, the investor could obtain overall a conservative portfolio, but with an expected return greater than what he might be able to obtain by investing directly in conservative assets themselves.

In short, an investor should be open to any type of investment regardless of his own goals. Just because the portfolio has risk characteristics that are unsuitable for a particular investor is no reason to discard it. The overall risk characteristics of a portfolio can easily be modified.

Determining the Optimal Portfolio

MPT uses the risk-free asset in conjunction with the efficient set of risky assets to determine the optimal set of portfolios which, at each level of risk, promise the greatest expected return. For concreteness, consider an investor who wants to invest assets in bonds, stocks, and risk-free or cash-equivalent investments. Although other types of assets might be included, these three types represent the bulk of institutional holdings and are the major holdings of many individual investors of substantial means. As mentioned, if bonds are interpreted

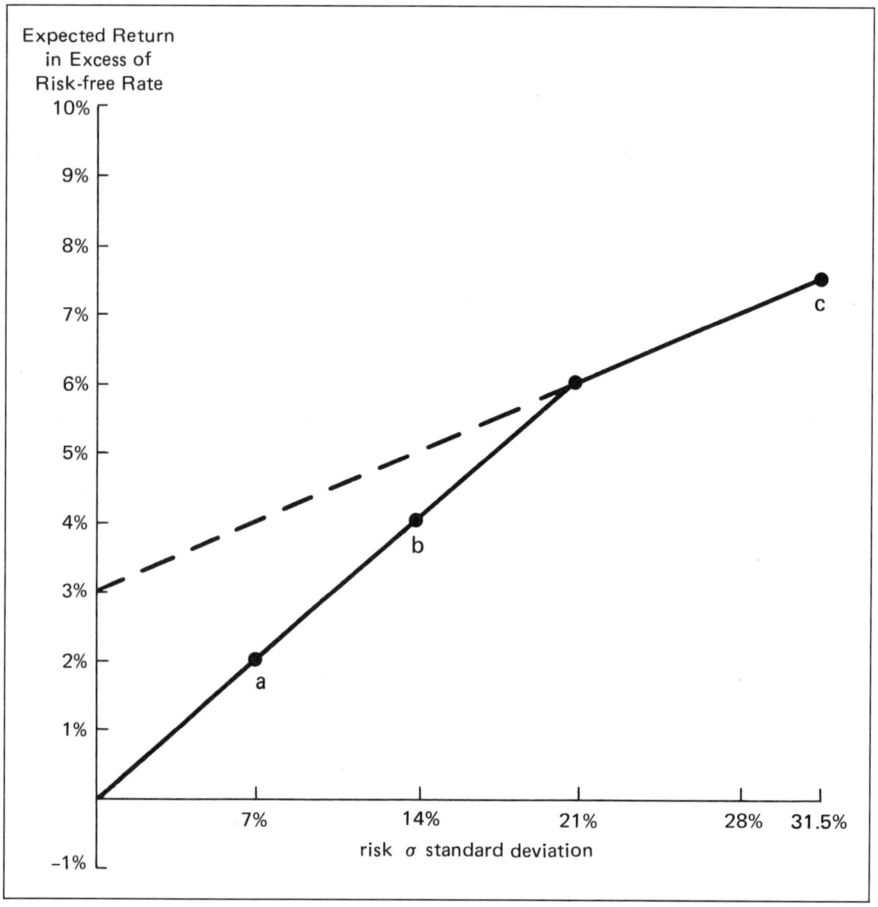

FIG. 4. Unequal Borrowing and Lending Rates With One Risky Portfolio

more generally as long-term fixed-interest obligations and stocks as equity investments, this classification is broader than it may appear on the surface.

To be even more concrete, assume that the investor is responsible for a profit-sharing plan whose participants are very risk-averse. They are willing to assume only modest risk in the expectation of receiving a return somewhat in excess of the return on the risk-free asset. Specifically, the participants will be satisfied in terms of expected return and standard deviation with a high-grade long-term bond portfolio. The question is whether some combination of investments in these bonds, stocks, and risk-free assets would lead to an increase in expected return with no increase in overall risk.

On the basis of the same assumptions as before, the bond fund would have an expected return in excess of the risk-free rate of one percent and a standard deviation of 7 percent. The stock fund would have an expected return in excess of the risk-free rate of 6 percent and a standard deviation of 21 percent. Assume that the correlation between the returns on these two funds is 0.3, a weak but positive correlation.

Indeed, the investor in this example could improve the portfolio's expected return without increasing the risk level from that implicit in the bond fund by exploiting the geometry of the efficient set. The approach is as follows: First, the investor who currently held a portfolio of bonds only should sell some bonds and invest the proceeds in common stock. Thus, the portfolio would be moving up the efficient set of risky assets in the direction indicated in Figure 5 on page 1022. He could continue to do this until reaching the portfolio designated in Figure 5 as the "optimal risky portfolio." It will soon be clear why this is the optimal risky portfolio. Since this portfolio contains more risk than the investor wants, he should then reduce the risk to which he is exposed by reducing his position in this optimal risky portfolio and investing the proceeds in the risk-free asset until the overall portfolio has a standard deviation of 7 percent.

Step one. The optimal risky portfolio is determined by drawing a line or ray from the risk-free rate (the origin in Figure 5) to that efficient portfolio of risky assets that maximizes the slope of the ray. Because the efficient set is, in general, curved and a ray is a straight line, the efficient portfolio that maximizes this slope will be at the tangency between the ray and the efficient set. Drawing the ray to any other efficient portfolio of risky assets will produce a lesser slope and thus create a lesser expected return for a given risk than that possible with the optimal risky portfolio.

For the assumed values of the expected returns and standard deviations, the optimal long-term portfolio would have 41.4 percent in the bond fund and 58.6 percent in the stock fund. This allocation to bonds and stocks was determined by a computer algorithm developed at the Rodney L. White Center for Financial Research. Since most of the readers of this article will probably not have such computer algorithms available to them, some examples of optimal risky portfolios for various scenarios will be presented below.

Step two. In this example, the optimal long-term portfolio would have an expected return in excess of the risk-free rate of 3.93 percent and a standard deviation of 13.47 percent. Since the investor wants a standard deviation of only 7.0 percent, he should expose 7 ÷ 13.47 or 52 percent of his assets to this optimal long-term portfolio and place the remaining funds or 48 percent in the risk-free asset. The resulting portfolio will have a standard deviation of 7.0 percent, but the expected return in excess of the risk-free rate will be 2.04 percent, for a gain of 1.04 percentage points with no additional risk. As a rough rule of thumb, a one-percentage-point increase in expected return will permit a reduction of 10 to 20 percent in contributions to a defined benefit plan. Thus, a gain of one percentage point is significant.

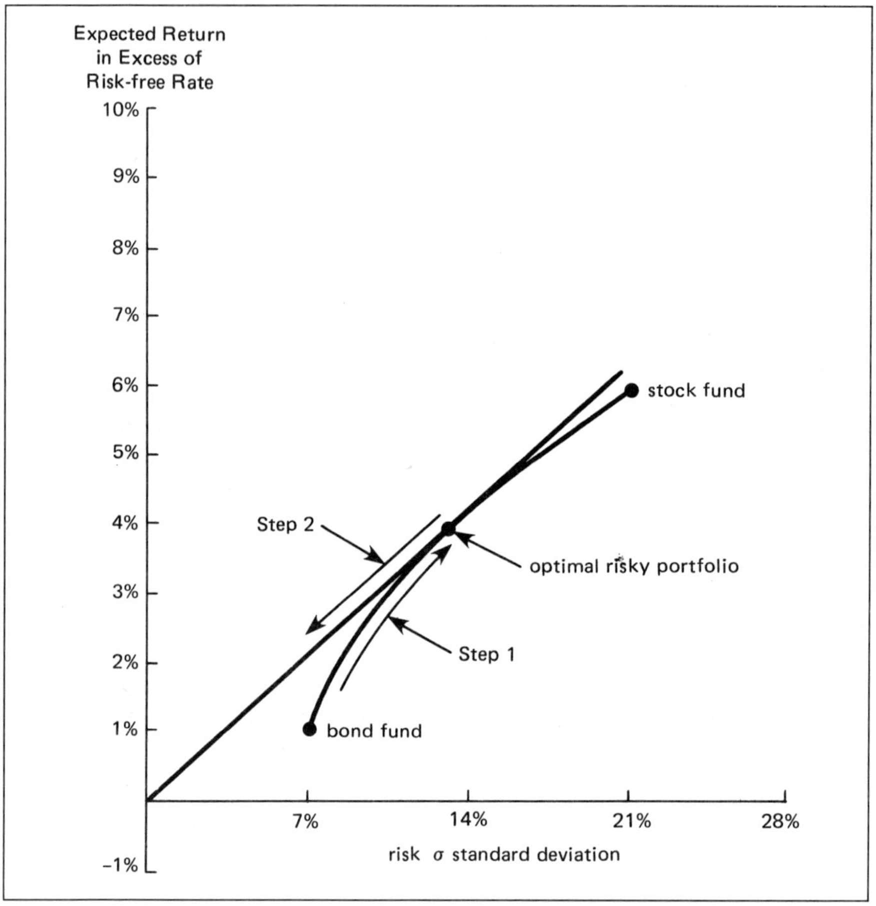

FIG. 5. Determining the Optimal Portfolio

The actual proportions to hold in the three types of asset for each $100 of wealth would be determined as follows:

$48 risk-free		$48.00 risk-free
$52 optimal risky portfolio:	41.4%	$21.50 bonds
	58.6%	$30.50 stocks

Although many investors probably would not intuitively construct a portfolio of moderate risk in this way, it is clear why such a portfolio has only a moderate level of risk. The high-risk component, represented by the common stock fund, has been offset by the zero risk of the risk-free asset. By holding a portfolio with both bonds and stocks, the investor has received some benefit from the diversification effect, a benefit that would not be present with an investment in only one kind of asset.

More generally, all investors who hold the same judgments as to the expected returns and risks of the bond and stock funds should hold the same optimal portfolio of risky assets. The investor's risk preferences should not affect the composition of this optimal long-term portfolio of risky assets. The investor's risk preferences enter in determining how he should allocate his wealth as between the optimal portfolio of risky assets and the risk-free asset. If an investor wanted a risk greater than 7 percent, he would invest less in the risk-free asset than would the investor in the above example. If he wanted a risk greater than 13.46 percent and could borrow and lend at the same risk-free rate, he should borrow and lever the optimal portfolio as discussed above.

If the investor were prohibited from borrowing to lever a portfolio, as some are, the only way to increase the expected return from that of the optimal portfolio would be to hold only risky assets and increase the proportion in equities from that implicit in the optimal portfolio of risky assets. As can be seen in Figure 5 on page 1022, the differences in expected returns from this latter strategy and the leverage strategy are not great. The efficient set of risky assets is relatively flat in its upper part.

Although a computer can give the optimal proportions in the risky funds to any apparent degree of accuracy, the real accuracy of the calculated proportions depends critically on the forecasted values of the expected returns and risks. If these are grossly in error, the proportions given by a computer will also be in error. Nonetheless, an examination of the geometry in Figure 5 indicates that if one is close to the optimal weights in the risky portfolio, the expected return on the overall portfolio with an appropriate position in the risk-free asset will be close to the maximum observable expected return. Thus, if the optimal proportion in bonds was 50 percent, but the actual percentage was 40 percent, an investor could obtain an expected return for a given level of risk almost as great as before.[6] Since the proportion held in bonds is less and the proportion in stocks is more than the optimal proportions, the portfolio of risky assets actually held would be more risky than the optimal portfolio. To maintain the same level of overall risk, the investor would have to take a greater position in risk-free assets than otherwise.

Use of Optimizing Procedures

Only a limited number of investors at the current time actually do undertake the formal optimization process implicit in MPT. This limited number would generally have substantial sums to invest and have the appropriate technical staff to perform the analysis. Nonetheless, the typical investor who would not undertake this formal process still can utilize some of the implications of MPT to obtain an overall portfolio that, though not optimal, is probably close to optimal.

Under normal circumstances, an investor should first construct a portfolio

[6] The ray connecting the risk-free asset to the suboptimal portfolio would be close to the best obtainable.

of risky assets. The risky assets should include assets of all types of risk, from the lowest risks to the greatest risks. In constructing this portfolio, the investor should make sure that it is well diversified to obtain the fullest possible benefits of diversification. He should not worry about the riskiness of the resulting portfolio in terms of his own goals. With an appropriate investment in a risk-free asset, an investor can modify the overall risk.

A risky portfolio consisting only of bonds or mortgages would generally be inconsistent with this principle of covering a broad range of risk. Likewise, a portfolio of a single stock would almost always be dominated by a well-diversified portfolio of different types of assets. It is sometimes alleged that an investor of modest means must of necessity hold a poorly diversified portfolio: An investor with, say, $4,000 can only realistically hold one or two stocks. This last statement is nonsense. Such an investor can most certainly hold two or three mutual funds, such as a bond fund and one or two stock funds.

Now that the investor has a well-diversified portfolio of assets spanning the whole range of risk, he should determine his position in the risk-free asset. According to surveys undertaken by the New York Stock Exchange and the Rodney L. White Center for Financial Research, most individual investors are highly risk-averse. Likewise, many pension plans and most profit-sharing plans do not want to expose their investments to extreme risk. For these investors, the usual question is how much to invest in risk-free assets. A very risk-averse investor might, for instance, place 75 percent of his wealth in risk-free assets and the remaining 25 percent in a well-diversified portfolio of risky assets. A less risk-averse investor might only place a third to a half of his overall portfolio in risk-free assets.

An investor who wanted to assume an extreme amount of risk in the hopes of realizing substantial returns should lever his portfolio through borrowings. The usual mechanism is for the investor to utilize a margin account at a brokerage house. Alternatively, the investor could tilt a well-diversified portfolio of risky assets towards the more risky assets in the portfolio.

Despite the logic of this two-step approach, the reader is cautioned that this approach may have to be modified for legal reasons in the case of personal trusts and certain other types of trusts. For such trusts, the trustee may be responsible for not only determining the appropriateness of the overall portfolio but also in some sense the appropriateness or suitability of each asset in the portfolio. In contrast, MPT evaluates a portfolio only in terms of the expected returns and risks of the total returns on the overall portfolio, whereas in managing a personal trust, the investor may also have to evaluate each of the individual assets on its own. As with any legal question, the investor is well advised to obtain expert legal advice.

Portfolio Selection — Two-Step Summary

MPT implies that an investor should select a portfolio in two steps:

1. Select a portfolio of risky assets that is well diversified over all types of risks. In

this step, do not consider the appropriateness of the expected returns and risks of the selected portfolio.

2. If the risk level of the selected portfolio of risky assets is too risky relative to the expected return, as is often the case, put a portion of the wealth in this risky portfolio and the remainder in a risk-free asset. If the risk level is too low, lever the portfolio with, for instance, a margin account, or tilt the portfolio towards the more risky components of the risky portfolio.

SELECTION OF A SPECIFIC PORTFOLIO

The use of MPT to select a specific portfolio involves two steps: First, determine the optimal portfolio of risky assets and, second, combine this portfolio with a position in the risk-free asset. The first part of this section will contain some numerical examples of this process. The purpose of these examples is to give the reader an intuitive feel of the composition of optimal portfolios at a low risk level and at a moderate risk level.

The second part of this section will contain an analysis of the long-term implications of various short-term strategies. As discussed above, most investors should probably view the investment decision in a short-term perspective by trying to obtain the best possible return each month or each year for the level of risk that has been assumed. However, the level of risk that an investor is willing to assume in the short term is dictated by long-term considerations.

Optimal Allocations

The first step in utilizing MPT to obtain an optimal portfolio is to identify those assets that an investor would consider and then to assess the expected returns and risks attached to these assets. For the purpose of this article, assume that the assets under consideration are a bond fund, a stock fund, and a risk-free asset. For many investors, particularly those of substantial means, these three types of assets would represent the bulk of their holdings. If bonds and stocks are interpreted more generally as long-term fixed-interest obligations and equity participations, respectively, real estate investments could be included in these categories.

Potential Risks

The specific allocations, shown in Table 2 on page 1026, are based upon the following assumptions: The standard deviation of the annual rate of return on the stock fund is 21 percent. The standard deviation of the annual rate of return on the bond fund is 7 percent. Thus, if an investor expected a return of 14 percent on bonds, there would be roughly a two-thirds probability that the realized return in the next year would be between 7 and 21 percent — 14 percent plus or minus 7 percent. The returns on the bond fund and the stock fund will be assumed to

TABLE 2. Optimal Portfolios of Bonds, Stocks, and Risk-Free Assets

Expected Annual Return in Excess of Risk-Free Rate		*Optimal Portfolios of Risky Assets*				*Portfolio With 5% Standard Deviation*				*Portfolio With 10% Standard Deviation*			
		Allocation				*Allocation*				*Allocation*			
Bonds	*Stocks*	*Bonds*	*Stocks*	*Expected Excess Return*	*Standard Deviation*	*Risk-Free*	*Bonds*	*Stocks*	*Expected Excess Return*	*Risk-Free*	*Bonds*	*Stocks*	*Expected Excess Return*
0.5%	1.0%	86.7%	13.3%	0.57%	7.40%	32.4%	58.6%	9.0%	0.38%	−35.1%	117.2%	17.9%	0.77%
0.5	2.0	63.5	36.5	1.05	9.94	49.7	31.9	18.3	0.53	− 0.6	63.9	36.7	1.05
0.5	3.0	41.4	58.6	1.97	13.47	62.9	15.4	21.8	0.73	25.7	30.7	43.5	1.46
0.5	4.0	20.2	79.8	3.29	17.23	71.0	5.9	23.1	0.96	42.0	11.7	46.3	1.91
0.5	5.0	0.0	100.0	5.00	21.00	76.2	0.0	23.8	1.19	52.4	0.0	47.6	2.38
1.0%	1.0%	98.8%	1.2%	1.00%	7.00%	28.5%	70.6%	0.9%	0.71%	−42.9%	141.2%	1.7%	1.43%
1.0	2.0	86.7	13.3	1.13	7.40	32.4	58.6	9.0	0.77	−35.1	117.2	17.9	1.53
1.0	3.0	75.0	25.0	1.50	8.47	40.9	44.3	14.8	0.89	−18.1	88.6	29.5	1.77
1.0	4.0	63.5	36.5	2.09	9.94	49.7	31.9	18.3	1.05	− 0.6	63.9	36.7	2.11
1.0	5.0	52.3	47.7	2.91	11.65	57.1	22.4	20.5	1.24	14.2	44.9	40.9	2.50
1.0	6.0	41.4	58.6	3.93	13.47	62.9	15.4	21.8	1.46	25.7	30.7	43.5	2.92
1.0	7.0	30.7	69.3	5.16	15.34	67.4	10.0	22.6	1.68	34.8	20.0	45.2	3.36
2.0%	2.0%	98.8%	1.2%	2.00%	7.00%	28.5%	70.6%	0.9%	1.43%	−42.9%	141.2%	1.7%	2.86%
2.0	3.0	92.7	7.3	2.07	7.10	29.6	65.3	5.1	1.46	−40.8	130.6	10.2	2.92
2.0	4.0	86.7	13.3	2.27	7.40	32.4	58.6	9.0	1.53	−35.1	117.2	17.9	3.07
2.0	5.0	80.8	19.2	2.57	7.87	36.4	51.4	12.2	1.64	−27.1	102.8	24.4	3.27
2.0	6.0	75.0	25.0	3.00	8.47	40.9	44.3	14.8	1.77	−18.1	88.6	29.5	3.54
2.0	7.0	69.2	30.8	3.54	9.17	45.5	37.8	16.8	1.93	−9.1	75.5	33.6	3.86
2.0	8.0	63.5	36.5	4.19	9.94	49.7	31.9	18.3	2.11	−0.6	63.9	36.7	4.21

be correlated with a correlation coefficient of 0.3. This correlation coefficient of 0.3 is virtually identical to its historical value in the post-World War II period, from 1945 to 1979.

For comparison purposes over the 1970-1979 period, the standard deviation of annual returns for the Standard & Poor's Composite Index of 500 stocks was 21.4, and the standard deviation of annual returns on a portfolio of high-grade industrial bonds managed so as to have a constant maturity of twenty years was 6.0.[7] Thus, the assumed standard deviation for the stock fund is very close to its historical value, while the assumed standard deviation for the bond fund is somewhat greater than its historical value. In view of the increased level of uncertainty associated with interest rates in the fall of 1981, the time at which the optimal allocations in Table 2 were determined, this assumption of a greater risk attached to bond investments seemed warranted.

One can be relatively confident in the estimates of the historical risk levels for stocks and bonds.[8] It doesn't take an investor long to learn that prices of stocks have fluctuated up and down by amounts considerably greater than those of the prices of bonds. Unless an investor has some explicit reason to believe that these relationships have changed, he should probably assume that in the future the risks associated with common stocks will be much greater than the risks associated with bonds.

Expected Returns

Unlike risks, an investor should be very cautious in extrapolating the past to assess future expected returns. In view of the greater risks attached to stocks, an investor is probably warranted in assuming that the marketplace expects a greater return on stocks than bonds although, of course, there is no certainty that stocks will outreturn bonds. It is probably also true that the marketplace expects a greater return on bonds than on risk-free assets.

The difficulty in assessing expected returns is that the historical evidence is so variable. Depending upon the period analyzed, one would find that the average return on long-term bonds was 0.5 to 2.0 percentage points in excess of the risk-free rate and that the average return on a composite index of stocks was from 3 to 8 percentage points greater than the average return on bonds.

Another approach to assessing the expected returns on bonds and stocks is to survey market participants to obtain their expectations. A survey in the beginning of 1980 of the 100 largest nonfinancial corporations found that these corporations judged that the market expected a return on their common stock of 5.3 percent more than the return on their bonds.[9] Another survey of the largest fifty

---

[7] These estimates were made by the Rodney L. White Center for Financial Research at the Wharton School, University of Pennsylvania.

[8] Merton, Robert C. "On Estimating the Expected Return on the Market: An Exploratory Investigation." *Journal of Financial Economics.* Vol. 8, No. 4, Dec. 1980, pages 323-362.

[9] Blume, Marshall E.; Friend, Irwin; Westerfield, Randolph. *Impediments to Capital Formation.*

institutional investors in December 1980 found that these institutions expected common stocks to return 17.5 to 18.0 percent when bonds were yielding 13 to 14 percent — a differential of 3.5 to 5.0 percent.[10]

In view of this evidence, particularly the survey data, it seems reasonable to assume that the marketplace in the fall of 1981 expected bonds to return from one to 2 percent more than risk-free assets, and stocks to return 3 to 4 percent more than bonds. Because of the uncertainty attached to these expectations and, further, to allow the interested reader to adjust for taxes and so on, optimal allocations have been determined for a large number of alternative assumptions. In the case of bonds, the example assumes an expected return in excess of the risk-free rate of from 0.5 to 2 percent, and in the case of stocks, an expected return in excess of the risk-free rate of from one to 8 percent.

The optimal allocations are shown in Table 2 under various assumptions. All returns have been measured in excess of the risk-free rate — in short, excess returns. These optimal allocations are only affected by the returns expected in excess of the risk-free rate, not by the level of the risk-free rate itself. The numbers in Table 2 are valid regardless of the risk-free return.

Specific Allocations

Table 2 and the subsequent tables contain a large amount of information and should be used as reference tables. As an example, if one expected an excess return on bonds of one percent and an excess return on stocks of 4 percent, one should go to the appropriate row as indicated by the first two columns of figures. The next four columns reveal that the optimal portfolio of risky assets would have 63.5 percent in bonds and 36.5 percent in stocks. The expected excess return on this portfolio would be 2.09 percent, and the standard deviation would be 9.94 percent. If the risk-free rate were 10 percent, the total expected return would be 12.09 percent.

If the investor wanted a portfolio with a risk level of 5 percent, which is a fairly low risk, the next four columns show that he should place 49.7 percent in the risk-free asset and the remainder in the optimal portfolio of risky assets resulting in 31.9 percent in bonds and 18.3 percent in stocks. The expected excess return would be 1.05 percent.

If the investor wanted a portfolio with a risk level of 10 percent, a moderate risk level, the last four columns show that he should borrow at the risk-free rate 0.6 percent of his net worth and invest this amount in addition to his net worth in the optimal portfolio of risky assets. Relative to his net worth, the investor would invest 63.9 percent in bonds and 36.7 percent in stocks for an expected excess return of 2.11 percent. If he could not borrow at the risk-free rate, the

Philadelphia: Rodney L. White Center for Financial Research, the Wharton School, University of Pennsylvania, 1980.

[10] This survey was conducted by the Rodney L. White Center for Financial Research.

alternative would be to increase the proportion in stocks and decrease the proportion in bonds from the proportions in the optimal portfolio of risky assets. Since the standard deviation of return for the optimal portfolio of risky assets is 9.94 percent, a very small shift would raise the risk to 10 percent, and there would be a marginal increase in expected return.

For pedagogical purposes, consider the two cases in which the expected excess returns are the same for bonds and stocks. Since the standard deviation of return for stocks is three times that of bonds, one might conclude that nothing should be invested in stocks, but the figures in Table 2 indicate in both cases that 1.2 percent should be placed in stocks. The reason is that stocks have the potential in combination with other risky assets to reduce overall risk, and as long as this diversification effect is greater than the inherent riskiness of stocks themselves, some investment in stock would be desirable. For the assumed values in Table 2, this diversification effect is so small, even though the effect is there, that it can, for practical purposes, be ignored.

Depending upon the assumed values for the expected excess returns on bonds and stocks, the expected excess returns on an optimally constructed portfolio with a standard deviation of 5 percent would range from roughly 0.5 to 2.0 percent. The expected excess returns on an optimally constructed portfolio with a standard deviation of 10 percent would range from 1.0 to 4.0 percent. The next part of this article will explore the long-term implications of different combinations of expected returns and standard deviations of annual returns.

Long-Term Implications

Although investment decisions are usually short-term in nature, the overall risk to which an investor exposes himself should be dictated by long-term considerations. In setting the risk level for the short term, the investor should be concerned with the implied probabilities of meeting his long-term goals. These probabilities will be related to the level of short-term risk to which an investor is exposed as well as the expected return associated with that level of risk.

By definition, for optimal portfolios, there will be a positive relationship between risks in the short term and expected returns in the short term. This statement does not imply that all investors will face the same trade-off. Some investors may be better able than others to find assets whose expected returns are greater than warranted by their underlying risks.

Potential Returns

Tables 3 and 4 contain various statistics pertaining to the potential returns of different combinations of short-term risks and expected returns for horizons from one to fifty years. In Table 3 on page 1030, the standard deviation of annual returns is assumed to be 10 percent per year, and in Table 4 on page 1031, the standard deviation is assumed to be 5 percent per year. Both tables assume that

TABLE 3. Potential Returns of Portfolios With Standard Deviations of 10 Percent Per Year

		Risk-Free Return		*Value of $1 Initial Investment*				*Annual Compounded Rate of Return*			
Annual Expected Return	*Horizon (Years)*	*Value of One Dollar*	*Probability of Lesser Return*	*5th Percentile*	*Median*	*Expected Return*	*95th Percentile*	*5th Percentile*	*Median*	*Expected Return*	*95th Percentile*
11%	1	$ 1.10	48%	$ 0.95	$ 1.11	$ 1.11	$ 1.28	−4.6%	10.6%	11.0%	28.2%
	5	1.61	45	1.19	1.65	1.68	2.30	3.5	10.6	11.0	18.1
	10	2.59	43	1.71	2.73	2.84	4.35	5.5	10.6	11.0	15.8
	20	6.73	40	3.84	7.43	8.06	14.40	6.9	10.6	11.0	14.3
	50	117.39	35	52.94	150.66	184.39	428.71	8.3	10.6	11.0	12.9
12%	1	$ 1.10	44%	$ 0.96	$ 1.12	$ 1.12	$ 1.29	−3.7%	11.6%	12.0%	29.2%
	5	1.61	33	1.24	1.73	1.76	2.40	4.5	11.6	12.0	19.1
	10	2.59	31	1.88	2.98	3.11	4.74	6.5	11.6	12.0	16.8
	20	6.73	24	4.62	8.91	9.64	17.16	7.9	11.6	12.0	15.3
	50	117.39	13	84.02	236.87	288.88	667.79	9.3	11.6	12.0	13.9
13%	1	$ 1.10	39%	$ 0.97	$ 1.13	$ 1.13	$ 1.30	−2.7%	12.6%	13.0%	30.2%
	5	1.61	28	1.31	1.81	1.84	2.50	5.5	12.6	13.0	20.1
	10	2.59	21	2.06	3.26	3.39	5.17	7.5	12.6	13.0	17.9
	20	6.73	12	5.57	10.66	11.52	20.41	9.0	12.6	13.0	16.3
	50	117.39	3	132.75	370.87	450.73	1036.10	10.3	12.6	13.0	14.9
14%	1	$ 1.10	36%	$ 0.98	$ 1.14	$ 1.14	$ 1.31	−1.7%	13.6%	14.0%	31.2%
	5	1.61	21	1.37	1.89	1.94	2.61	6.5	13.6	14.0	21.1
	10	2.59	13	2.26	3.57	3.71	5.63	8.5	13.6	14.0	18.9
	20	6.73	5	6.68	12.73	13.74	24.24	10.0	13.6	14.0	17.3
	50	117.39	1	208.80	578.12	700.23	1600.66	11.3	13.6	14.0	15.9

TABLE 4. Potential Returns of Portfolios With Standard Deviations of 5 Percent Per Year

		Risk-Free Return		*Value of $1 Initial Investment*				*Annual Compounded Rate of Return*			
Annual Expected Return	*Horizon (Years)*	*Value of One Dollar*	*Probability of Lesser Return*	*5th Percentile*	*Median*	*Expected Return*	*95th Percentile*	*5th Percentile*	*Median*	*Expected Return*	*95th Percentile*
10.5%	1	$ 1.10	47%	$ 1.02	$ 1.10	$ 1.11	$ 1.19	2.5%	10.4%	10.5%	18.9%
	5	1.61	43	1.39	1.64	1.65	1.94	6.8	10.4	10.5	14.1
	10	2.59	40	2.12	2.69	2.71	3.40	7.8	10.4	10.5	13.0
	20	6.73	36	5.17	7.22	7.37	10.03	8.6	10.4	10.5	12.2
	50	117.39	29	82.69	139.93	147.27	236.79	9.2	10.4	10.5	11.6
11.0%	1	$ 1.10	43%	$ 1.03	$ 1.11	$ 1.11	$ 1.19	2.9%	10.9%	11.0%	19.5%
	5	1.61	35	1.42	1.68	1.68	1.98	7.2	10.9	11.0	14.7
	10	2.59	29	2.22	2.81	2.84	3.56	8.3	10.9	11.0	13.6
	20	6.73	22	5.65	7.90	8.06	11.03	9.0	10.9	11.0	12.8
	50	117.39	11	103.33	175.28	184.56	297.33	9.7	10.9	11.0	12.1
12.0%	1	$ 1.10	35%	$ 1.04	$ 1.12	$ 1.12	$ 1.20	4.0%	11.9%	12.0%	20.4%
	5	1.61	20	1.49	1.75	1.76	2.07	8.3	11.9	12.0	15.6
	10	2.59	13	2.44	3.08	3.11	3.88	9.3	11.9	12.0	14.5
	20	6.73	4	6.81	9.46	9.65	13.13	10.0	11.9	12.0	13.7
	50	117.39	<1	163.63	274.97	289.00	462.05	10.7	11.9	12.0	13.1

the annual risk-free rate of return is 10 percent.[11]

If an investor expected an annual return of 3 percent in excess of the risk-free rate for a total expected return of 13 percent on a portfolio with a standard deviation of 10 percent, he should examine the third block of numbers in Table 3. For a horizon of ten years, the investor would see that an initial investment of one dollar would have appreciated to $2.59 if invested in the risk-free asset at 10 percent.

There would be a 21 percent probability that the realized return from the risky portfolio would be less than that obtainable through the risk-free strategy. Thus, in roughly one out of every five ten-year non-overlapping periods, the investor would have had greater wealth had he invested in the risk-free asset. Stated more positively, in four out of every five ten-year non-overlapping periods, the investor would be better off with the risky portfolio.

On the average, the investor will be better off with the risky portfolio. However, an investor who has only ten years to retirement and has realized a poor return from his investments may not receive much comfort from the knowledge that on average he would do better. He is only concerned with the immediate ten-year period.

The fifth percentile of the distribution of terminal values for a ten-year horizon from a risky portfolio with an expected return of 13 percent and a standard deviation of return of 10 percent is $2.06 for each dollar of initial investment. The fifth percentile should be interpreted as follows: There is a 5 percent probability that the realized terminal value will be less than $2.06 and, correspondingly, a 95 percent probability that the realized terminal value will be equal to or greater than $2.06. The ninety-fifth percentile is $5.17.

Median and Expected Values

The median terminal value after ten years for this risky portfolio is $3.26, while the expected terminal value is $3.39. The median value is the same as the fiftieth percentile, so that there is a 50 percent chance that the investor will realize a terminal value of $3.26 or more. The expected value is an average of the possible outcomes, weighted by the probabilities of each outcome. That the expected terminal value exceeds the median value implies that, on occasion, an investor will realize a return that is considerably greater than expected. In technical terminology, the distribution of potential terminal values is skewed just as the distribution of personal incomes in the United States is skewed. The average income, pulled up by the very high incomes of a few, is greater than the median income.

---

[11] The statistics in Tables 3 and 4 assume that annual returns R are distributed by a log normal distribution. The assumed numbers for the expected value and the standard deviation of R imply the expected values of the logarithm as well as the standard deviation of the logarithm of R. These latter two statistics were used to determine the statistical properties of the logarithm of R, from which the statistical properties of R were derived.

The implication for investing is that the probability is greater than 50 percent that an investor's realized returns will be less than expected. Occasionally, the realized returns will be much greater than expected. As an aside, the less diversified a portfolio, the greater the skewness. Thus, the probabilities of not meeting one's expectations increase as a portfolio becomes less diversified, but on occasion such a portfolio will produce much larger returns than expected. All this says is that the way to gain substantial wealth is to put everything into one highly risky venture and pray.

The last four columns contain the annual compounded rate of return, which would be equivalent to the terminal values in the prior four columns. As the number of years in the horizon increases, the compounded annual returns for the fifth and ninety-fifth percentile become closer to the expected returns. This tendency for the realized returns, expressed as compounded annual returns, to become less dispersed over time may have led some investors to the conclusion that high-risk investments will ultimately pay off. Such is not the case. The small deviations of the compounded annual returns from their expectations are not small when they are compounded over a large number of years.

A perusal of Tables 3 and 4 should give the reader a good understanding of the potential long-term implications of different short-term strategies. It has been this writer's experience that many investors who gain an appreciation of the long-term risks associated with different investment strategies tend to switch to safer strategies. Perhaps such a growing understanding of the underlying risks could explain the empirical finding that the risk levels of individual portfolios tend to decrease with the age of the investor.[12]

CONCLUSION

The basic idea underlying MPT is that an investor wants the greatest possible expected return for the risk to which he is exposed. For many investors, including most individual investors, it is possible to measure risk by the short-term volatility of a portfolio, even though most investors have a multi-year horizon. The reason is that the greater the short-term volatility, the greater the long-term volatility. The level of risk to which an investor will expose himself in the short term is directly related to long-term considerations.

At the cost of perhaps oversimplifying, any risky asset can be viewed as having three characteristics of importance to an investor: (1) its expected return, (2) its own volatility, and (3) its diversification potential. Portfolio theory is concerned with the balancing of these three characteristics in conjunction with a position in a risk-free asset, such as a Treasury bill, to obtain the greatest expected return for a given level of risk. As several examples showed, the diversifi-

[12] Blume, Marshall E., and Friend, Irwin. *The Changing Role of the Individual Investor.* New York: John Wiley & Sons, 1978.

cation effect can be very powerful. It is possible for a portfolio to be of very low risk even though each of the component assets is extremely volatile.

The role of the risk-free asset in this process is not generally well understood. But if properly used, a position in a risk-free asset in conjunction with an investment in a risky portfolio can lead to significant gains in expected returns at no increase in risk, particularly for portfolios of low to moderate risk. As an example, under normal market conditions, an investor who was satisfied with the risk and expected returns of a high-grade bond portfolio and currently held such a portfolio could obtain a greater expected return at no increase in risk. Specifically, the investor could buy some stock for diversification reasons and then shift some of his assets into risk-free assets to reduce the overall risk of the portfolio. The gain in expected return could be up to one percent per year. When compounded, a difference of one percent per year is substantial.

Although computer algorithms are available to determine optimal portfolios given an investor's judgments of the future, most investors, particularly those of modest means, would not have the resources to utilize these algorithms. Nonetheless, an investor can realize much of the potential diversification effects by merely holding a portfolio of a large number of different types of assets without too much invested in any one asset. Nonetheless, a surprising number of individual investors hold poorly diversified portfolios. According to a recent survey of stockholders,[13] the median number of issues held by a stockholding family, exclusive of mutual funds and personal trusts, was fewer than four, with 34 percent owning only one or two issues. Such poorly diversified portfolios inflict unnecessary risks upon these investors, and it is not surprising that many of these investors reported that their performance was worse than the market's.

In conclusion, one of the principal lessons of portfolio theory is the benefits of diversification. An undiversified portfolio does not increase expected returns; it only exposes an investor to unnecessary and avoidable risks.

---

13 *Id.*

Tax Considerations for Collector-Investors

Eugene M. Krader, Esq. *

INTRODUCTION

Collectors of the tangibles dealt with in this volume (Art Nouveau and Art Deco, books, collectibles, coins, gemstones, paintings, period furniture, photographs, porcelain, prints, rugs, sculpture, and stamps) should be aware of the tax benefits and limitations that may attach to the disposition of a piece or an entire collection, depending on such factors as timing, nature of disposition, and status of the collector as perceived by the tax authorities.

ESSENTIAL DISTINCTION BETWEEN COLLECTORS AND INVESTORS

There is a significant difference between an object bought primarily as an investment and one bought for personal pleasure from the tax standpoint. Taxation rules for the art investor differ from those for the art collector. Either can make a charitable gift or sell an object at a profit and incur the same tax treatment. But on a sale below cost, the investor can deduct his loss; the non-investor cannot. If the object is bought primarily for investment, many expenses are deductible, including the cost of insurance, restoration, cleaning, storage, and the installation of a home security system. Otherwise, these are simply non-deductible personal expenses.

The investor must prove a profit motive. On audit, the IRS will look for evidence of investment, such as turnover rate through sales and exchanges, as well as financial position. The IRS position may be interpreted to mean that the poorer a person is, the more likely he is to buy art for investment. Other important indications of investment purpose would be the routine hiring of experts when buying and selling; enrollment in educational programs relating to collectibles; the loan of works to museums; good business records; and financing through borrowing.

* Eugene M. Krader is Managing Editor of tax publications at Warren, Gorham & Lamont, Inc., New York. He acknowledges with thanks the material contributions to this article of Rotraut and Michele Beiny, and Paul Kunkel — authors of the articles on Porcelain and Period Furniture, respectively.

GOVERNING INCOME TAX ASPECTS

Capital Gains

When a collectible is purchased by an individual who is not a dealer, as defined by the IRS, he typically looks forward to a capital gain, as there is no periodic income. Under the Economic Recovery Tax Act of 1981, the maximum tax on a long-term capital gain was reduced to 20 percent, and the maximum tax on ordinary income was reduced to 50 percent. A long-term capital gain applies to property that has been owned for at least one year.

Fair Market Value

The concept of fair market value is a fluid one: what a willing buyer would pay a willing seller. This leaves a wide latitude to the owner who may want to maximize or minimize the value of his collection depending on the situation. If he is selling, of course, he wants the highest price; if he is giving to charity, he wants the highest deduction; on the other hand, in the estate and gift tax area, he will want the lowest possible value attached to his collection. It is an issue of some importance and delicacy in the areas in which the IRS may become involved. Among the relevant factors to be considered are the prices for which similar articles have been sold; whether the price trend for that type of work is upward; and the quality, condition, and provenance of the piece.

Charitable Contributions

An attractive tax aspect for the collector is the availability of deductions for income tax purposes on donations to charitable institutions. The basic rule, which is subject to certain limitations and complications, is that a taxpayer is allowed a deduction for the full fair market value of the property contributed at the time of the contribution. This is subject to a deduction ceiling of 50 percent of the taxpayer's adjusted gross income.

Nature of donee. The taxpayer must choose his charitable recipient carefully. This is because only certain organizations qualify for deductions of up to 50 percent of the donor's contribution base. In general, the 50-percent-ceiling applies to contributions made to publicly supported charities and to certain types of private foundations. This ceiling is consistent with the general purpose of the law, which favors contributions to recognized public charities but frowns upon gifts to certain private organizations.

The 50 percent ceiling applies to the familiar charities, such as churches, schools, hospitals, publicly supported organizations (Red Cross, community museums, and libraries), and governmental units. The ceiling also applies to certain types of private foundations referred to as operating foundations, pass-through foundations, and pooled-fund foundations. Private foundations that qualify for the 50 percent ceiling are defined so that gifts received by these qualifying private foundations will soon be used for the benefit of 50-percent-ceiling public charity organizations.

Twenty percent ceiling organizations. A charitable deduction of up to 20 percent of an individual's contribution base (adjusted gross income) is permitted for contributions to qualifying organizations that are not 50 percent organizations. Generally, these organizations include the usual type of private foundations that do not pass their contributions through to qualified charities within specified time limits.

When there are contributions to both 50 percent organizations and to 20 percent organizations, there may be an additional reduction affecting the 20 percent limitation. This is because there is an overall 50 percent annual limitation for all charitable contributions of which no more than 20 percent may consist of contributions to 20 percent organizations. Contributions to 20 percent organizations suffer since such contributions are taken into account only after deductions for contributions to 50 percent organizations. It should be noted that excess 20 percent contributions are not allowed to be carried over as deductions to succeeding taxable years. Therefore, careful tax planning of contributions to 20 percent organizations is recommended; otherwise such deductions may be lost forever.

Compatability of gift with donee organization. In order to qualify for the full deduction, the gift must relate to the exempt purpose or function of the institution. An allowable deduction will be drastically reduced if a collectible is donated to a hospital rather than a museum; while the function of a museum is the ownership and display of works of art, a hospital has a function unrelated to art. The deduction for a donation of a collectible to a hospital will be the fair market value reduced by 40 percent of the capital gain.

The objective is to reduce the deduction for the collectible, which the hospital is generally expected to sell, rather than retain. Since the application of this rule depends on the use made of the contributed property, it is important to ascertain what use will be made of the donated property by the charity.

Since very few museums have sufficient space to exhibit all their art properties at one time, the fact that a donor can anticipate that his gift may be placed in storage part or even most of the time will not cause the value of the gift to be reduced.

There are still unanswered questions concerning what is a related use. For example, it has been established that a gift of a painting to an art museum is related to the museum's exempt purpose. On the other hand, the same painting donated to a hospital generally will not be considered related to its exempt purpose, and, therefore, the amount of the contribution deduction must be reduced by 40 percent as noted above. If the same painting is donated to a university, the regulations state that it will be considered related to the university's exempt function if the painting is placed in the library for display and study by art students. If the university sells the painting and uses the proceeds to further its exempt purpose, then the use of the property is an unrelated use. But what position would the IRS take if the painting were placed outside the library for artistic display? This question and many similar issues still remain unanswered.

Property appreciation. Another limitation applies where the property has appreciated in value. Here it is important to distinguish between ordinary income property (dealer property) and capital gain property (investment property). In the former case, the charitable contribution is limited to the taxpayer's basis, that is, how much he originally paid for the object. In the case of capital gain property held for over one year, the deduction is the full fair market value subject to the 50 percent deduction ceiling, as discussed above.

If the fair market value is lower than the price originally paid, no loss deduction is allowed. But where a taxpayer has established himself as an investor as opposed to a collector, he could sell the object, realize the loss for tax purposes, and then make a gift of the proceeds.

Corporate donor. In the case of a corporate giver, the contribution deduction is limited to 5 percent of its taxable income before deducting the amount of the contribution. At the same time, the corporation is giving a significant boost to its public image. Many corporations have their own foundations to house their works of art.

In view of the obvious possibilities of exploitation, valuation of art objects is sometimes subject to Treasury scrutiny. Although only a small percentage of tax returns are actually audited because of the obvious possibilities of exploitation, the possibility of an audit must always be considered.

Tax-Free Exchanges

The tax law provides that if a property is held for investment and is exchanged for another property of like kind, no gain is recognized. Just what constitutes art investment is still an open question, a matter that tax courts have addressed but not finally settled. Similarly, when it comes to collectibles, the meaning of "like kind" is up in the air. The words "like kind" have reference to the nature or character of the property and not to its grade or quality. One kind or class of property may not, under Section 1031(a) of the Code, be exchanged for property of a different kind or class. The purpose of the like-kind requirement is to extend tax-free treatment only to those exchanges in which the taxpayer's position remains basically unaltered.

In the area of exchanges of real property, the courts have been quite liberal in their interpretation of what constitutes like-kind property. However, in the area of tangible personal property, such as art, there have been relatively few cases in which the IRS and the courts have considered what constitutes a like-kind exchange. With no parameters within which to work, it is unclear what art objects may be exchanged tax-free under Section 1031. Whether a Gainsborough oil painting may be exchanged tax-free for a modern sculpture or antique furniture is an open question. In such circumstances, an advance ruling from the IRS might be appropriate.

In Revenue Ruling 76-214, one of the few rulings in the personal property area, the IRS held that an exchange of Mexican gold coins and Austrian gold coins could be effected under Section 1031. In that ruling, the IRS stated:

> The differences between gold coins minted by one country and gold coins minted by another country where such coins are not used as a circulating medium of exchange, are primarily of size, shape, and amount of gold content. The nature or character of the gold coins, however, is the same, and thus they qualify as "like kind" property as such term is used in section 1.1031(a)-1(b) of the regulations.

Revenue Ruling 79-143 distinguished Revenue Ruling 76-214 in holding that the exchange of U.S. $20 (numismatic-type) gold coins and South African Krugerrand (bullion-type) gold coins did not qualify for nonrecognition of gain as a like-kind exchange under Section 1031. In Revenue Ruling 79-143, the IRS held the coins were not property of a like kind because the value of numismatic-type coins is determined by their age, number minted, history, art and aesthetics, condition, and metal content, while the value of the bullion-type coins is determined solely on the basis of their metal content. The coins, according to the IRS, represent totally different types of underlying investments and, therefore, are not of the same nature or character.

Exchanges for boot. If a collector exchanges an investment property for a combination of like-kind items and cash ("boot"), the gain will be taxable to the extent of the cash only. For example, assume that an investor has a chair originally purchased for $5,000, which is then exchanged for another piece of furniture appraised to be worth $6,000 plus $2,000 in cash. The actual gain is $3,000, but the taxable gain is only $2,000 (the amount of boot involved). If the $5,000 chair had been exchanged for a like-kind item appraised to be worth $8,000, the $3,000 gain would not be taxable.

As a result of this rule, a collector of tangibles could go through life trading up his like-kind investments without ever selling anything and thus never have to pay any capital gains tax. If the property were held until death, the estate's basis for computing gains on the eventual sale of the property would be the valuation placed at death. Thus, capital gains tax on the appreciation of the collectibles owned during the collector's lifetime would be eliminated. However, this whole area clearly shows the need for careful recordkeeping. If something obtained from a series of exchanges through the years is eventually sold, the burden of showing tax base cost is on the collector. If it cannot be shown, the collector risks having it assigned a value of zero and having to pay the maximum capital gains tax.

Depreciation

Though this may be obvious to many, one should not attempt to depreciate antique furniture for tax purposes the way some businesses depreciate office furniture and similar property over its useful life.

Generally, works of art are not depreciable. The position of the IRS regarding depreciation of art is set forth in Revenue Ruling 68-232:

> A valuable and treasured art piece does not have a determinable useful life. While the actual physical condition of the property may influence the value placed on the object, it will not ordinarily limit or determine the useful life. Accordingly, depreciation of works of art generally is not allowable.

Depreciating art and antiques for tax purposes may be considered equivalent to asking for an audit.

Deductions for Theft or Fire Losses

Many collectors take comfort in the idea that theft and fire losses not covered by insurance are fully tax-deductible. In fact, nothing could be farther from the truth. Such deductions are limited to tax cost or current value, whichever is less. Unless the market for a collectible takes a dramatic plunge, tax cost will nearly always be less than current value. Thus, if a collector paid $200 for a painting that is worth $2,000 on the open market, when it is lost by fire or theft he will get a deduction of only $200. For the individual in a 50 percent tax bracket, this saves only $100 in taxes. In other words, the IRS is one's co-insurer for only 5 percent of replacement cost. But even this understates the loss, since the first $100 of any such loss is nondeductible. Needless to say, this loss would pay for many years of insurance premiums on a sizeable collection.

In this example, if the theft or fire loss even on the basis of cost is so large as to reduce taxable income to below the 50 percent bracket, then the government bears even less than 5 percent loss in most cases. However, if the loss exceeds the collector's income for the entire year, it can be carried back against income for up to the preceding three years, starting with the immediately preceding tax year. And if even this does not absorb the taxpayer's loss, he can carry the excess forward for up to the succeeding seven years starting with the immediately succeeding year. The taxpaying collector can also elect to waive the three-year carryback and carry losses forward if doing so would yield greater tax benefits.

Most important, the collector should never lose sight of the fact that deductions are based on cost or market value, whichever is less.

Deducting Expenses of Collecting

As suggested earlier, deducting expenses of collecting is not easily accomplished by the individual collector. In the principal case in which this issue was raised, the court found that such expenses are not deductible for income tax purposes. However, the court was divided. The fact-finding commissioner before the U.S. Court of Claims who heard the case in 1971 recommended that the deductions be allowed. Subtle changes in the statutory law since the 1971 case, known in legal and collecting circles as the *Wrightsman* case, indicate that this question may still be subject to judicial clarification.

In *Wrightsman,* the question was to determine the primary reason for collecting. In today's climate, where investing in works of art has gained credibility from banks and investment firms, such decisions might well go the other way if the collector keeps excellent records and acts in a businesslike manner. In addition to good records, the collector should indicate in every possible way that his collection is an investment: Carry full insurance and provide for the orderly disposition of the investments in a will.

In addition to good records (which should include all basis attributes, including original costs, expenses, buildup costs when items are traded, and current market value), the collector should photograph all pieces, preferably from more than one angle. Periodic appraisals, proper insurance, and detailed instructions about disposition of the collection at death are all part of the documentation necessary for the collector to convince the IRS that acquiring and trading works of art is something more than an avocation.

Index

B

C

D

H

I

L

N

O

Q

R

S

T

U

V

W